gem
Collins
Portuguese Dictionary

HarperCollins Publishers
Westerhill Road
Bishopbriggs
Glasgow
G64 2QT

Seventh Edition 2013

10 9 8 7 6 5 4

ISBN 978-0-00-748551-2

Collins® and Collins Gem® are registered trademarks of HarperCollins Publishers Limited

www.collins.co.uk

A catalogue record for this book is available from the British Library

DISAL S.A.
Av. Marginal Direita do Tietê, 800
Jaguara – CEP 05118-100
São Paulo – SP – Brazil

www.disal.com.br

ISBN 978-0-00-751107-5 (vinyl)
ISBN 978-0-00-751106-8 (paperback)

Typeset by Davidson Publishing Solutions, Glasgow

Printed in Italy by Lego SpA, Lavis (Trento)

Acknowledgements
We would like to thank those authors And publishers who kindly gave permission for copyright material to be used in the Collins Corpus. We would also like to thank Times Newspapers Ltd for providing valuable data.

nas páginas pares) ou o último verbete (se for nas páginas ímpares) da página em questão. Informações sobre a utilização ou forma de certos verbetes são dadas entre parênteses e, em geral, aparecem em forma abreviada e em itálico (p. ex. *(fam)*, *(Com)*).

Quando for apropriado, palavras derivadas aparecem agrupadas no mesmo verbete (**abade, abadia; produce, producer**) num formato ligeiramente menor do que o verbete.

As expressões comuns nas quais o verbete aparece estão impressas em um tamanho diferente de negrito romano. O símbolo '**~**' usado nas expressões representa o verbete principal no começo de cada parágrafo. Por exemplo, na entrada '**cold**', a expressão '**to be ~**' equivale a '**to be cold**'.

SIGNIFICADOS

A tradução para o verbete aparece em letra normal e quando há mais de um significado ou utilização, estes estão separados por um ponto e vírgula. Frequentemente, você encontrará outras palavras em itálico e entre parênteses antes da tradução, sugerindo contextos nos quais o verbete pode aparecer (p. ex. **rough** *(voice)* ou *(weather)*), ou fornecendo sinônimos (p. ex. **rough** *(violent)*).

PALAVRAS-CHAVE

Atenção especial foi dada a certas palavras em inglês e em português consideradas 'palavras-chave' em cada língua. Elas podem, por exemplo, ser usadas com muita frequência ou ter muitos tipos de utilização (p. ex. **be, get**). Verbetes destacados com números ajudama a distinguir as

INTRODUÇÃO

Ficamos felizes com a sua decisão de comprar o Dicionário Inglês-Português Collins e esperamos que este lhe seja útil na escola, em casa, de férias ou no trabalho.

Esta introdução fornece algumas sugestões de como utilizar da melhor maneira possível o seu dicionário – não somente a partir da ampla lista de palavras mas também a partir das informações fornecidas em cada verbete. Este dicionário visa ajudá-lo a ler e a entender o inglês moderno assim como a exprimir-se corretamente.

No início do Dicionário Collins aparecem as abreviaturas utilizadas, e a ilustração dos sons através de símbolos fonéticos. Você encontrará, a seguir, verbos irregulares ingleses e quadros com verbos portugueses, seguidos por uma seção com números, horas e datas. E, por fim, o guia para viajantes fornece centenas de frases úteis que visam lhe dar ajuda prática em situações cotidianas durante uma viagem.

COMO UTILIZAR O DICIONÁRIO COLLINS

Um grande número de informações pode ser encontrado neste dicionário. Vários tipos e tamanhos de letras, símbolos, abreviaturas e parênteses foram utilizados. As convenções e símbolos usados são explicados nas seções seguintes.

VERBETES

As palavras que você procurar no dicionário – os verbetes – estão em ordem alfabética. Eles estão impressos **em cor** para uma rápida identificação. As palavras que aparecem no topo de cada página indicam o primeiro verbete (se for

GERÊNCIA DE PROJETO/PROJECT MANAGEMENT
Teresa Álvarez García
Carol McCann

COLABORADORES/CONTRIBUTORS
John Whitlam
Helen Newstead
Vitoria Davies
Mike Harland
Jane Horwood
Lígia Xavier
Gerard Breslin
Laura Neves
Emma McDade
Daniel Veloso
Orin Hargraves
Maggie Seaton
Cordelia Lilly

PARA A EDITORA/FOR THE PUBLISHER
Lucy Cooper
Kerry Ferguson
Ruth O'Donovan
Elaine Higgleton

ÍNDICE

CONTENTS

categorias gramaticais e diferentes significados. Informações complementares são fornecidas entre parênteses e em itálico na língua relevante para o usuário.

INFORMAÇÃO GRAMATICAL

As categorias gramaticais são dadas em versalete e abreviadas após a ortografia fonética do verbete (p. ex. VT, ADJ, VI).

Os adjetivos aparecem em ambos os gêneros quando forem diferentes (**interno, -a**). Esta distinção também é feita quando os adjetivos têm uma forma irregular no feminino ou no plural (p. ex. **ateu, atéia**). As formas irregulares de substantivos feminino ou plural também são indicadas (p. ex. **child** (*pl* **~ren**)).

INTRODUCTION

We are delighted you have decided to buy the Collins Portuguese Dictionary and hope you will enjoy and benefit from using it at school, at home, on holiday or at work.

This introduction gives you a few tips on how to get the most out of your dictionary – not simply from its comprehensive wordlist but also from the information provided in each entry. This will help you to read and understand modern Portuguese, as well as communicate and express yourself in the language.

The Collins Portuguese Dictionary begins by listing the abbreviations used in the text and illustrating the sounds shown by the phonetic symbols. Next you will find English irregular verbs and Portuguese verb tables followed by a section on numbers, time, and dates. Finally, the Phrasefinder supplement gives you hundreds of useful phrases which are intended to give you practical help in everyday situations when travelling.

USING YOUR COLLINS DICTIONARY

A wealth of information is presented in the dictionary, using various typefaces, sizes of type, symbols, abbreviations and brackets. The conventions and symbols used are explained in the following sections.

HEADWORDS

The words you look up in the dictionary – 'headwords' – are listed alphabetically. They are printed in **colour** for rapid identification. The headwords appearing at the top of each page indicate the first (if it appears on a left-hand page) and last word (if it appears on a right-hand page) dealt with on the page in question.

Information about the usage or form of certain headwords is given in brackets after the phonetic spelling. This usually appears in abbreviated form and in italics. (e.g. (*fam*), (*Comm*)).

Where appropriate, words related to headwords are grouped in the same entry (**abade, abadia; produce, producer**) in a slightly smaller bold type than the headword. Common expressions in which the headword appears are shown in a different size of bold roman type. The swung dash, **~**, represents the main headword at the start of each entry. For example, in the entry for '**caminho**', the phrase '**pôr-se a ~**' should be read '**pôr-se a caminho**'.

PHONETIC SPELLINGS

The phonetic spelling of each headword (indicating its pronunciation) is given in square brackets immediately after the headword (e.g. **grande** ['grãdʒi]). A list of these spellings is given on page xv.

MEANINGS

Headword translations are given in ordinary type and, where more than one meaning or usage exists, they are separated by a semicolon. You will often find other words in italics in brackets before the translations. These offer suggested contexts in which the headword might appear (e.g. **intenso** (*emoção*)) or provide synonyms (e.g. **cândido** (*inocente*)).

'KEY' WORDS

Special status is given to certain Portuguese and English words which are considered as 'key' words in each language. They may, for example, occur very frequently or have several types of usage (e.g. **bem, ficar**). A combination of lozenges and numbers helps you to distinguish different parts of speech and different meanings. Further helpful information is provided in brackets and in italics in the relevant language for the user.

GRAMMATICAL INFORMATION

Parts of speech are given in abbreviated form in small caps after the phonetic spellings of headwords (e.g. VT, ADJ, PREP).

Genders of Portuguese nouns are indicated as follows: *m* for a masculine and *f* for a feminine noun. Feminine and irregular plural forms of nouns are also shown next to the headword (**inglês, -esa; material** (*pl* **-ais**)). Adjectives are given in both masculine and feminine forms where these forms are different (**comilão, -lona**).

The gender of the Portuguese translation also appears in *italics* immediately following the key element of the translation, except where there is a regular masculine singular noun ending in 'o', or a regular feminine singular noun ending in 'a'.

ABREVIATURAS — ABBREVIATIONS

ABREVIATURAS		ABBREVIATIONS
abreviatura	AB(B)R	abbreviation
adjetivo	ADJ	adjective
administração	*Admin*	administration
advérbio, locução adverbial	ADV	adverb, adverbial phrase
aeronáutica	*Aer*	flying, air travel
agricultura	*Agr*	agriculture
anatomia	*Anat*	anatomy
arquitetura	*Arq, Arch*	architecture
artigo definido	ART DEF	definite article
artigo indefinido	ART INDEF	indefinite article
uso atributivo do substantivo	ATR	compound element
Austrália	*Aust*	Australia
automobilismo	*Aut(o)*	the motor car and motoring
auxiliar	AUX	auxiliary
aeronáutica	*Aviat*	flying, air travel
biologia	*Bio*	biology
botânica, flores	*Bot*	botany
português do Brasil	BR	Brazilian Portuguese
inglês britânico	BRIT	British English
química	*Chem*	chemistry
linguagem coloquial	*col*	colloquial
comércio, finanças, bancos	*Com(m)*	commerce, finance, banking
comparativo	*compar*	comparative
computação	*Comput*	computing
conjunção	CONJ	conjunction
construção	*Constr*	building
uso atributivo do substantivo	CPD	compound element
cozinha	*Culin*	cookery
artigo definido	DEF ART	definite article
economia	*Econ*	economics
educação, escola e universidade	*Educ*	schooling, schools and universities
eletricidade, eletrônica	*Elet, Elec*	electricity, electronics
especialmente	*esp*	especially
exclamação	*excl*	exclamation
feminino	*f*	feminine
ferrovia	*Ferro*	railways
uso figurado	*fig*	figurative use
física	*Fís*	physics

ABREVIATURAS		ABBREVIATIONS
fotografia	*Foto*	photography
(verbo inglês) do qual a partícula é inseparável	FUS	(phrasal verb) where the particle is inseparable
geralmente	*gen*	generally
geografia, geologia	*Geo*	geography, geology
geralmente	*ger*	generally
impessoal	IMPESS, IMPERS	impersonal
artigo indefinido	INDEF ART	indefinite article
linguagem coloquial	*inf*	colloquial
infinitivo	*infin*	infinitive
invariável	INV	invariable
irregular	*irreg*	irregular
jurídico	*Jur*	law
gramática, linguística	*Ling*	grammar, linguistics
masculino	*m*	masculine
matemática	*Mat(h)*	mathematics
medicina	*Med*	medicine
ou masculino ou feminino, dependendo do sexo da pessoa	*m/f*	masculine/feminine
militar, exército	*Mil*	military matters
música	*Mús, Mus*	music
substantivo	N	noun
navegação, náutica	*Náut, Naut*	sailing, navigation
adjetivo ou substantivo numérico	NUM	numeral adjective or noun
	o.s.	oneself
pejorativo	*pej*	pejorative
fotografia	*Phot*	photography
física	*Phys*	physics
fisiologia	*Physiol*	physiology
plural	*pl*	plural
política	*Pol*	politics
particípio passado	PP	past participle
preposição	PREP	preposition
pronome	PRON	pronoun
português de Portugal	*PT*	European Portuguese
pretérito	*pt*	past tense
química	*Quím*	chemistry
religião e cultos	*Rel*	religion, church services
	sb	somebody
educação, escola e universidade	*Sch*	schooling, schools and universities

ABREVIATURAS		ABBREVIATIONS
singular	*sg*	singular
	sth	something
sujeito (gramatical)	*su(b)j*	(grammatical) subject
subjuntivo, conjuntivo	*sub(jun)*	subjunctive
superlativo	*superl*	superlative
também	*tb*	also
técnica, tecnologia	*Tec(h)*	technical term, technology
telecomunicações	*Tel*	telecommunications
tipografia, imprensa	*Tip*	typography, printing
televisão	*TV*	television
tipografia, imprensa	*Typ*	typography, printing
inglês americano	*US*	American English
ver	*V*	see
verbo	VB	verb
verbo intransitivo	VI	intransitive verb
verbo reflexivo	VR	reflexive verb
verbo transitivo	VT	transitive verb
zoologia	*Zool*	zoology
marca registrada	®	registered trademark
equivalente cultural	≈	cultural equivalent
linguagem ofensiva	!	offensive

PRONÚNCIA INGLESA

VOGAIS

	Exemplo Inglês	*Explicação*
[aː]	father	Entre o *a* de padre e o *o* de nó; como em *fada*
[ʌ]	but, come	Aproximadamente como o primeiro *a* de cama
[æ]	man, cat	Som entre o *a* de *lá* e o *e* de *pé*
[ə]	father, ago	Som parecido com o *e* final pronunciado em Portugal
[əː]	bird, heard	Entre o *e* aberto e o *o* fechado
[ɛ]	get, bed	Como em *pé*
[ɪ]	it, big	Mais breve do que em *si*
[iː]	tea, see	Como em *fino*
[ɔ]	hot, wash	Como em *pó*
[ɔː]	saw, all	Como o *o* de *porte*
[u]	put, book	Som breve e mais fechado do que em *burro*
[uː]	too, you	Som aberto como em *juro*

DITONGOS

	Exemplo Inglês	*Explicação*
[aɪ]	fly, high	Como em *baile*
[au]	how, house	Como em *causa*
[ɛə]	there, bear	Como o *e* de *aeroporto*
[eɪ]	day, obey	Como o *ei* de *lei*
[ɪə]	here, hear	Como *ia* de *companhia*
[əu]	go, note	[ə] seguido de um *u* breve
[ɔɪ]	boy, oil	Como em *boia*
[uə]	poor, sure	Como *ua* em *sua*

CONSOANTES

	Exemplo Inglês	*Explicação*
[d]	mended	Como em *dado, andar*
[g]	get, big	Como em *grande*
[dʒ]	gin, judge	Como em *idade*
[˜]	sing	Como em *cinco*
[h]	house, he	*h* aspirado
[j]	young, yes	Como em *iogurte*
[k]	come, mock	Como em *cama*
[r]	red, tread	*r* como em *para*, mas pronunciado no céu da boca

[s]	sand, yes	Como em sala
[z]	rose, zebra	Como em zebra
[ʃ]	she, machine	Como em *ch*apéu
[tʃ]	chin, rich	Como *t* em timbre
[w]	water, which	Como o *u* em água
[ʒ]	vision	Como em *j*á
[θ]	think, myth	Sem equivalente, aproximadamente como um *s* pronunciado entre os dentes
[ð]	this, the	Sem equivalente, aproximadamente como um *z* pronunciado entre os dentes

b, f, l, m, n, p, t, v pronunciam-se como em português.

O sinal [*] indica que o r final escrito pronuncia-se apenas em inglês britânico, exceto quando a palavra seguinte começa por uma vogal. O sinal [ˈ] indica a sílaba acentuada.

BRAZILIAN PORTUGUESE PRONUNCIATION

CONSONANTS

c	[k]	café	*c* before *a*, *o*, *u* is pronounced as in *c*at
ce, ci	[s]	cego	*c* before *e* or *i*, as in re*c*eive
ç	[s]	raça	*ç* is pronounced as in re*c*eive
ch	[ʃ]	chave	*ch* is pronounced as in *sh*ock
d	[d]	data	as in English EXCEPT
de, di	[dʒ]	difícil cidade	*d* before an *i* sound or final unstressed *e* is pronounced as in ju*dg*e
g	[g]	gado	*g* before *a*, *o*, *u* as in *g*ap
ge, gi	[ʒ]	gíria	*g* before *e* or *i*, as *s* in lei*s*ure
h		humano	*h* is always silent in Portuguese
j	[ʒ]	jogo	*j* is pronounced as *s* in lei*s*ure
l	[l]	limpo, janela	as in English EXCEPT
	[w]	falta, total	*l* after a vowel tends to become *w*
lh	[ʎ]	trabalho	*lh* is pronounced like the *lli* in mi*lli*on
m	[m]	animal, massa	as in English EXCEPT
	[ãw]	cantam	*m* at the end of a syllable preceded by a vowel nasalizes the preceding vowel
	[ĩ]	sim	
n	[n]	nadar, penal	as in English EXCEPT
	[ã]	cansar	*n* at the end of a syllable, preceded by a vowel and followed by a consonant, nasalizes the preceding vowel
	[ẽ]	alento	
nh	[˜]	tamanho	*nh* is pronounced like the *ni* in o*ni*on
q	[k]	queijo	*qu* before *i* or *e* is usually pronounced as in *k*ick
q	[kw]	quanto cinquenta	*qu* before *a* or *o*, and sometimes before *e* or *i*, is pronounced as in *qu*een
-r-	[r]	compra	*r* preceded by a consonant (except *n*) and followed by a vowel is pronounced with a single trill
r-, -r-	[h]	rato, arpão	inital *r*, *r* followed by a consonant and
rr	[h]	borracha	*rr* are pronounced like *h* in *h*ouse
-r	[r]	pintar, dizer	word-final *r* can sometimes be heard as a single trill, but usually it is not pronounced at all in colloquial speech
s-	[s]	sol escada livros	as in English EXCEPT
-s-	[z]	mesa rasgar, desmaio	intervocalic *s* and *s* before *b*, *d*, *g*, *l*, *m*, *n*, *r*, and *v*, as in ro*s*e

-ss-	[s]	nosso	double *s* is always pronounced as in *boss*
t	[t]	todo	as in English EXCEPT
te, ti	[tʃ]	amante tipo	*t* followed by an *i* sound or final unstressed *e* is pronounced as *ch* in *cheer*
x-	[ʃ]	xarope	initial *x* is pronounced like *sh* in *ship*
-x-	[s]	exceto explorar	*x* before a consonant is pronounced like *s* in sail
ex-	[z]	exame	*x* in the prefix *ex* before a vowel is pronounced as *z* in squeeze
-x-	[ʃ] [ks] [s]	relaxar fixo auxiliar	*x* in any other position may be pronounced as in *ship*, axe or sail
z	[z]	zangar cartaz	as in English

b, f, k, p, v, w are pronounced as in English.

VOWELS

a, á, à, â	[a]	mata	*a* is normally pronounced as in f*a*ther
ã	[ã]	irmã	*ã* is pronounced approximately as in *sung*
e	[e]	vejo	unstressed (except final) *e* is pronounced like *e* in th*ey*, stressed *e* is pronounced either as in th*ey* or as in b*e*t
-e	[i]	fome	final *e* is pronounced as in mon*ey*
é	[ɛ]	miséria	*é* is pronounced as in b*e*t
ê	[e]	pêlo	*ê* is pronounced as in th*ey*
i	[i]	vida	*i* is pronounced as in m*ea*n
o	[o]	locomotiva	unstressed (except final) *o* is pronounced as in l*o*cal;
	[ɔ] [o]	loja globo	stressed *o* is pronounced either as in l*o*cal or as in r*o*ck
-o	[u]	livro	final *o* is pronounced as in f*oo*t
ó	[ɔ]	óleo	*ó* is pronounced as in r*o*ck
ô	[o]	colônia	*ô* is pronounced as in l*o*cal
u	[u]	luva	*u* is pronounced as in r*u*le
	[w]	linguiça frequente	it is usually silent as in *gue, gui, que, qui* but in some words it is pronounced as a *w* sound in this position

DIPHTHONGS

ãe	[ãj]	mãe	nasalized, approximately as in fl*y*ing
ai	[aj]	vai	as is r*i*de
ao, au	[aw]	aos, auxílio	as is sh*ou*t
ão	[ãw]	vão	nasalized, approximately as in r*ou*nd
ei	[ej]	feira	as is th*ey*
eu	[ew]	deusa	both elements pronounced
oi	[oj]	boi	as is t*oy*
ou	[o]	cenoura	as is l*o*cal
õe	[õj]	aviões	nasalized, approximately as in 'b*oi*ng!'

STRESS

The rules of stress in Portuguese are as follows:

(a) when a word ends in *a*, *e*, *o*, *m* (except *im*, *um* and their plural forms) or *s*, the second last syllable is stressed;
cama*ra*da; cama*ra*das
*par*te; *par*tem

(b) when a word ends in *i*, *u*, *im* (and plural), *um* (and plural), *n* or a consonant other than *m* or *s*, the stress falls on the last syllable:
ven*di*, al*gum*, al*guns*, fa*lar*

(c) when the rules set out in (a) and (b) are not applicable, an acute or circumflex accent appears over the stressed vowel:
*ó*tica, *â*nimo, ingl*ê*s

In the phonetic transcription, the symbol [ˈ] precedes the syllable on which the stress falls.

EUROPEAN PORTUGUESE PRONUNCIATION

The pronunciation of Brazilian Portuguese differs quite markedly from the Portuguese spoken in Portugal itself and in the African and island states. The more phonetic nature of Brazilian means that words nearly always retain their set pronunciation; in European Portuguese, on the other hand, vowels can often be unpronounced or weakened and consonants can change their sound, all depending on their position within a word or whether they are being elided with a following word. The major differences in pronunciation of European Portuguese are as follows:-

CONSONANTS: as in Brazilian, except:

-b-	[β]	cu**ba**	*b* between vowels is a softer sound, closer to *have*
d	[d]	**d**ança, **d**ifícil	as in English EXCEPT *d* between vowels is softer,
-d-	[ð]	fa**do**, ci**da**de	approximately as in *the*
-g-	[ɣ]	sa**ga**	*g* between vowels is a softer sound, approximately as in *lager*
gu	[ɣw]	a**gu**entar	in certain words *gu* is pronounced as in *Gwent*
qu	[kw]	tran**qu**ilo	in certain words *qu* is pronounced as in *quoits*
r-, rr	[ʀ]		initial *r* and double *r* are pronounced either like the
	[rr]		French *r* or strongly trilled as in Scottish *Rory*; pronunciation varies according to region
-r-, -r	[r]	**r**ato, a**rr**na	*r* in any other position is slightly trilled
t	[t]	**t**odo, aman**te**	*t* is pronounced as in English
z	[ʒ]	**z**angar	as in English EXCEPT final *z* is pronounced as *sh* in *flash*
	[ʃ]	carta**z**	

VOWELS: as in Brazilian, except:

a	[a]	fal**a**r	stressed *a* is pronounced either as in *father* or as
	[ɐ]	c**a**ma	*u* in *further*
-a-, -a	[ə]	f**a**lar, fal**a**	unstressed or final *a* is pronounced as *e* in *further*
e	[ə]	m**e**dir	unstressed *e* is a very short *i* sound as in *rabbit*
-e	[ə]	art**e**, regim**e**	final *e* is barely pronounced; these would sound like English *art* and *regime*
o	[u]	poç**o**, p**o**der	unstressed or final *o* is pronounced as in *foot*

PORTUGUESE SPELLING

In 2009, a spelling reform was introduced in all the Portuguese-speaking countries with the aim of eliminating the differences which existed between Brazilian and European Portuguese spelling. The following table summarizes these differences, which you will come across in texts written before the 2009 reform:

Description	**Brazilian spelling pre-2009**	**European Portuguese spelling pre-2009**	**Universal spelling post-2009**
The combinations *-gue-*, *-gui-*, *-que-*, *-qui-* when *u* is pronounced	With trema, e.g. *lingüiça*, *freqüente* etc.	Without trema, e.g. *linguiça*, *frequente* etc.	Without trema, e.g. *linguiça*, *frequente* etc.
Stressed *-ei-* and *-oi-* in penultimate syllables	With acute accent, e.g. *idéia*, *heróico*	Without acute accent, e.g. *ideia*, *heroico*	Without acute accent, e.g. *ideia*, *heroico*
Stressed *o* followed by unstressed *o*	First *o* has circumflex accent, e.g *vôo*, *abençôo*	No written accent, e.g. *voo*, *abençoo*	No written accent, e.g. *voo*, *abençoo*
First person plural preterite tense of *-ar* verbs	Without accent, e.g. *amamos*, *jogamos*	With acute accent, e.g. *amámos*, *jogámos*	Without accent, e.g. *amamos*, *jogamos*
comum + mente	*comumente*	*comummente*	*comumente*
com + nós	*conosco*	*connosco*	*conosco*
(h)úmido and derivatives	*úmido*, *umidade*	*húmido*, *humidade*	*úmido*, *umidade*
Latin consonant group *-ct-*	Simplified to *-c-/-ç-* or *-t-*, e.g. *acionar*, *ação*, *ator*	Silent *-c-* retained, e.g. *accionar*, *acção*, *actor*	Simplified spelling, e.g. *acionar*, *ação*, *ator*
Latin consonant group *-pt-*	Simplified to *-ç-* or *-t-*, e.g. *exceção*, *ótimo*	Silent *-p-* retained, e.g. *excepção*, *óptimo*	Simplified spelling, e.g. *exceção*, *ótimo*
Months of the year	e.g. *janeiro*, *dezembro*	e.g. *Janeiro*, *Dezembro*	e.g. *janeiro*, *dezembro*

One important difference between Brazilian and Portuguese spelling which still applies even after the reform is that, when a written accent is required on stressed *e* and *o* before *m* or *n*, Brazilian uses the circumflex while European uses the acute accent, reflecting the difference in the way the sounds are pronounced, e.g. *tênis* (BR), *ténis* (PT); *econômico* (BR), *económico* (PT). In addition, there are cases where two different spellings are permitted in European Portuguese to reflect two possible pronunciations, e.g. *súdito/súbdito*, *sutil/subtil*, *anistia/amnistia*.

VERBOS IRREGULARES EM INGLÊS

PRESENT	PT	PP
arise	arose	arisen
awake	awoke	awoken
be (am, is, are; being)	was, were	been
bear	bore	born(e)
beat	beat	beaten
begin	began	begun
bend	bent	bent
bet	bet, betted	bet, betted
bid *(at auction)*	bid	bid
bind	bound	bound
bite	bit	bitten
bleed	bled	bled
blow	blew	blown
break	broke	broken
breed	bred	bred
bring	brought	brought
build	built	built
burn	burnt, burned	burnt, burned
burst	burst	burst
buy	bought	bought
can	could	(been able)
cast	cast	cast
catch	caught	caught
choose	chose	chosen
cling	clung	clung
come	came	come
cost	cost	cost
creep	crept	crept
cut	cut	cut
deal	dealt	dealt
dig	dug	dug
do (does)	did	done
draw	drew	drawn
dream	dreamed, dreamt	dreamed, dreamt
drink	drank	drunk
drive	drove	driven
eat	ate	eaten
fall	fell	fallen
feed	fed	fed
feel	felt	felt

PRESENT	PT	PP
fight	fought	fought
find	found	found
fling	flung	flung
fly	flew	flown
forbid	forbad(e)	forbidden
forecast	forecast	forecast
forget	forgot	forgotten
forgive	forgave	forgiven
freeze	froze	frozen
get	got	got, *(US)* goten
give	gave	given
go (goes)	went	gone
grind	ground	ground
grow	grew	grown
hang	hung	hung
hang *(execute)*	hanged	hanged
have	had	had
hear	heard	heard
hide	hid	hidden
hit	hit	hit
hold	held	held
hurt	hurt	hurt
keep	kept	kept
kneel	knelt, kneeled	knelt, kneeled
know	knew	known
lay	laid	laid
lead	led	led
lean	leant, leaned	leant, leaned
leap	leapt, leaped	leapt, leaped
learn	learnt, learned	learnt, learned
leave	left	left
lend	lent	lent
let	let	let
lie (lying)	lay	lain
light	lit, lighted	lit, lighted
lose	lost	lost
make	made	made
may	might	–

PRESENT	PT	PP
mean	meant	meant
meet	met	met
mistake	mistook	mistaken
mow	mowed	mown, mowed
must	(had to)	(had to)
pay	paid	paid
put	put	put
quit	quit, quitted	quit, quitted
read	read	read
rid	rid	rid
ride	rode	ridden
ring	rang	rung
rise	rose	risen
run	ran	run
saw	sawed	sawed, sawn
say	said	said
see	saw	seen
sell	sold	sold
send	sent	sent
set	set	set
sew	sewed	sewn
shake	shook	shaken
shear	sheared	shorn, sheared
shed	shed	shed
shine	shone	shone
shoot	shot	shot
show	showed	shown
shrink	shrank	shrunk
shut	shut	shut
sing	sang	sung
sink	sank	sunk
sit	sat	sat
sleep	slept	slept
slide	slid	slid
sling	slung	slung
slit	slit	slit
smell	smelt, smelled	smelt, smelled
sow	sowed	sown, sowed

PRESENT	PT	PP
speak	spoke	spoken
speed	sped, speeded	sped, speeded
spell	spelt, spelled	spelt, spelled
spend	spent	spent
spill	spilt, spilled	spilt, spilled
spin	spun	spun
spit	spat	spat
spoil	spoiled, spoilt	spoiled, spoilt
spread	spread	spread
spring	sprang	sprung
stand	stood	stood
steal	stole	stolen
stick	stuck	stuck
sting	stung	stung
stink	stank	stunk
stride	strode	stridden
strike	struck	struck
swear	swore	sworn
sweep	swept	swept
swell	swelled	swollen, swelled
swim	swam	swum
swing	swung	swung
take	took	taken
teach	taught	taught
tear	tore	torn
tell	told	told
think	thought	thought
throw	threw	thrown
thrust	thrust	thrust
tread	trod	trodden
wake	woke, waked	woken, waked
wear	wore	worn
weave	wove	woven
weep	wept	wept
win	won	won
wind	wound	wound
wring	wrung	wrung
write	wrote	written

PORTUGUESE VERB FORMS

1 Gerund. 2 Imperative. 3 Present. 4 Imperfect. 5 Preterite. 6 Future. 7 Present subjunctive. 8 Imperfect subjunctive. 9 Future subjunctive. 10 Past participle. 11 Pluperfect. 12 Personal infinitive.

etc indicates that the irregular root is used for all persons of the tense, e.g. **ouvir** 7 ouça ouça, ouças, ouça, ouçamos, ouçais, ouçam.

abrir 10 aberto
acudir 2 acode 3 acudo, acodes, acode, acodem
aderir 3 adiro 7 adira
advertir 3 advirto 7 advirta *etc*
agir 3 ajo 7 aja *etc*
agradecer 3 agradeço 7 agradeça *etc*
agredir 2 agride 3 agrido, agrides, agride, agridem 7 agrida *etc*
AMAR 1 amando 2 ama, amai 3 amo, amas, ama, amamos, amais, amam 4 amava, amavas, amava, amávamos, amavéis, amavam 5 amei, amaste, amou, amamos amastes, amaram 6 amarei, amarás, amará, amaremos, amareis, amarão 7 ame, ames, ame, amemos, ameis, amem 8 amasse, amasses, amasse, amássemos, amásseis, amassem 9 amar, amares, amar, ámarmos, amardes, amarem 10 amado 11 amara, amaras, amara, amáramos, amáreis, amaram 12 amar, amares, amar, amarmos, amardes, amarem
ameaçar 5 ameacei 7 ameace *etc*
ansiar 2 anseia 3 anseio, anseias, anseia, anseiam 7 anseie *etc*
arrancar 7 arranque *etc*
arruinar 2 arruína 3 arruíno, arruínas, arruína, arruínam 7 arruíne, arruínes, arruíne, arruínem
atribuir 3 atribuo, atribuis, atribui, atribuímos, atribuís, atribuem
averiguar 7 averigúe, averigúes, averigúe, averigúem
bulir 2 bole 3 bulo, boles, bole, bolem
caber 3 caibo 5 coube *etc* 7 caiba *etc* 8 coubesse *etc* 9 couber *etc*
cair 2 cai 3 caio, cais, cai, caímos, caís, caem 4 caía *etc* 5 caí, caíste 7 caia *etc* 8 caisse *etc*
cobrir 3 cubro 7 cubra *etc* 10 coberto
compelir 3 compilo 7 compila *etc*
crer 2 crê 3 creio, crês, crê, cremos, credes, creem 5 cri, creste, creu, cremos, crestes, creram 7 creia *etc*
cuspir 2 cospe 3 cuspo, cospes, cospe, cospem
dar 2 dá 3 dou, dás, dá, damos, dais, dão 5 dei, deste, deu, demos, destes, deram 7 dê, dês, dê, demos, deis, deem 8 desse *etc* 9 der *etc* 11 dera *etc*
deduzir 2 deduz 3 deduzo, deduzes, deduz
denegrir 2 denigre 3 denigro, denigres, denigre, denigrem 7 denigre *etc*
despir 3 dispo 7 dispa *etc*
dizer 2 diz (dize) 3 digo, dizes, diz, dizemos, dizeis, dizem 5 disse *etc* 6 direi *etc* 7 diga *etc* 8 dissesse *etc* 9 disser *etc* 10 dito
doer 2 dói 3 doo, dóis, dói
dormir 3 durmo 7 durma *etc*
emergir 3 emirjo 7 emirja *etc*
escrever 10 escrito

ESTAR **2** está **3** estou, estás, está, estamos, estais, estão **4** estava *etc* **5** estive, estiveste, esteve, estivemos, estivestes, estiveram **7** esteja *etc* **8** estivesse *etc* **9** estiver *etc* **11** estivera *etc*
extorquir **3** exturco **7** exturca *etc*
FAZER **3** faço **5** fiz, fizeste, fez, fizemos, fizestes, fizeram **6** farei *etc* **7** faça *etc* **8** fizesse *etc* **9** fizer *etc* **10** feito **11** fizera *etc*
ferir **3** firo **7** fira *etc*
fluir **3** fluo, fluis, flui, fluímos, fluís, fluem
fugir **2** foge **3** fujo, foges, foge, fogem **7** fuja *etc*
ganhar **10** ganho
gastar **10** gasto
gerir **3** giro **7** gira *etc*
haver **2** há **3** hei, hás, há, havemos, haveis, hão **4** havia *etc* **5** houve, houveste, houve, houvemos, houvestes, houveram **7** haja *etc* **8** houvesse *etc* **9** houver *etc* **11** houvera *etc*
ir **1** indo **2** vai **3** vou, vais, vai, vamos, ides, vão **4** ia *etc* **5** fui, foste, foi, fomos, fostes, foram **7** vá, vás, vá, vamos, vades, vão **8** fosse, fosses, fosse, fôssemos, fôsseis, fossem **9** for *etc* **10** ido **11** fora *etc*
ler **2** lê **3** leio, lês, lê, lemos, ledes, leem **5** li, leste, leu, lemos, lestes, leram **7** leia *etc*
medir **3** meço, **7** meça *etc*
mentir **3** minto **7** minta *etc*
ouvir **3** ouço **7** ouça *etc*
pagar **10** pago
parar **2** pára **3** paro, paras, pára
parir **3** pairo **7** paira *etc*
pecar **7** peque *etc*
pedir **3** peço **7** peça *etc*
perder **3** perco **7** perca *etc*
poder **3** posso **5** pude, pudeste, pôde, pudemos, pudestes, puderam **7** possa *etc* **8** pudesse *etc* **9** puder *etc* **11** pudera *etc*
polir **2** pule **3** pulo, pules, pule, pulem **7** pula *etc*
pôr **1** pondo **2** põe **3** ponho, pões, põe, pomos, pondes, põem **4** punha *etc* **5** pus, puseste, pôs, pusemos, pusestes, puseram **6** porei *etc* **7** ponha *etc* **8** pusesse *etc* **9** puser *etc* **10** posto **11** pusera *etc*
preferir **3** prefiro **7** prefire *etc*
prevenir **2** previne **3** previno, prevines, previne, previnem **7** previna *etc*
prover **2** provê **3** provejo, provês, provê, provemos, provedes, proveem **5** provi, proveste, proveu, provemos, provestes, proveram **7** proveja *etc* **8** provesse *etc* **9** prover *etc*
querer **3** quero, queres, quer **5** quis, quiseste, quis, quisemos, quisestes, quiseram **7** queira *etc* **8** quisesse *etc* **9** quiser *etc* **11** quisera *etc*
refletir **3** reflito **7** reflita *etc*
repetir **3** repito **7** repita *etc*
requerer **3** requeiro, requeres, requer **7** requeira *etc*
reunir **2** reúne **3** reúno, reúnes, reúne, reúnem **7** reúna *etc*
rir **2** ri **3** rio, ris, ri, rimos, rides, ridem **5** ri, riste, riu, rimos, ristes, riram **7** ria *etc*
saber **3** sei, sabes, sabe, sabemos, sabeis, sabem **5** soube, soubeste, soube, soubemos, soubestes, souberam **7** saiba *etc* **8** soubesse *etc* **9** souber *etc* **11** soubera *etc*
seguir **3** sigo **7** siga *etc*
sentir **3** sinto **7** sinta *etc*
ser **2** sê **3** sou, és, é, somos, sois,

são **4** era *etc* **5** fui, foste, foi, fomos, fostes, foram **7** seja *etc* **8** fosse *etc* **9** for *etc* **11** fora *etc*
servir 3 sirvo **7** sirva *etc*
subir 2 sobe **3** subo, sobes, sobe, sobem
suster 2 sustém **3** sustenho, sustens, sustém, sustendes, sustêm **5** sustive, sustiveste, susteve, sustivemos, sustivestes, sustiveram **7** sustenha *etc*
ter 2 tem **3** tenho, tens, tem, temos, tendes, têm **4** tinha *etc* **5** tive, tiveste, teve, tivemos, tivestes, tiveram **6** terei *etc* **7** tenha *etc* **8** tivesse *etc* **9** tiver *etc* **11** tivera *etc*
torcer 3 torço **7** torça *etc*
tossir 3 tusso **7** tussa *etc*
trair 2 trai **3** traio, trais, trai, traímos, traís, traem **7** traia *etc*
trazer 2 (traze) traz **3** trago, trazes, traz, **5** trouxe, trouxeste, trouxe, trouxemos, trouxestes, trouxeram **6** trarei *etc* **7** traga *etc* **8** trouxesse *etc* **9** trouxer *etc* **11** trouxera *etc*
UNIR 1 unindo **2** une, uni **3** uno, unes, une, unimos, unis, unem **4** unia, unias, uníamos, uníeis, uniam **5** uni, uniste, uniu, unimos, unistes, uniram **6** unirei, unirás, unirá, uniremos, unireis, unirão **7** una, unas, una, unamos, unais, unam **8** unisse, unisses, unisse, uníssemos, unísseis, unissem **9** unir, unires, unir, unirmos, unirdes, unirem **10** unido **11** unira, uniras, unira, uníramos, uníreis, uniram **12** unir, unires, unir, unirmos, unirdes, unirem
valer 3 valho **7** valha *etc*
ver 2 vê **3** vejo, vês, vê, vemos, vedes, veem **4** via *etc* **5** vi, viste, viu, vimos, vistes, viram **7** veja *etc* **8** visse *etc* **9** vir *etc* **10** visto **11** vira
vir 1 vindo, **2** vem **3** venho, vens, vem, vimos, vindes, vêm **4** vinha *etc* **5** vim, vieste, veio, viemos, viestes, vieram **7** venha *etc* **8** viesse *etc* **9** vier *etc* **10** vindo **11** viera *etc*
VIVER 1 vivendo **2** vive, vivei **3** vivo, vives, vive, vivemos, viveis, vivem **4** vivia, vivias, vivia, vivíamos, vivíeis, viviam **5** vivi, viveste, viveu, vivemos, vivestes, viveram **6** viverei, viverás, viverá, viveremos, vivereis, viverão **7** viva, vivas, viva, vivamos, vivais, vivam **8** vivesse, vivesses, vivesse, vivêssemos, vivêsseis, vivessem **9** viver, viveres, viver, vivermos, viverdes, viverem **10** vivido **11** vivera, viveras, vivera, vivêramos, vivêreis, viveram **12** viver, viveres, viver, vivermos, viverdes, viverem

DATAS / DATES

DIAS DA SEMANA / DAYS OF THE WEEK

segunda(-feira)	Monday
terça(-feira)	Tuesday
quarta(-feira)	Wednesday
quinta(-feira)	Thursday
sexta(-feira)	Friday
sábado	Saturday
domingo	Sunday

MESES / MONTHS

janeiro	January
fevereiro	February
março	March
abril	April
maio	May
junho	June
julho	July
agosto	August
setembro	September
outubro	October
novembro	November
dezembro	December

VOCABULÁRIO ÚTIL / USEFUL VOCABULARY

Que dia é hoje?	What day is it today?
Hoje é dia 28.	Today is the 28th.
Quando?	When?
hoje	today
amanhã	tomorrow
ontem	yesterday
hoje de manhã/à tarde	this morning/afternoon
em duas semanas	in two weeks *ou* a fortnight
daqui a uma semana	in a week's time
o mês passado/que vem	last/next month

AS HORAS

THE TIME

QUE HORAS SÃO?

WHAT TIME IS IT?

É meio-dia /meia-noite.

It's noon (BRIT midday)/ midnight.

É uma e quinze.
É uma e um quarto *(PT)*.

It's a quarter past one.
(BRIT It's one fifteen.)

Faltam dez para as duas.
São duas menos dez *(PT)*.

It's ten to two.

São três e meia.

It's three-thirty.
(BRIT It's half past three.)

Faltam vinte para as oito.
São oito menos vinte *(PT)*.

It's twenty to eight.

São nove (horas) da manhã /da noite.

It's nine o'clock in the morning/at night.

NÚMEROS / NUMBERS

NÚMEROS CARDINAIS / CARDINAL NUMBERS

um (uma)	1	one
dois (duas)	2	two
três	3	three
quatro	4	four
cinco	5	five
seis	6	six
sete	7	seven
oito	8	eight
nove	9	nine
dez	10	ten
onze	11	eleven
doze	12	twelve
treze	13	thirteen
catorze	14	fourteen
quinze	15	fifteen
dezesseis *(BR)*, dezasseis *(PT)*	16	sixteen
dezessete *(BR)*, dezassete *(PT)*	17	seventeen
dezoito	18	eighteen
dezenove *(BR)*, dezanove *(PT)*	19	nineteen
vinte	20	twenty
vinte e um (uma)	21	twenty-one
trinta	30	thirty
quarenta	40	forty
cinquenta	50	fifty
sessenta	60	sixty
setenta	70	seventy
oitenta	80	eighty
noventa	90	ninety
cem	100	a hundred
cento e um (uma)	101	a hundred and one
duzentos(-as)	200	two hundred
trezentos(-as)	300	three hundred
quinhentos(-as)	500	five hundred
mil	1.000/1,000	a thousand
um milhão	1.000.000/1,000,000	a million

FRAÇÕES ETC		FRACTIONS ETC
zero vírgula cinco	0,5/0.5	zero point five
três vírgula quatro	3,4/3.4	three point four
dez por cento	10%	ten percent (BRIT per cent)
cem por cento	100%	a hundred percent (BRIT per cent)

NÚMEROS ORDINAIS		ORDINAL NUMBERS
primeiro	1°/1st	first
segundo	2°/2nd	second
terceiro	3°/3rd	third
quarto	4°/4th	fourth
quinto	5°/5th	fifth
sexto	6°/6th	sixth
sétimo	7°/7th	seventh
oitavo	8°/8th	eighth
nono	9°/9th	ninth
décimo	10°/10th	tenth
décimo primeiro	11°/11th	eleventh
vigésimo	20°/20th	twentieth
trigésimo	30°/30th	thirtieth
quadragésimo	40°/40th	fortieth
quinquagésimo	50°/50th	fiftieth
centésimo	100°/100th	hundredth
centésimo primeiro	101°/101st	hundred-and-first
milésimo	1000°/1000th	thousandth

a

A [eɪ] N (*Mus*) lá *m*

KEYWORD

a [eɪ, ə] INDEF ART (*before vowel or silent h*: **an**) **1** um(a); **a book/girl/mirror** um livro/uma menina/um espelho; **an apple** uma maçã; **she's a doctor** ela é médica **2** (*instead of the number "one"*) um(a); **a year ago** há um ano, um ano atrás; **a hundred/thousand** *etc* **pounds** cem/mil *etc* libras **3** (*in expressing ratios, prices etc*): **3 a day/week** 3 por dia/semana; **10 km an hour** 10 km por hora; **30p a kilo** 30p o quilo

aback [ə'bæk] ADV: **to be taken ~** ficar surpreendido, sobressaltar-se
abandon [ə'bændən] VT abandonar ▶ N: **with ~** com desenfreio
abbey ['æbɪ] N abadia, mosteiro
abbreviation N abreviatura
abdomen ['æbdəmən] N abdômen *m*
abduct [æb'dʌkt] VT sequestrar
ability [ə'bɪlɪtɪ] N habilidade *f*, capacidade *f*; (*talent*) talento
able ['eɪbl] ADJ capaz; (*skilled*) hábil, competente; **to be ~ to do sth** poder fazer algo
abnormal [æb'nɔːməl] ADJ anormal
aboard [ə'bɔːd] ADV a bordo ▶ PREP a bordo de
abolish [ə'bɔlɪʃ] VT abolir
aborigine [æbə'rɪdʒɪnɪ] N aborígene *m/f*
abort [ə'bɔːt] VT (*Med*) abortar; (*plan*) cancelar; **abortion** N aborto; **to have an abortion** fazer um aborto

KEYWORD

about [ə'baut] ADV **1** (*approximately*) aproximadamente; **it takes about 10 hours** leva mais ou menos 10 horas; **it's just about finished** está quase terminado **2** (*referring to place*) por toda parte, por todo lado; **to run/walk** *etc* **about** correr/andar *etc* por todos os lados **3**: **to be about to do sth** estar a ponto de fazer algo
▶ PREP **1** (*relating to*) acerca de, sobre; **what is it about?** do que se trata?, é sobre o quê?; **what** *or* **how about doing this?** que tal se fizermos isso? **2** (*place*) em redor de, por

above [ə'bʌv] ADV em *or* por cima, acima ▶ PREP acima de, por cima de; **costing ~ £10** que custa mais de £10; **~ all** sobretudo
abroad [ə'brɔːd] ADV (*be abroad*) no estrangeiro; (*go abroad*) ao estrangeiro

abrupt ['brʌpt] ADJ (*sudden*) brusco; (*curt*) ríspido
abscess ['æbsɪs] N abscesso (BR), abcesso (PT)
absence ['æbsəns] N ausência
absent ['æbsənt] ADJ ausente; **absent-minded** ADJ distraído
absolute ['æbsəlu:t] ADJ absoluto; **absolutely** [æbsə'lu:tlɪ] ADV absolutamente
absorb [əb'zɔ:b] VT absorver; (*group, business*) incorporar; (*changes*) assimilar; (*information*) digerir; **absorbent cotton** (US) N algodão *m* hidrófilo
abstain [əb'steɪn] VI: **to ~ (from)** abster-se (de)
abstract ['æbstrækt] ADJ abstrato
absurd [əb'sə:d] ADJ absurdo
abuse [*n* ə'bju:s, *vt* ə'bju:z] N (*insults*) insultos *mpl*; (*misuse*) abuso; (*ill-treatment*) maus-tratos *mpl* ▶ VT insultar; maltratar; abusar; **abusive** [ə'bju:sɪv] ADJ ofensivo
abysmal [ə'bɪzməl] ADJ (*ignorance*) profundo, total; (*very bad*) péssimo
academic [ækə'dɛmɪk] ADJ acadêmico; (*pej: issue*) teórico ▶ N universitário(-a)
academy [ə'kædəmɪ] N (*learned body*) academia; **~ of music** conservatório
accelerate [æk'sɛləreɪt] VT, VI acelerar; **accelerator** N acelerador *m*
accent ['æksɛnt] N (*written*) acento; (*pronunciation*) sotaque *m*; (*fig: emphasis*) ênfase *f*
accept [ək'sɛpt] VT aceitar; (*responsibility*) assumir; **acceptable** ADJ (*offer*) bem-vindo; (*risk*) aceitável; **acceptance** N aceitação *f*
access ['æksɛs] N acesso; **accessible** [æk'sɛsəbl] ADJ acessível; (*available*) disponível
accessory [æk'sɛsərɪ] N acessório; (*Jur*): **~ to** cúmplice *m/f* de
accident ['æksɪdənt] N acidente *m*; (*chance*) casualidade *f*; **by ~** (*unintentionally*) sem querer; (*by coincidence*) por acaso; **accidental** [æksɪ'dɛntl] ADJ acidental; **accidentally** [æksɪ'dɛntəlɪ] ADV sem querer; **Accident and Emergency Department** N (BRIT) pronto-socorro
acclaim [ə'kleɪm] N aclamação *f*
accommodate [ə'kɔmədeɪt] VT alojar; (*subj: car, hotel, etc*) acomodar; (*oblige, help*) comprazer a; **accommodation** [əkɔmə'deɪʃən] N, (US) **accomodations** NPL alojamento
accompany [ə'kʌmpənɪ] VT acompanhar
accomplice [ə'kʌmplɪs] N cúmplice *m/f*
accomplish [ə'kʌmplɪʃ] VT (*task*) concluir; (*goal*) alcançar; **accomplishment** N realização *f*
accord [ə'kɔ:d] N tratado ▶ VT conceder; **of his own ~** por sua iniciativa; **accordance** [ə'kɔ:dəns] N: **in accordance with** de acordo com; **according** PREP: **according to** segundo; (*in accordance with*) conforme; **accordingly** ADV por conseguinte; (*appropriately*) do modo devido
account [ə'kaunt] N conta; (*report*) relato; **accounts** NPL (*books, department*) contabilidade *f*; **of no ~** sem importância; **on ~** por conta; **on no ~** de modo nenhum; **on ~ of** por causa de; **to take into ~, take ~ of** levar em conta; **account for** VT

FUS (*explain*) explicar; (*represent*) representar; **accountant** N contador(a) *m/f* (BR), contabilista *m/f* (PT); **account number** N número de conta
accumulate [əˈkjuːmjuleɪt] VT acumular ▶ VI acumular-se
accuracy [ˈækjurəsɪ] N exatidão *f*, precisão *f*
accurate [ˈækjurɪt] ADJ (*description*) correto; (*person, device*) preciso; **accurately** ADV com precisão
accusation [ækjuˈzeɪʃən] N acusação *f*; (*instance*) incriminação *f*
accuse [əˈkjuːz] VT: **to ~ sb (of sth)** acusar alguém (de algo); **accused** N: **the accused** o/a acusado/a
ace [eɪs] N ás *m*
ache [eɪk] N dor *f* ▶ VI (*yearn*): **to ~ to do sth** ansiar por fazer algo; **my head ~s** dói-me a cabeça
achieve [əˈtʃiːv] VT alcançar; (*victory, success*) obter; **achievement** N realização *f*; (*success*) proeza
acid [ˈæsɪd] ADJ, N ácido
acknowledge [əkˈnɔlɪdʒ] VT (*fact*) reconhecer; (*also*: **~ receipt of**) acusar o recebimento de (BR) *or* a receção de (PT); **acknowledgement** N notificação *f* de recebimento
acne [ˈæknɪ] N acne *f*
acorn [ˈeɪkɔːn] N bolota
acoustic [əˈkuːstɪk] ADJ acústico
acquire [əˈkwaɪəʳ] VT adquirir
acquit [əˈkwɪt] VT absolver; **to ~ o.s. well** desempenhar-se bem
acre [ˈeɪkəʳ] N acre *m* (= $4047m^2$)
across [əˈkrɔs] PREP (*on the other side of*) no outro lado de; (*crosswise*) através de ▶ ADV: **to walk ~ (the road)** atravessar (a rua); **the lake is 12 km ~** o lago tem 12 km de largura; **~ from** em frente de
acrylic [əˈkrɪlɪk] ADJ acrílico ▶ N acrílico
act [ækt] N ação *f*; (*Theatre*) ato; (*in show*) número; (*Jur*) lei *f* ▶ VI tomar ação; (*behave, have effect*) agir; (*Theatre*) representar; (*pretend*) fingir ▶ VT (*part*) representar; **in the ~ of** no ato de; **to ~ as** servir de; **acting** ADJ interino ▶ N: **to do some acting** fazer teatro
action [ˈækʃən] N ação *f*; (*Mil*) batalha, combate *m*; (*Jur*) ação judicial; **out of ~** (*person*) fora de combate; (*thing*) com defeito; **to take ~** tomar atitude; **action replay** N (*TV*) replay *m*
activate [ˈæktɪveɪt] VT acionar
active [ˈæktɪv] ADJ ativo; (*volcano*) em atividade; **actively** ADV ativamente; **activity** [ækˈtɪvɪtɪ] N atividade *f*
actor [ˈæktəʳ] N ator *m*
actress [ˈæktrɪs] N atriz *f*
actual [ˈæktjuəl] ADJ real; **actually** ADV realmente; (*in fact*) na verdade; (*even*) mesmo
acute [əˈkjuːt] ADJ agudo; (*person*) perspicaz
ad [æd] N ABBR = **advertisement**
A.D. ADV ABBR (= *Anno Domini*) d.C.
adamant [ˈædəmənt] ADJ inflexível
adapt [əˈdæpt] VT adaptar ▶ VI: **to ~ (to)** adaptar-se (a)
add [æd] VT acrescentar; (*figures*: *also*: **~ up**) somar ▶ VI: **to ~ to** aumentar
addict [ˈædɪkt] N viciado(-a); **drug ~** toxicômano(-a); **addicted** [əˈdɪktɪd] ADJ: **to be/become addicted to** ser/ficar viciado em;

addiction N dependência; **addictive** ADJ que causa dependência
addition [ə'dɪʃən] N adição *f*; (*thing added*) acréscimo; **in ~** além disso; **in ~ to** além de; **additional** ADJ adicional
additive ['ædɪtɪv] N aditivo
address [ə'drɛs] N endereço; (*speech*) discurso ▸ VT (*letter*) endereçar; (*speak to*) dirigir-se a, dirigir a palavra a; **to ~ (o.s. to)** enfocar
adequate ['ædɪkwɪt] ADJ (*enough*) suficiente; (*satisfactory*) satisfatório
adhere [əd'hɪəʳ] VI: **to ~ to** aderir a; (*abide by*) ater-se a
adhesive [əd'hi:zɪv] N adesivo
adjective ['ædʒɛktɪv] N adjetivo
adjoining [ə'dʒɔɪnɪŋ] ADJ adjacente
adjourn [ə'dʒə:n] VT (*session*) suspender ▸ VI encerrar a sessão; (*go*) deslocar-se
adjust [ə'dʒʌst] VT (*change*) ajustar; (*clothes*) arrumar; (*machine*) regular ▸ VI: **to ~ (to)** adaptar-se (a); **adjustment** N ajuste *m*; (*of engine*) regulagem *f*; (*of prices, wages*) reajuste *m*; (*of person*) adaptação *f*
administer [əd'mɪnɪstəʳ] VT administrar; (*justice*) aplicar; (*drug*) ministrar; **administration** [ədmɪnɪs'treɪʃən] N administração *f*; (*US: government*) governo; **administrative** [əd'mɪnɪstrətɪv] ADJ administrativo
admiral ['ædmərəl] N almirante *m*
admire [əd'maɪəʳ] VT (*respect*) respeitar; (*appreciate*) admirar
admission [əd'mɪʃən] N (*admittance*) entrada; (*fee*) ingresso; (*confession*) confissão *f*
admit [əd'mɪt] VT admitir; (*accept*) aceitar; (*confess*) confessar; **admit to** VT FUS confessar; **admittance** N entrada; **admittedly** ADV evidentemente
adolescent [ædəu'lɛsnt] ADJ, N adolescente *m/f*
adopt [ə'dɔpt] VT adotar; **adopted** ADJ adotivo; **adoption** N adoção *f*
adore [ə'dɔ:ʳ] VT adorar
Adriatic [eɪdrɪ'ætɪk], **Adriatic Sea** N (mar *m*) Adriático
adrift [ə'drɪft] ADV à deriva
ADSL N ABBR (= *asymmetric digital subscriber line*) ADSL *m*
adult ['ædʌlt] N adulto(-a) ▸ ADJ adulto; (*literature, education*) para adultos
adultery [ə'dʌltərɪ] N adultério
advance [əd'vɑ:ns] N avanço; (*money*) adiantamento ▸ ADJ antecipado ▸ VT (*money*) adiantar ▸ VI (*move forward*) avançar; (*progress*) progredir; **in ~** com antecedência; **to make ~s to sb** fazer propostas a alguém; **advanced** ADJ adiantado
advantage [əd'vɑ:ntɪdʒ] N vantagem *f*; (*supremacy*) supremacia; vantagem *f*; **to take ~ of** aproveitar-se de
adventure [əd'vɛntʃəʳ] N aventura
adverb ['ædvə:b] N advérbio
adverse ['ædvə:s] ADJ (*effect*) contrário; (*weather, publicity*) desfavorável
advert ['ædvə:t] N ABBR = **advertisement**
advertise ['ædvətaɪz] VI anunciar ▸ VT (*event, job*) anunciar; (*product*) fazer a propaganda de; **to ~ for** (*staff*) procurar; **advertisement** [əd'və:tɪsmənt] N (*classified*) anúncio; (*display, TV*) propaganda, anúncio; **advertising** N publicidade *f*

advice [əd'vaɪs] N conselhos *mpl*; (*notification*) aviso; **piece of ~** conselho; **to take legal ~** consultar um advogado
advise [əd'vaɪz] VT aconselhar; (*inform*): **to ~ sb of sth** avisar alguém de algo; **to ~ sb against sth** desaconselhar algo a alguém; **to ~ sb against doing sth** aconselhar alguém a não fazer algo; **advisory** ADJ consultivo; **in an advisory capacity** na qualidade de assessor(a) *or* consultor(a)
advocate [*vt* 'ædvəkeɪt, *n* 'ædvəkɪt] VT defender; (*recommend*) advogar ▶ N advogado(-a); (*supporter*) defensor(a) *m/f*
Aegean [i:'dʒi:ən] N: **the ~ (Sea)** o (mar) Egeu
aerial ['ɛərɪəl] N antena ▶ ADJ aéreo
aerobics [ɛə'rəubɪks] N ginástica
aeroplane ['ɛərəpleɪn] (BRIT) N avião *m*
aerosol ['ɛərəsɔl] N aerossol *m*
affair [ə'fɛə^r] N (*matter*) assunto; (*business*) negócio; (*question*) questão *f*; (*also*: **love ~**) caso
affect [ə'fɛkt] VT afetar; (*move*) comover; **affected** ADJ afetado
affection [ə'fɛkʃən] N afeto, afeição *f*; **affectionate** ADJ afetuoso
afflict [ə'flɪkt] VT afligir
affluent ['æfluənt] ADJ rico; **the ~ society** a sociedade de abundância
afford [ə'fɔ:d] VT (*provide*) fornecer; (*goods etc*) ter dinheiro suficiente para; (*permit o.s.*): **I can't ~ the time** não tenho tempo; **affordable** ADJ acessível
afraid [ə'freɪd] ADJ assustado; **to be ~ of/to** ter medo de; **I am ~ that** lamento que; **I'm ~ so/not** receio que sim/não
Africa ['æfrɪkə] N África; **African** ADJ, N africano(-a)
after ['ɑ:ftə^r] PREP depois de ▶ ADV depois ▶ CONJ depois que; **a quarter ~ two** (US) duas e quinze; **what are you ~?** o que você quer?; **who are you ~?** quem procura?; **~ having done** tendo feito; **to ask ~ sb** perguntar por alguém; **~ all** afinal (de contas); **~ you!** passe primeiro!; **aftermath** N consequências *fpl*; **afternoon** N tarde *f*; **after-shave, after-shave lotion** N loção *f* após-barba; **aftersun** ['ɑ:ftəsʌn] N loção *f* pós-sol; **afterwards** ADV depois
again [ə'gɛn] ADV (*once more*) outra vez; (*repeatedly*) de novo; **to do sth ~** voltar a fazer algo; **~ and ~** repetidas vezes
against [ə'gɛnst] PREP contra; (*compared to*) em contraste com
age [eɪdʒ] N idade *f*; (*period*) época ▶ VT, VI envelhecer; **he's 20 years of ~** ele tem 20 anos de idade; **to come of ~** atingir a maioridade; **it's been ~s since I saw him** faz muito tempo que eu não o vejo; **~d 10** de 10 anos de idade; **aged** ['eɪdʒɪd] ADJ idoso ▶ NPL: **the aged** os idosos; **age group** N faixa etária; **age limit** N idade *f* mínima/máxima
agency ['eɪdʒənsɪ] N agência; (*government body*) órgão *m*
agenda [ə'dʒɛndə] N ordem *f* do dia
agent ['eɪdʒənt] N agente *m/f*
aggravate ['ægrəveɪt] VT agravar; (*annoy*) irritar

aggressive [əˈgrɛsɪv] ADJ agressivo
AGM N ABBR (= *annual general meeting*) AGO *f*
ago [əˈgəu] ADV: **2 days ~** há 2 dias (atrás); **not long ~** há pouco tempo; **how long ~?** há quanto tempo?
agony [ˈægənɪ] N (*pain*) dor *f*; **to be in ~** sofrer dores terríveis
agree [əˈgriː] VT combinar ▸VI (*correspond*) corresponder; **to ~ (with)** concordar (com); **to ~ to do** aceitar fazer; **to ~ to sth** consentir algo; **to ~ that** concordar *or* admitir que; **agreeable** ADJ agradável; (*willing*) disposto; **agreed** ADJ combinado; **agreement** N acordo; (*Comm*) contrato; **in agreement** de acordo
agricultural [ægrɪˈkʌltʃərəl] ADJ (*of crops*) agrícola; (*of crops and cattle*) agropecuário
agriculture [ˈægrɪkʌltʃəʳ] N (*of crops*) agricultura; (*of crops and cattle*) agropecuária
ahead [əˈhɛd] ADV adiante; **go right** *or* **straight ~** siga em frente; **go ~!** (*fig*) vá em frente!; **~ of** na frente de
aid [eɪd] N ajuda ▸VT ajudar; **in ~ of** em benefício de; **to ~ and abet** (*Jur*) ser cúmplice de
AIDS [eɪdz] N ABBR (= *acquired immune deficiency syndrome*) AIDS *f* (BR), SIDA *f* (PT)
aim [eɪm] VT: **to ~ sth (at)** apontar algo (para); (*missile, remark*) dirigir algo (a) ▸VI (*also*: **take ~**) apontar ▸N (*skill*) pontaria; (*objective*) objetivo; **to ~ at** mirar; **to ~ to do** pretender fazer
ain't [eɪnt] (*inf*) = **am not; aren't; isn't**
air [ɛəʳ] N ar *m*; (*appearance*) aparência, aspecto ▸VT arejar; (*grievances, ideas*) discutir ▸CPD aéreo; **to throw sth into the ~** jogar algo para cima; **by ~** (*travel*) de avião; **to be on the ~** (*Radio, TV*) estar no ar; **air bed** [ˈɛəbɛd] (BRIT) N colchão *m* de ar; **air conditioning** N ar-condicionado; **aircraft** N INV aeronave *f*; **airfield** N campo de aviação; **Air Force** N Força Aérea, Aeronáutica; **air hostess** (BRIT) N aeromoça (BR), hospedeira (PT); **airline** N linha aérea; **airliner** N avião *m* de passageiros; **airmail** N: **by airmail** por via aérea; **airplane** (US) N avião *m*; **airport** N aeroporto; **airsick** ADJ: **to be airsick** enjoar-se (no avião); **airtight** ADJ hermético; **airy** ADJ (*room*) arejado; (*manner*) leviano
aisle [aɪl] N (*of church*) nave *f*; (*of theatre etc*) corredor *m*
ajar [əˈdʒɑːʳ] ADJ entreaberto
alarm [əˈlɑːm] N alarme *m*; (*anxiety*) inquietação *f* ▸VT alarmar; **alarm clock** N despertador *m*
album [ˈælbəm] N (*for stamps etc*) álbum *m*; (*record*) elepê *m*
alcohol [ˈælkəhɔl] N álcool *m*; **alcohol-free** ADJ sem álcool; **alcoholic** [ælkəˈhɔlɪk] ADJ alcoólico ▸N alcoólatra *m/f*
ale [eɪl] N cerveja
alert [əˈləːt] ADJ atento; (*to danger, opportunity*) alerta ▸N alerta *m* ▸VT: **to ~ sb (to sth)** alertar alguém (de *or* sobre algo); **to be on the ~** estar alerta; (*Mil*) ficar de prontidão
Algarve [ælˈgɑːv] N: **the ~** o Algarve
algebra [ˈældʒɪbrə] N álgebra
Algeria [ælˈdʒɪərɪə] N Argélia
alias [ˈeɪlɪəs] ADV também chamado ▸N (*of criminal*) alcunha; (*of writer*) pseudônimo

alibi ['ælɪbaɪ] N álibi *m*
alien ['eɪlɪən] N estrangeiro(-a); (*from space*) alienígena *m/f* ▶ ADJ: **~ to** alheio a
alight [ə'laɪt] ADJ em chamas; (*eyes*) aceso; (*expression*) intento ▶ VI (*passenger*) descer (de um veículo); (*bird*) pousar
alike [ə'laɪk] ADJ semelhante ▶ ADV similamente, igualmente; **to look ~** parecer-se
alive [ə'laɪv] ADJ vivo; (*lively*) alegre

KEYWORD

all [ɔ:l] ADJ (*singular*) todo(-a); (*plural*) todos(-as); **all day/night** o dia inteiro/a noite inteira; **all five came** todos os cinco vieram; **all the books/food** todos os livros/toda a comida
▶ PRON **1** tudo; **all of us/the boys went** todos nós fomos/todos os meninos foram; **is that all?** é só isso?; (*in shop*) mais alguma coisa?
2 (*in phrases*): **above all** sobretudo; **after all** afinal (de contas); **not at all** (*in answer to question*) em absoluto, absolutamente não; **I'm not at all tired** não estou nada cansado; **anything at all will do** qualquer coisa serve; **all in all** ao todo
▶ ADV todo, completamente; **all alone** completamente só; **it's not as hard as all that** não é tão difícil assim; **all the more** ainda mais; **all the better** tanto melhor, melhor ainda; **all but** quase; **the score is 2 all** o jogo está empatado em 2 a 2

allegiance [ə'li:dʒəns] N lealdade *f*
allergic [ə'lə:dʒɪk] ADJ: **~ (to)** alérgico (a)
allergy ['ælədʒɪ] N alergia
alleviate [ə'li:vɪeɪt] VT (*pain*) aliviar; (*difficulty*) minorar
alley ['ælɪ] N viela
alliance [ə'laɪəns] N aliança
all-in (BRIT) ADJ, ADV (*charge*) tudo incluído
allocate ['æləkeɪt] VT destinar
allot [ə'lɔt] VT: **to ~ to** designar para
all-out ADJ (*effort etc*) máximo ▶ ADV: **all out** com toda a força
allow [ə'lau] VT permitir; (*claim, goal*) admitir; (*sum, time estimated*) calcular; (*concede*): **to ~ that** reconhecer que; **to ~ sb to do** permitir a alguém fazer; **allow for** VT FUS levar em conta; **allowance** [ə'lauəns] N ajuda de custo; (*welfare, payment*) pensão *f*, auxílio; (*Tax*) abatimento; **to make allowances for** levar em consideração
all right ADV (*well*) bem; (*correctly*) corretamente; (*as answer*) está bem!
ally [*n* 'ælaɪ, *vt* ə'laɪ] N aliado ▶ VT: **to ~ o.s. with** aliar-se com
almighty [ɔ:l'maɪtɪ] ADJ onipotente; (*row etc*) maior
almond ['ɑ:mənd] N amêndoa
almost ['ɔ:lməust] ADV quase
alone [ə'ləun] ADJ só, sozinho ▶ ADV só, somente; **to leave sb ~** deixar alguém em paz; **to leave sth ~** não tocar em algo; **let ~ ...** sem falar em ...
along [ə'lɔŋ] PREP por, ao longo de ▶ ADV: **is he coming ~?** ele vem conosco?; **he was hopping/limping ~** ele ia pulando/coxeando; **~ with** junto com; **all ~** o tempo tudo; **alongside** PREP ao lado de ▶ ADV encostado

aloof [ə'lu:f] ADJ afastado, altivo ▶ ADV: **to stand ~** afastar-se
aloud [ə'laud] ADV em voz alta
alphabet ['ælfəbɛt] N alfabeto
Alps [ælps] NPL: **the ~** os Alpes
already [ɔ:l'rɛdɪ] ADV já
alright ['ɔ:l'raɪt] (BRIT) ADV = **all right**
also ['ɔ:lsəu] ADV também; (*moreover*) além disso
altar ['ɔltə^r] N altar *m*
alter ['ɔltə^r] VT alterar ▶ VI modificar-se
alternate [*adj* ɔl'tə:nɪt, *vi* 'ɔltə:neɪt] ADJ alternado; (*US: alternative*) alternativo ▶ VI: **to ~ with** alternar-se (com)
alternative [ɔl'tə:nətɪv] ADJ alternativo ▶ N alternativa; **alternatively** ADV: **alternatively one could ...** por outro lado se podia ...
although [ɔ:l'ðəu] CONJ embora; (*given that*) se bem que
altitude ['æltɪtju:d] N altitude *f*
altogether [ɔ:ltə'gɛðə^r] ADV totalmente; (*on the whole*) no total
aluminium [ælju'mɪnɪəm] (BRIT) N alumínio
aluminum [ə'lu:mɪnəm] (US) N = **aluminium**
always ['ɔ:lweɪz] ADV sempre
Alzheimer's ['æltshaɪməz], **Alzheimer's disease** N mal *m* de Alzheimer
am [æm] VB *see* **be**
a.m. ADV ABBR (= *ante meridiem*) da manhã
amateur ['æmətə^r] ADJ, N amador(a) *m/f*
amaze [ə'meɪz] VT pasmar; **to be ~d (at)** espantar-se (de *or* com); **amazement** N pasmo, espanto; **amazing** ADJ surpreendente; (*fantastic*) fantástico
Amazon ['æməzən] N Amazonas *m*
ambassador [æm'bæsədə^r] N embaixador/embaixatriz *m/f*
amber ['æmbə^r] N âmbar *m*; **at ~** (BRIT *Aut*) em amarelo
ambiguous [æm'bɪgjuəs] ADJ ambíguo
ambition [æm'bɪʃən] N ambição *f*; **ambitious** ADJ ambicioso
ambulance ['æmbjuləns] N ambulância
ambush ['æmbuʃ] N emboscada ▶ VT emboscar
amend [ə'mɛnd] VT emendar; **to make ~s (for)** compensar
America [ə'mɛrɪkə] N (*continent*) América; (*USA*) Estados Unidos *mpl*; **American** ADJ americano; (*from USA*) norte-americano, estadunidense ▶ N americano(-a); (*from USA*) norte-americano(-a)
amicable ['æmɪkəbl] ADJ amigável
ammunition [æmju'nɪʃən] N munição *f*
among [ə'mʌŋ], **amongst** [ə'mʌŋst] PREP entre, no meio de
amount [ə'maunt] N quantidade *f*; (*of money etc*) quantia ▶ VI: **to ~ to** (*total*) montar a; (*be same as*) equivaler a, significar
amp ['æmp], **ampere** ['æmpɛə^r] N ampère *m*
ample ['æmpl] ADJ amplo; (*abundant*) abundante; (*enough*) suficiente
amplifier ['æmplɪfaɪə^r] N amplificador *m*
amuse [ə'mju:z] VT divertir; (*distract*) distrair; **amusement** N diversão *f*; (*pleasure*) divertimento; (*pastime*) passatempo; **amusement park** N parque *m* de diversões
an [æn, ən, n] INDEF ART *see* **a**

anaesthetic [ænɪs'θɛtɪk], (US) **anesthetic** N anestésico
analyse ['ænəlaɪz], (US) **analyze** VT analisar; **analysis** [ə'næləsɪs] (*pl* **analyses**) N análise *f*; **analyst** ['ænəlɪst] N analista *m/f*; (*psychoanalyst*) psicanalista *m/f*
analyze ['ænəlaɪz] (US) VT = **analyse**
anarchy ['ænəkɪ] N anarquia
anatomy [ə'nætəmɪ] N anatomia
ancestor ['ænsɪstə^r] N antepassado
anchor ['æŋkə^r] N âncora ▸ VI (*also*: **to drop ~**) ancorar, fundear ▸ VT (*fig*): **to ~ sth to** firmar algo em; **to weigh ~** levantar âncoras
anchovy ['æntʃəvɪ] N enchova
ancient ['eɪnʃənt] ADJ antigo; (*person, car*) velho
and [ænd] CONJ e; **~ so on** e assim por diante; **try ~ come** tente vir; **he talked ~ talked** ele falou sem parar; **better ~ better** cada vez melhor
Andes ['ændi:z] NPL: **the ~** os Andes
angel ['eɪndʒəl] N anjo
anger ['æŋgə^r] N raiva
angina [æn'dʒaɪnə] N angina (de peito)
angle ['æŋgl] N ângulo; (*viewpoint*): **from their ~** do ponto de vista deles
Anglican ['æŋglɪkən] ADJ, N anglicano(-a)
angling ['æŋglɪŋ] N pesca à vara (BR) *or* à linha (PT)
angry ['æŋgrɪ] ADJ zangado; **to be ~ with sb/at sth** estar zangado com alguém/algo; **to get ~** zangar-se
anguish ['æŋgwɪʃ] N (*physical*) dor *f*, sofrimento; (*mental*) angústia
animal ['ænɪməl] N animal *m*, bicho ▸ ADJ animal
aniseed ['ænɪsi:d] N erva-doce *f*, anis *f*
ankle ['æŋkl] N tornozelo
annex [*n* 'ænɛks, *vt* ə'nɛks] N (BRIT: *building*) anexo ▸ VT anexar
anniversary [ænɪ'və:sərɪ] N aniversário
announce [ə'nauns] VT anunciar; **announcement** N anúncio; (*official*) comunicação *f*; (*in letter etc*) aviso; **announcer** N (*Radio, TV*) locutor(a) *m/f*
annoy [ə'nɔɪ] VT aborrecer; **don't get ~ed!** não se aborreça!; **annoying** ADJ irritante
annual ['ænjuəl] ADJ anual ▸ N (*Bot*) anual *f*; (*book*) anuário
anonymous [ə'nɔnɪməs] ADJ anônimo
anorak ['ænəræk] N anoraque *m* (BR), anorak *m* (PT)
another [ə'nʌðə^r] ADJ: **~ book** (*one more*) outro livro, mais um livro; (*a different one*) um outro livro, um livro diferente ▸ PRON outro; *see also* **one**
answer ['ɑ:nsə^r] N resposta; (*to problem*) solução *f* ▸ VI responder ▸ VT (*reply to*) responder a; (*problem*) resolver; **in ~ to your letter** em resposta *or* respondendo à sua carta; **to ~ the phone** atender o telefone; **to ~ the bell** *or* **the door** atender à porta; **answer back** VI replicar, retrucar; **answer for** VT FUS responder por, responsabilizar-se por; **answer to** VT FUS (*description*) corresponder a; **answering machine** N secretária eletrônica; **answerphone** N (*esp* BRIT) secretária eletrônica

ant [ænt] N formiga
Antarctic [ænt'ɑ:ktɪk] N: **the ~** o Antártico
antenatal ['æntɪ'neɪtl] ADJ pré-natal
anthem ['ænθəm] N: **national ~** hino nacional
anticipate [æn'tɪsɪpeɪt] VT prever; (*expect*) esperar; (*look forward to*) aguardar, esperar; **anticipation** N expectativa; (*eagerness*) entusiasmo
anticlimax [æntɪ'klaɪmæks] N desapontamento
anticlockwise [æntɪ'klɔkwaɪz] (BRIT) ADV em sentido anti-horário
antics ['æntɪks] NPL bobices *fpl*; (*of child*) travessuras *fpl*
antifreeze ['æntɪfri:z] N anticongelante *m*
antihistamine [æntɪ'hɪstəmi:n] N anti-histamínico
antique [æn'ti:k] N antiguidade *f* ▸ ADJ antigo; **antique shop** N loja de antiguidades
antiseptic [æntɪ'sɛptɪk] N antisséptico
antisocial [æntɪ'səuʃəl] ADJ antissocial
antivirus ['æntɪ'vaɪərəs] ADJ antivírus *m inv*; **~ software** software antivírus
antlers ['æntləz] NPL esgalhos *mpl*, chifres *mpl*
anxiety [æŋ'zaɪətɪ] N (*worry*) inquietude *f*; (*eagerness*) ânsia; (*Med*) ansiedade *f*; **~ to do** ânsia de fazer
anxious ['æŋkʃəs] ADJ (*worried*) preocupado; (*worrying*) angustiante; (*keen*) ansioso; **~ to do/for sth** ansioso para fazer/por algo; **to be ~ that** desejar que

KEYWORD

any ['ɛnɪ] ADJ **1** (*in questions etc*) algum(a); **have you any butter/children?** você tem manteiga/filhos?; **if there are any tickets left** se houver alguns bilhetes sobrando
2 (*with negative*) nenhum(a); **I haven't any money/books** não tenho dinheiro/livros
3 (*no matter which*) qualquer; **choose any book you like** escolha qualquer livro que quiser
4 (*in phrases*): **in any case** em todo o caso; **any day now** qualquer dia desses; **at any moment** a qualquer momento; **at any rate** de qualquer modo; **any time** a qualquer momento; (*whenever*) quando quer que seja
▸ PRON **1** (*in questions etc*) algum(a); **have you got any?** tem algum?
2 (*with negative*) nenhum(a); **I haven't any (of them)** não tenho nenhum (deles)
3 (*no matter which one(s)*): **take any of those books (you like)** leve qualquer um desses livros (que você quiser)
▸ ADV **1** (*in questions etc*) algo; **do you want any more soup/sandwiches?** quer mais sopa/sanduíches?; **are you feeling any better?** você está se sentindo melhor?
2 (*with negative*) nada; **I can't hear him any more** não consigo mais ouvi-lo

anybody ['ɛnɪbɔdɪ] PRON qualquer um, qualquer pessoa; (*in interrogative sentences*) alguém
anyhow ['ɛnɪhau] ADV (*at any rate*) de qualquer modo, de qualquer

maneira; **I shall go ~** eu irei de qualquer jeito; **do it ~ you like** faça do jeito que você quiser; **she leaves things just ~** ela deixa as coisas de qualquer maneira

anyone ['ɛnɪwʌn] PRON (*in questions etc*) alguém; (*with negative*) ninguém; (*no matter who*) quem quer que seja; **can you see ~?** você pode ver alguém?; **if ~ should phone ...** se alguém telefonar; **~ could do it** qualquer um(a) poderia fazer isso

anything ['ɛnɪθɪŋ] PRON (*in questions etc*) alguma coisa; (*with negative*) nada; (*no matter what*) qualquer coisa; **can you see ~?** você pode ver alguma coisa?

anyway ['ɛnɪweɪ] ADV (*at any rate*) de qualquer modo; (*besides*) além disso; **I shall go ~** eu irei de qualquer jeito

anywhere ['ɛnɪwɛəʳ] ADV (*in questions etc*) em algum lugar; (*with negative*) em parte nenhuma; (*no matter where*) não importa onde, onde quer que seja; **can you see him ~?** você pode vê-lo em algum lugar?; **I can't see him ~** não o vejo em parte nenhuma; **~ in the world** em qualquer lugar do mundo

apart [ə'pɑːt] ADV à parte, à distância; (*separately*) separado; **10 miles ~** a uma distância de 10 milhas um do outro; **to take ~** desmontar; **~ from** além de, à parte de

apartment [ə'pɑːtmənt] (US) N apartamento

ape [eɪp] N macaco ▸VT macaquear, imitar

aperitif [ə'pɛrɪtɪv] N aperitivo

aperture ['æpətʃjuəʳ] N orifício; (*Phot*) abertura

APEX ['eɪpɛks] N (= *advance passenger excursion*) *tarifa aérea com desconto por compra antecipada*

apologize [ə'pɔlədʒaɪz] VI: **to ~ (for sth to sb)** desculpar-se *or* pedir desculpas (por *or* de algo a alguém); **apology** N desculpas *fpl*

apostrophe [ə'pɔstrəfɪ] N apóstrofo

app [æp] (*inf*) N ABBR (= *application program*) aplicativo (BR), aplicação *f* (PT)

appalling [ə'pɔːlɪŋ] ADJ (*shocking*) chocante; (*awful*) terrível

apparatus [æpə'reɪtəs] N aparelho; (*in gym*) aparelhos *mpl*; (*organization*) aparato

apparent [ə'pærənt] ADJ aparente; (*obvious*) claro, patente; **apparently** ADV aparentemente, pelo(s) visto(s)

appeal [ə'piːl] VI (*Jur*) apelar, recorrer ▸N (*Jur*) recurso, apelação *f*; (*request*) pedido; (*plea*) súplica; (*charm*) atração *f*; **to ~ (to sb) for** suplicar (a alguém); **to ~ to** atrair; **to ~ to sb for mercy** pedir misericórdia a alguém; **appealing** ADJ atraente

appear [ə'pɪəʳ] VI aparecer; (*Jur*) apresentar-se, comparecer; (*publication*) ser publicado; (*seem*) parecer; **to ~ in "Hamlet"** trabalhar em "Hamlet"; **to ~ on TV** (*person, news item*) sair na televisão; (*programme*) passar na televisão; **appearance** N aparecimento; (*presence*) comparecimento; (*look, aspect*) aparência

appendicitis [əpɛndɪ'saɪtɪs] N apendicite *f*

appendix [ə'pɛndɪks] (*pl* **appendices**) N apêndice *m*

appetite ['æpɪtaɪt] N apetite *m*; (*fig*) desejo
appetizer ['æpɪtaɪzəʳ] N (*food*) tira-gosto; (*drink*) aperitivo
applaud [ə'plɔːd] VI aplaudir ▶ VT aplaudir; (*praise*) admirar;
applause N aplausos *mpl*
apple ['æpl] N maçã *f*
appliance [ə'plaɪəns] N aparelho; **electrical** *or* **domestic ~s** eletrodomésticos *mpl*
applicant ['æplɪkənt] N: **~ (for)** (*for post*) candidato(-a) (a); (*Admin: for benefit etc*) requerente *m/f* (de)
application [æplɪ'keɪʃən] N aplicação *f*; (*for a job, a grant etc*) candidatura, requerimento; (*hard work*) empenho; **application form** N (formulário de) requerimento
apply [ə'plaɪ] VT (*paint etc*) usar; (*law etc*) pôr em prática ▶ VI: **to ~ to** (*be suitable for*) ser aplicável a; (*be relevant to*) valer para; (*ask*) pedir; **to ~ for** (*permit, grant*) solicitar, pedir; (*job*) candidatar-se a; **to ~ o.s. to** aplicar-se a, dedicar-se a
appoint [ə'pɔɪnt] VT (*to post*) nomear; **appointment** N (*engagement*) encontro, compromisso; (*at doctor's etc*) hora marcada; (*act*) nomeação *f*; (*post*) cargo; **to make an appointment (with sb)** marcar um encontro (com alguém)
appraisal [ə'preɪzl] N avaliação *f*
appreciate [ə'priːʃɪeɪt] VT (*like*) apreciar, estimar; (*be grateful for*) agradecer; (*understand*) compreender ▶ VI (*Comm*) valorizar-se; **appreciation** N apreciação *f*, estima; (*understanding*) compreensão *f*; (*gratitude*) agradecimento; (*Comm*) valorização *f*
apprehensive [æprɪ'hɛnsɪv] ADJ apreensivo, receoso
apprentice [ə'prɛntɪs] N aprendiz *m/f*
approach [ə'prəutʃ] VI aproximar-se ▶ VT aproximar-se de; (*ask, apply to*) dirigir-se a; (*subject, passer-by*) abordar ▶ N aproximação *f*; (*access*) acesso; (*to problem, situation*) enfoque *m*
appropriate [*adj* ə'prəuprɪɪt, *vt* ə'prəuprɪeɪt] ADJ (*apt*) apropriado; (*relevant*) adequado ▶ VT apropriar-se de
approval [ə'pruːvəl] N aprovação *f*; **on ~** (*Comm*) a contento
approve [ə'pruːv] VT (*publication, product*) autorizar; (*motion, decision*) aprovar; **approve of** VT FUS aprovar
approximate [ə'prɔksɪmɪt] ADJ aproximado; **approximately** ADV aproximadamente
apricot ['eɪprɪkɔt] N damasco
April ['eɪprəl] N abril *m*
apron ['eɪprən] N avental *m*
apt [æpt] ADJ (*suitable*) adequado; (*appropriate*) apropriado; (*likely*): **~ to do** sujeito a fazer
Aquarius [ə'kwɛərɪəs] N Aquário
Arab ['ærəb] ADJ, N árabe *m/f*
Arabian [ə'reɪbɪən] ADJ árabe
Arabic ['ærəbɪk] ADJ árabe; (*numerals*) arábico ▶ N (*Ling*) árabe *m*
arbitrary ['ɑːbɪtrərɪ] ADJ arbitrário
arbitration [ɑːbɪ'treɪʃən] N arbitragem *f*
arcade [ɑː'keɪd] N arcos *mpl*; (*passage with shops*) galeria
arch [ɑːtʃ] N arco; (*of foot*) curvatura ▶ VT arquear, curvar
archaeology [ɑːkɪ'ɔlədʒɪ], (US) **archeology** N arqueologia
archbishop [ɑːtʃ'bɪʃəp] N arcebispo

archeology [ɑːkɪ'ɔlədʒɪ] (US) N = **archaeology**
architect ['ɑːkɪtɛkt] N arquiteto(-a); **architecture** N arquitetura
Arctic ['ɑːktɪk] ADJ ártico ▶ N: **the ~** o Ártico
are [ɑːʳ] VB *see* **be**
area ['ɛərɪə] N (*zone*) zona, região *f*; (*part of place*) região; (*in room, of knowledge, experience*) área; (*Math*) superfície *f*, extensão *f*; **area code** (US) N (*Tel*) (código) DDD (BR), indicativo (PT)
aren't [ɑːnt] = **are not**
Argentina [ɑːdʒən'tiːnə] N Argentina
arguably ['ɑːgjuəblɪ] ADV possivelmente
argue ['ɑːgjuː] VI (*quarrel*) discutir; (*reason*) argumentar; **to ~ that** sustentar que
argument ['ɑːgjumənt] N (*reasons*) argumento; (*quarrel*) briga, discussão *f*
Aries ['ɛərɪz] N Áries *m*
arise [ə'raɪz] (*pt* **arose**, *pp* **arisen**) VI (*emerge*) surgir
arithmetic [ə'rɪθmətɪk] N aritmética
arm [ɑːm] N braço; (*of clothing*) manga; (*of organization etc*) divisão *f* ▶ VT armar; **arms** NPL (*weapons*) armas *fpl*; (*Heraldry*) brasão *m*; **~ in ~** de braços dados
armchair N poltrona
armed ADJ armado
armour ['ɑːməʳ], (US) **armor** N armadura
armpit ['ɑːmpɪt] N sovaco
armrest ['ɑːmrɛst] N braço (de poltrona)
army ['ɑːmɪ] N exército
aroma [ə'rəumə] N aroma; **aromatherapy** N aromaterapia
arose [ə'rəuz] PT *of* **arise**
around [ə'raund] ADV em volta; (*in the area*) perto ▶ PREP em volta de; (*near*) perto de; (*fig: about*) cerca de
arouse [ə'rauz] VT despertar; (*anger*) provocar
arrange [ə'reɪndʒ] VT (*organize*) organizar; (*put in order*) arrumar ▶ VI: **to ~ to do sth** combinar em *or* ficar de fazer algo; **arrangement** N (*agreement*) acordo; (*order, layout*) disposição *f*; **arrangements** NPL (*plans*) planos *mpl*; (*preparations*) preparativos *mpl*; **home deliveries by arrangement** entregas a domicílio por convênio; **I'll make all the necessary arrangements** eu vou tomar todas as providências necessárias
array [ə'reɪ] N: **~ of** variedade *f* de
arrears [ə'rɪəz] NPL atrasos *mpl*; **to be in ~ with one's rent** estar atrasado com o aluguel
arrest [ə'rɛst] VT prender, deter; (*sb's attention*) chamar, prender ▶ N detenção *f*, prisão *f*; **under ~** preso
arrival [ə'raɪvəl] N chegada; **new ~** recém-chegado; (*baby*) recém-nascido
arrive [ə'raɪv] VI chegar
arrogant ['ærəgənt] ADJ arrogante
arrow ['ærəu] N flecha; (*sign*) seta
arse [ɑːs] (BRIT!) N cu *m* (!)
arson ['ɑːsn] N incêndio premeditado
art [ɑːt] N arte *f*; (*skill*) habilidade *f*, jeito; **Arts** NPL (*Sch*) letras *fpl*
artery ['ɑːtərɪ] N (*Med*) artéria; (*fig*) estrada principal
art gallery N museu *m* de belas artes; (*small, private*) galeria de arte

arthritis [ɑːˈθraɪtɪs] N artrite *f*
artichoke [ˈɑːtɪtʃəuk] N (*globe artichoke*) alcachofra; (*also*: **Jerusalem ~**) topinambo
article [ˈɑːtɪkl] N artigo; **articles** NPL (BRIT *Jur*: *training*) contrato de aprendizagem; **~s of clothing** peças *fpl* de vestuário
articulate [*adj* ɑːˈtɪkjulɪt, *vt* ɑːˈtɪkjuleɪt] ADJ (*speech*) bem articulado; (*writing*) bem escrito; (*person*) eloquente ▶ VT expressar
artificial [ɑːtɪˈfɪʃəl] ADJ artificial; (*person, manner*) afetado
artist [ˈɑːtɪst] N artista *m/f*; (*Mus*) intérprete *m/f*; **artistic** [ɑːˈtɪstɪk] ADJ artístico
art school N ≈ escola de artes

KEYWORD

as [æz, əz] CONJ **1** (*referring to time*) quando; **as the years went by** no decorrer dos anos; **he came in as I was leaving** ele chegou quando eu estava saindo; **as from tomorrow** a partir de amanhã
2 (*in comparisons*) tão ... como, tanto(s) ... como; **as big as** tão grande como; **twice as big as** duas vezes maior que; **as much/many as** tanto/tantos como; **as much money/many books as** tanto dinheiro quanto/tantos livros quanto; **as soon as** logo que, assim que
3 (*since, because*) como
4 (*referring to manner, way*) como; **do as you wish** faça como quiser
5 (*concerning*): **as for** *or* **to that** quanto a isso
6: **as if** *or* **though** como se; **he looked as if he was ill** ele parecia doente
▶ PREP (*in the capacity of*): **he works as a driver** ele trabalha como motorista; **he gave it to me as a present** ele me deu isso de presente; *see also* **long, such, well**

a.s.a.p. ABBR = **as soon as possible**
asbestos [æzˈbɛstəs] N asbesto, amianto
ash [æʃ] N cinza; (*tree, wood*) freixo
ashamed [əˈʃeɪmd] ADJ envergonhado; **to be ~ of** ter vergonha de
ashore [əˈʃɔːʳ] ADV em terra; **to go ~** descer à terra, desembarcar
ashtray [ˈæʃtreɪ] N cinzeiro
Asia [ˈeɪʃə] N Ásia; **Asian** ADJ, N asiático(-a)
aside [əˈsaɪd] ADV à parte, de lado ▶ N aparte *m*
ask [ɑːsk] VT perguntar; (*invite*) convidar; **to ~ sb sth** perguntar algo a alguém; **to ~ sb to do sth** pedir para alguém fazer algo; **to ~ (sb) a question** fazer uma pergunta (a alguém); **to ~ sb out to dinner** convidar alguém para jantar; **ask after** VT FUS perguntar por; **ask for** VT FUS pedir; **it's just ~ing for it** *or* **trouble** é procurar encrenca
asleep [əˈsliːp] ADJ dormindo; **to fall ~** dormir, adormecer
asparagus [əsˈpærəgəs] N aspargo (BR), espargo (PT)
aspect [ˈæspɛkt] N aspecto; (*direction in which a building etc faces*) direção *f*
aspire [əsˈpaɪəʳ] VI: **to ~ to** aspirar a
aspirin [ˈæsprɪn] N aspirina
ass [æs] N jumento, burro; (*inf*) imbecil *m/f*; (*US !*) cu *m* (*!*)
assassinate [əˈsæsɪneɪt] VT assassinar

assault [ə'sɔ:lt] N assalto ▶ VT assaltar, atacar; (*sexually*) agredir, violar
assemble [ə'sɛmbl] VT (*people*) reunir; (*objects*) juntar; (*Tech*) montar ▶ VI reunir-se
assembly [ə'sɛmblɪ] N reunião *f*; (*institution*) assembleia
assert [ə'sə:t] VT afirmar
assess [ə'sɛs] VT avaliar; **assessment** N avaliação *f*
asset ['æsɛt] N vantagem *f*, trunfo; **assets** NPL (*property, funds*) bens *mpl*
assign [ə'saɪn] VT (*date*) fixar; **to ~ (to)** (*task*) designar (a); (*resources*) destinar (a); **assignment** N tarefa
assist [ə'sɪst] VT ajudar; **assistance** N ajuda, auxílio; **assistant** N assistente *m/f*, auxiliar *m/f*; (BRIT: *also*: **shop assistant**) vendedor(a) *m/f*
associate [*adj* ə'səuʃɪɪt, *vt, vi* ə'səuʃɪeɪt] ADJ associado; (*professor, director etc*) adjunto ▶ N sócio(-a) ▶ VI: **to ~ with sb** associar-se com alguém ▶ VT associar; **association** N associação *f*; (*link*) ligação *f*
assorted [ə'sɔ:tɪd] ADJ sortido
assortment [ə'sɔ:tmənt] N (*of shapes, colours*) sortimento; (*of books, people*) variedade *f*
assume [ə'sju:m] VT (*suppose*) supor, presumir; (*responsibilities etc*) assumir; (*attitude, name*) adotar, tomar; **assumption** [ə'sʌmpʃən] N suposição *f*, presunção *f*
assurance [ə'ʃuərəns] N garantia; (*confidence*) confiança; (*insurance*) seguro
assure [ə'ʃuəʳ] VT assegurar; (*guarantee*) garantir
asthma ['æsmə] N asma
astonish [ə'stɔnɪʃ] VT assombrar, espantar; **astonishment** N assombro, espanto
astound [ə'staund] VT pasmar, estarrecer
astray [ə'streɪ] ADV: **to go ~** extraviar-se; **to lead ~** desencaminhar
astrology [əs'trɔlədʒɪ] N astrologia
astronaut ['æstrənɔ:t] N astronauta *m/f*
astronomy [əs'trɔnəmɪ] N astronomia
asylum [ə'saɪləm] N (*refuge*) asilo; (*hospital*) manicômio; **asylum seeker** [-si:kəʳ] N solicitante *m/f* de asilo

KEYWORD

at [æt] PREP **1** (*referring to position*) em; (*referring to direction*) a; **at the top** em cima; **at home/school** em casa/ na escola; **to look at sth** olhar para algo
2 (*referring to time*): **at 4 o'clock** às quatro horas; **at night** à noite; **at Christmas** no Natal; **at times** às vezes
3 (*referring to rates, speed etc*): **at £1 a kilo** a uma libra o quilo; **two at a time** de dois em dois
4 (*referring to manner*): **at a stroke** de um golpe; **at peace** em paz
5 (*referring to activity*): **to be at work** estar no trabalho; **to play at cowboys** brincar de mocinho
6 (*referring to cause*): **to be shocked/surprised/annoyed at sth** ficar chocado/surpreso/ chateado com algo; **I went at his suggestion** eu fui por causa da sugestão dele
▶ N (*symbol @*) arroba

ate [eɪt] PT *of* **eat**
atheist ['eɪθɪɪst] N ateu/ateia *m/f*
Athens ['æθɪnz] N Atenas
athlete ['æθli:t] N atleta *m/f*; **athletic** [æθ'lɛtɪk] ADJ atlético; **athletics** N atletismo
Atlantic [ət'læntɪk] ADJ atlântico ▸N: **the ~ (Ocean)** o (oceano) Atlântico
atlas ['ætləs] N atlas *m inv*
ATM ABBR (= *automated teller machine*) caixa eletrônico *m*
atmosphere ['ætməsfɪəʳ] N atmosfera; (*fig*) ambiente *m*
atom ['ætəm] N átomo; **atomic** [ə'tɔmɪk] ADJ atômico
attach [ə'tætʃ] VT prender; (*document, letter*) juntar, anexar; (*importance etc*) dar; **to be ~ed to sb/sth** (*like*) ter afeição por alguém/algo; **to ~ a file to an email** anexar um arquivo a um e-mail
attachment [ə'tætʃmənt] N (*tool*) acessório; (*to email*) anexo; (*love*): **~ (to)** afeição *f* (por)
attack [ə'tæk] VT atacar; (*subj: criminal*) assaltar; (*task etc*) empreender ▸N ataque *m*; (*on sb's life*) atentado; **heart ~** ataque cardíaco *or* de coração
attain [ə'teɪn] VT (*also*: **~ to**: *happiness, results*) alcançar, atingir; (: *knowledge*) obter
attempt [ə'tɛmpt] N tentativa ▸VT tentar; **to make an ~ on sb's life** atentar contra a vida de alguém
attend [ə'tɛnd] VT (*lectures*) assistir a; (*school*) cursar; (*church*) ir a; (*course*) fazer; (*patient*) tratar; **attend to** VT FUS (*matter*) encarregar-se de; (*needs, customer*) atender a; (*patient*) tratar de; **attendance** N comparecimento; (*people present*) assistência;
attendant N servidor(a) *m/f* ▸ADJ concomitante
attention [ə'tɛnʃən] N atenção *f*; (*care*) cuidados *mpl* ▸EXCL (*Mil*) sentido!; **for the ~ of ...** (*Admin*) atenção ...
attic ['ætɪk] N sótão *m*
attitude ['ætɪtju:d] N atitude *f*
attorney [ə'tə:nɪ] N (*US*: *lawyer*) advogado(-a)
attract [ə'trækt] VT atrair, chamar; **attraction** N atração *f*; **attractive** ADJ atraente; (*idea, offer*) interessante
attribute [*n* 'ætrɪbju:t, *vt* ə'trɪbju:t] N atributo ▸VT: **to ~ sth to** atribuir algo a
aubergine ['əubəʒi:n] N beringela
auction ['ɔ:kʃən] N (*also*: **sale by ~**) leilão *m* ▸VT leiloar
audience ['ɔ:dɪəns] N (*in theatre, concert etc*) plateia; (*of writer, magazine*) público
audit ['ɔ:dɪt] VT fazer a auditoria de
audition [ɔ:'dɪʃən] N audição *f*
August ['ɔ:gəst] N agosto
aunt [ɑ:nt] N tia; **auntie** N titia; **aunty** N titia
au pair ['əu'pɛəʳ] N (*also*: **~ girl**) au pair *f*
Australia [ɔs'treɪlɪə] N Austrália; **Australian** ADJ, N australiano(-a)
Austria ['ɔstrɪə] N Áustria; **Austrian** ADJ, N austríaco(-a)
authentic [ɔ:'θɛntɪk] ADJ autêntico
author ['ɔ:θə] N autor(a) *m/f*
authority [ɔ:'θɔrɪtɪ] N autoridade *f*; (*government body*) jurisdição *f*; (*permission*) autorização *f*; **the authorities** NPL (*ruling body*) as autoridades
authorize ['ɔ:θəraɪz] VT autorizar
auto ['ɔ:təu] (*US*) N carro, automóvel *m*

autobiography [ɔːtəbaɪ'ɔgrəfɪ] N autobiografia

autograph ['ɔːtəgrɑːf] N autógrafo ▸VT (*photo etc*) autografar

automatic [ɔːtə'mætɪk] ADJ automático ▸N (*gun*) pistola automática; (*washing machine*) máquina de lavar roupa automática; (*car*) carro automático

automobile ['ɔːtəməbiːl] (US) N carro, automóvel *m*

autonomy [ɔː'tɔnəmɪ] N autonomia

autumn ['ɔːtəm] N outono

auxiliary [ɔːg'zɪlɪərɪ] ADJ, N auxiliar *m/f*

available [ə'veɪləbl] ADJ disponível; (*time*) livre

avalanche ['ævəlɑːnʃ] N avalanche *f*

Ave. ABBR (= *avenue*) Av., Avda.

avenue ['ævənjuː] N avenida; (*drive*) caminho; (*means*) solução *f*

average ['ævərɪdʒ] N média ▸ADJ (*mean*) médio; (*ordinary*) regular ▸VT alcançar uma média de; **on ~** em média; **average out** VI: **to ~ out at** dar uma média de

avert [ə'vəːt] VT prevenir; (*blow, one's eyes*) desviar

avocado [ævə'kɑːdəu] N (BRIT: *also*: **~ pear**) abacate *m*

avoid [ə'vɔɪd] VT evitar

await [ə'weɪt] VT esperar, aguardar

awake [ə'weɪk] (*pt* **awoke**, *pp* **awoken**) ADJ acordado ▸VT, VI despertar, acordar; **~ to** atento a

award [ə'wɔːd] N prêmio, condecoração *f*; (*Jur: damages*) sentença; (*act*) concessão *f* ▸VT outorgar, conceder; (*damages*) determinar o pagamento de

aware [ə'wɛəʳ] ADJ: **~ of** (*conscious*) consciente de; (*informed*) informado de *or* sobre; **to become ~ of** reparar em, saber de;

awareness N consciência

away [ə'weɪ] ADV fora; (*faraway*) muito longe; **two kilometres ~** a dois quilômetros de distância; **the holiday was two weeks ~** faltavam duas semanas para as férias; **he's ~ for a week** está ausente uma semana; **to take ~** levar; **to work/pedal** *etc* **~** trabalhar/pedalar *etc* sem parar; **to fade ~** (*colour*) desbotar; (*enthusiasm, sound*) diminuir

awe [ɔː] N temor *m* respeitoso

awful ['ɔːfəl] ADJ terrível, horrível; (*quantity*): **an ~ lot of** um monte de;

awfully ADV (*very*) muito

awkward ['ɔːkwəd] ADJ (*person, movement*) desajeitado; (*shape*) incômodo; (*problem*) difícil; (*situation*) embaraçoso, delicado

awoke [ə'wəuk] PT *of* **awake**;

awoken [ə'wəukən] PP *of* **awake**

axe [æks], (US) **ax** N machado ▸VT (*project etc*) abandonar; (*jobs*) reduzir

axle ['æksl] N (*Aut*) eixo

b

B [biː] N (*Mus*) si *m*
baby [ˈbeɪbɪ] N neném *m/f*, nenê *m/f*, bebê *m/f*; (*US inf*) querido(-a); **baby carriage** (US) N carrinho de bebê; **baby food** N papinha de bebê; **baby-sit** *irreg* VI tomar conta da(s) criança(s); **baby-sitter** N baby-sitter *m/f*; **baby wipe** N lenço umedecido
bachelor [ˈbætʃələʳ] N solteiro; **B~ of Arts** ≈ bacharel *m* em Letras; **B~ of Science** ≈ bacharel *m* em Ciências
back [bæk] N (*of person*) costas *fpl*; (*of animal*) lombo; (*of hand*) dorso; (*of car, train*) parte *f* traseira; (*of house*) fundos *mpl*; (*of chair*) encosto; (*of page*) verso; (*of book*) lombada; (*of crowd*) fundo; (*Football*) zagueiro (BR), defesa *m* (PT) ▶ VT (*candidate*: *also*: **~ up**) apoiar; (*horse*: *at races*) apostar em; (*car*) dar ré com ▶ VI (*car etc*: *also*: **~ up**) dar ré (BR), fazer marcha atrás (PT) ▶ CPD (*payment*) atrasado; (*Aut*: *seats, wheels*) de trás ▶ ADV (*not forward*) para trás; **he's ~** ele voltou; **throw the ball ~** devolva a bola; **he called ~** (*again*) chamou de novo; **he ran ~** voltou correndo; **back down** VI desistir; **back out** VI (*of promise*) voltar atrás, recuar; **back up** VT (*support*) apoiar; (*Comput*) fazer um backup de; **backache** N dor *f* nas costas; **backbone** N coluna vertebral; (*fig*) esteio; **backfire** VI (*Aut*) engasgar; (*plan*) sair pela culatra; **background** N fundo; (*of events*) antecedentes *mpl*; (*basic knowledge*) bases *fpl*; (*experience*) conhecimentos *mpl*, experiência; **family background** antecedentes *mpl* familiares; **backing** N (*fig*) apoio; **backlog** N: **backlog of work** atrasos *mpl*; **backpack** N mochila; **back pay** N salário atrasado; **backstage** ADV nos bastidores; **backstroke** N nado de costas; **backup** ADJ (*train, plane*) reserva *inv*; (*Comput*) de backup ▶ N (*support*) apoio; (*Comput*: *also*: **backup file**) backup *m*; **backward** ADJ (*movement*) para trás; (*person, country*) atrasado; **backwards** ADV (*move, go*) para trás; (*read a list*) às avessas; (*fall*) de costas; **backyard** N quintal *m*
bacon [ˈbeɪkən] N toucinho, bacon *m*
bacteria [bækˈtɪərɪə] NPL bactérias *fpl*
bad [bæd] ADJ mau/má, ruim; (*child*) levado; (*mistake, injury*) grave; (*meat, food*) estragado; **his ~ leg** sua perna machucada; **to go ~** estragar-se; **bad debt** N crédito duvidoso
badge [bædʒ] N (*of school etc*) emblema *m*; (*policeman's*) crachá *m*

badger ['bædʒəʳ] N texugo

badly ['bædlɪ] ADV mal; **~ wounded** gravemente ferido; **he needs it ~** faz-lhe grande falta; **to be ~ off (for money)** estar com pouco dinheiro

badminton ['bædmɪntən] N badminton *m*

bad-tempered ADJ mal humorado; (*temporary*) de mau humor

bag [bæg] N saco, bolsa; (*handbag*) bolsa; (*satchel, shopping bag*) sacola; (*case*) mala; **~s of ...** (*inf: lots of*) ... de sobra; **baggage** N bagagem *f*; **baggage allowance** N franquia de bagagem; **baggy** ADJ folgado, largo; **bagpipes** NPL gaita de foles

bail [beɪl] N (*payment*) fiança; (*release*) liberdade *f* sob fiança ▶ VT (*prisoner: grant bail to*) libertar sob fiança; (*boat: also:* **~ out**) baldear a água de; **on ~** sob fiança; **bail out** VT (*prisoner*) afiançar

bait [beɪt] N isca, engodo; (*for criminal etc*) atrativo, chamariz *m* ▶ VT iscar, cevar; (*person*) apoquentar

bake [beɪk] VT cozinhar ao forno; (*Tech: clay etc*) cozer ▶ VI assar; **baked beans** NPL feijão *m* cozido com molho de tomate; **baked potato** N batata assada com a casca; **baker** N padeiro(-a); **bakery** N (*for bread*) padaria; (*for cakes*) confeitaria; **baking** N (*act*) cozimento; (*batch*) fornada; **baking powder** N fermento em pó

balance ['bæləns] N equilíbrio; (*scales*) balança; (*Comm*) balanço; (*remainder*) resto, saldo ▶ VT equilibrar; (*budget*) nivelar; (*account*) fazer o balanço de; **~ of trade/payments** balança comercial/balanço de pagamentos; **balanced** ADJ (*report*) objetivo; (*personality, diet*) equilibrado; **balance sheet** N balanço geral

balcony ['bælkənɪ] N varanda; (*closed*) galeria; (*in theatre*) balcão *m*

bald [bɔːld] ADJ calvo, careca; (*tyre*) careca

ball [bɔːl] N bola; (*of wool, string*) novelo; (*dance*) baile *m*; **to play ~ with sb** jogar bola com alguém; (*fig*) fazer o jogo de alguém

ballerina [bæləˈriːnə] N bailarina

ballet ['bæleɪ] N balé *m*; **ballet dancer** N bailarino(-a)

balloon [bəˈluːn] N balão *m*

ballot ['bælət] N votação *f*

ballpoint ['bɔːlpɔɪnt], **ballpoint pen** N (caneta) esferográfica

ban [bæn] N proibição *f*, interdição *f*; (*suspension, exclusion*) exclusão *f* ▶ VT proibir, interditar; (*exclude*) excluir

banana [bəˈnɑːnə] N banana

band [bænd] N orquestra; (*Mil*) banda; (*strip*) faixa, cinta; **band together** VI juntar-se, associar-se

bandage ['bændɪdʒ] N atadura (BR), ligadura (PT) ▶ VT enfaixar

B & B N ABBR = **bed and breakfast**

bang [bæŋ] N estalo; (*of door*) estrondo; (*of gun, exhaust*) explosão *f*; (*blow*) pancada ▶ EXCL bum!, bumba! ▶ VT bater com força; (*door*) fechar com violência ▶ VI produzir estrondo; (*door*) bater; (*fireworks*) soltar

bangs [bæŋz] (US) NPL (*fringe*) franja

banish ['bænɪʃ] VT banir

banister ['bænɪstəʳ] N, **banisters** ['bænɪstəz] NPL corrimão *m*
bank [bæŋk] N banco; (*of river, lake*) margem *f*; (*of earth*) rampa, ladeira ▶VI (*Aviat*) ladear-se; **bank on** VT FUS contar com, apostar em; **bank account** N conta bancária; **bank card** N cartão *m* de garantia de cheques; **banker** N banqueiro(-a); **Bank holiday** (BRIT) N feriado nacional; **banking** N transações *fpl* bancárias; **banknote** N nota (bancária)
bankrupt ['bæŋkrʌpt] ADJ falido, quebrado; **to go ~** falir
bank statement N extrato bancário
banner ['bænəʳ] N faixa
baptism ['bæptɪzəm] N batismo
bar [bɑːʳ] N barra; (*rod*) vara; (*of window etc*) grade *f*; (*fig: hindrance*) obstáculo; (*prohibition*) impedimento; (*pub*) bar *m*; (*counter: in pub*) balcão *m* ▶VT (*road*) obstruir; (*person*) excluir; (*activity*) proibir ▶PREP: **~ none** sem exceção; **behind ~s** (*prisoner*) atrás das grades; **the B~** (*Jur*) a advocacia
barbaric [bɑː'bærɪk] ADJ bárbaro
barbecue ['bɑːbɪkjuː] N churrasco
barbed wire ['bɑːbd-] N arame *m* farpado
barber ['bɑːbəʳ] N barbeiro, cabeleireiro
bar code N código de barras
bare [bɛəʳ] ADJ despido; (*head*) descoberto; (*trees, vegetation*) sem vegetação; (*minimum*) básico ▶VT mostrar; **barefoot** ADJ, ADV descalço; **barely** ADV apenas, mal
bargain ['bɑːgɪn] N negócio; (*agreement*) acordo; (*good buy*) pechincha ▶VI (*haggle*) regatear; (*negotiate*): **to ~ (with sb)** pechinchar (com alguém); **into the ~** ainda por cima; **bargain for** VT FUS: **he got more than he ~ed for** ele conseguiu mais do que pediu
barge [bɑːdʒ] N barcaça; **barge in** VI irromper
bark [bɑːk] N (*of tree*) casca; (*of dog*) latido ▶VI latir
barley ['bɑːlɪ] N cevada
barmaid ['bɑːmeɪd] N garçonete *f* (BR), empregada (de bar) (PT)
barman ['bɑːmən] *irreg* N garçom *m* (BR), empregado (de bar) (PT)
barn [bɑːn] N celeiro
barometer [bə'rɔmɪtəʳ] N barômetro
baron ['bærən] N barão *m*; (*of press, industry*) magnata *m*; **baroness** ['bærənɪs] N baronesa
barracks ['bærəks] NPL quartel *m*, caserna
barrage ['bærɑːʒ] N (*Mil*) fogo de barragem; (*dam*) barragem *f*; (*fig*): **a ~ of questions** uma saraivada de perguntas
barrel ['bærəl] N barril *m*; (*of gun*) cano
barren ['bærən] ADJ (*land*) árido
barricade [bærɪ'keɪd] N barricada
barrier ['bærɪəʳ] N barreira; (*fig: to progress etc*) obstáculo
barrister ['bærɪstəʳ] (BRIT) N advogado(-a), causídico(-a)
barrow ['bærəu] N (*wheelbarrow*) carrinho (de mão)
bartender ['bɑːtɛndəʳ] (US) N garçom *m* (BR), empregado (de bar) (PT)
base [beɪs] N base *f* ▶VT (*opinion, belief*): **to ~ sth on** basear *or* fundamentar algo em ▶ADJ (*thoughts*) sujo; **baseball** N beisebol *m*
basement ['beɪsmənt] N porão *m*

bases¹ ['beɪsɪz] NPL *of* **base**
bases² ['beɪsi:z] NPL *of* **basis**
bash [bæʃ] (*inf*) VT (*with fist*) dar soco *or* murro em; (*with object*) bater em
basic ['beɪsɪk] ADJ básico; (*facilities*) mínimo; **basically** ADV basicamente; (*really*) no fundo; **basics** NPL: **the basics** o essencial
basin ['beɪsn] N bacia; (*also*: **wash~**) pia
basis ['beɪsɪs] (*pl* **bases**) N base *f*; **on a part-time ~** num esquema de meio-expediente; **on a trial ~** em experiência
basket ['bɑ:skɪt] N cesto; (*with handle*) cesta; **basketball** N basquete(bol) *m*
bass [beɪs] N (*Mus*) baixo
bastard ['bɑ:stəd] N bastardo(-a); (*!*) filho da puta *m* (*!*)
bat [bæt] N (*Zool*) morcego; (*for ball games*) bastão *m*; (BRIT: *for table tennis*) raquete *f* ▶ VT: **he didn't ~ an eyelid** ele nem pestanejou
batch [bætʃ] N (*of bread*) fornada; (*of papers*) monte *m*
bath [bɑ:θ] N banho; (*bathtub*) banheira ▶ VT banhar; **to have a ~** tomar banho (de banheira); *see also* **baths**
bathe [beɪð] VI banhar-se; (US: *have a bath*) tomar um banho ▶ VT (*wound*) lavar; **bathing** N banho; **bathing costume**, (US) **bathing suit** N (*woman's*) maiô *m* (BR), fato de banho (PT)
bathrobe ['bɑ:θrəub] N roupão *m* de banho
bathroom ['bɑ:θrum] N banheiro (BR), casa de banho (PT)
baths [bɑ:θs] NPL banhos *mpl* públicos
baton ['bætən] N (*Mus*) batuta; (*Athletics*) bastão *m*; (*truncheon*) cassetete *m*
batter ['bætə^r] VT espancar; (*subj*: *wind, rain*) castigar ▶ N massa (mole); **battered** ['bætəd] ADJ (*hat, pan*) amassado, surrado
battery ['bætərɪ] N bateria; (*of torch*) pilha
battle ['bætl] N batalha; (*fig*) luta ▶ VI lutar; **battlefield** N campo de batalha
bay [beɪ] N (*Geo*) baía; **to hold sb at ~** manter alguém a distância
bazaar [bə'zɑ:^r] N bazar *m*
BBC N ABBR (= *British Broadcasting Corporation*) *companhia britânica de rádio e televisão*
B.C. ADV ABBR (= *before Christ*) a.C. ▶ ABBR (CANADA) = **British Columbia**

KEYWORD

be [bi:] (*pt* **was** *or* **were**, *pp* **been**) AUX VB **1** (*with present participle, forming continuous tense*) estar; **what are you doing?** o que você está fazendo (BR) *or* a fazer (PT)?; **it is raining** está chovendo (BR) *or* a chover (PT); **I've been waiting for you for hours** há horas que eu espero por você
2 (*with pp, forming passives*): **to be killed** ser morto; **the box had been opened** a caixa tinha sido aberta; **the thief was nowhere to be seen** tinha sumido o ladrão
3 (*in tag questions*): **it was fun, wasn't it?** foi divertido, não foi?; **she's back again, is she?** ela voltou novamente, é?
4 (+ *to* + *infin*): **the house is to be sold** a casa está para ser vendida; **you're to be congratulated for**

all your work você devia ser cumprimentado pelo seu trabalho; **he's not to open it** ele não pode abrir isso
▶ VB + COMPLEMENT **1** (*gen*): **I'm English** sou inglês; **I'm tired** estou cansado; **2 and 2 are 4** dois e dois são quatro; **be careful!** tome cuidado!; **be quiet!** fique quieto!, fique calado!; **be good!** seja bonzinho!
2 (*of health*) estar; **how are you?** como está?
3 (*of age*): **how old are you?** quantos anos você tem?; **I'm twenty (years old)** tenho vinte anos
4 (*cost*) ser; **how much was the meal?** quanto foi a refeição?; **that'll be £5.75, please** são £5.75, por favor
▶ VI **1** (*exist, occur etc*) existir, haver; **the best singer that ever was** o maior cantor de todos os tempos; **is there a God?** Deus existe?; **be that as it may ...** de qualquer forma ...; **so be it** que seja assim
2 (*referring to place*) estar; **I won't be here tomorrow** eu não estarei aqui amanhã; **Edinburgh is in Scotland** Edinburgo é *or* fica na Escócia
3 (*referring to movement*) ir; **where have you been?** onde você foi?; **I've been in the garden** estava no quintal
▶ IMPERS VB **1** (*referring to time*) ser; **it's 8 o'clock** são 8 horas; **it's the 28th of April** é 28 de abril
2 (*referring to distance*) ficar; **it's 10 km to the village** o lugarejo fica a 10 km de distância
3 (*referring to the weather*) estar; **it's too hot/cold** está quente/frio demais
4 (*emphatic*): **it's only me** sou eu!; **it was Maria who paid the bill** foi Maria quem pagou a conta

beach [bi:tʃ] N praia ▶ VT puxar para a terra *or* praia, encalhar
beacon ['bi:kən] N (*lighthouse*) farol *m*; (*marker*) baliza
bead [bi:d] N (*of necklace*) conta; (*of sweat*) gota
beak [bi:k] N bico
beam [bi:m] N (*Arch*) viga; (*of light*) raio ▶ VI (*smile*) sorrir
bean [bi:n] N feijão *m*; (*of coffee*) grão *m*; **runner/broad ~** vagem *f*/fava
bear [bɛə^r] (*pt* **bore**, *pp* **borne**) N urso ▶ VT (*carry, support*) arcar com; (*tolerate*) suportar ▶ VI: **to ~ right/left** virar à direita/à esquerda; **bear out** VT (*theory, suspicion*) confirmar, corroborar; **bear up** VI aguentar, resistir
beard [bɪəd] N barba
bearing ['bɛərɪŋ] N porte *m*, comportamento; (*connection*) relação *f*; **bearings** NPL (*also*: **ball ~s**) rolimã *m*; **to take a ~** fazer marcação
beast [bi:st] N bicho; (*inf*) fera
beat [bi:t] (*pt* **beat**, *pp* **beaten**) N (*of heart*) batida; (*Mus*) ritmo, compasso; (*of policeman*) ronda ▶ VT (*hit*) bater em; (*eggs*) bater; (*defeat*) vencer, derrotar ▶ VI (*heart*) bater; **to ~ it** (*inf*) cair fora; **off the ~en track** fora de mão; **beat off** VT repelir; **beat up** VT (*inf*: *person*) espancar; (*eggs*) bater; **beating** N (*thrashing*) surra
beautiful ['bju:tɪful] ADJ belo, lindo, formoso
beauty ['bju:tɪ] N beleza; (*person*) beldade *f*, beleza

beaver ['bi:vəʳ] N castor *m*
because [bɪ'kɔz] CONJ porque; **~ of** por causa de
beckon ['bɛkən] VT (*also*: **~ to**) chamar com sinais, acenar para
become [bɪ'kʌm] (*irreg*: *like* **come**) VI (+ *n*) virar, fazer-se, tornar-se; (+ *adj*) tornar-se, ficar
bed [bɛd] N cama; (*of flowers*) canteiro; (*of coal, clay*) camada, base *f*; (*of sea, lake*) fundo; (*of river*) leito; **to go to ~** ir dormir, deitar(-se); **bed and breakfast** N (*place*) pensão *f*; (*terms*) cama e café da manhã (BR) *or* pequeno almoço (PT); **bedclothes** NPL roupa de cama; **bedding** N roupa de cama; **bedroom** N quarto, dormitório; **bedside** N: **at sb's bedside** à cabeceira de alguém ▶ CPD (*book, lamp*) de cabeceira; **bedsit** ['bɛdsɪt], **bedsitter** ['bɛdsɪtəʳ] (BRIT) N conjugado

Um **bedsit** é um quarto mobiliado cujo aluguel inclui uso de cozinha e banheiro comuns. Esse sistema de alojamento é muito comum na Grã-Bretanha entre estudantes, jovens profissionais liberais etc.

bedspread ['bɛdsprɛd] N colcha
bedtime ['bɛdtaɪm] N hora de ir para cama
bee [bi:] N abelha
beech [bi:tʃ] N faia
beef [bi:f] N carne *f* de vaca; **roast ~** rosbife *m*; **beefburger** N hambúrguer *m*
been [bi:n] PP *of* **be**
beer [bɪəʳ] N cerveja
beetle ['bi:tl] N besouro
beetroot ['bi:tru:t] (BRIT) N beterraba
before [bɪ'fɔ:ʳ] PREP (*of time*) antes de; (*of space*) diante de ▶ CONJ antes que ▶ ADV antes, anteriormente; à frente, na dianteira; **~ going** antes de ir; **the week ~** a semana anterior; **I've never seen it ~** nunca vi isso antes; **beforehand** ADV antes
beg [bɛg] VI mendigar, pedir esmola ▶ VT (*also*: **~ for**) mendigar; **to ~ sb to do sth** implorar a alguém para fazer algo; *see also* **pardon**
began [bɪ'gæn] PT *of* **begin**
beggar ['bɛgəʳ] N mendigo(-a)
begin [bɪ'gɪn] (*pt* **began**, *pp* **begun**) VT, VI começar, iniciar; **to ~ doing** *or* **to do sth** começar a fazer algo; **beginner** N principiante *m/f*; **beginning** N início, começo
behalf [bɪ'ha:f] N: **on** *or* **in** (*US*) **~ of** (*as representative of*) em nome de; (*for benefit of*) no interesse de
behave [bɪ'heɪv] VI comportar-se; (*well*: *also*: **~ o.s.**) comportar-se (bem); **behaviour**, (*US*) **behavior** N comportamento
behind [bɪ'haɪnd] PREP atrás de ▶ ADV atrás; (*move*) para trás ▶ N traseiro; **to be ~ (schedule) with sth** estar atrasado *or* com atraso em algo; **~ the scenes** nos bastidores
beige [beɪʒ] ADJ bege
Beijing [beɪ'ʒɪŋ] N Pequim
being ['bi:ɪŋ] N (*state*) existência; (*entity*) ser *m*
belated [bɪ'leɪtɪd] ADJ atrasado
belch [bɛltʃ] VI arrotar ▶ VT (*also*: **~ out**: *smoke etc*) vomitar
Belgian ['bɛldʒən] ADJ, N belga *m/f*
Belgium ['bɛldʒəm] N Bélgica

belief [bɪ'li:f] N *(opinion)* opinião *f*; *(trust, faith)* fé *f*
believe [bɪ'li:v] VT: **to ~ sth/sb** acreditar algo/em alguém ▶ VI: **to ~ in** *(God, ghosts)* crer em; *(method, person)* acreditar em;
believer N *(Rel)* crente *m/f*, fiel *m/f*
bell [bɛl] N sino; *(small, doorbell)* campainha
bellow ['bɛləu] VI mugir; *(person)* bramar
bell pepper N *(esp US)* pimentão *m*
belly ['bɛlɪ] N barriga, ventre *m*
belong [bɪ'lɔŋ] VI: **to ~ to** pertencer a; *(club etc)* ser sócio de; **the book ~s here** o livro fica guardado aqui; **belongings** NPL pertences *mpl*
beloved [bɪ'lʌvɪd] ADJ querido, amado
below [bɪ'ləu] PREP *(beneath)* embaixo de; *(lower than, less than)* abaixo de ▶ ADV em baixo; **see ~** ver abaixo
belt [bɛlt] N cinto; *(of land)* faixa; *(Tech)* correia ▶ VT *(thrash)* surrar;
beltway *(US)* N via circular
bemused [bɪ'mju:zd] ADJ bestificado, estupidificado
bench [bɛntʃ] N banco; *(work bench)* bancada (de carpinteiro); (BRIT *Pol*) assento num Parlamento; **the B~** *(Jur)* o tribunal; *(people)* os magistrados, o corpo de magistrados
bend [bɛnd] *(pt* **bent**, *pp* **bent**) VT *(leg, arm)* dobrar; *(pipe)* curvar ▶ VI dobrar-se, inclinar-se ▶ N curva; *(in pipe)* curvatura; **bend down** VI abaixar-se; **bend over** VI debruçar-se
beneath [bɪ'ni:θ] PREP abaixo de; *(unworthy of)* indigno de ▶ ADV em baixo
beneficial [bɛnɪ'fɪʃəl] ADJ: **~ (to)** benéfico (a)
benefit ['bɛnɪfɪt] N benefício, vantagem *f*; *(money)* subsídio, auxílio ▶ VT beneficiar ▶ VI: **to ~ from sth** beneficiar-se de algo
benign [bɪ'naɪn] ADJ *(person, smile)* afável, bondoso; *(Med)* benigno
bent [bɛnt] PT, PP *of* **bend** ▶ N inclinação *f* ▶ ADJ: **to be ~ on** estar empenhado em
bereaved [bɪ'ri:vd] NPL: **the ~** os enlutados
beret ['bɛreɪ] N boina
Berlin [bə:'lɪn] N Berlim
berry ['bɛrɪ] N baga
berth [bə:θ] N *(bed)* beliche *m*; *(cabin)* cabine *f*; *(on train)* leito; *(for ship)* ancoradouro ▶ VI *(in harbour)* atracar, encostar-se; *(at anchor)* ancorar
beside [bɪ'saɪd] PREP *(next to)* junto de, ao lado de, ao pé de; **to be ~ o.s. (with anger)** estar fora de si; **that's ~ the point** isso não tem nada a ver
besides [bɪ'saɪdz] ADV além disso ▶ PREP *(as well as)* além de
best [bɛst] ADJ melhor ▶ ADV (o) melhor; **the ~ part of** *(quantity)* a maior parte de; **at ~** na melhor das hipóteses; **to make the ~ of sth** tirar o maior partido possível de algo; **to do one's ~** fazer o possível; **to the ~ of my knowledge** que eu saiba; **to the ~ of my ability** o melhor que eu puder; **best-before date** N validade *f*; **best man** N padrinho de casamento
bet [bɛt] *(pt, pp* **bet** *or* **betted**) N aposta ▶ VI: **to ~ (on)** apostar (em)
betray [bɪ'treɪ] VT trair;

(*denounce*) delatar
better ['bɛtəʳ] ADJ, ADV melhor ▶ VT melhorar; (*go above*) superar ▶ N: **to get the ~ of sb** vencer alguém; **you had ~ do it** é melhor você fazer isso; **he thought ~ of it** pensou melhor, mudou de opinião; **to get ~** melhorar; **you'd be ~ off this way** seria melhor para você assim
betting ['bɛtɪŋ] N jogo; **betting shop** (BRIT) N agência de apostas
between [bɪ'twi:n] PREP no meio de, entre ▶ ADV no meio
beverage ['bɛvərɪdʒ] N bebida
beware [bɪ'wɛəʳ] VI: **to ~ (of)** precaver-se (de), ter cuidado (com); **"~ of the dog"** "cuidado com o cachorro"
bewildered [bɪ'wɪldəd] ADJ atordoado; (*confused*) confuso
beyond [bɪ'jɔnd] PREP (*in space, exceeding*) além de; (*exceeding*) acima de, fora de; (*date*) mais tarde que; (*above*) acima de ▶ ADV além; (*in time*) mais longe, mais adiante; **~ doubt** fora de qualquer dúvida; **to be ~ repair** não ter conserto
bias ['baɪəs] N parcialidade
bib [bɪb] N babadouro, babador *m*
Bible ['baɪbl] N Bíblia
bicycle ['baɪsɪkl] N bicicleta
bid [bɪd] (*pt* **bade** *or* **bid**, *pp* **bidden** *or* **bid**) N oferta; (*at auction*) lance *m*; (*attempt*) tentativa ▶ VI fazer lance ▶ VT oferecer; **to ~ sb good day** dar bom dia a alguém
big [bɪg] ADJ grande; (*bulky*) volumoso; **~ brother/sister** irmão/irmã mais velho/a
bigheaded ['bɪg'hɛdɪd] ADJ convencido
bike [baɪk] N bicicleta
bikini [bɪ'ki:nɪ] N biquíni *m*
bilingual [baɪ'lɪŋgwəl] ADJ bilíngue
bill [bɪl] N conta; (*invoice*) fatura; (*Pol*) projeto de lei; (*US: banknote*) bilhete *m*, nota; (*in restaurant*) conta, notinha; (*notice*) cartaz *m*; (*of bird*) bico; **to fit** *or* **fill the ~** (*fig*) servir; **billboard** N quadro para cartazes; **billfold** ['bɪlfəuld] (*US*) N carteira
billiards ['bɪlɪədz] N bilhar *m*
billion ['bɪlɪən] N bilhão *m* (BR), mil milhão *m* (PT)
bin [bɪn] N caixa; (BRIT: *also*: **dust~, litter ~**) lata de lixo
bind [baɪnd] (*pt, pp* **bound**) VT atar, amarrar; (*oblige*) obrigar; (*book*) encadernar ▶ N (*inf*) saco
binge [bɪndʒ] (*inf*) N: **to go on a ~** tomar uma bebedeira
bingo ['bɪŋgəu] N bingo
binoculars [bɪ'nɔkjuləz] NPL binóculo
bio ... [baɪəu] PREFIX bio ...; **biochemistry** N bioquímica; **biodiesel** ['baɪəudi:zl] N biodiesel *m*; **biodiversity** N biodiversidade *f*; **biofuel** N biocombustível *m*; **biography** N biografia; **biology** N biologia; **biometric** ADJ biométrico
birch [bə:tʃ] N bétula
bird [bə:d] N ave *f*, pássaro; (BRIT *inf*: *girl*) gatinha; **bird flu** N gripe *f* aviária
birth [bə:θ] N nascimento; **to give ~ to** dar à luz, parir; **birth certificate** N certidão *f* de nascimento; **birth control** N controle *m* de natalidade; (*methods*) métodos *mpl* anticoncepcionais; **birthday** N aniversário (BR), dia *m* de anos (PT) ▶ CPD de aniversário; *see also* **happy**

biscuit ['bɪskɪt] N (BRIT) bolacha, biscoito; (US) pão *m* doce
bishop ['bɪʃəp] N bispo
bit [bɪt] PT *of* **bite** ▸ N pedaço, bocado; (*of horse*) freio; (*Comput*) bit *m*; **a ~ of** (*a little*) um pouco de; **~ by ~** pouco a pouco
bitch [bɪtʃ] N (*dog*) cadela, cachorra; (!) cadela (!), vagabunda (!)
bite [baɪt] (*pt* **bit**, *pp* **bitten**) VT, VI morder; (*insect etc*) picar ▸ N (*insect bite*) picada; (*mouthful*) bocado; **to ~ one's nails** roer as unhas; **let's have a ~ (to eat)** (*inf*) vamos fazer uma boquinha
bitter ['bɪtə^r] ADJ amargo; (*wind, criticism*) cortante, penetrante ▸ N (BRIT: *beer*) cerveja amarga
black [blæk] ADJ preto; (*humour*) negro ▸ N (*colour*) cor *f* preta; (*person*): **B~** negro(-a) ▸ VT (BRIT *Industry*) boicotar; **to give sb a ~ eye** esmurrar alguém e deixá-lo de olho roxo; **~ and blue** contuso, contundido; **to be in the ~** (*in credit*) estar com saldo credor; **blackberry** N amora(-preta) (BR), amora silvestre (PT); **blackbird** N melro; **blackboard** N quadro(-negro); **black coffee** N café *m* preto; **blackcurrant** N groselha negra; **blackmail** N chantagem *f* ▸ VT fazer chantagem a; **black market** N mercado *or* câmbio negro; **blackout** N blecaute *m*; (*fainting*) desmaio; (*of radio signal*) desvanecimento; **Black Sea** N: **the Black Sea** o mar Negro
bladder ['blædə^r] N bexiga
blade [bleɪd] N lâmina; (*of oar, rotor*) pá *f*; **a ~ of grass** uma folha de relva
blame [bleɪm] N culpa ▸ VT: **to ~ sb for sth** culpar alguém por algo; **to be to ~** ter a culpa
bland [blænd] ADJ (*taste*) brando
blank [blæŋk] ADJ em branco; (*look*) sem expressão ▸ N (*of memory*): **to go ~** dar um branco; (*on form*) espaço em branco; (*cartridge*) bala de festim
blanket ['blæŋkɪt] N cobertor *m*
blast [blɑːst] N (*of wind*) rajada; (*of explosive*) explosão *f* ▸ VT fazer voar
blatant ['bleɪtənt] ADJ descarado
blaze [bleɪz] N (*fire*) fogo; (*in building etc*) incêndio; (*fig: of colour*) esplendor *m*; (: *of glory, publicity*) explosão *f* ▸ VI (*fire*) arder; (*guns*) descarregar; (*eyes*) brilhar ▸ VT: **to ~ a trail** (*fig*) abrir (um) caminho
blazer ['bleɪzə^r] N casaco esportivo, blazer *m*
bleach [bliːtʃ] N (*also*: **household ~**) água sanitária ▸ VT (*linen*) branquear
bleak [bliːk] ADJ (*countryside*) desolado; (*prospect*) desanimador(a), sombrio; (*weather*) ruim
bleed [bliːd] (*pt, pp* **bled**) VI sangrar
blemish ['blɛmɪʃ] N mancha; (*on reputation*) mácula
blend [blɛnd] N mistura ▸ VT misturar ▸ VI (*colours etc: also*: **~ in**) combinar-se, misturar-se; **blender** N liquidificador *m*
bless [blɛs] (*pt, pp* **blessed**) VT abençoar; **~ you!** (*after sneeze*) saúde!; **blessing** N bênção *f*; (*godsend*) graça, dádiva; (*approval*) aprovação *f*
blew [bluː] PT *of* **blow**
blind [blaɪnd] ADJ cego ▸ N (*for window*) persiana; (*also*: **Venetian ~**) veneziana ▸ VT cegar; (*dazzle*) deslumbrar; **the blind** NPL (*blind people*) os cegos; **blind alley** N beco sem saída *m*; **blindfold** N venda

▶ ADJ, ADV com os olhos vendados, às cegas ▶ VT vendar os olhos a
blink [blɪŋk] VI piscar
bliss [blɪs] N felicidade *f*
blister ['blɪstəʳ] N (*on skin*) bolha; (*in paint, rubber*) empola ▶ VI empolar-se
blizzard ['blɪzəd] N nevasca
bloated ['bləutɪd] ADJ (*swollen*) inchado; (*full*) empanturrado
blob [blɔb] N (*drop*) gota; (*indistinct shape*) ponto
block [blɔk] N (*of wood*) bloco; (*of stone*) laje *f*; (*in pipes*) entupimento; (*of buildings*) quarteirão *m* ▶ VT obstruir, bloquear; (*progress*) impedir; **~ of flats** (BRIT) prédio (de apartamentos); **mental ~** bloqueio; **blockade** [blɔ'keɪd] N bloqueio; **blockage** N obstrução *f*; **blockbuster** ['blɔkbʌstəʳ] N grande sucesso
blog ['blɔg] N blogue *m* ▶ VI blogar
blogger ['blɔgəʳ] N (*person*) blogueiro(-a); **blogosphere** ['blɔgəsfɪəʳ] N blogosfera
bloke [bləuk] (BRIT *inf*) N cara *m* (BR), gajo (PT)
blond, blonde [blɔnd] ADJ, N louro(-a)
blood [blʌd] N sangue *m*; **blood donor** N doador(a) *m/f* de sangue; **blood group** N grupo sanguíneo; **blood poisoning** N toxemia; **blood pressure** N pressão *f* arterial *or* sanguínea; **bloodshed** N matança, carnificina; **bloodshot** ADJ (*eyes*) injetado; **bloodstream** N corrente *f* sanguínea; **blood test** N exame *m* de sangue; **blood vessel** N vaso sanguíneo; **bloody** ADJ sangrento; (*nose*) ensanguentado; (BRIT *!*): **this bloody ...** essa droga de ..., esse maldito ...; **bloody** **strong/good** forte/bom pra burro (*inf*)
bloom [blu:m] N flor *f* ▶ VI florescer
blossom ['blɔsəm] N flor *f* ▶ VI florescer; **to ~ into** (*fig*) tornar-se
blot [blɔt] N borrão *m*; (*fig*) mancha ▶ VT borrar; **blot out** VT (*view*) tapar; (*memory*) apagar
blouse [blauz] N blusa
blow [bləu] (*pt* **blew**, *pp* **blown**) N golpe *m*; (*punch*) soco ▶ VI soprar ▶ VT (*subj: wind*) soprar; (*instrument*) tocar; (*fuse*) queimar; **to ~ one's nose** assoar o nariz; **blow away** VT levar, arrancar ▶ VI ser levado pelo vento; **blow down** VT derrubar; **blow off** VT levar; **blow out** VT (*candle*) apagar; **blow over** VI passar; **blow up** VI explodir ▶ VT explodir; (*tyre*) encher; (*Phot*) ampliar; **blow-dry** N escova; **blow-out** N (*of tyre*) furo
blue [blu:] ADJ azul; (*depressed*) deprimido; **blues** N (*Mus*): **the ~s** o blues; **out of the ~** (*fig*) de estalo, inesperadamente; **bluebell** N campainha
bluff [blʌf] VI blefar ▶ N blefe *m*; **to call sb's ~** pagar para ver alguém
blunder ['blʌndəʳ] N gafe *f* ▶ VI cometer *or* fazer uma gafe
blunt [blʌnt] ADJ (*knife*) cego; (*pencil*) rombudo; (*person*) franco, direto
blur [bləːʳ] N borrão *m* ▶ VT (*vision*) embaçar
blush [blʌʃ] VI corar, ruborizar-se ▶ N rubor *m*, vermelhidão *f*
board [bɔ:d] N tábua; (*blackboard*) quadro; (*notice board*) quadro de avisos; (*for chess etc*) tabuleiro; (*committee*) junta, conselho; (*in firm*) diretoria, conselho

administrativo; (*Naut, Aviat*): **on ~** a bordo ▶ VT embarcar em; **full ~** (BRIT) pensão *f* completa; **half ~** (BRIT) meia-pensão *f*; **~ and lodging** casa e comida; **to go by the ~** ficar abandonado, dançar (*inf*); **board up** VT entabuar; **boarding card** N = **boarding pass**; **boarding pass** (BRIT) N (*Aviat, Naut*) cartão *m* de embarque; **boarding school** N internato

boast [bəust] VI: **to ~ (about** *or* **of)** gabar-se (de), jactar-se (de)

boat [bəut] N barco *m*; (*ship*) navio

bob [bɔb] VI balouçar-se; **bob up** VI aparecer, surgir

body ['bɔdɪ] N corpo; (*corpse*) cadáver *m*; (*of car*) carroceria; (*fig: group*) grupo; (*: organization*) organização *f*; (*: quantity*) conjunto; (*: of wine*) corpo; **body-building** N musculação *f*; **bodyguard** N guarda-costas *m inv*; **bodywork** N lataria

bog [bɔg] N pântano, atoleiro ▶ VT: **to get ~ged down (in)** (*fig*) atolar-se (em)

bogus ['bəugəs] ADJ falso

boil [bɔɪl] VT ferver; (*eggs*) cozinhar ▶ VI ferver ▶ N (*Med*) furúnculo; **to come to the** (BRIT) *or* **a** (US) **~** começar a ferver; **boil down to** VT FUS (*fig*) reduzir-se a; **boil over** VI transbordar; **boiled egg** N ovo cozido; **boiled potatoes** NPL batatas *fpl* cozidas; **boiler** N caldeira; (*for central heating*) boiler *m*; **boiling point** N ponto de ebulição

bold [bəuld] ADJ corajoso; (*pej*) atrevido, insolente; (*outline, colour*) forte

Bolivia [bə'lɪvɪə] N Bolívia

bollard ['bɔləd] (BRIT) N (*Aut*) poste *m* de sinalização

bolt [bəult] N (*lock*) trinco, ferrolho; (*with nut*) parafuso, cavilha ▶ ADV: **~ upright** direito como um fuso ▶ VT (*door*) fechar a ferrolho, trancar; (*food*) engolir às pressas ▶ VI fugir; (*horse*) disparar

bomb [bɔm] N bomba ▶ VT bombardear; **bomb scare** N ameaça de bomba

bond [bɔnd] N (*binding promise*) compromisso; (*link*) vínculo, laço; (*Finance*) obrigação *f*; (*Comm*): **in ~** (*goods*) retido sob caução na alfândega

bone [bəun] N osso; (*of fish*) espinha ▶ VT desossar; tirar as espinhas de

bonfire ['bɔnfaɪə^r] N fogueira

bonnet ['bɔnɪt] N toucado; (BRIT: *of car*) capô *m*

bonus ['bəunəs] N (*payment*) bônus *m*; (*fig*) gratificação *f*

boo [bu:] VT vaiar ▶ EXCL ruuh!, bu!

book [buk] N livro; (*of stamps, tickets*) talão *m* ▶ VT reservar; (*driver*) autuar; (*football player*) mostrar o cartão amarelo a; **books** NPL (*Comm*) contas *fpl*, contabilidade *f*; **bookcase** N estante *f* (para livros); **booking office** (BRIT) N (*Rail, Theatre*) bilheteria (BR), bilheteira (PT); **book-keeping** N escrituração *f*, contabilidade *f*; **booklet** N livrinho, brochura; **bookmark** N (*for book*) marcador *m* de livro; (*Comput*) favorito, bookmark *m*; **bookshop, bookstore** N livraria

boom [bu:m] N (*noise*) barulho, estrondo; (*in sales etc*) aumento rápido ▶ VI retumbar; (*business*) tomar surto

boost [bu:st] N estímulo ▶ VT estimular

boot [bu:t] N bota; (*for football*) chuteira; (BRIT: *of car*) porta-malas *m*

(BR), porta-bagagem *m* (PT) ▶ VT (*Comput*) iniciar; **to ~ ...** (*in addition*) ainda por cima ...
booth [bu:ð] N (*at fair*) barraca; (*telephone booth, voting booth*) cabine *f*
booze [bu:z] (*inf*) N bebida alcoólica
border ['bɔ:dəʳ] N margem *f*; (*for flowers*) borda; (*of a country*) fronteira; (*on cloth etc*) debrum *m*, remate *m* ▶ VT (*also*: **~ on**) limitar-se com; **border on** VT FUS (*fig*) chegar às raias de; **borderline** N fronteira
bore [bɔ:ʳ] PT *of* **bear** ▶ VT (*hole*) abrir; (*well*) cavar; (*person*) aborrecer ▶ N (*person*) chato(-a), maçante *m/f*; (*of gun*) calibre *m*; **to be ~d to tears** *or* **~d to death** *or* **~d stiff** estar muito entediado; **boredom** N tédio, aborrecimento; **boring** ADJ chato, maçante
born [bɔ:n] ADJ: **to be ~** nascer
borne [bɔ:n] PP *of* **bear**
borough ['bʌrə] N município
borrow ['bɔrəu] VT: **to ~ sth (from sb)** pedir algo emprestado a alguém
bosom ['buzəm] N peito
boss [bɔs] N (*employer*) patrão(-troa) *m/f* ▶ VT (*also*: **~ about, ~ around**) mandar em; **bossy** ADJ mandão(-dona)
both [bəuθ] ADJ, PRON ambos(-as), os dois/as duas ▶ ADV: **~ A and B** tanto A como B; **~ of us went, we ~ went** nós dois fomos, ambos fomos
bother ['bɔðəʳ] VT (*worry*) preocupar; (*disturb*) atrapalhar ▶ VI (*also*: **~ o.s.**) preocupar-se ▶ N preocupação *f*; (*nuisance*) amolação *f*, inconveniente *m*
bottle ['bɔtl] N garrafa; (*of perfume, medicine*) frasco; (*baby's*) mamadeira (BR), biberão *m* (PT) ▶ VT engarrafar; **bottle up** VT conter, refrear; **bottle bank** N *depósito de vidro para reciclagem*, vidrão *m* (PT); **bottle-opener** N abridor *m* (de garrafas) (BR), abre-garrafas *m inv* (PT)
bottom ['bɔtəm] N fundo; (*buttocks*) traseiro; (*of page, list*) pé *m*; (*of class*) nível *m* mais baixo ▶ ADJ (*low*) inferior, mais baixo; (*last*) último
bought [bɔ:t] PT, PP *of* **buy**
boulder ['bəuldəʳ] N pedregulho, matacão *m*
bounce [bauns] VI saltar, quicar; (*cheque*) ser devolvido (*por insuficiência de fundos*) ▶ VT fazer saltar ▶ N (*rebound*) salto; **bouncer** (*inf*) N leão de chácara *m*
bound [baund] PT, PP *of* **bind** ▶ N (*leap*) pulo, salto; (*gen pl: limit*) limite *m* ▶ VI (*leap*) pular, saltar ▶ VT (*border*) demarcar ▶ ADJ: **~ by** limitado por; **to be ~ to do sth** (*obliged*) ter a obrigação de fazer algo; (*likely*) na certa ir fazer algo; **~ for** com destino a
boundary ['baundrɪ] N limite *m*, fronteira
bout [baut] N (*of malaria etc*) ataque *m*; (*of activity*) explosão *f*; (*Boxing etc*) combate *m*
bow[1] [bəu] N (*knot*) laço; (*weapon, Mus*) arco
bow[2] [bau] N (*of the body*) reverência; (*of the head*) inclinação *f*; (*Naut*: *also*: **~s**) proa ▶ VI curvar-se, fazer uma reverência; (*yield*): **to ~ to** *or* **before** ceder ante, submeter-se a

bowels ['bauəlz] NPL intestinos *mpl*, tripas *fpl*; (*fig*) entranhas *fpl*
bowl [bəul] N tigela; (*ball*) bola ▶ VI (*Cricket*) arremessar a bola
bowler ['bəulə^r] N (*Cricket*) lançador *m* (da bola); (BRIT: *also*: ~ **hat**) chapéu-coco *m*
bowling ['bəulɪŋ] N (*game*) boliche *m*; **bowling alley** N boliche *m*; **bowling green** N gramado (BR) *or* relvado (PT) para jogo de bolas
bowls [bəulz] N jogo de bolas
bow tie ['bəu-] N gravata-borboleta
box [bɔks] N caixa; (*Theatre*) camarote *m* ▶ VT encaixotar; (*Sport*) boxear contra ▶ VI (*Sport*) boxear; **boxer** N (*person*) boxeador *m*, pugilista *m*; **boxer shorts** NPL cueca samba-canção; **boxing** N (*Sport*) boxe *m*, pugilismo; **Boxing Day** (BRIT) N *Dia de Santo Estevão (26 de dezembro)*; **box office** N bilheteria (BR), bilheteira (PT)
boy [bɔɪ] N (*young*) menino, garoto; (*older*) moço, rapaz *m*; (*son*) filho
boycott ['bɔɪkɔt] N boicote *m*, boicotagem *f* ▶ VT boicotar
boyfriend ['bɔɪfrɛnd] N namorado
bra [brɑ:] N sutiã *m* (BR), soutien *m* (PT)
brace [breɪs] N (*on teeth*) aparelho; (*tool*) arco de pua ▶ VT retesar; **braces** NPL (BRIT) suspensórios *mpl*; **to ~ o.s.** (*for weight, fig*) preparar-se
bracelet ['breɪslɪt] N pulseira
bracket ['brækɪt] N (*Tech*) suporte *m*; (*group*) classe *f*, categoria; (*range*) faixa; (*also*: **round ~**) parêntese *m* ▶ VT pôr entre parênteses; (*fig*) agrupar
brag [bræg] VI gabar-se, contar vantagem
braid [breɪd] N (*trimming*) galão *m*; (*of hair*) trança
brain [breɪn] N cérebro; **brains** NPL (*Culin*) miolos *mpl*; (*intelligence*) inteligência, miolos
braise [breɪz] VT assar na panela
brake [breɪk] N freio (BR), travão *m* (PT) ▶ VT, VI frear (BR), travar (PT)
bran [bræn] N farelo
branch [brɑ:ntʃ] N ramo, galho; (*Comm*) sucursal *f*, filial *f*; **branch out** VI (*fig*) diversificar suas atividades; **to ~ out into** estender suas atividades a
brand [brænd] N marca; (*fig: type*) tipo ▶ VT (*cattle*) marcar com ferro quente; **brand-new** ADJ novo em folha, novinho
brandy ['brændɪ] N conhaque *m*
brash [bræʃ] ADJ (*forward*) descarado
brass [brɑ:s] N latão *m*; **the ~** (*Mus*) os metais; **brass band** N banda de música
brat [bræt] (*pej*) N pirralho(-a), fedelho(-a)
brave [breɪv] ADJ valente, corajoso ▶ VT (*face up to*) desafiar; **bravery** N coragem *f*, bravura
Brazil [brə'zɪl] N Brasil *m*; **Brazilian** ADJ, N brasileiro(-a)
breach [bri:tʃ] VT abrir brecha em ▶ N (*gap*) brecha; (*breaking*): **~ of contract** inadimplência (BR), inadimplemento (PT)
bread [brɛd] N pão *m*; **breadbin** (BRIT) N caixa de pão; **breadbox** (US) N caixa de pão; **breadcrumbs** NPL migalhas *fpl*; (*Culin*) farinha de rosca
breadth [brɛtθ] N largura; (*fig*) amplitude *f*
break [breɪk] (*pt* **broke**, *pp* **broken**) VT quebrar (BR), partir (PT); (*promise*) quebrar; (*law*) violar, transgredir; (*record*) bater ▶ VI

quebrar-se, partir-se; (*storm*) estourar; (*weather*) mudar; (*dawn*) amanhecer; (*story, news*) revelar ▶ N (*gap*) abertura; (*fracture*) fratura; (*rest*) descanso; (*interval*) intervalo; (*at school*) recreio; (*chance*) oportunidade *f*; **to ~ the news to sb** dar a notícia a alguém; **to ~ even** sair sem ganhar nem perder; **to ~ free** *or* **loose** soltar-se; **to ~ open** (*door etc*) arrombar; **break down** VT (*figures, data*) analisar ▶ VI (*machine, Aut*) enguiçar, pifar (*inf*); (*Med*) sofrer uma crise nervosa; (*person: cry*) desatar a chorar; (*talks*) fracassar; **break in** VT (*horse etc*) domar ▶ VI (*burglar*) forçar uma entrada; (*interrupt*) interromper; **break into** VT FUS (*house*) arrombar; **break off** VI (*speaker*) parar-se, deter-se; (*branch*) partir; **break out** VI (*war*) estourar; (*prisoner*) libertar-se; **to ~ out in spots/a rash** aparecer coberto de manchas/brotoejas; **break up** VI (*ship*) partir-se; (*partnership*) acabar; (*marriage*) desmanchar-se ▶ VT (*rocks*) partir; (*biscuit etc*) quebrar; (*journey*) romper; (*fight*) intervir em; **you're ~ing up** sua voz está falhando; **breakdown** N (*Aut*) enguiço, avaria; (*in communications*) interrupção *f*; (*of marriage*) fracasso, término; (*Med*: *also*: **nervous breakdown**) esgotamento nervoso; (*of figures*) discriminação *f*, desdobramento

breakfast ['brɛkfəst] N café *m* da manhã (BR), pequeno-almoço (PT)

break-in N roubo com arrombamento

breakthrough ['breɪkθruː] N (*fig*) avanço, novo progresso

breast [brɛst] N (*of woman*) peito, seio; (*chest, meat*) peito; **breast-feed** (*irreg*: *like* **feed**) VT, VI amamentar; **breaststroke** N nado de peito

breath [brɛθ] N fôlego, respiração *f*; **out of ~** ofegante, sem fôlego

breathe [briːð] VT, VI respirar; **breathe in** VT, VI inspirar; **breathe out** VT, VI expirar; **breathing** N respiração *f*

breathless ['brɛθlɪs] ADJ sem fôlego

breed [briːd] (*pt, pp* **bred**) VT (*animals*) criar; (*plants*) multiplicar ▶ VI acasalar-se ▶ N raça

breeze [briːz] N brisa, aragem *f*; **breezy** ADJ (*person*) despreocupado, animado; (*weather*) ventoso

brew [bruː] VT (*tea*) fazer; (*beer*) fermentar ▶ VI (*storm, fig*) armar-se; **brewery** N cervejaria

bribe [braɪb] N suborno ▶ VT subornar; **bribery** N suborno

brick [brɪk] N tijolo; **bricklayer** N pedreiro

bride [braɪd] N noiva; **bridegroom** N noivo; **bridesmaid** N dama de honra

bridge [brɪdʒ] N ponte *f*; (*Naut*) ponte de comando; (*Cards*) bridge *m*; (*of nose*) cavalete *m* ▶ VT transpor

bridle ['braɪdl] N cabeçada, freio

brief [briːf] ADJ breve ▶ N (*Jur*) causa; (*task*) tarefa ▶ VT (*inform*) informar; **briefs** N PL (*for men*) cueca (BR), cuecas *fpl* (PT); (*for women*) calcinha (BR), cuecas *fpl* (PT); **briefcase** N pasta; **briefly** ADV (*glance*) rapidamente; (*say*) em poucas palavras

bright [braɪt] ADJ claro, brilhante; (*weather*) resplandecente; (*person*:

clever) inteligente; (: *lively*) alegre, animado; (*colour*) vivo; (*future*) promissor(a), favorável
brilliant ['brɪljənt] ADJ brilhante; (*inf: great*) sensacional
brim [brɪm] N borda; (*of hat*) aba
brine [braɪn] N (*Culin*) salmoura
bring [brɪŋ] (*pt, pp* **brought**) VT trazer; **bring about** VT ocasionar, produzir; **bring back** VT restabelecer; (*return*) devolver; **bring down** VT (*price*) abaixar; (*government, plane*) derrubar; **bring forward** VT adiantar; **bring off** VT (*task, plan*) levar a cabo; **bring out** VT (*object*) tirar; (*meaning*) salientar; (*new product, book*) lançar; **bring round** VT fazer voltar a si; **bring up** VT (*person*) educar, criar; (*carry up*) subir; (*question*) introduzir; (*food*) vomitar
brisk [brɪsk] ADJ vigoroso; (*tone, person*) enérgico; (*trade, business*) ativo
bristle ['brɪsl] N (*of animal*) pelo rijo; (*of beard*) pelo de barba curta; (*of brush*) cerda ▶ VI (*in anger*) encolerizar-se
Britain ['brɪtən] N (*also*: **Great ~**) Grã-Bretanha
British ['brɪtɪʃ] ADJ britânico ▶ NPL: **the ~** os britânicos; **British Isles** NPL: **the British Isles** as ilhas Britânicas
Briton ['brɪtən] N britânico(-a)
brittle ['brɪtl] ADJ quebradiço, frágil
broad [brɔ:d] ADJ (*street, range*) amplo; (*shoulders, smile*) largo; (*distinction, outline*) geral; (*accent*) carregado; **in ~ daylight** em plena luz do dia; **broadband** N banda larga; **broadcast** (*pt, pp* **broadcast**) N transmissão *f* ▶ VT, VI transmitir; **broaden** VT alargar ▶ VI alargar-se; **to broaden one's mind** abrir os horizontes; **broadly** ADV em geral; **broad-minded** ADJ tolerante, liberal
broccoli ['brɔkəlɪ] N brócolis *mpl* (BR), brócolos *mpl* (PT)
brochure ['brəuʃjuə^r] N folheto, brochura
broke [brəuk] PT *of* **break** ▶ ADJ (*inf*) sem um vintém, duro; (: *company*): **to go ~** quebrar
broken ['brəukən] PP *of* **break** ▶ ADJ quebrado; **in ~ English** num inglês mascavado
broker ['brəukə^r] N corretor(a) *m/f*
bronchitis [brɔŋ'kaɪtɪs] N bronquite *f*
bronze [brɔnz] N bronze *m*
brooch [brəutʃ] N broche *m*
brood [bru:d] N ninhada ▶ VI (*person*) cismar, remoer
broom [brum] N vassoura; (*Bot*) giesta-das-vassouras *f*
Bros. ABBR (*Comm*: = *brothers*) Irmãos
broth [brɔθ] N caldo
brothel ['brɔθl] N bordel *m*
brother ['brʌðə^r] N irmão *m*; **brother-in-law** N cunhado
brought [brɔ:t] PT, PP *of* **bring**
brow [brau] N (*forehead*) fronte *f*, testa; (*eyebrow*) sobrancelha; (*of hill*) cimo, cume *m*
brown [braun] ADJ marrom (BR), castanho (PT); (*hair*) castanho; (*tanned*) bronzeado, moreno ▶ N (*colour*) cor *f* marrom (BR) *or* castanha (PT) ▶ VT (*Culin*) dourar; **brown bread** N pão *m* integral; **Brownie** N (*also*: **Brownie Guide**) fadinha de bandeirante; **brown sugar** N açúcar *m* mascavo
browse [brauz] VI (*in shop*) dar uma olhada; **to ~ through a book** folhear um livro; **browser** N (*Comput*) browser *m*

bruise [bru:z] N hematoma *m*, contusão *f* ▶ VT machucar
brunette [bru:'nɛt] N morena
brush [brʌʃ] N escova; (*for painting, shaving etc*) pincel *m*; (*quarrel*) bate-boca *m* ▶ VT varrer; (*groom*) escovar; (*also*: **~ against**) tocar ao passar, roçar; **brush aside** VT afastar, não fazer caso de; **brush up** VT retocar, revisar
Brussels ['brʌslz] N Bruxelas; **Brussels sprout** N couve-de-bruxelas *f*
brutal ['bru:tl] ADJ brutal
bubble ['bʌbl] N bolha (BR), borbulha (PT) ▶ VI borbulhar; **bubble bath** N banho de espuma; **bubble gum** N chiclete *m* (de bola) (BR), pastilha elástica (PT)
buck [bʌk] N (*rabbit*) macho; (*deer*) cervo; (*US inf*) dólar *m* ▶ VI corcovear; **to pass the ~** fazer o jogo de empurra; **buck up** VI (*cheer up*) animar-se, cobrar ânimo
bucket ['bʌkɪt] N balde *m*
buckle ['bʌkl] N fivela ▶ VT afivelar ▶ VI torcer-se, cambar-se
bud [bʌd] N broto; (*of flower*) botão *m* ▶ VI brotar, desabrochar
Buddhism ['budɪzəm] N budismo
buddy ['bʌdɪ] (*US*) N camarada *m*, companheiro
budge [bʌdʒ] VT mover ▶ VI mexer-se
budgerigar ['bʌdʒərɪgɑ:ʳ] N periquito
budget ['bʌdʒɪt] N orçamento ▶ VI: **to ~ for sth** incluir algo no orçamento
budgie ['bʌdʒɪ] N = **budgerigar**
buff [bʌf] ADJ (*colour*) cor de camurça ▶ N (*inf: enthusiast*) aficionado(-a)
buffalo ['bʌfələu] (**buffalo** *or pl* **buffaloes**) N (BRIT) búfalo; (*US: bison*) bisão *m*
buffer ['bʌfəʳ] N para-choque *m*; (*Comput*) buffer *m*
buffet[1] ['bufeɪ] (BRIT) N (*in station*) bar *m*; (*food*) bufê *m*
buffet[2] ['bʌfɪt] VT fustigar
buffet car (BRIT) N vagão-restaurante *m*
bug [bʌg] N (*esp US: insect*) bicho; (*fig: germ*) micróbio; (*spy device*) microfone *m* oculto; escuta clandestina; (*Comput: of program*) erro; (*: of equipment*) defeito ▶ VT (*inf: annoy*) apoquentar, incomodar; (*room*) colocar microfones em; (*phone*) grampear
build [bɪld] (*pt, pp* **built**) N (*of person*) talhe *m*, estatura ▶ VT construir, edificar; **build up** VT acumular; **builder** N construtor(a) *m/f*, empreiteiro(-a); **building** N construção *f*; (*residential, offices*) edifício, prédio; **building society** (BRIT) N sociedade *f* de crédito imobiliário, financiadora
built [bɪlt] PT, PP *of* **build** ▶ ADJ: **~-in** (*cupboard*) embutido
bulb [bʌlb] N (*Bot*) bulbo; (*Elec*) lâmpada
Bulgaria [bʌl'gɛərɪə] N Bulgária
bulge [bʌldʒ] N bojo, saliência ▶ VI inchar-se; (*pocket etc*) fazer bojo
bulimia [bu:'lɪmɪə] N bulimia
bulk [bʌlk] N volume *m*; **in ~** (*Comm*) a granel; **the ~ of** a maior parte de; **bulky** ADJ volumoso
bull [bul] N touro
bulldozer ['buldəuzəʳ] N buldôzer *m*, escavadora
bullet ['bulɪt] N bala
bulletin ['bulɪtɪn] N noticiário; (*journal*) boletim *m*

bullfight ['bulfaɪt] N tourada; **bullfighter** N toureiro; **bullfighting** N tauromaquia

bully ['bulɪ] N fanfarrão *m*, valentão *m* ▶ VT intimidar, tiranizar

bum [bʌm] N (*inf: backside*) bumbum *m*; (*esp US: tramp*) vagabundo(-a), vadio(-a)

bumblebee ['bʌmblbi:] N mamangaba

bump [bʌmp] N (*in car*) batida; (*jolt*) sacudida; (*on head*) galo; (*on road*) elevação *f* ▶ VT bater contra, dar encontrão em ▶ VI dar sacudidas; **bump into** VT FUS chocar-se com *or* contra, colidir com; (*inf: person*) dar com, topar com; **bumper** N (BRIT) para-choque *m* ▶ ADJ: **bumper crop/harvest** supersafra; **bumpy** ADJ (*road*) acidentado, cheio de altos e baixos

bun [bʌn] N pão *m* doce (BR), pãozinho (PT); (*in hair*) coque *m*

bunch [bʌntʃ] N (*of flowers*) ramo; (*of keys*) molho; (*of bananas, grapes*) cacho; (*of people*) grupo; **bunches** NPL (*in hair*) cachos *mpl*

bundle ['bʌndl] N trouxa, embrulho; (*of sticks*) feixe *m*; (*of papers*) maço ▶ VT (*also*: **~ up**) embrulhar, atar; (*put*): **to ~ sth/sb into** meter *or* enfiar algo/alguém correndo em

bungalow ['bʌŋgələu] N bangalô *m*, chalé *m*

bunion ['bʌnjən] N joanete *m*

bunk [bʌŋk] N beliche *m*; **bunk beds** NPL beliche *m*, cama-beliche *f*

bunker ['bʌŋkəʳ] N (*coal store*) carvoeira; (*Mil*) abrigo, casamata; (*Golf*) bunker *m*

buoy [bɔɪ] N boia; **buoy up** VT (*fig*) animar; **buoyant** ADJ flutuante; (*person*) alegre; (*market*) animado

burden ['bə:dn] N responsabilidade *f*, fardo; (*load*) carga ▶ VT sobrecarregar; (*trouble*): **to be a ~ to sb** ser um estorvo para alguém

bureau [bjuə'rəu] (*pl* **bureaux**) N (BRIT: *desk*) secretária, escrivaninha; (US: *chest of drawers*) cômoda; (*office*) escritório, agência

bureaucracy [bjuə'rɔkrəsɪ] N burocracia; **bureau de change** [-də'ʃɑ̃ʒ] (*pl* **bureaux de change**) N casa de câmbio

burger ['bə:gəʳ] N hambúrguer *m*

burglar ['bə:gləʳ] N ladrão/ladrona *m/f*; **burglar alarm** N alarma de roubo; **burglary** N roubo

burial ['bɛrɪəl] N enterro

burn [bə:n] (*pt, pp* **burned** *or* **burnt**) VT queimar; (*house*) incendiar ▶ VI queimar-se, arder; (*sting*) arder, picar ▶ N queimadura; **burn down** VT incendiar; **burning** ADJ ardente; (*hot: sand etc*) abrasador(a); (*ambition*) grande

burrow ['bʌrəu] N toca, lura ▶ VI fazer uma toca, cavar; (*rummage*) esquadrinhar

burst [bə:st] (*pt, pp* **burst**) VT arrebentar; (*banks etc*) romper ▶ VI estourar; (*tyre*) furar ▶ N rajada; **to ~ into flames** incendiar-se de repente; **to ~ into tears** desatar a chorar; **to ~ out laughing** cair na gargalhada; **to be ~ing with** (*emotion*) estar tomado de; (*subj: room, container*) estar abarrotado de; **a ~ of energy/speed/enthusiasm** uma explosão de energia/velocidade/entusiasmo; **burst into** VT FUS (*room etc*) irromper em

bury ['bɛrɪ] VT enterrar; (*at funeral*) sepultar; **to ~ one's head in one's hands** cobrir o rosto com as mãos; **to ~ one's head in the sand** (*fig*) bancar avestruz; **to ~ the hatchet** (*fig*) fazer as pazes

bus [bʌs] N ônibus *m inv* (BR), autocarro (PT); **bus conductor** N cobrador(a) *m/f* de ônibus

bush [buʃ] N arbusto, mata; (*scrubland*) sertão *m*; **to beat about the ~** ser evasivo

business ['bɪznɪs] N negócio; (*trading*) comércio, negócios *mpl*; (*firm*) empresa; (*occupation*) profissão *f*; **to be away on ~** estar fora a negócios; **it's my ~ to ...** encarrego-me de ...; **it's none of my ~** eu não tenho nada com isto; **he means ~** fala a sério; **business class** N (*on plane*) classe *f* executiva; **businesslike** ADJ eficiente, metódico; **businessman** *irreg* N homem *m* de negócios; **business trip** N viagem *f* de negócios; **businesswoman** *irreg* N mulher *f* de negócios

busker ['bʌskəʳ] (BRIT) N artista *m/f* de rua

bust [bʌst] N (*Anat*) busto ▶ ADJ (*inf: broken*) quebrado; **to go ~** falir

busy ['bɪzɪ] ADJ (*person*) ocupado, atarefado; (*shop, street*) animado, movimentado; (*US Tel*) ocupado (BR), impedido (PT) ▶ VT: **to ~ o.s. with** ocupar-se em *or* de

KEYWORD

but [bʌt] CONJ **1** (*yet*) mas, porém; **he's tired but Paul isn't** ele está cansado mas Paul não; **the trip was enjoyable but tiring** a viagem foi agradável porém cansativa

2 (*however*) mas; **I'd love to come, but I'm busy** eu adoraria vir, mas estou ocupado

3 (*showing disagreement, surprise etc*) mas; **but that's far too expensive!** mas isso é caro demais!

▶ PREP (*apart from, except*) exceto, menos; **he was/we've had nothing but trouble** ele só deu problema/nós só tivemos problema; **no-one but him** só ele, ninguém a não ser ele; **but for** sem, se não fosse; **(I'll do) anything but that** (eu faria) qualquer coisa menos isso

▶ ADV (*just, only*) apenas; **had I but known** se eu soubesse; **I can but try** a única coisa que eu posso fazer é tentar; **all but finished** quase acabado

butcher ['butʃəʳ] N açougueiro (BR), homem *m* do talho (PT) ▶ VT (*prisoners etc*) chacinar, massacrar; (*cattle etc for meat*) abater e carnear; **butcher's, butcher's shop** N açougue *m* (BR), talho (PT)

butler ['bʌtləʳ] N mordomo

butt [bʌt] N (*cask*) tonel *m*; (*of gun*) coronha; (*of cigarette*) toco (BR), ponta (PT); (BRIT *fig: target*) alvo ▶ VT (*subj: goat*) marrar; (*: person*) dar uma cabeçada em; **butt in** VI (*interrupt*) interromper

butter ['bʌtəʳ] N manteiga ▶ VT untar com manteiga

butterfly ['bʌtəflaɪ] N borboleta; (*Swimming: also:* **~ stroke**) nado borboleta

buttocks ['bʌtəks] NPL nádegas *fpl*

button ['bʌtn] N botão *m*; (*US: badge*) emblema *m* ▶ VT (*also:* **~ up**) abotoar ▶ VI ter botões

buy [baɪ] (*pt, pp* **bought**) VT comprar ▶ N compra; **to ~ sb sth/sth from sb** comprar algo para alguém/algo a alguém; **to ~ sb a drink** pagar um drinque para alguém; **buyer** N comprador(a) *m/f*

buzz [bʌz] N zumbido; (*inf: phone call*): **to give sb a ~** dar uma ligada para alguém ▶ VI zumbir; **buzzer** N cigarra, vibrador *m*

KEYWORD

by [baɪ] PREP **1** (*referring to cause, agent*) por, de; **killed by lightning** morto por um raio; **a painting by Picasso** um quadro de Picasso
2 (*referring to method, manner, means*) de, com; **by bus/car/train** de ônibus/carro/trem; **to pay by cheque** pagar com cheque; **by moonlight/candlelight** sob o luar/à luz de vela; **by saving hard, he ...** economizando muito, ele ...
3 (*via, through*) por, via; **we came by Dover** viemos por *or* via Dover
4 (*close to*) perto de, ao pé de; **a holiday by the sea** férias à beira-mar; **she sat by his bed** ela sentou-se ao lado de seu leito
5 (*past*) por; **she rushed by me** ela passou por mim correndo
6 (*not later than*): **by 4 o'clock** antes das quatro; **by this time tomorrow** esta mesma hora amanhã; **by the time I got here it was too late** quando eu cheguei aqui, já era tarde demais
7 (*during*): **by daylight** durante o dia
8 (*amount*) por; **by the kilometre** por quilômetro
9 (*Math, measure*) por; **it's broader by a metre** tem um metro a mais de largura
10 (*according to*) segundo, de acordo com; **it's all right by me** por mim tudo bem
11: **(all) by oneself** *etc* (completamente) só, sozinho; **he did it (all) by himself** ele fez tudo sozinho
12: **by the way** a propósito
▶ ADV **1** *see* **go, pass** *etc*
2: **by and by** logo, mais tarde; **by and large** em geral

bye ['baɪ], **bye-bye** ['baɪ'baɪ] EXCL até logo (BR), tchau (BR), adeus (PT)

bypass ['baɪpɑːs] N via secundária, desvio; (*Med*) ponte *f* de safena ▶ VT evitar

byte [baɪt] N (*Comput*) byte *m*

C

C [siː] N (*Mus*) dó *m*
cab [kæb] N táxi *m*; (*of truck etc*) boleia; (*of train*) cabina de maquinista
cabaret ['kæbəreɪ] N cabaré *m*
cabbage ['kæbɪdʒ] N repolho (BR), couve *f* (PT)
cabin ['kæbɪn] N cabana; (*on ship*) camarote *m*; (*on plane*) cabina de passageiros; **cabin crew** N (*Aviat*) tripulação *f*
cabinet ['kæbɪnɪt] N (*Pol*) gabinete *m*; (*furniture*) armário; (*also*: **display ~**) armário com vitrina
cable ['keɪbl] N cabo; (*telegram*) cabograma *m* ▶ VT enviar cabograma para; **cable television** N televisão *f* a cabo
cactus ['kæktəs] (*pl* **cacti**) N cacto
café ['kæfeɪ] N café *m*
cage [keɪdʒ] N (*bird cage*) gaiola; (*for large animals*) jaula; (*of lift*) cabina
cagoule [kə'guːl] N casaco de náilon
Cairo ['kaɪərəu] N o Cairo
cake [keɪk] N (*large*) bolo; (*small*) doce *m*, bolinho; **cake of soap** N sabonete *m*
calculate ['kælkjuleɪt] VT calcular; (*estimate*) avaliar; **calculation** N cálculo; **calculator** N calculador *m*
calendar ['kæləndə^r] N calendário; **calendar month** N mês *m* civil; **calendar year** N ano civil
calf [kɑːf] (*pl* **calves**) N (*of cow*) bezerro, vitela; (*of other animals*) cria; (*also*: **~skin**) pele *f* or couro de bezerro; (*Anat*) barriga da perna
calibre ['kælɪbə^r], (US) **caliber** N (*of person*) capacidade *f*, calibre *m*
call [kɔːl] VT chamar; (*label*) qualificar, descrever; (*Tel*) telefonar a, ligar para; (*witness*) citar; (*meeting, strike*) convocar ▶ VI chamar; (*shout*) gritar; (*Tel*) telefonar; (*visit*: *also*: **~ in, ~ round**) dar um pulo ▶ N (*shout, announcement*) chamada; (*also*: **telephone ~**) chamada, telefonema *m*; (*of bird*) canto; **to be ~ed** chamar-se; **on ~** de plantão; **call back** VI (*return*) voltar, passar de novo; (*Tel*) ligar de volta; **call for** VT FUS (*demand*) requerer, exigir; (*fetch*) ir buscar; **call off** VT (*cancel*) cancelar; **call on** VT FUS (*visit*) visitar; (*appeal to*) pedir; **call out** VI gritar, bradar; **call up** VT (*Mil*) chamar às fileiras; (*Tel*) ligar para; **call box** (BRIT) N cabine *f* telefônica; **call centre** (BRIT) N (*Tel*) central *f* de chamadas; **caller** N visita *m/f*; (*Tel*) chamador(a) *m/f*

callous ['kæləs] ADJ cruel, insensível
calm [kɑːm] ADJ calmo; (*peaceful*) tranquilo; (*weather*) estável ▸ N calma ▸ VT acalmar; (*fears, grief*) abrandar; **calm down** VT acalmar, tranquilizar ▸ VI acalmar-se
calorie ['kælərɪ] N caloria
calves [kɑːvz] NPL *of* **calf**
Cambodia [kæm'bəudjə] N Camboja
camcorder ['kæmkɔːdə^r] N filmadora, máquina de filmar
came [keɪm] PT *of* **come**
camel ['kæməl] N camelo
camera ['kæmərə] N máquina fotográfica; (*Cinema, TV*) câmera; **in ~** (*Jur*) em câmara; **camera phone** N celular *m* com câmera
camouflage ['kæməflɑːʒ] N camuflagem *f* ▸ VT camuflar
camp [kæmp] N campo, acampamento; (*Mil*) acampamento; (*for prisoners*) campo; (*faction*) facção *f* ▸ VI acampar ▸ ADJ afeminado
campaign [kæm'peɪn] N (*Mil, Pol etc*) campanha ▸ VI fazer campanha
camper ['kæmpə^r] N campista *m/f*; (*vehicle*) reboque *m*
camping ['kæmpɪŋ] N camping *m* (BR), campismo (PT); **to go ~** acampar
campsite ['kæmpsaɪt] N camping *m* (BR), parque *m* de campismo (PT)
campus ['kæmpəs] N campus *m*, cidade *f* universitária
can¹ [kæn] N lata ▸ VT enlatar

KEYWORD

can² [kæn] (*negative* **can't** *or* **cannot**, *pt, conditional* **could**) AUX VB **1** (*be able to*) poder; **you can do it if you try** se você tentar, você consegue fazê-lo; **I'll help you all I can** ajudarei você em tudo que eu puder; **she couldn't sleep that night** ela não conseguiu dormir aquela noite; **can you hear me?** você está me ouvindo?
2 (*know how to*) saber; **I can swim** sei nadar; **can you speak Portuguese?** você fala português?
3 (*may*): **could I have a word with you?** será que eu podia falar com você?
4 (*expressing disbelief, puzzlement*): **it CAN'T be true!** não pode ser verdade!; **what CAN he want?** o que é que ele quer?
5 (*expressing possibility, suggestion etc*): **he could be in the library** ele talvez esteja na biblioteca; **they could have forgotten** eles podiam ter esquecido

Canada ['kænədə] N Canadá *m*; **Canadian** [kə'neɪdɪən] ADJ, N canadense *m/f*
canal [kə'næl] N canal *m*
canary [kə'nɛərɪ] N canário
cancel ['kænsəl] VT cancelar; (*contract*) anular; (*cross out*) riscar, invalidar; **cancellation** [kænsə'leɪʃən] N cancelamento
cancer ['kænsə^r] N câncer *m* (BR), cancro (PT); **C~** (*Astrology*) Câncer
candidate ['kændɪdeɪt] N candidato(-a)
candle ['kændl] N vela; (*in church*) círio; **candlestick** N (*plain*) castiçal *m*; (*bigger, ornate*) candelabro, lustre *m*
candy ['kændɪ] N (*also*: **sugar ~**) açúcar *m* cristalizado; (US) bala (BR), rebuçado (PT)
cane [keɪn] N (*Bot*) cana; (*stick*) bengala ▸ VT (BRIT *Sch*) castigar (com bengala)

canister ['kænɪstəʳ] N lata
cannabis ['kænəbɪs] N maconha
canned [kænd] ADJ (*food*) em lata, enlatado
cannon ['kænən] (*pl inv or* **cannons**) N canhão *m*
cannot ['kænɔt] = **can not**
canoe [kə'nu:] N canoa
can't [kɑ:nt] = **can not**
canteen [kæn'ti:n] N cantina; (BRIT: *of cutlery*) jogo (de talheres)
canter ['kæntəʳ] VI ir a meio galope
canvas ['kænvəs] N (*material*) lona; (*for painting*) tela; (*Naut*) velas *fpl*
canvass ['kænvəs] VI (*Pol*): **to ~ for** fazer campanha por ▶ VT sondar
canyon ['kænjən] N canhão *m*, garganta, desfiladeiro
cap [kæp] N gorro; (*of pen, bottle*) tampa; (*contraceptive*: *also*: **Dutch ~**) diafragma *m*; (*for toy gun*) cartucho ▶ VT (*outdo*) superar; (*put limit on*) limitar
capable ['keɪpəbl] ADJ (*of sth*) capaz; (*competent*) competente, hábil
capacity [kə'pæsɪtɪ] N capacidade *f*; (*of stadium etc*) lotação *f*; (*role*) condição *f*, posição *f*
cape [keɪp] N capa; (*Geo*) cabo
caper ['keɪpəʳ] N (*Culin*: *gen pl*) alcaparra; (*prank*) travessura
capital ['kæpɪtl] N (*also*: **~ city**) capital *f*; (*money*) capital *m*; (*also*: **~ letter**) maiúscula; **capitalism** N capitalismo; **capitalist** ADJ, N capitalista *m/f*; **capital punishment** N pena de morte
Capitol ['kæpɪtl] N *ver nota*

> O Capitólio (**Capitol**) é a sede do Congresso dos Estados Unidos, localizado no monte Capitólio (*Capitol Hill*), em Washington.

Capricorn ['kæprɪkɔ:n] N Capricórnio
capsize [kæp'saɪz] VT, VI emborcar, virar
capsule ['kæpsju:l] N cápsula
captain ['kæptɪn] N capitão *m*
caption ['kæpʃən] N legenda
capture ['kæptʃəʳ] VT prender, aprisionar; (*person*) capturar; (*place*) tomar; (*attention*) atrair, chamar ▶ N captura; (*of place*) tomada
car [kɑ:ʳ] N carro, automóvel *m*; (*Rail*) vagão *m*
caramel ['kærəməl] N (*sweet*) caramelo; (*burnt sugar*) caramelado
caravan ['kærəvæn] N reboque *m* (BR), trailer *m* (BR), rulote *f* (PT); (*in desert*) caravana
carb [kɑ:b] (*inf*) N ABBR (= *carbohydrate*) carboidrato
carbohydrate [kɑ:bəu'haɪdreɪt] N hidrato de carbono; (*food*) carboidrato
carbon ['kɑ:bən] N carbono; **carbon copy** N cópia de papel carbono; **carbon dioxide** [-daɪ'ɔksaɪd] N dióxido de carbono; **carbon footprint** N pegada de carbono; **carbon monoxide** [-mə'nɔksaɪd] N monóxido de carbono; **carbon-neutral** ADJ sem emissão de carbono; **carbon offset** N compensação *f* de emissão de carbono
carburettor [kɑ:bju'rɛtəʳ], (US) **carburetor** N carburador *m*

C

card [kɑ:d] N (*also*: **playing ~**) carta; (*visiting card, postcard etc*) cartão *m*; (*thin cardboard*) cartolina;
cardboard N cartão *m*, papelão *m*
cardigan ['kɑ:dɪgən] N casaco de lã, cardigã *m*
cardinal ['kɑ:dɪnl] ADJ cardeal; (*Math*) cardinal ▶ N (*Rel*) cardeal *m*
care [kɛəʳ] N cuidado; (*worry*) preocupação *f*; (*charge*) encargo, custódia ▶ VI: **to ~ about** (*person, animal*) preocupar-se com; (*thing, idea*) ter interesse em; **~ of** (*on letter*) aos cuidados de; **in sb's ~** a cargo de alguém; **to take ~ (to do)** cuidar-se *or* ter o cuidado (de fazer); **to take ~ of** (*person*) cuidar de; (*situation*) encarregar-se de; **I don't ~** não me importa; **I couldn't ~ less** não dou a mínima; **care for** VT FUS cuidar de; (*like*) gostar de
career [kə'rɪəʳ] N carreira ▶ VI (*also*: **~ along**) correr a toda velocidade
carefree ['kɛəfri:] ADJ despreocupado
careful ['kɛəful] ADJ (*thorough*) cuidadoso; (*cautious*) cauteloso; **(be) ~!** tenha cuidado!; **carefully** ADV cuidadosamente; cautelosamente
careless ['kɛəlɪs] ADJ descuidado; (*heedless*) desatento
carer ['kɛərəʳ] N (*professional*) acompanhante *m/f*; (*unpaid*) cuidador(a) *m/f*
caretaker ['kɛəteɪkəʳ] N zelador(a) *m/f*
car-ferry N barca para carros (BR), barco de passagem (PT)
cargo ['kɑ:gəu] (*pl* **cargoes**) N carga
car hire (BRIT) N aluguel *m* (BR) *or* aluguer *m* (PT) de carros
Caribbean [kærɪ'bi:ən] N: **the ~ (Sea)** o Caribe
caring ['kɛərɪŋ] ADJ (*person*) bondoso; (*society*) humanitário
carnation [kɑ:'neɪʃən] N cravo
carnival ['kɑ:nɪvəl] N carnaval *m*; (US: *funfair*) parque *m* de diversões
carol ['kærəl] N: **(Christmas) ~** cântico de Natal
car park (BRIT) N estacionamento
carpenter ['kɑ:pɪntəʳ] N carpinteiro
carpet ['kɑ:pɪt] N tapete *m* ▶ VT atapetar
carriage ['kærɪdʒ] N carruagem *f*; (BRIT *Rail*) vagão *m*; (*of goods*) transporte *m*; (: *cost*) porte *m*;
carriageway (BRIT) N (*part of road*) pista
carrier ['kærɪəʳ] N transportador(a) *m/f*; (*company*) empresa de transportes, transportadora; (*Med*) portador(a) *m/f*; **carrier bag** (BRIT) N saco, sacola
carrot ['kærət] N cenoura
carry ['kærɪ] VT levar; (*transport*) transportar; (*involve: responsibilities etc*) implicar ▶ VI (*sound*) projetar-se; **to get carried away** (*fig*) exagerar; **carry on** VI seguir, continuar ▶ VT prosseguir, continuar; **carry out** VT (*orders*) cumprir; (*investigation*) levar a cabo, realizar
cart [kɑ:t] N carroça, carreta ▶ VT transportar (em carroça)
carton ['kɑ:tən] N (*box*) caixa (de papelão); (*of yogurt*) pote *m*; (*of milk*) caixa; (*packet*) pacote *m*
cartoon [kɑ:'tu:n] N (*drawing*) desenho; (BRIT: *comic strip*) história em quadrinhos (BR), banda desenhada (PT); (*film*) desenho animado
cartridge ['kɑ:trɪdʒ] N cartucho; (*of record player*) cápsula

carve [kɑːv] VT (*meat*) trinchar; (*wood, stone*) cinzelar, esculpir; (*initials, design*) gravar; **carve up** VT dividir, repartir; **carving** N (*object*) escultura; (*design*) talha, entalhe *m*

case [keɪs] N caso; (*for spectacles etc*) estojo; (*Jur*) causa; (BRIT: *also*: **suit~**) mala; (*of wine etc*) caixa; **in ~ (of)** em caso (de); **in any ~** em todo o caso; **just in ~** *conj* se por acaso; *adv* por via das dúvidas

cash [kæʃ] N dinheiro (em espécie) ▶ VT descontar; **to pay (in) ~** pagar em dinheiro; **~ on delivery** pagamento contra entrega; **cash card** (BRIT) N cartão *m* de saque; **cash desk** (BRIT) N caixa; **cash dispenser** N caixa automática *or* eletrônica

cashew [kæ'ʃuː] N (*also*: **~ nut**) castanha de caju

cashier [kæ'ʃɪəʳ] N caixa *m/f*

cash point N caixa *m* eletrônico

cash register N caixa registradora

casino [kə'siːnəu] N cassino

casket ['kɑːskɪt] N cofre *m*, porta-joias *m inv*; (US: *coffin*) caixão *m*

casserole ['kæsərəul] N panela de ir ao forno; (*food*) ensopado (BR) no forno, guisado (PT) no forno

cassette [kæ'sɛt] N fita-cassete *f*; **cassette player** N toca-fitas *m inv*

cast [kɑːst] (*pt, pp* **cast**) VT (*throw*) lançar, atirar; (*Theatre*): **to ~ sb as Hamlet** dar a alguém o papel de Hamlet ▶ N (*Theatre*) elenco; (*also*: **plaster ~**) gesso; **to ~ one's vote** votar; **cast off** VI (*Naut*) soltar o cabo; (*Knitting*) rematar os pontos; **cast on** VI montar os pontos

caster sugar ['kɑːstəʳ-] (BRIT) N açuçar *m* branco refinado

castle ['kɑːsl] N castelo; (*Chess*) torre *f*

casual ['kæʒjul] ADJ (*by chance*) fortuito; (*work etc*) eventual; (*unconcerned*) despreocupado; (*clothes etc*) descontraído, informal

casualty ['kæʒjultɪ] N ferido(-a); (*dead*) morto(-a); (*of situation*) vítima; (*department*) pronto-socorro

cat [kæt] N gato

catalogue ['kætəlɔg], (US) **catalog** N catálogo ▶ VT catalogar

catarrh [kə'tɑːʳ] N catarro

catastrophe [kə'tæstrəfɪ] N catástrofe *f*

catch [kætʃ] (*pt, pp* **caught**) VT pegar (BR), apanhar (PT); (*fish*) pescar; (*arrest*) prender, deter; (*person: by surprise*) flagrar, surpreender; (*attention*) atrair; (*hear*) ouvir; (*also*: **~ up**) alcançar ▶ VI (*fire*) pegar; (*in branches etc*) ficar preso, prender-se ▶ N (*fish etc*) pesca; (*game*) manha, armadilha; (*of lock*) trinco, lingueta; **to ~ fire** pegar fogo; (*building*) incendiar-se; **to ~ sight of** avistar; **catch on** VI (*understand*) entender (BR), perceber (PT); (*grow popular*) pegar; **catch up** VI equiparar-se ▶ VT (*also*: **~ up with**) alcançar; **catching** ADJ (*Med*) contagioso

category ['kætɪgərɪ] N categoria

cater ['keɪtəʳ] VI preparar comida; **cater for** VT FUS (*needs*) atender a; (*consumers*) satisfazer

caterpillar ['kætəpɪləʳ] N lagarta

cathedral [kə'θiːdrəl] N catedral *f*; **Catholic** ADJ, N (*Rel*) católico(-a)

catholic ['kæθəlɪk] ADJ eclético

cattle ['kætl] NPL gado

catwalk ['kætwɔːk] N passarela

C

caught [kɔ:t] PT, PP *of* **catch**
cauliflower ['kɔlɪflauəʳ] N couve-flor *f*
cause [kɔ:z] N causa; (*reason*) motivo, razão *f* ▶ VT causar, provocar
caution ['kɔ:ʃən] N cautela, prudência; (*warning*) aviso ▶ VT acautelar, avisar
cautious ['kɔ:ʃəs] ADJ cauteloso, prudente, precavido
cave [keɪv] N caverna, gruta; **cave in** VI ceder
cc ABBR (= *cubic centimetre*) cc; (*on letter etc*) = **carbon copy**
CCTV N ABBR (= *closed-circuit television*) CFTV; **CCTV camera** N câmera de segurança
CD N ABBR = **compact disc**; **CD burner, CD writer** N gravador *m* de CD; **CD-ROM** N ABBR (= *compact disc read-only memory*) CD-ROM *m*
cease [si:s] VT, VI cessar; **ceasefire** N cessar-fogo *m*
cedar ['si:dəʳ] N cedro
ceiling ['si:lɪŋ] N (*also fig*) teto
celebrate ['sɛlɪbreɪt] VT celebrar ▶ VI celebrar; (*birthday, anniversary etc*) festejar; (*Rel: mass*) rezar; **celebration** [sɛlɪ'breɪʃən] N (*party*) festa
celebrity [sɪ'lɛbrɪtɪ] N celebridade *f*
celery ['sɛlərɪ] N aipo
cell [sɛl] N cela; (*Bio*) célula; (*Elec*) pilha, elemento; (*US: cellphone*) celular *m* (BR), telemóvel *m* (PT)
cellar ['sɛləʳ] N porão *m*; (*for wine*) adega
cellphone ['sɛlfəun] N (telefone) celular *m* (BR), telemóvel *m* (PT)
cell tower (US) N (*Tel*) torre *f* de celular
cement [sə'mɛnt] N cimento
cemetery ['sɛmɪtrɪ] N cemitério
censor ['sɛnsəʳ] N censor(a) *m/f* ▶ VT censurar; **censorship** N censura
census ['sɛnsəs] N censo
cent [sɛnt] N cêntimo; *see also* **per cent**
centenary [sɛn'ti:nərɪ] N centenário
center ['sɛntəʳ] (US) = **centre**
centigrade ['sɛntɪgreɪd] ADJ centígrado
centimetre ['sɛntɪmi:təʳ], (US) **centimeter** N centímetro
central ['sɛntrəl] ADJ central; **Central America** N América Central; **central heating** N aquecimento central
centre ['sɛntəʳ], (US) **center** N centro; (*of room, circle etc*) meio ▶ VT centrar
century ['sɛntjurɪ] N século; **20th ~** século vinte
ceramic [sɪ'ræmɪk] ADJ cerâmico
cereal ['si:rɪəl] N cereal *m*
ceremony ['sɛrɪmənɪ] N cerimônia; (*ritual*) rito; **to stand on ~** fazer cerimônia
certain ['sə:tən] ADJ (*sure*) seguro; (*person*): **a ~ Mr Smith** um certo Sr. Smith; (*particular*): **~ days/places** certos dias/lugares; (*some*): **a ~ coldness/pleasure** uma certa frieza/um certo prazer; **for ~** com certeza; **certainly** ADV certamente, com certeza; **certainty** N certeza
certificate [sə'tɪfɪkɪt] N certidão *f*
certify ['sə:tɪfaɪ] VT certificar
cf. ABBR (= *compare*) cf
CFC N ABBR (= *chlorofluorocarbon*) CFC *m*
chain [tʃeɪn] N corrente *f*; (*of islands*) grupo; (*of mountains*) cordilheira; (*of shops*) cadeia; (*of events*) série *f* ▶ VT (*also*: **~ up**) acorrentar

chair [tʃɛəʳ] N cadeira; (*armchair*) poltrona; (*of university*) cátedra; (*of meeting*) presidência, mesa ▸VT (*meeting*) presidir; **chairlift** N teleférico; **chairman** *irreg* N presidente *m*
chalk [tʃɔːk] N (*Geo*) greda; (*for writing*) giz *m*
challenge [ˈtʃælɪndʒ] N desafio ▸VT desafiar; (*statement, right*) disputar, contestar; **challenging** ADJ desafiante; (*tone*) de desafio
chamber [ˈtʃeɪmbəʳ] N câmara; (BRIT *Jur: gen pl*) sala de audiências; **chambermaid** N arrumadeira (BR), empregada (PT); **chamber of commerce** N câmara de comércio
champagne [ʃæmˈpeɪn] N champanhe *m or f*
champion [ˈtʃæmpɪən] N campeão(-peã) *m/f*; (*of cause*) defensor(a) *m/f*; **championship** N campeonato
chance [tʃɑːns] N (*opportunity*) oportunidade, ocasião *f*; (*likelihood*) chance *f*; (*risk*) risco ▸VT arriscar ▸ADJ fortuito, casual; **to take a ~** arriscar-se; **by ~** por acaso; **to ~ it** arriscar-se
chancellor [ˈtʃɑːnsələʳ] N chanceler *m*; **C~ of the Exchequer** (BRIT) Ministro da Economia (Fazenda e Planejamento)
chandelier [ʃændəˈlɪəʳ] N lustre *m*
change [tʃeɪndʒ] VT (*alter*) mudar; (*wheel, bulb, money*) trocar; (*replace*) substituir; (*clothes, house*) mudar de, trocar de; (*nappy*) mudar, trocar; (*transform*): **to ~ sb into** transformar alguém em ▸VI mudar(-se); (*change clothes*) trocar-se; (*trains*) fazer baldeação (BR), mudar (PT); (*be transformed*): **to ~ into** transformar-se em ▸N mudança; (*exchange*) troca; (*difference*) diferença; (*of clothes*) muda; (*coins*) trocado; **to ~ gear** (*Aut*) trocar de marcha; **to ~ one's mind** mudar de ideia; **for a ~** para variar; **changeable** ADJ (*weather*) instável; (*mood*) inconstante
channel [ˈtʃænl] N canal *m*; (*of river*) leito; (*groove*) ranhura; (*fig: medium*) meio, via ▸VT: **to ~ (into)** canalizar (para); **the (English) C~** o Canal da Mancha
chant [tʃɑːnt] N canto; (*Rel*) cântico ▸VT cantar; (*word, slogan*) entoar
chaos [ˈkeɪɔs] N caos *m*
chap [tʃæp] N (BRIT *inf: man*) sujeito (BR), tipo (PT)
chapel [ˈtʃæpəl] N capela
chapter [ˈtʃæptəʳ] N capítulo
character [ˈkærɪktəʳ] N caráter *m*; (*in novel, film*) personagem *m/f*; (*letter*) letra; **characteristic** [kærɪktəˈrɪstɪk] ADJ característico
charcoal [ˈtʃɑːkəul] N carvão *m* de lenha; (*Art*) carvão *m*
charge [tʃɑːdʒ] N (*Jur*) encargo, acusação *f*; (*fee*) preço, custo; (*responsibility*) encargo ▸VT (*battery*) carregar; (*Mil*) atacar; (*customer*) cobrar dinheiro de; (*Jur*): **to ~ sb (with)** acusar alguém (de) ▸VI precipitar-se; **charges** NPL: **bank ~s** taxas *fpl* bancárias; **to reverse the ~s** (BRIT *Tel*) ligar a cobrar; **how much do you ~?** quanto você cobra?; **to ~ an expense (up) to sb's account** pôr a despesa na conta de alguém; **to take ~ of** encarregar-se de, tomar conta de; **to be in ~ of** estar a cargo de *or* encarregado de; **charge card** N cartão *m* de crédito (*emitido por uma loja*)

C

charity ['tʃærɪtɪ] N caridade *f*; (*organization*) obra de caridade; (*kindness*) compaixão *f*; (*money, gifts*) donativo

charm [tʃɑːm] N (*quality*) charme *m*; (*talisman*) amuleto; (*on bracelet*) berloque *m* ▸ VT encantar, deliciar; **charming** ADJ encantador(a)

chart [tʃɑːt] N (*graph*) gráfico; (*diagram*) diagrama *m*; (*map*) carta de navegação ▸ VT traçar; **charts** NPL (*hit parade*) paradas *fpl* (de sucesso)

charter ['tʃɑːtəʳ] VT fretar ▸ N (*document*) carta, alvará *m*; **chartered accountant** (BRIT) N perito-contador/perita-contadora *m/f*; **charter flight** N voo charter *or* fretado

chase [tʃeɪs] VT perseguir; (*also*: **~ away**) enxotar ▸ N perseguição *f*, caça

chat [tʃæt] VI (*also*: **have a ~**) conversar, bater papo (BR), cavaquear (PT) ▸ N conversa, bate-papo *m* (BR), cavaqueira (PT); **chatroom** N sala *f* de bate-papo; **chat show** (BRIT) N programa *m* de entrevistas

chatter ['tʃætəʳ] VI (*person*) tagarelar; (*animal*) emitir sons; (*teeth*) tiritar ▸ N tagarelice *f*; emissão *f* de sons; (*of birds*) chilro

chauvinist ['ʃəuvɪnɪst] N (*also*: **male ~**) machista *m*; (*nationalist*) chauvinista *m/f*

cheap [tʃiːp] ADJ barato; (*poor quality*) barato, de pouca qualidade; (*behaviour*) vulgar; (*joke*) de mau gosto ▸ ADV barato; **cheaply** ADV barato, por baixo preço

cheat [tʃiːt] VI trapacear; (*at cards*) roubar (BR), fazer batota (PT); (*in exam*) colar (BR), cabular (PT) ▸ N fraude *f*; (*person*) trapaceiro(-a); **to ~ sb out of sth** defraudar alguém de algo

check [tʃɛk] VT (*examine*) controlar; (*facts*) verificar; (*halt*) conter, impedir; (*restrain*) parar, refrear ▸ N controle *m*, inspeção *f*; (*curb*) freio; (US: *bill*) conta; (*pattern*: *gen pl*) xadrez *m*; (US) = **cheque** ▸ ADJ (*pattern, cloth*) xadrez *inv*; **check in** VI (*in hotel*) registrar-se; (*in airport*) apresentar-se ▸ VT (*luggage*) entregar; **check out** VI pagar a conta e sair; **check up** VI: **to ~ up on sth** verificar algo; **to ~ up on sb** investigar alguém; **checkers** (US) N (jogo de) damas *fpl*; **check-in, check-in desk** N check-in *m*; **checking account** (US) N conta corrente; **checkout** N caixa; **checkpoint** N (ponto de) controle *m*; **checkroom** (US) N depósito de bagagem; **checkup** N (*Med*) check-up *m*

cheek [tʃiːk] N bochecha; (*impudence*) folga, descaramento; **cheekbone** N maçã *f* do rosto; **cheeky** ADJ insolente, descarado

cheer [tʃɪəʳ] VT dar vivas a, aplaudir; (*gladden*) alegrar, animar ▸ VI gritar com entusiasmo ▸ N (*gen pl*) gritos *mpl* de entusiasmo; **cheers** NPL (*of crowd*) aplausos *mpl*; **~s!** saúde!; **cheer up** VI animar-se, alegrar-se ▸ VT alegrar, animar; **cheerful** ADJ alegre; **cheerio** (BRIT) EXCL tchau (BR), adeus (PT); **cheerleader** ['tʃɪəliːdəʳ] N animador(a) de torcida *m/f*

cheese [tʃiːz] N queijo

chef [ʃɛf] N cozinheiro-chefe/cozinheira-chefe *m/f*

chemical ['kɛmɪkəl] ADJ químico ▸ N produto químico

chemist ['kɛmɪst] N (BRIT: *pharmacist*) farmacêutico(-a); (*scientist*) químico(-a); **chemistry** N química; **chemist's, chemist's shop** (BRIT) N farmácia
cheque [tʃɛk] (BRIT) N cheque *m*; **chequebook** N talão *m* (BR) *or* livro (PT) de cheques; **cheque card** (BRIT) N cartão *m* (de garantia) de cheques
cherry ['tʃɛrɪ] N cereja; (*also*: **~ tree**) cerejeira
chess [tʃɛs] N xadrez *m*
chest [tʃɛst] N (*Anat*) peito; (*box*) caixa, cofre *m*
chestnut ['tʃɛsnʌt] N castanha
chest of drawers N cômoda
chew [tʃu:] VT mastigar; **chewing gum** N chiclete *m* (BR), pastilha elástica (PT)
chic [ʃɪk] ADJ elegante
chick [tʃɪk] N pinto; (*inf*: *girl*) broto
chicken ['tʃɪkɪn] N galinha; (*food*) galinha, frango; (*inf*: *coward*) covarde *m/f*, galinha; **chicken out** (*inf*) VI agalinhar-se; **chickenpox** N catapora (BR), varicela (PT)
chief [tʃi:f] N (*of tribe*) cacique *m*, morubixaba *m*; (*of organization*) chefe *m/f* ▶ ADJ principal; **chiefly** ADV principalmente
child [tʃaɪld] (*pl* **children**) N criança; (*offspring*) filho(-a); **childbirth** N parto; **childcare** N serviço de cuidado infantil; **childhood** N infância; **childish** ADJ infantil; **child minder** (BRIT) N cuidadora de crianças; **children** ['tʃɪldrən] NPL *of* **child**
Chile ['tʃɪlɪ] N Chile *m*
chill [tʃɪl] N frio, friagem *f*; (*Med*) resfriamento ▶ VT (*Culin*) semi-congelar; (*person*) congelar
chilli ['tʃɪlɪ], (US) **chili** N pimentão *m* picante
chilly ['tʃɪlɪ] ADJ frio; (*person*) friorento
chimpanzee [tʃɪmpæn'zi:] N chimpanzé *m*
chin [tʃɪn] N queixo
China ['tʃaɪnə] N China
china ['tʃaɪnə] N porcelana; (*crockery*) louça fina
Chinese [tʃaɪ'ni:z] ADJ chinês(-esa) ▶ N INV chinês(-esa) *m/f*; (*Ling*) chinês *m*
chip [tʃɪp] N (*gen pl*: BRIT *Culin*) batata frita; (: US: *also*: **potato ~**) batatinha frita; (*of wood*) lasca; (*of glass, stone*) lasca, pedaço; (*Comput*: *also*: **micro~**) chip *m* ▶ VT (*cup, plate*) lascar; **chip in** (*inf*) VI interromper; (*contribute*) compartilhar as despesas
chiropodist [kɪ'rɔpədɪst] (BRIT) N pedicuro(-a)
chisel ['tʃɪzl] N (*for wood*) formão *m*; (*for stone*) cinzel *m*
chives [tʃaɪvz] NPL cebolinha
chocolate ['tʃɔklɪt] N chocolate *m*
choice [tʃɔɪs] N (*selection*) seleção *f*; (*option*) escolha; (*preference*) preferência ▶ ADJ seleto, escolhido
choir ['kwaɪə^r] N coro
choke [tʃəuk] VI sufocar-se; (*on food*) engasgar ▶ VT estrangular; (*block*) obstruir ▶ N (*Aut*) afogador *m* (BR), ar *m* (PT)
cholesterol [kə'lɛstərɔl] N colesterol *m*
choose [tʃu:z] (*pt* **chose**, *pp* **chosen**) VT escolher; **to ~ to do** optar por fazer
chop [tʃɔp] VT (*wood*) cortar, talhar; (*Culin*: *also*: **~ up**) cortar em pedaços; (*meat*) picar ▶ N golpe *m*;

(*Culin*) costeleta; **chops** NPL (*inf: jaws*) beiços *mpl*
chopsticks ['tʃɔpstɪks] NPL pauzinhos *mpl*, palitos *mpl*
chord [kɔ:d] N (*Mus*) acorde *m*
chore [tʃɔ:ʳ] N tarefa; (*routine task*) trabalho de rotina
chorus ['kɔ:rəs] N (*group*) coro; (*song*) coral *m*; (*refrain*) estribilho
chose [tʃəuz] PT *of* **choose**; **chosen** PP *of* **choose**
Christ [kraɪst] N Cristo
christen ['krɪsn] VT batizar; (*nickname*) apelidar
Christian ['krɪstɪən] ADJ, N cristão(-tã) *m/f*; **Christianity** [krɪstɪ'ænɪtɪ] N cristianismo; **Christian name** N prenome *m*, nome *m* de batismo
Christmas ['krɪsməs] N Natal *m*; **Happy** *or* **Merry ~!** Feliz Natal!; **Christmas card** N cartão *m* de Natal; **Christmas cracker** N *ver nota*

Um **Christmas cracker** é um cilindro de papelão que ao ser aberto faz estourar uma bombinha. Contém um presente surpresa e um chapéu de papel que cada convidado coloca na cabeça durante a ceia de Natal.

Christmas: Christmas Day N dia *m* de Natal; **Christmas Eve** N véspera de Natal; **Christmas tree** N árvore *f* de Natal
chronic ['krɔnɪk] ADJ crônico; (*fig: drunkenness*) inveterado
chubby ['tʃʌbɪ] ADJ roliço, gorducho
chuck [tʃʌk] VT jogar (BR), deitar (PT); (BRIT: *also*: **~ up, ~ in**: *job*) largar; (: *person*) acabar com; **chuck out** VT (*thing*) jogar (BR) *or* deitar (PT) fora; (*person*) expulsar
chuckle ['tʃʌkl] VI rir
chuffed [tʃʌft] (*inf*) ADJ: **~ (about sth)** encantado (com algo)
chum [tʃʌm] N camarada *m/f*
church [tʃə:tʃ] N igreja; **churchyard** N adro, cemitério
churn [tʃə:n] N (*for butter*) batedeira; (*also*: **milk ~**) lata, vasilha; **churn out** VT produzir em série
chute [ʃu:t] N rampa; (*also*: **rubbish ~**) despejador *m*
CIA (US) N ABBR (= *Central Intelligence Agency*) CIA *f*
CID (BRIT) N ABBR = **Criminal Investigation Department**
cider ['saɪdəʳ] N sidra
cigar [sɪ'gɑ:ʳ] N charuto
cigarette [sɪgə'rɛt] N cigarro
cinema ['sɪnəmə] N cinema *m*
cinnamon ['sɪnəmən] N canela
circle ['sə:kl] N círculo; (*in cinema*) balcão *m* ▶ VI dar voltas ▶ VT (*surround*) rodear, cercar; (*move round*) dar a volta de
circuit ['sə:kɪt] N circuito; (*tour, lap*) volta; (*track*) pista
circular ['sə:kjuləʳ] ADJ circular ▶ N (carta) circular *f*
circulate ['sə:kjuleɪt] VT, VI circular; **circulation** [sə:kju'leɪʃən] N circulação *f*; (*of newspaper, book etc*) tiragem *f*
circumstances ['sə:kəmstənsɪz] NPL circunstâncias *fpl*; (*conditions*) condições *fpl*; (*financial condition*) situação *f* econômica
circus ['sə:kəs] N circo
citizen ['sɪtɪzn] N (*of country*) cidadão(-dã) *m/f*; (*of town*) habitante *m/f*; **citizenship** N cidadania
city ['sɪtɪ] N cidade *f*; **the C~** *centro financeiro de Londres*
civic ['sɪvɪk] ADJ cívico, municipal

civil ['sɪvɪl] ADJ civil; (*polite*) delicado, cortês; **civilian** [sɪ'vɪlɪən] ADJ, N civil *m/f*
civilized ['sɪvɪlaɪzd] ADJ civilizado
civil servant N funcionário(-a) público(-a)
Civil Service N administração *f* pública
civil war N guerra civil
claim [kleɪm] VT exigir, reclamar; (*rights etc*) reivindicar; (*responsibility*) assumir; (*assert*): **to ~ that/to be** afirmar que/ser ▶ VI (*for insurance*) reclamar ▶ N reclamação *f*; (*assertion*) afirmação *f*; (*wage claim etc*) reivindicação *f*
clam [klæm] N molusco
clamp [klæmp] N grampo ▶ VT prender; **clamp down on** VT FUS reprimir
clan [klæn] N clã *m*
clap [klæp] VI bater palmas, aplaudir
clarinet [klærɪ'nɛt] N clarinete *m*
clarity ['klærɪtɪ] N clareza
clash [klæʃ] N (*fight*) confronto; (*disagreement*) desavença; (*of beliefs*) divergência; (*of colours, styles*) choque *m*; (*of dates*) coincidência ▶ VI (*gangs, beliefs*) chocar-se; (*disagree*) entrar em conflito, ter uma desavença; (*colours*) não combinar; (*dates, events*) coincidir; (*weapons, cymbals etc*) ressoar
clasp [klɑ:sp] N fecho; (*embrace*) abraço ▶ VT prender; (*embrace*) abraçar
class [klɑ:s] N classe *f*; (*lesson*) aula; (*type*) tipo ▶ VT classificar
classic ['klæsɪk] ADJ clássico ▶ N clássico; **classical** ADJ clássico
classmate ['klæsmeɪt] N colega *m/f* de aula
classroom ['klæsrum] N sala de aula
clatter ['klætəʳ] N ruído, barulho; (*of hooves*) tropel *m* ▶ VI fazer barulho *or* ruído
clause [klɔ:z] N cláusula; (*Ling*) oração *f*
claw [klɔ:] N (*of animal*) pata; (*of bird of prey*) garra; (*of lobster*) pinça; **claw at** VT FUS arranhar; (*tear*) rasgar
clay [kleɪ] N argila
clean [kli:n] ADJ limpo ▶ VT limpar; (*hands, face etc*) lavar; **clean out** VT limpar; **clean up** VT limpar, assear; **cleaner** N faxineiro(-a); (*product*) limpador *m*; **cleaner's** N (*also*: **dry cleaner's**) tinturaria; **cleaning** N limpeza; **clean technology** N tecnologia limpa
clear [klɪəʳ] ADJ claro; (*footprint, photograph*) nétido; (*obvious*) evidente; (*glass, water*) transparente; (*road, way*) limpo, livre; (*conscience*) tranquilo; (*skin*) macio ▶ VT (*space*) abrir; (*room*) esvaziar; (*Jur: suspect*) absolver; (*fence, wall*) saltar, transpor; (*cheque*) compensar ▶ VI (*weather*) abrir; (*sky*) clarear; (*fog etc*) dissipar-se ▶ ADV: **~ of** a salvo de; **to ~ the table** tirar a mesa; **clear up** VT limpar; (*mystery*) resolver, esclarecer; **clearance** N remoção *f*; (*permission*) permissão *f*; **clear-cut** ADJ bem definido, nítido; **clearing** N (*in wood*) clareira; **clearly** ADV distintamente; (*obviously*) claramente; (*coherently*) coerentemente; **clearway** (BRIT) N *estrada onde não se pode estacionar*
clench [klɛntʃ] VT apertar, cerrar; (*teeth*) trincar

clerk [klɑ:k, (US) klə:rk] N auxiliar *m/f* de escritório; (US: *sales person*) balconista *m/f*
clever ['klɛvəʳ] ADJ inteligente; (*deft, crafty*) hábil; (*device, arrangement*) engenhoso
click [klɪk] VT (*tongue*) estalar; (*heels*) bater; (*Comput*) clicar em ▶ VI (*make sound*) estalar; (*Comput*) clicar
client ['klaɪənt] N cliente *m/f*
cliff [klɪf] N penhasco
climate ['klaɪmɪt] N clima *m*; **climate change** N mudanças *fpl* climáticas
climax ['klaɪmæks] N clímax *m*, ponto culminante; (*sexual*) clímax
climb [klaɪm] VI subir; (*plant*) trepar; (*plane*) ganhar altitude; (*prices etc*) escalar ▶ VT (*stairs*) subir; (*tree*) trepar em; (*hill*) escalar ▶ N subida; (*of prices etc*) escalada; **climber** N alpinista *m/f*; (*plant*) trepadeira; **climbing** N alpinismo
clinch [klɪntʃ] VT (*deal*) fechar; (*argument*) decidir, resolver
cling [klɪŋ] (*pt, pp* **clung**) VI: **to ~ to** pegar-se a, aderir a; (*support, idea*) agarrar-se a; (*clothes*) ajustar-se a
Clingfilm® ['klɪŋfɪlm] N papel *m* filme
clinic ['klɪnɪk] N clínica
clip [klɪp] N (*for hair*) grampo (BR), gancho (PT); (*also*: **paper ~**) mola, clipe *m*; (*TV, Cinema*) clipe ▶ VT (*cut*) aparar; (*papers*) grampear
cloak [kləuk] N capa, manto ▶ VT (*fig*) encobrir; **cloakroom** N vestiário; (BRIT: *WC*) sanitários *mpl* (BR), lavatórios *mpl* (PT)
clock [klɔk] N relógio; **clock in, clock on** (BRIT) VI assinar o ponto na entrada; **clock off, clock out** (BRIT) VI assinar o ponto na saída; **clockwise** ADV em sentido horário; **clockwork** N mecanismo de relógio ▶ ADJ de corda
clog [klɔg] N tamanco ▶ VT entupir ▶ VI (*also*: **~ up**) entupir-se
close [*adj, adv* kləus, *vb, n* kləuz] ADJ próximo; (*friend*) íntimo; (*examination*) minucioso; (*watch*) atento; (*contest*) apertado; (*weather*) abafado ▶ ADV perto ▶ VT fechar; (*end*) encerrar ▶ VI fechar; (*end*) concluir-se, terminar-se ▶ N (*end*) fim *m*, conclusão *f*, terminação *f*; **~ by, ~ at hand** perto, pertinho; **to have a ~ shave** (*fig*) livrar-se por um triz; **~ to** perto de; **close down** VI fechar definitivamente; **closed** [kləuzd] ADJ fechado
closely ['kləuslɪ] ADV (*watch*) de perto; **we are ~ related** somos parentes próximos
closet ['klɔzɪt] N (*cupboard*) armário
close-up [kləus-] N close *m*, close-up *m*
closure ['kləuʒəʳ] N fechamento
clot [klɔt] N (*gen*: *blood clot*) coágulo; (*inf*: *idiot*) imbecil *m/f* ▶ VI coagular-se
cloth [klɔθ] N (*material*) tecido, fazenda; (*rag*) pano
clothes [kləuðz] NPL roupa
clothing ['kləuðɪŋ] N = **clothes**
cloud [klaud] N nuvem *f*; **cloud computing** N computação *f* em nuvem; **cloudy** ADJ nublado; (*liquid*) turvo
clove [kləuv] N cravo; **clove of garlic** N dente *m* de alho
clown [klaun] N palhaço ▶ VI (*also*: **~ about, ~ around**) fazer palhaçadas
club [klʌb] N (*society*) clube *m*; (*weapon*) cacete *m*; (*also*: **golf ~**) taco ▶ VT esbordoar ▶ VI: **to ~ together** cotizar-se; **clubs** NPL (*Cards*) paus *mpl*

clue [klu:] N indício, pista; (*in crossword*) definição *f*; **I haven't a ~** não faço ideia
clumsy ['klʌmzɪ] ADJ (*person*) desajeitado; (*movement*) deselegante, mal-feito; (*attempt*) inábil
clung [klʌŋ] PT, PP *of* **cling**
cluster ['klʌstəʳ] N grupo; (*of flowers*) ramo ▸VI agrupar-se, apinhar-se
clutch [klʌtʃ] N (*grip, grasp*) garra; (*Aut*) embreagem *f* (BR), embraiagem *f* (PT) ▸VT empunhar, pegar em
Co. ABBR = **county**; (= *company*) Cia.
c/o ABBR (= *care of*) a/c
coach [kəutʃ] N (*bus*) ônibus *m* (BR), autocarro (PT); (*horse-drawn*) carruagem *f*, coche *m*; (*of train*) vagão *m*; (*Sport*) treinador(a) *m/f*, instrutor(a) *m/f*; (*tutor*) professor(a) *m/f* particular ▸VT (*Sport*) treinar; (*student*) preparar, ensinar; **coach station** (BRIT) N rodoviária; **coach trip** N passeio de ônibus (BR) *or* autocarro (PT)
coal [kəul] N carvão *m*
coalition [kəuə'lɪʃən] N coalizão *f*
coarse [kɔ:s] ADJ grosso, áspero; (*vulgar*) grosseiro, ordinário
coast [kəust] N costa, litoral *m* ▸VI (*Aut*) ir em ponto morto; **coastal** ADJ costeiro; **coastguard** N (*service*) guarda costeira; (*person*) guarda-costeira *m/f*; **coastline** N litoral *m*
coat [kəut] N (*overcoat*) sobretudo; (*of animal*) pelo; (*of paint*) demão *f*, camada ▸VT cobrir, revestir; **coat hanger** N cabide *m*; **coating** N camada
coax [kəuks] VT persuadir com meiguice
cobweb ['kɔbwɛb] N teia de aranha
cocaine [kɔ'keɪn] N cocaína
cock [kɔk] N (*rooster*) galo; (*male bird*) macho ▸VT (*gun*) engatilhar; **cockerel** N frango, galo pequeno
cockney ['kɔknɪ] N londrino(-a) (*nativo dos bairros populares do leste de Londres*)
cockpit ['kɔkpɪt] N (*in aircraft*) cabina
cockroach ['kɔkrəutʃ] N barata
cocktail ['kɔkteɪl] N coquetel *m* (BR), cocktail *m* (PT)
cocoa ['kəukəu] N cacau *m*; (*drink*) chocolate *m*
coconut ['kəukənʌt] N coco
cod [kɔd] N INV bacalhau *m*
code [kəud] N cifra; (*dialling code, post code*) código; **code of practice** N deontologia
coffee ['kɔfɪ] N café *m*; **coffee bar** (BRIT) N café *m*, lanchonete *f*; **coffee bean** N grão *m* de café; **coffeepot** N cafeteira; **coffee table** N mesinha de centro
coffin ['kɔfɪn] N caixão *m*
cognitive ['kɔgnɪtɪv] ADJ cognitivo
coil [kɔɪl] N rolo; (*Elec*) bobina; (*contraceptive*) DIU *m* ▸VT enrolar
coin [kɔɪn] N moeda ▸VT (*word*) cunhar, criar
coincide [kəuɪn'saɪd] VI coincidir; **coincidence** [kəu'ɪnsɪdəns] N coincidência
coke [kəuk] N (*coal*) coque *m*
colander ['kɔləndəʳ] N coador *m*, passador *m*
cold [kəuld] ADJ frio ▸N frio; (*Med*) resfriado (BR), constipação *f* (PT); **it's ~** está frio; **to be** *or* **feel ~** (*person*) estar com frio; (*object*) estar frio; **to catch ~** pegar

C

friagem; **to catch a ~** ficar resfriado (BR), apanhar uma constipação (PT); **in ~ blood** a sangue frio; **cold sore** N herpes *m* labial

coleslaw ['kəulslɔː] N salada de repolho cru

collapse [kə'læps] VI cair, tombar; (*building*) desabar; (*Med*) desmaiar ▶ N desabamento, desmoronamento; (*of government*) queda; (*Med*) colapso

collar ['kɔlər] N (*of shirt*) colarinho; (*of coat etc*) gola; (*for dog*) coleira; (*Tech*) aro, colar *m*; **collarbone** N clavícula

colleague ['kɔliːg] N colega *m/f*

collect [kə'lɛkt] VT (*as a hobby*) colecionar; (*gather*) recolher; (*wages, debts*) cobrar; (*donations, subscriptions*) colher; (*mail*) coletar; (BRIT: *call for*) (ir) buscar ▶ VI (*people*) reunir-se ▶ ADV: **to call ~** (US *Tel*) ligar a cobrar; **collection** N coleção *f*; (*of people*) grupo; (*of donations*) arrecadação *f*; (*of post, for charity*) coleta; (*of writings*) coletânea; **collector** N colecionador(a) *m/f*; (*of taxes etc*) cobrador(a) *m/f*

college ['kɔlɪdʒ] N (*of university*) faculdade *f*; (*of technology, agriculture*) escola profissionalizante

> Além de "universidade", **college** também se refere a um centro de educação superior para jovens que terminaram a educação obrigatória, *secondary school*. Alguns oferecem cursos de especialização em matérias técnicas, artísticas ou comerciais, outros oferecem disciplinas universitárias.

collide [kə'laɪd] VI: **to ~ (with)** colidir (com)

collision [kə'lɪʒən] N colisão *f*

Colombia [kə'lɔmbɪə] N Colômbia

colon ['kəulən] N (*sign*) dois pontos; (*Med*) cólon *m*

colonel ['kəːnl] N coronel *m*

colony ['kɔlənɪ] N colônia

colour ['kʌlər], (US) **color** N cor *f* ▶ VT colorir; (*with crayons*) colorir, pintar; (*dye*) tingir; (*fig: account*) falsear ▶ VI (*blush*) corar; **colours** NPL (*of party, club*) cores *fpl*; **in ~** (*photograph etc*) a cores; **colour in** VT (*drawing*) colorir; **colour-blind** ADJ daltônico; **coloured** ADJ colorido; (*person*) de cor; **colour film** N filme *m* a cores; **colourful** ADJ colorido; (*account*) vívido; (*personality*) vivo, animado; **colouring** N colorido; (*complexion*) tez *f*; (*in food*) colorante *m*; **colour television** N televisão *f* a cores

column ['kɔləm] N coluna; (*of smoke*) faixa; (*of people*) fila

coma ['kəumə] N coma *m*

comb [kəum] N pente *m*; (*ornamental*) crista ▶ VT pentear; (*area*) vasculhar

combat ['kɔmbæt] N combate *m* ▶ VT combater

combination [kɔmbɪ'neɪʃən] N combinação *f*; (*of safe*) segredo

combine [*vt, vi* kəm'baɪn, *n* 'kɔmbaɪn] VT combinar; (*qualities*) reunir ▶ VI combinar-se ▶ N (*Econ*) associação *f*

KEYWORD

come [kʌm] (*pt* **came**, *pp* **come**) VI

1 (*movement towards*) vir; **come with me** vem comigo; **to come running** vir correndo

2 (*arrive*) chegar; **she's come here to work** ela veio aqui para trabalhar; **to come home** chegar em casa

3 (*reach*): **to come to** chegar a; **the bill came to £40** a conta deu £40; **her hair came to her waist** o cabelo dela batia na cintura **4** (*occur*): **an idea came to me** uma ideia me ocorreu **5** (*be, become*) ficar; **to come loose/undone** soltar-se/desfazer-se; **I've come to like him** passei a gostar dele

come about VI suceder, acontecer

come across VT FUS (*person*) topar com; (*thing*) encontrar

come away VI (*leave*) ir-se embora; (*become detached*) desprender-se, soltar-se

come back VI (*return*) voltar

come by VT FUS (*acquire*) conseguir

come down VI (*price*) baixar; (*tree*) cair; (*building*) desmoronar-se

come forward VI apresentar-se

come from VT FUS (*subj: person*) ser de; (*: thing*) originar-se de

come in VI entrar; (*on deal etc*) participar; (*be involved*) estar envolvido

come in for VT FUS (*criticism etc*) receber

come into VT FUS (*money*) herdar; (*fashion*) ser; (*be involved*) estar envolvido em

come off VI (*button*) desprender-se, soltar-se; (*attempt*) dar certo

come on VI (*pupil, work, project*) avançar; (*lights, electricity*) ser ligado; **come on!** vamos!, vai!

come out VI (*fact*) vir à tona; (*book*) ser publicado; (*stain, sun*) sair

come round VI voltar a si

come to VI voltar a si

come up VI (*sun*) nascer; (*problem, subject*) surgir; (*event*) acontecer

come up against VT FUS (*resistance, difficulties*) enfrentar, esbarrar em

come upon VT FUS (*find*) encontrar, achar

come up with VT FUS (*idea*) propor, sugerir; (*money*) contribuir

C

comedian [kəˈmiːdɪən] N cômico, humorista *m*

comedy [ˈkɔmɪdɪ] N comédia

comfort [ˈkʌmfət] N (*well-being*) bem-estar *m*; (*relief*) alívio ▸ VT consolar, confortar; **comforts** NPL (*of home etc*) conforto; **comfortable** ADJ confortável; (*financially*) tranquilo; (*walk, climb etc*) fácil

comic [ˈkɔmɪk] ADJ (*also*: **~al**) cômico ▸ N (*person*) humorista *m/f*; (BRIT: *magazine*) revista em quadrinhos (BR), revista de banda desenhada (PT), gibi *m* (BR *inf*)

comma [ˈkɔmə] N vírgula

command [kəˈmɑːnd] N ordem *f*, mandado; (*control*) controle *m*; (*Mil: authority*) comando; (*mastery*) domínio ▸ VT mandar; **commander** N (*Mil*) comandante *m/f*

commemorate [kəˈmɛməreɪt] VT (*with monument*) comemorar; (*with celebration*) celebrar

commence [kəˈmɛns] VT, VI começar, iniciar

commend [kəˈmɛnd] VT elogiar, louvar; (*recommend*) recomendar

comment [ˈkɔmɛnt] N comentário ▸ VI comentar; **to ~ on sth** comentar algo; **"no ~"** "sem comentário"; **commentary** [ˈkɔməntərɪ] N comentário; **commentator** [ˈkɔmənteɪtəʳ] N comentarista *m/f*

commerce [ˈkɔməːs] N comércio

commercial [kəˈməːʃəl] ADJ comercial ▸ N anúncio, comercial *m*

commission [kə'mɪʃən] N comissão *f*; (*order for work of art etc*) empreitada, encomenda ▶ VT (*work of art*) encomendar; **out of ~** com defeito; **commissioner** N comissário(-a)
commit [kə'mɪt] VT cometer; (*money, resources*) alocar; (*to sb's care*) entregar; **to ~ o.s. (to do)** comprometer-se (a fazer); **to ~ suicide** suicidar-se; **commitment** N compromisso; (*political etc*) engajamento; (*undertaking*) promessa
committee [kə'mɪtɪ] N comitê *m*
commodity [kə'mɔdɪtɪ] N mercadoria
common ['kɔmən] ADJ comum; (*vulgar*) ordinário, vulgar ▶ N *área verde aberta ao público*; **Commons** NPL (BRIT *Pol*): **the (House of) C~s** a Câmara dos Comuns; **to have sth in ~ (with sb)** ter algo em comum (con alguém); **commonly** ADV geralmente; **commonplace** ADJ vulgar; **common sense** N bom senso; **Commonwealth** N: **the Commonwealth** a Comunidade Britânica
communal ['kɔmju:nl] ADJ comun
commune [*n* 'kɔmju:n, *vi* kə'mju:n] N (*group*) comuna ▶ VI: **to ~ with** comunicar-se com
communicate [kə'mju:nɪkeɪt] VT comunicar ▶ VI: **to ~ (with)** comunicar-se (com); **communication** [kəmju:nɪ'keɪʃən] N comunicação *f*; (*letter, call*) mensagem *f*
communion [kə'mju:nɪən] N (*also*: **Holy C~**) comunhão *f*
communism ['kɔmjunɪzəm] N comunismo; **communist** ADJ, N comunista *m/f*
community [kə'mju:nɪtɪ] N comunidade *f*; **community centre** N centro social
commute [kə'mju:t] VI viajar diariamente ▶ VT comutar; **commuter** N viajante *m/f* habitual
compact [*adj* kəm'pækt, *n* 'kɔmpækt] ADJ compacto ▶ N (*also*: **powder ~**) estojo; **compact disc** N disco laser; **compact disc player** N som cd *m*
companion [kəm'pænɪən] N companheiro(-a)
company ['kʌmpənɪ] N companhia; (*Comm*) sociedade *f*, companhia; **to keep sb ~** fazer companhia a alguém
comparative [kəm'pærətɪv] ADJ (*study*) comparativo; (*peace, safety*) relativo; **comparatively** ADJ relativamente
compare [kəm'pɛəʳ] VT comparar; **to ~ (to/with)** comparar (a/com) ▶ VI: **to ~ with** comparar-se com; **comparison** [kəm'pærɪsn] N comparação *f*
compartment [kəm'pɑ:tmənt] N compartimento; (*of wallet*) divisão *f*
compass ['kʌmpəs] N bússola; **compasses** NPL compasso
compassion [kəm'pæʃən] N compaixão *f*
compatible [kəm'pætɪbl] ADJ compatível
compel [kəm'pɛl] VT obrigar
compensate ['kɔmpənseɪt] VT indenizar ▶ VI: **to ~ for** compensar; **compensation** [kɔmpən'seɪʃən] N compensação *f*; (*damages*) indenização *f*
compete [kəm'pi:t] VI (*take part*) competir; (*vie*): **to ~ (with)** competir (com), fazer competição (com)

competent ['kɔmpɪtənt] ADJ competente

competition [kɔmpɪ'tɪʃən] N (*contest*) concurso; (*Econ*) concorrência; (*rivalry*) competição *f*

competitive [kəm'pɛtɪtɪv] ADJ competitivo; (*person*) competidor(a)

competitor [kəm'pɛtɪtə^r] N (*rival*) competidor(a) *m/f*; (*participant, Econ*) concorrente *m/f*

complain [kəm'pleɪn] VI queixar-se; **to ~ of** (*pain*) queixar-se de; **complaint** N (*objection*) objeção *f*; (*criticism*) queixa; (*Med*) achaque *m*, doença

complement ['kɔmplɪmənt] N complemento; (*esp ship's crew*) tripulação *f* ▶ VT complementar

complete [kəm'pli:t] ADJ completo; (*finished*) acabado ▶ VT (*finish: building, task*) acabar; (*set, group*) completar; (*a form*) preencher; **completely** ADV completamente; **completion** N conclusão *f*, término; (*of contract etc*) realização *f*

complex ['kɔmplɛks] ADJ complexo ▶ N complexo; (*of buildings*) conjunto

complexion [kəm'plɛkʃən] N (*of face*) cor *f*, tez *f*

complicate ['kɔmplɪkeɪt] VT complicar; **complicated** ADJ complicado; **complication** [kɔmplɪ'keɪʃən] N problema *m*; (*Med*) complicação *f*

compliment [*n* 'kɔmplɪmənt, *vt* 'kɔmplɪmɛnt] N (*praise*) elogio ▶ VT elogiar; **compliments** NPL cumprimentos *mpl*; **to pay sb a ~** elogiar alguém; **complimentary** [kɔmplɪ'mɛntərɪ] ADJ lisonjeiro; (*free*) gratuito

comply [kəm'plaɪ] VI: **to ~ with** cumprir com

component [kəm'pəunənt] ADJ componente ▶ N (*part*) peça

compose [kəm'pəuz] VT compor; **to be ~d of** compor-se de; **to ~ o.s.** tranquilizar-se; **composer** N (*Mus*) compositor(a) *m/f*; **composition** [kɔmpə'zɪʃən] N composição *f*

compound ['kɔmpaund] N (*Chem, Ling*) composto; (*enclosure*) recinto ▶ ADJ composto

comprehensive [kɔmprɪ'hɛnsɪv] ADJ abrangente; (*Insurance*) total; **comprehensive school** (BRIT) N *escola secundária de amplo programa*

> Criadas na década de 1960 pelo governo trabalhista da época, as **comprehensive schools** são estabelecimentos de ensino secundário polivalentes concebidos para acolher todos os alunos sem distinção e lhes oferecer oportunidades iguais, em oposição ao sistema seletivo das *grammar schools*. A maioria dos estudantes britânicos frequenta atualmente uma **comprehensive school**, mas as *grammar schools* não desapareceram de todo.

compress [*vt* kəm'prɛs, *n* 'kɔmprɛs] VT comprimir; (*text, information etc*) reduzir ▶ N (*Med*) compressa

comprise [kəm'praɪz] VT (*also*: **be ~d of**) compreender, constar de; (*constitute*) constituir

compromise ['kɔmprəmaɪz] N meio-termo ▶ VT comprometer ▶ VI chegar a um meio-termo

compulsive [kəm'pʌlsɪv] ADJ compulsório

C

compulsory [kəm'pʌlsərɪ] ADJ obrigatório; (*retirement*) compulsório
computer [kəm'pjuːtə^r] N computador *m*; **computer game** N game *m*; **computerize** VT informatizar, computadorizar; **computer literate** ADJ capaz de lidar com um computador; **computing** N computação *f*; (*science*) informática
conceal [kən'siːl] VT ocultar; (*information*) omitir
conceited [kən'siːtɪd] ADJ vaidoso
conceive [kən'siːv] VT conceber ▸VI conceber, engravidar
concentrate ['kɔnsəntreɪt] VI concentrar-se ▸VT concentrar; **concentration** N concentração *f*
concept ['kɔnsɛpt] N conceito
concern [kən'səːn] N (*Comm*) empresa; (*anxiety*) preocupação *f* ▸VT preocupar; (*involve*) envolver; (*relate to*) dizer respeito a; **to be ~ed (about)** preocupar-se (com); **concerning** PREP sobre, a respeito de, acerca de
concert ['kɔnsət] N concerto
concession [kən'sɛʃən] N concessão *f*; **tax ~** redução no imposto
conclude [kən'kluːd] VT (*finish*) acabar, concluir; (*treaty etc*) firmar; (*agreement*) chegar a; (*decide*) decidir
conclusion [kən'kluːʒən] N conclusão *f*
concrete ['kɔnkriːt] N concreto (BR), betão *m* (PT) ▸ADJ concreto
concussion [kən'kʌʃən] N (*Med*) concussão *f* cerebral
condemn [kən'dɛm] VT denunciar; (*prisoner, building*) condenar
condensation [kɔndɛn'seɪʃən] N condensação *f*
condense [kən'dɛns] VI condensar-se ▸VT condensar
condition [kən'dɪʃən] N condição *f*; (*Med: illness*) doença ▸VT condicionar; **conditions** NPL (*circumstances*) circunstâncias *fpl*; **on ~ that** com a condição (de) que; **conditioner** N (*for hair*) condicionador *m*; (*for fabrics*) amaciante *m*
condom ['kɔndɔm] N preservativo, camisinha
condominium [kɔndə'mɪnɪəm] (US) N (*building*) edifício
condone [kən'dəun] VT admitir, aceitar
conduct [*n* 'kɔndʌkt, *vt, vi* kən'dʌkt] N conduta, comportamento ▸VT (*research etc*) fazer; (*heat, electricity*) conduzir; (*Mus*) reger; **to ~ o.s.** comportar-se; **conducted tour** N viagem *f* organizada; **conductor** N (*of orchestra*) regente *m/f*; (*on bus*) cobrador(a) *m/f*; (US *Rail*) revisor(a) *m/f*; (*Elec*) condutor *m*
cone [kəun] N cone *m*; (*Bot*) pinha; (*for ice-cream*) casquinha
confectionery [kən'fɛkʃənrɪ] N (*sweets*) balas *fpl*; (*sweetmeats*) doces *mpl*
confer [kən'fəː^r] VT: **to ~ on** outorgar a ▸VI conferenciar
conference ['kɔnfərns] N congresso
confess [kən'fɛs] VT confessar ▸VI (*admit*) admitir; **confession** N admissão *f*; (*Rel*) confissão *f*
confide [kən'faɪd] VI: **to ~ in** confiar em, fiar-se em
confidence ['kɔnfɪdns] N confiança; (*faith*) fé *f*; (*secret*) confidência; **in ~** em confidência; **confident** ADJ confiante, convicto;

(*positive*) seguro; **confidential** [kɔnfɪ'dɛnʃəl] ADJ confidencial
confine [kən'faɪn] VT (*shut up*) encarcerar; (*limit*): **to ~ (to)** confinar (a); **confined** ADJ (*space*) reduzido
confirm [kən'fəːm] VT confirmar; **confirmation** [kɔnfə'meɪʃən] N confirmação *f*; (*Rel*) crisma
confiscate ['kɔnfɪskeɪt] VT confiscar
conflict [*n* 'kɔnflɪkt, *vi* kən'flɪkt] N (*disagreement*) divergência; (*of interests, loyalties*) conflito; (*fighting*) combate *m* ▶ VI estar em conflito; (*opinions*) divergir
conform [kən'fɔːm] VI conformar-se; **to ~ to** ajustar-se a, acomodar-se a
confront [kən'frʌnt] VT (*problems*) enfrentar; (*enemy, danger*) defrontar-se com; **confrontation** [kɔnfrən'teɪʃən] N confrontação *f*
confuse [kən'fjuːz] VT (*perplex*) desconcertar; (*mix up*) confundir, misturar; (*complicate*) complicar; **confused** ADJ confuso; **confusing** ADJ confuso; **confusion** [kən'fjuːʒən] N (*mix-up*) mal-entendido; (*perplexity*) perplexidade *f*; (*disorder*) confusão *f*
congestion [kən'dʒɛstʃən] N (*Med*) congestão *f*; (*traffic*) congestionamento
congratulate [kən'grætjuleɪt] VT parabenizar; **congratulations** [kəngrætju'leɪʃənz] NPL parabéns *mpl*
congress ['kɔŋgrɛs] N congresso; (*US*): **C~** Congresso

> O Congresso (**Congress**) é o Parlamento dos Estados Unidos. Consiste na *House of Representatives* e no Senado *Senate*. Os representantes e senadores são eleitos por sufrágio universal direto. O Congresso se reúne no *Capitol*, em Washington.

congressman (*US*) *irreg* N deputado
conjure ['kʌndʒəʳ] VI fazer truques; **conjure up** VT (*ghost, spirit*) fazer aparecer, invocar; (*memories*) evocar
connect [kə'nɛkt] VT (*Elec, Tel*) ligar; (*fig: associate*) associar; (*join*): **to ~ sth (to)** juntar *or* unir algo (a) ▶ VI: **to ~ with** (*train*) conectar com; **to be ~ed with** estar relacionado com; **I'm trying to ~ you** (*Tel*) estou tentando completar a ligação; **connecting flight** N conexão *f*; **connection** N ligação *f*; (*Elec, Rail*) conexão *f*; (*Tel*) ligação *f*
conquer ['kɔŋkəʳ] VT conquistar; (*enemy*) vencer; (*feelings*) superar; **conquest** ['kɔŋk] N conquista
conscience ['kɔnʃəns] N consciência; **conscientious** [kɔnʃɪ'ɛnʃəs] ADJ consciencioso
conscious ['kɔnʃəs] ADJ: **~ (of)** consciente (de); (*deliberate*) intencional; **consciousness** N consciência; **to lose/regain consciousness** perder/recuperar os sentidos
consent [kən'sɛnt] N consentimento ▶ VI: **to ~ to** consentir em
consequence ['kɔnsɪkwəns] N consequência; (*significance*): **of ~** de importância; **consequently** ADV por conseguinte
conservation [kɔnsə'veɪʃən] N conservação *f*; (*of the environment*) preservação *f*

conservative [kən'sə:vətɪv] ADJ conservador(a); (*cautious*) moderado; (BRIT *Pol*): **C~** conservador(a) ▶ N (BRIT *Pol*) conservador(a) *m/f*
conservatory [kən'sə:vətrɪ] N (*Mus*) conservatório; (*greenhouse*) estufa
consider [kən'sɪdə^r] VT considerar; (*take into account*) levar em consideração; (*study*) estudar, examinar; **to ~ doing sth** pensar em fazer algo
considerable [kən'sɪdərəbl] ADJ considerável; (*sum*) importante
considerate [kən'sɪdərɪt] ADJ atencioso; **consideration** [kənsɪdə'reɪʃən] N consideração *f*; (*deliberation*) deliberação *f*; (*factor*) fator *m*
considering [kən'sɪdərɪŋ] PREP em vista de
consist [kən'sɪst] VI: **to ~ of** (*comprise*) consistir em
consistency [kən'sɪstənsɪ] N coerência; (*thickness*) consistência
consistent [kən'sɪstənt] ADJ (*person*) coerente, estável; (*argument, idea*) sólido
consolation [kɔnsə'leɪʃən] N conforto
console [*vt* kən'səul, *n* 'kɔnsəul] VT confortar ▶ N consolo
consonant ['kɔnsənənt] N consoante *f*
conspicuous [kən'spɪkjuəs] ADJ conspícuo
conspiracy [kən'spɪrəsɪ] N conspiração *f*, trama
constable ['kʌnstəbl] (BRIT) N policial *m/f* (BR), polícia *m/f* (PT); **chief ~** chefe *m/f* de polícia
constant ['kɔnstənt] ADJ constante
constipated ['kɔnstɪpeɪtəd] ADJ com prisão de ventre
constipation [kɔnstɪ'peɪʃən] N prisão *f* de ventre
constituency [kən'stɪtjuənsɪ] N (*Pol*) distrito eleitoral; (*people*) eleitorado
constitution [kɔnstɪ'tju:ʃən] N constituição *f*; (*health*) compleição *f*
constraint [kən'streɪnt] N coação *f*, pressão *f*; (*restriction*) limitação *f*
construct [kən'strʌkt] VT construir; **construction** N construção *f*; (*structure*) estrutura
consul ['kɔnsl] N cônsul *m/f*; **consulate** ['kɔnsjulɪt] N consulado
consult [kən'sʌlt] VT consultar; **consultant** N (*Med*) (médico(-a)) especialista *m/f*; (*other specialist*) assessor(a) *m/f*, consultor(a) *m/f*; **consulting room** (BRIT) N consultório
consume [kən'sju:m] VT (*eat*) comer; (*drink*) beber; (*fire etc, Comm*) consumir; **consumer** N consumidor(a) *m/f*
consumption [kən'sʌmpʃən] N consumo
cont. ABBR = **continued**
contact ['kɔntækt] N contato ▶ VT entrar *or* pôr-se em contato com; **contact lenses** NPL lentes *fpl* de contato
contagious [kən'teɪdʒəs] ADJ contagioso; (*fig: laughter etc*) contagiante
contain [kən'teɪn] VT conter; **to ~ o.s.** conter-se; **container** N recipiente *m*; (*for shipping etc*) container *m*, cofre *m* de carga
contaminate [kən'tæmɪneɪt] VT contaminar
cont'd ABBR = **continued**

contemplate ['kɔntəmpleɪt] VT (*idea*) considerar; (*person, painting etc*) contemplar
contemporary [kən'tɛmpərərɪ] ADJ contemporâneo; (*design etc*) moderno ▸ N contemporâneo(-a)
contempt [kən'tɛmpt] N desprezo; **contempt of court** N (*Jur*) desacato à autoridade do tribunal
contend [kən'tɛnd] VT (*assert*): **to ~ that** afirmar que ▸ VI: **to ~ with** (*struggle*) lutar com; (*difficulty*) enfrentar; (*compete*): **to ~ for** competir por
content [*adj, vt* kən'tɛnt, *n* 'kɔntɛnt] ADJ (*happy*) contente; (*satisfied*) satisfeito ▸ VT contentar, satisfazer ▸ N conteúdo; (*fat content, moisture content etc*) quantidade *f*; **contents** NPL (*of packet, book*) conteúdo; **contented** ADJ contente, satisfeito
contest [*n* 'kɔntɛst, *vt* kən'tɛst] N contenda; (*competition*) concurso ▸ VT (*legal case*) defender; (*Pol*) ser candidato a; (*competition*) disputar; (*statement, decision*) contestar; **contestant** [kən'tɛstənt] N competidor(a) *m/f*; (*in fight*) adversário(-a)
context ['kɔntɛkst] N contexto
continent ['kɔntɪnənt] N continente *m*; **the C~** (BRIT) o continente europeu; **continental** [kɔntɪ'nɛntl] ADJ continental; **continental quilt** (BRIT) N edredom *m* (BR), edredão *m* (PT)
continual [kən'tɪnjuəl] ADJ contínuo
continue [kən'tɪnju:] VI prosseguir, continuar ▸ VT continuar; (*start again*) recomeçar, retomar; **continuous** [kən'tɪnjuəs] ADJ contínuo
contour ['kɔntuəʳ] N contorno; (*also*: **~ line**) curva de nível
contraceptive [kɔntrə'sɛptɪv] ADJ anticoncepcional ▸ N anticoncepcional *m*
contract [*n, cpd* 'kɔntrækt, *vt, vi* kən'trækt] N contrato ▸ CPD (*work*) de empreitada ▸ VI (*become smaller*) contrair-se, encolher-se; (*Comm*): **to ~ to do sth** comprometer-se por contrato a fazer algo ▸ VT contrair
contradict [kɔntrə'dɪkt] VT contradizer, desmentir
contrary¹ ['kɔntrərɪ] ADJ contrário ▸ N contrário; **on the ~** muito pelo contrário; **unless you hear to the ~** salvo aviso contrário
contrary² [kən'trɛərɪ] ADJ teimoso
contrast [*n* 'kɔntra:st, *vt* kən'tra:st] N contraste *m* ▸ VT comparar; **in ~ to** *or* **with** em contraste com, ao contrário de
contribute [kən'trɪbju:t] VT contribuir ▸ VI dar; **to ~ to** (*charity*) contribuir para; (*newspaper*) escrever para; (*discussion*) participar de; **contribution** [kɔntrɪ'bju:ʃən] N (*donation*) doação *f*; (BRIT: *for social security*) contribuição *f*; (*to debate*) intervenção *f*; (*to journal*) colaboração *f*; **contributor** [kən'trɪbjutəʳ] N (*to newspaper*) colaborador(a) *m/f*
control [kən'trəul] VT controlar; (*machinery*) regular; (*temper*) dominar ▸ N controle *m*; (*of car*) direção *f* (BR), condução *f* (PT); (*check*) freio, controle; **controls** NPL (*of vehicle*) comandos *mpl*; (*on radio, television etc*) controle; **to be in ~ of** ter o controle de; (*in charge of*) ser responsável por

controversial [kɔntrə'vəːʃl] ADJ controvertido, polêmico
controversy ['kɔntrəvəːsɪ] N controvérsia, polêmica
convenience [kən'viːnɪəns] N (*easiness*) facilidade *f*; (*suitability*) conveniência; (*advantage*) vantagem *f*, conveniência; **at your ~** quando lhe convier; **all modern ~s, all mod cons** (BRIT) com todos os confortos
convenient [kən'viːnɪənt] ADJ conveniente
convent ['kɔnvənt] N convento
convention [kən'vɛnʃən] N (*custom*) costume *m*; (*agreement*) convenção *f*; (*meeting*) assembleia; **conventional** ADJ convencional
conversation [kɔnvə'seɪʃən] N conversação *f*, conversa
convert [*vt* kən'vəːt, *n* 'kɔnvəːt] VT converter ▸ N convertido(-a); **convertible** [kən'vəːtəbl] N conversível *m*
convey [kən'veɪ] VT transportar, levar; (*thanks*) expressar; (*information*) passar; **conveyor belt** N correia transportadora
convict [*vt* kən'vɪkt, *n* 'kɔnvɪkt] VT condenar ▸ N presidiário(-a); **conviction** N condenação *f*; (*belief*) convicção *f*; (*certainty*) certeza
convince [kən'vɪns] VT (*assure*) assegurar; (*persuade*) convencer; **convincing** ADJ convincente
cook [kuk] VT cozinhar; (*meal*) preparar ▸ VI cozinhar ▸ N cozinheiro(-a); **cookbook** N livro de receitas; **cooker** N fogão *m*; **cookery** N culinária; **cookery book** (BRIT) N = **cookbook**; **cookie** (US) N bolacha, biscoito; **cooking** N cozinha
cool [kuːl] ADJ fresco; (*calm*) calmo; (*unfriendly*) frio ▸ VT resfriar ▸ VI esfriar
cop [kɔp] (*inf*) N policial *m/f* (BR), polícia *m/f* (PT), tira *m* (*inf*)
cope [kəup] VI: **to ~ with** poder com, arcar com; (*problem*) estar à altura de
copper ['kɔpəʳ] N (*metal*) cobre *m*; (BRIT *inf*: *policeman/woman*) policial *m/f* (BR), polícia *m/f* (PT); **coppers** NPL (*coins*) moedas *fpl* de pouco valor
copy ['kɔpɪ] N cópia; duplicata; (*of book etc*) exemplar *m* ▸ VT copiar; (*imitate*) imitar; **copyright** N direitos *mpl* autorais, copirraite *m*
coral ['kɔrəl] N coral *m*
cord [kɔːd] N corda; (*Elec*) fio, cabo; (*fabric*) veludo cotelê
corduroy ['kɔːdərɔɪ] N veludo cotelê
core [kɔːʳ] N centro; (*of fruit*) caroço; (*of problem*) âmago ▸ VT descaroçar
cork [kɔːk] N rolha; (*tree*) cortiça; **corkscrew** N saca-rolhas *m inv*
corn [kɔːn] N (BRIT) trigo; (US: *maize*) milho; (*on foot*) calo; **~ on the cob** (*Culin*) espiga de milho
corned beef ['kɔːnd-] N carne *f* de boi enlatada
corner ['kɔːnəʳ] N (*outside*) esquina; (*inside*) canto; (*in road*) curva; (*Football etc*) córner *m* ▸ VT (*trap*) encurralar; (*Comm*) açambarcar, monopolizar ▸ VI fazer uma curva
cornflakes ['kɔːnfleɪks] NPL flocos *mpl* de milho
cornflour ['kɔːnflauəʳ] (BRIT) N farinha de milho, maisena®
cornstarch ['kɔːnstɑːtʃ] (US) N = **cornflour**
Cornwall ['kɔːnwəl] N Cornualha

coronary ['kɔrənərɪ] N: **~ (thrombosis)** trombose *f* (coronária)
coronation [kɔrə'neɪʃən] N coroação *f*
coroner ['kɔrənəʳ] N *magistrado que investiga mortes suspeitas*
corporal ['kɔːpərl] N cabo ▶ ADJ: **~ punishment** castigo corporal
corporate ['kɔːpərɪt] ADJ (*finance*) corporativo; (*action*) coletivo; (*image*) da empresa
corporation [kɔːpə'reɪʃən] N (*of town*) município, junta; (*Comm*) sociedade *f*
corps [kɔːʳ] (*pl* **corps** [kɔːz]) N (*Mil*) unidade *f*; (*diplomatic*) corpo; **the press ~** a imprensa
corpse [kɔːps] N cadáver *m*
correct [kə'rɛkt] ADJ exato; (*proper*) correto ▶ VT corrigir; **correction** N correção *f*
correspond [kɔrɪs'pɔnd] VI (*write*): **to ~ (with)** corresponder-se (com); (*be equal to*): **to ~ to** corresponder a; (*be in accordance*): **to ~ (with)** corresponder (a); **correspondence** N correspondência; **correspondent** N correspondente *m/f*
corridor ['kɔrɪdɔːʳ] N corredor *m*
corrode [kə'rəud] VT corroer ▶ VI corroer-se
corrupt [kə'rʌpt] ADJ corrupto; (*Comput*) corrupto, danificado ▶ VT corromper; **corruption** N corrupção *f*
Corsica ['kɔːsɪkə] N Córsega
cosmetic [kɔz'mɛtɪk] N cosmético ▶ ADJ (*fig*) simbólico, superficial
cost [kɔst] (*pt, pp* **cost**) N (*price*) preço ▶ VT custar; **costs** NPL (*Comm*) custos *mpl*; (*Jur*) custas *fpl*; **at all ~s** custe o que custar
co-star [kəu-] N coestrela *m/f*
Costa Rica ['kɔstə'riːkə] N Costa Rica
costly ['kɔstlɪ] ADJ caro
costume ['kɔstjuːm] N traje *m*; (BRIT: *also*: **swimming ~**: *woman's*) maiô *m* (BR), fato de banho (PT); (: *man's*) calção *m* (de banho) (BR), calções *mpl* de banho (PT)
cosy ['kəuzɪ], (US) **cozy** ADJ aconchegante; (*life*) confortável
cot [kɔt] N (BRIT) cama (de criança), berço; (US) cama de lona
cottage ['kɔtɪdʒ] N casa de campo; **cottage cheese** N queijo tipo cottage (BR), queijo creme (PT)
cotton ['kɔtn] N algodão *m*; (*thread*) fio, linha; **cotton on** (*inf*) VI: **to ~ on (to sth)** sacar (algo); **cotton bud** (BRIT) N cotonete® *m*; **cotton candy** (US) N algodão *m* doce; **cotton wool** (BRIT) N algodão *m* (hidrófilo)
couch [kautʃ] N sofá *m*; (*doctor's*) cama; (*psychiatrist's*) divã *m*
cough [kɔf] VI tossir ▶ N tosse *f*
could [kud] PT, CONDITIONAL *of* **can²**
couldn't ['kudnt] = **could not**
council ['kaunsl] N conselho; **city** *or* **town ~** câmara municipal; **council estate** (BRIT) N conjunto habitacional; **council house** (BRIT) N casa popular; **councillor** N vereador(a) *m/f*
counsellor ['kaunsələʳ], (US) **counselor** N conselheiro(-a); (US *Jur*) advogado(-a)
count [kaunt] VT contar; (*include*) incluir ▶ VI contar ▶ N (*of votes etc*) contagem *f*; (*of pollen, alcohol*) nível *m*; (*nobleman*) conde *m*; **count on** VT FUS contar com; **countdown** N contagem *f* regressiva

counter ['kauntəʳ] N (*in shop*) balcão *m*; (*in post office etc*) guichê *m*; (*in games*) ficha ▶ VT contrariar ▶ ADV: **~ to** ao contrário de
counterfeit ['kauntəfɪt] N falsificação *f* ▶ VT falsificar ▶ ADJ falso, falsificado
counterpart ['kauntəpɑːt] N (*opposite number*) homólogo(-a); (*equivalent*) equivalente *m/f*; **counterterrorism** [kauntə'tɛrərɪzəm] N antiterrorismo
countess ['kauntɪs] N condessa
countless ['kauntlɪs] ADJ inumerável
country ['kʌntrɪ] N país *m*; (*nation*) nação *f*; (*native land*) terra; (*as opposed to town*) campo; (*region*) região *f*, terra; **countryside** N campo
county ['kauntɪ] N condado
coup [kuː] N golpe *m* de mestre; (*also*: **~ d'état**) golpe (de estado)
couple ['kʌpl] N (*of things, people*) par *m*; (*married couple, courting couple*) casal *m*; **a ~ of** um par de; (*a few*) alguns/algumas
coupon ['kuːpɔn] N cupom *m* (BR), cupão *m* (PT); (*voucher*) vale *m*
courage ['kʌrɪdʒ] N coragem *f*
courier ['kurɪəʳ] N correio; (*for tourists*) guia *m/f*, agente *m/f* de turismo
course [kɔːs] N (*direction*) direção *f*; (*process*) desenvolvimento; (*of river, Sch*) curso; (*of ship*) rumo; (*Golf*) campo; (*part of meal*) prato; **of ~** naturalmente; (*certainly*) certamente; **of ~!** claro!, lógico!
court [kɔːt] N (*royal*) corte *f*; (*Jur*) tribunal *m*; (*Tennis etc*) quadra ▶ VT (*woman*) cortejar, namorar; **to take to ~** demandar, levar a julgamento
courtesy ['kəːtəsɪ] N cortesia; **(by) ~ of** com permissão de
court-house (US) N palácio de justiça
courtroom ['kɔːtrum] N sala de tribunal
courtyard ['kɔːtjɑːd] N pátio
cousin ['kʌzn] N primo(-a) *m/f*; **first ~** primo-irmão/prima-irmã *m/f*
cover ['kʌvəʳ] VT cobrir; (*with lid*) tampar; (*chairs etc*) revestir; (*distance*) percorrer; (*include*) abranger; (*protect*) abrigar; (*issues*) tratar ▶ N (*lid*) tampa; (*for chair etc*) capa; (*for bed*) cobertor *m*; (*of book, magazine*) capa; (*shelter*) abrigo; (*Insurance*) cobertura; **to take ~** abrigar-se; **under ~** (*indoors*) abrigado; **under separate ~** (*Comm*) em separado; **cover up** VI: **to ~ up for sb** cobrir alguém; **coverage** N cobertura; **cover charge** N couvert *m*
cover-up N encobrimento (dos fatos)
cow [kau] N vaca ▶ VT intimidar
coward ['kauəd] N covarde *m/f*; **cowardly** ADJ covarde
cowboy ['kaubɔɪ] N vaqueiro
cozy ['kəuzɪ] (US) ADJ = **cosy**
crab [kræb] N caranguejo
crack [kræk] N rachadura; (*gap*) brecha; (*noise*) estalo; (*drug*) crack *m* ▶ VT quebrar; (*nut*) partir, descascar; (*wall*) rachar; (*whip etc*) estalar; (*joke*) soltar; (*mystery*) resolver; (*code*) decifrar ▶ ADJ (*expert*) de primeira classe; **crack down on** VT FUS (*crime*) ser linha dura com; **crack up** VI (*Psych*) sofrer um colapso nervoso; **cracker** N (*biscuit*) biscoito; (*Christmas cracker*) busca pé surpresa *m*

crackle ['krækl] VI crepitar
cradle ['kreɪdl] N berço
craft [krɑ:ft] N (*skill*) arte *f*; (*trade*) ofício; (*boat*) barco; **craftsman** *irreg* N artífice *m*, artesão *m*; **craftsmanship** N acabamento
cram [kræm] VT (*fill*): **to ~ sth with** encher *or* abarrotar algo de; (*put*): **to ~ sth into** enfiar algo em ▶ VI (*for exams*) estudar na última hora
cramp [kræmp] N (*Med*) cãibra; **cramped** ADJ apertado, confinado
cranberry ['krænbərɪ] N oxicoco
crane [kreɪn] N (*Tech*) guindaste *m*; (*bird*) grou *m*
crash [kræʃ] N (*noise*) estrondo; (*of car*) batida; (*of plane*) desastre *m* de avião; (*Comm*) falência, quebra; (*Stock Exchange*) craque *m* ▶ VT (*car*) bater com; (*plane*) jogar ▶ VI (*car*) bater; (*plane*) cair; (*two cars*) colidir, bater; (*Comm*) falir, quebrar; **crash course** N curso intensivo
crate [kreɪt] N caixote *m*; (*for bottles*) engradado
crave [kreɪv] VT, VI: **to ~ for** ansiar por
crawl [krɔ:l] VI arrastar-se; (*child*) engatinhar; (*insect*) andar; (*vehicle*) andar a passo de tartaruga ▶ N (*Swimming*) crawl *m*
crayfish ['kreɪfɪʃ] N INV (*freshwater*) camarão-d'água-doce *m*; (*saltwater*) lagostim *m*
crayon ['kreɪən] N lápis *m* de cera, crayon *m*
craze [kreɪz] N (*fashion*) moda
crazy ['kreɪzɪ] ADJ louco, maluco, doido
creak [kri:k] VI ranger
cream [kri:m] N (*of milk*) nata; (*artificial, cosmetic*) creme *m*; (*élite*): **the ~ of** a fina flor de ▶ ADJ (*colour*) creme *inv*; **cream cheese** N ricota (BR), queijo creme (PT); **creamy** ADJ (*colour*) creme *inv*; (*taste*) cremoso
crease [kri:s] N (*fold*) dobra, vinco; (*in trousers*) vinco; (*wrinkle*) ruga ▶ VT (*wrinkle*) amassar, amarrotar ▶ VI amassar-se, amarrotar-se
create [kri:'eɪt] VT criar; (*produce*) produzir
creature ['kri:tʃəʳ] N (*animal*) animal *m*, bicho; (*living thing*) criatura
credit ['krɛdɪt] N crédito; (*merit*) mérito ▶ VT (*also*: **give ~ to**) acreditar; (*Comm*) creditar; **credits** NPL (*Cinema, TV*) crédito; **to ~ sb with sth** (*fig*) atribuir algo a alguém; **to be in ~** ter fundos; **credit card** N cartão *m* de crédito; **credit crunch** N contração *f* do crédito
creek [kri:k] N enseada; (US) riacho
creep [kri:p] (*pt, pp* **crept**) VI (*animal*) rastejar; (*person*) deslizar(-se)
cremate [krɪ'meɪt] VT cremar; **crematorium** (*pl* **crematoria**) N crematório
crept [krɛpt] PT, PP *of* **creep**
crescent ['krɛsnt] N meia-lua; (*street*) rua semicircular
cress [krɛs] N agrião *m*
crest [krɛst] N (*of bird*) crista; (*of hill*) cimo, topo; (*of coat of arms*) timbre *m*
crew [kru:] N (*of ship etc*) tripulação *f*; (*Cinema*) equipe *f*
crib [krɪb] N manjedoira, presépio; (US: *cot*) berço ▶ VT (*inf*) colar
cricket ['krɪkɪt] N (*insect*) grilo; (*game*) criquete *m*, cricket *m*

C

crime [kraɪm] N (*no pl: illegal activities*) crime *m*; (*offence*) delito; (*fig*) pecado, maldade *f*; **criminal** ['krɪmɪnl] N criminoso ▶ ADJ criminal; (*morally wrong*) imoral
crimson ['krɪmzn] ADJ carmesim *inv*
cringe [krɪndʒ] VI encolher-se
cripple ['krɪpl] N aleijado(-a) ▶ VT aleijar
crisis ['kraɪsɪs] (*pl* **crises**) N crise *f*
crisp [krɪsp] ADJ fresco; (*bacon etc*) torrado; (*manner*) seco; **crisps** (BRIT) NPL batatinhas *fpl* fritas; **crispy** ADJ crocante
criterion [kraɪ'tɪərɪən] (*pl* **criteria**) N critério
critic ['krɪtɪk] N crítico(-a); **critical** ADJ crítico; (*illness*) grave; **to be critical of sth/sb** criticar algo/alguém; **criticism** ['krɪtɪsɪzm] N crítica; **criticize** ['krɪtɪsaɪz] VT criticar
Croatia [krəu'eɪʃə] N Croácia
crockery ['krɔkərɪ] N louça
crocodile ['krɔkədaɪl] N crocodilo
crocus ['krəukəs] N açafrão-da-primavera *m*
crook [kruk] N (*inf: criminal*) vigarista *m/f*; (*of shepherd*) cajado; **crooked** ['krukɪd] ADJ torto; (*dishonest*) desonesto
crop [krɔp] N (*produce*) colheita; (*amount produced*) safra; (*riding crop*) chicotinho ▶ VT cortar; **crop up** VI surgir
cross [krɔs] N cruz *f*; (*hybrid*) cruzamento ▶ VT cruzar; (*street etc*) atravessar; (*thwart*) contrariar ▶ ADJ zangado, mal-humorado; **cross out** VT riscar; **cross over** VI atravessar; **crossing** N (*sea passage*) travessia; (*also*: **pedestrian crossing**) faixa (para pedestres) (BR), passadeira (PT); **crossroads** N cruzamento; **crosswalk** (US) N faixa (para pedestres) (BR), passadeira (PT); **crossword** N palavras *fpl* cruzadas
crouch [krautʃ] VI agachar-se
crow [krəu] N (*bird*) corvo; (*of cock*) canto, cocoricó *m* ▶ VI (*cock*) cantar, cocoricar
crowd [kraud] N multidão *f* ▶ VT (*fill*) apinhar ▶ VI (*gather*) amontoar-se; (*cram*): **to ~ in** apinhar-se; **crowded** ADJ (*full*) lotado; (*densely populated*) superlotado
crown [kraun] N coroa; (*of head, hill*) topo ▶ VT coroar; (*fig*) rematar; **crown jewels** NPL joias *fpl* reais
crucial ['kru:ʃl] ADJ (*decision*) vital; (*vote*) decisivo
crucifix ['kru:sɪfɪks] N crucifixo
crude [kru:d] ADJ (*materials*) bruto; (*fig: basic*) tosco; (*: vulgar*) grosseiro
cruel ['kruəl] ADJ cruel
cruise [kru:z] N cruzeiro ▶ VI (*ship*) fazer um cruzeiro; (*car*): **to ~ at ... km/h** ir a ... km por hora
crumb [krʌm] N (*of bread*) migalha; (*of cake*) farelo
crumble ['krʌmbl] VT esfarelar ▶ VI (*building*) desmoronar-se; (*plaster, earth*) esfacelar-se; (*fig*) desintegrar-se
crumpet ['krʌmpɪt] N *bolo leve*
crumple ['krʌmpl] VT (*paper*) amassar; (*material*) amarrotar
crunch [krʌntʃ] VT (*food etc*) mastigar; (*underfoot*) esmagar ▶ N (*fig*): **the ~** o momento decisivo; **crunchy** ADJ crocante
crush [krʌʃ] N (*crowd*) aglomeração *f*; (*love*): **to have a ~ on sb** ter um rabicho por alguém; (*drink*): **lemon ~** limonada ▶ VT (*press*) esmagar;

(*squeeze*) espremer; (*paper*) amassar; (*cloth*) enrugar; (*army, opposition*) aniquilar; (*hopes*) destruir; (*person*) arrasar
crust [krʌst] N (*of bread*) casca; (*of snow, earth*) crosta
crutch [krʌtʃ] N muleta
cry [kraɪ] VI chorar; (*shout: also:* **~ out**) gritar ▸ N grito; (*of bird*) pio; (*of animal*) voz *f*; **cry off** VI desistir
crystal ['krɪstl] N cristal *m*
cub [kʌb] N filhote *m*; (*also:* **~ scout**) lobinho
Cuba ['kju:bə] N Cuba
cube [kju:b] N cubo ▸ VT (*Math*) elevar ao cubo; **cubic** ADJ cúbico
cubicle ['kju:bɪkl] N cubículo
cuckoo ['kuku:] N cuco
cucumber ['kju:kʌmbə^r] N pepino
cuddle ['kʌdl] VT abraçar ▸ VI abraçar-se
cue [kju:] N (*Snooker*) taco; (*Theatre etc*) deixa
cuff [kʌf] N (*of shirt, coat etc*) punho; (*US: on trousers*) bainha; (*blow*) bofetada; **off the ~** de improviso
cul-de-sac ['kʌldəsæk] N beco sem saída
cull [kʌl] VT (*story, idea*) escolher, selecionar ▸ N matança seletiva
culminate ['kʌlmɪneɪt] VI: **to ~ in** terminar em
culprit ['kʌlprɪt] N culpado(-a)
cult [kʌlt] N culto
cultivate ['kʌltɪveɪt] VT cultivar
cultural ['kʌltʃərəl] ADJ cultural
culture ['kʌltʃə[r]] N cultura
cunning ['kʌnɪŋ] N astúcia ▸ ADJ astuto, malandro; (*device, idea*) engenhoso
cup [kʌp] N xícara (BR), chávena (PT); (*prize, of bra*) taça
cupboard ['kʌbəd] N armário
curator [kjuə'reɪtə[r]] N diretor(a) *m/f*
curb [kə:b] VT refrear ▸ N freio; (*US*) = **kerb**
curdle ['kə:dl] VI coalhar
cure [kjuə[r]] VT curar ▸ N tratamento, cura
curfew ['kə:fju:] N toque *m* de recolher
curious ['kjuərɪəs] ADJ curioso; (*nosy*) abelhudo; (*unusual*) estranho
curl [kə:l] N (*of hair*) cacho ▸ VT (*loosely*) frisar; (*tightly*) encrespar ▸ VI (*hair*) encaracolar; **curl up** VI encaracolar-se; **curler** N rolo, bobe *m*; **curly** ADJ cacheado, crespo
currant ['kʌrnt] N passa de corinto; (*blackcurrant, redcurrant*) groselha
currency ['kʌrnsɪ] N moeda; **to gain ~** (*fig*) consagrar-se
current ['kʌrnt] N corrente *f* ▸ ADJ corrente; (*present*) atual; **current account** (BRIT) N conta corrente; **current affairs** NPL atualidades *fpl*; **currently** ADV atualmente
curriculum [kə'rɪkjuləm] (**curriculums** *or pl* **curricula**) N programa *m* de estudos; **curriculum vitae** [-'vi:taɪ] N currículo
curry ['kʌrɪ] N caril *m* ▸ VT: **to ~ favour with** captar simpatia de
curse [kə:s] VI xingar (BR), praguejar (PT) ▸ VT (*swear at*) xingar (BR), praguejar a (PT); (*bemoan*) amaldiçoar ▸ N maldição *f*; (*swearword*) palavrão *m* (BR), baixo calão *m* (PT); (*problem*) castigo
cursor ['kə:sə[r]] N (*Comput*) cursor *m*
curt [kə:t] ADJ seco, brusco

curtain ['kə:tn] N cortina; (*Theatre*) pano
curve [kə:v] N curva ▶ VI encurvar-se, torcer-se; (*road*) fazer (uma) curva
cushion ['kuʃən] N almofada ▶ VT amortecer
custard ['kʌstəd] N nata, creme *m*
custody ['kʌstədɪ] N custódia; **to take into ~** deter
custom ['kʌstəm] N (*tradition*) tradição *f*; (*convention*) costume *m*; (*habit*) hábito; (*Comm*) clientela; **customer** N cliente *m/f*; **customize** ['kʌstəmaɪz] VT personalizar
customs ['kʌstəmz] NPL alfândega; **customs officer** N inspetor(a) *m/f* da alfândega, aduaneiro(-a)
cut [kʌt] (*pt, pp* **cut**) VT cortar; (*reduce*) reduzir ▶ VI cortar ▶ N corte *m*; (*in spending*) redução *f*; (*of garment*) tacho; **cut down** VT (*tree*) derrubar; (*reduce*) reduzir; **cut off** VT (*piece, Tel*) cortar; (*person, village*) isolar; (*supply*) suspender; **cut out** VT (*shape*) recortar; (*activity etc*) suprimir; (*remove*) remover; **cut up** VT cortar em pedaços
cute [kju:t] ADJ bonitinho
cutlery ['kʌtlərɪ] N talheres *mpl*
cutlet ['kʌtlɪt] N costeleta
cut-price, (US) **cut-rate** ADJ a preço reduzido
cutting ADJ cortante ▶ N (BRIT: *from newspaper*) recorte *m*; (*from plant*) muda; **cutting-edge** ADJ (*technology, research*) de ponta
CV N ABBR = **curriculum vitae**
cyber attack ['saɪbərətæk] N ciberataque *m*
cybercafé ['saɪbəkæfeɪ] N cibercafé *m*
cyberspace ['saɪbəspeɪs] N ciberespaço
cycle ['saɪkl] N ciclo; (*bicycle*) bicicleta ▶ VI andar de bicicleta
cycling ['saɪklɪŋ] N ciclismo
cyclist ['saɪklɪst] N ciclista *m/f*
cylinder ['sɪlɪndəʳ] N cilindro; (*of gas*) bujão *m*
Cyprus ['saɪprəs] N Chipre *f*
cyst [sɪst] N cisto; **cystitis** N cistite *f*
czar [zɑːʳ] N czar *m*
Czech [tʃɛk] ADJ tcheco ▶ N tcheco(-a); (*Ling*) tcheco; **Czech Republic** N: **the Czech Republic** a República Tcheca

d

D¹ [diː] N (*Mus*) ré *m*
D² (*US*) ABBR (*Pol*) = **democrat, democratic**
dab [dæb] VT (*eyes, wound*) tocar (de leve); (*paint, cream*) aplicar de leve
dad [dæd] (*inf*) N papai *m*
daddy ['dædɪ] N = **dad**
daffodil ['dæfədɪl] N narciso-dos-prados *m*
daft [dɑːft] ADJ bobo, besta
dagger ['dægəʳ] N punhal *m*, adaga
daily ['deɪlɪ] ADJ diário ▶ N (*paper*) jornal *m*, diário ▶ ADV diariamente
dairy ['dɛərɪ] N leiteria
daisy ['deɪzɪ] N margarida
dam [dæm] N represa, barragem *f* ▶ VT represar
damage ['dæmɪdʒ] N (*harm*) prejuízo; (*dents etc*) avaria ▶ VT danificar; (*harm*) prejudicar; **damages** NPL (*Jur*) indenização *f* por perdas e danos
damn [dæm] VT condenar; (*curse*) maldizer ▶ N (*inf*): **I don't give a ~** não dou a mínima, estou me lixando ▶ ADJ (*inf*: *also*: **~ed**) danado, maldito; **~ (it)!** (que) droga!
damp [dæmp] ADJ úmido ▶ N umidade *f* ▶ VT (*also*: **~en**: *cloth, rag*) umedecer; (: *enthusiasm etc*) jogar água fria em
dance [dɑːns] N dança; (*party etc*) baile *m* ▶ VI dançar; **dancer** N dançarino(-a); (*professional*) bailarino(-a); **dancing** N dança
dandelion ['dændɪlaɪən] N dente-de-leão *m*
dandruff ['dændrəf] N caspa
Dane [deɪn] N dinamarquês(-esa) *m/f*
danger ['deɪndʒəʳ] N perigo; (*risk*) risco; **"~!"** (*on sign*) "perigo!"; **to be in ~ of** correr o risco de; **in ~** em perigo; **dangerous** ['deɪndʒərəs] ADJ perigoso
dangle ['dæŋgl] VT balançar ▶ VI pender balançando
Danish ['deɪnɪʃ] ADJ dinamarquês(-esa) ▶ N (*Ling*) dinamarquês *m*
dare [dɛəʳ] VT: **to ~ sb to do sth** desafiar alguém a fazer algo ▶ VI: **to ~ (to) do sth** atrever-se a fazer algo, ousar fazer algo; **I ~ say** (*I suppose*) acho provável que; **daring** ADJ audacioso; (*bold*) ousado ▶ N coragem *f*, destemor *m*
dark [dɑːk] ADJ escuro; (*complexion*) moreno ▶ N escuro; **in the ~ about** (*fig*) no escuro sobre; **after ~** depois de escurecer; **darken** VT escurecer; (*colour*) fazer mais escuro ▶ VI escurecer(-se); **darkness** N escuridão *f*; **darkroom** N câmara escura
darling ['dɑːlɪŋ] ADJ, N querido(-a)

dart [dɑːt] N dardo; (*in sewing*) alinhavo ▸ VI precipitar-se; **to ~ away/along** ir-se/seguir precipitadamente; **darts** N (*game*) jogo de dardos

dash [dæʃ] N (*sign*) hífen *m*; (: *long*) travessão *m*; (*small quantity*) pontinha ▸ VT arremessar; (*hopes*) frustrar ▸ VI precipitar-se, correr; **dash away** VI sair apressado; **dash off** VI = **dash away**

dashboard [ˈdæʃbɔːd] N painel *m* de instrumentos

data [ˈdeɪtə] NPL dados *mpl*; **database** N banco de dados; **data processing** N processamento de dados

date [deɪt] N data; (*with friend*) encontro; (*fruit*) tâmara ▸ VT datar; (*person*) namorar; **to ~** até agora; **out of ~** desatualizado; **up to ~** moderno; **dated** [ˈdeɪtɪd] ADJ antiquado

daughter [ˈdɔːtəʳ] N filha; **daughter-in-law** (*pl* **daughters-in-law**) N nora

daunting [ˈdɔːntɪŋ] ADJ desanimador(a)

dawn [dɔːn] N alvorada, amanhecer *m*; (*of period, situation*) surgimento, início ▸ VI (*day*) amanhecer; (*fig*): **it ~ed on him that ...** começou a perceber que ...

day [deɪ] N dia *m*; (*working day*) jornada, dia útil; **the ~ before/after** a véspera/o dia seguinte; **the ~ before yesterday** anteontem; **the ~ after tomorrow** depois de amanhã; **by ~** de dia; **day-care centre** [ˈdeɪkɛə-] N (*for elderly etc*) centro de convivência; (*for children*) creche *f*; **daydream** VI devanear; **daylight** N luz *f* (do dia); **day return** (BRIT) N bilhete *m* de ida e volta no mesmo dia; **daytime** N dia *m*; **day-to-day** ADJ cotidiano

dazzle [ˈdæzl] VT (*bewitch*) deslumbrar; (*blind*) ofuscar

dead [dɛd] ADJ morto; (*numb*) dormente; (*telephone*) cortado; (*Elec*) sem corrente ▸ ADV completamente; (*exactly*) absolutamente ▸ NPL: **the ~** os mortos; **to shoot sb ~** matar alguém a tiro; **~ tired** morto de cansado; **to stop ~** estacar; **dead end** N beco sem saída; **deadline** N prazo final; **deadly** ADJ mortal, fatal; (*weapon*) mortífero

deaf [dɛf] ADJ surdo; **deafen** VT ensurdecer

deal [diːl] (*pt, pp* **dealt**) N (*agreement*) acordo ▸ VT (*cards, blows*) dar; **a good** *or* **great ~ (of)** bastante, muito; **deal in** VT FUS (*Comm*) negociar em *or* com; **deal with** VT FUS (*people*) tratar com; (*problem*) ocupar-se de; (*subject*) tratar de; **dealer** N negociante *m/f*; **dealings** NPL transações *fpl*

dean [diːn] N (*Rel*) decano; (*Sch*: BRIT) reitor(a) *m/f*; (: US) orientador(a) *m/f* de estudos

dear [dɪəʳ] ADJ querido, caro; (*expensive*) caro ▸ N: **my ~** meu querido/minha querida ▸ EXCL: **~ me!** ai, meu Deus!; **D~ Sir/Madam** (*in letter*) Prezado Senhor/Prezada Senhora (BR), Exmo. Senhor/Exma. Senhora (PT); **D~ Mr/Mrs X** Prezado Sr. X/Prezada Sra. X; **dearly** ADV (*love*) ternamente; (*pay*) caro

death [dɛθ] N morte *f*; (*Admin*) óbito; **death penalty** N pena de morte; **death row** (US) N corredor *m* da morte

debate [dɪ'beɪt] N debate *m* ▶ VT debater
debit ['dɛbɪt] N débito ▶ VT: **to ~ a sum to sb** *or* **to sb's account** lançar uma quantia ao débito de alguém *or* à conta de alguém; *see also* **direct debit**; **debit card** N cartão *m* de débito
debt [dɛt] N dívida; (*state*) endividamento; **to be in ~** ter dívidas, estar endividado
decade ['dɛkeɪd] N década
decaffeinated [dɪ'kæfɪneɪtɪd] ADJ descafeinado
decay [dɪ'keɪ] N ruína; (*also*: **tooth ~**) cárie *f* ▶ VI (*rot*) apodrecer-se
deceased [dɪ'si:st] N: **the ~** o falecido/a falecida
deceit [dɪ'si:t] N engano; (*duplicity*) fraude *f*
deceive [dɪ'si:v] VT enganar
December [dɪ'sɛmbəʳ] N dezembro
decent ['di:sənt] ADJ (*proper*) decente; (*kind, honest*) honesto, amável
deception [dɪ'sɛpʃən] N engano; (*deceitful act*) fraude *f*; **deceptive** ADJ enganador(a)
decide [dɪ'saɪd] VT (*person*) convencer; (*question, argument*) resolver ▶ VI decidir; **to ~ on sth** decidir-se por algo
decimal ['dɛsɪməl] ADJ decimal ▶ N decimal *m*
decision [dɪ'sɪʒən] N (*choice*) escolha; (*act of choosing*) decisão *f*; (*decisiveness*) resolução *f*
decisive [dɪ'saɪsɪv] ADJ (*action*) decisivo; (*person*) decidido
deck [dɛk] N (*Naut*) convés *m*; (*of bus*): **top ~** andar *m* de cima; (*of cards*) baralho; **record/cassette ~** toca-discos *m inv*/toca-fitas *m inv*
declare [dɪ'klɛəʳ] VT (*intention*) revelar; (*result*) divulgar; (*income, at customs*) declarar
decline [dɪ'klaɪn] N declínio; (*lessening*) diminuição *f*, baixa ▶ VT recusar ▶ VI diminuir
decorate ['dɛkəreɪt] VT; **decoration** [dɛkə'reɪʃən] N enfeite *m*; (*act*) decoração; (*medal*) condecoração *f*; **decorator** N (*painter*) pintor(a) *m/f*
decrease [*n* 'di:kri:s, *vt, vi* di:'kri:s] N: **~ (in)** diminuição *f* (de) ▶ VT reduzir ▶ VI diminuir
decree [dɪ'kri:] N decreto
decrypt [di:'krɪpt] VT (*Comput, Tel*) desencriptar
dedicate ['dɛdɪkeɪt] VT dedicar; **dedication** [dɛdɪ'keɪʃən] N dedicação *f*; (*in book*) dedicatória; (*on radio*) mensagem *f*
deduce [dɪ'dju:s] VT deduzir
deduct [dɪ'dʌkt] VT deduzir; **deduction** N (*deducting*) redução *f*; (*amount*) subtração *f*; (*deducing*) dedução *f*
deed [di:d] N feito; (*Jur*) escritura, título
deep [di:p] ADJ profundo; (*voice*) baixo, grave; (*breath*) fundo; (*colour*) forte, carregado ▶ ADV: **the spectators stood 20 ~** havia 20 fileiras de espectadores; **to be 4 metres ~** ter 4 metros de profundidade; **deepen** VT aprofundar ▶ VI aumentar
deer [dɪəʳ] N INV veado, cervo
default [dɪ'fɔ:lt] N (*Comput*) default *m*, padrão *m*; **by ~** (*win*) por desistência
defeat [dɪ'fi:t] N derrota; (*failure*) malogro ▶ VT derrotar, vencer
defect [*n* 'di:fɛkt, *vi* dɪ'fɛkt] N defeito ▶ VI: **to ~ to the enemy**

d

desertar para se juntar ao inimigo;
defective [dɪ'fɛktɪv] ADJ defeituoso
defence [dɪ'fɛns], (US) **defense** N defesa
defend [dɪ'fɛnd] VT defender; (*Jur*) contestar; **defendant** N acusado(-a); (*in civil case*) réu/ré *m/f*; **defender** N defensor(a) *m/f*; (*Sport*) defesa
defer [dɪ'fəːʳ] VT (*postpone*) adiar
defiance [dɪ'faɪəns] N desafio; rebeldia; **in ~ of** a despeito de
defiant [dɪ'faɪənt] ADJ desafiador(a)
deficiency [dɪ'fɪʃənsɪ] N (*lack*) deficiência, falta; (*defect*) defeito
deficit ['dɛfɪsɪt] N déficit *m*
define [dɪ'faɪn] VT definir
definite ['dɛfɪnɪt] ADJ (*fixed*) definitivo; (*clear, obvious*) claro, categórico; (*certain*) certo; **he was ~ about it** ele foi categórico; **definitely** ADV sem dúvida
deflate [diː'fleɪt] VT esvaziar
deflect [dɪ'flɛkt] VT desviar
defraud [dɪ'frɔːd] VT: **to ~ sb (of sth)** trapacear alguém (por causa de algo)
defriend [diː'frɛnd] VT (*on social network*) excluir (*em rede social*)
defrost [diː'frɔst] VT descongelar
defuse [diː'fjuːz] VT tirar o estopim *or* a espoleta de; (*situation*) neutralizar
defy [dɪ'faɪ] VT desafiar; (*resist*) opor-se a
degree [dɪ'griː] N grau *m*; (*Sch*) diploma *m*, título; **~ in maths** formatura em matemática; **by ~s** (*gradually*) pouco a pouco; **to some ~, to a certain ~** até certo ponto
dehydrated [diːhaɪ'dreɪtɪd] ADJ desidratado; (*milk*) em pó
delay [dɪ'leɪ] VT (*decision etc*) retardar, atrasar; (*train, person*) atrasar ▶ VI hesitar ▶ N demora; (*postponement*) adiamento; **to be ~ed** estar atrasado; **without ~** sem demora *or* atraso
delegate [*n* 'dɛlɪgɪt, *vt* 'dɛlɪgeɪt] N delegado(-a) ▶ VT (*person*) autorizar; (*task*) delegar
delete [dɪ'liːt] VT eliminar, riscar; (*Comput*) deletar, excluir
deliberate [*adj* dɪ'lɪbərɪt, *vi* dɪ'lɪbəreɪt] ADJ (*intentional*) intencional; (*slow*) pausado, lento ▶ VI considerar; **deliberately** [dɪ'lɪbərɪtlɪ] ADV (*on purpose*) de propósito
delicacy ['dɛlɪkəsɪ] N delicadeza; (*of problem*) dificuldade *f*; (*choice food*) iguaria
delicate ['dɛlɪkɪt] ADJ delicado; (*health*) frágil
delicatessen [dɛlɪkə'tɛsn] N delicatessen *m*
delicious [dɪ'lɪʃəs] ADJ delicioso; (*food*) saboroso
delight [dɪ'laɪt] N prazer *m*, deleite *m*; (*person*) encanto; (*experience*) delícia ▶ VT encantar, deleitar; **to take (a) ~ in** deleitar-se com; **delighted** ADJ: **delighted (at** *or* **with sth)** encantado (com algo); **delightful** ADJ encantador(a), delicioso
delinquent [dɪ'lɪŋkwənt] ADJ, N delinquente *m/f*
deliver [dɪ'lɪvəʳ] VT (*distribute*) distribuir; (*hand over*) entregar; (*message*) comunicar; (*speech*) proferir; (*Med*) partejar; **delivery** N distribuição *f*; (*of speaker*) enunciação *f*; (*Med*) parto; **to take delivery of** receber
delusion [dɪ'luːʒən] N ilusão *f*

demand [dɪ'mɑ:nd] VT exigir; (*rights*) reivindicar, reclamar ▶ N exigência; (*claim*) reivindicação *f*; (*Econ*) procura; **to be in ~** estar em demanda; **on ~** à vista; **demanding** ADJ (*boss*) exigente; (*work*) absorvente

demise [dɪ'maɪz] N falecimento

demo ['dɛməu] (*inf*) N ABBR (= *demonstration*) passeata

democracy [dɪ'mɔkrəsɪ] N democracia; **democrat** ['dɛməkræt] N democrata *m/f*; **democratic** [dɛmə'krætɪk] ADJ democrático

demolish [dɪ'mɔlɪʃ] VT demolir, derrubar; (*argument*) refutar, contestar

demonstrate ['dɛmənstreɪt] VT demonstrar ▶ VI: **to ~ (for/against)** manifestar-se (a favor de/contra); **demonstration** [dɛmən'streɪʃən] N (*Pol*) manifestação *f*; (: *march*) passeata; (*proof*) demonstração *f*; (*exhibition*) exibição *f*; **demonstrator** N manifestante *m/f*

demote [dɪ'məut] VT rebaixar de posto

den [dɛn] N (*of animal*) covil *m*; (*of thieves*) antro, esconderijo; (*room*) aposento privado, cantinho

denial [dɪ'naɪəl] N refutação *f*; (*refusal*) negativa

denim ['dɛnɪm] N brim *m*, zuarte *m*; **denims** NPL jeans *m* (BR), jeans *mpl* (PT)

Denmark ['dɛnmɑ:k] N Dinamarca

denomination [dɪnɔmɪ'neɪʃən] N valor *m*, denominação *f*; (*Rel*) confissão *f*, seita

denounce [dɪ'nauns] VT denunciar

dense [dɛns] ADJ denso; (*inf: stupid*) estúpido, bronco

density ['dɛnsɪtɪ] N densidade *f*

dent [dɛnt] N amolgadura, depressão *f* ▶ VT amolgar, dentar

dental ['dɛntl] ADJ (*treatment*) dentário; (*hygiene*) dental; **dental floss** [-flɔs] N fio dental

dentist ['dɛntɪst] N dentista *m/f*

dentures ['dɛntʃəz] NPL dentadura

deny [dɪ'naɪ] VT negar; (*refuse*) recusar

deodorant [di:'əudərənt] N desodorante *m* (BR), desodorizante *m* (PT)

depart [dɪ'pɑ:t] VI ir-se, partir; (*train etc*) sair; **to ~ from** (*fig: differ from*) afastar-se de

department [dɪ'pɑ:tmənt] N (*Sch*) departamento; (*Comm*) seção *f*; (*Pol*) repartição *f*; **department store** N magazine *m* (BR), grande armazém *m* (PT)

departure [dɪ'pɑ:tʃə^r] N partida, ida; (*of train etc*) saída; (*of employee*) saída; **a new ~** uma nova orientação; **departure lounge** N sala de embarque

depend [dɪ'pɛnd] VI: **to ~ (up)on** depender de; (*rely on*) contar com; **it ~s** depende; **~ing on the result ...** dependendo do resultado ...; **dependant** N dependente *m/f*; **dependent** ADJ: **to be dependent (on)** depender (de), ser dependente (de) ▶ N = **dependant**

depict [dɪ'pɪkt] VT (*in picture*) retratar, representar; (*describe*) descrever

deport [dɪ'pɔ:t] VT deportar

deposit [dɪ'pɔzɪt] N (*Comm, Geo*) depósito; (*Chem*) sedimento;

d

(*of ore, oil*) jazida; (*down payment*) sinal *m* ▸ VT depositar; (*luggage*) guardar; **deposit account** N conta de depósito a prazo

depot ['dɛpəu] N (*storehouse*) depósito, armazém *m*; (*for vehicles*) garagem *f*, parque *m*; (US) estação *f*

depress [dɪ'prɛs] VT deprimir; (*press down*) apertar; **depressed** ADJ deprimido; (*area, market, trade*) em depressão; **depressing** ADJ deprimente; **depression** N depressão *f*; (*hollow*) achatamento

deprive [dɪ'praɪv] VT: **to ~ sb of** privar alguém de; **deprived** ADJ carente

depth [dɛpθ] N profundidade *f*; (*of feeling*) intensidade *f*; **in the ~s of despair** no auge do desespero; **to be out of one's ~** (BRIT: *swimmer*) estar sem pé; (*fig*) estar voando

deputy ['dɛpjutɪ] ADJ: **~ chairman** vice-presidente(-a) *m/f* ▸ N (*assistant*) adjunto; (*Pol: MP*) deputado(-a)

derail [dɪ'reɪl] VT: **to be ~ed** descarrilhar

derelict ['dɛrɪlɪkt] ADJ abandonado

derive [dɪ'raɪv] VT: **to ~ (from)** obter *or* tirar (de) ▸ VI: **to ~ from** derivar-se de

descend [dɪ'sɛnd] VT, VI descer; **to ~ from** descer de; **to ~ to** descambar em; **descent** N descida; (*origin*) descendência

describe [dɪs'kraɪb] VT descrever; **description** [dɪs'krɪpʃən] N descrição *f*; (*sort*) classe *f*, espécie *f*

desert [*n* 'dɛzət, *vt, vi* dɪ'zə:t] N deserto ▸ VT (*place*) desertar; (*partner, family*) abandonar ▸ VI (*Mil*) desertar

deserve [dɪ'zə:v] VT merecer

design [dɪ'zaɪn] N (*sketch*) desenho, esboço; (*layout, shape*) plano, projeto; (*pattern*) desenho, padrão *m*; (*art*) design *m*; (*intention*) propósito, intenção *f* ▸ VT (*plan*) projetar

designer [dɪ'zaɪnə^r] N (*Art*) artista *m/f* gráfico(-a); (*Tech*) desenhista *m/f*, projetista *m/f*; (*fashion designer*) estilista *m/f*

desire [dɪ'zaɪə^r] N anseio; (*sexual*) desejo ▸ VT querer; desejar, cobiçar

desk [dɛsk] N (*in office*) mesa, secretária; (*for pupil*) carteira *f*; (*at airport*) balcão *m*; (*in hotel*) recepção *f*; (BRIT: *in shop, restaurant*) caixa

despair [dɪs'pɛə^r] N desesperança ▸ VI: **to ~ of** desesperar-se de

despatch [dɪs'pætʃ] N, VT = **dispatch**

desperate ['dɛspərɪt] ADJ desesperado; (*situation*) desesperador(a); **to be ~ for sth/to do** estar louco por algo/para fazer; **desperately** ADV desesperadamente; (*very: unhappy*) terrívelmente; (*: ill*) gravemente; **desperation** [dɛspə'reɪʃən] N desespero, desesperança; **in (sheer) desperation** desesperado

despise [dɪs'paɪz] VT desprezar

despite [dɪs'paɪt] PREP apesar de, a despeito de

dessert [dɪ'zə:t] N sobremesa

destination [dɛstɪ'neɪʃən] N destino

destined ['dɛstɪnd] ADJ: **to be ~ to do sth** estar destinado a fazer algo; **~ for** com destino a

destiny ['dɛstɪnɪ] N destino

destroy [dɪs'trɔɪ] VT destruir; (*animal*) sacrificar; **destruction** N destruição *f*

detach [dɪ'tætʃ] VT separar; (*unstick*) desprender; **detached** ADJ (*attitude*) imparcial, objetivo; (*house*) independente, isolado
detail ['di:teɪl] N detalhe *m*; (*trifle*) bobagem *f* ▶ VT detalhar; **in ~** pormenorizado, em detalhe
detain [dɪ'teɪn] VT deter; (*in captivity*) prender; (*in hospital*) hospitalizar
detect [dɪ'tɛkt] VT perceber; (*Med, Police*) identificar; (*Mil, Radar, Tech*) detectar; **detection** N descoberta; **detective** N detetive *m/f*; **detective story** N romance *m* policial
detention [dɪ'tɛnʃən] N detenção *f*, prisão *f*; (*Sch*) castigo
deter [dɪ'tə:ʳ] VT (*discourage*) desanimar; (*dissuade*) dissuadir
detergent [dɪ'tə:dʒənt] N detergente *m*
deteriorate [dɪ'tɪərɪəreɪt] VI deteriorar-se
determine [dɪ'tə:mɪn] VT descobrir; (*limits etc*) demarcar; **determined** ADJ (*person*) resoluto; **determined to do** decidido a fazer
detour ['di:tuəʳ] N desvio
detract [dɪ'trækt] VI: **to ~ from** diminuir
detrimental [dɛtrɪ'mɛntl] ADJ: **~ (to)** prejudicial (a)
develop [dɪ'vɛləp] VT desenvolver; (*Phot*) revelar; (*disease*) contrair; (*resources*) explotar ▶ VI (*advance*) progredir; (*evolve*) evoluir; (*appear*) aparecer; **development** [dɪ'vɛləpmənt] N desenvolvimento; (*advance*) progresso; (*of land*) urbanização *f*
device [dɪ'vaɪs] N aparelho, dispositivo
devil ['dɛvl] N diabo
devious ['di:vɪəs] ADJ (*person*) malandro, esperto
devise [dɪ'vaɪz] VT (*plan*) criar; (*machine*) inventar
devote [dɪ'vəut] VT: **to ~ sth to** dedicar algo a; **devoted** [dɪ'vəutɪd] ADJ (*friendship*) leal; (*partner*) fiel; **to be devoted to** estar devotado a; **the book is devoted to politics** o livro trata de política; **devotion** N devoção *f*; (*to duty*) dedicação *f*
devour [dɪ'vauəʳ] VT devorar
devout [dɪ'vaut] ADJ devoto
dew [dju:] N orvalho
diabetes [daɪə'bi:ti:z] N diabete *f*
diagnosis [daɪəg'nəusɪs] (*pl* **diagnoses**) N diagnóstico
diagonal [daɪ'ægənl] ADJ diagonal ▶ N diagonal *f*
diagram ['daɪəgræm] N diagrama *m*, esquema *m*
dial ['daɪəl] N disco ▶ VT (*number*) discar (BR), marcar (PT)
dial code (US) N = **dialling code**
dialect ['daɪəlɛkt] N dialeto
dialling code ['daɪəlɪŋ-] (BRIT) N código de discagem
dialling tone ['daɪəlɪŋ-] (BRIT) N sinal *m* de discagem (BR) *or* de marcar (PT)
dialogue ['daɪəlɔg], (US) **dialog** N diálogo; (*conversation*) conversa
diameter [daɪ'æmɪtəʳ] N diâmetro
diamond ['daɪəmənd] N diamante *m*; (*shape*) losango, rombo; **diamonds** NPL (*Cards*) ouros *mpl*
diarrhoea [daɪə'ri:ə], (US) **diarrhea** N diarreia
diary ['daɪərɪ] N (*daily account*) diário; (*engagements book*) agenda

dice [daɪs] N INV dado ▶ VT (*Culin*) cortar em cubos
dictate [dɪk'teɪt] VT ditar; **dictation** N ditado
dictator [dɪk'teɪtəʳ] N ditador(a) *m/f*
dictionary ['dɪkʃənrɪ] N dicionário
did [dɪd] PT *of* **do**
didn't ['dɪdnt] = **did not**
die [daɪ] N, VI morrer; (*fig: fade*) murchar; **to be dying for sth/to do sth** estar louco por algo/para fazer algo; **die away** VI (*sound, light*) extinguir-se lentamente; **die down** VI (*fire*) apagar-se; (*wind*) abrandar; (*excitement*) diminuir; **die out** VI desaparecer
diesel ['di:zl] N diesel *m*; (*also*: **~ fuel, ~ oil**) óleo diesel
diet ['daɪət] N dieta; (*restricted food*) regime *m* ▶ VI (*also*: **be on a ~**) estar de dieta, fazer regime
differ ['dɪfəʳ] VI (*be different*): **to ~ from sth** ser diferente de algo, diferenciar-se de algo; (*disagree*): **to ~ (about)** discordar (sobre); **difference** N diferença; (*disagreement*) divergência; **different** ADJ diferente; **differentiate** [dɪfə'rɛnʃɪeɪt] VI: **to differentiate (between)** distinguir (entre)
difficult ['dɪfɪkəlt] ADJ difícil; **difficulty** N dificuldade *f*
dig [dɪg] (*pt, pp* **dug**) VT cavar ▶ N (*prod*) pontada; (*archaeological*) excavação *f*; (*remark*) alfinetada; **to ~ one's nails into** cravar as unhas em; **dig into** VT FUS (*savings*) gastar; **dig up** VT (*plant*) arrancar; (*information*) trazer à tona
digest [*vt* daɪ'dʒɛst, *n* 'daɪdʒɛst] VT (*food*) digerir; (*facts*) assimilar ▶ N sumário; **digestion** [dɪ'dʒɛstʃən] N digestão *f*
digit ['dɪdʒɪt] N (*Math*) dígito; (*finger*) dedo; **digital** ADJ digital; **digital camera** N câmara digital; **digital TV** N televisão *f* digital
dignified ['dɪgnɪfaɪd] ADJ digno
dignity ['dɪgnɪtɪ] N dignidade *f*
dilemma [daɪ'lɛmə] N dilema *m*
dilute [daɪ'lu:t] VT diluir
dim [dɪm] ADJ fraco; (*outline*) indistinto; (*room*) escuro; (*inf: person*) burro ▶ VT diminuir; (*US Aut*) baixar
dime [daɪm] (US) N (*moeda de*) *dez centavos*
dimension [dɪ'mɛnʃən] N dimensão *f*; (*measurement*) medida; (*also*: **~s**: *scale, size*) tamanho
diminish [dɪ'mɪnɪʃ] VI diminuir
din [dɪn] N zoeira
dine [daɪn] VI jantar; **diner** N comensal *m/f*; (*US: eating place*) lanchonete *f*
dinghy ['dɪŋgɪ] N dingue *m*, bote *m*; **rubber ~** bote de borracha
dingy ['dɪndʒɪ] ADJ (*room*) sombrio, lúgubre; (*clothes, curtains etc*) sujo
dining car ['daɪnɪŋ-] (BRIT) N (*Rail*) vagão-restaurante *m*
dining room ['daɪnɪŋ-] N sala de jantar
dinkum ['dɪŋkəm] (AUST *inf*) ADJ (*also*: **fair ~**) de verdade
dinner ['dɪnəʳ] N (*evening meal*) jantar *m*; (*lunch*) almoço; (*banquet*) banquete *m*; **dinner jacket** N smoking *m*; **dinner party** N jantar *m*; **dinner time** N (*midday*) hora de almoçar; (*evening*) hora de jantar
dip [dɪp] N (*slope*) inclinação *f*; (*in sea*) mergulho; (*Culin*) *pasta para servir com salgadinhos* ▶ VT (*in water*) mergulhar; (*ladle etc*) meter; (BRIT *Aut: lights*) baixar ▶ VI descer subitamente

diploma [dɪ'pləumə] N diploma *m*
diplomat ['dɪpləmæt] N diplomata *m/f*
dipstick ['dɪpstɪk] N (*Aut*) vareta medidora
dire [daɪə^r] ADJ terrível
direct [daɪ'rɛkt] ADJ direto; (*route*) reto; (*manner*) franco, sincero ▸VT dirigir; (*order*): **to ~ sb to do sth** ordenar alguém para fazer algo ▸ADV direto; **can you ~ me to ...?** pode me indicar o caminho a ...?; **direct debit** (BRIT) N (*Banking*) débito direto; **direction** N (*way*) indicação *f*; (*TV, Radio, Cinema*) direção *f*; **directions** NPL (*instructions*) instruções *fpl*; **directions for use** modo de usar; **directly** ADV diretamente; (*at once*) imediatamente; **director** N diretor(a) *m/f*
directory [dɪ'rɛktərɪ] N (*Tel*) lista (telefônica); (*Comm*) anuário comercial; (*Comput*) diretório; **directory enquiries**, (US) **directory assistance** N (serviço de) informações *fpl*
dirt [dəːt] N sujeira (BR), sujidade (PT); **dirty** ADJ sujo; (*joke*) indecente ▸VT sujar
disability [dɪsə'bɪlɪtɪ] N incapacidade *f*
disabled [dɪs'eɪbld] ADJ deficiente ▸NPL: **the ~** os deficientes
disadvantage [dɪsəd'vɑːntɪdʒ] N desvantagem *f*; (*prejudice*) inconveniente *m*
disagree [dɪsə'griː] VI (*differ*) diferir; (*be against, think otherwise*): **to ~ (with)** não concordar (com), discordar (de); **disagreeable** ADJ desagradável; **disagreement** N desacordo; (*quarrel*) desavença
disappear [dɪsə'pɪə^r] VI desaparecer, sumir; (*custom etc*) acabar; **disappearance** N desaparecimento, desaparição *f*
disappoint [dɪsə'pɔɪnt] VT decepcionar; **disappointed** ADJ decepcionado; **disappointment** N decepção *f*; (*cause*) desapontamento
disapproval [dɪsə'pruːvəl] N desaprovação *f*
disapprove [dɪsə'pruːv] VI: **to ~ of** desaprovar
disarmament N desarmamento
disaster [dɪ'zɑːstə^r] N (*accident*) desastre *m*; (*natural*) catástrofe *f*
disbelief [dɪsbə'liːf] N incredulidade *f*
disc [dɪsk] N disco; (*Comput*) = **disk**
discard [dɪs'kɑːd] VT (*old things*) desfazer-se de; (*fig*) descartar
discharge [*vt* dɪs'tʃɑːdʒ, *n* 'dɪstʃɑːdʒ] VT (*duties*) cumprir, desempenhar; (*patient*) dar alta a; (*employee*) despedir; (*soldier*) dar baixa em, dispensar; (*defendant*) pôr em liberdade; (*waste etc*) descarregar, despejar ▸N (*Elec*) descarga; (*dismissal*) despedida; (*of duty*) desempenho; (*of debt*) quitação *f*; (*from hospital*) alta; (*from army*) baixa; (*Jur*) absolvição *f*; (*Med*) secreção *f*
discipline ['dɪsɪplɪn] N disciplina ▸VT disciplinar; (*punish*) punir
disc jockey N (*on radio*) radialista *m/f*; (*in discotheque*) discotecário(-a)
disclose [dɪs'kləuz] VT revelar
disco ['dɪskəu] N ABBR = **discotheque**
discomfort [dɪs'kʌmfət] N (*unease*) inquietação *f*; (*physical*) desconforto

disconnect [dɪskə'nɛkt] VT desligar; (*pipe, tap*) desmembrar
discontent [dɪskən'tɛnt] N descontentamento
discontinue [dɪskən'tɪnju:] VT interromper; (*payments*) suspender; **"~d"** (*Comm*) "fora de linha"
discotheque ['dɪskəutɛk] N discoteca
discount [n 'dɪskaunt, vt dɪs'kaunt] N desconto ▸ VT descontar; (*idea*) ignorar
discourage [dɪs'kʌrɪdʒ] VT (*dishearten*) desanimar; (*advise against*): **to ~ sth/sb from doing** desaconselhar algo/alguém a fazer
discover [dɪs'kʌvə[r]] VT descobrir; (*missing person*) encontrar; (*mistake*) achar; **discovery** N descoberta
discredit [dɪs'krɛdɪt] VT desacreditar; (*claim*) desmerecer
discreet [dɪ'skri:t] ADJ discreto; (*careful*) cauteloso
discrepancy [dɪ'skrɛpənsɪ] N diferença
discretion [dɪ'skrɛʃən] N discrição *f*; **at the ~ of** ao arbítrio de
discriminate [dɪ'skrɪmɪneɪt] VI: **to ~ between** fazer distinção entre; **to ~ against** discriminar contra; **discrimination** [dɪskrɪmɪ'neɪʃən] N (*discernment*) discernimento; (*bias*) discriminação *f*
discuss [dɪ'skʌs] VT discutir; (*analyse*) analisar; **discussion** N discussão *f*; (*debate*) debate *m*
disease [dɪ'zi:z] N doença
disembark [dɪsɪm'bɑ:k] VT, VI desembarcar
disgrace [dɪs'greɪs] N ignomínia; (*shame*) desonra ▸ VT (*family*) envergonhar; (*name, country*) desonrar; **disgraceful** ADJ vergonhoso; (*behaviour*) escandaloso
disgruntled [dɪs'grʌntld] ADJ descontente
disguise [dɪs'gaɪz] N disfarce *m* ▸ VT: **to ~ o.s. (as)** disfarçar-se (de); **in ~** disfarçado
disgust [dɪs'gʌst] N repugnância ▸ VT repugnar a, dar nojo em; **disgusting** ADJ repugnante; (*unacceptable*) inaceitável
dish [dɪʃ] N prato; (*serving dish*) travessa; **to do** *or* **wash the ~es** lavar os pratos *or* a louça; **dish out** VT repartir; **dish up** VT servir; **dishcloth** N pano de prato *or* de louça
dishonest [dɪs'ɔnɪst] ADJ (*person*) desonesto; (*means*) fraudulento
dishwasher ['dɪʃwɔʃə[r]] N máquina de lavar louça *or* pratos
disillusion [dɪsɪ'lu:ʒən] VT desiludir
disinfectant [dɪsɪn'fɛktənt] N desinfetante *m*
disintegrate [dɪs'ɪntɪgreɪt] VI desintegrar-se
disk [dɪsk] N (*Comput*) disco; (*removable*) disquete *m*; **disk drive** N unidade *f* de disco; **diskette** [dɪs'kɛt] (US) N (*Comput*) disquete *m*
dislike [dɪs'laɪk] N desagrado ▸ VT antipatizar com, não gostar de
dislocate ['dɪsləkeɪt] VT deslocar
disloyal [dɪs'lɔɪəl] ADJ desleal
dismal ['dɪzml] ADJ (*depressing*) deprimente; (*very bad*) horrível
dismantle [dɪs'mæntl] VT desmontar, desmantelar
dismay [dɪs'meɪ] N consternação *f* ▸ VT consternar
dismiss [dɪs'mɪs] VT (*worker*) despedir; (*pupils*) dispensar; (*soldiers*) dar baixa a; (*Jur, possibility*) rejeitar; **dismissal** N demissão *f*
disobedient [dɪsə'bi:dɪənt] ADJ desobediente

disobey [dɪsə'beɪ] VT desobedecer a; (*rules*) transgredir
disorder [dɪs'ɔːdəʳ] N desordem *f*; (*rioting*) distúrbios *mpl*, tumulto; (*Med*) distúrbio
disown [dɪs'əun] VT repudiar; (*child*) rejeitar
dispatch [dɪs'pætʃ] VT (*send: parcel etc*) expedir; (: *messenger*) enviar ▸ N (*sending*) remessa; (*Press*) comunicado; (*Mil*) parte *f*
dispel [dɪs'pɛl] VT dissipar
dispense [dɪs'pɛns] VT (*medicine*) preparar (e vender); **dispense with** VT FUS prescindir de; **dispenser** N (*device*) distribuidor *m* automático
disperse [dɪs'pəːs] VT espalhar; (*crowd*) dispersar ▸ VI dispersar-se
display [dɪs'pleɪ] N (*in shop*) mostra; (*exhibition*) exposição *f*; (*Comput: information*) apresentação *f* visual; (: *device*) display *m*; (*of feeling*) manifestação *f* ▸ VT mostrar; (*ostentatiously*) ostentar
displease [dɪs'pliːz] VT (*offend*) ofender; (*annoy*) aborrecer
disposable [dɪs'pəuzəbl] ADJ descartável; (*income*) disponível
disposal [dɪs'pəuzl] N (*of rubbish*) destruição *f*; (*of property etc*) venda, traspasse *m*; **at sb's ~** à disposição de alguém;
disposition [dɪspə'zɪʃən] N disposição *f*; (*temperament*) índole *f*
dispute [dɪs'pjuːt] N (*domestic*) briga; (*also*: **industrial ~**) conflito, disputa ▸ VT disputar; (*question*) questionar
disqualify [dɪs'kwɔlɪfaɪ] VT (*Sport*) desclassificar; **to ~ sb for sth/from doing sth** desqualificar alguém para algo/de fazer algo
disregard [dɪsrɪ'gɑːd] VT ignorar
disrupt [dɪs'rʌpt] VT (*plans*) desfazer; (*conversation, proceedings*) perturbar, interromper
dissect [dɪ'sɛkt] VT dissecar
dissent [dɪ'sɛnt] N dissensão *f*
dissertation [dɪsə'teɪʃən] N (*also: Sch*) dissertação *f*, tese *f*
dissolve [dɪ'zɔlv] VT dissolver ▸ VI dissolver-se; **to ~ in(to) tears** debulhar-se em lágrimas
distance ['dɪstns] N distância; **in the ~** ao longe
distant ['dɪstnt] ADJ distante; (*manner*) afastado, reservado
distil [dɪs'tɪl], (US) **distill** VT destilar; **distillery** N destilaria
distinct [dɪs'tɪŋkt] ADJ distinto; (*clear*) claro; (*unmistakable*) nítido; **as ~ from** em oposição a; **distinction** N diferença; (*honour*) honra; (*in exam*) distinção *f*
distinguish [dɪs'tɪŋgwɪʃ] VT (*differentiate*) diferenciar; (*identify*) identificar; **to ~ o.s.** distinguir-se; **distinguished** ADJ (*eminent*) eminente; (*in appearance*) distinto
distort [dɪs'tɔːt] VT distorcer
distract [dɪs'trækt] VT distrair; (*attention*) desviar; **distracted** ADJ distraído; (*anxious*) aturdido; **distraction** N distração *f*; (*confusion*) aturdimento, perplexidade *f*; (*amusement*) divertimento
distraught [dɪs'trɔːt] ADJ desesperado
distress [dɪs'trɛs] N angústia ▸ VT afligir; **distressing** ADJ angustiante
distribute [dɪs'trɪbjuːt] VT distribuir; (*share out*) repartir, dividir; **distribution** [dɪstrɪ'bjuːʃən] N distribuição *f*; (*of profits etc*) repartição *f*;

d

distributor N (*Aut*) distribuidor *m*; (*Comm*) distribuidor(a) *m/f*
district ['dɪstrɪkt] N (*of country*) região *f*; (*of town*) zona; (*Admin*) distrito; **district attorney** (US) N promotor(a) *m/f* público(-a)
distrust [dɪs'trʌst] N desconfiança ▶VT desconfiar de
disturb [dɪs'tə:b] VT (*disorganize*) perturbar; (*upset*) incomodar; (*interrupt*) atrapalhar; **disturbance** N (*upheaval*) convulsão *f*; (*political, violent*) distúrbio; (*of mind*) transtorno; **disturbed** ADJ perturbado; (*child*) infeliz; **to be mentally/emotionally disturbed** ter problemas psicológicos/emocionais; **disturbing** ADJ perturbador(a)
ditch [dɪtʃ] N fosso; (*irrigation ditch*) rego ▶VT (*inf: partner*) abandonar; (*: car, plan etc*) desfazer-se de
ditto ['dɪtəu] ADV idem
dive [daɪv] N (*from board*) salto; (*underwater, of submarine*) mergulho ▶VI mergulhar; **to ~ into** (*bag, drawer etc*) enfiar a mão em; (*shop, car etc*) enfiar-se em; **diver** N mergulhador(a) *m/f*
diversion [daɪ'və:ʃən] N (BRIT *Aut*) desvio; (*distraction, Mil*) diversão *f*; (*of funds*) desvio
divert [daɪ'və:t] VT desviar
divide [dɪ'vaɪd] VT (*Math*) dividir; (*separate*) separar; (*share out*) repartir ▶VI dividir-se; (*road*) bifurcar-se; **divided highway** (US) N pista dupla
divine [dɪ'vaɪn] ADJ (*also fig*) divino
diving ['daɪvɪŋ] N salto; (*underwater*) mergulho; **diving board** N trampolim *m*
division [dɪ'vɪʒən] N divisão *f*; (*sharing out*) repartição *f*; (*disagreement*) discórdia; (*Football*) grupo
divorce [dɪ'vɔ:s] N divórcio ▶VT divorciar-se de; (*dissociate*) dissociar; **divorced** ADJ divorciado; **divorcee** N divorciado(-a)
DIY N ABBR = **do-it-yourself**
dizzy ['dɪzɪ] ADJ tonto
DJ N ABBR = **disc jockey**

KEYWORD

do [du:] (*pt* **did**, *pp* **done**) AUX VB **1** (*in negative constructions*): **I don't understand** eu não compreendo
2 (*to form questions*): **didn't you know?** você não sabia?; **what do you think?** o que você acha?
3 (*for emphasis, in polite expressions*): **she does seem rather late** ela está muito atrasada; **do sit down/help yourself** sente-se/sirva-se; **do take care!** tome cuidado!
4 (*used to avoid repeating vb*): **she swims better than I do** ela nada melhor que eu; **do you agree? — yes, I do/no, I don't** você concorda? — sim, concordo/não, não concordo; **she lives in Glasgow — so do I** ela mora em Glasgow — eu também; **who broke it? — I did** quem quebrou isso? — (fui) eu
5 (*in question tags*): **you like him, don't you?** você gosta dele, não é?; **he laughed, didn't he?** ele riu, não foi?
▶VT **1** (*gen: carry out, perform etc*) fazer; **what are you doing tonight?** o que você vai fazer hoje à noite?; **to do the washing-up/cooking** lavar a louça/cozinhar; **to do one's teeth/nails** escovar os dentes/fazer as unhas; **to do one's hair** (*comb*) pentear-se; (*style*) fazer

um penteado; **we're doing Othello at school** (*studying*) nós estamos estudando Otelo na escola; (*performing*) nós vamos encenar Otelo na escola
2 (*Aut etc*): **the car was doing 190** o carro andava a 190 por hora; **we've done 200 km already** já percorremos 200 km; **he can do 190 km/h in that car** ele consegue chegar a 190 km/h naquele carro
▸ VI **1** (*act, behave*) fazer; **do as I do** faça como eu faço
2 (*get on, fare*) ir; **how do you do?** como você está indo?
3 (*suit*) servir; **will it do?** serve?
4 (*be sufficient*) bastar; **will £10 do?** £10 dá?; **that'll do** é suficiente; **that'll do!** (*in annoyance*) basta!, chega!; **to make do (with)** contentar-se (com)
▸ N (*inf: party etc*) festa; **it was rather a do** foi uma festança
do away with VT FUS (*kill*) matar; (*law etc*) abolir; (*withdraw*) retirar
do up VT (*laces*) atar; (*zip*) fechar; (*dress, skirt*) abotoar; (*renovate, room, house*) arrumar, renovar
do with VT FUS (*be connected*) ter a ver com; (*need*): **I could do with a drink/some help** eu bem que gostaria de tomar alguma coisa/eu bem que precisaria de uma ajuda; **what has it got to do with you?** o que é que isso tem a ver com você?
do without VI: **if you're late for tea then you'll do without** se você chegar atrasado ficará sem almoço ▸ VT FUS passar sem

dock [dɔk] N (*Naut*) doca; (*Jur*) banco (dos réus) ▸ VI (*Naut: enter dock*) atracar; (*Space*) unir-se no espaço; **docks** NPL docas *fpl*
doctor ['dɔktəʳ] N médico(-a); (*PhD etc*) doutor(a) *m/f* ▸ VT (*drink etc*) falsificar
document ['dɔkjumənt] N documento; **documentary** [dɔkju'mɛntərɪ] ADJ documental ▸ N documentário
dodge [dɔdʒ] N (*trick*) trapaça ▸ VT esquivar-se de, evitar; (*tax*) sonegar; (*blow*) furtar-se a
does [dʌz] VB *see* **do**
doesn't ['dʌznt] = **does not**
dog [dɔg] N cachorro, cão *m* ▸ VT (*subj: person*) seguir; (*: bad luck*) perseguir; **doggy bag** ['dɔgɪ-] N quentinha
do-it-yourself N sistema *m* faça-você-mesmo
dole [dəul] (BRIT) N (*payment*) subsídio de desemprego; **on the ~** desempregado; **dole out** VT distribuir
doll [dɔl] N boneca; (*US inf: woman*) gatinha
dollar ['dɔləʳ] N dólar *m*
dolphin ['dɔlfɪn] N golfinho
dome [dəum] N (*Arch*) cúpula
domestic [də'mɛstɪk] ADJ doméstico; (*national*) nacional
dominate ['dɔmɪneɪt] VT dominar
domino ['dɔmɪnəu] (*pl* **dominoes**) N peça de dominó; **dominoes** N (*game*) dominó *m*
donate [də'neɪt] VT doar
done [dʌn] PP *of* **do**
donkey ['dɔŋkɪ] N burro
donor ['dəunəʳ] N doador(a) *m/f*; **donor card** N cartão *m* de doador
don't [dəunt] = **do not**
doodle ['du:dl] VI rabiscar

doom [du:m] N (*fate*) destino ▶ VT: **to be ~ed to failure** estar destinado *or* fadado ao fracasso

door [dɔ:ʳ] N porta; **doorbell** N campainha; **doorstep** N degrau *m* da porta, soleira; **doorway** N vão *m* da porta, entrada

dope [dəup] N (*inf: person*) imbecil *m/f*; (: *drugs*) maconha ▶ VT (*horse etc*) dopar

dormitory ['dɔ:mɪtrɪ] N dormitório; (US) *residência universitária*

dose [dəus] N dose *f*

dot [dɔt] N ponto; (*speck*) pontinho ▶ VT: **~ted with** salpicado de; **on the ~** em ponto

dotcom [dɔt'kɔm] N empresa pontocom

double ['dʌbl] ADJ duplo ▶ ADV (*twice*): **to cost ~ (sth)** custar o dobro (de algo) ▶ N (*person*) duplo(-a) ▶ VT dobrar ▶ VI dobrar; **at the ~** (BRIT), **on the ~** em passo acelerado; **double bass** N contrabaixo; **double bed** N cama de casal; **double-click** VI (*Comput*) clicar duas vezes; **double-decker** [dʌbl'dɛkəʳ] N ônibus *m* (BR) *or* autocarro (PT) de dois andares; **double room** N quarto de casal

doubt [daut] N dúvida ▶ VT duvidar; (*suspect*) desconfiar de; **to ~ that ...** duvidar que ...; **doubtful** ADJ duvidoso; **doubtless** ADV sem dúvida

dough [dəu] N massa; **doughnut**, (US) **donut** N sonho (BR), bola de Berlim (PT)

dove [dʌv] N pomba

down [daun] N (*feathers*) penugem *f* ▶ ADV (*downwards*) para baixo; (*on the ground*) por terra ▶ PREP por, abaixo ▶ VT (*inf: drink*) tomar de um gole só; **~ with X!** abaixo X!; **down-and-out** N (*tramp*) vagabundo(-a); **downfall** N queda, ruína; **downhill** ADV para baixo ▶ N (*Ski: also*: **downhill race**) descida; **to go downhill** descer, ir morro abaixo; (*fig: business*) degringolar

Downing Street ['daunɪŋ-] (BRIT) N *ver nota*

> **Downing Street** é a rua de Westminster (Londres) onde estão localizadas as residências oficiais do Primeiro-ministro (número 10) e do Ministro da Fazenda (número 11). O termo **Downing Street** é frequentemente utilizado para designar o governo britânico.

down: download ['daunləud] VT (*Comput*) baixar, fazer o download de; **downloadable** ADJ (*Comput*) baixável; **downright** ['daunraɪt] ADJ (*lie*) patente; (*refusal*) categórico

Down's syndrome [daunz-] N síndrome *f* de Down

down: downstairs ADV (*below*) lá em baixo; (*direction*) para baixo; **down-to-earth** ADJ prático, realista; **downtown** ADV no centro da cidade; **down under** ADV na Austrália (*or* Nova Zelândia); **downward** ['daunwəd] ADJ, ADV para baixo; **downwards** ADV = **downward**

doze [dəuz] VI dormitar; **doze off** VI cochilar

dozen ['dʌzn] N dúzia; **a ~ books** uma dúzia de livros; **~s of times** milhares de vezes

drab [dræb] ADJ sombrio

draft [dra:ft] N (*first copy*) rascunho; (*Pol: of bill*) projeto de lei; (*bank draft*) saque *m*, letra; (US: *call-up*)

recrutamento ▶ VT (*plan*) esboçar; (*speech, letter*) rascunhar; *see also* **draught**
drag [dræg] VT arrastar; (*river*) dragar ▶ VI arrastar-se ▶ N (*inf*) chatice *f* (BR), maçada (PT); (*women's clothing*): **in ~** em travesti;
drag on VI arrastar-se
dragon ['drægən] N dragão *m*
dragonfly ['drægənflaɪ] N libélula
drain [dreɪn] N bueiro; (*source of loss*) sorvedouro ▶ VT drenar; (*vegetables*) coar ▶ VI (*water*) escorrer, escoar-se; **drainage** N (*act*) drenagem *f*; (*system*) esgoto;
drainpipe N cano de esgoto
drama ['drɑːmə] N (*art*) teatro; (*play, event*) drama *m*; **dramatic** [drə'mætɪk] ADJ dramático; (*theatrical*) teatral
drank [dræŋk] PT *of* **drink**
drape [dreɪp] VT ornar, cobrir
drastic ['dræstɪk] ADJ drástico
draught [drɑːft], (US) **draft** N (*of air*) corrente *f*; (*Naut*) calado; (*beer*) chope *m*; **on ~** (*beer*) de barril;
draughts (BRIT) N (jogo de) damas *fpl*
draw [drɔː] (*pt* **drew**, *pp* **drawn**) VT desenhar; (*cart*) puxar; (*curtain*) fechar; (*gun*) sacar; (*attract*) atrair; (*money*) tirar; (*: from bank*) sacar ▶ VI empatar ▶ N empate *m*; (*lottery*) sorteio; **to ~ near** aproximar-se; **draw out** VT (*money*) sacar; **draw up** VI (*stop*) parar(-se) ▶ VT (*chair etc*) puxar; (*document*) redigir; **drawback** N inconveniente *m*, desvantagem *f*;
drawer [drɔː[r]] N gaveta; **drawing** N desenho; **drawing pin** (BRIT) N tachinha (BR), pionés *m* (PT);
drawing room N sala de visitas
drawn [drɔːn] PP *of* **draw**
dread [drɛd] N medo, pavor *m* ▶ VT temer, recear, ter medo de;
dreadful ADJ terrível
dream [driːm] (*pt, pp* **dreamed** *or* **dreamt**) N sonho ▶ VT, VI sonhar
dreary ['drɪərɪ] ADJ (*talk, time*) monótono; (*weather*) sombrio
drench [drɛntʃ] VT encharcar
dress [drɛs] N vestido; (*no pl: clothing*) traje *m* ▶ VT vestir; (*wound*) fazer curativo em ▶ VI vestir-se; **to get ~ed** vestir-se;
dress up VI vestir-se com elegância; (*in fancy dress*) fantasiar-se; **dress circle** (BRIT) N balcão *m* nobre; **dresser** N (BRIT: *cupboard*) aparador *m*; (US: *chest of drawers*) cômoda de espelho;
dressing N (*Med*) curativo; (*Culin*) molho; **dressing gown** (BRIT) N roupão *m*; (*woman's*) peignoir *m*;
dressing room N (*Theatre*) camarim *m*; (*Sport*) vestiário;
dressing table N penteadeira (BR), toucador *m* (PT); **dressmaker** N costureiro(-a)
drew [druː] PT *of* **draw**
dribble ['drɪbl] VI (*baby*) babar ▶ VT (*ball*) driblar
dried [draɪd] ADJ seco; (*eggs, milk*) em pó
drier ['draɪə[r]] N = **dryer**
drift [drɪft] N (*of current etc*) força; (*of snow, sand etc*) monte *m*; (*meaning*) sentido ▶ VI (*boat*) derivar; (*sand, snow*) amontoar-se
drill [drɪl] N furadeira; (*bit, of dentist*) broca; (*for mining etc*) broca, furadeira; (*Mil*) exercícios *mpl* militares ▶ VT furar, brocar; (*Mil*) exercitar ▶ VI (*for oil*) perfurar
drink [drɪŋk] (*pt* **drank**, *pp* **drunk**) N bebida ▶ VT, VI beber; **a ~ of**

d

water um copo d'água; **drinker** N bebedor(a) *m/f*; **drinking water** N água potável

drip [drɪp] N gotejar *m*; (*one drip*) gota, pingo; (*Med*) gota a gota *m* ▶ VI gotejar, pingar

drive [draɪv] (*pt* **drove**, *pp* **driven**) N passeio (de automóvel); (*journey*) trajeto, percurso; (*also*: **~way**) entrada; (*energy*) energia, vigor *m*; (*campaign*) campanha; (Comput) drive *m* ▶ VT (*car*) dirigir (BR), guiar (PT); (*push*) empurrar; (*Tech: motor*) acionar; (*nail*): **to ~ sth into** cravar algo em ▶ VI (*Aut: at controls*) dirigir (BR), guiar (PT); (: *travel*) ir de carro; **left-/right-hand ~** direção à esquerda/direita; **to ~ sb mad** deixar alguém louco

driver ['draɪvəʳ] N motorista *m/f*; (*Rail*) maquinista *m*; **driver's license** (US) N carteira de motorista (BR), carta de condução (PT)

driveway ['draɪvweɪ] N entrada

driving ['draɪvɪŋ] N direção *f* (BR), condução *f* (PT); **driving instructor** N instrutor(a) *m/f* de autoescola (BR) *or* de condução (PT); **driving licence** (BRIT) N carteira de motorista (BR), carta de condução (PT); **driving test** N exame *m* de motorista

drizzle ['drɪzl] N chuvisco

droop [dru:p] VI pender

drop [drɔp] N (*of water*) gota; (*lessening*) diminuição *f*; (*fall: distance*) declive *m* ▶ VT (*allow to fall*) deixar cair; (*voice, eyes, price*) baixar; (*set down from car*) deixar (saltar/descer); (*omit*) omitir ▶ VI cair; (*wind*) parar; **drops** NPL (*Med*) gotas *fpl*; **drop off** VI (*sleep*) cochilar ▶ VT (*passenger*) deixar; **drop out** VI (*withdraw*) retirar-se; **drop-out** N pessoa que abandona o trabalho, os estudos etc

drought [draut] N seca

drove [drəuv] PT *of* **drive**

drown [draun] VT afogar; (*also*: **~ out**: *sound*) encobrir ▶ VI afogar-se

drowsy ['drauzɪ] ADJ sonolento

drug [drʌg] N remédio, medicamento; (*narcotic*) droga ▶ VT drogar; **to be on ~s** (*an addict*) estar viciado em drogas; (*Med*) estar sob medicação; **drug addict** N toxicômano(-a); **druggist** (US) N farmacêutico(-a); **drugstore** (US) N drogaria

drum [drʌm] N tambor *m*; (*for oil, petrol*) tambor, barril *m*; **drums** NPL (*kit*) bateria; **drummer** N baterista *m/f*

drunk [drʌŋk] PP *of* **drink** ▶ ADJ bêbado ▶ N (*also*: **~ard**) bêbado(-a); **drunken** ADJ (*laughter*) de bêbado; (*party*) com muita bebida; (*person*) bêbado

dry [draɪ] ADJ seco; (*day*) sem chuva; (*humour*) irônico ▶ VT secar, enxugar; (*tears*) limpar ▶ VI secar; **dry up** VI secar completamente; **dry-cleaner's** N tinturaria; **dryer** N secador *m*; (*also*: **spin-dryer**) secadora

DSS (BRIT) N ABBR (= *Department of Social Security*) ≈ INAMPS *m*

DTP N ABBR (= *desktop publishing*) DTP *m*

dual ['djuəl] ADJ dual, duplo; **dual carriageway** (BRIT) N pista dupla

dubious ['dju:bɪəs] ADJ duvidoso; (*reputation, company*) suspeitoso

duck [dʌk] N pato ▶ VI abaixar-se repentinamente

due [dju:] ADJ (*proper*) devido; (*expected*) esperado ▶ N: **to give sb his** (*or* **her**) **~** ser justo com alguém

▶ ADV: **~ north** exatamente ao norte; **dues** NPL (*for club, union*) quota; (*in harbour*) direitos *mpl*; **in ~ course** no devido tempo; (*eventually*) no final; **~ to** devido a
duet [dju:'ɛt] N dueto
dug [dʌg] PT, PP *of* **dig**
duke [dju:k] N duque *m*
dull [dʌl] ADJ (*light*) sombrio; (*intelligence, wit*) lento; (*boring*) enfadonho; (*sound, pain*) surdo; (*weather, day*) nublado, carregado ▶ VT (*pain, grief*) aliviar; (*mind, senses*) entorpecer
dumb [dʌm] ADJ mudo; (*pej: stupid*) estúpido
dummy ['dʌmɪ] N (*tailor's model*) manequim *m*; (*mock-up*) modelo; (BRIT: *for baby*) chupeta ▶ ADJ falso
dump [dʌmp] N (*also*: **rubbish ~**) depósito de lixo; (*inf: place*) chiqueiro ▶ VT (*put down*) depositar, descarregar; (*get rid of*) desfazer-se de
dumpling ['dʌmplɪŋ] N bolinho cozido
dungarees [dʌŋgə'ri:z] NPL macacão *m* (BR), fato macaco (PT)
dungeon ['dʌndʒən] N calabouço
duplex ['dju:plɛks] (US) N casa geminada; (*also*: **~ apartment**) duplex *m*
duplicate [*n* 'dju:plɪkət, *vt* 'dju:plɪkeɪt] N (*of document*) duplicata; (*of key*) cópia ▶ VT duplicar; (*photocopy*) multigrafar; (*repeat*) reproduzir
durable ['djuərəbl] ADJ durável; (*clothes, metal*) resistente
during ['djuərɪŋ] PREP durante
dusk [dʌsk] N crepúsculo, anoitecer *m*
dust [dʌst] N pó *m*, poeira ▶ VT (*furniture*) tirar o pó de; (*cake etc*): **to ~ with** polvilhar com; **dustbin** N (BRIT) lata de lixo; **duster** N pano de pó; **dustman** (BRIT) *irreg* N lixeiro, gari *m* (BR *inf*); **dusty** ADJ empoeirado
Dutch [dʌtʃ] ADJ holandês(-esa) ▶ N (*Ling*) holandês *m* ▶ ADV: **let's go ~** (*inf*) cada um paga o seu, vamos rachar; **the Dutch** NPL (*people*) os holandeses; **Dutchman** *irreg* N holandês *m*; **Dutchwoman** *irreg* N holandesa
duty ['dju:tɪ] N dever *m*; (*tax*) taxa; **on ~** de serviço; **off ~** de folga; **duty-free** ADJ livre de impostos
duvet ['du:veɪ] (BRIT) N edredom *m* (BR), edredão *m* (PT)
DVD N ABBR (= *digital versatile* or *video disc*) DVD *m*; **DVD burner** N gravador *m* de DVD; **DVD player** N DVD player *m*; **DVD writer** N gravador *m* de DVD
dwarf [dwɔ:f] (*pl* **dwarves**) N anão/anã *m/f* ▶ VT ananicar
dwindle ['dwɪndl] VI diminuir
dye [daɪ] N tintura, tinta ▶ VT tingir
dynamite ['daɪnəmaɪt] N dinamite *f*
dyslexia [dɪs'lɛksɪə] N dislexia

d

e

E [iː] N (*Mus*) mi *m*

each [iːtʃ] ADJ cada *inv* ▶ PRON cada um(a); **~ other** um ao outro; **they hate ~ other** (eles) se odeiam

eager ['iːgəʳ] ADJ ávido; **to be ~ to do sth** ansiar por fazer algo; **to be ~ for** ansiar por

eagle ['iːgl] N águia

ear [ɪəʳ] N (*external*) orelha; (*inner, fig*) ouvido; (*of corn*) espiga; **earache** N dor *f* de ouvidos; **eardrum** N tímpano

earl [əːl] N conde *m*

earlier ['əːlɪəʳ] ADJ mais adiantado; (*edition etc*) anterior ▶ ADV mais cedo

early ['əːlɪ] ADV cedo; (*before time*) com antecedência ▶ ADJ (*sooner than expected*) prematuro; (*reply*) pronto; (*Christians, settlers*) primeiro; (*man*) primitivo; (*life, work*) juvenil; **in the ~** *or* **~ in the spring/19th century** no princípio da primavera/do século dezenove

earmark ['ɪəmɑːk] VT: **to ~ sth for** reservar *or* destinar algo para

earn [əːn] VT ganhar; (*Comm: interest*) render; (*praise, reward*) merecer

earnest ['əːnɪst] ADJ (*wish*) intenso; (*manner*) sério; **in ~** a sério

earnings ['əːnɪŋz] NPL (*personal*) vencimentos *mpl*, salário, ordenado; (*of company*) lucro

earphones NPL fones *mpl* de ouvido

earring N brinco

earth [əːθ] N terra; (BRIT *Elec*) fio terra ▶ VT (BRIT *Elec*) ligar à terra; **earthquake** N terremoto (BR), terramoto (PT)

ease [iːz] N facilidade *f*; (*relaxed state*) sossego ▶ VT facilitar; (*pain, tension*) aliviar; (*help pass*): **to ~ sth in/out** meter/tirar algo com cuidado; **at ~!** (*Mil*) descansar!; **ease off** VI acalmar-se; (*wind*) baixar; (*rain*) moderar-se; **ease up** VI = **ease off**

easily ['iːzɪlɪ] ADV facilmente, fácil (*inf*)

east [iːst] N leste *m* ▶ ADJ (*region*) leste; (*wind*) do leste ▶ ADV para o leste; **the E~** o Oriente; (*Pol*) o leste

Easter ['iːstəʳ] N Páscoa; **Easter egg** N ovo de Páscoa

eastern ['iːstən] ADJ do leste, oriental

easy ['iːzɪ] ADJ fácil; (*comfortable*) folgado, cômodo; (*relaxed*) natural, complacente; (*victim, prey*) desprotegido ▶ ADV: **to take it** *or* **things ~** (*not worry*) levar as coisas com calma; (*go slowly*) ir devagar; (*rest*) descansar; **easy-going** ADJ pacato, fácil

eat [iːt] (*pt* **ate**, *pp* **eaten**) VT, VI comer; **eat away** VT corroer;

eat away at VT FUS corroer;
eat into VT FUS = **eat away at**
eavesdrop ['i:vzdrɔp] VI: **to ~ (on)** escutar às escondidas
e-book ['i:buk] N livro eletrônico
e-card ['i:kɑ:d] N cartão *m* eletrônico
eccentric [ɪk'sɛntrɪk] ADJ, N excêntrico(-a)
echo ['ɛkəu] (*pl* **echoes**) N eco ▶ VT ecoar, repetir ▶ VI ressoar, repetir
eclipse [ɪ'klɪps] N eclipse *m*
eco-friendly [i:kəu'frɛndlɪ] ADJ ecológico
ecological [i:kə'lɔdʒɪkəl] ADJ ecológico
ecology [ɪ'kɔlədʒɪ] N ecologia
e-commerce N ABBR (= *electronic commerce*) comércio eletrônico
economic [i:kə'nɔmɪk] ADJ econômico; (*business etc*) rentável; **economical** ADJ econômico; **economics** N economia ▶ NPL aspectos *mpl* econômicos
economize [ɪ'kɔnəmaɪz] VI economizar, fazer economias
economy [ɪ'kɔnəmɪ] N economia; **economy class** N (*Aviat*) classe *f* econômica
ecstasy ['ɛkstəsɪ] N êxtase *m*; **ecstatic** [ɛks'tætɪk] ADJ extasiado
eczema ['ɛksɪmə] N eczema *m*
edge [ɛdʒ] N (*of knife etc*) fio; (*of table, chair etc*) borda; (*of lake etc*) margem *f* ▶ VT (*trim*) embainhar; **on ~** (*fig*) = **edgy**; **to ~ away from** afastar-se pouco a pouco de; **edgy** ADJ nervoso, inquieto
edible ['ɛdɪbl] ADJ comestível
Edinburgh ['ɛdɪnbərə] N Edimburgo
edit ['ɛdɪt] VT (*be editor of*) dirigir; (*cut*) cortar, redigir; (*Comput, TV*) editar; (*Cinema*) montar; **edition** [ɪ'dɪʃən] N edição *f*; **editor** N redator(a) *m/f*; (*of newspaper*) diretor(a) *m/f*; **editorial** [ɛdɪ'tɔ:rɪəl] ADJ editorial
educate ['ɛdjukeɪt] VT educar
education [ɛdju'keɪʃən] N educação *f*; (*schooling*) ensino; (*science*) pedagogia; **educational** ADJ (*policy, experience*) educacional; (*toy etc*) educativo
eel [i:l] N enguia
eerie ['ɪərɪ] ADJ (*strange*) estranho; (*mysterious*) misterioso
effect [ɪ'fɛkt] N efeito ▶ VT (*repairs*) fazer; (*savings*) efetuar; **to take ~** (*law*) entrar em vigor; (*drug*) fazer efeito; **in ~** na realidade; **effective** [ɪ'fɛktɪv] ADJ eficaz; (*actual*) efetivo
efficiency [ɪ'fɪʃənsɪ] N eficiência
efficient [ɪ'fɪʃənt] ADJ eficiente; (*machine*) rentável
effort ['ɛfət] N esforço; **effortless** ADJ fácil
e.g. ADV ABBR (= *exempli gratia*) p. ex.
egg [ɛg] N ovo; **hard-boiled/soft-boiled ~** ovo duro/mole; **egg on** VT incitar; **eggcup** N oveiro; **eggplant** (*esp US*) N beringela; **eggshell** N casca de ovo
ego ['i:gəu] N ego
Egypt ['i:dʒɪpt] N Egito; **Egyptian** [ɪ'dʒɪpʃən] ADJ, N egípcio(-a)
eight [eɪt] NUM oito; **eighteen** ['eɪ'ti:n] NUM dezoito; **eighteenth** NUM décimo oitavo; **eighth** [eɪtθ] NUM oitavo; **eightieth** ['eɪtɪɪθ] NUM octogésimo; **eighty** ['eɪtɪ] NUM oitenta
Eire ['ɛərə] N (República da) Irlanda
either ['aɪðə^r] ADJ (*one or other*) um ou outro; (*each*) cada; (*both*) ambos ▶ PRON: **~ (of them)**

qualquer (dos dois) ▶ADV: **no, I don't ~** eu também não ▶CONJ: **~ yes or no** ou sim ou não
eject [ɪ'dʒɛkt] VT expulsar
elaborate [*adj* ɪ'læbərɪt, *vt, vi* ɪ'læbəreɪt] ADJ complicado ▶VT (*expand*) expandir; (*refine*) aperfeiçoar ▶VI: **to ~ on** acrescentar detalhes a
elastic [ɪ'læstɪk] ADJ elástico; (*adaptable*) flexível, adaptável ▶N elástico; **elastic band** (BRIT) N elástico
elbow ['ɛlbəu] N cotovelo
elder ['ɛldə^r] ADJ mais velho ▶N (*tree*) sabugueiro; (*person*) o/a mais velho(-a); **elderly** ADJ idoso, de idade ▶NPL: **the elderly** as pessoas de idade, os idosos
eldest ['ɛldɪst] ADJ mais velho ▶N o/a mais velho(-a)
elect [ɪ'lɛkt] VT eleger ▶ADJ: **the president ~** o presidente eleito; **to ~ to do** (*choose*) optar por fazer; **election** N (*voting*) votação *f*; (*installation*) eleição *f*; **electorate** N eleitorado
electric [ɪ'lɛktrɪk] ADJ elétrico; **electrical** ADJ elétrico; **electric fire** N aquecedor *m* elétrico
electrician [ɪlɛk'trɪʃən] N eletricista *m/f*
electricity [ɪlɛk'trɪsɪtɪ] N eletricidade *f*
electrify [ɪ'lɛktrɪfaɪ] VT (*fence, Rail*) eletrificar; (*audience*) eletrizar
electronic [ɪlɛk'trɔnɪk] ADJ eletrônico; **electronic mail** N correio eletrônico; **electronics** N eletrônica
elegant ['ɛlɪgənt] ADJ (*person, building*) elegante; (*idea*) refinado
element ['ɛlɪmənt] N elemento; **elementary** [ɛlɪ'mɛntərɪ] ADJ (*gen*) elementar; (*primitive*) rudimentar; (*school, education*) primário; **elementary school** (US) N *ver nota*

> Nos Estados Unidos e no Canadá, uma **elementary school** (também chamada de *grade school* ou *grammar school* nos Estados Unidos) é uma escola pública onde os alunos passam de seis a oito dos primeiros anos escolares.

elephant ['ɛlɪfənt] N elefante *m*
elevator ['ɛlɪveɪtə^r] (US) N elevador *m*
eleven [ɪ'lɛvn] NUM onze; **eleventh** NUM décimo-primeiro
eligible ['ɛlɪdʒəbl] ADJ elegível, apto; **to be ~ for sth** (*job etc*) ter qualificações para algo
elm [ɛlm] N olmo
eloquent ['ɛləkwənt] ADJ eloquente
El Salvador [el'sælvədɔː^r] N El Salvador
else [ɛls] ADV outro, mais; **something ~** outra coisa; **nobody ~ spoke** ninguém mais falou; **elsewhere** ADV (*be*) em outro lugar (BR), noutro sítio (PT); (*go*) para outro lugar (BR), a outro sítio (PT)
elusive [ɪ'luːsɪv] ADJ esquivo; (*quality*) indescritível
email ['iːmeɪl] N e-mail *m*, correio eletrônico ▶VT (*person*) enviar um e-mail a; **email account** N conta de e-mail, conta de correio eletrônico; **email address** N e-mail *m*, endereço eletrônico
embark [ɪm'bɑːk] VI embarcar ▶VT embarcar; **to ~ on** (*fig*) empreender, começar
embarrass [ɪm'bærəs] VT (*politician*) embaraçar; (*emotionally*) constranger; **embarrassed** ADJ

descomfortável; **embarrassing** ADJ embaraçoso, constrangedor(a); **embarrassment** N embaraço, constrangimento
embassy ['ɛmbəsɪ] N embaixada
embrace [ɪm'breɪs] VT abraçar, dar um abraço em; (*include*) abarcar, abranger ▶ VI abraçar-se ▶ N abraço
embroider [ɪm'brɔɪdəʳ] VT bordar; **embroidery** N bordado
emerald ['ɛmərəld] N esmeralda
emerge [ɪ'mə:dʒ] VI sair; (*from sleep*) acordar; (*fact, idea*) emergir
emergency [ɪ'mə:dʒənsɪ] N emergência; **in an ~** em caso de urgência; **emergency exit** N saída de emergência; **emergency landing** N aterrissagem *f* forçada (BR), aterragem *f* forçosa (PT)
emigrate ['ɛmɪgreɪt] VI emigrar
eminent ['ɛmɪnənt] ADJ eminente
emit [ɪ'mɪt] VT (*smoke*) soltar; (*smell*) exalar; (*sound*) produzir
emoticon [ɪ'məutɪkɔn] N (*Comput*) emoticon *m*
emotion [ɪ'məuʃən] N emoção *f*; **emotional** ADJ (*needs, exhaustion*) emocional; (*person*) sentimental, emotivo; (*scene*) comovente; (*tone*) emocionante
emperor ['ɛmpərəʳ] N imperador *m*
emphasis ['ɛmfəsɪs] (*pl* **emphases**) N ênfase *f*
emphasize ['ɛmfəsaɪz] VT (*word, point*) enfatizar, acentuar; (*feature*) salientar
empire ['ɛmpaɪəʳ] N império
employ [ɪm'plɔɪ] VT empregar; (*tool*) utilizar; **employee** N empregado(-a); **employer** N empregador(a) *m/f*, patrão(-troa) *m/f*; **employment** N (*gen*) emprego; (*work*) trabalho
empress ['ɛmprɪs] N imperatriz *f*
emptiness ['ɛmptɪnɪs] N vazio, vácuo
empty ['ɛmptɪ] ADJ vazio; (*place*) deserto; (*house*) desocupado; (*threat*) vão/vã ▶ N, VT esvaziar; (*place*) evacuar ▶ VI esvaziar-se; (*place*) ficar deserto; **empty-handed** ADJ de mãos vazias
emulsion [ɪ'mʌlʃən] N emulsão *f*; (*also*: **~ paint**) tinta plástica
enable [ɪ'neɪbl] VT: **to ~ sb to do sth** (*allow*) permitir que alguém faça algo; (*prepare*) capacitar alguém para fazer algo
enamel [ɪ'næməl] N esmalte *m*
enclose [ɪn'kləuz] VT (*land*) cercar; (*with letter etc*) anexar (BR), enviar junto (PT); **please find ~d** segue junto
enclosure [ɪn'kləuʒəʳ] N cercado
encore [ɔŋ'kɔ:ʳ] EXCL bis!, outra! ▶ N bis *m*
encounter [ɪn'kauntəʳ] N encontro ▶ VT encontrar, topar com; (*difficulty*) enfrentar
encourage [ɪn'kʌrɪdʒ] VT (*activity*) encorajar; (*growth*) estimular; (*person*): **to ~ sb to do sth** animar alguém a fazer algo; **encouragement** N estímulo
encrypt [ɪn'krɪpt] VT (*Comput, Tel*) criptografar
encyclopaedia, encyclopedia [ɛnsaɪkləu'pi:dɪə] N enciclopédia
end [ɛnd] N fim *m*; (*of table, line, rope etc*) ponta; (*of street, town*) final *m* ▶ VT acabar, terminar; (*also*: **bring to an ~, put an ~ to**) acabar com, pôr fim a ▶ VI terminar, acabar; **in the ~** ao fim, por fim, finalmente; **on ~** na

ponta; **to stand on ~** (*hair*) arrepiar-se; **for hours on ~** por horas a fio; **end up** VI: **to ~ up in** terminar em; (*place*) ir parar em

endanger [ɪnˈdeɪndʒəʳ] VT pôr em perigo

endearing [ɪnˈdɪərɪŋ] ADJ simpático, atrativo

endeavour [ɪnˈdɛvəʳ], (US) **endeavor** N esforço; (*attempt*) tentativa ▶ VI: **to ~ to do** esforçar-se para fazer; (*try*) tentar fazer

ending [ˈɛndɪŋ] N fim *m*, conclusão *f*; (*of book*) desenlace *m*; (*Ling*) terminação *f*

endless [ˈɛndlɪs] ADJ interminável; (*possibilities*) infinito

endorse [ɪnˈdɔːs] VT (*cheque*) endossar; (*approve*) aprovar; **endorsement** N (BRIT: *on driving licence*) descrição *f* das multas; (*approval*) aval *m*

endure [ɪnˈdjuəʳ] VT (*bear*) aguentar, suportar ▶ VI (*last*) durar

enemy [ˈɛnəmɪ] ADJ, N inimigo(-a)

energy [ˈɛnədʒɪ] N energia; **energy drink** N energético, bebida energética

enforce [ɪnˈfɔːs] VT (*Jur*) fazer cumprir

engage [ɪnˈgeɪdʒ] VT (*attention*) chamar; (*interest*) atrair; (*lawyer*) contratar; (*clutch*) engrenar ▶ VI engrenar; **to ~ in** dedicar-se a, ocupar-se com; **to ~ sb in conversation** travar conversa com alguém; **engaged** ADJ (BRIT: *phone*) ocupado (BR), impedido (PT); (: *toilet*) ocupado; (*betrothed*) noivo; **to get engaged** ficar noivo; **engaged tone** (BRIT) N (*Tel*) sinal *m* de ocupado (BR) *or* de impedido (PT); **engagement** N encontro; (*booking*) contrato; (*to marry*) noivado; **engagement ring** N aliança de noivado

engine [ˈɛndʒɪn] N (*Aut*) motor *m*; (*Rail*) locomotiva

engineer [ɛndʒɪˈnɪəʳ] N engenheiro(-a); (US *Rail*) maquinista *m/f*; (BRIT: *for repairs*) técnico(-a); **engineering** N engenharia

England [ˈɪŋglənd] N Inglaterra

English [ˈɪŋglɪʃ] ADJ inglês(-esa) ▶ N (*Ling*) inglês *m*; **the English** NPL (*people*) os ingleses; **English Channel** N: **the English Channel** o Canal da Mancha

engraving [ɪnˈgreɪvɪŋ] N gravura

enhance [ɪnˈhɑːns] VT (*gen*) ressaltar, salientar; (*beauty*) realçar; (*position*) melhorar; (*add to*) aumentar

enjoy [ɪnˈdʒɔɪ] VT gostar de; (*health, privilege*) desfrutar de; **to ~ o.s.** divertir-se; **enjoyable** ADJ agradável; **enjoyment** N prazer *m*

enlarge [ɪnˈlɑːdʒ] VT aumentar; (*Phot*) ampliar ▶ VI: **to ~ on** (*subject*) desenvolver, estender-se sobre

enlist [ɪnˈlɪst] VT alistar; (*support*) conseguir, aliciar ▶ VI alistar-se

enormous [ɪˈnɔːməs] ADJ enorme

enough [ɪˈnʌf] ADJ: **~ time/books** tempo suficiente/livros suficientes ▶ PRON: **have you got ~?** você tem o suficiente? ▶ ADV: **big ~** suficientemente grande; **~!** basta!, chega!; **that's ~, thanks** chega, obrigado; **I've had ~ of him** estou farto dele; **which, funnily** *or* **oddly ~ …** o que, por estranho que pareça …

enquire [ɪnˈkwaɪəʳ] VT, VI = **inquire**

enrage [ɪnˈreɪdʒ] VT enfurecer, enraivecer

enrol [ɪn'rəul], (*US*) **enroll** VT inscrever; (*Sch*) matricular ▶ VI inscrever-se; matricular-se; **enrolment** N inscrição *f*; (*Sch*) matrícula

ensure [ɪn'ʃuəʳ] VT assegurar

entail [ɪn'teɪl] VT implicar

enter ['ɛntəʳ] VT entrar em; (*club*) ficar *or* fazer-se sócio de; (*army*) alistar-se em; (*competition*) inscrever-se em; (*sb for a competition*) inscrever; (*write down*) completar; (*Comput*) digitar ▶ VI entrar; **enter for** VT FUS inscrever-se em; **enter into** VT FUS estabelecer; (*plans*) fazer parte de; (*debate, negotiations*) entrar em; (*agreement*) chegar a, firmar

enterprise ['ɛntəpraɪz] N empresa; (*undertaking*) empreendimento; (*initiative*) iniciativa; **enterprising** ADJ empreendedor(a)

entertain [ɛntə'teɪn] VT divertir, entreter; (*guest*) receber (em casa); (*idea, plan*) estudar; **entertainer** N artista *m/f*; **entertaining** ADJ divertido; **entertainment** N (*amusement*) entretenimento, diversão *f*; (*show*) espetáculo

enthusiasm [ɪn'θu:zɪæzəm] N entusiasmo

enthusiast [ɪn'θu:zɪæst] N entusiasta *m/f*; **enthusiastic** [ɪnθu:zɪ'æstɪk] ADJ entusiasmado; **to be enthusiastic about** entusiasmar-se por

entire [ɪn'taɪəʳ] ADJ inteiro; **entirely** ADV totalmente, completamente

entitle [ɪn'taɪtl] VT: **to ~ sb to sth** dar a alguém direito a algo; **entitled** [ɪn'taɪtld] ADJ (*book etc*) intitulado; **to be entitled to sth/to do sth** ter direito a algo/de fazer algo

entrance [*n* 'ɛntrəns, *vt* ɪn'trɑ:ns] N entrada; (*arrival*) chegada ▶ VT encantar, fascinar; **to gain ~ to** (*university etc*) ser admitido em; **entrance examination** N exame *m* de admissão; **entrance fee** N joia

entrant ['ɛntrənt] N participante *m/f*; (BRIT: *in exam*) candidato(-a)

entrepreneur [ɔntrəprə'nə:ʳ] N empresário(-a)

entrust [ɪn'trʌst] VT: **to ~ sth to sb** confiar algo a alguém

entry ['ɛntrɪ] N entrada; (*in register*) registro, assentamento; (*in account*) lançamento; (*in dictionary*) verbete *m*; **"no ~"** "entrada proibida"; (*Aut*) "contramão" (BR), "entrada proibida" (PT); **entry phone** (BRIT) N interfone *m* (*em apartamento*)

envelope ['ɛnvələup] N envelope *m*

envious ['ɛnvɪəs] ADJ invejoso; (*look*) de inveja

environment [ɪn'vaɪərnmənt] N meio ambiente *m*; **environmental** [ɪnvaɪərn'mɛntl] ADJ ambiental

envisage [ɪn'vɪzɪdʒ] VT prever

envoy ['ɛnvɔɪ] N enviado(-a)

envy ['ɛnvɪ] N inveja ▶ VT ter inveja de; **to ~ sb sth** invejar alguém por algo, cobiçar algo de alguém

epic ['ɛpɪk] N epopeia ▶ ADJ épico

epidemic [ɛpɪ'dɛmɪk] N epidemia

epilepsy ['ɛpɪlɛpsɪ] N epilepsia

episode ['ɛpɪsəud] N episódio

equal ['i:kwl] ADJ igual; (*treatment*) equitativo, equivalente ▶ N igual *m/f* ▶ VT ser igual a; **to be ~ to** (*task*) estar à altura de; **equality** [i:'kwɔlɪtɪ] N igualdade *f*; **equalize**

vi igualar; (*Sport*) empatar; **equally** ADV igualmente; (*share etc*) por igual
equator [ɪ'kweɪtə^r] N equador *m*
equip [ɪ'kwɪp] VT equipar; (*person*) prover, munir; **to be well ~ped** estar bem preparado *or* equipado; **equipment** N equipamento; (*machines etc*) equipamentos *mpl*, aparelhagem *f*
equivalent [ɪ'kwɪvəlnt] ADJ equivalente ▶ N equivalente *m*
era ['ɪərə] N era, época
erase [ɪ'reɪz] VT apagar; **eraser** N borracha (de apagar)
e-reader ['iː'riːdə^r] N leitor *m* de livros digitais
erect [ɪ'rɛkt] ADJ (*posture*) ereto; (*tail, ears*) levantado ▶ VT erigir, levantar; (*assemble*) montar; **erection** N construção *f*; (*assembly*) montagem *f*; (*Physiol*) ereção *f*
erode [ɪ'rəud] VT (*Geo*) causar erosão em; (*confidence*) minar
erotic [ɪ'rɔtɪk] ADJ erótico
errand ['ɛrnd] N recado, mensagem *f*
erratic [ɪ'rætɪk] ADJ imprevisível
error ['ɛrə^r] N erro
erupt [ɪ'rʌpt] VI entrar em erupção; (*fig*) explodir, estourar; **eruption** N erupção *f*; (*fig*) explosão *f*
escalate ['ɛskəleɪt] VI intensificar-se
escalator ['ɛskəleɪtə^r] N escada rolante
escape [ɪ'skeɪp] N fuga; (*of gas*) escapatória ▶ VI escapar; (*flee*) fugir, evadir-se; (*leak*) vazar, escapar ▶ VT fugir de; (*elude*): **his name ~s me** o nome dele me foge a memória; **to ~ from** (*place*) escapar de; (*person*) escapulir de
escort [*n* 'ɛskɔːt, *vt* ɪ'skɔːt] N acompanhante *m/f*; (*Mil, Naut*) escolta ▶ VT acompanhar
especially [ɪ'spɛʃlɪ] ADV (*above all*) sobretudo; (*particularly*) em particular
espionage ['ɛspɪənɑːʒ] N espionagem *f*
essay ['ɛseɪ] N ensaio
essence ['ɛsns] N essência
essential [ɪ'sɛnʃl] ADJ (*necessary*) indispensável; (*basic*) essencial ▶ N elemento essencial
establish [ɪ'stæblɪʃ] VT estabelecer; (*facts*) verificar; (*proof*) demonstrar; (*reputation*) firmar; **establishment** N estabelecimento; **the Establishment** a classe dirigente
estate [ɪ'steɪt] N (*land*) fazenda (BR), propriedade *f* (PT); (*Jur*) herança; (*Pol*) estado; (BRIT: *also*: **housing ~**) conjunto habitacional; **estate agent** (BRIT) N corretor(a) *m/f* de imóveis (BR), agente *m/f* imobiliário(-a) (PT); **estate car** (BRIT) N perua (BR), canadiana (PT)
estimate [*n* 'ɛstɪmət, *vb* 'ɛstɪmeɪt] N (*assessment*) avaliação *f*; (*calculation*) cálculo; (*Comm*) orçamento ▶ VT estimar, avaliar, calcular
etc. ABBR (= *et cetera*) etc.
eternal [ɪ'təːnl] ADJ eterno
eternity [ɪ'təːnɪtɪ] N eternidade *f*
ethical ['ɛθɪkl] ADJ ético
ethics ['ɛθɪks] N ética ▶ NPL moral *f*
Ethiopia [iːθɪ'əupɪə] N Etiópia
ethnic ['ɛθnɪk] ADJ étnico; (*culture*) folclórico
e-ticket ['iːtɪkɪt] N bilhete *m* eletrônico
etiquette ['ɛtɪkɛt] N etiqueta
EU ABBR (= *European Union*) UE *f*
euro ['jʊərəʊ] N (*currency*) euro *m*

Europe ['juərəp] N Europa; **European** [juərə'pi:ən] ADJ, N europeu(-peia); **European Union** N: **the European Union** a União Europeia

evacuate [ɪ'vækjueɪt] VT evacuar

evade [ɪ'veɪd] VT (*person*) evitar; (*question, duties*) esquivar-se de; (*tax*) sonegar

evaporate [ɪ'væpəreɪt] VI evaporar-se

eve [i:v] N: **on the ~ of** na véspera de

even ['i:vn] ADJ (*level*) plano; (*smooth*) liso; (*equal, Sport*) igual; (*number*) par ▶ ADV até, mesmo; **~ if** mesmo que; **~ though** mesmo que, embora; **~ more** ainda mais; **~ so** mesmo assim; **not ~** nem; **to get ~ with sb** ficar quite com alguém; **even out** VI nivelar-se

evening ['i:vnɪŋ] N (*early*) tarde *f*; (*late*) noite *f*; (*event*) noitada; **in the ~** à noite; **evening class** N aula noturna

event [ɪ'vɛnt] N acontecimento; (*Sport*) prova; **in the ~ of** no caso de; **eventful** ADJ cheio de acontecimentos; (*game etc*) cheio de emoção, agitado

eventual [ɪ'vɛntʃuəl] ADJ final; **eventually** ADV finalmente; (*in time*) por fim

ever ['ɛvəʳ] ADV (*always*) sempre; (*at any time*) em qualquer momento; (*in question*): **why ~ not?** por que não, ora?; **the best ~** o melhor que já se viu; **have you ~ seen it?** você alguma vez já viu isto?; **better than ~** melhor que nunca; **~ since** *adv* desde então; *conj* depois que; **evergreen** N sempre-verde *f*

KEYWORD

every ['ɛvrɪ] ADJ **1** (*each*) cada; **every one of them** cada um deles; **every shop in the town was closed** todas as lojas da cidade estavam fechadas
2 (*all possible*) todo(-a); **I have every confidence in her** tenho absoluta confiança nela; **we wish you every success** desejamos-lhe o maior sucesso; **he's every bit as clever as his brother** ele é tão inteligente quanto o irmão
3 (*showing recurrence*) todo(-a); **every other car had been broken into** cada dois carros foram arrombados; **she visits me every other/third day** ele me visita cada dois/três dias; **every now and then** de vez em quando

everybody ['ɛvrɪbɔdɪ] PRON todos, todo mundo (BR), toda a gente (PT)

everyday ['ɛvrɪdeɪ] ADJ (*daily*) diário; (*usual*) corrente; (*common*) comum

everyone ['ɛvrɪwʌn] PRON = **everybody**

everything ['ɛvrɪθɪŋ] PRON tudo

everywhere ['ɛvrɪwɛəʳ] ADV (*be*) em todo lugar (BR), em toda a parte (PT); (*go*) a todo lugar (BR), a toda a parte (PT); (*wherever*): **~ you go you meet ...** aonde quer que se vá, encontra-se ...

evict [ɪ'vɪkt] VT despejar

evidence ['ɛvɪdəns] N (*proof*) prova(s) *f(pl)*; (*of witness*) testemunho, depoimento; (*indication*) sinal *m*; **to give ~** testemunhar, prestar depoimento

e

evident ['ɛvɪdənt] ADJ evidente; **evidently** ADV evidentemente; (*apparently*) aparentemente
evil ['i:vl] ADJ mau/má ▶ N mal *m*, maldade *f*
evoke [ɪ'vəuk] VT evocar
evolution [i:və'lu:ʃən] N evolução *f*; (*development*) desenvolvimento
evolve [ɪ'vɔlv] VT desenvolver ▶ VI desenvolver-se
exact [ɪg'zækt] ADJ exato; (*person*) meticuloso ▶ VT: **to ~ sth (from)** exigir algo (de); **exactly** ADV exatamente; (*indicating agreement*) isso mesmo
exaggerate [ɪg'zædʒəreɪt] VT, VI exagerar; **exaggeration** [ɪgzædʒə'reɪʃən] N exagero
exam [ɪg'zæm] N ABBR = **examination**
examination [ɪgzæmɪ'neɪʃən] N exame *m*; (*inquiry*) investigação *f*
examine [ɪg'zæmɪn] VT examinar; (*inspect*) inspecionar; **examiner** N examinador(a) *m/f*
example [ɪg'zɑ:mpl] N exemplo; **for ~** por exemplo
excavate ['ɛkskəveɪt] VT escavar
exceed [ɪk'si:d] VT exceder; (*number*) ser superior a; (*speed limit*) ultrapassar; (*limits*) ir além de; (*powers*) exceder-se em; (*hopes*) superar; **exceedingly** ADV extremamente
excellent ['ɛksələnt] ADJ excelente
except [ɪk'sɛpt] PREP (*also*: **~ for, ~ing**) exceto, a não ser ▶ VT: **to ~ sb from** excluir alguém de; **~ if/when** a menos que, a não ser que; **exception** N exceção *f*; **to take exception to** ressentir-se de
excerpt ['ɛksə:pt] N trecho
excess [ɪk'sɛs] N excesso; **excess baggage** N excesso de bagagem; **excessive** ADJ excessivo
exchange [ɪks'tʃeɪndʒ] N troca; (*of teachers, students*) intercâmbio; (*also*: **telephone ~**) estação *f* telefônica (BR), central *f* telefónica (PT) ▶ VT: **to ~ (for)** trocar (por); **exchange rate** N (taxa de) câmbio
excite [ɪk'saɪt] VT excitar; **to get ~d** entusiasmar-se; **excitement** N emoções *fpl*; (*agitation*) agitação *f*; **exciting** ADJ emocionante, empolgante
exclaim [ɪk'skleɪm] VI exclamar; **exclamation** [ɛksklə'meɪʃən] N exclamação *f*; **exclamation mark** N ponto de exclamação
exclude [ɪk'sklu:d] VT excluir
exclusive [ɪk'sklu:sɪv] ADJ exclusivo; **~ of tax** sem incluir os impostos
excruciating [ɪk'skru:ʃɪeɪtɪŋ] ADJ doloroso, martirizante
excursion [ɪk'skə:ʃən] N excursão *f*
excuse [*n* ɪk'skju:s, *vt* ɪk'skju:z] N desculpa ▶ VT desculpar, perdoar; **to ~ sb from doing sth** dispensar alguém de fazer algo; **~ me!** desculpe!; **if you will ~ me ...** com a sua licença ...
execute ['ɛksɪkju:t] VT (*plan*) realizar; (*order*) cumprir; (*person, movement*) executar; **execution** N realização *f*; (*killing*) execução *f*
executive [ɪg'zɛkjutɪv] N (*Comm, Pol*) executivo(-a) ▶ ADJ executivo
exempt [ɪg'zɛmpt] ADJ: **~ from** isento de ▶ VT: **to ~ sb from** dispensar *or* isentar alguém de
exercise ['ɛksəsaɪz] N exercício ▶ VT exercer; (*right*) valer-se de; (*dog*) levar para passear ▶ VI (*also*: **to take ~**) fazer exercício; **exercise book** N caderno

exert [ɪg'zəːt] VT exercer; **to ~ o.s.** esforçar-se, empenhar-se; **exertion** N esforço
exhale [ɛks'heɪl] VT, VI expirar
exhaust [ɪg'zɔːst] N (*Aut: also:* **~ pipe**) escape *m*, exaustor *m*; (*fumes*) escapamento (de gás) ▶ VT esgotar; **exhaustion** N exaustão *f*
exhibit [ɪg'zɪbɪt] N (*Art*) obra exposta; (*Jur*) objeto exposto ▶ VT (*courage etc*) manifestar, mostrar; (*quality, emotion*) demonstrar; (*paintings*) expor; **exhibition** [ɛksɪ'bɪʃən] N exposição *f*
exhilarating [ɪg'zɪləreɪtɪŋ] ADJ estimulante, tônico
exile ['ɛksaɪl] N exílio; (*person*) exilado(-a) ▶ VT desterrar, exilar
exist [ɪg'zɪst] VI existir; (*live*) viver; **existence** N existência; (*life*) vida; **existing** ADJ atual
exit ['ɛksɪt] N saída ▶ VI (*Comput, Theatre*) sair
exotic [ɪg'zɔtɪk] ADJ exótico
expand [ɪk'spænd] VT aumentar ▶ VI aumentar; (*trade, gas etc*) expandir-se; (*metal*) dilatar-se
expansion [ɪk'spænʃən] N (*of town*) desenvolvimento; (*of trade*) expansão *f*; (*of population*) aumento
expect [ɪk'spɛkt] VT esperar; (*suppose*) supor; (*require*) exigir ▶ VI: **to be ~ing** estar grávida; **expectation** [ɛkspɛk'teɪʃən] N esperança; (*belief*) expectativa
expedition [ɛkspə'dɪʃən] N expedição *f*
expel [ɪk'spɛl] VT expelir; (*from place, school*) expulsar
expense [ɪk'spɛns] N gasto, despesa; (*expenditure*) despesas *fpl*; **expenses** NPL (*costs*) despesas *fpl*; **at the ~ of** à custa de; **expense account** N relatório de despesas
expensive [ɪk'spɛnsɪv] ADJ caro
experience [ɪk'spɪərɪəns] N experiência ▶ VT (*situation*) enfrentar; (*feeling*) sentir; **experienced** ADJ experiente
experiment [ɪk'spɛrɪmənt] N experimento, experiência ▶ VI: **to ~ (with/on)** fazer experiências (com/em)
expert ['ɛkspəːt] ADJ hábil, perito ▶ N especialista *m/f*; **expertise** [ɛkspəː'tiːz] N perícia
expire [ɪk'spaɪə^r] VI expirar; (*run out*) vencer; **expiry** N expiração *f*, vencimento
explain [ɪk'spleɪn] VT explicar; (*clarify*) esclarecer; **explain away** VT justificar
explicit [ɪk'splɪsɪt] ADJ explícito
explode [ɪk'spləud] VI estourar, explodir
exploit [*n* 'ɛksplɔɪt, *vt* ɪk'splɔɪt] N façanha ▶ VT explorar; **exploitation** [ɛksplɔɪ'teɪʃən] N exploração *f*
explore [ɪk'splɔː^r] VT explorar; (*fig*) examinar, pesquisar; **explorer** N explorador(a) *m/f*
explosion [ɪk'spləuʒən] N explosão *f*
explosive [ɪk'spləusɪv] ADJ explosivo ▶ N explosivo
export [*vt* ɛk'spɔːt, *n, cpd* 'ɛkspɔːt] VT exportar ▶ N exportação *f* ▶ CPD de exportação; **exporter** N exportador(a) *m/f*
expose [ɪk'spəuz] VT expor; (*unmask*) desmascarar; **exposed** ADJ (*house etc*) desabrigado
exposure [ɪk'spəuʒə^r] N exposição *f*; (*publicity*) publicidade *f*; (*Phot*) revelação *f*; **to die from ~** (*Med*) morrer de frio

e

express [ɪk'sprɛs] ADJ expresso, explícito; (BRIT: *letter etc*) urgente ▶ N rápido ▶ VT exprimir, expressar; (*quantity*) representar; **expression** N expressão *f*; **expressway** (US) N rodovia (BR), autoestrada (PT)

extend [ɪk'stɛnd] VT (*visit, street*) prolongar; (*building*) aumentar; (*offer*) fazer; (*hand*) estender

extension [ɪk'stɛnʃən] N (*Elec*) extensão *f*; (*building*) acréscimo, expansão *f*; (*of rights*) ampliação *f*; (*Tel*) ramal *m* (BR), extensão *f* (PT); (*of deadline, campaign*) prolongamento, prorrogação *f*

extensive [ɪk'stɛnsɪv] ADJ extenso; (*damage*) considerável; (*broad*) vasto, amplo

extent [ɪk'stɛnt] N (*breadth*) extensão *f*; (*of damage etc*) dimensão *f*; (*scope*) alcance *m*; **to some** *or* **to a certain ~** até certo ponto

exterior [ɛk'stɪərɪə^r] ADJ externo ▶ N exterior *m*; (*appearance*) aspecto

external [ɛk'stə:nl] ADJ externo

extinct [ɪk'stɪŋkt] ADJ extinto

extinguish [ɪk'stɪŋgwɪʃ] VT extinguir

extra ['ɛkstrə] ADJ adicional ▶ ADV adicionalmente ▶ N (*surcharge*) extra *m*, suplemento; (*Cinema, Theatre*) figurante *m/f*

extract [*vt* ɪk'strækt, *n* 'ɛkstrækt] VT tirar, extrair; (*tooth*) arrancar; (*mineral*) extrair; (*money*) extorquir; (*promise*) conseguir, obter ▶ N extrato

extradite ['ɛkstrədaɪt] VT (*from country*) extraditar; (*to country*) obter a extradição de

extraordinary [ɪk'strɔ:dnrɪ] ADJ extraordinário; (*odd*) estranho

extravagance [ɪk'strævəgəns] N extravagância; (*no pl: spending*) esbanjamento

extravagant [ɪk'strævəgənt] ADJ (*lavish*) extravagante; (*wasteful*) gastador(a), esbanjador(a)

extreme [ɪk'stri:m] ADJ extremo ▶ N extremo; **extremely** ADV muito, extremamente

extrovert ['ɛkstrəvə:t] N extrovertido(-a)

eye [aɪ] N olho; (*of needle*) buraco ▶ VT olhar, observar; **to keep an ~ on** vigiar, ficar de olho em; **eyebrow** N sobrancelha; **eyedrops** NPL gotas *fpl* para os olhos; **eyelash** N cílio; **eyelid** N pálpebra; **eyeliner** N delineador *m*; **eye shadow** N sombra de olhos; **eyesight** N vista, visão *f*

f

F [ɛf] N (*Mus*) fá *m*
fabric ['fæbrɪk] N tecido, pano
face [feɪs] N cara, rosto; (*grimace*) careta; (*of clock*) mostrador *m*; (*side, surface*) superfície *f*; (*of building*) frente *f*, fachada ▶ VT (*facts, problem*) enfrentar; (*particular direction*) dar para; **~ down** de bruços; (*card*) virado para baixo; **to lose ~** perder o prestígio; **to save ~** salvar as aparências; **to make** *or* **pull a ~** fazer careta; **in the ~ of** diante de, à vista de; **on the ~ of it** a julgar pelas aparências, à primeira vista; **face up to** VT FUS enfrentar; **face cloth** (BRIT) N pano de rosto; **face pack** (BRIT) N máscara facial
facilities [fə'sɪlɪtɪz] NPL facilidades *fpl*, instalações *fpl*; **credit ~** crediário
fact [fækt] N fato; **in ~** realmente, na verdade
factor ['fæktə^r] N fator *m*
factory ['fæktərɪ] N fábrica
factual ['fæktjuəl] ADJ real, fatual
faculty ['fækəltɪ] N faculdade *f*; (US) corpo docente
fad [fæd] (*inf*) N mania, modismo
fade [feɪd] VI desbotar; (*sound, hope*) desvanecer-se; (*light*) apagar-se; (*flower*) murchar
fag [fæg] (*inf*) N cigarro
fail [feɪl] VT (*candidate*) reprovar; (*exam*) não passar em, ser reprovado em; (*subj: leader*) fracassar; (*: courage*) carecer; (*: memory*) falhar ▶ VI fracassar; (*engine, brakes, voice*) falhar; **to ~ to do sth** deixar de fazer algo; (*be unable*) não conseguir fazer algo; **without ~** sem falta; **failing** N defeito ▶ PREP na *or* à falta de; **failing that** senão; **failure** N fracasso; (*mechanical etc*) falha
faint [feɪnt] ADJ fraco; (*recollection*) vago; (*mark*) indistinto; (*smell, trace*) leve ▶ N desmaio ▶ VI desmaiar; **to feel ~** sentir tonteira
fair [fɛə^r] ADJ justo; (*hair*) louro; (*complexion*) branco; (*weather*) bom; (*good enough*) razoável; (*sizeable*) considerável ▶ ADV: **to play ~** fazer jogo limpo ▶ N (*also:* **trade ~**) feira; (BRIT: *funfair*) parque *m* de diversões; **fairly** ADV (*justly*) com justiça; (*quite*) bastante; **fair trade** N comércio justo
fairy ['fɛərɪ] N fada
faith [feɪθ] N fé *f*; (*trust*) confiança; (*denomination*) seita; **faithful** ADJ fiel; (*account*) exato; **faithfully** ADV fielmente; **yours faithfully** (BRIT: *in letters*) atenciosamente
fake [feɪk] N (*painting etc*) falsificação *f*; (*person*) impostor(a) *m/f* ▶ ADJ falso ▶ VT fingir; (*painting etc*) falsificar

falcon ['fɔːlkən] N falcão *m*
fall [fɔːl] (*pt* **fell**, *pp* **fallen**) N queda; (*US*: *autumn*) outono ▶ VI cair; (*price*) baixar; **falls** NPL (*waterfall*) cascata, queda d'água; **to ~ flat** cair de cara no chão; (*plan*) falhar; (*joke*) não agradar; **fall back** VI retroceder; **fall back on** VT FUS recorrer a; **fall behind** VI ficar para trás; **fall down** VI (*person*) cair; (*building*) desabar; **fall for** VT FUS (*trick*) cair em; (*person*) enamorar-se de; **fall in** VI ruir; (*Mil*) alinhar-se; **fall off** VI cair; (*diminish*) declinar, diminuir; **fall out** VI cair; (*friends etc*) brigar; **fall through** VI (*plan, project*) furar
fallout ['fɔːlaut] N chuva radioativa
false [fɔːls] ADJ falso; **false teeth** (BRIT) NPL dentadura postiça
fame [feɪm] N fama
familiar [fə'mɪlɪə^r] ADJ (*well-known*) conhecido; (*tone*) familiar, íntimo; **to be ~ with** (*subject*) estar familiarizado com
family ['fæmɪlɪ] N família
famine ['fæmɪn] N fome *f*
famous ['feɪməs] ADJ famoso, célebre
fan [fæn] N (*hand-held*) leque *m*; (*Elec*) ventilador *m*; (*person*) fã *m/f* ▶ VT abanar; (*fire, quarrel*) atiçar; **fan out** VI espalhar-se
fanatic [fə'nætɪk] N fanático(-a)
fan belt N correia do ventilador (BR) *or* da ventoinha (PT)
fan club N fã-clube *m*
fancy ['fænsɪ] N capricho; (*imagination*) imaginação *f*; (*fantasy*) fantasia ▶ ADJ ornamental; (*luxury*) luxuoso ▶ VT desejar, querer; (*imagine*) imaginar; (*think*) acreditar, achar; **to take a ~ to** tomar gosto por; **he fancies her** (*inf*) ele está a fim dela; **fancy dress** N fantasia
fantastic [fæn'tæstɪk] ADJ fantástico
fantasy ['fæntəsɪ] N (*dream*) sonho; (*unreality*) fantasia; (*imagination*) imaginação *f*
far [fɑː^r] ADJ (*distant*) distante ▶ ADV (*also*: **~ away, ~ off**) longe; **the ~ side/end** o lado de lá/a outra ponta; **~ better** muito melhor; **~ from** longe de; **by ~** de longe; **go as ~ as the farm** vá até a (BR) *or* à (PT) fazenda; **as ~ as I know** que eu saiba; **how ~?** até onde?; (*fig*) até que ponto?
farce [fɑːs] N farsa
fare [fɛə^r] N (*on trains, buses*) preço (da passagem); (*in taxi*: *cost*) tarifa; (*food*) comida; **half/full ~** meia/inteira passagem
Far East N: **the ~** o Extremo Oriente
farewell [fɛə'wɛl] EXCL adeus ▶ N despedida
farm [fɑːm] N fazenda (BR), quinta (PT) ▶ VT cultivar; **farmer** N fazendeiro(-a), agricultor *m*; **farmhouse** *irreg* N casa da fazenda (BR) *or* da quinta (PT); **farming** N agricultura; (*tilling*) cultura; (*of animals*) criação *f*; **farmyard** N curral *m*
far-reaching [-'riːtʃɪŋ] ADJ de grande alcance, abrangente
fart [fɑːt] (!) VI soltar um peido (!), peidar (!)
farther ['fɑːðə^r] ADV mais longe ▶ ADJ mais distante, mais afastado
farthest ['fɑːðɪst] SUPERL *of* **far**
fascinate ['fæsɪneɪt] VT fascinar
fashion ['fæʃən] N moda; (*fashion industry*) indústria da moda; (*manner*) maneira ▶ VT modelar, dar feitio a; **in ~** na moda; **fashionable**

ADJ da moda, elegante; **fashion show** N desfile *m* de modas
fast [fɑ:st] ADJ rápido; (*dye, colour*) firme, permanente; (*clock*): **to be ~** estar adiantado ▶ADV rápido, rapidamente, depressa; (*stuck, held*) firmemente ▶N jejum *m* ▶VI jejuar; **~ asleep** dormindo profundamente
fasten ['fɑ:sn] VT fixar, prender; (*coat*) fechar; (*belt*) apertar ▶VI prender-se, fixar-se
fast food N fast food *f*
fat [fæt] ADJ gordo; (*book*) grosso; (*wallet*) recheado; (*profit*) grande ▶N gordura; (*lard*) banha, gordura
fatal ['feɪtl] ADJ fatal; (*injury*) mortal
fate [feɪt] N destino; (*of person*) sorte *f*
father ['fɑ:ðəʳ] N pai *m*; **father-in-law** N sogro
fatigue [fə'ti:g] N fadiga, cansaço
fatty ['fætɪ] ADJ (*food*) gorduroso ▶N (*inf*) gorducho(-a)
fault [fɔ:lt] N (*blame*) culpa; (*defect*) defeito; (*Geo*) falha; (*Tennis*) falta, bola fora ▶VT criticar; **to find ~ with** criticar, queixar-se de; **at ~** culpado; **faulty** ADJ defeituoso
favour ['feɪvəʳ], (US) **favor** N favor *m* ▶VT favorecer; (*assist*) auxiliar; **to do sb a ~** fazer favor a alguém; **to find ~ with** cair nas boas graças de; **in ~ of** em favor de; **favourite** ['feɪvərɪt] ADJ predileto ▶N favorito(-a)
fawn [fɔ:n] N cervo novo, cervato ▶ADJ (*also*: **~-coloured**) castanho-claro *inv* ▶VI: **to ~ (up)on** bajular
fax [fæks] N fax *m*, fac-símile *m* ▶VT enviar por fax *or* fac-símile
FBI (US) N ABBR (= *Federal Bureau of Investigation*) FBI *m*
fear [fɪəʳ] N medo ▶VT ter medo de, temer; **for ~ of** com medo de; **fearful** ADJ medonho, temível; (*cowardly*) medroso; (*awful*) terrível
feasible ['fi:zəbl] ADJ viável
feast [fi:st] N banquete *m*; (*Rel*: *also*: **~ day**) festa ▶VI banquetear-se
feat [fi:t] N façanha, feito
feather ['fɛðəʳ] N pena, pluma
feature ['fi:tʃəʳ] N característica; (*article*) reportagem *f* ▶VT (*subj: film*) apresentar ▶VI figurar; **features** NPL (*of face*) feições *fpl*; **feature film** N longa-metragem *f*
February ['fɛbruərɪ] N fevereiro
fed [fɛd] PT, PP *of* **feed**
federal ['fɛdərəl] ADJ federal
fed up ADJ: **to be ~** estar (de saco) cheio (BR), estar farto (PT)
fee [fi:] N taxa (BR), propina (PT); (*of school*) matrícula; (*of doctor, lawyer*) honorários *mpl*
feeble ['fi:bl] ADJ fraco; (*attempt*) ineficaz
feed [fi:d] (*pt, pp* **fed**) N (*of baby*) alimento infantil; (*of animal*) ração *f*; (*on printer*) mecanismo alimentador ▶VT alimentar; (*baby*) amamentar; (*animal*) dar de comer a; (*data, information*): **to ~ into** introduzir em; **feed on** VT FUS alimentar-se de; **feedback** ['fi:dbæk] N reação *f*
feel [fi:l] (*pt, pp* **felt**) N sensação *f*; (*sense of touch*) tato; (*impression*) impressão *f* ▶VT tocar, apalpar; (*anger, pain etc*) sentir; (*think, believe*) achar, acreditar; **to ~ hungry/cold** estar com fome/frio (BR), ter fome/frio (PT); **to ~ lonely/better** sentir-se só/

melhor; **I don't ~ well** não estou me sentindo bem; **it ~s soft** é macio; **to ~ like** querer; **to ~ about** *or* **around** tatear; **feeling** N sensação *f*; (*emotion*) sentimento; (*impression*) impressão *f*

feet [fi:t] NPL *of* **foot**

fell [fɛl] PT *of* **fall** ▶VT (*tree*) lançar por terra, derrubar

fellow ['fɛləu] N camarada *m/f*; (*inf: man*) cara *m* (BR), tipo (PT); (*of learned society*) membro ▶CPD: **~ students** colegas *mpl/fpl* de curso; **fellowship** N amizade *f*; (*grant*) bolsa de estudo; (*society*) associação *f*

felony ['fɛlənɪ] N crime *m*

felt [fɛlt] PT, PP *of* **feel** ▶N feltro

female ['fi:meɪl] N (*pej: woman*) mulher *f*; (*Zool*) fêmea ▶ADJ fêmeo(-a); (*sex, character*) feminino; (*vote etc*) das mulheres; (*child etc*) do sexo feminino

feminine ['fɛmɪnɪn] ADJ feminino

feminist ['fɛmɪnɪst] N feminista *m/f*

fence [fɛns] N cerca ▶VT (*also*: **~ in**) cercar ▶VI esgrimir; **fencing** N (*sport*) esgrima

fend [fɛnd] VI: **to ~ for o.s.** defender-se, virar-se; **fend off** VT defender-se de

ferment [*vi* fə'mɛnt, *n* 'fə:mɛnt] VI fermentar ▶N (*fig*) agitação *f*

fern [fə:n] N samambaia (BR), feto (PT)

ferocious [fə'rəuʃəs] ADJ feroz

ferret ['fɛrɪt] N furão *m*; **ferret out** VT (*information*) desenterrar, descobrir

ferry ['fɛrɪ] N (*small*) barco (de travessia); (*large*: *also*: **~boat**) balsa ▶VT transportar

fertile ['fə:taɪl] ADJ fértil; (*Bio*) fecundo; **fertilizer** ['fə:tɪlaɪzə^r] N adubo, fertilizante *m*

festival ['fɛstɪvəl] N (*Rel*) festa; (*Art, Mus*) festival *m*

festive ['fɛstɪv] ADJ festivo; **the ~ season** (BRIT: *Christmas*) a época do Natal

fetch [fɛtʃ] VT ir buscar, trazer; (*sell for*) alcançar

fête [feɪt] N festa

feud [fju:d] N disputa, rixa

fever ['fi:və^r] N febre *f*; **feverish** ADJ febril

few [fju:] ADJ, PRON poucos(-as); **a ~ ...** alguns/algumas ...; **fewer** ['fju:ə^r] ADJ menos; **fewest** ['fju:ɪst] ADJ o menor número de

fib [fɪb] N lorota

fickle ['fɪkl] ADJ inconstante; (*weather*) instável

fiction ['fɪkʃən] N ficção *f*; **fictional** ADJ de ficção

fiddle ['fɪdl] N (*Mus*) violino; (*swindle*) trapaça ▶VT (BRIT: *accounts*) falsificar; **fiddle with** VT FUS brincar com

fidget ['fɪdʒɪt] VI estar irrequieto, mexer-se

field [fi:ld] N campo; (*fig*) área, esfera, especialidade *f*

fierce [fɪəs] ADJ feroz; (*wind, attack*) violento; (*heat*) intenso

fifteen [fɪf'ti:n] NUM quinze

fifth [fɪfθ] NUM quinto

fifty ['fɪftɪ] NUM cinquenta; **fifty-fifty** ADV: **to share** *or* **go fifty-fifty with sb** dividir meio a meio com alguém, rachar com alguém ▶ADJ: **to have a fifty-fifty chance** ter 50% de chance

fig [fɪg] N figo

fight [faɪt] (*pt, pp* **fought**) N briga; (*Mil*) combate *m*; (*struggle: against illness etc*) luta ▶VT lutar contra; (*cancer, alcoholism*) combater; (*election*) competir ▶VI brigar, bater-se

figure ['fɪgəʳ] N (*Drawing, Math*) figura, desenho; (*number, cipher*) número, cifra; (*outline*) forma; (*person*) personagem *m* ▶ VT (*esp US*) imaginar ▶ VI figurar; **figure out** VT compreender
file [faɪl] N (*tool*) lixa; (*dossier*) dossiê *m*, pasta; (*folder*) pasta; (*Comput*) arquivo; (*row*) fila, coluna ▶ VT (*wood, nails*) lixar; (*papers*) arquivar; (*Jur: claim*) apresentar, dar entrada em ▶ VI: **to ~ in/out** entrar/sair em fila; **file sharing** N (*Comput*) compartilhamento de arquivos
fill [fɪl] VT encher; (*vacancy*) preencher; (*need*) satisfazer ▶ N: **to eat one's ~** encher-se *or* fartar-se de comer; **fill in** VT (*form*) preencher; (*hole*) tapar; (*time*) encher; **fill up** VT encher ▶ VI (*Aut*) abastecer o carro
fillet ['fɪlɪt] N filete *m*, filé *m*; **fillet steak** N filé *m*
filling ['fɪlɪŋ] N (*Culin*) recheio; (*for tooth*) obturação *f* (BR), chumbo (PT); **filling station** N posto de gasolina
film [fɪlm] N filme *m*; (*of liquid etc*) camada fina, veu *m* ▶ VT rodar, filmar ▶ VI filmar; **film star** N astro/estrela do cinema
filter ['fɪltəʳ] N filtro ▶ VT filtrar
filth [fɪlθ] N sujeira (BR), sujidade *f* (PT); **filthy** ADJ sujo; (*language*) indecente, obsceno
fin [fɪn] N barbatana
final ['faɪnl] ADJ final, último; (*definitive*) definitivo ▶ N (*Sport*) final *f*; **finals** NPL (*Sch*) exames *mpl* finais; **finale** [fɪ'nɑːlɪ] N final *m*; **finalize** VT concluir, completar; **finally** ADV finalmente, por fim
finance [faɪ'næns] N fundos *mpl*; (*money management*) finanças *fpl* ▶ VT financiar; **finances** NPL (*personal finances*) finanças; **financial** [faɪ'nænʃəl] ADJ financeiro
find [faɪnd] (*pt, pp* **found**) VT encontrar, achar; (*discover*) descobrir ▶ N achado, descoberta; **to ~ sb guilty** (*Jur*) declarar alguém culpado; **find out** VT descobrir; (*person*) desmascarar ▶ VI: **to ~ out about** (*by chance*) saber de; **findings** NPL (*Jur*) veredito, decisão *f*; (*of report*) constatações *fpl*
fine [faɪn] ADJ fino; (*excellent*) excelente ▶ ADV muito bem ▶ N (*Jur*) multa ▶ VT (*Jur*) multar; **to be ~** (*person*) estar bem; (*weather*) estar bom; **fine arts** NPL belas artes *fpl*
finger ['fɪŋgəʳ] N dedo ▶ VT manusear; **fingernail** N unha; **fingerprint** N impressão *f* digital; **fingertip** N ponta do dedo
finish ['fɪnɪʃ] N fim *m*; (*Sport*) chegada; (*on wood etc*) acabamento ▶ VT, VI terminar, acabar; **to ~ doing sth** terminar de fazer algo; **to ~ third** chegar no terceiro lugar; **finish off** VT terminar; (*kill*) liquidar; **finish up** VT acabar ▶ VI ir parar
Finland ['fɪnlənd] N Finlândia
Finn [fɪn] N finlandês(-esa) *m/f*; **Finnish** ADJ finlandês(-esa) ▶ N (*Ling*) finlandês *m*
fir [fəːʳ] N abeto
fire ['faɪəʳ] N fogo; (*accidental*) incêndio; (*gas fire, electric fire*) aquecedor *m* ▶ VT (*gun*) disparar; (*arrow*) atirar; (*interest*) estimular; (*dismiss*) despedir ▶ VI disparar; **on ~** em chamas; **fire alarm** N alarme *m* de incêndio; **firearm** N arma de fogo; **fire brigade** N (corpo de)

bombeiros *mpl*; **fire engine** N carro de bombeiro; **fire escape** N escada de incêndio; **fire exit** N saída de emergência; **fire extinguisher** N extintor *m* de incêndio; **fireman** *irreg* N bombeiro; **fireplace** N lareira; **fire station** N posto de bombeiros; **firewall** N (*Comput*) firewall *m*; **firewood** N lenha; **fireworks** NPL fogos *mpl* de artifício

firm [fə:m] ADJ firme ▶ N firma

first [fə:st] ADJ primeiro ▶ ADV (*before others*) primeiro; (*when listing reasons etc*) em primeiro lugar ▶ N (*in race*) primeiro(-a); (*Aut*) primeira; (BRIT *Sch*) menção *f* honrosa; **at ~** no início; **~ of all** antes de tudo, antes de mais nada; **first aid** N primeiros socorros *mpl*; **first-aid kit** N estojo de primeiros socorros; **first-class** ADJ de primeira classe; **first-hand** ADJ de primeira mão; **first lady** (US) N primeira dama; **firstly** ADV primeiramente, em primeiro lugar; **first name** N primeiro nome *m*; **first-rate** ADJ de primeira categoria

fish [fɪʃ] N INV peixe *m* ▶ VT, VI pescar; **to go ~ing** ir pescar; **fisherman** *irreg* N pescador *m*; **fishing boat** N barco de pesca; **fishing line** N linha de pesca; **fishmonger** ['fɪʃmʌŋgə^r] N peixeiro(-a); **fishmonger's (shop)** peixaria; **fishy** (*inf*) ADJ (*tale*) suspeito

fist [fɪst] N punho

fit [fɪt] ADJ em (boa) forma; (*suitable*) adequado, apropriado ▶ VT (*subj: clothes*) caber em; (*put in, attach*) colocar; (*equip*) equipar ▶ VI (*clothes*) servir; (*parts*) ajustar-se; (*in space, gap*) caber ▶ N (*Med*) ataque *m*; **~ to** bom para; **~ for** adequado para; **a ~ of anger/pride** um acesso de raiva/orgulho; **by ~s and starts** espasmodicamente; **fit in** VI encaixar-se; (*person*) dar-se bem (com todos); **fitness** N (*Med*) saúde *f*, boa forma; **fitted kitchen** (BRIT) N cozinha planejada; **fitting** ADJ apropriado ▶ N (*of dress*) prova; **fittings** NPL (*in building*) instalações *fpl*, acessórios *mpl*

five [faɪv] NUM cinco; **fiver** (*inf*) N (BRIT) nota de cinco libras; (US) nota de cinco dólares

fix [fɪks] VT (*secure*) fixar, colocar; (*arrange*) arranjar; (*mend*) consertar; (*meal, drink*) preparar ▶ N: **to be in a ~** estar em apuros; **fix up** VT (*meeting*) marcar; **to ~ sb up with sth** arranjar algo para alguém; **fixed** ADJ (*prices, smile*) fixo; **fixture** N (*furniture*) móvel *m* fixo; (*Sport*) desafio, encontro

fizzy ['fɪzɪ] ADJ com gás, gasoso

flag [flæg] N bandeira; (*for signalling*) bandeirola; (*flagstone*) laje *f* ▶ VI acabar-se, descair; **flag down** VT: **to ~ sb down** fazer sinais a alguém para que pare

flagpole ['flægpəul] N mastro de bandeira

flair [flɛə^r] N (*talent*) talento; (*style*) habilidade *f*

flake [fleɪk] N (*of rust, paint*) lasca; (*of snow, soap powder*) floco ▶ VI (*also:* **~ off**) lascar, descamar-se

flamboyant [flæm'bɔɪənt] ADJ (*dress*) espalhafatoso; (*person*) extravagante

flame [fleɪm] N chama

flammable ['flæməbl] ADJ inflamável

flan [flæn] (BRIT) N torta

flannel ['flænl] N (BRIT: *also:* **face ~**) pano de rosto; (*fabric*) flanela; **flannels** NPL calça (BR) *or* calças *fpl* (PT) de flanela

flap [flæp] N (*of pocket, table*) aba; (*of envelope*) dobra ▶ VT (*arms*) oscilar; (*wings*) bater ▶ VI (*sail, flag*) ondular; (*inf: also:* **be in a ~**) estar atarantado

flare [flɛəʳ] N fogacho, chama; (*Mil*) foguete *m* sinalizador; (*in skirt etc*) folga; **flare up** VI chamejar; (*fig: person*) encolerizar-se; (*: violence*) irromper

flash [flæʃ] N (*of lightning*) clarão *m*; (*also:* **news ~**) notícias *fpl* de última hora; (*Phot*) flash *m* ▶ VT piscar; (*news, message*) transmitir; (*look, smile*) brilhar ▶ VI brilhar; (*light on ambulance, eyes etc*) piscar; **in a ~** num instante; **to ~ by** *or* **past** passar como um raio; **flash drive** N (*Comput*) pen drive *m*; **flashlight** N lanterna de bolso

flat [flæt] ADJ plano; (*battery*) descarregado; (*tyre*) vazio; (*beer*) choco; (*denial*) categórico; (*Mus*) abemolado; (*: voice*) desafinado; (*rate*) único; (*fee*) fixo ▶ N (BRIT: *apartment*) apartamento; (*Mus*) bemol *m*; (*Aut*) pneu *m* furado; **~ out** (*work*) a toque de caixa; **flatten** VT (*also:* **flatten out**) aplanar; (*demolish*) arrasar

flatter ['flætəʳ] VT lisonjear; **flattering** ADJ lisonjeiro; (*clothes etc*) favorecedor(a)

flaunt [flɔːnt] VT ostentar, pavonear

flavour ['fleɪvəʳ], (US) **flavor** N sabor *m* ▶ VT condimentar, aromatizar; **strawberry-~ed** com sabor de morango

flaw [flɔː] N defeito; (*in character*) falha; **flawless** ADJ impecável

flea [fliː] N pulga

flee [fliː] (*pt, pp* **fled**) VT fugir de ▶ VI fugir

fleece [fliːs] N tosão *m*; (*coat*) velo; (*wool*) lã *f* ▶ VT (*inf*) espoliar

fleet [fliːt] N (*gen, of lorries etc*) frota; (*of ships*) esquadra

fleeting ['fliːtɪŋ] ADJ fugaz

Flemish ['flɛmɪʃ] ADJ flamengo

flesh [flɛʃ] N carne *f*; (*of fruit*) polpa

flew [fluː] PT *of* **fly**

flex [flɛks] N fio ▶ VT (*muscles*) flexionar; **flexible** ADJ flexível

flick [flɪk] N pancada leve; (*with finger*) peteleco, piparote *m*; (*with whip*) chicotada ▶ VT dar um peteleo; (*switch*) apertar; **flick through** VT FUS folhear

flicker ['flɪkəʳ] VI tremular; (*eyelids*) tremer

flight [flaɪt] N voo *m*; (*escape*) fuga; (*of steps*) lance *m*; **flight attendant** (US) N comissário(-a) de bordo

flimsy ['flɪmzɪ] ADJ (*thin*) delgado, franzino; (*weak*) débil; (*excuse*) fraco

flinch [flɪntʃ] VI encolher-se; **to ~ from sth/from doing sth** vacilar diante de algo/em fazer algo

fling [flɪŋ] (*pt, pp* **flung**) VT lançar

flint [flɪnt] N pederneira; (*in lighter*) pedra

flip-flops ['flɪpflɔps] (*esp* BRIT) NPL chinelo (de dedo)

flipper ['flɪpəʳ] N (*of animal*) nadadeira; (*for swimmer*) pé de pato, nadadeira

flirt [fləːt] VI flertar ▶ N namorador(a) *m/f*, paquerador(a) *m/f*

float [fləut] N boia; (*in procession*) carro alegórico; (*sum of money*) caixa ▶ VI flutuar; (*swimmer*) boiar

f

flock [flɔk] N rebanho; *(of birds)* bando ▶ VI: **to ~ to** afluir a
flood [flʌd] N enchente *f*, inundação *f* ▶ VT inundar, alagar ▶ VI *(place)* alagar; *(people, goods)*: **to ~ into** inundar; **flooding** N inundação *f*; **floodlight** *irreg* N refletor *m*, holofote *m*
floor [flɔːʳ] N chão *m*; *(storey)* andar *m*; *(of sea)* fundo ▶ VT *(fig: confuse)* confundir, pasmar; **ground ~** (BRIT) *or* **first ~** (US) andar térreo (BR), rés-do-chão (PT); **first ~** (BRIT) *or* **second ~** (US) primeiro andar; **floorboard** N tábua de assoalho; **floor show** N show *m*
flop [flɔp] N fracasso ▶ VI fracassar; *(into chair etc)* cair pesadamente
floppy ['flɔpɪ] ADJ frouxo, mole ▶ N *(also: ~ disk)* disquete *m*
florist ['flɔrɪst] N florista *m/f*; **florist's, florist's shop** N floricultura
flour ['flauəʳ] N farinha
flourish ['flʌrɪʃ] VI florescer ▶ VT brandir, menear ▶ N: **with a ~** con gestos floreados
flow [fləu] N fluxo; *(of river, Elec)* corrente *f*; *(of blood)* circulação *f* ▶ VI correr; *(traffic)* fluir; *(blood, Elec)* circular; *(clothes, hair)* ondular
flower ['flauəʳ] N flor *f* ▶ VI florescer, florir; **flower bed** N canteiro; **flowerpot** N vaso
flown [fləun] PP *of* **fly**
flu [fluː] N gripe *f*
fluctuate ['flʌktjueɪt] VI flutuar; *(temperature)* variar
fluent ['fluːənt] ADJ fluente; **he speaks ~ French, he's ~ in French** ele fala francês fluentemente
fluff [flʌf] N felpa, penugem *f*; **fluffy** ADJ macio, fofo
fluid ['fluːɪd] ADJ fluido ▶ N fluido
fluke [fluːk] *(inf)* N sorte *f*
flung [flʌŋ] PT, PP *of* **fling**
fluoride ['fluəraɪd] N fluoreto
flurry ['flʌrɪ] N *(of snow)* lufada; **~ of activity/excitement** muita atividade/animação
flush [flʌʃ] N *(on face)* rubor *m* ▶ VT lavar com água ▶ VI ruborizar-se ▶ ADJ: **~ with** rente com; **to ~ the toilet** dar descarga; **flush out** VT levantar
flute [fluːt] N flauta
flutter ['flʌtəʳ] N agitação *f*; *(of wings)* bater *m* ▶ VI esvoaçar
fly [flaɪ] *(pt* **flew**, *pp* **flown**) N mosca; *(on trousers: also:* **flies**) braguilha ▶ VT *(plane)* pilotar; *(passengers, cargo)* transportar (de avião); *(distances)* percorrer ▶ VI voar; *(passengers)* ir de avião; *(escape)* fugir; *(flag)* hastear-se; **fly away** VI voar; **fly off** VI = **fly away**; **flying** N aviação *f* ▶ ADJ: **flying visit** visita de médico; **with flying colours** brilhantemente; **flying saucer** N disco voador; **flyover** (BRIT) N viaduto
foal [fəul] N potro
foam [fəum] N espuma ▶ VI espumar; **foam rubber** N espuma de borracha
focus ['fəukəs] *(pl* **focuses**) N foco ▶ VT enfocar ▶ VI: **to ~ on** enfocar, focalizar; **in/out of ~** em foco/fora de foco
fog [fɔg] N nevoeiro; **foggy** ADJ nevoento
foil [fɔɪl] VT frustrar ▶ N folha metálica; *(also:* **kitchen ~**) folha *or* papel *m* de alumínio; *(complement)* contraste *m*, complemento; *(Fencing)* florete *m*
fold [fəuld] N dobra, vinco, prega; *(of skin)* ruga; *(Agr)* redil *m*, curral *m*

▶ VT dobrar; **to ~ one's arms** cruzar os braços; **fold up** VI dobrar; (*business*) abrir falência ▶ VT dobrar; **folder** N pasta; **folding** ADJ dobrável

folk [fəuk] NPL gente *f* ▶ CPD popular, folclórico; **folks** NPL (*family*) família, parentes *mpl*; **folklore** ['fəuklɔːʳ] N folclore *m*

follow ['fɔləu] VT seguir ▶ VI seguir; (*result*) resultar; **I don't quite ~ you** não consigo acompanhar o seu raciocínio; **to ~ suit** fazer o mesmo; **follow up** VT (*letter*) responder a; (*offer*) levar adiante; (*case*) acompanhar; **follower** N seguidor(a) *m/f*; **following** ADJ seguinte ▶ N adeptos *mpl*

fond [fɔnd] ADJ carinhoso; (*hopes*) absurdo, descabido; **to be ~ of** gostar de

food [fuːd] N comida; **food mixer** N batedeira; **food poisoning** N intoxicação *f* alimentar; **food processor** N multiprocessador *m* de cozinha

fool [fuːl] N tolo(-a); (*Culin*) purê *m* de frutas com creme ▶ VT enganar ▶ VI (*gen*: *fool around*) brincar; **foolish** ADJ burro; (*careless*) imprudente; **foolproof** ADJ infalível

foot [fut] (*pl* **feet**) N pé *m*; (*of animal*) pata; (*measure*) pé (*304 mm; 12 inches*) ▶ VT (*bill*) pagar; **on ~** a pé; **footage** N (*Cinema*: *length*) ≈ metragem *f*; (: *material*) sequências *fpl*; **football** N bola; (*game*: BRIT) futebol *m*; (: US) futebol norte-americano; **footballer** N, **football player** N jogador *m* de futebol; **footbridge** N passarela; **foothold** N apoio para o pé; **footing** N (*fig*) posição *f*; **to lose one's footing** escorregar; **footnote** N nota ao pé da página, nota de rodapé; **footpath** N caminho, atalho; **footprint** N pegada; **footstep** N passo; **footwear** N calçados *mpl*

KEYWORD

for [fɔːʳ] PREP **1** (*indicating destination, direction*) para; **he went for the paper** foi pegar o jornal; **is this for me?** é para mim?; **it's time for lunch** é hora de almoçar

2 (*indicating purpose*) para; **what's it for?** para quê serve?; **to pray for peace** orar pela paz

3 (*on behalf of, representing*) por; **he works for the government/a local firm** ele trabalha para o governo/uma firma local; **G for George** G de George

4 (*because of*) por; **for this reason** por esta razão; **for fear of being criticized** com medo de ser criticado

5 (*with regard to*) para; **it's cold for July** está frio para julho

6 (*in exchange for*) por; **it was sold for £5** foi vendido por £5

7 (*in favour of*) a favor de; **are you for or against us?** você está a favor de ou contra nós?; **I'm all for it** concordo plenamente, tem todo o meu apoio; **vote for X** vote em X

8 (*referring to distance*): **there are road works for 5 km** há obras na estrada por 5 quilômetros; **we walked for miles** andamos quilômetros

9 (*referring to time*): **she will be away for a month** ela ficará fora um mês; **I have known her**

for years eu a conheço há anos; **can you do it for tomorrow?** você pode fazer isso para amanhã?
10 (*with infinite clause*): **it is not for me to decide** não cabe a mim decidir; **it would be best for you to leave** seria melhor que você fosse embora; **there is still time for you to do it** ainda há tempo para você fazer isso; **for this to be possible ...** para que isso seja possível ...
11 (*in spite of*) apesar de
▶ CONJ (*since, as: rather formal*) pois, porque

forbid [fə'bɪd] (*pt* **forbad(e)**, *pp* **forbidden**) VT proibir; **to ~ sb to do sth** proibir alguém de fazer algo
force [fɔːs] N força ▶ VT forçar; **the Forces** (BRIT) NPL as Forças Armadas; **in ~** em vigor; **forceful** ADJ enérgico, vigoroso
ford [fɔːd] N vau *m*
fore [fɔːʳ] N: **to come to the ~** salientar-se
forearm ['fɔːrɑːm] N antebraço
forecast ['fɔːkɑːst] (*irreg: like* **cast**) N previsão *f*; (*also*: **weather ~**) previsão do tempo ▶ VT prognosticar, prever
forefinger ['fɔːfɪŋgəʳ] N (dedo) indicador *m*
foreground ['fɔːgraund] N primeiro plano
forehead ['fɔrɪd] N testa
foreign ['fɔrɪn] ADJ estrangeiro; (*trade*) exterior; **foreigner** N estrangeiro(-a); **foreign exchange** N câmbio; **Foreign Office** (BRIT) N Ministério das Relações Exteriores
foreman ['fɔːmən] *irreg* N capataz *m*; (*in construction*) contramestre *m*; primeiro jurado
foremost ['fɔːməust] ADJ principal ▶ ADV: **first and ~** antes de mais nada
forensic [fə'rɛnsɪk] ADJ forense; **~ medicine** medicina legal
foresee [fɔː'siː] (*irreg: like* **see**) VT prever; **foreseeable** ADJ previsível
forest ['fɔrɪst] N floresta
forestry ['fɔrɪstrɪ] N silvicultura
forever [fə'rɛvəʳ] ADV para sempre
foreword ['fɔːwəːd] N prefácio
forfeit ['fɔːfɪt] VT perder (direito a)
forgave [fə'geɪv] PT *of* **forgive**
forge [fɔːdʒ] N ferraria ▶ VT falsificar; (*metal*) forjar; **forge ahead** VI avançar constantemente; **forger** N falsificador(a) *m/f*; **forgery** N falsificação *f*
forget [fə'gɛt] (*pt* **forgot**, *pp* **forgotten**) VT, VI esquecer; **forgetful** ADJ esquecido
forgive [fə'gɪv] (*pt* **forgave**, *pp* **forgiven**) VT perdoar; **to ~ sb for sth** perdoar algo a alguém, perdoar alguém de algo
forgot [fə'gɔt] PT *of* **forget**
forgotten [fə'gɔtn] PP *of* **forget**
fork [fɔːk] N (*for eating*) garfo; (*for gardening*) forquilha; (*of roads etc*) bifurcação *f* ▶ VI bifurcar-se; **fork out** (*inf*) VT (*pay*) desembolsar, morrer em
forlorn [fə'lɔːn] ADJ desolado; (*attempt*) desesperado; (*hope*) último
form [fɔːm] N forma; (*type*) tipo; (*Sch*) série *f*; (*questionnaire*) formulário ▶ VT formar; (*organization*) criar; **to ~ a queue** (BRIT) fazer fila; **in top ~** em plena forma
formal ['fɔːməl] ADJ (*offer, receipt*) oficial; (*person etc*) cerimonioso; (*occasion, education*) formal;

(*dress*) a rigor (BR), de cerimônia (PT); (*garden*) simétrico

format ['fɔ:mæt] N formato ▶ VT (*Comput*) formatar

former ['fɔ:məʳ] ADJ anterior; (*earlier*) antigo; **the ~ ... the latter ...** aquele ... este ...; **formerly** ADV anteriormente

formidable ['fɔ:mɪdəbl] ADJ terrível, temível

formula ['fɔ:mjulə] (*pl* **formulas** *or* **formulae**) N fórmula

fort [fɔ:t] N forte *m*

fortify ['fɔ:tɪfaɪ] VT (*city*) fortificar; (*person*) fortalecer

fortnight ['fɔ:tnaɪt] (BRIT) N quinzena, quinze dias *mpl*; **fortnightly** ADJ quinzenal ▶ ADV quinzenalmente

fortunate ['fɔ:tʃənɪt] ADJ (*event*) feliz; (*person*): **to be ~** ter sorte; **it is ~ that ...** é uma sorte que ...; **fortunately** ADV felizmente

fortune ['fɔ:tʃən] N sorte *f*; (*wealth*) fortuna; **fortune-teller** N adivinho(-a)

forty ['fɔ:tɪ] NUM quarenta

forward ['fɔ:wəd] ADJ (*movement*) para a frente; (*position*) avançado; (*not shy*) imodesto, presunçoso ▶ N (*Sport*) atacante *m* ▶ VT (*letter*) remeter; (*goods, parcel*) expedir; (*career*) promover; (*plans*) ativar; **to move ~** avançar; **~ planning** planejamento para o futuro; **forwards** ADV para a frente; **forward slash** N barra

foster ['fɔstəʳ] VT tutelar; (*activity*) promover; **foster child** *irreg* N tutelado(-a)

fought [fɔ:t] PT, PP *of* **fight**

foul [faul] ADJ horrível; (*language*) obsceno ▶ N (*Sport*) falta ▶ VT sujar; **foul play** N (*Jur*) crime *m*

found [faund] PT, PP *of* **find** ▶ VT (*establish*) fundar; **foundation** [faun'deɪʃən] N (*act*) fundação *f*; (*base*) base *f*; (*also*: **foundation cream**) creme *m* base; **foundations** NPL (*of building*) alicerces *mpl*

founder ['faundəʳ] N fundador(a) *m/f* ▶ VI naufragar

fountain ['fauntɪn] N chafariz *m*; **fountain pen** N caneta-tinteiro *f*

four [fɔ:ʳ] NUM quatro; **on all ~s** de quatro; **four-by-four** [fɔbaɪ'fɔʳ] N 4x4 *m* (*quatro por quatro*); **four-letter word** N palavrão *m*; **fourteen** NUM catorze; *see also* **five**; **fourth** NUM quarto

fowl [faul] N ave *f* (doméstica)

fox [fɔks] N raposa ▶ VT deixar perplexo

foyer ['fɔɪeɪ] N saguão *m*

fraction ['frækʃən] N fração *f*

fracture ['fræktʃəʳ] N fratura ▶ VT fraturar

fragile ['frædʒaɪl] ADJ frágil

fragment ['frægmənt] N fragmento

frail [freɪl] ADJ (*person*) fraco; (*structure*) frágil

frame [freɪm] N (*of building*) estrutura; (*body*) corpo; (*of picture, door*) moldura; (*of spectacles*: *also*: **~s**) armação *f*, aro ▶ VT (*picture*) emoldurar; **framework** N armação *f*

France [frɑ:ns] N França

frank [fræŋk] ADJ franco ▶ VT (*letter*) franquear; **frankly** ADV francamente; (*candidly*) abertamente

frantic ['fræntɪk] ADJ frenético; (*person*) fora de si

fraud [frɔ:d] N fraude *f*; (*person*) impostor(a) *m/f*

fraught [frɔːt] ADJ tenso; **~ with** repleto de
fray [freɪ] N combate *m*, luta ▸ VI esfiapar-se; **tempers were ~ed** estavam com os nervos em frangalhos
freak [friːk] N (*person*) anormal *m/f*; (*event*) anomalia
freckle ['frɛkl] N sarda
free [friː] ADJ livre; (*seat*) desocupado; (*costing nothing*) gratis, gratuito ▸ VT pôr em liberdade; (*jammed object*) soltar; **~ (of charge)** grátis, de graça; **freedom** N liberdade *f*; **freelance** ADJ freelance; **freely** ADV livremente; **free-range** N (*egg*) caseiro; **freeway** (US) N via expressa; **free will** N livre arbítrio; **of one's own free will** por sua própria vontade
freeze [friːz] (*pt* **froze**, *pp* **frozen**) VI gelar(-se), congelar-se ▸ VT congelar ▸ N geada; (*on arms, wages*) congelamento; **freezer** N congelador *m*, freezer *m* (BR); **freezing** ADJ: **freezing (cold)** (*weather*) glacial; (*water*) gelado; **3 degrees below freezing** 3 graus abaixo de zero; **freezing point** N ponto de congelamento
freight [freɪt] N (*goods*) carga; (*money charged*) frete *m*; **freight train** (US) N trem *m* de carga
French [frɛntʃ] ADJ francês(-esa) ▸ N (*Ling*) francês *m*; **the French** NPL os franceses; **French bean** (BRIT) N feijão *m* comum; **French fried potatoes** NPL batatas *fpl* fritas; **Frenchman** *irreg* N francês *m*; **Frenchwoman** *irreg* N francesa
frenzy ['frɛnzɪ] N frenesi *m*
frequent [*adj* 'friːkwənt, *vt* frɪ'kwɛnt] ADJ frequente ▸ VT frequentar; **frequently** ADV frequentemente, a miúdo
fresh [frɛʃ] ADJ fresco; (*new*) novo; (*cheeky*) atrevido; **freshen** VI (*wind, air*) tornar-se mais forte; **freshen up** VI (*person*) lavar-se, refrescar-se; **freshly** ADV recentemente, há pouco
fret [frɛt] VI afligir-se
friction ['frɪkʃən] N fricção *f*; (*between people*) atrito
Friday ['fraɪdɪ] N sexta-feira *f*
fridge [frɪdʒ] N geladeira (BR), frigorífico (PT)
fried [fraɪd] ADJ frito; **~ egg** ovo estrelado *or* frito
friend [frɛnd] N amigo(-a) ▸ VT (*on social network*) adicionar como amigo; **friendly** ADJ simpático ▸ N (*also*: **friendly match**) amistoso; **friendship** N amizade *f*
fries [fraɪz] (*esp* US) NPL = **French fried potatoes**
fright [fraɪt] N terror *m*; (*scare*) pavor *m*; **to take ~** assustar-se; **frighten** VT assustar; **frightened** ADJ: **to be frightened of** ter medo de; **frightening** ADJ assustador(a); **frightful** ADJ terrível, horrível
frill [frɪl] N babado
fringe [frɪndʒ] N franja; (*on shawl etc*) beira, orla; (*edge: of forest etc*) margem *f*
fritter ['frɪtə^r] N bolinho frito; **fritter away** VT desperdiçar
frivolous ['frɪvələs] ADJ frívolo; (*activity*) fútil
fro [frəu] ADJ *see* **to**
frock [frɔk] N vestido
frog [frɔg] N rã *f*; **frogman** *irreg* N homem-rã *m*

KEYWORD

from [frɔm] PREP **1** (*indicating starting place*) de; **where do you come from?** de onde você é?; **we**

flew from London to Glasgow fomos de avião de Londres para Glasgow; **to escape from sth/sb** escapar de algo/alguém
2 (*indicating origin etc*) de; **a letter/ telephone call from my sister** uma carta/um telefonema da minha irmã; **tell him from me that ...** diga a ele que da minha parte ...; **to drink from the bottle** beber na garrafa
3 (*indicating time*): **from one o'clock to** *or* **until** *or* **till two** da uma hora até às duas; **from January (on)** a partir de janeiro
4 (*indicating distance*) de; **we're still a long way from home** ainda estamos muito longe de casa
5 (*indicating price, number etc*) de; **prices range from £10 to £50** os preços vão de £10 a £50
6 (*indicating difference*) de; **he can't tell red from green** ele não pode diferenciar vermelho do verde
7 (*because of/on the basis of*): **from what he says** pelo que ele diz; **to act from conviction** agir por convicção; **weak from hunger** fraco de fome

front [frʌnt] N frente *f*; (*of vehicle*) parte *f* dianteira; (*of house*) fachada; (*also*: **sea ~**) orla marítima ▸ ADJ da frente; **in ~ (of)** em frente (de); **front door** N porta principal; **frontier** ['frʌntɪə^r] N fronteira; **front page** N primeira página
frost [frɔst] N geada; (*also*: **hoar~**) gelo; **frostbite** N ulceração *f* produzida pelo frio; **frosty** ADJ (*window*) coberto de geada; (*welcome*) glacial
froth [frɔθ] N espuma
frown [fraun] VI franzir as sobrancelhas, amarrar a cara
froze [frəuz] PT *of* **freeze**
frozen ['frəuzn] PP *of* **freeze**
fruit [fru:t] N INV fruta; (*fig*) fruto; **fruit juice** N suco (BR) *or* sumo (PT) de frutas; **fruit machine** (BRIT) N caça-níqueis *m inv* (BR), máquina de jogo (PT); **fruit salad** N salada de frutas
frustrate [frʌs'treɪt] VT frustrar
fry [fraɪ] (*pt, pp* **fried**) VT fritar; **frying pan** N frigideira
fudge [fʌdʒ] N (*Culin*) ≈ doce *m* de leite
fuel [fjuəl] N (*gen, for heating*) combustível *m*; (*for propelling*) carburante *m*; **fuel tank** N depósito de combustível
fulfil [ful'fɪl], (US) **fulfill** VT (*function*) cumprir; (*condition*) satisfazer; (*wish, desire*) realizar
full [ful] ADJ cheio; (*use, volume*) máximo; (*complete*) completo; (*information*) detalhado; (*price*) integral; (*skirt*) folgado ▸ ADV: **~ well** perfeitamente; **I'm ~ (up)** estou satisfeito; **~ employment** pleno emprego; **a ~ two hours** duas horas completas; **at ~ speed** a toda a velocidade; **in ~** integralmente; **full stop** N ponto (final); **full-time** ADJ (*work*) de tempo completo *or* integral; **fully** ADV completamente; (*at least*) pelo menos
fumble ['fʌmbl] VI atrapalhar-se; **fumble with** VT FUS atrapalhar-se com
fume [fju:m] VI fumegar; (*be angry*) estar com raiva; **fumes** NPL gases *mpl*
fun [fʌn] N divertimento; **to have ~** divertir-se; **for ~** de brincadeira;

to make ~ of fazer troça de, zombar de
function ['fʌŋkʃən] N função *f*; (*reception, dinner*) recepção *f* ▶ VI funcionar
fund [fʌnd] N fundo; (*source, store*) fonte *f*; **funds** NPL (*money*) fundos *mpl*
fundamental [fʌndə'mɛntl] ADJ fundamental
funeral ['fju:nərəl] N (*burial*) enterro
funfair ['fʌnfɛəʳ] (BRIT) N parque *m* de diversões
fungus ['fʌŋgəs] (*pl* **fungi**) N fungo; (*mould*) bolor *m*, mofo
funnel ['fʌnl] N funil *m*; (*of ship*) chaminé *f*
funny ['fʌnɪ] ADJ engraçado, divertido; (*strange*) esquisito, estranho
fur [fəːʳ] N pele *f*; (BRIT: *in kettle etc*) depósito, crosta
furious ['fjuərɪəs] ADJ furioso; (*effort*) incrível
furnish ['fəːnɪʃ] VT mobiliar (BR), mobilar (PT); (*supply*): **to ~ sb with sth** fornecer algo a alguém; **furnishings** NPL mobília
furniture ['fəːnɪtʃəʳ] N mobília, móveis *mpl*; **piece of ~** móvel *m*
furry ['fəːrɪ] ADJ peludo
further ['fəːðəʳ] ADJ novo, adicional ▶ ADV mais longe; (*more*) mais; (*moreover*) além disso ▶ VT promover; **further education** (BRIT) N educação *f* superior; **furthermore** ADV além disso
furthest ['fəːðɪst] SUPERL *of* **far**
fury ['fjuərɪ] N fúria
fuse [fjuːz] N fusível *m*; (*for bomb etc*) espoleta, mecha ▶ VT fundir; (*fig*) unir ▶ VI (*metal*) fundir-se; unir-se; **to ~ the lights** (BRIT *Elec*) queimar as luzes; **fuse box** N caixa de fusíveis
fuss [fʌs] N estardalhaço; (*complaining*) escândalo; **to make a ~** criar caso; **to make a ~ of sb** paparicar alguém; **fussy** ADJ (*person*) exigente; (*dress, style*) espalhafatoso
future ['fjuːtʃəʳ] ADJ futuro ▶ N futuro; **in (the) ~** no futuro
fuze [fjuːz] (US) = **fuse**
fuzzy ['fʌzɪ] ADJ (*Phot*) indistinto; (*hair*) frisado, encrespado

g

G [dʒiː] N (*Mus*) sol *m*
gadget ['gædʒɪt] N aparelho, engenhoca
Gaelic ['geɪlɪk] ADJ gaélico(-a) ▸ N (*Ling*) gaélico
gag [gæg] N (*on mouth*) mordaça; (*joke*) piada ▸ VT amordaçar
gain [geɪn] N ganho; (*profit*) lucro ▸ VT ganhar ▸ VI (*watch*) adiantar-se; (*benefit*): **to ~ from sth** tirar proveito de algo; **to ~ on sb** aproximar-se de alguém; **to ~ 3lbs (in weight)** engordar 3 libras
gal. ABBR = **gallon**
gale [geɪl] N ventania; **~ force 10** vento de força 10
gallery ['gælərɪ] N (*in theatre etc*) galeria; (*also*: **art ~**: *public*) museu *m*; (: *private*) galeria (de arte)
gallon ['gæln] N galão *m* (*Brit* = 4.5 *litros*, *US* = 3.8 *litros*)
gallop ['gæləp] N galope *m* ▸ VI galopar
gallstone ['gɔːlstəun] N cálculo biliar
gamble ['gæmbl] N risco ▸ VT, VI jogar, arriscar; **gambler** N jogador(a) *m/f*; **gambling** N jogo
game [geɪm] N jogo; (*match*) partida; (*Tennis*) jogada; (*strategy*) plano, esquema *m*; (*Hunting*) caça ▸ ADJ (*willing*): **to be ~ for anything** topar qualquer parada; **big ~** caça grossa; **games console** [geɪmz-] N console *m* de videogames (BR), consola de videojogos (PT); **game show** N game show *m*; **gaming** ['geɪmɪŋ] N (*with video games*) jogos *mpl* de computador
gang [gæŋ] N bando, grupo; (*of criminals*) gangue *f*; (*of workmen*) turma ▸ VI: **to ~ up on sb** conspirar contra alguém
gangster ['gæŋstə^r] N gângster *m*, bandido
gap [gæp] N brecha, fenda; (*in trees, traffic*) abertura; (*in time*) intervalo; (*difference*): **~ (between)** diferença (entre)
gape [geɪp] VI (*person*) estar *or* ficar boquiaberto; (*hole*) abrir-se
garage ['gærɑːʒ] N garagem *f*; (*for car repairs*) oficina (mecânica)
garbage ['gɑːbɪdʒ] N (*US*) lixo; (*inf: nonsense*) disparates *mpl*; **garbage can** (*US*) N lata de lixo; **garbage collector** (*US*) N lixeiro(-a)
garden ['gɑːdn] N jardim *m*; **gardens** NPL (*public park*) jardim público, parque *m*; **gardener** N jardineiro(-a); **gardening** N jardinagem *f*
garlic ['gɑːlɪk] N alho
garment ['gɑːmənt] N peça de roupa
garrison ['gærɪsn] N guarnição *f*

gas [gæs] N gás *m*; (*US: gasoline*) gasolina ▶ VT asfixiar com gás; **gas cooker** (BRIT) N fogão *m* a gás; **gas cylinder** N bujão *m* de gás; **gas fire** (BRIT) N aquecedor *m* a gás
gasket ['gæskɪt] N (*Aut*) junta, gaxeta
gasoline ['gæsəli:n] (US) N gasolina
gasp [gɑ:sp] N arfada ▶ VI arfar; **gasp out** VT dizer com voz entrecortada
gas station (US) N posto de gasolina
gastric ['gæstrɪk] ADJ gástrico; **gastric band** N (*Med*) banda gástrica
gate [geɪt] N portão *m*; **gate-crash** ['geɪtkræʃ] (BRIT) VT entrar de penetra em; **gated community** ['geɪtɪd-] N condomínio fechado; **gateway** N portão *m*, passagem *f*
gather ['gæðəʳ] VT colher; (*assemble*) reunir; (*Sewing*) franzir; (*understand*) compreender ▶ VI reunir-se; **to ~ speed** acelerar(-se); **gathering** N reunião *f*, assembleia
gauge [geɪdʒ] N (*instrument*) medidor *m* ▶ VT (*fig: sb's capabilities, character*) avaliar
gave [geɪv] PT *of* **give**
gay [geɪ] ADJ (*homosexual*) gay; (*old-fashioned: cheerful*) alegre; (*colour*) vistoso; (*music*) vivo
gaze [geɪz] N olhar *m* fixo ▶ VI: **to ~ at sth** fitar algo
GB ABBR = **Great Britain**
gear [gɪəʳ] N equipamento; (*Tech*) engrenagem *f*; (*Aut*) velocidade *f*, marcha (BR), mudança (PT) ▶ VT (*fig: adapt*): **to ~ sth to** preparar algo para; **top** (BRIT) *or* **high** (US)/**low ~** quinta/primeira (marcha); **in ~** engrenado
geese [gi:s] NPL *of* **goose**
gel [dʒɛl] N gel *m*
gem [dʒɛm] N joia, gema
Gemini ['dʒɛmɪnaɪ] N Gêminis *m*, Gêmeos *mpl*
gender ['dʒɛndəʳ] N gênero
general ['dʒɛnərl] N general *m* ▶ ADJ geral; **in ~** em geral; **general anaesthetic** N anestesia geral; **generally** ADV geralmente; **general practitioner** N clínico(-a) geral
generate ['dʒɛnəreɪt] VT gerar; **generator** N gerador *m*
generous ['dʒɛnərəs] ADJ generoso; (*measure etc*) abundante
genetically [dʒɪ'nɛtɪklɪ] ADV: **~ modified** (*food etc*) transgênico
Geneva [dʒɪ'ni:və] N Genebra
genitals ['dʒɛnɪtlz] NPL órgãos *mpl* genitais
genius ['dʒi:nɪəs] N gênio
genome ['dʒi:nəum] N genoma *m*
gentle ['dʒɛntl] ADJ (*touch, breeze*) leve, suave; (*landscape*) suave; (*animal*) manso
gentleman ['dʒɛntlmən] *irreg* N senhor *m*; (*referring to social position*) fidalgo; (*well-bred man*) cavalheiro
gently ['dʒɛntlɪ] ADV suavemente
gents [dʒɛnts] N banheiro de homens (BR), casa de banho dos homens (PT)
genuine ['dʒɛnjuɪn] ADJ autêntico; (*person*) sincero
geography [dʒɪ'ɔgrəfɪ] N geografia
geology [dʒɪ'ɔlədʒɪ] N geologia
geometry [dʒɪ'ɔmətrɪ] N geometria
geranium [dʒɪ'reɪnjəm] N gerânio
geriatric [dʒɛrɪ'ætrɪk] ADJ geriátrico
germ [dʒə:m] N micróbio, bacilo
German ['dʒə:mən] ADJ alemão(-mã) ▶ N alemão(-mã) *m/f*;

(*Ling*) alemão *m*; **German measles** N rubéola
Germany ['dʒəːmənɪ] N Alemanha
gesture ['dʒɛstjəʳ] N gesto

KEYWORD

get [gɛt] (*pt, pp* **got**, (*US*) *pp* **gotten**) VI **1** (*become, be*) ficar, tornar-se; **to get old/tired/cold** envelhecer/cansar-se/resfriar-se; **to get annoyed/bored** aborrecer-se/amuar-se; **to get drunk** embebedar-se; **to get dirty** sujar-se; **to get killed/married** ser morto/casar-se; **when do I get paid?** quando eu recebo?, quando eu vou ser pago?; **it's getting late** está ficando tarde
2 (*go*): **to get to/from** ir para/de; **to get home** chegar em casa
3 (*begin*) começar a; **to get to know sb** começar a conhecer alguém; **let's get going** *or* **started** vamos lá!
▸ MODAL AUX VB: **you've got to do it** você tem que fazê-lo
▸ VT **1**: **to get sth done** (*do*) fazer algo; (*have done*) mandar fazer algo; **to get one's hair cut** cortar o cabelo; **to get the car going** *or* **to go** fazer o carro andar; **to get sb to do sth** convencer alguém a fazer algo; **to get sth/sb ready** preparar algo/arrumar alguém
2 (*obtain*) ter; (*find*) achar; (*fetch*) buscar; **to get sth for sb** arranjar algo para alguém; (*fetch*) ir buscar algo para alguém; **get me Mr Harris, please** (*Tel*) pode chamar o Sr Harris, por favor; **can I get you a drink?** você está servido?
3 (*receive: present, letter*) receber; (*acquire: reputation, prize*) ganhar
4 (*catch*) agarrar; (*hit: target etc*) pegar; **to get sb by the arm/throat** agarrar alguém pelo braço/pela garganta; **get him!** pega ele!
5 (*take, move*) levar; **to get sth to sb** levar algo para alguém; **I can't get it in/out/through** não consigo enfiá-lo/tirá-lo/passá-lo; **do you think we'll get it through the door?** você acha que conseguiremos passar isto na porta?
6 (*plane, bus etc*) pegar, tomar; **where do I get the train to Birmingham?** onde eu pego o trem para Birmingham?
7 (*understand*) entender; (*hear*) ouvir; **I've got it** entendi; **I don't get your meaning** não entendo o que você quer dizer
8 (*have, possess*): **to have got** ter
get about VI (*news*) espalhar-se
get along VI (*agree*) entender-se; (*depart*) ir embora; (*manage*) = **get by**
get around = **get round**
get at VT FUS (*attack, criticize*) atacar; (*reach*) alcançar; **what are you getting at?** o que você está querendo dizer?
get away VI (*leave*) partir; (*escape*) escapar
get away with VT FUS conseguir fazer impunemente
get back VI (*return*) regressar, voltar ▸ VT receber de volta, recobrar
get by VI (*pass*) passar; (*manage*) virar-se
get down VI descer ▸ VT FUS abaixar ▸ VT (*object*) abaixar, descer; (*depress: person*) deprimir

get down to VT FUS (*work*) pôr-se a (fazer)
get in VI entrar; (*train*) chegar; (*arrive home*) voltar para casa
get into VT FUS entrar em; (*vehicle*) subir em; (*clothes*) pôr, vestir, enfiar; **to get into bed/a rage** meter-se na cama/ficar com raiva
get off VI (*from train etc*) saltar (BR), descer (PT); (*depart*) sair; (*escape*) escapar ▶ VT (*remove: clothes, stain*) tirar; (*send off*) mandar ▶ VT FUS (*train, bus*) saltar de (BR), sair de (PT)
get on VI (*at exam etc*): **how are you getting on?** como vai?; (*agree*): **to get on (with)** entender-se (com) ▶ VT FUS (*train etc*) subir em (BR), subir para (PT); (*horse*) montar em
get out VI (*of place, vehicle*) sair ▶ VT (*take out*) tirar
get out of VT FUS (*duty etc*) escapar de
get over VT FUS (*illness*) restabelecer-se de
get round VT FUS rodear; (*fig: person*) convencer
get through VI (*Tel*) completar a ligação
get through to VT FUS (*Tel*) comunicar-se com
get together VI (*people*) reunir-se ▶ VT reunir
get up VI levantar-se ▶ VT FUS levantar
get up to VT FUS (*reach*) chegar a; (BRIT: *prank etc*) fazer

getaway ['gɛtəweɪ] N fuga, escape *m*
ghastly ['gɑːstlɪ] ADJ horrível; (*building*) medonho; (*appearance*) horripilante; (*pale*) pálido
ghost [gəust] N fantasma *m*
giant ['dʒaɪənt] N gigante *m* ▶ ADJ gigantesco, gigante
gift [gɪft] N presente *m*, dádiva; (*ability*) dom *m*, talento; **gifted** ADJ bem-dotado; **gift shop**, (US) **gift store** N loja de presentes
gigabyte ['gɪgəbaɪt] N gigabyte *m*
gigantic [dʒaɪ'gæntɪk] ADJ gigantesco
giggle ['gɪgl] VI dar risadinha boba
gills [gɪlz] NPL (*of fish*) guelras *fpl*, brânquias *fpl*
gilt [gɪlt] ADJ dourado ▶ N dourado
gimmick ['gɪmɪk] N truque *m* or macete *m* (publicitário)
gin [dʒɪn] N gim *m*, genebra
ginger ['dʒɪndʒəʳ] N gengibre *m*
gipsy ['dʒɪpsɪ] N cigano
giraffe [dʒɪ'rɑːf] N girafa
girl [gəːl] N (*small*) menina (BR), rapariga (PT); (*young woman*) jovem *f*, moça; (*daughter*) filha; **girlfriend** N (*of girl*) amiga; (*of boy*) namorada; **Girl Guide** (BRIT) N bandeirante *f*
gist [dʒɪst] N essencial *m*

KEYWORD

give [gɪv] (*pt* **gave**, *pp* **given**) VT
1 (*hand over*) dar; **to give sb sth, give sth to sb** dar algo a alguém
2 (*used with n to replace a vb*): **to give a cry/sigh/push** *etc* dar um grito/suspiro/empurrão *etc*; **to give a speech/a lecture** fazer um discurso/uma palestra
3 (*tell, deliver: news, advice, message etc*) dar; **to give the right/wrong answer** dar a resposta certa/errada
4 (*supply, provide: opportunity, surprise, job etc*) dar; (*bestow: title, honour, right*) conceder; **the sun gives warmth and light** o sol fornece calor e luz

5 (*dedicate: time, one's life/attention*) dedicar; **she gave it all her attention** ela dedicou toda sua atenção a isto
6 (*organize*): **to give a party/dinner** *etc* dar uma festa/jantar *etc*
▸ VI **1** (*also*: **give way**: *break, collapse*) dar folga; **his legs gave beneath him** suas pernas bambearam; **the roof/floor gave as I stepped on it** o telhado/chão desabou quando eu pisei nele
2 (*stretch: fabric*) dar de si
give away VT (*money, opportunity*) dar; (*secret, information*) revelar
give back VT devolver
give in VI (*yield*) ceder ▸ VT (*essay etc*) entregar
give off VT (*heat, smoke*) soltar
give out VT (*distribute*) distribuir; (*make known*) divulgar
give up VI (*surrender*) desistir, dar-se por vencido ▸ VT (*job, boyfriend, habit*) renunciar a; (*idea, hope*) abandonar; **to give up smoking** deixar de fumar; **to give o.s. up** entregar-se
give way VI (*yield*) ceder; (*break, collapse: rope*) arrebentar; (*: ladder*) quebrar; (BRIT *Aut*) dar a preferência (BR), dar prioridade (PT)

glacier ['glæsɪəʳ] N glaciar *m*, geleira
glad [glæd] ADJ contente
gladly ['glædlɪ] ADV com muito prazer
glamorous ['glæmərəs] ADJ encantador(a), glamouroso
glamour ['glæməʳ] N encanto, glamour *m*
glance [glɑːns] N relance *m*, vista de olhos ▸ VI: **to ~ at** olhar (de relance); **glance off** VT FUS (*bullet*) ricochetear de
gland [glænd] N glândula
glare [glɛəʳ] N (*of anger*) olhar *m* furioso; (*of light*) luminosidade *f*; (*of publicity*) foco ▸ VI brilhar; **to ~ at** olhar furiosamente para;
glaring ADJ (*mistake*) notório
glass [glɑːs] N vidro, cristal *m*; (*for drinking*) copo; **glasses** NPL (*spectacles*) óculos *mpl*
glaze [gleɪz] VT (*door*) envidraçar; (*pottery*) vitrificar ▸ N verniz *m*
gleam [gliːm] VI brilhar
glide [glaɪd] VI deslizar; (*Aviat: birds*) planar; **glider** N (*Aviat*) planador *m*
glimmer ['glɪməʳ] N luz *f* trêmula; (*of interest, hope*) lampejo
glimpse [glɪmps] N vista rápida, vislumbre *m* ▸ VT vislumbrar, ver de relance
glint [glɪnt] VI cintilar
glisten ['glɪsn] VI brilhar
glitter ['glɪtəʳ] VI reluzir, brilhar
global ['gləubl] ADJ mundial;
globalization [gləubəlaɪ'zeɪʃən] N globalização *f*; **global warming** N aquecimento global
globe [gləub] N globo, esfera
gloom [gluːm] N escuridão *f*; (*sadness*) tristeza; **gloomy** ADJ escuro; (*sad*) triste
glorious ['glɔːrɪəs] ADJ (*weather*) magnífico; (*future*) glorioso
glory ['glɔːrɪ] N glória
gloss [glɔs] N (*shine*) brilho; (*also*: **~ paint**) pintura brilhante, esmalte *m*;
gloss over VT FUS encobrir
glossary ['glɔsərɪ] N glossário
glossy ['glɔsɪ] ADJ lustroso
glove [glʌv] N luva
glow [gləu] VI (*shine*) brilhar; (*fire*) arder

g

glucose ['glu:kəus] N glicose *f*
glue [glu:] N cola ▶ VT colar
GM ADJ ABBR (= *genetically modified*) geneticamente modificado; **GM crop** N plantação *f* geneticamente modificada; **GM foods** NPL alimentos *mpl* geneticamente modificados
gnaw [nɔ:] VT roer

KEYWORD

go [gəu] (*pt* **went**, *pp* **gone**, *pl* **goes**) VI **1** ir; (*travel, move*) viajar; **a car went by** um carro passou; **he has gone to Aberdeen** ele foi para Aberdeen
2 (*depart*) sair, ir embora
3 (*attend*) ir; **she went to university in Rio** ela fez universidade no Rio; **he goes to the local church** ele frequenta a igreja local
4 (*take part in an activity*) ir; **to go for a walk** ir passear
5 (*work*) funcionar; **the bell went just then** a campainha acabou de tocar
6 (*become*): **to go pale/mouldy** ficar pálido/mofado
7 (*be sold*): **to go for £10** ser vendido por £10
8 (*fit, suit*): **to go with** acompanhar, combinar com
9 (*be about to, intend to*): **he's going to do it** ele vai fazê-lo; **are you going to come?** você vem?
10 (*time*) passar
11 (*event, activity*) ser; **how did it go?** como foi?
12 (*be given*): **the job is to go to someone else** o emprego vai ser dado para outra pessoa
13 (*break*) romper-se; **the fuse went** o fusível queimou; **the leg of the chair went** a perna da cadeira quebrou
14 (*be placed*): **where does this cup go?** onde é que põe esta xícara?; **the milk goes in the fridge** pode guardar o leite na geladeira
▶ N **1** (*try*): **to have a go (at)** tentar
2 (*turn*) vez *f*
3 (*move*): **to be on the go** ter muito para fazer
go about VI (*also*: **go around**: *rumour*) espalhar-se ▶ VT FUS: **how do I go about this?** como é que eu faço isto?
go ahead VI (*make progress*) progredir; (*get going*) ir em frente
go along VI ir ▶ VT FUS ladear; **to go along with** concordar com
go away VI (*leave*) ir-se, ir embora
go back VI (*return*) voltar; (*go again*) ir de novo
go back on VT FUS (*promise*) faltar com
go by VI (*years, time*) passar ▶ VT FUS (*book, rule*) guiar-se por
go down VI (*descend*) descer, baixar; (*ship*) afundar; (*sun*) pôr-se ▶ VT FUS (*stairs, ladder*) descer
go for VT FUS (*fetch*) ir buscar; (*like*) gostar de; (*attack*) atacar
go in VI (*enter*) entrar
go in for VT FUS (*competition*) inscrever-se em; (*like*) gostar de
go into VT FUS (*enter*) entrar em; (*investigate*) investigar; (*embark on*) embarcar em
go off VI (*leave*) ir-se; (*food*) estragar, apodrecer; (*bomb, gun*) explodir; (*event*) realizar-se ▶ VT FUS (*person, place, food etc*) deixar de gostar de
go on VI (*continue*) seguir, continuar; (*happen*) acontecer, ocorrer
go out VI sair (*for entertainment*):

are you going out tonight? você vai sair hoje à noite?; (*couple*): **they went out for 3 years** eles namoraram durante 3 anos; (*fire, light*) apagar-se
go over VI (*ship*) soçobrar ▶ VT FUS (*check*) revisar
go round VI (*news, rumour*) circular
go through VT FUS (*town etc*) atravessar; (*search through*) vasculhar; (*examine*) percorrer de cabo a rabo
go up VI (*ascend*) subir; (*price, level*) aumentar
go without VT FUS passar sem

go-ahead ADJ empreendedor(a) ▶ N luz *f* verde
goal [gəul] N meta, alvo; (*Sport*) gol *m* (BR), golo (PT); **goalkeeper** N goleiro(-a) (BR), guarda-redes *m/f inv* (PT)
goat [gəut] N cabra
gobble ['gɔbl] VT (*also*: **~ down, ~ up**) engolir rapidamente, devorar
god [gɔd] N deus *m*; **G~** Deus; **godchild** *irreg* N afilhado(-a); **goddess** N deusa; **godfather** N padrinho; **godmother** N madrinha
goggles ['gɔglz] NPL óculos *mpl* de proteção
going ['gəuɪŋ] N (*conditions*) estado do terreno ▶ ADJ: **the ~ rate** tarifa corrente *or* em vigor
gold [gəuld] N ouro ▶ ADJ de ouro; **golden** ADJ (*made of gold*) de ouro; (*gold in colour*) dourado; **goldfish** N INV peixe-dourado *m*; **gold-plated** ADJ plaquê *inv*
golf [gɔlf] N golfe *m*; **golf ball** N bola de golfe; (*on typewriter*) esfera; **golf club** N clube *m* de golfe; (*stick*) taco; **golf course** N campo de golfe; **golfer** N jogador(a) *m/f* de golfe, golfista *m/f*
gone [gɔn] PP *of* **go**
gong [gɔŋ] N gongo
good [gud] ADJ bom/boa; (*kind*) bom, bondoso; (*well-behaved*) educado ▶ N bem *m*; **goods** NPL (*Comm*) mercadorias *fpl*; **~!** bom!; **to be ~ at** ser bom em; **to be ~ for** servir para; **it's ~ for you** faz-lhe bem; **a ~ deal (of)** muito; **a ~ many** muitos; **to make ~** reparar; **it's no ~ complaining** não adianta se queixar; **for ~** para sempre, definitivamente; **~ morning/afternoon!** bom dia/ boa tarde!; **~ evening!** boa noite!; **~ night!** boa noite!; **goodbye** EXCL até logo (BR), adeus (PT); **to say goodbye** despedir-se; **Good Friday** N Sexta-Feira Santa; **good-looking** ADJ bonito; **good-natured** ADJ (*person*) de bom gênio; (*pet*) de boa índole; **goodwill** N boa vontade *f*
Google® ['gu:gəl] VT, VI pesquisar no Google®
goose [gu:s] (*pl* **geese**) N ganso
gooseberry ['guzbərɪ] N groselha; **to play ~** (BRIT) ficar de vela
gorge [gɔ:dʒ] N desfiladeiro ▶ VT: **to ~ o.s. (on)** empanturrar-se (de)
gorgeous ['gɔ:dʒəs] ADJ magnífico, maravilhoso; (*person*) lindo
gorilla [gə'rɪlə] N gorila *m*
gosh [gɔʃ] (*inf*) EXCL puxa
gospel ['gɔspl] N evangelho
gossip ['gɔsɪp] N (*scandal*) fofocas *fpl* (BR), mexericos *mpl* (PT); (*chat*) conversa; (*scandalmonger*) fofoqueiro(-a) (BR), mexeriqueiro(-a) (PT) ▶ VI (*chat*) bater (um) papo (BR), cavaquear (PT)

got [gɔt] PT, PP *of* **get**
gotten ['gɔtn] (US) PP *of* **get**
govern ['gʌvən] VT governar; (*event*) controlar
government ['gʌvnmənt] N governo
governor ['gʌvənə^r] N governador(a) *m/f*; (*of school, hospital, jail*) diretor(a) *m/f*
gown [gaun] N vestido; (*of teacher, judge*) toga
GP N ABBR (*Med*) = **general practitioner**
GPS N ABBR (= *global positioning system*) GPS *m*
grab [græb] VT agarrar ▶ VI: **to ~ at** tentar agarrar
grace [greɪs] N (*Rel*) graça; (*gracefulness*) elegância, fineza ▶ VT (*honour*) honrar; (*adorn*) adornar; **5 days' ~** um prazo de 5 dias; **graceful** ADJ elegante, gracioso; **gracious** ['greɪʃəs] ADJ gracioso, afável
grade [greɪd] N (*quality*) classe *f*, qualidade *f*; (*degree*) grau *m*; (*US: Sch*) série *f*, classe ▶ VT classificar; **grade crossing** (US) N passagem *f* de nível; **grade school** (US) N escola primária
gradient ['greɪdɪənt] N declive *m*
gradual ['grædjuəl] ADJ gradual, gradativo; **gradually** ADV gradualmente, gradativamente, pouco a pouco
graduate [*n* 'grædjuɪt, *vi* 'grædjueɪt] N graduado, licenciado; (US) diplomado do colégio ▶ VI formar-se, licenciar-se; **graduation** [grædju'eɪʃən] N formatura
graffiti [grə'fi:tɪ] N, NPL pichações *fpl*
graft [grɑ:ft] N (*Agr, Med*) enxerto; (BRIT *inf*) trabalho pesado; (*bribery*) suborno ▶ VT enxertar
grain [greɪn] N grão *m*; (*no pl: cereals*) cereais *mpl*; (*in wood*) veio, fibra
gram [græm] N grama *m*
grammar ['græmə^r] N gramática; **grammar school** N (BRIT) ≈ liceo
gramme [græm] N = **gram**
gran [græn] (BRIT *inf*) N vó *f*
grand [grænd] ADJ grandioso; (*inf: wonderful*) ótimo; **granddad** N vovô *m*; **granddaughter** N neta; **grandfather** N avô *m*; **grandma** ['grænmɑ:] N avó *f*, vovó *f*; **grandmother** N avó *f*; **grandpa** ['grænpɑ:] N = **granddad**; **grandparents** NPL avós *mpl*; **grand piano** N piano de cauda; **grandson** N neto
granite ['grænɪt] N granito
granny ['grænɪ] (*inf*) N avó *f*, vovó *f*
grant [grɑ:nt] VT (*concede*) conceder; (*a request etc*) anuir a; (*admit*) admitir ▶ N (*Sch*) bolsa; (*Admin*) subvenção *f*, subsídio; **to take sth for ~ed** dar algo por certo
grape [greɪp] N uva
grapefruit ['greɪpfru:t] N toranja, grapefruit *m* (BR)
graph [grɑ:f] N gráfico; **graphic** ['græfɪk] ADJ gráfico; **graphics** N (*art*) artes *fpl* gráficas ▶ NPL (*drawings*) desenhos *mpl*
grasp [grɑ:sp] VT agarrar, segurar; (*understand*) compreender, entender ▶ N mão *f*; (*understanding*) compreensão *f*
grass [grɑ:s] N grama (BR), relva (PT); **grasshopper** N gafanhoto
grate [greɪt] N (*fireplace*) lareira ▶ VI ranger ▶ VT (*Culin*) ralar
grateful ['greɪtful] ADJ agradecido, grato

grater ['greɪtə^r] N ralador *m*
gratitude ['grætɪtju:d] N agradecimento
grave [greɪv] N cova, sepultura ▶ ADJ sério; (*mistake*) grave
gravestone ['greɪvstəun] N lápide *f*
graveyard ['greɪvjɑ:d] N cemitério
gravity ['grævɪtɪ] N (*Phys*) gravidade *f*; (*seriousness*) seriedade *f*, gravidade *f*
gravy ['greɪvɪ] N molho (de carne)
gray [greɪ] (*US*) ADJ = **grey**
graze [greɪz] VI pastar ▶ VT (*touch lightly*) roçar; (*scrape*) raspar ▶ N (*Med*) esfoladura, arranhadura
grease [gri:s] N (*fat*) gordura; (*lubricant*) graxa, lubrificante *m* ▶ VT (*dish*) untar; (*brakes etc*) lubrificar, engraxar; **greasy** ADJ gordurento, gorduroso; (*skin, hair*) oleoso
great [greɪt] ADJ grande; (*inf*) genial; (*pain, heat*) forte; (*important*) importante; **Great Britain** N Grã-Bretanha

> A Grã-Bretanha, **Great Britain** ou **Britain** em inglês, designa a maior das ilhas britânicas e, portanto, engloba a Escócia e o País de Gales. Junto com a Irlanda, a ilha de Man e as ilhas Anglo-normandas, a Grã-Bretanha forma as ilhas Britânicas, ou *British Isles*. Reino Unido, em inglês *United Kingdom* ou *UK*, é o nome oficial da entidade política que compreende a Grã-Bretanha e a Irlanda do Norte.

great: great-grandfather N bisavô *m*; **great-grandmother** N bisavó *f*; **greatly** ADV imensamente, muito
Greece [gri:s] N Grécia
greed [gri:d] N (*also*: **~iness**) avidez *f*, cobiça; **greedy** ADJ avarento; (*for food*) guloso
Greek [gri:k] ADJ grego ▶ N grego(-a); (*Ling*) grego
green [gri:n] ADJ verde; (*inexperienced*) inexperiente, ingênuo ▶ N verde *m*; (*stretch of grass*) gramado (BR), relvado (PT); (*on golf course*) green *m*; **greens** NPL (*vegetables*) verduras *fpl*; **greenhouse** N estufa; **greenhouse effect** N: **the greenhouse effect** o efeito estufa; **greenhouse gas** N gás *m* de efeito estufa
Greenland ['gri:nlənd] N Groenlândia
green tax N imposto ecológico
greet [gri:t] VT acolher; (*news*) receber; **greeting** N acolhimento; **greeting card, greetings card** N cartão *m* comemorativo
grew [gru:] PT *of* **grow**
grey [greɪ], (*US*) **gray** ADJ cinzento; (*dismal*) sombrio; **grey-haired** ADJ grisalho; **greyhound** N galgo; **grey vote** N voto dos idosos
grid [grɪd] N grade *f*; (*Elec*) rede *f*; **gridlock** N (*traffic jam*) paralisia do trânsito
grief [gri:f] N dor *f*, pesar *m*
grievance ['gri:vəns] N motivo de queixa, agravo
grieve [gri:v] VI sofrer ▶ VT dar pena a, afligir; **to ~ for** chorar por
grill [grɪl] N (*on cooker*) grelha; (*also*: **mixed ~**) prato de grelhados ▶ VT (BRIT) grelhar; (*question*) interrogar cerradamente
grille [grɪl] N grade *f*; (*Aut*) grelha

grim [grɪm] ADJ desagradável; (*unattractive*) feio; (*stern*) severo
grime [graɪm] N sujeira (BR), sujidade *f* (PT)
grin [grɪn] N sorriso largo ▶ VI: **to ~ (at)** dar um sorriso largo (para)
grind [graɪnd] (*pt, pp* **ground**) VT triturar; (*coffee, pepper etc*) moer; (*make sharp*) afiar; (*US: meat*) picar ▶ N (*work*) trabalho (repetitivo e maçante)
grip [grɪp] N (*of hands*) aperto; (*handle*) punho; (*of tyre, shoe*) aderência; (*holdall*) valise *f* ▶ VT agarrar; (*attention*) prender; **to come** *or* **get to ~s with** arcar com
gripping ['grɪpɪŋ] ADJ absorvente, emocionante
grit [grɪt] N areia, grão *m* de areia; (*courage*) coragem *f* ▶ VT (*road*) pôr areia em; **to ~ one's teeth** cerrar os dentes
groan [grəun] N gemido ▶ VI gemer
grocer ['grəusəʳ] N dono(-a) de mercearia; **grocer's, grocer's shop** N mercearia; **grocery** N mercearia; **groceries** NPL comestíveis *mpl*
groin [grɔɪn] N virilha
groom [gru:m] N cavalariço; (*also*: **bride~**) noivo ▶ VT (*horse*) tratar; (*fig*): **to ~ sb for sth** preparar alguém para algo; **well-~ed** bem-posto
groove [gru:v] N ranhura, entalhe *m*
grope [grəup] VI: **to ~ for** procurar às cegas
gross [grəus] ADJ (*flagrant*) grave; (*vulgar*) vulgar; (: *building*) de mau-gosto; (*Comm*) bruto
ground [graund] PT, PP *of* **grind** ▶ N terra, chão *m*; (*Sport*) campo; (*land*) terreno; (*reason: gen pl*) motivo, razão *f*; (*US: also*: **~ wire**) (ligação *f* à) terra, fio-terra *m* ▶ VT (*plane*) manter em terra; (*US Elec*) ligar à terra; **grounds** NPL (*of coffee etc*) borra; (*gardens etc*) jardins *mpl*, parque *m*; **on the ~** no chão; **to the ~** por terra; **groundsheet** (BRIT) N capa impermeável; **groundwork** N base *f*, preparação *f*
group [gru:p] N grupo; (*also*: **pop ~**) conjunto ▶ VT (*also*: **~ together**) agrupar ▶ VI (*also*: **~ together**) agrupar-se
grouse [graus] N INV (*bird*) tetraz *m*, galo-silvestre *m* ▶ VI (*complain*) queixar-se, resmungar
grovel ['grɔvl] VI: **to ~ (before)** abaixar-se (diante de)
grow [grəu] (*pt* **grew**, *pp* **grown**) VI crescer; (*increase*) aumentar; (*develop*): **to ~ (out of/from)** originar-se (de) ▶ VT plantar, cultivar; (*beard*) deixar crescer; **to ~ rich/weak** enriquecer(-se)/ enfraquecer-se; **grow up** VI crescer, fazer-se homem/mulher
growl [graul] VI rosnar
grown [grəun] PP *of* **grow**
grown-up N adulto(-a), pessoa mais velha
growth [grəuθ] N crescimento; (*increase*) aumento; (*Med*) abcesso, tumor *m*
grub [grʌb] N larva, lagarta; (*inf: food*) comida, rango (BR)
grubby ['grʌbɪ] ADJ encardido
grudge [grʌdʒ] N motivo de rancor ▶ VT: **to ~ sb sth** dar algo a alguém de má vontade, invejar algo a alguém; **to bear sb a ~ for sth** guardar rancor de alguém por algo
gruelling ['gruəlɪŋ], (*US*) **grueling** ADJ duro, árduo
gruesome ['gru:səm] ADJ horrível

grumble ['grʌmbl] VI resmungar, bufar
grumpy ['grʌmpɪ] ADJ rabugento
grunt [grʌnt] VI grunhir
guarantee [gærən'ti:] N garantia ▶VT garantir
guard [gɑ:d] N guarda; (*one person*) guarda *m*; (BRIT *Rail*) guarda-freio; (*on machine*) dispositivo de segurança; (*also*: **fire~**) guarda-fogo ▶VT (*protect*): **to ~ (against)** proteger (contra); (*prisoner*) vigiar; **to be on one's ~** estar prevenido; **guard against** VT FUS prevenir-se contra; **guardian** N protetor(a) *m/f*; (*of minor*) tutor(a) *m/f*
Guatemala [gwɔtə'mɑ:lə] N Guatemala
guerrilla [gə'rɪlə] N guerrilheiro(-a)
guess [gɛs] VT, VI (*estimate*) avaliar, conjeturar; (*correct answer*) adivinhar; (*US*) achar, supor ▶N suposição *f*, conjetura; **to take** *or* **have a ~** adivinhar, chutar (*inf*)
guest [gɛst] N convidado(-a); (*in hotel*) hóspede *m/f*
guidance ['gaɪdəns] N conselhos *mpl*
guide [gaɪd] N (*person*) guia *m/f*; (*book, fig*) guia *m*; (BRIT: *also*: **girl ~**) escoteira ▶VT guiar; **guidebook** N guia *m*; **guide dog** N cão *m* de guia; **guided tour** N visita guiada; **guidelines** NPL (*advice*) orientação *f*
guilt [gɪlt] N culpa; **guilty** ADJ culpado
guinea pig ['gɪnɪpɪg] N porquinho-da-Índia *m*, cobaia; (*fig*) cobaia
guitar [gɪ'tɑ:ʳ] N violão *m*
gulf [gʌlf] N golfo; (*abyss*: *also fig*) abismo
gull [gʌl] N gaivota
gulp [gʌlp] VI engolir em seco ▶VT (*also*: **~ down**) engolir
gum [gʌm] N (*Anat*) gengiva; (*glue*) goma; (*also*: **~ drop**) bala de goma; (*also*: **chewing-~**) chiclete *m* (BR), pastilha elástica (PT) ▶VT colar
gun [gʌn] N (*gen*) arma (de fogo); (*revolver*) revólver *m*; (*small*) pistola; (*rifle*) espingarda; (*cannon*) canhão *m*; **gunfire** N tiroteio; **gunman** *irreg* N pistoleiro; **gunpoint** N: **at gunpoint** sob a ameaça de uma arma; **gunpowder** N pólvora; **gunshot** N tiro (de arma de fogo)
gust [gʌst] N (*of wind*) rajada
gut [gʌt] N intestino, tripa; **guts** NPL (*Anat*) entranhas *fpl*; (*inf*: *courage*) coragem *f*, raça (*inf*)
gutter ['gʌtəʳ] N (*of roof*) calha; (*in street*) sarjeta
guy [gaɪ] N (*also*: **~rope**) corda; (*inf*: *man*) cara *m* (BR), tipo (PT); **Guy Fawkes' Night** N *ver nota*

> A **Guy Fawkes' Night**, também chamada de *bonfire night*, é a ocasião em que se comemora o fracasso da conspiração (a *Gunpowder Plot*) contra James I e o Parlamento, em 5 de novembro de 1605. Um dos conspiradores, Guy Fawkes, foi surpreendido no porão do Parlamento quando estava prestes a atear fogo a explosivos. Todo ano, no dia 5 de novembro, as crianças preparam antecipadamente um boneco de Guy Fawkes e pedem às pessoas que passam na rua *a penny for the Guy* (uma moedinha para o Guy), com o qual compram fogos de artifício.

gym [dʒɪm] N (*also*: **gymnasium**) ginásio; (*also*: **gymnastics**) ginástica
gymnast ['dʒɪmnæst] N ginasta *m/f*
gymnastics [dʒɪm'næstɪks] N ginástica
gynaecologist [gaɪnɪ'kɔlədʒɪst], (US) **gynecologist** N ginecologista *m/f*
gypsy ['dʒɪpsɪ] N = **gipsy**

h

haberdashery ['hæbə'dæʃərɪ] (BRIT) N armarinho
habit ['hæbɪt] N hábito, costume *m*; (*addiction*) vício; (*Rel*) hábito
hack [hæk] VT (*cut*) cortar; (*chop*) talhar ▸ N (*pej*: *writer*) escrevinhador(a) *m/f*; **hacker** N (*Comput*) hacker *m*
had [hæd] PT, PP *of* **have**
haddock ['hædək] (**haddocks** *or pl* **haddock**) N hadoque *m* (BR), eglefim *m* (PT)
hadn't ['hædnt] = **had not**
haemorrhage ['hɛmərɪdʒ], (US) **hemorrhage** N hemorragia
haemorrhoids ['hɛmərɔɪdz], (US) **hemorrhoids** NPL hemorróidas *fpl*
haggle ['hægl] VI pechinchar, regatear
hail [heɪl] N granizo; (*of objects*) chuva; (*of criticism*) torrente *f* ▸ VT (*greet*) cumprimentar, saudar; (*call*) chamar ▸ VI chover granizo; **hailstone** N pedra de granizo

hair [hɛəʳ] N (*of human*) cabelo; (*of animal, on legs*) pelo; **to do one's ~** pentear-se; **hairbrush** N escova de cabelo; **haircut** N corte *m* de cabelo; **hairdo** N penteado; **hairdresser** N cabeleireiro(-a); **hairdresser's** N cabeleireiro; **hair dryer** N secador *m* de cabelo; **hair gel** N gel *m* para o cabelo; **hair spray** N laquê *m* (BR), laca (PT); **hairstyle** N penteado; **hairy** ADJ cabeludo, peludo; (*inf: situation*) perigoso

hake [heɪk] (*pl* **hakes** *or* **hake**) N abrótea

half [hɑːf] (*pl* **halves**) N metade *f* ▸ ADJ meio ▸ ADV meio, pela metade; **~ a pound** meia libra; **two and a ~** dois e meio; **~ a dozen** meia-dúzia; **to cut sth in ~** cortar algo ao meio; **half-hearted** ADJ irresoluto, indiferente; **half-hour** N meia hora; **half-price** ADJ, ADV pela metade do preço; **half term** (BRIT) N (*Sch*) *dias de folga no meio do semestre*; **half-time** N meio tempo; **halfway** ADV a meio caminho; (*in time*) no meio

hall [hɔːl] N (*for concerts*) sala; (*entrance way*) hall *m*, entrada

hallmark ['hɔːlmɑːk] N (*also fig*) marca

hall of residence (BRIT) (*pl* **halls of residence**) N residência universitária

Hallowe'en ['hæləu'iːn] N Dia *m* das Bruxas (*31 de outubro*)

> Segundo a tradição, **Hallowe'en** é a noite dos fantasmas e dos bruxos. Na Escócia e nos Estados Unidos, sobretudo (bem menos na Inglaterra), as crianças, para festejar o **Hallowe'en**, se fantasiam e batem de porta em porta pedindo prendas (chocolates, maçãs etc).

hallway ['hɔːlweɪ] N hall *m*, entrada

halo ['heɪləu] N (*of saint etc*) auréola

halt [hɔːlt] N parada (BR), paragem *f* (PT) ▸ VI parar ▸ VT deter; (*process*) interromper

halve [hɑːv] VT (*divide*) dividir ao meio; (*reduce by half*) reduzir à metade

halves [hɑːvz] NPL *of* **half**

ham [hæm] N presunto, fiambre *m* (PT)

hamburger ['hæmbəːgəʳ] N hambúrguer *m*

hammer ['hæməʳ] N martelo ▸ VT martelar ▸ VI (*on door*) bater insistentemente

hammock ['hæmək] N rede *f*

hamper ['hæmpəʳ] VT dificultar, atrapalhar ▸ N cesto

hamster ['hæmstəʳ] N hamster *m*

hand [hænd] N mão *f*; (*of clock*) ponteiro; (*writing*) letra; (*of cards*) cartas *fpl*; (*worker*) trabalhador *m* ▸ VT dar, passar; **to give** *or* **lend sb a ~** dar uma mãozinha a alguém, dar uma ajuda a alguém; **at ~** à mão, disponível; **in ~** livre; (*situation*) sob controle; **to be on ~** (*person*) estar disponível; (*emergency services*) estar num estado de prontidão; **on the one ~ ..., on the other ~ ...** por um lado ..., por outro (lado) ...; **hand in** VT entregar; **hand out** VT distribuir; **hand over** VT entregar; (*powers etc*) transmitir; **handbag** N bolsa; **handbook** N manual *m*; **handbrake** N freio (BR) *or* travão *m* (PT) de mão; **handcuffs** NPL

h

algemas *fpl*; **handful** N punhado; (*of people*) grupo
handicap ['hændɪkæp] N (*Med*) incapacidade *f*; (*disadvantage*) desvantagem *f*; (*Sport*) handicap *m* ▸ VT prejudicar; **mentally/ physically ~ped** deficiente mental/físico
handkerchief ['hæŋkətʃɪf] N lenço
handle ['hændl] N (*of door etc*) maçaneta; (*of cup etc*) asa; (*of knife etc*) cabo; (*for winding*) manivela ▸ VT manusear; (*deal with*) tratar de; (*treat: people*) lidar com; **"~ with care"** "cuidado — frágil"; **to fly off the ~** perder as estribeiras;
handlebar N, **handlebars** ['hɑːndlbɑːz] NPL guidom *m* (BR), guidão *m* (PT)
handmade ['hændmeɪd] ADJ feito a mão
handout ['hændaut] N (*money, food*) doação *f*; (*leaflet*) folheto; (*at lecture*) apostila
hands-free kit ['hændzfriː-] N viva-voz *m*
handsome ['hænsəm] ADJ bonito; (*building*) elegante; (*profit*) considerável
handwriting ['hændraɪtɪŋ] N letra, caligrafia
handy ['hændɪ] ADJ (*close at hand*) à mão; (*useful*) útil; (*skilful*) habilidoso, hábil
hang [hæŋ] (*pt, pp* **hung**) VT pendurar; (*criminal*: *pt, pp* **hanged**) enforcar ▸ VI estar pendurado; (*hair, drapery*) cair ▸ N (*inf*): **to get the ~ of (doing) sth** pegar o jeito de (fazer) algo; **hang about** VI vadiar, vagabundear; **hang around** VI = **hang about**; **hang on** VI (*wait*) esperar; **hang up** VT (*coat*) pendurar ▸ VI (*Tel*) desligar; **to ~ up on sb** bater o telefone na cara de alguém
hanger ['hæŋər] N cabide *m*
hang-gliding N voo livre
hangover ['hæŋəuvər] N ressaca
happen ['hæpən] VI acontecer; **as it ~s ...** acontece que ...
happily ['hæpɪlɪ] ADV (*luckily*) felizmente; (*cheerfully*) alegremente
happiness ['hæpɪnɪs] N felicidade *f*
happy ['hæpɪ] ADJ feliz; (*cheerful*) contente; **to be ~ (with)** estar contente (com); **to be ~ to do** (*willing*) estar disposto a fazer; **~ birthday!** feliz aniversário
harass ['hærəs] VT importunar;
harassment N perseguição *f*
harbour ['hɑːbər], (US) **harbor** N porto ▸ VT (*hope etc*) abrigar; (*hide*) esconder
hard [hɑːd] ADJ duro; (*difficult*) difícil; (*work*) árduo; (*person*) severo, cruel; (*facts*) verdadeiro ▸ ADV (*work*) muito, diligentemente; (*think, try*) seriamente; **to look ~ at** olhar firme *or* fixamente para; **no ~ feelings!** sem ressentimentos!; **to be ~ of hearing** ser surdo; **to be ~ done by** ser tratado injustamente;
hardback N livro de capa dura;
hard disk N (*Comput*) disco rígido;
hard drive N (*Comput*) disco rígido;
harden VT endurecer; (*steel*) temperar; (*fig*) tornar insensível ▸ VI endurecer-se
hardly ['hɑːdlɪ] ADV (*scarcely*) apenas; (*no sooner*) mal; **~ ever** quase nunca
hardship ['hɑːdʃɪp] N privação *f*
hardware ['hɑːdwɛər] N ferragens *fpl*; (*Comput*) hardware *m*
hard-working ADJ trabalhador(a); (*student*) aplicado
hardy ['hɑːdɪ] ADJ forte; (*plant*) resistente

hare [hɛəʳ] N lebre *f*
harm [hɑːm] N mal *m*; (*damage*) dano ▶VT (*person*) fazer mal a, prejudicar; (*thing*) danificar; **out of ~'s way** a salvo; **harmful** ADJ prejudicial, nocivo; **harmless** ADJ inofensivo
harmony [ˈhɑːmənɪ] N harmonia
harness [ˈhɑːnɪs] N (*for horse*) arreios *mpl*; (*for child*) correia; (*safety harness*) correia de segurança ▶VT (*horse*) arrear, pôr arreios em; (*resources*) aproveitar
harp [hɑːp] N harpa ▶VI: **to ~ on about** bater sempre na mesma tecla sobre
harsh [hɑːʃ] ADJ (*life*) duro
harvest [ˈhɑːvɪst] N colheita ▶VT colher
has [hæz] VB *see* **have**
hash [hæʃ] N (*symbol*) sustenido; **hashtag** [ˈhæʃtæg] N (*on Twitter*) hashtag *f*
hasn't [ˈhæznt] = **has not**
hassle [ˈhæsl] (*inf*) N complicação *f*
haste [heɪst] N pressa; **hasten** [ˈheɪsn] VT acelerar ▶VI: **to hasten to do sth** apressar-se em fazer algo; **hastily** ADV depressa; **hasty** ADJ apressado; (*rash*) precipitado
hat [hæt] N chapéu *m*
hatch [hætʃ] N (*Naut*: *also*: **~way**) escotilha; (*also*: **service ~**) comunicação *f* entre a cozinha e a sala de jantar ▶VI sair do ovo, chocar
hate [heɪt] VT odiar, detestar ▶N ódio; **hatred** [ˈheɪtrɪd] N ódio
haul [hɔːl] VT puxar ▶N (*of fish*) redada; (*of stolen goods etc*) pilhagem *f*, presa
haunt [hɔːnt] VT (*subj*: *ghost*) assombrar; (: *problem, memory*) perseguir ▶N reduto; (*haunted house*) casa mal-assombrada

KEYWORD

have [hæv] (*pt, pp* **had**) AUX VB
1 (*gen*) ter; **to have arrived/gone/eaten/slept** ter chegado/ido/comido/dormido; **he has been kind/promoted** ele foi bondoso/promovido; **having finished** *or* **when he had finished, he left** quando ele terminou, foi embora
2 (*in tag questions*): **you've done it, haven't you?** você fez isto, não foi?; **he hasn't done it, has he?** ele não fez isto, fez?
3 (*in short questions and answers*): **you've made a mistake — no I haven't/so I have** você fez um erro — não, eu não fiz/sim, eu fiz; **I've been there before, have you?** eu já estive lá, e você?
▶MODAL AUX VB (*be obliged*): **to have (got) to do sth** ter que fazer algo; **I haven't got** *or* **I don't have to wear glasses** eu não preciso usar óculos
▶VT **1** (*possess*) ter; **he has (got) blue eyes/dark hair** ele tem olhos azuis/cabelo escuro
2 (*referring to meals etc*): **to have breakfast** tomar café (BR), tomar o pequeno almoço (PT); **to have lunch/dinner** almoçar/jantar; **to have a drink/a cigarette** tomar um drinque/fumar um cigarro
3 (*receive, obtain etc*): **may I have your address?** pode me dar seu endereço?; **you can have it for 5 pounds** você pode levá-lo por 5 libras; **to have a baby** dar à luz (BR), ter um nenê *or* bebê (PT)
4 (*maintain, allow*): **he will have it**

that he is right ele vai insistir que ele está certo; **I won't have it/this nonsense!** não vou aguentar isso/ este absurdo!; **we can't have that** não podemos permitir isto
5: **to have sth done** mandar fazer algo; **to have one's hair cut** ir cortar o cabelo; **to have sb do sth** mandar alguém fazer algo
6 (*experience, suffer*): **to have a cold/ flu** estar resfriado (BR) *or* constipado (PT)/com gripe; **she had her bag stolen/her arm broken** ela teve sua bolsa roubada/ ela quebrou o braço; **to have an operation** fazer uma operação
7 (+ *n: take, hold etc*): **to have a swim/walk/bath/rest** ir nadar/ passear/tomar um banho/ descansar; **let's have a look** vamos dar uma olhada; **to have a party** fazer uma festa
8 (*inf: dupe*): **he's been had** ele comprou gato por lebre
have out VT: **to have it out with sb** (*settle a problem*) explicar-se com alguém

haven ['heɪvn] N porto; (*fig*) abrigo, refúgio
haven't ['hævnt] = **have not**
havoc ['hævək] N destruição *f*; **to play ~ with** (*fig*) estragar
hawk [hɔːk] N falcão *m*
hay [heɪ] N feno; **hay fever** N febre *f* do feno; **haystack** N palheiro
hazard ['hæzəd] N perigo, risco ▶VT aventurar, arriscar; **hazard warning lights** NPL (*Aut*) pisca-alerta *m*
haze [heɪz] N névoa
hazelnut ['heɪzlnʌt] N avelã *f*
hazy ['heɪzɪ] ADJ nublado; (*idea*) confuso

he [hiː] PRON ele; **he who ...** quem ..., aquele que ...
head [hɛd] N cabeça; (*of table*) cabeceira; (*of queue*) frente *f*; (*of organization*) chefe *m/f*; (*of school*) diretor(a) *m/f* ▶VT (*list*) encabeçar; (*group*) liderar; **~s or tails** cara ou coroa; **~ first** de cabeça; **~ over heels** de pernas para o ar; **~ over heels in love** apaixonadíssimo; **to ~ the ball** cabecear a bola; **head for** VT FUS dirigir-se a; (*disaster*) estar procurando; **headache** N dor *f* de cabeça; **heading** N título, cabeçalho; **headlamp** (BRIT) N = **headlight**; **headlight** N farol *m*; **headline** N manchete *f*; **head office** N matriz *f*; **headphones** NPL fones *mpl* de ouvido; **headquarters** NPL sede *f*; (*Mil*) quartel *m* general; **headroom** N (*in car*) espaço (para a cabeça); (*under bridge*) vão *m* livre; **headscarf** *irreg* N lenço de cabeça
heal [hiːl] VT curar ▶VI cicatrizar
health [hɛlθ] N saúde *f*; **good ~!** saúde!; **health care** N assistência médica; **healthy** ADJ (*person*) saudável; (*air, walk*) sadio; (*economy*) próspero, forte
heap [hiːp] N pilha, montão *m* ▶VT (*plate*) encher; **~s (of)** (*inf*) um monte (de)
hear [hɪə[r]] (*pt, pp* **heard**) VT ouvir; (*listen to*) escutar; (*news*) saber; **to ~ about** ouvir falar de; **to ~ from sb** ter notícias de alguém; **hearing** N (*sense*) audição *f*; (*Jur*) audiência; **hearing aid** N aparelho para a surdez
hearse [həːs] N carro fúnebre
heart [hɑːt] N coração *m*; (*of problem, city*) centro; **hearts** NPL (*Cards*) copas *fpl*; **to lose/take ~**

perder o ânimo/criar coragem; **at ~** no fundo; **by ~** (*learn, know*) de cor; **heart attack** N ataque *m* de coração; **heartbeat** N batida do coração; **heartbroken** ADJ: **to be heartbroken** estar inconsolável; **heartburn** N azia

hearty ['hɑːtɪ] ADJ (*person*) energético; (*laugh*) animado; (*appetite*) bom/boa; (*welcome*) sincero; (*dislike*) absoluto

heat [hiːt] N calor *m*; (*excitement*) ardor *m*; (*Sport: also:* **qualifying ~**) (prova) eliminatória ▶ VT esquentar; (*room, house*) aquecer; **heat up** VI aquecer-se, esquentar ▶ VT esquentar; **heated** ADJ aquecido; (*fig*) acalorado; **heater** N aquecedor *m*

heather ['hɛðəʳ] N urze *f*

heating ['hiːtɪŋ] N aquecimento, calefação *f*

heaven ['hɛvn] N céu *m*, paraíso; **heavenly** ADJ celestial; (*Rel*) divino

heavily ['hɛvɪlɪ] ADV pesadamente; (*drink, smoke*) excessivamente; (*sleep, depend*) profundamente

heavy ['hɛvɪ] ADJ pesado; (*work*) duro; (*responsibility*) grande; (*rain, meal*) forte; (*drinker, smoker*) inveterado; (*weather*) carregado

Hebrew ['hiːbruː] ADJ hebreu/hebreia ▶ N (*Ling*) hebraico

Hebrides ['hɛbrɪdiːz] NPL: **the ~** as (ilhas) Hébridas

hectic ['hɛktɪk] ADJ agitado

he'd [hiːd] = **he would;** = **he had**

hedge [hɛdʒ] N cerca viva, sebe *f* ▶ VI dar evasivas ▶ VT: **to ~ one's bets** (*fig*) resguardar-se

hedgehog ['hɛdʒhɔg] N ouriço

heed [hiːd] VT (*also:* **take ~ of**) prestar atenção a

heel [hiːl] N (*of shoe*) salto; (*of foot*) calcanhar *m* ▶ VT (*shoe*) pôr salto em

hefty ['hɛftɪ] ADJ (*person*) robusto; (*parcel*) pesado; (*profit*) alto

height [haɪt] N (*of person*) estatura; (*of building, tree*) altura; (*of plane*) altitude *f*; (*high ground*) monte *m*; (*fig: of power*) auge *m*; (*: of luxury*) máximo; (*: of stupidity*) cúmulo; **heighten** VT elevar; (*fig*) aumentar

heir [ɛəʳ] N herdeiro; **heiress** N herdeira

held [hɛld] PT, PP *of* **hold**

helicopter ['hɛlɪkɔptəʳ] N helicóptero

hell [hɛl] N inferno; **~!** (*inf*) droga!

he'll [hiːl] = **he will;** = **he shall**

hello [hə'ləu] EXCL oi! (BR), olá! (PT); (*surprise*) ora essa!

helmet ['hɛlmɪt] N capacete *m*

help [hɛlp] N ajuda; (*charwoman*) faxineira ▶ VT ajudar; **~!** socorro!; **~ yourself** sirva-se; **he can't ~ it** não tem culpa; **help desk** N atendimento telefônico; **helper** N ajudante *m/f*; **helpful** ADJ prestativo; (*advice*) útil; **helping** N porção *f*; **helpless** ADJ (*incapable*) incapaz; (*defenceless*) indefeso; **helpline** N disque-ajuda *m* (BR), linha de apoio (PT)

hem [hɛm] N bainha ▶ VT embainhar; **hem in** VT cercar, encurralar

hemorrhage ['hɛmərɪdʒ] (US) N = **haemorrhage**

hemorrhoids ['hɛmərɔɪdz] (US) NPL = **haemorrhoids**

hen [hɛn] N galinha; (*female bird*) fêmea

hence [hɛns] ADV daí, portanto; **2 years ~** daqui a 2 anos

her [hə:ʳ] PRON (*direct*) a; (*indirect*) lhe; (*stressed, after prep*) ela ▸ ADJ seu/sua, dela; *see also* **me, my**

herb [hə:b] N erva

herd [hə:d] N rebanho

here [hɪəʳ] ADV aqui; (*at this point*) nesse ponto; **~!** (*present*) presente!; **~ is/are** aqui está/estão; **~ he/she is!** aqui está ele/ela!

heritage ['hɛrɪtɪdʒ] N patrimônio

hernia ['hə:nɪə] N hérnia

hero ['hɪərəu] (*pl* **heroes**) N herói *m*; (*of book, film*) protagonista *m*

heroin ['hɛrəuɪn] N heroína

heroine ['hɛrəuɪn] N heroína; (*of book, film*) protagonista

heron ['hɛrən] N garça

herring ['hɛrɪŋ] (*pl* **herrings** *or* **herring**) N arenque *m*

hers [hə:z] PRON (o) seu/(a) sua, (o/a) dela; *see also* **mine¹**

herself [hə:'sɛlf] PRON (*reflexive*) se; (*emphatic*) ela mesma; (*after prep*) si (mesma); *see also* **oneself**

he's [hi:z] = **he is**; = **he has**

hesitant ['hɛzɪtənt] ADJ hesitante, indeciso

hesitate ['hɛzɪteɪt] VI hesitar; **hesitation** [hɛzɪ'teɪʃən] N hesitação *f*, indecisão *f*

heterosexual ['hɛtərəu'sɛksjuəl] ADJ heterossexual

heyday ['heɪdeɪ] N: **the ~ of** o auge *or* apogeu de

hi [haɪ] EXCL oi!

hibernate ['haɪbəneɪt] VI hibernar

hiccup ['hɪkʌp] VI soluçar ▸ NPL: **~s** soluço; **to have (the) ~s** estar com soluço

hide [haɪd] (*pt* **hid**, *pp* **hidden**) N (*skin*) pele *f* ▸ VT esconder, ocultar; (*view*) obscurecer ▸ VI: **to ~ (from sb)** esconder-se *or* ocultar-se (de alguém)

hideous ['hɪdɪəs] ADJ horrível

hiding ['haɪdɪŋ] N (*beating*) surra; **to be in ~** (*concealed*) estar escondido

hi-fi ['haɪfaɪ] N alta-fidelidade *f*; (*system*) som *m* ▸ ADJ de alta-fidelidade

high [haɪ] ADJ alto, (*number*) grande; (*price*) alto, elevado; (*wind*) forte; (*voice*) agudo; (*opinion*) ótimo; (*principles*) nobre ▸ ADV alto, a grande altura; **it is 20 m ~** tem 20 m de altura; **~ in the air** nas alturas; **highchair** N cadeira alta (para criança); **higher education** N ensino superior; **high jump** N (*Sport*) salto em altura; **highlands** NPL: **the Highlands** (*in Scotland*) a Alta Escócia; **highlight** N (*fig*) ponto alto; (*in hair*) mecha ▸ VT realçar, ressaltar; **highly** ADV: **highly paid** muito bem pago; **to speak highly of** falar elogiosamente de; **high-rise** ADJ alto; **high school** N (BRIT) escola secundária; (US) científico

> Uma **high school** é um estabelecimento de ensino secundário. Nos Estados Unidos, existem a *Junior High School*, que equivale aproximadamente aos dois últimos anos do primeiro grau, e a *Senior High School*, que corresponde ao segundo grau. Na Grã-Bretanha, esse termo às vezes é utilizado para as escolas secundárias.

high street (BRIT) N rua principal

highway (US) N estrada; (*main road*) rodovia

hijack ['haɪdʒæk] VT sequestrar; **hijacker** N sequestrador(a) *m/f* (de avião)

hike [haɪk] VI caminhar ▶ N caminhada, excursão *f* a pé; **hiker** N caminhante *m/f*, andarilho(-a)
hilarious [hɪˈlɛərɪəs] ADJ hilariante
hill [hɪl] N colina; (*high*) montanha; (*slope*) ladeira, rampa; **hillside** N vertente *f*; **hilly** ADJ montanhoso
him [hɪm] PRON (*direct*) o; (*indirect*) lhe; (*stressed, after prep*) ele; *see also* **me**; **himself** PRON (*reflexive*) se; (*emphatic*) ele mesmo; (*after prep*) si (mesmo); *see also* **oneself**
hinder [ˈhɪndəʳ] VT retardar
hindsight [ˈhaɪndsaɪt] N: **with (the benefit of) ~** em retrospecto
Hindu [ˈhɪnduː] ADJ hindu
hinge [hɪndʒ] N dobradiça ▶ VI (*fig*): **to ~ on** depender de
hint [hɪnt] N (*suggestion*) indireta; (*advice*) dica; (*sign*) sinal *m* ▶ VT: **to ~ that** insinuar que ▶ VI: **to ~ at** fazer alusão a
hip [hɪp] N quadril *m*
hippopotamus [hɪpəˈpɔtəməs] (*pl* **hippopotamuses** *or* **hippopotami**) N hipopótamo
hire [ˈhaɪəʳ] VT (BRIT: *car, equipment*) alugar; (*worker*) contratar ▶ N aluguel *m*; **for ~** aluga-se; (*taxi*) livre; **hire purchase** (BRIT) N compra a prazo
his [hɪz] PRON (o) seu/(a) sua, (o/a) dele ▶ ADJ seu/sua, dele; *see also* **my, mine¹**
hiss [hɪs] VI (*snake, fat*) assoviar; (*gas*) silvar; (*boo*) vaiar
historic [hɪˈstɔrɪk], **historical** [hɪˈstɔrɪkl] ADJ histórico
history [ˈhɪstərɪ] N história
hit [hɪt] (*pt, pp* **hit**) VT bater em; (*target*) acertar, alcançar; (*car*) bater em, colidir com; (*fig: affect*) atingir ▶ N golpe *m*; (*success*) sucesso; (*internet visit*) visita; **to ~ it off with sb** dar-se bem com alguém
hitch [hɪtʃ] VT (*fasten*) atar, amarrar; (*also*: **~ up**) levantar ▶ N (*difficulty*) dificuldade *f*; **to ~ a lift** pegar carona (BR), arranjar uma boleia (PT)
hitch-hike VI pegar carona (BR), andar à boleia (PT); **hitch-hiker** N carona *m/f* (BR), viajante *m/f* à boleia (PT)
hi-tech ADJ tecnologicamente avançado ▶ N alta tecnologia
HIV ABBR: **~-negative/-positive** HIV negativo/positivo
hive [haɪv] N colmeia; **hive off** (*inf*) VT transferir
hoard [hɔːd] N provisão *f*; (*of money*) tesouro ▶ VT acumular
hoarse [hɔːs] ADJ rouco
hoax [həuks] N trote *m*
hob [hɔb] N *parte de cima do fogão*
hobble [ˈhɔbl] VI coxear
hobby [ˈhɔbɪ] N hobby *m*, passatempo predileto
hobo [ˈhəubəu] (US) N vagabundo
hockey [ˈhɔkɪ] N hóquei *m*
hog [hɔg] N porco ▶ VT (*fig*) monopolizar; **to go the whole ~** ir até o fim
hoist [hɔɪst] VT içar
hold [həuld] (*pt, pp* **held**) VT segurar; (*contain*) conter; (*have*) ter; (*meeting*) realizar; (*detain*) deter; (*consider*): **to ~ sb responsible (for sth)** responsabilizar alguém (por algo) ▶ VI (*withstand pressure*) resistir; (*be valid*) ser válido ▶ N (*fig*) influência, domínio; (*of ship*) porão *m*; (*of plane*) compartimento para cargo; **~ the line!** (*Tel*) não desligue!; **to ~ one's own** (*fig*) virar-se, sair-se

bem; **to catch** *or* **get (a) ~ of** agarrar, pegar; **hold back** VT reter; (*secret*) manter, guardar; **hold down** VT (*person*) segurar; (*job*) manter; **hold off** VT (*enemy*) afastar, repelir; **hold on** VI agarrar-se; (*wait*) esperar; **~ on!** espera aí!; (*Tel*) não desligue!; **hold on to** VT FUS agarrar-se a; (*keep*) guardar, ficar com; **hold out** VT estender ▶ VI (*resist*) resistir; **hold up** VT (*raise*) levantar; (*support*) apoiar; (*delay*) atrasar; (*rob*) assaltar; **holdall** (BRIT) N bolsa de viagem; **holder** N (*of ticket*) portador(a) *m/f*; (*of record*) detentor(a) *m/f*; (*of office, title etc*) titular *m/f*; **hold-up** N (*robbery*) assalto; (*delay*) demora; (BRIT: *in traffic*) engarrafamento

hole [həul] N buraco; (*small, in sock etc*) furo ▶ VT esburacar

holiday ['hɔlədɪ] N (BRIT: *vacation*) férias *fpl*; (*day off*) dia *m* de folga; (*public holiday*) feriado; **to be on ~** estar de férias; **holiday camp** (BRIT) N colônia de férias; **holiday-maker** (BRIT) N pessoa (que está) de férias; **holiday resort** N local *m* de férias

Holland ['hɔlənd] N Holanda

hollow ['hɔləu] ADJ oco, vazio; (*cheeks*) côncavo; (*eyes*) fundo; (*sound*) surdo; (*laugh, claim*) falso ▶ N (*in ground*) cavidade *f*, depressão *f* ▶ VT: **to ~ out** escavar

holly ['hɔlɪ] N azevinho

holy ['həulɪ] ADJ sagrado; (*person*) santo; bento

home [həum] N casa, lar *m*; (*country*) pátria; (*institution*) asilo ▶ CPD caseiro, doméstico; (*Econ, Pol*) nacional, interno; (*Sport: team*) de casa; (*: game*) no próprio campo ▶ ADV (*direction*) para casa; (*right in: nail etc*) até o fundo; **at ~** em casa; **make yourself at ~** fique à vontade; **home address** N endereço residencial; **homeland** N terra (natal); **homeless** ADJ sem casa, desabrigado; **homely** ADJ (*simple*) simples *inv*; **home-made** ADJ caseiro; **Home Office** (BRIT) N Ministério do Interior; **home page** N (*Comput*) página inicial; **Home Secretary** (BRIT) N Ministro(a) do Interior; **homesick** ADJ: **to be homesick** estar com saudades (do lar); **home town** N cidade *f* natal; **homework** N dever *m* de casa

homoeopathic [həumɪə'pæθɪk], (US) **homeopathic** ADJ homeopático

homosexual [hɔməu'sɛksjuəl] ADJ, N homossexual *m/f*

Honduras [hɔn'djuərəs] N Honduras *m* (*no article*)

honest ['ɔnɪst] ADJ (*truthful*) franco; (*trustworthy*) honesto; (*sincere*) sincero; **honestly** ADV honestamente; **honesty** N honestidade *f*, sinceridade *f*

honey ['hʌnɪ] N mel *m*; **honeymoon** N lua-de-mel *f*; (*trip*) viagem *f* de lua-de-mel

honorary ['ɔnərərɪ] ADJ (*unpaid*) não remunerado; (*duty, title*) honorário

honour ['ɔnə^r], (US) **honor** VT honrar ▶ N honra; **honourable** ADJ honrado

hood [hud] N capuz *m*; (*of cooker*) tampa; (BRIT *Aut*) capota; (US *Aut*) capô *m*

hoof [hu:f] (*pl* **hooves**) N casco, pata

hook [huk] N gancho; (*on dress*) colchete *m*; (*for fishing*) anzol *m* ▶ VT prender com gancho (*or* colchete); (*fish*) fisgar

hooligan ['hu:lɪgən] N desordeiro(-a), bagunceiro(-a)
hoop [hu:p] N arco
hooray [hu:'reɪ] EXCL = **hurrah**
hoot [hu:t] VI (*Aut*) buzinar; (*siren*) tocar; (*owl*) piar
hooves [hu:vz] NPL *of* **hoof**
hop [hɔp] VI saltar, pular; (*on one foot*) pular num pé só
hope [həup] VI esperar ▶ N esperança; **I ~ so/not** espero que sim/não; **hopeful** ADJ (*person*) otimista, esperançoso; (*situation*) promissor(a); **hopefully** ADV esperançosamente; **hopefully, they'll come back** é de esperar *or* esperamos que voltem; **hopeless** ADJ desesperado, irremediável; (*useless*) inútil
horizon [hə'raɪzn] N horizonte *m*; **horizontal** [hɔrɪ'zɔntl] ADJ horizontal
horn [hɔ:n] N corno, chifre *m*; (*material*) chifre; (*Mus*) trompa; (*Aut*) buzina
horoscope ['hɔrəskəup] N horóscopo
horrendous [hə'rɛndəs] ADJ horrendo
horrible ['hɔrɪbl] ADJ horrível; (*terrifying*) terrível
horrid ['hɔrɪd] ADJ horrível
horror ['hɔrə^r] N horror *m*; **horror film** N filme *m* de terror
horse [hɔ:s] N cavalo; **horseback**: **on horseback** ADJ, ADV a cavalo; **horse chestnut** N castanha-da-índia; **horsepower** N cavalo-vapor *m*; **horse-racing** N corridas *fpl* de cavalo, turfe *m*
hose [həuz] N (*also*: **~pipe**) mangueira
hospital ['hɔspɪtl] N hospital *m*
hospitality [hɔspɪ'tælɪtɪ] N hospitalidade *f*
host [həust] N anfitrião *m*; (*TV, Radio*) apresentador(a) *m/f*; (*Rel*) hóstia; (*large number*): **a ~ of** uma multidão de
hostage ['hɔstɪdʒ] N refém *m/f*
hostel ['hɔstl] N albergue *m*, abrigo; (*also*: **youth ~**) albergue da juventude
hostess ['həustɪs] N anfitriã *f*; (BRIT: *air hostess*) aeromoça (BR), hospedeira de bordo (PT); (*TV, Radio*) apresentadora
hostile ['hɔstaɪl] ADJ hostil
hostility [hɔ'stɪlɪtɪ] N hostilidade *f*
hot [hɔt] ADJ quente; (*as opposed to only warm*) muito quente; (*spicy*) picante; (*fierce*) ardente; **to be ~** (*person*) estar com calor; (*thing, weather*) estar quente; **hot dog** N cachorro-quente *m*
hotel [həu'tɛl] N hotel *m*
hotspot ['hɔtspɔt] N (*Comput*: *also*: **wireless ~**) hotspot *m* (*local público com acesso à Internet sem fio*)
hound [haund] VT acossar, perseguir ▶ N cão *m* de caça, sabujo
hour ['auə^r] N hora; **hourly** ADJ de hora em hora; (*rate*) por hora
house [*n* haus, *vt* hauz] N (*gen, firm*) casa; (*Pol*) câmara; (*Theatre*) assistência, lotação *f* ▶ VT (*person*) alojar; (*collection*) abrigar; **on the ~** (*fig*) por conta da casa; **household** N família; (*house*) casa; **housekeeper** N governanta; **housekeeping** N (*work*) trabalhos *mpl* domésticos; (*money*) economia doméstica; **housewife** *irreg* N dona de casa; **housework** N trabalhos *mpl* domésticos; **housing** N (*provision*) alojamento;

(*houses*) residências *fpl*; **housing development** N conjunto residencial; **housing estate** (BRIT) N = **housing development**

hover ['hɔvəʳ] VI pairar; **hovercraft** N aerobarco

KEYWORD

how [hau] ADV **1** (*in what way*) como; **how was the film?** que tal o filme?; **how are you?** como vai?
2 (*to what degree*) quanto; **how much milk/many people?** quanto de leite/quantas pessoas?; **how long have you been here?** há quanto tempo você está aqui?; **how old are you?** quantos anos você tem?; **how tall is he?** qual é a altura dele?; **how lovely/awful!** que ótimo/terrível!

however [hau'ɛvəʳ] ADV de qualquer modo; (+ *adj*) por mais ... que; (*in questions*) como ▶ CONJ no entanto, contudo

howl [haul] VI uivar

H.P. (BRIT) N ABBR = **hire purchase**

h.p. ABBR (*Aut*: = *horsepower*) CV

HQ N ABBR (= *headquarters*) QG *m*

HTML N ABBR (= *Hypertext Mark-up Language*) HTML *f*

huddle ['hʌdl] VI: **to ~ together** aconchegar-se

huff [hʌf] N: **in a ~** com raiva

hug [hʌg] VT abraçar; (*thing*) agarrar, prender

huge [hju:dʒ] ADJ enorme, imenso

hull [hʌl] N (*of ship*) casco

hum [hʌm] VT cantarolar ▶ VI cantarolar; (*insect, machine etc*) zumbir

human ['hju:mən] ADJ humano ▶ N (*also*: **~ being**) ser *m* humano

humane [hju:'meɪn] ADJ humano

humanitarian [hju:mænɪ'tɛərɪən] ADJ humanitário

humanity [hju:'mænɪtɪ] N humanidade *f*

human rights NPL direitos *mpl* humanos

humble ['hʌmbl] ADJ humilde ▶ VT humilhar

humid ['hju:mɪd] ADJ úmido

humiliate [hju:'mɪlɪeɪt] VT humilhar

humorous ['hju:mərəs] ADJ humorístico; (*person*) engraçado

humour ['hju:məʳ], (US) **humor** N humorismo, senso de humor; (*mood*) humor *m* ▶ VT fazer a vontade de

hump [hʌmp] N (*in ground*) elevação *f*; (*camel's*) corcova, giba; (*deformity*) corcunda

hunch [hʌntʃ] N (*premonition*) pressentimento, palpite *m*

hundred ['hʌndrəd] NUM cem; (*before lower numbers*) cento; **~s of people** centenas de pessoas; **hundredth** NUM centésimo

hung [hʌŋ] PT, PP *of* **hang**

Hungary ['hʌŋgərɪ] N Hungria

hunger ['hʌŋgəʳ] N fome *f* ▶ VI: **to ~ for** (*desire*) desejar ardentemente

hungry ['hʌŋgrɪ] ADJ faminto, esfomeado; (*keen*): **~ for** (*fig*) ávido de, ansioso por; **to be ~** estar com fome

hunt [hʌnt] VT buscar, perseguir; (*Sport*) caçar ▶ VI caçar ▶ N caça, caçada; **hunter** N caçador(a) *m/f*; **hunting** N caça

hurdle ['hə:dl] N (*Sport*) barreira; (*fig*) obstáculo

hurl [hə:l] VT arremessar, lançar; (*abuse*) gritar

hurrah [hu'rɑ:] EXCL oba!, viva!

hurray [hu'reɪ] EXCL = **hurrah**
hurricane ['hʌrɪkən] N furacão *m*
hurry ['hʌrɪ] N pressa ▸ VI (*also*: **~ up**) apressar-se ▸ VT (*also*: **~ up**: *person*) apressar; (: *work*) acelerar; **to be in a ~** estar com pressa
hurt [hə:t] (*pt, pp* **hurt**) VT machucar; (*injure*) ferir; (*fig*) magoar ▸ VI doer
husband ['hʌzbənd] N marido, esposo
hush [hʌʃ] N silêncio, quietude *f* ▸ VT silenciar, fazer calar; **~!** silêncio!, psiu!; **hush up** VT abafar, encobrir
husky ['hʌskɪ] ADJ rouco ▸ N cão *m* esquimó
hut [hʌt] N cabana, choupana; (*shed*) alpendre *m*
hyacinth ['haɪəsɪnθ] N jacinto
hydrofoil ['haɪdrəfɔɪl] N hidrofoil *m*, aliscafo
hydrogen ['haɪdrədʒən] N hidrogênio
hygiene ['haɪdʒi:n] N higiene *f*
hymn [hɪm] N hino
hype [haɪp] (*inf*) N tititi *m*, falatório
hyperlink ['haɪpəlɪŋk] N hiperlink *m*
hypermarket ['haɪpəma:kɪt] (BRIT) N hipermercado
hyphen ['haɪfn] N hífen *m*
hypnotize ['hɪpnətaɪz] VT hipnotizar
hypocrite ['hɪpəkrɪt] N hipócrita *m/f*; **hypocritical** ADJ hipócrita
hysterical [hɪ'stɛrɪkl] ADJ histérico; (*funny*) hilariante; **hysterics** NPL (*nervous*) crise *f* histérica; (*laughter*) ataque *m* de riso; **to be in** *or* **have hysterics** ter uma crise histérica

I

I [aɪ] PRON eu ▸ ABBR (= *island, isle*) I
ice [aɪs] N gelo; (*ice cream*) sorvete *m* ▸ VT (*cake*) cobrir com glacê ▸ VI (*also*: **~ over, ~ up**) gelar; **iceberg** N iceberg *m*; **ice cream** N sorvete *m* (BR), gelado (PT); **ice cube** N pedra de gelo; **ice hockey** N hóquei *m* sobre o gelo
Iceland ['aɪslənd] N Islândia
ice lolly (BRIT) N picolé *m*
ice rink N pista de gelo, rinque *m*
icing ['aɪsɪŋ] N (*Culin*) glacê *m*; **icing sugar** (BRIT) N açúcar *m* glacê
icon ['aɪkɔn] N (*gen, Comput*) ícone *m*
ICT N ABBR (= *Information and Communication(s) Technology*) TIC *f*
icy ['aɪsɪ] ADJ gelado
I'd [aɪd] = **I would**; = **I had**
idea [aɪ'dɪə] N ideia
ideal [aɪ'dɪəl] N ideal *m* ▸ ADJ ideal
identical [aɪ'dɛntɪkl] ADJ idêntico
identification [aɪdɛntɪfɪ'keɪʃən] N identificação *f*; **means of ~** documentos pessoais

identify [aɪ'dɛntɪfaɪ] VT identificar
identity [aɪ'dɛntɪtɪ] N identidade *f*; **identity card** N carteira de identidade; **identity theft** N roubo de identidade
idiom ['ɪdɪəm] N expressão *f* idiomática; (*style of speaking*) idioma *m*, linguagem *f*
idiot ['ɪdɪət] N idiota *m/f*
idle ['aɪdl] ADJ ocioso; (*lazy*) preguiçoso; (*unemployed*) desempregado; (*pointless*) inútil, vão/vã ▶ VI (*machine*) funcionar com a transmissão desligada; **idle away** VT: **to ~ away the time** perder *or* desperdiçar tempo
idol ['aɪdl] N ídolo
i.e. ABBR (= *id est*) i.e., isto é

KEYWORD

if [ɪf] CONJ **1** (*conditional use*) se; **if necessary** se necessário; **if I were you** se eu fôsse você
2 (*whenever*) quando
3 (*although*): **(even) if** mesmo que
4 (*whether*) se
5: **if so/not** sendo assim/do contrário; **if only** se pelo menos; *see also* **as**

ignition [ɪg'nɪʃən] N (*Aut*) ignição *f*; **to switch on/off the ~** ligar/desligar o motor
ignorant ['ɪgnərənt] ADJ ignorante; **to be ~ of** ignorar
ignore [ɪg'nɔːʳ] VT (*person*) não fazer caso de; (*fact*) não levar em consideração, ignorar
ill [ɪl] ADJ doente; (*harmful: effects*) nocivo ▶ N mal *m* ▶ ADV: **to speak/think ~ of sb** falar/pensar mal de alguém; **to take** *or* **be taken ~** ficar doente
I'll [aɪl] = **I will; = I shall**
illegal [ɪ'liːgl] ADJ ilegal
illegible [ɪ'lɛdʒɪbl] ADJ ilegível
illegitimate [ɪlɪ'dʒɪtɪmət] ADJ ilegítimo
illiterate [ɪ'lɪtərət] ADJ analfabeto
illness ['ɪlnɪs] N doença
illuminate [ɪ'luːmɪneɪt] VT iluminar, clarear
illusion [ɪ'luːʒən] N ilusão *f*
illustrate ['ɪləstreɪt] VT ilustrar; (*point*) exemplificar; **illustration** [ɪlə'streɪʃən] N ilustração *f*; (*example*) exemplo; (*explanation*) esclarecimento
I'm [aɪm] = **I am**
image ['ɪmɪdʒ] N imagem *f*
imaginary [ɪ'mædʒɪnərɪ] ADJ imaginário
imagination [ɪmædʒɪ'neɪʃən] N imaginação *f*; (*inventiveness*) inventividade *f*
imagine [ɪ'mædʒɪn] VT imaginar
imbalance [ɪm'bæləns] N desigualdade *f*
imitate ['ɪmɪteɪt] VT imitar; **imitation** [ɪmɪ'teɪʃən] N imitação *f*; (*copy*) cópia; (*mimicry*) mímica
immaculate [ɪ'mækjulət] ADJ impecável; (*Rel*) imaculado
immature [ɪmə'tjuəʳ] ADJ imaturo; (*fruit*) verde
immediate [ɪ'miːdɪət] ADJ imediato; (*pressing*) urgente, premente; (*neighbourhood, family*) próximo; **immediately** ADV imediatamente; **immediately next to** bem junto a
immense [ɪ'mɛns] ADJ imenso; (*importance*) enorme
immerse [ɪ'məːs] VT submergir; **to be ~d in** (*fig*) estar absorto em
immigrant ['ɪmɪgrənt] N imigrante *m/f*
immigration [ɪmɪ'greɪʃən] N imigração *f*

imminent ['ɪmɪnənt] ADJ iminente
immoral [ɪ'mɔrl] ADJ imoral
immortal [ɪ'mɔ:tl] ADJ imortal
immune [ɪ'mju:n] ADJ: **~ to** imune a, imunizado contra; **immune system** N sistema *m* imunológico
impact ['ɪmpækt] N impacto (BR), impacte *m* (PT)
impair [ɪm'pɛə^r] VT prejudicar
impartial [ɪm'pɑ:ʃl] ADJ imparcial
impatience [ɪm'peɪʃəns] N impaciência
impatient [ɪm'peɪʃənt] ADJ impaciente; **to get** *or* **grow ~** impacientar-se
impeccable [ɪm'pɛkəbl] ADJ impecável
impending [ɪm'pɛndɪŋ] ADJ iminente, próximo
imperative [ɪm'pɛrətɪv] ADJ (*tone*) imperioso, obrigatório; (*necessary*) indispensável ▶ N (*Ling*) imperativo
imperfect [ɪm'pə:fɪkt] ADJ imperfeito; (*goods etc*) defeituoso ▶ N (*Ling*: *also*: **~ tense**) imperfeito
imperial [ɪm'pɪərɪəl] ADJ imperial
impersonal [ɪm'pə:sənl] ADJ impessoal
impersonate [ɪm'pə:səneɪt] VT fazer-se passar por, personificar; (*Theatre*) imitar
implement [*n* 'ɪmplɪmənt, *vt* 'ɪmplɪmɛnt] N instrumento, ferramenta; (*for cooking*) utensílio ▶ VT efetivar
implicit [ɪm'plɪsɪt] ADJ implícito; (*complete*) absoluto
imply [ɪm'plaɪ] VT (*mean*) significar; (*hint*) dar a entender que
impolite [ɪmpə'laɪt] ADJ indelicado, mal-educado
import [*vt* ɪm'pɔ:t, *n*, *cpd* 'ɪmpɔ:t] VT importar ▶ N importação *f*; (*article*) mercadoria importada
importance [ɪm'pɔ:təns] N importância
important [ɪm'pɔ:tənt] ADJ importante; **it's not ~** não tem importância, não importa
impose [ɪm'pəuz] VT impor ▶ VI: **to ~ on sb** abusar de alguém; **imposing** ADJ imponente
impossible [ɪm'pɔsɪbl] ADJ impossível; (*situation*) inviável; (*person*) insuportável
impotent ['ɪmpətənt] ADJ impotente
impoverished [ɪm'pɔvərɪʃt] ADJ empobrecido; (*land*) esgotado
impractical [ɪm'præktɪkl] ADJ pouco prático
impress [ɪm'prɛs] VT impressionar; (*mark*) imprimir; **to ~ sth on sb** inculcar algo em alguém
impression [ɪm'prɛʃən] N impressão *f*; **to be under the ~ that** estar com a impressão de que
impressive [ɪm'prɛsɪv] ADJ impressionante
imprison [ɪm'prɪzn] VT encarcerar
improbable [ɪm'prɔbəbl] ADJ improvável; (*story*) inverossímil (BR), inverosímil (PT)
improper [ɪm'prɔpə^r] ADJ (*unsuitable*) impróprio; (*dishonest*) desonesto
improve [ɪm'pru:v] VT melhorar ▶ VI melhorar; (*pupils*) progredir; **improvement** N melhora; progresso
improvise ['ɪmprəvaɪz] VT, VI improvisar
impulse ['ɪmpʌls] N impulso, ímpeto; (*Elec*) impulso; **to act on ~** agir sem pensar *or* num impulso

KEYWORD

in [ɪn] PREP **1** (*indicating place, position*) em; **in the house/garden** na casa/no jardim; **I have the money in my hand** estou com o dinheiro na mão; **in here/there** aqui dentro/lá dentro
2 (*with place names: of town, country, region*) em; **in London** em Londres; **in England/Japan/Canada/the United States** na Inglaterra/no Japão/no Canadá/nos Estados Unidos; **in Rio** no Rio
3 (*indicating time: during*) em; **in spring/autumn** na primavera/no outono; **in 1988** em 1988; **in May** em maio; **I'll see you in July** até julho; **in the morning** de manhã; **at 4 o'clock in the afternoon** às 4 da tarde
4 (*indicating time: in the space of*) em; **I did it in 3 hours/days** fiz isto em 3 horas/dias; **in 2 weeks, in 2 weeks' time** daqui a 2 semanas
5 (*indicating manner etc*): **in a loud/soft voice** em voz alta/numa voz suave; **written in pencil/ink** escrito a lápis/à caneta; **in English/Portuguese** em inglês/português; **the boy in the blue shirt** o menino de camisa azul
6 (*indicating circumstances*): **in the sun** ao *or* sob o sol; **in the rain** na chuva; **a rise in prices** um aumento nos preços
7 (*indicating mood, state*): **in tears** aos prantos; **in anger/despair** com raiva/desesperado; **in good condition** em boas condições
8 (*with ratios, numbers*): **1 in 10** 1 em 10, 1 em cada 10; **20 pence in the pound** vinte pênis numa libra; **they lined up in twos** eles se alinharam dois a dois
9 (*referring to people, works*) em
10 (*indicating profession etc*): **to be in teaching/publishing** ser professor/trabalhar numa editora
11 (*after superl*): **the best pupil in the class** o melhor aluno da classe; **the biggest/smallest in Europe** o maior/menor na Europa
12 (*with present participle*): **in saying this** ao dizer isto
▶ ADV: **to be in** (*person: at home*) estar em casa; (*: at work*) estar no trabalho; (*fashion*) estar na moda; (*ship, plane, train*): **it's in** chegou; **is he in?** ele está?; **to ask sb in** convidar alguém para entrar; **to run/limp** *etc* **in** entrar correndo/mancando *etc*
▶ N: **the ins and outs** (*of proposal, situation etc*) os cantos e recantos, os pormenores

in. ABBR = **inch**
inability [ɪnə'bɪlɪtɪ] N: **~ (to do)** incapacidade *f* (de fazer)
inaccurate [ɪn'ækjurət] ADJ inexato, impreciso
inadequate [ɪn'ædɪkwət] ADJ insuficiente; (*person*) impróprio
inadvertently [ɪnəd'vəːtntlɪ] ADV inadvertidamente, sem querer
inappropriate [ɪnə'prəuprɪət] ADJ inadequado; (*word, expression*) impróprio
inbox ['ɪnbɔks] N (*Comput*) caixa de entrada; (*US: for papers*) cesta para correspondência de entrada
incapable [ɪn'keɪpəbl] ADJ incapaz
incense [*n* 'ɪnsɛns, *vt* ɪn'sɛns] N incenso ▶ VT (*anger*) exasperar, enraivecer
incentive [ɪn'sɛntɪv] N incentivo
inch [ɪntʃ] N polegada (*= 25 mm; 12 in a foot*); **to be within an ~ of** estar a

um passo de; **he didn't give an ~** ele não cedeu nem um milímetro; **inch forward** VI avançar palmo a palmo

incident ['ɪnsɪdnt] N incidente *m*, evento

inclination [ɪnklɪ'neɪʃən] N (*tendency*) tendência; (*disposition*) inclinação *f*

incline [*n* 'ɪnklaɪn, *vt, vi* ɪn'klaɪn] N inclinação *f*, ladeira ▶ VT curvar, inclinar ▶ VI inclinar-se; **to be ~d to** tender a, ser propenso a

include [ɪn'klu:d] VT incluir

including [ɪn'klu:dɪŋ] PREP inclusive

inclusive [ɪn'klu:sɪv] ADJ incluído, incluso; **~ of** incluindo

income ['ɪŋkʌm] N (*earnings*) renda, rendimentos *mpl*; (*unearned*) renda; **income tax** N imposto de renda (BR), imposto complementar (PT)

incoming ['ɪnkʌmɪŋ] ADJ (*flight, passenger*) de chegada; (*mail*) de entrada; (*government, tenant*) novo

incompetent [ɪn'kɔmpɪtənt] ADJ incompetente

incomplete [ɪnkəm'pli:t] ADJ incompleto; (*unfinished*) por terminar

inconsistent [ɪnkən'sɪstnt] ADJ inconsistente; **~ with** incompatível com

inconvenience [ɪnkən'vi:njəns] N (*quality*) inconveniência; (*problem*) inconveniente *m* ▶ VT incomodar

inconvenient [ɪnkən'vi:njənt] ADJ inconveniente, incômodo; (*time, place*) inoportuno

incorporate [ɪn'kɔ:pəreɪt] VT incorporar; (*contain*) compreender

incorrect [ɪnkə'rɛkt] ADJ incorreto

increase [*n* 'ɪnkri:s, *vi, vt* ɪn'kri:s] N aumento ▶ VI, VT aumentar

incredible [ɪn'krɛdɪbl] ADJ inacreditável; (*enormous*) incrível

incur [ɪn'kə:ʳ] VT incorrer em; (*expenses*) contrair

indecent [ɪn'di:snt] ADJ indecente

indeed [ɪn'di:d] ADV de fato; (*certainly*) certamente; (*furthermore*) aliás; **yes ~!** claro que sim!

indefinitely [ɪn'dɛfɪnɪtlɪ] ADV indefinidamente

independence [ɪndɪ'pɛndns] N independência; **Independence Day** N *ver nota*

> O dia da Independência **Independence Day** é a festa nacional dos Estados Unidos. Todo dia 4 de julho os americanos comemoram a adoção, em 1776, da declaração de Independência escrita por Thomas Jefferson que proclamava a separação das 13 colônias americanas da Grã-Bretanha.

independent [ɪndɪ'pɛndnt] ADJ independente; (*inquiry*) imparcial

index ['ɪndɛks] N (*pl* **indexes**) (*in book*) índice *m*; (*in library etc*) catálogo; (*pl* **indices**) (*ratio, sign*) índice *m*, expoente *m*

India ['ɪndɪə] N Índia; **Indian** ADJ, N (*from India*) indiano(-a); (*American, Brazilian*) índio(-a)

indicate ['ɪndɪkeɪt] VT (*show*) sugerir; (*point to*) indicar; **indication** [ɪndɪ'keɪʃən] N indício, sinal *m*; **indicative** [ɪn'dɪkətɪv] ADJ indicativo ▶ N (*Ling*) indicativo; **to be indicative of sth** ser sintomático de algo; **indicator** N indicador *m*; (*Aut*) pisca-pisca *m*

i

indices ['ɪndɪsiːz] NPL *of* **index**
indifferent [ɪn'dɪfrənt] ADJ indiferente; (*quality*) medíocre
indigenous [ɪn'dɪdʒɪnəs] ADJ indígena, nativo
indigestion [ɪndɪ'dʒɛstʃən] N indigestão *f*
indignant [ɪn'dɪgnənt] ADJ: **to be ~ about sth/with sb** estar indignado com algo/alguém, indignar-se de algo/alguém
indirect [ɪndɪ'rɛkt] ADJ indireto
individual [ɪndɪ'vɪdjuəl] N indivíduo ▶ ADJ individual, (*personal*) pessoal; (*characteristic*) particular
Indonesia [ɪndə'niːzɪə] N Indonésia
indoor ['ɪndɔːʳ] ADJ (*inner*) interno, interior; (*inside*) dentro de casa; (*swimming pool*) coberto; (*games, sport*) de salão; **indoors** ADV em lugar fechado
induce [ɪn'djuːs] VT (*Med*) induzir; (*bring about*) causar, produzir
indulge [ɪn'dʌldʒ] VT (*desire*) satisfazer; (*whim*) condescender com; (*person*) comprazer; (*child*) fazer a vontade de ▶ VI: **to ~ in** entregar-se a, satisfazer-se com; **indulgent** ADJ indulgente
industrial [ɪn'dʌstrɪəl] ADJ industrial
industry ['ɪndəstrɪ] N indústria; (*diligence*) aplicação *f*, diligência
inefficient [ɪnɪ'fɪʃənt] ADJ ineficiente
inequality [ɪnɪ'kwɔlɪtɪ] N desigualdade *f*
inevitable [ɪn'ɛvɪtəbl] ADJ inevitável; **inevitably** ADV inevitavelmente
inexpensive [ɪnɪk'spɛnsɪv] ADJ barato, econômico
inexperienced [ɪnɪk'spɪərɪənst] ADJ inexperiente
infamous ['ɪnfəməs] ADJ infame, abominável
infant ['ɪnfənt] N (*baby*) bebê *m*; (*young child*) criança
infant school (BRIT) N pré-escola
infect [ɪn'fɛkt] VT (*person*) contagiar; (*food*) contaminar; **infection** N infecção *f*; **infectious** ADJ contagioso; (*fig*) infeccioso
infer [ɪn'fəːʳ] VT deduzir, inferir
inferior [ɪn'fɪərɪəʳ] ADJ inferior; (*goods*) de qualidade inferior ▶ N inferior *m/f*; (*in rank*) subalterno(-a)
infertile [ɪn'fəːtaɪl] ADJ infértil; (*person, animal*) estéril
infinite ['ɪnfɪnɪt] ADJ infinito
infirmary [ɪn'fəːmərɪ] N enfermaria, hospital *m*
inflamed [ɪn'fleɪmd] ADJ inflamado
inflammation [ɪnflə'meɪʃən] N inflamação *f*
inflatable [ɪn'fleɪtəbl] ADJ inflável
inflate [ɪn'fleɪt] VT (*tyre, balloon*) inflar, encher; (*price*) inflar; **inflation** N (*Econ*) inflação *f*
inflict [ɪn'flɪkt] VT: **to ~ sth on sb** infligir algo em alguém
influence ['ɪnfluəns] N influência ▶ VT influir em, influenciar; **under the ~ of alcohol** sob o efeito do álcool; **influential** [ɪnflu'ɛnʃl] ADJ influente
influenza [ɪnflu'ɛnzə] N gripe *f*
inform [ɪn'fɔːm] VT: **to ~ sb of sth** informar alguém de algo ▶ VI: **to ~ on sb** delatar alguém
informal [ɪn'fɔːml] ADJ informal; (*visit, discussion*) extraoficial
information [ɪnfə'meɪʃən] N informação *f*, informações *fpl*; (*knowledge*) conhecimento; **a piece of ~** uma informação
informative [ɪn'fɔːmətɪv] ADJ informativo

infuriating [ɪn'fjuərɪeɪtɪŋ] ADJ de dar raiva, enfurecedor(a)
ingenious [ɪn'dʒi:njəs] ADJ engenhoso
ingredient [ɪn'gri:dɪənt] N ingrediente *m*; (*of situation*) fator *m*
inhabit [ɪn'hæbɪt] VT habitar; **inhabitant** N habitante *m/f*
inhale [ɪn'heɪl] VT inalar ▸ VI (*in smoking*) tragar; **inhaler** [ɪn'heɪlə^r] N inalador *m*
inherent [ɪn'hɪərənt] ADJ: **~ in** *or* **to** inerente a
inherit [ɪn'hɛrɪt] VT herdar; **inheritance** N herança
inhibit [ɪn'hɪbɪt] VT inibir; **inhibition** [ɪnhɪ'bɪʃən] N inibição *f*
initial [ɪ'nɪʃl] ADJ inicial ▸ N inicial *f* ▸ VT marcar com iniciais; **initials** NPL (*of name*) iniciais *fpl*; **initially** ADV inicialmente, no início
initiate [ɪ'nɪʃɪeɪt] VT (*start*) iniciar, começar; (*person*) iniciar; **to ~ sb into a secret** revelar um segredo a alguém; **to ~ proceedings against sb** (*Jur*) abrir um processo contra alguém
initiative [ɪ'nɪʃətɪv] N iniciativa
inject [ɪn'dʒɛkt] VT (*liquid, fig: money*) injetar; (*person*) dar uma injeção em; **injection** N injeção *f*
injure ['ɪndʒə^r] VT ferir; (*reputation etc*) prejudicar; (*offend*) ofender; **injured** ADJ ferido; (*feelings*) ofendido, magoado; **injury** N ferida
injustice [ɪn'dʒʌstɪs] N injustiça
ink [ɪŋk] N tinta
inland [*adj* 'ɪnlənd, *adv* ɪn'lænd] ADJ interior, interno ▸ ADV para o interior; **Inland Revenue** (BRIT) N ≈ fisco, ≈ receita federal (BR)
inmate ['ɪnmeɪt] N (*in prison*) presidiário(-a); (*in asylum*) internado(-a)
inn [ɪn] N hospedaria, taberna
inner ['ɪnə^r] ADJ (*place*) interno; (*feeling*) interior; **inner city** N aglomeração *f* urbana, metrópole *f*
innocent ['ɪnəsnt] ADJ inocente
in-patient N paciente *m/f* interno(-a)
input ['ɪnput] N entrada; (*resources*) investimento
inquest ['ɪnkwɛst] N inquérito judicial
inquire [ɪn'kwaɪə^r] VI pedir informação ▸ VT perguntar; **inquire into** VT FUS investigar, indagar; **inquiry** N pergunta; (*Jur*) investigação *f*, inquérito
ins. ABBR = **inches**
insane [ɪn'seɪn] ADJ louco, doido; (*Med*) demente, insano; **insanity** [ɪn'sænɪtɪ] N loucura; (*Med*) insanidade *f*, demência
inscrutable [ɪn'skru:təbl] ADJ inescrutável, impenetrável
insect ['ɪnsɛkt] N inseto
insecure [ɪnsɪ'kjuə^r] ADJ inseguro
insensitive [ɪn'sɛnsɪtɪv] ADJ insensível
insert [ɪn'sə:t] VT (*between things*) intercalar; (*into sth*) introduzir, inserir
inside ['ɪn'saɪd] N interior *m* ▸ ADJ interior, interno ▸ ADV (*be*) dentro; (*go*) para dentro ▸ PREP dentro de; (*of time*): **~ 10 minutes** em menos de 10 minutos; **insides** NPL (*inf*) entranhas *fpl*; **inside out** ADV às avessas; (*know*) muito bem; **to turn sth inside out** virar algo pelo avesso
insight ['ɪnsaɪt] N insight *m*
insignificant [ɪnsɪg'nɪfɪknt] ADJ insignificante
insincere [ɪnsɪn'sɪə^r] ADJ insincero

i

insist [ɪn'sɪst] VI insistir; **to ~ on doing** insistir em fazer; **to ~ that** insistir que; (*claim*) cismar que; **insistent** ADJ insistente, pertinaz; (*continual*) persistente
insomnia [ɪn'sɔmnɪə] N insônia
inspect [ɪn'spɛkt] VT inspecionar; (*building*) vistoriar; (BRIT: *tickets*) fiscalizar; (*troops*) passar revista em; **inspection** N inspeção *f*; (*of building*) vistoria; (BRIT: *of tickets*) fiscalização *f*; **inspector** N inspetor(a) *m/f*; (BRIT: *on buses, trains*) fiscal *m*
inspire [ɪn'spaɪəʳ] VT inspirar
install [ɪn'stɔːl] VT instalar; (*official*) nomear; **installation** [ɪnstə'leɪʃən] N instalação *f*
installment [ɪn'stɔːlmənt] (US) N = **instalment**
instalment [ɪn'stɔːlmənt] N (*of money*) prestação *f*; (*of story*) fascículo; (*of TV serial etc*) capítulo; **in ~s** (*pay*) a prestações; (*receive*) em várias vezes
instance ['ɪnstəns] N exemplo; **for ~** por exemplo; **in the first ~** em primeiro lugar
instant ['ɪnstənt] N instante *m*, momento ▶ ADJ imediato; (*coffee*) instantâneo; **instantly** ADV imediatamente; **instant message** N mensagem *f* instantânea; **instant messaging** N sistema *m* de mensagens instantâneas
instead [ɪn'stɛd] ADV em vez disso; **~ of** em vez de, em lugar de
instinct ['ɪnstɪŋkt] N instinto
institute ['ɪnstɪtjuːt] N instituto; (*professional body*) associação *f* ▶ VT (*inquiry*) começar, iniciar; (*proceedings*) instituir, estabelecer
institution [ɪnstɪ'tjuːʃən] N instituição *f*; (*organization*) instituto; (*Med: home*) asilo; (*asylum*) manicômio; (*custom*) costume *m*
instruct [ɪn'strʌkt] VT: **to ~ sb in sth** instruir alguém em *or* sobre algo; **to ~ sb to do sth** dar instruções a alguém para fazer algo; **instruction** N (*teaching*) instrução *f*; **instructions** NPL ordens *fpl*; **instructions (for use)** modo de usar; **instructor** N instrutor(a) *m/f*
instrument ['ɪnstrumənt] N instrumento
insufficient [ɪnsə'fɪʃənt] ADJ insuficiente
insulate ['ɪnsjuleɪt] VT isolar; (*protect*) segregar; **insulation** [ɪnsju'leɪʃən] N isolamento
insulin ['ɪnsjulɪn] N insulina
insult [*n* 'ɪnsʌlt, *vt* ɪn'sʌlt] N ofensa ▶ VT insultar, ofender
insurance [ɪn'ʃuərəns] N seguro; **fire/life ~** seguro contra incêndio/de vida
insure [ɪn'ʃuəʳ] VT segurar
intact [ɪn'tækt] ADJ intacto, íntegro; (*unharmed*) ileso, são e salvo
intake ['ɪnteɪk] N (*of food*) quantidade *f* ingerida; (BRIT *Sch*): **an ~ of 200 a year** 200 matriculados por ano
integral ['ɪntɪgrəl] ADJ (*part*) integrante, essencial
integrate ['ɪntɪgreɪt] VT integrar ▶ VI integrar-se
intellect ['ɪntəlɛkt] N intelecto; **intellectual** [ɪntə'lɛktjuəl] ADJ, N intelectual *m/f*
intelligence [ɪn'tɛlɪdʒəns] N inteligência; (*Mil etc*) informações *fpl*
intelligent [ɪn'tɛlɪdʒənt] ADJ inteligente

intend [ɪn'tɛnd] VT (*gift etc*): **to ~ sth for** destinar algo a; **to ~ to do sth** tencionar *or* pretender fazer algo; (*plan*) planejar fazer algo
intense [ɪn'tɛns] ADJ intenso; (*person*) muito emotivo
intensive [ɪn'tɛnsɪv] ADJ intensivo; **intensive care unit** N unidade *f* de tratamento intensivo
intent [ɪn'tɛnt] N intenção *f* ▸ ADJ: **to be ~ on doing sth** estar resolvido a fazer algo; **to all ~s and purposes** para todos os efeitos
intention [ɪn'tɛnʃən] N intenção *f*, propósito; **intentional** ADJ intencional, propositado
interact [ɪntər'ækt] VI interagir; **interactive** [ɪntər'æktɪv] ADJ interativo
interchange ['ɪntətʃeɪndʒ] N intercâmbio; (*exchange*) troca, permuta; (*on motorway*) trevo
intercourse ['ɪntəkɔ:s] N: **sexual ~** relações *fpl* sexuais
interest ['ɪntrɪst] N interesse *m*; (*Comm: sum of money*) juros *mpl*; (: *in company*) participação *f* ▸ VT interessar; **to be ~ed in** interessar-se por, estar interessado em; **interesting** ADJ interessante
interface ['ɪntəfeɪs] N (*Comput*) interface *f*
interfere [ɪntə'fɪə^r] VI: **to ~ in** interferir *or* intrometer-se em; **to ~ with** (*objects*) mexer em; (*hinder*) impedir; (*plans*) interferir em
interference [ɪntə'fɪərəns] N intromissão *f*; (*Radio, TV*) interferência
interior [ɪn'tɪərɪə^r] N interior *m* ▸ ADJ interno; (*ministry*) do interior
intermediate [ɪntə'mi:dɪət] ADJ intermediário
intermission [ɪntə'mɪʃən] N intervalo
intern [*vt* ɪn'tə:n, *n* 'ɪntə:n] VT internar ▸ N (*US: in hospital*) médico interno/médica interna; (*on work placement*) estagiário(-a)
internal [ɪn'tə:nl] ADJ interno
international [ɪntə'næʃənl] ADJ internacional ▸ N (BRIT *Sport: game*) jogo internacional
Internet ['ɪntənɛt] N: **the ~** a Internet; **Internet café** N cibercafé *m*; **Internet Service Provider** N provedor de acesso à Internet; **Internet user** N internauta *m/f*
interpret [ɪn'tə:prɪt] VT interpretar; (*translate*) traduzir ▸ VI interpretar; **interpreter** N intérprete *m/f*
interrogate [ɪn'tɛrəugeɪt] VT interrogar; **interrogation** [ɪntɛrə'geɪʃən] N interrogatório
interrupt [ɪntə'rʌpt] VT, VI interromper; **interruption** N interrupção *f*
interval ['ɪntəvl] N intervalo
intervene [ɪntə'vi:n] VI intervir; (*event*) ocorrer; (*time*) decorrer
interview ['ɪntəvju:] N entrevista ▸ VT entrevistar; **interviewer** N entrevistador(a) *m/f*
intimate [*adj* 'ɪntɪmət, *vt* 'ɪntɪmeɪt] ADJ íntimo; (*knowledge*) profundo ▸ VT insinuar, sugerir

KEYWORD

into ['ɪntu] PREP
1 (*indicating motion or direction*) em; **come into the house/garden** venha para dentro/o jardim; **research into cancer** pesquisa sobre o câncer; **he worked late**

into the night ele trabalhou até altas horas
2 (*indicating change of condition, result*): **she burst into tears** ela desatou a chorar; **he was shocked into silence** ele ficou mudo de choque; **into 3 pieces/French** em 3 pedaços/para o francês

intolerant [ɪn'tɔlərənt] ADJ: **~ (of)** intolerante (com *or* para com)
intranet ['ɪntrənet] N intranet *f*
intricate ['ɪntrɪkət] ADJ complexo, complicado
intrigue [ɪn'tri:g] N intriga ▶ VT intrigar; **intriguing** ADJ intrigante
introduce [ɪntrə'dju:s] VT introduzir; **to ~ sb (to sb)** apresentar alguém (a alguém); **to ~ sb to** (*pastime, technique*) iniciar alguém em; **introduction** N introdução *f*; (*of person*) apresentação *f*; **introductory** ADJ introdutório
intrude [ɪn'tru:d] VI: **to ~ (on** *or* **into)** intrometer-se (em); **intruder** N intruso(-a)
inundate ['ɪnʌndeɪt] VT: **to ~ with** inundar de
invade [ɪn'veɪd] VT invadir
invalid [*n* 'ɪnvəlɪd, *adj* ɪn'vælɪd] N inválido(-a) ▶ ADJ inválido, nulo
invaluable [ɪn'væljuəbl] ADJ valioso, inestimável
invariably [ɪn'vɛərɪəblɪ] ADV invariavelmente
invent [ɪn'vɛnt] VT inventar; **invention** N invenção *f*; (*inventiveness*) engenho; (*lie*) ficção *f*, mentira; **inventor** N inventor(a) *m/f*
inventory ['ɪnvəntrɪ] N inventário, relação *f*
invest [ɪn'vɛst] VT investir ▶ VI: **to ~ in** investir em; (*acquire*) comprar
investigate [ɪn'vɛstɪgeɪt] VT investigar; **investigation** [ɪnvɛstɪ'geɪʃən] N investigação *f*
investment [ɪn'vɛstmənt] N investimento
invisible [ɪn'vɪzɪbl] ADJ invisível
invitation [ɪnvɪ'teɪʃən] N convite *m*
invite [ɪn'vaɪt] VT convidar; (*opinions etc*) solicitar; **inviting** ADJ convidativo
invoice ['ɪnvɔɪs] N fatura ▶ VT faturar
involve [ɪn'vɔlv] VT (*entail*) implicar; (*require*) exigir; **to ~ sb (in)** envolver alguém (em); **involved** ADJ (*complex*) complexo; **to be/get involved in sth** estar/ficar envolvido em algo; **involvement** N envolvimento
inward ['ɪnwəd] ADJ (*movement*) interior, interno; (*thought, feeling*) íntimo ▶ ADV para dentro; **inwards** ADV para dentro
iPod® ['aɪpɔd] N iPod® *m*
IQ N ABBR (= *intelligence quotient*) QI *m*
IRA N ABBR (= *Irish Republican Army*) IRA *m*
Iran [ɪ'ra:n] N Irã *m* (BR), Irão *m* (PT)
Iraq [ɪ'ra:k] N Iraque *m*
Ireland ['aɪələnd] N Irlanda
iris ['aɪrɪs] (*pl* **irises**) N íris *f*
Irish ['aɪrɪʃ] ADJ irlandês(-esa); **the Irish** NPL os irlandeses; **Irishman** *irreg* N irlandês *m*; **Irish Sea** N: **the Irish Sea** o mar da Irlanda; **Irishwoman** *irreg* N irlandesa
iron ['aɪən] N ferro; (*for clothes*) ferro de passar roupa ▶ ADJ de ferro ▶ VT (*clothes*) passar; **iron out** VT (*problem*) resolver
ironic [aɪ'rɔnɪk], **ironical** [aɪ'rɔnɪkl] ADJ irônico
ironing ['aɪənɪŋ] N (*activity*) passar roupa; (*clothes*) roupa passada;

ironing board N tábua de passar roupa
irony ['aɪrənɪ] N ironia
irrational [ɪ'ræʃənl] ADJ irracional
irregular [ɪ'rɛgjuləʳ] ADJ irregular; (*surface*) desigual
irrelevant [ɪ'rɛləvənt] ADJ irrelevante
irresistible [ɪrɪ'zɪstɪbl] ADJ irresistível
irresponsible [ɪrɪ'spɔnsɪbl] ADJ irresponsável
irrigation [ɪrɪ'geɪʃən] N irrigação *f*
irritate ['ɪrɪteɪt] VT irritar; **irritating** ADJ irritante; **irritation** [ɪrɪ'teɪʃən] N irritação *f*
is [ɪz] VB *see* **be**
Islam ['ɪzlɑːm] N islamismo
island ['aɪlənd] N ilha; **islander** N ilhéu/ilhoa *m/f*
isle [aɪl] N ilhota, ilha
isn't ['ɪznt] = **is not**
ISP N ABBR (= *Internet Service Provider*) ISP *m*
Israel ['ɪzreɪl] N Israel; **Israeli** [ɪz'reɪlɪ] ADJ, N israelense *m/f*
issue ['ɪsjuː] N questão *f*, tema *m*; (*of book*) edição *f*; (*of stamps*) emissão *f* ▶ VT (*rations, equipment*) distribuir; (*orders*) dar; **at ~** em debate; **to take ~ with sb (over sth)** discordar de alguém (sobre algo); **to make an ~ of sth** criar caso com algo

KEYWORD

it [ɪt] PRON **1** (*specific: subject*) ele/ela; (: *direct object*) o/a; (: *indirect object*) lhe; **it's on the table** está em cima da mesa; **I can't find it** não consigo achá-lo; **give it to me** dê-mo; **about/from it** sobre/de isto; **did you go to it?** (*party, concert etc*) você foi?
2 (*impers*) isto, isso; (*after prep*) ele, ela; **it's raining** está chovendo (BR) *or* a chover (PT); **it's six o'clock/the 10th of August** são seis horas/hoje é (dia) 10 de agosto; **who is it? — it's me** quem é? — sou eu

Italian [ɪ'tæljən] ADJ italiano ▶ N italiano(-a); (*Ling*) italiano
italics [ɪ'tælɪks] NPL itálico
Italy ['ɪtəlɪ] N Itália
itch [ɪtʃ] N comichão *f*, coceira ▶ VI (*person*) estar com *or* sentir comichão *or* coceira; (*part of body*) comichar, coçar; **I'm ~ing to do something** estou louco para fazer algo; **itchy** ADJ que coça; **to be itchy** (*person*) estar com *or* sentir comichão *or* coceira; (*part of body*) comichar, coçar
it'd ['ɪtd] = **it would;** = **it had**
item ['aɪtəm] N item *m*; (*on agenda*) assunto; (*in programme*) número; (*also*: **news ~**) notícia
itinerary [aɪ'tɪnərərɪ] N itinerário
it'll ['ɪtl] = **it will;** = **it shall**
its [ɪts] ADJ seu/sua, dele/dela ▶ PRON o seu/a sua, o dele/a dela
it's [ɪts] = **it is;** = **it has**
itself [ɪt'sɛlf] PRON (*reflexive*) si mesmo(-a); (*emphatic*) ele mesmo/ela mesma
ITV (BRIT) N ABBR (= *Independent Television*) *canal de televisão comercial*
I've [aɪv] = **I have**
ivory ['aɪvərɪ] N marfim *m*
ivy ['aɪvɪ] N hera

j

jab [dʒæb] VT cutucar ▸ N cotovelada, murro; (*Med: inf*) injeção *f*; **to ~ sth into sth** cravar algo em algo
jack [dʒæk] N (*Aut*) macaco; (*Cards*) valete *m*; **jack up** VT (*Aut*) levantar com macaco
jacket ['dʒækɪt] N jaqueta, casaco curto; (*of boiler etc*) forro; (*of book*) sobrecapa
jackpot ['dʒækpɔt] N bolada, sorte *f* grande
jagged ['dʒægɪd] ADJ dentado, denteado
jail [dʒeɪl] N prisão *f*, cadeia ▸ VT encarcerar
jam [dʒæm] N geleia; (*also*: **traffic ~**) engarrafamento; (*inf*) apuro ▸ VT obstruir, atravancar; (*mechanism*) emperrar; (*Radio*) bloquear, interferir ▸ VI (*mechanism, drawer etc*) emperrar; **to ~ sth into sth** forçar algo dentro de algo
Jamaica [dʒə'meɪkə] N Jamaica
janitor ['dʒænɪtə^r] N zelador *m*
January ['dʒænjuərɪ] N janeiro
Japan [dʒə'pæn] N Japão *m*; **Japanese** [dʒæpə'ni:z] ADJ japonês(-esa) ▸ N INV japonês(-esa) *m/f*; (*Ling*) japonês *m*
jar [dʒɑ:^r] N jarro ▸ VI (*sound*) ranger, chiar; (*colours*) destoar
jargon ['dʒɑ:gən] N jargão *m*
javelin ['dʒævlɪn] N dardo de arremesso
jaw [dʒɔ:] N mandíbula, maxilar *m*
jazz [dʒæz] N jazz *m*; **jazz up** VT animar, avivar
jealous ['dʒɛləs] ADJ ciumento; **jealousy** N ciúmes *mpl*
jeans [dʒi:nz] NPL jeans *m* (BR), jeans *mpl* (PT)
jelly ['dʒɛlɪ] N (*jam*) geleia; **jellyfish** ['dʒɛlɪfɪʃ] N INV água-viva
jerk [dʒə:k] N solavanco, sacudida; (*wrench*) puxão *m*; (*inf: idiot*) babaca *m* ▸ VT sacudir ▸ VI dar um solavanco
jersey ['dʒə:zɪ] N suéter *m* (BR), camisola (PT); (*fabric*) jérsei *m*, malha
Jesus ['dʒi:zəs] N Jesus *m* (Cristo)
jet [dʒɛt] N (*of gas, liquid*) jato; (*Aviat*) (avião *m* a) jato; (*stone*) azeviche *m*; **jet lag** N cansaço devido à diferença de fuso horário
jetty ['dʒɛtɪ] N quebra-mar *m*, cais *m*
Jew [dʒu:] N judeu(-dia) *m/f*
jewel ['dʒu:əl] N joia; **jeweller**, (US) **jeweler** N joalheiro(-a); **jewellery**, (US) **jewelry** N joias *fpl*, pedrarias *fpl*
Jewish ['dʒu:ɪʃ] ADJ judeu/judia
jigsaw ['dʒɪgsɔ:] N (*also*: **~ puzzle**) quebra-cabeça *m*
job [dʒɔb] N trabalho; (*task*) tarefa; (*duty*) dever *m*; (*post*) emprego; **it's not my ~** não faz parte das minhas funções; **it's a good ~ that …** ainda bem que …; **just the ~!** justo

o que queria!; **jobless** ADJ desempregado

jockey ['dʒɔkɪ] N jóquei *m* ▶ VI: **to ~ for position** manobrar para conseguir uma posição

jog [dʒɔg] VT empurrar, sacudir ▶ VI fazer jogging *or* cooper; **jog along** VI ir levando; **jogging** N jogging *m*

john [dʒɔn] (*US inf*) N trono *m* (*inf*) (*no banheiro*)

join [dʒɔɪn] VT (*things*) juntar, unir; (*queue*) entrar em; (*become member of*) associar-se a; (*meet*) encontrar-se com; (*accompany*) juntar-se a ▶ VI (*roads, rivers*) confluir ▶ N junção *f*; **join in** VI participar ▶ VT FUS participar em; **join up** VI unir-se; (*Mil*) alistar-se

joint [dʒɔɪnt] N (*Tech*) junta, união *f*; (*wood*) encaixe *m*; (*Anat*) articulação *f*; (BRIT *Culin*) quarto; (*inf: place*) espelunca; (*: marijuana cigarette*) baseado ▶ ADJ comum; (*combined*) conjunto; (*committee*) misto

joke [dʒəuk] N piada; (*also:* **practical ~**) brincadeira, peça ▶ VI brincar; **to play a ~ on** pregar uma peça em; **joker** N (*Cards*) curingão *m*

jolly ['dʒɔlɪ] ADJ (*merry*) alegre; (*enjoyable*) divertido ▶ ADV (BRIT *inf*) muito, extremamente

jolt [dʒəult] N (*shake*) sacudida, solavanco; (*shock*) susto ▶ VT sacudir; (*emotionally*) abalar

Jordan ['dʒɔ:dən] N Jordânia; (*river*) Jordão *m*

journal ['dʒə:nl] N jornal *m*; (*magazine*) revista; (*diary*) diário; **journalism** N jornalismo; **journalist** N jornalista *m/f*

journey ['dʒə:nɪ] N viagem *f*; (*distance covered*) trajeto

joy [dʒɔɪ] N alegria

judge [dʒʌdʒ] N juiz/juíza *m/f*; (*in competition*) árbitro; (*fig: expert*) especialista *m/f*, conhecedor(a) *m/f* ▶ VT julgar; (*competition*) arbitrar; (*estimate*) avaliar; (*consider*) considerar

judo ['dʒu:dəu] N judô *m*

jug [dʒʌg] N jarro

juggle ['dʒʌgl] VI fazer malabarismos; **juggler** N malabarista *m/f*

juice [dʒu:s] N suco (BR), sumo (PT); **juicy** ADJ suculento

July [dʒu:'laɪ] N julho

jumble ['dʒʌmbl] N confusão *f*, mixórdia ▶ VT (*also:* **~ up**: *mix up*) misturar; **jumble sale** (BRIT) N bazar *m*

> As **jumble sales** têm lugar dentro de igrejas, salões de festa e escolas, onde são vendidos diversos tipos de mercadorias, em geral baratas e sobretudo de segunda mão, a fim de coletar dinheiro para uma obra de caridade, uma escola ou uma igreja.

jump [dʒʌmp] VI saltar, pular; (*start*) sobressaltar-se; (*increase*) disparar ▶ VT pular, saltar ▶ N pulo, salto; (*increase*) alta; (*fence*) obstáculo; **to ~ the queue** (BRIT) furar a fila (BR), pôr-se à frente (PT)

jumper ['dʒʌmpə^r] N (BRIT: *pullover*) suéter *m* (BR), camisola (PT); (US: *pinafore dress*) avental *m*; **jumper cables** (US) NPL = **jump leads**

jump leads, (US) **jumper cables** NPL cabos *mpl* para ligar a bateria

Jun. ABBR = **junior**

junction ['dʒʌŋkʃən] (BRIT) N (*of roads*) cruzamento; (*Rail*) entroncamento

June [dʒu:n] N junho
jungle ['dʒʌŋgl] N selva, mato
junior ['dʒu:nɪəʳ] ADJ (*in age*) mais novo *or* moço; (*position*) subalterno ▶ N jovem *m/f*
junk [dʒʌŋk] N (*cheap goods*) tranqueira, velharias *fpl*; (*rubbish*) lixo; **junk food** N *comida pronta de baixo valor nutritivo*; **junk mail** N correspondência não-solicitada
jury ['dʒuərɪ] N júri *m*
just [dʒʌst] ADJ justo ▶ ADV (*exactly*) justamente, exatamente; (*only*) apenas, somente; **he's ~ done it/left** ele acabou (BR) *or* acaba (PT) de fazê-lo/ir; **~ right** perfeito; **~ two o'clock** duas (horas) em ponto; **she's ~ as clever as you** ela é tão inteligente como você; **~ as well that ...** ainda bem que ...; **~ as he was leaving** no momento em que ele saía; **~ before/enough** justo antes/o suficiente; **~ here** bem aqui; **he ~ missed** falhou por pouco; **~ listen** escute aqui!
justice ['dʒʌstɪs] N justiça; (*US: judge*) juiz/juíza *m/f*; **to do ~ to** (*fig*) apreciar devidamente
justify ['dʒʌstɪfaɪ] VT justificar
jut [dʒʌt] VI (*also*: **~ out**) sobressair
juvenile ['dʒu:vənaɪl] ADJ juvenil; (*court*) de menores; (*books*) para adolescentes ▶ N menor *m/f* de idade

K

K ABBR (= *kilobyte*) K ▶ N ABBR (= *one thousand*) mil
kangaroo [kæŋgə'ru:] N canguru *m*
karate [kə'rɑ:tɪ] N karatê *m*
kebab [kə'bæb] N churrasquinho, espetinho
keen [ki:n] ADJ (*interest, desire*) grande, vivo; (*eye, intelligence*) penetrante; (*competition*) acirrado, intenso; (*edge*) afiado; (*eager*) entusiasmado; **to be ~ to do** *or* **on doing sth** sentir muita vontade de fazer algo; **to be ~ on sth/sb** gostar de algo/alguém
keep [ki:p] (*pt, pp* **kept**) VT ficar com; (*house etc*) cuidar; (*detain*) deter; (*shop etc*) tomar conta de; (*preserve*) conservar; (*family etc*) manter; (*promise*) cumprir; (*chickens, bees etc*) criar; (*prevent*): **to ~ sb from doing sth** impedir alguém de fazer algo ▶ VI (*food*) conservar-se; (*remain*) ficar ▶ N (*of castle*) torre *f* de menagem; (*food etc*): **to earn one's ~** ganhar a vida;

(*inf*): **for ~s** para sempre; **to ~ doing sth** continuar fazendo algo; **to ~ sb happy** manter alguém satisfeito; **to ~ a place tidy** manter um lugar limpo; **keep on** VI: **to ~ on doing** continuar fazendo; **keep out** VT impedir de entrar; **"~ out"** "entrada proibida"; **keep up** VT manter ▶ VI não atrasar-se, acompanhar; **to ~ up with** (*pace*) acompanhar; (*level*) manter-se ao nível de; **keeper** N guarda *m*, guardião(-diã) *m/f*

kennel ['kɛnl] N casa de cachorro; **kennels** N (*establishment*) canil *m*

kept [kɛpt] PT, PP *of* **keep**

kerb [kə:b] (BRIT) N meio-fio (BR), borda do passeio (PT)

kettle ['kɛtl] N chaleira

key [ki:] N chave *f*; (*Mus*) clave *f*; (*of piano, typewriter*) tecla ▶ CPD (*issue etc*) chave ▶ VT (*also*: **~ in**) digitar; **keyboard** N teclado; **keyhole** N buraco da fechadura; **keyring** N chaveiro

khaki ['kɑ:kɪ] ADJ cáqui

kick [kɪk] VT dar um pontapé em; (*ball*) chutar; (*inf: habit*) conseguir superar ▶ VI (*horse*) dar coices ▶ N (*from person*) pontapé *m*; (*from animal*) coice *m*, patada; (*to ball*) chute *m*; (*inf: thrill*): **he does it for ~s** faz isso para curtir; **kick off** VI (*Sport*) dar o chute inicial

kid [kɪd] N (*inf: child*) criança; (*animal*) cabrito; (*leather*) pelica ▶ VI (*inf*) brincar

kidnap ['kɪdnæp] VT sequestrar

kidney ['kɪdnɪ] N rim *m*

kill [kɪl] VT matar; (*murder*) assassinar ▶ N ato de matar; **killer** N assassino(-a); **killing** N assassinato; **to make a killing** (*inf*) faturar uma boa nota

kiln [kɪln] N forno

kilo ['ki:ləu] N quilo; **kilobyte** N kilobyte *m*; **kilogram, kilogramme** N quilograma *m*; **kilometre**, (US) **kilometer** N quilômetro; **kilowatt** N quilowatt *m*

kilt [kɪlt] N saiote *m* escocês

kin [kɪn] N *see* **next-of-kin**

kind [kaɪnd] ADJ (*friendly*) gentil; (*generous*) generoso; (*good*) bom/boa, bondoso, amável ▶ N espécie *f*, classe *f*; (*species*) gênero; **in ~** (*Comm*) em espécie

kindergarten ['kɪndəgɑ:tn] N jardim *m* de infância

kindly ['kaɪndlɪ] ADJ (*good*) bom/boa, bondoso; (*gentle*) gentil, carinhoso ▶ ADV bondosamente, amavelmente; **will you ~ ...** você pode fazer o favor de ...

kindness ['kaɪndnɪs] N bondade *f*, gentileza

king [kɪŋ] N rei *m*; **kingdom** N reino; **kingfisher** N martim-pescador *m*

kiosk ['ki:ɔsk] N banca (BR), quiosque *m* (PT); (BRIT: *also*: **telephone ~**) cabine *f*

kipper ['kɪpə^r] N *tipo de arenque defumado*

kiss [kɪs] N beijo ▶ VT beijar; **to ~ (each other)** beijar-se; **kiss of life** (BRIT) N respiração *f* boca-a-boca

kit [kɪt] N (*for sport etc*) kit *m*; (*equipment*) equipamento; (*set of tools etc*) caixa de ferramentas; (*for assembly*) kit *m* para montar

kitchen ['kɪtʃɪn] N cozinha

kite [kaɪt] N (*toy*) papagaio, pipa

kitten ['kɪtn] N gatinho

kitty ['kɪtɪ] N fundo comum, vaquinha

km ABBR (= *kilometre*) km

K

knack [næk] N: **there's a ~ (to it)** tem um jeito
knee [ni:] N joelho; **kneecap** N rótula
kneel [ni:l] (*pt, pp* **knelt**) VI (*also:* ~ **down**) ajoelhar-se
knew [nju:] PT *of* **know**
knickers ['nɪkəz] (BRIT) NPL calcinha (BR), cuecas *fpl* (PT)
knife [naɪf] (*pl* **knives**) N faca ▶ VT esfaquear
knight [naɪt] N cavaleiro; (*Chess*) cavalo
knit [nɪt] VT tricotar; (*brows*) franzir ▶ VI tricotar (BR), fazer malha (PT); (*bones*) consolidar-se; **knitting** N ato de tricotar, tricô (BR), malha (PT); **knitting needle** N agulha de tricô (BR) *or* de malha (PT); **knitwear** N roupa de malha
knives [naɪvz] NPL *of* **knife**
knob [nɔb] N (*of door*) maçaneta; (*of stick*) castão *m*; (*on radio, TV etc*) botão *m*
knock [nɔk] VT bater em; (*bump into*) colidir com; (*inf*) criticar, malhar ▶ N pancada, golpe *m*; (*on door*) batida ▶ VI: **to ~ at** *or* **on the door** bater à porta; **knock down** VT derrubar; (*pedestrian*) atropelar; **knock off** VI (*inf: finish*) terminar ▶ VT (*inf: steal*) abafar; (*from price*): **to ~ off £10** dar um desconto de £10; **knock out** VT pôr nocaute, nocautear; (*defeat*) eliminar; **knock over** VT derrubar; (*pedestrian*) atropelar
knot [nɔt] N nó *m* ▶ VT dar nó em
know [nəu] (*pt* **knew**, *pp* **known**) VT saber; (*person, author, place*) conhecer ▶ VI: **to ~ about** *or* **of sth** saber de algo; **to ~ how to swim** saber nadar; **know-how** N know-how *m*, experiência;
knowingly ADV (*purposely*) de propósito; (*spitefully*) maliciosamente
knowledge ['nɔlɪdʒ] N conhecimento; (*range of learning*) saber *m*, conhecimentos *mpl*; **knowledgeable** ADJ entendido, versado
known [nəun] PP *of* **know**
knuckle ['nʌkl] N nó *m*
Koran [kɔ'rɑ:n] N: **the ~** o Alcorão
Korea [kə'rɪə] N Coreia
kosher ['kəuʃə'] ADJ kosher *inv*
Kosovo ['kɒsəvəu] N Kosovo *m*

L ABBR (BRIT *Aut*: = *learner*) (condutor(a) *m/f*) aprendiz *m/f*
lab [læb] N ABBR = **laboratory**
label ['leɪbl] N etiqueta, rótulo ▶ VT etiquetar, rotular
labor ['leɪbəʳ] (US) = **labour**
laboratory [lə'bɔrətərɪ] N laboratório
labour ['leɪbəʳ], (US) **labor** N trabalho; (*work force*) mão-de-obra *f*; (*Med*): **to be in ~** estar em trabalho de parto ▶ VI: **to ~ (at)** trabalhar (em) ▶ VT insistir em; **the L~ Party** (BRIT) o Partido Trabalhista; **labourer** N operário; **farm labourer** trabalhador *m* rural, peão *m*
lace [leɪs] N renda; (*of shoe etc*) cadarço ▶ VT (*shoe*) amarrar
lack [læk] N falta ▶ VT (*money, confidence*) faltar; (*intelligence*) carecer de; **through** *or* **for ~ of** por falta de; **to be ~ing** faltar; **to be ~ing in** carecer de
lacquer ['lækəʳ] N laca; (*hair*) fixador *m*
lad [læd] N menino, rapaz *m*, moço
ladder ['lædəʳ] N escada *f* de mão; (BRIT: *in tights*) defeito (em forma de escada)
ladle ['leɪdl] N concha (de sopa)
lady ['leɪdɪ] N senhora; (*distinguished, noble*) dama; (*in address*): **ladies and gentlemen, ...** senhoras e senhores, ...; **young ~** senhorita; **"ladies' (toilets)"** "senhoras"; **ladybird**, (US) **ladybug** N joaninha
lag [læg] N atraso, retardamento ▶ VI (*also*: **~ behind**) ficar para trás ▶ VT (*pipes*) revestir com isolante térmico
lager ['lɑ:gəʳ] N *cerveja leve e clara*
lagoon [lə'gu:n] N lagoa
laid [leɪd] PT, PP *of* **lay**
lain [leɪn] PP *of* **lie**
lake [leɪk] N lago
lamb [læm] N cordeiro
lame [leɪm] ADJ coxo, manco; (*excuse, argument*) pouco convincente, fraco
lament [lə'mɛnt] N lamento, queixa ▶ VT lamentar-se de
lamp [læmp] N lâmpada; **lamppost** (BRIT) N poste *m*; **lampshade** N abajur *m*, quebra-luz *m*
land [lænd] N terra; (*country*) país *m*; (*piece of land*) terreno; (*estate*) terras *fpl*, propriedades *fpl* ▶ VI (*from ship*) desembarcar; (*Aviat*) pousar, aterrissar (BR), aterrar (PT); (*fig: arrive unexpectedly*) cair, terminar ▶ VT desembarcar; **to ~ sb with sth** (*inf*) sobrecarregar alguém com algo; **land up** VI: **to ~ up in/at** ir parar em; **landfill site** ['lændfɪl-] N aterro sanitário; **landing** N (*Aviat*) pouso, aterrissagem *f* (BR), aterragem *f* (PT); (*of staircase*)

patamar *m*; **landlady** N senhoria; (*of pub*) dona, proprietária; **landline** N telefone *m* fixo; **landlord** N senhorio, locador *m*; (*of pub etc*) dono, proprietário; **landmark** N lugar *m* conhecido; (*fig*) marco; **landowner** N latifundiário(-a)
landscape ['lændskeɪp] N paisagem *f*
landslide ['lændslaɪd] N (*Geo*) desmoronamento, desabamento; (*fig: Pol*) vitória esmagadora
lane [leɪn] N caminho, estrada estreita; (*Aut*) pista; (*in race*) raia
language ['læŋgwɪdʒ] N língua; (*way one speaks, Comput, style*) linguagem *f*; **bad ~** palavrões *mpl*; **language laboratory** N laboratório de línguas; **language school** N escola de línguas
lantern ['læntn] N lanterna
lap [læp] N (*of track*) volta; (*of person*) colo ▶ VT (*also*: **~ up**) lamber ▶ VI (*waves*) marulhar; **lap up** VT (*fig*) receber com sofreguidão
lapel [lə'pɛl] N lapela
lapse [læps] N lapso; (*bad behaviour*) deslize *m* ▶ VI (*law*) prescrever; **to ~ into bad habits** adquirir maus hábitos
laptop ['læptɔp], **laptop computer** N laptop *m*
lard [lɑ:d] N banha de porco
larder ['lɑ:dəʳ] N despensa
large [lɑ:dʒ] ADJ grande; **at ~** (*free*) em liberdade; (*generally*) em geral; **largely** ADV em grande parte; (*introducing reason*) principalmente; **large-scale** ADJ (*map*) em grande escala; (*fig*) importante, de grande alcance
lark [lɑ:k] N (*bird*) cotovia; (*joke*) brincadeira, peça; **lark about** VI divertir-se, brincar
laryngitis [lærɪn'dʒaɪtɪs] N laringite *f*
laser ['leɪzəʳ] N laser *m*; **laser printer** N impressora a laser
lash [læʃ] N (*blow*) chicotada; (*also*: **eye~**) pestana, cílio ▶ VT chicotear, açoitar; (*subj: rain, wind*) castigar; (*tie*) atar; **lash out** VI: **to ~ out (at sb)** atacar (alguém) violentamente; **to ~ out at** *or* **against sb** (*criticize*) atacer alguém verbalmente
lass [læs] (BRIT) N moça
last [lɑ:st] ADJ último; (*final*) derradeiro ▶ ADV em último lugar ▶ VI durar; (*continue*) continuar; **~ week** na semana passada; **~ night** ontem à noite; **at ~** finalmente; **~ but one** penúltimo; **lastly** ADV por fim, por último; (*finally*) finalmente; **last-minute** ADJ de última hora
latch [lætʃ] N trinco, fecho, tranca
late [leɪt] ADJ (*not on time*) atrasado; (*far on in day etc*) tardio; (*former*) antigo, ex-, anterior; (*dead*) falecido ▶ ADV tarde; (*behind time, schedule*) atrasado; **of ~** recentemente; **in ~ May** no final de maio; **latecomer** N retardatário(-a); **lately** ADV ultimamente; **later** ADJ (*date etc*) posterior; (*version etc*) mais recente ▶ ADV mais tarde, depois; **later on** mais tarde; **latest** ADJ último; **at the latest** no mais tardar
lather ['lɑ:ðəʳ] N espuma (de sabão) ▶ VT ensaboar
Latin ['lætɪn] N (*Ling*) latim *m* ▶ ADJ latino; **Latin America** N América Latina; **Latin American** ADJ, N latino-americano(-a)
latitude ['lætɪtju:d] N latitude *f*
latter ['lætəʳ] ADJ último; (*of two*) segundo ▶ N: **the ~** o último, este

laugh [lɑ:f] N riso, risada ▶VI rir, dar risada (*or* gargalhada); **(to do sth) for a ~** (fazer algo) só de curtição; **laugh at** VT FUS rir de; **laugh off** VT disfarçar sorrindo; **laughter** N riso, risada
launch [lɔ:ntʃ] N (*boat*) lancha; (*Comm, of rocket etc*) lançamento ▶VT lançar; **launch into** VT FUS lançar-se a
laundry ['lɔ:ndrɪ] N lavanderia; (*clothes*) roupa para lavar
lava ['lɑ:və] N lava
lavatory ['lævətərɪ] N privada (BR), casa de banho (PT)
lavender ['lævəndə^r] N lavanda
lavish ['lævɪʃ] ADJ (*amount*) generoso; (*person*): **~ with** pródigo em, generoso com ▶VT: **to ~ sth on sb** encher *or* cobrir alguém de algo
law [lɔ:] N lei *f*; (*rule*) regra; (*Sch*) direito; **lawful** ADJ legal, lícito
lawn [lɔ:n] N gramado (BR), relvado (PT); **lawnmower** N cortador *m* de grama (BR) *or* de relva (PT)
lawsuit ['lɔ:su:t] N ação *f* judicial, processo
lawyer ['lɔ:jə^r] N advogado(-a); (*for sales, wills etc*) notário(-a), tabelião(-liã) *m/f*
lax [læks] ADJ (*discipline*) relaxado; (*person*) negligente
laxative ['læksətɪv] N laxante *m*
lay [leɪ] (*pt, pp* **laid**) PT *of* **lie** ▶ADJ leigo ▶VT colocar; (*eggs, table*) pôr; **lay aside** VT pôr de lado; **lay by** VT = **lay aside**; **lay down** VT depositar; (*rules etc*) impor, estabelecer; **to ~ down the law** (*pej*) impor regras; **to ~ down one's life** sacrificar voluntariamenta a vida; **lay off** VT (*workers*) demitir; **lay on** VT (*meal, entertainment*) prover; **lay out** VT (*spread out*) dispor em ordem; **lay-by** (BRIT) N acostamento
layer ['leɪə^r] N camada
layman ['leɪmən] *irreg* N leigo
layout ['leɪaut] N (*of garden, building*) desenho; (*of piece of writing*) leiaute *m*
lazy ['leɪzɪ] ADJ preguiçoso; (*movement*) lento
lb. ABBR (*weight*) = **pound**
lead[1] [li:d] (*pt, pp* **led**) N (*front position*) dianteira; (*Sport*) liderança; (*fig*) vantagem *f*; (*clue*) pista; (*Elec*) fio; (*for dog*) correia; (*in play, film*) papel *m* principal ▶VT levar; (*be leader of*) chefiar; (*start, guide: activity*) encabeçar ▶VI encabeçar; **to be in the ~** (*Sport: in race*) estar na frente; (*: in match*) estar ganhando; **to ~ the way** assumir a direcão; **lead away** VT levar; **lead back** VT levar de volta; **lead on** VT (*tease*) provocar; **lead to** VT FUS levar a, conduzir a; **lead up to** VT FUS conduzir a
lead[2] [lɛd] N chumbo; (*in pencil*) grafite *f*
leader ['li:də^r] N líder *m/f*; **leadership** N liderança; (*quality*) poder *m* de liderança
lead-free [lɛd-] ADJ sem chumbo
leading ['li:dɪŋ] ADJ principal; (*role*) de destaque; (*first, front*) primeiro, dianteiro
lead singer [li:d-] N cantor(a) *m/f*
leaf [li:f] (*pl* **leaves**) N folha ▶VI: **to ~ through** (*book*) folhear; **to turn over a new ~** mudar de vida, partir para outra (*inf*)
leaflet ['li:flɪt] N folheto
league [li:g] N liga; **to be in ~ with** estar de comum acordo com

leak [li:k] N (*of liquid, gas*) escape *m*, vazamento; (*hole*) buraco, rombo; (*in roof*) goteira; (*fig: of information*) vazamento ▶ VI (*ship*) fazer água; (*shoe*) deixar entrar água; (*roof*) gotejar; (*pipe, container, liquid*) vazar; (*gas*) escapar ▶ VT (*news*) vazar

lean [li:n] (*pt, pp* **leaned** *or* **leant**) ADJ magro ▶ VT: **to ~ sth on** encostar *or* apoiar algo em ▶ VI inclinar-se; **to ~ against** encostar-se *or* apoiar-se contra; **to ~ on** encostar-se *or* apoiar-se em; **lean back** VI inclinar-se para trás; **lean forward** VI inclinar-se para frente; **lean out** VI: **to ~ out (of)** inclinar-se para fora (de); **lean over** VI debruçar-se ▶ VT FUS debruçar-se sobre

leap [li:p] (*pt, pp* **leaped** *or* **leapt**) N salto, pulo ▶ VI saltar; **leap year** N ano bissexto

learn [lə:n] (*pt, pp* **learned** *or* **learnt**) VT aprender; (*by heart*) decorar ▶ VI aprender; **to ~ about sth** (*hear, read*) saber de algo; **learner** N principiante *m/f*; (BRIT: *also*: **learner driver**) aprendiz *m/f* de motorista

lease [li:s] N arrendamento ▶ VT arrendar

leash [li:ʃ] N correia

least [li:st] ADJ: **the ~** (+ *n*) o/a menor; (*smallest amount of*) a menor quantidade de ▶ ADV: **the ~** (+ *adj*) o/a menos; **at ~** pelo menos; **not in the ~** de maneira nenhuma

leather ['lɛðə^r] N couro

leave [li:v] (*pt, pp* **left**) VT deixar; (*go away from*) abandonar ▶ VI ir-se, sair; (*train*) sair ▶ N licença; **to ~ sth to sb** deixar algo para alguém; **to be left** sobrar; **leave behind** VT deixar para trás; (*forget*) esquecer; **leave out** VT omitir

leaves [li:vz] NPL *of* **leaf**

Lebanon ['lɛbənən] N Líbano

lecture ['lɛktʃə^r] N conferência, palestra; (*Sch*) aula ▶ VI dar aulas, lecionar ▶ VT (*scold*) passar um sermão em; **lecturer** N (BRIT: *at university*) professor(a) *m/f*

led [lɛd] PT, PP *of* **lead¹**

ledge [lɛdʒ] N (*of window*) peitoril *m*; (*of mountain*) saliência, proeminência

leek [li:k] N alho-poró *m*

left [lɛft] PT, PP *of* **leave** ▶ ADJ esquerdo ▶ N esquerda ▶ ADV à esquerda; **on the ~** à esquerda; **to the ~** para a esquerda; **the L~** (*Pol*) a Esquerda; **left-handed** ADJ canhoto; **left-luggage**, (BRIT) **left-luggage office** N depósito de bagagem

left-wing ADJ (*Pol*) de esquerda, esquerdista

leg [lɛg] N perna; (*of animal*) pata; (*Culin: of meat*) perna; (*of journey*) etapa; **1st/2nd ~** (*Sport*) primeiro/segundo turno

legacy ['lɛgəsɪ] N legado; (*fig*) herança

legal ['li:gl] ADJ legal

legend ['lɛdʒənd] N lenda; (*person*) mito

leggings ['lɛgɪŋz] NPL legging *f*

legislation [lɛdʒɪs'leɪʃən] N legislação *f*

legitimate [lɪ'dʒɪtɪmət] ADJ legítimo

leisure ['lɛʒə^r] N lazer *m*; **at ~** desocupado, livre

lemon ['lɛmən] N limão(-galego) *m*; **lemonade** [lɛmə'neɪd] N limonada; **lemon tea** N chá *m* de limão

lend [lɛnd] (*pt, pp* **lent**) VT: **to ~ sth to sb** emprestar algo a alguém
length [lɛŋθ] N comprimento, extensão *f*; (*amount of time*) duração *f*; **at ~** (*at last*) finalmente, afinal; (*lengthily*) por extenso; **lengthen** VT encompridar, alongar ▸VI encompridar-se; **lengthways** ADV longitudinalmente, ao comprido; **lengthy** ADJ comprido, longo; (*meeting*) prolongado
lens [lɛnz] N (*of spectacles*) lente *f*; (*of camera*) objetiva
Lent [lɛnt] N Quaresma
lent [lɛnt] PT, PP *of* **lend**
lentil ['lɛntl] N lentilha
Leo ['li:əu] N Leão *m*
leotard ['li:ətɑ:d] N collant *m*
lesbian ['lɛzbɪən] N lésbica
less [lɛs] ADJ, PRON, ADV menos ▸PREP: **~ tax/10% discount** menos imposto/10% de desconto; **~ than ever** menos do que nunca; **~ and ~** cada vez menos; **the ~ he works ...** quanto menos trabalha ...
lessen ['lɛsn] VI diminuir, minguar ▸VT diminuir, reduzir
lesser ['lɛsə^r] ADJ menor; **to a ~ extent** *or* **degree** nem tanto
lesson ['lɛsn] N aula; (*example, warning*) lição *f*; **to teach sb a ~** (*fig*) dar uma lição em alguém
let [lɛt] (*pt, pp* **let**) VT (*allow*) deixar; (BRIT: *lease*) alugar; **to ~ sb know sth** avisar alguém de algo; **~'s go!** vamos!; **"to ~"** "aluga-se"; **let down** VT (*tyre*) esvaziar; (*disappoint*) desapontar; **let go** VT, VI soltar; **let in** VT deixar entrar; (*visitor etc*) fazer entrar; **let off** VT (*culprit*) perdoar; (*firework etc*) soltar; **let on** VI revelar; **let out** VT deixar sair; (*scream*) soltar; **let up** VI cessar, afrouxar
lethal ['li:θl] ADJ letal
letter ['lɛtə^r] N (*of alphabet*) letra; (*correspondence*) carta; **letterbox** (BRIT) N caixa do correio
lettuce ['lɛtɪs] N alface *f*
leukaemia [lu:'ki:mɪə], (US) **leukemia** N leucemia
level ['lɛvl] ADJ (*flat*) plano ▸ADV no mesmo nível ▸N nível *m*; (*height*) altura ▸VT aplanar; **"A" ~s** *npl* (BRIT) ≈ vestibular *m*; **"O" ~s** *npl* (BRIT) *provas prestadas no final do ensino fundamental*; **to be ~ with** estar no mesmo nível que; **on the ~** em nível; (*fig: honest*) sincero; **level off** VI (*prices etc*) estabilizar-se; **level out** VI, VT = **level off**; **level crossing** (BRIT) N passagem *f* de nível
lever ['li:və^r] N alavanca; (*fig*) estratagema *m*; **leverage** N força de uma alavanca; (*fig: influence*) influência
liability [laɪə'bɪlətɪ] N responsabilidade *f*; (*handicap*) desvantagem *f*; **liabilities** NPL (*Comm*) exigibilidades *fpl*, obrigações *fpl*
liable ['laɪəbl] ADJ (*subject*): **~ to** sujeito a; (*responsible*): **~ for** responsável por; (*likely*): **~ to do** capaz de fazer
liaise [li:'eɪz] VI: **to ~ (with)** cooperar (com)
liar ['laɪə^r] N mentiroso(-a)
libel ['laɪbl] N difamação *f* ▸VT caluniar, difamar
liberal ['lɪbərl] ADJ liberal; (*generous*) generoso
liberation N liberação *f*, libertação *f*
liberty ['lɪbətɪ] N liberdade *f*; (*criminal*): **to be at ~** estar livre; **to be at ~ to do** ser livre de fazer

Libra ['li:brə] N Libra, Balança
librarian [laɪ'brɛərɪən] N bibliotecário(-a)
library ['laɪbrərɪ] N biblioteca
Libya ['lɪbɪə] N Líbia
licence ['laɪsns], (US) **license** N (*gen, Comm*) licença; (*Aut*) carta de motorista (BR), carta de condução (PT)
license ['laɪsns] N (US) = **licence** ▶VT autorizar, dar licença a; **licensed** ADJ (*car*) autorizado oficialmente; (*for alcohol*) autorizado para vender bebidas alcoólicas; **license plate** (US) N (*Aut*) placa (de identificação) (*do carro*)
lick [lɪk] VT lamber; (*inf: defeat*) arrasar, surrar; **to ~ one's lips** (*also fig*) lamber os beiços
lid [lɪd] N tampa; (*eyelid*) pálpebra
lie [laɪ] VI (*pt* **lay**, *pp* **lain**) (*act*) deitar-se; (*state*) estar deitado; (*object: be situated*) estar, encontrar-se; (*fig: problem, cause*) residir; (*in race, league*) ocupar; (*pt, pt* **lied**) (*tell lies*) mentir ▶N mentira; **to ~ low** (*fig*) esconder-se; **lie about** VI (*things*) estar espalhado; (*people*) vadiar; **lie around** VI = **lie about**; **lie-in** (BRIT) N: **to have a lie-in** dormir até tarde
lieutenant [lɛf'tɛnənt, (US) lu:'tɛnənt] N (*Mil*) tenente *m*
life [laɪf] (*pl* **lives**) N vida; **to come to ~** animar-se; **lifeboat** N barco salva-vidas; **lifeguard** N salva-vidas *m/f*; **life jacket** N colete *m* salva-vidas; **lifelike** ADJ natural; (*realistic*) realista; **life preserver** (US) N = **life jacket**; **life sentence** N pena de prisão perpétua; **lifetime** N vida
lift [lɪft] VT levantar ▶VI (*fog*) dispersar-se, dissipar-se ▶N (BRIT: *elevator*) elevador *m*; **to give sb a ~** (BRIT) dar uma carona para alguém (BR), dar uma boleia a alguém (PT); **lift-off** N decolagem *f*
light [laɪt] (*pt, pp* **lit**) N luz *f*; (*Aut: headlight*) farol *m*; (*: rear light*) luz traseira; (*for cigarette etc*): **have you got a ~?** tem fogo? ▶VT acender; (*room*) iluminar ▶ADJ (*colour, room*) claro; (*not heavy, also fig*) leve; (*rain, traffic*) fraco; (*movement, action*) delicado; **lights** NPL (*Aut*) sinal *m* de trânsito; **to come to ~** vir à tona; **in the ~ of** à luz de; **light up** VI iluminar-se ▶VT iluminar; **light bulb** N lâmpada; **lighten** VT tornar mais leve; **lighter** N (*also*: **cigarette lighter**) isqueiro, acendedor *m*; **light-hearted** ADJ alegre, despreocupado; **lighthouse** N farol *m*; **lighting** N iluminação *f*; **lightly** ADV ligeiramente; **to get off lightly** conseguir se safar, livrar a cara (*inf*)
lightning ['laɪtnɪŋ] N relâmpago, raio
lightweight ['laɪtweɪt] ADJ (*suit*) leve; (*Boxing*) peso-leve
like [laɪk] VT gostar de ▶PREP como; (*such as*) tal qual ▶ADJ parecido, semelhante ▶N: **the ~** coisas *fpl* parecidas; **his ~s and dislikes** seus gostos e aversões; **I would ~, I'd ~** (eu) gostaria de; **to be** *or* **look ~ sb/sth** parecer-se com alguém/algo, parecer alguém/algo; **do it ~ this** faça isso assim; **it is nothing ~ ...** não se parece nada com ...; **likeable** ADJ simpático, agradável
likelihood ['laɪklɪhud] N probabilidade *f*
likely ['laɪklɪ] ADJ provável; **he's ~ to leave** é provável que ele se vá; **not ~!** (*inf*) nem morto!
likewise ['laɪkwaɪz] ADV igualmente; **to do ~** fazer o mesmo

liking ['laɪkɪŋ] N afeição *f*, simpatia; **to be to sb's ~** ser ao gosto de alguém
lilac ['laɪlək] N lilás *m*
lily ['lɪlɪ] N lírio, açucena
limb [lɪm] N membro
limbo ['lɪmbəu] N: **to be in ~** (*fig*) viver na expectativa
lime [laɪm] N (*tree*) limeira; (*fruit*) limão *m*; (*also*: **~ juice**) suco (BR) *or* sumo (PT) de limão; (*Geo*) cal *f*
limelight ['laɪmlaɪt] N: **to be in the ~** ser o centro das atenções
limestone ['laɪmstəun] N pedra calcária
limit ['lɪmɪt] N limite *m* ▶ VT limitar; **limited** ADJ limitado; **to be limited to** limitar-se a
limp [lɪmp] N: **to have a ~** mancar, ser coxo ▶ VI mancar ▶ ADJ frouxo
line [laɪn] N linha; (*rope*) corda; (*wire*) fio; (*row*) fila, fileira; (*on face*) ruga ▶ VT (*road, room*) encarreirar; (*container, clothing*): **to ~ sth (with)** forrar algo (de); **to ~ the streets** ladear as ruas; **in ~ with** de acordo com; **line up** VI enfileirar-se ▶ VT enfileirar; (*set up, have ready*) preparar, arranjar
linen ['lɪnɪn] N *artigos de cama e mesa*; (*cloth*) linho
liner ['laɪnəʳ] N navio de linha regular; (*also*: **bin ~**) saco para lata de lixo
linger ['lɪŋgəʳ] VI demorar-se, retardar-se; (*smell, tradition*) persistir
lining ['laɪnɪŋ] N forro; (*Anat*) parede *f*
link [lɪŋk] N (*of a chain*) elo; (*connection*) conexão *f* ▶ VT vincular, unir; (*associate*): **to ~ with** *or* **to** unir a; **links** NPL (*Golf*) campo de golfe; **link up** VT acoplar ▶ VI unir-se
lion ['laɪən] N leão *m*; **lioness** N leoa
lip [lɪp] N lábio; **lipread** *irreg* VI ler os lábios; **lip salve** N pomada para os lábios; **lipstick** N batom *m*
liqueur [lɪ'kjuəʳ] N licor *m*
liquid ['lɪkwɪd] ADJ líquido ▶ N líquido
liquor ['lɪkəʳ] N licor *m*, bebida alcoólica; **liquor store** (US) N loja que vende bebidas alcoólicas
Lisbon ['lɪzbən] N Lisboa
lisp [lɪsp] N ceceio ▶ VI cecear, falar com a língua presa
list [lɪst] N lista ▶ VT (*write down*) fazer uma lista *or* relação de; (*enumerate*) enumerar
listen ['lɪsn] VI escutar, ouvir; **to ~ to** escutar; **listener** N ouvinte *m/f*
lit [lɪt] PT, PP *of* **light**
liter ['li:təʳ] (US) N = **litre**
literacy ['lɪtərəsɪ] N capacidade *f* de ler e escrever, alfabetização *f*
literal ['lɪtərl] ADJ literal
literary ['lɪtərərɪ] ADJ literário
literate ['lɪtərət] ADJ alfabetizado, instruído; (*educated*) culto, letrado
literature ['lɪtərɪtʃəʳ] N literatura; (*brochures etc*) folhetos *mpl*
litre ['li:təʳ], (US) **liter** N litro
litter ['lɪtəʳ] N (*rubbish*) lixo; (*young animals*) ninhada; **litter bin** (BRIT) N lata de lixo
little ['lɪtl] ADJ (*small*) pequeno; (*not much*) pouco ▶ ADV pouco; **a ~** um pouco (de); **~ house** casinha; **for a ~ while** por um instante; **as ~ as possible** o menos possível; **~ by ~** pouco a pouco

live [*vi, vt* lɪv, *adj* laɪv] VI viver; (*reside*) morar ▶ ADJ vivo; (*wire*) eletrizado; (*broadcast*) ao vivo; (*shell*) carregado; **~ ammunition** munição de guerra; **live down** VT redimir; **live on** VT FUS viver de, alimentar-se de; **to ~ on £50 a week** viver com £50 por semana; **live together** VI viver juntos; **live up to** VT FUS (*fulfil*) cumprir

livelihood ['laɪvlɪhud] N meio de vida, subsistência

lively ['laɪvlɪ] ADJ vivo

liven up ['laɪvn-] VT animar ▶ VI animar-se

liver ['lɪvəʳ] N fígado

lives [laɪvz] NPL *of* **life**

living ['lɪvɪŋ] ADJ vivo ▶ N: **to earn** *or* **make a ~** ganhar a vida; **living room** N sala de estar; **living will** N testamento em vida

lizard ['lɪzəd] N lagarto

load [ləud] N carga; (*weight*) peso ▶ VT (*gen, Comput*) carregar; **a ~ of, ~s of** (*fig*) um monte de, uma porção de; **loaded** ADJ (*question, word*) intencionado; (*inf: rich*) cheio da nota; (*vehicle*): **to be loaded with** estar carregado de

loaf [ləuf] (*pl* **loaves**) N pão-de-forma *m*

loan [ləun] N empréstimo ▶ VT emprestar; **on ~** emprestado

loathe [ləuð] VT detestar, odiar

loaves [ləuvz] NPL *of* **loaf**

lobby ['lɔbɪ] N vestíbulo, saguão *m*; (*Pol: pressure group*) grupo de pressão, lobby *m* ▶ VT pressionar

lobster ['lɔbstəʳ] N lagostim *m*; (*large*) lagosta

local ['ləukl] ADJ local ▶ N (*pub*) bar *m* (local); **the locals** NPL (*local inhabitants*) os moradores locais; **local anaesthetic** N anestesia local

locate [ləu'keɪt] VT (*find*) localizar, situar; (*situate*): **to be ~d in** estar localizado em

location [ləu'keɪʃən] N local *m*, posição *f*; **on ~** (*Cinema*) em externas

loch [lɔx] N lago

lock [lɔk] N (*of door, box*) fechadura; (*of canal*) eclusa; (*of hair*) anel *m*, mecha ▶ VT (*with key*) trancar ▶ VI (*door etc*) fechar-se à chave; (*wheels*) travar-se; **lock in** VT trancar dentro; **lock out** VT trancar do lado de fora; **lock up** VT (*criminal, mental patient*) prender; (*house*) trancar ▶ VI fechar tudo

locker ['lɔkəʳ] N compartimento com chave; **locker-room** (US) N (*Sport*) vestiário

locksmith ['lɔksmɪθ] N serralheiro(-a)

lodge [lɔdʒ] N casa do guarda, guarita; (*hunting lodge*) pavilhão *m* de caça ▶ VI (*person*): **to ~ (with)** alojar-se (na casa de) ▶ VT (*complaint*) apresentar; **lodger** N inquilino(-a), hóspede *m/f*

loft [lɔft] N sótão *m*

log [lɔg] N (*of wood*) tora; (*book*) = **logbook** ▶ VT registrar; **logbook** N (*Naut*) diário de bordo; (*Aviat*) diário de voo; (*of car*) documentação *f* (do carro)

logic ['lɔdʒɪk] N lógica; **logical** ADJ lógico

login ['lɔgɪn] N (*Comput*) login *m*

LOL (*inf*) ABBR (= *laugh out loud*) rs, LOL

lollipop ['lɔlɪpɔp] N pirulito (BR), chupa-chupa *m* (PT); **lollipop lady** (BRIT) N *mulher que ajuda as crianças a atravessarem a rua*; **lollipop man** (BRIT) N *homem que ajuda as crianças a atravessarem a rua*

Lollipop men/ladies são as pessoas que ajudam as crianças a atravessar a rua nas proximidades das escolas na hora da entrada e da saída. São facilmente localizados graças a suas longas capas brancas e à placa redonda com a qual pedem aos motoristas que parem. São chamados assim por causa da forma circular da placa, que lembra um pirulito (*lollipop*).

lolly ['lɔlı] (*inf*) N (*ice*) picolé *m*; (*lollipop*) pirulito

London ['lʌndən] N Londres; **Londoner** N londrino(-a)

lone [ləun] ADJ (*person*) solitário; (*thing*) único

loneliness ['ləunlınıs] N solidão *f*, isolamento

lonely ['ləunlı] ADJ (*person*) só; (*place, childhood*) solitário, isolado

long [lɔŋ] ADJ longo; (*road, hair, table*) comprido ▸ADV muito tempo ▸VI: **to ~ for sth** ansiar *or* suspirar por algo; **how ~ is the street?** qual é a extensão da rua?; **how ~ is the lesson?** quanto dura a lição?; **all night ~** a noite inteira; **he no ~er comes** ele não vem mais; **~ before/after** muito antes/depois; **before ~** (+ *future*) dentro de pouco; (+ *past*) pouco tempo depois; **at ~ last** por fim, no final; **so** *or* **as ~ as** contanto que; **long-distance** ADJ (*travel*) de longa distância; (*call*) interurbano; **longing** N desejo, anseio

longitude ['lɔŋgıtju:d] N longitude *f*;

long: long jump N salto em distância; **long-sighted** ADJ presbita; **long-standing** ADJ de muito tempo; **long-term** ADJ a longo prazo

loo [lu:] (BRIT *inf*) N banheiro (BR), casa de banho (PT)

look [luk] VI olhar; (*seem*) parecer; (*building etc*): **to ~ south/(out) onto the sea** dar para o sul/o mar ▸N olhar *m*; (*glance*) olhada, vista de olhos; (*appearance*) aparência, aspecto; **looks** NPL (*good looks*) físico, aparência; **~ (here)!** (*annoyance*) escuta aqui!; **~!** (*surprise*) olha!; **look after** VT FUS cuidar de; (*deal with*) lidar com; **look at** VT FUS olhar (para); (*read quickly*) ler rapidamente; (*consider*) considerar; **look back** VI: **to ~ back on** (*remember*) recordar, rever; **look down on** VT FUS (*fig*) desdenhar, desprezar; **look for** VT FUS procurar; **look forward to** VT FUS aguardar com prazer, ansiar por; (*in letter*): **we ~ forward to hearing from you** no aguardo de suas notícias; **look into** VT FUS investigar; **look on** VI assistir; **look out** VI (*beware*): **to ~ out (for)** tomar cuidado (com); **look out for** VT FUS (*await*) esperar; **look round** VI virar a cabeça, voltar-se; **look through** VT FUS (*papers, book*) examinar; **look to** VT FUS (*rely on*) contar com; **look up** VI levantar os olhos; (*improve*) melhorar ▸VT (*word*) procurar

loop [lu:p] N laço ▸VT: **to ~ sth round sth** prender algo em torno de algo

loose [lu:s] ADJ solto; (*not tight*) frouxo ▸N: **to be on the ~** estar solto; **loosely** ADV frouxamente, folgadamente; **loosen** VT (*free*) soltar; (*slacken*) afrouxar

loot [lu:t] N saque *m*, despojo ▸VT saquear, pilhar

lord [lɔːd] N senhor *m*; **L~ Smith** Lord Smith; **the L~** (*Rel*) o Senhor; **good L~!** Deus meu!; **the (House of) L~s** (BRIT) a Câmara dos Lordes
lorry [ˈlɔrɪ] (BRIT) N caminhão *m* (BR), camião *m* (PT); **lorry driver** (BRIT) N caminhoneiro (BR), camionista *m/f* (PT)
lose [luːz] (*pt, pp* **lost**) VT, VI perder; **to ~ (time)** (*clock*) atrasar-se; **loser** N perdedor(a) *m/f*; (*inf: failure*) derrotado(-a), fracassado(-a)
loss [lɔs] N perda; (*Comm*): **to make a ~** sair com prejuízo; **heavy ~es** (*Mil*) grandes perdas; **to be at a ~** estar perplexo
lost [lɔst] PT, PP *of* **lose** ▶ ADJ perdido; **~ and found** (*US*) (seção *f* de) perdidos e achados *mpl*; **lost property** (BRIT) N (objetos *mpl*) perdidos e achados *mpl*
lot [lɔt] N (*set of things*) porção *f*; (*at auctions*) lote *m*; **the ~** tudo, todos(-as); **a ~** muito, bastante; **a ~ of, ~s of** muito(s); **I read a ~** leio bastante; **to draw ~s** tirar à sorte
lotion [ˈləuʃən] N loção *f*
lottery [ˈlɔtərɪ] N loteria
loud [laud] ADJ (*voice*) alto; (*shout*) forte; (*noise*) barulhento; (*support, condemnation*) veemente; (*gaudy*) berrante ▶ ADV alto; **out ~** em voz alta; **loudly** ADV ruidosamente; (*aloud*) em voz alta; **loudspeaker** N alto-falante *m*
lounge [laundʒ] N sala de estar *f*; (*of airport*) salão *m*; (BRIT: *also*: **~ bar**) bar *m* social ▶ VI recostar-se, espreguiçar-se; **lounge about, lounge around** VI ficar à-toa
lousy [ˈlauzɪ] (*inf*) ADJ ruim, péssimo; (*ill*): **to feel ~** sentir-se mal
love [lʌv] N amor *m* ▶ VT amar; (*like a lot*) adorar; **to ~ to do** adorar fazer; **~ (from) Anne** (*on letter*) um abraço *or* um beijo, Anne; **I ~ you** eu te amo; **I ~ coffee** adoro o café; **"15 ~"** (*Tennis*) "15 a zero"; **to be in ~ with** estar apaixonado por; **to fall in ~ with** apaixonar-se por; **to make ~** fazer amor; **love affair** N aventura (amorosa), caso (de amor); **love life** N vida sentimental
lovely [ˈlʌvlɪ] ADJ (*delightful*) encantador(a), delicioso; (*beautiful*) lindo, belo; (*holiday, surprise*) muito agradável, maravilhoso
lover [ˈlʌvəʳ] N amante *m/f*
loving [ˈlʌvɪŋ] ADJ carinhoso, afetuoso; (*actions*) dedicado
low [ləu] ADJ baixo; (*depressed*) deprimido; (*ill*) doente ▶ ADV baixo ▶ N (*Meteorology*) área de baixa pressão; **to be ~ on** (*supplies*) ter pouco; **to reach a new** *or* **an all-time ~** cair para o seu nível mais baixo; **low-alcohol** ADJ de baixo teor alcoólico; **low-calorie** ADJ de baixo teor calórico; **low-carb** (*inf*) ADJ (*diet, meal*) com baixo carboidrato; **lower** ADJ mais baixo; (*less important*) inferior ▶ VT abaixar; (*reduce*) reduzir, diminuir; **low-fat** ADJ magro
loyal [ˈlɔɪəl] ADJ leal; **loyalty** N lealdade *f*
loyalty card (BRIT) N cartão *m* de fidelidade
L-plates [ˈɛlpleɪts] (BRIT) NPL placas *fpl* de aprendiz de motorista

> As **L-plates** são placas quadradas com um "L" vermelho que são colocadas na parte de trás do carro para mostrar que a pessoa ao volante ainda não tem carteira de motorista. Até a

obtenção da carteira, o motorista aprendiz possui uma permissão provisória e não tem direito de dirigir sem um motorista qualificado ao lado. Os motoristas aprendizes não podem dirigir em estradas mesmo que estejam acompanhados.

Ltd (BRIT) ABBR (= *limited (liability) company*) SA

luck [lʌk] N sorte *f*; **bad ~** azar *m*; **good ~!** boa sorte!; **bad** *or* **hard** *or* **tough ~!** que azar!; **luckily** ADV por sorte, felizmente; **lucky** ADJ (*person*) sortudo; (*situation*) afortunado; (*object*) de sorte

ludicrous ['lu:dɪkrəs] ADJ ridículo

luggage ['lʌgɪdʒ] N bagagem *f*; **luggage rack** N porta-bagagem *m*, bagageiro

lukewarm ['lu:kwɔ:m] ADJ morno, tépido; (*fig*) indiferente

lull [lʌl] N pausa, interrupção *f* ▸VT: **to ~ sb to sleep** acalentar alguém; **to be ~ed into a false sense of security** ser acalmado com uma falsa sensação de segurança

lullaby ['lʌləbaɪ] N canção *f* de ninar

lumber ['lʌmbəʳ] N (*junk*) trastes *mpl* velhos; (*wood*) madeira serrada, tábua ▸VT: **to ~ sb with sth/sb** empurrar algo/alguém para cima de alguém

luminous ['lu:mɪnəs] ADJ luminoso

lump [lʌmp] N torrão *m*; (*fragment*) pedaço; (*on body*) galo, caroço; (*also*: **sugar ~**) cubo de açúcar ▸VT: **to ~ together** amontoar; **lump sum** N montante *m* único; **lumpy** ADJ encaroçado

lunatic ['lu:nətɪk] ADJ louco(-a)

lunch [lʌntʃ] N almoço; **lunch break, lunch hour** N hora do almoço

lung [lʌŋ] N pulmão *m*

lure [luəʳ] N isca ▸VT atrair, seduzir

lurk [lə:k] VI (*hide*) esconder-se; (*wait*) estar à espreita

lush [lʌʃ] ADJ exuberante

lust [lʌst] N luxúria; (*greed*) cobiça; **lust after** VT FUS cobiçar; **lust for** VT FUS = **lust after**

Luxembourg ['lʌksəmbə:g] N Luxemburgo

luxurious [lʌg'zjuərɪəs] ADJ luxuoso

luxury ['lʌkʃərɪ] N luxo ▸CPD de luxo

lying ['laɪɪŋ] N mentira(s) *f(pl)* ▸ADJ mentiroso, falso

lyrics ['lɪrɪks] NPL (*of song*) letra

m

M.A. ABBR (*Sch*) = **Master of Arts**
mac [mæk] (BRIT) N capa impermeável
macaroni [mækə'rəunɪ] N macarrão *m*
machine [mə'ʃiːn] N máquina ▶ VT (*dress etc*) costurar à máquina; (*Tech*) usinar; **machine gun** N metralhadora; **machinery** N maquinaria; (*fig*) máquina
mackerel ['mækrl] N INV cavala
mackintosh ['mækɪntɔʃ] (BRIT) N capa impermeável
mad [mæd] ADJ louco; (*foolish*) tolo; (*angry*) furioso, brabo; (*keen*): **to be ~ about** ser louco por
madam ['mædəm] N senhora, madame *f*
made [meɪd] PT, PP *of* **make**; **made-to-measure** (BRIT) ADJ feito sob medida; **made-up** ['meɪdʌp] ADJ (*story*) inventado
madly ['mædlɪ] ADV loucamente; **~ in love** louco de amor
madman ['mædmən] *irreg* N louco
madness ['mædnɪs] N loucura; (*foolishness*) tolice *f*
magazine [mægə'ziːn] N (*Press*) revista; (*Radio, TV*) programa *m* de atualidades
maggot ['mægət] N larva de inseto
magic ['mædʒɪk] N magia, mágica ▶ ADJ mágico; **magical** ADJ mágico; **magician** [mə'dʒɪʃən] N mago(-a); (*entertainer*) mágico(-a)
magistrate ['mædʒɪstreɪt] N magistrado(-a), juiz/juíza *m/f*
magnet ['mægnɪt] N ímã *m*; **magnetic** [mæg'nɛtɪk] ADJ magnético
magnificent [mæg'nɪfɪsnt] ADJ magnífico
magnify ['mægnɪfaɪ] VT aumentar; **magnifying glass** N lupa, lente *f* de aumento
magpie ['mægpaɪ] N pega
mahogany [mə'hɔgənɪ] N mogno, acaju *m*
maid [meɪd] N empregada; **old ~** (*pej*) solteirona
maiden name ['meɪdn-] N nome *m* de solteira
mail [meɪl] N correio; (*letters*) cartas *fpl* ▶ VT pôr no correio; **mailbox** N (US) caixa do correio; **mailing list** N lista de clientes, mailing list *m*
main [meɪn] ADJ principal ▶ N (*pipe*) cano *or* esgoto principal; **the mains** NPL (*Elec, gas, water*) a rede; **in the ~** na maior parte; **mainland** N: **the mainland** o continente; **mainly** ADV principalmente; **main road** N estrada principal; **mainstream** N corrente *f* principal
maintain [meɪn'teɪn] VT manter; (*keep up*) conservar (em bom estado); (*affirm*) sustentar, afirmar; **maintenance** ['meɪntənəns] N

manutenção *f*; (*alimony*) alimentos *mpl*, pensão *f* alimentícia
maize [meɪz] N milho
majesty ['mædʒɪstɪ] N majestade *f*
major ['meɪdʒə^r] N (*Mil*) major *m* ▶ ADJ (*main*) principal; (*considerable*) importante; (*Mus*) maior
Majorca [mə'jɔ:kə] N Maiorca
majority [mə'dʒɔrɪtɪ] N maioria
make [meɪk] (*pt, pp* **made**) VT fazer; (*manufacture*) fabricar, produzir; (*cause to be*): **to ~ sb sad** entristecer alguém, fazer alguém ficar triste; (*force*): **to ~ sb do sth** fazer com que alguém faça algo; (*equal*): **2 and 2 ~ 4** dois e dois são quatro ▶ N marca; **to ~ a profit/loss** ter um lucro/uma perda; **to ~ it** (*arrive*) chegar; (*succeed*) ter sucesso; **what time do you ~ it?** que horas você tem?; **to ~ do with** contentar-se com; **make for** VT FUS (*place*) dirigir-se a; **make out** VT (*decipher*) decifrar; (*understand*) compreender; (*see*) divisar, avistar; **make up** VT (*constitute*) constituir; (*invent*) inventar; (*parcel*) embrulhar ▶ VI reconciliar-se; (*with cosmetics*) maquilar-se (BR), maquilhar-se (PT); **make up for** VT FUS compensar; **maker** N (*of film, programme*) criador *m*; (*manufacturer*) fabricante *m/f*; **makeshift** ADJ provisório; **make-up** N maquilagem *f* (BR), maquilhagem *f* (PT)
malaria [mə'lɛərɪə] N malária
Malaysia [mə'leɪzɪə] N Malaísia (BR), Malásia (PT)
male [meɪl] N macho ▶ ADJ masculino; (*child etc*) do sexo masculino
malignant [mə'lɪgnənt] ADJ (*Med*) maligno
mall [mɔ:l] N (*also*: **shopping ~**) shopping *m*
mallet ['mælɪt] N maço, marreta
malt [mɔ:lt] N malte *m*
Malta ['mɔ:ltə] N Malta
malware ['mælwɛə^r] N (*Comput*) software *m* malicioso
mammal ['mæml] N mamífero
mammoth ['mæməθ] N mamute *m* ▶ ADJ gigantesco, imenso
man [mæn] (*pl* **men**) N homem *m* ▶ VT (*Naut*) tripular; (*Mil*) guarnecer; (*machine*) operar; **an old ~** um velho; **~ and wife** marido e mulher
manage ['mænɪdʒ] VI arranjar-se, virar-se ▶ VT (*be in charge of*) dirigir, administrar; (*business*) gerenciar; (*ship, person*) controlar; **manageable** ADJ manejável; (*task etc*) viável; **management** N administração *f*, direção *f*, gerência; **manager** N gerente *m/f*; (*Sport*) técnico(-a); **manageress** N gerente *f*; **managerial** [mænə'dʒɪə:rɪəl] ADJ administrativo, gerencial; **managing director** N diretor(a) *m/f*, diretor-gerente/diretora-gerente *m/f*
mandarin ['mændərɪn] N (*also*: **~ orange**) tangerina; (*person*) mandarim *m*
mandatory ['mændətərɪ] ADJ obrigatório
mane [meɪn] N (*of horse*) crina; (*of lion*) juba
maneuver [mə'nu:və^r] (US) = **manoeuvre**
mango ['mæŋgəu] (*pl* **mangoes**) N manga
manhole ['mænhəul] N poço de inspeção

manhood ['mænhud] N (*age*) idade *f* adulta; (*masculinity*) virilidade *f*
mania ['meɪnɪə] N mania; **maniac** ['meɪnɪæk] N maníaco(-a); (*fig*) louco(-a)
manic ['mænɪk] ADJ maníaco
manicure ['mænɪkjuəʳ] N manicure *f* (BR), manicura (PT)
manifest ['mænɪfɛst] VT manifestar, mostrar ▶ ADJ manifesto, evidente
manipulate [mə'nɪpjuleɪt] VT manipular
mankind [mæn'kaɪnd] N humanidade *f*, raça humana
man-made ADJ sintético, artificial
manner ['mænəʳ] N modo, maneira; (*behaviour*) conduta, comportamento; **manners** NPL (*conduct*) boas maneiras *fpl*, educação *f*; **bad ~s** falta de educação; **all ~ of** todo tipo de; **all ~ of things** todos os tipos de coisa
manoeuvre [mə'nu:vəʳ], (US) **maneuver** VT manobrar; (*manipulate*) manipular ▶ VI manobrar ▶ N manobra
manpower ['mænpauəʳ] N potencial *m* humano, mão-de-obra *f*
mansion ['mænʃən] N mansão *f*, palacete *m*
manslaughter ['mænslɔ:təʳ] N homicídio involuntário
mantelpiece ['mæntlpi:s] N consolo da lareira
manual ['mænjuəl] ADJ manual ▶ N manual *m*
manufacture [mænju'fæktʃəʳ] VT manufaturar, fabricar ▶ N fabricação *f*; **manufacturer** N fabricante *m/f*
manure [mə'njuəʳ] N estrume *m*, adubo
manuscript ['mænjuskrɪpt] N manuscrito
many ['mɛnɪ] ADJ, PRON muitos(-as); **a great ~** muitíssimos; **~ a time** muitas vezes
map [mæp] N mapa *m*; **map out** VT traçar
maple ['meɪpl] N bordo
mar [mɑ:ʳ] VT estragar
marathon ['mærəθən] N maratona
marble ['mɑ:bl] N mármore *m*; (*toy*) bola de gude
March [mɑ:tʃ] N março
march [mɑ:tʃ] VI marchar; (*demonstrators*) desfilar ▶ N marcha, passeata
mare [mɛəʳ] N égua
margarine [mɑ:dʒə'ri:n] N margarina
margin ['mɑ:dʒɪn] N margem *f*; **marginal** ADJ marginal; **marginal seat** (*Pol*) cadeira ganha por pequena maioria
marigold ['mærɪgəuld] N malmequer *m*
marijuana [mærɪ'wɑ:nə] N maconha
marine [mə'ri:n] ADJ marinho; (*engineer*) naval ▶ N fuzileiro naval
marital ['mærɪtl] ADJ matrimonial, marital; **~ status** estado civil
marjoram ['mɑ:dʒərəm] N manjerona
mark [mɑ:k] N marca, sinal *m*; (*imprint*) impressão *f*; (*stain*) mancha; (BRIT *Sch*) nota; (*currency*) marco ▶ VT marcar; (*stain*) manchar; (*indicate*) indicar; (*commemorate*) comemorar; (BRIT *Sch*) dar nota em; (: *correct*) corrigir; **to ~ time** marcar passo; **marker** N (*sign*) marcador *m*, marca; (*bookmark*) marcador

market ['mɑːkɪt] N mercado ▸ VT (*Comm*) comercializar; **marketing** N marketing *m*; **marketplace** N mercado; **market research** N pesquisa de mercado
marmalade ['mɑːməleɪd] N geleia de laranja
maroon [mə'ruːn] VT: **to be ~ed** ficar abandonado (numa ilha) ▸ ADJ vinho *inv*
marquee [mɑː'kiː] N toldo, tenda
marriage ['mærɪdʒ] N casamento
married ['mærɪd] ADJ casado; (*life, love*) conjugal
marrow ['mærəu] N medula; (*vegetable*) abóbora
marry ['mærɪ] VT casar(-se) com; (*subj: father, priest etc*) casar, unir ▸ VI (*also*: **get married**) casar(-se)
Mars [mɑːz] N Marte *m*
marsh [mɑːʃ] N pântano; (*salt marsh*) marisma
marshal ['mɑːʃl] N (*Mil: also*: **field ~**) marechal *m*; (*at sports meeting etc*) oficial *m* ▸ VT (*thoughts, support*) organizar; (*soldiers*) formar
martyr ['mɑːtəʳ] N mártir *m/f*
marvel ['mɑːvl] N maravilha ▸ VI: **to ~ (at)** maravilhar-se (de *or* com); **marvellous**, (*US*) **marvelous** ADJ maravilhoso
Marxist ['mɑːksɪst] ADJ, N marxista *m/f*
mascara [mæs'kɑːrə] N rímel *m*
masculine ['mæskjulɪn] ADJ masculino
mash [mæʃ] VT (*Culin*) fazer um purê de; (*crush*) amassar
mask [mɑːsk] N máscara ▸ VT (*face*) encobrir; (*feelings*) esconder, ocultar
mason ['meɪsn] N (*also*: **stone ~**) pedreiro(-a); (*also*: **free~**) maçom *m*; **masonry** N alvenaria
mass [mæs] N quantidade *f*; (*people*) multidão *f*; (*Phys*) massa; (*Rel*) missa; (*great quantity*) montão *m* ▸ CPD de massa ▸ VI reunir-se; (*Mil*) concentrar-se; **the masses** NPL (*ordinary people*) as massas; **~es of** (*inf*) montes de
massacre ['mæsəkəʳ] N massacre *m*, carnificina
massage ['mæsɑːʒ] N massagem *f*
massive ['mæsɪv] ADJ (*large*) enorme; (*support*) massivo
mass media NPL meios *mpl* de comunicação de massa, mídia
mast [mɑːst] N (*Naut*) mastro; (*Radio etc*) antena
master ['mɑːstəʳ] N mestre *m*; (*fig: of situation*) dono; (*in secondary school*) professor *m*; (*title for boys*): **M~ X** o menino X ▸ VT controlar; (*learn*) conhecer a fundo; **mastermind** N (*fig*) cabeça ▸ VT dirigir, planejar; **masterpiece** N obra-prima
mat [mæt] N esteira; (*also*: **door~**) capacho; (*also*: **table ~**) descanso
match [mætʃ] N fósforo; (*game*) jogo, partida; (*equal*) igual *m/f* ▸ VT (*also*: **~ up**) casar, emparelhar; (*go well with*) combinar com; (*equal*) igualar; (*correspond to*) corresponder a ▸ VI combinar; **to be a good ~** (*couple*) formar um bom casal; **matchbox** N caixa de fósforos; **matching** ADJ que combina (com)
mate [meɪt] N (*inf*) colega *m/f*; (*assistant*) ajudante *m/f*; (*animal*) macho/fêmea; (*in merchant navy*) imediato ▸ VI acasalar-se
material [mə'tɪərɪəl] N (*substance*) matéria; (*equipment*) material *m*; (*cloth*) pano, tecido;

(*data*) dados *mpl* ▶ ADJ material; **materials** NPL (*equipment*) material
maternal [mə'tə:nl] ADJ maternal
maternity [mə'tə:nɪtɪ] N maternidade *f*
mathematical [mæθə'mætɪkl] ADJ matemático
mathematics [mæθə'mætɪks] N matemática
maths [mæθs], (US) **math** N matemática
matron ['meɪtrən] N (*in hospital*) enfermeira chefe *f*; (*in school*) inspetora
matter ['mætə^r] N questão *f*, assunto; (*Phys*) matéria; (*substance*) substância; (*reading matter etc*) material *m*; (*Med: pus*) pus *m* ▶ VI importar; **matters** NPL (*affairs*) questões *fpl*; **it doesn't ~** não importa; (*I don't mind*) tanto faz; **what's the ~?** o que (é que) há?, qual é o problema?; **no ~ what** aconteça o que acontecer; **as a ~ of course** por rotina; **as a ~ of fact** na realidade, de fato
mattress ['mætrɪs] N colchão *m*
mature [mə'tjuə^r] ADJ maduro; (*cheese, wine*) amadurecido ▶ VI amadurecer
maul [mɔ:l] VT machucar, maltratar
mauve [məuv] ADJ cor de malva *inv*
maximum ['mæksɪməm] (*pl* **maxima** *or* **maximums**) ADJ máximo ▶ N máximo
May [meɪ] N maio
may [meɪ] (*conditional* **might**) AUX VB (*indicating possibility*): **he ~ come** pode ser que ele venha, é capaz de vir; (*be allowed to*): **~ I smoke?** posso fumar?; (*wishes*): **~ God bless you!** que Deus lhe abençoe
maybe ['meɪbi:] ADV talvez; **~ not** talvez não
mayhem ['meɪhɛm] N caos *m*
mayonnaise [meɪə'neɪz] N maionese *f*
mayor [mɛə^r] N prefeito (BR), presidente *m* do município (PT); **mayoress** N prefeita (BR), presidenta do município (PT)
maze [meɪz] N labirinto

KEYWORD

me [mi:] PRON **1** (*direct*) me; **he heard me** ele me ouviu; **it's me** sou eu
2 (*indirect*) me; **he gave me the money** ele me deu o dinheiro; **give it to me** dá isso para mim
3 (*stressed, after prep*) mim; **with me** comigo; **without me** sem mim

meadow ['mɛdəu] N prado, campina
meagre ['mi:gə^r], (US) **meager** ADJ escasso
meal [mi:l] N refeição *f*; (*flour*) farinha; **mealtime** N hora da refeição
mean [mi:n] (*pt, pp* **meant**) ADJ (*with money*) sovina, avarento, pão-duro *inv* (BR); (*unkind*) mesquinho; (*shabby*) malcuidado, dilapidado; (*average*) médio ▶ VT (*signify*) significar, querer dizer; (*refer to*): **I thought you ~t her** eu pensei que você estivesse se referindo a ela; (*intend*): **to ~ to do sth** pretender *or* tencionar fazer algo ▶ N meio, meio termo; **means** NPL (*way, money*) meio; **by ~s of** por meio de, mediante; **by all ~s!** claro que sim!, pois não; **do you ~ it?** você está falando sério?
meaning ['mi:nɪŋ] N sentido, significado; **meaningful** ADJ significativo; (*relationship*) sério; **meaningless** ADJ sem sentido

meant [mɛnt] PT, PP *of* **mean**
meantime ['mi:ntaɪm] ADV (*also*: **in the ~**) entretanto, enquanto isso
meanwhile ['mi:nwaɪl] ADV = **meantime**
measles ['mi:zlz] N sarampo
measure ['mɛʒəʳ] VT, VI medir ▶ N medida; (*also*: **tape ~**) fita métrica
measurement ['mɛʒəmənt] N medida; **measurements** NPL (*size*) medidas *fpl*
meat [mi:t] N carne *f*; **cold ~s** (BRIT) frios; **meatball** N almôndega
Mecca ['mɛkə] N Meca; (*fig*): **a ~ (for)** a meca (de)
mechanic [mɪ'kænɪk] N mecânico; **mechanical** ADJ mecânico
mechanism ['mɛkənɪzəm] N mecanismo
medal ['mɛdl] N medalha
meddle ['mɛdl] VI: **to ~ in** meter-se em, intrometer-se em; **to ~ with sth** mexer em algo
media ['mi:dɪə] NPL meios *mpl* de comunicação, mídia
mediaeval [mɛdɪ'i:vl] ADJ = **medieval**
mediate ['mi:dɪeɪt] VI mediar
medical ['mɛdɪkl] ADJ médico ▶ N (*examination*) exame *m* médico
medication [mɛdɪ'keɪʃən] N medicação *f*
medicine ['mɛdsɪn] N medicina; (*drug*) remédio, medicamento
medieval [mɛdɪ'i:vl] ADJ medieval
mediocre [mi:dɪ'əukəʳ] ADJ medíocre
meditate ['mɛdɪteɪt] VI meditar
Mediterranean [mɛdɪtə'reɪnɪən] ADJ mediterrâneo; **the ~ (Sea)** o (mar) Mediterrâneo
medium ['mi:dɪəm] (*pl* **media** *or* **mediums**) ADJ médio ▶ N (*means*) meio; (*pl* **mediums**: *person*) médium *m/f*
meek [mi:k] ADJ manso, dócil
meet [mi:t] (*pt, pp* **met**) VT encontrar; (*accidentally*) topar com, dar de cara com; (*by arrangement*) encontrar-se com, ir ao encontro de; (*for the first time*) conhecer; (*go and fetch*) ir buscar; (*opponent, problem*) enfrentar; (*obligations*) cumprir; (*need*) satisfazer ▶ VI encontrar-se; (*for talks*) reunir-se; (*join*) unir-se; (*get to know*) conhecer-se; **meet with** VT FUS reunir-se com; (*difficulty*) encontrar; **meeting** N encontro; (*session: of club, Comm*) reunião *f*; (*assembly*) assembleia; (*Sport*) corrida
megabyte ['mɛgəbaɪt] N (*Comput*) megabyte *m*
megaphone ['mɛgəfəun] N megafone *m*
megapixel ['mɛgəpɪksl] N megapixel *m*
melancholy ['mɛlənkəlɪ] N melancolia ▶ ADJ melancólico
melody ['mɛlədɪ] N melodia
melon ['mɛlən] N melão *m*
melt [mɛlt] VI (*metal*) fundir-se; (*snow*) derreter ▶ VT derreter; **melt down** VT fundir
member ['mɛmbəʳ] N membro(-a); (*of club*) sócio(-a); (*Anat*) membro; **M~ of Parliament** (BRIT) deputado(-a); **membership** N (*state*) adesão *f*; (*members*) número de sócios; **membership card** N carteira de sócio
memento [mə'mɛntəu] N lembrança

memo ['mɛməu] N memorando, nota

memorandum [mɛmə'rændəm] (*pl* **memoranda**) N memorando

memorial [mɪ'mɔːrɪəl] N monumento comemorativo ▸ ADJ comemorativo; **Memorial Day** (US) N *ver nota*

> **Memorial Day** é um feriado nos Estados Unidos, a última segunda-feira de maio na maior parte dos estados, em memória aos soldados americanos mortos em combate.

memorize ['mɛməraɪz] VT decorar, aprender de cor

memory ['mɛmərɪ] N memória; (*recollection*) lembrança; **memory stick** N (*Comput: flash pen*) pen drive *m*; (*card*) cartão *m* de memória

men [mɛn] NPL *of* **man**

menace ['mɛnəs] N ameaça; (*nuisance*) droga ▸ VT ameaçar

mend [mɛnd] VT consertar, reparar; (*darn*) remendar ▸ N: **to be on the ~** estar melhorando

meningitis [mɛnɪn'dʒaɪtɪs] N meningite *f*

menopause ['mɛnəupɔːz] N menopausa

menstruation [mɛnstru'eɪʃən] N menstruação *f*

mental ['mɛntl] ADJ mental; **mentality** [mɛn'tælɪtɪ] N mentalidade *f*

mention ['mɛnʃən] N menção *f* ▸ VT (*speak of*) falar de; **don't ~ it!** não tem de quê!, de nada!

menu ['mɛnjuː] N (*set menu, Comput*) menu *m*; (*printed*) cardápio (BR), ementa (PT)

MEP N ABBR (= *Member of the European Parliament*) deputado(-a)

mercenary ['məːsɪnərɪ] ADJ mercenário ▸ N mercenário

merchandise ['məːtʃəndaɪz] N mercadorias *fpl*

merchant ['məːtʃənt] N comerciante *m/f*

merciless ['məːsɪlɪs] ADJ desumano, inclemente

mercury ['məːkjurɪ] N mercúrio

mercy ['məːsɪ] N piedade *f*; (*Rel*) misericórdia; **at the ~ of** à mercê de

mere [mɪəʳ] ADJ mero, simples *inv*; **merely** ADV simplesmente, somente, apenas

merge [məːdʒ] VT unir ▸ VI unir-se; (*Comm*) fundir-se; **merger** N fusão *f*

meringue [mə'ræŋ] N suspiro, merengue *m*

merit ['mɛrɪt] N mérito; (*advantage*) vantagem *f* ▸ VT merecer

mermaid ['məːmeɪd] N sereia

merry ['mɛrɪ] ADJ alegre; **M~ Christmas!** Feliz Natal!; **merry-go-round** N carrossel *m*

mesh [mɛʃ] N malha

mess [mɛs] N confusão *f*; (*in room*) bagunça; (*Mil*) rancho; **to be in a ~** ser uma bagunça, estar numa bagunça; **mess about** (*inf*) VI perder tempo; (*pass the time*) vadiar; **mess about with** (*inf*) VT FUS mexer com; **mess around** (*inf*) VI = **mess about**; **mess up** VT (*spoil*) estragar; (*dirty*) sujar

message ['mɛsɪdʒ] N recado, mensagem *f* ▸ VT enviar uma mensagem para; **message board** N (*on internet*) fórum *m* de discussão

messenger ['mɛsɪndʒəʳ] N mensageiro(-a)

messy ['mɛsɪ] ADJ (*dirty*) sujo; (*untidy*) desarrumado

met [mɛt] PT, PP *of* **meet**

metal ['mɛtl] N metal *m*

meteorology [mi:tɪə'rɔlədʒɪ] N meteorologia
meter ['mi:tə^r] N (*instrument*) medidor *m*; (*also*: **parking ~**) parcômetro; (*us*: *unit*) = **metre**
method ['mɛθəd] N método; **methodical** [mɪ'θɔdɪkl] ADJ metódico
metre ['mi:tə^r], (*us*) **meter** N metro
metric ['mɛtrɪk] ADJ métrico
metropolitan [mɛtrə'pɔlɪtən] ADJ metropolitano
Mexico ['mɛksɪkəu] N México
mice [maɪs] NPL *of* **mouse**
micro... [maɪkrəu] PREFIX micro; **microblog** ['maɪkrəublɔg] N microblog(ue) *m*; **microchip** N microchip *m*; **microphone** N microfone *m*; **microscope** N microscópio; **microwave** N (*also*: **microwave oven**) micro-ondas *m inv*
mid [mɪd] ADJ: **in ~ May** em meados de maio; **in ~ afternoon** no meio da tarde; **in ~ air** em pleno ar; **midday** N meio-dia *m*
middle ['mɪdl] N meio; (*waist*) cintura ▶ ADJ meio; (*quantity, size*) médio, mediano; **middle-aged** ADJ de meia-idade; **Middle Ages** NPL: **the Middle Ages** a Idade Média; **Middle East** N: **the Middle East** o Oriente Médio; **middle name** N segundo nome *m*
midge [mɪdʒ] N mosquito
midget ['mɪdʒɪt] N anão(-anã) *m/f*
midnight ['mɪdnaɪt] N meia-noite *f*
midst [mɪdst] N: **in the ~ of** no meio de, entre
midsummer [mɪd'sʌmə^r] N: **a ~ day** um dia em pleno verão
midway [mɪd'weɪ] ADJ, ADV: **~ (between)** no meio do caminho (entre)
midweek [mɪd'wi:k] ADV no meio da semana
midwife ['mɪdwaɪf] (*pl* **midwives**) N parteira
might [maɪt] VB *see* **may** ▶ N poder *m*, força; **mighty** ADJ poderoso, forte
migraine ['mi:greɪn] N enxaqueca
migrant ['maɪgrənt] ADJ migratório; (*worker*) emigrante
migrate [maɪ'greɪt] VI emigrar; (*birds*) arribar
mike [maɪk] N ABBR = **microphone**
mild [maɪld] ADJ (*character*) pacífico; (*climate*) temperado; (*taste*) suave; (*illness*) leve, benigno; (*interest*) pequeno
mile [maɪl] N milha (1609 *m*); **mileage** N número de milhas; (*Aut*) ≈ quilometragem *f*; **milestone** ['maɪlstəun] N marco miliário
military ['mɪlɪtərɪ] ADJ militar
milk [mɪlk] N leite *m* ▶ VT (*cow*) ordenhar; (*fig*) explorar, chupar; **milk chocolate** N chocolate *m* de leite; **milkman** *irreg* N leiteiro; **milky** ADJ leitoso
mill [mɪl] N (*windmill etc*) moinho; (*coffee mill*) moedor *m* de café; (*factory*) moinho, engenho ▶ VT moer ▶ VI (*also*: **~ about**) aglomerar-se, remoinhar
millimetre, (*us*) **millimeter** ['mɪlɪmi:tə^r] N milímetro
million ['mɪljən] N milhão *m*; **a ~ times** um milhão de vezes; **millionaire** N milionário(-a); **millionth** NUM milionésimo
mime [maɪm] N mimo; (*actor*) mímico(-a), comediante *m/f* ▶ VT imitar ▶ VI fazer mímica

m

mimic ['mɪmɪk] N mímico(-a), imitador(a) *m/f* ▶ VT imitar, parodiar
min. ABBR (= *minute, minimum*) min
mince [mɪns] VT moer ▶ VI (*in walking*) andar com afetação ▶ N (BRIT *Culin*) carne *f* moída;
mincemeat N *recheio de sebo e frutas picadas*; (US: *meat*) carne *f* moída;
mince pie N *pastel com recheio de sebo e frutas picadas*
mind [maɪnd] N mente *f*; (*intellect*) intelecto; (*opinion*): **to my ~** a meu ver; (*sanity*): **to be out of one's ~** estar fora de si ▶ VT (*attend to, look after*) tomar conta de, cuidar de; (*be careful of*) ter cuidado com; (*object to*): **I don't ~ the noise** o barulho não me incomoda; **it is on my ~** não me sai da cabeça; **to keep** *or* **bear sth in ~** levar algo em consideração, não esquecer-se de algo; **to make up one's ~** decidir-se; **I don't ~** (*it doesn't worry me*) eu nem ligo; (*it's all the same to me*) para mim tanto faz; **~ you, ...** se bem que ...; **never ~!** não faz mal, não importa!; (*don't worry*) não se preocupe!; **"~ the step"** "cuidado com o degrau"; **mindless** ADJ (*violence, crime*) insensato; (*job*) monótono
mine¹ [maɪn] PRON o meu/a minha; **a friend of ~** um amigo meu
mine² [maɪn] N mina ▶ VT (*coal*) extrair, explorar; (*ship, beach*) minar
miner ['maɪnəʳ] N mineiro
mineral ['mɪnərəl] ADJ mineral ▶ N mineral *m*; **minerals** NPL (BRIT: *soft drinks*) refrigerantes *mpl*; **mineral water** N água mineral
mingle ['mɪŋgl] VI: **to ~ with** misturar-se com
miniature ['mɪnətʃəʳ] ADJ em miniatura ▶ N miniatura
minibus ['mɪnɪbʌs] N micro-ônibus *m*
minimal ['mɪnɪml] ADJ mínimo
minimum ['mɪnɪməm] (*pl* **minima**) ADJ mínimo ▶ N mínimo
mining ['maɪnɪŋ] N exploração *f* de minas
miniskirt ['mɪnɪskəːt] N minissaia
minister ['mɪnɪstəʳ] N (BRIT *Pol*) ministro(-a); (*Rel*) pastor *m* ▶ VI: **to ~ to sb** prestar assistência a alguém; **to ~ to sb's needs** atender às necessidades de alguém
ministry ['mɪnɪstrɪ] N (BRIT *Pol*) ministério; (*Rel*): **to go into the ~** ingressar no sacerdócio
minor ['maɪnəʳ] ADJ menor; (*unimportant*) de pouca importância; (*Mus*) menor ▶ N (*Jur*) menor *m/f* de idade
minority [maɪ'nɔrɪtɪ] N minoria
mint [mɪnt] N (*plant*) hortelã *f*; (*sweet*) bala de hortelã ▶ VT (*coins*) cunhar; **the (Royal) M~** (BRIT) *or* **the (US) M~** (US) ≈ a Casa da Moeda; **in ~ condition** em perfeito estado
minus ['maɪnəs] N (*also*: **~ sign**) sinal *m* de subtração ▶ PREP menos
minute¹ [maɪ'njuːt] ADJ miúdo, diminuto; (*search*) minucioso
minute² ['mɪnɪt] N minuto; **minutes** NPL (*of meeting*) atas *fpl*; **at the last ~** no último momento
miracle ['mɪrəkl] N milagre *m*
mirage ['mɪrɑːʒ] N miragem *f*
mirror ['mɪrəʳ] N espelho; (*in car*) retrovisor *m*
misbehave [mɪsbɪ'heɪv] VI comportar-se mal
miscarriage ['mɪskærɪdʒ] N (*Med*) aborto (espontâneo); (*failure*): **~ of justice** erro judicial

miscellaneous [mɪsɪ'leɪnɪəs] ADJ (*items, expenses*) diverso; (*selection*) variado

mischief ['mɪstʃɪf] N (*naughtiness*) travessura; (*fun*) diabrura; (*maliciousness*) malícia; **mischievous** ['mɪstʃɪvəs] ADJ (*naughty*) travesso; (*playful*) traquino

misconception [mɪskən'sɛpʃən] N concepção *f* errada, conceito errado

misconduct [mɪs'kɔndʌkt] N comportamento impróprio; **professional ~** má conduta profissional

miser ['maɪzəʳ] N avaro(-a), sovina *m/f*

miserable ['mɪzərəbl] ADJ triste; (*wretched*) miserável; (*weather, person*) deprimente; (*contemptible: offer*) desprezível; (*: failure*) humilhante

misery ['mɪzərɪ] N (*unhappiness*) tristeza; (*wretchedness*) miséria

misfortune [mɪs'fɔːtʃən] N desgraça, infortúnio

misguided [mɪs'gaɪdɪd] ADJ enganado

mishap ['mɪshæp] N desgraça, contratempo

misinterpret [mɪsɪn'təːprɪt] VT interpretar mal

misjudge [mɪs'dʒʌdʒ] VT fazer um juízo errado de, julgar mal

mislay [mɪs'leɪ] *irreg* VT extraviar, perder

mislead [mɪs'liːd] *irreg* VT induzir em erro, enganar; **misleading** ADJ enganoso, errôneo

misplace [mɪs'pleɪs] VT extraviar, perder

misprint ['mɪsprɪnt] N erro tipográfico

Miss [mɪs] N Senhorita (BR), a menina (PT)

miss [mɪs] VT (*train, class, opportunity*) perder; (*fail to hit*) errar, não acertar em; (*fail to see*): **you can't ~ it** é impossível não ver; (*regret the absence of*): **I ~ him** sinto a falta dele ▸ VI falhar ▸ N (*shot*) tiro perdido *or* errado; **miss out** (BRIT) VT omitir

missile ['mɪsaɪl] N míssil *m*; (*object thrown*) projétil *m*

missing ['mɪsɪŋ] ADJ (*pupil*) ausente; (*thing*) perdido; (*removed*) que está faltando; (*Mil*) desaparecido; **to be ~** estar desaparecido; **to go ~** desaparecer

mission ['mɪʃən] N missão *f*; (*official representatives*) delegação *f*

mist [mɪst] N (*light*) neblina; (*heavy*) névoa; (*at sea*) bruma ▸ VI (*eyes: also*: **~ over**) enevoar-se; (BRIT: *also*: **~ over, ~ up**: *windows*) embaçar

mistake [mɪs'teɪk] *irreg* N erro, engano ▸ VT entender *or* interpretar mal; **by ~** por engano; **to make a ~** fazer um erro; **to ~ A for B** confundir A com B; **mistaken** PP *of* **mistake** ▸ ADJ errado; **to be mistaken** enganar-se, equivocar-se

mister ['mɪstəʳ] (*inf*) N senhor *m*; *see* **Mr**

mistletoe ['mɪsltəu] N visco

mistook [mɪs'tuk] PT *of* **mistake**

mistress ['mɪstrɪs] N (*lover*) amante *f*; (*of house*) dona (da casa); (BRIT: *in school*) professora, mestra; (*of situation*) dona; *see* **Mrs**

mistrust [mɪs'trʌst] VT desconfiar de

misty ['mɪstɪ] ADJ (*day*) nublado; (*glasses etc*) embaçado

m

misunderstand [mɪsʌndə'stænd] *irreg* VT, VI entender *or* interpretar mal; **misunderstanding** N mal-entendido; (*disagreement*) desentendimento

misuse [*n* mɪs'ju:s, *vt* mɪs'ju:z] N uso impróprio; (*of power*) abuso; (*of funds*) desvio ▶ VT abusar de; desviar

mix [mɪks] VT misturar; (*combine*) combinar ▶ VI (*people*) entrosar-se ▶ N mistura; (*combination*) combinação *f*; **mix up** VT (*confuse*: *things*) misturar; (: *people*) confundir; **mixed** ADJ misto; **mixed-up** ADJ confuso; **mixer** N (*for food*) batedeira; (*person*) pessoa sociável; **mixture** N mistura; (*Med*) preparado; **mix-up** N trapalhada, confusão *f*

mm ABBR (= *millimetre*) mm

moan [məun] N gemido ▶ VI gemer; (*inf*: *complain*): **to ~ (about)** queixar-se (de), bufar (sobre) (*inf*)

moat [məut] N fosso

mob [mɔb] N multidão *f* ▶ VT cercar

mobile ['məubaɪl] ADJ móvel ▶ N móvel *m*; **mobile phone** N telefone *m* celular (BR), telemóvel *m* (PT)

mock [mɔk] VT ridicularizar; (*laugh at*) zombar de, gozar de ▶ ADJ falso, fingido; (*exam, battle*) simulado; **mockery** N zombaria; **to make a mockery of sth** ridicularizar algo

mode [məud] N modo; (*of transport*) meio

model ['mɔdl] N modelo; (*Arch*) maqueta; (*person*: *for fashion, Art*) modelo *m/f* ▶ ADJ exemplar ▶ VT modelar; **to ~ o.s. on** mirar-se em ▶ VI servir de modelo; (*in fashion*) trabalhar como modelo

modem ['məudɛm] N modem *m*

moderate [*adj, n* 'mɔdərət, *vi, vt* 'mɔdəreɪt] ADJ, N moderado(-a) ▶ VI moderar-se, acalmar-se ▶ VT moderar

modern ['mɔdən] ADJ moderno; **modernize** VT modernizar, atualizar

modest ['mɔdɪst] ADJ modesto; **modesty** N modéstia

modify ['mɔdɪfaɪ] VT modificar

moist [mɔɪst] ADJ úmido (BR), húmido (PT), molhado; **moisture** N umidade *f* (BR), humidade *f* (PT); **moisturizer** N creme *m* hidratante

mole [məul] N (*animal*) toupeira; (*spot*) sinal *m*, lunar *m*; (*fig*) espião(-piã) *m/f*

molest [məu'lɛst] VT molestar; (*attack sexually*) atacar sexualmente

molten ['məultən] ADJ fundido; (*lava*) liquefeito

mom [mɔm] (US) N = **mum**

moment ['məumənt] N momento; **at the ~** neste momento; **momentary** ADJ momentâneo; **momentous** [məu'mɛntəs] ADJ importantíssimo

momentum [məu'mɛntəm] N momento; (*fig*) ímpeto; **to gather ~** ganhar ímpeto

mommy ['mɔmɪ] (US) N = **mummy**

Monaco ['mɔnəkəu] N Mônaco (*no article*)

monarch ['mɔnək] N monarca *m/f*; **monarchy** N monarquia

monastery ['mɔnəstərɪ] N mosteiro, convento

Monday ['mʌndɪ] N segunda-feira

monetary ['mʌnɪtərɪ] ADJ monetário

money ['mʌnɪ] N dinheiro; (*currency*) moeda; **to make ~** ganhar dinheiro; **money order** N vale *m* (postal)

mongrel ['mʌŋgrəl] N (*dog*) vira-lata *m*

monitor ['mɔnɪtəʳ] N (*Comput*) monitor *m* ▶ VT (*heartbeat, pulse*) controlar; (*broadcasts, progress*) monitorar

monk [mʌŋk] N monge *m*

monkey ['mʌŋkɪ] N macaco

monopoly [mə'nɔpəlɪ] N monopólio

monotonous [mə'nɔtənəs] ADJ monótono

monsoon [mɔn'su:n] N monção *f*

monster ['mɔnstəʳ] N monstro

month [mʌnθ] N mês *m*; **monthly** ADJ mensal ▶ ADV mensalmente

monument ['mɔnjumənt] N monumento

mood [mu:d] N humor *m*; (*of crowd*) atmosfera; **to be in a good/bad ~** estar de bom/mau humor; **moody** ADJ (*variable*) caprichoso, de veneta; (*sullen*) rabugento

moon [mu:n] N lua; **moonlight** N luar *m* ▶ VI ter dois empregos, ter um bico

moor [muəʳ] N charneca ▶ VT (*ship*) amarrar ▶ VI fundear, atracar

moose [mu:s] N INV alce *m*

mop [mɔp] N esfregão *m*; (*for dishes*) esponja com cabeça; (*of hair*) grenha ▶ VT esfregar; **mop up** VT limpar

mope [məup] VI estar *or* andar deprimido *or* desanimado

moped ['məupɛd] N moto *f* pequena (BR), motorizada (PT)

moral ['mɔrl] ADJ moral ▶ N moral *f*; **morals** NPL (*principles*) moralidade *f*, costumes *mpl*

morale [mɔ'rɑ:l] N moral *f*, estado de espírito

morality [mə'rælɪtɪ] N moralidade *f*; (*correctness*) retidão *f*, probidade *f*

KEYWORD

more [mɔ:ʳ] ADJ **1** (*greater in number etc*) mais; **more people/work/letters than we expected** mais pessoas/trabalho/cartas do que esperávamos

2 (*additional*) mais; **do you want (some) more tea?** você quer mais chá?; **I have no** *or* **I don't have any more money** não tenho mais dinheiro

▶ PRON **1** (*greater amount*) mais; **more than 10** mais de 10; **it cost more than we expected** custou mais do que esperávamos

2 (*further or additional amount*) mais; **is there any more?** tem ainda mais?; **there's no more** não tem mais

▶ ADV mais; **more dangerous/difficult** *etc* **than** mais perigoso/difícil *etc* do que; **more easily/economically/quickly (than)** mais fácil/econômico/rápido (do que); **more and more** cada vez mais; **more or less** mais ou menos; **more than ever** mais do que nunca

moreover [mɔ:'rəuvəʳ] ADV além do mais, além disso

morning ['mɔ:nɪŋ] N manhã *f*; (*early morning*) madrugada ▶ CPD da manhã; **in the ~** de manhã; **7 o'clock in the ~** (as) 7 da manhã; **morning sickness** N náusea matinal

Morocco [mə'rɔkəu] N Marrocos *m*

moron ['mɔ:rɔn] (*inf*) N débil mental *m/f*, idiota *m/f*

Morse [mɔ:s] N (*also*: **~ code**) código Morse

mortar ['mɔ:təʳ] N (*cannon*) morteiro; (*Constr*) argamassa; (*dish*) pilão *m*, almofariz *m*

m

mortgage ['mɔːgɪdʒ] N hipoteca ▸ VT hipotecar
mortuary ['mɔːtjuərɪ] N necrotério
mosaic [məu'zeɪɪk] N mosaico
Moscow ['mɔskəu] N Moscou (BR), Moscovo (PT)
Moslem ['mɔzləm] ADJ, N = **Muslim**
mosque [mɔsk] N mesquita
mosquito [mɔs'kiːtəu] (*pl* **mosquitoes**) N mosquito
moss [mɔs] N musgo

KEYWORD

most [məust] ADJ **1** (*almost all: people, things etc*) a maior parte de, a maioria de; **most people** a maioria das pessoas
2 (*largest, greatest: interest*) máximo; (*money*): **who has (the) most money?** quem é que tem mais dinheiro?; **he derived the most pleasure from her visit** ele teve o maior prazer em recebê-la
▸ PRON (*greatest quantity, number*) a maior parte, a maioria; **most of it/them** a maioria dele/deles; **most of the money** a maior parte do dinheiro; **do the most you can** faça o máximo que você puder; **I saw the most** vi mais; **to make the most of sth** aproveitar algo ao máximo; **at the (very) most** quando muito, no máximo
▸ ADV (+ *vb, adj, adv*) o mais; **the most intelligent/expensive** *etc* o mais inteligente/caro *etc*; (*very: polite, interesting etc*) muito; **a most interesting book** um livro interessantíssimo

mostly ['məustlɪ] ADV principalmente, na maior parte

MOT (BRIT) N ABBR = **Ministry of Transport**; **the ~ (test)** *vistoria anual dos veículos automotores*
motel [məu'tɛl] N motel *m*
moth [mɔθ] N mariposa; (*clothes moth*) traça
mother ['mʌðəʳ] N mãe *f* ▸ ADJ materno ▸ VT (*care for*) cuidar de (como uma mãe); **motherhood** N maternidade *f*; **mother-in-law** N sogra; **mother-of-pearl** N madrepérola; **mother-to-be** N futura mamãe *f*; **mother tongue** N língua materna
motion ['məuʃən] N movimento; (*gesture*) gesto, sinal *m*; (*at meeting*) moção *f* ▸ VT, VI: **to ~ (to) sb to do sth** fazer sinal a alguém para que faça algo; **motionless** ADJ imóvel; **motion picture** N filme *m* (cinematográfico)
motive ['məutɪv] N motivo
motor ['məutəʳ] N motor *m*; (BRIT *inf: vehicle*) carro, automóvel *m* ▸ CPD (*industry*) de automóvel; **motorbike** N moto(cicleta) *f*, motoca (*inf*); **motorboat** N barco a motor; **motorcar** (BRIT) N carro, automóvel *m*; **motorcycle** N motocicleta; **motorist** N motorista *m/f*; **motor racing** (BRIT) N corrida de carros, automobilismo; **motorway** (BRIT) N rodovia (BR), autoestrada (PT)
motto ['mɔtəu] (*pl* **mottoes**) N lema *m*
mound [maund] N (*of earth*) monte *m*; (*of blankets, leaves etc*) pilha, montanha
mount [maunt] N monte *m* ▸ VT (*horse etc*) montar em, subir a; (*stairs*) subir; (*exhibition*) montar; (*picture*) emoldurar ▸ VI (*increase*) aumentar; **mount up** VI aumentar

mountain ['mauntɪn] N montanha ▸ CPD de montanha; **mountain bike** N mountain bike *f*; **mountaineer** [mauntɪ'nɪəʳ] N alpinista *m/f*, montanhista *m/f*; **mountaineering** N alpinismo; **mountainous** ADJ montanhoso

mourn [mɔːn] VT chorar, lamentar ▸ VI: **to ~ for** chorar *or* lamentar a morte de; **mourning** N luto; **(to be) in mourning** (estar) de luto

mouse [maus] (*pl* **mice**) N camundongo (BR), rato (PT); (*Comput*) mouse *m*; **mouse mat, mouse pad** N (*Comput*) mouse pad *m*

mousse [muːs] N musse *f*; (*for hair*) mousse *f*

moustache [məs'tɑːʃ], (US) **mustache** N bigode *m*

mouth [mauθ] N boca; (*of cave, hole*) entrada; (*of river*) desembocadura; **mouthful** N bocado; **mouth organ** N gaita; **mouthwash** N colutório

move [muːv] N movimento; (*in game*) lance *m*, jogada; (*: turn to play*) turno, vez *f*; (*of house, job*) mudança ▸ VT (*change position of*) mudar; (*in game*) jogar; (*emotionally*) comover; (*Pol: resolution etc*) propor ▸ VI mexer-se, mover-se; (*traffic*) circular; (*also:* **~ house**) mudar-se; (*develop: situation*) desenvolver; **to ~ sb to do sth** convencer alguém a fazer algo; **to get a ~ on** apressar-se; **move about** VI (*fidget*) mexer-se; (*travel*) deslocar-se; **move along** VI avançar; **move around** VI = **move about**; **move away** VI afastar-se; **move back** VI voltar; **move forward** VI avançar; **move in** VI (*to a house*) instalar-se (numa casa); **move on** VI ir andando; **move out** VI sair (de uma casa); **move over** VI afastar-se; **move up** VI ser promovido

movement ['muːvmənt] N movimento; (*gesture*) gesto; (*of goods*) transporte *m*; (*in attitude, policy*) mudança

movie ['muːvɪ] N filme *m*; **to go to the ~s** ir ao cinema

moving ['muːvɪŋ] ADJ (*emotional*) comovente; (*that moves*) móvel

mow [məu] (*pt* **mowed**, *pp* **mowed** *or* **mown**) VT (*grass*) cortar; (*corn*) ceifar; **mow down** VT (*massacre*) chacinar; **mower** N ceifeira; (*also:* **lawnmower**) cortador *m* de grama (BR) *or* de relva (PT)

Mozambique [məuzəm'biːk] N Moçambique *m* (*no article*)

MP N ABBR = **Member of Parliament**

MP3 player N tocador *m* de MP3

mph ABBR = **miles per hour**

Mr ['mɪstəʳ], (US) **Mr.** N: **Mr Smith** (o) Sr. Smith

Mrs ['mɪsɪz], (US) **Mrs.** N: **~ Smith** (a) Sra. Smith

Ms [mɪz], (US) **Ms.** N (= *Miss or Mrs*): **Ms X** (a) Sa X

> **Ms** é um título utilizado em lugar de *Mrs* (senhora) ou de *Miss* (senhorita) para evitar a distinção tradicional entre mulheres casadas e solteiras. É aceito, portanto, como o equivalente de *Mr* (senhor) para os homens. Muitas vezes reprovado por ter surgido como manifestação de um feminismo exacerbado, é uma forma de tratamento muito comum hoje em dia.

MSc N ABBR = **Master of Science**

KEYWORD

much [mʌtʃ] ADJ muito; **how much money/time do you need?** quanto dinheiro/tempo você precisa?; **he's done so much work for the charity** ele trabalhou muito para a obra de caridade; **as much as** tanto como
▶ PRON muito; **much has been gained from our discussions** nossas discussões foram muito proveitosas; **how much does it cost? — too much** quanto custa isso? — caro demais
▶ ADV **1** (*greatly, a great deal*) muito; **thank you very much** muito obrigado(-a); **we are very much looking forward to your visit** estamos aguardando a sua visita com muito ansiedade; **he is very much the gentleman/politician** ele é muito cavalheiro/político; **as much as** tanto como; **as much as you** tanto quanto você
2 (*by far*) de longe; **I'm much better now** estou bem melhor agora
3 (*almost*) quase; **how are you feeling? — much the same** como você está (se sentindo)? — do mesmo jeito

muck [mʌk] N (*dirt*) sujeira (BR), sujidade *f* (PT); **muck about** (*inf*) VI fazer besteiras; **muck around** VI = **muck about**; **muck up** (*inf*) VT estragar
mud [mʌd] N lama
muddle ['mʌdl] N confusão *f*, bagunça; (*mix-up*) trapalhada ▶ VT (*also*: **~ up**: *person, story*) confundir; (: *things*) misturar; **muddle through** VI virar-se
muddy ['mʌdɪ] ADJ (*road*) lamacento
mudguard ['mʌdgɑ:d] N para-lama *m*
muesli ['mju:zlɪ] N muesli *m*
muffin ['mʌfɪn] N *bolinho redondo e chato*
mug [mʌg] N (*cup*) caneca; (*for beer*) caneco, canecão; (*inf: face*) careta; (: *fool*) bobo(-a) ▶ VT (*assault*) assaltar; **mugging** N assalto
muggy ['mʌgɪ] ADJ abafado
mule [mju:l] N mula
multimedia [mʌltɪ'mi:dɪə] ADJ multimídia
multiple ['mʌltɪpl] ADJ múltiplo ▶ N múltiplo; **multiple sclerosis** [-sklɪ'rəusɪs] N esclerose *f* múltipla
multiply ['mʌltɪplaɪ] VT multiplicar ▶ VI multiplicar-se
multistorey ['mʌltɪ'stɔ:rɪ] (BRIT) ADJ de vários andares
mum [mʌm] N (BRIT *inf*) mamãe *f* ▶ ADJ: **to keep ~** ficar calado
mumble ['mʌmbl] VT, VI resmungar, murmurar
mummy ['mʌmɪ] N (BRIT: *mother*) mamãe *f*; (*embalmed*) múmia
mumps [mʌmps] N caxumba
municipal [mju:'nɪsɪpl] ADJ municipal
murder ['mə:də^r] N assassinato ▶ VT assassinar; **murderer** N assassino
murky ['mə:kɪ] ADJ escuro; (*water*) turvo
murmur ['mə:mə^r] N murmúrio ▶ VT, VI murmurar
muscle ['mʌsl] N músculo; (*fig: strength*) força (muscular); **muscle in** VI imiscuir-se, impor-se; **muscular** ['mʌskjulə^r] ADJ muscular; (*person*) musculoso
museum [mju:'zɪəm] N museu *m*
mushroom ['mʌʃrum] N cogumelo

▶ VI crescer da noite para o dia, pipocar
music ['mju:zɪk] N música; **musical** ADJ musical; (*harmonious*) melodioso ▶ N musical *m*; **musician** [mju:'zɪʃən] N músico(-a)
Muslim ['mʌzlɪm] ADJ, N muçulmano(-a)
mussel ['mʌsl] N mexilhão *m*
must [mʌst] AUX VB (*obligation*): **I ~ do it** tenho que *or* devo fazer isso; (*probability*): **he ~ be there by now** ele já deve estar lá; (*suggestion, invitation*): **you ~ come and see me soon** você tem que vir me ver em breve; (*indicating sth unwelcome*): **why ~ he behave so badly?** por que ele tem que se comportar tão mal? ▶ N necessidade *f*; **it's a ~** é imprescindível
mustache ['mʌstæʃ] (US) N = **moustache**
mustard ['mʌstəd] N mostarda
mustn't ['mʌsnt] = **must not**
mute [mju:t] ADJ, N mudo(-a)
mutiny ['mju:tɪnɪ] N motim *m*, rebelião *f*
mutter ['mʌtə[r]] VT, VI resmungar, murmurar
mutton ['mʌtn] N carne *f* de carneiro
mutual ['mju:tʃuəl] ADJ mútuo; (*shared*) comum
muzzle ['mʌzl] N (*of animal*) focinho; (*guard: for dog*) focinheira; (*of gun*) boca ▶ VT pôr focinheira em
my [maɪ] ADJ meu/minha; **this is my house/car/brother** esta é a minha casa/meu carro/meu irmão; **I've washed my hair/cut my finger** lavei meu cabelo/cortei meu dedo
myself [maɪ'sɛlf] PRON (*reflexive*) me; (*emphatic*) eu mesmo; (*after prep*) mim mesmo; *see also* **oneself**
mysterious [mɪs'tɪərɪəs] ADJ misterioso
mystery ['mɪstərɪ] N mistério
mystify ['mɪstɪfaɪ] VT mistificar
myth [mɪθ] N mito; **mythology** [mɪ'θɔlədʒɪ] N mitologia

m

n

nag [næg] VT ralhar, apoquentar
nail [neɪl] N (*human*) unha; (*metal*) prego ▶ VT pregar; **to ~ sb down to a date/price** conseguir que alguém se defina sobre a data/o preço; **nailbrush** N escova de unhas; **nailfile** N lixa de unhas; **nail polish** N esmalte *m* (BR) *or* verniz *m* (PT) de unhas; **nail polish remover** N removedor *m* de esmalte (BR) *or* verniz (PT); **nail scissors** NPL tesourinha de unhas; **nail varnish** (BRIT) N = **nail polish**
naïve [naɪ'i:v] ADJ ingênuo
naked ['neɪkɪd] ADJ nu(a)
name [neɪm] N nome *m*; (*surname*) sobrenome *m*; (*reputation*) reputação *f*, fama ▶ VT (*child*) pôr nome em; (*criminal*) apontar; (*price*) fixar; (*date*) marcar; **what's your ~?** qual é o seu nome?, como (você) se chama?; **by ~** de nome; **in the ~ of** em nome de; **namely** ADV a saber, isto é
nanny ['nænɪ] N babá *f*
nap [næp] N (*sleep*) soneca ▶ VI: **to be caught ~ping** ser pego de surpresa
napkin ['næpkɪn] N (*also*: **table ~**) guardanapo
nappy ['næpɪ] (BRIT) N fralda
narrative ['nærətɪv] N narrativa
narrow ['nærəu] ADJ estreito; (*fig: majority*) pequeno; (*: ideas*) tacanho ▶ VI (*road*) estreitar-se; (*difference*) diminuir; **to have a ~ escape** escapar por um triz; **to ~ sth down to** restringir *or* reduzir algo a; **narrowly** ADV (*miss*) por pouco; **narrow-minded** ADJ de visão limitada, bitolado
nasty ['nɑ:stɪ] ADJ (*unpleasant: remark*) desagradável; (*: person*) mau, ruim; (*malicious*) maldoso; (*rude*) grosseiro, obsceno; (*taste, smell*) repugnante, asqueroso; (*wound, disease etc*) grave, sério
nation ['neɪʃən] N nação *f*
national ['næʃənl] ADJ, N nacional *m/f*; **national anthem** N hino nacional; **National Health Service** (BRIT) N *serviço nacional de saúde*; **nationality** [næʃə'nælɪtɪ] N nacionalidade *f*; **nationalize** VT nacionalizar; **national park** N parque *m* nacional; **National Trust** (BRIT) N *ver nota*

> O **National Trust** é uma instituição independente, sem fins lucrativos, cuja missão é proteger e valorizar os monumentos e a paisagem da Grã-Bretanha devido a seu interesse histórico ou beleza natural.

nationwide ['neɪʃənwaɪd] ADJ de âmbito *or* a nível nacional ▶ ADV em todo o país

native ['neɪtɪv] N natural *m/f*, nativo(-a); (*in colonies*) indígena *m/f*, nativo(-a) ▶ ADJ (*indigenous*) indígena; (*of one's birth*) natal; (*language*) materno; (*innate*) inato, natural; **a ~ speaker of Portuguese** uma pessoa de língua (materna) portuguesa
NATO ['neɪtəu] N ABBR (= *North Atlantic Treaty Organization*) OTAN *f*
natural ['nætʃrəl] ADJ natural; **naturally** ADV naturalmente; (*of course*) claro, evidentemente
nature ['neɪtʃə^r] N natureza; (*character*) caráter *m*, índole *f*
naughty ['nɔːtɪ] ADJ travesso, levado
nausea ['nɔːsɪə] N náusea
naval ['neɪvl] ADJ naval
nave [neɪv] N nave *f*
navel ['neɪvl] N umbigo
navigate ['nævɪgeɪt] VI navegar; (*Aut*) ler o mapa; **navigation** [nævɪ'geɪʃən] N (*action*) navegação *f*; (*science*) náutica
navy ['neɪvɪ] N marinha (de guerra)
Nazi ['nɑːtsɪ] N nazista *m/f* (BR), nazi *m/f* (PT)
NB ABBR (= *nota bene*) NB
near [nɪə^r] ADJ (*place*) vizinho; (*time*) próximo; (*relation*) íntimo ▶ ADV perto ▶ PREP (*also*: **~ to**: *space*) perto de; (: *time*) perto de, quase ▶ VT aproximar-se de; **nearby** [nɪə'baɪ] ADJ próximo, vizinho ▶ ADV à mão, perto; **nearly** ADV quase; **I nearly fell** quase que caí; **near-sighted** ADJ míope
neat [niːt] ADJ (*place*) arrumado, em ordem; (*person*) asseado, arrumado; (*work*) caprichado; (*plan*) engenhoso, bem bolado; (*spirits*) puro; **neatly** ADV caprichosamente, com capricho; (*skilfully*) habilmente
necessarily ['nɛsɪsrɪlɪ] ADV necessariamente
necessary ['nɛsɪsrɪ] ADJ necessário
necessity [nɪ'sɛsɪtɪ] N (*thing needed*) necessidade *f*, requisito; (*compelling circumstances*) necessidade; **necessities** NPL (*essentials*) artigos *mpl* de primeira necessidade
neck [nɛk] N (*Anat*) pescoço; (*of garment*) gola; (*of bottle*) gargalo ▶ VI (*inf*) ficar de agarramento; **~ and ~** emparelhados
necklace ['nɛklɪs] N colar *m*
necktie ['nɛktaɪ] (*esp US*) N gravata
need [niːd] N (*lack*) falta, carência; (*necessity*) necessidade *f*; (*thing needed*) requisito, necessidade ▶ VT precisar de; **I ~ to do it** preciso fazê-lo
needle ['niːdl] N agulha ▶ VT (*inf*) provocar, alfinetar
needless ['niːdlɪs] ADJ inútil, desnecessário; **~ to say ...** desnecessário dizer que ...
needlework ['niːdlwəːk] N costura
needn't ['niːdnt] = **need not**
needy ['niːdɪ] ADJ necessitado, carente
negative ['nɛgətɪv] ADJ negativo ▶ N (*Phot*) negativo; (*Ling*) negativa
neglect [nɪ'glɛkt] VT (*one's duty*) negligenciar, não cumprir com; (*child*) descuidar, esquecer-se de ▶ N (*of child*) descuido, desatenção *f*; (*of house etc*) abandono; (*of duty*) negligência
negotiate [nɪ'gəuʃɪeɪt] VI negociar ▶ VT (*treaty, transaction*)

negociar; (*obstacle*) contornar; (*bend in road*) fazer; **negotiation** [nɪgəuʃɪ'eɪʃən] N negociação *f*

neighbour ['neɪbə^r], (US) **neighbor** N vizinho(-a); **neighbourhood** N (*place*) vizinhança, bairro; (*people*) vizinhos *mpl*; **neighbouring** ADJ vizinho

neither ['naɪðə^r] CONJ: **I didn't move and ~ did he** não me movi nem ele ▶ ADJ, PRON nenhum (dos dois), nem um nem outro ▶ ADV: **~ good nor bad** nem bom nem mau; **~ story is true** nenhuma das estórias é verdade

neon ['ni:ɔn] N neônio, néon *m*

nephew ['nɛvju:] N sobrinho

nerve [nə:v] N (*Anat*) nervo; (*courage*) coragem *f*; (*impudence*) descaramento, atrevimento; **to have a fit of ~s** ter uma crise nervosa

nervous ['nə:vəs] ADJ (*Anat*) nervoso; (*anxious*) apreensivo; (*timid*) tímido, acanhado; **nervous breakdown** N esgotamento nervoso

nest [nɛst] VI aninhar-se ▶ N (*of bird*) ninho; (*of wasp*) vespeiro

net [nɛt] N rede *f*; (*fabric*) filó *m* ▶ ADJ (*Comm*) líquido ▶ VT pegar na rede; (*money: subj: person*) faturar; (*: deal, sale*) render; **the Net** (*Internet*) a Rede; **netball** N *espécie de basquetebol*

Netherlands ['nɛðələndz] NPL: **the ~** os Países Baixos

nett [nɛt] ADJ = **net**

nettle ['nɛtl] N urtiga

network ['nɛtwə:k] N rede *f*; **there's no ~ coverage here** (*Tel*) aqui não tem cobertura

neurotic [njuə'rɔtɪk] ADJ, N neurótico(-a)

neuter ['nju:tə^r] ADJ neutro ▶ VT (*cat etc*) castrar, capar

neutral ['nju:trəl] ADJ neutro ▶ N (*Aut*) ponto morto

never ['nɛvə^r] ADV nunca; *see also* **mind**; **never-ending** ADJ sem fim, interminável; **nevertheless** ADV todavia, contudo

new [nju:] ADJ novo; **New Age** N esoterismo; **newborn** ADJ recém-nascido; **newcomer** N recém-chegado(-a), novato(-a); **newly** ADV recém, novamente

news [nju:z] N notícias *fpl*; (*Radio, TV*) noticiário; **a piece of ~** uma notícia; **newsagent** (BRIT) N jornaleiro(-a); **newscaster** N locutor(a) *m/f*; **newsletter** N boletim *m* informativo; **newspaper** N jornal *m*; **newsreader** N = **newscaster**

newt [nju:t] N tritão *m*

New Year N ano novo; **New Year's Day** N dia *m* de ano novo; **New Year's Eve** N véspera de ano novo

New Zealand [-'zi:lənd] N Nova Zelândia; **New Zealander** N neozelandês(-esa) *m/f*

next [nɛkst] ADJ (*in space*) próximo, vizinho; (*in time*) seguinte, próximo ▶ ADV depois; depois, logo; **~ time** na próxima vez; **~ year** o ano que vem; **~ to** ao lado de; **~ to nothing** quase nada; **next door** ADV na casa do lado ▶ ADJ vizinho; **next-of-kin** N parentes *mpl* mais próximos

NHS (BRIT) N ABBR = **National Health Service**

nibble ['nɪbl] VT mordiscar, beliscar

Nicaragua [nɪkə'rægjuə] N Nicarágua

nice [naɪs] ADJ (*likeable*) simpático; (*kind*) amável, atencioso; (*pleasant*) agradável; (*attractive*) bonito;

nicely ADV agradavelmente, bem
nick [nɪk] N (*wound*) corte *m*; (*cut, indentation*) entalhe *m*, incisão *f* ▸ VT (*inf: steal*) furtar; **in the ~ of time** na hora H, em cima da hora
nickel ['nɪkl] N níquel *m*; (US) moeda de 5 centavos
nickname ['nɪkneɪm] N apelido (BR), alcunha (PT) ▸ VT apelidar de (BR), alcunhar de (PT)
niece [ni:s] N sobrinha
Nigeria [naɪ'dʒɪərɪə] N Nigéria
night [naɪt] N noite *f*; **at** *or* **by ~** à *or* de noite; **the ~ before last** anteontem à noite; **nightclub** N boate *f*; **nightlife** ['naɪtlaɪf] N vida noturna; **nightly** ['naɪtlɪ] ADJ noturno, de noite ▸ ADV todas as noites, cada noite; **nightmare** ['naɪtmɛəʳ] N pesadelo; **night-time** N noite *f*
nil [nɪl] N nada; (BRIT *Sport*) zero
nine [naɪn] NUM nove; **nineteen** [naɪn'ti:n] NUM dezenove (BR), dezanove (PT); **nineteenth** [naɪn'ti:nθ] NUM décimo nono; **ninetieth** ['naɪntɪɪθ] NUM nonagésimo; **ninety** ['naɪntɪ] NUM noventa; **ninth** [naɪnθ] NUM nono
nip [nɪp] VT (*pinch*) beliscar; (*bite*) morder
nipple ['nɪpl] N (*Anat*) bico do seio, mamilo
nitrogen ['naɪtrədʒən] N nitrogênio

KEYWORD

no [nəu] (*pl* **noes**) ADV (*opposite of "yes"*) não; **are you coming? — no (I'm not)** você vem? — não (não vou)
▸ ADJ (*not any*) nenhum(a), não ... algum(a); **I have no more money/time/books** não tenho mais dinheiro/tempo/livros; **"no entry"** "entrada proibida"; **"no smoking"** "é proibido fumar"
▸ N não *m*, negativa

nobility [nəu'bɪlɪtɪ] N nobreza
noble ['nəubl] ADJ (*person*) nobre; (*title*) de nobreza
nobody ['nəubədɪ] PRON ninguém
no-brainer [nəu'breɪnəʳ] (*inf*) N: **it's a ~** isso é meio óbvio
nod [nɔd] VI (*greeting*) cumprimentar com a cabeça; (*in agreement*) acenar (que sim) com a cabeça; (*doze*) cochilar, dormitar ▸ VT: **to ~ one's head** inclinar a cabeça ▸ N inclinação *f* da cabeça; **nod off** VI cochilar
noise [nɔɪz] N barulho; **noisy** ADJ barulhento
nominate ['nɔmɪneɪt] VT (*propose*) propor; (*appoint*) nomear; **nominee** [nɔmɪ'ni:] N pessoa nomeada, candidato(-a)
none [nʌn] PRON (*person*) ninguém; (*thing*) nenhum(a), nada; **~ of you** nenhum de vocês; **I've ~ left** não tenho mais
nonetheless [nʌnðə'lɛs] ADV no entanto, apesar disso, contudo
non-fiction [nɔn-] N literatura de não-ficção
nonsense ['nɔnsəns] N disparate *m*, besteira, absurdo; **~!** bobagem!, que nada!
non-smoker N não-fumante *m/f*
non-stick ADJ tefal ®, não-aderente
noodles ['nu:dlz] NPL talharim *m*
noon [nu:n] N meio-dia *m*
no-one PRON = **nobody**
nor [nɔ:ʳ] CONJ = **neither** ▸ ADV *see* **neither**

norm [nɔ:m] N (*convention*) norma; (*requirement*) regra
normal ['nɔ:ml] ADJ normal
north [nɔ:θ] N norte *m* ▶ ADJ do norte, setentrional ▶ ADV ao *or* para o norte; **North America** N América do Norte; **north-east** N nordeste *m*; **northern** ['nɔ:ðən] ADJ do norte, setentrional; **Northern Ireland** N Irlanda do Norte; **North Pole** N: **the North Pole** o Pólo Norte; **North Sea** N: **the North Sea** o Mar do Norte; **north-west** N noroeste *m*
Norway ['nɔ:weɪ] N Noruega; **Norwegian** [nɔ:'wi:dʒən] ADJ norueguês(-esa) ▶ N norueguês(-esa) *m/f*; (*Ling*) norueguês *m*
nose [nəuz] N (*Anat*) nariz *m*; (*Zool*) focinho; (*sense of smell*: *of person*) olfato; (: *of animal*) faro; **nose about** VI bisbilhotar; **nose around** VI = **nose about**; **nosebleed** N hemorragia nasal; **nosey** (*inf*) ADJ = **nosy**
nostalgia [nɔs'tældʒɪə] N nostalgia
nostril ['nɔstrɪl] N narina
nosy ['nəuzɪ] (*inf*) ADJ intrometido, abelhudo
not [nɔt] ADV não; **he is ~** *or* **isn't here** ele não está aqui; **it's too late, isn't it?** é muito tarde, não?; **he asked me ~ to do it** ele me pediu para não fazer isto; **~ yet/now** ainda/agora não; *see also* **all, only**
notably ['nəutəblɪ] ADV (*particularly*) particularmente; (*markedly*) notavelmente
notch [nɔtʃ] N (*in wood*) entalhe *m*; (*in blade*) corte *m*
note [nəut] N (*Mus, banknote*) nota; (*letter*) nota, bilhete *m*; (*record*) nota, anotação *f*; (*tone*) tom *m* ▶ VT (*observe*) observar, reparar em; (*also*: **~ down**) anotar, tomar nota de; **notebook** N caderno; **notepad** N bloco de anotações; **notepaper** N papel *m* de carta
nothing ['nʌθɪŋ] N nada; (*zero*) zero; **he does ~** ele não faz nada; **~ new/much** nada de novo/de mais; **for ~** de graça, grátis; (*in vain*) à toa, por nada
notice ['nəutɪs] N (*sign*) aviso, anúncio; (*warning*) aviso; (*of leaving or losing job*) aviso prévio ▶ VT reparar em, notar; **at short ~** de repente, em cima da hora; **until further ~** até nova ordem; **to hand in** *or* **give one's ~** demitir, pedir a demissão; **to take ~ of** prestar atenção a, fazer caso de; **to bring sth to sb's ~** levar algo ao conhecimento de alguém; **noticeable** ADJ evidente, visível; **notice board** (BRIT) N quadro de avisos
notify ['nəutɪfaɪ] VT: **to ~ sb of sth** avisar alguém de algo
notion ['nəuʃən] N noção *f*, ideia
nought [nɔ:t] N zero
noun [naun] N substantivo
nourish ['nʌrɪʃ] VT nutrir, alimentar; (*fig*) fomentar, alentar; **nourishment** N alimento, nutrimento
novel ['nɔvl] N romance *m* ▶ ADJ novo, recente; **novelist** N romancista *m/f*; **novelty** N novidade *f*
November [nəu'vɛmbəʳ] N novembro
now [nau] ADV agora; (*these days*) atualmente, hoje em dia ▶ CONJ: **~ (that)** agora que; **right ~** agora

mesmo; **by ~** já; **just ~** agora; **~ and then, ~ and again** de vez em quando; **from ~ on** de agora em diante; **nowadays** ADV hoje em dia

nowhere ['nəuwɛəʳ] ADV (*go*) a lugar nenhum; (*be*) em nenhum lugar

nozzle ['nɔzl] N bocal *m*

nuclear ['nju:klɪəʳ] ADJ nuclear

nucleus ['nju:klɪəs] (*pl* **nuclei**) N núcleo

nude [nju:d] ADJ nu(a) ▶ N (*Art*) nu *m*; **in the ~** nu, pelado

nudge [nʌdʒ] VT acotovelar, cutucar (BR)

nudist ['nju:dɪst] N nudista *m/f*

nuisance ['nju:sns] N amolação *f*, aborrecimento; (*person*) chato; **what a ~!** que saco! (BR), que chatice! (PT)

numb [nʌm] ADJ dormente; **~ with cold** duro de frio; **~ with fear** paralisado de medo

number ['nʌmbəʳ] N número; (*numeral*) algarismo ▶ VT (*pages etc*) numerar; (*amount to*) montar a; **a ~ of** vários, muitos; **to be ~ed among** figurar entre; **they were ten in ~** eram em número de dez; **number plate** (BRIT) N placa (do carro)

numerous ['nju:mərəs] ADJ numeroso

nun [nʌn] N freira

nurse [nə:s] N enfermeiro(-a); (*also*: **~maid**) ama-seca, babá *f* ▶ VT (*patient*) cuidar de, tratar de

nursery ['nə:sərɪ] N (*institution*) creche *f*; (*room*) quarto das crianças; (*for plants*) viveiro; **nursery rhyme** N poesia infantil; **nursery school** N escola maternal

nursing ['nə:sɪŋ] N (*profession*) enfermagem *f*; (*care*) cuidado, assistência; **nursing home** N sanatório, clínica de repouso

nut [nʌt] N (*Tech*) porca; (*Bot*) noz *f*

nutmeg ['nʌtmɛg] N noz-moscada

nutritious [nju:'trɪʃəs] ADJ nutritivo

nuts [nʌts] (*inf*) ADJ: **he's ~** ele é doido

nylon ['naɪlɔn] N náilon *m* (BR), nylon *m* (PT) ▶ ADJ de náilon *or* nylon

O

oak [əuk] N carvalho ▶ ADJ de carvalho
OAP (BRIT) N ABBR = **old-age pensioner**
oar [ɔːʳ] N remo
oasis [əu'eɪsɪs] (*pl* **oases**) N oásis *m inv*
oath [əuθ] N juramento; (*swear word*) palavrão *m*
oatmeal ['əutmiːl] N farinha *or* mingau *m* de aveia
oats [əuts] N aveia
obedient [ə'biːdɪənt] ADJ obediente
obey [ə'beɪ] VT obedecer a; (*instructions, regulations*) cumprir
obituary [ə'bɪtjuərɪ] N necrológio
object [*n* 'ɔbdʒɪkt, *vi* əb'dʒɛkt] N objeto; (*purpose*) objetivo ▶ VI: **to ~ to** (*attitude*) desaprovar, objetar a; (*proposal*) opor-se a; **I ~!** protesto!; **he ~ed that ...** ele objetou que ...; **expense is no ~** o preço não é problema; **objection** [əb'dʒɛkʃən] N objeção *f*; **I have no objection to ...** não tenho nada contra ...; **objective** N objetivo
obligation [ɔblɪ'geɪʃən] N obrigação *f*; **without ~** sem compromisso
obligatory [ə'blɪgətərɪ] ADJ obrigatório
oblige [ə'blaɪdʒ] VT (*do a favour for*) obsequiar, fazer um favor a; (*force*) obrigar, forçar; **to be ~d to sb for doing sth** ficar agradecido por alguém fazer algo
oblong ['ɔblɔŋ] ADJ oblongo, retangular ▶ N retângulo
obnoxious [əb'nɔkʃəs] ADJ odioso, detestável; (*smell*) enjoativo
oboe ['əubəu] N oboé *m*
obscene [əb'siːn] ADJ obsceno
obscure [əb'skjuəʳ] ADJ obscuro, desconhecido; (*difficult to understand*) pouco claro ▶ VT ocultar, escurecer; (*hide: sun etc*) esconder
observant [əb'zəːvnt] ADJ observador(a)
observation [ɔbzə'veɪʃən] N observação *f*; (*Med*) exame *m*
observatory [əb'zəːvətrɪ] N observatório
observe [əb'zəːv] VT observar; (*rule*) cumprir; **observer** N observador(a) *m/f*
obsess [əb'sɛs] VT obsedar, obcecar
obsolete ['ɔbsəliːt] ADJ obsoleto
obstacle ['ɔbstəkl] N obstáculo; (*hindrance*) estorvo, impedimento
obstinate ['ɔbstɪnɪt] ADJ obstinado
obstruct [əb'strʌkt] VT obstruir; (*hinder*) estorvar
obtain [əb'teɪn] VT obter; (*achieve*) conseguir
obvious ['ɔbvɪəs] ADJ óbvio; **obviously** ADV evidentemente;

obviously not! (é)claro que não!
occasion [əˈkeɪʒən] N ocasião *f*; (*event*) acontecimento; **occasional** ADJ de vez em quando; **occasionally** ADV de vez em quando
occupation [ɔkjuˈpeɪʃən] N ocupação *f*; (*job*) profissão *f*
occupy [ˈɔkjupaɪ] VT ocupar; (*house*) morar em; **to ~ o.s. in doing** ocupar-se de fazer
occur [əˈkəːʳ] VI ocorrer; (*phenomenon*) acontecer; **to ~ to sb** ocorrer a alguém; **occurrence** N ocorrência, acontecimento; (*existence*) existência
ocean [ˈəuʃən] N oceano
o'clock [əˈklɔk] ADV: **it is 5 ~** são cinco horas
October [ɔkˈtəubəʳ] N outubro
octopus [ˈɔktəpəs] N polvo
odd [ɔd] ADJ (*strange*) estranho, esquisito; (*number*) ímpar; (*sock etc*) desemparelhado; **60-~** 60 e tantos; **at ~ times** às vezes, de vez em quando; **to be the ~ one out** ficar sobrando, ser a exceção; **oddly** ADV curiosamente; *see also* **enough**; **odds** NPL (*in betting*) pontos *mpl* de vantagem; **it makes no odds** dá no mesmo; **at odds** brigados(-as), de mal
odour [ˈəudəʳ], (*US*) **odor** N odor *m*, cheiro; (*unpleasant*) fedor *m*

KEYWORD

of [ɔv, əv] PREP **1** (*gen*) de; **a friend of ours** um amigo nosso; **a boy of 10** um menino de 10 anos; **that was very kind of you** foi muito gentil da sua parte
2 (*expressing quantity, amount, dates etc*) de; **how much of this do you need?** de quanto você precisa?; **3 of them** 3 deles; **3 of us went** 3 de nós foram; **the 5th of July** dia 5 de julho
3 (*from, out of*) de; **made of wood** feito de madeira

KEYWORD

off [ɔf] ADV **1** (*distance, time*): **it's a long way off** fica bem longe; **the game is 3 days off** o jogo é daqui a 3 dias
2 (*departure*): **I'm off** estou de partida; **to go off to Paris/Italy** ir para Paris/a Itália; **I must be off** devo ir-me
3 (*removal*): **to take off one's hat/coat/clothes** tirar o chapéu/o casaco/a roupa; **the button came off** o botão caiu; **10% off** (*Comm*) 10% de abatimento *or* desconto
4 (*not at work*): **to have a day off** tirar um dia de folga; (*: sick*): **to be off sick** estar ausente por motivo de saúde
▶ ADJ **1** (*not turned on: machine, water, gas*) desligado; (*: light*) apagado; (*: tap*) fechado
2 (*cancelled*) cancelado
3 (*not fresh: food*) passado; (*: milk*) talhado, anulado
4: **on the off chance** (*just in case*) ao acaso; **today I had an off day** (*not as good as usual*) hoje não foi o meu dia
▶ PREP **1** (*indicating motion, removal, etc*) de; **the button came off my coat** o botão do meu casaco caiu
2 (*distant from*) de; **5 km off (the road)** a 5 km (da estrada); **off the coast** em frente à costa
3: **to be off meat** (*no longer eat it*) não comer mais carne; (*no longer like it*) enjoar de carne

offence [ə'fɛns], (US) **offense** N (*crime*) delito; **to take ~ at** ofender-se com, melindrar-se com
offend [ə'fɛnd] VT ofender;
offender N delinquente *m/f*
offensive [ə'fɛnsɪv] ADJ (*weapon, remark*) ofensivo; (*smell etc*) repugnante ▶ N (*Mil*) ofensiva
offer ['ɔfəʳ] N oferta; (*proposal*) proposta ▶ VT oferecer; (*opportunity*) proporcionar; **"on ~"** (*Comm*) "em oferta"
office ['ɔfɪs] N (*place*) escritório; (*room*) gabinete *m*; (*position*) cargo, função *f*; **to take ~** tomar posse; **doctor's ~** (US) consultório; **office block**, (US) **office building** N conjunto de escritórios
officer ['ɔfɪsəʳ] N (*Mil etc*) oficial *m/f*; (*of organization*) diretor(a) *m/f*; (*also*: **police ~**) agente *m/f* policial *or* de polícia
office worker N empregado(-a) *or* funcionário(-a) de escritório
official [ə'fɪʃl] ADJ oficial ▶ N oficial *m/f*; (*civil servant*) funcionário(-a) público(-a)
off-licence (BRIT) N *loja de bebidas alcoólicas*

> Uma loja **off-licence** vende bebidas alcóolicas (para viagem) nos horários em que os pubs estão fechados. Nesses estabelecimentos também se pode comprar bebidas não-alcoólicas, cigarros, batatas fritas, balas, chocolates etc.

offline ADJ, ADV (*Comput*) off-line
off-peak ADJ (*heating etc*) de período de pouco consumo; (*ticket, train*) de período de pouco movimento
off-putting (BRIT) ADJ desconcertante
off-season ADJ, ADV fora de estação *or* temporada
offset ['ɔfsɛt] *irreg* VT compensar, contrabalançar
offshore [ɔf'ʃɔːʳ] ADJ (*breeze*) de terra; (*fishing*) costeiro; **~ oilfield** campo petrolífero ao largo
offside ['ɔf'saɪd] ADJ (*Sport*) impedido; (*Aut*) do lado do motorista
offspring ['ɔfsprɪŋ] N descendência, prole *f*
often ['ɔfn] ADV muitas vezes, frequentemente; **how ~ do you go?** com que frequência você vai?
oil [ɔɪl] N (*Culin*) azeite *m*; (*petroleum*) petróleo; (*for heating*) óleo ▶ VT (*machine*) lubrificar; **oil painting** N pintura a óleo; **oil rig** N torre *f* de perfuração; **oil slick** N mancha de óleo; **oil tanker** N (*ship*) petroleiro; (*truck*) carro-tanque *m* de petróleo; **oil well** N poço petrolífero; **oily** ADJ oleoso; (*food*) gorduroso
ointment ['ɔɪntmənt] N pomada
O.K. ['əu'keɪ] EXCL está bem, está bom, tá (bem *or* bom) (*inf*) ▶ ADJ bom; (*correct*) certo ▶ VT aprovar
old [əuld] ADJ velho; (*former*) antigo, anterior; **how ~ are you?** quantos anos você tem?; **he's 10 years ~** ele tem 10 anos; **~er brother** irmão mais velho; **old age** N velhice *f*; **old-age pensioner** (BRIT) N aposentado(-a) (BR), reformado(-a) (PT); **old-fashioned** ADJ fora de moda; (*person*) antiquado; (*values*) obsoleto, retrógrado
olive ['ɔlɪv] N (*fruit*) azeitona; (*tree*) oliveira ▶ ADJ (*also*: **~-green**) verde-oliva *inv*; **olive oil** N azeite *m* de oliva
Olympic [əu'lɪmpɪk] ADJ olímpico

omelette, (US) **omelet** ['ɔmlɪt] N omelete *f*

omen ['əumən] N presságio, agouro

OMG (*inf*) ABBR (= *Oh my God!*) OMG

ominous ['ɔmɪnəs] ADJ preocupante

omit [əu'mɪt] VT omitir

KEYWORD

on [ɔn] PREP **1** (*indicating position*) sobre, em (cima de); **on the wall** na parede; **on the left** à esquerda
2 (*indicating means, method, condition etc*): **on foot** a pé; **on the train/plane** no trem/avião; **on the telephone/radio** no telefone/rádio; **on television** na televisão; **to be on drugs** (*addicted*) ser viciado em drogas; (*Med*) estar sob medicação; **to be on holiday/business** estar de férias/a negócio
3 (*referring to time*): **on Friday** na sexta-feira; **a week on Friday** sem ser esta sexta-feira, a outra; **on arrival** ao chegar; **on seeing this** ao ver isto
4 (*about, concerning*) sobre
▶ ADV **1** (*referring to dress*): **to have one's coat on** estar de casaco; **what's she got on?** o que ela está usando?; **she put her boots on** ela calçou as botas; **he put his gloves/hat on** ele colocou as luvas/o chapéu
2: **screw the lid on tightly** atarraxar bem a tampa
3 (*further, continuously*): **to walk/drive on** continuar andando/dirigindo; **to go on** continuar (em frente); **to read on** continuar a ler
▶ ADJ **1** (*functioning, in operation: machine*) em funcionamento; (*: light*) aceso; (*: radio*) ligado; (*: tap*) aberto; (*: brakes: of car etc*): **to be on** estar freado; (*meeting*): **is the meeting still on?** (*in progress*) a reunião ainda está sendo realizada?; (*not cancelled*) ainda vai haver reunião?; **there's a good film on at the cinema** tem um bom filme passando no cinema
2: **that's not on!** (*inf: of behaviour*) isso não se faz!

once [wʌns] ADV uma vez; (*formerly*) outrora ▶ CONJ depois que; **~ he had left/it was done** depois que ele saiu/foi feito; **at ~** imediatamente; (*simultaneously*) de uma vez, ao mesmo tempo; **~ more** mais uma vez; **~ and for all** uma vez por todas; **~ upon a time** era uma vez

oncoming ['ɔnkʌmɪŋ] ADJ (*traffic*) que vem de frente

KEYWORD

one [wʌn] NUM um(a); **one hundred and fifty** cento e cinquenta; **one by one** um por um
▶ ADJ **1** (*sole*) único; **the one book which ...** o único livro que ...
2 (*same*) mesmo; **they came in the one car** eles vieram no mesmo carro
▶ PRON **1** um(a); **this one** este/esta; **that one** esse/essa, aquele/aquela; **I've already got one/a red one** eu já tenho um/um vermelho
2: **one another** um ao outro; **do you two ever see one another?** vocês dois se veem de vez em quando?

3 (*impers*): **one never knows** nunca se sabe; **to cut one's finger** cortar o dedo; **one needs to eat** é preciso comer

oneself [wʌn'sɛlf] PRON (*reflexive*) se; (*after prep, emphatic*) si (mesmo(-a)); **by ~** sozinho(-a); **to hurt ~** ferir-se; **to keep sth for ~** guardar algo para si mesmo; **to talk to ~** falar consigo mesmo

one-sided ADJ parcial

one-way ADJ (*street, traffic*) de mão única (BR), de sentido único (PT)

ongoing ['ɔngəuɪŋ] ADJ (*project*) em andamento; (*situation*) existente

onion ['ʌnjən] N cebola

online ADJ, ADV (*Comput*) on-line, online

onlooker ['ɔnlukəʳ] N espectador(a) *m/f*

only ['əunlɪ] ADV somente, apenas ▶ ADJ único, só ▶ CONJ só que, porém; **an ~ child** um filho único; **not ~ ... but also ...** não só ... mas também ...

onset ['ɔnsɛt] N começo

onto ['ɔntu] PREP = **on to**

onward ['ɔnwəd], **onwards** ['ɔnwədz] ADV (*move*) para diante, para a frente; **from this time ~(s)** de (ag)ora em diante

ooze [uːz] VI ressumar, filtrar-se

opaque [əu'peɪk] ADJ opaco, fosco

open ['əupn] ADJ aberto; (*car*) descoberto; (*road*) livre; (*fig: frank*) aberto, franco; (*meeting*) aberto, sem restrições ▶ VT abrir ▶ VI abrir(-se); (*book etc*) começar; **in the ~ (air)** ao ar livre; **open on to** VT FUS (*subj: room, door*) dar para; **open up** VT abrir; (*blocked road*) desobstruir ▶ VI (*Comm*) abrir; **opening** ADJ de abertura ▶ N abertura; (*start*) início; (*opportunity*) oportunidade *f*; **openly** ADV abertamente; **open-minded** ADJ aberto, imparcial; **open-necked** ADJ aberto no colo; **open-plan** ADJ sem paredes divisórias; **Open University** (BRIT) N *ver nota*

> Fundada em 1969, a **Open University** oferece um tipo de ensino que compreende cursos (alguns blocos da programação da TV e do rádio são reservados para esse fim), deveres que são enviados pelo aluno ao diretor ou diretora de estudos e uma estada obrigatória em uma universidade de verão. É preciso cumprir um certo número de unidades ao longo de um período determinado e obter a média em um certo número delas para receber o diploma almejado.

opera ['ɔpərə] N ópera

operate ['ɔpəreɪt] VT fazer funcionar, pôr em funcionamento ▶ VI funcionar; (*Med*): **to ~ on sb** operar alguém

operation [ɔpə'reɪʃən] N operação *f*; (*of machine*) funcionamento; **to be in ~** (*system*) estar em vigor

operator ['ɔpəreɪtəʳ] N (*of machine*) operador(a) *m/f*, manipulador(a) *m/f*; (*Tel*) telefonista *m/f*

opinion [ə'pɪnɪən] N opinião *f*; **in my ~** na minha opinião, a meu ver

opponent [ə'pəunənt] N oponente *m/f*; (*Mil, Sport*) adversário(-a)

opportunity [ɔpə'tjuːnɪtɪ] N oportunidade *f*; **to take the ~ of doing** aproveitar a oportunidade para fazer

oppose [ə'pəuz] VT opor-se a; **to be ~d to sth** opor-se a algo, estar

contra algo; **as ~d to** em oposição a
opposite ['ɔpəzɪt] ADJ oposto; (*house etc*) em frente ▶ ADV (lá) em frente ▶ PREP em frente de, defronte de ▶ N oposto, contrário
opposition [ɔpə'zɪʃən] N oposição *f*
opt [ɔpt] VI: **to ~ for** optar por; **to ~ to do** optar por fazer; **opt out** VI: **to ~ out of doing sth** optar por não fazer algo
optician [ɔp'tɪʃən] N oculista *m/f*
optimist ['ɔptɪmɪst] N otimista *m/f*; **optimistic** [ɔptɪ'mɪstɪk] ADJ otimista
option ['ɔpʃən] N opção *f*; **optional** ADJ opcional, facultativo
or [ɔː^r] CONJ ou; (*with negative*): **he hasn't seen or heard anything** ele não viu nem ouviu nada; **or else** senão
oral ['ɔːrəl] ADJ oral ▶ N prova *f* oral
orange ['ɔrɪndʒ] N (*fruit*) laranja ▶ ADJ cor de laranja *inv*, alaranjado
orbit ['ɔːbɪt] N órbita ▶ VT orbitar
orchard ['ɔːtʃəd] N pomar *m*
orchestra ['ɔːkɪstrə] N orquestra; (*US: seating*) plateia
orchid ['ɔːkɪd] N orquídea
ordeal [ɔː'diːl] N experiência penosa, provação *f*
order ['ɔːdə^r] N ordem *f*; (*Comm*) encomenda ▶ VT (*also*: **put in ~**) pôr em ordem, arrumar; (*in restaurant*) pedir; (*Comm*) encomendar; (*command*) mandar, ordenar; **in (working) ~** em bom estado; **in ~ to do/that** para fazer/que (+ *sub*); **good ~** bom estado; **on ~** (*Comm*) encomendado; **out of ~** com defeito, enguiçado; **order form** N impresso para encomendas;
orderly N (*Mil*) ordenança *m*; (*Med*) servente *m/f* ▶ ADJ (*room*) arrumado, ordenado; (*person*) metódico
ordinary ['ɔːdnrɪ] ADJ comum, usual; (*pej*) ordinário, medíocre; **out of the ~** fora do comum, extraordinário
ore [ɔː^r] N minério
organ ['ɔːgən] N órgão *m*; **organic** [ɔː'gænɪk] ADJ orgânico
organization [ɔːgənaɪ'zeɪʃən] N organização *f*
organize ['ɔːgənaɪz] VT organizar
orgasm ['ɔːgæzəm] N orgasmo
origin ['ɔrɪdʒɪn] N origem *f*
original [ə'rɪdʒɪnl] ADJ original ▶ N original *m*
originate [ə'rɪdʒɪneɪt] VI: **to ~ from** originar-se de, surgir de; **to ~ in** ter origem em
Orkney ['ɔːknɪ] N (*also*: **the ~ Islands, the ~s**) as ilhas Órcadas
ornament ['ɔːnəmənt] N ornamento; (*on dress*) enfeite *m*; **ornamental** [ɔːnə'mɛntl] ADJ decorativo, ornamental
ornate [ɔː'neɪt] ADJ enfeitado, requintado
orphan ['ɔːfn] N órfão/órfã *m/f*
orthopaedic [ɔːθə'piːdɪk], (*US*) **orthopedic** ADJ ortopédico
ostrich ['ɔstrɪtʃ] N avestruz *m/f*
other ['ʌðə^r] ADJ outro ▶ PRON: **the ~ (one)** o outro/a outra ▶ ADV (*usually in negatives*): **~ than** (*apart from*) além de; (*anything but*) exceto; **~s** (*other people*) outros; **otherwise** ADV (*in a different way*) de outra maneira; (*apart from that*) além disso ▶ CONJ (*if not*) senão
otter ['ɔtə^r] N lontra
ouch [autʃ] EXCL ai!

ought [ɔːt] (*pt* **ought**) AUX VB: **I ~ to do it** eu deveria fazê-lo; **he ~ to win** (*probability*) ele deve ganhar
ounce [auns] N onça (= 28.35g)
our ['auəʳ] ADJ nosso; *see also* **my**; **ours** PRON (o) nosso/(a) nossa *etc*; *see also* **mine¹**; **ourselves** [auə'sɛlvz] PRON PL (*reflexive, after prep*) nós; (*emphatic*) nós mesmos(-as); *see also* **oneself**
oust [aust] VT expulsar

KEYWORD

out [aut] ADV **1** (*not in*) fora; **(to stand) out in the rain/snow** (estar em pé) na chuva/neve; **out loud** em voz alta
2 (*not at home, absent*) fora (de casa); **Mr Green is out at the moment** Sr. Green não está no momento; **to have a day/night out** passar o dia fora/sair à noite
3 (*indicating distance*): **the boat was 10 km out** o barco estava a 10 km da costa
4 (*Sport*): **the ball is/has gone out** a bola caiu fora; **out!** (*Tennis etc*) fora!
▸ ADJ **1**: **to be out** (*unconscious*) estar inconsciente; (*out of game*) estar fora; (*out of fashion*) estar fora de moda
2 (*have appeared: news, secret*) do conhecimento público; **the flowers are out** as flores desabrocharam
3 (*extinguished: light, fire*) apagado; **before the week was out** (*finished*) antes da semana acabar
4: **to be out to do sth** (*intend*) pretender fazer algo; **to be out in one's calculations** (*wrong*) enganar-se nos cálculos
▸ **out of** PREP **1** (*outside, beyond*) fora de; **to go out of the house** sair da casa; **to look out of the window** olhar pela janela
2 (*cause, motive*) por
3 (*origin*): **to drink sth out of a cup** beber algo na xícara
4 (*from among*): **1 out of every 3 smokers** 1 entre 3 fumantes
5 (*without*) sem; **to be out of milk/sugar/petrol** *etc* não ter leite/açúcar/gasolina *etc*

outback ['autbæk] N (*in Australia*): **the ~** o interior; **outbox** ['autbɔks] N (*Comput*) caixa de saída; (*US: for papers*) cesta de saída
outbreak ['autbreɪk] N (*of war*) deflagração *f*; (*of disease*) surto; (*of violence etc*) explosão *f*
outburst ['autbəːst] N explosão *f*
outcast ['autkɑːst] N pária *m/f*
outcome ['autkʌm] N resultado
outcry ['autkraɪ] N clamor *m* (de protesto)
outdated [aut'deɪtɪd] ADJ antiquado, fora de moda
outdoor [aut'dɔːʳ] ADJ ao ar livre; (*clothes*) de sair; **outdoors** ADV ao ar livre
outer ['autəʳ] ADJ exterior, externo; **outer space** N espaço (exterior)
outfit ['autfɪt] N roupa, traje *m*
outgoing ['autgəuɪŋ] ADJ de saída; (*character*) extrovertido, sociável; **outgoings** (BRIT) NPL despesas *fpl*
outing ['autɪŋ] N excursão *f*
outlaw ['autlɔː] N fora-da-lei *m/f* ▸ VT (*person*) declarar fora da lei; (*practice*) declarar ilegal
outlay ['autleɪ] N despesas *fpl*
outlet ['autlɛt] N saída, escape *m*; (*of pipe*) desague *m*, escoadouro; (*US Elec*) tomada; (*also*: **retail ~**) posto de venda
outline ['autlaɪn] N (*shape*) contorno, perfil *m*; (*of plan*) traçado;

(*sketch*) esboço, linhas *fpl* gerais ▶ VT (*theory, plan*) traçar, delinear

outlook ['autluk] N (*attitude*) ponto de vista; (*fig: prospects*) perspectiva; (: *for weather*) previsão *f*

outnumber [aut'nʌmbəʳ] VT exceder em número

out-of-date ADJ (*passport, ticket*) sem validade; (*clothes*) fora de moda

out-of-the-way ADJ remoto, afastado

outpatient ['autpeɪʃənt] N paciente *m/f* externo(-a) *or* de ambulatório

outpost ['autpəust] N posto avançado

output ['autput] N (volume *m* de) produção *f*; (*Comput*) saída ▶ VT (*Comput*) dar saída em

outrage ['autreɪdʒ] N escândalo; (*atrocity*) atrocidade *f* ▶ VT ultrajar; **outrageous** [aut'reɪdʒəs] ADJ ultrajante, escandaloso

outright [*adv* aut'raɪt, *adj* 'autraɪt] ADV (*kill, win*) completamente; (*ask, refuse*) abertamente ▶ ADJ completo; franco

outset ['autsɛt] N início, princípio

outside [aut'saɪd] N exterior *m* ▶ ADJ exterior, externo ▶ ADV (lá) fora ▶ PREP fora de; (*beyond*) além (dos limites) de; **at the ~** (*fig*) no máximo; **outsider** N (*stranger*) estranho(-a), forasteiro(-a)

outsize ['autsaɪz] ADJ (*clothes*) de tamanho extra-grande *or* especial

outskirts ['autskə:ts] NPL arredores *mpl*, subúrbios *mpl*

outspoken [aut'spəukən] ADJ franco, sem rodeios

outstanding [aut'stændɪŋ] ADJ excepcional; (*work, debt*) pendente

outward ['autwəd] ADJ externo; (*journey*) de ida; **outwards** (*esp* BRIT) ADV para fora

outweigh [aut'weɪ] VT ter mais valor do que

oval ['əuvl] ADJ ovalado ▶ N oval *m*; **Oval Office** N *ver nota*

> O Salão Oval (**Oval Office**) é o escritório particular do presidente dos Estados Unidos na Casa Branca, assim chamado devido a sua forma oval. Por extensão, o termo se refere à presidência em si.

ovary ['əuvərɪ] N ovário

oven ['ʌvn] N forno

KEYWORD

over ['əuvəʳ] ADV **1** (*across: walk, jump, fly etc*) por cima; **to cross over to the other side of the road** atravessar para o outro lado da rua; **over here** por aqui, cá; **over there** por ali, lá; **to ask sb over** (*to one's home*) convidar alguém

2 to fall over cair; **to knock over** derrubar; **to turn over** virar; **to bend over** curvar-se, debruçar-se

3 (*finished*): **to be over** estar acabado

4 (*excessively: clever, rich, fat etc*) muito, demais; **she's not over intelligent** ela não é superdotada

5 (*remaining: money, food etc*): **there are 3 over** tem 3 sobrando/ sobraram 3

6: **all over** (*everywhere*) por todos os lados; **over and over (again)** repetidamente

▶ PREP **1** (*on top of*) sobre; (*above*) acima de

2 (*on the other side of*) no outro

lado de; **he jumped over the wall** ele pulou o muro
3 (*more than*) mais de; **over and above** além de
4 (*during*) durante

overall [*n, adj* 'əuvərɔ:l, *adv* əuvər'ɔ:l] ADJ (*length*) total; (*study*) global ▶ ADV (*view*) globalmente; (*measure, paint*) totalmente; **overalls** NPL macacão *m* (BR), (fato) macaco (PT)
overboard ['əuvəbɔ:d] ADV (*Naut*) ao mar
overcast ['əuvəkɑ:st] ADJ nublado, fechado
overcharge [əuvə'tʃɑ:dʒ] VT: **to ~ sb** cobrar em excesso a alguém
overcoat ['əuvəkəut] N sobretudo
overcome [əuvə'kʌm] *irreg* VT vencer, dominar; (*difficulty*) superar
overcrowded [əuvə'kraudɪd] ADJ superlotado
overdo [əuvə'du:] *irreg* VT exagerar; (*overcook*) cozinhar demais; **to ~ it** (*work too hard*) exceder-se
overdose ['əuvədəus] N overdose *f*, dose *f* excessiva
overdraft ['əuvədrɑ:ft] N saldo negativo
overdrawn [əuvə'drɔ:n] ADJ (*account*) sem fundos, a descoberto
overdue [əuvə'dju:] ADJ atrasado; (*change*) tardio
overestimate [əuvər'ɛstɪmeɪt] VT sobrestimar
overflow [*vi* əuvə'fləu, *n* 'əuvəfləu] VI transbordar ▶ N (*also*: **~ pipe**) tubo de descarga, ladrão *m*
overgrown [əuvə'grəun] ADJ (*garden*) coberto de vegetação
overhaul [*vt* əuvə'hɔ:l, *n* 'əuvəhɔ:l] VT revisar ▶ N revisão *f*
overhead [*adv* əuvə'hɛd, *adj, n* 'əuvəhɛd] ADV por cima, em cima; (*in the sky*) no céu ▶ ADJ (*lighting*) superior; (*railway*) suspenso ▶ N (US) = **overheads**; **overheads** NPL (*expenses*) despesas *fpl* gerais
overhear [əuvə'hɪə^r] *irreg* VT ouvir por acaso
overheat [əuvə'hi:t] VI (*engine*) aquecer demais
overland ['əuvəlænd] ADJ, ADV por terra
overlap [əuvə'læp] VI (*edges*) sobrepor-se em parte; (*fig*) coincidir
overload [əuvə'ləud] VT sobrecarregar
overlook [əuvə'luk] VT (*have view on*) dar para; (*miss*) omitir; (*forgive*) fazer vista grossa a
overnight [*adv* əuvə'naɪt, *adj* 'əuvənaɪt] ADV durante a noite; (*fig*) da noite para o dia ▶ ADJ de uma (*or* de) noite; **to stay ~** passar a noite, pernoitar
overpass ['əuvəpɑ:s] (*esp* US) N viaduto
overpower [əuvə'pauə^r] VT dominar, subjugar; (*fig*) assolar
overrule [əuvə'ru:l] VT (*decision*) anular; (*claim*) indeferir
overrun [əuvə'rʌn] *irreg* VT (*country etc*) invadir; (*time limit*) ultrapassar, exceder
overseas [əuvə'si:z] ADV (*abroad*) no estrangeiro, no exterior ▶ ADJ (*trade*) exterior; (*visitor*) estrangeiro
overshadow [əuvə'ʃædəu] VT ofuscar
oversight ['əuvəsaɪt] N descuido
oversleep [əuvə'sli:p] *irreg* VI dormir além da hora
overt [əu'və:t] ADJ aberto, indissimulado

overtake [əuvə'teɪk] *irreg* VT ultrapassar
overthrow [əuvə'θrəu] *irreg* VT (*government*) derrubar
overtime ['əuvətaɪm] N horas *fpl* extras
overturn [əuvə'tə:n] VT virar; (*system*) derrubar; (*decision*) anular ▶ VI capotar
overweight [əuvə'weɪt] ADJ acima do peso
overwhelm [əuvə'wɛlm] VT esmagar, assolar; **overwhelming** ADJ (*victory, defeat*) esmagador(a); (*heat*) sufocante; (*desire*) irresistível
owe [əu] VT: **to ~ sb sth, to ~ sth to sb** dever algo a alguém; **owing to** PREP devido a, por causa de
owl [aul] N coruja
own [əun] ADJ próprio ▶ VT possuir, ter; **a room of my ~** meu próprio quarto; **to get one's ~ back** ir à forra; **on one's ~** sozinho; **own up** VI: **to ~ up to sth** confessar algo; **owner** N dono(-a), proprietário(-a); **ownership** N posse *f*
ox [ɔks] (*pl* **oxen**) N boi *m*
oxygen ['ɔksɪdʒən] N oxigênio
oyster ['ɔɪstə^r] N ostra
oz. ABBR = **ounce**
ozone ['əuzəun] N ozônio

P

p [pi:] ABBR (= *page*) p; (BRIT) = **penny, pence**
p.a. ABBR (= *per annum*) por ano
pace [peɪs] N passo; (*speed*) velocidade *f* ▶ VI: **to ~ up and down** andar de um lado para o outro; **to keep ~ with** acompanhar o passo de; **pacemaker** N (*Med*) marcapasso *m*
Pacific [pə'sɪfɪk] N: **the ~ (Ocean)** o (Oceano) Pacífico
pack [pæk] N pacote *m*, embrulho; (*of hounds*) matilha; (*of thieves etc*) bando, quadrilha; (*of cards*) baralho; (*backpack*) mochila ▶ VT encher; (*in suitcase etc*) arrumar (na mala); (*cram*): **to ~ into** entupir de, entulhar com ▶ VI: **to ~ (one's bags)** fazer as malas; **~ it in!** para com isso!; **pack off** VT (*person*) despedir
package ['pækɪdʒ] N pacote *m*; (*bulky*) embrulho, fardo; (*also*: **~ deal**) pacote; **package tour** (BRIT) N excursão *f* organizada

packed lunch [pækt-] (BRIT) N merenda
packet ['pækɪt] N pacote *m*; (*of cigarettes*) maço; (*of washing powder etc*) caixa
packing ['pækɪŋ] N embalagem *f*; (*act*) empacotamento
pad [pæd] N (*of paper*) bloco; (*to prevent friction*) acolchoado; (*inf: home*) casa ▶ VT acolchoar, enchumaçar
paddle ['pædl] N remo curto; (*US: for table tennis*) raquete *f* ▶ VT remar ▶ VI patinhar; **paddling pool** (BRIT) N lago de recreação
paddock ['pædək] N cercado; (*at race course*) paddock *m*
padlock ['pædlɔk] N cadeado
paedophile, (US) **pedophile** ['pi:dəufaɪl] N pedófilo(-a)
page [peɪdʒ] N página; (*also*: **~ boy**) mensageiro ▶ VT mandar chamar
pager ['peɪdʒəʳ] N bip *m*
paid [peɪd] PT, PP *of* **pay** ▶ ADJ (*work*) remunerado; (*holiday*) pago; (*official*) assalariado; **to put ~ to** (BRIT) acabar com
pain [peɪn] N dor *f*; **to be in ~** sofrer *or* sentir dor; **to take ~s to do sth** dar-se ao trabalho de fazer algo; **painful** ADJ doloroso; (*laborious*) penoso; (*unpleasant*) desagradável; **painkiller** N analgésico; **painstaking** ['peɪnzteɪkɪŋ] ADJ (*work*) esmerado; (*person*) meticuloso
paint [peɪnt] N pintura ▶ VT pintar; **paintbrush** N (*artist's*) pincel *m*; (*decorator's*) broxa; **painter** N pintor(a) *m/f*; **painting** N pintura; (*picture*) tela, quadro
pair [pɛəʳ] N par *m*; **a ~ of scissors** uma tesoura; **a ~ of trousers** uma calça (BR), umas calças (PT)
pajamas [pɪ'dʒɑ:məz] (US) NPL pijama *m*
Pakistan [pɑ:kɪ'stɑ:n] N Paquistão *m*; **Pakistani** ADJ, N paquistanês(-esa) *m/f*
pal [pæl] (*inf*) N camarada *m/f*, colega *m/f*
palace ['pæləs] N palácio
pale [peɪl] ADJ pálido; (*colour*) claro; (*light*) fraco ▶ VI empalidecer ▶ N: **to be beyond the ~** passar dos limites
Palestine ['pælɪstaɪn] N Palestina; **Palestinian** [pælɪs'tɪnɪən] ADJ, N palestino(-a)
palm [pɑ:m] N (*hand, leaf*) palma; (*also*: **~ tree**) palmeira ▶ VT: **to ~ sth off on sb** (*inf*) impingir algo a alguém
pamper ['pæmpəʳ] VT paparicar, mimar
pamphlet ['pæmflət] N panfleto
pan [pæn] N (*also*: **sauce~**) panela (BR), caçarola (PT); (*also*: **frying ~**) frigideira
Panama ['pænəmɑ:] N Panamá *m*
pancake ['pænkeɪk] N panqueca
panda ['pændə] N panda *m/f*
pandemic [pæn'dɛmɪk] N pandemia
pane [peɪn] N vidraça, vidro
panel ['pænl] N (*of wood, Radio, TV*) painel *m*
panic ['pænɪk] N pânico ▶ VI entrar em pânico
pansy ['pænzɪ] N (*Bot*) amor-perfeito; (*inf, pej*) bicha (BR), maricas *m* (PT)
pant [pænt] VI arquejar, ofegar
panther ['pænθəʳ] N pantera
panties ['pæntɪz] NPL calcinha (BR), cuecas *fpl* (PT)
pantomime ['pæntəmaɪm] (BRIT) N pantomima

Uma **pantomime**, também chamada simplesmente de *panto*, é um gênero de comédia em que o personagem principal em geral é um rapaz e na qual há sempre uma *dame*, isto é, uma mulher idosa representada por um homem, e um vilão. Na maior parte das vezes, a história é baseada em um conto de fadas, como "A gata borralheira" ou "O gato de botas", e a plateia é encorajada a participar prevenindo os heróis dos perigos que estão por vir. Esse tipo de espetáculo, voltado sobretudo para as crianças, visa também ao público adulto por meio de diversas brincadeiras que fazem alusão aos fatos atuais.

pants [pænts] NPL (BRIT: *underwear: woman's*) calcinha (BR), cuecas *fpl* (PT); (: *man's*) cueca (BR), cuecas (PT); (US: *trousers*) calça (BR), calças *fpl* (PT)

paper ['peɪpəʳ] N papel *m*; (*also*: **news~**) jornal *m*; (*also*: **wall~**) papel de parede; (*study, article*) artigo, dissertação *f*; (*exam*) exame *m*, prova ▶ ADJ de papel ▶ VT (*room*) revestir (com papel de parede); **papers** NPL (*also*: **identity ~s**) documentos *mpl*; **paperback** N livro de capa mole; **paper bag** N saco de papel; **paper clip** N clipe *m*; **paperwork** N trabalho burocrático; (*pej*) papelada

par [pɑːʳ] N paridade *f*, igualdade *f*; (*Golf*) média *f*; **on a ~ with** em pé de igualdade com

parachute ['pærəʃuːt] N para-quedas *m inv*

parade [pə'reɪd] N desfile *m* ▶ VT (*show off*) exibir ▶ VI (*Mil*) passar revista

paradise ['pærədaɪs] N paraíso

paraffin ['pærəfɪn] (BRIT) N: **~ (oil)** querosene *m*

paragraph ['pærəgrɑːf] N parágrafo

Paraguay ['pærəgwaɪ] N Paraguai *m*

parallel ['pærəlɛl] ADJ (*lines etc*) paralelo; (*fig*) correspondente ▶ N paralela; correspondência

paralysis [pə'rælɪsɪs] (*pl* **paralyses**) N paralisia

paranoid ['pærənɔɪd] ADJ paranoico

parcel ['pɑːsl] N pacote *m* ▶ VT (*also*: **~ up**) embrulhar, empacotar

pardon ['pɑːdn] N (*Jur*) indulto ▶ VT perdoar; **~ me!, I beg your ~** (*apologizing*) desculpe(-me); **(I beg your) ~?** (BRIT), **~ me?** (US) (*not hearing*) como?, como disse?

parent ['pɛərənt] N (*father*) pai *m*; (*mother*) mãe *f*; **parents** NPL (*mother and father*) pais *mpl*

Paris ['pærɪs] N Paris

parish ['pærɪʃ] N paróquia, freguesia

park [pɑːk] N parque *m* ▶ VT, VI estacionar; **park and ride** N *esquema de transporte feito parcialmente com carro, que em seguida é estacionado para o uso de transporte público*

parking ['pɑːkɪŋ] N estacionamento; **"no ~"** "estacionamento proibido"; **parking lot** (US) N (parque *m* de) estacionamento; **parking meter** N parquímetro; **parking ticket** N multa por estacionamento proibido

parliament ['pɑːləmənt] (BRIT) N parlamento
parole [pə'rəul] N: **on ~** em liberdade condicional, sob promessa
parrot ['pærət] N papagaio
parsley ['pɑːslɪ] N salsa
parsnip ['pɑːsnɪp] N cherivia, pastinaga
parson ['pɑːsn] N padre *m*, clérigo; (*in Church of England*) pastor *m*
part [pɑːt] N parte *f*; (*of machine*) peça; (*Theatre etc*) papel *m*; (*of serial*) capítulo; (*US: in hair*) risca, repartido ▶ ADV = **partly** ▶ VT dividir; (*hair*) repartir ▶ VI (*people*) separar-se; (*crowd*) dispersar-se; **to take ~ in** participar de, tomar parte em; **to take sb's ~** defender alguém; **for my ~** pela minha parte; **for the most ~** na maior parte; **to take sth in good ~** não se ofender com algo; **part with** VT FUS ceder, entregar; (*money*) pagar
partial ['pɑːʃl] ADJ parcial; **to be ~ to** gostar de, ser apreciador(a) de
participate [pɑː'tɪsɪpeɪt] VI: **to ~ in** participar de
particle ['pɑːtɪkl] N partícula; (*of dust*) grão *m*
particular [pə'tɪkjulə^r] ADJ (*special*) especial; (*specific*) específico; (*fussy*) exigente, minucioso; **in ~** em particular; **particularly** ADV em particular, especialmente; **particulars** NPL detalhes *mpl*; (*personal details*) dados *mpl* pessoais
parting ['pɑːtɪŋ] N (*act*) separação *f*; (*farewell*) despedida; (BRIT: *in hair*) risca, repartido ▶ ADJ de despedida; **~ shot** (*fig*) flecha de parto
partition [pɑː'tɪʃən] N (*Pol*) divisão *f*; (*wall*) tabique *m*, divisória
partly ['pɑːtlɪ] ADV em parte
partner ['pɑːtnə^r] N (*Comm*) sócio(-a); (*Sport*) parceiro(-a); (*at dance*) par *m*; (*spouse*) cônjuge *m/f*; **partnership** N associação *f*, parceria; (*Comm*) sociedade *f*
partridge ['pɑːtrɪdʒ] N perdiz *f*
part-time ADJ, ADV de meio expediente
party ['pɑːtɪ] N (*Pol*) partido; (*celebration*) festa; (*group*) grupo; (*Jur*) parte *f* interessada, litigante *m/f* ▶ CPD (*Pol*) do partido, partidário
pass [pɑːs] VT passar; (*exam*) passar em; (*place*) passar por; (*overtake, surpass*) ultrapassar; (*approve*) aprovar ▶ VI passar; (*Sch*) ser aprovado, passar ▶ N (*permit*) passe *m*; (*membership card*) carteira; (*in mountains*) desfiladeiro; (*Sport*) passe *m*; (*Sch*): **to get a ~ in** ser aprovado em; **to make a ~ at sb** tomar liberdade com alguém; **pass away** VI falecer; **pass by** VI passar ▶ VT passar por cima de; **pass for** VT FUS passar por; **pass on** VT (*news, illness*) transmitir; (*object*) passar para; **pass out** VI desmaiar; **pass up** VT deixar passar; **passable** ADJ (*road*) transitável; (*work*) aceitável
passage ['pæsɪdʒ] N (*also*: **~way**: *indoors*) corredor *m*; (: *outdoors*) passagem *f*; (*Anat*) via; (*act of passing*) trânsito; (*in book*) trecho; (*by boat*) travessia; (*Mechanics, Med*) conduto
passenger ['pæsɪndʒə^r] N passageiro(-a)
passer-by ['pɑːsə^r-] (*pl* **passers-by**) N transeunte *m/f*
passion ['pæʃən] N paixão *f*; **passionate** ADJ apaixonado; **passion fruit** N maracujá *m*
passive ['pæsɪv] ADJ passivo

passport ['pɑːspɔːt] N passaporte *m*
password ['pɑːswəːd] N senha
past [pɑːst] PREP (*drive, walk etc: in front of*) por; (: *beyond*) mais além de; (*later than*) depois de ▶ ADJ passado; (*president etc*) ex-, anterior ▶ N passado; **he's ~ forty** ele tem mais de quarenta anos; **ten/quarter ~ four** quatro e dez/quinze; **for the ~ few/3 days** nos últimos/3 dias
pasta ['pæstə] N massa
paste [peɪst] N pasta; (*glue*) grude *m*, cola ▶ VT grudar; **tomato ~** massa de tomate
pasteurized ['pæstəraɪzd] ADJ pasteurizado
pastime ['pɑːstaɪm] N passatempo
pastry ['peɪstrɪ] N massa; (*cake*) bolo
pasture ['pɑːstʃəʳ] N pasto
pasty [*n* 'pæstɪ, *adj* 'peɪstɪ] N empadão *m* de carne ▶ ADJ (*complexion*) pálido
pat [pæt] VT dar palmadinhas em; (*dog etc*) fazer festa em
patch [pætʃ] N retalho; (*eye patch*) tapa-olho *m*; (*area*) aréa pequena; (*mend*) remendo ▶ VT remendar; **(to go through) a bad ~** (passar por) um mau pedaço; **patch up** VT consertar provisoriamente; (*quarrel*) resolver; **patchy** ADJ (*colour*) desigual; (*information*) incompleto
pâté ['pæteɪ] N patê *m*
patent ['peɪtnt] N patente *f* ▶ VT patentear ▶ ADJ patente, evidente
paternal [pə'təːnl] ADJ paternal; (*relation*) paterno
path [pɑːθ] N caminho; (*trail, track*) trilha, senda; (*trajectory*) trajetória
pathetic [pə'θɛtɪk] ADJ (*pitiful*) patético, digno de pena; (*very bad*) péssimo
pathway ['pɑːθweɪ] N caminho, trilha
patience ['peɪʃns] N paciência
patient ['peɪʃnt] ADJ, N paciente *m/f*
patio ['pætɪəu] N pátio
patrol [pə'trəul] N patrulha ▶ VT patrulhar; **patrol car** N carro de patrulha
patron ['peɪtrən] N (*customer*) cliente *m/f*, freguês(-esa) *m/f*; (*of charity*) benfeitor(a) *m/f*; **~ of the arts** mecenas *m*
pattern ['pætən] N (*Sewing*) molde *m*; (*design*) desenho
pause [pɔːz] N pausa ▶ VI fazer uma pausa
pave [peɪv] VT pavimentar; **to ~ the way for** preparar o terreno para
pavement ['peɪvmənt] N (BRIT) calçada (BR), passeio (PT)
pavilion [pə'vɪlɪən] N (*Sport*) barraca
paving ['peɪvɪŋ] N pavimento, calçamento
paw [pɔː] N pata; (*of cat*) garra
pawn [pɔːn] N (*Chess*) peão *m*; (*fig*) títere *m* ▶ VT empenhar;
pawnbroker N agiota *m/f*
pay [peɪ] (*pt, pp* **paid**) N salário; (*of manual worker*) paga ▶ VT pagar; (*debt*) liquidar, saldar; (*visit*) fazer ▶ VI valer a pena, render; **to ~ attention (to)** prestar atenção (a); **to ~ one's respects to sb** fazer uma visita de cortesia a alguém; **pay back** VT (*money*) devolver; (*person*) pagar; **pay for** VT FUS pagar a; (*fig*) recompensar; **pay in** VT depositar; **pay off** VT

P

(*debts*) saldar, liquidar; (*creditor*) pagar, reembolsar ▸ VI (*plan, patience*) valer a pena; **pay up** VT pagar; **payable** ADJ pagável; (*cheque*): **payable to** nominal em favor de; **payment** N pagamento; **monthly payment** pagamento mensal; **pay packet** (BRIT) N envelope *m* de pagamento; **pay phone** N telefone *m* público; **payroll** N folha de pagamento; **pay television** N televisão *f* por assinatura

PC N ABBR (= *personal computer*) PC *m*

PDA N ABBR (= *personal digital assistant*) PDA *m* (*assistente digital pessoal*)

pea [pi:] N ervilha

peace [pi:s] N paz *f*; (*calm*) tranquilidade *f*, quietude *f*; **peaceful** ADJ (*person*) tranquilo, pacífico; (*place, time*) tranquilo, sossegado

peach [pi:tʃ] N pêssego

peacock ['pi:kɔk] N pavão *m*

peak [pi:k] N (*of mountain: top*) cume *m*; (*of cap*) pala, viseira; (*fig*) apogeu *m*

peanut ['pi:nʌt] N amendoim *m*; **peanut butter** N manteiga de amendoim

pear [pɛəʳ] N pera

pearl [pə:l] N pérola

peasant ['pɛznt] N camponês(-esa) *m/f*

peat [pi:t] N turfa

pebble ['pɛbl] N seixo, calhau *m*

peck [pɛk] VT (*also*: **~ at**) bicar, dar bicadas em ▸ N bicada; (*kiss*) beijoca; **peckish** (BRIT *inf*) ADJ: **I feel peckish** estou a fim de comer alguma coisa

peculiar [pɪ'kju:lɪəʳ] ADJ (*strange*) estranho, esquisito; **~ to** (*belonging to*) próprio de

pedal ['pɛdl] N pedal *m* ▸ VI pedalar

pedestrian [pɪ'dɛstrɪən] N pedestre *m/f* (BR), peão *m* (PT) ▸ ADJ (*fig*) prosaico; **pedestrian crossing** (BRIT) N passagem *f* para pedestres (BR), passadeira (PT)

pedigree ['pɛdɪgri:] N raça; (*fig*) genealogia ▸ CPD (*animal*) de raça

pedophile ['pi:dəufaɪl] (US) N = **paedophile**

pee [pi:] (*inf*) VI fazer xixi, mijar

peek [pi:k] VI: **to ~ at** espiar, espreitar

peel [pi:l] N casca ▸ VT descascar ▸ VI (*paint, skin*) descascar; (*wallpaper*) desprender-se

peep [pi:p] N (BRIT: *look*) espiadela; (*sound*) pio ▸ VI espreitar; **peep out** (BRIT) VI mostrar-se, surgir

peer [pɪəʳ] VI: **to ~ at** perscrutar, fitar ▸ N (*noble*) par *m/f*; (*equal*) igual *m/f*; (*contemporary*) contemporâneo(-a)

peg [pɛg] N (*for coat etc*) cabide *m*; (BRIT: *also*: **clothes ~**) pregador *m*

pelican ['pɛlɪkən] N pelicano

pelt [pɛlt] VT: **to ~ sb with sth** atirar algo em alguém ▸ VI (*rain*: *also*: **~ down**) chover a cântaros; (*inf*: *run*) correr ▸ N pele *f* (não curtida)

pelvis ['pɛlvɪs] N pelvis *f*, bacia

pen [pɛn] N caneta; (*for sheep etc*) redil *m*, cercado

penalty ['pɛnltɪ] N pena, penalidade *f*; (*fine*) multa; (*Sport*) punição *f*

pence [pɛns] (BRIT) NPL *of* **penny**

pencil ['pɛnsl] N lápis *m*; **pencil case** N lapiseira, porta-lápis *m inv*; **pencil sharpener** N apontador *m* (de lápis) (BR), apara-lápis *m inv* (PT)

pendant ['pɛndnt] N pingente *m*

pending ['pɛndɪŋ] PREP até ▸ ADJ pendente

penetrate ['pɛnɪtreɪt] VT penetrar
penfriend ['pɛnfrɛnd] (BRIT) N amigo(-a) por correspondência
penguin ['pɛŋgwɪn] N pinguim *m*
peninsula [pə'nɪnsjulə] N península
penis ['pi:nɪs] N pênis *m*
penitentiary [pɛnɪ'tɛnʃərɪ] (US) N penitenciária, presídio
penknife ['pɛnnaɪf] *irreg* N canivete *m*
penniless ['pɛnɪlɪs] ADJ sem dinheiro, sem um tostão
penny ['pɛnɪ] (*pl* **pennies**, BRIT **pence**) N pêni *m*; (US) cêntimo
penpal ['pɛnpæl] N amigo(-a) por correspondência
pension ['pɛnʃən] N pensão *f*; (*old-age pension*) aposentadoria; **pensioner** (BRIT) N aposentado(-a) (BR), reformado(-a) (PT)
Pentagon ['pɛntəgən] N: **the ~** o Pentágono

> O Pentágono (**Pentagon**) é o nome dado aos escritórios do Ministério da Defesa americano, localizados em Arlington, no estado da Virgínia, por causa da forma pentagonal do edifício onde se encontram. Por extensão, o termo é utilizado também para se referir ao ministério.

penthouse ['pɛnthaus] N cobertura
people ['pi:pl] NPL gente *f*, pessoas *fpl*; (*inhabitants*) habitantes *mpl/fpl*; (*citizens*) povo; (*Pol*): **the ~** o povo ▶ N (*nation, race*) povo; **several ~ came** vieram várias pessoas; **~ say that ...** dizem que ...
pepper ['pɛpəʳ] N pimenta; (*vegetable*) pimentão *m* ▶ VT apimentar; (*fig*): **to ~ with** salpicar de; **peppermint** N (*sweet*) bala de hortelã
per [pə:ʳ] PREP por
perceive [pə'si:v] VT perceber; (*notice*) notar; (*realize*) compreender
per cent N por cento
percentage [pə'sɛntɪdʒ] N porcentagem *f*, percentagem *f*
perch [pə:tʃ] (*pl* **perches**) N (*for bird*) poleiro; (*fish*) perca ▶ VI: **to ~ (on)** (*bird*) empoleirar-se (em); (*person*) encarapitar-se (em)
perfect [*adj, n* 'pə:fɪkt, *vt* pə'fɛkt] ADJ perfeito; (*utter*) completo ▶ N (*also*: **~ tense**) perfeito ▶ VT aperfeiçoar; **perfectly** ADV perfeitamente
perform [pə'fɔ:m] VT (*carry out*) realizar, fazer; (*piece of music*) interpretar ▶ VI (*well, badly*) interpretar; **performance** N desempenho; (*of play, by artist*) atuação *f*; (*of car*) performance *f*; **performer** N (*actor*) artista *m/f*, ator/atriz *m/f*; (*Mus*) intérprete *m/f*
perfume ['pə:fju:m] N perfume *m*
perhaps [pə'hæps] ADV talvez
perimeter [pə'rɪmɪtəʳ] N perímetro
period ['pɪərɪəd] N período; (*Sch*) aula; (US: *full stop*) ponto final; (*Med*) menstruação *f*, regra ▶ ADJ (*costume, furniture*) da época
perish ['pɛrɪʃ] VI perecer; (*decay*) deteriorar-se
perjury ['pə:dʒərɪ] N (*Jur*) perjúrio, falso testemunho
perk [pə:k] (*inf*) N mordomia, regalia; **perk up** VI (*cheer up*) animar-se
perm [pə:m] N permanente *f*

permanent ['pə:mənənt] ADJ permanente
permission [pə'mɪʃən] N permissão *f*; (*authorization*) autorização *f*
permit [*n* 'pə:mɪt, *vt* pə'mɪt] N licença; (*to enter*) passe *m* ▶ VT permitir; (*authorize*) autorizar
perplex [pə'plɛks] VT deixar perplexo
persecute ['pə:sɪkju:t] VT perseguir
persevere [pə:sɪ'vɪə[r]] VI perseverar
Persian ['pə:ʃən] ADJ persa ▶ N (*Ling*) persa *m*; **the (~) Gulf** o golfo Pérsico
persist [pə'sɪst] VI: **to ~ (in doing sth)** persistir (em fazer algo);
persistent [pə'sɪstənt] ADJ persistente; (*determined*) teimoso
person ['pə:sn] N pessoa; **in ~** em pessoa; **personal** ADJ pessoal; (*private*) particular; (*visit*) em pessoa, pessoal; **personal assistant** N secretário(-a) particular; **personal computer** N computador *m* pessoal;
personality [pə:sə'nælɪtɪ] N personalidade *f*; **personal organizer** N agenda
personnel [pə:sə'nɛl] N pessoal *m*
perspective [pə'spɛktɪv] N perspectiva
perspiration [pə:spɪ'reɪʃən] N transpiração *f*
persuade [pə'sweɪd] VT: **to ~ sb to do sth** persuadir alguém a fazer algo
Peru [pə'ru:] N Peru *m*
pervert [*n* 'pə:və:t, *vt* pə'və:t] N pervertido(-a) ▶ VT perverter, corromper; (*truth*) distorcer
pessimist ['pɛsɪmɪst] N pessimista *m/f*; **pessimistic** [pɛsɪ'mɪstɪk] ADJ pessimista
pest [pɛst] N (*animal*) praga; (*fig*) peste *f*
pester ['pɛstə[r]] VT incomodar
pet [pɛt] N animal *m* de estimação ▶ CPD predileto ▶ VT acariciar ▶ VI (*inf*) acariciar-se; **teacher's ~** (*favourite*) preferido(-a) do professor
petal ['pɛtl] N pétala
petite [pə'ti:t] ADJ delicado, mignon
petition [pə'tɪʃən] N petição *f*; (*list of signatures*) abaixo-assinado
petrified ['pɛtrɪfaɪd] ADJ (*fig*) petrificado, paralisado
petrol ['pɛtrəl] (BRIT) N gasolina; **two/four-star ~** gasolina comum/premium
petroleum [pə'trəulɪəm] N petróleo
petrol: petrol pump (BRIT) N bomba de gasolina; **petrol station** (BRIT) N posto (BR) *or* bomba (PT) de gasolina; **petrol tank** (BRIT) N tanque *m* de gasolina
petticoat ['pɛtɪkəut] N anágua
petty ['pɛtɪ] ADJ (*mean*) mesquinho; (*unimportant*) insignificante
pew [pju:] N banco (de igreja)
pewter ['pju:tə[r]] N peltre *m*
phantom ['fæntəm] N fantasma *m*
pharmacy ['fɑ:məsɪ] N farmácia
phase [feɪz] N fase *f* ▶ VT: **to ~ in/out** introduzir/retirar por etapas
PhD N ABBR = **Doctor of Philosophy** ≈ doutorado
pheasant ['fɛznt] N faisão *m*
phenomenon [fə'nɔmɪnən] (*pl* **phenomena**) N fenômeno
philosophical [fɪlə'sɔfɪkl] ADJ filosófico; (*fig*) calmo, sereno
philosophy [fɪ'lɔsəfɪ] N filosofia
phishing ['fɪʃɪŋ] N phishing *m*; **~ attack** golpe *m* de phishing
phobia ['fəubjə] N fobia
phone [fəun] N telefone *m* ▶ VT telefonar para, ligar para; **to be on**

the ~ ter telefone; (*be calling*) estar no telefone; **phone back** VT, VI ligar de volta; **phone up** VT telefonar para ▸ VI telefonar; **phone book** N lista telefônica; **phone box** (BRIT) N cabine *f* telefônica; **phone call** N telefonema *m*, ligação *f*; **phone card** N cartão *m* telefônico; **phone number** N número de telefone

phonetics [fə'nɛtɪks] N fonética

phoney ['fəunɪ] ADJ falso; (*person*) fingido

photo ['fəutəu] N foto *f*

photo... ['fəutəu] PREFIX foto...; **photocopier** N fotocopiadora *f*; **photocopy** N fotocópia, xerox® *m* ▸ VT fotocopiar, xerocar

photograph ['fəutəgrɑ:f] N fotografia ▸ VT fotografar; **photographer** [fə'tɔgrəfəʳ] N fotógrafo(-a); **photography** [fə'tɔgrəfɪ] N fotografia

phrase [freɪz] N frase *f* ▸ VT expressar; **phrase book** N livro de expressões idiomáticas (para turistas)

physical ['fɪzɪkl] ADJ físico

physician [fɪ'zɪʃən] N médico(-a)

physics ['fɪzɪks] N física

physiotherapy [fɪzɪəu'θɛrəpɪ] N fisioterapia

physique [fɪ'zi:k] N físico

pianist ['pi:ənɪst] N pianista *m/f*

piano [pɪ'ænəu] N piano

pick [pɪk] N (*also*: **~axe**) picareta ▸ VT (*select*) escolher, selecionar; (*gather*) colher; (*remove*) tirar; (*lock*) forçar; **take your ~** escolha o que quiser; **the ~ of** o melhor de; **to ~ one's nose** colocar o dedo no nariz; **to ~ one's teeth** palitar os dentes; **to ~ a quarrel** *or* **a fight with sb** comprar uma briga com alguém; **pick at** VT FUS (*food*) beliscar; **pick on** VT FUS (*person: criticize*) criticar; (*: treat badly*) azucrinar, aporrinhar; **pick out** VT escolher; (*distinguish*) distinguir; **pick up** VI (*improve*) melhorar ▸ VT (*from floor, Aut*) apanhar; (*Police*) prender; (*collect*) buscar; (*for sexual encounter*) paquerar; (*learn*) aprender; (*Radio, TV, Tel*) pegar; **to ~ up speed** acelerar; **to ~ o.s. up** levantar-se

pickle ['pɪkl] N (*also*: **~s**: *as condiment*) picles *mpl*; (*fig: mess*) apuro ▸ VT (*in vinegar*) conservar em vinagre; (*in salt*) conservar em sal e água

pickpocket ['pɪkpɔkɪt] N batedor(a) *m/f* de carteira (BR), carteirista *m/f* (PT)

picnic ['pɪknɪk] N piquenique *m*

picture ['pɪktʃəʳ] N quadro; (*painting*) pintura; (*drawing*) desenho; (*etching*) água-forte *f*; (*photograph*) foto(grafia) *f*; (*TV*) imagem *f*; (*film*) filme *m*; (*fig: description*) descrição *f*; (*: situation*) conjuntura ▸ VT imaginar-se; **the pictures** NPL (BRIT *inf*) o cinema; **picture messaging** N serviço de mensagens multimídia

pie [paɪ] N (*vegetable*) pastelão *m*; (*fruit*) torta; (*meat*) empadão *m*

piece [pi:s] N pedaço; (*portion*) fatia; (*item*): **a ~ of clothing/furniture/advice** uma roupa/um móvel/um conselho ▸ VT: **to ~ together** juntar; **to take to ~s** desmontar

pie chart N gráfico de setores

pier [pɪəʳ] N cais *m*; (*jetty*) embarcadouro, molhe *m*

pierce [pɪəs] VT furar, perfurar

pig [pɪg] N porco; (*fig*)

porcalhão(-lhona) *m/f*; (*pej*: *unkind person*) grosseiro(-a); (: *greedy person*) ganancioso(-a)
pigeon ['pɪdʒən] N pombo
piggy bank ['pɪgɪ-] N *cofre em forma de porquinho*
pigsty ['pɪgstaɪ] N chiqueiro
pigtail ['pɪgteɪl] N rabo-de-cavalo, trança
pike [paɪk] (*pl* **pike** *or* **pikes**) N (*fish*) lúcio
pilchard ['pɪltʃəd] N sardinha
pile [paɪl] N (*heap*) monte *m*; (*of carpet*) pelo; (*of cloth*) lado felpudo ▶ VT (*also*: ~ **up**) empilhar ▶ VI (*also*: ~ **up**: *objects*) empilhar-se; (: *problems, work*) acumular-se; **pile into** VT FUS (*car*) apinhar-se
piles [paɪlz] NPL hemorróidas *fpl*
pile-up N (*Aut*) engavetamento
pilgrim ['pɪlgrɪm] N peregrino(-a)
pill [pɪl] N pílula; **the** ~ a pílula
pillar ['pɪlə^r] N pilar *m*; **pillar box** (BRIT) N caixa coletora (do correio) (BR), marco do correio (PT)
pillow ['pɪləu] N travesseiro (BR), almofada (PT); **pillowcase** N fronha
pilot ['paɪlət] N piloto(-a) ▶ CPD (*scheme etc*) piloto *inv* ▶ VT pilotar; **pilot light** N piloto
pimple ['pɪmpl] N espinha
PIN N ABBR (= *personal identification number*) senha
pin [pɪn] N alfinete *m* ▶ VT alfinetar; ~**s and needles** comichão *f*, sensação *f* de formigamento; **to** ~ **sth on sb** (*fig*) culpar alguém de algo; **pin down** VT (*fig*): **to** ~ **sb down** conseguir que alguém se defina *or* tome atitude
pinafore ['pɪnəfɔː^r] N (*also*: ~ **dress**) avental *m*
pinch [pɪntʃ] N (*of salt etc*) pitada ▶ VT beliscar; (*inf*: *steal*) afanar; **at a** ~ em último caso
pine [paɪn] N pinho ▶ VI: **to** ~ **for** ansiar por; **pine away** VI consumir-se, definhar
pineapple ['paɪnæpl] N abacaxi *m* (BR), ananás *m* (PT)
pink [pɪŋk] ADJ cor de rosa *inv* ▶ N (*colour*) cor *f* de rosa; (*Bot*) cravo, cravina
pinpoint ['pɪnpɔɪnt] VT (*discover*) descobrir; (*explain*) identificar; (*locate*) localizar com precisão
pint [paɪnt] N quartilho (*Brit* = *568cc, US* = *473cc*)
pioneer [paɪə'nɪə^r] N pioneiro(-a)
pious ['paɪəs] ADJ pio, devoto
pip [pɪp] N (*seed*) caroço, semente *f*; **the pips** NPL (BRIT: *time signal on radio*) ≈ o toque de seis segundos
pipe [paɪp] N cano; (*for smoking*) cachimbo ▶ VT canalizar, encanar; **pipes** NPL (*also*: **bag~s**) gaita de foles; **pipe down** (*inf*) VI calar o bico, meter a viola no saco; **pipeline** N (*for oil*) oleoduto; (*for gas*) gaseoduto
pirate ['paɪərət] N pirata *m* ▶ VT piratear
Pisces ['paɪsiːz] N Pisces *m*, Peixes *mpl*
piss [pɪs] (!) VI mijar; **pissed** (!) ADJ (*drunk*) bêbado, de porre
pistol ['pɪstl] N pistola
piston ['pɪstən] N pistão *m*, êmbolo
pit [pɪt] N cova, fossa; (*quarry, hole in surface of sth*) buraco; (*also*: **coal** ~) mina de carvão ▶ VT: **to** ~ **one's wits against sb** competir em conhecimento *or* inteligência contra alguém; **pits** NPL (*Aut*) box *m*
pitch [pɪtʃ] N (*Mus*) tom *m*; (*fig*: *degree*) intensidade *f*; (BRIT *Sport*) campo; (*tar*) piche *m*, breu *m* ▶ VT (*throw*) arremessar, lançar; (*tent*) armar ▶ VI (*fall forwards*) cair (para

frente); **pitch-black** ADJ escuro como o breu
pitfall ['pɪtfɔːl] N perigo (imprevisto), armadilha
pitiful ['pɪtɪful] ADJ comovente, tocante
pity ['pɪtɪ] N compaixão *f*, piedade *f* ▶ VT ter pena de, compadecer-se de
pixel ['pɪksl] N pixel *m*
pizza ['piːtsə] N pizza
placard ['plækɑːd] N placar *m*; (*in march etc*) cartaz *m*
place [pleɪs] N lugar *m*; (*rank, position*) posição *f*; (*post*) posto; (*role*) papel *m*; (*home*): **at/to his ~** na/para a casa dele ▶ VT pôr, colocar; (*identify*) identificar, situar; **to take ~** realizar-se; (*occur*) ocorrer; **out of ~** (*not suitable*) fora de lugar, deslocado; **in the first ~** em primeiro lugar; **to change ~s with sb** trocar de lugar com alguém; **to be ~d** (*in race, exam*) classificar-se
plague [pleɪg] N (*Med*) peste *f*; (*fig*) praga ▶ VT atormentar, importunar
plaice [pleɪs] N INV solha
plain [pleɪn] ADJ (*unpatterned*) liso; (*clear*) claro, evidente; (*simple*) simples *inv*, despretensioso; (*not handsome*) sem atrativos ▶ ADV claramente, com franqueza ▶ N planície *f*, campina; **plain chocolate** N chocolate *m* amargo; **plainly** ADV claramente, obviamente; (*hear, see*) facilmente; (*state*) francamente
plaintiff ['pleɪntɪf] N querelante *m/f*, queixoso(-a)
plait [plæt] N trança, dobra
plan [plæn] N plano; (*scheme*) projeto; (*schedule*) programa *m* ▶ VT planejar (BR), planear (PT) ▶ VI fazer planos; **to ~ to do** pretender fazer
plane [pleɪn] N (*Aviat*) avião *m*; (*also*: **~ tree**) plátano; (*fig: level*) nível *m*; (*tool*) plaina; (*Math*) plano
planet ['plænɪt] N planeta *m*
plank [plæŋk] N tábua
planning ['plænɪŋ] N planejamento (BR), planeamento (PT); **family ~** planejamento *or* planeamento familiar
plant [plɑːnt] N planta; (*machinery*) maquinaria; (*factory*) usina, fábrica ▶ VT plantar; (*field*) semear; (*bomb*) colocar, pôr
plaster ['plɑːstəʳ] N (*for walls*) reboco; (*also*: **~ of Paris**) gesso; (BRIT: *also*: **sticking ~**) esparadrapo, band-aid *m* ▶ VT rebocar; (*cover*): **to ~ with** encher *or* cobrir de
plastic ['plæstɪk] N plástico ▶ ADJ de plástico; **plastic bag** N sacola de plástico; **plastic surgery** N cirurgia plástica
plate [pleɪt] N prato; (*on door, Phot, dental*) chapa; (*in book*) gravura; **gold/silver ~** placa de ouro/prata
plateau ['plætəu] (*pl* **plateaus** *or* **plateaux**) N planalto
platform ['plætfɔːm] N (*Rail*) plataforma (BR), cais *m* (PT); (*at meeting*) tribuna; (*raised structure: for landing etc*) plataforma; (BRIT: *of bus*) plataforma; (*Pol*) programa *m* partidário
platinum ['plætɪnəm] N platina
plausible ['plɔːzɪbl] ADJ plausível; (*person*) convincente
play [pleɪ] N (*Theatre*) obra, peça ▶ VT jogar; (*team, opponent*) jogar contra; (*instrument, music, record*) tocar ▶ VI (*music*) tocar; (*frolic*) brincar; **to ~ safe** não se arriscar,

não correr riscos; **play down** VT minimizar; **play up** VI (*person*) dar trabalho; (*TV, car*) estar com defeito; **player** N jogador(a) *m/f*; (*Theatre*) ator/atriz *m/f*; (*Mus*) músico(-a); **playful** ADJ brincalhão(-lhona); **playground** N (*in park*) playground *m*; (*in school*) pátio de recreio; **playgroup** N *espécie de jardim de infância*; **playing card** N carta de baralho; **playing field** N campo de esportes (BR) *or* jogos (PT); **playtime** N (*Sch*) recreio; **playwright** N dramaturgo(-a)

plea [pli:] N (*request*) apelo, petição *f*; (*Jur*) defesa

plead [pli:d] VT (*Jur*) defender, advogar; (*give as excuse*) alegar ▶ VI (*Jur*) declarar-se; (*beg*): **to ~ with sb** suplicar *or* rogar a alguém

pleasant ['plɛznt] ADJ agradável; (*person*) simpático

please [pli:z] EXCL por favor ▶ VT agradar a, dar prazer a ▶ VI agradar, dar prazer; (*think fit*): **do as you ~** faça o que *or* como quiser; **~ yourself!** (*inf*) como você quiser!, você que sabe!; **pleased** ADJ: **pleased (with)** satisfeito (com); **pleased to meet you** prazer (em conhecê-lo)

pleasure ['plɛʒəʳ] N prazer *m*; **"it's a ~"** "não tem de quê"

pleat [pli:t] N prega

pledge [plɛdʒ] N (*promise*) promessa ▶ VT prometer; **to ~ support for sb** empenhar-se a apoiar alguém

plentiful ['plɛntɪful] ADJ abundante

plenty ['plɛntɪ] N: **~ of** (*food, money*) bastante; (*jobs, people*) muitos(-as)

pliers ['plaɪəz] NPL alicate *m*

plod [plɔd] VI caminhar pesadamente; (*fig*) trabalhar laboriosamente

plonk [plɔŋk] (*inf*) N (BRIT: *wine*) zurrapa ▶ VT: **to ~ sth down** deixar cair algo (pesadamente)

plot [plɔt] N (*scheme*) conspiração *f*, complô *m*; (*of story, play*) enredo, trama; (*of land*) lote *m* ▶ VT (*conspire*) tramar, planejar (BR), planear (PT); (*Aviat, Naut, Math*) plotar ▶ VI conspirar; **a vegetable ~** (BRIT) uma horta

plough [plau], (US) **plow** N arado ▶ VT arar; **to ~ money into** investir dinheiro em; **plough through** VT FUS abrir caminho por; **ploughman's lunch** (BRIT) N lanche de pão, queijo e picles

ploy [plɔɪ] N estratagema *m*

pls ABBR (= *please*) por favor

pluck [plʌk] VT (*fruit*) colher; (*musical instrument*) dedilhar; (*bird*) depenar ▶ N coragem *f*, puxão *m*; **to ~ one's eyebrows** fazer as sobrancelhas; **to ~ up courage** criar coragem

plug [plʌg] N (*Elec*) tomada (BR), ficha (PT); (*in sink*) tampa; (*Aut*: *also*: **spark(ing) ~**) vela (de ignição) ▶ VT (*hole*) tapar; (*inf*: *advertise*) fazer propaganda de; **plug in** VT (*Elec*) ligar; **plug-in** N (*Comput*) plug-in *m*

plum [plʌm] N (*fruit*) ameixa ▶ CPD (*inf*): **a ~ job** um emprego joia

plumber ['plʌməʳ] N bombeiro(-a) (BR), encanador(a) *m/f* (BR), canalizador(a) *m/f* (PT)

plumbing ['plʌmɪŋ] N (*trade*) ofício de encanador; (*piping*) encanamento

plummet ['plʌmɪt] VI: **to ~ (down)** (*bird, aircraft*) cair rapidamente; (*price*) baixar rapidamente

plump [plʌmp] ADJ roliço, rechonchudo ▶ VI: **to ~ for**

(*inf: choose*) escolher, optar por; **plump up** VT (*cushion*) afofar
plunge [plʌndʒ] N (*dive*) salto; (*fig*) queda ▸ VT (*hand, knife*) enfiar, meter ▸ VI (*fall, fig*) cair; (*dive*) mergulhar; **to take the ~** topar a parada
plural ['pluərl] ADJ plural ▸ N plural *m*
plus [plʌs] N (*also*: **~ sign**) sinal *m* de adição ▸ PREP mais; **ten/twenty ~** dez/vinte e tantos; **plus-one** ['plʌs'wʌn] (*inf*) N acompanhante *m/f*
ply [plaɪ] N (*of wool*) fio ▸ VT (*a trade*) exercer ▸ VI (*ship*) ir e vir; **to ~ sb with drink/questions** bombardear alguém com bebidas/perguntas; **plywood** N madeira compensada
p.m. ADV ABBR (= *post meridiem*) da tarde, da noite
PMT N ABBR (= *premenstrual tension*) TPM *f*, tensão *f* pré-menstrual
pneumatic drill [nju:mætɪk drɪl] N perfuratriz *f*
poach [pəutʃ] VT (*cook: fish*) escaldar; (: *eggs*) fazer pochê (BR), escalfar (PT); (*steal*) furtar ▸ VI caçar (*or* pescar) em propriedade alheia
pocket ['pɔkɪt] N bolso; (*fig: small area*) pedaço ▸ VT meter no bolso; (*steal*) embolsar; **to be out of ~** (BRIT) ter prejuízo; **pocketbook** (US) N carteira; **pocket money** N dinheiro para despesas miúdas; (*for child*) mesada
pod [pɔd] N vagem *f*
podcast ['pɔdka:st] N podcast *m*; **podcasting** N podcasting *m*
podiatrist [pɔ'di:ətrɪst] (US) N pedicuro(-a)
poem ['pəuɪm] N poema *m*
poet ['pəuɪt] N poeta/poetisa *m/f*; **poetic** [pəu'ɛtɪk] ADJ poético; **poetry** ['pəuɪtrɪ] N poesia
point [pɔɪnt] N ponto; (*of needle, knife etc*) ponta; (*purpose*) finalidade *f*; (*significant part*) ponto principal; (*position, place*) lugar *m*, posição *f*; (*moment*) momento; (*stage*) estágio; (*Elec: also*: **power ~**) tomada; (*also*: **decimal ~**): **2 ~ 3 (2.3)** dois vírgula três ▸ VT mostrar; (*gun etc*): **to ~ sth at sb** apontar algo para alguém ▸ VI apontar; **points** NPL (*Aut*) platinado, contato; (*Rail*) agulhas *fpl*; **to ~ at** apontar para; **to be on the ~ of doing sth** estar prestes a *or* a ponto de fazer algo; **to make a ~ of** fazer questão de, insistir em; **to get the ~** perceber; **to miss the ~** compreender mal; **to come to the ~** ir ao assunto; **there's no ~ (in doing)** não há razão (para fazer); **~ of view** ponto de vista; **point out** VT (*in debate etc*) ressaltar; **point to** VT FUS (*fig*) indicar; **point-blank** ADV categoricamente; (*also*: **at point-blank range**) à queima-roupa; **pointed** ADJ (*stick etc*) pontudo; (*remark*) mordaz; **pointer** N (*on chart*) indicador *m*; (*on machine*) ponteiro; (*fig*) dica; **pointless** ADJ (*useless*) inútil; (*senseless*) sem sentido
poison ['pɔɪzn] N veneno ▸ VT envenenar; **poisonous** ADJ venenoso; (*fumes etc*) tóxico
poke [pəuk] VT cutucar; (*put*): **to ~ sth in(to)** enfiar *or* meter algo em; **poke about** VI escarafunchar, espionar
poker ['pəukə^r] N atiçador *m* (de brasas); (*Cards*) pôquer *m*

P

Poland ['pəulənd] N Polônia
polar ['pəuləʳ] ADJ polar; **polar bear** N urso polar
Pole [pəul] N polonês(-esa) *m/f*
pole [pəul] N vara; (*Geo*) polo; (*telegraph pole*) poste *m*; (*flagpole*) mastro; **pole bean** (US) N feijão-trepador *m*; **pole vault** N salto com vara
police [pə'li:s] N polícia ▶ VT policiar; **police car** N rádio-patrulha *f*; **policeman** *irreg* N policial *m* (BR), polícia *m* (PT); **police station** N delegacia (de polícia) (BR), esquadra (PT); **policewoman** *irreg* N policial *f* (feminina) (BR), mulher *f* polícia (PT)
policy ['pɔlɪsɪ] N política; (*also*: **insurance ~**) apólice *f*
polio ['pəulɪəu] N polio(mielite) *f*
Polish ['pəulɪʃ] ADJ polonês(-esa) ▶ N (*Ling*) polonês *m*
polish ['pɔlɪʃ] N (*for shoes*) graxa; (*for floor*) cera (para encerar); (*shine*) brilho; (*fig*) refinamento, requinte *m* ▶ VT (*shoes*) engraxar; (*make shiny*) lustrar, dar brilho a; **polish off** VT (*work*) dar os arremates a; (*food*) raspar
polite [pə'laɪt] ADJ educado; **politeness** N gentileza, cortesia
political [pə'lɪtɪkl] ADJ político
politician [pɔlɪ'tɪʃən] N político(-a)
politics ['pɔlɪtɪks] N, NPL política
poll [pəul] N (*votes*) votação *f*; (*also*: **opinion ~**) pesquisa, sondagem *f* ▶ VT (*votes*) receber, obter
pollen ['pɔlən] N pólen *m*
pollute [pə'lu:t] VT poluir; **pollution** N poluição *f*
polyester [pɔlɪ'ɛstəʳ] N poliéster *m*
polystyrene [pɔlɪ'staɪri:n] N isopor ® *m*
polythene ['pɔlɪθi:n] N politeno
pomegranate ['pɔmɪgrænɪt] N romã *f*
pond [pɔnd] N (*natural*) lago pequeno; (*artificial*) tanque *m*
ponder ['pɔndəʳ] VT, VI ponderar, meditar (sobre)
pony ['pəunɪ] N pônei *m*; **ponytail** N rabo-de-cavalo; **pony trekking** (BRIT) N excursão *f* em pônei
poodle ['pu:dl] N cão-d'água *m*
pool [pu:l] N (*puddle*) poça, charco; (*pond*) lago; (*also*: **swimming ~**) piscina; (*fig*: *of light*) feixe *m*; (: *of liquid*) poça; (*Sport*) sinuca ▶ VT juntar; **pools** NPL (*football pools*) loteria esportiva (BR), totobola (PT); **typing** (BRIT) *or* **secretary** (US) **~** seção *f* de datilografia
poor [puəʳ] ADJ pobre; (*bad*) inferior, mau ▶ NPL: **the ~** os pobres; **~ in** (*resources etc*) deficiente em; **poorly** ADJ adoentado, indisposto ▶ ADV mal
pop [pɔp] N (*sound*) estalo, estouro; (*Mus*) pop *m*; (*US inf*: *father*) papai *m*; (*inf*: *fizzy drink*) bebida gasosa ▶ VT: **to ~ sth into/onto** *etc* (*put*) pôr algo em/sobre *etc* ▶ VI estourar; (*cork*) saltar; **pop in** VI dar um pulo; **pop out** VI dar uma saída; **pop up** VI surgir, aparecer inesperadamente; **popcorn** N pipoca
pope [pəup] N papa *m*
poplar ['pɔpləʳ] N álamo, choupo
poppy ['pɔpɪ] N papoula
popular ['pɔpjuləʳ] ADJ popular; (*person*) querido
population [pɔpju'leɪʃən] N população *f*
porcelain ['pɔ:slɪn] N porcelana
porch [pɔ:tʃ] N pórtico; (*US*: *verandah*) varanda
pore [pɔ:ʳ] N poro ▶ VI: **to ~ over** examinar minuciosamente

pork [pɔːk] N carne *f* de porco
pornography [pɔːˈnɔgrəfɪ] N pornografia
porridge [ˈpɔrɪdʒ] N mingau *m* (de aveia)
port [pɔːt] N (*harbour*) porto; (*Naut: left side*) bombordo; (*wine*) vinho do Porto; **~ of call** porto de escala
portable [ˈpɔːtəbl] ADJ portátil
porter [ˈpɔːtə^r] N (*for luggage*) carregador *m*; (*doorkeeper*) porteiro
portfolio [pɔːtˈfəulɪəu] N (*case*) pasta; (*Pol*) pasta ministerial; (*Finance*) carteira de ações ou títulos; (*of artist*) pasta, portfolió
portion [ˈpɔːʃən] N porção *f*, quinhão *m*; (*of food*) ração *f*
portrait [ˈpɔːtreɪt] N retrato
portray [pɔːˈtreɪ] VT retratar; (*act*) interpretar
Portugal [ˈpɔːtjugl] N Portugal *m* (*no article*)
Portuguese [pɔːtjuˈgiːz] ADJ português(-esa) ▸ N INV português(-esa) *m/f*; (*Ling*) português *m*
pose [pəuz] N postura, pose *f* ▸ VI (*pretend*): **to ~ as** fazer-se passar por ▸ VT (*question*) fazer; (*problem*) causar; **to ~ for** (*painting*) posar para
posh [pɔʃ] (*inf*) ADJ fino, chique; (*upper-class*) de classe alta
position [pəˈzɪʃən] N posição *f*; (*job*) cargo; (*situation*) situação *f* ▸ VT colocar, situar
positive [ˈpɔzɪtɪv] ADJ positivo; (*certain*) certo; (*definite*) definitivo
possess [pəˈzɛs] VT possuir;
possession N posse *f*, possessão *f*; **possessions** NPL (*belongings*) pertences *mpl*; **to take possession of sth** tomar posse de algo
possibility [pɔsɪˈbɪlɪtɪ] N possibilidade *f*; (*of sth happening*) probabilidade *f*
possible [ˈpɔsɪbl] ADJ possível; **possibly** ADV pode ser, talvez; (*surprise*): **what could they possibly want with me?** o que eles podem querer comigo?; (*emphasizing effort*): **they did everything they possibly could** eles fizeram tudo o que podiam; **I cannot possibly go** não posso ir de jeito nenhum
post [pəust] N (BRIT: *mail*) correio; (*job*) cargo, posto; (*pole*) poste *m*; (*on internet*) post *m*; (*Mil*) nomeação *f* ▸ VT (BRIT: *send by post*) pôr no correio; (*on internet*) postar; (BRIT: *appoint*): **to ~ to** destinar a;
postage N porte *m*, franquia;
postal order N vale *m* postal;
postbox (BRIT) N caixa de correio;
postcard N cartão *m* postal;
postcode (BRIT) N código postal, ≈ CEP *m* (BR)
poster [ˈpəustə^r] N cartaz *m*; (*as decoration*) pôster *m*
postman [ˈpəustmən] *irreg* N carteiro
postmark [ˈpəustmɑːk] N carimbo do correio
post office N (*building*) agência do correio, correio; (*organization*) ≈ Empresa Nacional dos Correios e Telégrafos (BR), ≈ Correios, Telégrafos e Telefones (PT)
postpone [pəsˈpəun] VT adiar
posture [ˈpɔstʃə^r] N postura; (*fig*) atitude *f*
pot [pɔt] N (*for cooking*) panela; (*for flowers*) vaso; (*container*) pote *m*; (*teapot*) bule *m*; (*inf: marijuana*)

P

maconha ▶ VT (*plant*) plantar em vaso; **to go to ~** (*inf*) arruinar-se, degringolar

potato [pə'teɪtəu] (*pl* **potatoes**) N batata; **potato peeler** N descascador *m* de batatas

potent ['pəutnt] ADJ poderoso; (*drink*) forte; (*man*) potente

potential [pə'tɛnʃl] ADJ potencial ▶ N potencial *m*

pothole ['pɔthəul] N (*in road*) buraco; (BRIT: *underground*) caldeirão *m*, cova

potter ['pɔtə^r] N (*artistic*) ceramista *m/f*; (*artisan*) oleiro(-a) ▶ VI (BRIT): **to ~ around, ~ about** ocupar-se com pequenos trabalhos; **pottery** N cerâmica; (*factory*) olaria

potty ['pɔtɪ] ADJ (*inf*: *mad*) maluco, doido ▶ N penico

pouch [pautʃ] N (*Zool*) bolsa; (*for tobacco*) tabaqueira

poultry ['pəultrɪ] N aves *fpl* domésticas; (*meat*) carne *f* de aves domésticas

pounce [pauns] VI: **to ~ on** lançar-se sobre; (*person*) agarrar em; (*fig*: *mistake etc*) apontar

pound [paund] N libra (*weight = 453g, 16 ounces; money = 100 pence*) ▶ VT (*beat*) socar, esmurrar; (*crush*) triturar ▶ VI (*heart*) bater

pour [pɔː^r] VT despejar; (*drink*) servir ▶ VI correr, jorrar; **pour away** VT esvaziar, decantar; **pour in** VI (*people*) entrar numa enxurrada; (*information*) chegar numa enxurrada; **pour off** VT esvaziar, decantar; **pour out** VI (*people*) sair aos borbotões ▶ VT (*drink*) servir; (*fig*) extravasar; **pouring** ['pɔːrɪŋ] ADJ: **pouring rain** chuva torrencial

pout [paut] VI fazer beicinho *or* biquinho

poverty ['pɔvətɪ] N pobreza, miséria

powder ['paudə^r] N pó *m*; (*face powder*) pó-de-arroz *m* ▶ VT (*face*) empoar, passar pó em; **powdered milk** N leite *m* em pó

power ['pauə^r] N poder *m*; (*of explosion, engine*) força, potência; (*ability, Pol*) poder; (*electricity*) força; **to be in ~** estar no poder; **power cut** (BRIT) N corte *m* de energia, blecaute *m* (BR); **powerful** ADJ poderoso; (*engine*) potente; (*body*) vigoroso; (*blow*) violento; (*argument*) convincente; (*emotion*) intenso; **powerless** ADJ impotente; **power point** (BRIT) N tomada; **power station** N central *f* elétrica

PR N ABBR = **public relations**

practical ['præktɪkl] ADJ prático; **practical joke** N brincadeira, peça

practice ['præktɪs] N (*habit, Rel*) costume *m*, hábito; (*exercise*) prática; (*of profession*) exercício; (*training*) treinamento; (*Med*) consultório; (*Jur*) escritório ▶ VT, VI (US) = **practise**; **in ~** na prática; **out of ~** destreinado

practise ['præktɪs], (US) **practice** VT praticar; (*profession*) exercer; (*sport*) treinar ▶ VI (*doctor*) ter consultório; (*lawyer*) ter escritório; (*train*) treinar, praticar

practitioner [præk'tɪʃənə^r] N (*Med*) médico(-a)

prairie ['prɛərɪ] N campina, pradaria

praise [preɪz] N louvor *m*; (*admiration*) elogio ▶ VT elogiar, louvar

pram [præm] (BRIT) N carrinho de bebê

prank [præŋk] N travessura, peça

prawn [prɔːn] N pitu *m*; (*small*) camarão *m*
pray [preɪ] VI: **to ~ for/that** rezar por/para que; **prayer** [prɛəʳ] N (*activity*) reza; (*words*) oração *f*, prece *f*
preach [priːtʃ] VT pregar ▸VI pregar; (*pej*) catequizar
precede [prɪ'siːd] VT preceder
precedent ['prɛsɪdənt] N precedente *m*
preceding [prɪ'siːdɪŋ] ADJ anterior
precinct ['priːsɪŋkt] N (*US: district*) distrito policial; **precincts** NPL (*of large building*) arredores *mpl*; **pedestrian ~** (BRIT) zona para pedestres (BR) *or* peões (PT); **shopping ~** (BRIT) zona comercial
precious ['prɛʃəs] ADJ precioso
precise [prɪ'saɪs] ADJ exato, preciso; (*plans*) detalhado
predecessor ['priːdɪsɛsəʳ] N predecessor(a) *m/f*, antepassado(-a)
predicament [prɪ'dɪkəmənt] N situação *f* difícil, apuro
predict [prɪ'dɪkt] VT prever, predizer, prognosticar; **predictable** ADJ previsível
predominantly [prɪ'dɔmɪnəntlɪ] ADV predominantemente; na maioria
preface ['prɛfəs] N prefácio
prefect ['priːfɛkt] N (BRIT *Sch*) monitor(a) *m/f*, tutor(a) *m/f*; (*in Brazil*) prefeito(-a)
prefer [prɪ'fəːʳ] VT preferir; **preferably** ['prɛfrəblɪ] ADV de preferência
prefix ['priːfɪks] N prefixo
pregnancy ['prɛgnənsɪ] N gravidez *f*; (*animal*) prenhez *f*
pregnant ['prɛgnənt] ADJ grávida; (*animal*) prenha
prehistoric [priːhɪs'tɔrɪk] ADJ pré-histórico
prejudice ['prɛdʒudɪs] N preconceito; **prejudiced** ADJ (*person*) preconceituoso
premature ['prɛmətʃuəʳ] ADJ prematuro
première ['prɛmɪɛəʳ] N estreia
premium ['priːmɪəm] N prêmio; **to be at a ~** ser caro
premonition [prɛmə'nɪʃən] N presságio, pressentimento
preoccupied [priː'ɔkjupaɪd] ADJ (*worried*) preocupado
prepaid [priː'peɪd] ADJ com porte pago
preparation [prɛpə'reɪʃən] N preparação *f*; **preparations** NPL (*arrangements*) preparativos *mpl*
prepare [prɪ'pɛəʳ] VT preparar ▸VI: **to ~ for** preparar-se *or* aprontar-se para; **~d to** disposto a; **~d for** pronto para
preposition [prɛpə'zɪʃən] N preposição *f*
prerequisite [priː'rɛkwɪzɪt] N pré-requisito, condição *f* prévia
prescribe [prɪ'skraɪb] VT prescrever; (*Med*) receitar
prescription [prɪ'skrɪpʃən] N receita
presence ['prɛzns] N presença; (*spirit*) espectro
present [*adj, n* 'prɛznt, *vt* prɪ'zɛnt] ADJ presente; (*current*) atual ▸N presente *m*; (*actuality*): **the ~** o presente ▸VT (*give*) entregar algo a alguém; (*describe*) descrever; **at ~** no momento, agora; **to give sb a ~** presentear alguém; **presentation** [prɛzn'teɪʃən] N apresentação *f*; (*ceremony*) entrega; (*of plan etc*) exposição *f*; **present-day** ADJ atual, de hoje;

P

presenter N apresentador(a) *m/f*; **presently** ADV (*soon after*) logo depois; (*soon*) logo, em breve; (*now*) atualmente
preservative [prɪ'zə:vətɪv] N conservante *m*
preserve [prɪ'zə:v] VT (*situation*) conservar, manter; (*building, manuscript*) preservar; (*food*) pôr em conserva ▸ N (*often pl: jam*) geleia; (*: fruit*) compota, conserva
president ['prɛzɪdənt] N presidente(-a) *m/f*; **presidential** [prɛzɪ'dɛnʃl] ADJ presidencial
press [prɛs] N (*printer's*) imprensa, prelo; (*newspapers*) imprensa; (*of switch*) pressão *f* ▸ VT apertar; (*clothes: iron*) passar; (*put pressure on: person*) pressionar; (*insist*): **to ~ sth on sb** insistir para que alguém aceite algo ▸ VI (*squeeze*) apertar; (*pressurize*): **to ~ for** pressionar por; **we are ~ed for time/money** estamos com pouco tempo/dinheiro; **press on** VI continuar; **pressing** ADJ urgente; **press stud** (BRIT) N botão *m* de pressão; **press-up** (BRIT) N flexão *f*
pressure ['prɛʃə^r] N pressão *f*; **to put ~ on sb (to do sth)** pressionar alguém (a fazer algo); **pressure cooker** N panela de pressão
prestige [prɛs'ti:ʒ] N prestígio
presume [prɪ'zju:m] VT supor
pretence [prɪ'tɛns], (US) **pretense** N pretensão *f*; **under false ~s** por meios fraudulentos
pretend [prɪ'tɛnd] VT, VI fingir
pretense [prɪ'tɛns] (US) N = **pretence**
pretty ['prɪtɪ] ADJ bonito ▸ ADV (*quite*) bastante
prevail [prɪ'veɪl] VI triunfar; (*be current*) imperar
prevalent ['prɛvələnt] ADJ (*common*) predominante
prevent [prɪ'vɛnt] VT impedir
preview ['pri:vju:] N pré-estreia
previous ['pri:vɪəs] ADJ (*earlier*) anterior; **previously** ADV (*before*) previamente; (*in the past*) anteriormente
prey [preɪ] N presa ▸ VI: **to ~ on** (*feed on*) alimentar-se de; **it was ~ing on his mind** preocupava-o, atormentava-o
price [praɪs] N preço ▸ VT fixar o preço de; **priceless** ADJ inestimável; (*inf: amusing*) impagável
prick [prɪk] N picada ▸ VT picar; (*make hole in*) furar; **to ~ up one's ears** aguçar os ouvidos
pride [praɪd] N orgulho; (*pej*) soberba ▸ VT: **to ~ o.s. on** orgulhar-se de
priest [pri:st] N (*Christian*) padre *m*; (*non-Christian*) sacerdote *m*
primarily ['praɪmərɪlɪ] ADV principalmente
primary ['praɪmərɪ] ADJ primário; (*first in importance*) principal ▸ N (*US: election*) eleição *f* primária; **primary school** (BRIT) N escola primária

> As **primary schools** da Grã-Bretanha acolhem crianças de 5 a 11 anos. Assinalam o início do ciclo escolar obrigatório e são compostas de duas partes: a pré-escola (*infant school*) e o primário (*junior school*).

prime [praɪm] ADJ primeiro, principal; (*excellent*) de primeira ▸ VT (*wood*) imprimar; (*fig*) preparar ▸ N: **in the ~ of life** na primavera da vida; **~ example** exemplo típico; **prime minister** N primeiro-ministro/primeira-ministra

primitive ['prɪmɪtɪv] ADJ primitivo; (*crude*) rudimentar
primrose ['prɪmrəuz] N prímula, primavera
prince [prɪns] N príncipe *m*
princess [prɪn'sɛs] N princesa
principal ['prɪnsɪpl] ADJ principal ▸ N (*of school, college*) diretor(a) *m/f*
principle ['prɪnsɪpl] N princípio; **in ~** em princípio; **on ~** por princípio
print [prɪnt] N (*letters*) letra de forma; (*fabric*) estampado; (*Art*) estampa, gravura; (*Phot*) cópia; (*footprint*) pegada; (*fingerprint*) impressão *f* digital ▸ VT imprimir; (*write in capitals*) escrever em letra de imprensa; **out of ~** esgotado; **printer** N (*person*) impressor(a) *m/f*; (*firm*) gráfica; (*machine*) impressora; **printout** N (*Comput*) cópia impressa
prior ['praɪəʳ] ADJ anterior, prévio; (*more important*) prioritário; **~ to doing** antes de fazer
priority [praɪ'ɔrɪtɪ] N prioridade *f*
prison ['prɪzn] N prisão *f* ▸ CPD carcerário; **prisoner** N (*in prison*) preso(-a), presidiário(-a); (*under arrest*) detido(-a)
privacy ['prɪvəsɪ] N isolamento, solidão *f*
private ['praɪvɪt] ADJ privado; (*personal*) particular; (*confidential*) confidencial, reservado; (*personal: belongings*) pessoal; (*: thoughts, plans*) secreto, íntimo; (*place*) isolado; (*quiet: person*) reservado; (*intimate*) íntimo ▸ N soldado raso; **"~"** (*on envelope*) "confidencial"; (*on door*) "privativo"; **in ~** em particular; **privatize** VT privatizar
privilege ['prɪvɪlɪdʒ] N privilégio
prize [praɪz] N prêmio ▸ ADJ de primeira classe ▸ VT valorizar; **prizewinner** N premiado(-a)
pro [prəu] N (*Sport*) profissional *m/f* ▸ PREP a favor de; **the ~s and cons** os prós e os contras
probability [prɔbə'bɪlɪtɪ] N probabilidade *f*
probable ['prɔbəbl] ADJ provável; (*plausible*) verossímil
probation [prə'beɪʃən] N: **on ~** (*employee*) em estágio probatório; (*Jur*) em liberdade condicional
probe [prəub] N (*Med, Space*) sonda; (*enquiry*) pesquisa ▸ VT investigar, esquadrinhar
problem ['prɔbləm] N problema *m*
procedure [prə'si:dʒəʳ] N procedimento; (*method*) método, processo
proceed [prə'si:d] VI (*do afterwards*): **to ~ to do sth** passar a fazer algo; (*continue*): **to ~ (with)** continuar *or* prosseguir (com); (*activity, event*) continuar; (*go*) ir em direção a, dirigir-se a; **proceedings** NPL evento, acontecimento; **proceeds** ['prəusi:dz] NPL produto, proventos *mpl*
process ['prəusɛs] N processo ▸ VT processar; **procession** [prə'sɛʃən] N desfile *m*, procissão *f*; **funeral procession** cortejo fúnebre
proclaim [prə'kleɪm] VT anunciar
prod [prɔd] VT empurrar; (*with finger, stick*) cutucar ▸ N empurrão *m*; cotovelada; espetada
produce [*n* 'prɔdju:s, *vt* prə'dju:s] N (*Agr*) produtos *mpl* agrícolas ▸ VT produzir; (*cause*) provocar; (*evidence, argument*) apresentar, mostrar; (*show*) apresentar, exibir; (*Theatre*) pôr em cena *or* em cartaz;

producer N (*Theatre*) diretor(a) *m/f*; (*Agr, Cinema, of record*) produtor(a) *m/f*; (*country*) produtor *m*
product ['prɔdʌkt] N produto
production [prə'dʌkʃən] N produção *f*; (*of electricity*) geração *f*; (*Theatre*) encenação *f*
profession [prə'fɛʃən] N profissão *f*; (*people*) classe *f*; **professional** N profissional *m/f* ▶ ADJ profissional; (*work*) de profissional
professor [prə'fɛsəʳ] N (BRIT) catedrático(-a); (US, CANADA) professor(a) *m/f*
profile ['prəufaɪl] N perfil *m*
profit ['prɔfɪt] N (*Comm*) lucro ▶ VI: **to ~ by** *or* **from** (*benefit*) aproveitar-se de, tirar proveito de; **profitable** ADJ (*Econ*) lucrativo, rendoso
profound [prə'faund] ADJ profundo
programme ['prəugræm], (*US or* COMPUT) **program** N programa *m* ▶ VT programar; **programming**, **programing** N programação *f*
progress [*n* 'prəugrɛs, *vi* prə'grɛs] N progresso ▶ VI progredir, avançar; **in ~** em andamento; **progressive** [prə'grɛsɪv] ADJ progressivo; (*person*) progressista
prohibit [prə'hɪbɪt] VT proibir
project [*n* 'prɔdʒɛkt, *vt, vi* prə'dʒɛkt] N projeto; (*Sch: research*) pesquisa ▶ VT projetar; (*figure*) estimar ▶ VI (*stick out*) ressaltar, sobressair
projection [prə'dʒɛkʃən] N projeção *f*; (*overhang*) saliência
projector [prə'dʒɛktəʳ] N projetor *m*
prolong [prə'lɔŋ] VT prolongar
prom [prɔm] N ABBR = **promenade**, **promenade concert**; (US: *ball*) baile *m* de estudantes
promenade [prɔmə'nɑːd] N (*by sea*) passeio (à orla marítima); **promenade concert** (BRIT) N concerto (de música clássica)

> Na Grã-Bretanha, um **promenade concert** (ou **prom**) é um concerto de música clássica, assim chamado porque originalmente o público não ficava sentado, mas de pé ou caminhando. Hoje em dia, uma parte do público permanece de pé, mas há também lugares sentados (mais caros). Os **Proms** mais conhecidos são os londrinos. A última sessão (*the Last Night of the Proms*) é um acontecimento carregado de emoção, quando são executadas árias tradicionais e patrióticas. Nos Estados Unidos e no Canadá, o **prom**, ou **promenade**, é um baile organizado pelas escolas secundárias.

prominent ['prɔmɪnənt] ADJ (*standing out*) proeminente; (*important*) eminente, notório
promise ['prɔmɪs] N promessa; (*hope*) esperança ▶ VT, VI prometer; **promising** ADJ promissor(a), prometedor(a)
promote [prə'məut] VT promover; (*product*) promover, fazer propaganda de; **promotion** N promoção *f*
prompt [prɔmpt] ADJ pronto, rápido ▶ ADV (*exactly*) em ponto, pontualmente ▶ N (*Comput*) sinal *m* de orientação, prompt *m* ▶ VT (*urge*) incitar, impelir; (*cause*) provocar, ocasionar; **to ~ sb to do sth** induzir alguém a fazer algo; **promptly** ADV imediatamente; (*exactly*) pontualmente

prone [prəun] ADJ (*lying*) de bruços; **~ to** propenso a, predisposto a
pronoun ['prəunaun] N pronome *m*
pronounce [prə'nauns] VT pronunciar; (*verdict, opinion*) declarar
pronunciation [prənʌnsɪ'eɪʃən] N pronúncia
proof [pru:f] N prova ▶ ADJ: **~ against** à prova de
prop [prɔp] N suporte *m*, escora; (*fig*) amparo, apoio ▶ VT (*also*: **~ up**) apoiar, escorar; (*lean*): **to ~ sth against** apoiar algo contra
propaganda [prɔpə'gændə] N propaganda
proper ['prɔpə[r]] ADJ (*correct*) correto; (*socially acceptable*) respeitável, digno; (*authentic*) genuíno, autêntico; (*referring to place*): **the village ~** a cidadezinha propriamente dita; **properly** ADV (*eat, study*) bem; (*behave*) decentemente
property ['prɔpətɪ] N propriedade *f*; (*goods*) posses *fpl*, bens *mpl*; (*buildings*) imóveis *mpl*
prophet ['prɔfɪt] N profeta *m/f*
proportion [prə'pɔ:ʃən] N proporção *f*; **proportional** ADJ proporcional
proposal [prə'pəuzl] N proposta; (*of marriage*) pedido
propose [prə'pəuz] VT propor; (*toast*) erguer ▶ VI propor casamento; **to ~ to do** propor-se fazer
proposition [prɔpə'zɪʃən] N proposta, proposição *f*; (*offer*) oferta
proprietor [prə'praɪətə[r]] N proprietário(-a), dono(-a)
prose [prəuz] N prosa
prosecute ['prɔsɪkju:t] VT processar; **prosecution** [prɔsɪ'kju:ʃən] N acusação *f*; (*accusing side*) autor *m* da demanda
prospect [*n* 'prɔspɛkt, *vt, vi* prə'spɛkt] N (*chance*) probabilidade *f*; (*outlook, potential*) perspectiva ▶ VI: **to ~ (for)** prospectar (por); **prospects** NPL (*for work etc*) perspectivas *fpl*
prospectus [prə'spɛktəs] N prospecto, programa *m*
prostitute ['prɔstɪtju:t] N prostituta; **male ~** prostituto
protect [prə'tɛkt] VT proteger; **protection** N proteção *f*; **protective** ADJ protetor(a)
protein ['prəuti:n] N proteína
protest [*n* 'prəutɛst, *vi, vt* prə'tɛst] N protesto ▶ VI protestar ▶ VT insistir
Protestant ['prɔtɪstənt] ADJ, N protestante *m/f*
protester [prə'tɛstə[r]] N manifestante *m/f*
proud [praud] ADJ orgulhoso; (*pej*) vaidoso, soberbo
prove [pru:v] VT comprovar ▶ VI: **to ~ (to be) correct** *etc* vir a ser correto *etc*; **to ~ o.s.** mostrar seu valor
proverb ['prɔvə:b] N provérbio
provide [prə'vaɪd] VT fornecer, proporcionar; **to ~ sb with sth** fornecer alguém de algo, fornecer algo a alguém; **provide for** VT FUS (*person*) prover à subsistência de
providing [prə'vaɪdɪŋ] CONJ: **~ (that)** contanto que (+ *sub*)
province ['prɔvɪns] N província; (*fig*) esfera; **provincial** [prə'vɪnʃəl] ADJ provincial; (*pej*) provinciano

P

provision [prəˈvɪʒən] N (*supplying*) abastecimento; (*in contract*) cláusula, condição *f*; **provisions** NPL (*food*) mantimentos *mpl*; **provisional** ADJ provisório, interino; (*agreement, licence*) provisório
provocative [prəˈvɔkətɪv] ADJ provocante; (*sexually*) excitante
provoke [prəˈvəuk] VT provocar; (*cause*) causar
prowl [praul] VI (*also*: **~ about, ~ around**) rondar, andar à espreita ▶ N: **on the ~** de ronda, rondando
proxy [ˈprɔksɪ] N: **by ~** por procuração
prudent [ˈpruːdənt] ADJ prudente
prune [pruːn] N ameixa seca ▶ VT podar
pry [praɪ] VI: **to ~ (into)** intrometer-se (em)
PS N ABBR (= *postscript*) PS *m*
pseudonym [ˈsjuːdənɪm] N pseudônimo
psychiatrist [saɪˈkaɪətrɪst] N psiquiatra *m/f*
psychic [ˈsaɪkɪk] ADJ psíquico; (*also*: **~al**: *person*) sensível a forças psíquicas
psychologist [saɪˈkɔlədʒɪst] N psicólogo(-a)
psychology [saɪˈkɔlədʒɪ] N psicologia
PTO ABBR (= *please turn over*) v.v., vire
pub [pʌb] N ABBR (= *public house*) pub *m*, bar *m*, botequim *m*

> Um **pub** geralmente consiste em duas salas: uma (*the lounge*) é bastante confortável, com poltronas e bancos estofados, enquanto a outra (*"the public bar"*) é simplesmente um bar onde a consumação é em geral mais barata. O (*"the public bar"*) é muitas vezes também um salão de jogos, dos quais os mais comuns são os dardos, dominó e bilhar. Atualmente muitos pubs servem refeições, sobretudo na hora do almoço, e essa é a única hora em que a entrada de crianças é permitida, desde que estejam acompanhadas por adultos. Em geral os pubs funcionam das 11 às 23 horas, mas isso pode variar de acordo com sua permissão de funcionamento; alguns pubs fecham à tarde.

public [ˈpʌblɪk] ADJ público ▶ N público; **in ~** em público; **to make ~** tornar público; **public convenience** (BRIT) N banheiro público; **public holiday** N feriado; **public house** (BRIT) N pub *m*, bar *m*, taberna
publicity [pʌbˈlɪsɪtɪ] N publicidade *f*
publicize [ˈpʌblɪsaɪz] VT divulgar
public: public relations N relações *fpl* públicas; **public school** N (BRIT) escola particular; (US) escola pública; **public transport**, (US) **public transportation** N transporte *m* coletivo
publish [ˈpʌblɪʃ] VT publicar; **publisher** N editor(a) *m/f*; (*company*) editora; **publishing** N a indústria editorial
pudding [ˈpudɪŋ] N (BRIT: *dessert*) sobremesa; (*cake*) pudim *m*, doce *m*; **black** (BRIT) *or* **blood** (US) **~** morcela
puddle [ˈpʌdl] N poça
puff [pʌf] N sopro; (*of cigarette*) baforada; (*of air, smoke*) lufada ▶ VT: **to ~ one's pipe** tirar baforadas do cachimbo ▶ VI (*pant*) arquejar; **puff out** VT (*cheeks*) encher; **puff pastry**, (US) **puff paste** N massa folhada

pull [pul] N (*tug*): **to give sth a ~** dar um puxão em algo ▶ VT puxar; (*trigger*) apertar; (*curtain, blind*) fechar ▶ VI puxar, dar um puxão; **to ~ to pieces** picar em pedacinhos; **to ~ one's punches** não usar toda a força; **to ~ one's weight** fazer a sua parte; **to ~ o.s. together** recompor-se; **to ~ sb's leg** (*fig*) brincar com alguém, sacanear alguém (*inf*); **pull apart** VT (*break*) romper; **pull down** VT (*building*) demolir, derrubar; **pull in** VI (*Aut: at the kerb*) encostar; (*Rail*) chegar (na plataforma); **pull off** VT tirar; (*fig: deal etc*) acertar; **pull out** VI (*Aut: from kerb*) sair; (*Rail*) partir ▶ VT tirar, arrancar; **pull over** VI (*Aut*) encostar; **pull through** VI (*Med*) sobreviver; **pull up** VI (*stop*) deter-se, parar ▶ VT levantar; (*uproot*) desarraigar, arrancar

pulley ['pulɪ] N roldana

pullover ['puləuvəʳ] N pulôver *m*

pulp [pʌlp] N (*of fruit*) polpa

pulse [pʌls] N (*Anat*) pulso; (*of music, engine*) cadência; (*Bot*) legume *m*

pump [pʌmp] N bomba; (*shoe*) sapatilha (de dança) ▶ VT bombear; **pump up** VT encher

pumpkin ['pʌmpkɪn] N abóbora

pun [pʌn] N jogo de palavras, trocadilho

punch [pʌntʃ] N (*blow*) soco, murro; (*tool*) punção *m*; (*drink*) ponche *m* ▶ VT (*hit*): **to ~ sb/sth** esmurrar *or* socar alguém/algo

punctual ['pʌŋktjuəl] ADJ pontual

punish ['pʌnɪʃ] VT punir, castigar; **punishment** N castigo, punição *f*

punk [pʌŋk] N (*also*: **~ rocker**) punk *m/f*; (*also*: **~ rock**) punk *m*; (*US inf: hoodlum*) pinta-brava *m*

pupil ['pju:pl] N aluno(-a); (*of eye*) pupila

puppet ['pʌpɪt] N marionete *f*, títere *m*; (*fig*) fantoche *m*

puppy ['pʌpɪ] N cachorrinho (BR), cachorro (PT)

purchase ['pə:tʃɪs] N compra ▶ VT comprar

pure [pjuəʳ] ADJ puro

purple ['pə:pl] ADJ roxo, purpúreo

purpose ['pə:pəs] N propósito, objetivo; **on ~** de propósito

purse [pə:s] N (BRIT) carteira; (US) bolsa ▶ VT enrugar, franzir

pursue [pə'sju:] VT perseguir; (*fig: activity*) exercer; (*: interest, plan*) dedicar-se a; (*: result*) lutar por

pursuit [pə'sju:t] N perseguição *f*; (*fig*) busca

push [puʃ] N empurrão *m*; (*of button*) aperto ▶ VT empurrar; (*button*) apertar; (*promote*) promover ▶ VI empurrar; (*press*) apertar; (*fig*): **to ~ for** reivindicar; **push aside** VT afastar com a mão; **push off** (*inf*) VI dar o fora; **push on** VI prosseguir; **push through** VI abrir caminho ▶ VT (*measure*) forçar a aceitação de; **push up** VT forçar a alta de; **pushchair** (BRIT) N carrinho; **pusher** N (*also*: **drug pusher**) traficante *m/f*; **push-up** (US) N flexão *f*

put [put] (*pt, pp* **put**) VT pôr, colocar; (*put into*) meter; (*person: in institution etc*) internar; (*say*) dizer, expressar; (*case*) expor; (*question*) fazer; (*estimate*) avaliar, calcular; (*write, type etc*) colocar; **put about** VT (*rumour*) espalhar; **put across** VT (*ideas*) comunicar; **put away** VT guardar; **put back** VT (*replace*) repor; (*postpone*) adiar; (*delay*) atrasar; **put by** VT

P

(*money etc*) poupar, pôr de lado; **put down** VT pôr em; (*animal*) sacrificar; (*in writing*) anotar, inscrever; (*revolt etc*) sufocar; (*attribute*): **to ~ sth down to** atribuir algo a; **put forward** VT apresentar, propor; **put in** VT (*application, complaint*) apresentar; (*time, effort*) investir, gastar; **put off** VT adiar, protelar; (*discourage*) desanimar; **put on** VT (*clothes, make-up, dinner*) pôr; (*light*) acender; (*play*) encenar; (*weight*) ganhar; (*brake*) aplicar; (*record, video, kettle*) ligar; (*accent, manner*) assumir; **put out** VT (*take out*) colocar fora; (*fire, cigarette, light*) apagar; (*one's hand*) estender; (*inf: person*): **to be ~ out** estar aborrecido; **put through** VT (*call*) transferir; (*plan*) aprovar; **put up** VT (*raise*) levantar, erguer; (*hang*) prender; (*build*) construir, edificar; (*tent*) armar; (*increase*) aumentar; (*accommodate*) hospedar; **put up with** VT FUS suportar, aguentar

puzzle ['pʌzl] N charada; (*jigsaw*) quebra-cabeça *m*; (*also*: **crossword ~**) palavras cruzadas *fpl*; (*mystery*) mistério ▸ VT desconcertar, confundir ▸ VI: **to ~ over sth** tentar entender algo; **puzzling** ADJ intrigante, confuso

pyjamas [pɪ'dʒɑːməz], (US) **pajamas** NPL pijama *m or f*

pylon ['paɪlən] N pilono, poste *m*, torre *f*

pyramid ['pɪrəmɪd] N pirâmide *f*

Pyrenees [pɪrə'niːz] NPL: **the ~** os Pirineus

q

quack [kwæk] N grasnido; (*pej: doctor*) curandeiro(-a), charlatão(-tã) *m/f*

quaint [kweɪnt] ADJ (*ideas*) curioso, esquisito; (*village etc*) pitoresco

quake [kweɪk] VI (*with fear*) tremer ▸ N ABBR = **earthquake**

qualification [kwɔlɪfɪ'keɪʃən] N (*skill, quality*) qualificação *f*; (*reservation*) restrição *f*, ressalva; (*modification*) modificação *f*; (*often pl: degree, training*) título, qualificação

qualified ['kwɔlɪfaɪd] ADJ (*trained*) habilitado, qualificado; (*professionally*) diplomado; (*fit*): **~ to** apto para, capaz de; (*limited*) limitado

qualify ['kwɔlɪfaɪ] VT (*modify*) modificar ▸ VI: **to ~ (for)** reunir os requisitos (para)

quality ['kwɔlɪtɪ] N qualidade *f*; **quality (news)papers** (BRIT) NPL *ver nota*

Os **quality (news)papers** (ou **quality press**) englobam os jornais "sérios", diários ou semanais, em oposição aos jornais populares (**tabloid press**). Esses jornais visam a um público que procura informações detalhadas sobre uma grande variedade de assuntos e que está disposto a dedicar um bom tempo à leitura. Geralmente os *quality newspapers* são publicados em formato grande.

quantify ['kwɔntɪfaɪ] VT quantificar

quantity ['kwɔntɪtɪ] N quantidade *f*

quarantine ['kwɔrnti:n] N quarentena

quarrel ['kwɔrl] N (*argument*) discussão *f* ▶ VI: **to ~ (with)** brigar (com)

quarry ['kwɔrɪ] N (*for stone*) pedreira; (*animal*) presa, caça

quart [kwɔ:t] N quarto de galão (1.136 *l*)

quarter ['kwɔ:tə'] N quarto, quarta parte *f*; (*of year*) trimestre *m*; (*district*) bairro; (*US: 25 cents*) (moeda de) 25 centavos *mpl* de dólar ▶ VT dividir em quatro; (*Mil: lodge*) aquartelar; **quarters** NPL (*Mil*) quartel *m*; (*living quarters*) alojamento; **a ~ of an hour** um quarto de hora; **quarter final** N quarta de final; **quarterly** ADJ trimestral ▶ ADV trimestralmente

quay [ki:] N (*also*: **~side**) cais *m*

queasy ['kwi:zɪ] ADJ (*sickly*) enjoado

queen [kwi:n] N rainha; (*also*: **~ bee**) abelha-mestra, rainha; (*Cards etc*) dama

queer [kwɪə'] ADJ (*odd*) esquisito, estranho ▶ N (*inf: homosexual*) bicha *m* (BR), maricas *m inv* (PT)

quench [kwɛntʃ] VT: **to ~ one's thirst** matar a sede

query ['kwɪərɪ] N pergunta ▶ VT questionar

quest [kwɛst] N busca

question ['kwɛstʃən] N pergunta; (*doubt*) dúvida; (*issue, in test*) questão *f* ▶ VT (*doubt*) duvidar; (*interrogate*) interrogar, inquirir; **beyond ~** sem dúvida; **out of the ~** fora de cogitação, impossível; **questionable** ADJ discutível; (*doubtful*) duvidoso; **question mark** N ponto de interrogação; **questionnaire** [kwɛstʃə'nɛə'] N questionário

queue [kju:] (BRIT) N fila (BR), bicha (PT) ▶ VI (*also*: **~ up**) fazer fila (BR) *or* bicha (PT)

quick [kwɪk] ADJ rápido; (*agile*) ágil; (*mind*) sagaz, despachado ▶ N: **to cut sb to the ~** ferir alguém; **be ~!** ande depressa!, vai rápido!; **quickly** ADV rapidamente, depressa

quid [kwɪd] (BRIT *inf*) N INV libra

quiet ['kwaɪət] ADJ (*voice, music*) baixo; (*peaceful: place*) tranquilo; (*calm: person*) calmo; (*not noisy: place*) silencioso; (*not talkative: person*) calado; (*silent*) silencioso; (*ceremony*) discreto ▶ N (*peacefulness*) sossego; (*silence*) quietude *f* ▶ VT, VI (US) = **quieten**; **quieten, quieten down** VI (*grow calm*) acalmar-se; (*grow silent*) calar-se ▶ VT tranquilizar; fazer calar; **quietly** ADV silenciosamente; (*talk*) baixo

quilt [kwɪlt] N acolchoado, colcha; (BRIT: *also* **continental ~**) edredom *m* (BR), edredão *m* (PT)

q

quit [kwɪt] (*pt, pp* **quit** *or* **quitted**) VT (*smoking etc*) parar; (*job*) deixar; (*premises*) desocupar ▶ VI desistir; (*resign*) pedir demissão

quite [kwaɪt] ADV (*rather*) bastante; (*entirely*) completamente, totalmente; **that's not ~ big enough** não é suficientemente grande; **~ a few of them** um bom número deles; **~ (so)!** exatamente!, isso mesmo!

quiver ['kwɪvə^r] VI estremecer

quiz [kwɪz] N concurso (de cultura geral) ▶ VT interrogar

quota ['kwəutə] N cota, quota

quotation [kwəu'teɪʃən] N citação *f*; (*estimate*) orçamento; **quotation marks** NPL aspas *fpl*

quote [kwəut] N citação *f*; (*estimate*) orçamento ▶ VT citar; (*price*) propor; (*figure, example*) citar, dar; **quotes** NPL aspas *fpl*

r

rabbi ['ræbaɪ] N rabino

rabbit ['ræbɪt] N coelho

rabies ['reɪbi:z] N raiva

RAC (BRIT) N ABBR (= *Royal Automobile Club*) ≈ TCB *m* (BR), ≈ ACP *m* (PT)

race [reɪs] N corrida; (*species*) raça ▶ VT (*horse*) fazer correr ▶ VI (*compete*) competir; (*run*) correr; (*pulse*) bater rapidamente; **race car** (US) N = **racing car**; **racecourse** N hipódromo; **racehorse** N cavalo de corridas; **racetrack** N pista de corridas; (*for cars*) autódromo

racing ['reɪsɪŋ] N corrida; **racing car** (BRIT) N carro de corrida; **racing driver** (BRIT) N piloto(-a) de corrida

racism ['reɪsɪzəm] N racismo; **racist** (*pej*) ADJ, N racista *m/f*

rack [ræk] N (*also*: **luggage ~**) bagageiro; (*shelf*) estante *f*; (*also*: **roof ~**) xalmas *fpl*, porta-bagagem *m*; (*also*: **dish ~**) secador *m* de prato ▶ VT: **~ed by** (*pain, anxiety*) tomado por; **to ~ one's brains** quebrar a cabeça

racket ['rækɪt] N (*for tennis*) raquete *f* (BR), raqueta (PT); (*noise*) barulheira, zoeira; (*swindle*) negócio ilegal, fraude *f*

racquet ['rækɪt] N raquete *f* (BR), raqueta (PT)

radiation [reɪdɪ'eɪʃən] N radiação *f*

radiator ['reɪdɪeɪtə^r] N radiador *m*

radical ['rædɪkl] ADJ radical

radio ['reɪdɪəu] N rádio ▶VT: **to ~ sb** comunicar-se por rádio com alguém

radio... [reɪdɪəu] PREFIX radio...; **radioactive** ['reɪdɪəu'æktɪv] ADJ radioativo; **radio station** N emissora, estação *f* de rádio

radish ['rædɪʃ] N rabanete *m*

raffle ['ræfl] N rifa

raft [rɑːft] N balsa

rag [ræg] N trapo; (*torn cloth*) farrapo; (*pej: newspaper*) jornaleco; (*University*) *atividades estudantis beneficentes*; **rags** NPL (*torn clothes*) trapos *mpl*, farrapos *mpl*

rage [reɪdʒ] N (*fury*) raiva, furor *m* ▶VI (*person*) estar furioso; (*storm*) assolar; (*debate*) continuar calorosamente; **it's all the ~** é a última moda

ragged ['rægɪd] ADJ (*edge*) irregular, desigual; (*clothes*) puído, gasto; (*appearance*) esfarrapado, andrajoso

raid [reɪd] N (*Mil*) incursão *f*; (*criminal*) assalto; (*attack*) ataque *m*; (*by police*) batida ▶VT invadir, atacar; assaltar; atacar; fazer uma batida em

rail [reɪl] N (*on stair*) corrimão *m*; (*on bridge, balcony*) parapeito, anteparo; (*of ship*) amurada; **rails** NPL (*for train*) trilhos *mpl*; **by ~** de trem (BR), por caminho de ferro (PT); **railing** N, **railings** NPL grade *f*; **railroad** (US) N = **railway**; **railway** N estrada (BR) *or* caminho (PT) de ferro; **railway line** (BRIT) N linha de trem (BR) *or* de comboio (PT); **railway station** (BRIT) N estação *f* ferroviária (BR) *or* de caminho de ferro (PT)

rain [reɪn] N chuva ▶VI chover; **it's ~ing** está chovendo (BR), está a chover (PT); **rainbow** N arco-íris *m inv*; **raincoat** N impermeável *m*, capa de chuva; **raindrop** N gota de chuva; **rainfall** N chuva; (*measurement*) pluviosidade *f*; **rainforest** N floresta tropical; **rainy** ADJ chuvoso; **a rainy day** um dia de chuva

raise [reɪz] N aumento ▶VT levantar; (*salary, production*) aumentar; (*morale, standards*) melhorar; (*doubts*) suscitar, despertar; (*cattle, family*) criar; (*crop*) cultivar, plantar; (*army*) recrutar, alistar; (*funds*) angariar; (*loan*) levantar, obter; **to ~ one's voice** levantar a voz

raisin ['reɪzn] N passa, uva seca

rake [reɪk] N ancinho ▶VT (*garden*) revolver *or* limpar com o ancinho; (*with machine gun*) varrer

rally ['rælɪ] N (*Pol etc*) comício; (*Aut*) rally *m*, rali *m*; (*Tennis*) rebatida ▶VT reunir ▶VI reorganizar-se; (*sick person, stock exchange*) recuperar-se; **rally round** VT FUS dar apoio a

RAM [ræm] N ABBR (*Comput: = random access memory*) RAM *f*

ram [ræm] N carneiro ▶VT (*push*) cravar; (*crash into*) colidir com

ramble ['ræmbl] N caminhada, excursão *f* a pé ▶VI caminhar; (*talk: also:* **~ on**) divagar; **rambler**

r

N caminhante *m/f*; (*Bot*) roseira trepadeira; **rambling** ADJ (*speech*) desconexo, incoerente; (*house*) cheio de recantos; (*plant*) rastejante
ramp [ræmp] N (*incline*) rampa; **on/off ~** (*US Aut*) entrada (para a rodovia)/saída da rodovia
rampage [ræm'peɪdʒ] N: **to be on the ~** alvoroçar-se
ran [ræn] PT *of* **run**
ranch [rɑːntʃ] N rancho, fazenda, estância
random ['rændəm] ADJ ao acaso, casual, fortuito; (*Comput, Math*) aleatório ▶ N: **at ~** a esmo, aleatoriamente
rang [ræŋ] PT *of* **ring**
range [reɪndʒ] N (*of mountains*) cadeia, cordilheira; (*of missile*) alcance *m*; (*of voice*) extensão *f*; (*series*) série *f*; (*of products*) gama, sortimento; (*Mil*: *also*: **shooting ~**) estande *m*; (*also*: **kitchen ~**) fogão *m* ▶ VT (*place*) colocar; (*arrange*) arrumar, ordenar ▶ VI: **to ~ over** (*extend*) estender-se por; **to ~ from ... to ...** variar de ... a ..., oscilar entre ... e ...
rank [ræŋk] N (*row*) fila, fileira; (*Mil*) posto; (*status*) categoria, posição *f*; (BRIT: *also*: **taxi ~**) ponto de táxi ▶ VI: **to ~ among** figurar entre ▶ ADJ fétido, malcheiroso; **the ~ and file** (*fig*) a gente comum
ransom ['rænsəm] N resgate *m*; **to hold sb to ~** (*fig*) encostar alguém contra a parede
rant [rænt] VI arengar
rap [ræp] N, VT bater de leve; (*also*: **~ music**) rap *m*
rape [reɪp] N estupro; (*Bot*) colza ▶ VT violentar, estuprar
rapid ['ræpɪd] ADJ rápido
rapids ['ræpɪdz] NPL (*Geo*) cachoeira
rapist ['reɪpɪst] N estuprador *m*
rapport [ræ'pɔːʳ] N harmonia, afinidade *f*
rare [rɛəʳ] ADJ raro; (*Culin: steak*) mal passado
rascal ['rɑːskl] N maroto, malandro
rash [ræʃ] ADJ impetuoso, precipitado ▶ N (*Med*) exantema *m*, erupção *f* cutânea; (*of events*) série *f*, torrente *f*
rasher ['ræʃəʳ] N fatia fina
raspberry ['rɑːzbərɪ] N framboesa
rat [ræt] N rato (BR), ratazana (PT)
rate [reɪt] N (*ratio*) razão *f*; (*price*) preço, taxa; (*: of hotel*) diária; (*of interest, change*) taxa; (*speed*) velocidade *f* ▶ VT (*value*) taxar; (*estimate*) avaliar; **rates** NPL (BRIT) imposto predial e territorial; (*fees*) pagamento; **to ~ sb/sth as** considerar alguém/algo como
rather ['rɑːðəʳ] ADV (*somewhat*) um tanto, meio; (*to some extent*) até certo ponto; (*more accurately*): **or ~** ou melhor; **it's ~ expensive** (*quite*) é meio caro; (*too*) é caro demais; **there's ~ a lot** há bastante *or* muito; **I would** *or* **I'd ~ go** preferiria *or* preferia ir; **or ~** ou melhor
ratio ['reɪʃɪəu] N razão *f*, proporção *f*
ration ['ræʃən] N ração *f* ▶ VT racionar; **rations** NPL (*Mil*) mantimentos *mpl*, víveres *mpl*
rational ['ræʃənl] ADJ lógico; (*person*) sensato, razoável
rat race N: **the ~** a competição acirrada na vida moderna
rattle ['rætl] N (*of door*) batida; (*of train etc*) chocalhada; (*of coins*) chocalhar *m*; (*object: for baby*) chocalho ▶ VI (*small objects*) tamborilar; (*vehicle*): **to ~ along** mover-se ruidosamente ▶ VT sacudir, fazer bater; (*unnerve*) perturbar

rave [reɪv] VI (*in anger*) encolerizar-se; (*Med*) delirar; (*with enthusiasm*): **to ~ about** vibrar com
raven ['reɪvən] N corvo
ravine [rə'vi:n] N ravina, barranco
raw [rɔ:] ADJ (*uncooked*) cru(a); (*not processed*) bruto; (*sore*) vivo; (*inexperienced*) inexperiente, novato; (*weather*) muito frio
ray [reɪ] N raio; **~ of hope** fio de esperança
razor ['reɪzəʳ] N (*open*) navalha; (*safety razor*) aparelho de barbear; (*electric*) aparelho de barbear elétrico; **razor blade** N gilete *m* (BR), lâmina de barbear (PT)
Rd ABBR = **road**
re [ri:] PREP referente a
reach [ri:tʃ] N alcance *m*; (*of river etc*) extensão *f* ▸ VT alcançar; (*arrive at: place*) chegar em; (*: agreement, conclusion*) chegar a; (*by telephone*) conseguir falar com ▸ VI (*stretch out*) esticar-se; **within ~** ao alcance (da mão); **out of** *or* **beyond ~** fora de alcance; **reach out** VT (*hand*) esticar ▸ VI: **to ~ out for sth** estender *or* esticar a mão para pegar (em) algo
react [ri:'ækt] VI reagir; **reaction** N reação *f*; **reactions** NPL (*reflexes*) reflexos *mpl*
reactor [ri:'æktəʳ] N (*also: **nuclear ~***) reator *m* nuclear
read [ri:d] (*pt, pp* **read** [rɛd]) VI ler ▸ VT ler; (*understand*) compreender; (*study*) estudar; **read out** VT ler em voz alta; **reader** N leitor(a) *m/f*; (*book*) livro de leituras; (BRIT: *at university*) professor(a) *m/f* adjunto(-a)
readily ['rɛdɪlɪ] ADV (*willingly*) de boa vontade; (*easily*) facilmente; (*quickly*) sem demora, prontamente
reading ['ri:dɪŋ] N leitura; (*on instrument*) indicação *f*, registro (BR), registo (PT)
ready ['rɛdɪ] ADJ pronto, preparado; (*willing*) disposto; (*available*) disponível ▸ N: **at the ~** (*Mil*) pronto para atirar; **to get ~** *vi* preparar-se; *vt* preparar; **ready-made** ADJ (já) feito; (*clothes*) pronto
real [rɪəl] ADJ real; (*genuine*) verdadeiro, autêntico; **in ~ terms** em termos reais; **real estate** N bens *mpl* imobiliários *or* de raiz; **realistic** [rɪə'lɪstɪk] ADJ realista
reality [ri:'ælɪtɪ] N realidade *f*; **reality TV** N reality TV *f*
realization [rɪəlaɪ'zeɪʃən] N (*fulfilment*) realização *f*; (*understanding*) compreensão *f*; (*Comm*) conversão *f* em dinheiro, realização
realize ['rɪəlaɪz] VT (*understand*) perceber; (*fulfil, Comm*) realizar
really ['rɪəlɪ] ADV (*for emphasis*) realmente; (*actually*): **what ~ happened?** o que aconteceu na verdade?; **~?** (*interest*) é mesmo?; (*surprise*) verdade!; **~!** (*annoyance*) realmente!
realm [rɛlm] N reino; (*fig*) esfera, domínio
realtor ['rɪəltəʳ] (US) N corretor(a) *m/f* de imóveis (BR), agente *m/f* imobiliário(-a) (PT)
reappear [ri:ə'pɪəʳ] VI reaparecer
rear [rɪəʳ] ADJ traseiro, de trás ▸ N traseira ▸ VT criar ▸ VI (*also: **~ up***) empinar-se
reason ['ri:zn] N (*cause*) razão *f*; (*ability to think*) raciocínio; (*sense*) bom-senso ▸ VI: **to ~ with sb** argumentar com alguém, persuadir alguém; **it stands to ~**

r

that é razoável *or* lógico que; **reasonable** ADJ (*fair*) razoável; (*sensible*) sensato; **reasonably** ADV razoavelmente; (*sensibly*) sensatamente; **reasoning** N raciocínio

reassurance [ri:əˈʃuərəns] N garantia

reassure [ri:əˈʃuəʳ] VT tranquilizar; **to ~ sb of** reafirmar a confiança de alguém acerca de

rebate [ˈri:beɪt] N devolução *f*

rebel [*n* ˈrɛbl, *vi* rɪˈbɛl] N rebelde *m/f* ▶ VI rebelar-se; **rebellious** [rɪˈbɛljəs] ADJ insurreto; (*behaviour*) rebelde

recall [rɪˈkɔ:l] VT (*remember*) recordar, lembrar; (*parliament*) reunir de volta; (*ambassador etc*) chamar de volta ▶ N (*memory*) recordação *f*, lembrança; (*of ambassador etc*) chamada (de volta)

receipt [rɪˈsi:t] N recibo; (*act of receiving*) recebimento (BR), receção *f* (PT); **receipts** NPL (*Comm*) receitas *fpl*

receive [rɪˈsi:v] VT receber; (*guest*) acolher; (*wound, criticism*) sofrer; **receiver** N (*Tel*) fone *m* (BR), auscultador *m* (PT); (*Radio, TV*) receptor *m*; (*of stolen goods*) receptador(a) *m/f*; (*Comm*) curador(a) *m/f* síndico(-a) de massa falida

recent [ˈri:snt] ADJ recente; **recently** ADV recentemente; (*in recent times*) ultimamente

reception [rɪˈsɛpʃən] N recepção *f*; (*welcome*) acolhida; **reception desk** N (mesa de) recepção *f*; **receptionist** N recepcionista *m/f*

recession [rɪˈsɛʃən] N recessão *f*

recipe [ˈrɛsɪpɪ] N receita

recipient [rɪˈsɪpɪənt] N recipiente *m/f*, recebedor(a) *m/f*; (*of letter*) destinatário(-a)

recite [rɪˈsaɪt] VT recitar

reckless [ˈrɛkləs] ADJ (*driver*) imprudente; (*speed*) imprudente, excessivo; (*spending*) irresponsável

reckon [ˈrɛkən] VT (*calculate*) calcular, contar; (*think*): **I ~ that ...** acho que ...; **reckon on** VT FUS contar com

reclaim [rɪˈkleɪm] VT (*demand back*) reivindicar; (*waste materials*) reaproveitar

recline [rɪˈklaɪn] VI reclinar-se

recognition [rɛkəgˈnɪʃən] N reconhecimento

recognize [ˈrɛkəgnaɪz] VT reconhecer

recommend [rɛkəˈmɛnd] VT recomendar

reconcile [ˈrɛkənsaɪl] VT reconciliar; (*two facts*) conciliar, harmonizar; **to ~ o.s. to sth** resignar-se a *or* conformar-se com algo

reconsider [ri:kənˈsɪdəʳ] VT reconsiderar

reconstruct [ri:kənˈstrʌkt] VT reconstruir; (*event*) reconstituir

record [*n, adj* ˈrɛkɔ:d, *vt* rɪˈkɔ:d] N (*Mus*) disco; (*of meeting etc*) ata, minuta; (*Comput, of attendance*) registro (BR), registo (PT); (*written*) história; (*also*: **criminal ~**) antecedentes *mpl*; (*Sport*) recorde *m* ▶ VT (*write down*) anotar; (*temperature, speed*) registrar (BR), registar (PT); (*Mus: song etc*) gravar ▶ ADJ: **in ~ time** num tempo recorde; **off the ~** *adj* confidencial; *adv* confidencialmente; **recorder** N (*Mus*) flauta; **recording** N (*Mus*) gravação *f*; **record player** N toca-discos *m inv* (BR), gira-discos *m inv* (PT)

recover [rɪ'kʌvəʳ] VT recuperar ▶ VI (*from illness*) recuperar-se; (*from shock*) refazer-se; **recovery** N recuperação *f*; (*Med*) recuperação, melhora

recreation [rɛkrɪ'eɪʃən] N recreio; **recreational drug** N droga recreacional

recruit [rɪ'kru:t] N recruta *m/f*; (*in company*) novato(-a) ▶ VT recrutar

rectangle ['rɛktæŋgl] N retângulo

rector ['rɛktəʳ] N (*Rel*) pároco

recur [rɪ'kə:ʳ] VI repetir-se, ocorrer outra vez; (*symptoms*) reaparecer

recyclable [ri:'saɪkləbl] ADJ reciclável; **recycle** VT reciclar; **recycling** N reciclagem *f*

red [rɛd] N vermelho; (*Pol: pej*) vermelho(-a) ▶ ADJ vermelho; (*hair*) ruivo; (*wine*) tinto; **to be in the ~** não ter fundos; **Red Cross** N Cruz *f* Vermelha

redeem [rɪ'di:m] VT (*Rel*) redimir; (*sth in pawn*) tirar do prego; (*loan, fig: situation*) salvar

red: red-haired ADJ ruivo; **redhead** ['rɛdhɛd] N ruivo(-a); **red-hot** ADJ incandescente; **red-light district** N zona (de meretrício)

reduce [rɪ'dju:s] VT reduzir; (*lower*) rebaixar; **"~ speed now"** (*Aut*) "diminua a velocidade"; **to ~ sb to** (*silence, begging*) levar alguém a; (*tears*) reduzir alguém a; **reduction** [rɪ'dʌkʃən] N redução *f*; (*of price*) abatimento

redundancy [rɪ'dʌndənsɪ] N (BRIT: *dismissal*) demissão *f*; (*unemployment*) desemprego

redundant [rɪ'dʌndnt] ADJ (BRIT: *worker*) desempregado; (*detail, object*) redundante, supérfluo; **to be made ~** ficar desempregado *or* sem trabalho

reed [ri:d] N (*Bot*) junco; (*Mus: of clarinet etc*) palheta

reef [ri:f] N (*at sea*) recife *m*

reel [ri:l] N carretel *m*, bobina; (*of film*) rolo, filme *m*; (*on fishing-rod*) carretilha; (*dance*) *dança típica da Escócia* ▶ VI (*sway*) cambalear, oscilar; **reel in** VT puxar enrolando a linha

ref [rɛf] (*inf*) N ABBR = **referee**

refectory [rɪ'fɛktərɪ] N refeitório

refer [rɪ'fə:ʳ] VT (*matter, problem*): **to ~ sth to** submeter algo à apreciação de; (*person, patient*): **to ~ sb to** encaminhar alguém a ▶ VI: **to ~ to** referir-se *or* aludir a; (*consult*) recorrer a

referee [rɛfə'ri:] N árbitro(-a); (BRIT: *for job application*) referência ▶ VT apitar

reference ['rɛfrəns] N referência; (*mention*) menção *f*; **with ~ to** com relação a; (*Comm: in letter*) com referência a; **"please quote this ~"** (*Comm*) "queira citar esta referência"

refill [*vt* ri:'fɪl, *n* 'ri:fɪl] VT reencher; (*lighter etc*) reabastecer ▶ N (*for pen*) carga nova

refine [rɪ'faɪn] VT refinar; **refined** ADJ refinado, culto

reflect [rɪ'flɛkt] VT refletir ▶ VI (*think*) refletir, meditar; **it ~s badly/well on him** isso repercute mal/bem para ele; **reflection** N reflexo; (*thought, act*) reflexão *f*; (*criticism*): **reflection on** crítica de; **on reflection** pensando bem

reflex ['ri:flɛks] ADJ, N reflexo

reform [rɪ'fɔ:m] N reforma ▶ VT reformar

r

refrain [rɪ'freɪn] VI: **to ~ from doing** abster-se de fazer ▶N estribilho, refrão *m*
refresh [rɪ'frɛʃ] VT refrescar; **refreshing** ADJ refrescante; (*sleep*) repousante
refreshment [rɪ'frɛʃmənt] N (*eating*): **for some ~** para comer alguma coisa; **refreshments** NPL comes e bebes *mpl*
refrigerator [rɪ'frɪdʒəreɪtə^r] N refrigerador *m*, geladeira (BR), frigorífico (PT)
refuel [ri:'fjuəl] VI reabastecer
refuge ['rɛfju:dʒ] N refúgio; **to take ~ in** refugiar-se em
refugee [rɛfju'dʒi:] N refugiado(-a)
refund [*n* 'ri:fʌnd, *vt* rɪ'fʌnd] N reembolso ▶VT devolver, reembolsar
refurbish [ri:'fə:bɪʃ] VT renovar
refusal [rɪ'fju:zəl] N recusa, negativa; **first ~** primeira opção
refuse¹ [rɪ'fju:z] VT recusar; (*order*) recusar-se a ▶VI recusar-se, negar-se; (*horse*) recusar-se a pular a cerca
refuse² ['rɛfju:s] N refugo, lixo
regain [rɪ'geɪn] VT recuperar, recobrar
regard [rɪ'gɑ:d] N (*gaze*) olhar *m* firme; (*attention*) atenção *f*; (*esteem*) estima, consideração *f* ▶VT (*consider*) considerar; **to give one's ~s to** dar lembranças a; **"with kindest ~s"** "cordialmente"; **as ~s, with ~ to** com relação a, com respeito a, quanto a; **regarding** PREP com relação a; **regardless** ADV apesar de tudo; **regardless of** apesar de
regiment ['rɛdʒɪmənt] N regimento
region ['ri:dʒən] N região *f*; **in the ~ of** (*fig*) por volta de, ao redor de; **regional** ADJ regional
register ['rɛdʒɪstə^r] N registro (BR), registo (PT); (*Sch*) chamada ▶VT registrar (BR), registar (PT); (*subj: instrument*) marcar, indicar ▶VI (*at hotel*) registrar-se (BR), registar-se (PT); (*for work*) candidatar-se; (*as student*) inscrever-se; (*make impression*) causar impressão; **registered** ADJ (*letter, parcel*) registrado (BR), registado (PT)
registrar ['rɛdʒɪstrɑ:^r] N oficial *m/f* de registro (BR) *or* registo (PT), escrivão(-vã) *m/f*; (*in college*) funcionário(-a) administrativo(-a) sênior; (*in hospital*) médico(-a) sênior
registration [rɛdʒɪs'treɪʃən] N (*act*) registro (BR), registo (PT); (*Aut: also*: **~ number**) número da placa
regret [rɪ'grɛt] N desgosto, pesar *m* ▶VT lamentar; (*repent of*) arrepender-se de
regular ['rɛgjulə^r] ADJ regular; (*frequent*) frequente; (*usual*) habitual; (*soldier*) de linha ▶N habitual *m/f*; **regularly** ADV regularmente; (*shaped*) simetricamente; (*often*) frequentemente
regulate ['rɛgjuleɪt] VT (*speed*) regular; (*spending*) controlar; (*Tech*) regular, ajustar; **regulation** [rɛgju'leɪʃən] N (*rule*) regra, regulamento; (*adjustment*) ajuste *m*
rehearsal [rɪ'hə:səl] N ensaio
rehearse [rɪ'hə:s] VT ensaiar
reign [reɪn] N reinado; (*fig*) domínio ▶VI reinar; imperar
reimburse [ri:ɪm'bə:s] VT reembolsar
rein [reɪn] N (*for horse*) rédea
reindeer ['reɪndɪə^r] N INV rena
reinforce [ri:ɪn'fɔ:s] VT reforçar

reinstate [riːɪnˈsteɪt] VT (*worker*) readmitir; (*tax, law*) reintroduzir
reject [*n* ˈriːdʒɛkt, *vt* rɪˈdʒɛkt] N (*Comm*) artigo defeituoso ▶ VT rejeitar; (*offer of help*) recusar; (*goods*) refugar; **rejection** N rejeição *f*; (*of offer of help*) recusa
rejoice [rɪˈdʒɔɪs] VI: **to ~ at** *or* **over** regozijar-se *or* alegrar-se de
relate [rɪˈleɪt] VT (*tell*) contar, relatar; (*connect*): **to ~ sth to** relacionar algo com ▶ VI: **to ~ to** relacionar-se com; **~d to** ligado a, relacionado a
relation [rɪˈleɪʃən] N (*person*) parente *m/f*; (*link*) relação *f*; **relations** NPL (*dealings*) relações *fpl*; (*relatives*) parentes *mpl*; **relationship** N relacionamento; (*between two things*) relação *f*; (*also*: **family relationship**) parentesco
relative [ˈrɛlətɪv] N parente *m/f* ▶ ADJ relativo; **relatively** ADV relativamente
relax [rɪˈlæks] VI (*unwind*) descontrair-se; (*muscle*) relaxar-se ▶ VT (*grip*) afrouxar; (*control*) relaxar; (*mind, person*) descansar; **relaxation** [riːlækˈseɪʃən] N (*rest*) descanso; (*of muscle, control*) relaxamento; (*of grip*) afrouxamento; (*recreation*) lazer *m*; **relaxed** ADJ relaxado; (*tranquil*) descontraído
relay [ˈriːleɪ] N (*race*) (corrida de) revezamento ▶ VT (*message*) retransmitir
release [rɪˈliːs] N (*from prison*) libertação *f*; (*from obligation*) liberação *f*; (*of gas*) escape *m*; (*of water*) despejo; (*of film, book etc*) lançamento ▶ VT (*prisoner*) pôr em liberdade; (*book, film*) lançar; (*report, news*) publicar; (*gas etc*) soltar; (*free: from wreckage etc*) soltar; (*Tech: catch, spring etc*) desengatar, desapertar
relegate [ˈrɛləgeɪt] VT relegar; (*Sport*): **to be ~d** ser rebaixado
relent [rɪˈlɛnt] VI (*yield*) ceder; **relentless** ADJ (*unceasing*) contínuo; (*determined*) implacável
relevant [ˈrɛləvənt] ADJ pertinente; **~ to** relacionado com
reliable [rɪˈlaɪəbl] ADJ (*person, firm*) de confiança, confiável, sério; (*method, machine*) seguro; (*news*) fidedigno
relic [ˈrɛlɪk] N (*Rel*) relíquia; (*of the past*) vestígio
relief [rɪˈliːf] N alívio; (*help, supplies*) ajuda, socorro; (*Art, Geo*) relevo
relieve [rɪˈliːv] VT (*pain, fear*) aliviar; (*bring help to*) ajudar, socorrer; (*take over from: gen*) substituir, revezar; (*: guard*) render; **to ~ sb of sth** (*load*) tirar algo de alguém; (*duties*) destituir alguém de algo; **to ~ o.s.** fazer as necessidades
religion [rɪˈlɪdʒən] N religião *f*; **religious** ADJ religioso
relish [ˈrɛlɪʃ] N (*Culin*) condimento, tempero; (*enjoyment*) entusiasmo ▶ VT (*food etc*) saborear; (*thought*) ver com satisfação
reluctant [rɪˈlʌktənt] ADJ relutante; **reluctantly** ADV relutantemente, de má vontade
rely on [rɪˈlaɪ-] VT FUS confiar em, contar com; (*be dependent on*) depender de
remain [rɪˈmeɪn] VI (*survive*) sobreviver; (*stay*) ficar, permanecer; (*be left*) sobrar; (*continue*) continuar; **remainder** N resto, restante *m*; **remaining** ADJ

restante; **remains** NPL (*of body*) restos *mpl*; (*of meal*) sobras *fpl*; (*of building*) ruínas *fpl*

remand [rɪ'mɑːnd] N: **on ~** sob prisão preventiva ▸VT: **to be ~ed in custody** continuar sob prisão preventiva, manter sob custódia

remark [rɪ'mɑːk] N observação *f*, comentário ▸VT comentar; **remarkable** ADJ (*outstanding*) extraordinário

remarry [riː'mærɪ] VI casar-se de novo

remedy ['rɛmədɪ] N: **~ (for)** remédio (contra *or* a) ▸VT remediar

remember [rɪ'mɛmbəʳ] VT lembrar-se de, lembrar; (*bear in mind*) ter em mente; (*send greetings*): **~ me to her** dê lembranças a ela

remembrance [rɪ'mɛmbrəns] N (*memory*) memória; (*souvenir*) lembrança, recordação *f*; **Remembrance Sunday** N *ver nota*

> **Remembrance Sunday** ou **Remembrance Day** é o domingo mais próximo do dia 11 de novembro, dia em que a Primeira Guerra Mundial terminou oficialmente e no qual se homenageia as vítimas das duas guerras mundiais. Nessa ocasião são observados dois minutos de silêncio às 11 horas, horário da assinatura do armistício com a Alemanha em 1918. Nos dias anteriores, papoulas de papel são vendidas por associações de caridade e a renda é revertida aos ex-combatentes e suas famílias.

remind [rɪ'maɪnd] VT: **to ~ sb to do sth** lembrar a alguém que tem de fazer algo; **to ~ sb of sth** lembrar algo a alguém, lembrar alguém de algo; **reminder** N lembrança; (*letter*) carta de advertência

remnant ['rɛmnənt] N resto; (*of cloth*) retalho; **remnants** NPL (*Comm*) retalhos *mpl*

remorse [rɪ'mɔːs] N remorso

remote [rɪ'məut] ADJ remoto; (*person*) reservado, afastado; **remote control** N controle *m* remoto; **remotely** ADV remotamente; (*slightly*) levemente

removal [rɪ'muːvəl] N (*taking away*) remoção *f*; (BRIT: *from house*) mudança; (*from office: sacking*) afastamento, demissão *f*; (*Med*) extração *f*; **removal van** (BRIT) N caminhão *m* (BR) *or* camião *m* (PT) de mudanças

remove [rɪ'muːv] VT tirar, retirar; (*clothing*) tirar; (*stain*) remover; (*employee*) afastar, demitir; (*name from list, obstacle*) eliminar, remover; (*doubt, abuse*) afastar; (*Med*) extrair, extirpar

render ['rɛndəʳ] VT (*thanks*) trazer; (*service*) prestar; (*make*) fazer, tornar

rendezvous ['rɔndɪvuː] N encontro; (*place*) ponto de encontro

renew [rɪ'njuː] VT retomar, recomeçar; (*loan etc*) prorrogar; (*negotiations, acquaintance*) reatar

renovate ['rɛnəveɪt] VT renovar; (*house, room*) reformar

rent [rɛnt] N aluguel *m* (BR), aluguer *m* (PT) ▸VT (*also*: **~ out**) alugar; **rental** N (*for television, car*) aluguel *m* (BR), aluguer *m* (PT)

rep [rɛp] N ABBR (*Comm*) = **representative**

repair [rɪ'pɛəʳ] N reparação *f*, conserto ▸VT consertar; **in good/bad ~** em bom/mau estado; **repair kit** N caixa de ferramentas

repay [ri:'peɪ] *irreg* VT (*money*) reembolsar, restituir; (*person*) pagar de volta; (*debt*) saldar, liquidar; (*sb's efforts*) corresponder, retribuir; (*favour*) retribuir; **repayment** N reembolso; (*of debt*) pagamento

repeat [rɪ'pi:t] N (*Radio, TV*) repetição *f* ▶ VT repetir; (*Comm: order*) renovar ▶ VI repetir-se

repetitive [rɪ'pɛtɪtɪv] ADJ repetitivo

replace [rɪ'pleɪs] VT (*put back*) repor, devolver; (*take the place of*) substituir; **replacement** N (*substitution*) substituição *f*; (*substitute*) substituto(-a)

replay ['ri:pleɪ] N (*of match*) partida decisiva; (*TV: also*: **action ~**) replay *m*

replica ['rɛplɪkə] N réplica, cópia, reprodução *f*

reply [rɪ'plaɪ] N resposta ▶ VI responder

report [rɪ'pɔ:t] N relatório; (*Press etc*) reportagem *f*; (BRIT: *also*: **school ~**) boletim *m* escolar; (*of gun*) estampido, detonação *f* ▶ VT informar sobre; (*Press etc*) fazer uma reportagem sobre; (*bring to notice*) comunicar, anunciar ▶ VI (*make a report*): **to ~ (on)** apresentar um relatório (sobre); (*present o.s.*): **to ~ (to sb)** apresentar-se (a alguém); (*be responsible to*): **to ~ to sb** obedecer as ordens de alguém; **report card** (US, SCOTLAND) N boletim *m* escolar; **reportedly** ADV: **she is reportedly living in Spain** dizem que ela mora na Espanha; **reporter** N repórter *m/f*

represent [rɛprɪ'zɛnt] VT representar; (*constitute*) constituir; (*Comm*) ser representante de; **representation** [rɛprɪzɛn'teɪʃən] N representação *f*; (*picture, statue*) representação, retrato; (*petition*) petição *f*; **representations** NPL (*protest*) reclamação *f*, protesto; **representative** [rɛprɪ'zɛntətɪv] N representante *m/f*; (US *Pol*) deputado(-a) ▶ ADJ: **representative (of)** representativo (de)

repress [rɪ'prɛs] VT reprimir; **repression** N repressão *f*

reproduce [ri:prə'dju:s] VT reproduzir ▶ VI reproduzir-se

reptile ['rɛptaɪl] N réptil *m*

republic [rɪ'pʌblɪk] N república; **republican** ADJ, N republicano(-a); (US *Pol*): **Republican** membro(-a) do Partido Republicano

reputable ['rɛpjutəbl] ADJ (*make etc*) bem conceituado, de confiança; (*person*) honrado, respeitável

reputation [rɛpju'teɪʃən] N reputação *f*

request [rɪ'kwɛst] N pedido; (*formal*) petição *f* ▶ VT: **to ~ sth of** *or* **from sb** pedir algo a alguém; (*formally*) solicitar algo a alguém; **request stop** (BRIT) N (*for bus*) parada não obrigatória

require [rɪ'kwaɪə^r] VT (*need: subj: person*) precisar de, necessitar; (: *thing, situation*) requerer, exigir; (*want*) pedir; (*order*): **to ~ sb to do sth/sth of sb** exigir que alguém faça algo/algo de alguém; **requirement** N (*need*) necessidade *f*; (*want*) pedido

rescue ['rɛskju:] N salvamento, resgate *m* ▶ VT: **to ~ (from)** resgatar (de); (*save, fig*) salvar (de)

r

research [rɪ'sə:tʃ] N pesquisa ▶ VT pesquisar
resemblance [rɪ'zɛmbləns] N semelhança
resemble [rɪ'zɛmbl] VT parecer-se com
resent [rɪ'zɛnt] VT (*attitude*) ressentir-se de; (*person*) estar ressentido com; **resentful** ADJ ressentido
reservation [rɛzə'veɪʃən] N reserva
reserve [rɪ'zə:v] N reserva; (*Sport*) suplente *m/f*, reserva *m/f* (BR) ▶ VT reservar; **reserves** NPL (*Mil*) (tropas *fpl* da) reserva; (*Comm*) reserva; **in ~** de reserva; **reserved** ADJ reservado
residence ['rɛzɪdəns] N residência; (*formal: home*) domicílio; **residence permit** (BRIT) N autorização *f* de residência
resident ['rɛzɪdənt] N (*of country, town*) habitante *m/f*; (*in hotel*) hóspede *m/f* ▶ ADJ (*population*) permanente; (*doctor*) interno, residente; **residential** [rɛzɪ'dɛnʃəl] ADJ residencial
residue ['rɛzɪdju:] N resto
resign [rɪ'zaɪn] VT renunciar a, demitir-se de ▶ VI: **to ~ (from)** demitir-se (de); **to ~ o.s. to** resignar-se a; **resignation** [rɛzɪg'neɪʃən] N demissão *f*; (*state of mind*) resignação *f*
resist [rɪ'zɪst] VT resistir a
resolution [rɛzə'lu:ʃən] N resolução *f*; (*of problem*) solução *f*
resolve [rɪ'zɔlv] N resolução *f* ▶ VT resolver ▶ VI: **to ~ to do** resolver-se a fazer
resort [rɪ'zɔ:t] N local *m* turístico, estação *f* de veraneio; (*recourse*) recurso ▶ VI: **to ~ to** recorrer a; **in the last ~** em último caso, em última instância
resource [rɪ'sɔ:s] N (*raw material*) recurso natural; **resources** NPL (*coal, money, energy*) recursos *mpl*; **resourceful** ADJ engenhoso, habilidoso
respect [rɪs'pɛkt] N respeito ▶ VT respeitar; **respects** NPL (*greetings*) cumprimentos *mpl*; **respectable** ADJ respeitável; (*large*) considerável; (*result, player*) razoável; **respectful** ADJ respeitoso
respond [rɪs'pɔnd] VI (*answer*) responder; (*react*) reagir; **response** N resposta; (*reaction*) reação *f*
responsibility [rɪspɔnsɪ'bɪlɪtɪ] N responsabilidade *f*; (*duty*) dever *m*
responsible [rɪs'pɔnsɪbl] ADJ sério, responsável; (*job*) de responsabilidade; (*liable*): **~ (for)** responsável (por)
responsive [rɪs'pɔnsɪv] ADJ receptivo
rest [rɛst] N descanso, repouso; (*pause*) pausa, intervalo; (*support*) apoio; (*remainder*) resto; (*Mus*) pausa ▶ VI descansar; (*stop*) parar; (*be supported*): **to ~ on** apoiar-se em ▶ VT descansar; (*lean*): **to ~ sth on/against** apoiar algo em *or* sobre/contra; **the ~ of them** os outros; **it ~s with him to do it** cabe a ele fazê-lo
restaurant ['rɛstərɔŋ] N restaurante *m*; **restaurant car** (BRIT) N vagão-restaurante *m*
restless ['rɛstlɪs] ADJ desassossegado, irrequieto
restore [rɪ'stɔ:ʳ] VT (*building, order*) restaurar; (*sth stolen*) restituir; (*peace, health*) restabelecer
restrain [rɪs'treɪn] VT (*feeling*) reprimir; (*growth, inflation*) refrear; (*person*): **to ~ (from doing)** impedir (de fazer); **restraint** N (*restriction*)

restrição *f*; (*moderation*) moderação *f*, comedimento; (*of style*) sobriedade *f*
restrict [rɪs'trɪkt] VT restringir, limitar; (*people, animals*) confinar; (*activities*) limitar; **restriction** N restrição *f*, limitação *f*
rest room (US) N banheiro (BR), lavabo (PT)
result [rɪ'zʌlt] N resultado ▶ VI: **to ~ in** resultar em; **as a ~ of** como resultado *or* consequência de
resume [rɪ'zju:m] VT (*work, journey*) retomar, recomeçar ▶ VI recomeçar
résumé ['reɪzju:meɪ] N (*summary*) resumo; (*US: curriculum vitae*) curriculum vitae *m*, currículo
resuscitate [rɪ'sʌsɪteɪt] VT (*Med*) ressuscitar, reanimar
retail ['ri:teɪl] ADJ a varejo (BR), a retalho (PT) ▶ ADV a varejo (BR), a retalho (PT); **retailer** N varejista *m/f* (BR), retalhista *m/f* (PT)
retain [rɪ'teɪn] VT (*keep*) reter, conservar
retire [rɪ'taɪə[r]] VI aposentar-se; (*withdraw*) retirar-se; (*go to bed*) deitar-se; **retired** ADJ aposentado (BR), reformado (PT); **retirement** N aposentadoria (BR), reforma (PT)
retort [rɪ'tɔ:t] VI replicar, retrucar
retreat [rɪ'tri:t] N (*place*) retiro; (*act*) retirada ▶ VI retirar-se
retrieve [rɪ'tri:v] VT (*sth lost*) reaver, recuperar; (*situation, honour*) salvar; (*error, loss*) reparar
retrospect ['rɛtrəspɛkt] N: **in ~** retrospectivamente, em retrospecto; **retrospective** [rɛtrə'spɛktɪv] ADJ retrospectivo; (*law*) retroativo
return [rɪ'tə:n] N regresso, volta; (*of sth stolen etc*) devolução *f*; (*Finance: from land, shares*) rendimento ▶ CPD (*journey*) de volta; (BRIT: *ticket*) de ida e volta; (*match*) de revanche ▶ VI voltar, regressar; (*symptoms etc*) voltar; (*regain*): **to ~ to** (*consciousness*) recobrar; (*power*) retornar a ▶ VT devolver; (*favour, love etc*) retribuir; (*verdict*) proferir, anunciar; (*Pol: candidate*) eleger; **returns** NPL (*Comm*) receita; **in ~ (for)** em troca (de); **many happy ~s (of the day)!** parabéns!; **by ~ (of post)** por volta do correio
retweet [ri:'twi:t] N (*on Twitter*) retweet *m*
reunion [ri:'ju:nɪən] N (*family*) reunião *f*; (*two people, class*) reencontro
reunite [ri:ju:'naɪt] VT reunir; (*reconcile*) reconciliar
revamp ['ri:'væmp] VT dar um jeito em
reveal [rɪ'vi:l] VT revelar; (*make visible*) mostrar; **revealing** ADJ revelador(a)
revel ['rɛvl] VI: **to ~ in sth/in doing sth** deleitar-se com algo/em fazer algo
revenge [rɪ'vɛndʒ] N vingança, desforra; **to take ~ on** vingar-se de
revenue ['rɛvənju:] N receita, renda
reversal [rɪ'və:sl] N (*of order*) reversão *f*; (*of direction*) mudança em sentido contrário; (*of decision*) revogação *f*; (*of roles*) inversão *f*
reverse [rɪ'və:s] N (*opposite*) contrário; (*back: of cloth*) avesso; (*: of coin*) reverso; (*: of paper*) dorso; (*Aut: also:* **~ gear**) marcha à ré (BR), marcha atrás (PT); (*setback*) revés *m*, derrota ▶ ADJ (*order*) inverso, oposto; (*direction*) contrário;

(*process*) inverso ▸VT inverter; (*position*) mudar; (*process, decision*) revogar; (*car*) dar ré com ▸VI (BRIT *Aut*) dar (marcha à) ré (BR), fazer marcha atrás (PT); **reverse-charge call** (BRIT) N (*Tel*) ligação *f* a cobrar
revert [rɪ'vəːt] VI: **to ~ to** voltar a; (*Jur*) reverter a
review [rɪ'vjuː] N (*magazine, Mil*) revista; (*of book, film*) crítica, resenha; (*examination*) recapitulação *f*, exame *m* ▸VT rever, examinar; (*Mil*) passar em revista; (*book, film*) fazer a crítica *or* resenha de
revise [rɪ'vaɪz] VT (*manuscript*) corrigir; (*opinion, procedure*) alterar; (*price*) revisar; **revision** [rɪ'vɪʒən] N correção *f*; (*for exam*) revisão *f*
revival [rɪ'vaɪvəl] N (*recovery*) restabelecimento; (*of interest*) renascença, renascimento; (*Theatre*) reestreia; (*of faith*) despertar *m*
revive [rɪ'vaɪv] VT (*person*) reanimar, ressuscitar; (*economy*) recuperar; (*custom*) restabelecer, restaurar; (*hope, courage*) despertar; (*play*) reapresentar ▸VI (*person: from faint*) voltar a si, recuperar os sentidos; (*: from ill-health*) recuperar-se; (*activity, economy*) reativar-se; (*hope, interest*) renascer
revolt [rɪ'vəult] N revolta, rebelião *f*, insurreição *f* ▸VI revoltar-se ▸VT causar aversão a, repugnar; **revolting** ADJ revoltante, repulsivo
revolution [rɛvə'luːʃən] N revolução *f*; (*of wheel, earth*) rotação *f*
revolve [rɪ'vɔlv] VI girar
revolver [rɪ'vɔlvə^r] N revólver *m*
reward [rɪ'wɔːd] N recompensa ▸VT: **to ~ (for)** recompensar *or* premiar (por); **rewarding** ADJ (*fig*) gratificante, compensador(a)
rewind [riː'waɪnd] *irreg* VT (*tape*) voltar para trás
rewritable [riː'raɪtəbl] ADJ regravável
rheumatism ['ruːmətɪzəm] N reumatismo
rhinoceros [raɪ'nɔsərəs] N rinoceronte *m*
rhubarb ['ruːbɑːb] N ruibarbo
rhyme [raɪm] N rima; (*verse*) verso(s) *m(pl)* rimado(s), poesia
rhythm ['rɪðm] N ritmo
rib [rɪb] N (*Anat*) costela ▸VT (*mock*) zombar de, encarnar em
ribbon ['rɪbən] N fita; **in ~s** (*torn*) em tirinhas, esfarrapado
rice [raɪs] N arroz *m*; **rice pudding** N arroz *m* doce
rich [rɪtʃ] ADJ rico; (*clothes*) valioso; (*soil*) fértil; (*food*) suculento, forte; (*colour*) intenso; (*voice*) suave, cheio ▸NPL: **the ~** os ricos; **riches** NPL (*wealth*) riquezas *fpl*
rid [rɪd] (*pt, pp* **rid**) VT: **to ~ sb of sth** livrar alguém de algo; **to get ~ of** livrar-se de; (*sth no longer required*) desfazer-se de
riddle ['rɪdl] N (*conundrum*) adivinhação *f*; (*mystery*) enigma *m*, charada ▸VT: **to be ~d with** estar cheio de
ride [raɪd] (*pt* **rode**, *pp* **ridden**) N (*gen*) passeio; (*on horse*) passeio a cavalo; (*distance covered*) percurso, trajeto ▸VI (*as sport*) montar; (*go somewhere: on horse, bicycle*) ir (a cavalo, de bicicleta); (*journey: on bicycle, motorcycle, bus*) viajar ▸VT (*a horse*) montar a; (*bicycle, motorcycle*) andar de; (*distance*) percorrer; **to ~ at anchor** (*Naut*) estar ancorado; **to take sb for a ~** (*fig*) enganar alguém; **rider** N (*on horse: male*) cavaleiro; (*: female*)

amazona; (*on bicycle*) ciclista *m/f*; (*on motorcycle*) motociclista *m/f*
ridge [rɪdʒ] N (*of hill*) cume *m*, topo; (*of roof*) cumeeira; (*wrinkle*) ruga
ridicule ['rɪdɪkju:l] N escárnio, zombaria, mofa ▶ VT ridicularizar, zombar de; **ridiculous** ADJ ridículo
riding ['raɪdɪŋ] N equitação *f*
rife [raɪf] ADJ: **to be ~** ser comum; **to be ~ with** estar repleto de, abundar em
rifle ['raɪfl] N rifle *m*, fuzil *m* ▶ VT saquear; **rifle through** VT FUS vasculhar
rift [rɪft] N fenda, fratura; (*in clouds*) brecha; (*fig: between friends*) desentendimento; (*: in party*) rompimento, divergência
rig [rɪg] N (*also*: **oil ~**) torre *f* de perfuração ▶ VT adulterar *or* falsificar os resultados de; **rig out** (BRIT) VT: **to ~ out as/in** ataviar *or* vestir como/com; **rig up** VT instalar, montar, improvisar
right [raɪt] ADJ certo, correto; (*suitable*) adequado, conveniente; (*: decision*) certo; (*just*) justo; (*morally good*) bom; (*not left*) direito ▶ N direito; (*not left*) direita ▶ ADV bem, corretamente; (*fairly*) adequadamente, justamente; (*not on the left*) à direita; (*exactly*): **~ now** agora mesmo ▶ VT colocar em pé; (*correct*) corrigir, indireitar ▶ EXCL bom!; **to be ~** (*person*) ter razão; (*answer, clock*) estar certo; **by ~s** por direito; **on the ~** à direita; **to be in the ~** ter razão; **~ away** imediatamente, logo, já; **~ in the middle** bem no meio; **rightful** ADJ (*heir*) legítimo; (*place*) justo, legítimo; **right-handed** ADJ destro; **rightly** ADV (*with reason*) com razão; **right of way** N prioridade *f* de passagem; (*Aut*) preferência; **right-wing** ADJ de direita
rigid ['rɪdʒɪd] ADJ rígido; (*principle*) inflexível
rim [rɪm] N borda, beira; (*of spectacles, wheel*) aro
rind [raɪnd] N (*of bacon*) pele *f*; (*of lemon etc*) casca; (*of cheese*) crosta, casca
ring [rɪŋ] (*pt* **rang**, *pp* **rung**) N (*of metal*) aro; (*on finger*) anel *m*; (*of people, objects*) círculo, grupo; (*for boxing*) ringue *m*; (*of circus*) pista, picadeiro; (*bullring*) picadeiro, arena; (*of light, smoke*) círculo; (*sound: of small bell*) toque *m*; (*: of large bell*) badalada, repique *m* ▶ VI (*on telephone*) telefonar; (*bell*) tocar; (*also*: **~ out**) soar; (*ears*) zumbir ▶ VT (BRIT *Tel*) telefonar a, ligar para; (*bell etc*) badalar; (*doorbell*) tocar; **to give sb a ~** (BRIT *Tel*) dar uma ligada *or* ligar para alguém; **ring back** (BRIT) VI (*Tel*) telefonar *or* ligar de volta ▶ VT telefonar *or* ligar de volta para; **ring off** (BRIT) VI (*Tel*) desligar; **ring up** (BRIT) VT (*Tel*) telefonar a, ligar para; **ring-fence** VT (*money, tax*) restringir (o uso de alguma verba); **ringing tone** (BRIT) N (*Tel*) sinal *m* de chamada; **ringleader** N cabeça *m/f*, cérebro; **ring road** (BRIT) N estrada periférica *or* perimetral; **ringtone** N (*on cellphone*) toque *m*
rink [rɪŋk] N (*also*: **ice ~**) pista de patinação, rinque *m*
rinse [rɪns] N enxaguada ▶ VT enxaguar; (*also*: **~ out**: *mouth*) bochechar
riot ['raɪət] N distúrbio, motim *m*, desordem *f*; (*of colour*) festival *m*,

profusão *f* ▶ VI provocar distúrbios, amotinar-se; **to run ~** desenfrear-se

rip [rɪp] N rasgão *m* ▶ VT rasgar ▶ VI rasgar-se

ripe [raɪp] ADJ maduro

ripple ['rɪpl] N ondulação *f*, encrespação *f*; (*of laughter etc*) onda ▶ VI encrespar-se

rise [raɪz] (*pt* **rose**, *pp* **risen**) N elevação *f*, ladeira; (*hill*) colina, rampa; (*increase*: BRIT: *in wages*) aumento; (: *in prices, temperature*) subida; (*to power etc*) ascensão *f* ▶ VI levantar-se, erguer-se; (*prices, waters*) subir; (*sun*) nascer; (*from bed etc*) levantar(-se); (*sound, voice*) aumentar, erguer-se; (*also*: **~ up**; *building*) erguer-se; (: *rebel*) sublevar-se; (*in rank*) ascender, subir; **to give ~ to** ocasionar, dar origem a; **to ~ to the occasion** mostrar-se à altura da situação; **rising** ADJ (*increasing*: *prices*) em alta; (: *number*) crescente, cada vez maior; (*tide*) montante; (*sun, moon*) nascente

risk [rɪsk] N risco, perigo; (*Insurance*) risco ▶ VT pôr em risco; (*chance*) arriscar, aventurar; **to take** *or* **run the ~ of doing** correr o risco de fazer; **at ~** em perigo; **at one's own ~** por sua própria conta e risco; **risky** ADJ perigoso

rite [raɪt] N rito; **last ~s** últimos sacramentos

ritual ['rɪtjuəl] ADJ ritual ▶ N ritual *m*; (*of initiation*) rito

rival ['raɪvl] ADJ, N rival *m/f*; (*in business*) concorrente *m/f* ▶ VT competir com; **rivalry** N rivalidade *f*

river ['rɪvə^r] N rio ▶ CPD (*port, traffic*) fluvial; **up/down ~** rio acima/abaixo; **riverbank** N margem *f* (do rio)

road [rəud] N via; (*motorway etc*) estrada (de rodagem); (*in town*) rua ▶ CPD rodoviário; **road accident** N acidente *m* de trânsito; **roadblock** N barricada; **road map** N mapa *m* rodoviário; **road rage** N *conduta agressiva dos motoristas no trânsito*; **roadside** N beira da estrada; **road sign** N placa de sinalização; **roadworks** ['rəudwə:ks] NPL obras *fpl* de estrada

roam [rəum] VI vagar, perambular, errar

roar [rɔ:^r] N (*of animal*) rugido, urro; (*of crowd*) bramido; (*of vehicle, storm*) estrondo; (*of laughter*) barulho ▶ VI (*animal, engine*) rugir; (*person, crowd*) bradar; **to ~ with laughter** dar gargalhadas

roast [rəust] N carne *f* assada, assado ▶ VT assar; (*coffee*) torrar; **roast beef** N rosbife *m*

rob [rɔb] VT roubar; (*bank*) assaltar; **to ~ sb of sth** roubar algo de alguém; (*fig*: *deprive*) despojar alguém de algo; **robber** N ladrão/ladra *m/f*; **robbery** N roubo

robe [rəub] N toga, beca; (*also*: **bath ~**) roupão *m* (de banho)

robin ['rɔbɪn] N pisco-de-peito-ruivo (BR), pintarroxo (PT)

robot ['rəubɔt] N robô *m*

robust [rəu'bʌst] ADJ robusto, forte; (*appetite*) sadio; (*economy*) forte

rock [rɔk] N rocha; (*boulder*) penhasco, rochedo; (*US*: *small stone*) cascalho; (BRIT: *sweet*) pirulito ▶ VT (*swing gently*: *cradle*) balançar, oscilar; (: *child*) embalar, acalentar; (*shake*) sacudir ▶ VI (*object*) balançar-se; (*person*) embalar-se; **on the ~s** (*drink*) com gelo; (*marriage etc*) arruinado, em dificuldades; **rock and roll** N rock-and-roll *m*

rocket ['rɔkɪt] N foguete *m*
rocky ['rɔkɪ] ADJ rochoso; bambo, instável; (*marriage etc*) instável
rod [rɔd] N vara, varinha; (*also*: **fishing ~**) vara de pescar
rode [rəud] PT *of* **ride**
rodent ['rəudnt] N roedor *m*
rogue [rəug] N velhaco, maroto
role [rəul] N papel *m*; **role model** N modelo
roll [rəul] N rolo; (*of banknotes*) maço; (*also*: **bread ~**) pãozinho; (*register*) rol *m*, lista; (*of drums etc*) rufar *m* ▶ VT rolar; (*also*: **~ up**: *string*) enrolar; (: *sleeves*) arregaçar; (*cigarette*) enrolar; (*eyes*) virar; (*also*: **~ out**: *pastry*) esticar; (*lawn, road etc*) aplanar ▶ VI rolar; (*drum*) rufar; (*vehicle*: *also*: **~ along**) rodar; (*ship*) balançar, jogar; **roll about** VI ficar rolando; **roll around** VI = **roll about**; **roll by** VI (*time*) passar; **roll in** VI (*mail, cash*) chegar em grande quantidade; **roll over** VI dar uma volta; **roll up** VI (*inf*) pintar, chegar, aparecer ▶ VT (*carpet etc*) enrolar; **roller** N (*in machine*) rolo, cilindro; (*wheel*) roda, roldana; (*for lawn, road*) rolo compressor; (*for hair*) rolo; **roller coaster** N montanha-russa; **roller skates** NPL patins *mpl* de roda
rolling pin N rolo de pastel
ROM [rɔm] N ABBR (*Comput*: = *read-only memory*) ROM *f*
Roman ['rəumən] ADJ, N romano(-a); **Roman Catholic** ADJ, N católico(-a) (romano(-a))
romance [rə'mæns] N aventura amorosa, romance *m*; (*book etc*) história de amor; (*charm*) romantismo
Romania [ru:'meɪnɪə] N Romênia; **Romanian** ADJ romeno ▶ N romeno(-a); (*Ling*) romeno
romantic [rə'mæntɪk] ADJ romântico
Rome [rəum] N Roma
roof [ru:f] N (*of house*) telhado; (*of car*) capota, teto ▶ VT telhar, cobrir com telhas; **the ~ of the mouth** o céu da boca; **roof rack** N (*Aut*) bagageiro
rook [ruk] N (*bird*) gralha; (*Chess*) torre *f*
room [ru:m] N (*in house*) quarto, aposento; (*also*: **bed~**) quarto, dormitório; (*in school etc*) sala; (*space*) espaço, lugar *m*; (*scope*: *for improvement etc*) espaço; **rooms** NPL (*lodging*) alojamento; **"~s to let"** (BRIT), **"~s for rent"** (US) "alugam-se quartos *or* apartamentos"; **roommate** N companheiro(-a) de quarto; **room service** N serviço de quarto; **roomy** ADJ espaçoso; (*garment*) folgado
rooster ['ru:stəʳ] N galo
root [ru:t] N raiz *f*; (*fig*) origem *f* ▶ VI enraizar, arraigar; **roots** NPL (*family origins*) raízes *fpl*; **root about** VI (*fig*): **to ~ about in** (*drawer*) vasculhar; (*house*) esquadrinhar; **root for** VT FUS torcer por; **root out** VT extirpar
rope [rəup] N corda; (*Naut*) cabo ▶ VT (*tie*) amarrar; (*climbers*: *also*: **~ together**) amarrar *or* atar com uma corda; (*area*: *also*: **~ off**) isolar; **to know the ~s** (*fig*) estar por dentro (do assunto); **rope in** VT (*fig*): **to ~ sb in** persuadir alguém a tomar parte
rose [rəuz] PT *of* **rise** ▶ N rosa; (*also*: **~bush**) roseira; (*on watering can*) crivo
rosé ['rəuzeɪ] N rosado, rosé *m*
rosemary ['rəuzmərɪ] N alecrim *m*

r

rosy ['rəuzɪ] ADJ rosado, rosáceo; (*cheeks*) rosado; (*situation*) cor-de-rosa *inv*; **a ~ future** um futuro promissor

rot [rɔt] N (*decay*) putrefação *f*, podridão *f*; (*fig: pej*) besteira ▶ VT, VI apodrecer

rota ['rəutə] N lista de tarefas, escala de serviço

rotate [rəu'teɪt] VT fazer girar, dar voltas em ▶ VI girar, dar voltas

rotten ['rɔtn] ADJ podre; (*wood*) carcomido; (*fig*) corrupto; (*inf: bad*) péssimo; **to feel ~** (*ill*) sentir-se podre

rough [rʌf] ADJ (*skin, surface*) áspero; (*terrain*) acidentado; (*road*) desigual; (*voice*) áspero, rouco; (*weather*) tempestuoso; (*treatment*) brutal, mau/má; (*sea*) agitado; (*district*) violento; (*plan*) preliminar; (*work, cloth*) grosseiro; (*guess*) aproximado ▶ N (*Golf*): **in the ~** na grama crescida; **to sleep ~** (BRIT) dormir na rua; **roughly** ADV bruscamente; (*make*) toscamente; (*approximately*) aproximadamente

roulette [ru:'lɛt] N roleta

round [raund] ADJ redondo ▶ N (BRIT: *of toast*) rodela; (*of policeman*) ronda; (*of milkman*) trajeto; (*of doctor*) visitas *fpl*; (*game: of cards, golf, in competition*) partida; (*of ammunition*) cartucho; (*Boxing*) round *m*, assalto; (*of talks*) ciclo ▶ VT virar, dobrar ▶ PREP (*surrounding*): **~ his neck/the table** em volta de seu pescoço/ao redor da mesa; (*in a circular movement*): **to go ~ the world** dar a volta ao mundo; (*in various directions*): **to move ~ a house** mover-se por uma casa; (*approximately*): **~ about** aproximadamente ▶ ADV: **all ~** por todos os lados; **the long way ~** o caminho mais comprido; **all the year ~** durante todo o ano; **it's just ~ the corner** (*fig*) está pertinho; **~ the clock** ininterrupto; **to go ~ the back** passar por detrás; **to go ~ a house** visitar uma casa; **enough to go ~** suficiente para todos; **a ~ of applause** uma salva de palmas; **a ~ of drinks** uma rodada de bebidas; **~ of sandwiches** sanduíche *m* (BR), sandes *f inv* (PT); **round off** VT terminar, completar; **round up** VT (*cattle*) encurralar; (*people*) reunir; (*price, figure*) arredondar; **roundabout** N (BRIT: *Aut*) rotatória; (*: at fair*) carrossel *m* ▶ ADJ indireto; **round trip** N viagem *f* de ida e volta

rouse [rauz] VT (*wake up*) despertar, acordar; (*stir up*) suscitar

route [ru:t] N caminho, rota; (*of bus*) trajeto; (*of shipping*) rumo, rota; (*of procession*) rota

routine [ru:'ti:n] ADJ (*work*) rotineiro; (*procedure*) de rotina ▶ N rotina; (*Theatre*) número

row¹ [rəu] N (*line*) fila, fileira; (*in theatre, boat*) fileira; (*Knitting*) carreira, fileira ▶ VI, VT remar; **in a ~** (*fig*) a fio, seguido

row² [rau] N barulho, balbúrdia; (*dispute*) discussão *f*, briga; (*scolding*) repreensão *f* ▶ VI brigar; **to have a ~** ter uma briga

rowboat ['rəubəut] (US) N barco a remo

rowing ['rəuɪŋ] N remo; **rowing boat** (BRIT) N barco a remo

royal ['rɔɪəl] ADJ real

Royal Academy (BRIT) N *ver nota*

> A **Royal Academy**, ou **Royal Academy of Arts**, fundada em 1768 por George III para desenvolver a pintura, a escultura e a arquitetura,

situa-se em Burlington House, Piccadilly. A cada verão há uma exposição de obras de artistas contemporâneos. A **Royal Academy** também oferece cursos de pintura, escultura e arquitetura.

royalty N família real, realeza; (*payment: to author*) direitos *mpl* autorais

rpm ABBR (= *revolutions per minute*) rpm

rub [rʌb] VT (*part of body*) esfregar; (*object*) friccionar ▸ N: **to give sth a ~** dar uma esfregada em algo; **to ~ sb up** (BRIT) *or* **~ sb** (US) **the wrong way** irritar alguém; **rub off** VI sair esfregando; **rub off on** VT FUS transmitir-se para, influir sobre; **rub out** VT apagar

rubber ['rʌbəʳ] N borracha; (BRIT: *eraser*) borracha; **rubber band** N elástico, tira elástica

rubbish ['rʌbɪʃ] N (*waste*) refugo; (*from household, in street*) lixo; (*junk*) coisas *fpl* sem valor; (*fig: pej: nonsense*) disparates *mpl*, asneiras *fpl*; **rubbish bin** (BRIT) N lata de lixo; **rubbish dump** N (*in town*) depósito (de lixo)

rubble ['rʌbl] N (*debris*) entulho; (*Constr*) escombros *mpl*

ruby ['ru:bɪ] N rubi *m*

rucksack ['rʌksæk] N mochila

rudder ['rʌdəʳ] N leme *m*; (*of plane*) leme de direção

rude [ru:d] ADJ (*person*) grosso, mal-educado; (*word, manners*) grosseiro; (*shocking*) obsceno, chocante

rug [rʌg] N tapete *m*; (BRIT: *for knees*) manta (de viagem)

rugby ['rʌgbɪ] N (*also:* **~ football**) rúgbi *m* (BR), râguebi *m* (PT)

rugged ['rʌgɪd] ADJ (*landscape*) acidentado, irregular; (*features*) marcado; (*character*) severo, austero

ruin ['ru:ɪn] N ruína; (*of plans*) destruição *f*; (*downfall*) queda; (*bankruptcy*) bancarrota ▸ VT destruir; (*future, person*) arruinar; (*spoil*) estragar; **ruins** NPL (*of building*) ruínas *fpl*

rule [ru:l] N (*norm*) regra; (*regulation*) regulamento; (*government*) governo, domínio; (*ruler*) régua ▸ VT governar ▸ VI governar; (*monarch*) reger; (*Jur*): **to ~ in favour of/against** decidir oficialmente a favor de/contra; **as a ~** por via de regra, geralmente; **rule out** VT excluir; **ruler** N (*sovereign*) soberano(-a); (*for measuring*) régua; **ruling** ADJ (*party*) dominante; (*class*) dirigente ▸ N (*Jur*) parecer *m*, decisão *f*

rum [rʌm] N rum *m*

rumble ['rʌmbl] N ruído surdo, barulho; (*of thunder*) estrondo, ribombo ▸ VI ribombar, ressoar; (*stomach*) roncar; (*pipe*) fazer barulho; (*thunder*) ribombar

rumour ['ru:məʳ], (US) **rumor** N rumor *m*, boato ▸ VT: **it is ~ed that ...** corre o boato de que ...

rump steak [rʌmp-] N alcatra

run [rʌn] (*pt* **ran**, *pp* **run**) N corrida; (*in car*) passeio (de carro); (*distance travelled*) trajeto, percurso; (*journey*) viagem *f*; (*series*) série *f*; (*Theatre*) temporada; (*Ski*) pista; (*in stockings*) fio puxado ▸ VT (*race*) correr; (*operate: business*) dirigir; (*: competition, course*) organizar; (*: hotel, house*) administrar; (*water*) deixar correr; (*bath*) encher; (*Press: feature*) publicar; (*Comput*) rodar;

(*hand, finger*) passar ▶ VI correr; (*work: machine*) funcionar; (*bus, train: operate*) circular; (: *travel*) ir; (*continue: play*) continuar em cartaz; (: *contract*) ser válido; (*river, bath*) fluir, correr; (*colours, washing*) desbotar; (*in election*) candidatar-se; (*nose*) escorrer; **there was a ~ on** houve muita procura de; **in the long ~** no final das contas, mais cedo ou mais tarde; **on the ~** em fuga, foragido; **run about** VI correr por todos os lados; **run across** VT FUS encontrar por acaso, topar com, dar com; **run around** VI = **run about**; **run away** VI fugir; **run down** VT (*Aut*) atropelar; (*production*) reduzir; (*criticize*) criticar; **to be ~ down** estar enfraquecido *or* exausto; **run in** (BRIT) VT (*car*) rodar; **run into** VT FUS (*meet: person*) dar com, topar com; (: *trouble*) esbarrar em; (*collide with*) bater em; **run off** VI fugir; **run out** VI (*person*) sair correndo; (*liquid*) escorrer, esgotar-se; (*lease, passport*) caducar, vencer; (*money*) acabar; **run out of** VT FUS ficar sem; **run over** VT (*Aut*) atropelar ▶ VT FUS (*revise*) recapitular; **run through** VT FUS (*instructions*) recapitular; **run up** VT (*debt*) acumular ▶ VI: **to ~ up against** esbarrar em; **runaway** ADJ (*horse*) desembestado; (*truck*) desgovernado; (*person*) fugitivo

rung [rʌŋ] PP *of* **ring** ▶ N (*of ladder*) degrau *m*

runner ['rʌnə^r] N (*in race*) corredor(a) *m/f*; (: *horse*) corredor *m*; (*on sledge*) patim *m*, lâmina; (*for drawer*) corrediça; **runner bean** (BRIT) N (*Bot*) vagem *f* (BR), feijão *m* verde (PT); **runner-up** N segundo(-a) colocado(-a)

running ['rʌnɪŋ] N (*sport, race*) corrida; (*of business*) direção *f* ▶ ADJ (*water*) corrente; (*commentary*) contínuo, seguido; **6 days ~** 6 dias seguidos *or* consecutivos; **to be in/out of the ~ for sth** disputar algo/estar fora da disputa por algo

runny ['rʌnɪ] ADJ aguado; (*egg*) mole; **to have a ~ nose** estar com coriza, estar com o nariz escorrendo

run-up N: **~ to sth** (*election etc*) período que antecede algo; **during** *or* **in the ~ to** nas vésperas de

runway ['rʌnweɪ] N (*Aviat*) pista (de decolagem *or* de pouso)

rupture ['rʌptʃə^r] N (*Med*) hérnia

rural ['ruərl] ADJ rural

rush [rʌʃ] N (*hurry*) pressa; (*Comm*) grande procura *or* demanda; (*Bot*) junco; (*current*) torrente *f*; (*of emotion*) ímpeto ▶ VT apressar ▶ VI apressar-se, precipitar-se; **rush hour** N rush *m* (BR), hora de ponta (PT)

Russia ['rʌʃə] N Rússia; **Russian** ADJ russo ▶ N russo(-a); (*Ling*) russo

rust [rʌst] N ferrugem *f* ▶ VI enferrujar

rusty ['rʌstɪ] ADJ enferrujado

ruthless ['ru:θlɪs] ADJ implacável, sem piedade

rye [raɪ] N centeio

S

Sabbath ['sæbəθ] N (*Christian*) domingo; (*Jewish*) sábado
sabotage ['sæbətɑːʒ] N sabotagem *f* ▸ VT sabotar
saccharin, saccharine ['sækərɪn] N sacarina
sachet ['sæʃeɪ] N sachê *m*
sack [sæk] N (*bag*) saco, saca ▸ VT (*dismiss*) despedir; (*plunder*) saquear; **to get the ~** ser demitido
sacred ['seɪkrɪd] ADJ sagrado
sacrifice ['sækrɪfaɪs] N sacrifício ▸ VT sacrificar
sad [sæd] ADJ triste; (*deplorable*) deplorável, triste
saddle ['sædl] N sela; (*of cycle*) selim *m* ▸ VT selar; **to ~ sb with sth** (*inf: task, bill*) pôr algo nas costas de alguém; (*: responsibility*) sobrecarregar alguém com algo
sadistic [sə'dɪstɪk] ADJ sádico
sadly ['sædlɪ] ADV tristemente; (*regrettably*) infelizmente; (*mistaken, neglected*) gravemente; **~ lacking (in)** muito carente (de)
sadness ['sædnɪs] N tristeza
safe [seɪf] ADJ seguro; (*out of danger*) fora de perigo; (*unharmed*) ileso, incólume ▸ N cofre *m*, caixa-forte *f*; **~ from** protegido de; **~ and sound** são e salvo; **(just) to be on the ~ side** por via das dúvidas; **safely** ADV com segurança, a salvo; (*without mishap*) sem perigo
safety ['seɪftɪ] N segurança; **safety belt** N cinto de segurança; **safety pin** N alfinete *m* de segurança
sag [sæg] VI (*breasts*) cair; (*roof*) afundar; (*hem*) desmanchar
sage [seɪdʒ] N salva; (*man*) sábio
Sagittarius [sædʒɪ'tɛərɪəs] N Sagitário
Sahara [sə'hɑːrə] N: **the ~ (Desert)** o Saara
said [sɛd] PT, PP *of* **say**
sail [seɪl] N (*on boat*) vela; (*trip*): **to go for a ~** dar um passeio de barco a vela ▸ VT (*boat*) governar ▸ VI (*travel: ship*) navegar, velejar; (*: passenger*) ir de barco; (*Sport*) velejar; (*set off*) zarpar; **they ~ed into Rio de Janeiro** entraram no porto do Rio de Janeiro; **sail through** VT FUS (*fig*) fazer com facilidade; **sailboat** (US) N barco a vela; **sailing** N (*Sport*) navegação *f* a vela, vela; **to go sailing** ir velejar
sailor ['seɪləʳ] N marinheiro, marujo
saint [seɪnt] N santo(-a)
sake [seɪk] N: **for the ~ of** por (causa de), em consideração a; **for sb's/sth's ~** pelo bem de alguém/algo
salad ['sæləd] N salada; **salad cream** (BRIT) N maionese *f*; **salad dressing** N tempero *or* molho da salada

salami [sə'lɑːmɪ] N salame *m*
salary ['sælərɪ] N salário
sale [seɪl] N venda; (*at reduced prices*) liquidação *f*, saldo; (*auction*) leilão *m*; **sales** NPL (*total amount sold*) vendas *fpl*; **"for ~"** "vende-se"; **on ~** à venda; **on ~ or return** em consignação; **sales assistant**, (US) **sales clerk** N vendedor(a) *m/f*
salmon ['sæmən] N INV salmão *m*
salon ['sælɔn] N (*hairdressing salon*) salão *m* (de cabeleireiro); (*beauty salon*) salão (de beleza)
saloon [sə'luːn] N (US) bar *m*, botequim *m*; (BRIT *Aut*) sedã *m*; (*ship's lounge*) salão *m*
salt [sɔːlt] N sal *m* ▶ VT salgar; **saltwater** ADJ de água salgada; **salty** ADJ salgado
salute [sə'luːt] N (*greeting*) saudação *f*; (*of guns*) salva; (*Mil*) continência ▶ VT saudar; (*Mil*) fazer continência a
salvage ['sælvɪdʒ] N (*saving*) salvamento, recuperação *f*; (*things saved*) salvados *mpl* ▶ VT salvar
same [seɪm] ADJ mesmo ▶ PRON: **the ~** o mesmo/a mesma; **the ~ book as** o mesmo livro que; **all** *or* **just the ~** apesar de tudo, mesmo assim; **the ~ to you!** igualmente!
sample ['sɑːmpl] N amostra ▶ VT (*food, wine*) provar, experimentar
sanction ['sæŋkʃən] N sanção *f* ▶ VT sancionar
sanctuary ['sæŋktjuərɪ] N (*holy place*) santuário; (*refuge*) refúgio, asilo; (*for animals*) reserva
sand [sænd] N areia; (*beach*: *also*: **~s**) praia ▶ VT (*also*: **~ down**) lixar
sandal ['sændl] N sandália
sand: sandbox ['sændbɔks] (US) N (*for children*) caixa de areia; **sand castle** N castelo de areia; **sandpaper** ['sændpeɪpə^r] N lixa; **sandpit** ['sændpɪt] (BRIT) N (*for children*) caixa de areia; **sandstone** ['sændstəun] N arenito, grés *m*
sandwich ['sændwɪtʃ] N sanduíche *m* (BR), sandes *f inv* (PT) ▶ VT: **~ed between** encaixado entre
sandy ['sændɪ] ADJ arenoso; (*colour*) vermelho amarelado
sane [seɪn] ADJ são/sã do juízo; (*sensible*) ajuizado, sensato
sang [sæŋ] PT *of* **sing**
sanity ['sænɪtɪ] N sanidade *f*, equilíbrio mental; (*common sense*) juízo, sensatez *f*
sank [sæŋk] PT *of* **sink**
Santa Claus [sæntə'klɔːz] N Papai Noel *m*
sap [sæp] N (*of plants*) seiva ▶ VT (*strength*) esgotar, minar
sapphire ['sæfaɪə^r] N safira
sarcasm ['sɑːkæzm] N sarcasmo
sardine [sɑː'diːn] N sardinha
Sardinia [sɑː'dɪnɪə] N Sardenha
sat [sæt] PT, PP *of* **sit**
satchel ['sætʃl] N sacola
satellite ['sætəlaɪt] N satélite *m*; **satellite dish** N antena parabólica; **satellite television** N televisão *f* via satélite
satin ['sætɪn] N cetim *m* ▶ ADJ acetinado
satire ['sætaɪə^r] N sátira
satisfaction [sætɪs'fækʃən] N satisfação *f*; (*refund, apology etc*) compensação *f*; **satisfactory** ADJ satisfatório
satisfy ['sætɪsfaɪ] VT satisfazer; (*convince*) convencer, persuadir
Saturday ['sætədɪ] N sábado
sauce [sɔːs] N molho; (*sweet*) calda; **saucepan** N panela (BR), caçarola (PT)
saucer ['sɔːsə^r] N pires *m inv*

Saudi ['saudɪ] ADJ, N (*also*: **~ Arabia**) Arábia Saudita; (*also*: **~ Arabian**) saudita *m/f*
sauna ['sɔːnə] N sauna
sausage ['sɔsɪdʒ] N salsicha, linguiça; (*cold meat*) frios *mpl*; **sausage roll** N folheado de salsicha
savage ['sævɪdʒ] ADJ (*cruel, fierce*) cruel, feroz; (*primitive*) selvagem ▸ N selvagem *m/f*
save [seɪv] VT (*rescue, Comput*) salvar; (*money*) poupar, economizar; (*time*) ganhar; (*Sport*) impedir; (*avoid: trouble*) evitar; (*keep: seat*) guardar ▸ VI (*also*: **~ up**) poupar ▸ N (*Sport*) salvamento ▸ PREP salvo, exceto
saw [sɔː] (*pt* **sawed**, *pp* **sawed** *or* **sawn**) PT *of* **see** ▸ N (*tool*) serra ▸ VT serrar; **sawdust** N serragem *f*, pó *m* de serra
saxophone ['sæksəfəun] N saxofone *m*
say [seɪ] (*pt, pp* **said**) N: **to have one's ~** exprimir sua opinião, vender seu peixe (*inf*) ▸ VT dizer, falar; **to have a** *or* **some ~ in sth** opinar sobre algo, ter que ver com algo; **could you ~ that again?** poderia repetir?; **that is to ~** ou seja; **saying** N ditado, provérbio
scab [skæb] N casca, crosta (de ferida); (*pej*) fura-greve *m/f inv*
scald [skɔːld] N escaldadura ▸ VT escaldar, queimar
scale [skeɪl] N escala; (*of fish*) escama; (*of salaries, fees etc*) tabela ▸ VT (*mountain*) escalar; **scales** NPL (*for weighing*) balança; **~ of charges** tarifa, lista de preços; **scale down** VT reduzir
scallop ['skɔləp] N (*Zool*) vieira, venera; (*Sewing*) barra, arremate *m*
scalp [skælp] N couro cabeludo ▸ VT escalpar
scam [skæm] (*inf*) N maracutaia, falcatrua
scampi ['skæmpɪ] NPL camarões *mpl* fritos
scan [skæn] VT (*examine*) esquadrinhar, perscrutar; (*glance at quickly*) passar uma vista de olhos por; (*TV, Radar*) explorar ▸ N (*Med*) exame *m*
scandal ['skændl] N escândalo; (*gossip*) fofocas *fpl*; (*fig: disgrace*) vergonha
Scandinavian [skændɪ'neɪvɪən] ADJ, N escandinavo(-a)
scanner ['skænəʳ] N (*Med, Comput*) scanner *m*
scapegoat ['skeɪpgəut] N bode *m* expiatório
scar [skɑː] N cicatriz *f* ▸ VT marcar (com uma cicatriz)
scarce [skɛəs] ADJ escasso, raro; **to make o.s. ~** (*inf*) dar o fora, cair fora; **scarcely** ADV mal, quase não; (*barely*) apenas
scare [skɛəʳ] N susto; (*panic*) pânico ▸ VT assustar; **to ~ sb stiff** deixar alguém morrendo de medo; **bomb ~** alarme de bomba; **scare away** VT espantar; **scare off** VT = **scare away**; **scarecrow** N espantalho; **scared** ADJ: **to be scared** estar assustado *or* com medo
scarf [skɑːf] (*pl* **scarfs** *or* **scarves**) N cachecol *m*; (*square*) lenço (de cabeça)
scarlet ['skɑːlɪt] ADJ escarlate
scary ['skɛərɪ] (*inf*) ADJ assustador(a)
scatter ['skætəʳ] VT espalhar; (*put to flight*) dispersar ▸ VI espalhar-se

scene [si:n] N (*Theatre, fig*) cena; (*of crime, accident*) cenário; (*sight*) vista, panorama *m*; (*fuss*) escândalo; **scenery** ['si:nərɪ] N (*Theatre*) cenário; (*landscape*) paisagem *f*; **scenic** ADJ pitoresco

scent [sɛnt] N perfume *m*; (*smell*) aroma; (*track, fig*) pista, rastro

schedule [(BRIT) 'ʃɛdju:l, (US) 'skɛdju:l] N (*of trains*) horário; (*of events*) programa *m*; (*list*) lista ▸ VT (*timetable*) planejar; (*visit*) marcar (a hora de); **on ~** na hora, sem atraso; **to be ahead of/behind ~** estar adiantado/atrasado

scheme [ski:m] N (*plan, plot*) maquinação *f*; (*pension scheme etc*) projeto; (*arrangement*) arranjo ▸ VI conspirar

scholar ['skɔlə[r]] N aluno(-a), estudante *m/f*; (*learned person*) sábio(-a), erudito(-a); **scholarship** N erudição *f*; (*grant*) bolsa de estudos

school [sku:l] N escola; (*secondary school*) colégio; (*US: university*) universidade *f* ▸ CPD escolar; **schoolboy** N aluno; **schoolchildren** NPL alunos *mpl*; **schoolgirl** N aluna; **schoolteacher** N professor(a) *m/f*

science ['saɪəns] N ciência; **science fiction** N ficção *f* científica; **scientific** [saɪən'tɪfɪk] ADJ científico; **scientist** N cientista *m/f*

scissors ['sɪzəz] NPL tesoura; **a pair of ~** uma tesoura

scold [skəuld] VT ralhar

scone [skɔn] N *bolinho de trigo*

scoop [sku:p] N colherona; (*for flour etc*) pá *f*; (*Press*) furo (jornalístico); **scoop out** VT escavar; **scoop up** VT recolher

scooter ['sku:tə[r]] N (*also*: **motor ~**) lambreta; (*toy*) patinete *m*

scope [skəup] N liberdade *f* de ação; (*of plan, undertaking*) âmbito; (*of person*) competência; (*opportunity*) oportunidade *f*

score [skɔ:[r]] N (*points etc*) escore *m*, contagem *f*; (*Mus*) partitura; (*twenty*) vintena ▸ VT (*goal, point*) fazer; (*mark*) marcar, entalhar; (*success*) alcançar ▸ VI (*in game*) marcar; (*Football*) marcar *or* fazer um gol; (*keep score*) marcar o escore; **on that ~** a esse respeito, por esse motivo; **~s of** (*fig*) um monte de; **to ~ 6 out of 10** tirar nota 6 num total de 10; **score out** VT riscar; **scoreboard** N marcador *m*, placar *m*

scorn [skɔ:n] N desprezo ▸ VT desprezar, rejeitar

Scorpio ['skɔ:pɪəu] N Escorpião *m*

Scot [skɔt] N escocês(-esa) *m/f*

Scotch [skɔtʃ] N uísque *m* (BR) *or* whisky *m* (PT) escocês

Scotland ['skɔtlənd] N Escócia; **Scots** ADJ escocês(-esa); **Scotsman** *irreg* N escocês *m*; **Scotswoman** *irreg* N escocesa; **Scottish** ADJ escocês(-esa)

scout [skaut] N (*Mil*) explorador *m*, batedor *m*; (*also*: **boy ~**) escoteiro; **girl ~** (US) escoteira; **scout around** VI explorar

scowl [skaul] VI franzir a testa; **to ~ at sb** olhar de cara feia para alguém

scramble ['skræmbl] N (*climb*) escalada (difícil); (*struggle*) luta ▸ VI: **to ~ out/through** conseguir sair com dificuldade; **to ~ for** lutar por; **scrambled eggs** NPL ovos *mpl* mexidos

scrap [skræp] N (*of paper*) pedacinho; (*of material*) fragmento; (*fig: of truth*) mínimo; (*fight*) rixa, luta; (*also*: **~ iron**) ferro velho, sucata ▸ VT sucatar, jogar no ferro velho; (*fig*) descartar, abolir ▶ VI brigar; **scraps** N PL (*leftovers*) sobras *fpl*, restos *mpl*; **scrapbook** N álbum *m* de recortes

scrape [skreɪp] N (*fig*): **to get into a ~** meter-se numa enrascada ▶ VT raspar; (*also*: **~ against**: *hand, car*) arranhar, roçar ▶ VI: **to ~ through** (*in exam*) passar raspando; **scrape together** VT (*money*) juntar com dificuldade

scrap paper N papel *m* de rascunho

scratch [skrætʃ] N arranhão *m*; (*from claw*) arranhadura ▶ CPD: **~ team** time *m* improvisado, escrete *m* ▶ VT (*rub*) coçar; (*with claw, nail*) arranhar, unhar; (*damage*) arranhar ▶ VI coçar(-se); **to start from ~** partir do zero; **to be up to ~** estar à altura (das circunstâncias)

scream [skri:m] N grito ▶ VI gritar

screen [skri:n] N (*Cinema, TV, Comput*) tela (BR), ecrã *m* (PT); (*movable*) biombo; (*fig*) cortina ▶ VT (*conceal*) esconder, tapar; (*from the wind etc*) proteger; (*film*) projetar; (*candidates etc, Med*) examinar; **screenplay** N roteiro; **screensaver** ['skri:nseɪvəʳ] N protetor *m* de tela; **screenshot** N (*Comput*) captura de tela

screw [skru:] N parafuso ▶ VT aparafusar; (*also*: **~ in**) apertar, atarraxar; **screw up** VT (*paper etc*) amassar; **to ~ up one's eyes** franzir os olhos; **screwdriver** N chave *f* de fenda *or* de parafuso

scribble ['skrɪbl] N garrancho ▶ VT escrevinhar ▶ VI rabiscar

script [skrɪpt] N (*Cinema etc*) roteiro, script *m*; (*writing*) escrita, caligrafia

scroll [skrəul] N rolo de pergaminho

scrub [skrʌb] N mato, cerrado ▶ VT esfregar; (*inf*) cancelar, eliminar

scruffy ['skrʌfɪ] ADJ desmazelado

scrutiny ['skru:tɪnɪ] N escrutínio, exame *m* cuidadoso

sculptor ['skʌlptəʳ] N escultor(a) *m/f*

sculpture ['skʌlptʃəʳ] N escultura

scum [skʌm] N (*on liquid*) espuma; (*pej*: *people*) ralé *f*, gentinha

scurry ['skʌrɪ] VI sair correndo; **scurry off** VI sair correndo, dar no pé

sea [si:] N mar *m* ▶ CPD do mar, marino; **on the ~** (*boat*) no mar; (*town*) junto ao mar; **to go by ~** viajar por mar; **out to** *or* **at ~** em alto mar; **to be all at ~** (*fig*) estar confuso *or* desorientado; **seafood** N mariscos *mpl*; **seagull** N gaivota

seal [si:l] N (*animal*) foca; (*stamp*) selo ▶ VT fechar; **seal off** VT fechar

sea level N nível *m* do mar

seam [si:m] N costura; (*where edges meet*) junta; (*of coal*) veio, filão *m*

search [sə:tʃ] N busca, procura; (*Comput*) busca; (*inspection*) exame *m*, investigação *f* ▶ VT (*look in*) procurar em; (*examine*) examinar; (*person, place*) revistar ▶ VI: **to ~ for** procurar; **in ~ of** à procura de; **search through** VT FUS dar busca em; **search engine** N (*on Internet*) site *m* de busca; **search party** N equipe *f* de salvamento

sea: seashore N praia, beira-mar *f*, litoral *m*; **seasick** ADJ: **to be** *or* **get seasick** enjoar; **seaside** N praia; **seaside resort** N balneário

season ['si:zn] N (*of year*) estação *f*; (*sporting etc*) temporada; (*of films*

S

etc) série *f* ▶ VT (*food*) temperar; **to be in/out of ~** (*fruit*) estar na época/fora de época; **season ticket** N bilhete *m* de temporada

seat [si:t] N (*in bus, train: place*) assento; (*chair*) cadeira; (*Pol*) lugar *m*, cadeira; (*buttocks*) traseiro, nádegas *fpl*; (*of trousers*) fundilhos *mpl* ▶ VT sentar; (*have room for*) ter capacidade para; **to be ~ed** estar sentado; **seat belt** N cinto de segurança

sea water N água do mar

seaweed ['si:wi:d] N alga marinha

sec. ABBR (= *second*) seg.

secluded [sɪ'klu:dɪd] ADJ (*place*) afastado; (*life*) solitário

second¹ [sɪ'kɔnd] (BRIT) VT (*employee*) transferir temporariamente

second² ['sɛkənd] ADJ segundo ▶ ADV (*in race etc*) em segundo lugar ▶ N segundo; (*Aut: also:* **~ gear**) segunda; (*Comm*) artigo defeituoso; (BRIT *Sch: degree*) *uma qualificação boa mas sem distinção* ▶ VT (*motion*) apoiar, secundar; **secondary** ADJ secundário; **secondary school** N escola secundária, colégio

> Na Grã-Bretanha, uma **secondary school** é um estabelecimento de ensino para alunos de 11 a 18 anos, alguns dos quais interrompem os estudos aos 16 anos.

second: second-class ADV em segunda classe; **secondhand** ADJ de (BR) *or* em (PT) segunda mão, usado; **second hand** N (*on clock*) ponteiro de segundos; **secondly** ADV em segundo lugar; **second-rate** ADJ de segunda categoria; **second thoughts** NPL, (US) **second thought**: **to have second thoughts (about doing sth)** pensar duas vezes (antes de fazer algo); **on second thoughts** pensando bem

secrecy ['si:krəsɪ] N sigilo

secret ['si:krɪt] ADJ secreto ▶ N segredo

secretary ['sɛkrətərɪ] N secretário(-a); (BRIT *Pol*): **S~ of State** Ministro(-a) de Estado

secretive ['si:krətɪv] ADJ sigiloso, reservado

section ['sɛkʃən] N seção *f*; (*part*) parte *f*, porção *f*; (*of document*) parágrafo, artigo; (*of opinion*) setor *m*; **cross-~** corte *m* transversal

sector ['sɛktə^r] N setor *m*

secular ['sɛkjulə^r] ADJ (*priest*) secular; (*music, society*) leigo

secure [sɪ'kjuə^r] ADJ (*safe*) seguro; (*firmly fixed*) firme, rígido ▶ VT (*fix*) prender; (*get*) conseguir, obter; **security** N segurança; (*for loan*) fiança, garantia; **security guard** N segurança *m/f*

sedate [sɪ'deɪt] ADJ calmo ▶ VT sedar, tratar com calmantes; **sedative** N calmante *m*, sedativo

seduce [sɪ'dju:s] VT seduzir; **seductive** ADJ sedutor(a)

see [si:] (*pt* **saw**, *pp* **seen**) VT ver; (*understand*) entender; (*accompany*): **to ~ sb to the door** acompanhar *or* levar alguém até a porta ▶ VI ver; (*find out*) achar ▶ N sé *f*, sede *f*; **to ~ that** (*ensure*) assegurar que; **~ you soon/later/tomorrow!** até logo/mais tarde/amanhã!; **see about** VT FUS tratar de; **see off** VT despedir-se de; **see through** VT FUS enxergar através de ▶ VT levar a cabo; **see to** VT FUS providenciar

seed [si:d] N semente *f*; (*sperm*) esperma *m*; (*fig: gen pl*) germe *m*;

(*Tennis*) pré-selecionado(-a); **to go to ~** produzir sementes; (*fig*) deteriorar-se
seeing ['si:ɪŋ] CONJ: **~ (that)** visto (que), considerando (que)
seek [si:k] (*pt, pp* **sought**) VT procurar; (*post*) solicitar
seem [si:m] VI parecer; **there ~s to be ...** parece que há ...
seen [si:n] PP *of* **see**
seesaw ['si:sɔ:] N gangorra, balanço
segment ['sɛgmənt] N segmento; (*of orange*) gomo
seize [si:z] VT agarrar, pegar; (*power, hostage*) apoderar-se de, confiscar; (*territory*) tomar posse de; (*opportunity*) aproveitar; **seize on** VT FUS valer-se de; **seize up** VI (*Tech*) gripar; **seize upon** VT FUS = **seize on**; **seizure** N (*Med*) ataque *m*, acesso; (*Jur, of power*) confisco, embargo
seldom ['sɛldəm] ADV raramente
select [sɪ'lɛkt] ADJ seleto, fino ▸ VT escolher, selecionar; (*Sport*) selecionar, escalar; **selection** N seleção *f*, escolha; (*Comm*) sortimento
self [sɛlf] (*pl* **selves**) PRON *see* **herself, himself, itself, myself, oneself, ourselves, themselves, yourself** ▸ N: **the ~** o eu; **self-assured** ADJ seguro de si; **self-catering** (BRIT) ADJ (*flat*) com cozinha; (*holiday*) em casa alugada; **self-centred**, (US) **self-centered** ADJ egocêntrico; **self-confidence** N autoconfiança, confiança em si; **self-conscious** ADJ inibido, constrangido; **self-control** N autocontrole *m*, autodomínio; **self-defence**, (US) **self-defense** N legítima defesa, autodefesa; **in self-defence** em legítima defesa; **self-employed** ADJ autônomo; **self-harm** N autoimolação *f*; **self-interest** N egoísmo; **selfish** ADJ egoísta; **self-pity** N pena de si mesmo; **self-respect** N amor *m* próprio; **self-service** ADJ de autosserviço
sell [sɛl] (*pt, pp* **sold**) VT vender; (*fig*): **to ~ sb an idea** convencer alguém de uma ideia ▸ VI vender-se; **to ~ at** *or* **for £10** vender a *or* por £10; **sell off** VT liquidar; **sell out** VI vender todo o estoque ▸ VT: **the tickets are all sold out** todos os ingressos já foram vendidos; **sell-by date** N vencimento; **seller** N vendedor(a) *m/f*
selves [sɛlvz] PL *of* **self**
semi... [sɛmɪ] PREFIX semi..., meio...; **semicircle** N semicírculo; **semidetached**, **semidetached house** (BRIT) N (casa) geminada
seminar ['sɛmɪnɑ:ʳ] N seminário
senate ['sɛnɪt] N senado; **senator** N senador(a) *m/f*
send [sɛnd] (*pt, pp* **sent**) VT mandar, enviar; (*dispatch*) expedir, remeter; (*transmit*) transmitir; **send away** VT (*letter, goods*) expedir, mandar; (*unwelcome visitor*) mandar embora; **send away for** VT FUS encomendar, pedir pelo correio; **send back** VT devolver, mandar de volta; **send for** VT FUS mandar buscar; (*by post*) pedir pelo correio, encomendar; **send off** VT (*goods*) despachar, expedir; (BRIT *Sport: player*) expulsar; **send on** VT (BRIT: *letter*) remeter; (*luggage etc: in advance*) mandar com antecedência; **send out** VT (*invitation*) distribuir;

S

(*signal*) emitir; **send up** VT (*person, price*) fazer subir; (BRIT: *parody*) parodiar; **sender** N remetente *m/f*; **send-off** N: **a good send-off** uma boa despedida
senior ['si:nɪə^r] ADJ (*older*) mais velho *or* idoso; (*on staff*) mais antigo; (*of higher rank*) superior; **senior citizen** N idoso(-a)
sensation [sɛn'seɪʃən] N sensação *f*; **sensational** ADJ sensacional; (*headlines, result*) sensacionalista
sense [sɛns] N sentido; (*feeling*) sensação *f*; (*good sense*) bom senso ▶ VT sentir, perceber; **it makes ~** faz sentido; **senseless** ADJ insensato, estúpido; (*unconscious*) sem sentidos, inconsciente; **sensible** ADJ sensato, de bom senso; (*reasonable: price*) razoável; (: *advice, decision*) sensato
sensitive ['sɛnsɪtɪv] ADJ sensível; (*fig: touchy*) suscetível
sensual ['sɛnsjuəl] ADJ sensual
sensuous ['sɛnsjuəs] ADJ sensual
sent [sɛnt] PT, PP *of* **send**
sentence ['sɛntəns] N (*Ling*) frase *f*, oração *f*; (*Jur*) sentença ▶ VT: **to ~ sb to death/to 5 years** condenar alguém à morte/a 5 anos de prisão
sentiment ['sɛntɪmənt] N sentimento; (*opinion: also pl*) opinião *f*; **sentimental** [sɛntɪ'mɛntl] ADJ sentimental
separate [*adj* 'sɛprɪt, *vt, vi* 'sɛpəreɪt] ADJ separado; (*distinct*) diferente ▶ VT separar; (*part*) dividir ▶ VI separar-se; **separately** ADV separadamente
September [sɛp'tɛmbə^r] N setembro
septic ['sɛptɪk] ADJ sético; (*wound*) infeccionado
sequel ['si:kwl] N consequência, resultado; (*of film, story*) continuação *f*
sequence ['si:kwəns] N série *f*, sequência; (*Cinema*) série
sequin ['si:kwɪn] N lantejoula, paetê *m*
sergeant ['sɑ:dʒənt] N sargento
serial ['sɪərɪəl] N seriado; **serial killer** N assassino(-a) em série, serial killer *m/f*; **serial number** N número de série
series ['sɪəri:z] N INV série *f*
serious ['sɪərɪəs] ADJ sério; (*matter*) importante; (*illness*) grave; **seriously** ADV a sério, com seriedade; (*hurt*) gravemente
sermon ['sə:mən] N sermão *m*
servant ['sə:vənt] N empregado(-a); (*fig*) servidor(a) *m/f*
serve [sə:v] VT servir; (*customer*) atender; (*subj: train*) passar por; (*apprenticeship*) fazer; (*prison term*) cumprir ▶ VI (*at table*) servir-se; (*Tennis*) sacar; (*be useful*): **to ~ as/for/to do** servir como/para/para fazer ▶ N (*Tennis*) saque *m*; **it ~s him right** é bem feito para ele; **serve out** VT (*food*) servir; **serve up** VT = **serve out**; **server** ['sə:və^r] N (*Comput*) servidor *m*
service ['sə:vɪs] N serviço; (*Rel*) culto; (*Aut*) revisão *f*; (*Tennis*) saque *m*; (*also*: **dinner ~**) aparelho de jantar ▶ VT (*car, washing machine*) fazer a revisão de, revisar; **the Services** NPL (*army, navy etc*) as Forças Armadas; **to be of ~ to sb** ser útil a alguém; **service area** N (*on motorway*) *posto de gasolina com bar, restaurante etc*; **service charge** (BRIT) N serviço; **serviceman** *irreg* N militar *m*; **service station** N posto de gasolina (BR), estação *f* de serviço (PT)

serviette [sə:vɪ'ɛt] (BRIT) N guardanapo
session ['sɛʃən] N sessão *f*; **to be in ~** estar reunido em sessão
set [sɛt] (*pt, pp* **set**) N (*collection of things*) jogo; (*radio set, TV set*) aparelho; (*of utensils*) bateria de cozinha; (*of cutlery*) talher *m*; (*of books*) coleção *f*; (*group of people*) grupo; (*Tennis*) set *m*; (*Theatre, Cinema*) cenário; (*Hairdressing*) penteado; (*Math*) conjunto ▶ ADJ fixo; (*ready*) pronto ▶ VT pôr, colocar; (*table*) pôr; (*price*) fixar; (*rules etc*) estabelecer, decidir; (*record*) estabelecer; (*time*) marcar; (*adjust*) ajustar; (*task, exam*) passar ▶ VI (*sun*) pôr-se; (*jam, jelly, concrete*) endurecer, solidificar-se; **to be ~ on doing sth** estar decidido a fazer algo; **to ~ to music** musicar, pôr música em; **to ~ on fire** botar fogo em, incendiar; **to ~ free** libertar; **to ~ sth going** pôr algo em movimento; **set about** VT FUS começar com; **set aside** VT deixar de lado; **set back** VT (*cost*): **it ~ me back £50** custou £50; (*in time*): **to ~ sb back (by)** atrasar alguém (em); **set off** VI partir, ir indo ▶ VT (*bomb*) fazer explodir; (*alarm*) disparar; (*chain of events*) iniciar; (*show up well*) ressaltar; **set out** VI partir ▶ VT (*arrange*) colocar, dispor; (*state*) expor, explicar; **to ~ out to do sth** pretender fazer algo; **set up** VT fundar, estabelecer;
setback N revés *m*, contratempo;
set menu N refeição *f* a preço fixo
settee [sɛ'ti:] N sofá *m*
setting ['sɛtɪŋ] N (*background*) cenário; (*position*) posição *f*; (*of sun*) pôr(-do-sol) *m*; (*of jewel*) engaste *m*
settle ['sɛtl] VT (*argument, matter*) resolver, esclarecer; (*accounts*) ajustar, liquidar; (*Med: calm*) acalmar, tranquilizar ▶ VI (*dust etc*) assentar; (*calm down: children*) acalmar-se; (*also*: **~ down**) instalar-se, estabilizar-se; **to ~ for sth** concordar em aceitar algo; **to ~ on sth** optar por algo; **settle in** VI instalar-se; **settle up** VI: **to ~ up with sb** ajustar as contas com alguém; **settlement** N (*payment*) liquidação *f*; (*agreement*) acordo, convênio; (*village etc*) povoado, povoação *f*
setup ['sɛtʌp] N (*organization*) organização *f*; (*situation*) situação *f*
seven ['sɛvn] NUM sete;
seventeen ['sɛvn'ti:n] NUM dezessete; **seventeenth** [sevn'ti:nθ] NUM décimo sétimo;
seventh ['sɛvnθ] NUM sétimo;
seventieth ['sevntɪɪθ] NUM septuagésimo; **seventy** ['sɛvntɪ] NUM setenta
sever ['sɛvəʳ] VT cortar; (*relations*) romper
several ['sɛvərl] ADJ, PRON vários(-as); **~ of us** vários de nós
severe [sɪ'vɪəʳ] ADJ severo; (*serious*) grave; (*hard*) duro; (*pain*) intenso; (*dress*) austero
sew [səu] (*pt* **sewed**, *pp* **sewn**) VT coser, costurar; **sew up** VT coser, costurar
sewage ['su:ɪdʒ] N detritos *mpl*
sewer ['su:əʳ] N (cano do) esgoto, bueiro
sewing ['səuɪŋ] N costura;
sewing machine N máquina de costura
sewn [səun] PP *of* **sew**
sex [sɛks] N sexo; **sexist** ADJ sexista

sexual ['sɛksjuəl] ADJ sexual; **sexuality** [seksju'ælɪtɪ] N sexualidade *f*
sexy ['sɛksɪ] ADJ sexy
shabby ['ʃæbɪ] ADJ (*person*) esfarrapado, maltrapilho; (*clothes*) usado, surrado; (*behaviour*) indigno
shack [ʃæk] N choupana, barraca
shade [ʃeɪd] N sombra; (*for lamp*) quebra-luz *m*; (*of colour*) tom *m*, tonalidade *f*; (*small quantity*): **a ~ (more/too big)** um pouquinho (mais/grande) ▸ VT dar sombra a; (*eyes*) sombrear; **in the ~** à sombra
shadow ['ʃædəu] N sombra ▸ VT (*follow*) seguir de perto (sem ser visto)
shady ['ʃeɪdɪ] ADJ à sombra; (*fig: dishonest: person*) suspeito, duvidoso; (*: deal*) desonesto
shaft [ʃɑ:ft] N (*of arrow, spear*) haste *f*; (*Aut, Tech*) eixo, manivela; (*of mine, of lift*) poço; (*of light*) raio
shake [ʃeɪk] (*pt* **shook**, *pp* **shaken**) VT sacudir; (*building, confidence*) abalar; (*surprise*) surpreender ▸ VI tremer; **to ~ hands with sb** apertar a mão de alguém; **to ~ one's head** (*in refusal etc*) dizer não com a cabeça; (*in dismay*) sacudir a cabeça; **shake off** VT sacudir; (*fig*) livrar-se de; **shake up** VT sacudir; (*fig*) reorganizar; **shaky** ADJ (*hand, voice*) trêmulo; (*table*) instável; (*building*) abalado
shall [ʃæl] AUX VB: **I ~ go** irei; **~ I open the door?** posso abrir a porta?; **I'll get some, ~ I?** eu vou pegar algum, está bem?
shallow ['ʃæləu] ADJ raso; (*breathing*) fraco; (*fig*) superficial
sham [ʃæm] N fraude *f*, fingimento ▸ VT fingir, simular
shambles ['ʃæmblz] N confusão *f*
shame [ʃeɪm] N vergonha ▸ VT envergonhar; **it is a ~ (that/to do)** é (uma) pena (que/fazer); **what a ~!** que pena!; **shameful** ADJ vergonhoso; **shameless** ADJ sem vergonha, descarado
shampoo [ʃæm'pu:] N xampu *m* (BR), champô *m* (PT) ▸ VT lavar o cabelo (com xampu *or* champô)
shandy ['ʃændɪ] N *mistura de cerveja com refresco gaseificado*
shan't [ʃɑ:nt] = **shall not**
shape [ʃeɪp] N forma ▸ VT (*form*) moldar; (*sb's ideas*) formar; (*sb's life*) definir, determinar; **to take ~** tomar forma; **shape up** VI (*events*) desenrolar-se; (*person*) tomar jeito
share [ʃɛəʳ] N parte *f*; (*contribution*) cota; (*Comm*) ação *f* ▸ VT dividir; (*have in common*) compartilhar; **share out** VI distribuir; **shareholder** N acionista *m/f*
shark [ʃɑ:k] N tubarão *m*
sharp [ʃɑ:p] ADJ (*razor, knife*) afiado; (*point, features*) pontiagudo; (*outline*) definido, bem marcado; (*pain, voice*) agudo; (*taste*) acre; (*Mus*) desafinado; (*contrast*) marcado; (*quick-witted*) perspicaz; (*dishonest*) desonesto ▸ N (*Mus*) sustenido ▸ ADV: **at 2 o'clock ~** às 2 (horas) em ponto; **sharpen** VT afiar; (*pencil*) apontar, fazer a ponta de; (*fig*) aguçar; **sharpener** N (*also*: **pencil sharpener**) apontador *m* (BR), apara-lápis *m inv* (PT); **sharply** ADV (*abruptly*) bruscamente; (*clearly*) claramente; (*harshly*) severamente
shatter ['ʃætəʳ] VT despedaçar, estilhaçar; (*fig: ruin*) destruir, acabar com; (*: upset*) arrasar ▸ VI despedaçar-se, estilhaçar-se
shave [ʃeɪv] VT barbear, fazer a barba de ▸ VI fazer a barba,

barbear-se ▶ N: **to have a ~** fazer a barba; **shaver** N barbeador *m*; **electric shaver** barbeador elétrico; **shaving cream** N creme *m* de barbear; **shaving foam** N espuma de barbear
shawl [ʃɔːl] N xale *m*
she [ʃiː] PRON ela ▶ PREFIX: **~-elephant** *etc* elefante *etc* fêmea
sheath [ʃiːθ] N bainha; (*contraceptive*) camisa-de-vênus *f*, camisinha
shed [ʃɛd] (*pt, pp* **shed**) N alpendre *m*, galpão *m* ▶ VT (*skin*) mudar; (*load, leaves, fur*) perder; (*tears, blood*) derramar; (*workers*) despedir
she'd [ʃiːd] = **she had;** = **she would**
sheep [ʃiːp] N INV ovelha; **sheepdog** N cão *m* pastor; **sheepskin** N pele *f* de carneiro, pelego
sheer [ʃɪəʳ] ADJ (*utter*) puro, completo; (*steep*) íngreme, empinado; (*almost transparent*) fino, translúcido ▶ ADV a pique
sheet [ʃiːt] N (*on bed*) lençol *m*; (*of paper*) folha; (*of glass, metal*) lâmina, chapa; (*of ice*) camada
sheik, sheikh [ʃeɪk] N xeque *m*
shelf [ʃɛlf] (*pl* **shelves**) N prateleira
shell [ʃɛl] N (*on beach*) concha; (*of egg, nut etc*) casca; (*explosive*) obus *m*; (*of building*) armação *f*, esqueleto ▶ VT (*peas*) descascar; (*Mil*) bombardear
she'll [ʃiːl] = **she will;** = **she shall**
shellfish [ˈʃɛlfɪʃ] N INV crustáceo; (*as food*) frutos *mpl* do mar, mariscos *mpl*
shelter [ˈʃɛltəʳ] N (*building*) abrigo; (*protection*) refúgio ▶ VT (*protect*) proteger; (*give lodging to*) abrigar ▶ VI abrigar-se, refugiar-se
shepherd [ˈʃɛpəd] N pastor *m* ▶ VT guiar, conduzir; **shepherd's pie** (BRIT) N empadão *m* de carne e batata
sheriff [ˈʃɛrɪf] (US) N xerife *m*
sherry [ˈʃɛrɪ] N (vinho de) Xerez *m*
she's [ʃiːz] = **she is;** = **she has**
Shetland [ˈʃɛtlənd] N (*also*: **the ~s, the ~ Isles**) as ilhas Shetland
shield [ʃiːld] N escudo; (*Sport*) escudo, brasão *m*; (*protection*) proteção *f* ▶ VT: **to ~ (from)** proteger (contra)
shift [ʃɪft] N mudança; (*of work*) turno; (*of workers*) turma ▶ VT transferir; (*remove*) tirar ▶ VI mudar
shin [ʃɪn] N canela (da perna)
shine [ʃaɪn] (*pt, pp* **shone**) N brilho, lustre *m* ▶ VI brilhar ▶ VT (*shoes*: *pt, pp* **shined**) lustrar; **to ~ a torch on sth** apontar uma lanterna para algo
shingles [ˈʃɪŋglz] N (*Med*) herpes-zoster *m*
shiny [ˈʃaɪnɪ] ADJ brilhante, lustroso
ship [ʃɪp] N barco ▶ VT (*goods*) embarcar; (*send*) transportar *or* mandar (por via marítima); **shipment** N carregamento; **shipping** N (*ships*) navios *mpl*; (*cargo*) transporte *m* de mercadorias (por via marítima); (*traffic*) navegação *f*; **shipwreck** N (*event*) malogro; (*ship*) naufrágio ▶ VT: **to be shipwrecked** naufragar; **shipyard** N estaleiro
shirt [ʃəːt] N (*man's*) camisa; (*woman's*) blusa; **in ~ sleeves** em manga de camisa
shit [ʃɪt] (!) EXCL merda (!)
shiver [ˈʃɪvəʳ] N tremor *m*, arrepio ▶ VI tremer, estremecer, tiritar

shock [ʃɔk] N (*impact*) choque *m*; (*Elec*) descarga; (*emotional*) comoção *f*, abalo; (*start*) susto, sobressalto; (*Med*) trauma *m* ▶ VT dar um susto em, chocar; (*offend*) escandalizar; **shocking** ADJ chocante, lamentável; (*outrageous*) revoltante, chocante

shoe [ʃu:] (*pt, pp* **shod**) N sapato; (*for horse*) ferradura ▶ VT (*horse*) ferrar; **shoelace** N cadarço, cordão *m* (de sapato); **shoe polish** N graxa de sapato; **shoeshop** N sapataria

shone [ʃɔn] PT, PP *of* **shine**

shook [ʃuk] PT *of* **shake**

shoot [ʃu:t] (*pt, pp* **shot**) N (*on branch, seedling*) broto ▶ VT disparar; (*kill*) matar à bala, balear; (*wound*) ferir à bala, balear; (*execute*) fuzilar; (*film*) filmar, rodar ▶ VI: **to ~ (at)** atirar (em); (*Football*) chutar; **shoot down** VT (*plane*) derrubar, abater; **shoot in** VI entrar correndo; **shoot out** VI sair correndo; **shoot up** VI (*fig*) subir vertiginosamente

shop [ʃɔp] N loja; (*workshop*) oficina ▶ VI (*also*: **go ~ping**) ir fazer compras; **shop assistant** (BRIT) N vendedor(a) *m/f*; **shopkeeper** N lojista *m/f*; **shoplifting** N furto (em lojas); **shopping** N (*goods*) compras *fpl*; **shopping bag** N bolsa (de compras); **shopping cart** (US) N carrinho de compras; **shopping centre**, (US) **shopping center** N shopping (center) *m*; **shopping mall** N shopping *m*; **shopping trolley** (BRIT) N carrinho de compras; **shop window** N vitrine *f* (BR), montra (PT)

shore [ʃɔ:ʳ] N (*of sea*) costa, praia; (*of lake*) margem *f* ▶ VT: **to ~ (up)** reforçar, escorar; **on ~** em terra

short [ʃɔ:t] ADJ curto; (*in time*) breve, de curta duração; (*person*) baixo; (*curt*) seco, brusco; (*insufficient*) insuficiente, em falta; **to be ~ of sth** estar em falta de algo; **in ~** em resumo; **~ of doing ...** a não ser fazer ...; **everything ~ of ...** tudo a não ser ...; **it is ~ for** é a abreviatura de; **to cut ~** (*speech, visit*) encurtar; **to fall ~ of** não ser à altura de; **to run ~ of sth** ficar sem algo; **to stop ~** parar de repente; **to stop ~ of** chegar quase a; **shortage** N escassez *f*, falta; **shortbread** N biscoito amanteigado; **shortcoming** N defeito, imperfeição *f*, falha; **shortcrust pastry**, (BRIT) **short pastry** N massa amanteigada; **shortcut** N atalho; **shorten** VT encurtar; (*visit*) abreviar; **shorthand** (BRIT) N estenografia; **shortly** ADV em breve, dentro em pouco; **shorts** NPL: **(a pair of) shorts** um calção (BR), um short (BR), uns calções (PT); **short-sighted** (BRIT) ADJ míope; (*fig*) imprevidente; **short story** N conto; **short-tempered** ADJ irritadiço; **short-term** ADJ a curto prazo

shot [ʃɔt] PT, PP *of* **shoot** ▶ N (*of gun*) tiro; (*pellets*) chumbo; (*try, Football*) tentativa; (*injection*) injeção *f*; (*Phot*) fotografia; **to be a good/bad ~** (*person*) ter boa/má pontaria; **like a ~** como um relâmpago, de repente; **shotgun** N espingarda

should [ʃud] AUX VB: **I ~ go now** devo ir embora agora; **he ~ be there now** ele já deve ter chegado; **I ~ go if I were you** se eu fosse você eu iria; **I ~ like to** eu gostaria de

shoulder [ˈʃəuldəʳ] N ombro ▶ VT (*fig*) arcar com; **shoulder blade** N omoplata *m*

shouldn't ['ʃudnt] = **should not**
shout [ʃaut] N grito ▶ VT gritar ▶ VI (*also*: ~ **out**) gritar, berrar; **shout down** VT fazer calar com gritos
shove [ʃʌv] VT empurrar; (*inf*: *put*): **to ~ sth in** botar algo em; **shove off** VI (*inf*) dar o fora
shovel ['ʃʌvl] N pá *f*; (*mechanical*) escavadeira ▶ VT cavar com pá
show [ʃəu] (*pt* **showed**, *pp* **shown**) N (*of emotion*) demonstração *f*; (*semblance*) aparência; (*exhibition*) exibição *f*; (*Theatre*) espetáculo, representação *f*; (*Cinema*) sessão *f* ▶ VT mostrar; (*courage etc*) demonstrar, dar prova de; (*exhibit*) exibir, expor; (*depict*) ilustrar; (*film*) exibir ▶ VI mostrar-se; (*appear*) aparecer; **to be on ~** estar em exposição; **show in** VT mandar entrar; **show off** VI (*pej*) mostrar-se, exibir-se ▶ VT (*display*) exibir, mostrar; **show out** VT levar até a porta; **show up** VI (*stand out*) destacar-se; (*inf*: *turn up*) aparecer, pintar ▶ VT descobrir; **show business** N o mundo do espetáculo
shower ['ʃauə^r] N (*rain*) pancada de chuva; (*of stones etc*) chuva, enxurrada; (*also*: ~ **bath**) chuveiro ▶ VI tomar banho (de chuveiro) ▶ VT: **to ~ sb with** (*gifts etc*) cumular alguém de; **to have** *or* **take a ~** tomar banho (de chuveiro)
showing ['ʃəuɪŋ] N (*of film*) projeção *f*, exibição *f*
show jumping [-'dʒʌmpɪŋ] N hipismo
shown [ʃəun] PP *of* **show**
show-off (*inf*) N (*person*) exibicionista *m/f*, faroleiro(-a)
showpiece ['ʃəupi:s] N (*of exhibition etc*) obra mais importante
showroom ['ʃəurum] N sala de exposição
shrank [ʃræŋk] PT *of* **shrink**
shred [ʃrɛd] N (*gen pl*) tira, pedaço ▶ VT rasgar em tiras, retalhar; (*Culin*) desfiar, picar
shrewd [ʃru:d] ADJ perspicaz
shriek [ʃri:k] N grito ▶ VI gritar, berrar
shrimp [ʃrɪmp] N camarão *m*
shrine [ʃraɪn] N santuário
shrink [ʃrɪŋk] (*pt* **shrank**, *pp* **shrunk**) VI encolher; (*be reduced*) reduzir-se; (*also*: ~ **away**) encolher-se ▶ VT (*cloth*) fazer encolher ▶ N (*inf*, *pej*) psicanalista *m/f*; **to ~ from doing sth** não se atrever a fazer algo
shrivel ['ʃrɪvl] VT (*also*: ~ **up**: *dry*) secar; (: *crease*) enrugar ▶ VI secar-se; enrugar-se, murchar
Shrove Tuesday [ʃrəuv-] N terça-feira gorda
shrub [ʃrʌb] N arbusto
shrug [ʃrʌg] N encolhimento dos ombros ▶ VT, VI: **to ~ (one's shoulders)** encolher os ombros, dar de ombros (BR); **shrug off** VT negar a importância de
shrunk [ʃrʌŋk] PP *of* **shrink**
shudder ['ʃʌdə^r] N estremecimento, tremor *m* ▶ VI estremecer, tremer de medo
shuffle ['ʃʌfl] VT (*cards*) embaralhar ▶ VI: **to ~ (one's feet)** arrastar os pés
shun [ʃʌn] VT evitar, afastar-se de
shut [ʃʌt] (*pt*, *pp* **shut**) VT fechar ▶ VI fechar(-se); **shut down** VT, VI fechar; **shut off** VT cortar, interromper; **shut up** VI (*inf*: *keep*

quiet) calar-se, calar a boca ▶ VT (*close*) fechar; (*silence*) calar; **shutter** N veneziana; (*Phot*) obturador *m*

shuttle [ˈʃʌtl] N (*plane: also:* **~ service**) ponte *f* aérea; (*space shuttle*) ônibus *m* espacial

shuttlecock [ˈʃʌtlkɔk] N peteca

shy [ʃaɪ] ADJ tímido; (*reserved*) reservado

sick [sɪk] ADJ (*ill*) doente; (*nauseated*) enjoado; (*humour*) negro; (*vomiting*): **to be ~** vomitar; **to feel ~** estar enjoado; **to be ~ of** (*fig*) estar cheio *or* farto de; **sickening** ADJ (*fig*) repugnante; **sick leave** N licença por doença; **sickly** ADJ doentio; (*causing nausea*) nauseante; **sickness** N doença, indisposição *f*; (*vomiting*) náusea, enjoo

side [saɪd] N lado; (*of body*) flanco; (*of lake*) margem *f*; (*aspect*) aspecto; (*team*) time *m* (BR), equipa (PT); (*of hill*) declive *m* ▶ CPD (*door, entrance*) lateral ▶ VI: **to ~ with sb** tomar o partido de alguém; **by the ~ of** ao lado de; **~ by ~** lado a lado, juntos; **from ~ to ~** para lá e para cá; **to take ~s with** pôr-se ao lado de; **sideboard** N aparador *m*; **sideboards** NPL (BRIT) = **sideburns**; **sideburns** NPL suiças *fpl*, costeletas *fpl*; **side effect** N efeito colateral; **sidelight** N (*Aut*) luz *f* lateral; **side order** N acompanhamento; **sidetrack** VT (*fig*) desviar (do seu propósito); **sidewalk** (US) N calçada; **sideways** ADV de lado

siege [si:dʒ] N sítio, assédio

sieve [sɪv] N peneira ▶ VT peneirar

sift [sɪft] VT peneirar; (*fig*) esquadrinhar, analisar minuciosamente

sigh [saɪ] N suspiro ▶ VI suspirar

sight [saɪt] N (*faculty*) vista, visão *f*; (*spectacle*) espetáculo; (*on gun*) mira ▶ VT avistar; **in ~** à vista; **on ~** (*shoot*) no local; **out of ~** longe dos olhos; **sightseeing** N turismo; **to go sightseeing** fazer turismo, passear

sign [saɪn] N (*with hand*) sinal *m*, aceno; (*indication*) indício; (*notice*) letreiro, tabuleta; (*written, of zodiac*) signo ▶ VT assinar; **to ~ sth over to sb** assinar a transferência de algo para alguém; **sign on** VI (*Mil*) alistar-se; (BRIT: *as unemployed*) cadastrar-se para receber auxílio-desemprego; (*for course*) inscrever-se ▶ VT (*Mil*) alistar; (*employee*) efetivar; **sign up** VI (*Mil*) alistar-se; (*for course*) inscrever-se ▶ VT recrutar

signal [ˈsɪgnl] N sinal *m*, aviso ▶ VI (*also: Aut*) sinalizar, dar sinal ▶ VT (*person*) fazer sinais para; (*message*) transmitir

signature [ˈsɪgnətʃəʳ] N assinatura

significance [sɪgˈnɪfɪkəns] N importância; **significant** ADJ significativo; (*important*) importante

sign language N mímica, linguagem *f* através de sinais

silence [ˈsaɪləns] N silêncio ▶ VT silenciar, impor silêncio a

silent [ˈsaɪlənt] ADJ silencioso; (*not speaking*) calado; (*film*) mudo; **to keep** *or* **remain ~** manter-se em silêncio

silhouette [sɪlu:ˈɛt] N silhueta

silicon chip [ˈsɪlɪkən tʃɪp] N placa *or* chip *m* de silício

silk [sɪlk] N seda ▶ ADJ de seda

silly [ˈsɪlɪ] ADJ (*person*) bobo, idiota, imbecil; (*idea*) absurdo, ridículo

silver ['sɪlvəʳ] N prata; (*money*) moedas *fpl*; (*also*: **~ware**) prataria ▶ ADJ de prata; **silver-plated** ADJ prateado, banhado a prata
SIM card ['sɪm-] N (*Tel*) cartão *m* SIM, chip *m*
similar ['sɪmɪləʳ] ADJ: **~ to** parecido com, semelhante a
simmer ['sɪməʳ] VI cozer em fogo lento, ferver lentamente
simple ['sɪmpl] ADJ simples *inv*; (*foolish*) ingênuo; **simply** ADV de maneira simples; (*merely*) simplesmente
simultaneous [sɪməl'teɪnɪəs] ADJ simultâneo
sin [sɪn] N pecado ▶ VI pecar
since [sɪns] ADV desde então, depois ▶ PREP desde ▶ CONJ (*time*) desde que; (*because*) porque, visto que, já que; **~ then** desde então; **(ever) ~ I arrived** desde que eu cheguei
sincere [sɪn'sɪəʳ] ADJ sincero; **sincerely** ADV: **yours sincerely** (BRIT), **sincerely yours** (US) (*at end of letter*) atenciosamente
sing [sɪŋ] (*pt* **sang**, *pp* **sung**) VT, VI cantar
Singapore [sɪŋgə'pɔːʳ] N Cingapura (*no article*)
singer ['sɪŋəʳ] N cantor(a) *m/f*
singing ['sɪŋɪŋ] N canto; (*songs*) canções *fpl*
single ['sɪŋgl] ADJ único, só; (*unmarried*) solteiro; (*not double*) simples *inv* ▶ N (BRIT: *also*: **~ ticket**) passagem *f* de ida; (*record*) compacto; **single out** VT (*choose*) escolher; (*distinguish*) distinguir; **single file** N: **in single file** em fila indiana; **single-handed** ADV sem ajuda, sozinho; **single-minded** ADJ determinado; **single room** N quarto individual
singular ['sɪŋgjuləʳ] ADJ (*odd*) esquisito; (*outstanding*) extraordinário, excepcional; (*Ling*) singular ▶ N (*Ling*) singular *m*
sinister ['sɪnɪstəʳ] ADJ sinistro
sink [sɪŋk] (*pt* **sank**, *pp* **sunk**) N pia ▶ VT (*ship*) afundar; (*foundations*) escavar ▶ VI afundar-se; (*heart*) partir; (*spirits*) ficar deprimido; (*also*: **~ back, ~ down**) cair *or* mergulhar gradativamente; **to ~ sth into** enterrar algo em; **sink in** VI (*fig*) penetrar
sinus ['saɪnəs] N (*Anat*) seio (paranasal)
sip [sɪp] N gole *m* ▶ VT sorver, bebericar
sir [səʳ] N senhor *m*; **S~ John Smith** Sir John Smith; **yes, ~** sim, senhor
siren ['saɪərn] N sirena
sirloin ['səːlɔɪn] N lombo de vaca
sister ['sɪstəʳ] N irmã *f*; (BRIT: *nurse*) enfermeira-chefe *f*; (*nun*) freira; **sister-in-law** N cunhada
sit [sɪt] (*pt, pp* **sat**) VI sentar-se; (*be sitting*) estar sentado; (*assembly*) reunir-se; (*for painter*) posar ▶ VT (*exam*) prestar; **sit down** VI sentar-se; **sit in on** VT FUS assistir a; **sit up** VI (*after lying*) levantar-se; (*straight*) endireitar-se; (*not go to bed*) aguardar acordado, velar
sitcom ['sɪtkɔm] N ABBR (= *situation comedy*) comédia de costumes
site [saɪt] N local *m*, sítio; (*also*: **building ~**) lote *m* (de terreno) ▶ VT situar, localizar
sitting ['sɪtɪŋ] N (*in canteen*) turno; **sitting room** N sala de estar
situation [sɪtju'eɪʃən] N situação *f*; (*job*) posição *f*; (*location*) local *m*; **"~s vacant/wanted"**

S

(BRIT) "empregos oferecem-se/ procurados"
six [sɪks] NUM seis; **sixteen** NUM dezesseis; **sixteenth** [sɪks'ti:nθ] NUM décimo sexto; **sixth** NUM sexto; **sixtieth** ['sɪkstɪɪθ] NUM sexagésimo; **sixty** NUM sessenta
size [saɪz] N tamanho; (*extent*) extensão *f*; (*of clothing*) tamanho, medida; (*of shoes*) número; **size up** VT avaliar, formar uma opinião sobre; **sizeable** ADJ considerável, importante
sizzle ['sɪzl] VI chiar
skate [skeɪt] N patim *m*; (*fish: pl inv*) arraia ▶ VI patinar; **skateboard** N skate *m*, patim-tábua *m*; **skating** N patinação *f*; **skating rink** N rinque *m* de patinação
skeleton ['skɛlɪtn] N esqueleto; (*Tech*) armação *f*; (*outline*) esquema *m*, esboço
sketch [skɛtʃ] N (*drawing*) desenho; (*outline*) esboço, croqui *m*; (*Theatre*) quadro, esquete *m* ▶ VT desenhar, esboçar; (*ideas: also*: **~ out**) esboçar
skewer ['skju:əʳ] N espetinho
ski [ski:] N esqui *m* ▶ VI esquiar; **ski boot** N bota de esquiar
skid [skɪd] N derrapagem *f* ▶ VI deslizar; (*Aut*) derrapar
skier ['ski:əʳ] N esquiador(a) *m/f*
skiing ['ski:ɪŋ] N esqui *m*
skilful ['skɪlful], (US) **skillful** ADJ habilidoso, jeitoso
ski lift N ski lift *m*
skill [skɪl] N habilidade *f*, perícia; (*for work*) técnica; **skilled** ADJ hábil, perito; (*worker*) especializado, qualificado
skim [skɪm] VT (*milk*) desnatar; (*glide over*) roçar ▶ VI: **to ~ through** (*book*) folhear; **skimmed milk** N leite *m* desnatado
skin [skɪn] N pele *f*; (*of fruit, vegetable*) casca ▶ VT (*fruit etc*) descascar; (*animal*) tirar a pele de; **skinny** ADJ magro, descarnado
skip [skɪp] N salto, pulo; (BRIT: *container*) balde *m* ▶ VI saltar; (*with rope*) pular corda ▶ VT (*pass over*) omitir, saltar; (*miss*) deixar de
skipper ['skɪpəʳ] N capitão *m*
skipping rope ['skɪpɪŋ-] (BRIT) N corda (de pular)
skirt [skə:t] N saia ▶ VT orlar, circundar; **skirting board** (BRIT) N rodapé *m*
skull [skʌl] N caveira; (*Anat*) crânio
skunk [skʌŋk] N gambá *m*
sky [skaɪ] N céu *m*; **skyscraper** N arranha-céu *m*
slab [slæb] N (*stone*) bloco; (*flat*) laje *f*; (*of cake*) fatia grossa
slack [slæk] ADJ (*loose*) frouxo; (*slow*) lerdo; (*careless*) descuidoso, desmazelado; **slacks** NPL (*trousers*) calça (BR), calças *fpl* (PT)
slain [sleɪn] PP *of* **slay**
slam [slæm] VT (*door*) bater *or* fechar (com violência); (*throw*) atirar violentamente; (*criticize*) malhar, criticar ▶ VI fechar-se (com violência)
slander ['slɑ:ndəʳ] N calúnia, difamação *f*
slang [slæŋ] N gíria; (*jargon*) jargão *m*
slant [slɑ:nt] N declive *m*, inclinação *f*; (*fig*) ponto de vista
slap [slæp] N tapa *m or f* ▶ VT dar um(a) tapa em; (*paint etc*): **to ~ sth on sth** passar algo em algo descuidadamente ▶ ADV diretamente, exatamente
slash [slæʃ] VT cortar, talhar; (*fig: prices*) cortar
slate [sleɪt] N ardósia ▶ VT (*fig: criticize*) criticar duramente, arrasar

slaughter ['slɔːtəʳ] N (*of animals*) matança; (*of people*) carnificina ▶ VT abater; matar, massacrar; **slaughterhouse** N matadouro
slave [sleɪv] N escravo(-a) ▶ VI (*also*: **~ away**) trabalhar como escravo; **slavery** N escravidão *f*
slay [sleɪ] (*pt* **slew**, *pp* **slain**) VT (*literary*) matar
sleazy ['sliːzɪ] ADJ sórdido
sledge [slɛdʒ] N trenó *m*
sleek [sliːk] ADJ (*hair, fur*) macio, lustroso; (*car, boat*) aerodinâmico
sleep [sliːp] (*pt, pp* **slept**) N sono ▶ VI dormir; **to go to ~** dormir, adormecer; **sleep around** VI ser promíscuo sexualmente; **sleep in** VI (*oversleep*) dormir demais; **sleeper** N (*Rail: train*) vagão-leitos *m* (BR), carruagem-camas (PT); **sleeping bag** N saco de dormir; **sleeping car** N vagão-leitos *m* (BR), carruagem-camas *f* (PT); **sleeping pill** N pílula para dormir; **sleepy** ADJ sonolento; (*fig*) morto
sleet [sliːt] N chuva com neve *or* granizo
sleeve [sliːv] N manga; (*of record*) capa
sleigh [sleɪ] N trenó *m*
slender ['slɛndəʳ] ADJ esbelto, delgado; (*means*) escasso, insuficiente
slept [slɛpt] PT, PP *of* **sleep**
slew [sluː] PT *of* **slay**
slice [slaɪs] N (*of meat, bread*) fatia; (*of lemon*) rodela; (*utensil*) pá *f or* espátula de bolo ▶ VT cortar em fatias
slick [slɪk] ADJ (*skilful*) jeitoso, ágil, engenhoso; (*clever*) esperto, astuto ▶ N (*also*: **oil ~**) mancha de óleo
slide [slaɪd] (*pt, pp* **slid**) N deslizamento, escorregão *m*; (*in playground*) escorregador *m*; (*Phot*) slide *m*; (BRIT: *also*: **hair ~**) passador *m* ▶ VT deslizar ▶ VI escorregar; **slide show** N apresentação *f* de slides; **sliding** ADJ (*door*) corrediço
slight [slaɪt] ADJ (*slim*) fraco, franzino; (*frail*) delicado; (*error, pain, increase*) pequeno; (*trivial*) insignificante ▶ N desfeita, desconsideração *f*; **not in the ~est** em absoluto, de maneira alguma; **slightly** ADV ligeiramente, um pouco
slim [slɪm] ADJ esbelto, delgado; (*chance*) pequeno ▶ VI emagrecer
slimming N emagrecimento
sling [slɪŋ] (*pt, pp* **slung**) N (*Med*) tipoia; (*for baby*) bebêbag *m*; (*weapon*) estilingue *m*, funda ▶ VT atirar, arremessar, lançar
slip [slɪp] N (*fall*) escorregão *m*; (*mistake*) erro, lapso; (*underskirt*) combinação *f*; (*of paper*) tira ▶ VT deslizar ▶ VI (*slide*) deslizar; (*lose balance*) escorregar; (*decline*) decair; (*move smoothly*): **to ~ into/ out of** entrar furtivamente em/ sair furtivamente de; **to ~ sth on/ off** enfiar/tirar algo; **to give sb the ~** esgueirar-se de alguém; **a ~ of the tongue** um lapso da língua; **slip away** VI escapulir; **slip in** VT meter ▶ VI (*errors*) surgir; **slip out** VI (*go out*) sair (um momento); **slip up** VI cometer um erro
slipper ['slɪpəʳ] N chinelo
slippery ['slɪpərɪ] ADJ escorregadio
slip-up N equívoco, mancada
slit [slɪt] (*pt, pp* **slit**) N fenda; (*cut*) corte *m* ▶ VT (*cut*) rachar, cortar; (*open*) abrir

slog [slɔg] (BRIT) VI mourejar ▶ N: **it was a ~** deu um trabalho louco
slogan ['sləugən] N lema *m*, slogan *m*
slope [sləup] N ladeira; (*side of mountain*) encosta, vertente *f*; (*ski slope*) pista; (*slant*) inclinação *f*, declive *m* ▶ VI: **to ~ down** estar em declive; **to ~ up** inclinar-se; **sloping** ADJ inclinado, em declive; (*handwriting*) torto
sloppy ['slɔpɪ] ADJ (*work*) descuidado; (*appearance*) relaxado
slot [slɔt] N (*in machine*) fenda ▶ VT: **to ~ into** encaixar em
slow [sləu] ADJ lento; (*not clever*) bronco, de raciocínio lento; (*watch*): **to be ~** atrasar ▶ ADV lentamente, devagar ▶ VT, VI ir (mais) devagar; **"~"** (*road sign*) "devagar"; **slowly** ADV lentamente, devagar; **slow motion** N: **in slow motion** em câmara lenta
slug [slʌg] N lesma; **sluggish** ADJ vagaroso; (*business*) lento
slum [slʌm] N (*area*) favela; (*house*) cortiço, barraco
slump [slʌmp] N (*economic*) depressão *f*; (*Comm*) baixa, queda ▶ VI (*person*) cair; (*prices*) baixar repentinamente
slung [slʌŋ] PT, PP *of* **sling**
slur [slə:ʳ] N calúnia ▶ VT pronunciar indistintamente
slush [slʌʃ] N neve *f* meio derretida
sly [slaɪ] ADJ (*person*) astuto; (*smile, remark*) malicioso, velhaco
smack [smæk] N palmada ▶ VT bater; (*child*) dar uma palmada em; (*on face*) dar um tabefe em ▶ VI: **to ~ of** cheirar a, saber a
small [smɔ:l] ADJ pequeno; **small change** N trocado
smart [smɑ:t] ADJ elegante; (*clever*) inteligente, astuto; (*quick*) vivo, esperto ▶ VI sofrer; **SMART Board®** N quadro interativo; **smart phone** N smartphone *m*
smash [smæʃ] N (*also*: **~-up**) colisão *f*, choque *m*; (*smash hit*) sucesso de bilheteira ▶ VT (*break*) escangalhar, despedaçar; (*car etc*) bater com; (*Sport: record*) quebrar ▶ VI despedaçar-se; (*against wall etc*) espatifar-se; **smashing** (*inf*) ADJ excelente
smear [smɪəʳ] N mancha, nódoa; (*Med*) esfregaço ▶ VT untar; (*to make dirty*) lambuzar
smell [smɛl] (*pt, pp* **smelt** *or* **smelled**) N cheiro; (*sense*) olfato ▶ VT cheirar ▶ VI (*food etc*) cheirar; (*pej*) cheirar mal; **to ~ of** cheirar a; **smelly** (*pej*) ADJ fedorento, malcheiroso
smile [smaɪl] N sorriso ▶ VI sorrir
smirk [smə:k] (*pej*) N sorriso falso *or* afetado
smog [smɔg] N nevoeiro com fumaça (BR) *or* fumo (PT)
smoke [sməuk] N fumaça (BR), fumo (PT) ▶ VI fumar; (*chimney*) fumegar ▶ VT (*cigarettes*) fumar; **smoked** ADJ (*bacon*) defumado; (*glass*) fumée; **smoker** N (*person*) fumante *m/f*; (*Rail*) vagão *m* para fumantes; **smoking** N: **"no smoking"** (*sign*) "proibido fumar"; **he's given up smoking** ele deixou de fumar; **smoky** ADJ enfumaçado; (*taste*) defumado
smooth [smu:ð] ADJ liso, macio; (*sauce*) cremoso; (*sea*) tranquilo, calmo; (*flavour, movement*) suave ▶ VT (*also*: **~ out**) alisar; (*: difficulties*) aplainar
smother ['smʌðəʳ] VT (*fire*) abafar; (*person*) sufocar; (*emotions*) reprimir

SMS N ABBR (= *short message service*) SMS *m*
smudge [smʌdʒ] N mancha ▶ VT manchar, sujar
smug [smʌg] (*pej*) ADJ convencido
smuggle ['smʌgl] VT contrabandear; **smuggling** N contrabando
snack [snæk] N lanche *m* (BR), merenda (PT); **snack bar** N lanchonete *f* (BR), snackbar *m* (PT)
snag [snæg] N dificuldade *f*, obstáculo
snail [sneɪl] N caracol *m*
snake [sneɪk] N cobra
snap [snæp] N (*sound*) estalo; (*photograph*) foto *f* ▶ ADJ repentino ▶ VT quebrar; (*fingers, whip*) estalar ▶ VI quebrar; (*fig: person*) retrucar asperamente; **to ~ shut** fechar com um estalo; **snap at** VT FUS (*subj: dog*) tentar morder; **snap off** VT (*break*) partir; **snap up** VT arrebatar, comprar rapidamente; **snapshot** N foto *f* (instantânea)
snarl [snɑ:l] VI grunhir
snatch [snætʃ] N (*small piece*) trecho ▶ VT agarrar; (*fig: look*) roubar
sneak [sni:k] VI: **to ~ in/out** entrar/sair furtivamente ▶ N (*inf*) dedo-duro; **to ~ up on sb** chegar de mansinho perto de alguém; **sneakers** NPL tênis *m* (BR), sapatos *mpl* de treino (PT)
sneer [snɪə^r] VI rir-se com desdém; (*mock*): **to ~ at** zombar de, desprezar
sneeze [sni:z] N espirro ▶ VI espirrar
sniff [snɪf] N fungada; (*of dog*) farejada; (*of person*) fungadela ▶ VI fungar ▶ VT fungar, farejar; (*glue, drug*) cheirar
snigger ['snɪgə^r] VI rir-se com dissimulação
snip [snɪp] N tesourada; (BRIT *inf*) pechincha ▶ VT cortar com tesoura
sniper ['snaɪpə^r] N franco-atirador(a) *m/f*
snob [snɔb] N esnobe *m/f*
snooker ['snu:kə^r] N sinuca
snoop [snu:p] VI: **to ~ about** bisbilhotar
snooze [snu:z] N soneca ▶ VI tirar uma soneca, dormitar
snore [snɔ:^r] VI roncar ▶ N ronco
snorkel ['snɔ:kl] N tubo snorkel
snort [snɔ:t] N bufo, bufido ▶ VI bufar
snow [snəu] N neve *f* ▶ VI nevar; **snowball** N bola de neve ▶ VI (*fig*) aumentar (como bola de neve); **snowboarding** ['snəubɔ:dɪŋ] N snowboard *m*; **snowdrift** N monte *m* de neve (formado pelo vento); **snowman** *irreg* N boneco de neve; **snowplough**, (US) **snowplow** N máquina limpa-neve, removedor *m* de neve; **snowstorm** N nevasca, tempestade *f* de neve
snub [snʌb] VT desdenhar, menosprezar ▶ N repulsa
snug [snʌg] ADJ (*sheltered*) abrigado, protegido; (*fitted*) justo, cômodo

KEYWORD

so [səu] ADV **1** (*thus, likewise*) assim, deste modo; **so saying he walked away** falou isto e foi embora; **if so** se for assim, se assim é; **I didn't do it — you did so** não fiz isso — você fez!; **so do I, so am I** *etc* eu também; **so it is!** é verdade!; **I hope/think so** espero/acho que sim; **so far** até aqui
2 (*in comparisons etc: to such a degree*) tão; **so big/quickly (that)**

tão grande/rápido (que)
3: **so much** (*adj, adv*) tanto; **I've got so much work** tenho tanto trabalho; **so many** tantos(-as); **there are so many people to see** tem tanta gente para ver
4 (*phrases*): **10 or so** uns 10; **so long!** (*inf: goodbye*) tchau!
▶ CONJ 1 (*expressing purpose*): **so as to do** para fazer; **we hurried so as not to be late** nós nos apressamos para não chegarmos atrasados; **so (that)** para que, a fim de que
2 (*result*) de modo que; **he didn't arrive so I left** como ele não chegou, eu fui embora; **so I was right after all** então eu estava certo no final das contas

soak [səuk] VT embeber, ensopar; (*put in water*) pôr de molho ▶ VI estar de molho, impregnar-se; **soak in** VI infiltrar; **soak up** VT absorver

soap [səup] N sabão *m*; **soap opera** N novela; **soap powder** N sabão *m* em pó

soar [sɔ:ʳ] VI (*on wings*) elevar-se em voo; (*rocket, temperature*) subir; (*building etc*) levantar-se; (*price, production*) disparar

sob [sɔb] N soluço ▶ VI soluçar

sober [ˈsəubəʳ] ADJ (*serious*) sério; (*not drunk*) sóbrio; (*colour, style*) discreto; **sober up** VI ficar sóbrio

so-called [-kɔ:ld] ADJ chamado

soccer [ˈsɔkəʳ] N futebol *m*

social [ˈsəuʃl] ADJ social ▶ N reunião *f* social; **socialism** N socialismo; **socialist** ADJ, N socialista *m/f*; **socialize** VI: **to socialize (with)** socializar (com); **social media** N PL mídias *fpl* sociais (BR), meios *mpl* de comunicação social (PT); **social networking** [-ˈnɛtwə:kɪŋ] N redes *fpl* sociais; **social networking site** N rede *f* social; **social security** (BRIT) N previdência social; **social work** N assistência social, serviço social; **social worker** N assistente *m/f* social

society [səˈsaɪətɪ] N sociedade *f*; (*club*) associação *f*; (*also*: **high ~**) alta sociedade

sociology [səusɪˈɔlədʒɪ] N sociologia

sock [sɔk] N meia (BR), peúga (PT)

socket [ˈsɔkɪt] N bocal *m*, encaixe *m*; (BRIT *Elec*) tomada

soda [ˈsəudə] N (*Chem*) soda; (*also*: **~ water**) água com gás; (*US*: *also*: **~ pop**) soda

sofa [ˈsəufə] N sofá *m*

soft [sɔft] ADJ mole; (*voice, music, light*) suave; (*kind*) meigo, bondoso; **soft drink** N refrigerante *m*; **soften** VT amolecer, amaciar; (*effect*) abrandar; (*expression*) suavizar ▶ VI amolecer-se; (*voice, expression*) suavizar-se; **softly** ADV suavemente; (*gently*) delicadamente; **software** N software *m*

soggy [ˈsɔgɪ] ADJ ensopado, encharcado

soil [sɔɪl] N terra, solo; (*territory*) território ▶ VT sujar, manchar

solar [ˈsəuləʳ] ADJ solar; **solar panel** N painel *m* solar; **solar power** N energia solar

sold [səuld] PT, PP *of* **sell** ▶ ADJ: **~ out** (*Comm*) esgotado

soldier [ˈsəuldʒəʳ] N soldado; (*army man*) militar *m*

sole [səul] N (*of foot, shoe*) sola; (*fish: pl inv*) solha, linguado ▶ ADJ único

solicitor [səˈlɪsɪtəʳ] (BRIT) N (*for wills etc*) tabelião(-lioa) *m/f*; (*in court*) ≈ advogado(-a)

solid ['sɔlɪd] ADJ sólido; (*gold etc*) maciço; (*person*) sério ▶ N sólido; **solids** NPL (*food*) comida sólida
solitary ['sɔlɪtərɪ] ADJ solitário, só; (*walk*) só; (*isolated*) isolado, retirado; (*single*) único
solo ['səuləu] N, ADV solo; **soloist** N solista *m/f*
solution [sə'lu:ʃən] N solução *f*
solve [sɔlv] VT resolver, solucionar
solvent ['sɔlvənt] ADJ (*Comm*) solvente ▶ N (*Chem*) solvente *m*

KEYWORD

some [sʌm] ADJ **1** (*a certain number or amount*): **some tea/water/biscuits** um pouco de chá/água/uns biscoitos; **some children came** algumas crianças vieram
2 (*certain: in contrasts*) algum(a); **some people say that ...** algumas pessoas dizem que ...
3 (*unspecified*) um pouco de; **some woman was asking for you** uma mulher estava perguntando por você; **some day** um dia
▶ PRON **1** (*a certain number*) alguns/algumas; **I've got some** (*books etc*) tenho alguns; **some went for a taxi and some walked** alguns foram pegar um táxi e outros foram andando
2 (*a certain amount*) um pouco; **I've got some** (*milk, money etc*) tenho um pouco
▶ ADV: **some 10 people** umas 10 pessoas

somebody ['sʌmbədɪ] PRON = **someone**
somehow ['sʌmhau] ADV de alguma maneira; (*for some reason*) por uma razão ou outra
someone ['sʌmwʌn] PRON alguém
someplace ['sʌmpleɪs] (US) ADV = **somewhere**
something ['sʌmθɪŋ] PRON alguma coisa, algo (BR)
sometime ['sʌmtaɪm] ADV (*in future*) algum dia, em outra oportunidade; (*in past*): **~ last month** durante o mês passado
sometimes ['sʌmtaɪmz] ADV às vezes, de vez em quando
somewhat ['sʌmwɔt] ADV um tanto
somewhere ['sʌmwɛə^r] ADV (*be*) em algum lugar; (*go*) para algum lugar; **~ else** (*be*) em outro lugar; (*go*) para outro lugar
son [sʌn] N filho
song [sɔŋ] N canção *f*; (*of bird*) canto
son-in-law ['sʌnɪnlɔ:] N genro
soon [su:n] ADV logo, brevemente; (*a short time after*) logo após; (*early*) cedo; **~ afterwards** pouco depois; *see also* **as**; **sooner** ADV antes, mais cedo; (*preference*): **I would sooner do that** preferia fazer isso; **sooner or later** mais cedo ou mais tarde
soothe [su:ð] VT acalmar, sossegar; (*pain*) aliviar, suavizar
soprano [sə'prɑ:nəu] N soprano *m/f*
sore [sɔ:^r] ADJ dolorido ▶ N chaga, ferida
sorrow ['sɔrəu] N tristeza, mágoa, dor *f*; **sorrows** NPL (*causes of grief*) tristezas *fpl*
sorry ['sɔrɪ] ADJ (*regretful*) arrependido; (*condition, excuse*) lamentável; **~!** desculpe!, perdão!, sinto muito!; **to feel ~ for sb** sentir pena de alguém

S

sort [sɔ:t] N tipo ▶ VT (*also*: **~ out**: *papers*) classificar; (: *problems*) solucionar, resolver
SOS N ABBR (= *save our souls*) S.O.S. *m*
so-so ADV mais ou menos, regular
sought [sɔ:t] PT, PP *of* **seek**
soul [səul] N alma; (*person*) criatura
sound [saund] ADJ (*healthy*) saudável, sadio; (*safe, not damaged*) sólido, completo; (*secure*) seguro; (*reliable*) confiável; (*sensible*) sensato ▶ ADV: **~ asleep** dormindo profundamente ▶ N (*noise*) som *m*, ruído, barulho; (*volume: on TV etc*) volume *m*; (*Geo*) estreito, braço (de mar) ▶ VT (*alarm*) soar ▶ VI soar, tocar; (*fig: seem*) parecer; **to ~ like** parecer; **sound out** VI sondar; **soundtrack** N trilha sonora
soup [su:p] N sopa; **in the ~** (*fig*) numa encrenca
sour ['sauəʳ] ADJ azedo, ácido; (*milk*) talhado; (*fig*) mal-humorado, rabugento; **it's ~ grapes!** (*fig*) é despeito!
source [sɔ:s] N fonte *f*
south [sauθ] N sul *m* ▶ ADJ do sul, meridional ▶ ADV ao *or* para o sul; **South Africa** N África do Sul; **South African** ADJ, N sul-africano(-a); **South America** N América do Sul; **South American** ADJ, N sul-americano(-a); **south-east** N sudeste *m*; **southern** ['sʌðən] ADJ (*to the south*) para o sul, em direção do sul; (*from the south*) do sul, sulista; **the southern hemisphere** o Hemisfério Sul; **South Pole** N Pólo Sul; **southward, southwards** ADV para o sul; **south-west** N sudoeste *m*
souvenir [su:və'nɪəʳ] N lembrança
sovereign ['sɔvrɪn] N soberano(-a)
sow¹ [sau] N porca
sow² [səu] (*pt* **sowed**, *pp* **sown**) VT semear; (*fig: spread*) disseminar, espalhar
soya ['sɔɪə], (US) **soy** [sɔɪ] N soja; **soya bean**, (US) **soybean** N semente *f* de soja; **soya sauce**, (US) **soy sauce** N molho de soja
spa [spɑ:] N (*town*) estância hidro-mineral; (US: *also*: **health ~**) estância balnear
space [speɪs] N (*gen*) espaço; (*room*) lugar *m* ▶ CPD espacial ▶ VT (*also*: **~ out**) espaçar; **spacecraft** N nave *f* espacial; **spaceship** N = **spacecraft**; **spacious** ['speɪʃəs] ADJ espaçoso
spade [speɪd] N pá *f*; **spades** NPL (*Cards*) espadas *fpl*
Spain [speɪn] N Espanha
spam ['spæm] N (*junk email*) spam *m*
span [spæn] N (*also*: **wing~**) envergadura; (*of arch*) vão *m*; (*in time*) lapso, espaço ▶ VT estender-se sobre, atravessar; (*fig*) abarcar
Spaniard ['spænjəd] N espanhol(a) *m/f*
Spanish ['spænɪʃ] ADJ espanhol(a) ▶ N (*Ling*) espanhol *m*, castelhano; **the Spanish** NPL os espanhóis
spanner ['spænəʳ] (BRIT) N chave *f* inglesa
spare [spɛəʳ] ADJ vago, desocupado; (*surplus*) de sobra, a mais ▶ N = **spare part** ▶ VT dispensar, passar sem; (*make available*) dispor de; (*refrain from hurting*) perdoar, poupar; **to ~** de sobra; **spare part** N peça sobressalente; **spare time** N tempo livre; **spare wheel** N estepe *m*
spark [spɑ:k] N chispa, faísca; (*fig*) centelha
sparkle ['spɑ:kl] N cintilação *f*, brilho ▶ VI (*shine*) brilhar, faiscar;

sparkling ADJ (*mineral water*) gasoso; (*wine*) espumante; (*conversation*) animado; (*performance*) brilhante

sparrow ['spærəu] N pardal *m*

sparse [spɑːs] ADJ escasso; (*hair*) ralo

spasm ['spæzəm] N (*Med*) espasmo

spat [spæt] PT, PP *of* **spit**

speak [spiːk] (*pt* **spoke**, *pp* **spoken**) VT (*language*) falar; (*truth*) dizer ▶ VI falar; (*make a speech*) discursar; **~ up!** fale alto!; **speaker** N (*in public*) orador(a) *m/f*; (*also*: **loudspeaker**) alto-falante *m*; (*Pol*): **the Speaker** o Presidente da Câmara

spear [spɪəʳ] N lança ▶ VT lancear, arpoar

special ['spɛʃl] ADJ especial; (*edition etc*) extra; (*delivery*) rápido; **specialist** N especialista *m/f*; **speciality** [spɛʃɪ'ælɪtɪ] N especialidade *f*; **specialize** VI: **to specialize (in)** especializar-se (em); **specially** ADV especialmente; **specialty** ['spɛʃəltɪ] (*esp US*) N = **speciality**

species ['spiːʃiːz] N INV espécie *f*

specific [spə'sɪfɪk] ADJ específico

specimen ['spɛsɪmən] N espécime *m*, amostra; (*for testing, Med*) espécime

speck [spɛk] N mancha, pinta

spectacle ['spɛktəkl] N espetáculo; **spectacles** NPL (*glasses*) óculos *mpl*; **spectacular** [spɛk'tækjuləʳ] ADJ espetacular ▶ N (*Cinema etc*) superprodução *f*

spectator [spɛk'teɪtəʳ] N espectador(a) *m/f*

spectrum ['spɛktrəm] (*pl* **spectra**) N espectro

sped [spɛd] PT, PP *of* **speed**

speech [spiːtʃ] N (*faculty, Theatre*) fala; (*formal talk*) discurso; **speechless** ADJ estupefato, emudecido

speed [spiːd] (*pt, pp* **sped**) N velocidade *f*; (*rate*) rapidez *f*; (*haste*) pressa; (*promptness*) prontidão *f*; **at full** *or* **top ~** a toda a velocidade; **speed up** (*pt, pp* **speeded up**) VT, VI acelerar; **speedboat** N lancha; **speed camera** N radar *m* de velocidade; **speeding** N (*Aut*) excesso de velocidade; **speed limit** N limite *m* de velocidade, velocidade *f* máxima; **speedometer** [spɪ'dɔmɪtəʳ] N velocímetro; **speedy** ADJ veloz, rápido; (*prompt*) pronto, imediato

spell [spɛl] (*pt, pp* **spelled** *or* **spelt**) N (*also*: **magic ~**) encanto, feitiço; (*period of time*) período, temporada ▶ VT (*also*: **~ out**) soletrar; (*fig*) pressagiar, ser sinal de; **to cast a ~ on sb** enfeitiçar alguém; **he can't ~** não sabe escrever bem, comete erros de ortografia; **spellchecker** ['speltʃekəʳ] N (*Comput*) corretor *m* ortográfico

spend [spɛnd] (*pt, pp* **spent**) VT (*money*) gastar; (*time*) passar

sperm [spəːm] N esperma

sphere [sfɪəʳ] N esfera

spice [spaɪs] N especiaria ▶ VT condimentar

spicy ['spaɪsɪ] ADJ condimentado

spider ['spaɪdəʳ] N aranha

spike [spaɪk] N (*point*) ponta, espigão *m*; (*Bot*) espiga

spill [spɪl] (*pt, pp* **spilt** *or* **spilled**) VT entornar, derramar ▶ VI derramar-se; **spill over** VI transbordar

S

spin [spɪn] (*pt, pp* **spun**) N (*Aviat*) parafuso; (*trip in car*) volta *or* passeio de carro; (*ball*): **to put ~ on** fazer rolar ▸ VT (*wool etc*) fiar, tecer ▸ VI girar, rodar; (*make thread*) tecer; **spin out** VT prolongar; (*money*) fazer render
spinach ['spɪnɪtʃ] N espinafre *m*
spinal cord ['spaɪnl kɔːd] N espinha dorsal
spin doctor (*inf*) N marqueteiro(-a)
spin-dryer (BRIT) N secadora
spine [spaɪn] N espinha dorsal; (*thorn*) espinho
spiral ['spaɪərl] N espiral *f* ▸ VI (*prices*) disparar
spire ['spaɪəʳ] N flecha, agulha
spirit ['spɪrɪt] N (*soul*) alma; (*ghost*) fantasma *m*; (*courage*) coragem *f*, ânimo; (*frame of mind*) estado de espírito; (*sense*) sentido; **spirits** NPL (*drink*) álcool *m*; **in good ~s** alegre, de bom humor; **spiritual** ADJ espiritual ▸ N (*also*: **Negro spiritual**) *canto religioso dos negros*
spit [spɪt] (*pt, pp* **spat**) N (*for roasting*) espeto; (*saliva*) saliva ▸ VI cuspir; (*sound*) escarrar; (*rain*) chuviscar
spite [spaɪt] N rancor *m*, ressentimento ▸ VT contrariar; **in ~ of** apesar de, a despeito de; **spiteful** ADJ maldoso, malévolo
splash [splæʃ] N (*sound*) borrifo, respingo; (*of colour*) mancha ▸ VT: **to ~ (with)** salpicar (de) ▸ VI (*also*: **~ about**) borrifar, respingar
splendid ['splɛndɪd] ADJ esplêndido; (*impressive*) impressionante
splinter ['splɪntəʳ] N (*of wood, glass*) lasca; (*in finger*) farpa ▸ VI lascar-se, estilhaçar-se, despedaçar-se
split [splɪt] (*pt, pp* **split**) N fenda, brecha; (*fig: division*) rompimento; (: *difference*) diferença; (*Pol*) divisão *f* ▸ VT partir, fender; (*party, work*) dividir; (*profits*) repartir ▸ VI (*divide*) dividir-se, repartir-se; **split up** VI (*couple*) separar-se, acabar; (*meeting*) terminar
spoil [spɔɪl] (*pt, pp* **spoilt** *or* **spoiled**) VT (*damage*) danificar; (*mar*) estragar, arruinar; (*child*) mimar
spoke [spəuk] PT *of* **speak** ▸ N raio
spoken ['spəukn] PP *of* **speak**
spokesman ['spəuksmən] *irreg* N porta-voz *m*
spokeswoman ['spəukswumən] *irreg* N porta-voz *f*
sponge [spʌndʒ] N esponja; (*cake*) pão de ló *m* ▸ VT lavar com esponja ▸ VI: **to ~ on sb** viver às custas de alguém; **sponge bag** (BRIT) N bolsa de toalete
sponsor ['spɔnsəʳ] N patrocinador(a) *m/f* ▸ VT patrocinar; apadrinhar; fiar; (*applicant, proposal*) apoiar, defender; **sponsorship** N patrocínio
spontaneous [spɔn'teɪnɪəs] ADJ espontâneo
spooky ['spuːkɪ] (*inf*) ADJ arrepiante
spoon [spuːn] N colher *f*; **spoonful** N colherada
sport [spɔːt] N esporte *m* (BR), desporto (PT); (*person*) bom perdedor/boa perdedora *m/f* ▸ VT (*wear*) exibir; **sport jacket** (US) N = **sports jacket**; **sports car** N carro esporte (BR), carro de sport (PT); **sports drink** N isotônico; **sports jacket** (BRIT) N casaco esportivo (BR) *or* desportivo (PT); **sportsman** *irreg* N esportista *m* (BR), desportista *m* (PT); **sportswear** N roupa esportiva (BR) *or* desportiva (PT) *or* esporte; **sportswoman** *irreg* N esportista (BR), desportista (PT);

sporty ADJ esportivo (BR), desportivo (PT)
spot [spɔt] N (*mark*) marca; (*place*) lugar *m*, local *m*; (*dot: on pattern*) mancha, ponto; (*on skin*) espinha; (*Radio, TV*) hora; (*small amount*): **a ~ of** um pouquinho de ▶ VT notar; **on the ~** na hora; (*there*) ali mesmo; (*in difficulty*) em apuros; **spotless** ADJ sem mancha, imaculado; **spotlight** N holofote *m*, refletor *m*
spouse [spauz] N cônjuge *m/f*
sprain [spreɪn] N distensão *f*, torcedura ▶ VT torcer
sprang [spræŋ] PT *of* **spring**
sprawl [sprɔːl] VI esparramar-se
spray [spreɪ] N borrifo; (*container*) spray *m*, atomizador *m*; (*garden spray*) vaporizador *m*; (*of flowers*) ramalhete *m* ▶ VT pulverizar; (*crops*) borrifar, regar
spread [sprɛd] (*pt, pp* **spread**) N extensão *f*; (*distribution*) expansão *f*, difusão *f*; (*Culin*) pasta; (*inf: food*) banquete *m* ▶ VT espalhar; (*butter*) untar, passar; (*wings, sails*) abrir, desdobrar; (*workload, wealth*) distribuir; (*scatter*) disseminar ▶ VI (*news, stain*) espalhar-se; (*disease*) alastrar-se; **spread out** VI dispersar-se; **spreadsheet** N (*Comput*) planilha
spree [spriː] N: **to go on a ~** cair na farra
spring [sprɪŋ] (*pt* **sprang**, *pp* **sprung**) N salto, pulo; (*coiled metal*) mola; (*season*) primavera; (*of water*) fonte *f*; **spring up** VI aparecer de repente
sprinkle ['sprɪŋkl] VT (*liquid*) salpicar; (*salt, sugar*) borrifar; **to ~ water on, ~ with water** salpicar de água
sprint [sprɪnt] N corrida de pequena distância ▶ VI correr a toda velocidade
sprung [sprʌŋ] PP *of* **spring**
spun [spʌn] PT, PP *of* **spin**
spur [spəːʳ] N espora; (*fig*) estímulo ▶ VT (*also*: **~ on**) incitar, estimular; **on the ~ of the moment** de improviso, de repente
spurt [spəːt] N (*of energy*) acesso; (*of blood etc*) jorro ▶ VI jorrar
spy [spaɪ] N espião/espiã *m/f* ▶ VI: **to ~ on** espiar, espionar ▶ VT enxergar, avistar; **spyware** ['spaɪwɛəʳ] N (*Comput*) spyware *m*, software *m* espião
sq. ABBR (*Math etc*) = **square**
squabble ['skwɔbl] VI brigar, discutir
squad [skwɔd] N (*Mil, Police*) pelotão *m*, esquadra; (*Football*) seleção *f*
squadron ['skwɔdrən] N (*Mil*) esquadrão *m*; (*Aviat*) esquadrilha; (*Naut*) esquadra
squander ['skwɔndəʳ] VT esbanjar, dissipar; (*chances*) desperdiçar
square [skwɛəʳ] N quadrado; (*in town*) praça; (*inf: person*) quadrado(-a), careta *m/f* ▶ ADJ quadrado; (*inf: ideas, tastes*) careta, antiquado ▶ VT (*arrange*) ajustar, acertar; (*Math*) elevar ao quadrado; (*reconcile*) conciliar; **all ~** igual, quite; **a ~ meal** uma refeição substancial; **2 metres ~** um quadrado de dois metros de lado; **2 ~ metres** 2 metros quadrados
squash [skwɔʃ] N (BRIT: *drink*): **lemon/orange ~** limonada/laranjada concentrada; (*Sport*) squash *m*; (US: *vegetable*) abóbora ▶ VT esmagar

S

squat [skwɔt] ADJ atarracado ▸ VI (*also*: **~ down**) agachar-se, acocorar-se; **squatter** N posseiro(-a)

squeak [skwi:k] VI (*door*) ranger; (*mouse*) guinchar

squeal [skwi:l] VI guinchar, gritar agudamente

squeeze [skwi:z] N (*gen, of hand*) aperto; (*Econ*) arrocho ▸ VT comprimir, socar; (*hand, arm*) apertar; **squeeze out** VT espremer; (*fig*) extorquir

squid [skwɪd] (*pl* **squids** *or* **squid**) N lula

squint [skwɪnt] VI olhar *or* ser vesgo ▸ N (*Med*) estrabismo

squirm [skwə:m] VI retorcer-se

squirrel ['skwɪrəl] N esquilo

squirt [skwə:t] VI, VT jorrar, esguichar

Sr ABBR = **senior**

St ABBR (= *saint*) S.; = **street**

stab [stæb] N (*with knife etc*) punhalada; (*of pain*) pontada; (*inf*: *try*): **to have a ~ at (doing) sth** tentar (fazer) algo ▸ VT apunhalar

stable ['steɪbl] ADJ estável ▸ N estábulo, cavalariça

stack [stæk] N montão *m*, pilha ▸ VT amontoar, empilhar

stadium ['steɪdɪəm] (*pl* **stadia** *or* **stadiums**) N estádio

staff [stɑ:f] N (*work force*) pessoal *m*, quadro; (BRIT *Sch*: *also*: **teaching ~**) corpo docente ▸ VT prover de pessoal

stag [stæg] N veado, cervo

stage [steɪdʒ] N palco, cena; (*point*) etapa, fase *f*; (*platform*) plataforma, estrado; (*profession*): **the ~** o palco, o teatro ▸ VT pôr em cena, representar; (*demonstration*) montar, organizar; **in ~s** por etapas

stagger ['stægəʳ] VI cambalear ▸ VT (*amaze*) surpreender, chocar; (*hours, holidays*) escalonar; **staggering** ADJ (*amazing*) surpreendente, chocante

stain [steɪn] N mancha; (*colouring*) tinta, tintura ▸ VT manchar; (*wood*) tingir

stair [stɛəʳ] N (*step*) degrau *m*; **stairs** NPL (*flight of steps*) escada; **staircase** N escadaria, escada; **stairway** N = **staircase**

stake [steɪk] N estaca, poste *m*; (*Comm*: *interest*) interesse *m*, participação *f*; (*Betting*: *gen pl*) aposta ▸ VT apostar; (*claim*) reivindicar; **to be at ~** estar em jogo

stale [steɪl] ADJ (*bread*) dormido; (*food*) estragado; (*air*) viciado; (*smell*) mofado; (*beer*) velho

stalk [stɔ:k] N talo, haste *f* ▸ VT caçar de tocaia; **to ~ in/out** entrar/sair silenciosamente; **to ~ off** andar com arrogância

stall [stɔ:l] N (BRIT: *in market*) barraca; (*in stable*) baia ▸ VT (*Aut*) fazer morrer; (*fig*: *delay*) impedir, atrasar ▸ VI morrer; esquivar-se, ganhar tempo; **stalls** NPL (BRIT: *in cinema, theatre*) plateia

stamina ['stæmɪnə] N resistência

stammer ['stæməʳ] N gagueira ▸ VI gaguejar, balbuciar

stamp [stæmp] N selo; (*rubber stamp*) carimbo, timbre *m*; (*mark, also fig*) marca, impressão *f* ▸ VI (*also*: **~ one's foot**) bater com o pé ▸ VT (*letter*) selar; (*mark*) marcar; (*with rubber stamp*) carimbar

stampede [stæm'pi:d] N debandada, estouro (da boiada)

stance [stæns] N postura, posição *f*

stand [stænd] (*pt, pp* **stood**) N posição *f*, postura; (*for taxis*) ponto;

(*also*: **hall ~**) pedestal *m*; (*also*: **music ~**) estante *f*; (*Sport*) tribuna, palanque *m*; (*stall*) barraca ▶ VI (*be*) estar, encontrar-se; (*be on foot*) estar em pé; (*rise*) levantar-se; (*remain: decision, offer*) estar de pé; (*in election*) candidatar-se ▶ VT (*place*) pôr, colocar; (*tolerate, withstand*) aguentar, suportar; (*cost*) pagar; **to make a ~** resistir; (*fig*) ater-se a um princípio; **to ~ for parliament** (BRIT) apresentar-se como candidato ao parlamento; **stand by** VI estar a postos ▶ VT FUS (*opinion*) aferrar-se a; (*person*) ficar ao lado de; **stand down** VI retirar-se; **stand for** VT FUS (*signify*) significar; (*represent*) representar; (*tolerate*) tolerar, permitir; **stand in for** VT FUS substituir; **stand out** VI (*be prominent*) destacar-se; **stand up** VI levantar-se; **stand up for** VT FUS defender; **stand up to** VT FUS enfrentar

standard ['stændəd] N padrão *m*, critério; (*flag*) estandarte *m*; (*level*) nível *m* ▶ ADJ padronizado, regular, normal; **standards** NPL (*morals*) valores *mpl* morais; **standard of living** N padrão *m* de vida (BR), nível *m* de vida (PT)

stand-by ADJ de reserva ▶ N: **to be on ~** estar de sobreaviso *or* de prontidão; **stand-by ticket** N bilhete *m* de stand-by

standing ['stændɪŋ] ADJ (*on foot*) em pé; (*permanent*) permanente ▶ N posição *f*, reputação *f*; **of many years' ~** de muitos anos

standpoint ['stændpɔɪnt] N ponto de vista

standstill ['stændstɪl] N: **at a ~** paralisado, parado; **to come to a ~** (*car*) parar; (*factory, traffic*) ficar paralisado

stank [stæŋk] PT *of* **stink**

staple ['steɪpl] N (*for papers*) grampo ▶ ADJ (*food etc*) básico ▶ VT grampear

star [stɑːʳ] N estrela; (*celebrity*) astro/estrela ▶ VI: **to ~ in** ser a estrela em, estrelar ▶ VT (*Cinema*) ser estrelado por; **the stars** NPL (*horoscope*) o horóscopo

starboard ['stɑːbəd] N estibordo

starch [stɑːtʃ] N (*in food*) amido, fécula; (*for clothes*) goma

stardom ['stɑːdəm] N estrelato

stare [stɛəʳ] N olhar *m* fixo ▶ VI: **to ~ at** olhar fixamente, fitar

stark [stɑːk] ADJ severo, áspero ▶ ADV: **~ naked** completamente nu, em pelo

start [stɑːt] N princípio, começo; (*departure*) partida; (*sudden movement*) sobressalto, susto; (*advantage*) vantagem *f* ▶ VT começar, iniciar; (*cause*) causar; (*found*) fundar; (*engine*) ligar ▶ VI começar, iniciar; (*with fright*) sobressaltar-se, assustar-se; (*train etc*) sair; **start off** VI começar, principiar; (*leave*) sair, pôr-se a caminho; **start up** VI começar; (*car*) pegar, pôr-se em marcha ▶ VT começar; (*car*) ligar; **starter** N (*Aut*) arranque *m*; (*Sport: official*) juiz/juíza *m/f* da partida; **starting point** N ponto de partida

startle ['stɑːtl] VT assustar, aterrar; **startling** ADJ surpreendente

starvation [stɑː'veɪʃən] N fome *f*

starve ['stɑːv] VI passar fome; (*to death*) morrer de fome ▶ VT fazer passar fome; (*fig*): **to ~ (of)** privar (de)

S

state [steɪt] N estado ▶ VT afirmar, declarar; **the States** NPL (*Geo*) os Estados Unidos; **to be in a ~** estar agitado; **statement** N declaração *f*; **statesman** *irreg* N estadista *m*
static ['stætɪk] N (*Radio, TV*) interferência ▶ ADJ estático
station ['steɪʃən] N estação *f*; (*Police*) delegacia; (*Radio*) emissora ▶ VT colocar
stationary ['steɪʃnərɪ] ADJ estacionário
station wagon (US) N perua (BR), canadiana (PT)
statistic [stə'tɪstɪk] N estatística; **statistics** [stə'tɪstɪks] N (*science*) estatística
statue ['stætju:] N estátua
status ['steɪtəs] N posição *f*; (*official classification*) categoria; (*importance*) status *m*
staunch [stɔ:ntʃ] ADJ fiel
stay [steɪ] N estadia, estada ▶ VI ficar; (*as guest*) hospedar-se; (*spend some time*) demorar-se; **to ~ put** não se mexer; **to ~ the night** pernoitar; **stay behind** VI ficar atrás; **stay in** VI ficar em casa; **stay on** VI ficar; **stay out** VI ficar fora de casa; **stay up** VI (*at night*) velar, ficar acordado
steadily ['stɛdɪlɪ] ADV (*firmly*) firmemente; (*unceasingly*) sem parar, constantemente; (*walk*) regularmente
steady ['stɛdɪ] ADJ (*job, boyfriend*) constante; (*speed*) fixo; (*regular*) regular; (*person, character*) sensato; (*calm*) calmo, sereno ▶ VT (*stabilize*) estabilizar; (*nerves*) acalmar
steak [steɪk] N filé *m*; (*beef*) bife *m*
steal [sti:l] (*pt* **stole**, *pp* **stolen**) VT roubar ▶ VI mover-se furtivamente
steam [sti:m] N vapor *m* ▶ VT (*Culin*) cozinhar no vapor ▶ VI fumegar; **steamy** ADJ vaporoso; (*room*) cheio de vapor, úmido (BR), húmido (PT); (*heat, atmosphere*) vaporoso
steel [sti:l] N aço ▶ ADJ de aço
steep [sti:p] ADJ íngreme; (*increase*) acentuado; (*price*) exorbitante ▶ VT (*food*) colocar de molho; (*cloth*) ensopar, encharcar
steeple ['sti:pl] N campanário, torre *f*
steer [stɪə^r] VT (*person*) guiar; (*vehicle*) dirigir ▶ VI conduzir; **steering** N (*Aut*) direção *f*; **steering wheel** N volante *m*
stem [stɛm] N (*of plant*) caule *m*, haste *f*; (*of glass*) pé *m* ▶ VT deter, reter; (*blood*) estancar; **stem from** VT FUS originar-se de
step [stɛp] N passo; (*stair*) degrau *m* ▶ VI: **to ~ forward** dar um passo a frente/atrás; **steps** NPL (BRIT) = **stepladder**; **to be in ~ (with)** (*fig*) manter a paridade (com); **to be out of ~ (with)** (*fig*) estar em disparidade (com); **step down** VI (*fig*) renunciar; **step on** VT FUS pisar; **step up** VT aumentar; **stepbrother** N meio-irmão *m*; **stepdaughter** N enteada; **stepfather** N padrasto; **stepladder** (BRIT) N escada portátil *or* de abrir; **stepmother** N madrasta; **stepsister** N meia-irmã *f*; **stepson** N enteado
stereo ['stɛrɪəu] N estéreo; (*record player*) (aparelho de) som *m* ▶ ADJ (*also*: **~phonic**) estereofônico
sterile ['stɛraɪl] ADJ esterelizado; (*barren*) estéril; **sterilize** ['stɛrɪlaɪz] VT esterilizar
sterling ['stə:lɪŋ] ADJ esterlino; (*silver*) de lei ▶ N (*currency*) libra esterlina; **one pound ~** uma libra esterlina

stern [stəːn] ADJ severo, austero ▸ N (*Naut*) popa, ré *f*

stew [stjuː] N guisado, ensopado ▸ VT guisar, ensopar; (*fruit*) cozinhar

steward ['stjuːəd] N (*Aviat*) comissário de bordo; **stewardess** N aeromoça (BR), hospedeira de bordo (PT)

stick [stɪk] (*pt, pp* **stuck**) N pau *m*; (*as weapon*) cacete *m*; (*walking stick*) bengala, cajado ▸ VT (*glue*) colar; (*inf: put*) meter; (*: tolerate*) aguentar, suportar; (*thrust*): **to ~ sth into** cravar *or* enfiar algo em ▸ VI (*become attached*) colar-se; (*be unmoveable*) emperrar; (*in mind etc*) gravar-se; **stick out** VI estar saliente, projetar-se; **stick up** VI estar saliente, projetar-se; **stick up for** VT FUS defender; **sticker** N adesivo; **sticking plaster** N esparadrapo

sticky ['stɪkɪ] ADJ pegajoso; (*label*) adesivo; (*fig*) delicado

stiff [stɪf] ADJ (*strong*) forte; (*hard*) duro; (*difficult*) difícil; (*moving with difficulty: person*) teso; (*: door, zip*) empenado; (*formal*) formal ▸ ADV (*bored, worried*) extremamente

stigma ['stɪgmə] N estigma *m*

stiletto [stɪ'lɛtəu] (BRIT) N (*also:* **~ heel**) salto alto e fino

still [stɪl] ADJ parado ▸ ADV (*up to this time*) ainda; (*even, yet*) ainda; (*nonetheless*) entretanto, contudo

stimulate ['stɪmjuleɪt] VT estimular

stimulus ['stɪmjuləs] (*pl* **stimuli**) N estímulo, incentivo

sting [stɪŋ] (*pt, pp* **stung**) N (*wound*) picada; (*pain*) ardência; (*of insect*) ferrão *m* ▸ VT arguilhar ▸ VI (*insect, animal*) picar; (*eyes, ointment*) queimar

stink [stɪŋk] (*pt* **stank**, *pp* **stunk**) N fedor *m*, catinga ▸ VI feder, cheirar mal

stir [stəːʳ] N (*fig*) comoção *f*, rebuliço ▸ VT mexer; (*fig*) comover ▸ VI mover-se, remexer-se; **stir up** VT excitar; (*trouble*) provocar

stitch [stɪtʃ] N (*Sewing, Knitting, Med*) ponto; (*pain*) pontada ▸ VT costurar; (*Med*) dar pontos em, suturar

stock [stɔk] N suprimento; (*Comm: reserves*) estoque *m*, provisão *f*; (*: selection*) sortimento; (*Agr*) gado; (*Culin*) caldo; (*lineage*) estirpe *f*, linhagem *f*; (*Finance*) valores *mpl*, títulos *mpl* ▸ ADJ (*reply etc*) de sempre, costumeiro ▸ VT ter em estoque, estocar; **in ~** em estoque; **out of ~** esgotado; **to take ~ of** (*fig*) fazer um balanço de; **~s and shares** valores e títulos mobiliários; **stock up** VI: **to ~ up (with)** abastecer-se (de); **stockbroker** N corretor(a) *m/f* de valores; **stock cube** (BRIT) N cubo de caldo; **stock exchange** N Bolsa de Valores

stocking ['stɔkɪŋ] N meia

stock market (BRIT) N Bolsa, mercado de valores

stole [stəul] PT *of* **steal** ▸ N estola

stolen ['stəuln] PP *of* **steal**

stomach ['stʌmək] N (*Anat*) estômago; (*belly*) barriga, ventre *m* ▸ VT suportar, tolerar

stone [stəun] N pedra; (*pebble*) pedrinha; (*in fruit*) caroço; (*Med*) pedra, cálculo; (BRIT: *weight*) = 6.348kg; 14 pounds ▸ ADJ de pedra ▸ VT apedrejar; (*fruit*) tirar o(s) caroço(s) de

stood [stud] PT, PP *of* **stand**

S

stool [stu:l] N tamborete *m*, banco
stoop [stu:p] VI (*also*: **have a ~**) ser corcunda; (*also*: **~ down**) debruçar-se, curvar-se
stop [stɔp] N parada, interrupção *f*; (*for bus etc*) parada (BR), ponto (BR), paragem *f* (PT); (*also*: **full ~**) ponto ▸ VT parar, deter; (*break off*) interromper; (*pay, cheque*) sustar, suspender; (*also*: **put a ~ to**) impedir ▸ VI parar, deter-se; (*watch, noise*) parar; (*end*) acabar; **to ~ doing sth** deixar de fazer algo; **stop dead** VI parar de repente; **stop off** VI dar uma parada; **stop up** VT tapar; **stopover** N parada rápida; (*Aviat*) escala
storage ['stɔ:rɪdʒ] N armazenagem *f*
store [stɔ:ʳ] N (*stock*) suprimento; (*depot*) armazém *m*; (*reserve*) estoque *m*; (BRIT: *large shop*) loja de departamentos; (US: *shop*) loja ▸ VT armazenar; **stores** NPL (*provisions*) víveres *mpl*, provisões *fpl*; **who knows what is in ~ for us?** quem sabe o que nos espera?; **store up** VT acumular
storey ['stɔ:rɪ], (US) **story** N andar *m*
storm [stɔ:m] N tempestade *f*; (*fig*) tumulto ▸ VI (*fig*) enfurecer-se ▸ VT tomar de assalto, assaltar; **stormy** ADJ tempestuoso
story ['stɔ:rɪ] N história, estória; (*lie*) mentira; (US) = **storey**
stout [staut] ADJ sólido, forte; (*fat*) gordo, corpulento; (*resolute*) decidido, resoluto ▸ N cerveja preta
stove [stəuv] N (*for cooking*) fogão *m*; (*for heating*) estufa, fogareiro
straight [streɪt] ADJ reto; (*back*) esticado; (*hair*) liso; (*honest*) honesto; (*simple*) simples *inv* ▸ ADV reto; (*drink*) puro; **to put** *or* **get sth ~** esclarecer algo; **~ away, ~ off** (*at once*) imediatamente; **straighten** VT arrumar; **to straighten things out** arrumar as coisas; **straighten out** VT endireitar; (*fig*) esclarecer; **straightforward** ADJ (*simple*) simples *inv*, direto; (*honest*) honesto, franco
strain [streɪn] N tensão *f*; (*Tech*) esforço; (*Med: back strain*) distensão *f*; (*: tension*) luxação *f*; (*breed*) raça, estirpe *f* ▸ VT forçar, torcer, distender; (*stretch*) puxar, estirar; (*Culin*) coar; **strains** NPL (*Mus*) acordes *mpl*; **strained** ADJ distendido; (*laugh*) forçado; (*relations*) tenso; **strainer** N coador *m*; (*sieve*) peneira
strait [streɪt] N estreito; **straits** NPL: **to be in dire ~s** estar em apuros
strand [strænd] N (*of thread, hair*) fio; (*of rope*) tira; **stranded** ADJ preso
strange [streɪndʒ] ADJ (*not known*) desconhecido; (*odd*) estranho, esquisito; **strangely** ADV estranhamente; **stranger** N desconhecido(-a); (*from another area*) forasteiro(-a)
strangle ['stræŋgl] VT estrangular; (*fig*) sufocar
strap [stræp] N correia; (*of slip, dress*) alça
strategic [strə'ti:dʒɪk] ADJ estratégico
strategy ['strætɪdʒɪ] N estratégia
straw [strɔ:] N palha; (*drinking straw*) canudo; **that's the last ~!** essa foi a última gota!
strawberry ['strɔ:bərɪ] N morango
stray [streɪ] ADJ (*animal*) extraviado; (*bullet*) perdido; (*scattered*) espalhado ▸ VI perder-se

streak [stri:k] N listra, traço; (*in hair*) mecha ▸VT listrar ▸VI: **to ~ past** passar como um raio
stream [stri:m] N riacho, córrego; (*of people, vehicles*) fluxo; (*of smoke*) rastro; (*of questions etc*) torrente *f* ▸VT (*Sch*) classificar ▸VI correr, fluir; **to ~ in/out** entrar/sair em massa
street [stri:t] N rua; **streetcar** (US) N bonde *m* (BR), eléctrico (PT); **street plan** N mapa *m*
strength [strɛŋθ] N força; (*of girder, knot etc*) firmeza, resistência; (*fig*) poder *m*; **strengthen** VT fortificar; (*fig*) fortalecer
strenuous ['strɛnjuəs] ADJ enérgico; (*determined*) tenaz
stress [strɛs] N pressão *f*; (*mental strain*) tensão *f*, stress *m*; (*emphasis*) ênfase *f*; (*Tech*) tensão ▸VT realçar, dar ênfase a; (*syllable*) acentuar; **stressed** ADJ (*tense*) estressado; (*syllable*) tônico
stretch [strɛtʃ] N (*of sand etc*) trecho, extensão *f* ▸VI espreguiçar-se; (*extend*): **to ~ to** *or* **as far as** estender-se até ▸VT estirar, esticar; (*fig: subj: job, task*) exigir o máximo de; **stretch out** VI esticar-se ▸VT (*arm etc*) esticar; (*spread*) estirar
stretcher ['strɛtʃə[r]] N maca, padiola
strict [strɪkt] ADJ (*person*) severo, rigoroso; (*meaning*) exato, estrito
stride [straɪd] (*pt* **strode**, *pp* **stridden**) N passo largo ▸VI andar a passos largos
strike [straɪk] (*pt, pp* **struck**) N greve *f*; (*of oil etc*) descoberta; (*attack*) ataque *m* ▸VT bater em; (*oil etc*) descobrir; (*deal*) fechar, acertar; (*fig*): **the thought** *or* **it ~s me that ...** me ocorre que ...; ▸VI estar em greve; (*attack: soldiers, illness*) atacar; (*: disaster*) assolar; (*clock*) bater; **on ~** em greve; **to ~ a match** acender um fósforo; **strike down** VT derrubar; **strike up** VT (*Mus*) começar a tocar; (*conversation, friendship*) travar; **striker** N grevista *m/f*; (*Sport*) atacante *m/f*; **striking** ADJ impressionante
string [strɪŋ] (*pt, pp* **strung**) N (*cord*) barbante *m* (BR), cordel *m* (PT); (*of beads*) cordão *m*; (*of onions*) réstia; (*Mus*) corda ▸VT: **to ~ out** esticar; **the strings** NPL (*Mus*) os instrumentos de corda; **to ~ together** (*words*) unir; (*ideas*) concatenar; **to get a job by pulling ~s** (*fig*) usar pistolão
strip [strɪp] N tira; (*of land*) faixa; (*of metal*) lâmina, tira ▸VT despir ▸VI despir-se
stripe [straɪp] N listra; (*Mil*) galão *m*; **striped** ADJ listrado, com listras
strive [straɪv] (*pt* **strove**, *pp* **striven**) VI: **to ~ for sth/to do sth** esforçar-se por *or* batalhar para algo/para fazer algo
strode [strəud] PT *of* **stride**
stroke [strəuk] N (*blow*) golpe *m*; (*Med*) derrame *m* cerebral; (*of paintbrush*) pincelada; (*Swimming: style*) nado ▸VT acariciar, afagar; **at a ~** de repente, de golpe
stroll [strəul] N volta, passeio ▸VI passear, dar uma volta; **stroller** (US) N carrinho (de criança)
strong [strɔŋ] ADJ forte; (*imagination*) fértil; (*personality*) forte, dominante; (*nerves*) de aço; **they are 50 ~** são em 50 pessoas; **stronghold** N fortaleza; (*fig*) baluarte *m*; **strongly** ADV

S

firmemente; (*push, defend*) vigorosamente; (*believe*) profundamente
strove [strəuv] PT *of* **strive**
struck [strʌk] PT, PP *of* **strike**
structure ['strʌktʃə'] N estrutura; (*building*) construção *f*
struggle ['strʌgl] N luta, contenda ▶ VI (*fight*) lutar; (*try hard*) batalhar
strung [strʌŋ] PT, PP *of* **string**
stub [stʌb] N (*of ticket etc*) canhoto; (*of cigarette*) toco, ponta; **to ~ one's toe** dar uma topada; **stub out** VT apagar
stubble ['stʌbl] N restolho; (*on chin*) barba por fazer
stubborn ['stʌbən] ADJ teimoso, cabeçudo, obstinado
stuck [stʌk] PT, PP *of* **stick** ▶ ADJ (*jammed*) emperrado
stud [stʌd] N (*shirt stud*) botão *m*; (*earring*) tarraxa, rosca; (*of boot*) cravo; (*also*: **~ farm**) fazenda de cavalos; (*also*: **~ horse**) garanhão *m* ▶ VT (*fig*): **~ded with** salpicado de
student ['stju:dənt] N estudante *m/f* ▶ ADJ estudantil; **student driver** (US) N aprendiz *m/f*
studio ['stju:dɪəu] N estúdio; (*sculptor's*) ateliê *m*
study ['stʌdɪ] N estudo; (*room*) sala de leitura *or* estudo ▶ VT estudar; (*examine*) examinar, investigar ▶ VI estudar; **studies** NPL (*subjects*) estudos *mpl*, matérias *fpl*
stuff [stʌf] N (*substance*) troço; (*things*) troços *mpl*, coisas *fpl* ▶ VT (*Culin*) rechear; (*animals*) empalhar; (*inf: push*) enfiar; **~ed toy** brinquedo de pelúcia; **stuffing** N recheio; **stuffy** ADJ (*room*) abafado, mal ventilado; (*person*) rabujento, melindroso
stumble ['stʌmbl] VI tropeçar; **to ~ across** *or* **on** (*fig*) topar com
stump [stʌmp] N (*of tree*) toco; (*of limb*) coto ▶ VT: **to be ~ed** ficar perplexo
stun [stʌn] VT (*subj: blow*) aturdir; (*: news*) pasmar
stung [stʌŋ] PT, PP *of* **sting**
stunk [stʌŋk] PP *of* **stink**
stunning ['stʌnɪŋ] ADJ (*news*) atordoante; (*appearance*) maravilhoso
stunt [stʌnt] N façanha sensacional; (*publicity stunt*) truque *m* publicitário
stupid ['stju:pɪd] ADJ estúpido, idiota
sturdy ['stə:dɪ] ADJ (*person*) robusto, firme; (*thing*) sólido
stutter ['stʌtə'] N gagueira, gaguez *f* ▶ VI gaguejar
style [staɪl] N estilo; (*elegance*) elegância; **stylish** ADJ elegante, chique
subconscious [sʌb'kɔnʃəs] ADJ do subconsciente
subject [*n* 'sʌbdʒɪkt, *vt* səb'dʒɛkt] N (*of king*) súdito(-a); (*theme*) assunto; (*Sch*) matéria; (*Ling*) sujeito ▶ VT: **to ~ sb to sth** submeter alguém a algo; **to be ~ to** estar sujeito a; **subjective** [səb'dʒɛktɪv] ADJ subjetivo; **subject matter** N assunto; (*content*) conteúdo
submarine ['sʌbməri:n] N submarino
submission [səb'mɪʃən] N submissão *f*; (*to committee*) petição *f*; (*of plan*) apresentação *f*, exposição *f*
submit [səb'mɪt] VT submeter ▶ VI submeter-se
subordinate [sə'bɔ:dɪnət] ADJ, N subordinado(-a)
subscribe [səb'skraɪb] VI subscrever; **to ~ to** (*opinion*) concordar com; (*fund*) contribuir para; (*newspaper*) assinar;

subscription [səb'skrɪpʃən] N assinatura
subsequent ['sʌbsɪkwənt] ADJ subsequente, posterior; **subsequently** ADV posteriormente, depois
subside [səb'saɪd] VI (*feeling, wind*) acalmar-se; (*flood*) baixar
subsidiary [səb'sɪdɪərɪ] ADJ secundário ▶ N (*also:* **~ company**) subsidiária
subsidize ['sʌbsɪdaɪz] VT subsidiar
subsidy ['sʌbsɪdɪ] N subsídio
substance ['sʌbstəns] N substância
substantial [səb'stænʃl] ADJ (*solid*) sólido; (*reward, meal*) substancial
substitute ['sʌbstɪtju:t] N substituto(-a); (*person*) suplente *m/f* ▶ VT: **to ~ A for B** substituir B por A
subtitled ['sʌbtaɪtld] ADJ (*film*) legendado
subtle ['sʌtl] ADJ sutil
subtract [səb'trækt] VT subtrair, deduzir
suburb ['sʌbə:b] N subúrbio; **suburban** [sə'bə:bən] ADJ suburbano; (*train etc*) de subúrbio
subway ['sʌbweɪ] N (BRIT) passagem *f* subterrânea; (US) metrô *m* (BR), metro(-politano) (PT)
succeed [sək'si:d] VI (*person*) ser bem sucedido, ter êxito; (*plan*) sair bem ▶ VT suceder a; **to ~ in doing** conseguir fazer
success [sək'sɛs] N êxito; (*hit, person*) sucesso; **successful** ADJ (*venture*) bem sucedido; (*writer*) de sucesso, bem sucedido; **to be successful (in doing)** conseguir (fazer); **successfully** ADV com sucesso, com êxito
succession [sək'sɛʃən] N sucessão *f*, série *f*; (*to throne*) sucessão
such [sʌtʃ] ADJ tal, semelhante; (*of that kind: singular*): **~ a book** um livro parecido, tal livro; (*: plural*): **~ books** tais livros; (*so much*): **~ courage** tanta coragem ▶ ADV tão; **~ a long trip** uma viagem tão longa; **~ a lot of** tanto; **~ as** tal como; **as ~** como tal; **such-and-such** ADJ tal e qual
suck [sʌk] VT chupar; (*breast*) mamar
sudden ['sʌdn] ADJ (*rapid*) repentino, súbito; (*unexpected*) imprevisto; **all of a ~** inesperadamente; **suddenly** ADV inesperadamente
sudoku [su'dəuku:] N sudoku *m*
sue [su:] VT processar
suede [sweɪd] N camurça
suffer ['sʌfəʳ] VT sofrer; (*bear*) aguentar, suportar ▶ VI sofrer, padecer; **to ~ from** sofrer de, estar com; **suffering** N sofrimento
sufficient [sə'fɪʃənt] ADJ suficiente, bastante
suffocate ['sʌfəkeɪt] VI sufocar(-se), asfixiar(-se)
sugar ['ʃugəʳ] N açúcar *m* ▶ VT pôr açúcar em, açucarar
suggest [sə'dʒɛst] VT sugerir; (*indicate*) indicar; **suggestion** N sugestão *f*; (*indication*) indicação *f*
suicide ['suɪsaɪd] N suicídio; (*person*) suicida *m/f*; *see also* **commit**; **suicide attack** N ataque *m* suicida, atentado suicida; **suicide bomber** N homem-bomba *m*, mulher-bomba *f*; **suicide bombing** N ataque *m* suicida
suit [su:t] N (*man's*) terno (BR), fato (PT); (*woman's*) conjunto;

S

(*Jur*) processo; (*Cards*) naipe *m* ▶ VT convir a; (*clothes*) ficar bem a; (*adapt*): **to ~ sth to** adaptar *or* acomodar algo a; **they are well ~ed** fazem um bom par; **suitable** ADJ conveniente; (*appropriate*) apropriado

suitcase ['su:tkeɪs] N mala

suite [swi:t] N (*of rooms*) conjunto de salas; (*Mus*) suite *f*; **a three-piece ~** um conjunto estofado (sofá e duas poltronas)

sulfur ['sʌlfə^r] (*US*) = **sulphur**

sulk [sʌlk] VI ficar emburrado, fazer beicinho *or* biquinho (*inf*)

sulphur ['sʌlfə^r], (*US*) **sulfur** N enxofre *m*

sultana [sʌl'tɑ:nə] N passa branca

sum [sʌm] N soma; (*calculation*) cálculo; **sum up** VT, VI resumir

summarize ['sʌməraɪz] VT resumir

summary ['sʌmərɪ] N resumo

summer ['sʌmə^r] N verão *m* ▶ ADJ de verão; **in (the) ~** no verão; **summertime** N (*season*) verão *m*

summit ['sʌmɪt] N topo, cume *m*; (*also*: **~ conference**) (conferência de) cúpula

summon ['sʌmən] VT (*person*) mandar chamar; (*meeting*) convocar; (*Jur: witness*) convocar; **summon up** VT concentrar

sun [sʌn] N sol *m*; **sunbathe** VI tomar sol; **sunblock** N bloqueador *m* solar; **sunburn** N queimadura do sol

Sunday ['sʌndɪ] N domingo

sunflower ['sʌnflauə^r] N girassol *m*

sung [sʌŋ] PP *of* **sing**

sunglasses ['sʌnglɑ:sɪz] NPL óculos *mpl* de sol

sunk [sʌŋk] PP *of* **sink**

sun: sunlight N (luz *f* do) sol *m*; **sunny** ADJ cheio de sol; (*day*) ensolarado, de sol; **sunrise** N nascer *m* do sol; **sun roof** N (*Aut*) teto solar; **sunscreen** N protetor *m* solar; **sunset** N pôr *m* do sol; **sunshade** N para-sol *m*; **sunshine** N (luz *f* do) sol *m*; **sunstroke** N insolação *f*; **suntan** N bronzeado; **suntan lotion** N loção *f* de bronzear

super ['su:pə^r] (*inf*) ADJ bacana (BR), muito giro (PT)

superb [su:'pə:b] ADJ excelente

superintendent [su:pərɪn'tɛndənt] N superintendente *m/f*; (*Police*) chefe *m/f* de polícia

superior [su'pɪərɪə^r] ADJ superior; (*smug*) desdenhoso ▶ N superior *m*

supermarket ['su:pəmɑ:kɪt] N supermercado

supernatural [su:pə'nætʃərəl] ADJ sobrenatural ▶ N: **the ~** o sobrenatural

superpower ['su:pəpauə^r] N (*Pol*) superpotência

superstitious [su:pə'stɪʃəs] ADJ supersticioso

supervise ['su:pəvaɪz] VT supervisar, supervisionar; **supervision** [su:pə'vɪʒən] N supervisão *f*; **supervisor** N supervisor(a) *m/f*; (*academic*) orientador(a) *m/f*

supper ['sʌpə^r] N jantar *m*; (*late evening*) ceia

supple ['sʌpl] ADJ flexível

supplement [*n* 'sʌplɪmənt, *vt* sʌplɪ'mɛnt] N suplemento ▶ VT suprir, completar

supplier [sə'plaɪə^r] N abastecedor(a) *m/f*, fornecedor(a) *m/f*

supply [sə'plaɪ] VT (*provide*): **to ~ sth (to sb)** fornecer algo (a alguém); (*equip*): **to ~ (with)** suprir (de) ▶ N fornecimento, provisão *f*;

(*stock*) estoque *m*; (*supplying*) abastecimento

support [sə'pɔ:t] N (*moral, financial etc*) apoio; (*Tech*) suporte *m* ▶ VT apoiar; (*financially*) manter; (*Tech: hold up*) sustentar; (*theory etc*) defender; **supporter** N (*Pol etc*) partidário(-a); (*Sport*) torcedor(a) *m/f*

suppose [sə'pəuz] VT supor; (*imagine*) imaginar; (*duty*): **to be ~d to do sth** dever fazer algo; **supposedly** [sə'pəuzɪdlɪ] ADV supostamente, pretensamente; **supposing** CONJ caso, supondo-se que

suppress [sə'prɛs] VT (*information*) suprimir; (*feelings, revolt*) reprimir; (*yawn*) conter

supreme [su'pri:m] ADJ supremo

surcharge ['sə:tʃɑ:dʒ] N sobretaxa

sure [ʃuəʳ] ADJ seguro; (*definite*) certo; (*aim*) certeiro; **to make ~ of sth/that** assegurar-se de algo/que; **~!** (*of course*) claro que sim!; **~ enough** efetivamente; **surely** ADV (*certainly*: US: *also*: **sure**) certamente

surf [sə:f] N (*waves*) ondas *fpl*, arrebentação *f*

surface ['sə:fɪs] N superfície *f* ▶ VT (*road*) revestir ▶ VI vir à superfície *or* à tona; (*fig: news, feeling*) vir à tona

surfboard ['sə:fbɔ:d] N prancha de surfe

surfer ['sə:fəʳ] N surfista *m/f*; (*on the Internet*) internauta *m/f*

surfing ['sə:fɪŋ] N surfe *m*

surge [sə:dʒ] N onda ▶ VI (*sea*) encapelar-se; (*people, vehicles*) precipitar-se; (*feeling*) aumentar repentinamente

surgeon ['sə:dʒən] N cirurgião(-giã) *m/f*

surgery ['sə:dʒərɪ] N cirurgia; (BRIT: *room*) consultório; (*also*: **~ hours**) horas *fpl* de consulta

surname ['sə:neɪm] N sobrenome *m* (BR), apelido (PT)

surplus ['sə:pləs] N excedente *m*; (*Comm*) superávit *m* ▶ ADJ excedente, de sobra

surprise [sə'praɪz] N surpresa ▶ VT surpreender; **surprising** ADJ surpreendente

surrender [sə'rɛndəʳ] N rendição *f*, entrega ▶ VI render-se, entregar-se

surround [sə'raund] VT circundar, rodear; (*Mil etc*) cercar; **surrounding** ADJ circundante, adjacente; **surroundings** NPL arredores *mpl*, cercanias *fpl*

surveillance [sə:'veɪləns] N vigilância

survey [*n* 'sə:veɪ, *vt* sə:'veɪ] N inspeção *f*; (*of habits etc*) pesquisa; (*of house*) inspeção *f*; (*of land*) levantamento ▶ VT observar, contemplar; (*land*) fazer um levantamento de; **surveyor** N (*of land*) agrimensor(a) *m/f*; (*of building*) inspetor(a) *m/f*

survival [sə'vaɪvl] N sobrevivência; (*relic*) remanescente *m*

survive [sə'vaɪv] VI sobreviver; (*custom etc*) perdurar ▶ VT sobreviver a; **survivor** N sobrevivente *m/f*

suspect [*adj, n* 'sʌspɛkt, *vt* səs'pɛkt] ADJ, N suspeito(-a) ▶ VT suspeitar, desconfiar

suspend [səs'pɛnd] VT suspender; **suspenders** NPL (BRIT) ligas *fpl*; (US) suspensórios *mpl*

suspense [səs'pɛns] N incerteza, ansiedade *f*; (*in film etc*) suspense *m*;

to keep sb in ~ manter alguém em suspense *or* na expectativa
suspension [səs'pɛnʃən] N suspensão *f*; (*of driving licence*) cassação *f*
suspicion [səs'pɪʃən] N suspeita; **suspicious** ADJ (*suspecting*) suspeitoso; (*causing suspicion*) suspeito
sustain [səs'teɪn] VT sustentar; (*suffer*) sofrer; **sustainable** ADJ sustentável
SUV N ABBR (= *sports utility vehicle*) SUV *m*
swallow ['swɔləu] N (*bird*) andorinha ▶ VT engolir, tragar; (*fig: story*) engolir; (*pride*) pôr de lado; (*one's words*) retirar; **swallow up** VT (*savings etc*) consumir
swam [swæm] PT *of* **swim**
swamp [swɔmp] N pântano, brejo ▶ VT atolar, inundar; (*fig*) assoberbar
swan [swɔn] N cisne *m*
swap [swɔp] N troca, permuta ▶ VT: **to ~ (for)** trocar (por); (*replace (with)*) substituir (por)
swarm [swɔ:m] N (*of bees*) enxame *m*; (*of people*) multidão *f* ▶ VI enxamear; aglomerar-se; (*place*): **to be ~ing with** estar apinhado de
sway [sweɪ] VI balançar-se, oscilar ▶ VT (*influence*) influenciar
swear [swɛə^r] (*pt* **swore**, *pp* **sworn**) VI (*curse*) xingar ▶ VT (*promise*) jurar; **swearword** N palavrão *m*
sweat [swɛt] N suor *m* ▶ VI suar
sweater N suéter *m or f* (BR), camisola (PT)
sweaty ADJ suado
Swede [swi:d] N sueco(-a)
swede [swi:d] N *tipo de nabo*
Sweden ['swi:dən] N Suécia; **Swedish** ADJ sueco ▶ N (*Ling*) sueco
sweep [swi:p] (*pt, pp* **swept**) N (*act*) varredura; (*also*: **chimney ~**) limpador *m* de chaminés ▶ VT varrer; (*with arm*) empurrar; (*subj: current*) arrastar; (*: fashion, craze*) espalhar-se por ▶ VI varrer; **sweep away** VT varrer; **sweep past** VI passar rapidamente; **sweep up** VI varrer
sweet [swi:t] N (*candy*) bala (BR), rebuçado (PT); (BRIT: *pudding*) sobremesa ▶ ADJ doce; (*fig: air*) fresco; (*: water, smell*) doce; (*: sound*) suave; (*: baby, kitten*) bonitinho; (*kind*) meigo; **sweetheart** N namorado(-a)
swell [swɛl] (*pt* **swelled**, *pp* **swollen** *or* **swelled**) N (*of sea*) vaga, onda ▶ ADJ (*US inf: excellent*) bacana ▶ VI (*increase*) aumentar; (*get stronger*) intensificar-se; (*also*: **~ up**) inchar(-se); **swelling** N (*Med*) inchação *f*
swept [swɛpt] PT, PP *of* **sweep**
swerve [swə:v] VI desviar-se
swift [swɪft] N (*bird*) andorinhão *m* ▶ ADJ rápido
swim [swɪm] (*pt* **swam**, *pp* **swum**) N: **to go for a ~** ir nadar ▶ VI nadar; (*head, room*) rodar ▶ VT atravessar a nado; (*distance*) percorrer (a nado); **swimmer** N nadador(a) *m/f*; **swimming** N natação *f*; **swimming costume** (BRIT) N (*woman's*) maiô *m* (BR), fato de banho (PT); (*man's*) calção *m* de banho (BR), calções *mpl* de banho (PT); **swimming pool** N piscina; **swimming trunks** NPL sunga (BR), calções *mpl* de banho (PT); **swimsuit** N maiô *m* (BR), fato de banho (PT)
swine flu ['swaɪn-] N gripe *f* suína
swing [swɪŋ] (*pt, pp* **swung**) N (*in playground*) balanço; (*movement*)

balanceio, oscilação *f*; (*change: in opinion*) mudança; virada; (*rhythm*) ritmo ▸ VT balançar; (*also*: **~ round**) girar, rodar ▸ VI oscilar; (*on swing*) balançar; (*also*: **~ round**) voltar-se bruscamente; **to be in full ~** estar a todo vapor
swirl [swəːl] VI redemoinhar
Swiss [swɪs] ADJ, N INV suíço(-a)
switch [swɪtʃ] N (*for light, radio etc*) interruptor *m*; (*change*) mudança ▸ VT (*change*) trocar; **switch off** VT apagar; (*engine*) desligar; **switch on** VT acender; ligar; **switchboard** N (*Tel*) mesa telefônica
Switzerland ['swɪtsələnd] N Suíça
swollen ['swəulən] PP *of* **swell**
swoop [swuːp] N (*by police etc*) batida ▸ VI (*also*: **~ down**) precipitar-se, cair
swop [swɔp] N, VT = **swap**
sword [sɔːd] N espada
swore [swɔːʳ] PT *of* **swear**
sworn [swɔːn] PP *of* **swear** ▸ ADJ (*statement*) sob juramento; (*enemy*) declarado
swum [swʌm] PP *of* **swim**
swung [swʌŋ] PT, PP *of* **swing**
syllable ['sɪləbl] N sílaba
syllabus ['sɪləbəs] N programa *m* de estudos
symbol ['sɪmbl] N símbolo
sympathetic [sɪmpə'θɛtɪk] ADJ (*understanding*) compreensivo; (*likeable*) agradável; (*supportive*): **~ to(wards)** solidário com
sympathize ['sɪmpəθaɪz] VI: **to ~ with** (*person*) compadecer-se de; (*sb's feelings*) compreender; (*cause*) simpatizar com
sympathy ['sɪmpəθɪ] N compaixão *f*; **sympathies** NPL (*tendencies*) simpatia; **in ~ with** em acordo com; (*strike*) em solidariedade com; **with our deepest ~** com nossos mais profundos pêsames
symphony ['sɪmfənɪ] N sinfonia
symptom ['sɪmptəm] N sintoma *m*; (*sign*) indício
syndicate ['sɪndɪkɪt] N sindicato; (*of newspapers*) cadeia
synthetic [sɪn'θɛtɪk] ADJ sintético
Syria ['sɪrɪə] N Síria
syringe [sɪ'rɪndʒ] N seringa
syrup ['sɪrəp] N xarope *m*; (*also*: **golden ~**) melaço
system ['sɪstəm] N sistema *m*; (*method*) método; (*Anat*) organismo; **systematic** [sɪstə'mætɪk] ADJ sistemático

S

t

tab [tæb] N lingueta, aba; (*label*) etiqueta; **to keep ~s on** (*fig*) vigiar

table ['teɪbl] N mesa ▶ VT (*motion etc*) apresentar; **to lay** *or* **set the ~** pôr a mesa; **~ of contents** índice *m*, sumário; **tablecloth** N toalha de mesa; **tablespoon** N colher *f* de sopa; (*also*: **tablespoonful**: *as measurement*) colherada

tablet ['tæblɪt] N (*Med*) comprimido; (*also*: **~ computer**) tablet *m*; (*of stone*) lápide *f*

table tennis N pingue-pongue *m*, tênis *m* de mesa

tabloid ['tæblɔɪd] N tabloide *m*; **tabloid press** N *ver nota*

O termo **tabloid press** refere-se aos jornais populares de formato meio jornal que apresentam muitas fotografias e adotam um estilo bastante conciso. O público-alvo desses jornais é composto por leitores que se interessam pelos fatos do dia que contenham um certo toque de escândalo; veja **quality (news)papers**.

tack [tæk] N (*nail*) tachinha, percevejo ▶ VT prender com tachinha; (*stitch*) alinhavar ▶ VI virar de bordo

tackle ['tækl] N (*gear*) equipamento; (*also*: **fishing ~**) apetrechos *mpl*; (*for lifting*) guincho; (*Football*) ato de tirar a bola de adversário ▶ VT (*difficulty*) atacar; (*challenge*: *person*) desafiar; (*grapple with*) atracar-se com; (*Football*) tirar a bola de

tacky ['tækɪ] ADJ pegajoso, grudento; (*inf*: *tasteless*) cafona

tact [tækt] N tato, diplomacia; **tactful** ADJ diplomático

tactics ['tæktɪks] N, NPL tática

tactless ['tæktlɪs] ADJ sem diplomacia

tag [tæg] N (*label*) etiqueta; **tag along** VI seguir

tail [teɪl] N rabo; (*of bird, comet, plane*) cauda; (*of shirt, coat*) aba ▶ VT (*follow*) seguir bem de perto; *see also* **head**; **tail away** VI diminuir gradualmente; **tail off** VI diminuir gradualmente

tailor ['teɪləʳ] N alfaiate *m*

take [teɪk] (*pt* **took**, *pp* **taken**) VT tomar; (*photo, holiday*) tirar; (*grab*) pegar (em); (*prize*) ganhar; (*effort, courage*) requerer, exigir; (*tolerate*) aguentar; (*accompany, bring, carry*: *person*) acompanhar, trazer; (: *thing*) trazer, carregar; (*exam*) fazer; (*passengers etc*): **it ~s 50 people** cabem 50 pessoas; **to ~ sth from** (*drawer etc*) tirar algo de; (*person*) pegar algo de; **I ~ it that ...** suponho que ...; **take after** VT FUS parecer-se com; **take apart** VT desmontar; **take away** VT (*extract*) tirar; (*carry off*) levar; (*subtract*) subtrair; **take back** VT (*return*) devolver; (*one's words*) retirar; **take down** VT (*building*) demolir; (*dismantle*) desmontar; (*letter etc*) tomar por escrito; **take in** VT (*deceive*) enganar; (*understand*) compreender; (*include*) abranger; (*lodger*) receber; **take off** VI (*Aviat*) decolar; (*go away*) ir-se ▶ VT (*remove*) tirar; **take on** VT (*work*) empreender; (*employee*) empregar; (*opponent*) desafiar; **take out** VT tirar; (*extract*) extrair; (*invite*) acompanhar; **take over** VT (*business*) assumir; (*country*) tomar posse de ▶ VI: **to ~ over from sb** suceder a alguém; **take to** VT FUS (*person*) simpatizar com; (*activity*) afeiçoar-se a; **to ~ to doing sth** criar o hábito de fazer algo; **take up** VT (*dress*) encurtar; (*time, space*) ocupar; (*hobby etc*) dedicar-se a; (*offer, challenge*) aceitar; **to ~ sb up on a suggestion/offer** aceitar a oferta/sugestão de alguém sobre algo; **takeaway** (BRIT) ADJ (*food*) para levar; **takeoff** N (*Aviat*) decolagem *f*; **takeover** N (*Comm*) aquisição *f* de controle; **takings** NPL (*Comm*) receita, renda

talc [tælk] N (*also*: **talcum powder**) talco

tale [teɪl] N (*story*) conto; (*account*) narrativa; **to tell ~s** (*fig: lie*) dizer mentiras

talent ['tælənt] N talento; **talented** ADJ talentoso

talk [tɔ:k] N conversa, fala; (*gossip*) mexerico, fofocas *fpl*; (*conversation*) conversa, conversação *f* ▶ VI falar; **talks** NPL (*Pol etc*) negociações *fpl*; **to ~ about** falar sobre; **to ~ sb into doing sth** convencer alguém a fazer algo; **to ~ sb out of doing sth** dissuadir alguém de fazer algo; **to ~ shop** falar sobre negócios/questões profissionais; **talk over** VT discutir

tall [tɔ:l] ADJ alto; **to be 6 feet ~** medir 6 pés, ter 6 pés de altura

tame [teɪm] ADJ domesticado; (*fig: story, style*) sem graça, insípido

tamper ['tæmpə^r] VI: **to ~ with** mexer em

tampon ['tæmpɔn] N tampão *m*

tan [tæn] N (*also*: **sun~**) bronzeado ▶ VI bronzear-se ▶ ADJ (*colour*) bronzeado, marrom claro

tangerine [tændʒə'ri:n] N tangerina, mexerica

tangle ['tæŋgl] N emaranhado; **to get in(to) a ~** meter-se num rolo

tank [tæŋk] N depósito, tanque *m*; (*for fish*) aquário; (*Mil*) tanque *m*

tanker ['tæŋkə^r] N (*ship*) navio-tanque *m*; (*truck*) caminhão-tanque *m*

tantrum ['tæntrəm] N chilique *m*, acesso (de raiva)

tap [tæp] N (*on sink etc*) torneira; (*gentle blow*) palmadinha; (*gas tap*) chave *f* ▶ VT dar palmadinha em, bater de leve; (*resources*) utilizar, explorar; (*telephone*) grampear; **on ~** disponível

tape [teɪp] N fita; (*also*: **magnetic ~**) fita magnética; (*sticky tape*) fita adesiva ▶ VT (*record*) gravar (em fita); (*stick with tape*) colar; **tape measure** N fita métrica, trena

tar [tɑ:^r] N alcatrão *m*

target ['tɑ:gɪt] N alvo

tariff ['tærɪf] N tarifa

tarmac ['tɑ:mæk] N (BRIT: *on road*) macadame *m*; (*Aviat*) pista

tarpaulin [tɑ:'pɔ:lɪn] N lona alcatroada

t

tart [tɑ:t] N (*Culin*) torta; (BRIT *inf, pej: woman*) piranha ▶ ADJ (*flavour*) ácido, azedo; **tart up** (*inf*) VT arrumar, dar um jeito em; **to ~ o.s. up** arrumar-se; (*pej*) empetecar-se
tartan ['tɑ:tn] N pano escocês axadrezado, tartan *m* ▶ ADJ axadrezado
tartar ['tɑ:tər] N (*on teeth*) tártaro
taste [teɪst] N gosto; (*also*: **after~**) gosto residual; (*sample, fig*) amostra, ideia ▶ VT provar; (*test*) experimentar ▶ VI: **to ~ of** *or* **like** ter gosto *or* sabor de; **you can ~ the garlic (in it)** sente-se o gosto de alho; **in good/bad ~** de bom/mau gosto; **tasteful** ADJ de bom gosto; **tasteless** ADJ insípido, insosso; (*remark*) de mau gosto; **tasty** ADJ saboroso, delicioso
tatters ['tætəz] NPL: **in ~** (*clothes*) em farrapos; (*papers etc*) em pedaços
tattoo [tə'tu:] N tatuagem *f*; (*spectacle*) espetáculo militar ▶ VT tatuar
taught [tɔ:t] PT, PP *of* **teach**
taunt [tɔ:nt] N zombaria, escárnio ▶ VT zombar de, mofar de
Taurus ['tɔ:rəs] N Touro
taut [tɔ:t] ADJ esticado
tax [tæks] N imposto ▶ VT tributar; (*fig: test*) sobrecarregar; (*: patience*) esgotar; **tax-free** ADJ isento de impostos
taxi ['tæksɪ] N táxi *m* ▶ VI (*Aviat*) taxiar; **taxi driver** N motorista *m/f* de táxi; **taxi rank** (BRIT) N ponto de táxi; **taxi stand** N ponto de táxi
tax: tax payer N contribuinte *m/f*; **tax return** N declaração *f* de rendimentos
TB ABBR *of* **tuberculosis**
tea [ti:] N chá *m*; (BRIT: *meal*) refeição *f* à noite; **high ~** (BRIT) ajantarado; **tea bag** N saquinho (BR) *or* carteira (PT) de chá; **tea break** (BRIT) N pausa (para o chá)
teach [ti:tʃ] (*pt, pp* **taught**) VT: **to ~ sb sth, ~ sth to sb** ensinar algo a alguém; (*in school*) lecionar ▶ VI ensinar; (*be a teacher*) lecionar; **teacher** N professor(a) *m/f*; **teaching** N ensino; (*as profession*) magistério
teacup ['ti:kʌp] N xícara (BR) *or* chávena (PT) de chá
team [ti:m] N (*Sport*) time *m* (BR), equipa (PT); (*group*) equipe *f* (BR), equipa (PT); (*of animals*) parelha
teapot ['ti:pɔt] N bule *m* de chá
tear¹ [tɪər] N lágrima; **in ~s** chorando, em lágrimas
tear² [tɛər] (*pt* **tore**, *pp* **torn**) N rasgão *m* ▶ VT rasgar ▶ VI rasgar-se; **tear along** VI (*rush*) precipitar-se; **tear up** VT rasgar
tearful ['tɪəful] ADJ choroso
tear gas N gás *m* lacrimogênio
tearoom ['ti:ru:m] N salão *m* de chá
tease [ti:z] VT implicar com
teaspoon ['ti:spu:n] N colher *f* de chá; (*also*: **~ful**: *as measurement*) (conteúdo de) colher de chá
teatime ['ti:taɪm] N hora do chá
tea towel (BRIT) N pano de prato
technical ['tɛknɪkl] ADJ técnico
technician [tɛk'nɪʃn] N técnico(-a)
technique [tɛk'ni:k] N técnica
technology [tɛk'nɔlədʒɪ] N tecnologia
teddy ['tɛdɪ], **teddy bear** N ursinho de pelúcia
tedious ['ti:dɪəs] ADJ maçante, chato
teenage ['ti:neɪdʒ] ADJ (*fashions etc*) de *or* para adolescentes; **teenager** N adolescente *m/f*, jovem *m/f*

teens [ti:nz] NPL: **to be in one's ~** estar entre os 13 e 19 anos, estar na adolescência
teeth [ti:θ] NPL *of* **tooth**
teetotal ['ti:'təutl] ADJ abstêmio
teleconferencing ['telıkɔnfərənsıŋ] N teleconferência *f*
telegram ['tɛlıgræm] N telegrama *m*
telephone ['tɛlıfəun] N telefone *m* ▶ VT (*person*) telefonar para; (*message*) telefonar; **to be on the ~** (BRIT), **to have a ~** (*subscriber*) ter telefone; **to be on the ~** (*be speaking*) estar falando no telefone; **telephone booth**, (BRIT) **telephone box** N cabine *f* telefônica; **telephone call** N telefonema *m*; **telephone directory** N lista telefônica, catálogo (BR); **telephone number** N (número de) telefone *m*
telesales ['tɛlıseılz] NPL televendas *fpl*
telescope ['tɛlıskəup] N telescópio
television ['tɛlıvıʒən] N televisão *f*; **on ~** na televisão
tell [tɛl] (*pt, pp* **told**) VT dizer; (*relate: story*) contar; (*distinguish*): **to ~ sth from** distinguir algo de ▶ VI (*have effect*) ter efeito; (*talk*): **to ~ (of)** falar (de *or* em); **to ~ sb to do sth** dizer para alguém fazer algo; **tell off** VT repreender
telly ['tɛlı] (BRIT *inf*) N ABBR = **television**
temp [tɛmp] (BRIT *inf*) N temporário(-a) ▶ VI trabalhar como temporário(-a)
temper ['tɛmpəʳ] N (*nature*) temperamento; (*mood*) humor *m*; (*fit of anger*) cólera ▶ VT (*moderate*) moderar; **to be in a ~** estar de mau humor; **to lose one's ~** perder a paciência *or* a calma, ficar zangado
temperament ['tɛmprəmənt] N temperamento; **temperamental** [tɛmprə'mɛntl] ADJ temperamental
temperature ['tɛmprətʃəʳ] N temperatura; **to have** *or* **run a ~** ter febre
temple ['tɛmpl] N (*building*) templo; (*Anat*) têmpora
temporary ['tɛmpərərı] ADJ temporário; (*passing*) transitório
tempt [tɛmpt] VT tentar; **tempting** ['tɛmptıŋ] ADJ tentador(a)
ten [tɛn] NUM dez; *see also* **five**
tenant ['tɛnənt] N inquilino(-a), locatário(-a)
tend [tɛnd] VT (*sick etc*) cuidar de ▶ VI: **to ~ to do sth** tender a fazer algo
tendency ['tɛndənsı] N tendência
tender ['tɛndəʳ] ADJ terno; (*age*) tenro; (*sore*) sensível, dolorido; (*meat*) macio ▶ N (*Comm: offer*) oferta, proposta; (*money*): **legal ~** moeda corrente *or* legal ▶ VT oferecer; **to ~ one's resignation** pedir demissão
tennis ['tɛnıs] N tênis *m*; **tennis ball** N bola de tênis; **tennis court** N quadra de tênis; **tennis player** N jogador(a) *m/f* de tênis; **tennis racket** N raquete *f* de tênis
tenor ['tɛnəʳ] N (*Mus*) tenor *m*
tense [tɛns] ADJ tenso; (*muscle*) rígido, teso ▶ N (*Ling*) tempo
tension ['tɛnʃən] N tensão *f*
tent [tɛnt] N tenda, barraca
tentative ['tɛntətıv] ADJ provisório, tentativo; (*person*) hesitante, indeciso

tenth [tɛnθ] NUM décimo
tent peg N estaca
tent pole N pau *m*
tepid ['tɛpɪd] ADJ tépido, morno
term [tə:m] N (*word, expression*) termo, expressão *f*; (*period*) período; (*Sch*) trimestre *m* ▶ VT denominar; **terms** NPL (*conditions*) condições *fpl*; (*Comm*) cláusulas *fpl*, termos *mpl*; **in the short/long ~** a curto/longo prazo; **to be on good ~s with sb** dar-se bem com alguém; **to come to ~s with** aceitar
terminal ['tə:mɪnl] ADJ incurável ▶ N (*Elec*) borne *m*; (BRIT: *also*: **air ~**) terminal *m*; (*for oil, ore etc, also: Comput*) terminal *m*; (BRIT: *also*: **coach ~**) estação *f* rodoviária
terminate ['tə:mɪneɪt] VT terminar; **to ~ a pregnancy** fazer um aborto
terminus ['tə:mɪnəs] (*pl* **termini**) N terminal *m*
terrace ['tɛrəs] N terraço; (BRIT: *row of houses*) lance *m* de casas; **the terraces** NPL (BRIT *Sport*) a arquibancada (BR), a geral (PT); **terraced** ADJ (*house*) ladeado por outras casas; (*garden*) em dois níveis
terrain [tɛ'reɪn] N terreno
terrible ['tɛrɪbl] ADJ terrível, horroroso; (*conditions*) precário; (*inf: awful*) terrível; **terribly** ADV terrivelmente; (*very badly*) pessimamente
terrific [tə'rɪfɪk] ADJ terrível, magnífico; (*wonderful*) maravilhoso, sensacional
terrify ['tɛrɪfaɪ] VT apavorar
territory ['tɛrɪtərɪ] N território
terror ['tɛrə^r] N terror *m*; **terrorist** N terrorista *m/f*
test [tɛst] N (*trial, check*) prova, ensaio; (*of courage etc, Chem*) prova; (*Med*) exame *m*; (*exam*) teste *m*, prova; (*also*: **driving ~**) exame de motorista ▶ VT testar, pôr à prova
testicle ['tɛstɪkl] N testículo
testify ['tɛstɪfaɪ] VI (*Jur*) depor, testemunhar; **to ~ to sth** atestar algo; testemunhar algo
testimony ['tɛstɪmənɪ] N (*Jur*) testemunho, depoimento; **to be (a) ~ to** ser uma prova de
test match N (*Cricket, Rugby*) jogo internacional
test tube N proveta, tubo de ensaio
tetanus ['tɛtənəs] N tétano
text [tɛkst] N texto; (*also*: **~ message**) mensagem *f* de texto, torpedo (*inf*) ▶ VT mandar uma mensagem de texto *or* (*inf*) um torpedo para; **textbook** N livro didático; (*Sch*) livro escolar; **text message** N mensagem *f* de texto, torpedo (*inf*)
texture ['tɛkstʃə^r] N textura
Thailand ['taɪlænd] N Tailândia
Thames [tɛmz] N: **the ~** o Tâmisa (BR), o Tamisa (PT)
than [ðæn, ðən] CONJ (*in comparisons*) do que; **more ~ 10** mais de 10; **I have more/less ~ you** tenho mais/menos do que você; **she has more apples ~ pears** ela tem mais maçãs do que peras; **she is older ~ you think** ela é mais velha do que você pensa
thank [θæŋk] VT agradecer; **~ you (very much)** muito obrigado(-a); **thanks** NPL agradecimentos *mpl* ▶ EXCL obrigado(-a)!
Thanksgiving ['θæŋksgɪvɪŋ], **Thanksgiving Day** N Dia *m* de Ação de Graças

> O feriado de Ação de graças (**Thanksgiving Day**) nos Estados Unidos, quarta quinta-feira do mês de

novembro, é o dia em que se comemora a boa colheita feita pelos peregrinos originários da Grã-Bretanha em 1621; tradicionalmente, é um dia em que se agradece a Deus e se organiza um grande banquete. Uma festa semelhante é celebrada no Canadá na segunda segunda-feira de outubro.

KEYWORD

that [ðæt, ðət] (*pl* **those**) ADJ (*demonstrative*) esse/essa; (*more remote*) aquele/aquela; **that man/woman/book** aquele homem/aquela mulher/aquele livro; **that one** esse/essa
▶ PRON **1** (*demonstrative*) esse/essa, aquele/aquela; (*neuter*) isso, aquilo; **who's/what's that?** quem é?/o que é isso?; **is that you?** é você?; **I prefer this to that** eu prefiro isto a aquilo; **that's what he said** foi isso o que ele disse; **that is (to say)** isto é, quer dizer
2 (*relative, direct: thing, person*) que; (*: person*) quem; (*relative, indirect: thing, person*) o/a qual *sg*, os/as quais *pl*; (*: person*) quem; **the book (that) I read** o livro que eu li; **the box (that) I put it in** a caixa na qual eu o coloquei; **the man (that) I spoke to** o homem com quem *or* o qual falei
3 (*relative, of time*): **on the day that he came** no dia em que ele veio
▶ CONJ que; **she suggested that I phone you** ela sugeriu que eu telefonasse para você
▶ ADV (*demonstrative*): **I can't work that much** não posso trabalhar tanto; **I didn't realize it was that bad** não pensei que fôsse tão ruim; **that high** dessa altura, até essa altura

thatched [θætʃt] ADJ (*roof*) de sapê; **~ cottage** chalé *m* com telhado de sapê *or* de colmo
thaw [θɔː] N degelo ▶ VI (*ice*) derreter-se; (*food*) descongelar-se ▶ VT (*food*) descongelar

KEYWORD

the [ðiː, ðə] DEF ART **1** (*gen: singular*) o/a; (*: plural*) os/as; **the books/children are in the library** os livros/as crianças estão na biblioteca; **she put it on the table** ela colocou-o na mesa; **he took it from the drawer** ele tirou isto da gaveta; **to play the piano/violin** tocar piano/violino; **I'm going to the cinema** vou ao cinema
2 (+ *adj to form n*): **the rich and the poor** os ricos e os pobres; **to attempt the impossible** tentar o impossível
3 (*in titles*): **Richard the Second** Ricardo II; **Peter the Great** Pedro o Grande
4 (*in comparisons*): **the more he works, the more he earns** quanto mais ele trabalha, mais ele ganha

theatre [ˈθɪətəʳ], (*US*) **theater** N teatro; (*Med: also*: **operating ~**) sala de operação
theft [θɛft] N roubo
their [ðɛəʳ] ADJ seu/sua, deles/delas; **theirs** PRON (o) seu/(a) sua
them [ðɛm, ðəm] PRON (*direct*) os/as; (*indirect*) lhes; (*stressed, after prep*) a eles/a elas

t

theme [θi:m] N tema *m*; **theme park** N *parque de diversões em torno de um único tema*
themselves [ðəm'sɛlvz] PRON (*subject*) eles mesmos/elas mesmas; se; (*after prep*) si (mesmos/as)
then [ðɛn] ADV (*at that time*) então; (*next*) em seguida; (*later*) logo, depois; (*and also*) além disso ▶ CONJ (*therefore*) então, nesse caso, portanto ▶ ADJ: **the ~ president** o então presidente; **by ~** (*past*) até então; (*future*) até lá; **from ~ on** a partir de então
theology [θɪ'ɔlədʒɪ] N teologia
theory ['θɪərɪ] N teoria; **in ~** em teoria, teoricamente
therapy ['θɛrəpɪ] N terapia

KEYWORD

there [ðɛə^r] ADV **1**: **there is, there are** há, tem; **there are 3 of them** são três; **there is no-one here/no bread left** não tem ninguém aqui/não tem mais pão; **there has been an accident** houve um acidente
2 (*referring to place*) aí, ali, lá; **put it in/on/up/down there** põe isto lá dentro/cima/em cima/embaixo; **I want that book there** quero aquele livro lá; **there he is!** lá está ele!
3: **there, there!** (*esp to child*) calma!

thereabouts ['ðɛərəbauts] ADV por aí; (*amount*) aproximadamente
thereafter [ðɛər'ɑ:ftə^r] ADV depois disso
thereby ['ðɛəbaɪ] ADV assim, deste modo
therefore ['ðɛəfɔ:] ADV portanto
there's [ðɛəz] = **there is**; = **there has**
thermal ['θə:ml] ADJ térmico
thermometer [θə'mɔmɪtə^r] N termômetro
thermostat ['θə:məustæt] N termostato
these [ði:z] PL ADJ, PRON estes/estas
thesis ['θi:sɪs] (*pl* **theses**) N tese *f*
they [ðeɪ] PRON PL eles/elas; **~ say that ...** (*it is said that*) diz-se que ..., dizem que ...; **they'd** = **they had**; = **they would**; **they'll** = **they shall**; = **they will**; **they've** = **they have**
thick [θɪk] ADJ espesso; (*mud, fog, forest*) denso; (*sauce*) grosso; (*stupid*) burro ▶ N: **in the ~ of the battle** em plena batalha; **it's 20 cm ~** tem 20 cm de espessura;
thicken VI (*fog*) adensar-se; (*plot etc*) complicar-se ▶ VT engrossar;
thickness N espessura, grossura
thief [θi:f] (*pl* **thieves**) N ladrão/ladra *m/f*
thigh [θaɪ] N coxa
thin [θɪn] ADJ magro; (*slice, line, book*) fino; (*light*) leve; (*hair*) ralo; (*crowd*) pequeno; (*soup, sauce*) aguado ▶ VT (*also*: **~ down**) diluir
thing [θɪŋ] N coisa; (*object*) negócio; (*matter*) assunto, negócio; (*mania*) mania; **things** NPL (*belongings*) pertences *mpl*; **to have a ~ about sb/sth** ser vidrado em alguém/algo; **the best ~ would be to ...** o melhor seria ...; **how are ~s?** como vai?, tudo bem?; **she's got a ~ about ...** ela detesta ...; **poor ~!** coitadinho(-a)!
think [θɪŋk] (*pt, pp* **thought**) VI pensar; (*believe*) achar ▶ VT pensar, achar; (*imagine*) imaginar; **what did you ~ of them?** o que você achou deles?; **to ~ about sth/sb** pensar em algo/alguém; **I'll ~ about it** vou pensar sobre isso;

to ~ of doing sth pensar em fazer algo; **I ~ so/not** acho que sim/não; **to ~ well of sb** fazer bom juízo de alguém; **think over** VT refletir sobre, meditar sobre; **think up** VT inventar, bolar

third [θə:d] ADJ terceiro ▶ N terceiro(-a); (*fraction*) terço; (*Aut*) terceira; (*Sch: degree*) terceira categoria; **thirdly** ADV em terceiro lugar; **third party insurance** N seguro contra terceiros; **Third World** N: **the Third World** o Terceiro Mundo

thirst [θə:st] N sede *f*; **thirsty** ADJ (*person*) sedento, com sede; (*work*) que dá sede; **to be thirsty** estar com sede

thirteen ['θə:'ti:n] NUM treze

thirty ['θə:tɪ] NUM trinta

KEYWORD

this [ðɪs] (*pl* **these**) ADJ (*demonstrative*) este/esta; **this man/woman/book** este homem/esta mulher/este livro; **these people/children/records** estas pessoas/crianças/estes discos; **this one** este aqui ▶ PRON (*demonstrative*) este/esta; (*neuter*) isto; **who/what is this?** quem é esse?/o que é isso?; **this is where I live** é aqui que eu moro; **this is Mr Brown** este é o Sr Brown; (*on phone*) aqui é o Sr Brown ▶ ADV (*demonstrative*): **this high** desta altura; **this long** deste comprimento; **we can't stop now we've gone this far** não podemos parar agora que fomos tão longe

thistle ['θɪsl] N cardo

thorn [θɔ:n] N espinho

thorough ['θʌrə] ADJ (*search*) minucioso; (*knowledge, research, person*) metódico, profundo; **thoroughly** ADV minuciosamente; (*search*) profundamente; (*wash*) completamente; (*very*) muito

those [ðəuz] PRON PL, ADJ esses/essas

though [ðəu] CONJ embora, se bem que ▶ ADV no entanto

thought [θɔ:t] PT, PP *of* **think** ▶ N pensamento; (*idea*) ideia; (*opinion*) opinião *f*; (*reflection*) reflexão *f*; **thoughtful** ADJ pensativo; (*serious*) sério; (*considerate*) atencioso; **thoughtless** ADJ desatencioso; (*words, person*) inconsequente

thousand ['θauzənd] NUM mil; **two ~** dois mil; **~s (of)** milhares *mpl* (de); **thousandth** ADJ milésimo

thrash [θræʃ] VT surrar, malhar; (*defeat*) derrotar; **thrash about** VI debater-se; **thrash out** VT discutir exaustivamente

thread [θrɛd] N fio, linha; (*of screw*) rosca ▶ VT (*needle*) enfiar

threat [θrɛt] N ameaça; **threaten** VI ameaçar ▶ VT: **to threaten sb with sth/to do** ameaçar alguém com algo/de fazer

three [θri:] NUM três; **three-dimensional** ADJ tridimensional, em três dimensões; **three-piece suit** N terno (3 peças) (BR), fato de 3 peças (PT)

threshold ['θrɛʃhəuld] N limiar *m*

threw [θru:] PT *of* **throw**

thrill [θrɪl] N emoção *f*; (*shudder*) estremecimento ▶ VT emocionar, vibrar; **to be ~ed** (*with gift etc*) estar emocionado; **thriller** N romance *m or* filme *m* de suspense; **thrilling** ADJ emocionante

throat [θrəut] N garganta; **to have a sore ~** estar com dor de garganta

throb [θrɔb] N (*of heart*) batida; (*of engine*) vibração *f*; (*of pain*) latejo ▶ VI (*heart*) bater, palpitar; (*pain*) dar pontadas; (*engine*) vibrar

throne [θrəun] N trono

through [θru:] PREP por, através de; (*time*) durante; (*by means of*) por meio de, por intermédio de; (*owing to*) devido a ▶ ADJ (*ticket, train*) direto ▶ ADV através; **to put sb ~ to sb** (*Tel*) ligar alguém com alguém; **to be ~** (*Tel*) estar na linha; (*have finished*) acabar; **"no ~ road"** "rua sem saída"; **I'm halfway ~ the book** estou na metade do livro; **throughout** PREP (*place*) por todo(-a); (*time*) durante todo(-a) ▶ ADV por *or* em todas as partes

throw [θrəu] (*pt* **threw**, *pp* **thrown**) N arremesso, tiro; (*Sport*) lançamento ▶ VT jogar, atirar; (*Sport*) lançar; (*rider*) derrubar; (*fig*) desconcertar; **to ~ a party** dar uma festa; **throw away** VT (*dispose of*) jogar fora; (*waste*) desperdiçar; **throw off** VT desfazer-se de; (*habit, cold*) livrar-se; **throw out** VT expulsar; (*rubbish*) jogar fora; (*idea*) rejeitar; **throw up** VI vomitar, botar para fora

thru [θru:] (US) PREP, ADJ, ADV = **through**

thrush [θrʌʃ] N (*Zool*) tordo

thrust [θrʌst] (*pt, pp* **thrust**) N impulso; (*Tech*) empuxo ▶ VT empurrar

thud [θʌd] N baque *m*, som *m* surdo

thug [θʌg] N facínora *m/f*

thumb [θʌm] N (*Anat*) polegar *m*; **to ~ a lift** pegar carona (BR), arranjar uma boleia (PT); **thumb through** VT FUS folhear; **thumbtack** (US) N percevejo, tachinha

thump [θʌmp] N murro, pancada; (*sound*) baque *m* ▶ VT dar um murro em ▶ VI bater

thunder ['θʌndə^r] N trovão *m* ▶ VI trovejar; (*train etc*): **to ~ past** passar como um raio; **thunderstorm** N tempestade *f* com trovoada, temporal *m*

Thursday ['θə:zdɪ] N quinta-feira

thyme [taɪm] N tomilho

tick [tɪk] N (*of clock*) tique-taque *m*; (*mark*) tique *m*, marca; (*Zool*) carrapato; (BRIT *inf*): **in a ~** num instante ▶ VI fazer tique-taque ▶ VT marcar, ticar; **tick off** VT assinalar, ticar; (*person*) dar uma bronca em; **tick over** (BRIT) VI (*engine*) funcionar em marcha lenta; (*fig*) ir indo

ticket ['tɪkɪt] N (*for bus, plane*) passagem *f*; (*for theatre, raffle*) bilhete *m*; (*for cinema*) entrada; (*in shop: on goods*) etiqueta; (*for library*) cartão *m*; (*also*: **parking ~**: *fine*) multa; **to get a (parking) ~** (*Aut*) ganhar uma multa (por estacionamento ilegal); **ticket barrier** (BRIT) N (*Rail*) catraca de embarque/desembarque; **ticket collector** N revisor(a) *m/f*; **ticket office** N bilheteria (BR), bilheteira (PT)

tickle ['tɪkl] VT fazer cócegas em ▶ VI fazer cócegas; **ticklish** ADJ coceguento; (*problem*) delicado

tide [taɪd] N maré *f*; (*fig*) curso; **high/low ~** maré alta/baixa; **the ~ of public opinion** a corrente da opinião pública; **tide over** VT ajudar num período difícil

tidy ['taɪdɪ] ADJ (*room*) arrumado; (*dress, work*) limpo; (*person*) bem arrumado ▶ VT (*also*: ~ **up**) pôr em ordem, arrumar

tie [taɪ] N (*string etc*) fita, corda; (BRIT: *also*: **neck~**) gravata; (*fig: link*) vínculo, laço; (*Sport: draw*) empate *m* ▶ VT amarrar ▶ VI (*Sport*) empatar; **to ~ in a bow** dar um laço em; **to ~ a knot in sth** dar um nó em algo; **tie down** VT amarrar; (*fig: restrict*) limitar, restringir; (: *to date, price etc*) obrigar; **tie up** VT embrulhar; (*dog*) prender; (*boat, prisoner etc*) amarrar; (*arrangements*) concluir; **to be ~d up** estar ocupado

tier [tɪəʳ] N fileira; (*of cake*) camada

tiger ['taɪgəʳ] N tigre *m*

tight [taɪt] ADJ (*rope*) esticado, firme; (*money*) escasso; (*clothes, shoes*) justo; (*bend*) fechado; rigoroso; (*inf: drunk*) bêbado ▶ ADV (*squeeze*) bem forte; (*shut*) hermeticamente; **tighten** VT (*rope*) esticar; (*screw, grip*) apertar; (*security*) aumentar ▶ VI esticar-se; apertar-se; **tightly** ADV firmemente

tile [taɪl] N (*on roof*) telha; (*on floor*) ladrilho; (*on wall*) azulejo, ladrilho

till [tɪl] N caixa (registradora) ▶ VT (*land*) cultivar ▶ PREP, CONJ = **until**

tilt [tɪlt] VT inclinar ▶ VI inclinar-se

timber ['tɪmbəʳ] N (*material*) madeira; (*trees*) mata, floresta

time [taɪm] N tempo; (*epoch: often pl*) época; (*by clock*) hora; (*moment*) momento; (*occasion*) vez *f*; (*Mus*) compasso ▶ VT calcular *or* medir o tempo de; (*visit etc*) escolher o momento para; **a long ~** muito tempo; **4 at a ~** quatro de uma vez; **for the ~ being** por enquanto; **from ~ to ~** de vez em quando; **at ~s** às vezes; **in ~** (*soon enough*) a tempo; (*after some time*) com o tempo; (*Mus*) no compasso; **in a week's ~** dentro de uma semana; **in no ~** num abrir e fechar de olhos; **any ~** a qualquer hora; **on ~** na hora; **5 ~s 5 is 25** 5 vezes 5 são 25; **what ~ is it?** que horas são?; **to have a good ~** divertir-se; **timely** ADJ oportuno; **timetable** N horário; **time zone** N fuso horário

timid ['tɪmɪd] ADJ tímido

timing ['taɪmɪŋ] N escolha do momento; (*Sport*) cronometragem *f*; **the ~ of his resignation** o momento que escolheu para se demitir

tin [tɪn] N estanho; (*also*: ~ **plate**) folha-de-flandres *f*; (BRIT: *can*) lata

tingle ['tɪŋgl] VI formigar

tinned [tɪnd] (BRIT) ADJ (*food*) em lata, em conserva

tin opener (BRIT) N abridor *m* de latas (BR), abre-latas *m inv* (PT)

tinsel ['tɪnsl] N ouropel *m*

tint [tɪnt] N matiz *m*; (*for hair*) tintura, tinta; **tinted** ADJ (*hair*) pintado; (*spectacles, glass*) fumê *inv*

tiny ['taɪnɪ] ADJ pequenininho, minúsculo

tip [tɪp] N ponta; (*gratuity*) gorjeta; (BRIT: *for rubbish*) depósito; (*advice*) dica ▶ VT dar uma gorjeta a; (*tilt*) inclinar; (*overturn: also*: ~ **over**) virar, emborcar; (*empty: also*: ~ **out**) esvaziar, entornar

tiptoe ['tɪptəu] N: **on ~** na ponta dos pés

tire ['taɪəʳ] N (US) = **tyre** ▶ VT cansar ▶ VI cansar-se; (*become bored*) chatear-se; **tired** ADJ cansado; **to be tired of sth** estar farto *or* cheio de algo; **tiring** ADJ cansativo

t

tissue ['tɪʃu:] N tecido; (*paper handkerchief*) lenço de papel; **tissue paper** N papel *m* de seda

tit [tɪt] N (*bird*) passarinho; **to give ~ for tat** pagar na mesma moeda

title ['taɪtl] N título

TM N ABBR = **trademark**

KEYWORD

to [tu:, tə] PREP **1** (*direction*) a, para; (*towards*) para; **to go to France/London/school/the station** ir à França/a Londres/ao colégio/à estação; **to go to Lígia's/the doctor's** ir à casa da Lígia/ao médico; **the road to Edinburgh** a estrada para Edinburgo; **to the left/right** à esquerda/direita
2 (*as far as*) até; **to count to 10** contar até 10; **from 40 to 50 people** de 40 a 50 pessoas
3 (*with expressions of time*): **a quarter to 5** quinze para as 5 (BR), 5 menos um quarto (PT)
4 (*for, or*) de, para; **the key to the front door** a chave da porta da frente; **a letter to his wife** uma carta para a sua mulher
5 (*expressing indirect object*): **to give sth to sb** dar algo a alguém; **to talk to sb** falar com alguém; **I sold it to a friend** vendi isto para um amigo; **to cause damage to sth** causar danos em algo
6 (*in relation to*) para; **3 goals to 2** 3 a 2; **8 apples to the kilo** 8 maçãs por quilo
7 (*purpose, result*) para; **to come to sb's aid** prestar ajuda a alguém; **to sentence sb to death** condenar alguém à morte; **to my surprise** para minha surpresa
▶ WITH VB **1** (*simple infin*): **to go/eat** ir/comer
2 (*following another vb*): **to want/try to do** querer/tentar fazer; **to start to do** começar a fazer
3 (*with vb omitted*): **I don't want to** eu não quero; **you ought to** você deve
4 (*purpose, result*) para
5 (*equivalent to relative clause*) para, a; **I have things to do** eu tenho coisas para fazer; **the main thing is to try** o principal é tentar
6 (*after adj etc*) para; **ready to go** pronto para ir; **too old/young to ...** muito velho/jovem para ...
▶ ADV: **pull/push the door to** puxar/empurrar a porta

toad [təud] N sapo

toadstool ['təudstu:l] N chapéu-de-cobra *m*, cogumelo venenoso

toast [təust] N (*Culin*) torradas *fpl*; (*drink, speech*) brinde *m* ▶ VT torrar; (*drink to*) brindar; **toaster** N torradeira

tobacco [tə'bækəu] N tabaco, fumo (BR)

today [tə'deɪ] ADV, N hoje *m*

toddler ['tɔdləʳ] N *criança que começa a andar*

toe [təu] N dedo do pé; (*of shoe*) bico ▶ VT: **to ~ the line** (*fig*) conformar-se, cumprir as obrigações

toffee ['tɔfɪ] N puxa-puxa *m* (BR), caramelo (PT)

together [tə'gɛðəʳ] ADV juntos; (*at same time*) ao mesmo tempo; **~ with** junto com

toilet ['tɔɪlət] N privada, vaso sanitário; (BRIT: *lavatory*) banheiro (BR), casa de banho (PT) ▶ CPD de toalete; **toilet paper** N papel *m* higiênico; **toiletries** NPL artigos *mpl* de toalete; **toilet roll** N rolo de papel higiênico

token ['təukən] N (*sign*) sinal *m*, símbolo, prova; (*souvenir*) lembrança; (*substitute coin*) ficha ▶ CPD simbólico; **book/record ~** (BRIT) vale para comprar livros/ discos

told [təuld] PT, PP *of* **tell**

tolerant ['tɔlərənt] ADJ: **~ of** tolerante com

tolerate ['tɔləreɪt] VT suportar; (*Med, Tech*) tolerar

toll [təul] N (*of casualties*) número de baixas; (*tax, charge*) pedágio (BR), portagem *f* (PT) ▶ VI dobrar, tanger

tomato [tə'mɑːtəu] (*pl* **tomatoes**) N tomate *m*

tomb [tuːm] N tumba

tombstone ['tuːmstəun] N lápide *f*

tomorrow [tə'mɔrəu] ADV, N amanhã *m*; **the day after ~** depois de amanhã; **~ morning** amanhã de manhã

ton [tʌn] N tonelada; **~s of** (*inf*) um monte de

tone [təun] N tom *m* ▶ VI harmonizar; **tone down** VT (*colour, criticism*) suavizar; (*sound*) baixar; (*Mus*) entoar; **tone up** VT (*muscles*) tonificar

tongs [tɔŋz] NPL (*for coal*) tenaz *f*; (*for hair*) ferros *mpl* de frisar cabelo

tongue [tʌŋ] N língua; **~ in cheek** ironicamente

tonic ['tɔnɪk] N (*Med*) tônico; (*also*: **~ water**) (água) tônica

tonight [tə'naɪt] ADV, N esta noite, hoje à noite

tonsil ['tɔnsəl] N amígdala; **tonsillitis** [tɔnsɪ'laɪtɪs] N amigdalite *f*

too [tuː] ADV (*excessively*) demais; muito; (*also*) também; **~ much** (*adv*) demais; (*adj*) demasiado; **~ many** demasiados(-as)

took [tuk] PT *of* **take**

tool [tuːl] N ferramenta

tooth [tuːθ] (*pl* **teeth**) N (*Anat, Tech*) dente *m*; (*molar*) molar *m*; **toothache** N dor *f* de dente; **to have toothache** estar com dor de dente; **toothbrush** N escova de dentes; **toothpaste** N pasta de dentes, creme *m* dental; **toothpick** N palito

top [tɔp] N (*of mountain*) cume *m*, cimo; (*of tree*) topo; (*of head*) cocuruto; (*of cupboard, table*) superfície *f*, topo; (*of box, jar, bottle*) tampa; (*of ladder, page*) topo; (*toy*) pião *m*; (*blouse etc*) top *m*, blusa ▶ ADJ (*highest: shelf, step*) mais alto; (*: marks*) máximo; (*in rank*) principal, superior ▶ VT exceder; (*be first in*) estar à cabeça de; **on ~ of** sobre, em cima de; (*in addition to*) além de; **from ~ to toe** (BRIT) da cabeça aos pés; **from ~ to bottom** de cima abaixo; **top up**, (US) **top off** VT completar; (*mobile phone*) recarregar; **top floor** N último andar *m*

topic ['tɔpɪk] N tópico, assunto; **topical** ADJ atual

topless ['tɔplɪs] ADJ (*bather etc*) topless *inv, sem a parte superior do biquíni*

topple ['tɔpl] VT derrubar ▶ VI cair para frente

top-up card N cartão de recarga (para celular)

torch [tɔːtʃ] N (BRIT) lanterna

tore [tɔːʳ] PT *of* **tear²**

torment [*n* 'tɔːmɛnt, *vt* tɔː'mɛnt] N tormento, suplício ▶ VT

t

atormentar; (*fig: annoy*) chatear, aborrecer

torn [tɔ:n] PP *of* **tear²**

tornado [tɔ:'neɪdəu] (*pl* **tornadoes**) N tornado

torrent ['tɔrənt] N torrente *f*

tortoise ['tɔ:təs] N tartaruga

torture ['tɔ:tʃəʳ] N tortura ▶ VT torturar; (*fig*) atormentar

Tory ['tɔ:rɪ] (BRIT) ADJ, N (*Pol*) conservador(a) *m/f*

toss [tɔs] VT atirar, arremessar; (*head*) lançar para trás ▶ VI: **to ~ and turn in bed** virar de um lado para o outro na cama; **to ~ a coin** tirar cara ou coroa; **to ~ up for sth** (BRIT) jogar cara ou coroa por algo

total ['təutl] ADJ total ▶ N total *m*, soma ▶ VT (*add up*) somar; (*amount to*) montar a

touch [tʌtʃ] N (*sense*) toque *m*; (*contact*) contato ▶ VT tocar (em); (*tamper with*) mexer com; (*make contact with*) fazer contato com; (*emotionally*) comover; **a ~ of** (*fig*) um traço de; **to get in ~ with sb** entrar em contato com alguém; **to lose ~** perder o contato; **touch on** VT FUS (*topic*) tocar em, fazer menção de; **touch up** VT (*paint*) retocar; **touchdown** N aterrissagem *f* (BR), aterragem *f* (PT); (*on sea*) amerissagem *f* (BR), amaragem *f* (PT); (*US Football*) touchdown *m* (*colocação da bola no chão atrás da linha de gol*); **touching** ADJ comovedor(a); **touch screen** N (*Comput*) touch screen *m*, ecrã táctil (PT)

tough [tʌf] ADJ duro; (*difficult*) difícil; (*resistant*) resistente; (*person: physically*) forte; (: *mentally*) tenaz; (*firm*) firme, inflexível

tour ['tuəʳ] N viagem *f*, excursão *f*; (*also*: **package ~**) excursão organizada; (*of town, museum*) visita; (*by artist*) turnê *f* ▶ VT (*country, city*) excursionar por; (*factory*) visitar

tourism ['tuərɪzm] N turismo

tourist ['tuərɪst] N turista *m/f* ▶ CPD turístico; **tourist office** N (*in country*) escritório de turismo; (*in embassy etc*) departamento de turismo

tournament ['tuənəmənt] N torneio

tow [təu] VT rebocar; **"on ~"** (BRIT), **"in ~"** (US) (*Aut*) "rebocado"

toward [tə'wɔ:d], **towards** [tə'wɔ:dz] PREP em direção a; (*of attitude*) para com; (*of purpose*) para; **~(s) noon/the end of the year** perto do meio-dia/do fim do ano

towel ['tauəl] N toalha; **towelling** N (*fabric*) tecido para toalhas

tower ['tauəʳ] N torre *f*; **tower block** (BRIT) N prédio alto, espigão *m*, cortiço (BR)

town [taun] N cidade *f*; **to go to ~** ir à cidade; (*fig*) fazer com entusiasmo, mandar brasa (BR); **town centre** N centro (da cidade); **town hall** N prefeitura (BR), concelho (PT)

toy [tɔɪ] N brinquedo; **toy with** VT FUS brincar com; (*idea*) contemplar

trace [treɪs] N (*sign*) sinal *m*; (*small amount*) traço ▶ VT (*draw*) traçar, esboçar; (*follow*) seguir a pista de; (*locate*) encontrar

track [træk] N (*mark*) pegada, vestígio; (*path: gen*) caminho, vereda; (: *of bullet etc*) trajetória; (: *of suspect, animal*) pista, rasto; (*Rail*) trilhos (BR), carris *mpl* (PT); (*on tape*) trilha; (*Sport*) pista; (*on record*) faixa ▶ VT seguir a pista de; **to keep ~ of** não perder de vista; (*fig*)

manter-se informado sobre; **track down** VT (*prey*) seguir a pista de; (*sth lost*) procurar e encontrar
tractor ['træktəʳ] N trator *m*
trade [treɪd] N comércio; (*skill, job*) ofício ▸VI negociar, comerciar ▸VT: **to ~ sth (for sth)** trocar algo (por algo); **trade in** VT dar como parte do pagamento; **trademark** N marca registrada; **trader** N comerciante *m/f*; **tradesman** *irreg* N lojista *m*; **trade union** N sindicato
tradition [trə'dɪʃən] N tradição *f*; **traditional** ADJ tradicional
traffic ['træfɪk] N trânsito; (*air traffic etc*) tráfego; (*illegal*) tráfico ▸VI: **to ~ in** (*pej: liquor, drugs*) traficar com, fazer tráfico com; **traffic circle** (US) N rotatória; **traffic jam** N engarrafamento, congestionamento; **traffic lights** NPL sinal *m* luminoso; **traffic warden** N guarda *m/f* de trânsito
tragedy ['trædʒədɪ] N tragédia
tragic ['trædʒɪk] ADJ trágico
trail [treɪl] N (*tracks*) rasto, pista; (*path*) caminho, trilha; (*of smoke, dust*) rasto ▸VT (*drag*) arrastar; (*follow*) seguir a pista de ▸VI arrastar-se; (*hang loosely*) pender; (*in game, contest*) ficar para trás; **trail behind** VI atrasar-se; **trailer** N (*Aut*) reboque *m*; (US: *caravan*) trailer *m* (BR), rulote *f* (PT); (*Cinema*) trailer
train [treɪn] N trem *m* (BR), comboio (PT); (*of dress*) cauda ▸VT formar; (*teach skills to*) instruir; (*Sport*) treinar; (*dog*) adestrar, amestrar; (*point: gun etc*): **to ~ on** apontar para ▸VI (*learn a skill*) instruir-se; (*Sport*) treinar; (*be educated*) ser treinado; **to lose one's ~ of thought** perder o fio; **trainee** [treɪ'ni:] N estagiário(-a); **trainer** N (*Sport*) treinador(a) *m/f*; (*of animals*) adestrador(a) *m/f*; **trainers** NPL (*shoes*) tênis *m*; **training** N instrução *f*; (*Sport, for occupation*) treinamento; (*professional*) formação
trait [treɪt] N traço
traitor ['treɪtəʳ] N traidor(a) *m/f*
tram [træm] (BRIT) N (*also*: **~car**) bonde *m* (BR), eléctrico (PT)
tramp [træmp] N (*person*) vagabundo(-a); (*inf, pej: woman*) piranha ▸VI caminhar pesadamente
trample ['træmpl] VT: **to ~ (underfoot)** calcar aos pés
trampoline ['træmpəli:n] N trampolim *m*
tranquil ['træŋkwɪl] ADJ tranquilo; **tranquillizer** N (*Med*) tranquilizante *m*
transfer [*n* 'trænsfəʳ, *vt* træns'fə:ʳ] N transferência; (*picture, design*) decalcomania ▸VT transferir; **to ~ the charges** (BRIT *Tel*) ligar a cobrar
transform [træns'fɔ:m] VT transformar
transfusion [træns'fju:ʒən] N (*also*: **blood ~**) transfusão *f* (de sangue)
transit ['trænzɪt] N: **in ~** em trânsito, de passagem
translate [trænz'leɪt] VT traduzir; **translation** N tradução *f*; **translator** N tradutor(a) *m/f*
transmission [trænz'mɪʃən] N transmissão *f*
transmit [trænz'mɪt] VT transmitir
transparent [træns'pærnt] ADJ transparente

t

transplant [*vt* træns'plɑ:nt, *n* 'trænsplɑ:nt] VT transplantar ▸ N (*Med*) transplante *m*

transport [*n* 'trænspɔ:t, *vt* træns'pɔ:t] N transporte *m* ▸ VT transportar; (*carry*) acarretar; **transportation** [trænspɔ:'teɪʃən] N transporte *m*

trap [træp] N (*snare*) armadilha, cilada; (*trick*) cilada; (*carriage*) aranha, charrete *f* ▸ VT (*animal, person*) pegar numa armadilha; (*immobilize*) bloquear; **to be ~ped** (*in bad marriage, fire*) estar preso(-a)

trash [træʃ] N (*US: rubbish*) lixo; **trash can** (US) N lata de lixo

trauma ['trɔ:mə] N trauma *m*

travel ['trævl] N viagem *f* ▸ VI viajar; (*sound*) propagar-se; (*news*) levar; (*wine*): **this wine ~s well** este vinho não sofre alteração ao ser transportado ▸ VT percorrer; **travels** NPL (*journeys*) viagens *fpl*; **travel agent** N agente *m/f* de viagens; **traveller**, (US) **traveler** N viajante *m/f*; (*Comm*) caixeiro(-a) viajante; **traveller's cheque**, (US) **traveler's check** N cheque *m* de viagem; **travelling**, (US) **traveling** N as viagens, viajar *m* ▸ ADJ (*circus, exhibition*) itinerante; (*salesman*) viajante ▸ CPD de viagem; **travel sickness** N enjoo

tray [treɪ] N bandeja; (*on desk*) cesta

treacherous ['trɛtʃərəs] ADJ traiçoeiro; (*ground, tide*) perigoso

treacle ['tri:kl] N melado

tread [trɛd] (*pt* **trod**, *pp* **trodden**) N (*step*) passo, pisada; (*sound*) passada; (*of stair*) piso; (*of tyre*) banda de rodagem ▸ VI pisar; **tread on** VT FUS pisar (em)

treasure ['trɛʒə^r] N tesouro; (*person*) joia ▸ VT (*value*) apreciar, estimar; **treasures** NPL (*art treasures etc*) preciosidades *fpl*

treasurer ['trɛʒərə^r] N tesoureiro(-a)

treasury ['trɛʒərɪ] N tesouraria

treat [tri:t] N regalo, deleite *m* ▸ VT tratar; **to ~ sb to sth** convidar alguém para algo

treatment ['tri:tmənt] N tratamento

treaty ['tri:tɪ] N tratado, acordo

treble ['trɛbl] ADJ tríplice ▸ VT triplicar ▸ VI triplicar(-se)

tree [tri:] N árvore *f*

trek [trɛk] N (*long journey*) jornada; (*walk*) caminhada

tremble ['trɛmbl] VI tremer

tremendous [trɪ'mɛndəs] ADJ tremendo; (*enormous*) enorme; (*excellent*) sensacional, fantástico

trench [trɛntʃ] N trincheira

trend [trɛnd] N (*tendency*) tendência; (*of events*) curso; (*fashion*) modismo, tendência; (*on social network: also:* **~ing topic**) trending topic *m* ▸ VI (*on social network*) ser compartilhado no Twitter até virar trending topic; **trendy** ADJ (*idea*) de acordo com a tendência atual; (*clothes*) da última moda

trespass ['trɛspəs] VI: **to ~ on** invadir; **"no ~ing"** "entrada proibida"

trial ['traɪəl] N (*Jur*) processo; (*test: of machine etc*) prova, teste *m*; **trials** NPL (*unpleasant experiences*) dissabores *mpl*; **by ~ and error** por tentativas; **to be on ~** ser julgado; **trial period** N período de experiência

triangle ['traɪæŋgl] N (*Math, Mus*) triângulo

tribe [traɪb] N tribo *f*

tribunal [traɪ'bjuːnl] N tribunal *m*
tribute ['trɪbjuːt] N homenagem *f*; **to pay ~ to** prestar homenagem a, homenagear
trick [trɪk] N truque *m*; (*joke*) peça, brincadeira; (*skill, knack*) habilidade *f*; (*Cards*) vaza ▶ VT enganar; **to play a ~ on sb** pregar uma peça em alguém; **that should do the ~** (*inf*) isso deveria dar resultado
trickle ['trɪkl] N (*of water etc*) fio (de água) ▶ VI gotejar, pingar
tricky ['trɪkɪ] ADJ difícil, complicado
trifle ['traɪfl] N bobagem *f*, besteira; (*Culin*) *tipo de bolo com fruta e creme* ▶ ADV: **a ~ long** um pouquinho longo
trigger ['trɪgə^r] N (*of gun*) gatilho; **trigger off** VT desencadear
trim [trɪm] ADJ (*figure*) elegante; (*house*) arrumado; (*garden*) bem cuidado ▶ N (*haircut etc*) aparada; (*on car*) estofamento ▶ VT aparar, cortar; (*decorate*): **to ~ (with)** enfeitar (com); (*Naut: sail*) ajustar
trip [trɪp] N viagem *f*; (*outing*) excursão *f*; (*stumble*) tropeção *m* ▶ VI tropeçar; (*go lightly*) andar com passos ligeiros; **on a ~** de viagem; **trip up** VI tropeçar ▶ VT passar uma rasteira em
triple ['trɪpl] ADJ triplo, tríplice; **triplets** NPL trigêmeos(-as) *mpl/fpl*
tripod ['traɪpɔd] N tripé *m*
triumph ['traɪʌmf] N (*satisfaction*) satisfação *f*; (*great achievement*) triunfo ▶ VI: **to ~ (over)** triunfar (sobre)
trivial ['trɪvɪəl] ADJ insignificante; (*commonplace*) trivial
trod [trɔd] PT *of* **tread**; **trodden** PP *of* **tread**
troll [trɔl, trəul] (*inf: Comput*) N troll *m* ▶ VI trollar
trolley ['trɔlɪ] N carrinho; (*table on wheels*) mesa volante
trombone [trɔm'bəun] N trombone *m*
troop [truːp] N bando, grupo ▶ VI: **to ~ in/out** entrar/sair em bando; **troops** NPL (*Mil*) tropas *fpl*; **~ing the colour** (BRIT) *saudação da bandeira*
trophy ['trəufɪ] N troféu *m*
tropic ['trɔpɪk] N trópico; **tropical** ADJ tropical
trot [trɔt] N trote *m*; (*fast pace*) passo rápido ▶ VI trotar; (*person*) andar rapidamente; **on the ~** (*fig: inf*) a fio
trouble ['trʌbl] N problema(s) *m(pl)*, dificuldade(s) *f(pl)*; (*worry*) preocupação *f*; (*bother, effort*) incômodo, trabalho; (*Pol*) distúrbios *mpl*; (*Med*): **stomach ~** *etc* problemas *mpl* gástricos *etc* ▶ VT perturbar; (*worry*) preocupar, incomodar ▶ VI: **to ~ to do sth** incomodar-se *or* preocupar-se de fazer algo; **troubles** NPL (*Pol etc*) distúrbios *mpl*; **to be in ~** estar num aperto; (*ship, climber etc*) estar em dificuldade; **what's the ~?** qual é o problema?; **troubled** ADJ preocupado; (*epoch, life*) agitado; **troublemaker** N criador(a)-de-casos *m/f*; (*child*) encrenqueiro(-a); **troublesome** ADJ importuno; (*child, cough*) incômodo
trough [trɔf] N (*also*: **drinking ~**) bebedouro, cocho; (*also*: **feeding ~**) gamela; (*depression*) depressão *f*
trousers ['trauzəz] NPL calça (BR), calças *fpl* (PT)
trout [traut] N INV truta
truant ['truənt] (BRIT) N: **to play ~** matar aula (BR), fazer gazeta (PT)

truce [tru:s] N trégua, armistício
truck [trʌk] N caminhão *m* (BR), camião *m* (PT); (*Rail*) vagão *m*; **truck driver** N caminhoneiro(-a)(BR), camionista *m/f* (PT)
true [tru:] ADJ verdadeiro; (*accurate*) exato; (*genuine*) autêntico; (*faithful*) fiel, leal; **to come ~** realizar-se, tornar-se realidade
truly ['tru:lɪ] ADV realmente; (*truthfully*) verdadeiramente; (*faithfully*) fielmente; **yours ~** (*in letter*) atenciosamente
trumpet ['trʌmpɪt] N trombeta
trunk [trʌŋk] N tronco; (*of elephant*) tromba; (*case*) baú *m*; (US *Aut*) mala (BR), porta-bagagens *m* (PT); **trunks** NPL (*also*: **swimming ~s**) sunga (BR), calções *mpl* de banho (PT)
trust [trʌst] N confiança; (*responsibility*) responsibilidade *f*; (*Jur*) fideicomisso ▶ VT (*rely on*) confiar em; (*entrust*): **to ~ sth to sb** confiar algo a alguém; (*hope*): **to ~ (that)** esperar que; **to take sth on ~** aceitar algo sem verificação prévia; **trusted** ADJ de confiança; **trustworthy** ADJ digno de confiança
truth [tru:θ] N verdade *f*; **truthful** ADJ (*person*) sincero, honesto
try [traɪ] N tentativa; (*Rugby*) ensaio ▶ VT (*Jur*) julgar; (*test: sth new*) provar, pôr à prova; (*strain*) cansar ▶ VI tentar; **to have a ~** fazer uma tentativa; **to ~ to do sth** tentar fazer algo; **try on** VT (*clothes*) experimentar, provar; **trying** ADJ exasperante
T-shirt N camiseta (BR), T-shirt *f* (PT)
tub [tʌb] N tina; (*bath*) banheira
tube [tju:b] N tubo; (*pipe*) cano; (BRIT: *underground*) metrô *m* (BR), metro(-politano) (PT); (*for tyre*) câmara-de-ar *f*
tuberculosis [tjubə:kju'ləusɪs] N tuberculose *f*
tuck [tʌk] VT (*put*) enfiar, meter; **tuck away** VT esconder; **to be ~ed away** estar escondido; **tuck in** VT enfiar para dentro; (*child*) aconchegar ▶ VI (*eat*) comer com apetite; **tuck up** VT (*child*) aconchegar
Tuesday ['tju:zdɪ] N terça-feira
tug [tʌg] N (*ship*) rebocador *m* ▶ VT puxar
tuition [tju:'ɪʃən] N ensino; (*private tuition*) aulas *fpl* particulares; (US: *fees*) taxas *fpl* escolares
tulip ['tju:lɪp] N tulipa
tumble ['tʌmbl] N (*fall*) queda ▶ VI cair, tombar; **to ~ to sth** (*inf*) sacar algo
tumbler ['tʌmblə^r] N copo
tummy ['tʌmɪ] (*inf*) N (*belly*) barriga; (*stomach*) estômago
tumour ['tju:mə^r], (US) **tumor** N tumor *m*
tuna ['tju:nə] N INV (*also*: **~ fish**) atum *m*
tune [tju:n] N melodia ▶ VT (*Mus*) afinar; (*Radio, TV*) sintonizar; (*Aut*) regular; **to be in/out of ~** (*instrument*) estar afinado/ desafinado; (*singer*) cantar afinado/ desafinar; **to be in/out of ~ with** (*fig*) harmonizar-se com/destoar de; **tune in** VI (*Radio, TV*): **to ~ in (to)** sintonizar (com); **tune up** VI (*musician*) afinar (seu instrumento)
tunic ['tju:nɪk] N túnica
Tunisia [tju:'nɪzɪə] N Tunísia
tunnel ['tʌnl] N túnel *m*; (*in mine*) galeria ▶ VI abrir um túnel (*or* uma galeria)
turbulence ['tə:bjuləns] N (*Aviat*) turbulência

turf [tə:f] N torrão *m* ▶ VT relvar, gramar; **turf out** (*inf*) VT (*person*) pôr no olho da rua
Turk [tə:k] N turco(-a)
Turkey ['tə:kɪ] N Turquia
turkey ['tə:kɪ] N peru(a) *m/f*
Turkish ['tə:kɪʃ] ADJ turco(-a) ▶ N (*Ling*) turco
turmoil ['tə:mɔɪl] N tumulto, distúrbio, agitação *f*; **in ~** agitado, tumultuado
turn [tə:n] N volta, turno; (*in road*) curva; (*of mind, events*) propensão *f*, tendência; (*Theatre*) número; (*Med*) choque *m* ▶ VT dar volta a, fazer girar; (*collar*) virar; (*change*): **to ~ sth into** converter algo em ▶ VI virar; (*person: look back*) voltar-se; (*reverse direction*) mudar de direção; (*milk*) azedar; (*become*) tornar-se, virar; **to ~ nasty** engrossar; **to ~ forty** fazer quarenta anos; **a good ~** um favor; **it gave me quite a ~** me deu um susto enorme; **"no left ~"** (*Aut*) "proibido virar à esquerda"; **it's your ~** é a sua vez; **in ~** por sua vez; **to take ~s (at)** revezar (em); **turn away** VI virar a cabeça ▶ VT (*business, applicants*) recusar; **turn back** VI voltar atrás ▶ VT voltar para trás; (*clock*) atrasar; **turn down** VT (*refuse*) recusar; (*reduce*) baixar; (*fold*) dobrar, virar para baixo; **turn in** VI (*inf: go to bed*) ir dormir ▶ VT (*fold*) dobrar para dentro; **turn off** VI (*from road*) virar, sair do caminho ▶ VT (*light, radio etc*) apagar; (*engine*) desligar; **turn on** VT (*light*) acender; (*engine, radio*) ligar; (*tap*) abrir; **turn out** VT (*light, gas*) apagar; (*produce*) produzir ▶ VI (*troops*) ser mobilizado; **to ~ out to be ...** revelar-se (ser) ..., resultar (ser) ..., vir a ser ...; **turn over** VI (*person*) virar-se ▶ VT (*object*) virar; **turn round** VI voltar-se, virar-se; **turn up** VI (*person*) aparecer, pintar; (*lost object*) aparecer ▶ VT (*collar*) subir; (*volume, radio etc*) aumentar; **turning** N (*in road*) via lateral
turnip ['tə:nɪp] N nabo
turnout ['tə:naut] N assistência; (*in election*) comparecimento às urnas
turnover ['tə:nəuvəʳ] N (*Comm: amount of money*) volume *m* de negócios; (*: of goods*) movimento; (*of staff*) rotatividade *f*
turn-up (BRIT) N (*on trousers*) volta, dobra
turquoise ['tə:kwɔɪz] N (*stone*) turquesa ▶ ADJ azul-turquesa *inv*
turtle ['tə:tl] N tartaruga, cágado
tusk [tʌsk] N defesa (de elefante)
tutor ['tju:təʳ] N professor(a) *m/f*; (*private tutor*) professor(a) *m/f* particular; **tutorial** [tju:'tɔ:rɪəl] N (*Sch*) seminário
tuxedo [tʌk'si:dəu] (US) N smoking *m*
TV N ABBR (= *television*) TV *f*
tweed [twi:d] N tweed *m*, *pano grosso de lã*
tweet [twi:t] (*on Twitter*) N tweet *m* ▶ VT, VI tuitar
tweezers ['twi:zəz] NPL pinça (pequena)
twelfth [twɛlfθ] NUM décimo segundo
twelve [twɛlv] NUM doze; **at ~ (o'clock)** (*midday*) ao meio-dia; (*midnight*) à meia-noite
twentieth ['twɛntɪɪθ] NUM vigésimo
twenty ['twɛntɪ] NUM vinte
twice [twaɪs] ADV duas vezes; **~ as much** duas vezes mais

twig [twɪg] N graveto, varinha ▸ VI (*inf*) sacar
twilight ['twaɪlaɪt] N crepúsculo, meia-luz *f*
twin [twɪn] ADJ gêmeo(-a); (*beds*) separado ▸ N gêmeo(-a) ▸ VT irmanar; **twin-bedded room** N quarto com duas camas
twinkle ['twɪŋkl] VI cintilar; (*eyes*) pestanejar
twist [twɪst] N torção *f*; (*in road, coil*) curva; (*in wire, flex*) virada; (*in story*) mudança imprevista ▸ VT torcer, retorcer; (*ankle*) torcer; (*weave*) entrelaçar; (*roll around*) enrolar; (*fig*) deturpar ▸ VI serpentear
twit [twɪt] (*inf*) N idiota *m/f*, bobo(-a)
twitch [twɪtʃ] N puxão *m*; (*nervous*) tique *m* nervoso ▸ VI contrair-se
two [tu:] NUM dois; **to put ~ and ~ together** (*fig*) tirar conclusões;
two-way ADJ: **two-way traffic** trânsito em mão dupla
type [taɪp] N (*category*) tipo, espécie *f*; (*model*) modelo; (*Typ*) tipo, letra ▸ VT (*letter etc*) datilografar, bater (à máquina);
typewriter N máquina de escrever
typhoid ['taɪfɔɪd] N febre *f* tifoide
typical ['tɪpɪkl] ADJ típico
typing ['taɪpɪŋ] N datilografia
typist ['taɪpɪst] N datilógrafo(-a) *m/f*
tyre ['taɪə^r], (US) **tire** N pneu *m*

U

UFO ['ju:fəu] N ABBR (= *unidentified flying object*) óvni *m*
Uganda [ju:'gændə] N Uganda (*no article*)
ugly ['ʌglɪ] ADJ feio; (*dangerous*) perigoso
UK N ABBR = **United Kingdom**
ulcer ['ʌlsə^r] N úlcera; **mouth ~** afta
ultimate ['ʌltɪmət] ADJ último, final; (*authority*) máximo;
ultimately ADV (*in the end*) no final, por último; (*fundamentally*) no fundo
ultrasound ['ʌltrəsaund] N (*Med*) ultrassom *m*
umbrella [ʌm'brɛlə] N guarda-chuva *m*; (*for sun*) guarda-sol *m*, barraca (da praia)
umpire ['ʌmpaɪə^r] N árbitro ▸ VT arbitrar
UN N ABBR (= *United Nations*) ONU *f*
unable [ʌn'eɪbl] ADJ: **to be ~ to do sth** não poder fazer algo
unanimous [ju:'nænɪməs] ADJ unânime

unarmed [ʌn'ɑːmd] ADJ (*without a weapon*) desarmado; (*defenceless*) indefeso
unattended [ʌnə'tɛndɪd] ADJ (*car, luggage*) abandonado
unattractive [ʌnə'træktɪv] ADJ sem atrativos; (*building, appearance, idea*) pouco atraente
unavoidable [ʌnə'vɔɪdəbl] ADJ inevitável
unaware [ʌnə'wɛəʳ] ADJ: **to be ~ of** ignorar, não perceber
unawares [ʌnə'wɛəz] ADV improvisadamente, de surpresa
unbearable [ʌn'bɛərəbl] ADJ insuportável
unbeatable [ʌn'biːtəbl] ADJ (*team*) invencível; (*price*) sem igual
unbelievable [ʌnbɪ'liːvəbl] ADJ inacreditável; (*amazing*) incrível
unborn [ʌn'bɔːn] ADJ por nascer
unbutton [ʌn'bʌtn] VT desabotoar
uncalled-for [ʌn'kɔːld-] ADJ desnecessário, gratuito
uncanny [ʌn'kænɪ] ADJ estranho; (*knack*) excepcional
uncertain [ʌn'səːtn] ADJ incerto; (*character*) indeciso; (*unsure*): **~ about** inseguro sobre; **in no ~ terms** em termos precisos; **uncertainty** N incerteza; (*also pl: doubts*) dúvidas *fpl*
uncle ['ʌŋkl] N tio
uncomfortable [ʌn'kʌmfətəbl] ADJ incômodo; (*uneasy*) pouco à vontade; (*situation*) desagradável
uncommon [ʌn'kɔmən] ADJ raro, incomum, excepcional
unconditional [ʌnkən'dɪʃənl] ADJ incondicional
unconscious [ʌn'kɔnʃəs] ADJ sem sentidos, desacordado; (*unaware*): **~ of** inconsciente de ▸ N: **the ~** o inconsciente
uncontrollable [ʌnkən'trəuləbl] ADJ (*temper*) ingovernável; (*child, animal, laughter*) incontrolável
unconventional [ʌnkən'vɛnʃənl] ADJ inconvencional
uncover [ʌn'kʌvəʳ] VT descobrir; (*take lid off*) destapar, destampar
undecided [ʌndɪ'saɪdɪd] ADJ indeciso; (*question*) não respondido, pendente
under ['ʌndəʳ] PREP embaixo de (BR), debaixo de (PT); (*fig*) sob; (*less than*) menos de; (*according to*) segundo, de acordo com ▸ ADV embaixo; (*movement*) por baixo; **~ there** ali embaixo; **~ repair** em conserto; **undercover** ADJ secreto, clandestino; **underdog** N o mais fraco; **underdone** ADJ (*Culin*) mal passado; **underestimate** VT subestimar; **undergo** *irreg* VT sofrer; (*test*) passar por; (*operation, treatment*) ser submetido a; **undergraduate** N universitário(-a); **underground** N (BRIT) metrô *m* (BR), metro(-politano) (PT); (*Pol*) organização *f* clandestina ▸ ADJ subterrâneo; (*fig*) clandestino ▸ ADV (*work*) embaixo da terra; (*fig*) na clandestinidade; **undergrowth** N vegetação *f* rasteira; **underline** VT sublinhar; **undermine** VT minar, solapar; **underneath** ADV embaixo, debaixo, por baixo ▸ PREP embaixo de (BR), debaixo de (PT); **underpaid** ADJ mal pago; **underpants** (BRIT) NPL cueca (BR), cuecas *fpl* (PT); **underpass** (BRIT) N passagem *f* inferior; **underprivileged** ADJ menos favorecido

understand [ʌndəˈstænd] *irreg* VT entender, compreender ▶VI: **to ~ that** acreditar que; **understandable** ADJ compreensível; **understanding** ADJ compreensivo ▶N compreensão *f*; (*knowledge*) entendimento; (*agreement*) acordo

understatement [ʌndəˈsteɪtmənt] N (*quality*) subestimação *f*; (*euphemism*) eufemismo; **it's an ~ to say that ...** é uma subestimação dizer que ...

understood [ʌndəˈstud] PT, PP *of* **understand** ▶ADJ entendido; (*implied*) subentendido, implícito

undertake [ʌndəˈteɪk] (*irreg: like* **take**) VT incumbir-se de, encarregar-se de; **to ~ to do sth** comprometer-se a fazer algo

undertaking [ˈʌndəteɪkɪŋ] N empreendimento; (*promise*) promessa

underwater [ʌndəˈwɔːtəʳ] ADV sob a água ▶ADJ subaquático

underwear [ˈʌndəwɛəʳ] N roupa de baixo

underworld [ˈʌndəwəːld] N (*of crime*) submundo

undo [ʌnˈduː] (*irreg: like* **do**) VT (*unfasten*) desatar; (*spoil*) desmanchar

undress [ʌnˈdrɛs] VI despir-se, tirar a roupa

unearth [ʌnˈəːθ] VT desenterrar; (*fig*) revelar

uneasy [ʌnˈiːzɪ] ADJ (*person*) preocupado; (*feeling*) incômodo; (*peace, truce*) desconfortável

uneducated [ʌnˈɛdjukeɪtɪd] ADJ inculto, sem instrução, não escolarizado

unemployed [ʌnɪmˈplɔɪd] ADJ desempregado ▶NPL: **the ~** os desempregados

unemployment [ʌnɪmˈplɔɪmənt] N desemprego

uneven [ʌnˈiːvn] ADJ desigual; (*road etc*) irregular, acidentado

unexpected [ʌnɪkˈspɛktɪd] ADJ inesperado; **unexpectedly** [ʌnɪkˈspɛktɪdlɪ] ADV inesperadamente

unfair [ʌnˈfɛəʳ] ADJ: **~ (to)** injusto (com); **it's ~ that ...** não é justo que ...

unfaithful [ʌnˈfeɪθful] ADJ infiel

unfamiliar [ʌnfəˈmɪlɪəʳ] ADJ pouco familiar, desconhecido; **to be ~ with sth** não estar familiarizado com algo

unfashionable [ʌnˈfæʃnəbl] ADJ fora da moda

unfasten [ʌnˈfɑːsn] VT desatar; (*open*) abrir

unfavourable [ʌnˈfeɪvərəbl], (US) **unfavorable** ADJ desfavorável

unfinished [ʌnˈfɪnɪʃt] ADJ incompleto, inacabado

unfit [ʌnˈfɪt] ADJ sem preparo físico; (*incompetent*) incompetente, incapaz; **~ for work** inapto para trabalhar

unfold [ʌnˈfəuld] VT desdobrar ▶VI (*story, situation*) desdobrar-se

unfortunate [ʌnˈfɔːtʃənət] ADJ infeliz; (*event, remark*) inoportuno

unfriend [ʌnˈfrɛnd] VT excluir (em rede social)

unfriendly [ʌnˈfrɛndlɪ] ADJ antipático

unhappiness [ʌnˈhæpɪnɪs] N infelicidade *f*

unhappy [ʌnˈhæpɪ] ADJ triste; (*unfortunate*) desventurado; (*childhood*) infeliz; (*dissatisfied*): **~ with** descontente com, insatisfeito com

unhealthy [ʌn'hɛlθɪ] ADJ insalubre; (*person*) doentio; (*fig*) anormal
unheard-of [ʌn'hə:d-] ADJ insólito
unhurt [ʌn'hə:t] ADJ ileso
uniform ['ju:nɪfɔ:m] N uniforme *m* ▶ ADJ uniforme
uninhabited [ʌnɪn'hæbɪtɪd] ADJ inabitado
uninstall ['ʌnɪnstɔ:l] VT (*Comput*) desinstalar
unintentional [ʌnɪn'tɛnʃənəl] ADJ involuntário, não intencional
union ['ju:njən] N união *f*; (*also*: **trade ~**) sindicato (de trabalhadores) ▶ CPD sindical; **Union Jack** N bandeira britânica
unique [ju:'ni:k] ADJ único, sem igual
unit ['ju:nɪt] N unidade *f*; (*of furniture etc*) segão *f*; (*team, squad*) equipe *f*; **kitchen ~** armário de cozinha
unite [ju:'naɪt] VT unir ▶ VI unir-se; **united** ADJ unido; (*effort*) conjunto; **United Kingdom** N Reino Unido; **United Nations, United Nations Organization** N (Organização *f* das) Nações *fpl* Unidas; **United States, United States of America** N Estados Unidos *mpl* (da América)
universal [ju:nɪ'və:sl] ADJ universal
universe ['ju:nɪvə:s] N universo
university [ju:nɪ'və:sɪtɪ] N universidade *f*
unjust [ʌn'dʒʌst] ADJ injusto
unkind [ʌn'kaɪnd] ADJ maldoso; (*comment etc*) cruel
unknown [ʌn'nəun] ADJ desconhecido
unlawful [ʌn'lɔ:ful] ADJ ilegal
unleaded [ʌn'lɛdɪd] ADJ (*petrol, fuel*) sem chumbo
unleash [ʌn'li:ʃ] VT (*fig*) desencadear
unless [ʌn'lɛs] CONJ a menos que, a não ser que; **~ he comes** a menos que ele venha
unlike [ʌn'laɪk] ADJ diferente ▶ PREP diferentemente de, ao contrário de
unlikely [ʌn'laɪklɪ] ADJ (*not likely*) improvável; (*unexpected*) inesperado
unlisted [ʌn'lɪstɪd] ADJ (*US Tel*): **an ~ number** um número que não consta na lista telefônica
unload [ʌn'ləud] VT descarregar
unlock [ʌn'lɔk] VT destrancar
unlucky [ʌn'lʌkɪ] ADJ infeliz; (*object, number*) de mau agouro; **to be ~** ser azarado, ter azar
unmarried [ʌn'mærɪd] ADJ solteiro
unmistakable, unmistakeable [ʌnmɪs'teɪkəbl] ADJ inconfundível
unnatural [ʌn'nætʃrəl] ADJ antinatural, artificial; (*manner*) afetado; (*habit*) depravado
unnecessary [ʌn'nɛsəsərɪ] ADJ desnecessário, inútil
UNO ['ju:nəu] N ABBR (= *United Nations Organization*) ONU *f*
unofficial [ʌnə'fɪʃl] ADJ não-oficial, informal; (*strike*) desautorizado
unpack [ʌn'pæk] VI desembrulhar ▶ VT desfazer
unpleasant [ʌn'plɛznt] ADJ desagradável; (*person, manner*) antipático
unplug [ʌn'plʌg] VT desligar
unpopular [ʌn'pɔpjulə^r] ADJ impopular
unprecedented [ʌn'prɛsɪdəntɪd] ADJ sem precedentes
unpredictable [ʌnprɪ'dɪktəbl] ADJ imprevisível

U

unravel [ʌn'rævl] VT desemaranhar; (*mystery*) desvendar
unreal [ʌn'rɪəl] ADJ irreal, ilusório; (*extraordinary*) extraordinário
unrealistic [ʌnrɪə'lɪstɪk] ADJ pouco realista
unreasonable [ʌn'ri:znəbl] ADJ insensato; (*demand*) absurdo
unrelated [ʌnrɪ'leɪtɪd] ADJ sem relação; (*family*) sem parentesco
unreliable [ʌnrɪ'laɪəbl] ADJ (*person*) indigno de confiança; (*machine*) incerto, perigoso
unrest [ʌn'rɛst] N inquietação *f*, desassossego; (*Pol*) distúrbios *mpl*
unroll [ʌn'rəul] VT desenrolar
unruly [ʌn'ru:lɪ] ADJ indisciplinado; (*hair*) desalinhado
unsafe [ʌn'seɪf] ADJ perigoso
unsatisfactory [ʌnsætɪs'fæktərɪ] ADJ insatisfatório
unscrew [ʌn'skru:] VT desparafusar
unsettled [ʌn'sɛtld] ADJ (*weather*) instável; (*person*) inquieto
unsightly [ʌn'saɪtlɪ] ADJ feio, disforme
unskilled [ʌn'skɪld] ADJ não-especializado
unstable [ʌn'steɪbl] ADJ em falso; (*government, mentally*) instável
unsteady [ʌn'stɛdɪ] ADJ (*hand, person*) trêmulo; (*ladder*) instável
unsuccessful [ʌnsək'sɛsful] ADJ (*attempt*) frustrado, vão/vã; (*writer, proposal*) sem êxito; **to be ~** (*in attempting sth*) ser mal sucedido, não conseguir; (*application*) ser recusado
unsuitable [ʌn'su:təbl] ADJ inadequado; (*time, moment*) inconveniente
unsure [ʌn'ʃuə^r] ADJ inseguro, incerto; **to be ~ of o.s.** não ser seguro de si
untidy [ʌn'taɪdɪ] ADJ (*room*) desarrumado, desleixado; (*appearance*) desmazelado, desalinhado
untie [ʌn'taɪ] VT desatar, desfazer; (*dog, prisoner*) soltar
until [ən'tɪl] PREP até ▸ CONJ até que; **~ he comes** até que ele venha; **~ now** até agora; **~ then** até então
unused[1] [ʌn'ju:zd] ADJ novo, sem uso
unused[2] [ʌn'ju:st] ADJ: **to be ~ to sth/to doing sth** não estar acostumado com algo/a fazer algo
unusual [ʌn'ju:ʒuəl] ADJ (*strange*) estranho; (*rare*) incomum; (*exceptional*) extraordinário
unveil [ʌn'veɪl] VT desvelar, descobrir
unwanted [ʌn'wɔntɪd] ADJ não desejado, indesejável
unwell [ʌn'wɛl] ADJ: **to be ~** estar doente; **to feel ~** estar indisposto
unwilling [ʌn'wɪlɪŋ] ADJ: **to be ~ to do sth** relutar em fazer algo, não querer fazer algo
unwind [ʌn'waɪnd] *irreg* VT desenrolar ▸ VI (*relax*) relaxar-se
unwise [ʌn'waɪz] ADJ imprudente
unwrap [ʌn'ræp] VT desembrulhar

KEYWORD

up [ʌp] PREP: **to go/be up sth** subir algo/estar em cima de algo; **we climbed/walked up the hill** nós subimos/andamos até em cima da colina; **they live further up the street** eles moram mais adiante nesta rua
▸ ADV **1** (*upwards, higher*) em cima, para cima; **up in the sky/the mountains** lá no céu/nas montanhas; **up there** lá em cima; **up above** em cima

2: **to be up** (*out of bed*) estar de pé; (*prices, level*) estar elevado; (*building, tent*) estar erguido
3: **up to** (*as far as*) até; **up to now** até agora
4: **to be up to** (*depending on*): **it is up to you** você é quem sabe, você decide
5: **to be up to** (*equal to*) estar à altura de; **he's not up to it** (*job, task etc*) ele não é capaz de fazê-lo; **his work is not up to the required standard** seu trabalho não atende aos padrões exigidos
6: **to be up to** (*inf: be doing*) estar fazendo (BR) *or* a fazer (PT); **what is he up to?** o que ele está querendo?, o que ele está tramando?
▶ N: **ups and downs** altos *mpl* e baixos

upbringing ['ʌpbrɪŋɪŋ] N educação *f*, criação *f*
update [ʌp'deɪt] VT atualizar, pôr em dia
upgrade [ʌp'greɪd] VT (*person*) promover; (*job*) melhorar; (*house*) reformar
upheaval [ʌp'hiːvl] N transtorno; (*unrest*) convulsão *f*
uphill [ʌp'hɪl] ADJ ladeira acima; (*fig: task*) trabalhoso, árduo ▶ ADV: **to go ~** ir morro acima
upload ['ʌpləud] VT (*Comput*) fazer upload, transferir
upon [ə'pɔn] PREP sobre
upper ['ʌpə^r] ADJ superior, de cima ▶ N (*of shoe*) gáspea, parte *f* superior; **upper-class** ADJ de classe alta
upright ['ʌpraɪt] ADJ vertical; (*straight*) reto; (*fig*) honesto
uprising ['ʌpraɪzɪŋ] N revolta, rebelião *f*, sublevação *f*
uproar ['ʌprɔː^r] N tumulto, algazarra
upset [*n* 'ʌpsɛt, *vt, adj* ʌp'sɛt] (*irreg: like* **set**) N (*to plan etc*) revés *m*, reviravolta; (*stomach upset*) indisposição *f* ▶ VT (*glass etc*) virar; (*plan*) perturbar; (*person: annoy*) aborrecer ▶ ADJ aflito; (*stomach*) indisposto
upside down ['ʌpsaɪd-] ADV de cabeça para baixo; **to turn a place ~** (*fig*) deixar um lugar de cabeça para baixo
upstairs [ʌp'stɛəz] ADV (*be*) em cima; (*go*) lá em cima ▶ ADJ (*room*) de cima ▶ N andar *m* de cima
up-to-date ADJ (*person*) moderno, atualizado; (*information*) atualizado
upward ['ʌpwəd] ADJ ascendente, para cima ▶ ADV para cima
upwards ['ʌpwədz] ADV = **upward**
urban ['əːbən] ADJ urbano, da cidade
urge [əːdʒ] N desejo ▶ VT: **to ~ sb to do sth** incitar alguém a fazer algo
urgent ['əːdʒənt] ADJ urgente; (*tone, plea*) insistente
urinal [ju'raɪnl] (BRIT) N (*vessel*) urinol *m*; (*building*) mictório
urine ['juərɪn] N urina
URL ABBR (= *uniform resource locator*) URL *m*
Uruguay ['juərəgwaɪ] N Uruguai *m*
US N ABBR (= *United States*) EUA *mpl*
us [ʌs] PRON nos; (*after prep*) nós; *see also* **me**
USA N ABBR (= *United States of America*) EUA *mpl*
USB ABBR (*Comput*) (= *universal serial bus*) USB *m*; **USB stick** N (*Comput*) pen drive *m*

use [*n* juːs, *vt* juːz] N uso, emprego; (*usefulness*) utilidade *f* ▶ VT usar, utilizar; (*phrase*) empregar; **in ~** em uso; **out of ~** fora de uso; **to be of ~** ser útil; **it's no ~** (*pointless*) é inútil; (*not useful*) não serve; **to be ~d to** estar acostumado a; **she ~d to do it** ela costumava fazê-lo; **use up** VT esgotar, consumir; (*money*) gastar; **used** [juːzd] ADJ usado; **useful** ['juːsful] ADJ útil; **useless** ['juːslɪs] ADJ inútil; (*person*) incapaz; **user** ['juːzəʳ] N usuário(-a) (BR), utente *m/f* (PT); **user-friendly** ADJ de fácil utilização

USP N ABBR (= *unique selling proposition*) *proposta única de valor*

usual ['juːʒuəl] ADJ usual, habitual; **as ~** como de hábito, como sempre; **usually** ['juːʒuəlɪ] ADV normalmente

utensil [juː'tɛnsl] N utensílio

utmost ['ʌtməust] ADJ maior ▶ N: **to do one's ~** fazer todo o possível

utter ['ʌtəʳ] ADJ total ▶ VT (*sounds*) emitir; (*words*) proferir, pronunciar; **utterly** ADV completamente, totalmente

U-turn N retorno

V

vacancy ['veɪkənsɪ] N (BRIT: *job*) vaga; (*room*) quarto livre

vacant ['veɪkənt] ADJ desocupado, livre; (*expression*) distraído

vacate [və'keɪt] VT (*house*) desocupar; (*job*) deixar

vacation [və'keɪʃən] (*esp US*) N férias *fpl*

vacuum ['vækjum] N vácuo *m*; **vacuum cleaner** N aspirador *m* de pó

vagina [və'dʒaɪnə] N vagina

vague [veɪg] ADJ vago; (*blurred: memory*) fraco

vain [veɪn] ADJ vaidoso; (*useless*) vão/vã, inútil; **in ~** em vão

valentine ['væləntaɪn] N (*also*: **~ card**) cartão *m* do Dia dos Namorados; (*person*) namorado

valid ['vælɪd] ADJ válido

valley ['vælɪ] N vale *m*

valuable ['væljuəbl] ADJ (*jewel*) de valor; (*time*) valioso; (*help*) precioso; **valuables** NPL objetos *mpl* de valor

value ['væljuː] N valor *m*;

(*importance*) importância ▶ VT (*fix price of*) avaliar; (*appreciate*) valorizar, estimar; **values** NPL (*principles*) valores *mpl*
valve [vælv] N válvula
van [væn] N (*Aut*) camionete *f* (BR), camioneta (PT)
vandal ['vændl] N vândalo(-a); **vandalize** VT destruir, depredar
vanilla [və'nɪlə] N baunilha
vanish ['vænɪʃ] VI desaparecer, sumir
vanity ['vænɪtɪ] N vaidade *f*
vapour ['veɪpə^r], (US) **vapor** N vapor *m*
variety [və'raɪətɪ] N variedade *f*, diversidade *f*; (*type, quantity*) variedade
various ['vɛərɪəs] ADJ vários(-as), diversos(-as); (*several*) vários(-as)
varnish ['vɑːnɪʃ] N verniz *m*; (*nail varnish*) esmalte *m* ▶ VT envernizar; (*nails*) pintar (com esmalte)
vary ['vɛərɪ] VT mudar ▶ VI variar; (*become different*): **to ~ with** *or* **according to** variar de acordo com
vase [vɑːz] N vaso
vast [vɑːst] ADJ enorme
VAT [væt] (BRIT) N ABBR (= *value added tax*) ≈ ICM *m* (BR), IVA *m* (PT)
vault [vɔːlt] N (*of roof*) abóbada; (*tomb*) sepulcro; (*in bank*) caixa-forte *f* ▶ VT (*also*: **~ over**) saltar (por cima de)
veal [viːl] N carne *f* de vitela
vegan ['viːgən] N vegetalista *m/f*
vegetable ['vɛdʒtəbl] N (*Bot*) vegetal *m*; (*edible plant*) legume *m*, hortaliça ▶ ADJ vegetal
vegetarian [vɛdʒɪ'tɛərɪən] ADJ, N vegetariano(-a)
vehicle ['viːɪkl] N veículo
veil [veɪl] N véu *m* ▶ VT velar
vein [veɪn] N veia; (*of ore etc*) filão *m*; (*on leaf*) nervura
velvet ['vɛlvɪt] N veludo ▶ ADJ aveludado
vending machine ['vɛndɪŋ-] N vendedor *m* automático
Venezuela [vɛnɛ'zweɪlə] N Venezuela
vengeance ['vɛndʒəns] N vingança; **with a ~** (*fig*) para valer
venison ['vɛnɪsn] N carne *f* de veado
venom ['vɛnəm] N veneno; (*bitterness*) malevolência
vent [vɛnt] N (*opening, in jacket*) abertura; (*also*: **air ~**) respiradouro ▶ VT (*fig: feelings*) desabafar, descarregar
venture ['vɛntʃə^r] N empreendimento ▶ VT (*opinion*) arriscar ▶ VI arriscar-se; **business ~** empreendimento comercial
venue ['vɛnjuː] N local *m*
verb [vəːb] N verbo
verdict ['vəːdɪkt] N veredicto, decisão *f*; (*fig*) opinião *f*, parecer *m*
verge [vəːdʒ] N beira, margem *f*; (*on road*) acostamento (BR), berma (PT); **"soft ~s"** (BRIT *Aut*) "acostamento mole"; **to be on the ~ of doing sth** estar a ponto *or* à beira de fazer algo; **verge on** VT FUS beirar em
versatile ['vəːsətaɪl] ADJ (*person*) versátil; (*machine, tool etc*) polivalente
verse [vəːs] N verso, poesia; (*stanza*) estrofe *f*; (*in bible*) versículo
version ['vəːʃən] N versão *f*
versus ['vəːsəs] PREP contra, versus
vertical ['vəːtɪkl] ADJ vertical
very ['vɛrɪ] ADV muito ▶ ADJ: **the ~ book which** o mesmo livro que;

the ~ last o último (de todos), bem o último; **at the ~ least** no mínimo; **~ much** muitíssimo
vessel ['vɛsl] N (*Naut*) navio, barco; (*container*) vaso, vasilha
vest [vɛst] N (BRIT) camiseta (BR), camisola interior (PT); (US: *waistcoat*) colete *m*
vet [vɛt] N ABBR (= *veterinary surgeon*) veterinário(-a) ▶ VT examinar
veteran ['vɛtərn] N (*also*: **war ~**) veterano de guerra
veto ['vi:təu] (*pl* **vetoes**) N veto ▶ VT vetar
via ['vaɪə] PREP por, via
vibrate [vaɪ'breɪt] VI vibrar
vicar ['vɪkəʳ] N vigário
vice [vaɪs] N (*evil*) vício; (*Tech*) torno mecânico
vice- [vaɪs] PREFIX vice-
vice versa ['vaɪsɪ'və:sə] ADV vice-versa
vicinity [vɪ'sɪnɪtɪ] N proximidade *f*; **in the ~ of** nas proximidades de
vicious ['vɪʃəs] ADJ violento; (*cruel*) cruel
victim ['vɪktɪm] N vítima *f*
victor ['vɪktəʳ] N vencedor(a) *m/f*
Victorian [vɪk'tɔ:rɪən] ADJ vitoriano
victory ['vɪktərɪ] N vitória
video ['vɪdɪəu] N (*video film*) vídeo; (*also*: **~ cassette**) videocassete *m*; (*also*: **~ cassette recorder**) videocassete *m*; **video camera** N filmadora; **videophone** N videofone *m*
Vienna [vɪ'ɛnə] N Viena
Vietnam ['vjɛt'næm] N Vietnã *m* (BR), Vietname *m* (PT); **Vietnamese** [vjɛtnə'mi:z] ADJ vietnamita ▶ N INV vietnamita *m/f*; (*Ling*) vietnamita *m*
view [vju:] N vista; (*outlook*) perspectiva; (*opinion*) opinião *f*, parecer *m* ▶ VT olhar; **in full ~ (of)** à plena vista (de); **in my ~** na minha opinião; **in ~ of the weather/the fact that** em vista do tempo/do fato de que; **viewer** N telespectador(a) *m/f*; **viewpoint** N ponto de vista; (*place*) lugar *m*
vigorous ['vɪgərəs] ADJ vigoroso; (*plant*) vigoso
vile [vaɪl] ADJ vil, infame; (*smell*) repugnante, repulsivo; (*temper*) violento
villa ['vɪlə] N (*country house*) casa de campo; (*suburban house*) vila, quinta
village ['vɪlɪdʒ] N aldeia, povoado; **villager** N aldeão/aldeã *m/f*
villain ['vɪlən] N (*scoundrel*) patife *m*; (BRIT: *in novel etc*) vilão *m*; (*criminal*) marginal *m/f*
vine [vaɪn] N planta trepadeira
vinegar ['vɪnɪgəʳ] N vinagre *m*
vineyard ['vɪnjɑ:d] N vinha, vinhedo
vintage ['vɪntɪdʒ] N vindima; (*year*) safra, colheita ▶ CPD (*comedy*) de época; (*performance*) clássico; **the 1970 ~** a safra de 1970
viola [vɪ'əulə] N viola
violate ['vaɪəleɪt] VT violar
violence ['vaɪələns] N violência; (*strength*) força
violent ['vaɪələnt] ADJ violento; (*intense*) intenso
violet ['vaɪələt] ADJ violeta ▶ N violeta
violin [vaɪə'lɪn] N violino
VIP N ABBR (= *very important person*) VIP *m/f*
viral ['vaɪərəl] ADJ (*Med*) viral; **to go ~** (*Comput*) propagar-se rapidamente
virgin ['və:dʒɪn] N virgem *m/f* ▶ ADJ virgem
Virgo ['və:gəu] N Virgem *f*

virtually ['vəːtjuəlɪ] ADV praticamente
virtual reality ['vəːtjuəl-] N (*Comput*) realidade *f* virtual
virtue ['vəːtjuː] N virtude *f*; (*advantage*) vantagem *f*; **by ~ of** em virtude de
virus ['vaɪərəs] N vírus *m*
visa ['viːzə] N visto
visible ['vɪzəbl] ADJ visível
vision ['vɪʒən] N (*sight*) vista, visão *f*; (*foresight, in dream*) visão *f*
visit ['vɪzɪt] N visita ▶ VT (*person*: *US*: *also*: **~ with**) visitar, fazer uma visita a; (*place*) ir a, ir conhecer; **visiting hours** NPL horário de visita; **visitor** N visitante *m/f*; (*to a house*) visita; (*tourist*) turista *m/f*
visual ['vɪzjuəl] ADJ visual; **visualize** VT visualizar
vital ['vaɪtl] ADJ essencial, indispensável; (*important*) de importância vital; (*crucial*) crucial; (*person*) vivo; (*of life*) vital
vitamin ['vɪtəmɪn] N vitamina
vivid ['vɪvɪd] ADJ (*account*) vívido; (*light*) claro, brilhante; (*imagination, colour*) vivo
V-neck N (*also*: **~ jumper, ~ pullover**) suéter *f* com decote em V
vocabulary [vəu'kæbjulərɪ] N vocabulário
vocal ['vəukl] ADJ vocal; (*noisy*) clamoroso; (*articulate*) claro, eloquente
vodka ['vɔdkə] N vodca
vogue [vəug] N voga, moda; **to be in ~** estar na moda
voice [vɔɪs] N voz *f* ▶ VT expressar; **voice mail** N (*system*) correio *m* de voz; (*device*) caixa *f* postal
void [vɔɪd] N vazio; (*hole*) oco ▶ ADJ nulo; (*empty*): **~ of** destituído de
volatile ['vɔlətaɪl] ADJ volátil; (*situation, person*) imprevisível
volcano [vɔl'keɪnəu] (*pl* **volcanoes**) N vulcão *m*
volt [vəult] N volt *m*
volume ['vɔljuːm] N volume *m*; (*of tank*) capacidade *f*
voluntarily ['vɔləntrɪlɪ] ADV livremente, voluntariamente
voluntary ['vɔləntərɪ] ADJ voluntário; (*unpaid*) (a título) gratuito
volunteer [vɔlən'tɪə^r^] N voluntário(-a) ▶ VT oferecer voluntariamente ▶ VI (*Mil*) alistar-se voluntariamente; **to ~ to do** oferecer-se voluntariamente para fazer
vomit ['vɔmɪt] N vômito ▶ VT, VI vomitar
vote [vəut] N voto; (*votes cast*) votação *f*; (*right to vote*) direito de votar ▶ VT: **to be ~d chairman** *etc* ser eleito presidente *etc*; (*propose*): **to ~ that** propor que; (*in election*) votar ▶ VI votar; **voter** N votante *m/f*, eleitor(a) *m/f*
voucher ['vautʃə^r^] N (*with petrol etc*) vale *m*; (*gift voucher*) vale *m* para presente
vow [vau] N voto ▶ VT: **to ~ to do/ that** prometer solenemente fazer/ que
vowel ['vauəl] N vogal *f*
voyage ['vɔɪɪdʒ] N viagem *f*
vulgar ['vʌlgə^r^] ADJ grosseiro, ordinário; (*in bad taste*) vulgar, baixo
vulture ['vʌltʃə^r^] N abutre *m*, urubu *m*

W

wade [weɪd] VI: **to ~ through** andar em; (*fig: a book*) ler com dificuldade
wafer ['weɪfəʳ] N (*biscuit*) bolacha
waffle ['wɔfl] N (*Culin*) waffle *m*; (*empty talk*) lengalenga ▸ VI encher linguiça
wag [wæg] VT (*tail*) sacudir; (*finger*) menear ▸ VI abanar
wage [weɪdʒ] N (*also*: **~s**) salário, ordenado ▸ VT: **to ~ war** empreender *or* fazer guerra
waggon, wagon ['wægən] N (*horse-drawn*) carroça; (BRIT *Rail*) vagão *m*
wail [weɪl] N lamento, gemido ▸ VI lamentar-se, gemer; (*siren*) tocar
waist [weɪst] N cintura; **waistcoat** N colete *m*
wait [weɪt] N espera ▸ VI esperar; **I can't ~ to** (*fig*) estou morrendo de vontade de; **to ~ for sb/sth** esperar por alguém/algo; **wait behind** VI ficar para trás; **wait on** VT FUS servir; **waiter** N garçom *m* (BR), empregado (PT); **waiting list** N lista de espera; **waiting room** N sala de espera; **waitress** N garçonete *f* (BR), empregada (PT)
waive [weɪv] VT abrir mão de
wake [weɪk] (*pt* **woke**, *pp* **woken**) VT (*also*: **~ up**) acordar ▸ VI acordar ▸ N (*for dead person*) velório; (*Naut*) esteira
Wales [weɪlz] N País *m* de Gales
walk [wɔːk] N passeio; (*hike*) excursão *f* a pé, caminhada; (*gait*) passo, modo de andar; (*in park etc*) alameda, passeio ▸ VI andar; (*for pleasure, exercise*) passear ▸ VT (*distance*) percorrer a pé, andar; (*dog*) levar para passear; **it's 10 minutes' ~ from here** daqui são 10 minutos a pé; **people from all ~s of life** pessoas de todos os níveis; **walk out** VI sair; (*audience*) retirar-se; (*strike*) entrar em greve; **walk out on** VT FUS abandonar; **walkie-talkie** ['wɔːkɪ'tɔːkɪ] N transmissor-receptor *m* portátil, walkie-talkie *m*; **walking** N o andar; **walking shoes** NPL sapatos *mpl* de caminhada; **walking stick** N bengala; **walkway** N passeio, passadiço
wall [wɔːl] N parede *f*; (*exterior*) muro; (*city wall etc*) muralha
wallet ['wɔlɪt] N carteira
wallpaper ['wɔːlpeɪpəʳ] N papel *m* de parede ▸ VT colocar papel de parede em
walnut ['wɔːlnʌt] N noz *f*; (*tree, wood*) nogueira
walrus ['wɔːlrəs] (*pl* **walrus** *or* **walruses**) N morsa
waltz [wɔːlts] N valsa ▸ VI valsar
wand [wɔnd] N (*also*: **magic ~**) varinha de condão

wander ['wɔndəʳ] VI (*person*) vagar, perambular; (*thoughts*) divagar ▶ VT perambular
want [wɔnt] VT querer; (*demand*) exigir; (*need*) precisar de, necessitar; **wanted** ADJ (*criminal etc*) procurado (pela polícia); **"cook wanted"** (*in advertisement*) "precisa-se cozinheiro"
war [wɔːʳ] N guerra; **to make ~ (on)** fazer guerra (contra)
ward [wɔːd] N (*in hospital*) ala; (*Pol*) distrito eleitoral; (*Jur: child*) tutelado(-a), pupilo(-a); **ward off** VT desviar, aparar; (*attack*) repelir
warden ['wɔːdn] N (BRIT: *of institution*) diretor(a) *m/f*; (*of park, game reserve*) administrador(a) *m/f*; (BRIT: *also*: **traffic ~**) guarda *m/f*
wardrobe ['wɔːdrəub] N guarda-roupa *m*
warehouse ['wɛəhaus] N armazém *m*, depósito
warfare ['wɔːfɛəʳ] N guerra, combate *m*
warhead ['wɔːhɛd] N ogiva
warm [wɔːm] ADJ quente; (*thanks, welcome*) caloroso; **it's ~** está quente; **I'm ~** estou com calor; **warm up** VI esquentar ▶ VT esquentar; **warmly** ADV calorosamente; **warmth** N calor *m*; (*friendliness*) calor humano
warn [wɔːn] VT prevenir, avisar; **to ~ sb that/of/(not) to do** prevenir alguém de que/de/para (não) fazer
warning ['wɔːnɪŋ] N advertência; (*in writing*) aviso; (*signal*) sinal *m*
warrant ['wɔrnt] N (*voucher*) comprovante *m*; (*Jur: to arrest*) mandado de prisão; (: *to search*) mandado de busca; **warranty** N garantia
warrior ['wɔrɪəʳ] N guerreiro(-a)
Warsaw ['wɔːsɔː] N Varsóvia
warship ['wɔːʃɪp] N navio de guerra
wart [wɔːt] N verruga
wartime ['wɔːtaɪm] N: **in ~** em tempo de guerra
wary ['wɛərɪ] ADJ cauteloso, precavido
was [wɔz] PT *of* **be**
wash [wɔʃ] VT lavar ▶ VI lavar-se; (*sea etc*): **to ~ over/against sth** bater/chocar-se contra algo ▶ N (*clothes etc*) lavagem *f*; (*of ship*) esteira; **to have a ~** lavar-se; **wash away** VT (*stain*) tirar ao lavar; (*subj: river etc*) levar, arrastar; **wash off** VT tirar lavando ▶ VI sair ao lavar; **wash up** VI (BRIT) lavar a louça; (US) lavar-se; **washbasin** N pia (BR), lavatório (PT); **washing** (BRIT) N (*dirty*) roupa suja; (*clean*) roupa lavada; **washing machine** N máquina de lavar roupa, lavadora; **washing powder** (BRIT) N sabão *m* em pó; **washing-up** N: **to do the washing-up** lavar a louça; **washing-up liquid** N detergente *m*; **washroom** (US) N banheiro (BR), casa de banho (PT)
wasn't ['wɔznt] = **was not**
wasp [wɔsp] N vespa
waste [weɪst] N desperdício, esbanjamento; (*of time*) perda; (*also*: **household ~**) detritos *mpl* domésticos; (*rubbish*) lixo ▶ ADJ (*material*) de refugo; (*left over*) de sobra; (*land*) baldio ▶ VT (*squander*) esbanjar, desperdiçar; (*time, opportunity*) perder; **wastes** NPL ermos *mpl*; **to lay ~** devastar; **waste away** VI definhar
watch [wɔtʃ] N (*clock*) relógio; (*also*: **wrist~**) relógio de pulso;

(*act of watching*) vigia; (*guard: Mil*) sentinela; (*Naut: spell of duty*) quarto ▶ VT (*look at*) observar, olhar; (*programme, match*) assistir a; (*television*) ver; (*spy on, guard*) vigiar; (*be careful of*) tomar cuidado com ▶ VI ver, olhar; (*keep guard*) montar guarda; **watch out** VI ter cuidado; **watchdog** N cão *m* de guarda; (*fig*) vigia *m/f*

water ['wɔːtəʳ] N água ▶ VT (*plant*) regar ▶ VI (*eyes*) lacrimejar; (*mouth*) salivar; **in British ~s** nas águas territoriais britânicas; **water down** VT (*milk*) aguar; (*fig*) diluir; **watercolour**, (US) **watercolor** N aquarela; **waterfall** N cascata, cachoeira; **watering can** N regador *m*; **watermelon** N melancia; **waterproof** ADJ impermeável; **water-skiing** N esqui *m* aquático

watt [wɔt] N watt *m*

wave [weɪv] N onda; (*of hand*) aceno, sinal *m*; (*in hair*) onda, ondulação *f* ▶ VI acenar com a mão; (*flag, grass, branches*) tremular ▶ VT (*hand*) acenar; (*handkerchief*) acenar com; (*weapon*) brandir; **wavelength** N comprimento de onda; **to be on the same wavelength as** ter os mesmos gostos e atitudes que

waver ['weɪvəʳ] VI vacilar; (*voice, eyes, love*) hesitar

wavy ['weɪvɪ] ADJ (*hair*) ondulado; (*line*) ondulante

wax [wæks] N cera ▶ VT encerar; (*car*) polir ▶ VI (*moon*) crescer

way [weɪ] N caminho; (*distance*) percurso; (*direction*) direção *f*, sentido; (*manner*) maneira, modo; (*habit*) costume *m*; **which ~? — this ~** por onde? — por aqui; **on the ~ (to)** a caminho (de); **to be on one's ~** estar a caminho; **to be in the ~** atrapalhar; **to go out of one's ~ to do sth** dar-se ao trabalho de fazer algo; **to lose one's ~** perder-se; **to be under ~** estar em andamento; **in a ~** de certo modo, até certo ponto; **in some ~s** a certos respeitos; **by the ~** a propósito; **"~ in"** (BRIT) "entrada"; **"~ out"** (BRIT) "saída"; **the ~ back** o caminho de volta; **"give ~"** (BRIT *Aut*) "dê a preferência"; **no ~!** (*inf*) de jeito nenhum!

WC ['dʌblju'siː] N ABBR (= *water closet*) privada

we [wiː] PRON PL nós

weak [wiːk] ADJ fraco, débil; (*morally, currency*) fraco; (*excuse*) pouco convincente; (*tea*) aguado, ralo; **weaken** VI enfraquecer(-se); (*give way*) ceder; (*influence, power*) diminuir ▶ VT enfraquecer; **weakness** N fraqueza; (*fault*) ponto fraco; **to have a weakness for** ter uma queda por

wealth [wɛlθ] N riqueza; (*of details*) abundância; **wealthy** ADJ rico, abastado; (*country*) rico

weapon ['wɛpən] N arma; **~s of mass destruction** armas de destruição em massa

wear [wɛəʳ] (*pt* **wore**, *pp* **worn**) N (*use*) uso; (*deterioration through use*) desgaste *m*; (*clothing*): **baby/sports ~** roupa infantil/de esporte ▶ VT (*clothes*) usar; (*shoes*) usar, calçar; (*put on*) vestir; (*damage: through use*) desgastar ▶ VI (*last*) durar; (*rub through etc*) gastar-se; **town/evening ~** traje *m* de passeio/de gala; **wear away** VT gastar ▶ VI desgastar-se; **wear down** VT gastar; (*strength*) esgotar;

wear off VI (*pain etc*) passar; **wear out** VT desgastar; (*person, strength*) esgotar
weary ['wɪərɪ] ADJ cansado; (*dispirited*) deprimido ▶ VI: **to ~ of** cansar-se de
weasel ['wi:zl] N (*Zool*) doninha
weather ['wɛðə^r] N tempo ▶ VT (*storm, crisis*) resistir a; **under the ~** (*fig: ill*) doente; **weather forecast** N previsão *f* do tempo
weave [wi:v] (*pt, pp* **wove** *or* **woven**) VT tecer
web [wɛb] N (*of spider*) teia; (*on foot*) membrana; (*network*) rede *f*; **the (World Wide) W~** a (World Wide) Web; **web address** N endereço web; **webcam** ['wɛbkæm] N webcam *f*; **webinar** ['wɛbɪnɑ:^r] N seminário online, webinar *m*; **weblog** N weblog *m*; **webmail** N (serviço *m* de) webmail *m*; **web page** N página (da) web; **website** N site *m*, website *m*
wed [wɛd] (*pt, pp* **wedded**) VT casar ▶ VI casar-se
we'd [wi:d] = **we had;** = **we would**
wedding ['wɛdɪŋ] N casamento, núpcias *fpl*; **wedding dress** N vestido de noiva; **wedding ring** N anel *m or* aliança de casamento
wedge [wɛdʒ] N (*of wood etc*) cunha, calço; (*of cake*) fatia ▶ VT (*pack tightly*) apinhar; (*door*) pôr calço em
Wednesday ['wɛdnzdɪ] N quarta-feira
wee [wi:] (SCOTLAND) ADJ pequeno, pequenino
weed [wi:d] N erva daninha ▶ VT capinar; **weedkiller** N herbicida *m*
week [wi:k] N semana; **a ~ today** daqui a uma semana; **a ~ on Tuesday** sem ser essa terça-feira, a outra; **every other ~** uma semana sim, uma semana não; **weekday** N dia *m* de semana; (*Comm*) dia útil; **weekend** N fim *m* de semana; **weekly** ADV semanalmente ▶ ADJ semanal ▶ N semanário
weep [wi:p] (*pt, pp* **wept**) VI (*person*) chorar
weigh [weɪ] VT, VI pesar; **to ~ anchor** levantar ferro; **weigh down** VT sobrecarregar; (*fig: with worry*) deprimir, acabrunhar; **weigh up** VT ponderar, avaliar
weight [weɪt] N peso; **to lose/put on ~** emagrecer/engordar
weird [wɪəd] ADJ esquisito, estranho
welcome ['wɛlkəm] ADJ bem-vindo ▶ N acolhimento, recepção *f* ▶ VT dar as boas-vindas a; (*be glad of*) saudar; **you're ~** (*after thanks*) de nada
weld [wɛld] N solda ▶ VT soldar, unir
welfare ['wɛlfɛə^r] N bem-estar *m*; (*social aid*) assistência social; **welfare state** N *país auto-financiador da sua assistência social*
well [wɛl] N poço ▶ ADV bem ▶ ADJ: **to be ~** estar bem (de saúde) ▶ EXCL bem!, então!; **as ~** também; **as ~ as** assim como; **~ done!** muito bem!; **get ~ soon!** melhoras!; **to do ~** ir *or* sair-se bem; (*business*) ir bem; **well up** VI brotar
we'll [wi:l] = **we will;** = **we shall**
well: well-behaved [-bɪ'heɪvd] ADJ bem comportado; **well-built** ADJ robusto; (*house*) bem construído; **well-dressed** [-drɛst] ADJ bem vestido

W

wellingtons ['wɛlɪŋtənz] N (*also:* **wellington boots**) *botas de borracha até os joelhos*
well-known ADJ conhecido
well-off ADJ próspero, rico
Welsh [wɛlʃ] ADJ galês/galesa ▶ N (*Ling*) galês *m*; **the Welsh** NPL (*people*) os galeses; **Welshman** *irreg* N galês *m*; **Welshwoman** *irreg* N galesa
went [wɛnt] PT *of* **go**
wept [wɛpt] PT, PP *of* **weep**
were [wəːʳ] PT *of* **be**
we're [wɪəʳ] = **we are**
weren't [wəːnt] = **were not**
west [wɛst] N oeste *m* ▶ ADJ ocidental, do oeste ▶ ADV para o oeste *or* ao oeste; **the W~** (*Pol*) o Oeste, o Ocidente; **western** ADJ ocidental ▶ N (*Cinema*) western *m*, bangue-bangue (BR *inf*); **West Indian** ADJ, N antilhano(-a); **West Indies** NPL Antilhas *fpl*
wet [wɛt] ADJ molhado; (*damp*) úmido; (*wet through*) encharcado; (*rainy*) chuvoso ▶ N (BRIT *Pol*) político de tendência moderada; **to get ~** molhar-se; **"~ paint"** "tinta fresca"; **wetsuit** N roupa de mergulho
we've [wiːv] = **we have**
whale [weɪl] N (*Zool*) baleia
wharf [wɔːf] (*pl* **wharves**) N cais *m inv*

KEYWORD

what [wɔt] ADJ **1** (*in direct/indirect questions*) que, qual; **what size is it?** que tamanho é este?; **what colour/shape is it?** qual é a cor/o formato?; **he asked me what books I needed** ele me perguntou de quais os livros eu precisava
2 (*in exclamations*) quê!, como!; **what a mess!** que bagunça!
▶ PRON **1** (*interrogative*) que, o que; **what are you doing?** o que é que você está fazendo?; **what is it called?** como se chama?; **what about me?** e eu?; **what about doing ...?** que tal fazer ...?
2 (*relative*) o que; **I saw what you did/was on the table** eu vi o que você fez/estava na mesa; **he asked me what she had said** ele me perguntou o que ela tinha dito
▶ EXCL (*disbelieving*): **what, no coffee?** ué, não tem café?

whatever [wɔt'ɛvəʳ] ADJ: **~ book you choose** qualquer livro que você escolha ▶ PRON: **do ~ is necessary/you want** faça tudo o que for preciso/o que você quiser; **~ happens** aconteça o que acontecer; **no reason ~** *or* **whatsoever** nenhuma razão seja qual for *or* em absoluto; **nothing ~** nada em absoluto
whatsoever [wɔtsəu'ɛvəʳ] ADJ = **whatever**
wheat [wiːt] N trigo
wheel [wiːl] N roda; (*also:* **steering ~**) volante *m*; (*Naut*) roda do leme ▶ VT (*pram etc*) empurrar ▶ VI (*birds*) dar voltas; (*also:* **~ round**) girar, dar voltas, virar-se; **wheelbarrow** N carrinho de mão; **wheelchair** N cadeira de rodas; **wheel clamp** N (*Aut*) *grampo com que se imobiliza carros estacionados ilegalmente*
wheeze [wiːz] VI respirar ruidosamente

KEYWORD

when [wɛn] ADV quando
▶ CONJ **1** (*at, during, after the time that*) quando; **when you've read it, tell me what you think** depois

que você tiver lido isto, diga-me o que acha; **that was when I needed you** foi quando eu precisei de você
2 (*on, at which*) quando, em que; **on the day when I met him** no dia em que o conheci; **one day when it was raining** um dia quando estava chovendo
3 (*whereas*) ao passo que; **you said I was wrong when in fact I was right** você disse que eu estava errado quando, na verdade, eu estava certo

whenever [wɛn'ɛvəʳ] CONJ quando, quando quer que; (*every time that*) sempre que ▶ ADV quando você quiser
where [wɛəʳ] ADV onde ▶ CONJ onde, aonde; **this is ~ ...** aqui é onde ...; **whereabouts** ['wɛərəbauts] ADV (por) onde ▶ N: **nobody knows his whereabouts** ninguém sabe o seu paradeiro; **whereas** [wɛər'æz] CONJ uma vez que, ao passo que; **whereby** ADV (*formal*) pelo qual (*or* pela qual *etc*); **wherever** [wɛər'ɛvəʳ] CONJ onde quer que ▶ ADV (*interrogative*) onde?
whether ['wɛðəʳ] CONJ se; **I don't know ~ to accept or not** não sei se aceito ou não; **~ you go or not** quer você vá quer não; **it's doubtful ~ ...** não é certo que ...

KEYWORD

which [wɪtʃ] ADJ **1** (*interrogative*) que, qual; **which picture do you want?** que quadro você quer?; **which books are yours?** quais são os seus livros?; **which one?** qual?
2: **in which case** em cujo caso; **by which time** momento em que
▶ PRON **1** (*interrogative*) qual; **which (of these) are yours?** quais (destes) são seus?
2 (*relative*) que, o que, o qual *etc*; **the apple which you ate** a maçã que você comeu; **the chair on which you are sitting** a cadeira na qual você está sentado; **he said he knew, which is true** ele disse que sabia, o que é verdade; **after which** depois do que

whichever [wɪtʃ'ɛvəʳ] ADJ: **take ~ book you prefer** pegue o livro que preferir; **~ book you take** qualquer livro que você pegue
while [waɪl] N tempo, momento ▶ CONJ enquanto, ao mesmo tempo que; (*as long as*) contanto que; (*although*) embora; **for a ~** durante algum tempo; **while away** VT (*time*) encher
whim [wɪm] N capricho, veneta
whine [waɪn] N (*of pain*) gemido; (*of engine, siren*) zunido ▶ VI gemer; zunir; (*fig*) lamuriar-se
whip [wɪp] N açoite *m*; (*for riding*) chicote *m*; (*Pol*) líder *m/f* da bancada ▶ VT chicotear; (*snatch*) apanhar de repente; (*cream, eggs*) bater; (*move quickly*): **to ~ sth out/off/away** *etc* arrancar algo; **whipped cream** [wɪpt-] N creme *m* chantilly
whirl [wəːl] VT fazer girar ▶ VI (*dancers*) rodopiar; (*leaves, water etc*) redemoinhar
whisk [wɪsk] N (*Culin*) batedeira ▶ VT bater; **to ~ sb away** *or* **off** levar alguém rapidamente
whiskers ['wɪskəz] NPL (*of animal*) bigodes *mpl*; (*of man*) suíças *fpl*
whisky ['wɪskɪ], (US, IRELAND) **whiskey** N uísque *m* (BR), whisky *m* (PT)

W

whisper ['wɪspəʳ] N sussurro, murmúrio ▶ VT, VI sussurrar
whistle ['wɪsl] N (*sound*) assobio; (*object*) apito ▶ VT, VI assobiar
white [waɪt] ADJ branco; (*pale*) pálido ▶ N branco; (*of egg*) clara; **whiteboard** N quadro branco; **interactive whiteboard** quadro interativo; **white coffee** N café *m* com leite; **White House** N *ver nota*

A Casa Branca (**White House**) é um grande edifício branco situado em Washington D.C. onde reside o presidente dos Estados Unidos. Por extensão, o termo se refere também ao poder executivo americano.

whitewash ['waɪtwɔʃ] N (*paint*) cal *f* ▶ VT caiar; (*fig*) encobrir
whiting ['waɪtɪŋ] N INV pescada-marlonga
Whitsun ['wɪtsn] N Pentecostes *m*
whizz [wɪz] VI: **to ~ past** *or* **by** passar a toda velocidade

KEYWORD

who [hu:] PRON **1** (*interrogative*) quem?; **who is it?** quem é?
2 (*relative*) que, o qual *etc*, quem; **my cousin, who lives in New York** meu primo que mora em Nova Iorque; **the man/woman who spoke to me** o homem/a mulher que falou comigo

whole [həul] ADJ (*complete*) todo, inteiro; (*not broken*) intacto ▶ N (*all*): **the ~ of the time** o tempo todo; (*entire unit*) conjunto; **on the ~, as a ~** como um todo, no conjunto; **wholemeal** (BRIT) ADJ integral; **wholesale** N venda por atacado ▶ ADJ por atacado; (*destruction*) em grande escala ▶ ADV por atacado; **wholewheat** ADJ = **wholemeal**;
wholly ['həulɪ] ADV totalmente, completamente

KEYWORD

whom [hu:m] PRON **1** (*interrogative*) quem?; **to whom did you give it?** para quem você deu isto?
2 (*relative*) que, quem; **the man whom I saw/to whom I spoke** o homem que eu vi/com quem eu falei

whore [hɔ:ʳ] (*inf, pej*) N puta

KEYWORD

whose [hu:z] ADJ **1** (*possessive, interrogative*): **whose book is this?, whose is this book?** de quem é este livro?; **I don't know whose it is** eu não sei de quem é isto
2 (*possessive, relative*): **the man whose son you rescued** o homem cujo filho você salvou; **the woman whose car was stolen** a mulher de quem o carro foi roubado
▶ PRON de quem

KEYWORD

why [waɪ] ADV por que (BR), porque (PT); (*at end of sentence*) por quê (BR), porquê (PT)
▶ CONJ por que; **that's not why I'm here** não é por isso que estou aqui; **the reason why** a razão por que
▶ EXCL (*expressing surprise, shock, annoyance*) ora essa!; (*explaining*) bem!; **why, it's you!** ora, é você!

wicked ['wɪkɪd] ADJ perverso; (*smile*) malicioso
wicket ['wɪkɪt] N (*Cricket*) arco

wide [waɪd] ADJ largo; (*area, publicity, knowledge*) amplo ▶ ADV: **to open ~** abrir totalmente; **to shoot ~** atirar longe do alvo; **widely** ADV extremamente; (*travelled, spaced*) muito; (*believed, known*) ampliamente; **widen** VT alargar; (*one's experience*) aumentar ▶ VI alargar-se; **wide open** ADJ (*eyes*) arregalado; (*door*) escancarado; **widespread** ADJ (*belief etc*) difundido, comum

widget ['wɪdʒɪt] N (*Comput*) widget *m*

widow ['wɪdəu] N viúva; **widower** N viúvo

width [wɪdθ] N largura

wield [wi:ld] VT (*sword*) brandir, empunhar; (*power*) exercer

wife [waɪf] (*pl* **wives**) N mulher *f*, esposa

Wi-Fi ['waɪfaɪ] N Wi-Fi *m*

wig [wɪg] N peruca

wild [waɪld] ADJ (*animal*) selvagem; (*plant*) silvestre; (*rough*) violento, furioso; (*idea*) disparatado, extravagante; (*person*) insensato; **wilderness** ['wɪldənɪs] N ermo; **wildlife** N animais *mpl* (e plantas *fpl*) selvagens; **wildly** ADV (*behave*) freneticamente; (*hit, guess*) irrefletidamente; (*happy*) extremamente

KEYWORD

will [wɪl] (*pt, pp* **willed**) AUX VB

1 (*forming future tense*): **I will finish it tomorrow** vou acabar isto amanhã; **I will have finished it by tomorrow** até amanhã eu terei terminado isto; **will you do it? — yes I will/no I won't** você vai fazer isto? — sim, vou/não eu não vou

2 (*in conjectures, predictions*): **he will come** ele virá; **he will** *or* **he'll be there by now** nesta altura ele está lá; **that will be the postman** deve ser o carteiro; **this medicine will/won't help you** este remédio vai/não vai fazer efeito em você

3 (*in commands, requests, offers*): **will you be quiet!** fique quieto, por favor!; **will you come?** você vem?; **will you help me?** você pode me ajudar?; **will you have a cup of tea?** você vai querer uma xícara de chá *or* um chá?; **I won't put up with it** eu não vou tolerar isto

▶ VT: **to will sb to do sth** desejar que alguém faça algo; **he willed himself to go on** reuniu grande força de vontade para continuar

▶ N (*volition*) vontade *f*; (*testament*) testamento

willing ['wɪlɪŋ] ADJ disposto, pronto; (*enthusiastic*) entusiasmado; **willingly** ADV de bom grado, de boa vontade

willow ['wɪləu] N salgueiro

willpower ['wɪlpauəʳ] N força de vontade

wilt [wɪlt] VI (*flower*) murchar; (*plant*) morrer

win [wɪn] (*pt, pp* **won**) N vitória ▶ VT ganhar, vencer; (*obtain*) conseguir, obter; (*support*) alcançar ▶ VI ganhar; **win over** VT conquistar; **win round** (BRIT) VT = **win over**

wince [wɪns] VI encolher-se, estremecer

wind¹ [wɪnd] N vento; (*Med*) gases *mpl*, flatulência; (*breath*) fôlego ▶ VT deixar sem fôlego

wind² [waɪnd] (*pt, pp* **wound**) VT enrolar, bobinar; (*wrap*) envolver;

(*clock, toy*) dar corda a ▸VI (*road, river*) serpentear; **wind up** VT (*clock*) dar corda em; (*debate*) rematar, concluir
windfall ['wɪndfɔːl] N golpe *m* de sorte
wind farm N parque *m* eólico
winding ['waɪndɪŋ] ADJ (*road*) sinuoso, tortuoso; (*staircase*) de caracol, em espiral
windmill ['wɪndmɪl] N moinho de vento
window ['wɪndəu] N janela; (*in shop etc*) vitrine *f* (BR), montra (PT); **window box** N jardineira (no peitoril da janela); **window cleaner** N limpador(a) *m/f* de janelas; **window-shopping** N: **to go window-shopping** ir ver vitrines
windscreen ['wɪndskriːn] (BRIT) N para-brisa *m*; **windscreen wiper** (BRIT) N limpador *m* de para-brisa
windshield ['wɪndʃiːld] (US) N = **windscreen**
wind turbine ['wɪndtəːbaɪn] N turbina eólica
windy ['wɪndɪ] ADJ com muito vento, batido pelo vento; **it's ~** está ventando (BR), faz vento (PT)
wine [waɪn] N vinho; **wine bar** N bar *m* para degustação de vinhos; **wine glass** N cálice *m* (de vinho); **wine list** N lista de vinhos
wing [wɪŋ] N asa; (*of building*) ala; (*Aut*) aleta, para-lamas *m inv*; **wings** NPL (*Theatre*) bastidores *mpl*
wink [wɪŋk] N piscadela ▸VI piscar o olho; (*light etc*) piscar
winner ['wɪnəʳ] N vencedor(a) *m/f*
winning ['wɪnɪŋ] ADJ (*team*) vencedor(a); (*goal*) decisivo; (*smile*) sedutor(a)
winter ['wɪntəʳ] N inverno; **winter sports** NPL esportes *mpl* (BR) *or* desportos *mpl* (PT) de inverno
wipe [waɪp] N: **to give sth a ~** limpar algo com um pano ▸VT limpar; (*rub*) esfregar; (*erase: tape*) apagar; **wipe off** VT remover esfregando; **wipe out** VT (*debt*) liquidar; (*memory*) apagar; (*destroy*) exterminar; **wipe up** VT limpar
wire ['waɪəʳ] N arame *m*; (*Elec*) fio (elétrico); (*telegram*) telegrama *m* ▸VT (*house*) instalar a rede elétrica em; (*also*: **~ up**) conectar; (*telegram*) telegrafar para
wireless ['waɪəlɪs] ADJ sem fio (BR), sem fios (PT)
wiring ['waɪərɪŋ] N instalação *f* elétrica
wisdom ['wɪzdəm] N prudência; (*of action, remark*) bom-senso, sabedoria; **wisdom tooth** *irreg* N dente *m* do siso
wise [waɪz] ADJ prudente; (*action, remark*) sensato
wish [wɪʃ] N desejo ▸VT (*want*) querer; **best ~es** (*on birthday etc*) parabéns *mpl*, felicidades *fpl*; **with best ~es** (*in letter*) cumprimentos; **to ~ sb goodbye** despedir-se de alguém; **he ~ed me well** me desejou boa sorte; **to ~ to do/sb to do sth** querer fazer/que alguém faça algo; **to ~ for** desejar
wistful ['wɪstful] ADJ melancólico
wit [wɪt] N (*wittiness*) presença de espírito, engenho; (*intelligence*: *also*: **~s**) entendimento; (*person*) espirituoso(-a)
witch [wɪtʃ] N bruxa

KEYWORD

with [wɪð, wɪθ] PREP **1** (*accompanying, in the company of*) com; **I was with him** eu estava com ele; **to stay overnight with friends** dormir na casa de amigos; **we'll take the**

children with us vamos levar as crianças conosco; **I'll be with you in a minute** vou vê-lo num minuto; **I'm with you** (*I understand*) compreendo; **to be with it** (*inf*) estar por dentro; (: *aware*) estar a par da situação; (: *up-to-date*) estar atualizado com
2 (*descriptive*) com, de; **a room with a view** um quarto com vista; **the man with the grey hat/blue eyes** o homem do chapéu cinza/ de olhos azuis
3 (*indicating manner, means, cause*) com, de; **with tears in her eyes** com os olhos cheios de lágrimas; **to fill sth with water** encher algo de água

withdraw [wɪð'drɔ:] *irreg* VT tirar, remover; (*offer*) retirar ▸VI retirar-se; **to ~ money (from the bank)** retirar dinheiro (do banco); **withdrawal** N retirada; **withdrawal symptoms** NPL síndrome *f* de abstinência; **withdrawn** ADJ (*person*) reservado, introvertido
wither ['wɪðəʳ] VI murchar
withhold [wɪð'həuld] (*irreg*: *like* **hold**) VT (*money*) reter; (*permission*) negar; (*information*) esconder
within [wɪð'ɪn] PREP dentro de ▸ADV dentro; **~ reach** ao alcance da mão; **~ sight** à vista; **~ the week** antes do fim da semana; **~ a mile of** a uma milha de
without [wɪð'aut] PREP sem; **~ anybody knowing** sem ninguém saber; **to go** *or* **do ~ sth** passar sem algo
withstand [wɪð'stænd] (*irreg*: *like* **stand**) VT resistir a
witness ['wɪtnɪs] N testemunha ▸VT testemunhar, presenciar; (*document*) legalizar; **to bear ~ to sth** (*fig*) testemunhar algo
witty ['wɪtɪ] ADJ espirituoso
wives [waɪvz] NPL *of* **wife**
wizard ['wɪzəd] N feiticeiro, mago
wk ABBR = **week**
wobble ['wɔbl] VI oscilar; (*chair*) balançar
woe [wəu] N dor *f*, mágoa
woke [wəuk] PT *of* **wake**; **woken** PP *of* **wake**
wolf [wulf] (*pl* **wolves**) N lobo
woman ['wumən] (*pl* **women**) N mulher *f*; **~ doctor** médica
womb [wu:m] N (*Anat*) matriz *f*, útero
women ['wɪmɪn] NPL *of* **woman**
won [wʌn] PT, PP *of* **win**
wonder ['wʌndəʳ] N maravilha, prodígio; (*feeling*) espanto ▸VI: **to ~ whether/why** perguntar-se a si mesmo se/por quê; **to ~ at** admirar-se de; **to ~ about** pensar sobre *or* em; **it's no ~ that** não é de admirar que; **wonderful** ADJ maravilhoso; (*miraculous*) impressionante
won't [wəunt] = **will not**
wood [wud] N (*timber*) madeira; (*forest*) floresta, bosque *m*; **wooden** ADJ de madeira; (*fig*) inexpressivo; **woodwind** N (*Mus*) instrumentos *mpl* de sopro de madeira; **woodwork** N carpintaria
wool [wul] N lã *f*; **to pull the ~ over sb's eyes** (*fig*) enganar alguém, vender a alguém gato por lebre; **woollen** ADJ de lã; **woolly**, (US) **wooly** ADJ de lã; (*fig*) confuso
word [wə:d] N palavra; (*news*) notícia ▸VT redigir; **in other ~s** em outras palavras, ou seja; **to break/keep one's ~** faltar à palavra/cumprir a promessa;

to have ~s with sb discutir com alguém; **wording** N fraseado; **word processing** N processamento de textos; **word processor** N processador *m* de textos
wore [wɔːʳ] PT *of* **wear**
work [wəːk] N trabalho; (*job*) emprego, trabalho; (*Art, Literature*) obra ▶ VI trabalhar; (*mechanism*) funcionar; (*medicine etc*) surtir efeito, ser eficaz ▶ VT (*clay*) moldar; (*wood etc*) talhar; (*mine etc*) explorar; (*machine*) fazer trabalhar, manejar; (*effect, miracle*) causar; **to ~ loose** (*part*) soltar-se; (*knot*) afrouxar-se; **work on** VT FUS trabalhar em, dedicar-se a; (*principle*) basear-se em; **work out** VI dar certo, surtir efeito ▶ VT (*problem*) resolver; (*plan*) elaborar, formular; **it ~s out at £100** dá £100; **worker** N trabalhador(a) *m/f*, operário(-a); **working class** N proletariado, classe *f* operária ▶ ADJ: **working-class** do proletariado, da classe operária; **workman** *irreg* N operário, trabalhador *m*; **worksheet** N (*with exercises*) folha de exercícios; **workshop** N oficina; (*practical session*) aula prática
world [wəːld] N mundo ▶ CPD mundial; **to think the ~ of sb** (*fig*) ter alguém em alto conceito
worm [wəːm] N (*also*: **earth~**) minhoca, lombriga
worn [wɔːn] PP *of* **wear** ▶ ADJ gasto; **worn-out** ADJ (*object*) gasto; (*person*) esgotado, exausto
worry [ˈwʌrɪ] N preocupação *f* ▶ VT preocupar, inquietar ▶ VI preocupar-se, afligir-se
worse [wəːs] ADJ, ADV pior ▶ N o pior; **a change for the ~** uma mudança para pior, uma piora; **worsen** VT, VI piorar; **worse off** ADJ com menos dinheiro; (*fig*): **you'll be worse off this way** assim você ficará pior que nunca
worship [ˈwəːʃɪp] N adoração *f* ▶ VT adorar, venerar; (*person, thing*) adorar; **Your W~** (BRIT: *to mayor*) vossa Excelência; (: *to judge*) senhor Juiz
worst [wəːst] ADJ (o/a) pior ▶ ADV pior ▶ N o pior; **at ~** na pior das hipóteses
worth [wəːθ] N valor *m*, mérito ▶ ADJ: **to be ~** valer; **it's ~ it** vale a pena; **to be ~ one's while (to do)** valer a pena (fazer); **worthless** ADJ (*person*) imprestável; (*thing*) inútil; **worthwhile** ADJ (*activity*) que vale a pena; (*cause*) de mérito, louvável
worthy [ˈwəːðɪ] ADJ (*person*) merecedor(a), respeitável; (*motive*) justo; **~ of** digno de

KEYWORD

would [wud] AUX VB **1** (*conditional tense*): **if you asked him, he would do it** se você pedisse, ele faria isto; **if you had asked him, he would have done it** se você tivesse pedido, ele teria feito isto
2 (*in offers, invitations, requests*): **would you like a biscuit?** você quer um biscoito?; **would you ask him to come in?** pode pedir a ele para entrar?; **would you close the door, please?** quer fechar a porta por favor?
3 (*in indirect speech*): **I said I would do it** eu disse que eu faria isto
4 (*emphatic*): **you WOULD say that, wouldn't you?** é lógico que você vai dizer isso
5 (*insistence*): **she wouldn't behave** não houve jeito dela se comportar

6 (*conjecture*): **it would have been midnight** devia ser meia-noite; **it would seem so** parece que sim 7 (*indicating habit*): **he would go on Mondays** costumava ir nas segundas-feiras

wouldn't ['wudnt] = **would not**
wound[1] [waund] PT, PP *of* **wind**[2]
wound[2] [wu:nd] N ferida ▶ VT ferir
wove [wəuv] PT *of* **weave**; **woven** PP *of* **weave**
wrap [ræp] N (*stole*) xale *m*; (*cape*) capa ▶ VT (*cover*) envolver; (*also*: **~ up**) embrulhar; **wrapper** N invólucro; (BRIT: *of book*) capa; **wrapping paper** N papel *m* de embrulho; (*fancy*) papel de presente
wreath [ri:θ] N coroa
wreck [rɛk] N (*of vehicle*) destroços *mpl*; (*ship*) restos *mpl* do naufrágio; (*pej: person*) caco ▶ VT destruir, danificar; (*fig*) arruinar, arrasar; **wreckage** N (*of car, plane*) destroços *mpl*; (*of ship*) restos *mpl*; (*of building*) escombros *mpl*
wren [rɛn] N (*Zool*) carriça
wrench [rɛntʃ] N (*Tech*) chave *f* inglesa; (*tug*) puxão *m*; (*fig*) separação *f* penosa ▶ VT torcer com força; **to ~ sth from sb** arrancar algo de alguém
wrestle ['rɛsl] VI: **to ~ (with sb)** lutar (com *or* contra alguém); **wrestler** N lutador *m*; **wrestling** N luta (livre)
wretched ['rɛtʃɪd] ADJ desventurado, infeliz; (*inf*) maldito
wriggle ['rɪgl] VI (*also*: **~ about**) retorcer-se, contorcer-se
wring [rɪŋ] (*pt, pp* **wrung**) VT (*clothes, neck*) torcer; (*hands*) apertar; (*fig*): **to ~ sth out of sb** arrancar algo de alguém
wrinkle ['rɪŋkl] N (*on skin*) ruga; (*on paper*) prega ▶ VT franzir ▶ VI enrugar-se
wrist [rɪst] N pulso
write [raɪt] (*pt* **wrote**, *pp* **written**) VT escrever; (*cheque, prescription*) passar ▶ VI escrever; **to ~ to sb** escrever para alguém; **write down** VT (*note*) anotar; (*put on paper*) pôr no papel; **write off** VT cancelar; **write out** VT escrever por extenso; (*cheque etc*) passar; **write up** VT redigir; **write-off** N perda total; **writer** N escritor(a) *m/f*
writing ['raɪtɪŋ] N escrita; (*handwriting*) caligrafia, letra; (*of author*) obra; **in ~** por escrito
wrong [rɔŋ] ADJ (*bad*) errado, mau; (*unfair*) injusto; (*incorrect*) errado, equivocado; (*inappropriate*) impróprio ▶ ADV mal, errado ▶ N injustiça ▶ VT ser injusto com; **you are ~ to do it** você se engana ao fazê-lo; **you are ~ about that, you've got it ~** você está enganado sobre isso; **to be in the ~** não ter razão; **what's ~?** o que é que há?; **to go ~** (*person*) desencaminhar-se; (*plan*) dar errado; (*machine*) sofrer uma avaria; **wrongly** ADV errado
wrote [rəut] PT *of* **write**
wrung [rʌŋ] PT, PP *of* **wring**
WWW N ABBR = **World Wide Web**; **the ~** a WWW

X

Y

Xmas ['ɛksməs] N ABBR = **Christmas**

X-ray [ɛks'reɪ] N radiografia ▸ VT radiografar, tirar uma chapa de

yacht [jɔt] N iate *m*; **yachting** N iatismo

yard [jɑːd] N pátio, quintal *m*; (*measure*) jarda (*914 mm; 3 feet*)

yarn [jɑːn] N fio; (*tale*) história inverossímil

yawn [jɔːn] N bocejo ▸ VI bocejar

yeah [jɛə] (*inf*) ADV é

year [jɪəʳ] N ano; **to be 8 ~s old** ter 8 anos; **an eight-~-old child** uma criança de oito anos (de idade); **yearly** ADJ anual ▸ ADV anualmente

yearn [jəːn] VI: **to ~ to do/for sth** ansiar fazer/por algo

yeast [jiːst] N levedura, fermento

yell [jɛl] N grito, berro ▸ VI gritar, berrar

yellow ['jɛləu] ADJ amarelo; **Yellow Pages**® NPL (*Tel*) Páginas Amarelas *fpl*

yes [jɛs] ADV, N sim *m*

yesterday ['jɛstədɪ] ADV, N ontem *m*

yet [jɛt] ADV ainda ▸ CONJ porém, no entanto; **the best ~** o melhor até agora; **as ~** até agora, ainda

yew [ju:] N teixo
yield [ji:ld] N (*Agr*) colheita; (*Comm*) rendimento ▸ VT produzir; (*profit*) render; (*surrender*) ceder ▸ VI render-se, ceder; (*US Aut*) ceder
yoghurt, yogurt ['jəugət] N iogurte *m*
yolk [jəuk] N gema (do ovo)

KEYWORD

you [ju:] PRON **1** (*subj: singular*) tu, você; (: *plural*) vós, vocês; **you French enjoy your food** vocês franceses gostam de comer; **you and I will go** nós iremos
2 (*direct object: singular*) te, o/a; (: *plural*) vos, os/as; (*indirect object: singular*) te, lhe; (: *plural*) vos, lhes; **I know you** eu lhe conheço; **I gave it to you** dei isto para você
3 (*stressed*) você; **I told YOU to do it** eu disse para você fazer isto
4 (*after prep, in comparisons: singular*) ti, você; (: *plural*) vós, vocês; (*polite form: singular*) o senhor/a senhora; (: *plural*) os senhores/as senhoras; **it's for you** é para você; **with you** contigo, com você; convosco, com vocês; com o senhor *etc*
5 (*impers: one*): **you never know** nunca se sabe; **apples do you good** as maçãs fazem bem à saúde

you'd [ju:d] = **you had;** = **you would**
you'll [ju:l] = **you will;** = **you shall**
young [jʌŋ] ADJ jovem ▸ NPL (*of animal*) filhotes *mpl*, crias *fpl*; (*people*): **the ~** a juventude, os jovens; **younger** ADJ mais novo
your [jɔ:ʳ] ADJ teu/tua, seu/sua; (*plural*) vosso, seu/sua; (*formal*) do senhor/da senhora; *see also* **my**
you're [juəʳ] = **you are**
yours [jɔ:z] PRON teu/tua, seu/sua; (*plural*) vosso, seu/sua; (*formal*) do senhor/da senhora; **~ sincerely** *or* **faithfully** atenciosamente; *see also* **mine¹**
yourself [jɔ:'sɛlf] PRON (*emphatic*) tu mesmo, você mesmo; (*object, reflexive*) te, se; (*after prep*) ti mesmo, si mesmo; (*formal*) o senhor mesmo/a senhora mesma; **yourselves** PRON vós mesmos, vocês mesmos; (*object, reflexive*) vos, se; (*after prep*) vós mesmos, vôces mesmos; (*formal*) os senhores mesmos/as senhoras mesmas; *see also* **oneself**
youth [ju:θ] N mocidade *f*, juventude *f*; (*young man*) jovem *m*; **youth club** N associação *f* de juventude; **youthful** ADJ juvenil; **youth hostel** N albergue *m* da juventude
you've [ju:v] = **you have**

Z

zebra ['zi:brə] N zebra; **zebra crossing** (BRIT) N faixa (para pedestres) (BR), passadeira (PT)
zero ['zɪərəu] N zero
zest [zɛst] N vivacidade *f*, entusiasmo; (*of lemon etc*) zesto
zigzag ['zɪgzæg] N ziguezague *m* ▶ VI ziguezaguear
zinc [zɪŋk] N zinco
zip [zɪp] N (*also*: **~ fastener**) fecho ecler (BR) *or* éclair (PT) ▶ VT (*also*: **~ up**) fechar o fecho ecler de, subir o fecho ecler de; **zip code** (US) N código postal; **zip file** N arquivo zipado; **zipper** (US) N = **zip**
zit [zɪt] (*inf*) N espinha
zodiac ['zəudɪæk] N zodíaco
zone [zəun] N zona
zoo [zu:] N (jardim *m*) zoológico
zoom [zu:m] VI: **to ~ past** passar zunindo; **zoom lens** N zoom *m*, zum *m*
zucchini [zu:'ki:nɪ] (US) NPL abobrinha

Phrasefinder

Guia do viajante

TOPICS | TEMAS

TOPICS | TEMAS

MEETING PEOPLE | SAUDAÇÕES/ APRESENTAÇÕES

Hello!	Olá!/Oi!
Good evening!	Boa noite!
Good night!	Boa noite!
Goodbye!	Até logo!
What's your name?	Qual é seu nome? / Como você se chama?
My name is ...	Meu nome é ... / Eu me chamo ...
This is ...	Esta é ... / Este é ...
my wife.	*a minha mulher.*
my husband.	*o meu marido.*
my partner.	*o meu companheiro/a minha companheira.*
Pleased to meet you.	Muito prazer.
Where are you from?	De onde você é?
I come from ...	Sou de/da/do ...
How are you?	Como vai você?
Fine, thanks.	Vou bem, obrigado.
And you?	E você?
Do you speak English?	Você fala inglês?
I don't understand Portuguese.	Não entendo português.
Thanks very much!	Muito obrigado!

GETTING AROUND | TRASLADOS

Asking the Way	Perguntando a direção
Where is the nearest ...?	Onde é o/a ... mais perto daqui?
How do I get to ...?	Como faço para ir à/ao ...?
Is it far?	É longe?
How far is it from here?	Fica a que distância daqui?
Is this the right way to ...?	Este é o caminho certo para ...?
I'm lost.	Estou perdido(-da).
Can you show me on the map?	Você poderia me mostrar no mapa?
You have to turn round.	Você tem que dar a volta.
Go straight on.	Siga reto.
Turn left/right.	Vire à esquerda/direita.
Take the second street on the left/right.	Pegue a segunda rua à esquerda/direita.

Car Rental (BRIT Car Hire)	Aluguel de carro
I want to rent (BRIT hire) ...	Eu gostaria de alugar ...
a car.	*um carro.*
a moped.	*uma lambreta.*
a motorbike.	*uma motocicleta.*
How much is it for ...?	Quanto é ...?
one day	*por um dia*
a week	*por uma semana*
I'd like a child seat for a *...-year-old child.*	Eu gostaria de uma cadeira para carro para uma *criança de ... anos.*
What do I do if I have an accident/if I break down?	O que devo fazer em caso de acidente/avaria?

Breakdowns	Avarias
My car has broken down.	Meu carro enguiçou.

GETTING AROUND | TRASLADOS

Where is the next garage?	Onde é a oficina mais perto daqui?
The exhaust	*O cano de escapamento*
The gearbox	*A caixa de marchas*
... is broken.	... quebrou.
The brakes	*Os freios*
The headlights	*Os faróis*
***The windshield wipers* (BRIT *windscreen wipers*)**	*Os limpadores de para-brisa*
... are not working.	... não estão funcionando.
The battery is dead (BRIT flat).	A bateria arriou.
The car won't start.	O motor não dá partida.
The engine is overheating.	O motor está aquecendo demais.
I have a flat tyre.	Furou um pneu.
Can you repair it?	Você pode consertá-lo?
When will the car be ready?	Quando o carro vai ficar pronto?

Parking | Estacionamento

Can I park here?	Posso estacionar aqui?
Do I need to buy a (car-parking) ticket?	Preciso comprar um tíquete (de estacionamento)?
Where is the ticket machine?	Onde fica o parquímetro?
The ticket machine isn't working.	O parquímetro não funciona.

Gas Station (BRIT Petrol Station) | Posto de gasolina

Where is the nearest gas station (BRIT petrol station)?	Onde é o posto de gasolina mais próximo?
Fill it up, please.	Pode completar, por favor.
30 pounds worth of ..., please.	30 libras de ..., por favor.
diesel	*diesel*
(unleaded) economy petrol	*gasolina comum*

GETTING AROUND | TRASLADOS

premium unleaded	*gasolina premium*
Pump number ..., please.	Bomba número ..., por favor.
Please check ...	Por favor, verifique ...
the tyre pressure.	*a pressão dos pneus.*
the oil.	*o óleo.*
the water.	*a água.*

Accident | Acidentes

Please call ...	Por favor, chame ...
the police.	*a polícia.*
an ambulance.	*uma ambulância.*
Here are my insurance details.	Aqui estão os dados do meu seguro.
Give me your insurance details, please.	Me dê os dados do seu seguro, por favor.
Can you be a witness for me?	Você poderia servir de testemunha para mim?
You were driving too fast.	Você vinha a uma velocidade muito alta.
It wasn't your right of way.	A preferencial não era sua.

Travelling by Car | Viajando de carro

What's the best route to ...?	Qual o melhor caminho para ir para ...?
Where can I pay the toll?	Onde eu pago o pedágio?
Do you have a road map of this area?	Você tem um mapa rodoviário desta região?

Cycling | Ciclismo

Where is the cycle path to ...?	Onde fica a ciclovia para ...?
Can I keep my bike here?	Posso deixar minha bicicleta aqui?

GETTING AROUND | TRASLADOS

My bike has been stolen.	Roubaram minha bicicleta.
Where is the nearest bike repair shop?	Onde fica a loja de conserto de bicicletas mais próxima?
The brakes/the gears aren't working.	Os freios/as marchas não estão funcionando.
The chain is broken.	A corrente quebrou.
I've got a flat tyre.	Furou um pneu.
I need a flat (BRIT **puncture**) **repair kit.**	Eu preciso de um kit de ferramentas para reparo de pneu.

Train | Trem

A one-way (BRIT **single**) **to ..., please.**	Uma passagem de ida para ..., por favor.
I would like to travel ... first/second class.	Eu gostaria de viajar ... na primeira/segunda classe.
Two round trips (BRIT **returns**) **to ..., please.**	Duas passagens de ida e volta para ..., por favor.
Is there a discount ...?	Há desconto ...?
for students	*para estudantes*
for seniors (BRIT ***pensioners***)	*para idosos*
for children	*para crianças*
with this pass	*com este passe*
I'd like to reserve a seat on the train to ... please.	Eu gostaria de fazer uma reserva no trem que vai para ..., por favor.
Non smoking/smoking, please.	Para não fumantes/fumantes, por favor.
I want to book a sleeper to ...	Eu gostaria de fazer uma reserva no vagão-leito para ...
When is the next train to ...?	A que horas parte o próximo trem para ...?

GETTING AROUND | TRASLADOS

Is there a supplement to pay?	Tenho que pagar algum suplemento?
Do I need to change?	Vou precisar trocar de trem?
Where do I change?	Onde faço o traslado?
Is this the train for ...?	Este é o trem para ...?
Excuse me, that's my seat.	Desculpe, este assento é o meu.
I have a reservation.	Tenho uma reserva.
Is this seat free?	Este assento está livre?
Please let me know when we get to ...	Por favor, me avise quando chegarmos em ...
Where is the buffet car?	Onde é o vagão-restaurante?
Where is coach number ...?	Onde é o vagão número ...?

Ferry | Barca

Is there a ferry to ...?	Há uma barca para ...?
When is the next/first/last ferry to ...?	A que horas sai a próxima/primeira/última barca para ...?
How much is it for a car/camper with ... people?	Quanto é para um carro/motor home com ... pessoas?
How long does the crossing take?	Quanto tempo leva a travessia?
Where is ...?	Onde é ...?
the restaurant	*o restaurante*
the bar	*o bar*
Where is cabin number ...?	Onde é a cabine número ...?
Do you have anything for seasickness?	Você tem algum remédio para enjoo?

Plane | Avião

Where is ...?	Onde é ...?
the taxi stand **(BRIT *rank*)**	*o ponto de táxi*

GETTING AROUND | TRASLADOS

the bus stop	*o ponto de ônibus*
the information office	*o setor de informações*
Where do I check in for the flight to ...?	Onde faço o check-in para o voo para ...?
Which gate for the flight to ...?	Qual o portão de embarque do voo para ...?
When is the latest I can check in?	Até que horas posso fazer o check-in?
When does boarding begin?	A que horas começa o embarque?
Window/aisle, please.	Janela/corredor, por favor.
I've lost ...	Perdi ...
my boarding pass.	*meu cartão de embarque.*
my ticket.	*minha passagem.*
Where is the baggage (BRIT luggage) for the flight from ...?	Em que esteira está a bagagem do voo procedente de ...?
My luggage hasn't arrived.	Minha bagagem não chegou.

Local Public Transport | Transporte Público Municipal

How do I get to ...?	Como faço para ir a/à/ao ...?
Which number goes to ...?	Que linha vai para ...?
Where is the nearest ...?	Onde fica ... mais perto daqui?
bus stop	*o ponto de ônibus*
tram stop	*a parada de bonde*
metro (BRIT underground) station	*a estação de metrô/o metrô*
Where is the bus station?	Onde fica a estação rodoviária/o terminal de ônibus?
A ticket to ..., please.	Uma passagem/um bilhete para ..., por favor.

GETTING AROUND | TRASLADOS

Is there a discount ...?	Há desconto ...?
for students	*para estudantes*
***for seniors* (BRIT *pensioners*)**	*para idosos*
for children	*para crianças*
for the unemployed	*para desempregados*
with this pass	*com este passe*
Do you have multi-trip (BRIT multi-journey) tickets?	Vocês têm bilhetes múltiplos?
Do you have a map of the metro (BRIT underground)?	Você tem um mapa do metrô?
Please tell me when to get off.	Você podia me avisar quando devo descer?
What is the next stop?	Qual é a próxima parada?

Taxi | Táxi

Where can I get a taxi?	Onde posso pegar um táxi?
Call me a taxi, please.	Você podia chamar um táxi para mim, por favor?
To the airport/station, please.	Para o aeroporto/a estação, por favor.
To the ... hotel, please.	Para o hotel ..., por favor.
To this address, please.	Para este endereço, por favor.
I'm in a hurry.	Estou com pressa.
How much is it?	Quanto é?
I need a receipt.	Preciso de um recibo.
Keep the change.	Pode ficar com o troco.
Stop here, please.	Pode parar aqui, por favor.

ACCOMMODATION | HOSPEDAGEM

Camping	**Camping**
Is there a campsite here?	Há algum camping por aqui?
We'd like a site for ...	Gostaríamos de uma área para ...
a tent.	*uma barraca.*
a camper **(BRIT** ***caravan*****).**	*um trailer.*
We'd like to stay one night/ ... nights.	Gostaríamos de ficar uma noite/ ... noites.
How much is it per night?	Quanto é por noite?
Where are ...?	Onde ficam ...?
the toilets	*os banheiros*
the showers	*os chuveiros*
Where is ...?	Onde fica ...?
the site office	*a recepção*
Can we camp/park here overnight?	Podemos acampar/estacionar o carro aqui esta noite?
Self-Catering	**Apartamento alugado/ casa alugada para férias**
Where do we get the key for the apartment/house?	Onde devemos pegar a chave do apartamento/da casa?
Do we have to pay extra for electricity/gas?	Temos que pagar a eletricidade/o gás à parte?
How does the range (BRIT cooker) work?	Como funciona o fogão?
Who do I contact if there are any problems?	Com quem devo falar se houver algum problema?
We need ...	Precisamos de ...
a second key.	*outra cópia da chave.*
more sheets.	*mais lençóis.*
The gas has run out.	Acabou o gás.
There is no electricity.	Não há eletricidade.

Do we have to clean the apartment/the house before we leave?	Temos que limpar o apartamento/a casa antes de partir?

Hotel	**Hotel**
Do you have a ... for tonight?	Vocês têm um ... para esta noite?
single room	*quarto de solteiro*
double room	*quarto de casal*
with bathroom	*com banheiro*
with shower	*com chuveiro*
I want to stay for one night/ ... nights.	Eu gostaria de ficar por uma noite/ ... noites.
I booked a room in the name of ...	Reservei um quarto em nome de ...
I'd like another room.	Eu gostaria de um quarto differente.
What time is breakfast?	A que horas é servido o café da manhã?
Can I have breakfast in my room?	Vocês servem o café da manhã no quarto?
Where is ...?	Onde fica ...?
the gym	*a academia de ginástica*
I'd like an alarm call for tomorrow morning at ...	Eu gostaria de ser acordado(-da) amanhã às ...
I'd like to get these things washed/cleaned.	Eu gostaria que essas coisas fossem lavadas/limpas.
Please bring me ...	Você podia me trazer ..., por favor?
... doesn't work.	... não funciona.
Room number ...	Quarto número ...
Are there any messages for me?	Tem algum recado para mim?

SHOPPING | COMPRAS

I'd like ...	Eu gostaria de ...
Do you have ...?	Vocês têm ...?
Do you have this ...?	Você tem esse/essa ...?
in another size	*em outro tamanho*
in another colour	*em outra cor*
I take size ...	Meu tamanho é ...
My feet are a size 5½.	Eu calço número 37.
I'll take it.	Vou levar isto.
Do you have anything else?	Você tem outras coisas para me mostrar?
That's too expensive.	É muito caro.
I'm just looking.	Estou só olhando.
Do you take credit cards?	Vocês aceitam cartões de crédito?

Food Shopping | Compra de alimentos

Where is the nearest ...?	Onde é ... mais perto daqui?
supermarket	*o supermercado*
bakery (BRIT ***baker's***)	*a padaria*
butcher (BRIT ***butcher's***)	*o açougue*
Where is the market?	Onde é o mercado?
What are the hours of the market? (BRIT **When is the market on?**)	Qual o horário de funcionamento do mercado?
a kilo/pound of ...	um quilo/meio quilo de ...
200 grams of ...	200 gramas de ...
... slices of ...	... fatias de ...
a litre/bottle of ...	um litro/uma garrafa de ...
a bag/box of ...	um saco/uma caixa de ...

Post Office | Correio

Where is the nearest post office?	Onde é o correio mais perto daqui?

When does the post office open?	A que horas abre o correio?
Where can I buy stamps?	Onde posso comprar selos?
I'd like ... stamps for *postcards/letters to* Britain/the United States.	Eu gostaria de ... selos para *cartões-postais/cartas para a* Grã-Bretanha/os Estados Unidos
I'd like to post/send ...	Eu gostaria de enviar ...
this letter.	*esta carta.*
this parcel.	*esta encomenda.*
by airmail/express mail/ registered mail	por via aérea/expressa por Sedex/registrada
Is there any mail for me?	Chegou alguma correspondência para mim?
Where is the nearest postbox?	Onde fica a caixa de correio mais próxima?

LEISURE | LAZER

Sightseeing	Passeios turísticos
Where is the tourist office?	Onde fica o posto de informações turísticas?
Do you have any brochures (BRIT leaflets) about ...?	Você tem algum panfleto sobre ...?
Are there any sightseeing tours of ...	Há algum passeio turístico ...
the town?	*da cidade?*
When is ... open?	Qual é o horário de visitação ...?
the museum	*do museu*
the church	*da igreja*
the castle	*do castelo*
How much does it cost to get in?	Quanto custa o ingresso?
Is there a discount ...?	Há desconto ...?
for students	*para estudantes*
for children	*para crianças*
for seniors (BRIT *pensioners*)	*para idosos*
for the over-sixties	*para maiores de 60 anos*
Is there a guided tour in English?	Há visita guiada em inglês?
Can I take photos here?	É permitido tirar fotos aqui?
Can I film here?	É permitido filmar aqui?

Entertainment	Entretenimento
What is there to do here?	O que tem para fazer aqui?
Where can we ...?	Onde podemos ...?
go dancing	*ir dançar*
hear live music	*ouvir música ao vivo*
Where is there ...?	Onde tem ...?
a nice bar	*um bom bar*
a good club	*uma boa discoteca*

LEISURE | LAZER

What's on tonight ...?	Qual é a programação para hoje à noite ...?
at the cinema	*no cinema*
at the theatre	*no teatro*
at the opera	*na ópera*
at the concert hall	*na sala de concerto*
Where can I buy tickets for ...?	Onde posso comprar entradas para ...?
the theatre	*o teatro*
the concert	*o concerto*
the opera	*a ópera*
the ballet	*o balé*
How much is it to get in?	Quanto é a entrada?
I'd like a ticket/... tickets for ...	Eu gostaria de uma entrada/ ... entradas para ...
Is there a discount ...?	Há desconto ...?
for children	*para crianças*
for students	*para estudantes*
for the over-sixties	*para maiores de 60 anos*
for pensioners	*para idosos*

At the Beach | Na praia

Where is the nearest beach?	Onde é a praia mais perto daqui?
Is it safe to swim here?	É seguro nadar aqui?
How deep is the water?	Qual é a profundidade da água?
Is there a lifeguard?	Tem salva-vidas aqui?
Where can you ...?	Onde se pode ...?
go surfing	*fazer surfe*
go waterskiing	*fazer esqui aquático*

LEISURE | LAZER

go diving	*fazer mergulho*
go paragliding	*voar de parapente*
I'd like to rent (BRIT **hire**) ...	Eu gostaria de alugar ...
a deckchair.	*uma cadeira.*
a sunshade.	*uma barraca.*
a surfboard.	*uma prancha de surfe.*
a jet-ski.	*um jet-ski.*
a rowboat (BRIT *rowing boat*).	*um barco a remo.*
a pedal boat.	*um pedalinho.*

Sport | Esporte

Where can we ...?	Onde podemos ...?
play tennis/golf	*jogar tênis/golfe*
go swimming	*nadar*
go riding	*andar a cavalo*
go fishing	*pescar*
How much is it per hour?	Quanto custa por hora?
Where can I book a court?	Onde posso reservar uma quadra?
Where can I rent (BRIT **hire**) **rackets?**	Onde posso alugar raquetes?
Where can I hire a rowboat (BRIT **rowing boat**)**/a pedal boat?**	Onde posso alugar um barco a remo/pedalinho?
Do you need a fishing permit?	É preciso uma licença para pescar?

FOOD AND DRINK | COMIDA E BEBIDA

A table for ... people, please.	Uma mesa para ... pessoas, por favor.
The ... please.	Por favor, ...
menu	*o cardápio*
wine list	*a carta de vinhos*
What do you recommend?	O que você recomenda?
Do you have ...?	Vocês têm ...?
any vegetarian dishes	*pratos vegetarianos*
children's portions	*prato infantil*
Does that contain ...?	Isto contém ...?
peanuts	*amendoim*
alcohol	*bebida alcoólica*
Can you bring (more) ... please?	Você poderia trazer (mais) ... por favor?
I'll have ...	Eu vou comer ...
The check (BRIT **bill**)**, please.**	A conta, por favor.
All together, please.	Tudo junto, por favor.
Separate checks (BRIT **bills**)**, please.**	Contas separadas, por favor.
Keep the change.	Pode ficar com o troco.
This isn't what I ordered.	Não foi isto que pedi.
The check (BRIT **bill**) **is wrong.**	Esta conta está errada.
The food is cold/too salty.	A comida está fria/salgada demais.

TELEPHONE | TELEFONE

Where can I make a phone call?	De onde eu poderia dar um telefonema?
Where is the nearest card phone?	Onde tem um telefone público a cartão perto daqui?
Where is the nearest phone booth (BRIT phone box)?	Onde tem um telefone público a moeda perto daqui?
I'd like a twenty-five euro phone card.	Eu gostaria de um cartão telefônico de vinte e cinco euros.
I'd like some coins for the phone, please.	Eu gostaria de moedas para o telefone, por favor.
I'd like to make a ... reverse charge call.	Eu gostaria de fazer uma ... chamada a cobrar.
Hello.	Alô.
This is ...	Aqui fala ...
Who's speaking, please?	Com quem falo?
Can I speak to Mr/Ms ..., please?	Posso falar com o Sr./a Sra. ..., por favor?
Extension ..., please.	Ramal ..., por favor.
I'll phone back later.	Volto a ligar mais tarde.
Can you text me your answer?	Você poderia me responder com uma mensagem de texto?
Where can I charge my mobile phone?	Onde posso carregar meu celular?
I need a new battery.	Preciso de uma bateria nova.
Where can I buy a top-up card?	Onde posso comprar cartão para celular?
I can't get a network.	Aqui não tem cobertura.

PRACTICALITIES | PRATICIDADES

Passport/Customs	Passaporte/Alfândega
Here is ...	Aqui está ...
my passport.	*o meu passaporte.*
my identity card.	*a minha carteira de identidade.*
my driving licence.	*a minha carteira de motorista.*
Here are my vehicle documents.	Aqui estão os documentos do meu carro.
This is a present.	Isto é um presente.
This is for personal use.	Isto é para uso pessoal.

At the Bank	No Banco
Where can I change money?	Onde posso trocar dinheiro?
Is there a bank/bureau de change here?	Há um banco/uma casa de câmbio por aqui?
When is the bank open?	Qual é o horário de atendimento do banco?
I'd like ... Brazilian reais.	Eu gostaria de ... reais.
I'd like to cash these traveller's cheques.	Eu gostaria de trocar estes cheques de viagem.
What's the commission?	Quanto é a comissão?
Can I use my card to get cash?	Posso usar meu cartão para sacar dinheiro?
Is there an ATM (BRIT a cash machine) here?	Há um caixa eletrônico aqui?
The ATM (BRIT cash machine) swallowed my card.	O caixa eletrônico engoliu meu cartão.

Repairs	Consertos
Where can I get this repaired?	Onde posso consertar isto?
Can you repair ...?	Você poderia consertar ...?
these shoes	*estes sapatos*
this watch	*este relógio*

PRACTICALITIES | PRATICIDADES

How much will the repairs cost?	Quanto vão custar os consertos?

Emergency Services | Serviços de emergência

Help!	Socorro!
Fire!	Incêndio!
Please call ...	Por favor, chame ...
the emergency doctor.	*um serviço médico de urgência.*
the fire brigade.	*o corpo de bombeiros.*
the police.	*a polícia.*
I need to make an urgent phone call.	Preciso fazer um telefonema urgente.
I need an interpreter.	Preciso de um intérprete.
Where is the police station?	Onde é a delegacia?
Where is the hospital?	Onde é o hospital?
I want to report a theft.	Quero fazer a ocorrência de um roubo.
... has been stolen.	... foi roubado(-da).
There's been an accident.	Houve um acidente.
There are ... people injured.	Há ... pessoas feridas.
I've been ...	Fui ...
robbed.	*roubado(-da).*
attacked.	*assaltado(-da).*
raped.	*estuprado(-da).*
I'd like to phone my embassy.	Eu gostaria de ligar para a minha embaixada.

HEALTH | SAÚDE

Pharmacy	Farmácia
Where is the nearest pharmacy?	Onde é a farmácia mais perto daqui?
Which pharmacy is open 24 hours?	Que farmácia fica aberta 24 horas?
I'd like something ...	Eu gostaria de alguma coisa ...
for diarrhoea.	*para diarreia.*
for a temperature.	*para febre.*
for travel sickness.	*para enjoo.*
for a headache.	*para dor de cabeça.*
for a cold.	*para resfriado.*
I'd like ...	Eu gostaria de ...
Band-aids (BRIT ***plasters***).	Band-Aids.
a bandage.	*uma gaze*
some acetaminophen (BRIT ***paracetamol***).	*paracetamol.*
I can't take ...	Não posso tomar ...
aspirin.	*aspirina.*
penicillin.	*penicilina.*
Is it safe to give to children?	Pode-se dar isso para crianças?

At the Doctor (BRIT At the Doctor's)	No médico
I need a doctor.	Preciso de um médico.
Where is the ER (BRIT **casualty**)?	Onde é o pronto-socorro?
I have a pain here.	Sinto dor aqui.
I feel ...	Sinto ...
hot.	*calor.*
cold.	*frio.*
I feel sick.	Sinto enjoo.
I feel dizzy.	Sinto tonteira.
I'm allergic to ...	Sou alérgico(-ca) a ...

HEALTH | SAÚDE

I am pregnant.	Estou grávida.
I am diabetic.	Sou diabético(-ca).
I am HIV-positive.	Sou soropositivo(-va).
I'm on this medication.	Estou tomando este remédio.
My blood group is ...	Meu tipo sanguineo é ...

At the Hospital | No hospital

Which ward is ... in?	Em que enfermaria está ...?
When are visiting hours?	Qual é o horário de visitas?
I'd like to speak to ...	Eu gostaria de falar com ...
a doctor.	*um médico.*
a nurse.	*uma enfermeira.*
When will I be discharged?	Quando terei alta?

At the Dentist (BRIT At the Dentist's) | No dentista

I need a dentist.	Preciso de um dentista.
This tooth hurts.	Este dente está doendo.
One of my fillings has fallen out.	Uma das minhas obturações caiu.
I have an abscess.	Estou com um abcesso.
Can you repair my dentures?	Você poderia consertar minha dentadura?
I need a receipt for the insurance.	Preciso de um recibo para o seguro.

Business Travel	Viagem de negócios
I'd like to arrange a meeting with Mr/Ms ...	Eu gostaria de marcar uma reunião com o Sr./a Sra. ...
I have an appointment with Mr/Ms ...	Tenho um encontro marcado com o Sr./a Sra. ...
Here is my card.	Aqui está o meu cartão.
I work for ...	Trabalho no/na ...
Shall I come to your office?	Quer que eu vá ao seu escritório?
How do I get to ...?	Como faço para chegar ...?
your office	*no seu escritório*
Mr/Ms ...'s office	*no escritório do Sr./da Sra. ...*
I need an interpreter.	Preciso de um intérprete.
May I use ...?	Posso usar ...?
your phone	*seu telefone*
your computer	*seu computador*
your desk	*sua mesa*
What is your ...?	Qual é o seu ...?
email address	*e-mail*
fax number	*número de fax*
telephone extension	*ramal*
Is there an internet connection in the room?	O quarto tem acesso à internet?
Where can I charge my laptop?	Onde posso carregar meu laptop?
Is there a fax machine I can use?	Há um fax que eu possa usar?
I wondered if you'd received a fax for me.	Eu queria saber se chegou um fax para mim.
I'd like to have a conference call at ... o'clock.	Eu gostaria de fazer uma audioconferência a/às ... hora(s).

Is there anywhere I can charge up my mobile phone?	Há alguma tomada onde eu possa carregar a bateria do meu celular?
Is there somewhere where I can make photocopies?	Há algum lugar onde eu possa fazer fotocópias?
Is there a projector in the conference room?	Há um retroprojetor na sala de conferências?
Would someone be able to help me set up the projector?	Alguém poderia me ajudar a preparar o retroprojetor?
How do I get an outside line?	Como consigo linha para discar para fora?
What prefix do I need to dial when making an international call?	Que prefixo devo discar para fazer uma chamada internacional?
If anyone should phone me, can you tell them I'll be back at the hotel at 6pm?	Se alguém me ligar, por favor diga que estarei de volta ao hotel às 6 da tarde?

Disabled Travellers | Viajantes portadores de deficiência física

Is it possible to visit ... with a wheelchair?	É possível visitar ... em cadeira de rodas?
Where is the wheelchair-accessible entrance?	Por onde se pode entrar com a cadeira de rodas?
Is your hotel accessible to wheelchairs?	Há acesso para cadeira de rodas no seu hotel?
I need a room ...	Preciso de um quarto
on the ground floor.	*no andar térreo.*
with wheelchair access.	*com acesso para cadeira de rodas.*
Do you have an elevator (BRIT a lift) for wheelchairs?	Vocês têm um elevador para cadeira de rodas?

Where is the disabled toilet?	Onde é o toalete para deficientes?
Can you help me get on/off please?	Você poderia me ajudar a subir/descer, por favor?
The tyre has burst.	O pneu furou.
The battery is dead (BRIT **flat**).	A bateria descarregou.

Travelling with children | Viajando com crianças

Is it OK to bring children here?	É permitida a entrada de crianças aqui?
Is there a discount for children?	Há desconto para crianças?
Do you have children's portions?	Vocês servem prato infantil?
Do you have ...?	Vocês têm ...?
a high chair	*uma cadeira alta (para refeição)*
a crib (BRIT ***cot***)	*um berço*
a child's seat	*uma cadeira para carro*
Where can I change the baby?	Onde posso trocar a fralda do bebê?
Where can I breastfeed the baby?	Onde posso dar de mamar ao bebê?
Can you warm this up, please?	Você poderia aquecer isto, por favor?
What is there for children to do?	O que tem aqui para as crianças fazerem?
Where is the nearest playground?	Onde fica a pracinha mais perto daqui?
Is there a babysitting (BRIT **child-minding**) **service?**	Há serviço de babá?

COMPLAINTS | RECLAMAÇÕES

I'd like to make a complaint.	Eu gostaria de fazer uma reclamação.
To whom can I complain?	Com quem eu falo para fazer uma reclamação?
I'd like to speak to the manager, please.	Eu gostaria de falar com o gerente, por favor.
The heating	*O aquecimento*
The shower	*O chuveiro*
... doesn't work.	... não está funcionando.
The light doesn't work.	A luz não está acendendo.
The room is dirty	O quarto está sujo.
The room is too small.	O quarto é pequeno demais.
The room is too cold.	O quarto é frio demais.
Can you clean the room, please?	Você poderia limpar o quarto, por favor?
Can you turn down the TV/the radio, please?	Você poderia abaixar o volume da tevê/do rádio, por favor?
The food is ...	A comida está ...
cold.	*fria.*
too salty.	*muito salgada.*
This isn't what I ordered.	Isto não foi o que pedi.
We've been waiting for a very long time.	Nós já estamos esperando há muito tempo.
The amount is wrong.	A conta está errada.
I want my money back.	Eu quero meu dinheiro de volta.
I'd like to exchange this.	Eu gostaria de trocar isto.
I'm not satisfied with this.	Não estou satisfeito(-ta) com isto.

bangers and mash (*BRIT*) = **sausages and mashed potatoes** (*US*) linguiça com purê de batata, cebola frita e molho de carne assada
banoffee pie torta de banana com caramelo e chantilly
BLT (sandwich) sanduíche de bacon, alface, tomate e maionese
burrito burrito
butternut squash tipo de abóbora
Caesar salad salada César: alface romana, *croutons* e parmesão ralado, às vezes com anchovas ou frango grelhado
chocolate brownie brownie: bolo de chocolate e nozes
chowder sopa de mariscos ou peixe engrossada com batata
chicken Kiev frango à Kiev: peito de frango com recheio de manteiga, alho e salsinha
chicken nuggets pedaços de frango empanados
chili chili
club sandwich sanduíche quente de três andares, geralmente com recheio de carne, queijo, alface, tomate e cebola
cottage pie (*BRIT*) = **shepherd's pie** (*US*) carne moída e vegetais com cobertura de batata e queijo
English breakfast café da manhã inglês: ovos, bacon, linguiça, feijão branco com molho de tomate, pão frito e cogumelos
filo pastry massa filo: tipo de massa folhada finíssima
fried chicken (*US*) frango frito
haggis (*BRIT*) prato escocês a base de fígado e coração de cordeiro, aveia e outros temperos, cozidos na bolsa estomacal do animal
hamburger hambúrguer
hash browns cubinhos de batata refogados com cebola
hotdog cachorro-quente
hotpot (*BRIT*) ensopado de carne, vegetais e batatas
Irish stew ensopado irlandês, a base de cordeiro, batata e cebola
Jell-O (*US*) gelatina
monkfish tamboril, peixe-sapo
oatcake biscoito de aveia

pavlova (BRIT) sobremesa de suspiro com frutas e chantilly
ploughman's lunch (BRIT) almoço servido em *pubs* a base de pão, queijo e picles
purée purê
Quorn® (BRIT) proteína vegetal usada como substituto de carne
Savoy cabbage couve-lombarda
sea bass robalo
Scotch broth sopa de carne, cevada e vegetais
Scotch egg (BRIT) ovo cozido envolto em carne de linguiça e empanado
spare ribs costelinhas de porco
spring roll rolinho de primavera
Stilton queijo inglês tipo roquefort
sundae sorvete com calda, nozes e chantilly
taco taco
Thousand Island dressing molho de ketchup e maionese
toad in the hole (BRIT) linguiças assadas numa massa de ovos, leite e farinha
Waldorf salad salada Waldorf: maçã fatiada, aipo, nozes e maionese
Welsh rarebit torrada com cobertura de queijo derretido e ovo
Yorkshire pudding tipo de suflê salgado, às vezes recheado de vegetais, que acompanha o rosbife

acarajé (BR) fried bean cake served with a spicy shrimp sauce
açorda (PT) stew made with bread
amêijoas à Bulhão Pato (PT) clams with garlic and coriander
arroz doce rice pudding
arroz e feijão (BR) rice and beans
assado roasted, baked
bacalhau à brás (PT) dish with salt cod, onion and potatoes all bound with scrambled eggs
bifana (PT) thin pork tenderloin steak
bife à café (PT) steak in cream sauce topped with a fried egg with fries (BRIT chips)
bitoque (PT) small steak with fried egg and fries (BRIT chips)
brasa, ... na grilled over charcoal
broa (PT) rustic corn bread (BRIT rustic maize bread)
caldo verde (PT) soup made with shredded kale and potatoes with *chouriço* and olive oil
caruru (BR) dish made with okra, prawns, cashew nuts and palm oil
cataplana, ... na (PT) cooked with potatoes and a tomato sauce in a cataplana pot
chapa, ... na grilled over charcoal
coxinha (BR) deep-fried savoury snack made with chicken mince
cozido à portuguesa (PT) boiled meat and vegetable stew, served with rice
espeto, ... no kebab/on the spit
farofa (BR) side dish based on toasted manioc flour, often served with *feijoada*
feijoada bean stew with pork and sausage
folhado de carne meat in puff pastry
forno, ... no roasted or cooked in the oven
frango ao molho pardo (BR) chicken cooked in its own blood with vegetables

goiabada (BR) guava jelly
milanesa, ... à breaded
pão de queijo (BR) snack made with cheese, cassava and eggs
papos de anjo small egg cakes with syrup
pastéis de bacalhau (PT) salt cod cakes
porco à alentejana (PT) traditional dish with pork, clams and herbs
prego no pão (PT) steak roll
pudim de leite (BR) flan made with condensed milk
pudim flan (PT) crème caramel
queijo Minas (BR) soft white cheese
quibe (BR) kibbeh, dish made with bulgar wheat, meat and spices
quindim (BR) baked dessert made from sugar, eggs and coconut
recheado com ... stuffed/filled with ...
rodízio type of restaurant at which, for a fixed price, you are served several courses of food on an all-you-can-eat basis
tripas à modo do Porto (PT) tripe stew with beans and various meats
tucupi (BR) sauce made from the manioc root
xinxim de galinha (BR) chicken with a shrimp and peanut sauce

BR = Brazilian dish
BRIT = British dish
PT = Portuguese dish
US = American dish

a

PALAVRA-CHAVE

a [a] ART DEF the; *ver tb* **o**
▶ PRON (*ela*) her; (*você*) you; (*coisa*) it; *ver tb* **o**
▶ PREP (*a + o(s) = ao(s); a + a(s) = à(s); a + aquele/a(s) = àquele/a(s)*)
1 (*direção*) to; **à direita/esquerda** to *ou* on the right/left
2 (*distância*): **está a 15 km daqui** it's 15 km from here
3 (*posição*): **ao lado de** beside, at the side of
4 (*tempo*) at; **a que horas?** at what time?; **às 5 horas** at 5 o'clock; **à noite** at night; **aos 15 anos** at 15 years of age
5 (*maneira*): **à francesa** in the French way; **a cavalo/pé** on horseback/foot
6 (*meio, instrumento*): **à força** by force; **a mão** by hand; **a lápis** in pencil; **fogão a gás** gas stove
7 (*razão*): **a R$10 o quilo** at R$10 a kilo; **a mais de 100 km/h** at over 100 km/h
8 (*depois de certos verbos*): **começou a nevar** it started snowing *ou* to snow; **passar a fazer** to become
9 (*+ infin*): **ao vê-lo, reconheci-o imediatamente** when I saw him, I recognized him immediately; **ele ficou muito nervoso ao falar com o professor** he became very nervous while he was talking to the teacher
10 (PT: *+ infin, gerúndio*): **a correr** running; **estou a trabalhar** I'm working

à [a] = **a + a**; *ver* **a**
(a) ABR (= *assinado*) signed
aba ['aba] F (*de chapéu*) brim; (*de casaco*) tail; (*de montanha*) foot
abacate [aba'katʃi] M avocado (pear)
abacaxi [abaka'ʃi] (BR) M pineapple
abafado, -a [aba'fadu, a] ADJ (*ar*) stuffy; (*tempo*) humid, close; (*ocupado*) (extremely) busy; (*angustiado*) anxious
abaixar [abaj'ʃar] VT to lower; (*luz, som*) to turn down; **abaixar-se** VR to stoop
abaixo [a'bajʃu] ADV down ▶ PREP: **~ de** below; **~ o governo!** down with the government!; **morro ~** downhill; **rio ~** downstream; **mais ~** further down; **~ e acima** up and down; **~ assinado** undersigned; **abaixo-assinado** [-asi'nadu] (*pl* **-s**) M petition
abalado, -a [aba'ladu, a] ADJ unstable, unsteady; (*fig*) shaken
abalar [aba'lar] VT to shake; (*fig: comover*) to affect ▶ VI to shake; **abalar-se** VR to be moved

abalo [a'balu] M (*comoção*) shock; (*ação*) shaking; **~ sísmico** earth tremor
abanar [aba'nar] VT to shake; (*rabo*) to wag; (*com leque*) to fan
abandonar [abãdo'nar] VT to leave; (*ideia*) to reject; (*esperança*) to give up; (*descuidar*) to neglect
abarrotado, -a [abaho'tadu, a] ADJ (*gaveta*) crammed full; (*lugar*) packed
abastecer [abaste'ser] VT to supply; (*motor*) to fuel; (*Auto*) to fill up; (*Aer*) to refuel; **abastecer-se** VR: **~-se de** to stock up with
abastecimento [abastesi'mẽtu] M supply; (*comestíveis*) provisions *pl*; (*ato*) supplying; **abastecimentos** MPL (*suprimentos*) supplies
abater [aba'ter] VT (*gado*) to slaughter; (*preço*) to reduce; (*desalentar*) to upset; **abatido, -a** [aba'tʃidu, a] ADJ depressed, downcast; **abatimento** [abatʃi'mẽtu] M (*fraqueza*) weakness; (*de preço*) reduction; (*prostração*) depression; **fazer um abatimento em** to give a discount on
abdômen [ab'domẽ] M abdomen
á-bê-cê [abe'se] M alphabet
abecedário [abese'darju] M alphabet, ABC
abelha [a'beʎa] F bee
abelhudo, -a [abe'ʎudu, a] ADJ nosy
abençoar [abẽ'swar] VT to bless
aberto, -a [a'bɛrtu, a] PP *de* **abrir** ▸ ADJ open; (*céu*) clear; (*sinal*) green; (*torneira*) on
abestalhado, -a [abesta'ʎadu, a] ADJ stupid
abismado, -a [abiz'madu, a] ADJ astonished
ABL ABR F = **Academia Brasileira de Letras**
abnegado, -a [abne'gadu, a] ADJ self-sacrificing
abnegar [abne'gar] VT to renounce
abóbada [a'bɔbada] F vault; (*telhado*) arched roof
abobalhado, -a [aboba'ʎadu, a] ADJ (*criança*) simple
abóbora [a'bɔbora] F pumpkin
abobrinha [abo'briɲa] F courgette (BRIT), zucchini (US)
abolir [abo'lir] VT to abolish
aborrecer [abohe'ser] VT (*chatear*) to annoy; (*maçar*) to bore; **aborrecer-se** VR to get upset; to get bored; **aborrecido, -a** [abohe'sidu, a] ADJ boring; (*chateado*) annoyed;
aborrecimento [abohesi'mẽtu] M boredom; (*chateação*) annoyance
abortar [abor'tar] VI (*Med*) to have a miscarriage; (*: de propósito*) to have an abortion; **aborto** [a'bortu] M miscarriage; (*forçado*) abortion; **fazer/ter um aborto** to have an abortion/a miscarriage
abotoadura [abotwa'dura] F cufflink
abotoar [abo'twar] VT to button up ▸ VI (*Bot*) to bud
abraçar [abra'sar] VT to hug; (*causa*) to embrace; **abraçar-se** VR to embrace; **ele abraçou-se a mim** he embraced me; **abraço** [a'brasu] M embrace, hug; **com um abraço** (*em carta*) with best wishes
abre-garrafas ['abri-] (PT) M INV bottle opener
abre-latas ['abri-] (PT) M INV tin (BRIT) *ou* can opener
abreviar [abre'vjar] VT to abbreviate; (*texto*) to abridge; **abreviatura** [abrevja'tura] F abbreviation
abridor [abri'dor] (BR) M: **~ (de**

lata) tin (BRIT) *ou* can opener; **~ de garrafa** bottle opener

abrigar [abri'gar] VT to shelter; (*proteger*) to protect; **abrigar-se** VR to take shelter

abrigo [a'brigu] M shelter, cover; **~ antiaéreo** air-raid shelter; **~ antinuclear** fall-out shelter

abril [a'briw] M April

On 25 April (**25 de abril**) 1974 in Portugal, the MAF (Armed Forces Movement) instigated the bloodless revolution that was to topple the 48-year-old dictatorship presided over until 1968 by António de Oliveira Salazar. The red carnation has come to symbolize the coup, as it is said that the Armed Forces took to the streets with carnations in the barrels of their rifles. 25 April is now a public holiday in Portugal.

abrir [a'brir] VT to open; (*fechadura*) to unlock; (*vestuário*) to unfasten; (*torneira*) to turn on; (*buraco, exceção*) to make ▸ VI to open; (*sinal*) to go green; **abrir-se** VR: **~-se com alguém** to confide in sb

abrupto, -a [a'bruptu, a] ADJ abrupt; (*repentino*) sudden

absolutamente [absoluta'mẽtʃi] ADV absolutely; (*em resposta*) absolutely not, not at all

absoluto, -a [abso'lutu, a] ADJ absolute; **em ~** absolutely not, not at all

absorto, -a [ab'sortu, a] PP *de* **absorver** ▸ ADJ absorbed, engrossed

absorvente [absor'vẽtʃi] ADJ (*papel etc*) absorbent; (*livro etc*) absorbing

absorver [absor'ver] VT to absorb; **absorver-se** VR: **~-se em** to concentrate on

abstêmio, -a [abs'temju, a] ADJ abstemious; (*álcool*) teetotal ▸ M/F abstainer; teetotaller (BRIT), teetotaler (US)

abster-se [ab'stersi] (*irreg: como* **ter**) VR: **~ de** to abstain *ou* refrain from

abstinência [abstʃi'nẽsja] F abstinence; (*jejum*) fasting

abstrato, -a [abs'tratu, a] ADJ abstract

absurdo, -a [abi'surdu, a] ADJ absurd ▸ M nonsense

abundante [abũ'dãtʃi] ADJ abundant; **abundar** [abũ'dar] VI to abound

abusar [abu'zar] VI to go too far; **~ de** to abuse

abuso [a'buzu] M abuse; (*Jur*) indecent assault

a.C. ABR (= *antes de Cristo*) B.C.

a/c ABR (= *aos cuidados de*) Attn:

acabado, -a [aka'badu, a] ADJ finished; (*esgotado*) worn out

acabamento [akaba'mẽtu] M finish

acabar [aka'bar] VT to finish, complete; (*consumir*) to use up; (*rematar*) to finish off ▸ VI to finish, end; **acabar-se** VR to be over; (*prazo*) to expire; (*esgotar-se*) to run out; **~ com** to put an end to; **~ de chegar** to have just arrived; **~ por fazer** to end up (by) doing; **acabou-se!** it's all over!; (*basta!*) that's enough!

academia [akade'mia] F academy; **Academia Brasileira de Letras** *see note*

Founded in 1896 in Rio de Janeiro, on the initiative of the author Machado de Assis, the

Academia Brasileira de Letras, or ABL, aims to preserve and develop the Portuguese language and Brazilian literature. Machado de Assis was its president until 1908. It is made up of forty life members known as the *imortais*. The Academia's activities include publication of reference books, promotion of literary prizes, and running a library, museum and archive.

acadêmico, -a [aka'demiku, a] ADJ, M/F academic
açafrão [asa'frãw] M saffron
acalmar [akaw'mar] VT to calm ▶ VI (*vento etc*) to abate; **acalmar-se** VR to calm down
acampamento [akãpa'mẽtu] M camping; (*Mil*) camp, encampment
acampar [akã'par] VI to camp
acanhado, -a [aka'ɲadu, a] ADJ shy
acanhamento [akaɲa'mẽtu] M shyness
acanhar-se [aka'ɲarsi] VR to be shy
ação [a'sãw] (*pl* **-ões**) F action; (*ato*) act, deed; (*Mil*) battle; (*enredo*) plot; (*Jur*) lawsuit; (*Com*) share; **~ ordinária/preferencial** (*Com*) ordinary/preference share
acarajé [akara'ʒɛ] M (*Culin*) *beans fried in palm oil*
acarretar [akahe'tar] VT to result in, bring about
acaso [a'kazu] M chance; **ao ~** at random; **por ~** by chance
acatar [aka'tar] VT to respect; (*lei*) to obey
aceitação [asejta'sãw] F acceptance; (*aprovação*) approval
aceitar [asej'tar] VT to accept; (*aprovar*) to approve; **aceitável** [asej'tavew] (*pl* **-eis**) ADJ acceptable;
aceito, -a [a'sejtu, a] PP *de* **aceitar**
acelerador [aselera'dor] M accelerator
acelerar [asele'rar] VT, VI to accelerate; **~ o passo** to go faster
acenar [ase'nar] VI (*com a mão*) to wave; (*com a cabeça*) to nod
acender [asẽ'der] VT (*cigarro, fogo*) to light; (*luz*) to switch on; (*fig*) to excite, inflame
acento [a'sẽtu] M accent; (*de intensidade*) stress; **acentuar** [asẽ'twar] VT to accent; (*salientar*) to stress, emphasize
acepção [asep'sãw] (*pl* **-ões**) F (*de uma palavra*) sense
acerca [a'serka] ADV: **~ de** about, concerning
acertado, -a [aser'tadu, a] ADJ right, correct; (*sensato*) sensible
acertar [aser'tar] VT (*ajustar*) to put right; (*relógio*) to set; (*alvo*) to hit; (*acordo*) to reach; (*pergunta*) to get right ▶ VI to get it right, be right; **~ o caminho** to find the right way; **~ com** to hit upon
aceso, -a [a'sezu, a] PP *de* **acender** ▶ ADJ (*luz, gás, TV*) on; (*fogo*) alight; (*excitado*) excited; (*furioso*) furious
acessar [ase'sar] VT (*Comput*) to access
acessível [ase'sivew] (*pl* **-eis**) ADJ accessible; (*pessoa*) approachable; (*preço*) reasonable, affordable
acesso [a'sɛsu] M access; (*Med*) fit, attack
acessório, -a [ase'sɔrju, a] ADJ (*máquina, equipamento*) backup ▶ M accessory
achado [a'ʃadu] M find, discovery; (*pechincha*) bargain; (*sorte*) godsend
achar [a'ʃar] VT (*descobrir*) to find; (*pensar*) to think; **achar-se** VR to think (that) one is; (*encontrar-se*) to be; **~ de fazer** (*resolver*) to decide to

do; **o que é que você acha disso?** what do you think of it?; **acho que sim** I think so
achatar [aʃa'tar] VT to squash, flatten
acidentado, -a [asidẽ'tadu, a] ADJ (*terreno*) rough; (*estrada*) bumpy; (*viagem*) eventful; (*vida*) difficult ▶ M/F injured person
acidental [asidẽ'taw] (*pl* **-ais**) ADJ accidental
acidente [asi'dẽtʃi] M accident; **por ~** by accident; **~ de trânsito** road accident
acidez [asi'dez] F acidity
ácido, -a ['asidu, a] ADJ acid; (*azedo*) sour ▶ M acid
acima [a'sima] ADV above; (*para cima*) up ▶ PREP: **~ de** above; (*além de*) beyond; **mais ~** higher up; **rio ~** up river; **passar rua ~** to go up the street; **~ de 1000** more than 1000
acionar [asjo'nar] VT to set in motion; (*máquina*) to operate; (*Jur*) to sue
acionista [asjo'nista] M/F shareholder
acirrado, -a [asi'hadu, a] ADJ (*luta, competição*) tough
acirrar [asi'har] VT to incite, stir up
aclamar [akla'mar] VT to acclaim; (*aplaudir*) to applaud
aço ['asu] M steel
acocorar-se [akoko'rarsi] VR to squat, crouch
acode [a'kɔdʒi] VB *ver* **acudir**
ações [a'sõjs] FPL *de* **ação**
acolá [ako'la] ADV over there
acolchoado [akow'ʃwadu] M quilt
acolhedor, a [akoʎe'dor(a)] ADJ welcoming; (*hospitaleiro*) hospitable
acolher [ako'ʎer] VT to welcome; (*abrigar*) to shelter; (*aceitar*) to accept; **acolher-se** VR to shelter;
acolhida [ako'ʎida] F (*recepção*) reception, welcome; (*refúgio*) refuge; **acolhimento** [akoʎi'mẽtu] M = **acolhida**
acomodação [akomoda'sãw] (*pl* **-ões**) F accommodation; (*arranjo*) arrangement; (*adaptação*) adaptation
acomodar [akomo'dar] VT to accommodate; (*arrumar*) to arrange; (*adaptar*) to adapt
acompanhamento [akõpaɲa'mẽtu] M attendance; (*cortejo*) procession; (*Mús*) accompaniment; (*Culin*) side dish
acompanhante [akõpa'ɲãtʃi] M/F companion; (*Mús*) accompanist; (*de idoso, doente*) carer (BRIT), caregiver (US)
acompanhar [akõpa'ɲar] VT to accompany
aconchegante [akõʃe'gãtʃi] ADJ cosy (BRIT), cozy (US)
aconselhar [akõse'ʎar] VT to advise; **aconselhar-se** VR: **~-se com** to consult
acontecer [akõte'ser] VI to happen; **acontecimento** [akõtesi'mẽtu] M event
acordar [akor'dar] VT to wake (up); (*concordar*) to agree (on) ▶ VI to wake up
acorde [a'kɔrdʒi] M chord
acordo [a'kordu] M agreement; **"de ~!"** "agreed!"; **de ~ com** (*pessoa*) in agreement with; (*conforme*) in accordance with; **estar de ~** to agree
Açores [a'soris] MPL: **os ~** the Azores; **açoriano, -a** [aso'rjanu, a] ADJ, M/F Azorean

acossar [ako'sar] VT (*perseguir*) to pursue; (*atormentar*) to harass
acostamento [akosta'mẽtu] M hard shoulder (BRIT), berm (US)
acostumado, -a [akostu'madu, a] ADJ usual, customary; **estar ~ a algo** to be used to sth
acostumar [akostu'mar] VT to accustom; **acostumar-se** VR: **~-se a** to get used to
açougue [a'sogi] M butcher's (shop); **açougueiro** [aso'gejru] M butcher
acovardar-se [akovar'darsi] VR (*desanimar*) to lose courage; (*amedrontar-se*) to flinch, cower
acreditado, -a [akredʒi'tadu, a] ADJ accredited
acreditar [akredʒi'tar] VT to believe; (*Com*) to credit; (*afiançar*) to guarantee ▶ VI: **~ em** to believe in
acrescentar [akresẽ'tar] VT to add
açúcar [a'sukar] M sugar; **açucareiro** [asuka'rejru] M sugar bowl
açude [a'sudʒi] M dam
acudir [aku'dʒir] VT (*ir em socorro*) to help, assist ▶ VI (*responder*) to reply, respond; **~ a** to come to the aid of
acumular [akumu'lar] VT to accumulate; (*reunir*) to collect; (*funções*) to combine
acusação [akuza'sãw] (*pl* **-ões**) F accusation, charge; (*Jur*) prosecution
acusar [aku'zar] VT to accuse; (*revelar*) to reveal; (*culpar*) to blame; **~ o recebimento de** to acknowledge receipt of
acústico, -a [a'kustʃiku, a] ADJ acoustic
adaptar [adap'tar] VT to adapt; (*acomodar*) to fit; **adaptar-se** VR: **~-se a** to adapt to
adega [a'dɛga] F cellar
ademais [adʒi'majs] ADV besides, moreover
adentro [a'dẽtru] ADV inside, in; **mata ~** into the woods
adequado, -a [ade'kwadu, a] ADJ appropriate
adereço [ade'resu] M adornment; **adereços** MPL (*Teatro*) stage props
aderente [ade'rẽtʃi] ADJ adhesive, sticky ▶ M/F supporter
aderir [ade'rir] VI to adhere
adesão [ade'zãw] F adhesion; (*patrocínio*) support
adesivo, -a [ade'zivu, a] ADJ adhesive, sticky ▶ M adhesive tape; (*Med*) sticking plaster
adestrar [ades'trar] VT to train; (*cavalo*) to break in
adeus [a'dews] EXCL goodbye!
adiantado, -a [adʒjã'tadu, a] ADJ advanced; (*relógio*) fast; **chegar ~** to arrive ahead of time; **pagar ~** to pay in advance
adiantamento [adʒjãta'mẽtu] M progress; (*dinheiro*) advance (payment)
adiantar [adʒjã'tar] VT (*dinheiro, salário*) to advance; (*relógio*) to put forward; **não adianta reclamar/insistir** there's no point *ou* it's no use complaining/insisting
adiante [a'dʒjãtʃi] ADV (*na frente*) in front; (*para a frente*) forward; **mais ~** further on; (*no futuro*) later on
adiar [a'dʒjar] VT to postpone, put off; (*sessão*) to adjourn
adição [adʒi'sãw] (*pl* **-ões**) F addition; (*Mat*) sum; **adicionar** [adʒisjo'nar] VT to add
adido, -a [a'dʒidu, a] M/F attaché
adiro [a'diru] VB *ver* **aderir**
adivinhar [adʒivi'ɲar] VT to guess; (*ler a sorte*) to foretell ▶ VI to guess;

a

~ o pensamento de alguém to read sb's mind; **adivinho, -a** [adʒi'viɲu, a] M/F fortune-teller
adjetivo [adʒe'tʃivu] M adjective
adjudicar [adʒudʒi'kar] VT to award, grant
administração [adʒiministra'sãw] (*pl* **-ões**) F administration; (*direção*) management; (*comissão*) board
administrador, a [adʒiministra'dor(a)] M/F administrator; (*diretor*) director; (*gerente*) manager
administrar [adʒiminis'trar] VT to administer, manage; (*governar*) to govern
admiração [adʒimira'sãw] F wonder; (*estima*) admiration; **ponto de ~** (PT) exclamation mark
admirado, -a [adʒimi'radu, a] ADJ astonished, surprised
admirar [adʒimi'rar] VT to admire; **admirar-se** VR: **~-se de** to be astonished *ou* surprised at; **admirável** [adʒimi'ravew] (*pl* **-eis**) ADJ amazing
admissão [adʒimi'sãw] (*pl* **-ões**) F admission; (*consentimento para entrar*) admittance; (*de escola*) intake
admitir [adʒimi'tʃir] VT to admit; (*permitir*) to allow; (*funcionário*) to take on
adoção [ado'sãw] F adoption
adoçar [ado'sar] VT to sweeten
adoecer [adoe'ser] VI to fall ill ▸VT to make ill; **~ de** *ou* **com** to fall ill with
adoidado, -a [adoj'dadu, a] ADJ crazy
adolescente [adole'sẽtʃi] ADJ, M/F adolescent
adorar [ado'rar] VT to adore; (*venerar*) to worship
adormecer [adorme'ser] VI to fall asleep; (*entorpecer-se*) to go numb; **adormecido, -a** [adorme'sidu, a] ADJ sleeping ▸M/F sleeper
adorno [a'dornu] M adornment
adotar [ado'tar] VT to adopt; **adotivo, -a** [ado'tʃivu, a] ADJ (*filho*) adopted
adquirir [adʒiki'rir] VT to acquire
Adriático, -a [a'drjatʃiku, a] ADJ: **o (mar) ~** the Adriatic (Sea)
adro ['adru] M (church) forecourt; (*em volta da igreja*) churchyard
adulação [adula'sãw] F flattery
adulterar [aduwte'rar] VT to adulterate; (*contas*) to falsify ▸VI to commit adultery
adultério [aduw'tɛrju] M adultery
adulto, -a [a'duwtu, a] ADJ, M/F adult
advento [ad'vẽtu] M advent; **o A~** Advent
advérbio [adʒ'vɛrbju] M adverb
adverso, -a [adʒi'vɛrsu, a] ADJ adverse; (*oposto*): **~ a** opposed to
advertência [adʒiver'tẽsja] F warning
advertir [adʒiver'tʃir] VT to warn; (*repreender*) to reprimand; (*chamar a atenção a*) to draw attention to
advogado, -a [adʒivo'gadu, a] M/F lawyer
advogar [adʒivo'gar] VT to advocate; (*Jur*) to plead ▸VI to practise (BRIT) *ou* practice (US) law
aéreo, -a [a'erju, a] ADJ air *atr*
aerobarco [aero'barku] M jetfoil
aeromoço, -a [aero'mosu, a] (BR) M/F flight attendant
aeronáutica [aero'nawtʃika] F air force; (*ciência*) aeronautics *sg*
aeronave [aero'navi] F aircraft

aeroporto [aero'portu] M airport
aerossol [aero'sɔw] (*pl* **-óis**) M aerosol
afã [a'fã] M (*entusiasmo*) enthusiasm; (*diligência*) diligence; (*ânsia*) eagerness; (*esforço*) effort
afagar [afa'gar] VT to caress; (*cabelo*) to stroke
afastado, -a [afas'tadu, a] ADJ (*distante*) remote; (*isolado*) secluded; **manter-se ~** to keep to o.s.
afastamento [afasta'mẽtu] M removal; (*distância*) distance; (*de pessoal*) lay-off
afastar [afas'tar] VT to remove; (*separar*) to separate; (*ideia*) to put out of one's mind; (*pessoal*) to lay off; **afastar-se** VR to move away
afável [a'favew] (*pl* **-eis**) ADJ friendly
afazeres [afa'zeris] MPL business *sg*; (*dever*) duties, tasks; **~ domésticos** household chores
afeição [afej'sãw] F affection, fondness; (*dedicação*) devotion; **afeiçoado, -a** [afej'swadu, a] ADJ: **afeiçoado a** (*amoroso*) fond of; (*devotado*) devoted to; **afeiçoar-se** [afej'swarsi] VR: **afeiçoar-se a** to take a liking to
afeito, -a [a'fejtu, a] ADJ: **~ a** accustomed to, used to
aferrado, -a [afe'hadu, a] ADJ obstinate, stubborn
afetar [afe'tar] VT to affect; (*fingir*) to feign
afetivo, -a [afe'tʃivu, a] ADJ affectionate; (*problema*) emotional
afeto [a'fɛtu] M affection; **afetuoso, -a** [afe'twozu, ɔza] ADJ affectionate
afiado, -a [a'fjadu, a] ADJ sharp; (*pessoa*) well-trained
afiar [a'fjar] VT to sharpen
aficionado, -a [afisjo'nadu, a] M/F enthusiast
afilhado, -a [afi'ʎadu, a] M/F godson/goddaughter
afim [a'fĩ] (*pl* **-ns**) ADJ (*semelhante*) similar; (*consanguíneo*) related ▶ M/F relative, relation
afinado, -a [afi'nadu, a] ADJ in tune
afinal [afi'naw] ADV at last, finally; **~ (de contas)** after all
afinar [afi'nar] VT (*Mús*) to tune
afinco [a'fĩku] M tenacity, persistence
afins [a'fĩs] PL *de* **afim**
afirmação [afirma'sãw] (*pl* **-ões**) F affirmation; (*declaração*) statement
afirmar [afir'mar] VT, VI to affirm, assert; (*declarar*) to declare
afirmativo, -a [afirma'tʃivu, a] ADJ affirmative
afixar [afik'sar] VT (*cartazes*) to stick, post
aflição [afli'sãw] F affliction; (*ansiedade*) anxiety; (*angústia*) anguish
afligir [afli'ʒir] VT to distress; (*atormentar*) to torment; (*inquietar*) to worry; **afligir-se** VR: **~-se com** to worry about; **aflito, -a** [a'flitu, a] PP *de* **afligir** ▶ ADJ distressed, anxious
afluência [a'flwẽsja] F affluence; (*corrente copiosa*) flow; (*de pessoas*) stream; **afluente** [a'flwẽtʃi] ADJ copious; (*rico*) affluent ▶ M tributary
afobação [afoba'sãw] F fluster; (*ansiedade*) panic
afobado, -a [afo'badu, a] ADJ flustered; (*ansioso*) panicky, nervous
afobar [afo'bar] VT to fluster; (*deixar ansioso*) to make nervous *ou* panicky ▶ VI to get flustered; to panic, get nervous; **afobar-se** VR to get flustered

afogar [afo'gar] VT to drown ▸ VI (*Auto*) to flood; **afogar-se** VR to drown
afoito, -a [a'fojtu, a] ADJ bold, daring
afortunado, -a [afortu'nadu, a] ADJ fortunate, lucky
África ['afrika] F: **a ~** Africa; **a ~ do Sul** South Africa; **africano, -a** [afri'kanu, a] ADJ, M/F African
afro-brasileiro, -a ['afru-] (*pl* **-s**) ADJ Afro-Brazilian
afronta [a'frõta] F insult, affront; **afrontar** [afrõ'tar] VT to insult; (*ofender*) to offend
afrouxar [afro'ʃar] VT (*desapertar*) to slacken; (*soltar*) to loosen ▸ VI to come loose
afta ['afta] F (mouth) ulcer
afugentar [afuʒẽ'tar] VT to drive away, put to flight
afundar [afũ'dar] VT to sink; (*cavidade*) to deepen; **afundar-se** VR to sink
agachar-se [aga'ʃarsi] VR (*acaçapar-se*) to crouch, squat; (*curvar-se*) to stoop
agarrar [aga'har] VT to seize, grasp; **agarrar-se** VR: **~-se a** to cling to, hold on to
agasalhar [agaza'ʎar] VT to dress warmly, wrap up; **agasalhar-se** VR to wrap o.s. up
agasalho [aga'zaʎu] M (*casaco*) coat; (*suéter*) sweater
ágeis ['aʒejs] PL *de* **ágil**
agência [a'ʒẽsja] F agency; (*escritório*) office; **~ de correio** (BR) post office; **~ de viagens** travel agency
agenda [a'ʒẽda] F diary; **~ eletrônica** personal organizer
agente [a'ʒẽtʃi] M/F agent; (*de polícia*) policeman/woman
ágil ['aʒiw] (*pl* **-eis**) ADJ agile
agir [a'ʒir] VI to act
agitação [aʒita'sãw] (*pl* **-ões**) F agitation; (*perturbação*) disturbance; (*inquietação*) restlessness
agitado, -a [aʒi'tadu, a] ADJ agitated, disturbed; (*inquieto*) restless
agitar [aʒi'tar] VT to agitate, disturb; (*sacudir*) to shake; (*cauda*) to wag; (*mexer*) to stir; **agitar-se** VR to get upset; (*mar*) to get rough
aglomeração [aglomera'sãw] (*pl* **-ões**) F gathering; (*multidão*) crowd
aglomerar [aglome'rar] VT to heap up, pile up; **aglomerar-se** VR (*multidão*) to crowd together
agonia [ago'nia] F agony, anguish; (*ânsia da morte*) death throes *pl*; **agonizante** [agoni'zãtʃi] ADJ dying ▸ M/F dying person; **agonizar** [agoni'zar] VI to be dying; (*afligir-se*) to agonize
agora [a'gɔra] ADV now; **~ mesmo** right now; (*há pouco*) a moment ago; **até ~** so far, up to now; **por ~** for now
agosto [a'gostu] M August
agouro [a'goru] M omen
agraciar [agra'sjar] VT to decorate
agradar [agra'dar] VT to please; (*fazer agrados a*) to be nice to ▸ VI to be pleasing; (*satisfazer*) to go down well
agradável [agra'davew] (*pl* **-eis**) ADJ pleasant
agradecer [agrade'ser] VT: **~ algo a alguém, ~ a alguém por algo** to thank sb for sth; **agradecido, -a** [agrade'sidu, a] ADJ grateful; **mal agradecido** ungrateful;

agradecimento [agradesi'mẽtu] M gratitude; **agradecimentos** MPL (*gratidão*) thanks

agrado [a'gradu] M: **fazer um ~ a alguém** (*afagar*) to be affectionate with sb; (*ser agradável*) to be nice to sb

agrário, -a [a'grarju, a] ADJ agrarian; **reforma agrária** land reform

agravante [agra'vãtʃi] ADJ aggravating ▶ F aggravating circumstance

agravar [agra'var] VT to aggravate, make worse; **agravar-se** VR (*piorar*) to get worse

agredir [agre'dʒir] VT to attack; (*insultar*) to insult

agregar [agre'gar] VT (*juntar*) to collect; (*acrescentar*) to add

agressão [agre'sãw] (*pl* **-ões**) F aggression; (*ataque*) attack; (*assalto*) assault

agressivo, -a [agre'sivu, a] ADJ aggressive

agressões [agre'sõjs] FPL *de* **agressão**

agreste [a'grɛstʃi] ADJ rural, rustic; (*terreno*) wild

agrião [a'grjãw] M watercress

agrícola [a'grikola] ADJ agricultural

agricultor [agrikuw'tor] M farmer

agricultura [agrikuw'tura] F agriculture, farming

agrido [a'gridu] VB *ver* **agredir**

agridoce [agri'dosi] ADJ bittersweet

agronegócio [agrone'gɔsju] M agribusiness

agronomia [agrono'mia] F agronomy

agropecuária [agrope'kwarja] F farming, agriculture

agrupar [agru'par] VT to group; **agrupar-se** VR to group together

agrura [a'grura] F bitterness

água ['agwa] F water; **águas** FPL (*mar*) waters; (*chuvas*) rain *sg*; (*maré*) tides; **~ abaixo/acima** downstream/upstream; **dar ~ na boca** (*comida*) to be mouthwatering; **estar na ~** (*bêbado*) to be drunk; **fazer ~** (*Náut*) to leak; **~ benta** holy water; **~ corrente** running water; **~ de coco** coconut water; **~ doce** fresh water; **~ dura/leve** hard/soft water; **~ mineral** mineral water; **~ oxigenada** peroxide; **~ salgada** salt water; **~ sanitária** household bleach

água-de-colônia (*pl* **águas-de-colônia**) F eau-de-cologne

aguado, -a [a'gwadu, a] ADJ watery

aguardar [agwar'dar] VT to wait for; (*contar com*) to expect ▶ VI to wait

aguardente [agwar'dẽtʃi] M spirit (BRIT), liquor (US)

aguçado, -a [agu'sadu, a] ADJ pointed; (*espírito, sentidos*) acute

agudo, -a [a'gudu, a] ADJ sharp; shrill; (*intenso*) acute

aguentar [agwẽ'tar] VT (*muro etc*) to hold up; (*dor, injustiças*) to stand, put up with; (*peso*) to withstand ▶ VI to last; **aguentar-se** VR to remain, hold on; **~ fazer algo** to manage to do sth; **não ~ de** not to be able to stand

águia ['agja] F eagle; (*fig*) genius

agulha [a'guʎa] F (*de coser, tricô*) needle; (*Náut*) compass; (*Ferro*) points *pl* (BRIT), switch (US); **trabalho de ~** needlework

ai [aj] EXCL (*suspiro*) oh!; (*de dor*) ouch! ▶ M (*suspiro*) sigh; (*gemido*) groan; **ai de mim** poor me!

algo ['awgu] ADV somewhat, rather ▶ PRON something; (*qualquer coisa*) anything

algodão [awgo'dãw] M cotton; **~ (hidrófilo)** cotton wool (BRIT), absorbent cotton (US)

alguém [aw'gẽj] PRON someone, somebody; (*em frases interrogativas ou negativas*) anyone, anybody

algum, a [aw'gũ, 'guma] ADJ some; (*em frases interrogativas ou negativas*) any ▶ PRON one; (*no plural*) some; (*negativa*): **de modo ~** in no way; **coisa ~a** nothing; **~ dia** one day; **~ tempo** for a while; **~a coisa** something; **~a vez** sometime

alheio, -a [a'ʎeju, a] ADJ (*de outra pessoa*) someone else's; (*de outras pessoas*) other people's; (*estranho*) alien; (*estrangeiro*) foreign; (*impróprio*) irrelevant

alho ['aʎu] M garlic

ali [a'li] ADV there; **até ~** up to there; **por ~** around there; (*direção*) that way; **~ por** (*tempo*) round about; **de ~ por diante** from then on; **~ dentro** in there

aliado, -a [a'ljadu, a] ADJ allied ▶ M/F ally

aliança [a'ljãsa] F alliance; (*anel*) wedding ring

aliar [a'ljar] VT to ally; **aliar-se** VR to form an alliance

aliás [a'ljajs] ADV (*a propósito*) as a matter of fact; (*ou seja*) rather, that is; (*contudo*) nevertheless; (*diga-se de passagem*) incidentally

álibi ['alibi] M alibi

alicate [ali'katʃi] M pliers *pl*; **~ de unhas** nail clippers *pl*

alienação [aljena'sãw] F alienation; (*de bens*) transfer (of property); **~ mental** insanity

alienado, -a [alje'nadu, a] ADJ alienated; (*demente*) insane; (*bens*) transferred ▶ M/F lunatic

alienar [alje'nar] VT (*bens*) to transfer; (*afastar*) to alienate

alimentação [alimẽta'sãw] F (*alimentos*) food; (*ação*) feeding; (*nutrição*) nourishment; (*Elet*) supply

alimentar [alimẽ'tar] VT to feed; (*fig*) to nurture ▶ ADJ (*produto*) food *atr*; (*hábitos*) eating *atr*; **alimentar-se** VR: **~-se de** to feed on

alimento [ali'mẽtu] M food; (*nutrição*) nourishment

alisar [ali'zar] VT to smooth; (*cabelo*) to straighten; (*acariciar*) to stroke

aliviar [ali'vjar] VT to relieve

alívio [a'livju] M relief

alma ['awma] F soul; (*entusiasmo*) enthusiasm; (*caráter*) character

almejar [awme'ʒar] VT to long for, yearn for

almirante [awmi'rãtʃi] M admiral

almoçar [awmo'sar] VI to have lunch ▶ VT: **~ peixe** to have fish for lunch

almoço [aw'mosu] M lunch; **pequeno ~** (PT) breakfast

almofada [awmo'fada] F cushion; (PT: *travesseiro*) pillow

almoxarifado [awmoʃari'fadu] M storeroom

alô [a'lo] (BR) EXCL (*Tel*) hello!

alocar [alo'kar] VT to allocate

alojamento [aloʒa'mẽtu] M accommodation (BRIT), accommodations *pl* (US); (*habitação*) housing

alojar [alo'ʒar] VT to lodge; (*Mil*) to billet; **alojar-se** VR to stay

alongar [alõ'gar] VT to lengthen; (*prazo*) to extend; (*prolongar*) to

prolong; (*braço*) to stretch out; **alongar-se** VR (*sobre um assunto*) to dwell
aloprado, -a [alo'pradu, a] (*col*) ADJ nutty
alpendre [aw'pẽdri] M (*telheiro*) shed; (*pórtico*) porch
Alpes ['awpis] MPL: **os ~** the Alps
alpinismo [awpi'nizmu] M mountaineering, climbing; **alpinista** [awpi'nista] M/F mountaineer, climber
alta ['awta] F (*de preços*) rise; (*de hospital*) discharge
altar [aw'tar] M altar
alterado, -a [awte'radu, a] ADJ bad-tempered, irritated
alterar [awte'rar] VT to alter; (*falsificar*) to falsify; **alterar-se** VR (*mudar-se*) to change; (*enfurecer-se*) to lose one's temper
alternar [awter'nar] VT, VI to alternate; **alternar-se** VR to alternate; (*por turnos*) to take turns
alternativa [awterna'tʃiva] F alternative
alternativo, -a [awterna'tʃivu, a] ADJ alternative; (*Elet*) alternating
alteza [aw'teza] F highness
altitude [awtʃi'tudʒi] F altitude
alto, -a ['awtu, a] ADJ high; (*pessoa*) tall; (*som*) loud; (*Geo*) upper ▶ ADV (*falar*) loudly, loud; (*voar*) high ▶ EXCL halt! ▶ M top, summit; **do ~** from above; **por ~** superficially; **alta fidelidade** high fidelity, hi-fi; **alta noite** dead of night
alto-falante (*pl* **-s**) M loudspeaker
altura [aw'tura] F height; (*momento*) point, juncture; (*altitude*) altitude; (*de um som*) pitch; **em que ~ da Rio Branco fica a livraria?** whereabouts in Rio Branco is the bookshop?; **nesta ~** at this juncture; **estar à ~ de** (*ser capaz de*) to be up to; **ter 1.80 metros de ~** to be 1.80 metres (BRIT) *ou* meters (US) tall
alucinado, -a [alusi'nadu, a] ADJ crazy
alugar [alu'gar] VT (*tomar de aluguel*) to rent, hire; (*dar de aluguel*) to let, rent out; **alugar-se** VR to let; **aluguel** [alu'gɛw] (*pl* **-éis**) (BR) M rent; (*ação*) renting; **aluguel de carro** car hire (BRIT) *ou* rental (US); **aluguer** [alu'gɛr] (PT) M = **aluguel**
alumínio [alu'minju] M aluminium (BRIT), aluminum (US)
aluno, -a [a'lunu, a] M/F pupil, student
alvejar [awve'ʒar] VT (*tomar como alvo*) to aim at; (*branquear*) bleach
alvenaria [awvena'ria] F masonry; **de ~** brick *atr*, brick-built
alvéolo [aw'vɛolu] M cavity
alvo, -a ['awvu, a] ADJ white ▶ M target
alvorada [awvo'rada] F dawn
alvorecer [awvore'ser] VI to dawn
alvoroço [awvo'rosu] M commotion; (*entusiasmo*) enthusiasm
amabilidade [amabili'dadʒi] F kindness; (*simpatia*) friendliness
amaciante [ama'sjãtʃi] M: **~ (de roupa)** fabric conditioner
amaciar [ama'sjar] VT (*tornar macio*) to soften; (*carro*) to run in
amado, -a [a'madu, a] M/F beloved, sweetheart
amador, a [ama'dor(a)] ADJ, M/F amateur
amadurecer [amadure'ser] VT, VI (*frutos*) to ripen; (*fig*) to mature
âmago ['amagu] M (*centro*) heart, core; (*medula*) pith; (*essência*) essence

...mar [amawga'mar] VT ...amalgamate; (*combinar*) to fuse (BRIT), fuze (US), blend
amalucado, -a [amalu'kadu, a] ADJ crazy, whacky
amamentar [amamẽ'tar] VT, VI to breast-feed
amanhã [ama'ɲã] ADV, M tomorrow
amanhecer [amaɲe'ser] VI (*alvorecer*) to dawn; (*encontrar-se pela manhã*): **amanhecemos em Paris** we were in Paris at daybreak ▸ M dawn; **ao ~** at daybreak
amansar [amã'sar] VT (*animais*) to tame; (*cavalos*) to break in; (*aplacar*) to placate
amante [a'mãtʃi] M/F lover
amar [a'mar] VT to love; **eu te amo** I love you
amarelo, -a [ama'rɛlu, a] ADJ yellow ▸ M yellow
amargar [amar'gar] VT to make bitter; (*fig*) to embitter
amargo, -a [a'margu, a] ADJ bitter; **amargura** [amar'gura] F bitterness
amarrar [ama'har] VT to tie (up); (*Náut*) to moor; **~ a cara** to frown, scowl
amarrotar [amaho'tar] VT to crease
amassar [ama'sar] VT (*pão*) to knead; (*misturar*) to mix; (*papel*) to screw up; (*roupa*) to crease; (*carro*) to dent
amável [a'mavew] (*pl* **-eis**) ADJ kind
Amazonas [ama'zɔnas] M: **o ~** the Amazon
Amazônia [ama'zonja] F: **a ~** the Amazon region

> **Amazônia** is the region formed by the basin of the river Amazon (the river with the largest volume of water in the world) and its tributaries. With a total area of almost 7 million square kilometres, it stretches from the Atlantic to the Andes. Most of **Amazônia** is in Brazilian territory, although it also extends into Peru, Colombia, Venezuela and Bolivia. It contains the richest biodiversity and largest area of tropical rainforest in the world.

ambição [ambi'sãw] (*pl* **-ões**) F ambition; **ambicionar** [ãbisjo'nar] VT to aspire to; **ambicioso, -a** [ãbi'sjozu, ɔza] ADJ ambitious
ambidestro, -a [ãbi'destru, a] ADJ ambidextrous
ambientar [ãbjẽ'tar] VT (*filme etc*) to set; (*adaptar*): **~ alguém a algo** to get sb used to sth; **ambientar-se** VR to fit in
ambiente [ã'bjẽtʃi] M atmosphere; (*meio, Comput*) environment; **meio ~** environment; **temperatura ~** room temperature
ambíguo, -a [ã'bigwu, a] ADJ ambiguous
âmbito ['ãbitu] M extent; (*campo de ação*) scope, range
ambos, ambas ['ãbus, as] ADJ PL both
ambulância [ãbu'lãsja] F ambulance
ambulante [ãbu'lãtʃi] ADJ walking; (*errante*) wandering; (*biblioteca*) mobile
ambulatório [ãbula'tɔrju] M outpatient department
ameaça [ame'asa] F threat; **~ de bomba** bomb scare; **ameaçar** [amea'sar] VT to threaten

amedrontar [amedrõ'tar] VT to scare, intimidate; **amedrontar-se** VR to be frightened
ameixa [a'mejʃa] F plum; (*passa*) prune
amém [a'mẽj] EXCL amen!
amêndoa [a'mẽdwa] F almond; **amendoeira** [amẽ'dwejra] F almond tree
amendoim [amẽdo'ĩ] (*pl* **-ns**) M peanut
amenidade [ameni'dadʒi] F wellbeing; **amenidades** FPL (*assuntos superficiais*) small talk *sg*
amenizar [ameni'zar] VT (*abrandar*) to soften; (*tornar agradável*) to make pleasant; (*facilitar*) to ease
ameno, -a [a'mɛnu, a] ADJ pleasant; (*clima*) mild
América [a'mɛrika] F: **a ~** America; **a ~ do Norte/do Sul** North/South America; **a ~ Central/Latina** Central/Latin America; **americano, -a** [ameri'kanu, a] ADJ, M/F American
amestrar [ames'trar] VT to train
amianto [a'mjãtu] M asbestos
amido [a'midu] M starch
amigável [ami'gavew] (*pl* **-eis**) ADJ amicable
amígdala [a'migdala] F tonsil; **amigdalite** [amigda'litʃi] F tonsillitis
amigo, -a [a'migu, a] ADJ friendly ▶ M/F friend; **ser ~ de** to be friends with
amistoso, -a [amis'tozu, ɔza] ADJ friendly, cordial ▶ M (*jogo*) friendly
amiúde [a'mjudʒi] ADV often, frequently
amizade [ami'zadʒi] F (*relação*) friendship; (*simpatia*) friendliness
amnistia [amnis'tia] (PT) F = **anistia**
amolação [amola'sãw] (*pl* **-ões**) F bother, annoyance
amolar [amo'lar] VT to sharpen; (*aborrecer*) to annoy, bother ▶ VI to be annoying
amolecer [amole'ser] VT to soften ▶ VI to soften; (*abrandar-se*) to relent
amônia [a'monja] F ammonia
amoníaco [amo'niaku] M ammonia
amontoar [amõ'twar] VT to pile up, accumulate; **~ riquezas** to amass a fortune
amor [a'mor] M love; **por ~ de** for the sake of; **fazer ~** to make love
amora [a'mɔra] F (*amora-preta*) blackberry; **~ silvestre** blackberry
amordaçar [amorda'sar] VT to gag
amoroso, -a [amo'rozu, ɔza] ADJ loving, affectionate
amor-perfeito (*pl* **amores-perfeitos**) M pansy
amortização [amortʃiza'sãw] F payment in instalments (BRIT) *ou* installments (US)
amortizar [amortʃi'zar] VT to pay in instalments (BRIT) *ou* installments (US)
amostra [a'mɔstra] F sample
amparar [ãpa'rar] VT to support; (*ajudar*) to assist; **amparar-se** VR: **~-se em/contra** to lean on/against
amparo [ã'paru] M support; (*auxílio*) help, assistance
ampliação [amplja'sãw] (*pl* **-ões**) F enlargement; (*extensão*) extension
ampliar [ã'pljar] VT to enlarge; (*conhecimento*) to broaden
amplificador [ãplifika'dor] M amplifier
amplificar [ãplifi'kar] VT to amplify
amplitude [ãpli'tudʒi] F (*espaço*) spaciousness; (*fig: extensão*) extent

amplo, -a ['ãplu, a] ADJ (*sala*) spacious; (*conhecimento, sentido*) broad; (*possibilidade*) ample
amputar [ãpu'tar] VT to amputate
Amsterdã [amister'dã] (BR) N Amsterdam
Amsterdão [amister'dãw] (PT) N = **Amsterdã**
amuado, -a [a'mwadu, a] ADJ sulky
anã [a'nã] F *de* **anão**
anais [a'najs] MPL annals
analfabeto, -a [anawfa'bɛtu, a] ADJ, M/F illiterate
analgésico, -a [anaw'ʒɛziku, a] ADJ analgesic ▶ M painkiller
analisar [anali'zar] VT to analyse; **análise** [a'nalizi] F analysis; **analista** [ana'lista] M/F analyst
ananás [ana'nas] (*pl* **ananases**) M (BR) *variety of pineapple*; (PT) pineapple
anão, anã [a'nãw, a'nã] (*pl* **-ões/-s**) M/F dwarf
anarquia [anar'kia] F anarchy; **anarquista** [anar'kista] M/F anarchist
anatomia [anato'mia] F anatomy
anca ['ãka] F (*de pessoa*) hip; (*de animal*) rump
ancião, anciã [ã'sjãw, ã'sjã] (*pl* **-ões/-s**) ADJ old ▶ M/F old man/woman; (*de uma tribo*) elder
anciões [a'sjõjs] MPL *de* **ancião**
âncora ['ãkora] F anchor; **ancorar** [ãko'rar] VT, VI to anchor
andaime [ã'dajmi] M (*Arq*) scaffolding
andamento [ãda'mẽtu] M (*progresso*) progress; (*rumo*) course; (*Mús*) tempo; **em ~** in progress
andar [ã'dar] VI to walk; (*máquina*) to work; (*progredir*) to progress; (*estar*): **ela anda triste** she's been sad lately ▶ M gait; (*pavimento*) floor, storey (BRIT), story (US); **anda!** hurry up!; **~ a cavalo** to ride; **~ de trem/avião/bicicleta** to travel by train/to fly/to ride a bike
Andes ['ãdʒis] MPL: **os ~** the Andes
andorinha [ãdo'riɲa] F (*pássaro*) swallow
anedota [ane'dɔta] F anecdote
anel [a'nɛw] (*pl* **-éis**) M ring; (*elo*) link; (*de cabelo*) curl; **~ de casamento** wedding ring
anestesia [aneste'zia] F anaesthesia (BRIT), anesthesia (US); (*anestésico*) anaesthetic (BRIT), anesthetic (US)
anexar [anek'sar] VT to annex; (*juntar*) to attach; (*documento*) to enclose; **anexo, -a** [a'nɛksu, a] ADJ attached ▶ M annexe; (*em carta*) enclosure; (*em e-mail*) attachment; **segue em anexo** please find enclosed
anfitrião, -triã [ãfi'trjãw, 'trjã] (*pl* **-ões/-s**) M/F host/hostess
angina [ã'ʒina] F: **~ do peito** angina (pectoris)
Angola [ã'gɔla] F Angola
angu [ã'gu] M corn-meal purée
ângulo ['ãgulu] M angle; (*canto*) corner
angústia [ã'gustʃja] F anguish, distress
animado, -a [ani'madu, a] ADJ lively; (*alegre*) cheerful; **~ com** enthusiastic about
animador, a [anima'dor(a)] ADJ encouraging ▶ M/F (BR TV) presenter; (*de festa*) entertainer; **~(a) de torcida** cheerleader
animal [ani'maw] (*pl* **-ais**) ADJ, M

animal; **~ de estimação** pet (animal)
animar [ani'mar] VT to liven up; (*encorajar*) to encourage;
animar-se VR to cheer up; (*festa etc*) to liven up; **~-se a** to bring o.s. to
ânimo ['animu] M (*coragem*) courage; **~!** cheer up!; **perder o ~** to lose heart; **recobrar o ~** to pluck up courage; (*alegrar-se*) to cheer up
aninhar [ani'ɲar] VT to nestle;
aninhar-se VR to nestle
anis [a'nis] M aniseed
anistia [anis'tʃia] F amnesty
aniversário [aniver'sarju] M anniversary; (*de nascimento*) birthday; (: *festa*) birthday party
anjo ['ãʒu] M angel; **~ da guarda** guardian angel
ano ['anu] M year; **Feliz A~ Novo!** Happy New Year!; **o ~ que vem** next year; **por ~** per annum; **fazer ~s** to have a birthday; **ter dez ~s** to be ten (years old); **dia de ~s** (PT) birthday; **~ letivo** academic year; (*da escola*) school year
anões [a'nõjs] MPL *de* **anão**
anoitecer [anojte'ser] VI to grow dark ▸ M nightfall
anomalia [anoma'lia] F anomaly
anônimo, -a [a'nonimu, a] ADJ anonymous
anoraque [ano'raki] M anorak
anormal [anor'maw] (*pl* **-ais**) ADJ abnormal; (*excepcional*) handicapped; **anormalidade** [anormali'dadʒi] F abnormality
anotação [anota'sãw] (*pl* **-ões**) F annotation; (*nota*) note
anotar [ano'tar] VT (*tomar nota*) to note down; (*esclarecer*) to annotate
anseio [ã'seju] VB *ver* **ansiar**
ânsia ['ãsja] F anxiety; (*desejo*): **~ (de)** longing (for); **ter ~s (de vômito)** to feel sick
ansiar [ã'sjar] VI: **~ por** (*desejar*) to yearn for; **~ por fazer** to long to do
ansiedade [ãsje'dadʒi] F anxiety; (*desejo*) eagerness
ansioso, -a [ã'sjozu, ɔza] ADJ anxious; (*desejoso*) eager
antártico, -a [ã'tartʃiku, a] ADJ antarctic ▸ M: **o A~** the Antarctic
ante ['ãtʃi] PREP (*na presença de*) before; (*em vista de*) in view of, faced with
antecedência [ãtese'dẽsja] F: **com ~** in advance; **3 dias de ~** three days' notice
antecedente [ãtese'dẽtʃi] ADJ preceding ▸ M antecedent; **antecedentes** MPL (*registro*) record *sg*; (*passado*) background *sg*
anteceder [ãtese'der] VT to precede
antecipação [ãtesipa'sãw] F anticipation; **com um mês de ~** a month in advance; **~ de pagamento** advance (payment)
antecipadamente [ãtesipada'mẽtʃi] ADV in advance, beforehand
antecipado, -a [ãtesi'padu, a] ADJ (*pagamento*) (in) advance
antecipar [ãtesi'par] VT to anticipate, forestall; (*adiantar*) to bring forward
antemão [ante'mãw] ADV: **de ~** beforehand
antena [ã'tɛna] F (*Bio*) antenna, feeler; (*Rádio, TV*) aerial
anteontem [ãtʃi'õtẽ] ADV the day before yesterday
antepassado [ãtʃipa'sadu] M ancestor
anterior [ãte'rjor] ADJ previous; (*antigo*) former; (*de posição*) front
antes ['ãtʃis] ADV before;

(*antigamente*) formerly; (*ao contrário*) rather ▶ PREP: **~ de** before; **o quanto ~** as soon as possible; **~ de partir** before leaving; **~ de tudo** above all; **~ que** before

anti- [ãtʃi] PREFIXO anti-

antiácido, -a [ã'tʃjasidu, a] ADJ, M antacid

antibiótico, -a [ãtʃi'bjɔtʃiku, a] ADJ, M antibiotic

anticaspa [ãtʃi'kaspa] ADJ INV anti-dandruff

anticlímax [ãtʃi'klimaks] M anticlimax

anticoncepcional [ãtʃikõsepsjo'naw] (*pl* **-ais**) ADJ, M contraceptive

antidepressivo, -a [ãtʃidepre'sivu, a] ADJ, M anti-depressant

antigamente [ãtʃiga'mẽtʃi] ADV formerly; (*no passado*) in the past

antiglobalização [ãtʃiglobaliza'sãw] F antiglobalization

antigo, -a [ã'tʃigu, a] ADJ old; (*histórico*) ancient; (*de estilo*) antique; (*chefe etc*) former

antiguidade [ãtʃigwi'dadʒi] F antiquity, ancient times *pl*; (*de emprego*) seniority; **antiguidades** FPL (*monumentos*) ancient monuments; (*artigos*) antiques

anti-horário, -a ADJ anticlockwise

antilhano, -a [ãtʃi'ʎanu, a] ADJ, M/F West Indian

Antilhas [ã'tʃiʎas] FPL: **as ~** the West Indies

antipatia [ãtʃipa'tʃia] F dislike; **antipático, -a** [ãtʃi'patʃiku, a] ADJ unpleasant, unfriendly

antipatizar [ãtʃipatʃi'zar] VI: **~ com alguém** to dislike sb

antiquado, -a [ãtʃi'kwadu, a] ADJ antiquated; (*fora de moda*) out of date, old-fashioned

antiquário, -a [ãtʃi'kwarju, a] M/F antique dealer ▶ M (*loja*) antique shop

antissemita ADJ anti-Semitic

antisséptico, -a ADJ, M antiseptic

antissocial (*pl* **-ais**) ADJ antisocial

antivírus [ãtʃi'virus] M INV (*Comput*) antivirus

antologia [ãtolo'ʒia] F anthology

anual [a'nwaw] (*pl* **-ais**) ADJ annual, yearly

anulação [anula'sãw] (*pl* **-ões**) F cancellation; (*de contrato, casamento*) annulment

anunciante [anũ'sjãtʃi] M (*Com*) advertiser

anunciar [anũ'sjar] VT to announce; (*Com*) to advertise

anúncio [a'nũsju] M announcement; (*Com*) advertisement; (*cartaz*) notice; **~s classificados** small *ou* classified ads

ânus ['anus] M INV anus

anzol [ã'zɔw] (*pl* **-óis**) M fish-hook

ao [aw] = **a + o**; *ver* **a**

aonde [a'õdʒi] ADV where; **~ quer que** wherever

aos [aws] = **a + os**; *ver* **a**

Ap. ABR = **apartamento**

apagado, -a [apa'gadu, a] ADJ (*fogo*) out; (*luz elétrica*) off

apagão [apa'gãw] (*pl* **-ões**) M power cut (BRIT), power outage (US)

apagar [apa'gar] VT to put out; (*luz elétrica*) to switch off; (*vela*) to blow out; (*com borracha*) to rub out, erase; **apagar-se** VR to go out

apaixonado, -a [apajʃo'nadu, a]

ADJ (*discurso*) impassioned; (*pessoa*): **ele está ~ por ela** he is in love with her; **ele é ~ por tênis** he's mad about tennis

apaixonar-se [apajʃo'narsi] VR: **~ por** to fall in love with

apalpar [apaw'par] VT to touch, feel; (*Med*) to examine

apanhado [apa'ɲadu] M (*de flores*) bunch; (*resumo*) summary

apanhar [apa'ɲar] VT to catch; (*algo à mão, do chão*) to pick up; (*ir buscar, surra, táxi*) to get; (*flores, frutas*) to pick; (*agarrar*) to grab ▸ VI to get a beating; **~ sol/chuva** to sunbathe/get soaked

aparador [apara'dor] M sideboard

apara-lápis [apara'lapis] (PT) M INV pencil sharpener

aparar [apa'rar] VT (*cabelo*) to trim; (*lápis*) to sharpen; (*algo arremessado*) to catch

aparato [apa'ratu] M pomp; (*coleção*) array

aparecer [apare'ser] VI to appear; (*apresentar-se*) to turn up; (*ser publicado*) to be published; **~ em casa de alguém** to call on sb;

aparecimento [aparesi'mẽtu] M appearance; (*publicação*) publication

aparelho [apa'reʎu] M apparatus; (*equipamento*) equipment; (*Pesca*) tackle; (*máquina*) machine; (BR: *fone*) telephone; **~ de barbear** electric shaver; **~ de chá** tea set; **~ de rádio/TV** radio/TV set; **~ doméstico** domestic appliance

aparência [apa'rẽsja] F appearance; **na ~** apparently; **sob a ~ de** under the guise of; **ter ~ de** to look like, seem

aparentar [aparẽ'tar] VT (*fingir*) to feign; (*parecer*) to give the appearance of

aparente [apa'rẽtʃi] ADJ apparent

aparição [apari'sãw] (*pl* **-ões**) F (*visão*) apparition; (*fantasma*) ghost

apartamento [aparta'mẽtu] M apartment, flat (BRIT)

apartar [apar'tar] VT to separate;

apartar-se VR to separate

apatia [apa'tʃia] F apathy

apático, -a [a'patʃiku, a] ADJ apathetic

apavorado, -a [apavo'radu, a] ADJ terrified

apavorante [apavo'rãtʃi] ADJ terrifying

apavorar [apavo'rar] VT to terrify ▸ VI to be terrifying; **apavorar-se** VR to be terrified

apear-se [a'pjarsi] VR: **~ de** (*cavalo*) to dismount from

apegado, -a [ape'gadu, a] ADJ: **ser ~ a** (*gostar de*) to be attached to

apegar-se [ape'garsi] VR: **~ a** (*afeiçoar-se*) to become attached to

apego [a'pegu] M (*afeição*) attachment

apelar [ape'lar] VI to appeal; **~ da sentença** (*Jur*) to appeal against the sentence; **~ para** to appeal to; **~ para a ignorância/violência** to resort to abuse/violence

apelido [ape'lidu] M (PT: *nome de família*) surname; (BR: *alcunha*) nickname

apelo [a'pelu] M appeal

apenas [a'pɛnas] ADV only

apendicite [apẽdʒi'sitʃi] F appendicitis

aperfeiçoar [aperfej'swar] VT to perfect; (*melhorar*) to improve

apertado, -a [aper'tadu, a] ADJ tight; (*estreito*) narrow; (*sem dinheiro*) hard-up; (*vida*) hard

apertar [aper'tar] VT (*agarrar*) to hold tight; (*roupa*) to take in;

(*esponja*) to squeeze; (*botão*) to press; (*despesas*) to limit; (*vigilância*) to step up; (*coração*) to break; (*fig: pessoa*) to put pressure on ▶VI (*sapatos*) to pinch; (*chuva, frio*) to get worse; (*estrada*) to narrow; **~ em** (*insistir*) to insist on; **~ a mão de alguém** to shake hands with sb

aperto [a'pertu] M (*pressão*) pressure; (*situação difícil*) spot of bother, jam; **um ~ de mãos** a handshake

apesar [ape'zar] PREP: **~ de** in spite of, despite; **~ disso** nevertheless; **~ de que** even though

apetecer [apete'ser] VI (*comida*) to be appetizing

apetite [ape'tʃitʃi] M appetite; **bom ~!** enjoy your meal!

apetrechos [ape'treʃus] MPL gear *sg*; (*Pesca*) tackle *sg*

apinhado, -a [api'ɲadu, a] ADJ crowded

apitar [api'tar] VI to whistle;

apito [a'pitu] M whistle

aplacar [apla'kar] VT to placate ▶VI to calm down; **aplacar-se** VR to calm down

aplaudir [aplaw'dʒir] VT to applaud

aplauso [a'plawzu] M applause; (*apoio*) support; (*elogio*) praise; (*aprovação*) approval

aplicação [aplika'sãw] (*pl* **-ões**) F application; (*esforço*) effort; (*da lei*) enforcement; (*de dinheiro*) investment; (PT *Comput*) application, app (*col*)

aplicado, -a [apli'kadu, a] ADJ hard-working

aplicar [apli'kar] VT to apply; (*lei*) to enforce; (*dinheiro*) to invest;

aplicar-se VR: **~-se a** to devote o.s. to

aplicativo [aplika'tʃivu] M (BR *Comput*) application, app (*col*)

apoderar-se [apode'rarsi] VR: **~ de** to seize, take possession of

apodrecer [apodre'ser] VT to rot; (*dente*) to decay ▶VI to rot; to decay

apogeu [apo'ʒew] M (*fig*) height, peak

apoiar [apo'jar] VT to support; (*basear*) to base; (*moção*) to second;

apoiar-se VR: **~-se em** to rest on

apoio [a'poju] M support; (*financeiro*) backing

apólice [a'pɔlisi] F (*certificado*) policy, certificate; (*ação*) share, bond; **~ de seguro** insurance policy

apontamento [apõta'mẽtu] M (*nota*) note

apontar [apõ'tar] VT (*fusil*) to aim; (*erro*) to point out; (*com o dedo*) to point at *ou* to; (*razão*) to put forward ▶VI to begin to appear; (*brotar*) to sprout; (*com o dedo*) to point; **~ para** to point to; (*com arma*) to aim at

após [a'pɔjs] PREP after

aposentado, -a [apozẽ'tadu, a] ADJ retired ▶M/F retired person, pensioner; **ser ~** to be retired;

aposentadoria [apozẽtado'ria] F retirement; (*dinheiro*) pension

aposentar [apozẽ'tar] VT to retire; **aposentar-se** VR to retire

aposento [apo'zẽtu] M room

apossar-se [apo'sarsi] VR: **~ de** to take possession of, seize

apostar [apos'tar] VT to bet ▶VI: **~ em** to bet on

apóstrofo [a'pɔstrofu] M apostrophe

apreciar [apre'sjar] VT to appreciate; (*gostar de*) to enjoy
apreço [a'presu] M esteem, regard; (*consideração*) consideration; **em ~** in question
apreender [aprjẽ'der] VT to apprehend; (*tomar*) to seize; (*entender*) to grasp
apreensão [aprjẽ'sãw] (*pl* **-ões**) F (*percepção*) perception; (*tomada*) seizure; (*receio*) apprehension
apreensivo, -a [aprjẽ'sivu, a] ADJ apprehensive
apreensões [aprjẽ'sõjs] FPL *de* **apreensão**
apregoar [apre'gwar] VT to proclaim, announce; (*mercadorias*) to cry
aprender [aprẽ'der] VT, VI to learn; **~ a ler** to learn to read; **~ de cor** to learn by heart
aprendizagem [aprẽdʒi'zaʒẽ] F (*num ofício*) apprenticeship; (*numa profissão*) training; (*escolar*) learning
apresentação [aprezẽta'sãw] (*pl* **-ões**) F presentation; (*de peça, filme*) performance; (*de pessoas*) introduction; (*porte pessoal*) appearance
apresentador, a [aprezẽta'dor(a)] M/F presenter
apresentar [aprezẽ'tar] VT to present; (*pessoas*) to introduce; **apresentar-se** VR to introduce o.s.; (*problema*) to present itself; (*à polícia etc*) to report; **quero ~-lhe ...** may I introduce you to ...
apressado, -a [apre'sadu, a] ADJ hurried, hasty; **estar ~** to be in a hurry
apressar [apre'sar] VT to hurry; **apressar-se** VR to hurry (up)
aprisionar [aprizjo'nar] VT (*cativar*) to capture; (*encarcerar*) to imprison
aprontar [aprõ'tar] VT to get ready, prepare; **aprontar-se** VR to get ready
apropriado, -a [apro'prjadu, a] ADJ appropriate, suitable
aprovado, -a [apro'vadu, a] ADJ approved; **ser ~ num exame** to pass an exam
aprovar [apro'var] VT to approve of; (*exame*) to pass ▶ VI to make the grade
aproveitador, a [aprovejta'dor(a)] M/F opportunist
aproveitamento [aprovejta'mẽtu] M use, utilization; (*nos estudos*) progress
aproveitar [aprovej'tar] VT to take advantage of; (*utilizar*) to use; (*oportunidade*) to take ▶ VI to make the most of it; (PT) to be of use; **aproveite!** enjoy yourself!
aproximação [aprosima'sãw] (*pl* **-ões**) F approximation; (*chegada*) approach; (*proximidade*) nearness
aproximar [aprosi'mar] VT to bring near; (*aliar*) to bring together; **aproximar-se** VR: **~-se de** (*acercar-se*) to approach
aptidão [aptʃi'dãw] F aptitude; (*jeito*) knack; **~ física** physical fitness
apto, -a ['aptu, a] ADJ apt; (*capaz*) capable
apto. ABR = **apartamento**
apunhalar [apuɲa'lar] VT to stab
apurado, -a [apu'radu, a] ADJ refined
apurar [apu'rar] VT to perfect; (*averiguar*) to investigate; (*dinheiro*) to raise, get; (*votos*) to count; **apurar-se** VR to dress up
aquarela [akwa'rɛla] F watercolour (BRIT), watercolor (US)
aquário [a'kwarju] M aquarium;

A~ (*Astrologia*) Aquarius

aquático, -a [a'kwatʃiku, a] ADJ aquatic, water *atr*

aquecer [ake'ser] VT to heat ▶ VI to heat up; **aquecer-se** VR to heat up; **aquecido, -a** [ake'sidu, a] ADJ heated; **aquecimento** [akesi'mẽtu] M heating; **aquecimento central** central heating; **aquecimento global** global warming

aquele, -ela [a'keli, ɛla] ADJ (*sg*) that; (*pl*) those ▶ PRON (*sg*) that one; (*pl*) those (ones)

àquele, -ela [a'keli, ɛla] = **a + aquele, -ela**

aquém [a'kẽj] ADV on this side; **~ de** on this side of

aqui [a'ki] ADV here; **eis ~** here is/are; **~ mesmo** right here; **até ~** up to here; **por ~** hereabouts; (*nesta direção*) this way

aquilo [a'kilu] PRON that; **~ que** what

àquilo [a'kilu] = **a + aquilo**

aquisição [akizi'sãw] (*pl* **-ões**) F acquisition

ar [ar] M air; (*aspecto*) look; (*brisa*) breeze; (PT *Auto*) choke; **ares** MPL (*atitude*) airs; (*clima*) climate *sg*; **ao ar livre** in the open air; **no ar** (*TV, Rádio*) on air; (*fig: planos*) up in the air; **dar-se ares** to put on airs

árabe ['arabi] ADJ, M/F Arab ▶ M (*Ling*) Arabic

Arábia [a'rabja] F: **a ~ Saudita** Saudi Arabia

arame [a'rami] M wire

aranha [a'raɲa] F spider

arara [a'rara] F macaw

arbitragem [arbi'traʒẽ] F arbitration

arbitrar [arbi'trar] VT to arbitrate; (*Esporte*) to referee

arbitrário, -a [arbi'trarju, a] ADJ arbitrary

arbítrio [ar'bitrju] M decision; **ao ~ de** at the discretion of

árbitro ['arbitru] M (*juiz*) arbiter; (*Jur*) arbitrator; (*Futebol*) referee; (*Tênis*) umpire

arbusto [ar'bustu] M shrub, bush

arca ['arka] F chest, trunk; **~ de Noé** Noah's Ark

arcar [ar'kar] VT: **~ com** (*responsabilidades*) to shoulder; (*despesas*) to handle; (*consequencias*) to take

arcebispo [arse'bispu] M archbishop

arco ['arku] M (*Arq*) arch; (*Mil, Mús*) bow; (*Elet, Mat*) arc

arco-íris (*pl* **arcos-íris**) M rainbow

ar-condicionado (*pl* **ares-condicionados**) M (*aparelho*) air conditioner; (*sistema*) air conditioning

arder [ar'der] VI to burn; (*pele, olhos*) to sting; **~ de raiva** to seethe (with rage)

ardiloso, -a [ardʒi'lozu, ɔza] ADJ cunning

ardor [ar'dor] M ardour (BRIT), ardor (US); **ardoroso, -a** [ardo'rozu, ɔza] ADJ ardent

árduo, -a ['ardwu, a] ADJ arduous; (*difícil*) hard, difficult

área ['arja] F area; (*Esporte*) penalty area; (*fig*) field; **~ (de serviço)** balcony (*for hanging washing etc*)

areia [a'reja] F sand; **~ movediça** quicksand

arejar [are'ʒar] VT to air ▶ VI to get some air; (*descansar*) to have a breather; **arejar-se** VR to get some air; to have a break

arena [a'rɛna] F arena; (*de circo*) ring

Argélia [ar'ʒɛlja] F: **a ~** Algeria
Argentina [arʒẽ'tʃina] F: **a ~** Argentina
argila [ar'ʒila] F clay
argola [ar'gɔla] F ring; **argolas** FPL (*brincos*) hooped earrings; **~ (de porta)** door-knocker
argumentação [argumẽta'sãw] F line of argument
argumentar [argumẽ'tar] VT, VI to argue
argumento [argu'mẽtu] M argument; (*de obra*) theme
aridez [ari'dez] F dryness; (*esterilidade*) barrenness; (*falta de interesse*) dullness
árido, -a ['aridu, a] ADJ arid, dry; (*estéril*) barren; (*maçante*) dull
Áries ['aris] F Aries
aritmética [aritʃ'mɛtʃika] F arithmetic
arma ['arma] F weapon; **armas** FPL (*nucleares etc*) arms; (*brasão*) coat *sg* of arms; **passar pelas ~s** to shoot, execute; **~ convencional/nuclear** conventional/nuclear weapon; **~s de destruição em massa** weapons of mass destruction; **~ de fogo** firearm
armação [arma'sãw] (*pl* **-ões**) F (*armadura*) frame; (*Pesca*) tackle; (*Náut*) rigging; (*de óculos*) frames *pl*
armado, -a [ar'madu, a] ADJ armed
armar [ar'mar] VT to arm; (*montar*) to assemble; (*barraca*) to pitch; (*um aparelho*) to set up; (*armadilha*) to set; (*Náut*) to fit out; **armar-se** VR to arm o.s.; **~ uma briga com** to pick a quarrel with
armarinho [arma'riɲu] M haberdashery (BRIT), notions *pl* (US)
armário [ar'marju] M cupboard; (*de roupa*) wardrobe
armazém [arma'zẽj] (*pl* **-ns**) M (*depósito*) warehouse; (*loja*) grocery store; **armazenar** [armaze'nar] VT to store; (*provisões*) to stock
aro ['aru] M (*argola*) ring; (*de óculos, roda*) rim; (*de porta*) frame
aroma [a'rɔma] M aroma; **aromático, -a** [aro'matʃiku, a] ADJ (*comida*) aromatic; (*perfume*) fragrant
arpão [ar'pãw] (*pl* **-ões**) M harpoon
arqueiro, -a [ar'kejru, a] M/F archer; (*goleiro*) goalkeeper
arqueologia [arkjolo'ʒia] F archaeology (BRIT), archeology (US); **arqueólogo, -a** [ar'kjɔlogu, a] M/F archaeologist (BRIT), archeologist (US)
arquiteto, -a [arki'tɛtu, a] M/F architect; **arquitetónico, -a** [arkite'toniku, a] ADJ architectural; **arquitetura** [arkite'tura] F architecture
arquivar [arki'var] VT to file; (*projeto*) to shelve
arquivo [ar'kivu] M (*ger, Comput*) file; (*lugar*) archive; (*de empresa*) files *pl*; (*móvel*) filing cabinet; **~ zipado** (*Comput*) zip file
arraial [aha'jaw] (*pl* **-ais**) M (PT: *festa*) fair
arrancada [ahã'kada] F (*puxão*) jerk; **dar uma ~** (*em carro*) to pull away (suddenly)
arrancar [ahã'kar] VT to pull out; (*botão etc*) to pull off; (*arrebatar*) to snatch (away); (*fig: confissão*) to extract ▸ VI to start (off); **arrancar-se** VR to leave; (*fugir*) to run off
arranha-céu [a'haɲa-] (*pl* **-s**) M skyscraper
arranhão [aha'ɲãw] (*pl* **-ões**) M scratch
arranhar [aha'ɲar] VT to scratch
arranjar [ahã'ʒar] VT to arrange;

(*emprego etc*) to get, find; (*doença*) to get, catch; (*questão*) to settle; **arranjar-se** VR to manage; (*conseguir emprego*) to get a job; **~-se sem** to do without

arranjo [a'hãʒu] M arrangement

arrasar [aha'zar] VT to devastate; (*demolir*) to demolish; (*estragar*) to ruin; **arrasar-se** VR to be devastated; (*destruir-se*) to destroy o.s.; (*arruinar-se*) to lose everything

arrastão [ahas'tãw] (*pl* **-ões**) M tug; (*rede*) dragnet

arrastar [ahas'tar] VT to drag; (*atrair*) to draw ▶ VI to trail; **arrastar-se** VR to crawl; (*tempo*) to drag; (*processo*) to drag on

arrebatado, -a [aheba'tadu, a] ADJ rash, impetuous

arrebatar [aheba'tar] VT to snatch (away); (*levar*) to carry off; (*enlevar*) to entrance; (*enfurecer*) to enrage; **arrebatar-se** VR to be entranced

arrebentado, -a [ahebẽ'tadu, a] ADJ broken; (*estafado*) worn out

arrebentar [ahebẽ'tar] VT to break; (*porta*) to break down; (*corda*) to snap ▶ VI to break; to snap; (*guerra*) to break out

arrebitado, -a [ahebi'tadu, a] ADJ turned-up; (*nariz*) snub

arrecadar [aheka'dar] VT (*impostos etc*) to collect

arredondado, -a [ahedõ'dadu, a] ADJ round, rounded

arredondar [ahedõ'dar] VT to round (off); (*conta*) to round up

arredores [ahe'dɔris] MPL suburbs; (*cercanias*) outskirts

arrefecer [ahefe'ser] VT to cool; (*febre*) to lower; (*desanimar*) to discourage ▶ VI to cool (off); to get discouraged

arregaçar [ahega'sar] VT to roll up

arregalado, -a [ahega'ladu, a] ADJ (*olhos*) wide

arregalar [ahega'lar] VT: **~ os olhos** to stare in amazement

arrematar [ahema'tar] VT (*dizer concluindo*) to conclude; (*comprar*) to buy by auction; (*vender*) to sell by auction; (*Costura*) to finish off

arremessar [aheme'sar] VT to throw, hurl; **arremesso** [ahe'mesu] M throw

arremeter [aheme'ter] VI to lunge; **~ contra** (*acometer*) to attack, assail

arrendar [ahẽ'dar] VT to lease

arrepender-se [ahepẽ'dersi] VR to repent; (*mudar de opinião*) to change one's mind; **~ de** to regret, be sorry for; **arrependido, -a** [ahepẽ'dʒidu, a] ADJ (*pessoa*) sorry; **arrependimento** [ahepẽdʒi'mẽtu] M regret; (*Rel, de crime*) repentance

arrepiar [ahe'pjar] VT (*amedrontar*) to horrify; (*cabelo*) to cause to stand on end; **arrepiar-se** VR to shiver; (*cabelo*) to stand on end; **(ser) de ~ os cabelos** (to be) hair-raising

arrepio [ahe'piu] M shiver; (*de frio*) chill; **isso me dá ~s** it gives me the creeps

arriar [a'hjar] VT to lower; (*depor*) to lay down ▶ VI to drop; (*vergar*) to sag; (*desistir*) to give up; (*fig*) to collapse

arriscado, -a [ahis'kadu, a] ADJ risky; (*audacioso*) daring

arriscar [ahis'kar] VT to risk; (*pôr em perigo*) to endanger, jeopardize; **arriscar-se** VR to take a risk; **~-se a fazer** to risk doing

arrogante [aho'gãtʃi] ADJ arrogant
arrojado, -a [aho'ʒadu, a] ADJ (*design*) bold; (*temerário*) rash; (*ousado*) daring
arrolar [aho'lar] VT to list
arrombar [ahõ'bar] VT (*porta*) to break down; (*cofre*) to crack
arrotar [aho'tar] VI to belch ▶ VT (*alardear*) to boast of
arroz [a'hoz] M rice; ~ **doce** rice pudding
arruinar [ahwi'nar] VT to ruin; (*destruir*) to destroy; **arruinar-se** VR to be ruined; (*perder a saúde*) to ruin one's health
arrumação [ahuma'sãw] F arrangement; (*de um quarto etc*) tidying up; (*de malas*) packing
arrumadeira [ahuma'dejra] F cleaning lady; (*num hotel*) chambermaid
arrumar [ahu'mar] VT to put in order, arrange; (*quarto etc*) to tidy up; (*malas*) to pack; (*emprego*) to get; (*vestir*) to dress up; (*desculpa*) to make up, find; (*vida*) to sort out; **arrumar-se** VR (*aprontar-se*) to get dressed, get ready; (*na vida*) to sort o.s. out; (*virar-se*) to manage
arte ['artʃi] F art; (*habilidade*) skill; (*ofício*) trade, craft
artefato [artʃi'fatu], (PT) **artefacto** M (manufactured) article
artéria [ar'tɛrja] F (*Anat*) artery
artesão, -sã [arte'zãw, zã] (*pl* **-s/-s**) M/F artisan, craftsman/woman
ártico, -a ['artʃiku, a] ADJ Arctic ▶ M: **o Á~** the Arctic
artificial [artʃifi'sjaw] (*pl* **-ais**) ADJ artificial
artifício [artʃi'fisju] M stratagem, trick
artigo [ar'tʃigu] M article; (*Com*) item; **artigos** MPL (*produtos*) goods
artista [ar'tʃista] M/F artist; **artístico, -a** [ar'tʃistʃiku, a] ADJ artistic
artrite [ar'tritʃi] F (*Med*) arthritis
árvore ['arvori] F tree; (*Tec*) shaft; ~ **de Natal** Christmas tree
as [as] ART DEF *ver* **a**
ás [ajs] M ace
às [as] = **a** + **as**; *ver* **a**
asa ['aza] F wing; (*de xícara etc*) handle
ascendência [asẽ'dẽsja] F (*antepassados*) ancestry; (*domínio*) ascendancy, sway; **ascendente** [asẽ'dẽtʃi] ADJ rising, upward
ascender [asẽ'der] VI to rise, ascend
ascensão [asẽ'sãw] (*pl* **-ões**) F ascent; (*Rel*): **dia da A~** Ascension Day
asco ['asku] M loathing, revulsion; **dar ~ a** to revolt, disgust
asfalto [as'fawtu] M asphalt
asfixia [asfik'sia] F asphyxia, suffocation
Ásia ['azja] F: **a ~** Asia
asiático, -a [a'zjatʃiku, a] ADJ, M/F Asian
asilo [a'zilu] M (*refúgio*) refuge; (*estabelecimento*) home; ~ **político** political asylum
asma ['azma] F asthma
asneira [az'nejra] F (*tolice*) stupidity; (*ato, dito*) stupid thing
asno ['aznu] M donkey; (*fig*) ass
aspas ['aspas] FPL inverted commas
aspecto [as'pɛktu] M aspect; (*aparência*) look, appearance; (*característica*) feature; (*ponto de vista*) point of view
aspereza [aspe'reza] F roughness; (*severidade*) harshness; (*rudeza*) rudeness

áspero, -a ['asperu, a] ADJ rough; (*severo*) harsh; (*rude*) rude
aspiração [aspira'sãw] (*pl* **-ões**) F aspiration; (*inalação*) inhalation
aspirador [aspira'dor] M: **~ (de pó)** vacuum cleaner; **passar o ~ (em)** to vacuum
aspirante [aspi'rãtʃi] ADJ aspiring ▶ M/F candidate
aspirar [aspi'rar] VT to breathe in; (*bombear*) to suck up ▶ VI to breathe; (*soprar*) to blow; (*desejar*): **~ a algo** to aspire to sth
aspirina [aspi'rina] F aspirin
asqueroso, -a [aske'rozu, ɔza] ADJ disgusting, revolting
assado, -a [a'sadu, a] ADJ roasted; (*Culin*) roast ▶ M roast; **carne assada** roast beef
assaltante [asaw'tãtʃi] M/F assailant; (*de banco*) robber; (*de casa*) burglar; (*na rua*) mugger
assaltar [asaw'tar] VT to attack; (*casa*) to break into; (*banco*) to rob; (*pessoa na rua*) to mug; **assalto** [a'sawtu] M attack, raid; (*a um banco etc*) robbery; (*a uma casa*) burglary, break-in; (*a uma pessoa na rua*) mugging; (*Boxe*) round
assar [a'sar] VT to roast; (*na grelha*) to grill
assassinar [asasi'nar] VT to murder, kill; (*Pol*) to assassinate; **assassinato** [asasi'natu] M murder, killing; (*Pol*) assassination; **assassino, -a** [asa'sinu, a] M/F murderer; (*Pol*) assassin; **assassino em série** serial killer
assaz [a'saz] ADV (*suficientemente*) sufficiently; (*muito*) rather
assediar [ase'dʒjar] VT (*sitiar*) to besiege; (*importunar*) to pester; **assédio** [a'sɛdʒu] M siege; (*insistência*) insistence
assegurar [asegu'rar] VT to secure; (*garantir*) to ensure; (*afirmar*) to assure; **assegurar-se** VR: **~-se de** to make sure of
asseio [a'seju] M cleanliness
assembleia [asẽ'blɛja] F assembly; (*reunião*) meeting; **~ geral (ordinária)** annual general meeting
assentar [asẽ'tar] VT (*fazer sentar*) to seat; (*colocar*) to place; (*estabelecer*) to establish; (*decidir*) to decide upon ▶ VI (*pó etc*) to settle; **assentar-se** VR to sit down; **~ em** *ou* **a** (*roupa*) to suit
assentir [asẽ'tʃir] VI: **~ (em)** to consent *ou* agree (to)
assento [a'sẽtu] M seat; (*base*) base
assíduo, -a [a'sidwu, a] ADJ (*aluno*) who attends regularly; (*diligente*) assiduous; (*constante*) constant; **ser ~ num lugar** to be a regular visitor to a place
assim [a'sĩ] ADV (*deste modo*) like this, in this way, thus; (*portanto*) therefore; (*igualmente*) likewise; **~ ~** so-so; **~ mesmo** in any case; **e ~ por diante** and so on; **~ como** as well as; **como ~?** how do you mean?; **~ que** (*logo que*) as soon as
assimilar [asimi'lar] VT to assimilate; (*apreender*) to take in; (*assemelhar*) to compare
assinante [asi'nãtʃi] M/F (*de jornal etc*) subscriber
assinar [asi'nar] VT to sign
assinatura [asina'tura] F (*nome*) signature; (*de jornal etc*) subscription; (*Teatro*) season ticket
assinto [a'sĩtu] VB *ver* **assentir**
assistência [asis'tẽsja] F (*presença*) presence; (*público*) audience; (*auxílio*) aid; **~ médica**

medical aid; **~ social** social work
assistente [asis'tẽtʃi] ADJ assistant ▸ M/F spectator, onlooker; (*ajudante*) assistant; **~ social** social worker
assistir [asis'tʃir] VT, VI: **~ (a)** (*Med*) to attend (to); **~ a** to assist; (*TV, filme, jogo*) to watch; (*reunião*) to attend
assoar [aso'ar] VT: **~ o nariz** to blow one's nose; **assoar-se** VR (PT) to blow one's nose
assobiar [aso'bjar] VI to whistle
assobio [aso'biu] M whistle
associação [asosja'sãw] (*pl* **-ões**) F association; (*organização*) society; (*parceria*) partnership
associado, -a [aso'sjadu, a] ADJ associate ▸ M/F associate, member; (*Com*) associate; (*sócio*) partner
associar [aso'sjar] VT to associate; **associar-se** VR: **~-se a** to associate with
assombração [asõbra'sãw] (*pl* **-ões**) F ghost
assombro [a'sõbru] M amazement, astonishment; (*maravilha*) marvel; **assombroso, -a** [asõ'brozu, ɔza] ADJ astonishing, amazing
assoviar [aso'vjar] VT = **assobiar**
assovio [aso'viu] M = **assobio**
assumir [asu'mir] VT to assume, take on; (*reconhecer*) to accept
assunto [a'sũtu] M subject, matter; (*enredo*) plot
assustador, a [asusta'dor(a)] ADJ (*alarmante*) startling; (*amedrontador*) frightening
assustar [asus'tar] VT to frighten, startle; **assustar-se** VR to be frightened
asteca [as'tɛka] ADJ, M/F Aztec
astral [as'traw] (*pl* **-ais**) M mood; **bom ~** good vibe; **alto ~** upbeat mood; **baixo ~** gloom; **estar de baixo ~** to be feeling glum
astrologia [astrolo'ʒia] F astrology
astronauta [astro'nawta] M/F astronaut
astronave [astro'navi] F spaceship
astronomia [astrono'mia] F astronomy
astúcia [as'tusja] F cunning
ata ['ata] F (*de reunião*) minutes *pl*
atacado, -a [ata'kadu, a] ADJ (*col: pessoa*) in a bad mood ▸ M: **por ~** wholesale
atacante [ata'kãtʃi] ADJ attacking ▸ M/F attacker, assailant ▸ M (*Futebol*) forward
atacar [ata'kar] VT to attack; (*problema etc*) to tackle
atado, -a [a'tadu, a] ADJ (*desajeitado*) clumsy, awkward; (*perplexo*) puzzled
atalho [a'taʎu] M (*caminho*) short cut
ataque [a'taki] M attack; **~ aéreo** air raid; **~ suicida** suicide attack
atar [a'tar] VT to tie (up), fasten; **não ~ nem desatar** (*pessoa*) to waver; (*negócio*) to be in the air
atarefado, -a [atare'fadu, a] ADJ busy
atarracado, -a [ataha'kadu, a] ADJ stocky
até [a'tɛ] PREP (PT: + *a: lugar*) up to, as far as; (*tempo etc*) until, till ▸ ADV (*tb*: **~ mesmo**) even; **~ certo ponto** to a certain extent; **~ em cima** to the top; **~ já** see you soon; **~ logo** bye!; **~ onde** as far as; **~ que** until; **~ que enfim!** at last!
atear [ate'ar] VT (*fogo*) to kindle; (*fig*) to incite, inflame; **atear-se** VR to blaze; (*paixões*) to flare up
ateia [a'tɛja] F *de* **ateu**

atemorizar [atemori'zar] VT to frighten; (*intimidar*) to intimidate
Atenas [a'tenas] N Athens
atenção [atẽ'sãw] (*pl* **-ões**) F attention; (*cortesia*) courtesy; (*bondade*) kindness; **~!** be careful!; **chamar a ~** to attract attention; **atencioso, -a** [atẽ'sjozu, ɔza] ADJ considerate
atender [atẽ'der] VT: **~ (a)** to attend to; (*receber*) to receive; (*deferir*) to grant; (*telefone etc*) to answer; (*paciente*) to see ▶ VI to answer; (*dar atenção*) to pay attention; **atendimento** [atẽdʒi'mẽtu] M service; (*recepção*) reception; **horário de atendimento** opening hours; (*em consultório*) surgery (BRIT) *ou* office (US) hours
atentado [atẽ'tadu] M attack; (*crime*) crime; (*contra a vida de alguém*) attempt on sb's life; **~ suicida** suicide attack
atento, -a [a'tẽtu, a] ADJ attentive; **estar ~ a** to be aware *ou* mindful of
atenuante [ate'nwãtʃi] ADJ extenuating ▶ M extenuating circumstance
atenuar [ate'nwar] VT to reduce, lessen
aterragem [ate'haʒẽj] (PT) (*pl* **-ns**) F (*Aer*) landing
aterrar [ate'har] VI (PT *Aer*) to land
aterrissagem [atehi'saʒẽ] (BR) (*pl* **-ns**) F (*Aer*) landing
aterrissar [atehi'sar] (BR) VI (*Aer*) to land
aterro [a'tehu] M: **~ sanitário** landfill (site)
aterrorizante [atehori'zãtʃi] ADJ terrifying
aterrorizar [atehori'zar] VT to terrorize
atestado, -a [ates'tadu, a] ADJ certified ▶ M certificate; (*prova*) proof; (*Jur*) testimony
ateu, ateia [a'tew, a'tɛja] ADJ, M/F atheist
atinar [atʃi'nar] VT (*acertar*) to guess correctly ▶ VI: **~ com** (*solução*) to find; **~ em** to notice; **~ a fazer algo** to succeed in doing sth
atingir [atʃĩ'ʒir] VT to reach; (*acertar*) to hit; (*afetar*) to affect; (*objetivo*) to achieve; (*compreender*) to grasp
atirador, a [atʃira'dor(a)] M/F marksman/woman; **~ de tocaia** sniper
atirar [atʃi'rar] VT to throw, fling ▶ VI (*arma*) to shoot; **atirar-se** VR: **~-se a** to hurl o.s. at
atitude [atʃi'tudʒi] F attitude; (*postura*) posture
atividade [atʃivi'dadʒi] F activity
ativo, -a [a'tʃivu, a] ADJ active ▶ M (*Com*) assets *pl*
atlântico, -a [at'lãtʃiku, a] ADJ Atlantic ▶ M: **o (Oceano) A~** the Atlantic (Ocean)
atlas ['atlas] M INV atlas
atleta [at'lɛta] M/F athlete; **atlético, -a** [at'lɛtʃiku, a] ADJ athletic; **atletismo** [atle'tʃizmu] M athletics *sg*
atmosfera [atmos'fɛra] F atmosphere
ato ['atu] M act, action; (*cerimônia*) ceremony; (*Teatro*) act; **em ~ contínuo** straight after; **no ~** on the spot; **no mesmo ~** at the same time
atômico, -a [a'tomiku, a] ADJ atomic
átomo ['atomu] M atom
atônito, -a [a'tonitu, a] ADJ astonished, amazed

ator [a'tor] M actor
atordoado, -a [ator'dwadu, a] ADJ dazed
atordoar [ator'dwar] VT to daze, stun
atormentar [atormẽ'tar] VT to torment
atração [atra'sãw] (*pl* **-ões**) F attraction
atracar [atra'kar] VT, VI (*Náut*) to moor; **atracar-se** VR to grapple
atrações [atra'sõjs] FPL *de* **atração**
atraente [atra'ẽtʃi] ADJ attractive
atrair [atra'ir] VT to attract; (*fascinar*) to fascinate
atrapalhar [atrapa'ʎar] VT to confuse; (*perturbar*) to disturb; (*dificultar*) to hinder ▶ VI to be a nuisance
atrás [a'trajs] ADV behind; (*no fundo*) at the back ▶ PREP: **~ de** behind; (*no tempo*) after; **dois meses ~** two months ago
atrasado, -a [atra'zadu, a] ADJ late; (*país etc*) backward; (*relógio etc*) slow; (*pagamento*) overdue; **atrasados** [atra'zadus] MPL (*Com*) arrears
atrasar [atra'zar] VT to delay; (*progresso, desenvolvimento*) to hold back; (*relógio*) to put back; (*pagamento*) to be late with ▶ VI (*relógio etc*) to be slow; (*avião, pessoa*) to be late; **atrasar-se** VR to be late; (*num trabalho*) to fall behind; (*num pagamento*) to get into arrears
atraso [a'trazu] M delay; (*de país etc*) backwardness; **atrasos** MPL (*Com*) arrears; **com 20 minutos de ~** 20 minutes late
atrativo, -a [atra'tʃivu, a] ADJ attractive ▶ M attraction; (*incentivo*) incentive; **atrativos** MPL (*encantos*) charms
através [atra'vɛs] ADV across; **~ de** across; (*pelo centro de*) through
atravessar [atrave'sar] VT to cross; (*pôr ao través*) to put *ou* lay across; (*traspassar*) to pass through
atrever-se [atre'versi] VR: **~ a** to dare to; **atrevido, -a** [atre'vidu, a] ADJ cheeky; (*corajoso*) bold; **atrevimento** [atrevi'mẽtu] M (*ousadia*) boldness; (*insolência*) cheek
atribuir [atri'bwir] VT: **~ algo a** to attribute sth to; (*prêmios, regalias*) to confer sth on
atributo [atri'butu] M attribute
átrio ['atrju] M hall; (*pátio*) courtyard
atrito [a'tritu] M (*fricção*) friction; (*desentendimento*) disagreement
atriz [a'triz] F actress
atropelamento [atropela'mẽtu] M (*de pedestre*) accident involving a pedestrian
atropelar [atrope'lar] VT to knock down, run over; (*empurrar*) to jostle
atuação [atwa'sãw] (*pl* **-ões**) F acting; (*de ator etc*) performance
atual [a'twaw] (*pl* **-ais**) ADJ current; (*pessoa, carro*) modern; **atualidade** [atwali'dadʒi] F present (time); **atualidades** FPL (*notícias*) news *sg*; **atualizar** [atwali'zar] VT to update; **atualmente** [atwaw'mẽtʃi] ADV at present, currently; (*hoje em dia*) nowadays
atuante [a'twãtʃi] ADJ active
atuar [a'twar] VI to act; **~ para** to contribute to; **~ sobre** to influence
atum [a'tũ] (*pl* **-ns**) M tuna (fish)
aturdido, -a [atur'dʒidu, a] ADJ stunned; (*com barulho*) deafened; (*com confusão, movimento*) bewildered
audácia [aw'dasja] F boldness;

a

(*insolência*) insolence; **audacioso, -a** [awda'sjozu, ɔza] ADJ daring; (*insolente*) insolent
audição [awdʒi'sãw] (*pl* **-ões**) F audition
audiência [aw'dʒjẽsja] F audience; (*de tribunal*) session, hearing
auditar [awdʒi'tar] VT to audit
auditor, a [awdʒi'tor(a)] M/F auditor; (*juiz*) judge; (*ouvinte*) listener
auditoria [awdʒito'ria] F: **fazer a ~ de** to audit
auditório [awdʒi'tɔrju] M audience; (*recinto*) auditorium
auge ['awʒi] M height, peak
aula ['awla] F (PT: *sala*) classroom; (*lição*) lesson, class; **dar ~** to teach
aumentar [awmẽ'tar] VT to increase; (*salários, preços*) to raise; (*sala, casa*) to expand, extend; (*suj: lente*) to magnify; (*acrescentar*) to add ▸VI to increase; (*preço, salário*) to rise, go up
aumento [aw'mẽtu] M increase; (*de preços*) rise; (*ampliação*) enlargement; (*crescimento*) growth
ausência [aw'zẽsja] F absence
ausentar-se [awzẽ'tarsi] VR (*ir-se*) to go away; (*afastar-se*) to stay away
ausente [aw'zẽtʃi] ADJ absent
austral [aws'traw] (*pl* **-ais**) ADJ southern
Austrália [aws'tralja] F: **a ~** Australia; **australiano, -a** [awstra'ljanu, a] ADJ, M/F Australian
Áustria ['awstrja] F: **a ~** Austria; **austríaco, -a** [aws'triaku, a] ADJ, M/F Austrian
autêntico, -a [aw'tẽtʃiku, a] ADJ authentic; (*pessoa*) genuine; (*verdadeiro*) true, real
auto ['awtu] M car; **autos** MPL (*Jur: processo*) legal proceedings; (*documentos*) legal papers
autobiografia [awtobjogra'fia] F autobiography
autobronzeador [awtobrõzja'dor] ADJ self-tanning
autocarro [awto'kahu] (PT) M bus
autodefesa [awtode'feza] F self-defence (BRIT), self-defense (US)
autódromo [aw'tɔdromu] M race track
autoestrada [awtois'trada] F motorway (BRIT), expressway (US)
autografar [awtogra'far] VT to autograph
autógrafo [aw'tɔgrafu] M autograph
automático, -a [awto'matʃiku, a] ADJ automatic
automobilismo [awtomobi'lizmu] M motoring; (*Esporte*) motor car racing
automóvel [awto'mɔvew] (*pl* **-eis**) M motor car (BRIT), automobile (US)
autonomia [awtono'mia] F autonomy
autor, a [aw'tor(a)] M/F author; (*de um crime*) perpetrator; (*Jur*) plaintiff
autoral [awto'raw] (*pl* **-ais**) ADJ: **direitos autorais** copyright *sg*
autoridade [awtori'dadʒi] F authority
autorização [awtoriza'sãw] (*pl* **-ões**) F permission, authorization; **dar ~ a alguém para** to authorize sb to
autorizar [awtori'zar] VT to authorize
autosserviço [awtoser'visu] M self-service

auxiliar [awsi'ljar] ADJ auxiliary ▶ M/F assistant ▶ VT to help; **auxílio** [aw'silju] M help, assistance
Av. ABR (= *avenida*) Ave.
aval [a'vaw] (*pl* **-ais**) M guarantee
avalancha [ava'lãʃa] F avalanche
avaliar [ava'ljar] VT to value; to assess
avançado, -a [avã'sadu, a] ADJ advanced; (*ideias, pessoa*) progressive
avançar [avã'sar] VT to move forward ▶ VI to advance; **avanço** [a'vãsu] M advancement; (*progresso*) progress
avaria [ava'ria] F (*Tec*) breakdown; **avariado, -a** [ava'rjadu, a] ADJ (*máquina*) out of order; (*carro*) broken down; **avariar** [ava'rjar] VT to damage ▶ VI to suffer damage; (*Tec*) to break down
ave ['avi] F bird
aveia [a'veja] F oats *pl*
avelã [ave'lã] F hazelnut
avenida [ave'nida] F avenue
avental [avẽ'taw] (*pl* **-ais**) M apron; (*vestido*) pinafore dress (BRIT), jumper (US)
averiguar [averi'gwar] VT to investigate; (*verificar*) to verify
avermelhado, -a [averme'ʎadu, a] ADJ reddish
avesso, -a [a'vesu, a] ADJ (*lado*) opposite, reverse ▶ M wrong side, reverse; **ao ~** inside out; **às avessas** (*inverso*) upside down; (*oposto*) the wrong way round
avestruz [aves'truz] M ostrich
aviação [avja'sãw] F aviation, flying
aviador, a [avja'dor(a)] M/F aviator, airman/woman
avião [a'vjãw] (*pl* **-ões**) M aeroplane; **~ a jato** jet
ávido, -a ['avidu, a] ADJ greedy; (*desejoso*) eager
aviões [a'vjõjs] MPL *de* **avião**
avisar [avi'zar] VT to warn; (*informar*) to tell, let know; **aviso** [a'vizu] M (*comunicação*) notice
avistar [avis'tar] VT to catch sight of
avô, avó [a'vo, a'vɔ] M/F grandfather/mother; **avós** MPL grandparents
avulso, -a [a'vuwsu, a] ADJ separate, detached
axila [ak'sila] F armpit
azar [a'zar] M bad luck; **~!** too bad!, bad luck!; **estar com ~, ter ~** to be unlucky; **azarento, -a** [aza'rẽtu, a] ADJ unlucky
azedar [aze'dar] VT to turn sour ▶ VI to turn sour; (*leite*) to go off; **azedo, -a** [a'zedu, a] ADJ sour; (*leite*) off; (*fig*) grumpy
azeite [a'zejtʃi] M oil; (*de oliva*) olive oil
azeitona [azej'tɔna] F olive
azia [a'zia] F heartburn
azougue [a'zogi] M (*Quím*) mercury
azul [a'zuw] (*pl* **-uis**) ADJ blue
azulejo [azu'leʒu] M (glazed) tile
azul-marinho ADJ INV navy blue
azul-turquesa ADJ INV turquoise

b

baba ['baba] F dribble
babá [ba'ba] F nanny
babado [ba'badu] M frill; (*col*) piece of gossip
babador [baba'dor] M bib
babar [ba'bar] VI to dribble; **babar-se** VR to dribble
baby-sitter ['bejbisiter] (*pl* **-s**) M/F baby-sitter
bacalhau [baka'ʎaw] M (dried) cod
bacana [ba'kana] (*col*) ADJ great
bacharel [baʃa'rɛw] (*pl* **-éis**) M graduate
bacia [ba'sia] F basin; (*Anat*) pelvis
backup [ba'kapi] (*pl* **-s**) M (*Comput*) back-up; **fazer um ~ de** to back up
bactéria [bak'tɛrja] F germ, bacterium; **bactérias** MPL bacteria *pl*
badalar [bada'lar] VT, VI to ring
baderna [ba'dɛrna] F commotion
bafo ['bafu] M (bad) breath
bagaço [ba'gasu] M (*de frutos*) pulp; (PT: *cachaça*) brandy; **estar/ficar um ~** (*fig: pessoa*) to be/get run down
bagageiro [baga'ʒejru] M (*Auto*) roof rack; (PT) porter
bagagem [ba'gaʒẽ] F luggage; (*fig*) baggage; **recebimento de ~** (*Aer*) baggage reclaim
bagulho [ba'guʎu] M (*objeto*) piece of junk
bagunça [ba'gũsa] F mess, shambles *sg*; **bagunçado, -a** [bagũ'sadu, a] ADJ messy; **bagunçar** [bagũ'sar] VT to mess up; **bagunceiro, -a** [bagũ'sejru, a] ADJ messy
baía [ba'ia] F bay
bailado [baj'ladu] M dance; (*balé*) ballet
bailarino, -a [bajla'rinu, a] M/F ballet dancer
baile ['bajli] M dance; (*formal*) ball; **~ à fantasia** fancy-dress ball
bainha [ba'iɲa] F (*de arma*) sheath; (*de costura*) hem
bairro ['bajhu] M district
baixa ['bajʃa] F decrease; (*de preço*) reduction, fall; drop; (*em combate*) casualty; (*do serviço*) discharge
baixar [baj'ʃar] VT to lower; (*ordem*) to issue; (*lei*) to pass; (*Comput*) to download ▸ VI to go (*ou* come) down; (*temperatura, preço*) to drop, fall
baixinho [baj'ʃiɲu] ADV (*falar*) softly, quietly; (*em segredo*) secretly
baixo, -a ['bajʃu, a] ADJ low; (*pessoa*) short, small; (*rio*) shallow; (*linguagem*) common; (*olhos*) lowered; (*atitude*) mean; (*metal*) base ▸ ADV low; (*em posição baixa*) low down; (*falar*) softly ▸ M (*Mús*) bass; **em ~** below; (*em casa*) downstairs; **em voz baixa** in a quiet voice; **para ~** down,

downwards; (*em casa*) downstairs; **por ~ de** under, underneath
bala ['bala] F bullet; (BR: *doce*) sweet
balança [ba'lãsa] F scales *pl*; **B~** (*Astrologia*) Libra; **~ comercial** balance of trade; **~ de pagamentos** balance of payments
balançar [balã'sar] VT to swing; (*pesar*) to weigh (up) ▶ VI to swing; (*carro, avião*) to shake; (*em cadeira*) to rock; **balançar-se** VR to swing; **balanço** [ba'lãsu] M (*movimento*) swinging; (*brinquedo*) swing; (*de carro, avião*) shaking; (*Com: registro*) balance (sheet); (: *verificação*) audit; **fazer um balanço de** (*fig*) to take stock of
balão [ba'lãw] (*pl* **-ões**) M balloon
balbúrdia [baw'burdʒja] F uproar, bedlam
balcão [baw'kãw] (*pl* **-ões**) M balcony; (*de loja*) counter; (*Teatro*) circle; **balconista** [bawko'nista] M/F shop assistant
balde ['bawdʒi] M bucket, pail
balé [ba'lɛ] M ballet
baleia [ba'leja] F whale
baliza [ba'liza] F (*estaca*) post; (*boia*) buoy; (*luminosa*) beacon; (*Esporte*) goal
balneário [baw'njarju] M bathing resort
balões [ba'lõjs] MPL *de* **balão**
baloiço [ba'lojsu] (PT) M (*de criança*) swing; (*ação*) swinging
balsa ['bawsa] F raft; (*barca*) ferry
bamba ['bãba] ADJ, M/F expert
bambo, -a ['bãbu, a] ADJ slack, loose
banana [ba'nana] F banana; **bananeira** [bana'nejra] F banana tree
banca ['bãka] F bench; (*escritório*) office; (*em jogo*) bank; **~ (de jornais)** newsstand; **bancada** [bã'kada] F (*banco, Pol*) bench; (*de cozinha*) worktop
bancar [bã'kar] VT to finance ▶ VI (*fingir*): **~ que** to pretend that;
bancário, -a [bã'karju, a] ADJ bank *atr* ▶ M/F bank employee
bancarrota [bãka'hota] F bankruptcy; **ir à ~** to go bankrupt
banco ['bãku] M (*assento*) bench; (*Com*) bank; **~ de areia** sandbank; **~ de dados** (*Comput*) database
banda ['bãda] F band; (*lado*) side; (*cinto*) sash; **de ~** sideways; **pôr de ~** to put aside; **~ desenhada** (PT) cartoon; **~ larga** (*Tel*) broadband
bandeira [bã'dejra] F flag; (*estandarte, fig*) banner; **bandeirinha** [bãdej'riɲa] M (*Esporte*) linesman
bandeja [bã'deʒa] F tray
bandido [bã'dʒidu] M bandit
bando ['bãdu] M band; (*grupo*) group; (*de malfeitores*) gang; (*de ovelhas*) flock; (*de gado*) herd; (*de livros etc*) pile
banha ['baɲa] F fat; (*de porco*) lard
banhar [ba'ɲar] VT to wet; (*mergulhar*) to dip; (*lavar*) to wash; **banhar-se** VR to bathe
banheira [ba'ɲejra] F bath
banheiro [ba'ɲejru] M bathroom
banho ['baɲu] M bath; (*mergulho*) dip; **tomar ~** to have a bath; (*de chuveiro*) to have a shower; **~ de chuveiro** shower; **~ de sol** sunbathing
banir [ba'nir] VT to banish
banqueiro, -a [bã'kejru, a] M/F banker
banquete [bã'ketʃi] M banquet
bar [bar] M bar
baralho [ba'raʎu] M pack of cards
barata [ba'rata] F cockroach

barateiro, -a [bara'tejru, a] ADJ cheap

barato, -a [ba'ratu, a] ADJ cheap ▸ ADV cheaply

barba ['barba] F beard; **fazer a ~** to shave

bárbaro, -a ['barbaru, a] ADJ barbaric; (*dor, calor*) terrible; (*maravilhoso*) great

barbeador [barbja'dor] M razor; (*tb*: **~ elétrico**) shaver

barbear [bar'bjar] VT to shave; **barbear-se** VR to shave; **barbearia** [barbja'ria] F barber's (shop)

barbeiro [bar'bejru] M barber; (*loja*) barber's

barca ['barka] F barge; (*de travessia*) ferry

barco ['barku] M boat; **~ a motor** motorboat; **~ a remo** rowing boat; **~ a vela** sailing boat

barganha [bar'gaɲa] F bargain; **barganhar** [barga'ɲar] VT, VI to negotiate

barman [bar'mã] (*pl* **-men**) M barman

barra ['baha] F bar; (*faixa*) strip; (*traço*) stroke; (*alavanca*) lever; (*em endereço web*) forward slash

barraca [ba'haka] F (*tenda*) tent; (*de feira*) stall; (*de madeira*) hut; (*de praia*) sunshade; **barracão** [baha'kãw] (*pl* **-ões**) M shed; **barraco** [ba'haku] M shack, shanty; (*col: confusão*) scene

barragem [ba'haʒẽ] (*pl* **-ns**) F dam; (*impedimento*) barrier

barrar [ba'har] VT to bar

barreira [ba'hejra] F barrier; (*cerca*) fence; (*Esporte*) hurdle

barricada [bahi'kada] F barricade

barriga [ba'higa] F belly; **estar de ~** to be pregnant; **~ da perna** calf;

barrigudo, -a [bahi'gudu, a] ADJ paunchy, pot-bellied

barril [ba'hiw] (*pl* **-is**) M barrel, cask

barro ['bahu] M clay; (*lama*) mud

barulhento, -a [baru'ʎẽtu, a] ADJ noisy

barulho [ba'ruʎu] M (*ruído*) noise; (*tumulto*) din

base ['bazi] F base; (*fig*) basis; **sem ~** groundless; **com ~ em** based on; **na ~ de** by means of

basear [ba'zjar] VT to base; **basear-se** VR: **~-se em** to be based on

básico, -a ['baziku, a] ADJ basic

basquete [bas'kɛtʃi] M = **basquetebol**

basquetebol [baskete'bɔw] M basketball

basta ['basta] M: **dar um ~ em** to call a halt to

bastante [bas'tãtʃi] ADJ (*suficiente*) enough; (*muito*) quite a lot (of) ▸ ADV enough; a lot

bastão [bas'tãw] (*pl* **-ões**) M stick

bastar [bas'tar] VI to be enough, be sufficient; **bastar-se** VR to be self-sufficient; **basta!** (that's) enough!; **~ para** to be enough to

bastardo, -a [bas'tardu, a] ADJ, M/F bastard

bastões [bas'tõjs] MPL *de* **bastão**

bata ['bata] F (*de mulher*) smock; (*de médico*) overall

batalha [ba'taʎa] F battle; **batalhador, a** [bataʎa'dor(a)] ADJ struggling ▸ M/F fighter; **batalhão** [bata'ʎãw] (*pl* **-ões**) M battalion; **batalhar** [bata'ʎar] VI to battle, fight; (*esforçar-se*) to make an effort, try hard ▸ VT (*emprego*) to go after

batata [ba'tata] F potato; **~ doce**

sweet potato; **~ frita** chips *pl* (BRIT), French fries *pl*; (*de pacote*) crisps *pl* (BRIT), (potato) chips *pl* (US)
bate-boca ['batʃi-] (*pl* **-s**) M row, quarrel
batedeira [bate'dejra] F beater; (*de manteiga*) churn; **~ elétrica** mixer
batente [ba'tẽtʃi] M doorpost
bate-papo ['batʃi-] (*pl* **-s**) (BR) M chat
bater [ba'ter] VT to beat; to strike; (*pé*) to stamp; (*foto*) to take; (*porta*) to slam; (*asas*) to flap; (*recorde*) to break; (*roupa*) to wear all the time ▶ VI to slam; (*sino*) to ring; (*janela*) to bang; (*coração*) to beat; (*sol*) to beat down; **bater-se** VR: **~-se para fazer/por** to fight to do/for; **~ (à porta)** to knock (at the door); **~ à maquina** to type; **~ em** to hit; **~ com o carro** to crash one's car; **~ com a cabeça** to bang one's head; **~ com o pé (em)** to kick
bateria [bate'ria] F battery; (*Mús*) drums *pl*; **~ de cozinha** kitchen utensils *pl*; **baterista** [bate'rista] M/F drummer
batida [ba'tʃida] F beat; (*da porta*) slam; (*à porta*) knock; (*da polícia*) raid; (*Auto*) crash; (*bebida*) *cocktail of cachaça, fruit and sugar*
batido, -a [ba'tʃidu, a] ADJ beaten; (*roupa*) worn ▶ M: **~ de leite** (PT) milk shake
batina [ba'tʃina] F (*Rel*) cassock
batismo [ba'tʃizmu] M baptism, christening
batizar [batʃi'zar] VT to baptize, christen
batom [ba'tõ] (*pl* **-ns**) M lipstick
batucada [batu'kada] F dance percussion group
batucar [batu'kar] VT, VI to drum
baú [ba'u] M trunk
baunilha [baw'niʎa] F vanilla
bazar [ba'zar] M bazaar; (*loja*) shop
bêbado, -a ['bebadu, a] ADJ, M/F drunk
bebê [be'be] M baby
bebedeira [bebe'dejra] F drunkenness; **tomar uma ~** to get drunk
bêbedo, -a ['bebedu, a] ADJ, M/F = **bêbado**
bebedouro [bebe'douru] M drinking fountain
beber [be'ber] VT to drink; (*absorver*) to soak up ▶ VI to drink; **bebida** [be'bida] F drink
beça ['bɛsa] (*col*) F: **à ~** (*com vb*) a lot; (*com n*) a lot of
beco ['beku] M alley, lane; **~ sem saída** cul-de-sac
bege ['bɛʒi] ADJ INV beige
beija-flor [bejʒa'flɔr] (*pl* **-es**) M hummingbird
beijar [bej'ʒar] VT to kiss; **beijar-se** VR to kiss (one another); **beijo** ['bejʒu] M kiss; **dar beijos em alguém** to kiss sb
beira ['bejra] F edge; (*de rio*) bank; (*orla*) border; **à ~ de** on the edge of; (*ao lado de*) beside, by; (*fig*) on the verge of; **~ do telhado** eaves *pl*; **beira-mar** F seaside
belas-artes FPL fine arts
beldade [bew'dadʒi] F beauty
beleza [be'leza] F beauty; **que ~!** how lovely!
belga ['bɛwga] ADJ, M/F Belgian
Bélgica ['bɛwʒika] F: **a ~** Belgium
beliche [be'liʃi] M bunk
beliscão [belis'kãw] (*pl* **-ões**) M pinch; **beliscar** [belis'kar] VT to pinch, nip; (*comida*) to nibble
Belize [be'lizi] M Belize
belo, -a ['bɛlu, a] ADJ beautiful

PALAVRA-CHAVE

bem [bẽj] ADV **1** (*de maneira satisfatória, correta etc*) well; **trabalha/come bem** she works/ eats well; **respondeu bem** he answered correctly; **me sinto/ não me sinto bem** I feel fine/I don't feel very well; **tudo bem? — tudo bem** how's it going? — fine
2 (*valor intensivo*) very; **um quarto bem quente** a nice warm room; **bem se vê que ...** it's clear that ...
3 (*bastante*) quite, fairly; **a casa é bem grande** the house is quite big
4 (*exatamente*): **bem ali** right there; **não é bem assim** it's not quite like that
5 (*estar bem*): **estou muito bem aqui** I feel very happy here; **está bem! vou fazê-lo** oh all right, I'll do it!
6 (*de bom grado*): **eu bem que iria mas ...** I'd gladly go but ...
7 (*cheirar*) good, nice
▶ M **1** (*bem-estar*) good; **estou dizendo isso para o seu bem** I'm telling you for your own good; **o bem e o mal** good and evil
2 (*posses*): **bens** goods, property *sg*; **bens de consumo** consumer goods; **bens de família** family possessions; **bens móveis/ imóveis** moveable property *sg*/ real estate *sg*
▶ EXCL **1** (*aprovação*): **bem!** OK!; **muito bem!** well done!
2 (*desaprovação*): **bem feito!** it serves you right!
▶ ADJ INV (*tom depreciativo*): **gente bem** posh people
▶ CONJ **1**: **nem bem** as soon as, no sooner than; **nem bem ela chegou começou a dar ordens** as soon as she arrived she started to give orders, no sooner had she arrived than she started to give orders
2: **se bem que** though; **gostaria de ir se bem que não tenho dinheiro** I'd like to go even though I've got no money
3: **bem como** as well as; **o livro bem como a peça foram escritos por ele** the book as well as the play was written by him

bem-conceituado, -a [-kõsej'twadu, a] ADJ highly regarded
bem-disposto, -a [-dʒis'postu, 'pɔsta] ADJ well, in good form
bem-me-quer (*pl* **-es**) M daisy
bem-vindo, -a ADJ welcome
bênção ['bẽsãw] (*pl* **-s**) F blessing
beneficência [benefi'sẽsja] F kindness; (*caridade*) charity
beneficiar [benefi'sjar] VT to benefit; (*melhorar*) to improve; **beneficiar-se** VR to benefit
benefício [bene'fisju] M benefit, profit; (*favor*) favour (BRIT), favor (US); **em ~ de** in aid of; **benéfico, -a** [be'nɛfiku, a] ADJ beneficial; (*generoso*) generous
bengala [bẽ'gala] F walking stick
benigno, -a [be'nignu, a] ADJ kind; (*agradável*) pleasant; (*Med*) benign
bens [bẽjs] MPL *de* **bem**
bento, -a ['bẽtu, a] PP *de* **benzer**
▶ ADJ blessed; (*água*) holy
benzer [bẽ'zer] VT to bless; **benzer-se** VR to cross o.s.
berço ['bersu] M cradle; (*cama*) cot; (*origem*) birthplace
Berlim [ber'lĩ] N Berlin
berma ['bɛrma] (PT) F hard shoulder (BRIT), berm (US)

berrar [be'har] VI to bellow; (*criança*) to bawl; **berreiro** [be'hejru] M: **abrir o berreiro** to burst out crying; **berro** ['bɛhu] M yell

besta ['besta] ADJ stupid; (*convencido*) full of oneself; **~ de carga** beast of burden; **besteira** [bes'tejra] F foolishness; **dizer besteiras** to talk nonsense; **fazer uma besteira** to do something silly; **bestial** [bes'tʃjaw] (*pl* **-ais**) ADJ bestial; (*repugnante*) repulsive

best-seller [bɛst'sɛler] (*pl* **-s**) M best seller

betão [be'tãw] (PT) M concrete

beterraba [bete'haba] F beetroot

bexiga [be'ʃiga] F bladder

bezerro, -a [be'zehu, a] M/F calf

BI ABR M *see note*

> All Portuguese citizens are required to carry an identity card, known as the **BI** or *bilhete de identidade*. The photocard, which gives the holder's name, date of birth, marital status, height and a fingerprint, can be used instead of a passport for travel within the European Union. Failure to produce a valid identity card when stopped by the police can result in a fine.

Bíblia ['biblja] F Bible

bibliografia [bibljogra'fia] F bibliography

biblioteca [bibljo'tɛka] F library; (*estante*) bookcase; **bibliotecário, -a** [bibljote'karju, a] M/F librarian

bica ['bika] F tap; (PT) black coffee, expresso

bicha ['biʃa] F (*lombriga*) worm; (PT: *fila*) queue

bicho ['biʃu] M animal; (*inseto*) insect, bug

bicicleta [bisi'klɛta] F bicycle; (*col*) bike; **andar de ~** to cycle

bico ['biku] M (*de ave*) beak; (*ponta*) point; (*de chaleira*) spout; (*boca*) mouth; (*de pena*) nib; (*do peito*) nipple; (*de gás*) jet; (*col: emprego*) casual job; (*chupeta*) dummy; **calar o ~** to shut up

bidê [bi'de] M bidet

bife ['bifi] M (beef) steak; **~ a cavalo** steak with fried eggs; **~ à milanesa** beef escalope; **~ de panela** beef stew

bifurcação [bifurka'sãw] (*pl* **-ões**) F fork

bifurcar-se [bifur'karsi] VR to fork, divide

bigode [bi'gɔdʒi] M moustache

bijuteria [biʒute'ria] F (costume) jewellery (BRIT) *ou* jewelry (US)

bilhão [bi'ʎãw] (*pl* **-ões**) M billion

bilhar [bi'ʎar] M (*jogo*) billiards *sg*

bilhete [bi'ʎetʃi] M ticket; (*cartinha*) note; **~ eletrônico** e-ticket; **~ de ida** single (BRIT) *ou* one-way ticket; **~ de ida e volta** return (BRIT) *ou* round-trip (US) ticket; **bilheteira** [biʎe'tejra] (PT) F ticket office; (*Teatro*) box office; **bilheteiro, -a** [biʎe'tejru, a] M/F ticket seller; **bilheteria** [biʎete'ria] F ticket office

bilhões [bi'ʎõjs] MPL *de* **bilhão**

bilíngue [bi'lĩgwi] ADJ bilingual

binóculo [bi'nɔkulu] M binoculars *pl*; (*para teatro*) opera glasses *pl*

biocombustível [bjokõbus'tʃivew] (*pl* **-eis**) M biofuel

biodiesel [bjo'dʒizew] M biodiesel

biodiversidade [bjodʒiversi'dadʒi] F biodiversity

biografia [bjogra'fia] F biography

biologia [bjolo'ʒia] F biology

biombo ['bjõbu] M screen

b

bioterrorismo [bjoteho'rizmu] M bioterrorism
bip [bip] N pager
biquíni [bi'kini] M bikini
birita [bi'rita] (*col*) F drink
biruta [bi'ruta] ADJ crazy ▶ F windsock
bis [bis] EXCL encore!
bisavô, -vó [biza'vo, vɔ] M/F great-grandfather/great-grandmother; **bisavós** [biza'vɔs] MPL great-grandparents
biscate [bis'katʃi] M odd job
biscoito [bis'kojtu] M biscuit (BRIT), cookie (US)
bispo ['bispu] M bishop
bissexto, -a [bi'sestu, a] ADJ: **ano ~** leap year
bit ['bitʃi] M (*Comput*) bit
bizarro, -a [bi'zahu, a] ADJ bizarre
blasfemar [blasfe'mar] VT to curse ▶ VI to blaspheme; **blasfêmia** [blas'femja] F blasphemy
blazer ['blejzer] (*pl* **-s**) M blazer
blecaute [ble'kawtʃi] M power cut
blindado, -a [blĩ'dadu, a] ADJ armoured (BRIT), armored (US)
blitz [blits] F police road block
bloco ['blɔku] M block; (*Pol*) bloc; (*de escrever*) writing pad; **~ de carnaval** carnival troupe
blog ['blɔgi] M blog; **blogar** [blɔ'gar] VI to blog; **blogosfera** [blɔgos'fɛra] F blogosphere; **blogue** ['blɔgi] M blog; **blogueiro, -a** [blo'gejru, a] M/F blogger
bloqueador [blokja'dor] M: **~ solar** sunblock
bloquear [blo'kjar] VT to blockade; (*obstruir*) to block; **bloqueio** [blo'keju] M (*Mil*) blockade; (*obstrução*) blockage
blusa ['bluza] F (*de mulher*) blouse; (*de homem*) shirt; **~ de lã** jumper; **blusão** [blu'zãw] (*pl* **-ões**) M jacket
boa ['boa] ADJ F *de* **bom** ▶ F boa constrictor
boate ['bwatʃi] F nightclub
boato ['bwatu] M rumour (BRIT), rumor (US)
bobagem [bo'baʒẽ] (*pl* **-ns**) F silliness, nonsense; (*dito, ato*) silly thing
bobo, -a ['bobu, a] ADJ silly, daft ▶ M/F fool ▶ M (*de corte*) jester; **fazer-se de ~** to act the fool
bobó [bo'bɔ] M *beans, palm oil and manioc*
boca ['boka] F mouth; (*entrada*) entrance; (*de fogão*) ring; **de ~ aberta** amazed; **bater ~** to argue
bocadinho [boka'dʒiɲu] M: **um ~** (*pouco tempo*) a little while; (*pouquinho*) a little bit
bocado [bo'kadu] M mouthful, bite; (*pedaço*) piece, bit; **um ~ de tempo** quite some time
boçal [bo'saw] (*pl* **-ais**) ADJ ignorant; (*grosseiro*) uncouth
bocejar [bose'ʒar] VI to yawn; **bocejo** [bo'seʒu] M yawn
bochecha [bo'ʃeʃa] F cheek; **bochecho** [bo'ʃeʃu] M mouthwash
boda ['boda] F wedding; **bodas** FPL (*aniversário de casamento*) wedding anniversary *sg*
bode ['bɔdʒɪ] M goat; **~ expiatório** scapegoat
bofetada [bofe'tada] F slap
bofetão [bofe'tãw] (*pl* **-ões**) M punch
boi [boj] M ox
boia ['bɔja] F buoy; (*col*) grub; (*de braço*) armband, water wing
boiar [bo'jar] VT, VI to float
boi-bumbá [-bũ'ba] N *see note*

The **boi-bumbá**, or *bumba-meu-boi*, is a traditional folk dance from north-eastern Brazil, which brings together human, animal and mythological characters in a theatrical performance. The ox, which the dance is named after, is played by a dancer wearing an iron frame covered in pieces of colourful fabric. Eventually the beast is "killed" and its meat is symbolically shared out before it comes back to life in the finale.

boicotar [bojko'tar] VT to boycott;
boicote [boj'kɔtʃi] M boycott
bola ['bɔla] F ball; **dar ~ para** (*flertar*) to flirt with; **ela não dá a menor ~ (para isso)** she couldn't care less (about it); **não ser certo da ~** (*col*) not to be right in the head
bolacha [bo'laʃa] F biscuit (BRIT), cookie (US); (*col: bofetada*) wallop; (*para chope*) beer mat
boleia [bo'leja] F (*de caminhão*) cab; (PT: *carona*) lift; **dar uma ~ a alguém** (PT) to give sb a lift
boletim [bole'tʃĩ] (*pl* **-ns**) M report; (*publicação*) newsletter; **~ meteorológico** weather forecast
bolha ['boʎa] F (*na pele*) blister; (*de ar, sabão*) bubble
boliche [bo'liʃi] M bowling, skittles *sg*
bolinho [bo'liɲu] M: **~ de carne** meat ball; **~ de arroz/bacalhau** rice/dry cod cake
Bolívia [bo'livja] F: **a ~** Bolivia
bolo ['bolu] M cake; (*monte: de gente*) bunch; (*: de papéis*) bundle; **dar o ~ em alguém** to stand sb up; **vai dar ~** (*col*) there's going to be trouble
bolor [bo'lor] M mould (BRIT), mold (US); (*nas plantas*) mildew; (*bafio*) mustiness
bolota [bo'lɔta] F acorn
bolsa ['bowsa] F bag; (*Com: tb:* **~ de valores**) stock exchange; **~ (de estudos)** scholarship
bolso ['bowsu] M pocket; **de ~** pocket *atr*

PALAVRA-CHAVE

bom, boa [bõ, 'boa] (*pl* **bons/boas**) ADJ **1** (*ótimo*) good; **é um livro bom** *ou* **um bom livro** it's a good book; **a comida está boa** the food is delicious; **o tempo está bom** the weather's fine; **ele foi muito bom comigo** he was very nice *ou* kind to me
2 (*apropriado*): **ser bom para** to be good for; **acho bom você não ir** I think it's better if you don't go
3 (*irônico*): **um bom quarto de hora** a good quarter of an hour; **que bom motorista você é!** a fine *ou* some driver you are!; **seria bom que ...!** a fine thing it would be if ...!; **essa é boa!** what a cheek!
4 (*saudação*): **bom dia!** good morning!; **boa tarde!** good afternoon!; **boa noite!** good evening!; (*ao deitar-se*) good night!; **tudo bom?** how's it going?
5 (*outras frases*): **está bom?** OK?
▶ EXCL: **bom!** all right!; **bom, ...** right, ...

bomba ['bõba] F bomb; (*Tec*) pump; (*fig*) bombshell; **~ atômica/relógio/de fumaça** atomic/time/smoke bomb; **~ de gasolina** petrol (BRIT) *ou* gas (US) pump; **~ de incêndio** fire extinguisher
bombardear [bõbar'dʒjar] VT to bomb; (*fig*) to bombard;

bombardeio [bõbar'deju] M bombing, bombardment; **bombardeio suicida** suicide bombing
bombeiro [bõ'bejru] M fireman; (BR: *encanador*) plumber; **o corpo de ~s** fire brigade
bombom [bõ'bõ] (*pl* **-ns**) M chocolate
bondade [bõ'dadʒi] F goodness, kindness; **tenha a ~ de vir** would you please come
bonde ['bõdʒi] (BR) M tram
bondoso, -a [bõ'dozu, ɔza] ADJ kind, good
boné [bo'nɛ] M cap
boneca [bo'nɛka] F doll
boneco [bo'neku] M dummy
bonito, -a [bo'nitu, a] ADJ pretty; (*gesto, dia*) nice ▶ M (*peixe*) tuna (fish), tunny
bônus ['bonus] M INV bonus
boquiaberto, -a [bokja'bɛrtu, a] ADJ dumbfounded, astonished
borboleta [borbo'leta] F butterfly; (BR: *roleta*) turnstile
borbotão [borbo'tãw] (*pl* **-ões**) M gush, spurt; **sair aos borbotões** to gush out
borbulhar [borbu'ʎar] VI to bubble
borda ['bɔrda] F edge; (*do rio*) bank; **à ~ de** on the edge of
bordado [bor'dadu] M embroidery
bordar [bor'dar] VT to embroider
bordo ['bɔrdu] M (*de navio*) side; **a ~** on board
borra ['boha] F dregs *pl*
borracha [bo'haʃa] F rubber;
borracheiro [boha'ʃejru] M tyre (BRIT) *ou* tire (US) specialist
borrão [bo'hãw] (*pl* **-ões**) M (*rascunho*) rough draft; (*mancha*) blot
borrifar [bohi'far] VT to sprinkle;
borrifo [bo'hifu] M spray
borrões [bo'hõjs] MPL *de* **borrão**
bosque ['bɔski] M wood, forest
bossa ['bɔsa] F charm; (*inchaço*) swelling; **Bossa nova** (*Mús*) *see note*

> **Bossa nova** is a type of music invented by young, middle-class inhabitants of Rio de Janeiro at the end of the 1950s. It has an obvious jazz influence, an unusual, rhythmic beat and lyrics praising beauty and love. **Bossa nova** became known around the world through the work of the conductor and composer Antônio Carlos Jobim, whose compositions, working with the poet Vinícius de Morais, include the famous song "The Girl from Ipanema".

bota ['bɔta] F boot; **~s de borracha** wellingtons
botânica [bo'tanika] F botany
botão [bo'tãw] (*pl* **-ões**) M button; (*flor*) bud
botar [bo'tar] VT to put; (*roupa, sapatos*) to put on; (*mesa*) to set; (*defeito*) to find; (*ovos*) to lay
bote ['bɔtʃi] M boat; (*com arma*) thrust; (*salto*) spring
botequim [botʃi'kĩ] (*pl* **-ns**) M bar
botija [bo'tʃiʒa] F (earthenware) jug
botões [bo'tõjs] MPL *de* **botão**
boxe ['bɔksi] M boxing
brabo, -a ['brabu, a] ADJ fierce; (*zangado*) angry; (*ruim*) bad; (*calor*) unbearable
braçada [bra'sada] F armful; (*Natação*) stroke
bracelete [brase'letʃi] M bracelet

braço ['brasu] M arm; **de ~s cruzados** with arms folded; (*fig*) without lifting a finger; **de ~ dado** arm-in-arm
bradar [bra'dar] VT, VI to shout, yell; **brado** ['bradu] M shout, yell
braguilha [bra'giʎa] F flies *pl*
branco, -a ['brãku, a] ADJ white ▶ M/F white man/woman ▶ M (*espaço*) blank; **em ~** blank; **noite em ~** sleepless night; **brancura** [brã'kura] F whiteness
brando, -a ['brãdu, a] ADJ gentle; (*mole*) soft
brasão [bra'zãw] (*pl* **-ões**) M coat of arms
braseiro [bra'zejru] M brazier
Brasil [bra'ziw] M: **o ~** Brazil; **brasileiro, -a** [brazi'lejru, a] ADJ, M/F Brazilian
Brasília [bra'zilja] N Brasília
brasões [bra'zõjs] MPL *de* **brasão**
bravata [bra'vata] F bravado, boasting
bravio, -a [bra'viu, a] ADJ (*selvagem*) wild; (*feroz*) ferocious
bravo, -a ['bravu, a] ADJ brave; (*furioso*) angry; (*mar*) rough ▶ M brave man; **~!** bravo!; **bravura** [bra'vura] F courage, bravery
brecar [bre'kar] VT (*carro*) to stop; (*reprimir*) to curb ▶ VI to brake
breu [brew] M tar, pitch
breve ['brɛvi] ADJ short; (*conciso, rápido*) brief ▶ ADV soon; **em ~** soon, shortly; **até ~** see you soon
bridge ['bridʒi] M bridge
briga ['briga] F fight; (*verbal*) quarrel
brigada [bri'gada] F brigade
brigão, -gona [bri'gãw, ɔna] (*pl* **-ões/-s**) ADJ quarrelsome ▶ M/F troublemaker
brigar [bri'gar] VI to fight; (*altercar*) to quarrel
brigões [bri'gõjs] MPL *de* **brigão**
brigona [bri'gɔna] F *de* **brigão**
brilhante [bri'ʎãtʃi] ADJ brilliant ▶ M diamond
brilhar [bri'ʎar] VI to shine
brincadeira [brĩka'dejra] F fun; (*gracejo*) joke; (*de criança*) game; **deixe de ~s!** stop fooling!; **de ~** for fun
brincalhão, -lhona [brĩka'ʎãw, ɔna] (*pl* **-ões/-s**) ADJ playful ▶ M/F joker, teaser
brincar [brĩ'kar] VI to play; (*gracejar*) to joke; **estou brincando** I'm only kidding; **~ de soldados** to play (at) soldiers; **~ com alguém** to tease sb
brinco ['brĩku] M (*joia*) earring
brindar [brĩ'dar] VT to drink to; (*presentear*) to give a present to; **brinde** ['brĩdʒi] M toast; (*presente*) free gift
brinquedo [brĩ'kedu] M toy
brio ['briu] M self-respect, dignity
brisa ['briza] F breeze
britânico, -a [bri'taniku, a] ADJ British ▶ M/F Briton
broche ['brɔʃi] M brooch
brochura [bro'ʃura] F (*livro*) paperback; (*folheto*) brochure, pamphlet
brócolis ['brɔkolis] MPL broccoli *sg*
bronca ['brõka] (*col*) F telling off; **dar uma ~ em** to tell off; **levar uma ~** to get told off
bronco, -a ['brõku, a] ADJ (*rude*) coarse; (*burro*) thick
bronquite [brõ'kitʃi] F bronchitis
bronze ['brõzi] M bronze; **bronzear** [brõ'zjar] VT to tan; **bronzear-se** VR to get a tan
broto ['brotu] M bud; (*fig*) youngster
broxa ['brɔʃa] F (large) paint brush

bruços ['brusus] MPL: **de ~** face down
bruma ['bruma] F mist, haze
brusco, -a ['brusku, a] ADJ brusque; (*súbito*) sudden
brutal [bru'taw] (*pl* **-ais**) ADJ brutal
bruto, -a ['brutu, a] ADJ brutish; (*grosseiro*) coarse; (*móvel*) heavy; (*petróleo*) crude; (*peso, Com*) gross ▶ M brute; **em ~** raw, unworked
bruxa ['bruʃa] F witch; **bruxaria** [bruʃa'ria] F witchcraft
Bruxelas [bru'ʃelas] N Brussels
bruxo ['bruʃu] M wizard
budismo [bu'dʒizmu] M Buddhism
bufar [bu'far] VI to puff, pant; (*com raiva*) to snort; (*reclamar*) to moan, grumble
bufê [bu'fe] M sideboard; (*comida*) buffet
buffer ['bafer] (*pl* **-s**) M (*Comput*) buffer
bula ['bula] F (*Med*) directions *pl* for use
bule ['buli] M (*de chá*) teapot; (*de café*) coffeepot
Bulgária [buw'garja] F: **a ~** Bulgaria; **búlgaro, -a** ['buwgaru, a] ADJ, M/F Bulgarian ▶ M (*Ling*) Bulgarian
bulimia [buli'mia] F bulimia
bunda ['bũda] (*col*) F bottom, backside
buquê [bu'ke] M bouquet
buraco [bu'raku] M hole; (*de agulha*) eye; **ser um ~** to be tough; **~ da fechadura** keyhole
burguês, -guesa [bur'ges, 'geza] ADJ middle-class, bourgeois; **burguesia** [burge'zia] F middle class, bourgeoisie
burocracia [burokra'sia] F bureaucracy
burro, -a ['buhu, a] ADJ stupid ▶ M/F (*Zool*) donkey; (*pessoa*) fool, idiot; **pra ~** (*col*) a lot; (*com adj*) really; **~ de carga** (*fig*) hard worker
busca ['buska] F search; **em ~ de** in search of; **dar ~ a** to search for
buscador [buska'dor] M search engine
buscar [bus'kar] VT to fetch; (*procurar*) to look *ou* search for; **ir ~** to fetch, go for; **mandar ~** to send for
bússola ['busola] F compass
busto ['bustu] M bust
buzina [bu'zina] F horn; **buzinar** [buzi'nar] VI to sound one's horn, toot the horn ▶ VT to hoot
búzio ['buzju] M conch

C

c/ ABR = **com**
cá [ka] ADV here; **de cá** on this side; **para cá** here, over here; **para lá e para cá** back and forth; **de lá para cá** since then
caatinga [ka'tʃĩga] (BR) F scrub(-land)
cabana [ka'bana] F hut
cabeça [ka'besa] F head; (*inteligência*) brain; (*de uma lista*) top ▶ M/F leader; **de ~** off the top of one's head; (*calcular*) in one's head; **de ~ para baixo** upside down; **por ~** per person, per head; **cabeçada** [kabe'sada] F (*pancada com cabeça*) butt; (*Futebol*) header; (*asneira*) blunder; **cabeçalho** [kabe'saʎu] M (*de livro*) title page; (*de página, capítulo*) heading
cabeceira [kabe'sejra] F (*de cama*) head
cabeçudo, -a [kabe'sudu, a] ADJ with a big head; (*teimoso*) headstrong
cabeleira [kabe'lejra] F head of hair; (*postiça*) wig; **cabeleireiro, -a** [kabelej'rejru, a] M/F hairdresser
cabelo [ka'belu] M hair; **cortar/fazer o ~** to have one's hair cut/done; **cabeludo, -a** [kabe'ludu, a] ADJ hairy
caber [ka'ber] VI: **~ (em)** to fit; (*ser compatível*) to be appropriate (in); **~ a** (*em partilha*) to fall to; **cabe a alguém fazer** it is up to sb to do; **não cabe aqui fazer comentários** this is not the time or place to comment
cabide [ka'bidʒi] M (coat) hanger; (*móvel*) hat stand; (*fixo à parede*) coat rack
cabine [ka'bini] F cabin; (*em loja*) fitting room; **~ do piloto** (*Aer*) cockpit; **~ telefônica** telephone box (BRIT) *ou* booth
cabo ['kabu] M (*extremidade*) end; (*de faca, vassoura etc*) handle; (*corda*) rope; (*elétrico etc*) cable; (*Geo*) cape; (*Mil*) corporal; **ao ~ de** at the end of; **de ~ a rabo** from beginning to end; **levar a ~** to carry out; **dar ~ de** to do away with
caboclo, -a [ka'boklu, a] (BR) M/F mestizo
cabra ['kabra] F goat
cabreiro, -a [ka'brejru, a] (*col*) ADJ suspicious
cabrito [ka'britu] M kid
caça ['kasa] F hunting; (*busca*) hunt; (*animal*) quarry, game ▶ M (*Aer*) fighter (plane); **caçador, a** [kasa'dor(a)] M/F hunter
cação [ka'sãw] (*pl* **-ões**) M shark
caçar [ka'sar] VT to hunt; (*com espingarda*) to shoot; (*procurar*) to seek ▶ VI to hunt, go hunting
caçarola [kasa'rɔla] F (sauce)pan
cacau [ka'kaw] M cocoa; (*Bot*) cacao

cacetada [kase'tada] F blow (with a stick)
cachaça [ka'ʃasa] F (white) rum
cachaceiro, -a [kaʃa'sejru, a] ADJ drunk ▶ M/F drunkard
cachê [ka'ʃe] M fee
cachecol [kaʃe'kɔw] (*pl* **-óis**) M scarf
cachimbo [ka'ʃĩbu] M pipe
cacho ['kaʃu] M bunch; (*de cabelo*) curl; (*longo*) ringlet
cachoeira [kaʃ'wejra] F waterfall
cachorra [ka'ʃoha] F bitch, (female) puppy
cachorrinho, -a [kaʃo'hiɲu, a] M/F puppy
cachorro [ka'ʃohu] M dog, puppy; **cachorro-quente** (*pl* **cachorros-quentes**) M hot dog
cacique [ka'siki] M (Indian) chief; (*mandachuva*) local boss
caco ['kaku] M bit, fragment; (*pessoa velha*) old relic
caçoar [ka'swar] VT, VI to mock
cacoete [ka'kwetʃi] M twitch, tic
cacto ['kaktu] M cactus
cada ['kada] ADJ INV each; (*todo*) every; **~ um** each one; **~ semana** each week; **a ~ 3 horas** every 3 hours; **~ vez mais** more and more
cadastrar [kadas'trar] VT to register; **cadastrar-se** VR to register
cadastro [ka'dastru] M register; (*ato*) registration; (*de criminosos*) criminal record
cadáver [ka'daver] M corpse, (dead) body
cadê [ka'de] (*col*) ADV: **~ ...?** where's/where are ...?, what's happened to ...?
cadeado [ka'dʒjadu] M padlock
cadeia [ka'deja] F chain; (*prisão*) prison; (*rede*) network
cadeira [ka'dejra] F chair; (*disciplina*) subject; (*Teatro*) stall; (*função*) post; **cadeiras** FPL (*Anat*) hips; **~ de balanço** rocking chair; **~ de rodas** wheelchair
cadela [ka'dɛla] F (*cão*) bitch
caderneta [kader'neta] F notebook; **~ de poupança** savings account
caderno [ka'dɛrnu] M exercise book; (*de notas*) notebook; (*de jornal*) section
caducar [kadu'kar] VI to lapse, expire; **caduco, -a** [ka'duku, a] ADJ invalid, expired; (*senil*) senile; (*Bot*) deciduous
cães [kãjs] MPL *de* **cão**
cafajeste [kafa'ʒɛstʃi] (*col*) ADJ roguish; (*vulgar*) vulgar, coarse ▶ M/F rogue; rough customer
café [ka'fɛ] M coffee; (*estabelecimento*) café; **~ com leite** white coffee (BRIT), coffee with cream (US); **~ preto** black coffee; **~ da manhã** (BR) breakfast
cafeteira [kafe'tejra] F coffeepot; (*máquina*) percolator; **cafezal** [kafe'zaw] (*pl* **-ais**) M coffee plantation; **cafezinho** [kafe'ziɲu] M *small black coffee*
cagada [ka'gada] (*!*) F shit (*!*)
cágado ['kagadu] M turtle
cagar [ka'gar] (*!*) VI to (have a) shit (*!*)
caguetar [kagwe'tar] VT to inform on; **caguete** [ka'gwetʃi] M informer
caiba ['kajba] VB *ver* **caber**
cãibra ['kãjbra] F (*Med*) cramp
caída [ka'ida] F = **queda**
caído, -a [ka'idu, a] ADJ dejected; (*derrubado*) fallen; (*pendente*) droopy; **~ por** (*apaixonado*) in love with

câimbra ['kãjbra] F = **câibra**

caipirinha [kajpi'riɲa] F *cocktail of cachaça, lemon and sugar*

cair [ka'ir] VI to fall; **~ bem/mal** (*roupa*) to fit well/badly; (*col: pessoa*) to look good/bad; **~ em si** to come to one's senses; **ao ~ da noite** at nightfall; **essa comida me caiu mal** that food did not agree with me

Cairo ['kajru] M: **o ~** Cairo

cais [kajs] M (*Náut*) quay; (PT *Ferro*) platform

caixa ['kajʃa] F box; (*cofre*) safe; (*de uma loja*) cash desk ▶ M/F (*pessoa*) cashier; **~ automática** *ou* **eletrônico** cash machine; **pequena ~** petty cash; **~ de correio** letter box; **~ de mudanças** (BR) *ou* **de velocidades** gear box; **~ econômica** savings bank; **~ postal** P.O. box; **~ registradora** cash register; **caixa-forte** (*pl* **caixas-fortes**) F vault

caixão [kaj'ʃãw] (*pl* **-ões**) M (*ataúde*) coffin; (*caixa grande*) large box

caixeiro-viajante, caixeira-viajante (*pl* **caixeiros-viajantes/caixeiras-viajantes**) M/F commercial traveller (BRIT) *ou* traveler (US)

caixilho [kaj'ʃiʎu] M (*moldura*) frame

caixões [kaj'ʃõjs] MPL *de* **caixão**

caixote [kaj'ʃɔtʃi] M packing case; **~ do lixo** (PT) dustbin (BRIT), garbage can (US)

caju [ka'ʒu] M cashew fruit

cal [kaw] F lime; (*na água*) chalk; (*para caiar*) whitewash

calabouço [kala'bosu] M dungeon

calado, -a [ka'ladu, a] ADJ quiet

calafrio [kala'friu] M shiver; **ter ~s** to shiver

calamidade [kalami'dadʒi] F calamity, disaster

calão [ka'lãw] M: **(baixo) ~** slang

calar [ka'lar] VT (*não dizer*) to keep quiet about; (*impor silêncio a*) to silence ▶ VI to go quiet; (*manter-se calado*) to keep quiet; **calar-se** VR to go quiet; to keep quiet; **cala a boca!** shut up!

calça ['kawsa] F (*tb*: **~s**) trousers *pl* (BRIT), pants *pl* (US)

calçada [kaw'sada] F (PT: *rua*) roadway; (BR: *passeio*) pavement (BRIT), sidewalk (US)

calçadão [kawsa'dãw] (*pl* **-ões**) M pedestrian precinct (BRIT), pedestrian zone (US)

calçado, -a [kaw'sadu, a] ADJ (*rua*) paved ▶ M shoe; **calçados** MPL (*para os pés*) footwear *sg*

calçadões [kawsa'dõjs] MPL *de* **calçadão**

calçamento [kawsa'mẽtu] M paving

calcanhar [kawka'ɲar] M (*Anat*) heel

calção [kaw'sãw] (*pl* **-ões**) M shorts *pl*; **~ de banho** swimming trunks *pl*

calcar [kaw'kar] VT to tread on; (*espezinhar*) to trample (on)

calçar [kaw'sar] VT (*sapatos, luvas*) to put on; (*pavimentar*) to pave; **calçar-se** VR to put on one's shoes; **ela calça (número) 28** she takes size 28 (in shoes)

calcário, -a [kaw'karju, a] ADJ (*água*) hard ▶ M limestone

calcinha [kaw'siɲa] F panties *pl*

calço ['kawsu] M wedge

calções [kaw'sõjs] MPL *de* **calção**

calculador [kawkula'dor] M = **calculadora**

calculadora [kawkula'dora] F calculator

calcular [kawku'lar] VT to calculate; (*imaginar*) to imagine; **~ que** to reckon that
cálculo ['kawkulu] M calculation; (*Mat*) calculus; (*Med*) stone
calda ['kawda] F (*de doce*) syrup; **caldas** FPL (*águas termais*) hot springs
caldeirada [kawdej'rada] (PT) F (*guisado*) fish stew
caldo ['kawdu] M broth; (*de fruta*) juice; **~ de carne/galinha** beef/ chicken stock; **~ verde** potato and cabbage broth
calendário [kalẽ'darju] M calendar
calhar [ka'ʎar] VI: **calhou viajarmos no mesmo avião** we happened to travel on the same plane; **calhou que** it so happened that; **~ a** (*cair bem*) to suit; **se ~** (PT) perhaps, maybe
calibre [ka'libri] M (*de cano*) calibre (BRIT), caliber (US)
cálice ['kalisi] M wine glass; (*Rel*) chalice
calista [ka'lista] M/F chiropodist (BRIT), podiatrist (US)
calma ['kawma] F calm
calmante [kaw'mãtʃi] ADJ soothing ▸ M (*Med*) tranquillizer
calmo, -a ['kawmu, a] ADJ calm
calo ['kalu] M callus; (*no pé*) corn
calor [ka'lor] M heat; (*fig*) warmth; **está** *ou* **faz ~** it is hot; **estar com ~** to be hot
calorento, -a [kalo'rẽtu, a] ADJ (*pessoa*) sensitive to heat; (*lugar*) hot
caloria [calo'ria] F calorie
caloroso, -a [kalo'rozu, ɔza] ADJ warm; (*entusiástico*) enthusiastic
calouro, -a [ka'loru, a] M/F (*Educ*) fresher (BRIT), freshman (US)
calúnia [ka'lunja] F slander
calvo, -a ['kawvu, a] ADJ bald
cama ['kama] F bed; **~ de casal** double bed; **~ de solteiro** single bed; **de ~** (*doente*) ill (in bed)
camada [ka'mada] F layer; (*de tinta*) coat
câmara ['kamara] F chamber; (PT *Foto*) camera; **~ de ar** inner tube; **~ municipal** (BR) town council; (PT) town hall
camarão [kama'rãw] (*pl* **-ões**) M shrimp; (*graúdo*) prawn
camarões [kama'rõjs] MPL *de* **camarão**
camarote [kama'rɔtʃi] M (*Náut*) cabin; (*Teatro*) box
cambaleante [kãba'ljãtʃi] ADJ unsteady (on one's feet)
cambalhota [kãba'ʎɔta] F somersault
câmbio ['kãbju] M (*dinheiro etc*) exchange; (*preço de câmbio*) rate of exchange; **~ livre** free trade; **~ oficial/paralelo** official/black market
cambista [kã'bista] M money changer
Camboja [kã'bɔja] M: **o ~** Cambodia
camelo [ka'melu] M camel
câmera ['kamera] (BR) F camera; **em ~ lenta** in slow motion; **~ de segurança** security camera, CCTV camera; **~ digital** digital camera
camião [ka'mjãw] (*pl* **-ões**) (PT) M lorry (BRIT), truck (US)
caminhada [kami'ɲada] F walk
caminhão [kami'ɲãw] (*pl* **-ões**) (BR) M lorry (BRIT), truck (US)
caminhar [kami'ɲar] VI to walk; (*processo*) to get under way; (*negócios*) to progress
caminho [ka'miɲu] M way;

(*vereda*) road, path; **~ de ferro** (PT) railway (BRIT), railroad (US); **a ~** on the way, en route; **cortar ~** to take a short cut; **pôr-se a ~** to set off
caminhões [kami'ɲõjs] MPL *de* **caminhão**
caminhoneiro, -a [kamiɲo'nejru, a] M/F lorry driver (BRIT), truck driver (US)
camiões [ka'mjõjs] MPL *de* **camião**
camioneta [kamjo'neta] (PT) F (*para passageiros*) coach; (*comercial*) van
camionista [kamjo'nista] (PT) M/F lorry driver (BRIT), truck driver (US)
camisa [ka'miza] F shirt; **~ de dormir** nightshirt; **~ de força** straitjacket; **~ esporte/polo/social** sports/polo/dress shirt
camiseta [kami'zɛta] (BR) F T-shirt; (*interior*) vest
camisinha [kami'ziɲa] (*col*) F condom
camisola [kami'zɔla] F (BR) nightdress; (PT: *pulôver*) sweater; **~ interior** (PT) vest
campainha [kampa'iɲa] F bell
campanário [kãpa'narju] M church tower, steeple
campeão, -peã [kã'pjãw, 'pjã] (*pl* **-ões/-s**) M/F champion;
campeonato [kãpjo'natu] M championship
campestre [kã'pɛstri] ADJ rural, rustic
camping ['kãpĩŋ] (BR) (*pl* **-s**) M camping; (*lugar*) campsite
campismo [kã'pizmu] M camping; **parque de ~** campsite
campista [kã'pista] M/F camper
campo [kãpu] M field; (*fora da cidade*) countryside; (*Esporte*) ground; (*acampamento*) camp; (*Tênis*) court
camponês, -esa [kãpo'nes, eza] M/F countryman/woman; (*agricultor*) farmer
campus ['kãpus] M INV campus
camuflagem [kamu'flaʒẽ] F camouflage
camundongo [kamũ'dõgu] (BR) M mouse
camurça [ka'mursa] F suede
cana ['kana] F cane; (*col: cadeia*) nick; (*de açúcar*) sugar cane
Canadá [kana'da] M: **o ~** Canada;
canadense [kana'dẽsi] ADJ, M/F Canadian
canal [ka'naw] (*pl* **-ais**) M channel; (*de navegação*) canal; (*Anat*) duct
canalização [kanaliza'sãw] F plumbing
canalizador, a [kanaliza'dor(a)] (PT) M/F plumber
canário [ka'narju] M canary
canastra [ka'nastra] F (big) basket
canção [kã'sãw] (*pl* **-ões**) F song; **~ de ninar** lullaby
cancela [kã'sɛla] F gate
cancelamento [kãsela'mẽtu] M cancellation
cancelar [kãse'lar] VT to cancel; (*riscar*) to cross out
câncer ['kãser] M cancer; **C~** (*Astrologia*) Cancer
canções [kã'sõjs] FPL *de* **canção**
cancro ['kãkru] (PT) M cancer
candelabro [kãde'labru] M candlestick; (*lustre*) chandelier
candidato, -a [kãdʒi'datu, a] M/F candidate; (*a cargo*) applicant
cândido, -a ['kãdʒidu, a] ADJ naive; (*inocente*) innocent
candomblé [kãdõ'blɛ] M *see note*

Candomblé is Brazil's most influential Afro-Brazilian religion. Practised mainly in Bahia, it mixes catholicism with

Yoruba traditions. According to **candomblé**, believers become possessed by spirits and thus become an instrument of communication between divine and mortal forces. **Candomblé** ceremonies are great spectacles of African rhythm and dance held in *terreiros*.

caneca [ka'nɛka] F mug
canela [ka'nɛla] F cinnamon; (*Anat*) shin
caneta [ka'neta] F pen; **~ esferográfica** ballpoint pen; **~ pilot** felt-tip pen
cangaceiro [kãga'sejru] (BR) M bandit
canguru [kãgu'ru] M kangaroo
canhão [ka'ɲãw] (*pl* **-ões**) M cannon; (*Geo*) canyon
canhoto, -a [ka'ɲotu, a] ADJ left-handed ▶ M/F left-handed person ▶ M (*de cheque*) stub
canibal [kani'baw] (*pl* **-ais**) M/F cannibal
canil [ka'niw] (*pl* **-is**) M kennel
canja ['kãʒa] F chicken broth; (*col*) cinch, pushover
canjica [kã'ʒika] F maize porridge
cano ['kanu] M pipe; (*tubo*) tube; (*de arma de fogo*) barrel; (*de bota*) top; **~ de esgoto** sewer
canoa [ka'noa] F canoe
cansaço [kã'sasu] M tiredness
cansado, -a [kã'sadu, a] ADJ tired
cansar [kã'sar] VT to tire; (*entediar*) to bore ▶ VI to get tired; **cansar-se** VR to get tired; **cansativo, -a** [kãsa'tʃivu, a] ADJ tiring; (*tedioso*) tedious
cantar [kã'tar] VT, VI to sing ▶ M song
canteiro [kã'tejru] M stonemason; (*de flores*) flower bed
cantiga [kã'tʃiga] F ballad; **~ de ninar** lullaby
cantil [kã'tʃiw] (*pl* **-is**) M canteen
cantina [kã'tʃina] F canteen
cantis [kã'tʃis] MPL *de* **cantil**
canto ['kãtu] M corner; (*lugar*) place; (*canção*) song
cantor, a [kã'tor(a)] M/F singer
cão [kãw] (*pl* **cães**) M dog
caolho, -a [ka'oʎu, a] ADJ cross-eyed
caos ['kaos] M chaos
capa ['kapa] F cape; (*cobertura*) cover; **livro de ~ dura/mole** hardback/paperback (book)
capacete [kapa'setʃi] M helmet
capacidade [kapasi'dadʒi] F capacity; (*aptidão*) ability, competence
capaz [ka'paz] ADJ able, capable; **ser ~ de** to be able to (*ou* capable of); **sou ~ de ...** (*talvez*) I might ...; **é ~ de chover hoje** it might rain today
capela [ka'pɛla] F chapel
capim [ka'pĩ] M grass
capitães [kapi'tãjs] MPL *de* **capitão**
capital [kapi'taw] (*pl* **-ais**) ADJ, M capital ▶ F (*cidade*) capital; **~ (em) ações** (*Com*) share capital
capitalismo [kapita'lizmu] M capitalism; **capitalista** [kapita'lista] M/F capitalist
capitalizar [kapitali'zar] VT to capitalize on; (*Com*) to capitalize
capitão [kapi'tãw] (*pl* **-ães**) M captain
capítulo [ka'pitulu] M chapter
capô [ka'po] M (*Auto*) bonnet (BRIT), hood (US)
capoeira [ka'pwejra] F (PT) hencoop

> **Capoeira** is a fusion of martial arts and dance which originated among African slaves in colonial Brazil. It is danced in a circle to the sound of the *berimbau*, a percussion instrument of African origin. Opposed by the Brazilian authorities until the beginning of the twentieth century, today **capoeira** is regarded as a national sport.

capota [ka'pɔta] F (*Auto*) hood, top
capotar [kapo'tar] VI to overturn
capricho [ka'priʃu] M whim, caprice; (*teimosia*) obstinacy; (*apuro*) care; **caprichoso, -a** [kapri'ʃozu, ɔza] ADJ capricious; (*com apuro*) meticulous
Capricórnio [kapri'kɔrnju] M Capricorn
cápsula ['kapsula] F capsule
captar [kap'tar] VT (*atrair*) to win; (*Rádio*) to pick up
captura [kap'tura] F capture; **~ de tela** (*Comput*) screenshot; **capturar** [kaptu'rar] VT to capture
capuz [ka'puz] M hood
cáqui ['kaki] ADJ khaki
cara ['kara] F face; (*aspecto*) appearance ▶ M (*col*) guy; **~ ou coroa?** heads or tails?; **de ~** straightaway; **dar de ~ com** to bump into; **ser a ~ de** (*col*) to be the spitting image of; **ter ~ de** to look (like)
caracol [kara'kɔw] (*pl* **-óis**) M snail; (*de cabelo*) curl; **escada em ~** spiral staircase
caracteres [karak'tɛris] MPL *de* **caráter**
característica [karakte'ristʃika] F characteristic, feature
característico, -a [karakte'ristʃiku, a] ADJ characteristic
cara de pau F cheek ▶ ADJ INV brazen
caramelo [kara'mɛlu] M caramel; (*bala*) toffee
caranguejo [karã'geʒu] M crab
caratê [kara'te] M karate
caráter [ka'rater] (*pl* **caracteres**) M character
caravana [kara'vana] F caravan
carboidrato [karboi'dratu] M carbohydrate
cardápio [kar'dapju] (BR) M menu
cardeal [kar'dʒjaw] (*pl* **-ais**) ADJ, M cardinal
cardigã [kardʒi'gã] M cardigan
careca [ka'rɛka] ADJ bald
carecer [kare'ser] VI: **~ de** to lack; (*precisar*) to need
carência [ka'rẽsja] F lack; (*necessidade*) need; (*privação*) deprivation; **carente** [ka'rẽtʃi] ADJ wanting; (*pessoa*) needy, deprived
carga ['karga] F load; (*de navio, avião*) cargo; (*ato de carregar*) loading; (*Elet*) charge; (*fig: peso*) burden; (*Mil*) attack, charge
cargo ['kargu] M responsibility; (*função*) post; **a ~ de** in charge of; **ter a ~** to be in charge of; **tomar a ~** to take charge of
Caribe [ka'ribi] M: **o ~** the Caribbean (Sea)
caridade [kari'dadʒi] F charity; **obra de ~** charity
cárie ['kari] F tooth decay
carimbar [karĩ'bar] VT to stamp; (*no correio*) to postmark
carimbo [ka'rĩbu] M stamp; (*postal*) postmark
carinho [ka'riɲu] M affection, fondness; (*carícia*) caress; **fazer ~** to caress; **com ~** affectionately; (*com cuidado*) with care; **carinhoso, -a** [kari'ɲozu, ɔza] ADJ affectionate

carioca [ka'rjɔka] ADJ of Rio de Janeiro ▶ M/F native of Rio de Janeiro ▶ M (*café*) *type of weak coffee*
carnal [kar'naw] (*pl* **-ais**) ADJ carnal; **primo ~** first cousin
carnaval [karna'vaw] (*pl* **-ais**) M carnival

In Brazil, **Carnaval** is the popular festival held each year in the four days before Lent. It is celebrated in very different ways in different parts of the country. In Rio de Janeiro, for example, the big attraction is the parades of the *escolas de samba*, in Salvador the *trios elétricos*, in Recife the *frevo* and, in Olinda, the giant figures, such as the *Homen da meia-noite* and *Mulher do meio-dia*. In Portugal, **Carnaval** is celebrated on Shrove Tuesday, with street parties and processions taking place throughout the country.

carne ['karni] F flesh; (*Culin*) meat; **em ~ e osso** in the flesh
carnê [kar'ne] M (*para compras*) payment book
carneiro [kar'nejru] M sheep; (*macho*) ram; **perna/costeleta de ~** leg of lamb/lamb chop
carnificina [karnifi'sina] F slaughter
caro, -a ['karu, a] ADJ dear; **cobrar/pagar ~** to charge a lot/ pay dearly
carochinha [karo'ʃiɲa] F: **conto da ~** fairy tale
caroço [ka'rosu] M (*de frutos*) stone; (*endurecimento*) lump
carona [ka'rɔna] F lift; **viajar de ~** to hitchhike; **pegar uma ~** to get a lift
carpete [kar'pɛtʃi] M (fitted) carpet
carpinteiro [karpĩ'tejru] M carpenter
carrapato [kaha'patu] M (*inseto*) tick
carrasco [ka'hasku] M executioner; (*fig*) tyrant
carregado, -a [kahe'gadu, a] ADJ loaded; (*semblante*) sullen; (*céu*) dark; (*ambiente*) tense
carregador [kahega'dor] M porter
carregamento [kahega'mẽtu] M (*ação*) loading; (*carga*) load, cargo
carregar [kahe'gar] VT to load; (*levar*) to carry; (*bateria*) to charge; (PT: *apertar*) to press; (*levar para longe*) to take away ▶ VI: **~ em** to overdo; (*pôr enfase*) to bring out
carreira [ka'hejra] F run, running; (*profissão*) career; (*Turfe*) race; (*Náut*) slipway; (*fileira*) row; **às ~s** in a hurry
carretel [kahe'tɛw] (*pl* **-éis**) M spool, reel
carrinho [ka'hiɲu] M trolley; (*brinquedo*) toy car; **~ (de criança)** pram; **~ de mão** wheelbarrow; **~ de compras** shopping trolley (BRIT), shopping cart (US)
carro ['kaho] M car; (*de bois*) cart; (*de mão*) barrow; (*de máquina de escrever*) carriage; **~ de corrida** racing car; **~ de passeio** saloon car; **~ de praça** cab; **~ de bombeiro** fire engine; **~ esporte** sports car
carroça [ka'hɔsa] F cart, wagon
carroçeria [kahose'ria] F (*Auto*) bodywork
carro-chefe (*pl* **carros-chefe(s)**) M (*de desfile*) main float; (*fig*) flagship, centrepiece (BRIT), centerpiece (US)

carrossel [kaho'sɛw] (*pl* **-éis**) M merry-go-round
carruagem [ka'hwaʒẽ] (*pl* **-ns**) F carriage, coach
carta ['karta] F letter; (*de jogar*) card; (*mapa*) chart; **~ aérea** airmail letter; **~ registrada** registered letter; **~ de condução** (PT) driving licence (BRIT), driver's license (US); **dar as ~s** to deal
cartão [kar'tãw] (*pl* **-ões**) M card; (PT: *material*) cardboard; **~ de crédito** credit card; **~ de débito** debit card; **~ de memória** memory card; **~ de recarga** (*para celular*) top-up card; **~ telefônico** phone card; **cartão-postal** (*pl* **cartões-postais**) M postcard; (*lugar turístico*) sight
cartaz [kar'taz] M poster, bill (US); **(estar) em ~** (*Teatro, Cinema*) (to be) showing
carteira [kar'tejra] F desk; (*para dinheiro*) wallet; (*de ações*) portfolio; **~ de identidade** identity card; **~ de motorista** driving licence (BRIT), driver's license (US)
carteiro [kar'tejru] M postman (BRIT), mailman (US)
cartões [kar'tõjs] MPL *de* **cartão**
cartola [kar'tɔla] F top hat
cartolina [karto'lina] F card
cartório [kar'tɔrju] M registry office
cartucho [kar'tuʃu] M cartridge; (*saco de papel*) packet
cartum [kar'tũ] (*pl* **-ns**) M cartoon
carvalho [kar'vaʎu] M oak
carvão [kar'vãw] (*pl* **-ões**) M coal; (*de madeira*) charcoal
casa ['kaza] F house; (*lar*) home; (*Com*) firm; (*Mat: decimal*) place; **em/para ~** (at) home/home; **~ de saúde** hospital; **~ da moeda** mint; **~ de banho** (PT) bathroom; **~ e comida** board and lodging; **~ de câmbio** bureau de change; **~ de cômodos** tenement; **~ de repouso** old people's home (BRIT), retirement home (US); **~ popular** ≈ council house
casacão [kaza'kãw] (*pl* **-ões**) M overcoat
casaco [ka'zaku] M coat; (*paletó*) jacket
casacões [kaza'kõjs] MPL *de* **casacão**
casado, -a [ka'zadu, a] ADJ married
casal [ka'zaw] (*pl* **-ais**) M couple
casamento [kaza'mẽtu] M marriage; (*boda*) wedding
casar [ka'zar] VT to marry; (*combinar*) to match (up); **casar-se** VR to get married; (*harmonizar-se*) to combine well
casarão [kaza'rãw] (*pl* **-ões**) M mansion
casca ['kaska] F (*de árvore*) bark; (*de banana*) skin; (*de ferida*) scab; (*de laranja*) peel; (*de nozes, ovos*) shell; (*de milho etc*) husk; (*de pão*) crust
cascata [kas'kata] F waterfall
casco ['kasku] M skull; (*de animal*) hoof; (*de navio*) hull; (*para bebidas*) empty bottle; (*de tartaruga*) shell
caseiro, -a [ka'zejru, a] ADJ home-made; (*pessoa, vida*) domestic ▶ M/F housekeeper
caso ['kazu] M case; (*tb*: **~ amoroso**) affair; (*estória*) story ▶ CONJ in case, if; **no ~ de** in case (of); **em todo ~** in any case; **neste ~** in that case; **~ necessário** if necessary; **criar ~** to cause trouble; **não fazer ~ de** to ignore; **~ de emergência** emergency
caspa ['kaspa] F dandruff
casquinha [kas'kiɲa] F (*de sorvete*)

cone; (*pele*) skin
cassar [ka'sar] VT (*direitos, licença*) to cancel, withhold; (*políticos*) to ban
cassete [ka'sɛtʃi] M cassette
cassino [ka'sinu] M casino
castanha [kas'taɲa] F chestnut; **~ de caju** cashew nut;
castanha-do-pará [-pa'ra] (*pl* **castanhas-do-pará**) F Brazil nut
castanheiro [kasta'ɲejru] M chestnut tree
castanho, -a [kas'taɲu, a] ADJ brown
castelo [kas'tɛlu] M castle
castiçal [kastʃi'saw] (*pl* **-ais**) M candlestick
castiço, -a [kas'tʃisu, a] ADJ pure
castidade [kastʃi'dadʒi] F chastity
castigar [kastʃi'gar] VT to punish;
castigo [kas'tʃigu] M punishment; (*fig: mortificação*) pain
casto, -a ['kastu, a] ADJ chaste
casual [ka'zwaw] (*pl* **-ais**) ADJ chance *atr*, accidental; (*fortuito*) fortuitous; **casualidade** [kazwali'dadʒi] F chance; (*acidente*) accident
cata ['kata] F: **à ~ de** in search of
catalizador, a [kataliza'dor(a)] ADJ catalytic ▶ M catalyst
catalogar [katalo'gar] VT to catalogue (BRIT), catalog (US)
catálogo [ka'talogu] M catalogue (BRIT), catalog (US); **~ (telefônico)** telephone directory
catapora [kata'pɔra] (BR) F chickenpox
catar [ka'tar] VT to pick (up); (*procurar*) to look for, search for; (*recolher*) to collect, gather
catarata [kata'rata] F waterfall; (*Med*) cataract
catarro [ka'tahu] M catarrh
catástrofe [ka'tastrofi] F catastrophe
cata-vento M weathercock
catedral [kate'draw] (*pl* **-ais**) F cathedral
categoria [katego'ria] F category; (*social*) rank; (*qualidade*) quality; **de alta ~** first-rate
cativar [katʃi'var] VT to enslave; (*fascinar*) to captivate; (*atrair*) to charm
cativeiro [katʃi'vejru] M captivity; (*escravidão*) slavery; (*cadeia*) prison
católico, -a [ka'tɔliku, a] ADJ, M/F Catholic
catorze [ka'torzi] NUM fourteen
catraca [ka'traka] F turnstile; **~ de embarque/desembarque** (*em estação*) ticket barrier
caução [kaw'sãw] (*pl* **-ões**) F security, guarantee; (*Jur*) bail; **sob ~** on bail
caule ['kauli] M stalk, stem
causa ['kawza] F cause; (*motivo*) motive, reason; (*Jur*) lawsuit, case; **por ~ de** because of; **causador, a** [kawza'dor(a)] ADJ which caused ▶ M cause; **causar** [kaw'zar] VT to cause, bring about
cautela [kaw'tɛla] F caution; (*senha*) ticket; **~ (de penhor)** pawn ticket; **cauteloso, -a** [kawte'lozu, ɔza] ADJ cautious, wary
cavado, -a [ka'vadu, a] ADJ (*olhos*) sunken; (*roupa*) low-cut
cavala [ka'vala] F mackerel
cavaleiro [kava'lejru] M rider, horseman; (*medieval*) knight
cavalheiro, -a [kava'ʎejru, a] ADJ courteous, gallant ▶ M gentleman
cavalo [ka'valu] M horse; (*Xadrez*) knight; **a ~** on horseback;

50 ~s(-vapor), 50 ~s de força 50 horsepower; **~ de corrida** racehorse
cavaquinho [kava'kiɲu] M small guitar
cavar [ka'var] VT to dig; (*esforçar-se para obter*) to try to get ▸ VI to dig; (*fig*) to delve; (*animal*) to burrow
cave ['kavi] (PT) F wine cellar
caveira [ka'vejra] F skull
cavidade [kavi'dadʒi] F cavity
caxumba [ka'ʃũba] F mumps *sg*
CD ABR M CD
cê [se] (*col*) PRON = **você**
cear [sjar] VT to have for supper ▸ VI to dine
cebola [se'bola] F onion; **cebolinha** [sebo'liɲa] F spring onion
ceder [se'der] VT to give up; (*dar*) to hand over; (*emprestar*) to lend ▸ VI to give in, yield; (*porta etc*) to give (way)
cedilha [se'dʒiʎa] F cedilla
cedo ['sedu] ADV early; (*em breve*) soon
cedro ['sɛdru] M cedar
cédula ['sɛdula] F banknote; (*eleitoral*) ballot paper
CEE ABR F (= *Comunidade Econômica Europeia*) EEC
cegar [se'gar] VT to blind; (*ofuscar*) to dazzle ▸ VI to be dazzling
cego, -a ['sɛgu, a] ADJ blind; (*total*) complete, total; (*tesoura*) blunt ▸ M/F blind man/woman; **às cegas** blindly
ceia ['seja] F supper
cela ['sɛla] F cell
celebração [selebra'sãw] (*pl* **-ões**) F celebration
celebrar [sele'brar] VT to celebrate; (*exaltar*) to praise; (*acordo*) to seal
celebridade [selebri'dadʒi] F celebrity
celeiro [se'lejru] M granary; (*depósito*) barn
celeste [se'lɛstʃi] ADJ celestial, heavenly
celibatário, -a [seliba'tarju, a] ADJ unmarried, single ▸ M/F bachelor/spinster
celofane [selo'fani] M cellophane; **papel ~** cling film
célula ['sɛlula] F (*Bio, Elet*) cell;
celular [selu'lar] ADJ cellular ▸ N: **(telefone) celular** mobile (phone) (BRIT), cellphone (US); **celular com câmera** camera phone
cem [sẽ] NUM hundred
cemitério [semi'tɛrju] M cemetery, graveyard
cena ['sɛna] F scene; (*palco*) stage
cenário [se'narju] M scenery; (*Cinema*) scenario; (*de um acontecimento*) setting
cenoura [se'nora] F carrot
censo ['sẽsu] M census
censor, a [sẽ'sor(a)] M/F censor
censura [sẽ'sura] F censorship; (*reprovação*) censure, criticism;
censurar [sẽsu'rar] VT to censure; (*filme, livro etc*) to censor
centavo [sẽ'tavu] M cent; **estar sem um ~** to be penniless
centeio [sẽ'teju] M rye
centelha [sẽ'teʎa] F spark
centena [sẽ'tɛna] F hundred; **às ~s** in hundreds
centenário, -a [sẽte'narju, a] ADJ centenary ▸ M centenary
centígrado [sẽ'tʃigradu] M centigrade
centímetro [sẽ'tʃimetru] M centimetre (BRIT), centimeter (US)
cento ['sẽtu] M: **~ e um** one hundred and one; **por ~** per cent
centopeia [sẽto'peja] F centipede
central [sẽ'traw] (*pl* **-ais**) ADJ

central ▶ F (*de polícia etc*) head office; **~ elétrica** (electric) power station; **~ telefônica** telephone exchange; **centralizar** [sẽtrali'zar] VT to centralize
centrar [sẽ'trar] VT to centre (BRIT), center (US)
centro ['sẽtru] M centre (BRIT), center (US); (*de uma cidade*) town centre; **centroavante** [sẽtroa'vãtʃi] M (*Futebol*) centre forward
CEP ['sɛpi] (BR) ABR M (= *Código de Endereçamento Postal*) postcode (BRIT), zip code (US)
cera ['sera] F wax
cerâmica [se'ramika] F pottery
cerca ['serka] F fence ▶ PREP: **~ de** (*aproximadamente*) around, about; **~ viva** hedge
cercado, -a [ser'kadu, a] ADJ surrounded ▶ M enclosure; (*para animais*) pen; (*para crianças*) playpen
cercanias [serka'nias] FPL outskirts; (*vizinhança*) neighbourhood *sg* (BRIT), neighborhood *sg* (US)
cerco ['serku] M siege; **pôr ~ a** to besiege
cereal [se'rjaw] (*pl* **-ais**) M cereal
cérebro ['sɛrebru] M brain; (*fig*) brains *pl*
cereja [se'reʒa] F cherry
cerimônia [seri'monja] F ceremony
cerração [seha'sãw] F fog
cerrado, -a [se'hadu, a] ADJ shut, closed; (*denso*) thick ▶ M scrub(land)
certeza [ser'teza] F certainty; **com ~** certainly, surely; (*provavelmente*) probably; **ter ~ de** to be certain *ou* sure of; **ter ~ de que** to be sure that
certidão [sertʃi'dãw] (*pl* **-ões**) F certificate
certificado [sertʃifi'kadu] M certificate
certificar [sertʃifi'kar] VT to certify; (*assegurar*) to assure; **certificar-se** VR: **~-se de** to make sure of
certo, -a ['sɛrtu, a] ADJ certain, sure; (*exato, direito*) right; (*um, algum*) a certain ▶ ADV correctly; **na certa** certainly; **ao ~** for certain; **está ~** okay, all right
cerveja [ser'veʒa] F beer; **cervejaria** [serveʒa'ria] F (*fábrica*) brewery; (*bar*) bar, public house
cervical [servi'kaw] (*pl* **-ais**) ADJ cervical
cessação [sesa'sãw] F halting, ceasing
cessão [se'sãw] (*pl* **-ões**) F surrender
cessar [se'sar] VI to cease, stop; **sem ~** continually; **cessar-fogo** M INV cease-fire
cessões [se'sõjs] FPL *de* **cessão**
cesta ['sesta] F basket; **~ básica** food parcel
cesto ['sestu] M basket; (*com tampa*) hamper
cético, -a ['sɛtʃiku, a] M/F sceptic (BRIT), skeptic (US)
cetim [se'tʃĩ] M satin
céu [sɛw] M sky; (*Rel*) heaven; (*da boca*) roof
cevada [se'vada] F barley
CFTV ABR M (= *circuito fechado de TV*) CCTV
chá [ʃa] M tea
chácara ['ʃakara] F farm; (*casa de campo*) country house
chacina [ʃa'sina] F slaughter; **chacinar** [ʃasi'nar] VT (*matar*) to slaughter

chacota [ʃa'kɔta] F mockery
chafariz [ʃafa'riz] M fountain
chalé [ʃa'lɛ] M chalet
chaleira [ʃa'lejra] F kettle; (*bajulador*) crawler, toady
chama ['ʃama] F flame
chamada [ʃa'mada] F call; (*Mil*) roll call; (*Educ*) register; (*no jornal*) headline; **dar uma ~ em alguém** to tell sb off
chamar [ʃa'mar] VT to call; (*convidar*) to invite; (*atenção*) to attract ▶ VI to call; (*telefone*) to ring; **chamar-se** VR to be called; **chamo-me João** my name is John; **~ alguém de idiota/Dudu** to call sb an idiot/Dudu; **mandar ~** to summon, send for
chamariz [ʃama'riz] M decoy
chamativo, -a [ʃama'tʃivu, a] ADJ showy, flashy
chaminé [ʃami'nɛ] F chimney; (*de navio*) funnel
champanha [ʃã'paɲa] M *ou* F champagne
champanhe [ʃã'paɲi] M *ou* F = **champanha**
champu [ʃã'pu] (PT) M shampoo
chance ['ʃãsi] F chance
chantagear [ʃãta'ʒjar] VT to blackmail
chantagem [ʃã'taʒẽ] F blackmail
chão [ʃãw] (*pl* **chãos**) M ground; (*terra*) soil; (*piso*) floor
chapa ['ʃapa] F (*placa*) plate; (*eleitoral*) list; **~ de matrícula** (PT *Auto*) number (BRIT) *ou* license (US) plate; **oi, meu ~!** hi, mate!
chapéu [ʃa'pɛw] M hat
charco ['ʃarku] M marsh, bog
charme ['ʃarmi] M charm; **fazer ~** to be nice, use one's charm; **charmoso, -a** [ʃar'mozu, ɔza] ADJ charming
charrete [ʃa'hɛtʃi] F cart
charuto [ʃa'rutu] M cigar
chassi [ʃa'si] M (*Auto, Elet*) chassis
chata ['ʃata] F barge; *ver tb* **chato**
chateação [ʃatʃja'sãw] (*pl* **-ões**) F bother, hassle; (*maçada*) bore
chatear [ʃa'tʃjar] VT to bother, upset; (*importunar*) to pester; (*entediar*) to bore; (*irritar*) to annoy ▶ VI to be upsetting; to be boring; to be annoying; **chatear-se** VR to get upset; to get bored; to get annoyed
chatice [ʃa'tʃisi] F nuisance
chato, -a ['ʃatu, a] ADJ flat; (*tedioso*) boring; (*irritante*) annoying; (*que fica mal*) rude ▶ M/F bore; (*quem irrita*) pain
chauvinista [ʃawvi'nista] ADJ chauvinistic ▶ M/F chauvinist
chavão [ʃa'vãw] (*pl* **-ões**) M cliché
chave ['ʃavi] F key; (*Elet*) switch; **~ de porcas** spanner; **~ inglesa** (monkey) wrench; **~ de fenda** screwdriver
chávena ['ʃavena] (PT) F cup
checar [ʃe'kar] VT to check
check-up [tʃe'kapi] (*pl* **-s**) M check-up
chefe ['ʃɛfi] M/F head, chief; (*patrão*) boss; **~ de estação** stationmaster; **chefia** [ʃe'fia] F leadership; (*direção*) management; (*repartição*) headquarters *sg*; **chefiar** [ʃe'fjar] VT to lead
chegada [ʃe'gada] F arrival
chegado, -a [ʃe'gadu, a] ADJ near; (*íntimo*) close
chegar [ʃe'gar] VT to bring near ▶ VI to arrive; (*ser suficiente*) to be enough; **chegar-se** VR: **~-se a** to approach; **chega!** that's enough!; **~ a** (*atingir*) to reach; (*conseguir*) to manage to

cheio, -a [ˈʃeju, a] ADJ full; (*repleto*) full up; (*col: farto*) fed up

cheirar [ʃejˈrar] VT, VI to smell; **~ a** to smell of; **cheiro** [ˈʃejru] M smell; **ter cheiro de** to smell of; **cheiroso, -a** [ʃejˈrozu, ɔza] ADJ: **ser** *ou* **estar cheiroso** to smell nice

cheque [ˈʃɛki] M cheque (BRIT), check (US); **~ de viagem** traveller's cheque (BRIT), traveler's check (US)

chiar [ʃjar] VI to squeak; (*porta*) to creak; (*vapor*) to hiss; (*col: reclamar*) to grumble

chiclete [ʃiˈklɛtʃi] M chewing gum

chicória [ʃiˈkɔrja] F chicory

chicote [ʃiˈkɔtʃi] M whip

chifre [ˈʃifri] M horn

Chile [ˈʃili] M: **o ~** Chile

chimarrão [ʃimaˈhãw] (*pl* **-ões**) M *mate tea without sugar taken from a pipe-like cup*

chimpanzé [ʃĩpãˈzɛ] M chimpanzee

China [ˈʃina] F: **a ~** China

chinelo [ʃiˈnɛlu] M slipper; **~ (de dedo)** flip-flop

chinês, -esa [ʃiˈnes, eza] ADJ, M/F Chinese ▸ M (*Ling*) Chinese

chip [ˈʃipi] M (*Comput*) chip

Chipre [ˈʃipri] F Cyprus

chique [ˈʃiki] ADJ stylish, chic

chocalho [ʃoˈkaʎu] M (*Mús, brinquedo*) rattle; (*para animais*) bell

chocante [ʃoˈkãtʃi] ADJ shocking; (*col*) amazing

chocar [ʃoˈkar] VT to hatch, incubate; (*ofender*) to shock, offend ▸ VI to shock; **chocar-se** VR to crash, collide; to be shocked

chocho, -a [ˈʃoʃu, a] ADJ hollow, empty; (*fraco*) weak; (*sem graça*) dull

chocolate [ʃokoˈlatʃi] M chocolate

chofer [ʃoˈfer] M driver

chope [ˈʃopi] M draught beer

choque[1] [ˈʃɔki] M shock; (*colisão*) collision; (*impacto*) impact; (*conflito*) clash

choque[2] [ˈʃɔki] VB *ver* **chocar**

choramingar [ʃoramĩˈgar] VI to whine, whimper

chorão, -rona [ʃoˈrãw, rɔna] (*pl* **-ões/-s**) ADJ tearful ▸ M/F crybaby ▸ M (*Bot*) weeping willow

chorar [ʃoˈrar] VT, VI to weep, cry

chorinho [ʃoˈriɲu] M *type of Brazilian music*

choro [ˈʃoru] M crying; (*Mús*) *type of Brazilian music*

choupana [ʃoˈpana] F shack, hut

chouriço [ʃoˈrisu] M (BR) black pudding; (PT) spicy sausage

chover [ʃoˈver] VI to rain; **~ a cântaros** to rain cats and dogs

chulé [ʃuˈlɛ] M foot odour (BRIT) *ou* odor (US)

chulo, -a [ˈʃulu, a] ADJ vulgar

chumbo [ˈʃũbu] M lead; (*de caça*) gunshot; (PT: *de dente*) filling; **sem ~** (*gasolina*) unleaded

chupar [ʃuˈpar] VT to suck

chupeta [ʃuˈpeta] F dummy (BRIT), pacifier (US)

churrasco [ʃuˈhasku] M barbecue; **churrasqueira** [ʃuhasˈkejra] F barbecue

churrasquinho [ʃuhasˈkiɲu] M kebab

chutar [ʃuˈtar] VT to kick; (*col: adivinhar*) to guess at; (*: dar o fora em*) to dump ▸ VI to kick; to guess; (*col: mentir*) to lie

chute [ˈʃutʃi] M kick; (*col: mentira*) lie; **dar o ~ em alguém** (*col*) to give sb the boot

chuteira [ʃuˈtejra] F football boot

chuva ['ʃuva] F rain; **chuveiro** [ʃu'vejru] M shower
chuviscar [ʃuvis'kar] VI to drizzle; **chuvisco** [ʃu'visku] M drizzle
chuvoso, -a [ʃu'vozu, ɔza] ADJ rainy
Cia. ABR (= *companhia*) Co
cibercafé [siberka'fɛ] M cybercafé
ciberespaço [siberis'pasu] M cyberspace
cicatriz [sika'triz] F scar; **cicatrizar** [sikatri'zar] VI to heal; (*rosto*) to scar
cicerone [sise'rɔni] M tourist guide
ciclismo [si'klizmu] M cycling
ciclista [si'klista] M/F cyclist
ciclo ['siklu] M cycle
ciclovia [siklo'via] F cycle path
cidadã [sida'dã] F *de* **cidadão**
cidadania [sidada'nia] F citizenship
cidadão, cidadã [sida'dãw] (*pl* **-s/-s**) M/F citizen
cidade [si'dadʒi] F town; (*grande*) city
ciência ['sjẽsja] F science
ciente ['sjẽtʃi] ADJ aware
científico, -a [sjẽ'tʃifiku, a] ADJ scientific
cientista [sjẽ'tʃista] M/F scientist
cifra ['sifra] F cipher; (*algarismo*) number, figure; (*total*) sum
cigano, -a [si'ganu, a] ADJ, M/F gypsy
cigarra [si'gaha] F cicada; (*Elet*) buzzer
cigarrilha [siga'hiʎa] F cheroot
cigarro [si'gahu] M cigarette
cilada [si'lada] F ambush; (*armadilha*) trap; (*embuste*) trick
cilindro [si'lĩdru] M cylinder; (*rolo*) roller
cima ['sima] F: **de ~ para baixo** from top to bottom; **para ~** up; **em ~ de** on, on top of; **por ~ de** over; **de ~** from above; **lá em ~** up there; (*em casa*) upstairs; **ainda por ~** on top of that
cimento [si'mẽtu] M cement; (*fig*) foundation
cimo ['simu] M top, summit
cinco ['sĩku] NUM five
cineasta [sine'asta] M/F film maker
cinema [si'nɛma] F cinema
Cingapura [sĩga'pura] F Singapore
cinquenta [sĩ'kwẽta] NUM fifty
cinta ['sĩta] F sash; (*de mulher*) girdle
cinto ['sĩtu] M belt; **~ de segurança** safety belt; (*Auto*) seat belt
cintura [sĩ'tura] F waist; (*linha*) waistline
cinza ['sĩza] ADJ INV grey (BRIT), gray (US) ▶ F ash, ashes *pl*
cinzeiro [sĩ'zejru] M ashtray
cinzento, -a [sĩ'zẽtu, a] ADJ grey (BRIT), gray (US)
cio [siu] M: **no ~** on heat, in season
cipreste [si'prɛstʃi] M cypress (tree)
cipriota [si'prjɔta] ADJ, M/F Cypriot
circo ['sirku] M circus
circuito [sir'kwitu] M circuit
circulação [sirkula'sãw] F circulation
circular [sirku'lar] ADJ circular ▶ F (*carta*) circular ▶ VI to circulate; (*girar, andar*) to go round ▶ VT to circulate; (*estar em volta de*) to surround; (*percorrer em roda*) to go round
círculo ['sirkulu] M circle
circundar [sirkũ'dar] VT to surround
circunferência [sirkũfe'rẽsja] F circumference
circunflexo, -a [sirkũ'flɛksu, a] ADJ circumflex ▶ M circumflex (accent)
circunstância [sirkũ'stãsja] F

circumstance; **~s atenuantes** mitigating circumstances

cirurgia [sirur'ʒia] F surgery; **~ plástica/estética** plastic/cosmetic surgery

cirurgião, -giã [sirur'ʒjãw, 'ʒjã] (*pl* **-ões/-s**) M/F surgeon

cisco ['sisku] M speck

cismado, -a [siz'madu, a] ADJ with fixed ideas

cismar [siz'mar] VI (*pensar*): **~ em** to brood over; (*antipatizar*): **~ com** to take a dislike to ▶ VT: **~ que** to be convinced that; **~ de** *ou* **em fazer** (*meter na cabeça*) to get into one's head to do; (*insistir*) to insist on doing

cisne ['sizni] M swan

cisterna [sis'tɛrna] F cistern, tank

citação [sita'sãw] (*pl* **-ões**) F quotation; (*Jur*) summons *sg*

citar [si'tar] VT to quote; (*Jur*) to summon

ciúme ['sjumi] M jealousy; **ter ~s de** to be jealous of; **ciumento, -a** [sju'mẽtu, a] ADJ jealous

cívico, -a ['siviku, a] ADJ civic

civil [si'viw] (*pl* **-is**) ADJ civil ▶ M/F civilian; **civilidade** [sivili'dadʒi] F politeness

civilização [siviliza'sãw] (*pl* **-ões**) F civilization

civis [si'vis] PL *de* **civil**

clamar [kla'mar] VT to clamour (BRIT) *ou* clamor (US) for ▶ VI to cry out, clamo(u)r

clamor [kla'mor] M outcry, uproar

clandestino, -a [klãdes'tʃinu, a] ADJ clandestine; (*ilegal*) underground

clara ['klara] F egg white

clarão [kla'rãw] (*pl* **-ões**) M (*cintilação*) flash; (*claridade*) gleam

clarear [kla'rjar] VI (*dia*) to dawn; (*tempo*) to clear up, brighten up ▶ VT to clarify

claridade [klari'dadʒi] F brightness

clarim [kla'rĩ] (*pl* **-ns**) M bugle

clarinete [klari'netʃi] M clarinet

clarins [kla'rĩs] MPL *de* **clarim**

claro, -a ['klaru, a] ADJ clear; (*luminoso*) bright; (*cor*) light; (*evidente*) clear, evident ▶ M (*na escrita*) space; (*clareira*) clearing ▶ ADV clearly; **~!** of course!; **~ que sim!/não!** of course!/of course not!; **às claras** openly

classe ['klasi] F class; **~ econômica/executiva** economy/business class

clássico, -a ['klasiku, a] ADJ classical; (*fig*) classic; (*habitual*) usual ▶ M classic

classificação [klasifika'sãw] (*pl* **-ões**) F classification; (*Esporte*) place, placing

classificado, -a [klasifi'kadu, a] ADJ (*em exame*) successful; (*anúncio*) classified; (*Esporte*) placed ▶ M classified ad

classificar [klasifi'kar] VT to classify; **classificar-se** VR: **~-se de algo** to call o.s. sth, describe o.s. as sth

cláusula ['klawzula] F clause

clausura [klaw'zura] F enclosure

clavícula [kla'vikula] F collar bone

clemência [kle'mẽsja] F mercy

clero ['klɛru] M clergy

clicar [kli'kar] VI (*Comput*) to click; **~ duas vezes em** to double-click on

cliente ['kljẽtʃi] M client; customer; (*de médico*) patient; **clientela** [kljẽ'tɛla] F clientele; (*de loja*) customers *pl*

C

clima ['klima] M climate
clímax ['klimaks] M INV climax
clipe ['klipi] M clip; (*para papéis*) paper clip
clique ['kliki] M (*Comput*) click
cloro ['klɔru] M chlorine
close ['klozi] M close-up
clube ['klubi] M club
coadjuvante [koadʒu'vãtʃi] ADJ supporting ▶ M/F (*num crime*) accomplice; (*Teatro, Cinema*) co-star
coador [koa'dor] M strainer; (*de café*) filter bag; (*para legumes*) colander
coalhada [koa'ʎada] F curd
coalizão [koali'zãw] (*pl* **-ões**) F coalition
coar [ko'ar] VT (*líquido*) to strain
coberta [ko'bɛrta] F cover, covering; (*Náut*) deck
cobertor [kober'tor] M blanket
cobertura [kober'tura] F covering; (*telhado*) roof; (*apartamento*) penthouse; (*TV, Rádio, Jornalismo*) coverage; (*Seguros*) cover; (*Tel*) network coverage; **aqui não tem ~** there's no network coverage here
cobiça [ko'bisa] F greed
cobra ['kɔbra] F snake
cobrador, a [kobra'dor(a)] M/F collector; (*em transporte*) conductor; **~ de ônibus** bus conductor
cobrança [ko'brãsa] F collection; (*ato de cobrar*) charging
cobrar [ko'brar] VT to collect; (*preço*) to charge
cobre ['kɔbri] M copper; **cobres** MPL (*dinheiro*) money *sg*
cobrir [ko'brir] VT to cover
cocada [ko'kada] F coconut sweet
cocaína [koka'ina] F cocaine
coçar [ko'sar] VT to scratch ▶ VI to itch; **coçar-se** VR to scratch o.s.
cócegas ['kɔsegas] FPL: **fazer ~ em** to tickle; **tenho ~ nos pés** I have tickly feet; **sentir ~** to be ticklish
coceira [ko'sejra] F itch; (*qualidade*) itchiness
cochichar [koʃi'ʃar] VI to whisper; **cochicho** [ko'ʃiʃu] M whispering
cochilar [koʃi'lar] VI to snooze, doze; **cochilo** [ko'ʃilu] M nap
coco ['koku] M coconut
cócoras ['kɔkoras] FPL: **de ~** squatting; **ficar de ~** to squat (down)
código ['kɔdʒigu] M code; **~ de barras** bar code
coelho [ko'eʎu] M rabbit
coerente [koe'rẽtʃi] ADJ coherent; (*consequente*) consistent
cofre ['kɔfri] M safe; (*caixa*) strongbox; **os ~s públicos** public funds
cogitar [koʒi'tar] VT, VI to contemplate
cognitivo, -a [kogni'tʃivu, a] ADJ cognitive
cogumelo [kogu'mɛlu] M mushroom; **~ venenoso** toadstool
coice ['kojsi] M kick; (*de arma*) recoil; **dar ~s em** to kick
coincidência [koĩsi'dẽsja] F coincidence
coincidir [koĩsi'dʒir] VI to coincide; (*concordar*) to agree
coisa ['kojza] F thing; (*assunto*) matter; **~ de** about
coitado, -a [koj'tadu, a] ADJ poor, wretched
cola ['kɔla] F glue
colaborador, a [kolabora'dor(a)] M/F collaborator; (*em jornal*) contributor
colaborar [kolabo'rar] VI to collaborate; (*ajudar*) to help; (*escrever artigos etc*) to contribute
colante [ko'lãtʃi] ADJ (*roupa*) skin-tight

colapso [ko'lapsu] M collapse; **~ cardíaco** heart failure
colar [ko'lar] VT to stick, glue; (BR: *copiar*) to crib ▶ VI to stick; to cheat ▶ M necklace
colarinho [kola'riɲu] M collar
colarinho-branco (*pl* **colarinhos-brancos**) M white-collar worker
colcha ['kowʃa] F bedspread
colchão [kow'ʃãw] (*pl* **-ões**) M mattress
colchete [kow'ʃetʃi] M clasp, fastening; (*parêntese*) square bracket; **~ de gancho** hook and eye; **~ de pressão** press stud, popper
colchões [kow'ʃõjs] MPL *de* **colchão**
coleção [kole'sãw] (*pl* **coleções**) F collection; **colecionador, a** [kolesjona'dor(a)] M/F collector; **colecionar** [kolesjo'nar] VT to collect
colega [ko'lɛga] M/F colleague; (*de escola*) classmate
colegial [kole'ʒjaw] (*pl* **-ais**) M/F schoolboy/girl
colégio [ko'lɛʒu] M school
coleira [ko'lejra] F collar
cólera ['kɔlera] F anger ▶ M *ou* F (*Med*) cholera
colesterol [koleste'rɔw] M cholesterol
colete [ko'letʃi] M waistcoat (BRIT), vest (US); **~ salva-vidas** life jacket (BRIT), life preserver (US)
coletivo, -a [kole'tʃivu, a] ADJ collective; (*transportes*) public ▶ M bus
colheita [ko'ʎejta] F harvest
colher [ko'ʎer] VT to gather, pick; (*dados*) to gather ▶ F spoon; **~ de chá/sopa** teaspoon/tablespoon
colidir [koli'dʒir] VI: **~ com** to collide with, crash into
coligação [koliga'sãw] (*pl* **-ões**) F coalition
colina [ko'lina] F hill
colisão [koli'zãw] (*pl* **-ões**) F collision
collant [ko'lã] (*pl* **-s**) M tights *pl* (BRIT), pantihose (US); (*blusa*) leotard
colmeia [kow'meja] F beehive
colo ['kɔlu] M neck; (*regaço*) lap
colocar [kolo'kar] VT to put, place; (*empregar*) to find a job for, place; (*Com*) to market; (*pneus, tapetes*) to fit; (*questão, ideia*) to put forward
Colômbia [ko'lõbja] F: **a ~** Colombia
colônia [ko'lonja] F colony; (*perfume*) cologne; **colonial** [kolo'njaw] (*pl* **-ais**) ADJ colonial
colonizador, a [koloniza'dor(a)] M/F colonist, settler
coloquial [kolo'kjaw] (*pl* **-ais**) ADJ colloquial
colóquio [ko'lɔkju] M conversation; (*congresso*) conference
colorido, -a [kolo'ridu, a] ADJ colourful (BRIT), colorful (US) ▶ M colouring (BRIT), coloring (US)
colorir [kolo'rir] VT to colour (BRIT), color (US)
coluna [ko'luna] F column; (*pilar*) pillar; **~ dorsal** *ou* **vertebral** spine; **colunável** [kolu'navew] (*pl* **-eis**) ADJ famous ▶ M/F celebrity; **colunista** [kolu'nista] M/F columnist
com [kõ] PREP with; **estar ~ fome** to be hungry; **~ cuidado** carefully; **estar ~ dinheiro/câncer** to have some money on one/have cancer
coma ['kɔma] F coma
comandante [komã'dãtʃi] M

commander; (*Mil*) commandant; (*Náut*) captain
comandar [komã'dar] VT to command
comando [ko'mãdu] M command
combate [kõ'batʃi] M combat;
combater [kõba'ter] VT to fight; (*opor-se a*) to oppose ▶ VI to fight; **combater-se** VR to fight
combinação [kõbina'sãw] (*pl* **-ões**) F combination; (*Quím*) compound; (*acordo*) arrangement; (*plano*) scheme; (*roupa*) slip
combinar [kõbi'nar] VT to combine; (*jantar etc*) to arrange; (*fuga etc*) to plan ▶ VI (*roupas etc*) to go together; **combinar-se** VR to combine; (*pessoas*) to get on well together; **~ com** (*harmonizar-se*) to go with; **~ de fazer** to arrange to do; **combinado!** agreed!
comboio [kõ'boju] M (PT) train; (*de navios, carros*) convoy
combustível [kõbus'tʃivew] M fuel
começar [kome'sar] VT, VI to begin, start; **~ a fazer** to begin *ou* start to do
começo [ko'mesu] M beginning, start
comédia [ko'mɛdʒja] F comedy
comemorar [komemo'rar] VT to commemorate, celebrate
comentar [komẽ'tar] VT to comment on; (*maliciosamente*) to make comments about
comentário [komẽ'tarju] M comment, remark; (*análise*) commentary
comer [ko'mer] VT to eat; (*Damas, Xadrez*) to take, capture ▶ VI to eat; **dar de ~ a** to feed
comercial [komer'sjaw] (*pl* **-ais**) ADJ commercial; (*relativo ao negócio*) business *atr* ▶ M commercial
comercializar [komersjali'zar] VT to market
comerciante [komer'sjãtʃi] M/F trader
comércio [ko'mɛrsju] M commerce; (*tráfico*) trade; (*negócio*) business; (*lojas*) shops *pl*; **~ eletrônico** e-commerce; **~ justo** fair trade
comes ['kɔmis] MPL: **~ e bebes** food and drink
comestíveis [komes'tʃiveis] MPL foodstuffs, food *sg*
comestível [komes'tʃivew] (*pl* **-eis**) ADJ edible
cometer [kome'ter] VT to commit
comício [ko'misju] M (*Pol*) rally, meeting; (*assembleia*) assembly
cômico, -a ['komiku, a] ADJ comic(al) ▶ M comedian; (*de teatro*) actor
comida [ko'mida] F (*alimento*) food; (*refeição*) meal; **~ pronta** ready meal (BRIT), TV dinner (US)
comigo [ko'migu] PRON with me
comilão, -lona [komi'lãw, lɔna] (*pl* **-ões/-s**) ADJ greedy ▶ M/F glutton
comiserar [komize'rar] VT to move to pity; **comiserar-se** VR: **~-se (de)** to sympathize (with)
comissão [komi'sãw] (*pl* **-ões**) F commission; (*comitê*) committee
comissário [komi'sarju] M commissioner; (*Com*) agent; **~ de bordo** (*Aer*) steward; (*Náut*) purser
comissões [komi'sõjs] FPL *de* **comissão**
comitê [komi'te] M committee

PALAVRA-CHAVE

como ['kɔmu] ADV **1** (*modo*) as; **ela fez como eu pedi** she did as I asked; **como se** as if; **como quiser**

as you wish; **seja como for** be that as it may
2 (*assim como*) like; **ela tem olhos azuis como o pai** she has blue eyes like her father's; **ela trabalha numa loja, como a mãe** she works in a shop, as does her mother
3 (*de que maneira*) how; **como?** pardon?; **como!** what!; **como assim?** what do you mean?; **como não!** of course!
▶ CONJ (*porque*) as, since; **como estava tarde ele dormiu aqui** since it was late he slept here

comoção [komo'sãw] (*pl* **-ões**) F distress; (*revolta*) commotion
cômoda ['komoda] F chest of drawers (BRIT), bureau (US)
comodidade [komodʒi'dadʒi] F comfort; (*conveniência*) convenience
comodismo [komo'dʒizmu] M complacency
cômodo, -a ['komodu, a] ADJ comfortable; (*conveniente*) convenient ▶ M room
comovente [komo'vẽtʃi] ADJ moving, touching
comover [komo'ver] VT to move ▶ VI to be moving; **comover-se** VR to be moved
compacto, -a [kõ'paktu, a] ADJ compact; (*espesso*) thick; (*sólido*) solid ▶ M (*disco*) single
compadecer-se [kõpade'sersi] VR: **~ de** to pity
compadre [kõ'padri] M (*col*: *companheiro*) buddy, pal
compaixão [kõpaj'ʃãw] M compassion; (*misericórdia*) mercy
companheiro, -a [kõpa'ɲejru, a] M/F companion; (*colega*) friend; (*col*) buddy, mate
companhia [kõpa'ɲia] F company
comparação [kõpara'sãw] (*pl* **-ões**) F comparison
comparar [kõpa'rar] VT to compare; **~ com** to compare with; **~ a** to liken to
comparecer [kõpare'ser] VI to appear, make an appearance; **~ a uma reunião** to attend a meeting
comparsa [kõ'parsa] M/F (*Teatro*) extra; (*cúmplice*) accomplice
compartilhar [kõpartʃi'ʎar] VT to share ▶ VI: **~ de** to share in, participate in
compartimento [kõpartʃi'mẽtu] M compartment; (*aposento*) room
compasso [kõ'pasu] M (*instrumento*) pair of compasses; (*Mús*) time; (*ritmo*) beat
compatível [kõpa'tʃivew] (*pl* **-eis**) ADJ compatible
compensar [kõpẽ'sar] VT to make up for, compensate for; (*equilibrar*) to offset; (*cheque*) to clear
competência [kõpe'tẽsja] F competence, ability; (*responsabilidade*) responsibility;
competente [kõpe'tẽtʃi] ADJ competent; (*apropriado*) appropriate; (*responsável*) responsible
competição [kõpetʃi'sãw] (*pl* **-ões**) F competition
competidor, a [kõpetʃi'dor(a)] M/F competitor
competir [kõpe'tʃir] VI to compete; **~ a alguém** to be sb's responsibility; (*caber*) to be up to sb
competitivo, -a [kõpetʃi'tʃivu, a] ADJ competitive
compito [kõ'pitu] VB *ver* **competir**

complementar [kõplemẽ'tar] ADJ complementary ▸VT to supplement
complemento [kõple'mẽtu] M complement
completamente [kõpleta'mẽtʃi] ADV completely, quite
completar [kõple'tar] VT to complete; to fill up; **~ dez anos** to be ten
completo, -a [kõ'plɛtu, a] ADJ complete; (*cheio*) full (up); **por ~** completely
complexo, -a [kõ'plɛksu, a] ADJ complex ▸M complex
complicação [kõplika'sãw] (*pl* **-ões**) F complication
complicado, -a [kõpli'kadu, a] ADJ complicated
complicar [kõpli'kar] VT to complicate
complô [kõ'plo] M plot, conspiracy
componente [kõpo'nẽtʃi] ADJ, M component
compor [kõ'por] (*irreg: como* **pôr**) VT to compose; (*discurso, livro*) to write; (*arranjar*) to arrange ▸VI to compose; **compor-se** VR (*controlar-se*) to compose o.s.; **~-se de** to consist of
comportamento [kõporta'mẽtu] M behaviour (BRIT), behavior (US)
comportar [kõpor'tar] VT to put up with; **comportar-se** VR (*portar-se*) to behave; **~-se mal** to misbehave, behave badly
composição [kõpozi'sãw] (*pl* **-ões**) F composition; (*Tip*) typesetting
compositor, a [kõpozi'tor(a)] M/F composer; (*Tip*) typesetter
compota [kõ'pɔta] F fruit in syrup
compra ['kõpra] F purchase; **fazer ~s** to go shopping; **comprador, a** [kõpra'dor(a)] M/F buyer, purchaser
comprar [kõ'prar] VT to buy
compreender [kõprjen'der] VT to understand; (*constar de*) to comprise, consist of, be composed of; (*abranger*) to cover
compreensão [kõprjẽ'sãw] F understanding, comprehension; **compreensivo, -a** [kõprjẽ'sivu, a] ADJ understanding
compressa [kõ'prɛsa] F compress
comprido, -a [kõ'pridu, a] ADJ long; (*alto*) tall; **ao ~** lengthways
comprimento [kõpri'mẽtu] M length
comprimido, -a [kõpri'midu, a] ADJ compressed ▸M pill; tablet
comprimir [kõpri'mir] VT to compress
comprometer [kõprome'ter] VT to compromise; (*envolver*) to involve; (*arriscar*) to jeopardize; (*empenhar*) to pledge; **comprometer-se** VR: **~-se a** to undertake to, promise to
compromisso [kõpro'misu] M promise; (*obrigação*) commitment; (*hora marcada*) appointment; (*acordo*) agreement
comprovante [kõpro'vãtʃi] M receipt; **~ de residência** proof of address
comprovar [kõpro'var] VT to prove; (*confirmar*) to confirm
compulsivo, -a [kõpuw'sivu, a] ADJ compulsive
compulsório, -a [kõpuw'sɔrju, a] ADJ compulsory
computação [kõputa'sãw] F computer science, computing; **~ em nuvem** cloud computing
computador [kõputa'dor] M computer
computar [kõpu'tar] VT (*calcular*) to calculate; (*contar*) to count
comum [ko'mũ] (*pl* **-ns**) ADJ

ordinary, common; (*habitual*) usual; **em ~** in common
comungar [komũ'gar] VI to take communion
comunhão [komu'ɲãw] (*pl* **-ões**) F communion
comunicação [komunika'sãw] (*pl* **-ões**) F communication; (*mensagem*) message; (*acesso*) access
comunicado [komuni'kadu] M notice
comunicar [komuni'kar] VT, VI to communicate; **comunicar-se** VR to communicate; **~-se com** (*entrar em contato*) to get in touch with
comunidade [komuni'dadʒi] F community; **C~ (Econômica) Europeia** European (Economic) Community
comunismo [komu'nizmu] M communism; **comunista** [komu'nista] ADJ, M/F communist
comuns [ko'mũs] PL *de* **comum**
conceber [kõse'ber] VT, VI to conceive
conceder [kõse'der] VT to allow; (*outorgar*) to grant; (*dar*) to give ▶ VI: **~ em** to agree to
conceito [kõ'sejtu] M concept, idea; (*fama*) reputation; (*opinião*) opinion; **conceituado, -a** [kõsej'twadu, a] ADJ well thought of, highly regarded
concentração [kõsẽtra'sãw] (*pl* **-ões**) F concentration
concepção [kõsep'sãw] (*pl* **-ões**) F (*geração*) conception; (*noção*) idea, concept; (*opinião*) opinion
concerto [kõ'sertu] M concert
concessão [kõse'sãw] (*pl* **-ões**) F concession; (*permissão*) permission
concha ['kõʃa] F shell; (*para líquidos*) ladle
conchavo [kõ'ʃavu] M conspiracy
conciliar [kõsi'ljar] VT to reconcile
concluir [kõ'klwir] VT, VI to conclude
conclusão [kõklu'zãw] (*pl* **-ões**) F end; (*dedução*) conclusion
conclusões [kõklu'zõjs] FPL *de* **conclusão**
concordância [kõkor'dãsja] F agreement
concordar [kõkor'dar] VI, VT to agree
concorrência [kõko'hẽsja] F competition; (*a um cargo*) application
concorrente [kõko'hẽtʃi] M/F contestant; (*candidato*) candidate
concorrer [kõko'her] VI to compete; **~ a** to apply for
concretizar [kõkretʃi'zar] VT to make real; **concretizar-se** VR (*sonho*) to come true; (*ambições*) to be realized
concreto, -a [kõ'krɛtu, a] ADJ concrete ▶ M concrete
concurso [kõ'kursu] M contest; (*exame*) competition
conde ['kõdʒi] M count
condenar [kõde'nar] VT to condemn; (*Jur: sentenciar*) to sentence; (*: declarar culpado*) to convict
condensar [kõdẽ'sar] VT to condense; **condensar-se** VR to condense
condessa [kõ'desa] F countess
condimento [kõdʒi'mẽtu] M seasoning
condomínio [kõdo'minju] M condominium; **~ fechado** gated community
condução [kõdu'sãw] F driving; (*transporte*) transport; (*ônibus*) bus
condutor, a [kõdu'tor(a)] M/F (*de*

veículo) driver ▶ M (*Elet*) conductor
conduzir [kõdu'zir] VT (*levar*) to lead; (*Fís*) to conduct; **conduzir-se** VR to behave; **~ a** to lead to
cone ['kɔni] M cone
conectar [konek'tar] VT to connect
conexão [konek'sãw] (*pl* **-ões**) F connection; (*voo*) connecting flight
confecção [kõfek'sãw] (*pl* **-ões**) F making; (*de um boletim*) production; (*roupa*) ready-to-wear clothes *pl*; (*negócio*) *business selling ready-to-wear clothes*
confeccionar [kõfeksjo'nar] VT to make; (*fabricar*) to manufacture
confecções [kõfek'sõjs] FPL *de* **confecção**
confeitaria [kõfejta'ria] F patisserie
conferência [kõfe'rẽsja] F conference; (*discurso*) lecture
conferir [kõfe'rir] VT to check; (*comparar*) to compare; (*outorgar*) to grant ▶ VI to tally
confessar [kõfe'sar] VT, VI to confess; **confessar-se** VR to confess
confiança [kõ'fjãsa] F confidence; (*fé*) trust; **de ~** reliable; **ter ~ em alguém** to trust sb
confiar [kõ'fjar] VT to entrust; (*segredo*) to confide ▶ VI: **~ em** to trust; (*ter fé*) to have faith in
confiável [kõ'fjavew] (*pl* **-eis**) ADJ reliable
confidência [kõfi'dẽsja] F secret; **em ~** in confidence; **confidencial** [kõfidẽ'sjaw] (*pl* **-ais**) ADJ confidential
confirmação [kõfirma'sãw] (*pl* **-ões**) F confirmation
confirmar [kõfir'mar] VT to confirm
confiro [kõ'firu] VB *ver* **conferir**
confissão [kõfi'sãw] (*pl* **-ões**) F confession
conformar [kõfor'mar] VT to form ▶ VI: **~ com** to conform to; **conformar-se** VR: **~-se com** to resign o.s. to; (*acomodar-se*) to conform to
conforme [kõ'fɔrmi] PREP according to; (*dependendo de*) depending on ▶ CONJ (*logo que*) as soon as; (*como*) as, according to what; (*à medida que*) as; **você vai? — ~** are you going? — it depends
conformidade [kõformi'dadʒi] F agreement; **em ~ com** in accordance with
confortar [kõfor'tar] VT to comfort, console
confortável [kõfor'tavew] (*pl* **-eis**) ADJ comfortable
conforto [kõ'fortu] M comfort
confrontar [kõfrõ'tar] VT to confront; (*comparar*) to compare
confronto [kõ'frõtu] M confrontation; (*comparação*) comparison
confusão [kõfu'zãw] (*pl* **-ões**) F confusion; (*tumulto*) uproar; (*problemas*) trouble
confuso, -a [kõ'fuzu, a] ADJ confused; (*problema*) confusing
confusões [kõfu'zõjs] FPL *de* **confusão**
congelador [kõʒela'dor] M freezer, deep freeze
congelamento [kõʒela'mẽtu] M freezing; (*Econ*) freeze
congelar [kõʒe'lar] VT to freeze; **congelar-se** VR to freeze
congestão [kõʒes'tãw] F congestion; **congestionado, -a** [kõʒestʃjo'nadu, a] ADJ congested; (*olhos*) bloodshot; (*rosto*) flushed; **congestionamento** [kõʒestʃjona'mẽtu] M congestion; **um congestionamento (de**

tráfego) a traffic jam
congestionar [kõʒestʃjo'nar] VT to congest; **congestionar-se** VR (*rosto*) to go red
congressista [kõgre'sista] M/F congressman/woman
congresso [kõ'grɛsu] M congress, conference
conhaque [ko'ɲaki] M cognac, brandy
conhecedor, a [koɲese'dor(a)] ADJ knowing ▶ M/F connoisseur, expert
conhecer [koɲe'ser] VT to know; (*travar conhecimento com*) to meet; (*descobrir*) to discover; **conhecer-se** VR to meet; (*ter conhecimento*) to know each other
conhecido, -a [koɲe'sidu, a] ADJ known; (*célebre*) well-known ▶ M/F acquaintance
conhecimento [koɲesi'mẽtu] M knowledge; (*ideia*) idea; (*conhecido*) acquaintance; (*Com*) bill of lading; **conhecimentos** MPL (*informações*) knowledge *sg*; **levar ao ~ de alguém** to bring to sb's notice
conjugado [kõʒu'gadu] M studio
cônjuge ['kõʒuʒi] M spouse
conjunção [kõʒũ'sãw] (*pl* **-ões**) F union; (*Ling*) conjunction
conjuntivo [kõʒũ'tʃivu] (PT) M (*Ling*) subjunctive
conosco [ko'nosku] PRON with us
conquista [kõ'kista] F conquest; **conquistador, a** [kõkista'dor(a)] ADJ conquering ▶ M conqueror; **conquistar** [kõkis'tar] VT to conquer; (*alcançar*) to achieve; (*ganhar*) to win
consciência [kõ'sjẽsja] F conscience; (*percepção*) awareness; (*senso de responsabilidade*) conscientiousness
consciente [kõ'sjẽtʃi] ADJ conscious
conseguinte [kõse'gĩtʃi] ADJ: **por ~** consequently
conseguir [kõse'gir] VT to get, obtain; **~ fazer** to manage to do, succeed in doing
conselho [kõ'seʎu] M piece of advice; (*corporação*) council; **conselhos** MPL (*advertência*) advice *sg*; **~ de guerra** court martial; **C~ de ministros** (*Pol*) Cabinet
consentimento [kõsẽtʃi'mẽtu] M consent
consentir [kõsẽ'tʃir] VT to allow, permit; (*aprovar*) to agree to ▶ VI: **~ em** to agree to
consequência [kõse'kwẽsja] F consequence; **por ~** consequently
consertar [kõser'tar] VT to mend, repair; (*remediar*) to put right; **conserto** [kõ'sertu] M repair
conserva [kõ'serva] F pickle; **em ~** pickled
conservação [kõserva'sãw] F conservation; (*de vida, alimentos*) preservation
conservador, a [kõserva'dor(a)] ADJ conservative ▶ M/F (*Pol*) conservative
conservante [kõser'vãtʃi] M preservative
conservar [kõser'var] VT to preserve, maintain; (*reter, manter*) to keep, retain; **conservar-se** VR to keep
conservatório [kõserva'tɔrju] M conservatory
consideração [kõsidera'sãw] (*pl* **-ões**) F consideration; (*estima*) respect, esteem; **levar em ~** to take into account
considerar [kõside'rar] VT to

consider; (*prezar*) to respect ▶ VI to consider
considerável [kõside'ravew] (*pl* **-eis**) ADJ considerable
consigo¹ [kõ'sigu] PRON (*m*) with him; (*f*) with her; (*pl*) with them; (*com você*) with you
consigo² VB *ver* **conseguir**
consinto [kõ'sĩtu] VB *ver* **consentir**
consistente [kõsis'tẽtʃi] ADJ solid; (*espesso*) thick
consistir [kõsis'tʃir] VI: **~ em** to be made up of, consist of
consoante [kõso'ãtʃi] F consonant ▶ PREP according to ▶ CONJ: **~ prometera** as he had promised
consolação [kõsola'sãw] (*pl* **-ões**) F consolation
consolar [kõso'lar] VT to console
console [kõ'sɔli], **consola** [kõ'sɔla] F (*Comput*) console
consolidar [kõsoli'dar] VT to consolidate; (*fratura*) to knit ▶ VI to become solid; to knit together
consolo [kõ'solu] M consolation
consome [kõ'somi] VB *ver* **consumir**
consórcio [kõ'sɔrsju] M (*união*) partnership; (*Com*) consortium
conspiração [kõspira'sãw] (*pl* **-ões**) F plot, conspiracy
conspirar [kõspi'rar] VT, VI to plot
constante [kõs'tãtʃi] ADJ constant
constar [kõs'tar] VI to be in; **ao que me consta** as far as I know
constatar [kõsta'tar] VT to establish; (*notar*) to notice; (*evidenciar*) to show up
consternado, -a [kõster'nadu, a] ADJ depressed; (*desolado*) distressed
constipação [kõstʃipa'sãw] (*pl* **-ões**) F (PT) cold
constipado, -a [kõstʃi'padu, a] (PT) ADJ: **estar ~** to have a cold
constituição [kõstʃitwi'sãw] (*pl* **-ões**) F constitution
constituinte [kõstʃi'twĩtʃi] M/F (*deputado*) member ▶ F: **a C~** the Constituent Assembly
constituir [kõstʃi'twir] VT to constitute; (*formar*) to form; (*estabelecer*) to establish; (*nomear*) to appoint
constrangimento [kõstrãʒi'mẽtu] M constraint; (*acanhamento*) embarrassment
construção [kõstru'sãw] (*pl* **-ões**) F building, construction
construir [kõs'trwir] VT to build, construct
construtivo, -a [kõstru'tʃivu, a] ADJ constructive
construtor, a [kõstru'tor(a)] M/F builder
cônsul ['kõsuw] (*pl* **cônsules**) M consul; **consulado** [kõsu'ladu] M consulate
consulta [kõ'suwta] F consultation; **livro de ~** reference book; **horário de ~** surgery hours *pl* (BRIT), office hours *pl* (US); **consultar** [kõsuw'tar] VT to consult; **consultor, a** [kõsuw'tor(a)] M/F consultant
consultório [kõsuw'tɔrju] M surgery
consumidor, a [kõsumi'dor(a)] ADJ consumer *atr* ▶ M/F consumer
consumir [kõsu'mir] VT to consume; (*gastar*) to use up; **consumir-se** VR to waste away
consumo [kõ'sumu] M consumption; **artigos de ~** consumer goods
conta ['kõta] F count; (*em restaurante*) bill; (*fatura*) invoice; (*bancária*) account; (*de colar*) bead; **contas** FPL (*Com*) accounts; **levar**

ou **ter em ~** to take into account; **tomar ~ de** to take care of; (*dominar*) to take hold of; **afinal de ~s** after all; **dar-se ~ de** to realize; (*notar*) to notice; **~ corrente** current account; **~ de e-mail** *ou* **de correio eletrônico** email account

contabilista [kõtabi'lista] (PT) M/F accountant

contabilizar [kõtabili'zar] VT to write up, book

contacto [kõ'tatu] (PT) M = **contato**

contador, a [kõta'dor(a)] M/F (*Com*) accountant ▶ M (*Tec: medidor*) meter

contagiante [kõta'ʒjãtʃi] ADJ (*alegria*) contagious

contagiar [kõta'ʒjar] VT to infect

contágio [kõ'taʒju] M infection

contagioso, -a [kõta'ʒjozu, ɔza] ADJ (*doença*) contagious

contaminar [kõtami'nar] VT to contaminate

contanto que [kõ'tãtu ki] CONJ provided that

conta-quilómetros (PT) M INV speedometer

contar [kõ'tar] VT to count; (*narrar*) to tell; (*pretender*) to intend ▶ VI to count; **~ com** to count on; (*esperar*) to expect; **~ em fazer** to count on doing, expect to do

contatar [kõta'tar] VT to contact;

contato [kõ'tatu] M contact; **entrar em contato com** to get in touch with, contact

contemplar [kõtẽ'plar] VT to contemplate; (*olhar*) to gaze at

contemplativo, -a [kõtẽpla'tʃivu, a] ADJ (*pessoa*) thoughtful

contemporâneo, -a [kõtẽpo'ranju, a] ADJ, M/F contemporary

contentamento [kõtẽta'mẽtu] M (*felicidade*) happiness; (*satisfação*) contentment

contente [kõ'tẽtʃi] ADJ happy; (*satisfeito*) pleased, satisfied

contento [kõ'tẽtu] M: **a ~** satisfactorily

conter [kõ'ter] (*irreg: como* **ter**) VT to contain, hold; (*refrear*) to restrain, hold back; (*gastos*) to curb

contestação [kõtesta'sãw] (*pl* **-ões**) F challenge; (*negação*) denial

contestar [kõtes'tar] VT to dispute, contest; (*impugnar*) to challenge

conteúdo [kõte'udu] M contents *pl*; (*de um texto*) content

contexto [kõ'testu] M context

contigo [kõ'tʃigu] PRON with you

contíguo, -a [kõ'tʃigwu, a] ADJ: **~ a** next to

continental [kõtʃinẽ'taw] (*pl* **-ais**) ADJ continental

continente [kõtʃi'nẽtʃi] M continent

continuação [kõtʃinwa'sãw] F continuation

continuar [kõtʃi'nwar] VT, VI to continue; **~ falando** *ou* **a falar** to go on talking; **ela continua doente** she is still sick

continuidade [kõtʃinwi'dadʒi] F continuity

conto ['kõtu] M story, tale; (PT: *dinheiro*) 1000 escudos

contorcer [kõtor'ser] VT to twist;

contorcer-se VR to writhe

contornar [kõtor'nar] VT (*rodear*) to go round; (*ladear*) to skirt; (*fig: problema*) to get round

contorno [kõ'tornu] M outline; (*da terra*) contour; (*do rosto*) profile

contra ['kõtra] PREP against ▸ M: **os prós e os ~s** the pros and cons; **dar o ~ (a)** to be opposed (to)
contra-ataque M counterattack
contrabandear [kõtrabã'dʒjar] VT to smuggle; **contrabandista** [kõtrabã'dʒista] M/F smuggler; **contrabando** [kõtra'bãdu] M smuggling; (*artigos*) contraband
contraceptivo, -a [kõtrasep'tʃivu, a] ADJ contraceptive ▸ M contraceptive
contracheque [kõtra'ʃɛki] M pay slip (BRIT), check stub (US)
contradição [kõtradʒi'sãw] (*pl* **-ões**) F contradiction
contraditório, -a [kõtradʒi'tɔrju, a] ADJ contradictory
contradizer [kõtradʒi'zer] (*irreg: como* **dizer**) VT to contradict
contragosto [kõtra'gostu] M: **a ~** against one's will, unwillingly
contrair [kõtra'ir] VT to contract; (*hábito*) to form
contramão [kõtra'mãw] ADJ one-way ▸ F: **na ~** the wrong way down a one-way street
contraproducente [kõtraprodu'sẽtʃi] ADJ counterproductive
contrário, -a [kõ'trarju, a] ADJ (*oposto*) opposite; (*pessoa*) opposed; (*desfavorável*) unfavourable (BRIT), unfavorable (US), adverse ▸ M opposite; **do ~** otherwise; **pelo** *ou* **ao ~** on the contrary; **ao ~** the other way round
contrassenso M nonsense
contrastar [kõtras'tar] VT to contrast; **contraste** [kõ'trastʃi] M contrast
contratação [kõtrata'sãw] F (*de pessoal*) employment
contratar [kõtra'tar] VT (*serviços*) to contract; (*pessoal*) to employ, take on
contratempo [kõtra'tẽpu] M setback; (*aborrecimento*) upset; (*dificuldade*) difficulty
contrato [kõ'tratu] M contract; (*acordo*) agreement
contribuição [kõtribwi'sãw] (*pl* **-ões**) F contribution; (*imposto*) tax
contribuinte [kõtri'bwĩtʃi] M/F contributor; (*que paga impostos*) taxpayer
contribuir [kõtri'bwir] VT to contribute ▸ VI to contribute; (*pagar impostos*) to pay taxes
controlar [kõtro'lar] VT to control
controle [kõ'troli] M control; **~ remoto** remote control; **~ de crédito** (*Com*) credit control; **~ de qualidade** (*Com*) quality control
controvérsia [kõtro'vɛrsja] F controversy; (*discussão*) debate; **controverso, -a** [kõtro'vɛrsu, a] ADJ controversial
contudo [kõ'tudu] CONJ nevertheless, however
contumaz [kõtu'majz] ADJ obstinate, stubborn
contusão [kõtu'zãw] (*pl* **-ões**) F bruise
convenção [kõvẽ'sãw] (*pl* **-ões**) F convention; (*acordo*) agreement
convencer [kõvẽ'ser] VT to convince; (*persuadir*) to persuade; **convencer-se** VR: **~-se de** to be convinced about; **convencido, -a** [kõvẽ'sidu, a] ADJ convinced; (*col: imodesto*) conceited, smug
convencional [kõvẽsjo'naw] (*pl* **-ais**) ADJ conventional
convenções [kõvẽ'sõjs] FPL *de* **convenção**
conveniência [kõve'njẽsja] F convenience

conveniente [kõve'njẽtʃi] ADJ convenient, suitable; (*vantajoso*) advantageous
convênio [kõ'venju] M (*reunião*) convention; (*acordo*) agreement
convento [kõ'vẽtu] M convent
conversa [kõ'vɛrsa] F conversation; **~ fiada** idle talk; (*promessa falsa*) hot air
conversão [kõver'sãw] (*pl* **-ões**) F conversion
conversar [kõver'sar] VI to talk; to chat
conversões [kõver'sõjs] FPL *de* **conversão**
converter [kõver'ter] VT to convert
convés [kõ'vɛs] (*pl* **-eses**) M (*Náut*) deck
convexo, -a [kõ'vɛksu, a] ADJ convex
convicção [kõvik'sãw] (*pl* **-ões**) F conviction
convidado, -a [kõvi'dadu, a] M/F guest
convidar [kõvi'dar] VT to invite
convincente [kõvĩ'sẽtʃi] ADJ convincing
convir [kõ'vir] (*irreg*: *como* **vir**) VI to suit, be convenient; (*ficar bem*) to be appropriate; (*concordar*) to agree; **convém fazer isso o mais rápido possível** we must do this as soon as possible
convite [kõ'vitʃi] M invitation
convivência [kõvi'vẽsja] F living together; (*familiaridade*) familiarity, intimacy
conviver [kõvi'ver] VI: **~ com** (*viver em comum*) to live with; (*ter familiaridade*) to get on with;
convívio [kõ'vivju] M living together; (*familiaridade*) familiarity
convocar [kõvo'kar] VT to summon, call upon; (*reunião, eleições*) to call; (*para o serviço militar*) to call up
convosco [kõ'vosku] ADV with you
convulsão [kõvuw'sãw] (*pl* **-ões**) F convulsion
cooper ['kuper] M jogging; **fazer ~** to go jogging *ou* running
cooperação [koopera'sãw] F cooperation
cooperar [koope'rar] VI to cooperate
coordenada [koorde'nada] F coordinate
copa ['kɔpa] F (*de árvore*) top; (*torneio*) cup; **copas** FPL (*Cartas*) hearts
cópia ['kɔpja] F copy; **tirar ~ de** to copy; **copiadora** [kopja'dora] F duplicating machine
copiar [ko'pjar] VT to copy
copo ['kɔpu] M glass
coque ['kɔki] M (*penteado*) bun
coqueiro [ko'kejru] M (*Bot*) coconut palm
coquetel [koke'tɛw] (*pl* **-éis**) M cocktail; (*festa*) cocktail party
cor[1] [kɔr] M: **de ~** by heart
cor[2] [kor] F colour (BRIT), color (US); **de ~** colo(u)red
coração [kora'sãw] (*pl* **-ões**) M heart; **de bom ~** kind-hearted; **de todo o ~** wholeheartedly
corado, -a [ko'radu, a] ADJ ruddy
coragem [ko'raʒẽ] F courage; (*atrevimento*) nerve
corais [ko'rajs] MPL *de* **coral**
corajoso, -a [kora'ʒozu, ɔza] ADJ courageous
coral [ko'raw] (*pl* **-ais**) M (*Mús*) choir; (*Zool*) coral
corar [ko'rar] VT (*roupa*) to bleach (in the sun) ▶ VI to blush; (*tornar-se*

branco) to bleach
corda ['kɔrda] F rope, line; (*Mús*) string; (*varal*) clothes line; (*de relógio*) spring; **dar ~ em** to wind up; **~s vocais** vocal chords
cordão [kor'dãw] (*pl* **-ões**) M string, twine; (*joia*) chain; (*no carnaval*) group; (*Elet*) lead; (*fileira*) row
cordeiro [kor'dejru] M lamb
cordel [kor'dɛw] (*pl* **-éis**) M string; **literatura de ~** pamphlet literature
cor-de-rosa ADJ INV pink
cordões [kor'dõjs] MPL *de* **cordão**
coreano, -a [ko'rjanu, a] ADJ Korean ▶ M/F Korean ▶ M (*Ling*) Korean
Coreia [ko'rɛja] F: **a ~** Korea
coreto [ko'retu] M bandstand
córner ['kɔrner] M (*Futebol*) corner
coro ['koru] M chorus; (*conjunto de cantores*) choir
coroa [ko'roa] F crown; (*de flores*) garland ▶ M/F (BR *col*) old timer
coroar [koro'ar] VT to crown; (*premiar*) to reward
coronel [koro'nɛw] (*pl* **-éis**) M colonel; (*político*) local political boss
corpo ['korpu] M body; (*aparência física*) figure; (: *de homem*) build; (*de vestido*) bodice; (*Mil*) corps *sg*; **de ~ e alma** (*fig*) wholeheartedly; **~ diplomático** diplomatic corps *sg*
corpulento, -a [korpu'lẽtu, a] ADJ stout
correção [kohe'sãw] (*pl* **-ões**) F correction; (*exatidão*) correctness; **casa de ~** reformatory
corre-corre [kɔhi'kɔhi] (*pl* **-s**) M (*pressa*) scramble; (*de muitas pessoas*) stampede
corredor, a [kohe'dor(a)] M/F runner ▶ M corridor; (*em avião etc*) aisle; (*cavalo*) racehorse
correia [ko'heja] F strap; (*de máquina*) belt; (*para cachorro*) leash
correio [ko'heju] M mail, post; (*local*) post office; (*carteiro*) postman (BRIT), mailman (US); **~ aéreo** air mail; **pôr no ~** to post; **~ eletrônico** email; **~ de voz** voice mail
corrente [ko'hẽtʃi] ADJ (*atual*) current; (*águas*) running; (*comum*) usual, common ▶ F current; (*cadeia, joia*) chain; **~ de ar** draught (BRIT), draft (US); **correnteza** [kohẽ'teza] F (*de ar*) draught (BRIT), draft (US); (*de rio*) current
correr [ko'her] VT to run; (*viajar por*) to travel across ▶ VI to run; (*em carro*) to drive fast, speed; (*o tempo*) to elapse; (*boato*) to go round; (*atuar com rapidez*) to rush; **correria** [kohe'ria] F rush
correspondência [kohespõ'dẽsja] F correspondence;
correspondente [kohespõ'dẽtʃi] ADJ corresponding ▶ M correspondent
corresponder [kohespõ'der] VI: **~ a** to correspond to; (*ser igual*) to match (up to); **corresponder-se** VR: **~-se com** to correspond with
correto, -a [ko'hɛtu, a] ADJ correct; (*conduta*) right; (*pessoa*) straight, honest
corretor, a [kohe'tor(a)] M/F broker; **~ de fundos** *ou* **de bolsa** stockbroker; **~ de imóveis** estate agent (BRIT), realtor (US); **~ ortográfico** spellchecker
corrida [ko'hida] F running; (*certame*) race; (*de taxi*) fare; **~ de cavalos** horse race
corrido, -a [ko'hidu, a] ADJ quick; (*expulso*) driven out ▶ ADV quickly
corrigir [kohi'ʒir] VT to correct
corriqueiro, -a [kohi'kejru, a] ADJ

common; (*problema*) trivial
corromper [koho͂'per] VT to corrupt; (*subornar*) to bribe; **corromper-se** VR to be corrupted
corrosão [koho'zãw] F corrosion; (*fig*) erosion
corrosivo, -a [koho'zivu, a] ADJ corrosive
corrupção [kohup'sãw] F corruption
corrupto, -a [ko'huptu, a] ADJ corrupt
Córsega ['kɔrsega] F: **a ~** Corsica
cortada [kor'tada] F: **dar uma ~ em alguém** (*fig*) to cut sb short
cortante [kor'tãtʃi] ADJ cutting
cortar [kor'tar] VT to cut; (*eliminar*) to cut out; (*água, telefone etc*) to cut off; (*efeito*) to stop ▶ VI to cut; (*encurtar caminho*) to take a short cut; **~ o cabelo** (*no cabeleireiro*) to have one's hair cut; **~ a palavra de alguém** to interrupt sb
corte[1] ['kɔrtʃi] M cut; (*de luz*) power cut; **sem ~** (*tesoura etc*) blunt; **~ de cabelo** haircut
corte[2] ['kortʃi] F court; **cortes** FPL (PT) parliament *sg*
cortejo [kor'teʒu] M procession
cortesia [korte'zia] F politeness; (*de empresa*) free offer
cortiça [kor'tʃisa] F cork
cortiço [kor'tʃisu] M slum tenement
cortina [kor'tʃina] F curtain
coruja [ko'ruʒa] F owl
corvo ['korvu] M crow
coser [ko'zer] VT, VI to sew
cosmético, -a [koz'mɛtʃiku, a] ADJ, M cosmetic
cospe ['kɔspi] VB *ver* **cuspir**
costa ['kɔsta] F coast; **costas** FPL (*dorso*) back *sg*; **dar as ~s a** to turn one's back on
Costa Rica F: **a ~** Costa Rica
costela [kos'tɛla] F rib
costeleta [koste'leta] F chop, cutlet; **costeletas** FPL (*suíças*) side-whiskers
costumar [kostu'mar] VT (*habituar*) to accustom ▶ VI: **ele costuma chegar às 6.00** he usually arrives at 6.00; **costumava dizer ...** he used to say ...
costume [kos'tumi] M custom, habit; (*traje*) costume; **costumes** MPL (*comportamento*) behaviour *sg* (BRIT), behavior *sg* (US); (*conduta*) conduct *sg*; (*de um povo*) customs; **de ~** usual; **como de ~** as usual
costura [kos'tura] F sewing; (*sutura*) seam; **costurar** [kostu'rar] VT, VI to sew; **costureira** [kostu'rejra] F dressmaker
cota ['kɔta] F quota, share
cotação [kota'sãw] (*pl* **-ões**) F (*de preços*) list, quotation; (*Bolsa*) price; (*consideração*) esteem; **~ bancária** bank rate
cotado, -a [ko'tadu, a] ADJ (*Com: ação*) quoted; (*bem-conceituado*) well thought of; (*num concurso*) fancied
cotar [ko'tar] VT (*ações*) to quote; **~ algo em** to value sth at
cotejar [kote'ʒar] VT to compare
cotidiano, -a [kotʃi'dʒjanu, a] ADJ daily, everyday ▶ M: **o ~** daily life
cotonete® [koto'nɛtʃi] M cotton bud (BRIT)
cotovelada [kotove'lada] F shove; (*cutucada*) nudge
cotovelo [koto'velu] M (*Anat*) elbow; (*curva*) bend; **falar pelos ~s** to talk non-stop

coube ['kobi] VB *ver* **caber**
couro ['koru] M leather; (*de um animal*) hide
couve ['kovi] F spring greens *pl*; **couve-flor** (*pl* **couves-flor(es)**) F cauliflower
couvert [ku'vɛr] M cover charge
cova ['kɔva] F pit; (*caverna*) cavern; (*sepultura*) grave
covarde [ko'vardʒi] ADJ cowardly ▶ M/F coward; **covardia** [kovar'dʒia] F cowardice
covil [ko'viw] (*pl* **-is**) M den, lair
covis [ko'vis] MPL *de* **covil**
coxa ['koʃa] F thigh
coxear [ko'ʃjar] VI to limp
coxia [ko'ʃia] F aisle, gangway
coxo, -a ['koʃu, a] ADJ lame
cozer [ko'zer] VT, VI to cook
cozido [ko'zidu] M stew
cozinha [ko'ziɲa] F kitchen; (*arte*) cookery; **~ planejada** fitted kitchen
cozinhar [kozi'ɲar] VT, VI to cook
cozinheiro, -a [kozi'ɲejru, a] M/F cook
CP ABR = **Caminhos de Ferro Portugueses**
CPF (BR) ABR M (= *Cadastro de Pessoa Física*) identification number
CPLP ABR F *see note*

> The **CPLP** o the *Comunidade de Países de Língua Portuguesa* was set up in 1996 to establish economic and diplomatic links between all countries where the official language is Portuguese. The members are Brazil, Portugal, Angola, Mozambique, Guinea-Bissau, Cape Verde and São Tomé e Príncipe. Portuguese is spoken by around 170 million people around the world today.

crachá [kra'ʃa] M badge
crânio ['kranju] M skull
craque ['kraki] M/F ace, expert
crasso, -a ['krasu, a] ADJ crass
cratera [kra'tɛra] F crater
cravar [kra'var] VT (*prego etc*) to drive (in); (*com os olhos*) to stare at; **cravar-se** VR to penetrate
cravo ['kravu] M carnation; (*Mús*) harpsichord; (*especiaria*) clove; (*na pele*) blackhead; (*prego*) nail
creche ['krɛʃi] F crèche, day-care centre
credenciais [kredẽ'sjajs] FPL credentials
creditar [kredʒi'tar] VT to guarantee; (*Com*) to credit; **~ algo a alguém** to credit sb with sth; (*garantir*) to assure sb of sth
crédito ['krɛdʒitu] M credit; **digno de ~** reliable
creme ['krɛmi] ADJ INV cream ▶ M cream; (*Culin: doce*) custard; **~ dental** toothpaste; **cremoso, -a** [kre'mozu, ɔza] ADJ creamy
crença ['krẽsa] F belief
crente ['krẽtʃi] M/F believer
crepúsculo [kre'puskulu] M dusk, twilight
crer [krer] VT, VI to believe; **crer-se** VR to believe o.s. to be; **~ em** to believe in; **creio que sim** I think so
crescer [kre'ser] VI to grow; **crescimento** [kresi'mẽtu] M growth
crespo, -a ['krespu, a] ADJ (*cabelo*) curly
cretinice [kretʃi'nisi] F stupidity; (*ato, dito*) stupid thing
cretino [kre'tʃinu] M cretin, imbecile
cria ['kria] F (*animal: sg*) baby animal; (*: pl*) young *pl*
criação [krja'sãw] (*pl* **-ões**) F creation; (*de animais*) raising,

breeding; *(educação)* upbringing; *(animais domésticos)* livestock *pl*; **filho de ~** adopted child
criado, -a ['krjadu, a] M/F servant
criador, a [krja'dor(a)] M/F creator; **~ de gado** cattle breeder
criança ['krjãsa] ADJ childish ▶ F child; **criançada** [krjã'sada] F: **a criançada** the kids
criar [krjar] VT to create; *(crianças)* to bring up; *(animais)* to raise; *(amamentar)* to suckle, nurse; *(planta)* to grow; **criar-se** VR: **~-se (com)** to grow up (with); **~ caso** to make trouble
criatura [kria'tura] F creature; *(indivíduo)* individual
crime ['krimi] M crime; **criminal** [krimi'naw] (*pl* **-ais**) ADJ criminal; **criminalidade** [kriminali'dadʒi] F crime; **criminoso, -a** [krimi'nozu, ɔza] ADJ, M/F criminal
crina ['krina] F mane
crioulo, -a ['krjolu, a] ADJ creole ▶ M/F creole; (BR: *negro*) Black (person)
criptografar [kriptogra'far] VT *Comput* to encrypt
crise ['krizi] F crisis; *(escassez)* shortage; *(Med)* attack, fit
crista ['krista] F *(de serra, onda)* crest; *(de galo)* cock's comb
cristal [kris'taw] (*pl* **-ais**) M crystal; *(vidro)* glass; **cristais** MPL *(copos)* glassware *sg*; **cristalino, -a** [krista'linu, a] ADJ crystal-clear
cristão, -tã [kris'tãw, 'tã] (*pl* **-s/-s**) ADJ, M/F Christian
cristianismo [kristʃja'nizmu] M Christianity
Cristo ['kristu] M Christ
critério [kri'tɛrju] M criterion; *(juízo)* discretion, judgement;
criterioso, -a [krite'rjozu, ɔza] ADJ thoughtful, careful
crítica ['kritʃika] F criticism; *ver tb* **crítico**
criticar [kritʃi'kar] VT to criticize; *(um livro)* to review
crítico, -a ['kritʃiku, a] ADJ critical ▶ M/F critic
crivar [kri'var] VT *(com balas etc)* to riddle
crivo ['krivu] M sieve
crocante [kro'kãtʃi] ADJ *(pão, alface)* crispy; *(nozes, chocolate)* crunchy
crônica ['kronika] F chronicle; *(coluna de jornal)* newspaper column; *(texto jornalístico)* feature; *(conto)* short story
crônico, -a ['kroniku, a] ADJ chronic
cronológico, -a [krono'lɔʒiku, a] ADJ chronological
croquete [kro'kɛtʃi] M croquette
cru, a [kru, 'krua] ADJ raw; *(não refinado)* crude
crucial [kru'sjaw] (*pl* **-ais**) ADJ crucial
crucificar [krusifi'kar] VT to crucify
crucifixo [krusi'fiksu] M crucifix
cruel [kru'ɛw] (*pl* **-éis**) ADJ cruel; **crueldade** [kruew'dadʒi] F cruelty
cruz [kruz] F cross; **C~ Vermelha** Red Cross
cruzado, -a [kru'zadu, a] ADJ crossed ▶ M *(moeda)* cruzado
cruzamento [kruza'mẽtu] M crossroads
cruzar [kru'zar] VT to cross ▶ VI *(Náut)* to cruise; *(pessoas)* to pass each other by; **~ com** to meet
cruzeiro [kru'zejru] M *(cruz)* *(monumental)* cross; *(moeda)* cruzeiro; *(viagem de navio)* cruise

cu [ku] (!) M arse (!); **vai tomar no cu** fuck off (!)
Cuba ['kuba] F Cuba
cubro ['kubru] VB *ver* **cobrir**
cuca ['kuka] (*col*) F head; **fundir a ~** (*quebrar a cabeça*) to rack one's brain; (*baratinar*) to boggle the mind; (*perturbar*) to drive crazy
cuco ['kuku] M cuckoo
cueca ['kwɛka] F (BR) underpants *pl*; **cuecas** FPL (PT) underpants *pl*; (*para mulheres*) panties *pl*
cuíca ['kwika] F *kind of musical instrument*
cuidado [kwi'dadu] M care; **aos ~s de** in the care of; **ter ~** to be careful; **~!** watch out!, be careful!; **tomar ~ (de)** to be careful (of); **cuidadoso, -a** [kwida'dozu, ɔza] ADJ careful
cuidar [kwi'dar] VI: **~ de** to take care of, look after; **cuidar-se** VR to look after o.s.
cujo, -a ['kuʒu, a] PRON (*de quem*) whose; (*de que*) of which
culinária [kuli'narja] F cookery
culpa ['kuwpa] F fault; (*Jur*) guilt; **ter ~ de** to be to blame for; **por ~ de** because of; **culpado, -a** [kuw'padu, a] ADJ guilty ▶ M/F culprit; **culpar** [kuw'par] VT to blame; (*acusar*) to accuse; **culpar-se** VR to take the blame; **culpável** [kuw'pavew] (*pl* **-eis**) ADJ guilty
cultivar [kuwtʃi'var] VT to cultivate; (*plantas*) to grow; **cultivo** [kuw'tʃivu] M cultivation
culto, -a ['kuwtu, a] ADJ cultured ▶ M (*homenagem*) worship; (*religião*) cult
cultura [kuw'tura] F culture; (*da terra*) cultivation; **cultural** [kuwtu'raw] (*pl* **culturais**) ADJ cultural
cume ['kumi] M top, summit; (*fig*) climax
cúmplice ['kũplisi] M/F accomplice
cumprimentar [kũprimẽ'tar] VT to greet; (*dar parabéns*) to congratulate
cumprimento [kũpri'mẽtu] M fulfilment; (*saudação*) greeting; (*elogio*) compliment; **cumprimentos** MPL (*saudações*) best wishes; **~ de uma lei/ordem** compliance with a law/an order
cumprir [kũ'prir] VT (*desempenhar*) to carry out; (*promessa*) to keep; (*lei*) to obey; (*pena*) to serve ▶ VI to be necessary; **~ a palavra** to keep one's word; **fazer ~** to enforce
cúmulo ['kumulu] M height; **é o ~!** that's the limit!
cunha ['kuɲa] F wedge
cunhado, -a [ku'ɲadu, a] M/F brother-in-law/sister-in-law
cunho ['kuɲu] M (*marca*) hallmark; (*caráter*) nature
cupim [ku'pĩ] (*pl* **-ns**) M termite
cupins [ku'pĩs] MPL *de* **cupim**
cúpula ['kupula] F dome; (*de abajur*) shade; (*de partido etc*) leadership; **(reunião de) ~** summit (meeting)
cura ['kura] F cure; (*tratamento*) treatment; (*de carnes etc*) curing, preservation ▶ M priest
curar [ku'rar] VT (*doença*) to cure; (*ferida*) to treat; **curar-se** VR to get well
curativo [kura'tʃivu] M dressing
curiosidade [kurjozi'dadʒi] F curiosity; (*objeto raro*) curio
curioso, -a [ku'rjozu, ɔza] ADJ curious ▶ M/F snooper, inquisitive person; **curiosos** MPL (*espectadores*) onlookers

curral [ku'haw] (*pl* **-ais**) M pen, enclosure

currículo [ku'hikulu] M (*curriculum*) curriculum vitae

cursar [kur'sar] VT (*aulas, escola*) to attend; (*cursos*) to follow; **ele está cursando História** he's studying *ou* doing history

curso ['kursu] M course; (*direção*) direction; **em ~** (*ano etc*) current; (*processo*) in progress

cursor [kur'sor] M (*Comput*) cursor

curtição [kurtʃi'sãw] F fun

curtir [kur'tʃir] VT (*couro*) to tan; (*tornar rijo*) to toughen up; (*padecer*) to suffer, endure; (*col*) to enjoy

curto, -a ['kurtu, a] ADJ short ▶ M (*Elet*) short (circuit); **curto-circuito** (*pl* **curtos-circuitos**) M short circuit

curva ['kurva] F curve; (*de estrada, rio*) bend; **~ fechada** hairpin bend

curvo, -a ['kurvu, a] ADJ curved; (*estrada*) winding

cuscuz [kus'kuz] M couscous

cuspe ['kuspi] M spit, spittle

cuspir [kus'pir] VT, VI to spit

custa ['kusta] F: **à ~ de** at the expense of; **custas** FPL (*Jur*) costs

custar [kus'tar] VI to cost; **~ a fazer** to have trouble doing; (*demorar*) to take a long time to do

custo ['kustu] M cost; **a ~** with difficulty; **a todo ~** at all costs

cutelo [ku'tɛlu] M cleaver

cutícula [ku'tʃikula] F cuticle

cutucar [kutu'kar] VT (*com o dedo*) to prod, poke; (*com o cotovelo*) to nudge

d

D ABR = **Dona**; (= *direito*) r; (= *deve*) d

d/ ABR = **dia**

da [da] = **de + a**

dá [da] VB *ver* **dar**

dactilografar [datilogra'far] (PT) = **datilografar** *etc*

dado, -a ['dadu, a] ADJ given; (*sociável*) sociable ▶ M (*em jogo*) die; (*fato*) fact; **dados** MPL dice; (*fatos, Comput*) data *sg*; **~ que** supposing that; (*uma vez que*) given that

daí [da'ji] ADV (= **de + aí**) (*desse lugar*) from there; (*desse momento*) from then; **~ a um mês** a month later

dali [da'li] ADV = **de + ali**

daltônico, -a [daw'toniku, a] ADJ colour-blind (BRIT), color-blind (US)

dama ['dama] F lady; (*Xadrez, Cartas*) queen; **damas** FPL (*jogo*) draughts (BRIT), checkers (US); **~ de honra** bridesmaid

damasco [da'masku] M apricot

danado, -a [da'nadu, a] ADJ damned; (*zangado*) furious;

(*menino*) mischievous

dança ['dãsa] F dance; **dançar** [dã'sar] VI to dance

danificar [danifi'kar] VT to damage

dano ['danu] M (*tb*: **~s**) damage; harm; (*a uma pessoa*) injury

dantes ['dãtʃis] ADV before, formerly

daquele, -a [da'kele, 'kɛla] = **de + aquele**

daqui [da'ki] ADV (= **de + aqui**) (*deste lugar*) from here; **~ a pouco** soon, in a little while; **~ a uma semana** a week from now; **~ em diante** from now on

daquilo [da'kilu] = **de + aquilo**

PALAVRA-CHAVE

dar [dar] VT **1** (*ger*) to give; (*festa*) to hold; (*problemas*) to cause; **dar algo a alguém** to give sb sth, give sth to sb; **dar de beber a alguém** to give sb a drink; **dar aula de francês** to teach French

2 (*produzir: fruta etc*) to produce

3 (*notícias no jornal*) to publish

4 (*cartas*) to deal

5 (*+ n, perífrase de vb*): **me dá medo/pena** it frightens/upsets me

▶ VI **1**: **dar com** (*coisa*) to find; (*pessoa*) to meet

2: **dar em** (*bater*) to hit; (*resultar*) to lead to; (*lugar*) to come to

3: **dá no mesmo** it's all the same

4: **dar de si** (*sapatos etc*) to stretch, give

5: **dar para** (*impess: ser possível*) to be able to; **dá para trocar dinheiro aqui?** can I change money here?; **vai dar para eu ir amanhã** I'll be able to go tomorrow; **dá para você vir amanhã? — não, amanhã não vai dar** can you come tomorrow? — no, I can't

6 (*ser suficiente*): **dar para/para fazer** to be enough for/to do; **dá para todo mundo?** is there enough for everyone?

dar-se VR **1** (*sair-se*): **dar-se bem/mal** to do well/badly

2: **dar-se (com alguém)** to be acquainted (with sb); **dar-se bem (com alguém)** to get on well (with sb)

3: **dar-se por vencido** to give up

das [das] = **de + as**

data ['data] F date; (*época*) time; **datar** [da'tar] VT to date ▶ VI: **datar de** to date from

datilografar [datʃilogra'far] VT to type; **datilografia** [datʃilogra'fia] F typing; **datilógrafo, -a** [datʃi'lɔgrafu, a] M/F typist (BRIT), stenographer (US)

d.C. ABR (= *depois de Cristo*) A.D.

DDD ABR F (= *discagem direta a distância*) *direct long-distance dialling* ▶ ABR M (*código*) dialling code (BRIT), area code (US)

DDI ABR F (= *discagem direta internacional*) IDD ▶ ABR M (*código de país*) country code

PALAVRA-CHAVE

de [dʒi] (*de + o(s)/a(s) = do(s)/da(s); + ele(s)/a(s) = dele(s)/a(s); + esse(s)/a(s) = desse(s)/a(s); + isso = disso; + este(s)/a(s) = deste(s)/a(s); + isto = disto; + aquele(s)/a(s) = daquele(s)/a(s); + aquilo = daquilo*) PREP **1** (*posse*) of; **a casa de João/da irmã** João's/my sister's house; **é dele** it's his; **um romance de** a novel by

2 (*origem, distância, com números*) from; **sou de São Paulo** I'm from

São Paulo; **de 8 a 20** from 8 to 20; **sair do cinema** to leave the cinema; **de dois em dois** two by two, two at a time
3 (*valor descritivo*): **um copo de vinho** a glass of wine; **um homem de cabelo comprido** a man with long hair; **o infeliz do homem** (*col*) the poor man; **um bilhete de avião** an air ticket; **uma criança de três anos** a three-year-old (child); **uma máquina de costurar** a sewing machine; **aulas de inglês** English lessons; **feito de madeira** made of wood; **vestido de branco** dressed in white
4 (*modo*): **de trem/avião** by train/plane; **de lado** sideways
5 (*hora, tempo*): **às 8 da manhã** at 8 o'clock in the morning; **de dia/noite** by day/night; **de hoje a oito dias** a week from now; **de dois em dois dias** every other day
6 (*comparações*): **mais/menos de cem pessoas** more/less than a hundred people; **é o mais caro da loja** it's the most expensive in the shop; **ela é mais bonita do que sua irmã** she's prettier than her sister; **gastei mais do que pretendia** I spent more than I intended
7 (*causa*): **estou morto de calor** I'm boiling hot; **ela morreu de câncer** she died of cancer
8 (*adj + de + infin*): **fácil de entender** easy to understand

dê [de] VB *ver* **dar**
debaixo [de'bajʃu] ADV below, underneath ▸ PREP: **~ de** under, beneath
debate [de'batʃi] M discussion, debate; (*disputa*) argument; **debater** [deba'ter] VT to debate; (*discutir*) to discuss; **debater-se** VR to struggle
débil ['debiw] (*pl* **-eis**) ADJ weak, feeble ▸ M: **~ mental** mentally handicapped person; **debilidade** [debili'dadʒi] F weakness; **debilidade mental** mental handicap; **debilitar** [debili'tar] VT to weaken; **debilitar-se** VR to become weak, weaken; **debiloide** [debi'lɔjdʒi] (*col*) ADJ idiotic ▸ M/F idiot
debitar [debi'tar] VT: **~ $40 à** *ou* **na conta de alguém** to debit $40 to sb's account; **débito** ['dɛbitu] M debit
debochado, -a [debo'ʃadu, a] ADJ (*pessoa*) sardonic; (*jeito, tom*) mocking
década ['dɛkada] F decade
decadência [deka'dẽsja] F decadence
decair [deka'ir] VI to decline
decente [de'sẽtʃi] ADJ decent; (*apropriado*) proper; (*honrado*) honourable (BRIT), honorable (US); (*trabalho*) neat; **decentemente** [desẽtʃi'mẽtʃi] ADV decently; (*apropriadamente*) properly; (*honradamente*) honourably (BRIT), honorably (US)
decepção [desep'sãw] (*pl* **-ões**) F disappointment; **decepcionar** [desepsjo'nar] VT to disappoint; (*desiludir*) to disillusion; **decepcionar-se** VR to be disappointed; to be disillusioned
decidir [desi'dʒir] VT to decide; (*solucionar*) to resolve; **decidir-se** VR: **~-se a** to make up one's mind to; **~-se por** to decide on, go for
decifrar [desi'frar] VT to decipher;

d

(*futuro*) to foretell; (*compreender*) to understand
decimal [desi'maw] (*pl* **-ais**) ADJ, M decimal
décimo, -a ['dɛsimu, a] ADJ tenth ▶ M tenth; *ver tb* **quinto**
decisão [desi'zãw] (*pl* **-ões**) F decision; **decisivo, -a** [desi'zivu, a] ADJ (*fator*) decisive; (*jogo*) deciding
declaração [deklara'sãw] (*pl* **-ões**) F declaration; (*depoimento*) statement
declarado, -a [dekla'radu, a] ADJ (*intenção*) declared; (*opinião*) professed; (*inimigo*) sworn; (*alcoólatra*) self-confessed; (*cristão etc*) avowed
declarar [dekla'rar] VT to declare; (*confessar*) to confess
declinar [dekli'nar] VT to decline ▶ VI (*sol*) to go down; (*terreno*) to slope down; **declínio** [de'klinju] M decline
declive [de'klivi] M slope, incline
decolagem [deko'laʒẽ] (*pl* **-ns**) F (*Aer*) take-off
decolar [deko'lar] VI (*Aer*) to take off
decompor [dekõ'por] (*irreg: como* **pôr**) VT to analyse; (*apodrecer*) to rot; **decompor-se** VR to rot, decompose
decomposição [dekõpozi'sãw] (*pl* **-ões**) F decomposition; (*análise*) dissection
decorar [deko'rar] VT to decorate; (*aprender*) to learn by heart; **decorativo, -a** [dekora'tʃivu, a] ADJ decorative
decoro [de'koru] M decency; (*dignidade*) decorum
decorrente [deko'hẽtʃi] ADJ: **~ de** resulting from
decorrer [deko'her] VI (*tempo*) to pass; (*acontecer*) to take place, happen ▶ M: **no ~ de** in the course of; **~ de** to result from
decrescer [dekre'ser] VI to decrease, diminish
decretar [dekre'tar] VT to decree, order; **decreto** [de'krɛtu] M decree, order; **decreto-lei** (*pl* **decretos-leis**) M act, law
dedetizar [dedetʃi'zar] VT to spray with insecticide
dedicação [dedʒika'sãw] F dedication; (*devotamento*) devotion
dedicar [dedʒi'kar] VT to dedicate; (*tempo, atenção*) to devote; **dedicar-se** VR: **~-se a** to devote o.s. to; **dedicatória** [dedʒika'tɔrja] F (*de obra*) dedication
dedo ['dedu] M finger; (*do pé*) toe; **~ anular** ring finger; **~ indicador** index finger; **~ mínimo** *ou* **mindinho** little finger
dedução [dedu'sãw] (*pl* **-ões**) F deduction
deduzir [dedu'zir] VT (*concluir*): **~ (de)** to deduce (from), infer (from); (*quantia*) to deduct
defasagem [defa'zaʒẽ] (*pl* **-ns**) F discrepancy
defeito [de'fejtu] M defect, flaw; **pôr ~s em** to find fault with; **com ~** broken, out of order; **para ninguém botar ~** (*col*) perfect; **defeituoso, -a** [defej'twozu, ɔza] ADJ defective, faulty
defender [defẽ'der] VT to defend; **defender-se** VR to stand up for o.s.; (*numa língua*) to get by
defensiva [defẽ'siva] F: **estar** *ou* **ficar na ~** to be on the defensive
defensor, a [defẽ'sor(a)] M/F defender; (*Jur*) defending counsel
defesa [de'feza] F defence (BRIT), defense (US); (*Jur*) counsel for the

defence ▶ M (*Futebol*) back
deficiente [defi'sjẽtʃi] ADJ (*imperfeito*) defective; (*carente*): **~ (em)** deficient (in)
déficit ['dɛfisitʃi] (*pl* **-s**) M deficit
definição [defini'sãw] (*pl* **-ões**) F definition
definir [defi'nir] VT to define; **definir-se** VR to make a decision; (*explicar-se*) to make one's position clear; **~-se a favor de/contra algo** to come out in favo(u)r of/against sth
definitivamente [definitʃiva'mẽtʃi] ADV definitively; (*permanentemente*) for good; (*sem dúvida*) definitely
definitivo, -a [defini'tʃivu, a] ADJ final, definitive; (*permanente*) permanent; (*resposta, data*) definite
defronte [de'frõtʃi] ADV opposite ▶ PREP: **~ de** opposite
defumar [defu'mar] VT (*presunto*) to smoke; (*perfumar*) to perfume
defunto, -a [de'fũtu, a] ADJ dead ▶ M/F dead person
degelar [deʒe'lar] VT to thaw; (*geladeira*) to defrost ▶ VI to thaw out; to defrost
degradar [degra'dar] VT to degrade, debase; **degradar-se** VR to demean o.s.
degrau [de'graw] M step; (*de escada de mão*) rung
degustação [degusta'sãw] (*pl* **-ões**) F tasting, sampling; (*saborear*) savouring (BRIT), savoring (US)
degustar [degus'tar] VT (*provar*) to taste; (*saborear*) to savour (BRIT), savor (US)
dei [dej] VB *ver* **dar**
deitada [dej'tada] (*col*) F: **dar uma ~** to have a lie-down
deitado, -a [dej'tadu, a] ADJ (*estendido*) lying down; (*na cama*) in bed
deitar [dej'tar] VT to lay down; (*na cama*) to put to bed; (*colocar*) to put, place; (*lançar*) to cast; (PT: *líquido*) to pour; **deitar-se** VR to lie down; to go to bed; **~ sangue** (PT) to bleed; **~ abaixo** to knock down, flatten; **~ a fazer algo** to start doing sth; **~ uma carta** (PT) to post a letter; **~ fora** (PT) to throw away *ou* out; **~ e rolar** (*col*) to do as one likes
deixa ['dejʃa] F clue, hint; (*Teatro*) cue; (*chance*) chance
deixar [dej'ʃar] VT to leave; (*abandonar*) to abandon; (*permitir*) to let, allow ▶ VI: **~ de** (*parar*) to stop; (*não fazer*) to fail to; **não posso ~ de ir** I must go; **~ cair** to drop; **~ alguém louco** to drive sb crazy *ou* mad; **~ alguém cansado/nervoso** *etc* to make sb tired/nervous *etc*; **deixa disso!** (*col*) come off it!; **deixa para lá!** (*col*) forget it!
dela ['dɛla] = **de + ela**
delatar [dela'tar] VT (*pessoa*) to inform on; (*abusos*) to reveal; (*à polícia*) to report; **delator, a** [dela'tor(a)] M/F informer
dele ['deli] = **de + ele**
delegacia [delega'sia] F office; **~ de polícia** police station
delegado, -a [dele'gadu, a] M/F delegate, representative; **~ de polícia** police chief
delegar [dele'gar] VT to delegate
deleitar [delej'tar] VT to delight; **deleitar-se** VR: **~-se com** to delight in
delgado, -a [dew'gadu, a] ADJ

thin; (*esbelto*) slim; (*fino*) fine
deliberação [delibera'sãw] (*pl* **-ões**) F deliberation; (*decisão*) decision
deliberar [delibe'rar] VT to decide, resolve ▶ VI to deliberate
delicadeza [delika'deza] F delicacy; (*cortesia*) kindness
delicado, -a [deli'kadu, a] ADJ delicate; (*frágil*) fragile; (*cortês*) polite; (*sensível*) sensitive
delícia [de'lisja] F delight; (*prazer*) pleasure; **que ~!** how lovely!; **deliciar** [deli'sjar] VT to delight; **deliciar-se** VR: **deliciar-se com algo** to take delight in sth
delicioso, -a [deli'sjozu, ɔza] ADJ lovely; (*comida, bebida*) delicious
delinear [deli'njar] VT to outline
delinquente [delĩ'kwẽtʃi] ADJ, M/F delinquent, criminal
delirar [deli'rar] VI (*com febre*) to be delirious; (*de ódio, prazer*) to go mad, go wild
delírio [de'lirju] M (*Med*) delirium; (*êxtase*) ecstasy; (*excitação*) excitement
delito [de'litu] M (*crime*) crime; (*falta*) offence (BRIT), offense (US)
demais [dʒi'majs] ADV (*em demasia*) too much; (*muitíssimo*) a lot, very much ▶ PRON: **os/as ~** the rest (of them); **já é ~!** this is too much!; **é bom ~** it's really good; **foi ~** (*col: bacana*) it was great
demanda [de'mãda] F lawsuit; (*disputa*) claim; (*requisição*) request; (*Econ*) demand; **em ~ de** in search of; **demandar** [demã'dar] VT (*Jur*) to sue; (*exigir, reclamar*) to demand
demasia [dema'zia] F excess, surplus; (*imoderação*) lack of moderation; **em ~** (*dinheiro, comida etc*) too much; (*cartas, problemas etc*) too many
demasiadamente [demazjada'mẽtʃi] ADV too much; (*com adj*) too
demasiado, -a [dema'zjadu, a] ADJ too much; (*pl*) too many ▶ ADV too much; (*com adj*) too
demitir [demi'tʃir] VT to dismiss; (*col*) to sack, fire; **demitir-se** VR to resign
democracia [demokra'sia] F democracy
democrático, -a [demo'kratʃiku, a] ADJ democratic
demolir [demo'lir] VT to demolish, knock down; (*fig*) to destroy
demonstração [demõstra'sãw] (*pl* **-ões**) F demonstration; (*de amizade*) show, display; (*prova*) proof
demonstrar [demõs'trar] VT to demonstrate; (*provar*) to prove; (*amizade etc*) to show
demora [de'mɔra] F delay; (*parada*) stop; **sem ~** at once, without delay; **qual é a ~ disso?** how long will this take?; **demorado, -a** [demo'radu, a] ADJ slow; **demorar** [demo'rar] VT to delay, slow down ▶ VI (*permanecer*) to stay; (*tardar a vir*) to be late; (*conserto*) to take (a long) time; **demorar-se** VR to stay for a long time, linger; **demorar a chegar** to be a long time coming; **vai demorar muito?** will it take long?; **não vou demorar** I won't be long
dendê [dẽ'de] M (*Culin: óleo*) palm oil; (*Bot*) oil palm
dengoso, -a [dẽ'gozu, ɔza] ADJ coy; (*criança: choraminguento*): **ser ~** to be a crybaby
dengue ['dẽgi] F (*Med*) dengue
denominar [denomi'nar] VT: **~ algo/alguém ...** to call sth/sb ...; **denominar-se** VR to be called; (*a si mesmo*) to call o.s.

denotar [deno'tar] VT (*indicar*) to show, indicate; (*significar*) to signify
densidade [dẽsi'dadʒi] F density
denso, -a [dẽsu, a] ADJ dense; (*espesso*) thick; (*compacto*) compact
dentada [dẽ'tada] F bite
dentadura [dẽta'dura] F teeth *pl*, set of teeth; (*artificial*) dentures *pl*
dente ['dẽtʃi] M tooth; (*de animal*) fang; (*de elefante*) tusk; (*de alho*) clove; **falar entre os ~s** to mutter, mumble; **~ de leite/do siso** milk/wisdom tooth; **~s postiços** false teeth
dentista [dẽ'tʃista] M/F dentist
dentre ['dẽtri] PREP (from) among
dentro ['dẽtru] ADV inside ▶ PREP: **~ de** inside; (*tempo*) (with)in; **de ~ para fora** inside out; **dar uma ~** (*col*) to get it right; **aí ~** in there; **por ~** on the inside; **estar por ~** (*col: fig*) to be in the know
denúncia [de'nũsja] F denunciation; (*acusação*) accusation; (*de roubo*) report;
denunciar [denũ'sjar] VT (*acusar*) to denounce; (*delatar*) to inform on; (*revelar*) to reveal
deparar [depa'rar] VT to reveal; (*fazer aparecer*) to present ▶ VI: **~ com** to come across, meet;
deparar-se VR: **~-se com** to come across, meet
departamento [departa'mẽtu] M department
dependência [depẽ'dẽsja] F dependence; (*edificação*) annexe (BRIT), annex (US); (*colonial*) dependency; (*cômodo*) room
dependente [depẽ'dẽtʃi] M/F dependant
depender [depẽ'der] VI: **~ de** to depend on
depilar [depi'lar] VT to wax;
depilatório [depila'tɔrju] M hair-remover
deplorável [deplo'ravew] (*pl* **-eis**) ADJ deplorable; (*lamentável*) regrettable
depoimento [depoj'mẽtu] M testimony, evidence; (*na polícia*) statement
depois [de'pojs] ADV afterwards ▶ PREP: **~ de** after; **~ de comer** after eating; **~ que** after
depor [de'por] (*irreg: como* **pôr**) VT (*pôr*) to place; (*indicar*) to indicate; (*rei*) to depose; (*governo*) to overthrow ▶ VI (*Jur*) to testify, give evidence; (*na polícia*) to give a statement
depositar [depozi'tar] VT to deposit; (*voto*) to cast; (*colocar*) to place
depósito [de'pɔzitu] M deposit; (*armazém*) warehouse, depot; (*de lixo*) dump; (*reservatório*) tank; **~ de bagagens** left-luggage office (BRIT), checkroom (US)
depreciação [depresja'sãw] F depreciation
depredar [depre'dar] VT to wreck
depressa [dʒi'prɛsa] ADV fast, quickly; **vamos ~** let's get a move on!
depressão [depre'sãw] (*pl* **-ões**) F depression
deprimente [depri'mẽtʃi] ADJ depressing
deprimido, -a [depri'midu, a] ADJ depressed
deprimir [depri'mir] VT to depress; **deprimir-se** VR to get depressed
deputado, -a [depu'tadu, a] M/F deputy; (*agente*) agent; (*Pol*)

≈ Member of Parliament (BRIT), ≈ Representative (US)

der [der] VB *ver* **dar**

deriva [de'riva] F drift; **ir à ~** to drift; **ficar à ~** to be adrift

derivar [deri'var] VT to divert; (*Ling*) to derive ▶ VI to drift; **derivar-se** VR to be derived; (*ir à deriva*) to drift; (*provir*): **~(-se) (de)** to derive *ou* be derived (from)

derradeiro, -a [deha'dejru, a] ADJ last, final

derramamento [dehama'mẽtu] M spilling; (*de sangue, lágrimas*) shedding

derramar [deha'mar] VT to spill; (*entornar*) to pour; (*sangue, lágrimas*) to shed; **derramar-se** VR to pour out

derrame [de'hami] M haemorrhage (BRIT), hemorrhage (US)

derrapar [deha'par] VI to skid

derreter [dehe'ter] VT to melt; **derreter-se** VR to melt; (*coisa congelada*) to thaw; (*enternecer-se*) to be touched

derrota [de'hɔta] F defeat, rout; (*Náut*) route; **derrotar** [deho'tar] VT (*vencer*) to defeat; (*em jogo*) to beat

derrubar [dehu'bar] VT to knock down; (*governo*) to bring down; (*suj: doença*) to lay low; (*col: prejudicar*) to put down

desabafar [dʒizaba'far] VT (*sentimentos*) to give vent to ▶ VI: **~ (com)** to unburden o.s. (to); **desabafar-se** VR: **~-se (com)** to unburden o.s. (to); **desabafo** [dʒiza'bafu] M confession

desabamento [dʒizaba'mẽtu] M collapse

desabar [dʒiza'bar] VI (*edifício, ponte*) to collapse; (*chuva*) to pour down; (*tempestade*) to break

desabitado, -a [dʒizabi'tadu, a] ADJ uninhabited

desabotoar [dʒizabo'twar] VT to unbutton

desabrigado, -a [dʒizabri'gadu, a] ADJ (*sem casa*) homeless; (*exposto*) exposed

desabrochar [dʒizabro'ʃar] VI (*flores, fig*) to blossom

desacatar [dʒizaka'tar] VT (*desrespeitar*) to have *ou* show no respect for; (*afrontar*) to defy; (*desprezar*) to scorn; **desacato** [dʒiza'katu] M disrespect; (*desprezo*) disregard

desaconselhar [dʒizakõse'ʎar] VT: **~ algo (a alguém)** to advise (sb) against sth

desacordado, -a [dʒizakor'dadu, a] ADJ unconscious

desacordo [dʒiza'kordu] M disagreement; (*desarmonia*) discord

desacostumado, -a [dʒizakostumadu, a] ADJ: **~ (a)** unaccustomed (to)

desacreditar [dʒizakredʒi'tar] VT to discredit; **desacreditar-se** VR to lose one's reputation

desafiador, a [dʒizafja'dor(a)] ADJ challenging; (*pessoa*) defiant ▶ M/F challenger

desafiar [dʒiza'fjar] VT to challenge; (*afrontar*) to defy

desafinado, -a [dʒizafi'nadu, a] ADJ out of tune

desafio [dʒiza'fiu] M challenge; (PT *Esporte*) match, game

desaforado, -a [dʒizafo'radu, a] ADJ rude, insolent

desaforo [dʒiza'foru] M insolence, abuse

desafortunado, -a

[dʒizafortu'nadu, a] ADJ unfortunate, unlucky
desagradar [dʒizagra'dar] VT to displease ▶ VI: **~ a alguém** to displease sb; **desagradável** [dʒizagra'davew] (*pl* **-eis**) ADJ unpleasant; **desagrado** [dʒiza'gradu] M displeasure
desaguar [dʒiza'gwar] VT to drain ▶ VI: **~ (em)** to flow *ou* empty (into)
desajeitado, -a [dʒizaʒej'tadu, a] ADJ clumsy, awkward
desalentado, -a [dʒizalẽ'tadu, a] ADJ disheartened
desalentar [dʒizalẽ'tar] VT to discourage; (*deprimir*) to depress; **desalento** [dʒiza'lẽtu] M discouragement
desalmado, -a [dʒizaw'madu, a] ADJ cruel, inhuman
desalojar [dʒizalo'ʒar] VT (*expulsar*) to oust; **desalojar-se** VR to move out
desamarrar [dʒizama'har] VT to untie ▶ VI (*Náut*) to cast off
desamor [dʒiza'mor] M dislike
desamparado, -a [dʒizãpa'radu, a] ADJ abandoned; (*sem apoio*) helpless
desanimação [dʒizanima'sãw] F dejection
desanimado, -a [dʒizani'madu, a] ADJ (*pessoa*) fed up, dispirited; (*festa*) dull; **ser ~** (*pessoa*) to be apathetic
desanuviar [dʒizanu'vjar] VT (*céu*) to clear; **desanuviar-se** VR to clear; (*fig*) to stop; **~ alguém** to put sb's mind at rest
desaparafusar [dʒizaparafu'zar] VT to unscrew
desaparecer [dʒizapare'ser] VI to disappear, vanish; **desaparecido, -a** [dʒizapare'sidu, a] ADJ lost, missing ▶ M/F missing person;
desaparecimento [dʒizaparesi'mẽtu] M disappearance; (*falecimento*) death
desapego [dʒiza'pegu] M indifference, detachment
desapercebido, -a [dʒizaperse'bidu, a] ADJ unnoticed
desapertar [dʒizaper'tar] VT to loosen; (*livrar*) to free
desapontamento [dʒizapõta'mẽtu] M disappointment
desapontar [dʒizapõ'tar] VT to disappoint
desapropriar [dʒizapro'prjar] VT (*bens*) to expropriate; (*pessoa*) to dispossess
desaprovar [dʒizapro'var] VT to disapprove of; (*censurar*) to object to
desarmamento [dʒizarma'mẽtu] M disarmament
desarmar [dʒizar'mar] VT to disarm; (*desmontar*) to dismantle; (*bomba*) to defuse
desarmonia [dʒizarmo'nia] F discord
desarranjo [dʒiza'hãʒu] M disorder; (*enguiço*) breakdown; (*diarreia*) diarrhoea (BRIT), diarrhea (US)
desarrumado, -a [dʒizahu'madu, a] ADJ untidy, messy
desarrumar [dʒizahu'mar] VT to mess up; (*mala*) to unpack
desassossego [dʒizaso'segu] M (*inquietação*) disquiet; (*perturbação*) restlessness
desastrado, -a [dʒizas'tradu, a] ADJ clumsy
desastre [dʒi'zastri] M disaster;

(*acidente*) accident; (*de avião*) crash
desatar [dʒiza'tar] VT (*nó*) to undo, untie ▶ VI: **~ a fazer** to begin to do; **~ a chorar** to burst into tears; **~ a rir** to burst out laughing
desatento, -a [dʒiza'tẽtu, a] ADJ inattentive
desatinado, -a [dʒizatʃi'nadu, a] ADJ crazy, wild ▶ M/F lunatic
desatino [dʒiza'tʃinu] M madness; (*ato*) folly
desativar [dʒizatʃi'var] VT (*firma, usina*) to shut down; (*veículos*) to withdraw from service; (*bomba*) to deactivate, defuse
desatualizado, -a [dʒizatwali'zadu, a] ADJ out of date; (*pessoa*) out of touch
desavença [dʒiza'vẽsa] F (*briga*) quarrel; (*discórdia*) disagreement; **em ~** at loggerheads
desavergonhado, -a [dʒizavergo'ɲadu, a] ADJ shameless
desavisado, -a [dʒizavi'zadu, a] ADJ careless
desbastar [dʒizbas'tar] VT (*cabelo, plantas*) to thin (out); (*vegetação*) to trim
desbocado, -a [dʒizbo'kadu, a] ADJ foul-mouthed
desbotar [dʒizbo'tar] VT to discolour (BRIT), discolor (US) ▶ VI to fade
desbragadamente [dʒizbragada'mẽtʃi] ADV (*beber*) to excess; (*mentir*) blatantly
desbravar [dʒizbra'var] VT (*terras desconhecidas*) to explore
descabelar [dʒiskabe'lar] VT: **~ alguém** to mess up sb's hair; **descabelar-se** VR to get one's hair messed up
descabido, -a [dʒiska'bidu, a] ADJ improper; (*inoportuno*) inappropriate
descafeinado [dʒiskafej'nadu] ADJ decaffeinated ▶ N decaf
descalçar [dʒiskaw'sar] VT (*sapatos*) to take off; **descalçar-se** VR to take off one's shoes
descalço, -a [dʒis'kawsu, a] ADJ barefoot
descansado, -a [dʒiskã'sadu, a] ADJ calm, quiet; (*vagaroso*) slow; **fique ~** don't worry; **pode ficar ~ que ...** you can rest assured that ...
descansar [dʒiskã'sar] VT to rest; (*apoiar*) to lean ▶ VI to rest; to lean; **descanso** [dʒis'kãsu] M rest; (*folga*) break; (*para prato*) mat
descarregamento [dʒiskahega'mẽtu] M (*de carga*) unloading; (*Elet*) discharge
descarregar [dʒiskahe'gar] VT (*carga*) to unload; (*Elet*) to discharge; (*aliviar*) to relieve; (*raiva*) to vent, give vent to; (*arma*) to fire ▶ VI to unload; (*bateria*) to run out; **~ a raiva em alguém** to take it out on sb
descartar [dʒiskar'tar] VT to discard; **descartar-se** VR: **~-se de** to get rid of; **descartável** [dʒiskar'tavew] (*pl* **-eis**) ADJ disposable
descascar [dʒiskas'kar] VT (*fruta*) to peel; (*ervilhas*) to shell ▶ VI (*depois do sol*) to peel; (*cobra*) to shed its skin
descaso [dʒis'kazu] M disregard
descendência [desẽ'dẽsja] F descendants *pl*, offspring *pl*
descendente [desẽ'dẽtʃi] ADJ descending, going down ▶ M/F descendant
descer [de'ser] VT (*escada*) to go (*ou* come) down; (*bagagem*) to take down ▶ VI (*saltar*) to get off; (*baixar*) to go (*ou* come) down; **descida** [de'sida] F descent; (*declive*) slope;

...to) fall, drop
...ficar [dʒisklasifi'kar]
...isqualify; (*desacreditar*) to
...edit
...coberta [dʒisko'bɛrta] F
...iscovery; (*invenção*) invention
...escoberto, -a [dʒisko'bɛrtu, a]
PP *de* **descobrir** ▶ ADJ bare, naked; (*exposto*) exposed ▶ M overdraft; **a ~** openly; **conta a ~** overdrawn account; **pôr** *ou* **sacar a ~** (*conta*) to overdraw
descobridor, a [dʒiskobri'dor(a)] M/F discoverer; (*explorador*) explorer
descobrimento [dʒiskobri'mẽtu] M discovery; **Descobrimentos** MPL *see note*

Mainly due to the seafaring expertise of Henry the Navigator, Portugal enjoyed a period of unrivalled overseas expansion during the 15th century. He organized and financed several voyages to Africa, which eventually led to the rounding of the Cape of Good Hope in 1488 by Bartolomeu Dias. In 1497, Vasco da Gama became the first European to travel by sea to India, where he established a lucrative spice trade, and a few years later, in 1500, Pedro Álvares Cabral reached Brazil, which he claimed for Portugal. Brazil remained under Portuguese rule until 1822.

descobrir [dʒisko'brir] VT to discover; (*tirar a cobertura de*) to uncover; (*panela*) to take the lid off; (*averiguar*) to find out; (*enigma*) to solve
descolar [dʒisko'lar] VT to unstick ▶ VI: **a criança não descola da mãe** the child won't leave its mother's side
descolorante [dʒiskolo'rãtʃi] M bleach
descolorir [dʒiskolo'rir] VT to discolour (BRIT), discolor (US); (*cabelo*) to bleach ▶ VI to fade
descompostura [dʒiskõpos'tura] F (*repreensão*) dressing-down; (*insulto*) abuse; **passar uma ~ em alguém** to give sb a dressing-down; to hurl abuse at sb
desconcentrar [dʒiskõsẽ'trar] VT to distract; **desconcentrar-se** VR to lose one's concentration
desconfiado, -a [dʒiskõ'fjadu, a] ADJ suspicious, distrustful ▶ M/F suspicious person
desconfiança [dʒiskõ'fjãsa] F suspicion, distrust
desconfiar [dʒiskõ'fjar] VI to be suspicious; **~ de alguém** (*não ter confiança em*) to distrust sb; (*suspeitar*) to suspect sb; **~ que ...** to have the feeling that ...
desconfortável [dʒiskõfor'tavew] (*pl* **-eis**) ADJ uncomfortable
desconforto [dʒiskõ'fortu] M discomfort
desconhecer [dʒiskoɲe'ser] VT (*ignorar*) not to know; (*não reconhecer*) not to recognize; (*um benefício*) not to acknowledge; (*não admitir*) not to accept;
desconhecido, -a [dʒiskoɲe'sidu, a] ADJ unknown ▶ M/F stranger;
desconhecimento [dʒiskoɲesi'mẽtu] M ignorance
desconsolado, -a [dʒiskõso'ladu, a] ADJ miserable, disconsolate

d

descontar [dʒiskõ'tar] VT to deduct; (*não levar em conta*) to discount; (*não fazer caso de*) to make light of
descontentamento [dʒiskõtẽta'mẽtu] M discontent; (*desprazer*) displeasure
desconto [dʒis'kõtu] M discount; **com ~** at a discount; **dar um ~ (para)** (*fig*) to make allowances (for)
descontraído, -a [dʒiskõtra'idu, a] ADJ casual, relaxed
descontrair [dʒiskõtra'ir] VT to relax; **descontrair-se** VR to relax
descontrolar-se [dʒiskõtro'larsi] VR (*situação*) to get out of control; (*pessoa*) to lose one's self-control
desconversar [dʒiskõver'sar] VI to change the subject
descortesia [dʒiskorte'zia] F rudeness, impoliteness
descoser [dʒisko'zer] VT (*descosturar*) to unstitch; (*rasgar*) to rip apart; **descoser-se** VR to come apart at the seams
descrença [dʒis'krẽsa] F disbelief, incredulity
descrente [dʒis'krẽtʃi] ADJ sceptical (BRIT), skeptical (US) ▸ M/F sceptic (BRIT), skeptic (US)
descrever [dʒiskre'ver] VT to describe
descrição [dʒiskri'sãw] (*pl* **-ões**) F description
descriptografar [dʒiskrɪptogra'far] VT *Comput* to decrypt
descritivo, -a [dʒiskri'tʃivu, a] ADJ descriptive
descrito, -a [dʒis'kritu, a] PP *de* **descrever**
descubro [dʒis'kubru] VB *ver* **descobrir**
descuidar [dʒiskwi'dar] VT to neglect ▸ VI: **~ de** to neglect, disregard; **descuido** [dʒis'kwidu] M carelessness; (*negligência*) neglect; (*erro*) oversight, slip; **por descuido** inadvertently
desculpa [dʒis'kuwpa] F excuse; (*perdão*) pardon; **pedir ~s a alguém por** *ou* **de algo** to apologize to sb for sth; **desculpar** [dʒiskuw'par] VT to excuse; (*perdoar*) to pardon, forgive; **desculpar-se** VR to apologize; **desculpar algo a alguém** to forgive sb for sth; **desculpe!** (I'm) sorry, I beg your pardon; **desculpável** [dʒiskuw'pavew] (*pl* **-eis**) ADJ forgivable

PALAVRA-CHAVE

desde ['dezdʒi] PREP **1** (*lugar*): **desde ... até ...** from ... to ...; **andamos desde a praia até o restaurante** we walked from the beach to the restaurant
2 (*tempo, + adv, n*): **desde então** from then on, ever since; **desde já** (*de agora*) from now on; (*imediatamente*) at once, right now; **desde o casamento** since the wedding
3 (*tempo, + vb*) since; for; **conhecemo-nos desde 1978/há 20 anos** we've known each other since 1978/for 20 years; **não o vejo desde 1983** I haven't seen him since 1983
4 (*variedade*): **desde os mais baratos até os mais luxuosos** from the cheapest to the most luxurious
▸ CONJ: **desde que** since; **desde que comecei a trabalhar não o vi mais** I haven't seen him since I started work; **não saiu de casa**

desde que chegou he hasn't been out since he arrived

desdizer [dʒizdʒi'zer] (*irreg*: *como* **dizer**) VT to contradict; **desdizer-se** VR to go back on one's word

desdobrar [dʒizdo'brar] VT (*abrir*) to unfold; (*esforços*) to increase, redouble; (*tropas*) to deploy; (*bandeira*) to unfurl; (*dividir em grupos*) to split up; **desdobrar-se** VR to unfold; (*empenhar-se*) to work hard, make a big effort

desejar [dese'ʒar] VT to want, desire

desejo [de'zeʒu] M wish, desire; **desejoso, -a** [deze'ʒozu, ɔza] ADJ: **desejoso de algo** wishing for sth; **desejoso de fazer** keen to do

desembaraçar [dʒizẽbara'sar] VT (*livrar*) to free; (*cabelo*) to untangle; **desembaraçar-se** VR (*desinibir-se*) to lose one's inhibitions; **~-se de** to get rid of

desembaraço [dʒizẽba'rasu] M liveliness; (*facilidade*) ease; (*confiança*) self-assurance

desembarcar [dʒizẽbar'kar] VT (*carga*) to unload; (*passageiros*) to let off ▸ VI to disembark; **desembarque** [dʒizẽ'barki] M landing, disembarkation; **"desembarque"** (*no aeroporto*) "arrivals"

desembolsar [dʒizẽbow'sar] VT to spend

desembrulhar [dʒizẽbru'ʎar] VT to unwrap

desempacotar [dʒizẽpako'tar] VT to unpack

desempatar [dʒizẽpa'tar] VT to decide ▸ VI to decide the match (*ou* race *etc*); **desempate** [dʒizẽ'patʃi] M: **partida de desempate** (*jogo*) play-off, decider

desempenhar [dʒizẽpe'ɲar] VT (*cumprir*) to carry out, fulfil (BRIT), fulfill (US); (*papel*) to play; **desempenho** [dʒizẽ'pɛɲu] M performance; (*de obrigações etc*) fulfilment (BRIT), fulfillment (US)

desempregado, -a [dʒizẽpre'gadu, a] ADJ unemployed ▸ M/F unemployed person

desempregar-se [dʒizẽpre'garsi] VR to lose one's job

desemprego [dʒizẽ'pregu] M unemployment

desencadear [dʒizẽka'dʒjar] VT to unleash; (*despertar*) to provoke, trigger off ▸ VI (*chuva*) to pour; **desencadear-se** VR to break loose; (*tempestade*) to break

desencaixar [dʒizẽkaj'ʃar] VT to put out of joint; (*deslocar*) to dislodge; **desencaixar-se** VR to become dislodged

desencaixotar [dʒizẽkajʃo'tar] VT to unpack

desencarregar-se [dʒizẽkahe'garsi] VR (*de obrigação*) to discharge o.s.

desencontrar [dʒizẽkõ'trar] VT to keep apart; **desencontrar-se** VR (*não se encontrar*) to miss each other; (*perder-se um do outro*) to lose each other; **~-se de** to miss; to get separated from

desencorajar [dʒizẽkora'ʒar] VT to discourage

desencostar [dʒizẽkos'tar] VT to move away; **desencostar-se** VR: **~-se de** to move away from

desencriptar [dʒizẽkrip'tar] VT (*Comput, Tel*) to decrypt

d

desenfreado, -a [dʒizẽ'frjadu, a] ADJ wild
desenganado, -a [dʒizẽga'nadu, a] ADJ incurable; (*desiludido*) disillusioned
desenganar [dʒizẽga'nar] VT: **~ alguém** to disillusion sb; (*de falsas crenças*) to open sb's eyes; (*doente*) to give up hope of curing; **desenganar-se** VR to become disillusioned; (*sair de erro*) to realize the truth; **desengano** [dʒizẽ'ganu] M disillusionment; (*desapontamento*) disappointment
desengonçado, -a [dʒizẽgõ'sadu, a] ADJ (*malseguro*) rickety; (*pessoa*) ungainly
desenhar [deze'ɲar] VT to draw; (*Tec*) to design; **desenhar-se** VR (*destacar-se*) to stand out; (*figurar-se*) to take shape; **desenhista** [deze'ɲista] M/F (*Tec*) designer
desenho [de'zɛɲu] M drawing; (*modelo*) design; (*esboço*) sketch; (*plano*) plan; **~ animado** cartoon
desenlace [dʒizẽ'lasi] M outcome
desenrolar [dʒizẽho'lar] VT to unroll; (*narrativa*) to develop; **desenrolar-se** VR to unfold
desentender [dʒizẽtẽ'der] VT to misunderstand; **desentender-se** VR: **~-se com** to have a disagreement with; **desentendido, -a** [dʒizẽtẽ'dʒidu, a] ADJ: **fazer-se de desentendido** to pretend not to understand; **desentendimento** [dʒizẽtẽdʒi'mẽtu] M misunderstanding
desenterrar [dʒizẽte'har] VT (*cadáver*) to exhume; (*tesouro*) to dig up; (*descobrir*) to bring to light
desentupir [dʒizẽtu'pir] VT to unblock
desenvoltura [dʒizẽvow'tura] F self-confidence
desenvolver [dʒizẽvow'ver] VT to develop; **desenvolver-se** VR to develop; **desenvolvimento** [dʒizẽvowvi'mẽtu] M development; (*crescimento*) growth; **país em desenvolvimento** developing country
deserção [dezer'sãw] F desertion
desertar [deser'tar] VT to desert, abandon ▶ VI to desert; **deserto, -a** [de'zɛrtu, a] ADJ deserted ▶ M desert; **desertor, a** [dezer'tor(a)] M/F deserter
desesperado, -a [dʒizespe'radu, a] ADJ desperate; (*furioso*) furious
desesperador, a [dʒizespera'dor(a)] ADJ desperate; (*enfurecedor*) maddening
desesperança [dʒizespe'rãsa] F despair
desesperar [dʒizespe'rar] VT to drive to despair; (*enfurecer*) to infuriate; **desesperar-se** VR to despair; (*enfurecer-se*) to become infuriated; **desespero** [dʒizes'peru] M despair, desperation; (*raiva*) fury
desestimular [dʒizestʃimu'lar] VT to discourage
desfalcar [dʒisfaw'kar] VT (*dinheiro*) to embezzle; (*reduzir*): **~ (de)** to reduce (by); **o jogo está desfalcado** the game is incomplete
desfalecer [dʒisfale'ser] VT (*enfraquecer*) to weaken ▶ VI (*enfraquecer*) to weaken; (*desmaiar*) to faint
desfalque [dʒis'fawki] M (*de dinheiro*) embezzlement; (*diminuição*) reduction
desfavorável [dʒisfavo'ravew] (*pl* **-eis**) ADJ unfavourable (BRIT), unfavorable (US)

desfazer [dʒisfa'zer] (*irreg: como* **fazer**) VT (*costura*) to undo; (*dúvidas*) to dispel; (*agravo*) to redress; (*grupo*) to break up; (*contrato*) to dissolve; (*noivado*) to break off ▶VI: **~ de alguém** to belittle sb; **desfazer-se** VR to vanish; (*tecido*) to come to pieces; (*grupo*) to break up; (*vaso*) to break; **~-se de** (*livrar-se*) to get rid of; **~-se em lágrimas/gentilezas** to burst into tears/go out of one's way to please

desfecho [dʒis'feʃu] M ending, outcome

desfeito, -a [dʒis'fejtu, a] ADJ undone; (*cama*) unmade; (*contrato*) broken

desfilar [dʒisfi'lar] VI to parade; **desfile** [dʒis'fili] M parade, procession

desforra [dʒis'fɔha] F revenge; (*reparação*) redress; **tirar ~** to get even

desfrutar [dʒisfru'tar] VT to enjoy ▶VI: **~ de** to enjoy

desgarrado, -a [dʒizga'hadu, a] ADJ stray; (*navio*) off course

desgastante [dʒizgas'tãtʃi] ADJ (*fig*) stressful

desgrudar [dʒizgru'dar] VT to unstick ▶VI: **~ de** to tear o.s. away from; **~ algo de algo** to take sth off sth

desidratar [dʒizidra'tar] VT to dehydrate

design [dʒi'zãjn] M design

designar [dezig'nar] VT to designate; (*nomear*) to name, appoint; (*dia, data*) to fix

desigual [dezi'gwaw] (*pl* **-ais**) ADJ unequal; (*terreno*) uneven; **desigualdade** [dʒizigwaw'dadʒi] F inequality

desiludir [dʒizilu'dʒir] VT to disillusion; (*causar decepção a*) to disappoint; **desiludir-se** VR to lose one's illusions

desimpedido, -a [dʒizĩpe'dʒidu, a] ADJ free

desinfetante [dʒizĩfe'tãtʃi] ADJ, M disinfectant

desinfetar [dʒizĩfe'tar] VT to disinfect

desinstalar [dʒizĩsta'lar] VT (*Comput*) to uninstall

desintegração [dʒizintegra'sãw] F disintegration, break-up

desintegrar [dʒizĩte'grar] VT to separate; **desintegrar-se** VR to disintegrate, fall to pieces

desistir [dezis'tʃir] VI to give up; **~ de fumar** to stop smoking; **ele ia, mas no final desistiu** he was going, but in the end he gave up the idea *ou* he decided not to

desjejum [dʒizʒe'ʒũ] M breakfast

deslavado, -a [dʒizla'vadu, a] ADJ (*pessoa, atitude*) shameless; (*mentira*) blatant

desleal [dʒizle'aw] (*pl* **-ais**) ADJ disloyal

desleixo [dʒiz'lejʃu] M sloppiness

desligado, -a [dʒizli'gadu, a] ADJ (*eletricidade*) off; (*pessoa*) absent-minded; **estar ~** to be miles away

desligar [dʒizli'gar] VT (*Tec*) to disconnect; (*luz, TV, motor*) to switch off; (*telefone*) to hang up; **desligar-se** VR: **~-se de algo** (*afastar-se*) to leave sth; (*problemas etc*) to turn one's back on sth; **não desligue** (*Tel*) hold the line

deslizar [dʒizli'zar] VI to slide; (*por acidente*) to slip; (*passar de leve*) to glide; **deslize** [dʒiz'lizi] M lapse; (*escorregadela*) slip

deslocado, -a [dʒizlo'kadu, a] ADJ (*membro*) dislocated; (*desambientado*) out of place
deslumbramento [dʒizlũbra'mẽtu] M dazzle; (*fascinação*) fascination
deslumbrante [dʒizlũ'brãtʃi] ADJ dazzling; (*casa, festa*) amazing
deslumbrar [dʒizlũ'brar] VT to dazzle; (*maravilhar*) to amaze; (*fascinar*) to fascinate ▸ VI to be dazzling; to be amazing; **deslumbrar-se** VR: **~-se com** to be fascinated by
desmaiado, -a [dʒizma'jadu, a] ADJ unconscious; (*cor*) pale
desmaiar [dʒizma'jar] VI to faint; **desmaio** [dʒiz'maju] M faint
desmanchar [dʒizman'ʃar] VT (*costura*) to undo; (*contrato*) to break; (*noivado*) to break off; (*penteado*) to mess up; **desmanchar-se** VR (*costura*) to come undone
desmarcar [dʒizmar'kar] VT (*compromisso*) to cancel
desmascarar [dʒizmaska'rar] VT to unmask
desmazelado, -a [dʒizmaze'ladu, a] ADJ slovenly, untidy
desmedido, -a [dʒizme'dʒidu, a] ADJ excessive
desmentido [dʒizmẽ'tʃidu] M (*negação*) denial; (*contradição*) contradiction
desmentir [dʒizmẽ'tʃir] VT (*contradizer*) to contradict; (*negar*) to deny
desmiolado, -a [dʒizmjo'ladu, a] ADJ brainless; (*esquecido*) forgetful
desmoronamento [dʒizmorona'mẽtu] M collapse
desmoronar [dʒizmoro'nar] VT to knock down ▸ VI to collapse
desnatado, -a [dʒizna'tadu, a] ADJ (*leite*) skimmed
desnaturado, -a [dʒiznatu'radu, a] ADJ inhumane ▸ M/F monster
desnecessário, -a [dʒiznese'sarju, a] ADJ unnecessary
desnutrição [dʒiznutri'sãw] F malnutrition
desobedecer [dʒizobede'ser] VT to disobey; **desobediência** [dʒizobe'dʒjẽsja] F disobedience; **desobediente** [dʒizobe'dʒjẽtʃi] ADJ disobedient
desobstruir [dʒizobis'trwir] VT to unblock
desocupado, -a [dʒizoku'padu, a] ADJ (*casa*) empty, vacant; (*disponível*) free; (*sem trabalho*) unemployed
desocupar [dʒizoku'par] VT (*casa*) to vacate; (*liberar*) to free
desodorante [dʒizodo'rãtʃi], (PT) **desodorizante** [dʒizodori'zãtʃi] M deodorant
desolação [dezola'sãw] F (*consternação*) grief; (*de um lugar*) desolation; **desolado, -a** [dezo'ladu, a] ADJ distressed; (*lugar*) desolate
desonesto, -a [dezo'nɛstu, a] ADJ dishonest
desordem [dʒi'zordẽ] F disorder, confusion; **em ~** (*casa*) untidy
desorganizar [dʒizorgani'zar] VT to disorganize; (*dissolver*) to break up; **desorganizar-se** VR to become disorganized; to break up
desorientação [dʒizorjẽta'sãw] F bewilderment, confusion
desorientar [dʒizorjẽ'tar] VT (*desnortear*) to throw off course; (*perturbar*) to confuse; (*desvairar*) to unhinge; **desorientar-se** VR to lose one's way; to get confused; to go mad

desovar [dʒizo'var] VT to lay; (*peixe*) to spawn
despachado, -a [dʒispa'ʃadu, a] ADJ (*pessoa*) efficient
despachar [dʒispa'ʃar] VT to dispatch, send off; (*atender, resolver*) to deal with; (*despedir*) to sack; **despachar-se** VR to hurry (up); **despacho** [dʒis'paʃu] M dispatch; (*de negócios*) handling; (*nota em requerimento*) ruling; (*reunião*) consultation; (*macumba*) witchcraft
despeço [dʒis'pɛsu] VB *ver* **despedir**
despedaçar [dʒispeda'sar] VT (*quebrar*) to smash; (*rasgar*) to tear apart; **despedaçar-se** VR to smash; to tear
despedida [dʒispe'dʒida] F farewell; (*de trabalhador*) dismissal
despedir [dʒispe'dʒir] VT (*de emprego*) to dismiss, sack; **despedir-se** VR: **~-se (de)** to say goodbye (to)
despeitado, -a [dʒispej'tadu, a] ADJ spiteful; (*ressentido*) resentful
despeito [dʒis'pejtu] M spite; **a ~ de** in spite of, despite
despejar [dʒispe'ʒar] VT (*água*) to pour; (*esvaziar*) to empty; (*inquilino*) to evict; **despejo** [dʒis'peʒu] M eviction; **quarto de despejo** junk room
despencar [dʒispẽ'kar] VI to fall down, tumble down
despentear [dʒispẽ'tʃjar] VT (*cabelo: sem querer*) to mess up; (*: de propósito*) to let down; **despentear-se** VR to mess one's hair up; to let one's hair down
despercebido, -a [dʒisperse'bidu, a] ADJ unnoticed
desperdiçar [dʒisperdʒi'sar] VT to waste; (*dinheiro*) to squander;
desperdício [dʒisper'dʒisju] M waste
despertador [dʒisperta'dor] M (*tb*: **relógio ~**) alarm clock
despertar [dʒisper'tar] VT to wake; (*suspeitas, interesse*) to arouse; (*reminiscências*) to revive; (*apetite*) to whet ▶ VI to wake up ▶ M awakening; **desperto, -a** [dʒis'pɛrtu, a] ADJ awake
despesa [dʒis'peza] F expense; **despesas** FPL (*de uma empresa*) expenses, costs; **~s gerais** (*Com*) overheads
despido, -a [dʒis'pidu, a] ADJ naked, bare; (*livre*) free
despir [dʒis'pir] VT (*roupa*) to take off; (*pessoa*) to undress; (*despojar*) to strip; **despir-se** VR to undress
despojar [dʒispo'ʒar] VT (*casas*) to loot, sack; (*pessoas*) to rob
despontar [dʒispõ'tar] VI to emerge; (*sol*) to come out; (*: ao amanhecer*) to come up; **ao ~ do dia** at daybreak
desporto [dʒis'portu] M sport
desprender [dʒisprẽ'der] VT to loosen; (*desatar*) to unfasten; (*emitir*) to emit; **desprender-se** VR (*botão*) to come off; (*cheiro*) to be given off
desprezar [dʒispre'zar] VT to despise, disdain; (*não dar importância a*) to disregard, ignore; **desprezível** [dʒispre'zivew] (*pl* **-eis**) ADJ despicable; **desprezo** [dʒis'prezu] M scorn, contempt; **dar ao desprezo** to ignore
desproporcional [dʒisproporsjo'naw] ADJ disproportionate
despropósito [dʒispro'pɔzitu] M nonsense

d

desprovido, -a [dʒispro'vidu, a] ADJ deprived; **~ de** without
desqualificar [dʒiskwalifi'kar] VT (*Esporte etc*) to disqualify; (*tornar indigno*) to disgrace, lower
desregrado, -a [dʒizhe'gradu, a] ADJ disorderly, unruly; (*devasso*) immoderate
desrespeito [dʒizhe'spejtu] M disrespect
desse[1], -a ['desi, a] = **de + esse, ~ a**
desse[2] VB *ver* **dar**
destacar [dʒista'kar] VT (*Mil*) to detail; (*separar*) to detach; (*enfatizar*) to emphasize ▶VI to stand out; **destacar-se** VR to stand out; (*pessoa*) to be outstanding
destampar [dʒistã'par] VT to take the lid off
destapar [dʒista'par] VT to uncover
destaque [dʒis'taki] M distinction; (*pessoa, coisa*) highlight
deste, -a ['destʃi, a] = **de + este, ~ a**
destemido, -a [deste'midu, a] ADJ fearless, intrepid
destilar [destʃi'lar] VT to distil (BRIT), distill (US)
destinação [destʃina'sãw] (*pl* **-ões**) F destination
destinar [des'tʃinar] VT to destine; (*dinheiro*): **~ (para)** to set aside (for); **destinar-se** VR: **~-se a** to be intended for; (*carta*) to be addressed to
destinatário, -a [destʃina'tarju, a] M/F addressee
destino [des'tʃinu] M destiny, fate; (*lugar*) destination; **com ~ a** bound for
destituir [destʃi'twir] VT to dismiss; **~ de** (*privar de*) to deprive of
destrancar [dʒistrã'kar] VT to unlock
destratar [dʒistra'tar] VT to abuse, insult
destreza [des'treza] F skill; (*agilidade*) dexterity
destro, -a ['dɛstru, a] ADJ skilful (BRIT), skillful (US); (*ágil*) agile; (*não canhoto*) right-handed
destrocar [dʒistro'kar] VT to give back, return
destroçar [dʒistro'sar] VT to destroy; (*quebrar*) to smash, break;
destroços [dʒis'trɔsus] MPL wreckage *sg*
destruição [dʒistrwi'sãw] F destruction
destruir [dʒis'trwir] VT to destroy
desvairado, -a [dʒizvaj'radu, a] ADJ (*louco*) crazy, demented; (*desorientado*) bewildered
desvalorizar [dʒizvalori'zar] VT to devalue
desvantagem [dʒizvã'taʒẽ] (*pl* **-ns**) F disadvantage
desvão [dʒiz'vãw] (*pl* **-s**) M loft
desventura [dʒizvẽ'tura] F misfortune; (*infelicidade*) unhappiness
desvio [dʒiz'viu] M diversion, detour; (*curva*) bend; (*fig*) deviation; (*de dinheiro*) embezzlement
detalhadamente [detaʎada'mẽtʃi] ADV in detail
detalhado, -a [deta'ʎadu, a] ADJ detailed
detalhe [de'taʎi] M detail
detectar [detek'tar] VT to detect
detector [detek'tor] M detector
detenção [detẽ'sãw] (*pl* **-ões**) F detention
deter [de'ter] (*irreg: como* **ter**) VT to stop; (*prender*) to arrest, detain; (*reter*) to keep; (*conter: riso*) to contain; **deter-se** VR to stop; (*ficar*) to stay; (*conter-se*) to restrain o.s.

detergente [deter'ʒẽtʃi] M detergent
deteriorar [deterjo'rar] VT to spoil, damage; **deteriorar-se** VR to deteriorate; (*relações*) to worsen
determinação [determina'sãw] F determination; (*decisão*) decision; (*ordem*) order
determinado, -a [determi'nadu, a] ADJ determined; (*certo*) certain, given
determinar [determi'nar] VT to determine; (*decretar*) to order; (*resolver*) to decide (on); (*causar*) to cause
detestar [detes'tar] VT to hate; **detestável** [detes'tavew] (*pl* **-eis**) ADJ horrible, hateful
detetive [dete'tʃivi] M/F detective
detido, -a [de'tʃidu, a] ADJ (*preso*) under arrest; (*minucioso*) thorough ▶ M/F person under arrest, prisoner
detonação [detona'sãw] (*pl* **-ões**) F explosion
detonar [deto'nar] VI, VT to detonate
detrás [de'trajs] ADV behind ▶ PREP: **~ de** behind
detrimento [detri'mẽtu] M: **em ~ de** to the detriment of
detrito [de'tritu] M debris *sg*; (*de comida*) remains *pl*; (*resíduo*) dregs *pl*
deturpação [deturpa'sãw] F corruption; (*de palavras*) distortion
deturpar [detur'par] VT to corrupt; (*desfigurar*) to disfigure; (*palavras*) to twist
deu [dew] VB *ver* **dar**
deus, a [dews, 'dewza] M/F god/goddess; **D~ me livre!** God forbid!; **graças a D~** thank goodness; **meu D~!** good Lord!
devagar [dʒiva'gar] ADV slowly
devaneio [deva'neju] M daydream
devassa [de'vasa] F investigation, inquiry
devassidão [devasi'dãw] F debauchery
devasso, -a [de'vasu, a] ADJ dissolute
deve ['dɛvi] M debit
dever [de'ver] M duty ▶ VT to owe ▶ VI (*suposição*): **deve (de) estar doente** he must be ill; (*obrigação*): **devo partir às oito** I must go at eight; **você devia ir ao médico** you should go to the doctor; **que devo fazer?** what shall I do?
devido, -a [de'vidu, a] ADJ (*maneira*) proper; (*respeito*) due; **~ a** due to, owing to; **no ~ tempo** in due course
devoção [devo'sãw] F devotion
devolução [devolu'sãw] F devolution; (*restituição*) return; (*reembolso*) refund; **~ de impostos** tax rebate
devolver [devow'ver] VT to give back, return; (*Com*) to refund
devorar [devo'rar] VT to devour; (*destruir*) to destroy
devotar [devo'tar] VT to devote
dez [dɛz] NUM ten
dezanove [deza'nɔvə] (PT) NUM = **dezenove**
dezasseis [deza'sejs] (PT) NUM = **dezesseis**
dezassete [deza'setə] (PT) NUM = **dezessete**
dezembro [de'zẽbru] M December
dezena [de'zena] F: **uma ~** ten
dezenove [deze'nɔvi] NUM nineteen
dezesseis [deze'sejs] NUM sixteen

dezessete [dezi'setʃi] NUM seventeen
dezoito [dʒi'zojtu] NUM eighteen
dia ['dʒia] M day; (*claridade*) daylight; **~ a ~** day by day; **~ santo** holy day; **~ útil** weekday; **estar** *ou* **andar em ~ (com)** to be up to date (with); **de ~** in the daytime, by day; **mais ~ menos ~** sooner or later; **~ sim, ~ não** every other day; **no ~ seguinte** the next day; **bom ~** good morning; **um ~ desses** one of these days; **~s a fio** days on end; **~ cheio/morto** busy/quiet *ou* slow day; **todo santo ~** (*col*) every single day, day after day; **recebo por ~** I'm paid by the day; **um bebê de ~s** a newborn baby; **ele está com os ~s contados** his days are numbered; **dia a dia** M daily life, everyday life
diabete, diabetes [dʒja'bɛtʃi(s)] F diabetes *sg*; **diabético, -a** [dʒja'bɛtʃiku, a] ADJ, M/F diabetic
diabo ['dʒjabu] M devil; **que ~!** (*col*) damn it!
diabrura [dʒja'brura] F prank; **diabruras** FPL (*travessura*) mischief *sg*
diagnóstico [dʒjag'nɔstʃiku] M diagnosis
diagonal [dʒjago'naw] (*pl* **-ais**) ADJ, F diagonal
diagrama [dʒja'grama] M diagram
dialeto [dʒja'lɛtu] M dialect
dialogar [dʒjalo'gar] VI: **~ (com alguém)** to talk (to sb); (*Pol*) to have *ou* hold talks (with sb)
diálogo ['dʒjalogu] M dialogue; (*conversa*) talk, conversation
diamante [dʒja'mãtʃi] M diamond
diâmetro ['dʒjametru] M diameter
diante ['dʒjãtʃi] PREP: **~ de** before; (*na frente de*) in front of; (*problemas etc*) in the face of; **e assim por ~** and so on; **para ~** forward
dianteira [dʒjã'tejra] F front, vanguard; **tomar a ~** to get ahead
dianteiro, -a [dʒjã'tejru, a] ADJ front
diapositivo [dʒjapozi'tʃivu] M (*Foto*) slide
diária ['dʒjarja] F (*de hotel*) daily rate
diário, -a ['dʒjarju, a] ADJ daily ▶ M diary; (*jornal*) (daily) newspaper; **~ de bordo** (*Aer*) logbook
diarreia [dʒja'hɛja] F diarrhoea (BRIT), diarrhea (US)
dica ['dʒika] (*col*) F hint
dicionário [dʒisjo'narju] M dictionary
dieta ['dʒjɛta] F diet; **fazer ~** to go on a diet
diferença [dʒife'rẽsa] F difference; **ela tem uma ~ comigo** she's got something against me
diferenciar [dʒiferẽ'sjar] VT to differentiate
diferente [dʒife'rẽtʃi] ADJ different; **estar ~ com alguém** to be at odds with sb
difícil [dʒi'fisiw] (*pl* **-eis**) ADJ difficult; (*improvável*) unlikely; **o ~ é ...** the difficult thing is ...; **acho ~ ela aceitar nossa proposta** I think it's unlikely she will accept our proposal; **dificilmente** [dʒifisiw'mẽtʃi] ADV with difficulty; (*mal*) hardly; (*raramente*) hardly ever
dificuldade [dʒifikuw'dadʒi] F difficulty; **em ~s** in trouble
dificultar [dʒifikuw'tar] VT to make difficult; (*complicar*) to complicate
difundir [dʒifũ'dʒir] VT to diffuse; to spread
digerir [dʒiʒe'rir] VT, VI to digest
digestão [dʒiʒes'tãw] F digestion
digital [dʒiʒi'taw] (*pl* **-ais**) ADJ:

impressão ~ fingerprint
digitar [dʒiʒi'tar] VT (*Comput: dados*) to key (in)
dígito ['dʒiʒitu] M digit
dignidade [dʒigni'dadʒi] F dignity
digno, -a ['dʒignu, a] ADJ (*merecedor*) worthy; (*nobre*) dignified
digo ['dʒigu] VB *ver* **dizer**
dilatar [dʒila'tar] VT to dilate, expand; (*prolongar*) to prolong; (*retardar*) to delay
dilema [dʒi'lɛma] M dilemma
diluir [dʒi'lwir] VT to dilute
dilúvio [dʒi'luvju] M flood
dimensão [dʒimẽ'sãw] (*pl* **-ões**) F dimension; **dimensões** FPL (*medidas*) measurements
diminuição [dʒiminwi'sãw] F reduction
diminuir [dʒimi'nwir] VT to reduce; (*som*) to turn down; (*interesse*) to lessen ▶ VI to lessen, diminish; (*preço*) to go down; (*dor*) to wear off; (*barulho*) to die down
diminutivo, -a [dʒiminu'tʃivu, a] ADJ diminutive ▶ M (*Ling*) diminutive
Dinamarca [dʒina'marka] F Denmark; **dinamarquês, -quesa** [dʒinamar'kes, 'keza] ADJ Danish ▶ M/F Dane ▶ M (*Ling*) Danish
dinâmico, -a [dʒi'namiku, a] ADJ dynamic
dínamo ['dʒinamu] M dynamo
dinheirão [dʒiɲej'rãw] M: **um ~** loads *pl* of money
dinheiro [dʒi'ɲejru] M money; **~ à vista** cash for paying in cash; **~ em caixa** money in the till; **~ em espécie** cash
dinossauro [dʒino'sawru] M dinosaur
diploma [dʒip'lɔma] M diploma
diplomacia [dʒiploma'sia] F diplomacy; (*fig*) tact
diplomata [dʒiplo'mata] M/F diplomat; **diplomático, -a** [dʒiplo'matʃiku, a] ADJ diplomatic
dique ['dʒiki] M dam; (*Geo*) dyke
direção [dʒire'sãw] (*pl* **-ões**) F direction; (*endereço*) address; (*Auto*) steering; (*administração*) management; (*comando*) leadership; (*diretoria*) board of directors; **em ~ a** towards
direi [dʒi'rej] VB *ver* **dizer**
direita [dʒi'rejta] F (*mão*) right hand; (*lado*) right-hand side; (*Pol*) right wing; **à ~** on the right
direito, -a [dʒi'rejtu, a] ADJ (*lado*) right-hand; (*mão*) right; (*honesto*) honest; (*devido*) proper; (*justo*) right, just ▶ M right; (*Jur*) law ▶ ADV straight; (*bem*) right; (*de maneira certa*) properly; **direitos** MPL (*humanos*) rights; (*alfandegários*) duty *sg*
direto, -a [dʒi'rɛtu, a] ADJ direct ▶ ADV straight; **transmissão direta** (*TV*) live broadcast
diretor, a [dʒire'tor(a)] ADJ directing, guiding ▶ M/F director; (*de jornal*) editor; (*de escola*) head teacher; **diretoria** [dʒireto'ria] F (*Com*) management
dirigente [dʒiri'ʒẽtʃi] M/F (*de país, partido*) leader; (*diretor*) director; (*gerente*) manager
dirigir [dʒiri'ʒir] VT to direct; (*Com*) to manage; (*veículo*) to drive ▶ VI to drive; **dirigir-se** VR: **~-se a** (*falar com*) to speak to; (*ir, recorrer*) to go to; (*esforços*) to be directed towards
discagem [dʒis'kaʒẽ] F (*Tel*) dialling

discar [dʒis'kar] VT to dial
disciplina [dʒisi'plina] F discipline; **disciplinar** [dʒisipli'nar] VT to discipline
discípulo, -a [dʒi'sipulu, a] M/F disciple; (*aluno*) pupil
disco ['dʒisku] M disc; (*Comput*) disk; (*Mús*) record; (*de telefone*) dial; **~ rígido** (*Comput*) hard drive, hard disk; **~ do sistema** system disk; **~ voador** flying saucer
discordar [dʒiskor'dar] VI: **~ de alguém em algo** to disagree with sb on sth
discórdia [dʒis'kɔrdʒja] F discord, strife
discoteca [dʒisko'tɛka] F discotheque, disco (*col*)
discrepância [dʒiskre'pãsja] F discrepancy; (*desacordo*) disagreement; **discrepante** [dʒiskre'pãtʃi] ADJ conflicting
discreto, -a [dʒis'krɛtu, a] ADJ discreet; (*modesto*) modest; (*prudente*) shrewd; (*roupa*) plain; **discrição** [dʒiskri'sãw] F discretion
discriminação [dʒiskrimina'sãw] F discrimination
discriminar [dʒiskrimi'nar] VT to distinguish ▶ VI: **~ entre** to discriminate between
discurso [dʒis'kursu] M speech
discussão [dʒisku'sãw] (*pl* **-ões**) F discussion; (*contenda*) argument
discutir [dʒisku'tʃir] VT to discuss ▶ VI: **~ (sobre algo)** to talk (about sth); (*contender*) to argue (about sth)
disenteria [dʒizẽte'ria] F dysentery
disfarçar [dʒisfar'sar] VT to disguise ▶ VI to pretend; **disfarçar-se** VR: **~-se em** *ou* **de algo** to disguise o.s. as sth; **disfarce** [dʒis'farsi] M disguise; (*máscara*) mask
dislexia [dʒizlek'sia] F dyslexia
disparar [dʒispa'rar] VT to shoot, fire ▶ VI to fire; (*arma*) to go off; (*correr*) to shoot off, bolt
disparatado, -a [dʒispara'tadu, a] ADJ silly, absurd
disparate [dʒispa'ratʃi] M nonsense, rubbish
disparidade [dʒispari'dadʒi] F disparity
dispensar [dʒispẽ'sar] VT to excuse; (*prescindir de*) to do without; (*conferir*) to grant; **dispensável** [dʒispẽ'savew] (*pl* **-eis**) ADJ expendable
dispersar [dʒisper'sar] VT, VI to disperse; **disperso, -a** [dʒis'pɛrsu, a] ADJ scattered
displicência [dʒispli'sensja] (BR) F negligence, carelessness; **displicente** [dʒispli'sẽtʃi] ADJ careless
dispo ['dʒispu] VB *ver* **despir**
disponível [dʒispo'nivew] (*pl* **-eis**) ADJ available
dispor [dʒis'por] (*irreg: como* **pôr**) VT to arrange ▶ VI: **~ de** to have the use of; (*ter*) to have, own; (*pessoas*) to have at one's disposal; **dispor-se** VR: **~-se a** (*estar pronto a*) to be prepared to, be willing to; (*decidir*) to decide to; **~ sobre** to talk about; **disponha!** feel free!
disposição [dʒispozi'sãw] (*pl* **-ões**) F arrangement; (*humor*) disposition; (*inclinação*) inclination; **à sua ~** at your disposal
dispositivo [dʒispozi'tʃivu] M gadget, device; (*determinação de lei*) provision
disputa [dʒis'puta] F dispute, argument; (*competição*) contest; **disputar** [dʒispu'tar] VT to dispute;

(*concorrer a*) to compete for; (*lutar por*) to fight over ▸ VI to quarrel, argue; to compete; **disputar uma corrida** to run a race
disquete [dʒis'ketʃi] M (*Comput*) diskette
disse ['dʒisi] VB *ver* **dizer**
disseminar [dʒisemi'nar] VT to disseminate; (*espalhar*) to spread
dissertar [dʒiser'tar] VI to speak
dissidência [dʒisi'dẽsja] F (*cisão*) difference of opinion
disso ['dʒisu] = **de + isso**
dissolução [dʒisolu'sãw] F (*libertinagem*) debauchery; (*de casamento*) dissolution
dissolver [dʒisow'ver] VT to dissolve; (*dispersar*) to disperse; (*motim*) to break up
dissuadir [dʒiswa'dʒir] VT to dissuade; **~ alguém de fazer algo** to talk sb out of doing sth, dissuade sb from doing sth
distância [dʒis'tãsja] F distance; **a 3 quilômetros de ~** 3 kilometres (BRIT) *ou* kilometers (US) away
distanciar [dʒistã'sjar] VT to distance, set apart; (*colocar por intervalos*) to space out; **distanciar-se** VR to move away; (*fig*) to distance o.s.
distante [dʒis'tãtʃi] ADJ distant
distender [dʒistẽ'der] VT to expand; (*estirar*) to stretch; (*dilatar*) to distend; (*músculo*) to pull; **distender-se** VR to expand; to distend
distinção [dʒistʃĩ'sãw] (*pl* **-ões**) F distinction; **fazer ~** to make a distinction
distinguir [dʒistʃĩ'gir] VT to distinguish; (*avistar, ouvir*) to make out; **distinguir-se** VR to stand out
distinto, -a [dʒis'tʃĩtu, a] ADJ different; (*eminente*) distinguished; (*claro*) distinct; (*refinado*) refined
disto ['dʒistu] = **de + isto**
distorcer [dʒistor'ser] VT to distort
distração [dʒistra'sãw] (*pl* **-ões**) F (*alheamento*) absent-mindedness; (*divertimento*) pastime; (*descuido*) oversight
distraído, -a [dʒistra'idu, a] ADJ absent-minded; (*não atento*) inattentive
distrair [dʒistra'ir] VT to distract; (*divertir*) to amuse
distribuição [dʒistribwi'sãw] F distribution; (*de cartas*) delivery
distribuidor, a [dʒistribwi'dor(a)] M/F distributor ▸ M (*Auto*) distributor ▸ F (*Com*) distribution company, distributor
distribuir [dʒistri'bwir] VT to distribute; (*repartir*) to share out; (*cartas*) to deliver
distrito [dʒis'tritu] M district; (*delegacia*) police station; **~ eleitoral** constituency; **~ federal** federal area
distúrbio [dʒis'turbju] M disturbance
ditado [dʒi'tadu] M dictation; (*provérbio*) saying
ditador [dʒita'dor] M dictator; **ditadura** [dʒita'dura] F dictatorship
ditar [dʒi'tar] VT to dictate; (*impor*) to impose
dito, -a ['dʒitu, a] PP *de* **dizer**; **~ e feito** no sooner said than done
diurno, -a ['dʒjurnu, a] ADJ daytime *atr*
divã [dʒi'vã] M couch, divan
divergir [dʒiver'ʒir] VI to diverge; (*discordar*): **~ (de alguém)** to

d

disagree (with sb)
diversão [dʒiver'sãw] (*pl* **-ões**) F amusement; (*passatempo*) pastime
diverso, -a [dʒi'vɛrsu, a] ADJ different; (*pl*) various
diversões [diver'sõjs] FPL *de* **diversão**
diversos [dʒi'vɛrsus] MPL sundries
divertido, -a [dʒiver'tʃidu, a] ADJ amusing, funny
divertimento [dʒivertʃi'mẽtu] M amusement, entertainment
divertir [dʒiver'tʃir] VT to amuse, entertain; **divertir-se** VR to enjoy o.s., have a good time
dívida ['dʒivida] F debt; **contrair ~s** to run into debt; **~ externa** foreign debt
dividir [dʒivi'dʒir] VT to divide; (*despesas, lucro, comida etc*) to share; (*separar*) to separate ▶ VI (*Mat*) to divide; **dividir-se** VR to divide, split up
divino, -a [dʒi'vinu, a] ADJ divine ▶ M Holy Ghost
divirjo [dʒi'virʒu] VB *ver* **divergir**
divisa [dʒi'viza] F emblem; (*frase*) slogan; (*fronteira*) border; (*Mil*) stripe; **divisas** FPL (*câmbio*) foreign exchange *sg*
divisão [dʒivi'zãw] (*pl* **-ões**) F division; (*discórdia*) split; (*partilha*) sharing
divisões [dʒivi'zõjs] FPL *de* **divisão**
divisória [dʒivi'zɔrja] F partition
divorciado, -a [dʒivor'sjadu, a] ADJ divorced ▶ M/F divorcé(e)
divorciar [dʒivor'sjar] VT to divorce; **divorciar-se** VR to get divorced; **divórcio** [dʒi'vɔrsju] M divorce
divulgar [dʒivuw'gar] VT (*notícias*) to spread; (*segredo*) to divulge; (*produto*) to market; (*livro*) to publish; **divulgar-se** VR to leak out
dizer [dʒi'zer] VT to say ▶ M saying; **dizer-se** VR to claim to be; **diz-se** *ou* **dizem que ...** it is said that ...; **~ algo a alguém** to tell sb sth; (*falar*) to say sth to sb; **~ a alguém que ...** to tell sb that ...; **o que você diz da minha sugestão?** what do you think of my suggestion?; **querer ~** to mean; **quer ~** that is to say; **digo** (*ou seja*) I mean; **não diga!** you don't say!; **por assim ~** so to speak; **até ~ chega** as much as possible
do [du] = **de + o**
doação [doa'sãw] (*pl* **-ões**) F donation
doador, a [doa'dor(a)] M/F donor
doar [do'ar] VT to donate, give
dobra ['dɔbra] F fold; (*prega*) pleat; (*de calças*) turn-up
dobradiça [dobra'dʒisa] F hinge
dobradinha [dobra'dʒiɲa] F (*Culin*) tripe stew
dobrar [do'brar] VT to double; (*papel*) to fold; (*joelho*) to bend; (*esquina*) to turn, go round; (*fazer ceder*): **~ alguém** to talk sb round ▶ VI to double; (*sino*) to toll; (*vergar*) to bend; **dobrar-se** VR to double (up)
dobro ['dobru] M double
doce ['dosi] ADJ sweet; (*terno*) gentle ▶ M sweet
dóceis ['dɔsejs] ADJ PL *de* **dócil**
dócil ['dɔsiw] (*pl* **-eis**) ADJ docile
documentação [dokumẽta'sãw] F documentation; (*documentos*) papers *pl*
documentário, -a [dokumẽ'tarju, a] ADJ, M documentary
documento [doku'mẽtu] M document

doçura [do'sura] F sweetness; (*brandura*) gentleness
doença [do'ẽsa] F illness
doente [do'ẽtʃi] ADJ ill, sick ▶ M/F sick person; (*cliente*) patient
doentio, -a [doẽ'tʃiu, a] ADJ (*pessoa*) sickly; (*clima*) unhealthy; (*curiosidade*) morbid
doer [do'er] VI to hurt, ache; **~ a alguém** (*pesar*) to grieve sb
doido, -a ['dojdu, a] ADJ mad, crazy ▶ M/F madman/woman
doído, -a [do'idu, a] ADJ painful; (*moralmente*) hurt; (*que causa dor*) painful
dois, duas [dojs, 'duas] NUM two; **conversa a ~** tête-à-tête
dólar ['dɔlar] M dollar; **~ oficial** dollar at the official rate; **~ turismo** dollar at the special tourist rate; **doleiro, -a** [do'lejru, a] M/F (black market) dollar dealer
dolorido, -a [dolo'ridu, a] ADJ painful, sore
dom [dõ] M gift; (*aptidão*) knack
domar [do'mar] VT to tame
doméstica [do'mɛstʃika] F maid
domesticar [domestʃi'kar] VT to domesticate; (*povo*) to tame
doméstico, -a [do'mɛstʃiku, a] ADJ domestic; (*vida*) home *atr*
domicílio [domi'silju] M home, residence; **"entregamos a ~"** "we deliver"
dominador, a [domina'dor(a)] ADJ (*pessoa*) domineering; (*olhar*) imposing ▶ M/F ruler
dominar [domi'nar] VT to dominate; (*reprimir*) to overcome ▶ VI to dominate; **dominar-se** VR to control o.s.
domingo [do'mĩgu] M Sunday
domínio [do'minju] M power; (*dominação*) control; (*território*) domain; (*esfera*) sphere; **~ próprio** self-control
dona ['dɔna] F owner; (*col: mulher*) lady; **~ de casa** housewife; **D~ Lígia** Lígia; **D~ Luísa Souza** Mrs Luísa Souza
donde ['dõdə] (PT) ADV from where; (*daí*) thus
dono ['donu] M owner
dopar [do'par] VT (*cavalo*) to dope
dor [dor] F ache; (*aguda*) pain; (*fig*) grief, sorrow; **~ de cabeça** headache; **~ de dentes** toothache; **~ de estômago** stomachache
dormente [dor'mẽtʃi] ADJ numb ▶ M (*Ferro*) sleeper
dormir [dor'mir] VI to sleep; **~ fora** to spend the night away
dormitório [dormi'tɔrju] M bedroom; (*coletivo*) dormitory
dorso ['dorsu] M back
dos [dus] = **de + os**
dosagem [do'zaʒẽ] M dosage
dose ['dɔzi] F dose
dossiê [do'sje] M dossier, file
dotado, -a [do'tadu, a] ADJ gifted; **~ de** endowed with
dotar [do'tar] VT to endow
dou [do] VB *ver* **dar**
dourado, -a [do'radu, a] ADJ golden; (*com camada de ouro*) gilt ▶ M gilt
doutor, a [do'tor(a)] M/F doctor; **D~** (*forma de tratamento*) Sir; **D~ Eduardo Souza** Mr Eduardo Souza
doutrina [do'trina] F doctrine
doze ['dozi] NUM twelve
Dr. ABR (= *Doutor*) Dr
Dra. ABR (= *Doutora*) Dr
dragão [dra'gãw] (*pl* **-ões**) M dragon
dragões [dra'gõjs] MPL *de* **dragão**

drama ['drama] M drama; **dramático, -a** [dra'matʃiku, a] ADJ dramatic; **dramatizar** [dramatʃi'zar] VT, VI to dramatize
drástico, -a ['drastʃiku, a] ADJ drastic
dreno ['drɛnu] M drain
driblar [dri'blar] VT (*Futebol*) to dribble
drinque ['drĩki] M drink
droga ['drɔga] F drug; (*fig*) rubbish; **drogado, -a** [dro'gadu, a] M/F drug addict; **drogar** [dro'gar] VT to drug; **drogar-se** VR to take drugs
drogaria [droga'ria] F chemist's shop (BRIT), drugstore (US)
duas ['duas] F *de* **dois**
ducha ['duʃa] F shower
dueto ['dwetu] M duet
duna ['duna] F dune
dupla ['dupla] F pair; (*Esporte*): **~ masculina/feminina/mista** men's/women's/mixed doubles
duplicar [dupli'kar] VT to duplicate ▸ VI to double; **duplicata** [dupli'kata] F duplicate; (*título*) trade note, bill
duplo, -a ['duplu, a] ADJ, M double
duque ['duki] M duke
duração [dura'sãw] F duration; **de pouca ~** short-lived
durante [du'rãtʃi] PREP during; **~ uma hora** for an hour
durar [du'rar] VI to last
durável [du'ravew] (*pl* **-eis**) ADJ lasting
durex® [du'rɛks] ADJ: **fita ~** adhesive tape, Sellotape® (BRIT), Scotch tape® (US)
durmo ['durmu] VB *ver* **dormir**
duro, -a ['duru, a] ADJ hard; (*severo*) harsh; (*resistente, fig*) tough; **estar ~** (*col*) to be broke
dúvida ['duvida] F doubt; **sem ~** undoubtedly, without a doubt; **duvidar** [duvi'dar] VT to doubt ▸ VI to have one's doubts; **duvidar de alguém/algo** to doubt sb/sth; **duvidar que …** to doubt that …; **duvido!** I doubt it!; **duvidoso, -a** [duvi'dozu, ɔza] ADJ doubtful; (*suspeito*) dubious
duzentos, -as [du'zẽtus, as] NUM two hundred
dúzia ['duzja] F dozen; **meia ~** half a dozen
DVD ABR M (= *disco digital versátil*) DVD
dz. ABR = **dúzia**

e

e [i] CONJ and; **e a bagagem?** what about the luggage?
é [ɛ] VB *ver* **ser**
eclipse [e'klipsi] M eclipse
eco ['ɛku] M echo; **ter ~** to catch on; **ecoar** [e'kwar] VT to echo ▶ VI (*ressoar*) to echo
ecologia [ekolo'ʒia] F ecology
ecológico, -a [eko'lɔʒiku, a] ADJ ecological, eco-friendly
economia [ekono'mia] F economy; (*ciência*) economics *sg*; **economias** FPL (*poupanças*) savings; **fazer ~ (de)** to economize (with)
econômico, -a [eko'nomiku, a] ADJ economical; (*pessoa*) thrifty; (*Com*) economic
economizar [ekonomi'zar] VT (*gastar com economia*) to economize on; (*poupar*) to save (up) ▶ VI to economize; to save up
ecrã, écran ['ɛkrã] (PT) M screen; **~ tactil** touch screen
edição [ɛdʒi'sãw] (*pl* **-ões**) F publication; (*conjunto de exemplares*) edition; (*TV, Cinema*) editing
edifício [edʒi'fisju] M building; **~ garagem** multistorey car park (BRIT), multistory parking lot (US)
Edimburgo [edʒĩ'burgu] N Edinburgh
editar [edʒi'tar] VT to publish; (*Comput etc*) to edit
editor, a [edʒi'tor(a)] ADJ publishing *atr* ▶ M/F publisher; (*redator*) editor ▶ F publishing company; **casa ~a** publishing house
editoração [edʒitora'sãw] F: **~ eletrônica** desktop publishing; **editorial** [edʒitor'jaw] (*pl* **-ais**) ADJ publishing *atr* ▶ M editorial
edredão [ədrə'dãw] (*pl* **-ões**) (PT) M = **edredom**
edredom [edre'dõ] (*pl* **-ns**) M eiderdown
educação [eduka'sãw] F education; (*criação*) upbringing; (*de animais*) training; (*maneiras*) good manners *pl*; **educacional** [edukasjo'naw] (*pl* **-ais**) ADJ education *atr*
educar [edu'kar] VT to educate; (*criar*) to bring up; (*animal*) to train
efeito [e'fejtu] M effect; **fazer ~** to work; **levar a ~** to put into effect; **com ~** indeed
efeminado, -a [efemi'nadu, a] ADJ effeminate
efervescente [eferve'sẽtʃi] ADJ fizzy
efetivamente [efetʃiva'mẽtʃi] ADV effectively; (*realmente*) really, in fact
efetivo, -a [efe'tʃivu, a] ADJ effective; (*real*) actual, real; (*cargo, funcionário*) permanent

efetuar [efe'twar] VT to carry out; (*soma*) to do, perform
eficaz [efi'kaz] ADJ (*pessoa*) efficient; (*tratamento*) effective
eficiência [efi'sjẽsja] F efficiency; **eficiente** [efi'sjẽtʃi] ADJ efficient
egípcio, -a [e'ʒipsju, a] ADJ, M/F Egyptian
Egito [e'ʒitu] M: **o ~** Egypt
egoísmo [ego'izmu] M selfishness, egoism; **egoísta** [ego'ista] ADJ selfish, egoistic ▶ M/F egoist
égua ['ɛgwa] F mare
ei [ej] EXCL hey!
ei-lo = **eis + o**
eis [ejs] ADV (*sg*) here is; (*pl*) here are; **~ aí** there is; there are
ejacular [eʒaku'lar] VT (*sêmen*) to ejaculate; (*líquido*) to spurt ▶ VI to ejaculate
ela ['ɛla] PRON (*pessoa*) she; (*coisa*) it; (*com prep*) her; it; **elas** FPL they; (*com prep*) them; **~s por ~s** (*col*) tit for tat
elaboração [elabora'sãw] (*pl* **-ões**) F (*de uma teoria*) working out; (*preparo*) preparation
elaborar [elabo'rar] VT to prepare; (*fazer*) to make
elástico, -a [e'lastʃiku, a] ADJ elastic; (*flexível*) flexible; (*colchão*) springy ▶ M elastic band
ele ['elɪ] PRON he; (*coisa*) it; (*com prep*) him; it; **eles** MPL they; (*com prep*) them
elefante, -ta [ele'fãtʃi, ta] M/F elephant
elegante [ele'gãtʃi] ADJ elegant; (*da moda*) fashionable
eleger [ele'ʒer] VT to elect; (*escolher*) to choose
eleição [elej'sãw] (*pl* **-ões**) F election; (*escolha*) choice
eleito, -a [e'lejtu, a] PP *de* **eleger** ▶ ADJ elected; (*escolhido*) chosen
eleitor, a [elej'tor(a)] M/F voter
elejo [e'leʒu] VB *ver* **eleger**
elementar [elemẽ'tar] ADJ elementary; (*fundamental*) basic, fundamental
elemento [ele'mẽtu] M element; (*parte*) component; (*recurso*) means; (*informação*) grounds *pl*; **elementos** MPL (*rudimentos*) rudiments
elenco [e'lẽku] M list; (*de atores*) cast
eletricidade [eletrisi'dadʒi] F electricity
eletricista [eletri'sista] M/F electrician
elétrico, -a [e'lɛtriku, a] ADJ electric; (*fig: agitado*) worked up ▶ M tram (BRIT), streetcar (US)
eletrificar [eletrifi'kar] VT to electrify
eletrizar [eletri'zar] VT to electrify; (*fig*) to thrill
eletro... [eletru] PREFIXO electro...; **eletrocutar** [eletroku'tar] VT to electrocute; **eletrodo** [ele'trodu], (PT) **elétrodo** [e'letrodu] M electrode; **eletrodomésticos** [eletrodo'mɛstʃikus] (BR) MPL (electrical) household appliances
eletrônica [ele'tronika] F electronics *sg*
eletrônico, -a [ele'troniku, a] ADJ electronic
elevação [eleva'sãw] (*pl* **-ões**) F (*Arq*) elevation; (*aumento*) rise; (*ato*) raising; (*altura*) height; (*promoção*) promotion; (*ponto elevado*) bump
elevador [eleva'dor] M lift (BRIT), elevator (US)
elevar [ele'var] VT to lift up; (*voz, preço*) to raise; (*exaltar*) to exalt; (*promover*) to promote; **elevar-se** VR to rise

eliminar [elimi'nar] VT to remove; (*suprimir*) to delete; (*possibilidade*) to rule out; (*Med, banir*) to expel; (*Esporte*) to eliminate; **eliminatória** [elimina'tɔrja] F (*Esporte*) heat, preliminary round; (*exame*) test
elite [e'litʃi] F elite
elogiar [elo'ʒjar] VT to praise; **elogio** [elo'ʒiu] M praise; (*cumprimento*) compliment
El Salvador [ew-] N El Salvador

PALAVRA-CHAVE

em [ẽ] (*em + o(s)/a(s) = no(s)/na(s); + ele(s)/a(s) = nele(s)/a(s); + esse(s)/a(s) = nesse(s)/a(s); + isso = nisso; + este(s)/a(s) = neste(s)/a(s); + isto = nisto; + aquele(s)/a(s) = naquele(s)/a(s); + aquilo = naquilo*) PREP **1** (*posição*) in; (: *sobre*) on; **está na gaveta/no bolso** it's in the drawer/pocket; **está na mesa/no chão** it's on the table/ floor
2 (*lugar*) in; (: *casa, escritório etc*) at; (: *andar, meio de transporte*) on; **no Brasil/em São Paulo** in Brazil/ São Paulo; **em casa/no dentista** at home/the dentist; **no avião** on the plane; **no quinto andar** on the fifth floor
3 (*ação*) into; **ela entrou na sala de aula** she went into the classroom; **colocar algo na bolsa** to put sth into one's bag
4 (*tempo*) in; on; **em 1962/3 semanas** in 1962/3 weeks; **no inverno** in the winter; **em janeiro, no mês de janeiro** in January; **nessa ocasião/altura** on that occasion/at that time; **em breve** soon
5 (*diferença*): **reduzir/aumentar em 20%** to reduce/increase by 20%
6 (*modo*): **escrito em inglês** written in English
7 (*após vb que indica gastar etc*) on; **a metade do seu salário vai em comida** he spends half his salary on food
8 (*tema, ocupação*): **especialista no assunto** expert on the subject; **ele trabalha na construção civil** he works in the building industry

emagrecer [imagre'ser] VT to make thin ▶ VI to grow thin; (*mediante regime*) to slim; **emagrecimento** [imagresi'mẽtu] M (*mediante regime*) slimming
e-mail [i'mew] M email; **mandar um ~ para alguém** to email sb; **mandar algo por ~** to email sth
emaranhado, -a [imara'ɲadu, a] ADJ tangled ▶ M tangle
embaixada [ẽbaj'ʃada] F embassy
embaixador, a [ẽbajʃa'dor(a)] M/F ambassador
embaixatriz [ẽbajʃa'triz] F ambassador; (*mulher de embaixador*) ambassador's wife
embaixo [ẽ'bajʃu] ADV below, underneath ▶ PREP: **~ de** under, underneath; **(lá) ~** (*em andar inferior*) downstairs
embalagem [ẽba'laʒẽ] F packing; (*de produto: caixa etc*) packaging
embalar [ẽba'lar] VT to pack; (*balançar*) to rock
embaraçar [ẽbara'sar] VT to hinder; (*complicar*) to complicate; (*encabular*) to embarrass; (*confundir*) to confuse; (*obstruir*) to block; **embaraçar-se** VR to become embarrassed

embaraço [ẽba'rasu] M hindrance; (*cábula*) embarrassment;
embaraçoso, -a [ẽbara'sozu, ɔza] ADJ embarrassing
embarcação [ẽbarka'sãw] (*pl* **-ões**) F vessel
embarcar [ẽbar'kar] VT to embark, put on board; (*mercadorias*) to ship, stow ▸VI to go on board, embark
embarque [ẽ'barkɪ] M (*de pessoas*) boarding, embarkation; (*de mercadorias*) shipment
embebedar [ẽbebe'dar] VT to make drunk ▸VI: **o vinho embebeda** wine makes you drunk;
embebedar-se VR to get drunk
emblema [ẽ'blɛma] M emblem; (*na roupa*) badge
êmbolo ['ẽbolu] M piston
embolsar [ẽbow'sar] VT to pocket; (*herança etc*) to come into
embora [ẽ'bɔra] CONJ though, although ▸EXCL even so; **ir(-se) ~** to go away
emboscada [ẽbos'kada] F ambush
embriagar [ẽbrja'gar] VT to make drunk, intoxicate; **embriagar-se** VR to get drunk; **embriaguez** [ẽbrja'gez] F drunkenness; (*fig*) rapture
embrião [e'brjãw] (*pl* **-ões**) M embryo
embromar [ẽbro'mar] VT (*adiar*) to put off; (*enganar*) to cheat ▸VI (*prometer e não cumprir*) to make empty promises, be all talk (and no action); (*protelar*) to stall; (*falar em rodeios*) to beat about the bush
embrulhar [ẽbru'ʎar] VT (*pacote*) to wrap; (*enrolar*) to roll up; (*confundir*) to muddle up; (*enganar*) to cheat; (*estômago*) to upset; **embrulhar-se** VR to get into a muddle
embrulho [ẽ'bruʎu] M package, parcel; (*confusão*) mix-up
emburrar [ẽbu'har] VI to sulk
embutido, -a [ẽbu'tʃidu, a] ADJ (*armário*) built-in, fitted
emenda [e'mẽda] F correction; (*Jur*) amendment; (*de uma pessoa*) improvement; (*ligação*) join; (*sambladura*) joint; (*Costura*) seam
emendar [emẽ'dar] VT to correct; (*reparar*) to mend; (*injustiças*) to make amends for; (*Jur*) to amend; (*ajuntar*) to put together;
emendar-se VR to mend one's ways
ementa [e'mẽta] (PT) F menu
emergência [imer'ʒẽsja] F emergence; (*crise*) emergency
emigrado, -a [emi'gradu, a] ADJ emigrant
emigrante [emi'grãtʃi] M/F emigrant
emigrar [emi'grar] VI to emigrate; (*aves*) to migrate
eminência [emi'nẽsja] F eminence; (*altura*) height;
eminente [emi'nẽtʃi] ADJ eminent, distinguished; (*Geo*) high
emissão [emi'sãw] (*pl* **-ões**) F emission; (*Rádio*) broadcast; (*de moeda, ações*) issue; **emissões de carbono** carbon emissions
emissor, a [emi'sor(a)] ADJ (*de moeda-papel*) issuing ▸M (*Rádio*) transmitter ▸F (*estação*) broadcasting station; (*empresa*) broadcasting company
emitir [emi'tʃir] VT (*som*) to give out; (*cheiro*) to give off; (*moeda, ações*) to issue; (*Rádio*) to broadcast; (*opinião*) to express ▸VI (*emitir moeda*) to print money
emoção [emo'sãw] (*pl* **-ões**) F emotion; (*excitação*) excitement;
emocional [imosjo'naw] (*pl* **-ais**) ADJ emotional; **emocionante**

[imosjo'nãtʃi] ADJ moving; (*excitante*) exciting; **emocionar** [imosjo'nar] VT to move; (*perturbar*) to upset; (*excitar*) to excite, thrill ▶ VI to be exciting; (*comover*) to be moving; **emocionar-se** VR to get emotional

emotivo, -a [emo'tʃivu, a] ADJ emotional

empacotar [ẽpako'tar] VT to pack, wrap up

empada [ẽ'pada] F pie

empadão [ẽpa'dãw] (*pl* **-ões**) M pie

empalidecer [ẽpalide'ser] VI to turn pale

empanturrar [ẽpãtu'har] VT: **~ alguém de algo** to stuff sb full of sth

empatar [ẽpa'tar] VT to hinder; (*dinheiro*) to tie up; (*no jogo*) to draw; (*tempo*) to take up ▶ VI (*no jogo*): **~ (com)** to draw (with); **empate** [ẽ'patʃi] M draw; (*numa corrida etc*) tie; (*Xadrez*) stalemate; (*em negociações*) deadlock

empecilho [ẽpe'siʎu] M obstacle; (*col*) snag

empenhar [ẽpe'ɲar] VT (*objeto*) to pawn; (*palavra*) to pledge; (*empregar*) to exert; (*compelir*) to oblige; **empenhar-se** VR: **~-se em fazer** to strive to do, do one's utmost to do; **empenho** [ẽ'peɲu] M pawning; (*palavra*) pledge; (*insistência*): **empenho (em)** commitment (to)

empilhar [ẽpi'ʎar] VT to pile up

empinado, -a [ẽpi'nadu, a] ADJ upright; (*cavalo*) rearing; (*colina*) steep

empinar [ẽpi'nar] VT to raise, uplift

empobrecer [ẽpobre'ser] VT to impoverish ▶ VI to become poor; **empobrecimento** [ẽpobresi'mẽtu] M impoverishment

empolgação [ẽpowga'sãw] F excitement; (*entusiasmo*) enthusiasm

empolgante [ẽpow'gãtʃi] ADJ exciting

empolgar [ẽpow'gar] VT to stimulate, fill with enthusiasm; (*prender a atenção de*): **~ alguém** to keep sb riveted

empossar [ẽpo'sar] VT to appoint

empreendedor, a [ẽprjẽde'dor(a)] ADJ enterprising ▶ M/F entrepreneur

empreender [ẽprjẽ'der] VT to undertake; **empreendimento** [ẽprjẽdʒi'mẽtu] M undertaking

empregada [ẽpre'gada] F (BR: *doméstica*) maid; (PT: *de restaurante*) waitress; *ver tb* **empregado**

empregado, -a [ẽpre'gadu, a] M/F employee; (*em escritório*) clerk ▶ M (PT: *de restaurante*) waiter

empregador, a [ẽprega'dor(a)] M/F employer

empregar [ẽpre'gar] VT (*pessoa*) to employ; (*coisa*) to use; **empregar-se** VR to get a job

emprego [ẽ'pregu] M job; (*uso*) use

empreiteiro [ẽprej'tejru] M contractor

empresa [ẽ'preza] F undertaking; (*Com*) enterprise, firm; **~ pontocom** dotcom; **empresário, -a** [ẽpre'zarju, a] M/F businessman/woman; (*de cantor, boxeador etc*) manager

emprestado, -a [ẽpres'tadu, a] ADJ on loan; **pedir ~** to borrow; **tomar algo ~** to borrow sth

e

emprestar [ẽpres'tar] VT to lend; **empréstimo** [ẽ'prɛstʃimu] M loan
empunhar [ẽpu'ɲar] VT to grasp, seize
empurrão [ẽpu'hãw] (*pl* **-ões**) M push, shove; **aos empurrões** jostling
empurrar [ẽpu'har] VT to push
empurrões [ẽpu'hõjs] MPL *de* **empurrão**
emudecer [emude'ser] VT to silence ▶VI to fall silent, go quiet
enamorado, -a [enamo'radu, a] ADJ enchanted; (*apaixonado*) in love
encabulado, -a [ẽkabu'ladu, a] ADJ shy
encadernação [ẽkaderna'sãw] (*pl* **-ões**) F (*de livro*) binding
encadernado, -a [ẽkader'nadu, a] ADJ bound; (*de capa dura*) hardback
encadernar [ẽkader'nar] VT to bind
encaixar [ẽkaj'ʃar] VT (*colocar*) to fit in; (*inserir*) to insert ▶VI to fit; **encaixe** [ẽ'kajʃi] M (*ato*) fitting; (*ranhura*) groove; (*buraco*) socket
encalço [ẽ'kawsu] M pursuit; **ir no ~ de** to pursue
encaminhar [ẽkami'ɲar] VT to direct; (*no bom caminho*) to put on the right path; (*processo*) to set in motion; **encaminhar-se** VR: **~-se para/a** to set out for/to
encanar [ẽka'nar] VT to channel
encantado, -a [ẽkã'tadu, a] ADJ delighted; (*castelo etc*) enchanted; (*fascinado*): **~ (por alguém/algo)** smitten (with sb/sth)
encantamento [ẽkãta'mẽtu] M (*magia*) spell; (*fascinação*) charm
encanto [ẽ'kãtu] M delight; (*fascinação*) charm
encarar [ẽka'rar] VT to face; (*olhar*) to look at; (*considerar*) to consider
encargo [ẽ'kargu] M responsibility; (*ocupação*) job, assignment; (*oneroso*) burden
encarnação [ẽkarna'sãw] (*pl* **-ões**) F incarnation
encarnado, -a [ẽkar'nadu, a] ADJ red, scarlet
encarnar [ẽkar'nar] VT to embody, personify; (*Teatro*) to play
encarregado, -a [ẽkahe'gadu, a] ADJ: **~ de** in charge of ▶M/F person in charge ▶M (*de operários*) foreman
encarregar [ẽkahe'gar] VT: **~ alguém de algo** to put sb in charge of sth; **encarregar-se** VR: **~-se de fazer** to undertake to do
encenação [ẽsena'sãw] (*pl* **-ões**) F (*de peça*) staging, putting on; (*produção*) production; (*fingimento*) play-acting; (*atitude fingida*) put-on
encerar [ẽse'rar] VT to wax
encerramento [ẽseha'mẽtu] M close, end
encerrar [ẽse'har] VT to shut in, lock up; (*conter*) to contain; (*concluir*) to close
encharcar [ẽʃar'kar] VT to flood; (*ensopar*) to soak, drench; **encharcar-se** VR to get soaked *ou* drenched
enchente [ẽ'ʃẽtʃi] F flood
encher [ẽ'ʃer] VT to fill (up); (*balão*) to blow up; (*tempo*) to fill, take up ▶VI (*col*) to be annoying; **encher-se** VR to fill up; **~-se (de)** (*col*) to get fed up (with); **enchimento** [ẽʃi'mẽtu] M filling
enciclopédia [ẽsiklo'pɛdʒja] F encyclopedia, encyclopaedia (BRIT)
encoberto, -a [ẽko'bɛrtu, a] PP *de* **encobrir** ▶ADJ concealed; (*tempo*) overcast
encobrir [ẽko'brir] VT to conceal, hide

encolher [ẽko'ʎer] VT (*pernas*) to draw up; (*os ombros*) to shrug; (*roupa*) to shrink ▶ VI to shrink; **encolher-se** VR (*de frio*) to huddle
encomenda [ẽko'mẽda] F order; **feito de ~** made to order, custom-made; **encomendar** [ẽkomẽ'dar] VT: **encomendar algo a alguém** to order sth from sb
encontrar [ẽkõ'trar] VT to find; (*inesperadamente*) to come across, meet; (*dar com*) to bump into ▶ VI: **~ com** to bump into; **encontrar-se** VR (*achar-se*) to be; (*ter encontro*): **~-se (com alguém)** to meet (sb)
encontro [ẽ'kõtru] M (*de pessoas*) meeting; (*Mil*) encounter; **~ marcado** appointment; **ir/vir ao ~ de** to go/come and meet; (*aspirações*) to meet, fulfil (BRIT), fulfill (US)
encorajar [ẽkora'ʒar] VT to encourage
encosta [ẽ'kɔsta] F slope
encostar [ẽkos'tar] VT (*cabeça*) to put down; (*carro*) to park; (*pôr de lado*) to put to one side; (*pôr junto*) to put side by side; (*porta*) to leave ajar ▶ VI to pull in; **encostar-se** VR: **~-se em** to lean against; (*deitar-se*) to lie down on; **~ em** to lean against; **~ a mão em** (*bater*) to hit
encosto [ẽ'kostu] M (*arrimo*) support; (*de cadeira*) back
encrencar [ẽkrẽ'kar] (*col*) VT (*situação*) to complicate; (*pessoa*) to get into trouble ▶ VI to get complicated; (*carro*) to break down; **encrencar-se** VR to get complicated; to get into trouble
encriptar [ẽkrip'tar] VT (*Comput, Tel*) to encrypt
encruzilhada [ẽkruzi'ʎada] F crossroads *sg*
encurtar [ẽkur'tar] VT to shorten
endereçar [ẽdere'sar] VT (*carta*) to address; (*encaminhar*) to direct
endereço [ẽde'resu] M address; **~ de e-mail** email address; **~ web** web address
endiabrado, -a [ẽdʒja'bradu, a] ADJ devilish; (*travesso*) mischievous
endinheirado, -a [ẽdʒiɲej'radu, a] ADJ rich, wealthy
endireitar [ẽdʒirej'tar] VT (*objeto*) to straighten; (*retificar*) to put right; **endireitar-se** VR to straighten up
endividar [ẽdʒivi'dar] VT to put into debt; **endividar-se** VR to run into debt
endossar [ẽdo'sar] VT to endorse
endurecer [ẽdure'ser] VT, VI to harden
energético, -a [ener'ʒɛtʃiku, a] ADJ energy *atr* ▶ M energy source; (*tb*: **bebida energética**) energy drink
energia [enɛr'ʒia] F energy, drive; (*Tec*) power, energy; **~ solar** solar power; **enérgico, -a** [e'nɛrʒiku, a] ADJ energetic, vigorous
enervante [ener'vãtʃi] ADJ annoying
enevoado, -a [ene'vwadu, a] ADJ misty, hazy
enfado [ẽ'fadu] M annoyance
ênfase ['ẽfazi] F emphasis, stress
enfastiado, -a [ẽfas'tʃjadu, a] ADJ bored
enfático, -a [ẽ'fatʃiku, a] ADJ emphatic
enfatizar [ẽfatʃi'zar] VT to emphasize
enfeitar [ẽfej'tar] VT to decorate; **enfeitar-se** VR to dress up;

enfeite [ẽ'fejtʃi] M decoration
enfermeiro, -a [ẽfer'mejru, a] M/F nurse
enfermidade [ẽfermi'dadʒi] F illness
enfermo, -a [ẽ'fermu, a] ADJ ill, sick ▶ M/F sick person, patient
enferrujar [ẽfehu'ʒar] VT to rust, corrode ▶ VI to go rusty
enfiar [ẽ'fjar] VT (*meter*) to put; (*agulha*) to thread; (*vestir*) to slip on; **enfiar-se** VR: **~-se em** to slip into
enfim [ẽ'fĩ] ADV finally, at last; (*em suma*) in short; **até que ~!** at last!
enfoque [ẽ'fɔki] M approach
enforcar [ẽfor'kar] VT to hang; (*trabalho, aulas*) to skip; **enforcar-se** VR to hang o.s.
enfraquecer [ẽfrake'ser] VT to weaken ▶ VI to grow weak
enfrentar [ẽfrẽ'tar] VT to face; (*confrontar*) to confront; (*problemas*) to face up to
enfurecer [ẽfure'ser] VT to infuriate; **enfurecer-se** VR to get furious
enganado, -a [ẽga'nadu, a] ADJ mistaken; (*traído*) deceived
enganar [ẽga'nar] VT to deceive; (*desonrar*) to seduce; (*cônjuge*) to be unfaithful to; (*fome*) to stave off; **enganar-se** VR to be wrong, be mistaken; (*iludir-se*) to deceive o.s.
engano [ẽ'gãnu] M mistake; (*ilusão*) deception; (*logro*) trick; **é ~** (*Tel*) I've (*ou* you've) got the wrong number
engarrafamento [ẽgahafa'mẽtu] M bottling; (*de trânsito*) traffic jam
engarrafar [ẽgaha'far] VT to bottle; (*trânsito*) to block
engasgar [ẽgaz'gar] VT to choke ▶ VI to choke; (*máquina*) to splutter; **engasgar-se** VR to choke
engatinhar [ẽgatʃi'ɲar] VI to crawl
engenharia [ẽʒeɲa'ria] F engineering; **engenheiro, -a** [ẽʒe'ɲejru, a] M/F engineer
engenhoso, -a [ẽʒe'ɲozu, ɔza] ADJ clever, ingenious
engessar [ẽʒe'sar] VT (*perna*) to put in plaster; (*parede*) to plaster
englobar [ẽglo'bar] VT to include
engodo [ẽ'godu] M bait
engolir [ẽgo'lir] VT to swallow
engordar [ẽgor'dar] VT to fatten ▶ VI to put on weight
engraçado, -a [ẽgra'sadu, a] ADJ funny, amusing
engradado [ẽgra'dadu] M crate
engraxador [ẽgraʃa'dor] (PT) M shoe shiner
engraxar [ẽgra'ʃar] VT to polish
engrenagem [ẽgre'naʒẽ] (*pl* **-ns**) F (*Auto*) gear
engrenar [ẽgre'nar] VT to put into gear; (*fig: conversa*) to strike up ▶ VI: **~ com alguém** to get on with sb
engrossar [ẽgro'sar] VT (*sopa*) to thicken; (*aumentar*) to swell; (*voz*) to raise ▶ VI to thicken; to swell; to rise; (*col: pessoa, conversa*) to turn nasty
enguia [ẽ'gia] F eel
enguiçar [ẽgi'sar] VI (*máquina*) to break down ▶ VT to cause to break down; **enguiço** [ẽ'gisu] M snag; (*desarranjo*) breakdown
enigma [e'nigima] M enigma; (*mistério*) mystery
enjeitado, -a [ẽʒej'tadu, a] M/F foundling, waif
enjoado, -a [ẽ'ʒwadu, a] ADJ sick; (*enfastiado*) bored; (*enfadonho*) boring; (*mal-humorado*) in a bad mood
enjoar [ẽ'ʒwar] VT to make sick; (*enfastiar*) to bore ▶ VI (*pessoa*) to be

sick; (*remédio, comida*) to cause nausea; **enjoar-se** VR: **~-se de** to get sick of
enjoo [ẽ'ʒou] M sickness; (*em carro*) travel sickness; (*em navio*) seasickness; (*aborrecimento*) boredom
enlatado, -a [ẽla'tadu, a] ADJ tinned (BRIT), canned ▶ M (*pej: filme*) foreign import; **enlatados** MPL (*comida*) tinned (BRIT) *ou* canned foods
enlouquecer [ẽloke'ser] VT to drive mad ▶ VI to go mad
enlutado, -a [ẽlu'tadu, a] ADJ in mourning
enorme [e'nɔrmi] ADJ enormous, huge; **enormidade** [enormi'dadʒi] F enormity; **uma enormidade (de)** (*col*) a hell of a lot (of)
enquanto [ẽ'kwãtu] CONJ while; (*considerado como*) as; **~ isso** meanwhile; **por ~** for the time being; **~ ele não vem** until he comes; **~ que** whereas
enquete [ẽ'kɛtʃi] F survey
enraivecer [ẽhajve'ser] VT to enrage
enredo [ẽ'hedu] M (*de uma obra*) plot; (*intriga*) intrigue
enriquecer [ẽhike'ser] VT to make rich; (*fig*) to enrich ▶ VI to get rich; **enriquecer-se** VR to get rich
enrolar [ẽho'lar] VT to roll up; (*agasalhar*) to wrap up; (*col: enganar*) to con ▶ VI (*col*) to waffle; **enrolar-se** VR to roll up; to wrap up; (*col: confundir-se*) to get mixed *ou* muddled up
enroscar [ẽhos'kar] VT (*torcer*) to twist, wind (round); **enroscar-se** VR to coil up
enrugar [ẽhu'gar] VT (*pele*) to wrinkle; (*testa*) to furrow; (*tecido*) to crease ▶ VI (*pele, mãos*) to go wrinkly; (*pessoa*) to get wrinkles
ensaiar [ẽsa'jar] VT to test, try out; (*treinar*) to practise (BRIT), practice (US); (*Teatro*) to rehearse
ensaio [ẽ'saju] M test; (*tentativa*) attempt; (*treino*) practice; (*Teatro*) rehearsal; (*literário*) essay
enseada [ẽ'sjada] F inlet, cove; (*baía*) bay
ensejo [ẽ'seʒu] M chance, opportunity
ensinamento [ẽsina'mẽtu] M teaching; (*exemplo*) lesson
ensinar [ẽsi'nar] VT, VI to teach
ensino [ẽ'sinu] M teaching, tuition; (*educação*) education; **~ fundamental** primary education; **~ médio** secondary education
ensopado, -a [ẽso'padu, a] ADJ soaked ▶ M stew
ensurdecer [ẽsurde'ser] VT to deafen ▶ VI to go deaf
entalar [ẽta'lar] VT to wedge, jam; (*encher*): **ela me entalou de comida** she stuffed me full of food
entalhar [ẽta'ʎar] VT to carve; **entalhe** [ẽ'taʎi] M groove, notch
entanto [ẽ'tãtu] ADV: **no ~** yet, however
então [ẽ'tãw] ADV then; **até ~** up to that time; **desde ~** ever since; **e ~?** well then?; **para ~** so that; **pois ~** in that case; **~, você vai ou não?** so, are you going or not?
entardecer [ẽtarde'ser] VI to get late ▶ M sunset
ente ['ẽtʃi] M being
enteado, -a [ẽ'tʃjadu, a] M/F stepson/stepdaughter
entediar [ẽte'dʒjar] VT to bore; **entediar-se** VR to get bored

entender [ẽtẽ'der] VT to understand; (*pensar*) to think; (*ouvir*) to hear; **entender-se** VR to understand one another; **dar a ~** to imply; **no meu ~** in my opinion; **~ de música** to know about music; **~ de fazer** to decide to do; **~-se por** to be meant by; **~-se com alguém** to get along with sb; (*dialogar*) to sort things out with sb

entendimento [ẽtẽdʒi'mẽtu] M understanding

enterrar [ẽte'har] VT to bury; (*faca*) to plunge; (*levar à ruína*) to ruin; (*assunto*) to close

enterro [ẽ'tehu] M burial; (*funeral*) funeral

entidade [ẽtʃi'dadʒi] F (*ser*) being; (*corporação*) body; (*coisa que existe*) entity

entornar [ẽtor'nar] VT to spill; (*fig: copo*) to drink ▶ VI to drink a lot

entorpecente [ẽtorpe'sẽtʃi] M narcotic

entorpecimento [ẽtorpesi'mẽtu] M numbness; (*torpor*) lethargy

entorse [ẽ'tɔrsi] F sprain

entortar [ẽtor'tar] VT (*curvar*) to bend; (*empenar*) to warp; **~ os olhos** to squint

entrada [ẽ'trada] F (*ato*) entry; (*lugar*) entrance; (*Tec*) inlet; (*de casa*) doorway; (*começo*) beginning; (*bilhete*) ticket; (*Culin*) starter, entrée; (*Comput*) input; (*pagamento inicial*) down payment; (*corredor de casa*) hall; **entradas** FPL (*no cabelo*) receding hairline; **~ gratuita** admission free; **"~ proibida"** "no entry", "no admittance"; **meia ~** half-price ticket

entra e sai ['ẽtrai'saj] M comings and goings *pl*

entranhado, -a [ẽtra'ɲadu, a] ADJ deep-rooted

entranhas [ẽ'traɲas] FPL bowels, entrails; (*sentimentos*) feelings; (*centro*) heart *sg*

entrar [ẽ'trar] VI to go (*ou* come) in, enter; **~ com** (*Comput: dados etc*) to enter; **eu entrei com £100** I put in £100; **~ de férias/licença** to start one's holiday (BRIT) *ou* vacation (US)/leave; **~ em** to go (*ou* come) into, enter; (*assunto*) to get onto; (*comida, bebida*) to start in on

entrave [ẽ'travi] M (*fig*) impediment

entre ['ẽtri] PREP (*dois*) between; (*mais de dois*) among(st); **~ si** amongst themselves

entreaberto, -a [ẽtrja'bɛrtu, a] ADJ half-open; (*porta*) ajar

entrega [ẽ'trɛga] F (*de mercadorias*) delivery; (*a alguém*) handing over; (*rendição*) surrender; **~ rápida** special delivery

entregar [ẽtre'gar] VT to hand over; (*mercadorias*) to deliver; (*confiar*) to entrust; (*devolver*) to return; **entregar-se** VR (*render-se*) to give o.s. up; (*dedicar-se*) to devote o.s.

entregue [ẽ'trɛgi] PP *de* **entregar**

entrelinha [ẽtre'liɲa] F line space; **ler nas ~s** to read between the lines

entreolhar-se [ẽtrio'ʎarsɪ] VR to exchange glances

entretanto [ẽtri'tãtu] CONJ however

entretenimento [ẽtriteni'mẽtu] M entertainment; (*distração*) pastime

entreter [ẽtri'ter] (*irreg: como* **ter**) VT to entertain, amuse; (*ocupar*) to occupy; (*manter*) to keep up; (*esperanças*) to cherish; **entreter-se** VR to amuse o.s.; to occupy o.s.

entrevista [ẽtre'vista] F interview;

~ coletiva (à imprensa) press conference; **entrevistar** [ẽtrevis'tar] VT to interview; **entrevistar-se** VR to have an interview
entristecer [ẽtriste'ser] VT to sadden, grieve ▶ VI to feel sad; **entristecer-se** VR to feel sad
entroncamento [ẽtrõka'mẽtu] M junction
entrudo [ẽ'trudu] (PT) M carnival; (*Rel*) Shrovetide
entulhar [ẽtu'ʎar] VT to cram full; (*suj: multidão*) to pack
entupido, -a [ẽtu'pidu, a] ADJ blocked; **estar ~** (*col: congestionado*) to have a blocked-up nose; (*de comida*) to be fit to burst, be full up
entupimento [ẽtupi'mẽtu] M blockage
entupir [ẽtu'pir] VT to block, clog; **entupir-se** VR to become blocked; (*de comida*) to stuff o.s.
entusiasmar [ẽtuzjaz'mar] VT to fill with enthusiasm; (*animar*) to excite; **entusiasmar-se** VR to get excited
entusiasmo [ẽtu'zjazmu] M enthusiasm; (*júbilo*) excitement
entusiasta [ẽtu'zjasta] ADJ enthusiastic ▶ M/F enthusiast
enumerar [enume'rar] VT to enumerate; (*com números*) to number
envelhecer [ẽveʎe'ser] VT to age ▶ VI to grow old, age
envelope [ẽve'lɔpi] M envelope
envenenamento [ẽvenena'mẽtu] M poisoning; **~ do sangue** blood poisoning
envenenar [ẽvene'nar] VT to poison; (*fig*) to corrupt; (*: declaração, palavras*) to distort, twist; (*tornar amargo*) to sour ▶ VI to be poisonous; **envenenar-se** VR to poison o.s.
envergonhado, -a [ẽvergo'ɲadu, a] ADJ ashamed; (*tímido*) shy
envergonhar [ẽvergo'ɲar] VT to shame; (*degradar*) to disgrace; **envergonhar-se** VR to be ashamed
enviado, -a [ẽ'vjadu, a] M/F envoy, messenger
enviar [ẽ'vjar] VT to send
envio [ẽ'viu] M sending; (*expedição*) dispatch; (*remessa*) remittance; (*de mercadorias*) consignment
enviuvar [ẽvju'var] VI to be widowed
envolver [ẽvow'ver] VT to wrap (up); (*cobrir*) to cover; (*comprometer, acarretar*) to involve; (*nos braços*) to embrace; **envolver-se** VR (*intrometer-se*) to become involved; (*cobrir-se*) to wrap o.s. up; **envolvimento** [ẽvowvi'mẽtu] M involvement
enxada [ẽ'ʃada] F hoe
enxaguar [ẽʃa'gwar] VT to rinse
enxame [ẽ'ʃami] M swarm
enxaqueca [ẽʃa'keka] F migraine
enxergar [ẽʃer'gar] VT (*avistar*) to catch sight of; (*divisar*) to make out; (*notar*) to observe, see
enxofre [ẽ'ʃofri] M sulphur (BRIT), sulfur (US)
enxotar [ẽʃo'tar] VT to drive out
enxoval [ẽʃo'vaw] (*pl* **-ais**) M (*de noiva*) trousseau; (*de recém-nascido*) layette
enxugar [ẽʃu'gar] VT to dry; (*fig: texto*) to tidy up
enxurrada [ẽʃu'hada] F (*de água*) torrent; (*fig*) spate

enxuto, -a [ẽ'ʃutu, a] ADJ dry; (*corpo*) shapely; (*bonito*) good-looking
épico, -a ['ɛpiku, a] ADJ epic ▶ M epic poet
epidemia [epide'mia] F epidemic
epilepsia [epile'psia] F epilepsy
episódio [epi'zɔdʒu] M episode
época ['ɛpoka] F time, period; (*da história*) age, epoch; **naquela ~** at that time; **fazer ~** to be epoch-making
equação [ekwa'sãw] (*pl* **-ões**) F equation
Equador [ekwa'dor] M: **o ~** Ecuador
equador [ekwa'dor] M equator
equilibrar [ekili'brar] VT to balance; **equilibrar-se** VR to balance; **equilíbrio** [eki'librju] M balance
equipa [e'kipa] (PT) F team
equipamento [ekipa'mẽtu] M equipment, kit
equipar [eki'par] VT (*navio*) to fit out; (*prover*) to equip
equipe [e'kipi] (BR) F team
equitação [ekita'sãw] F (*ato*) riding; (*arte*) horsemanship
equivalente [ekiva'lẽtʃi] ADJ, M equivalent
equivaler [ekiva'ler] VI: **~ a** to be the same as, equal
equivocado, -a [ekivo'kadu, a] ADJ mistaken, wrong
equivocar-se [ekivo'karsi] VR to make a mistake, be wrong
era[1] ['ɛra] F era, age
era[2] VB *ver* **ser**
erário [e'rarju] M exchequer
ereto, -a [e'rɛtu, a] ADJ upright, erect
erguer [er'ger] VT to raise, lift; (*edificar*) to build, erect; **erguer-se** VR to rise; (*pessoa*) to stand up
eriçar [eri'sar] VT: **~ o cabelo de alguém** to make sb's hair stand on end; **eriçar-se** VR to bristle; (*cabelos*) to stand on end
erigir [eri'ʒir] VT to erect
erosão [ero'zãw] F erosion
erótico, -a [e'rɔtʃiku, a] ADJ erotic
errado, -a [e'hadu, a] ADJ wrong; **dar ~** to go wrong
errar [e'har] VT (*alvo*) to miss; (*conta*) to get wrong ▶ VI to wander, roam; (*enganar-se*) to be wrong, make a mistake; **~ o caminho** to lose one's way
erro ['ehu] M mistake; **salvo ~** unless I am mistaken; **~ de imprensa** misprint
errôneo, -a [e'honju, a] ADJ wrong, mistaken; (*falso*) false, untrue
erva ['ɛrva] F herb; **~ daninha** weed; (*col: dinheiro*) dosh; (*: maconha*) dope
erva-mate (*pl* **ervas-mate(s)**) F maté
ervilha [er'viʎa] F pea
esbanjar [izbã'ʒar] VT to squander, waste
esbarrar [izba'har] VI: **~ em** to bump into; (*obstáculo, problema*) to come up against
esbelto, -a [iz'bɛwtu, a] ADJ slim, slender
esboçar [izbo'sar] VT to sketch; (*delinear*) to outline; (*plano*) to draw up; **esboço** [iz'bosu] M sketch; (*primeira versão*) draft; (*fig: resumo*) outline
esbofetear [izbofe'tʃjar] VT to slap, hit
esburacar [izbura'kar] VT to make holes (*ou* a hole) in
esc (PT) ABR = **escudo**
escabroso, -a [iska'brozu, ɔza] ADJ

(*difícil*) tough; (*indecoroso*) indecent
escada [is'kada] F (*dentro da casa*) staircase, stairs *pl*; (*fora da casa*) steps *pl*; (*de mão*) ladder; **~ de incêndio** fire escape; **~ rolante** escalator; **escadaria** [iskada'ria] F staircase
escala [is'kala] F scale; (*Náut*) port of call; (*parada*) stop; **fazer ~ em** to call at; **sem ~** non-stop
escalada [iska'lada] F (*de guerra*) escalation
escalão [eska'lãw] (*pl* **-ões**) M step; (*Mil*) echelon
escalar [iska'lar] VT (*montanha*) to climb; (*muro*) to scale; (*designar*) to select
escaldar [iskaw'dar] VT to scald; **escaldar-se** VR to scald o.s.
escalões [ɛska'lõjs] MPL *de* **escalão**
escama [is'kama] F (*de peixe*) scale; (*de pele*) flake
escancarado, -a [iskãka'radu, a] ADJ wide open
escandalizar [iskãdali'zar] VT to shock; **escandalizar-se** VR to be shocked; (*ofender-se*) to be offended
escândalo [is'kãdalu] M scandal; (*indignação*) outrage; **fazer** *ou* **dar um ~** to make a scene;
escandaloso, -a [iskãda'lozu, ɔza] ADJ shocking, scandalous
Escandinávia [iskãdʒi'navja] F: **a ~** Scandinavia; **escandinavo, -a** [iskãdʒi'navu, a] ADJ, M/F Scandinavian
escangalhar [iskãga'ʎar] VT to break, smash (up); **escangalhar-se** VR: **~-se de rir** to split one's sides laughing
escapar [iska'par] VI: **~ a** *ou* **de** to escape from; (*fugir*) to run away from; **escapar-se** VR to run away, flee; **deixar ~** (*uma oportunidade*) to miss; (*palavras*) to blurt out; **~ de boa** (*col*) to have a close shave
escapatória [iskapa'tɔrja] F way out; (*desculpa*) excuse
escape [is'kapi] M (*de gás*) leak; (*Auto*) exhaust
escapulir [iskapu'lir] VI: **~ (de)** to get away (from); (*suj: coisa*) to slip (from)
escarrar [iska'har] VT to spit, cough up ▶ VI to spit
escarro [is'kahu] M phlegm, spit
escassear [iska'sjar] VT to skimp on ▶ VI to become scarce
escassez [iska'sez] F (*falta*) shortage
escavar [iska'var] VT to excavate
esclarecer [isklare'ser] VT (*situação*) to explain; (*mistério*) to clear up, explain; **esclarecer-se** VR: **~-se (sobre algo)** to find out (about sth); **esclarecimento** [isklaresi'mẽtu] M explanation; (*informação*) information
escoadouro [iskoa'doru] M drain; (*cano*) drainpipe
escocês, -esa [isko'ses, seza] ADJ Scottish, Scots ▶ M/F Scot, Scotsman/woman
Escócia [is'kɔsja] F Scotland
escola [is'kɔla] F school; **~ de línguas** language school; **~ naval** naval college; **~ primária/secundária** primary (BRIT) *ou* elementary (US) /secondary (BRIT) *ou* high (US) school; **~ particular/pública** private/state (BRIT) *ou* public (US) school; **~ superior** college

Escolas de samba are musical and recreational associations made up, among others, of samba dancers, percussionists and carnival dancers. Although they exist throughout Brazil, the most famous schools are in Rio de Janeiro. The schools in Rio rehearse all year long for the **carnaval**, when they parade along the *Sambódromo*, a purpose-built avenue flanked by stands for spectators, and compete for the samba school championship. Characterised by their extravagance, the biggest schools have up to 4,000 members and are one of Brazil's major tourist attractions.

escolar [isko'lar] ADJ school *atr* ▶ M/F schoolboy/girl

escolha [is'koʎa] F choice

escolher [isko'ʎer] VT to choose, select

escolho [is'koʎu] M (*recife*) reef; (*rocha*) rock

escolta [is'kɔwta] F escort; **escoltar** [iskow'tar] VT to escort

escombros [is'kõbrus] MPL ruins, debris *sg*

esconde-esconde [iskõdʒis'kõdʒi] M hide-and-seek

esconder [iskõ'der] VT to hide, conceal; **esconder-se** VR to hide

escondidas [iskõ'dʒidas] FPL: **às ~** secretly

escopo [is'kopu] M aim, purpose

escorar [isko'rar] VT to prop (up); (*amparar*) to support; (*esperar de espreita*) to lie in wait for ▶ VI to lie in wait; **escorar-se** VR: **~-se em** (*fundamentar-se*) to go by; (*amparar-se*) to live off

escore [is'kɔri] M score

escoriação [iskorja'sãw] (*pl* **-ões**) F abrasion, scratch

escorpião [iskorpi'ãw] (*pl* **-ões**) M scorpion; **E~** (*Astrologia*) Scorpio

escorrega [isko'hɛga] F slide; **escorregadela** [iskohega'dɛla] F slip; **escorregadio, -a** [iskohega'dʒiu, a] ADJ slippery; **escorregão** [iskohe'gãw] (*pl* **-ões**) M slip; (*fig*) slip(-up); **escorregar** [iskohe'gar] VI to slip; (*errar*) to slip up

escorrer [isko'her] VT to drain (off); (*verter*) to pour out ▶ VI (*pingar*) to drip; (*correr em fio*) to trickle

escoteiro [isko'tejru] M scout

escova [is'kova] F brush; (*penteado*) blow-dry; **~ de dentes** toothbrush; **~ progressiva** keratin straightening; **escovar** [isko'var] VT to brush

escravatura [iskrava'tura] F (*tráfico*) slave trade; (*escravidão*) slavery

escravidão [iskravi'dãw] F slavery

escravizar [iskravi'zar] VT to enslave; (*cativar*) to captivate

escravo, -a [is'kravu, a] ADJ captive ▶ M/F slave

escrever [iskre'ver] VT, VI to write; **escrever-se** VR to write to each other; **~ à máquina** to type

escrita [es'krita] F writing; (*pessoal*) handwriting

escrito, -a [es'kritu, a] PP *de* **escrever** ▶ ADJ written ▶ M piece of writing; **~ à mão** handwritten; **dar por ~** to put in writing

escritor, a [iskri'tor(a)] M/F writer; (*autor*) author

escritório [iskri'tɔrju] M office; (*em casa*) study

escritura [iskri'tura] F (*Jur*) deed; (*na compra de imóveis*) ≈ exchange of contracts; **as Sagradas E~s** the Scriptures

escrivã [iskri'vã] F *de* **escrivão**

escrivaninha [iskriva'niɲa] F writing desk
escrivão, -vã [iskri'vãw, vã] (*pl* **-ões/-s**) M/F registrar, recorder
escrupuloso, -a [iskrupu'lozu, ɔza] ADJ scrupulous; (*cuidadoso*) careful
escudo [is'kudu] M shield; (*moeda*) escudo
esculhambado, -a [iskuʎã'badu, a] (*!*) ADJ shabby, slovenly; (*estragado*) knackered
esculhambar [iskuʎã'bar] (*!*) VT to mess up, fuck up (*!*); **~ alguém** (*criticar*) to give sb stick; (*descompor*) to give sb a bollocking (*!*)
esculpir [iskuw'pir] VT to carve, sculpt; (*gravar*) to engrave
escultor, a [iskuw'tor(a)] M/F sculptor
escultura [iskuw'tura] F sculpture
escuras [is'kuras] FPL: **às ~** in the dark
escurecer [iskure'ser] VT to darken ▶ VI to get dark; **ao ~** at dusk
escuridão [iskuri'dãw] F (*trevas*) darkness
escuro, -a [is'kuru, a] ADJ dark; (*dia*) overcast; (*pessoa*) swarthy ▶ M dark
escuso, -a [is'kuzu, a] ADJ shady
escuta [is'kuta] F listening; **à ~** listening out; **ficar na ~** to stand by
escutar [isku'tar] VT to listen to; (*sem prestar atenção*) to hear ▶ VI to listen; to hear
esfacelar [isfase'lar] VT to destroy
esfaquear [isfaki'ar] VT to stab
esfarrapado, -a [isfaha'padu, a] ADJ (*roupa*) ragged, tattered; (*desculpa*) lame
esfera [is'fɛra] F sphere; (*globo*) globe
esfolar [isfo'lar] VT to skin; (*arranhar*) to graze; (*cobrar demais a*) to overcharge, fleece
esfomeado, -a [isfo'mjadu, a] ADJ famished, starving
esforçado, -a [isfor'sadu, a] ADJ committed, dedicated
esforçar-se [isfor'sarsi] VR: **~ para** to try hard to, strive to
esforço [is'forsu] M effort
esfregar [isfre'gar] VT to rub; (*com água*) to scrub
esfriar [is'frjar] VT to cool, chill ▶ VI to get cold; (*fig*) to cool off
esganar [izga'nar] VT to strangle, choke
esgotado, -a [izgo'tadu, a] ADJ exhausted; (*consumido*) used up; (*livros*) out of print; **os ingressos estão ~s** the tickets are sold out
esgotamento [izgota'mẽtu] M exhaustion
esgotar [izgo'tar] VT to drain, empty; (*recursos*) to use up; (*pessoa, assunto*) to exhaust; **esgotar-se** VR to become exhausted; (*mercadorias, edição*) to be sold out; (*recursos*) to run out
esgoto [iz'gotu] M drain; (*público*) sewer
esgrima [iz'grima] F (*Esporte*) fencing
esgueirar-se [izgej'rarsi] VR to slip away, sneak off
esguelha [iz'geʎa] F slant; **olhar alguém de ~** to look at sb out of the corner of one's eye
esguio, -a [ez'giu, a] ADJ slender
esmagador, a [izmaga'dor(a)] ADJ crushing; (*provas*) irrefutable; (*maioria*) overwhelming
esmalte [iz'mawtʃi] M enamel;

(*de unhas*) nail polish
esmeralda [izme'rawda] F emerald
esmerar-se [izme'rarsi] VR: **~ em** to take great care to
esmigalhar [izmiga'ʎar] VT to crumble; (*despedaçar*) to shatter; (*esmagar*) to crush; **esmigalhar-se** VR to crumble; (*vaso*) to smash, shatter
esmo ['ezmu] M: **a ~** at random; **falar a ~** to prattle
esmola [iz'mɔla] F alms *pl*; **pedir ~s** to beg
esmurrar [izmu'har] VT to punch
esoterismo [ezote'rizmu] M New Age
espacial [ispa'sjaw] (*pl* **-ais**) ADJ space *atr*; **nave ~** spaceship
espaço [is'pasu] M space; (*tempo*) period; **~ para 3 pessoas** room for 3 people; **a ~s** from time to time; **espaçoso, -a** [ispa'sozu, ɔza] ADJ spacious, roomy
espada [is'pada] F sword; **espadas** FPL (*Cartas*) spades
espadarte [ispa'dartʃi] M swordfish
espairecer [ispajre'ser] VT to amuse, entertain ▶ VI to relax; **espairecer-se** VR to relax
espaldar [ispaw'dar] M (chair) back
espalhafato [ispaʎa'fatu] M din, commotion
espalhar [ispa'ʎar] VT to scatter; (*boato, medo*) to spread; (*luz*) to shed; **espalhar-se** VR to spread; (*refestelar-se*) to lounge
espanador [ispana'dor] M duster
espancar [ispã'kar] VT to beat up
Espanha [is'paɲa] F: **a ~** Spain; **espanhol, a** [ispa'ɲɔw, ɔla] (*pl* **-óis/-s**) ADJ Spanish ▶ M/F Spaniard ▶ M (*Ling*) Spanish; **os espanhóis** MPL the Spanish
espantado, -a [ispã'tadu, a] ADJ astonished
espantalho [ispã'taʎu] M scarecrow
espantar [ispã'tar] VT to frighten; (*admirar*) to amaze, astonish; (*afugentar*) to frighten away ▶ VI to be amazing; **espantar-se** VR to be amazed; (*assustar-se*) to be frightened
espanto [is'pãtu] M fright, fear; (*admiração*) amazement; **espantoso, -a** [ispã'tozu, ɔza] ADJ amazing
esparadrapo [ispara'drapu] M (sticking) plaster (BRIT), bandaid® (US)
esparramar [ispaha'mar] VT to splash; (*espalhar*) to scatter
esparso, -a [is'parsu, a] ADJ scattered; (*solto*) loose
espasmo [is'pazmu] M spasm, convulsion
espatifar [ispatʃi'far] VT to smash; **espatifar-se** VR to smash; (*avião*) to crash
especial [ispe'sjaw] (*pl* **-ais**) ADJ special; **em ~** especially; **especialidade** [ispesjali'dadʒi] F speciality (BRIT), specialty (US); (*ramo de atividades*) specialization; **especialista** [ispesja'lista] M/F specialist; (*perito*) expert; **especializar-se** [ispesjali'zarsi] VR: **especializar-se (em)** to specialize (in)
espécie [is'pɛsi] F (*Bio*) species; (*tipo*) sort, kind; **causar ~** to be surprising; **pagar em ~** to pay in cash
especificar [ispesifi'kar] VT to specify; **específico, -a** [ispe'sifiku, a] ADJ specific

espécime [is'pɛsimi] M specimen
espécimen [is'pɛsimẽ] (*pl* **-s**) M = **espécime**
espectador, a [ispekta'dor(a)] M/F onlooker; (*TV*) viewer; (*Esporte*) spectator; (*Teatro*) member of the audience; **espectadores** MPL audience *sg*
especular [ispeku'lar] VI: **~ (sobre)** to speculate (on)
espelho [is'peʎu] M mirror; (*fig*) model; **~ retrovisor** (*Auto*) rear-view mirror
espera [is'pɛra] F (*demora*) wait; (*expectativa*) expectation; **à ~ de** waiting for; **à minha ~** waiting for me
esperança [ispe'rãsa] F hope; (*expectativa*) expectation; **dar ~s a alguém** to get sb's hopes up; **esperançoso, -a** [isperã'sozu, ɔza] ADJ hopeful
esperar [ispe'rar] VT to wait for; (*desejar*) to hope for; (*contar com, bebê*) to expect ▸ VI to wait; to hope; to expect
esperma [is'pɛrma] M sperm
espertalhão, -lhona [isperta'ʎãw, ʎɔna] (*pl* **-ões/-s**) ADJ crafty, shrewd
esperteza [isper'teza] F cleverness; (*astúcia*) cunning
esperto, -a [is'pɛrtu, a] ADJ clever; (*espertalhão*) crafty
espetacular [ispetaku'lar] ADJ spectacular
espetáculo [ispe'takulu] M (*Teatro*) show; (*vista*) sight; (*cena ridícula*) spectacle; **dar ~** to make a spectacle of o.s.
espetar [ispe'tar] VT (*carne*) to put on a spit; (*cravar*) to stick; **espetar-se** VR to prick o.s.; **~ algo em algo** to pin sth to sth
espeto [is'petu] M spit; (*pau*) pointed stick; **ser um ~** (*ser difícil*) to be awkward
espevitado, -a [ispevi'tadu, a] ADJ (*fig: vivo*) lively
espiã [is'pjã] F *de* **espião**
espiada [is'pjada] F: **dar uma ~** to have a look
espião, -piã [is'pjãw, 'pjã] (*pl* **-ões/-s**) M/F spy
espiar [is'pjar] VT to spy on; (*uma ocasião*) to watch out for; (*olhar*) to watch ▸ VI to spy; (*olhar*) to peer
espiga [is'piga] F (*de milho*) ear
espinafre [ispi'nafri] M spinach
espingarda [ispĩ'garda] F shotgun, rifle
espinha [is'piɲa] F (*de peixe*) bone; (*na pele*) spot, zit (*col*); (*coluna vertebral*) spine
espinho [is'piɲu] M thorn; (*de animal*) spine; (*fig: dificuldade*) snag; **espinhoso, -a** [ispi'ɲozu, ɔza] ADJ (*planta*) prickly, thorny; (*fig: difícil*) difficult; (*: problema*) thorny
espiões [is'pjõjs] MPL *de* **espião**
espionar [ispjo'nar] VT to spy on ▸ VI to spy, snoop
espírito [is'piritu] M spirit; (*pensamento*) mind; **~ esportivo** sense of humo(u)r; **E~ Santo** Holy Spirit
espiritual [ispiri'twaw] (*pl* **-ais**) ADJ spiritual
espirituoso, -a [ispiri'twozu, ɔza] ADJ witty
espirrar [ispi'har] VI to sneeze; (*jorrar*) to spurt out ▸ VT (*água*) to spurt; **espirro** [is'pihu] M sneeze
esplêndido, -a [is'plẽdʒidu, a] ADJ splendid
esplendor [isplẽ'dor] M splendour (BRIT), splendor (US)

e

esponja [is'põʒa] F sponge
espontâneo, -a [ispõ'tanju, a] ADJ spontaneous; (*pessoa*) straightforward
esporádico, -a [ispo'radʒiku, a] ADJ sporadic
esporte [is'pɔrtʃi] (BR) M sport; **esportista** [ispor'tʃista] ADJ sporting ▶ M/F sportsman/woman; **esportivo, -a** [ispor'tʃivu, a] ADJ sporting
esposa [is'poza] F wife
esposo [is'pozu] M husband
espreguiçadeira [ispregisa'dejra] F deck chair; (*com lugar para as pernas*) lounger
espreguiçar-se [ispregi'sarsi] VR to stretch
espreita [is'prejta] F: **ficar à ~** to keep watch
espreitar [isprej'tar] VT to spy on; (*observar*) to observe, watch
espremer [ispre'mer] VT (*fruta*) to squeeze; (*roupa molhada*) to wring out; (*pessoas*) to squash; **espremer-se** VR (*multidão*) to be squashed together; (*uma pessoa*) to squash up
espuma [is'puma] F foam; (*de cerveja*) froth, head; (*de sabão*) lather; (*de ondas*) surf; **~ de borracha** foam rubber; **espumante** [ispu'mãtʃi] ADJ frothy, foamy; (*vinho*) sparkling
esq. ABR (= *esquerdo*) l.; = **esquina**
esquadra [is'kwadra] F (*Náut*) fleet; (PT: *da polícia*) police station
esquadrão [iskwa'drãw] (*pl* **-ões**) M squadron
esquadrilha [iskwa'driʎa] F squadron
esquadrões [iskwa'drõjs] MPL *de* **esquadrão**
esquartejar [iskwarte'ʒar] VT to quarter
esquecer [iske'ser] VT, VI to forget; **esquecer-se** VR: **~-se de** to forget; **esquecido, -a** [iske'sidu, a] ADJ forgotten; (*pessoa*) forgetful
esqueleto [iske'letu] M skeleton; (*arcabouço*) framework
esquema [is'kɛma] M outline; (*plano*) scheme; (*diagrama*) diagram, plan
esquentar [iskẽ'tar] VT to heat (up), warm (up); (*fig: irritar*) to annoy ▶ VI to warm up; (*casaco*) to be warm; **esquentar-se** VR to get annoyed
esquerda [is'kerda] F (*tb Pol*) left; **à ~** on the left
esquerdista [isker'dʒista] ADJ left-wing ▶ M/F left-winger
esquerdo, -a [is'kerdu, a] ADJ left
esqui [is'ki] M (*patim*) ski; (*esporte*) skiing; **~ aquático** water skiing; **fazer ~** to go skiing; **esquiar** [is'kjar] VI to ski
esquilo [is'kilu] M squirrel
esquina [is'kina] F corner
esquisito, -a [iski'zitu, a] ADJ strange, odd
esquivar-se [iski'varsi] VR: **~ de** to escape from, get away from; (*deveres*) to get out of
esquivo, -a [is'kivu, a] ADJ aloof, standoffish
essa ['ɛsa] PRON: **~ é/foi boa** that is/was a good one; **~ não, sem ~** come off it!; **vamos nessa** let's go!; **ainda mais ~!** that's all I need!; **corta ~!** cut it out!; **por ~s e outras** for these and other reasons; **~ de fazer ...** this business of doing ...
esse ['esi] ADJ (*sg*) that; (*pl*) those; (BR: *este: sg*) this; (*: pl*) these ▶ PRON (*sg*) that one; (*pl*) those (ones); (BR: *este: sg*) this one; (*: pl*) these (ones)
essência [e'sẽsja] F essence;

essencial [esẽ'sjaw] (*pl* **-ais**) ADJ essential; (*principal*) main ▶ M: **o essencial** the main thing

esta ['ɛsta] F *de* **este²**

estabelecer [istabele'ser] VT to establish; (*fundar*) to set up

estabelecimento [istabelesi'mẽtu] M establishment; (*casa comercial*) business

estábulo [is'tabulu] M cow-shed

estaca [is'taka] F post, stake; (*de barraca*) peg

estação [ista'sãw] (*pl* **-ões**) F station; (*do ano*) season; **~ de águas** spa; **~ balneária** seaside resort; **~ emissora** broadcasting station

estacionamento [istasjona'mẽtu] M (*ato*) parking; (*lugar*) car park (BRIT), parking lot (US)

estacionar [istasjo'nar] VT to park ▶ VI to park; (*não mover*) to remain stationary

estacionário, -a [istasjo'narju, a] ADJ (*veículo*) stationary; (*Com*) slack

estações [ista'sõjs] FPL *de* **estação**

estada [is'tada] F stay

estadia [ista'dʒia] F = **estada**

estádio [is'tadʒu] M stadium

estadista [ista'dʒista] M/F statesman/woman

estado [i'stadu] M state; **E~s Unidos (da América)** United States (of America); **~ civil** marital status; **~ de espírito** state of mind; **~ maior** staff; **estadual** [ista'dwaw] (*pl* **-ais**) ADJ state *atr*

estafa [is'tafa] F fatigue; (*esgotamento*) nervous exhaustion

estagiário, -a [ista'ʒjarju, a] M/F (*empregado*) trainee; (*estudante*) intern; (*professor*) student teacher; (*médico*) junior doctor

estágio [is'taʒu] M (*aprendizado: de empregado*) traineeship; (: *de estudante*) internship; (*fase*) stage

estagnado, -a [istag'nadu, a] ADJ stagnant

estalar [ista'lar] VT to break; (*os dedos*) to snap ▶ VI to split, crack; (*crepitar*) to crackle

estalido [ista'lidu] M pop

estalo [is'talu] M (*do chicote*) crack; (*dos dedos*) snap; (*dos lábios*) smack; (*de foguete*) bang; **~ de trovão** thunderclap; **de ~** suddenly

estampa [is'tãpa] F (*figura impressa*) print; (*ilustração*) picture

estampado, -a [istã'padu, a] ADJ printed ▶ M (*tecido*) print; (*num tecido*) pattern

estampar [istã'par] VT to print; (*marcar*) to stamp

estancar [istã'kar] VT to staunch; (*fazer cessar*) to stop; **estancar-se** VR to stop

estância [is'tãsja] F ranch, farm

estandarte [istã'dartʃi] M standard, banner

estanho [is'taɲu] M (*metal*) tin

estante [is'tãtʃi] F bookcase; (*suporte*) stand

PALAVRA-CHAVE

estar [is'tar] VI **1** (*lugar*) to be; (*em casa*) to be in; (*no telefone*): **a Lúcia está? — não, ela não está** is Lúcia there? — no, she's not in

2 (*estado*) to be; **estar doente** to be ill; **estar bem** (*de saúde*) to be well; (*financeiramente*) to be well off; **estar calor/frio** to be hot/cold; **estar com fome/sede/medo** to be hungry/thirsty/afraid

3 (*ação contínua*): **estar fazendo**

(BR) *ou* **a fazer** (PT) to be doing
4 (+ *pp, como adj*): **estar sentado/ cansado** to be sitting down/tired
5 (+ *pp, uso passivo*): **está condenado à morte** he's been condemned to death; **o livro está emprestado** the book's been borrowed
6: **estar de férias/licença** to be on holiday (BRIT) *ou* vacation (US)/ leave; **ela estava de chapéu** she had a hat on, she was wearing a hat
7: **estar para fazer** to be about to do; **ele está para chegar a qualquer momento** he'll be here any minute; **não estar para conversas** not to be in the mood for talking
8: **estar por fazer** to be still to be done
9: **estar sem dinheiro** to have no money; **estar sem dormir** not to have slept; **estou sem dormir há três dias** I haven't slept for three days; **está sem terminar** it isn't finished yet
10 (*frases*): **tá (bem)** (*col*) OK; **estar bem com** to be on good terms with

estardalhaço [istarda'ʎasu] M fuss; (*ostentação*) ostentation
estas ['ɛstas] FPL *de* **este²**
estatal [ista'taw] (*pl* **-ais**) ADJ nationalized, state-owned ▸ F state-owned company
estático, -a [is'tatʃiku, a] ADJ static
estatística [ista'tʃistʃika] F statistic; (*ciência*) statistics *sg*
estatizar [istatʃi'zar] VT to nationalize
estátua [is'tatwa] F statue
estatura [ista'tura] F stature
estável [is'tavew] (*pl* **-eis**) ADJ stable
este¹ ['ɛstʃi] M east ▸ ADJ INV (*região*) eastern; (*vento, direção*) easterly
este², esta ['estʃi, 'ɛsta] ADJ (*sg*) this; (*pl*) these ▸ PRON this one; (*pl*) these; (*a quem/que se referiu por último*) the latter; **esta noite** (*noite passada*) last night; (*noite de hoje*) tonight
esteira [is'tejra] F mat; (*de navio*) wake; (*rumo*) path
esteja [is'teʒa] VB *ver* **estar**
estelionato [isteljo'natu] M fraud
estender [istẽ'der] VT to extend; (*mapa*) to spread out; (*pernas*) to stretch; (*massa*) to roll out; (*conversa*) to draw out; (*corda*) to pull tight; (*roupa molhada*) to hang out; **estender-se** VR to lie down; (*fila, terreno*) to stretch, extend; **~-se sobre algo** to dwell on sth, expand on sth; **~ a mão** to hold out one's hand
estéreis [is'tɛrejs] ADJ PL *de* **estéril**
estereo... [isterju] PREFIXO stereo...; **estereofônico, -a** [isterjo'foniku, a] ADJ stereo(phonic); **estereótipo** [iste'rjɔtʃipu] M stereotype
estéril [is'tɛriw] (*pl* **-eis**) ADJ sterile; (*terra*) infertile; (*fig*) futile;
esterilizar [isterili'zar] VT to sterilize
esteve [is'tevi] VB *ver* **estar**
esticar [istʃi'kar] VT to stretch; **esticar-se** VR to stretch out
estigma [is'tʃigima] M mark, scar; (*fig*) stigma
estilhaçar [istʃiʎa'sar] VT to splinter; (*despedaçar*) to shatter; **estilhaçar-se** VR to shatter;
estilhaço [istʃi'ʎasu] M fragment; (*de pedra*) chip; (*de madeira, metal*) splinter
estilo [is'tʃilu] M style; (*Tec*) stylus;

~ de vida way of life
estima [is'tʃima] F esteem; (*afeto*) affection
estimação [istʃima'sãw] F: **... de ~** favourite (BRIT) ..., favorite (US) ...
estimado, -a [istʃi'madu, a] ADJ respected; (*em cartas*): **E~ Senhor** Dear Sir
estimar [istʃi'mar] VT to appreciate; (*avaliar*) to value; (*ter estima a*) to have a high regard for; (*calcular aproximadamente*) to estimate
estimativa [istʃima'tʃiva] F estimate
estimulante [istʃimu'lãtʃi] ADJ stimulating ▶ M stimulant
estimular [istʃimu'lar] VT to stimulate; (*incentivar*) to encourage; **estímulo** [is'tʃimulu] M stimulus; (*ânimo*) encouragement
estipular [istʃipu'lar] VT to stipulate
estirar [istʃi'rar] VT to stretch (out); **estirar-se** VR to stretch
estive [is'tʃivi] VB *ver* **estar**
estocada [isto'kada] F stab, thrust
estocar [isto'kar] VT to stock
estofo [is'tofu] M (*tecido*) material; (*para acolchoar*) padding, stuffing
estojo [is'toʒu] M case; **~ de ferramentas** tool kit; **~ de unhas** manicure set
estômago [is'tomagu] M stomach; **ter ~ para (fazer) algo** to be up to (doing) sth
estontear [istõ'tʃjar] VT to stun, daze
estoque [is'tɔki] M (*Com*) stock
estourado, -a [isto'radu, a] ADJ (*temperamental*) explosive; (*col: cansado*) knackered, worn out
estourar [isto'rar] VI to explode; (*pneu*) to burst; (*escândalo*) to blow up; (*guerra*) to break out; (BR: *chegar*) to turn up, arrive; **~ (com alguém)** (*zangar-se*) to blow up (at sb)
estouro [is'toru] M explosion; **dar o ~** (*fig: zangar-se*) to blow up, blow one's top
estrábico, -a [is'trabiku, a] ADJ cross-eyed
estraçalhar [istrasa'ʎar] VT (*livro, objeto*) to pull to pieces; (*pessoa*) to tear to pieces
estrada [is'trada] F road; **~ de ferro** (BR) railway (BRIT), railroad (US); **~ principal** main road (BRIT), state highway (US)
estrado [is'tradu] M (*tablado*) platform; (*de cama*) base
estragado, -a [istra'gadu, a] ADJ ruined; (*fruta*) rotten; (*muito mimado*) spoiled, spoilt (BRIT)
estraga-prazeres [istraga-] M/F INV spoilsport
estragar [istra'gar] VT to spoil; (*arruinar*) to ruin, wreck; (*desperdiçar*) to waste; (*saúde*) to damage; (*mimar*) to spoil; **estrago** [is'tragu] M destruction; (*desperdício*) waste; (*dano*) damage; **os estragos da guerra** the ravages of war
estrangeiro, -a [istrã'ʒejru, a] ADJ foreign ▶ M/F foreigner; **no ~** abroad
estrangular [istrãgu'lar] VT to strangle
estranhar [istra'ɲar] VT to be surprised at; (*achar estranho*): **~ algo** to find sth strange; **estranhei o clima** the climate did not agree with me; **não é de se ~** it's not surprising

estranho, -a [is'traɲu, a] ADJ strange, odd; (*influências*) outside ▶ M/F (*desconhecido*) stranger; (*de fora*) outsider
estratégia [istra'tɛʒa] F strategy
estrear [is'trjar] VT (*vestido*) to wear for the first time; (*peça de teatro*) to perform for the first time; (*veículo*) to use for the first time; (*filme*) to show for the first time, première; (*iniciar*): **~ uma carreira** to embark on *ou* begin a career ▶ VI (*ator, jogador*) to make one's first appearance; (*filme, peça*) to open
estrebaria [istreba'ria] F stable
estreia [is'treja] F (*de artista*) debut; (*de uma peça*) first night; (*de um filme*) première, opening
estreitar [istrej'tar] VT to narrow; (*roupa*) to take in; (*abraçar*) to hug; (*laços de amizade*) to strengthen ▶ VI (*estrada*) to narrow
estreito, -a [is'trejtu, a] ADJ narrow; (*saia*) straight; (*vínculo, relação*) close; (*medida*) strict ▶ M strait
estrela [is'trela] F star; **~ cadente** falling star; **estrelado, -a** [istre'ladu, a] ADJ (*céu*) starry; (*ovo*) fried
estremecer [istreme'ser] VT to shake; (*amizade*) to strain; (*fazer tremer*): **~ alguém** to make sb shudder ▶ VI to shake; (*tremer*) to tremble; (*horrorizar-se*) to shudder; (*amizade*) to be strained
estremecimento [istremesi'mẽtu] M shaking, trembling; (*tremor*) tremor; (*numa amizade*) tension
estresse [is'trɛsi] M stress
estribeira [istri'bejra] F: **perder as ~s** (*col*) to fly off the handle, lose one's temper
estridente [istri'dẽtʃi] ADJ shrill, piercing
estrofe [is'trɔfi] F stanza
estrondo [is'trõdu] M (*de trovão*) rumble; (*de armas*) din
estrutura [istru'tura] F structure; (*armação*) framework; (*de edifício*) fabric
estudante [istu'dãtʃi] M/F student; **estudantil** [istudã'tʃiw] (*pl* **-is**) ADJ student *atr*
estudar [istu'dar] VT, VI to study
estúdio [is'tudʒu] M studio
estudo [is'tudu] M study
estufa [is'tufa] F (*fogão*) stove; (*de plantas*) greenhouse; (*de fogão*) plate warmer; **efeito ~** greenhouse effect
estufado [istu'fadu] (PT) M stew
estupefato, -a [istupe'fatu, a], (PT) **estupefacto** ADJ dumbfounded
estupendo, -a [istu'pẽdu, a] ADJ wonderful; (*col*) terrific
estupidez [istupi'dez] F stupidity; (*ato, dito*) stupid thing; (*grosseria*) rudeness
estúpido, -a [is'tupidu, a] ADJ stupid; (*grosseiro*) rude, churlish ▶ M/F idiot; (*grosseiro*) oaf
estuprar [istu'prar] VT to rape; **estupro** [is'tupru] M rape
esvaziar [izva'zjar] VT to empty; **esvaziar-se** VR to empty
etapa [e'tapa] F stage
etc. ABR (= *et cetera*) etc
eternidade [eterni'dadʒi] F eternity
ética ['ɛtʃika] F ethics *pl*
ético, -a ['ɛtʃiku, a] ADJ ethical
Etiópia [e'tʃjɔpja] F: **a ~** Ethiopia
etiqueta [etʃi'keta] F etiquette; (*rótulo, em roupa*) label; (*que se amarra*) tag

étnico, -a ['ɛtʃniku, a] ADJ ethnic
etos ['ɛtus] M INV ethos
eu [ew] PRON I ▶ M self; **sou eu** it's me
EUA ABR MPL (= *Estados Unidos da América*) USA
eucaristia [ewkaris'tʃia] F Holy Communion
euro ['ewru] M (*moeda*) euro
Europa [ew'rɔpa] F: **a ~** Europe; **europeu, -peia** [ewro'peu, 'pɛja] ADJ, M/F European
evacuar [eva'kwar] VT to evacuate; (*sair de*) to leave; (*Med*) to discharge ▶ VI to defecate
evadir [eva'dʒir] VT to evade; **evadir-se** VR to escape
evangelho [evã'ʒeʎu] M gospel
evaporar [evapo'rar] VT, VI to evaporate; **evaporar-se** VR to evaporate; (*desaparecer*) to vanish
evasão [eva'zãw] (*pl* **-ões**) F escape, flight; (*fig*) evasion
evasiva [eva'ziva] F excuse
evasivo, -a [eva'zivu, a] ADJ evasive
evasões [eva'zõjs] FPL *de* **evasão**
evento [e'vẽtu] M event; (*eventualidade*) eventuality
eventual [evẽ'tuaw] (*pl* **-ais**) ADJ fortuitous, accidental; **eventualidade** [evẽtwali'dadʒi] F eventuality
evidência [evi'dẽsja] F evidence, proof; **evidenciar** [evidẽ'sjar] VT to prove; (*mostrar*) to show; **evidenciar-se** VR to be evident, be obvious
evidente [evi'dẽtʃi] ADJ obvious, evident
evitar [evi'tar] VT to avoid; **~ de fazer algo** to avoid doing sth
evocar [evo'kar] VT to evoke; (*espíritos*) to invoke
evolução [evolu'sãw] (*pl* **-ões**) F development; (*Mil*) manoeuvre (BRIT), maneuver (US); (*movimento*) movement; (*Bio*) evolution
evoluir [evo'lwir] VI to evolve; **~ para** to evolve into
Ex.a ABR = **excelência**
exagerar [ezaʒe'rar] VT to exaggerate ▶ VI to exaggerate; (*agir com exagero*) to overdo it; **exagero** [eza'ʒeru] M exaggeration
exalar [eza'lar] VT (*odor*) to give off
exaltado, -a [ezaw'tadu, a] ADJ fanatical; (*apaixonado*) overexcited
exaltar [ezaw'tar] VT (*elevar: pessoa, virtude*) to exalt; (*louvar*) to praise; (*excitar*) to excite; (*irritar*) to annoy; **exaltar-se** VR (*irritar-se*) to get worked up; (*arrebatar-se*) to get carried away
exame [e'zami] M (*Educ*) examination, exam; (*Med etc*) examination; **fazer um ~** (*Educ*) to take an exam; (*Med*) to have an examination
examinar [ezami'nar] VT to examine
exatidão [ezatʃi'dãw] F accuracy; (*perfeição*) correctness
exato, -a [e'zatu, a] ADJ right, correct; (*preciso*) exact; **~!** exactly!
exaustão [ezaw'stãw] F exhaustion; **exausto, -a** [e'zawstu, a] ADJ exhausted
exaustor [ezaw'stor] M extractor fan
exceção [ese'sãw] (*pl* **-ões**) F exception; **com ~ de** with the exception of; **abrir ~** to make an exception
excecional (PT) ADJ = **excepcional**
excedente [ese'dẽtʃi] ADJ excess; (*Com*) surplus ▶ M (*Com*) surplus

exceder [ese'der] VT to exceed; (*superar*) to surpass; **exceder-se** VR (*cometer excessos*) to go too far; (*cansar-se*) to overdo things
excelência [ese'lẽsja] F excellence; **por ~** par excellence; **Vossa E~** Your Excellency; **excelente** [ese'lẽtʃi] ADJ excellent
excêntrico, -a [e'sẽtriku, a] ADJ, M/F eccentric
excepcional [esepsjo'naw] (*pl* **-ais**) ADJ exceptional; (*especial*) special; (*Med*) handicapped
excesso [e'sɛsu] M excess; (*Com*) surplus
exceto [e'sɛtu] PREP except (for), apart from
excitação [esita'sãw] F excitement
excitado, -a [esi'tadu, a] ADJ excited; (*estimulado*) aroused
excitante [esi'tãtʃi] ADJ exciting
exclamação [isklama'sãw] (*pl* **-ões**) F exclamation
exclamar [iskla'mar] VI to exclaim
excluir [is'klwir] VT to exclude, leave out; (*eliminar*) to rule out; (*ser incompatível com*) to preclude; **exclusão** [isklu'zãw] F exclusion; **exclusivo, -a** [isklu'zivu, a] ADJ exclusive
excursão [iskur'sãw] (*pl* **-ões**) F outing; excursion; **~ a pé** hike; **excursionista** [iskursjo'nista] M/F tourist; (*para o dia*) day-tripper; (*a pé*) hiker
execução [ezeku'sãw] (*pl* **-ões**) F execution; (*de música*) performance
executar [ezeku'tar] VT to execute; (*Mús*) to perform; (*plano*) to carry out; (*papel teatral*) to play
executivo, -a [ezeku'tʃivu, a] ADJ, M/F executive
exemplar [ezẽ'plar] ADJ exemplary ▸ M model, example; (*Bio*) specimen; (*livro*) copy; (*peça*) piece
exemplo [e'zẽplu] M example; **por ~** for example
exercer [ezer'ser] VT to exercise; (*influência, pressão*) to exert; (*função*) to perform; (*profissão*) to practise (BRIT), practice (US); (*obrigações*) to carry out
exercício [ezer'sisju] M exercise; (*de medicina*) practice; (*Mil*) drill; (*Com*) financial year
exercitar [ezersi'tar] VT (*profissão*) to practise (BRIT), practice (US); (*direitos, músculos*) to exercise; (*adestrar*) to train
exército [e'zɛrsitu] M army
exibição [ezibi'sãw] (*pl* **-ões**) F show, display; (*de filme*) showing
exibir [ezi'bir] VT to show, display; (*alardear*) to show off; (*filme*) to show, screen; **exibir-se** VR to show off; (*indecentemente*) to expose o.s.
exigência [ezi'ʒẽsja] F demand; (*o necessário*) requirement; **exigente** [ezi'ʒẽtʃi] ADJ demanding
exigir [ezi'ʒir] VT to demand
exíguo, -a [e'zigwu, a] ADJ (*diminuto*) small; (*escasso*) scanty
exilado, -a [ezi'ladu, a] M/F exile
exilar [ezi'lar] VT to exile; **exilar-se** VR to go into exile; **exílio** [e'zilju] M exile; (*forçado*) deportation
existência [ezis'tẽsja] F existence; (*vida*) life
existir [ezis'tʃir] VI to exist; **existe/existem ...** (*há*) there is/are ...
êxito ['ezitu] M result; (*sucesso*) success; (*música, filme etc*) hit; **ter ~ (em)** to succeed (in), be successful (in)
Exmo, -a (*pl* **-s/-s**) ABR (= *Excelentíssimo*) Dear
êxodo ['ezodu] M exodus
exorcista [ezor'sista] M/F exorcist

exótico, -a [e'zɔtʃiku, a] ADJ exotic
expandir [ispã'dʒir] VT to expand; (*espalhar*) to spread; **expandir-se** VR to expand; **~-se com alguém** to be frank with sb
expansão [ispã'sãw] F expansion, spread; (*de alegria*) effusiveness
expansivo, -a [ispã'sivu, a] ADJ (*pessoa*) outgoing
expeça [is'pɛsa] VB *ver* **expedir**
expectativa [ispekta'tʃiva] F expectation
expedição [ispedʒi'sãw] (*pl* **-ões**) F (*viagem*) expedition; (*de mercadorias*) despatch; (*por navio*) shipment; (*de passaporte etc*) issue
expediente [ispe'dʒẽtʃi] M means; (*serviço*) working day; (*correspondência*) correspondence ▶ ADJ expedient; **~ bancário** banking hours *pl*; **~ do escritório** office hours *pl*
expedir [ispe'dʒir] VT to send, despatch; (*bilhete, passaporte, decreto*) to issue
expelir [ispe'lir] VT to expel; (*sangue*) to spit
experiência [ispe'rjẽsja] F experience; (*prova*) experiment, test; **em ~** on trial
experimentar [isperimẽ'tar] VT (*comida*) to taste; (*vestido*) to try on; (*pôr à prova*) to try out, test; (*conhecer pela experiência*) to experience; (*sofrer*) to suffer, undergo; **experimento** [isperi'mẽtu] M experiment
expilo [is'pilu] VB *ver* **expelir**
expirar [ispi'rar] VT to exhale, breathe out ▶ VI to die; (*terminar*) to end
explicação [isplika'sãw] (*pl* **-ões**) F explanation
explicar [ispli'kar] VT, VI to explain; **explicar-se** VR to explain o.s.
explícito, -a [is'plisitu, a] ADJ explicit, clear
explodir [isplo'dʒir] VT, VI to explode
exploração [isplora'sãw] F exploration; (*abuso*) exploitation; (*de uma mina*) running
explorador, a [isplora'dor(a)] M/F explorer; (*de outros*) exploiter
explorar [isplo'rar] VT (*região*) to explore; (*mina*) to work, run; (*ferida*) to probe; (*trabalhadores etc*) to exploit
explosão [isplo'zãw] (*pl* **-ões**) F explosion; (*fig*) outburst;
explosivo, -a [isplo'zivu, a] ADJ explosive; (*pessoa*) hot-headed ▶ M explosive
expor [is'por] (*irreg: como* **pôr**) VT to expose; (*a vida*) to risk; (*teoria*) to explain; (*revelar*) to reveal; (*mercadorias*) to display; (*quadros*) to exhibit; **expor-se** VR to expose o.s.
exportação [isporta'sãw] F (*ato*) export(ing); (*mercadorias*) exports *pl*
exportador, a [isporta'dor(a)] ADJ exporting ▶ M/F exporter
exportar [ispor'tar] VT to export
exposição [ispozi'sãw] (*pl* **-ões**) F exhibition; (*explicação*) explanation; (*declaração*) statement; (*narração*) account; (*Foto*) exposure
exposto, -a [is'postu, 'pɔsta] ADJ (*lugar*) exposed; (*quadro, mercadoria*) on show *ou* display ▶ M: **o acima ~** the above
expressão [ispre'sãw] (*pl* **-ões**) F expression
expressar [ispre'sar] VT to express;

expressivo, -a [ispre'sivu, a] ADJ expressive; (*pessoa*) demonstrative
expresso, -a [is'prɛsu, a] PP *de* **exprimir** ▶ ADJ definite, clear; (*trem, ordem, carta*) express ▶ M express
expressões [ispre'sõjs] FPL *de* **expressão**
exprimir [ispri'mir] VT to express
expulsão [ispu'sãw] (*pl* **-ões**) F expulsion; (*Esporte*) sending off
expulsar [ispuw'sar] VT to expel; (*de uma festa, clube etc*) to throw out; (*inimigo*) to drive out; (*estrangeiro*) to expel, deport; (*jogador*) to send off
expulso, -a [is'puwsu, a] PP *de* **expulsar**
expulsões [ispul'sõjs] FPL *de* **expulsão**
êxtase ['estazi] M ecstasy
extenso, -a [is'tẽsu, a] ADJ extensive; (*comprido*) long; (*artigo*) full, comprehensive; **por ~** in full
extenuante [iste'nwãtʃi] ADJ exhausting; (*debilitante*) debilitating
exterior [iste'rjor] ADJ (*de fora*) outside, exterior; (*aparência*) outward; (*comércio*) foreign ▶ M (*da casa*) outside; (*aspecto*) outward appearance; **do ~** (*do estrangeiro*) from abroad; **no ~** abroad
exterminar [istermi'nar] VT (*inimigo*) to wipe out, exterminate; (*acabar com*) to do away with
externo, -a [is'tɛrnu, a] ADJ external; (*aparente*) outward; **aluno ~** day pupil
extinguir [istʃĩ'gir] VT (*fogo*) to put out, extinguish; (*um povo*) to wipe out; **extinguir-se** VR (*fogo, luz*) to go out; (*Bio*) to become extinct
extinto, -a [is'tʃĩtu, a] ADJ (*fogo*) extinguished; (*língua*) dead; (*animal, vulcão*) extinct; (*associação etc*) defunct; **extintor** [istʃĩ'tor] M (fire) extinguisher
extorsão [istor'sãw] F extortion
extra ['ɛstra] ADJ extra ▶ M/F extra person; (*Teatro*) extra
extração [istra'sãw] (*pl* **-ões**) F extraction; (*de loteria*) draw
extrair [istra'jir] VT to extract, take out
extraordinário, -a [istraordʒi'narju, a] ADJ extraordinary; (*despesa*) extra; (*reunião*) special
extrato [is'tratu] M extract; (*resumo*) summary; **~ (bancário)** (bank) statement
extravagância [istrava'gãsja] F extravagance; **extravagante** [istrava'gãtʃi] ADJ extravagant; (*roupa*) outlandish; (*conduta*) wild
extravasar [istrava'zar] VI to overflow
extraviado, -a [istra'vjadu, a] ADJ lost, missing
extraviar [istra'vjar] VT to mislay; (*pessoa*) to lead astray; (*dinheiro*) to embezzle; **extraviar-se** VR to get lost; **extravio** [istra'viu] M loss; (*roubo*) embezzlement; (*fig*) deviation
extremado, -a [istre'madu, a] ADJ extreme
extremidade [istremi'dadʒi] F extremity; (*do dedo*) tip; (*ponta*) end; (*beira*) edge
extremo, -a [is'trɛmu, a] ADJ extreme ▶ M extreme; **ao ~** extremely
extrovertido, -a [estrover'tʃidu, a] ADJ extrovert, outgoing ▶ M/F extrovert
exultante [ezuw'tãtʃi] ADJ jubilant, exultant

f

fã [fã] (*col*) M/F fan

fábrica ['fabrika] F factory; **~ de cerveja** brewery; **a preço de ~** wholesale

fabricação [fabrika'sãw] F manufacture; **~ em série** mass production

fabuloso, -a [fabu'lozu, ɔza] ADJ fabulous

faca ['faka] F knife; **facada** [fa'kada] F stab, cut

façanha [fa'saɲa] F exploit, deed

facção [fak'sãw] (*pl* **-ões**) F faction

face ['fasi] F face; (*bochecha*) cheek; **em ~ de** in view of; **fazer ~ a** to face up to

fáceis ['fasejs] ADJ PL *de* **fácil**

faceta [fa'seta] F facet

fachada [fa'ʃada] F façade, front

fácil ['fasiw] (*pl* **-eis**) ADJ easy; (*temperamento, pessoa*) easy-going ▶ ADV easily; **facilidade** [fasili'dadʒi] F ease; (*jeito*) facility; **facilidades** FPL (*recursos*) facilities; **ter facilidade para algo** to have a talent *ou* a facility for sth

facilitar [fasili'tar] VT to facilitate, make easy; (*fornecer*): **~ algo a alguém** to provide sb with sth

fã-clube [fã'klubi] (*pl* **-s**) M fan club

faço ['fasu] VB *ver* **fazer**

facto ['faktu] (PT) M = **fato**

factual [fak'twaw] (*pl* **-ais**) ADJ factual

faculdade [fakuw'dadʒi] F faculty; (*poder*) power

facultativo, -a [fakuwta'tʃivu, a] ADJ optional ▶ M/F doctor

fadado, -a [fa'dadu, a] ADJ destined

fadiga [fa'dʒiga] F fatigue

fadista [fa'dʒista] M/F "fado" singer ▶ M (PT) ruffian

fado ['fadu] M fate; (*canção*) *traditional song of Portugal*

> The best-known musical form in Portugal is the melancholic **fado**, which is traditionally sung by a soloist (known as a *fadista*) accompanied by the Portuguese *guitarra*. There are two main types of **fado**: Coimbra **fado** is traditionally sung by men, and is considered to be more cerebral than the **fado** from Lisbon, which is sung by both men and women. The theme is nearly always one of deep nostalgia known as *saudade*, and the harsh reality of life.

faia ['faja] F beech (tree)

faisão [faj'zãw] (*pl* **-ões**) M pheasant

faísca [fa'iska] F spark; (*brilho*) flash

faisões [faj'zõjs] MPL *de* **faisão**

faixa ['fajʃa] F (*cinto, Judô*) belt;

(*tira*) strip; (*área*) zone; (*Auto: pista*) lane; (BR: *para pedestres*) zebra crossing (BRIT), crosswalk (US); (*Med*) bandage; (*num disco*) track

fala ['fala] F speech; **chamar às ~s** to call to account; **sem ~** speechless

falante [fa'lãtʃi] ADJ talkative

falar [fa'lar] VT (*língua*) to speak; (*besteira etc*) to talk; (*dizer*) to say; (*verdade, mentira*) to tell ▶ VI to speak; **~ algo a alguém** to tell sb sth; **~ de** *ou* **em algo** to talk about sth; **~ com alguém** to talk to sb; **por ~ em** speaking of; **sem ~ em** not to mention; **falou!, 'tá falado!** (*col*) OK!

falcão [faw'kãw] (*pl* **-ões**) M falcon

falcatrua [fawka'trua] F (*col*) scam

falecer [fale'ser] VI to die;

falecimento [falesi'mẽtu] M death

falência [fa'lẽsja] F bankruptcy; **abrir ~** to declare o.s. bankrupt; **ir à ~** to go bankrupt; **levar à ~** to bankrupt

falésia [fa'lɛzja] F cliff

falha ['faʎa] F fault; (*lacuna*) omission; (*de caráter*) flaw

falhar [fa'ʎar] VI to fail; (*não acertar*) to miss; (*errar*) to be wrong; **sua voz está falhando** you're breaking up

falho, -a ['faʎu, a] ADJ faulty; (*deficiente*) wanting

falido, -a [fa'lidu, a] ADJ, M/F bankrupt

falir [fa'lir] VI to fail; (*Com*) to go bankrupt

falsário, -a [faw'sarju, a] M/F forger

falsidade [fawsi'dadʒi] F falsehood; (*fingimento*) pretence (BRIT), pretense (US)

falsificar [fawsifi'kar] VT (*forjar*) to forge; (*falsear*) to falsify; (*adulterar*) to adulterate; (*desvirtuar*) to misrepresent

falso, -a ['fawsu, a] ADJ false; (*fraudulento*) dishonest; (*errôneo*) wrong; (*joia, moeda, quadro*) fake; **pisar em ~** to blunder

falta ['fawta] F (*carência*) lack; (*ausência*) absence; (*defeito, culpa*) fault; (*Futebol*) foul; **por** *ou* **na ~ de** for lack of; **sem ~** without fail; **fazer ~** to be lacking, be needed; **sentir ~ de alguém/algo** to miss sb/sth; **ter ~ de** to lack, be in need of

faltar [faw'tar] VI to be lacking, be wanting; (*pessoa*) to be absent; (*falhar*) to fail; **~ ao trabalho** to be absent from work; **~ à palavra** to break one's word; **falta pouco para ...** it won't be long until ...

fama ['fama] F (*renome*) fame; (*reputação*) reputation

família [fa'milja] F family

familiar [fami'ljar] ADJ (*da família*) family *atr*; (*conhecido*) familiar ▶ M/F relation, relative;

familiaridade [familjari'dadʒi] F familiarity; (*sem-cerimônia*) informality

famoso, -a [fa'mozu, ɔza] ADJ famous

fanático, -a [fa'natʃiku, a] ADJ fanatical ▶ M/F fanatic

fantasia [fãta'zia] F fantasy; (*imaginação*) imagination; (*capricho*) fancy; (*traje*) fancy dress

fantasiar [fãta'zjar] VT to imagine ▶ VI to daydream; **fantasiar-se** VR to dress up (in fancy dress)

fantasma [fã'tazma] M ghost; (*alucinação*) illusion

fantástico, -a [fã'tastʃiku, a] ADJ fantastic; (*ilusório*) imaginary; (*incrível*) unbelievable

fantoche [fã'toʃi] M puppet
farda ['farda] F uniform
farei [fa'rej] VB *ver* **fazer**
farinha [fa'riɲa] F: **~ (de mesa)** (manioc) flour; **~ de rosca** breadcrumbs *pl*; **~ de trigo** plain flour
farmacêutico, -a [farma'sewtʃiku, a] ADJ pharmaceutical ▶ M/F pharmacist, chemist (BRIT)
farmácia [far'masja] F pharmacy, chemist's (shop) (BRIT)
faro ['faru] M sense of smell; (*fig*) flair
farofa [fa'rɔfa] F (*Culin*) *side dish based on manioc flour*
farol [fa'rɔw] (*pl* **-óis**) M lighthouse; (*Auto*) headlight; **~ alto** (*Auto*) full (BRIT) *ou* high (US) beam; **~ baixo** dipped headlights *pl* (BRIT), dimmed beam (US)
farra ['faha] F binge, spree
farrapo [fa'hapu] M rag
farsa ['farsa] F farce; **farsante** [far'sãtʃi] M/F joker
fartar [far'tar] VT to satiate; (*encher*) to fill up; **fartar-se** VR to gorge o.s.
farto, -a ['fartu, a] ADJ full, satiated; (*abundante*) plentiful; (*aborrecido*) fed up
fartura [far'tura] F abundance
fascinante [fasi'nãtʃi] ADJ fascinating
fascinar [fasi'nar] VT to fascinate; (*encantar*) to charm; **fascínio** [fa'sinju] M fascination
fase ['fazi] F phase
fashion ['fɛʃjõ] (*col*) ADJ trendy
fatal [fa'taw] (*pl* **-ais**) ADJ (*mortal*) fatal; (*inevitável*) fateful; **fatalidade** [fatali'dadʒi] F fate; (*desgraça*) disaster
fatia [fa'tʃia] F slice
fatigante [fatʃi'gãtʃi] ADJ tiring; (*aborrecido*) tiresome
fatigar [fatʃi'gar] VT to tire; (*aborrecer*) to bore; **fatigar-se** VR to get tired
Fátima ['fatʃima] F *see note*

> **Fátima**, situated in central Portugal, is known worldwide as a site of pilgrimage for Catholics. It is said that, in 1917, the Virgin Mary appeared six times to three shepherd children (*os três pastorinhos*). Millions of pilgrims visit Fátima every year.

fato ['fatu] M fact; (*acontecimento*) event; (PT: *traje*) suit; **~ de banho** (PT) swimming costume (BRIT), bathing suit (US); **de ~** in fact, really
fator [fa'tor] M factor
fatura [fa'tura] F bill, invoice; **faturar** [fatu'rar] VT to invoice; (*dinheiro*) to make ▶ VI (*col: ganhar dinheiro*): **faturar (alto)** to rake it in
fava ['fava] F broad bean; **mandar alguém às ~s** to send sb packing
favela [fa'vɛla] F slum
favor [fa'vor] M favour (BRIT), favor (US); **a ~ de** in favo(u)r of; **por ~** please; **se faz ~** (PT) please; **faça** *ou* **faz o ~ de ...** would you be so good as to ..., kindly ...; **favorável** [favo'ravew] (*pl* **-eis**) ADJ: **favorável (a)** favourable (BRIT) *ou* favorable (US) (to); **favorecer** [favore'ser] VT to favour (BRIT), favor (US); (*beneficiar*) to benefit; (*suj: vestido*) to suit; (: *retrato*) to flatter; **favorito, -a** [favo'ritu, a] ADJ, M/F (*tb Comput*) favourite (BRIT), favorite (US)

f

fax [faks] M fax; **enviar por ~** to fax
faxina [fa'ʃina] F: **fazer ~** to clean up; **faxineiro, -a** [faʃi'nejru, a] M/F cleaner
fazenda [fa'zẽda] F farm; (*de café*) plantation; (*de gado*) ranch; (*pano*) cloth, fabric; (*Econ*) treasury; **fazendeiro** [fazẽ'dejru] M farmer; (*de café*) plantation-owner; (*de gado*) rancher, ranch-owner

PALAVRA-CHAVE

fazer [fa'zer] VT
1 (*fabricar, produzir*) to make; (*construir*) to build; (*pergunta*) to ask; (*poema, música*) to write; **fazer um filme/ruído** to make a film/noise
2 (*executar*) to do; **o que você está fazendo?** what are you doing?; **fazer a comida** to do the cooking; **fazer o papel de** (*Teatro*) to play
3 (*estudos, alguns esportes*) to do; **fazer medicina/direito** to do *ou* study medicine/law; **fazer ioga/ginástica** to do yoga/keep-fit
4 (*transformar, tornar*): **sair o fará sentir melhor** going out will make him feel better; **sua partida fará o trabalho mais difícil** his departure will make work more difficult
5 (*como sustituto de vb*): **ele bebeu e eu fiz o mesmo** he drank and I did likewise
6: **ele faz anos hoje** it's his birthday today; **fiz 30 anos ontem** I was 30 yesterday
▸ VI **1** (*portar-se*) to act, behave; **fazer bem/mal** to do the right/wrong thing; **não fiz por mal** I didn't mean it; **faz como quem não sabe** act as if you don't know anything
2: **fazer com que alguém faça algo** to make sb do sth
▸ VB IMPESS **1**: **faz calor/frio** it's hot/cold
2 (*tempo*): **faz um ano** a year ago; **faz dois anos que ele se formou** it's two years since he graduated; **faz três meses que ele está aqui** he's been here for three months
3: **não faz mal** never mind; **tanto faz** it's all the same
fazer-se VR **1**: **fazer-se de desentendido** to pretend not to understand
2: **faz-se com ovos e leite** it's made with eggs and milk; **isso não se faz** that's not done

fé [fɛ] F faith; (*crença*) belief; (*confiança*) trust; **de boa/má fé** in good/bad faith
febre ['fɛbri] F fever; (*fig*) excitement; **~ do feno** hay fever; **febril** [fe'briw] (*pl* **-is**) ADJ feverish
fechado, -a [fe'ʃadu, a] ADJ shut, closed; (*pessoa*) reserved; (*sinal*) red; (*luz, torneira*) off; (*tempo*) overcast; (*cara*) stern
fechadura [feʃa'dura] F (*de porta*) lock
fechar [fe'ʃar] VT to close, shut; (*concluir*) to finish, conclude; (*luz, torneira*) to turn off; (*rua*) to close off; (*ferida*) to close up; (*bar, loja*) to close down ▸ VI to close (up), shut; to close down; (*tempo*) to cloud over; **fechar-se** VR to close, shut; (*pessoa*) to withdraw; **~ à chave** to lock
fecho ['feʃu] M fastening; (*trinco*) latch; (*término*) close; **~ ecler** zip fastener (BRIT), zipper (US)
fécula ['fɛkula] F starch
feder [fe'der] VI to stink
federação [federa'sãw] (*pl* **-ões**) F federation

federal [fede'raw] (*pl* **-ais**) ADJ federal; (*col: grande*) huge
fedor [fe'dor] M stench
feijão [fej'ʒãw] (*pl* **-ões**) M bean(s) (*pl*); (*preto*) black bean(s) (*pl*); **feijoada** [fej'ʒwada] F (*Culin*) meat, rice and black beans
feio, -a ['feju, a] ADJ ugly; (*situação*) grim; (*atitude*) bad; (*tempo*) horrible ▶ ADV (*perder*) badly
feira ['fejra] F fair; (*mercado*) market
feiticeira [fejtʃi'sejra] F witch
feiticeiro, -a [fejtʃi'sejru, a] ADJ bewitching, enchanting ▶ M wizard
feitiço [fej'tʃisu] M charm, spell
feitio [fej'tʃiu] M shape, pattern; (*caráter*) nature, manner; (*Tec*) workmanship
feito, -a ['fejtu, a] PP *de* **fazer** ▶ ADJ finished, ready ▶ M act, deed; (*façanha*) feat ▶ CONJ like; **~ a mão** hand-made; **homem ~** grown man
feiura [fe'jura] F ugliness
felicidade [felisi'dadʒi] F happiness; (*sorte*) good luck; (*êxito*) success; **felicidades** FPL (*congratulações*) congratulations
felicitações [felisita'sõjs] FPL congratulations, best wishes
feliz [fe'liz] ADJ happy; (*afortunado*) lucky; **felizmente** [feliz'mẽtʃi] ADV fortunately
feltro ['fewtru] M felt
fêmea ['femja] F female
feminino, -a [femi'ninu, a] ADJ feminine; (*sexo*) female; (*equipe, roupa*) women's ▶ M (*Ling*) feminine
feminista [femi'nista] ADJ, M/F feminist
feno ['fenu] M hay
fenomenal [fenome'naw] (*pl* **-ais**) ADJ phenomenal; (*espantoso*) amazing; (*pessoa*) brilliant
fenômeno [fe'nomenu] M phenomenon
fera ['fɛra] F wild animal
feriado [fe'rjadu] M (public) holiday (BRIT), vacation (US)
férias ['fɛrjas] FPL holiday(s) (BRIT), vacation *sg* (US); **de ~** on holiday (BRIT) *ou* vacation (US); **tirar ~** to have *ou* take a holiday (BRIT) *ou* vacation (US)
ferida [fe'rida] F wound, injury; *ver tb* **ferido**
ferido, -a [fe'ridu, a] ADJ injured; (*em batalha*) wounded; (*magoado*) hurt ▶ M/F casualty
ferimento [feri'mẽtu] M injury; (*em batalha*) wound
ferir [fe'rir] VT to injure; (*tb fig*) to hurt; (*em batalha*) to wound; (*ofender*) to offend
fermentar [fermẽ'tar] VI to ferment
fermento [fer'mẽtu] M yeast; **~ em pó** baking powder
feroz [fe'roz] ADJ fierce, ferocious; (*cruel*) cruel
ferragem [fe'haʒẽ] (*pl* **-ns**) F (*peças*) hardware; (*guarnição*) metalwork; **loja de ferragens** ironmonger's (BRIT), hardware store (US)
ferramenta [feha'mẽta] F tool; (*caixa de ferramentas*) tool kit
ferrão [fe'hãw] (*pl* **-ões**) M goad; (*de inseto*) sting
ferrenho, -a [fe'heɲu, a] ADJ (*vontade*) iron
ferro ['fɛhu] M iron; **ferros** MPL (*algemas*) shackles, chains; **~ batido** wrought iron; **~ de**

passar iron; **~ fundido** cast iron; **~ ondulado** corrugated iron
ferrões [fe'hõjs] MPL *de* **ferrão**
ferrolho [fe'hoʎu] M (*trinco*) bolt
ferrovia [feho'via] F railway (BRIT), railroad (US); **ferroviário, -a** [feho'vjarju, a] ADJ railway *atr* (BRIT), railroad *atr* (US) ▶ M/F railway *ou* railroad worker
ferrugem [fe'huʒẽ] F rust
fértil ['fɛrtʃiw] (*pl* **-eis**) ADJ fertile; **fertilizante** [fertʃili'zãtʃi] M fertilizer; **fertilizar** [fertʃili'zar] VT to fertilize
ferver [fer'ver] VT, VI to boil; **~ de raiva/indignação** to seethe with rage/indignation; **~ em fogo baixo** (*Culin*) to simmer
fervilhar [fervi'ʎar] VI to simmer; (*com atividade*) to hum; (*pulular*): **~ de** to swarm with
fervor [fer'vor] M fervour (BRIT), fervor (US)
festa ['fɛsta] F (*reunião*) party; (*conjunto de cerimônias*) festival; **festas** FPL (*carícia*) embrace; **boas ~s** Merry Christmas and a Happy New Year; **dia de ~** public holiday
festejar [feste'ʒar] VT to celebrate; (*acolher*) to welcome, greet; **festejo** [fes'teʒu] M festivity; (*ato*) celebration
festival [festʃi'vaw] (*pl* **-ais**) M festival
festividade [festʃivi'dadʒi] F festivity
festivo, -a [fes'tʃivu, a] ADJ festive
fetiche [fe'tʃiʃi] M fetish
feto ['fɛtu] M (*Med*) foetus (BRIT), fetus (US)
fevereiro [feve'rejru] M February
fez [fez] VB *ver* **fazer**
fezes ['fɛzis] FPL faeces (BRIT), feces (US)
fiado, -a ['fjadu, a] ADV: **comprar/vender ~** to buy/sell on credit
fiador, a [fja'dor(a)] M/F (*Jur*) guarantor; (*Com*) backer
fiambre ['fjãbri] M cold meat; (*presunto*) ham
fiança ['fjãsa] F guarantee; (*Jur*) bail; **prestar ~ por** to stand bail for; **sob ~** on bail
fiar ['fjar] VT (*algodão etc*) to spin; (*confiar*) to entrust; (*vender a crédito*) to sell on credit; **fiar-se** VR: **~-se em** to trust
fibra ['fibra] F fibre (BRIT), fiber (US)

PALAVRA-CHAVE

ficar [fi'kar] VI **1** (*permanecer*) to stay; (*sobrar*) to be left; **ficar perguntando/olhando** *etc* to keep asking/looking *etc*; **ficar por fazer** to have still to be done; **ficar para trás** to be left behind
2 (*tornar-se*) to become; **ficar cego/surdo/louco** to go blind/deaf/mad; **fiquei contente ao saber da notícia** I was happy when I heard the news; **ficar com raiva/medo** to get angry/frightened; **ficar de bem/mal com alguém** (*col*) to make up/fall out with sb
3 (*posição*) to be; **a casa fica ao lado da igreja** the house is next to the church; **ficar sentado/deitado** to be sitting down/lying down
4 (*tempo: durar*): **ele ficou duas horas para resolver** he took two hours to decide; (*: ser adiado*): **a reunião ficou para amanhã** the meeting has been postponed until tomorrow
5 (*comportamento*): **sua atitude não ficou bem** his (*ou* her *etc*) behaviour was inappropriate; (*cor*): **você fica bem em azul** blue suits

you, you look good in blue; (*roupa*): **ficar bem para** to suit
6: **ficar bom** (*de saúde*) to be cured; (*trabalho, foto etc*) to turn out well
7: **ficar de fazer algo** (*combinar*) to arrange to do sth; (*prometer*) to promise to do sth
8: **ficar de pé** to stand up

ficção [fik'sãw] F fiction
ficha ['fiʃa] F (*tb*: **~ de telefone**) token; (*tb*: **~ de jogo**) chip; (*de fichário*) (index) card; (*Polícia*) record; (PT *Elet*) plug; (*em loja, lanchonete*) ticket
fichário [fi'ʃarju] M filing cabinet; (*caixa*) card index; (*caderno*) file
ficheiro [fi'ʃejru] (PT) M = **fichário**
fidelidade [fideli'dadʒi] F fidelity, loyalty; (*exatidão*) accuracy
fiel [fjɛw] (*pl* **-éis**) ADJ (*leal*) faithful, loyal; (*acurado*) accurate; (*que não falha*) reliable
figa ['figa] F talisman; **fazer uma ~** to make a *figa*, ≈ cross one's fingers; **de uma ~** (*col*) damned
fígado ['figadu] M liver
figo ['figu] M fig; **figueira** [fi'gejra] F fig tree
figura [fi'gura] F figure; (*forma*) form, shape; (*Ling*) figure of speech; (*aspecto*) appearance
figurino [figu'rinu] M model; (*revista*) fashion magazine
fila ['fila] F row, line; (BR: *fileira de pessoas*) queue (BRIT), line (US); (*num teatro, cinema*) row; **em ~** in a row; **fazer ~** to form a line, queue; **~ indiana** single file
filé [fi'lɛ] M (*bife*) steak; (*peixe*) fillet
fileira [fi'lejru] F row, line; **fileiras** FPL (*serviço militar*) military service *sg*
filho, -a ['fiʎu, a] M/F son/daughter; **filhos** MPL children; (*de animais*) young; **~ da mãe, ~ da puta** (!) bastard (!)
filhote [fi'ʎɔtʃi] M (*de leão, urso etc*) cub; (*cachorro*) pup(py)
filial [fi'ljaw] (*pl* **-ais**) F (*sucursal*) branch
filipeta [fili'peta] F flyer
Filipinas [fili'pinas] FPL: **as ~** the Philippines
filmadora [fiwma'dora] F video camera
filmar [fiw'mar] VT, VI to film
filme ['fiwmi] M film (BRIT), movie (US)
filosofia [filozo'fia] F philosophy; **filósofo, -a** [fi'lɔzofu, a] M/F philosopher
filtrar [fiw'trar] VT to filter; **filtrar-se** VR to filter; (*infiltrar-se*) to infiltrate
filtro ['fiwtru] M (*Tec*) filter
fim [fĩ] (*pl* **-ns**) M end; (*motivo*) aim, purpose; (*de história, filme*) ending; **a ~ de** in order to; **no ~ das contas** after all; **por ~** finally; **sem ~** endless; **levar ao ~** to carry through; **pôr** *ou* **dar ~ a** to put an end to; **ter ~** to come to an end; **~ de semana** weekend
finado, -a [fi'nadu, a] ADJ, M/F deceased

> The day of **Finados**, 2 November, a holiday throughout Brazil, is dedicated to remembering the dead. On this day, people usually gather in cemeteries to remember their family dead, and also to worship at the graves of popular figures from Brazilian culture and society, such as singers, actors and other personalities. It is popularly believed that these people can work miracles.

f

final [fi'naw] (*pl* **-ais**) ADJ final, last ▶ M end; (*Mús*) finale ▶ F (*Esporte*) final; **finalista** [fina'lista] M/F finalist; **finalizar** [finali'zar] VT to finish, conclude

finanças [fi'nãsas] FPL finance *sg*; **financeiro, -a** [finã'sejru, a] ADJ financial ▶ M/F financier; **financiar** [finã'sjar] VT to finance

fingimento [fĩʒi'mẽtu] M pretence (BRIT), pretense (US)

fingir [fĩ'ʒir] VT to feign ▶ VI to pretend; **fingir-se** VR: **~-se de** to pretend to be

finito, -a [fi'nitu, a] ADJ finite

finlandês, -esa [fĩlã'des, eza] ADJ Finnish ▶ M/F Finn ▶ M (*Ling*) Finnish

Finlândia [fĩ'lãdʒja] F: **a ~** Finland

fino, -a ['finu, a] ADJ fine; (*delgado*) slender; (*educado*) polite; (*som, voz*) shrill; (*elegante*) refined ▶ ADV: **falar ~** to talk in a high voice

fins [fĩs] MPL *de* **fim**

fio ['fiu] M thread; (*Bot*) fibre (BRIT), fiber (US); (*Elet*) wire; (*Tel*) line; (*de líquido*) trickle; (*gume*) edge; (*encadeamento*) series; **horas/dias a ~** hours/days on end; **sem ~** (*Comput*) wireless

firewall [faja'aw] M firewall

firma ['firma] F signature; (*Com*) firm, company

firmar [fir'mar] VT to secure, make firm; (*assinar*) to sign; (*estabelecer*) to establish; (*basear*) to base ▶ VI (*tempo*) to settle; **firmar-se** VR: **~-se em** (*basear-se*) to rest on, be based on

firme ['firmi] ADJ firm; (*estável*) stable; (*sólido*) solid; (*tempo*) settled ▶ ADV firmly; **firmeza** [fir'meza] F firmness; (*estabilidade*) stability; (*solidez*) solidity

fiscal [fis'kaw] (*pl* **-ais**) M/F supervisor; (*aduaneiro*) customs officer; (*de impostos*) tax inspector; **fiscalizar** [fiskali'zar] VT to supervise; (*examinar*) to inspect, check

fisco ['fisku] M: **o ~** ≈ the Inland Revenue (BRIT), ≈ the Internal Revenue Service (US)

física ['fizika] F physics *sg*; *ver tb* **físico**

físico, -a ['fiziku, a] ADJ physical ▶ M/F (*cientista*) physicist ▶ M (*corpo*) physique

fisionomia [fizjono'mia] F (*rosto*) face; (*ar*) expression, look; (*aspecto de algo*) appearance

fissura [fi'sura] F crack

fita ['fita] F (*tira*) strip, band; (*filme*) film; (*para máquina de escrever*) ribbon; (*magnética, adesiva*) tape; **~ durex®** adhesive tape, Sellotape® (BRIT), Scotch tape® (US); **~ métrica** tape measure

fitar [fi'tar] VT to stare at, gaze at

fivela [fi'vɛla] F buckle

fixar [fik'sar] VT to fix; (*colar, prender*) to stick; (*data, prazo, regras*) to set; (*atenção*) to concentrate; **fixar-se** VR: **~-se em** (*assunto*) to concentrate on; (*detalhe*) to fix on; (*apegar-se a*) to be attached to; **~ os olhos em** to stare at; **~ residência** to set up house

fixo, -a ['fiksu, a] ADJ fixed; (*firme*) firm; (*permanente*) permanent; (*cor*) fast ▶ M (*tb*: **telefone ~**) landline

fiz [fiz] VB *ver* **fazer**

flagelado, -a [flaʒe'ladu, a] M/F: **os ~s** the afflicted, the victims

flagrante [fla'grãtʃi] ADJ flagrant; **apanhar em ~ (delito)** to catch red-handed *ou* in the act

flagrar [fla'grar] VT to catch

flanela [fla'nɛla] F flannel
flash [flaʃ] M (*Foto*) flash
flauta ['flawta] F flute
flecha ['flɛʃa] F arrow
fleuma ['flewma] F phlegm
floco ['flɔku] M flake; **~ de milho** cornflake; **~ de neve** snowflake
flor [flor] F flower; (*o melhor*) cream, pick; **em ~** in bloom; **à ~ da pele** on edge
florescente [flore'sẽtʃi] ADJ (*Bot*) in flower; (*próspero*) flourishing
florescer [flore'ser] VI (*Bot*) to flower; (*prosperar*) to flourish
floresta [flo'rɛsta] F forest; **florestal** [flores'taw] (*pl* **florestais**) ADJ forest *atr*
florido, -a [flo'ridu, a] ADJ (*jardim*) in flower
fluente [flu'ẽtʃi] ADJ fluent
fluido, -a ['flwidu, a] ADJ fluid ▶ M fluid
fluir [flwir] VI to flow
fluminense [flumi'nẽsi] ADJ from the state of Rio de Janeiro ▶ M/F native *ou* inhabitant of the state of Rio de Janeiro
flutuar [flu'twar] VI to float; (*bandeira*) to flutter; (*fig: vacilar*) to waver
fluvial [flu'vjaw] (*pl* **-ais**) ADJ river *atr*
fluxo ['fluksu] M (*corrente*) flow; (*Elet*) flux; **~ de caixa** (*Com*) cash flow
fobia [fo'bia] F phobia
foca ['fɔka] F seal
foco ['fɔku] M focus; (*Med, fig*) seat, centre (BRIT), center (US); **fora de ~** out of focus
fofo, -a ['fofu, a] ADJ soft; (*col: pessoa*) cute
fofoca [fo'fɔka] F piece of gossip; **fofocas** FPL (*mexericos*) gossip *sg*;
fofocar [fofo'kar] VI to gossip
fogão [fo'gãw] (*pl* **-ões**) M stove, cooker
fogareiro [foga'rejru] M stove
foge ['fɔʒi] VB *ver* **fugir**
fogo ['fogu] M fire; (*fig*) ardour (BRIT), ardor (US); **você tem ~?** have you got a light?; **~s de artifício** fireworks; **pôr ~ a** to set fire to
fogões [fo'gõjs] MPL *de* **fogão**
fogueira [fo'gejra] F bonfire
foguete [fo'getʃi] M rocket
foi [foj] VB *ver* **ir, ser**
folclore [fowk'lɔri] M folklore
folclórico, -a [fowk'lɔriku, a] ADJ (*música etc*) folk *atr*; (*comida, roupa*) ethnic
fôlego ['folegu] M breath; (*folga*) breathing space; **perder o ~** to get out of breath
folga ['fɔwga] F rest, break; (*espaço livre*) clearance; (*ócio*) inactivity; (*col: atrevimento*) cheek; **dia de ~** day off; **folgado, -a** [fow'gadu, a] ADJ (*roupa*) loose; (*vida*) leisurely; (*col: atrevido*) cheeky; **folgar** [fow'gar] VT to loosen ▶ VI (*descansar*) to rest; (*divertir-se*) to have fun
folha ['foʎa] F leaf; (*de papel, de metal*) sheet; (*página*) page; (*de faca*) blade; (*jornal*) paper; **novo em ~** brand new; **~ de estanho** tinfoil (BRIT), aluminum foil (US); **~ de exercícios** worksheet
folhagem [fo'ʎaʒẽ] F foliage
folheto [fo'ʎetu] M booklet, pamphlet
fome ['fɔmi] F hunger; (*escassez*) famine; (*fig: avidez*) longing; **passar ~** to go hungry; **estar com** *ou* **ter ~** to be hungry
fone ['fɔni] M telephone, phone; (*peça do telefone*) receiver

f

fonte ['fõtʃi] F (*nascente*) spring; (*chafariz*) fountain; (*origem*) source; (*Anat*) temple
for [for] VB *ver* **ir, ser**
fora[1] ['fɔra] ADV out, outside ▶ PREP (*além de*) apart from ▶ M: **dar o ~** (*bateria, radio*) to give out; (*pessoa*) to leave, be off; **dar um ~** to slip up; **dar um ~ em alguém** (*namorado*) to chuck sb, dump sb; (*esnobar*) to snub sb; **levar um ~** (*de namorado*) to be given the boot; (*ser esnobado*) to get the brush-off; **~ de** outside; **~ de si** beside o.s.; **estar ~** (*viajando*) to be away; **estar ~ (de casa)** to be out; **lá ~** outside; (*no exterior*) abroad; **jantar ~** to eat out; **com os braços de ~** with bare arms; **ser de ~** to be from out of town; **ficar de ~** not to join in; **lá para ~** outside; **ir para ~** (*viajar*) to go out of town; **com a cabeça para ~ da janela** with one's head sticking out of the window; **costurar/cozinhar para ~** to do sewing/cooking for other people; **por ~** on the outside; **cobrar por ~** to charge extra; **~ de dúvida** beyond doubt; **~ de propósito** irrelevant
fora[2] VB *ver* **ir, ser**
foragido, -a [fora'ʒidu, a] ADJ, M/F fugitive; **estar ~** to be on the run
forasteiro, -a [foras'tejru, a] M/F outsider, stranger; (*de outro país*) foreigner
força ['forsa] F strength; (*Tec, Elet*) power; (*esforço*) effort; (*coerção*) force; **à ~** by force; **à ~ de** by dint of; **com ~** hard; **por ~** of necessity; **fazer ~** to try (hard); **~ de trabalho** workforce
forçado, -a [for'sadu, a] ADJ forced; (*afetado*) false
forçar [for'sar] VT to force; (*olhos, voz*) to strain
forma ['fɔrma] F form; (*de um objeto*) shape; (*físico*) figure; (*maneira*) way; (*Med*) fitness; **desta ~** in this way; **de qualquer ~** anyway; **manter a ~** to keep fit
fôrma ['forma] F (*Culin*) cake tin; (*molde*) mould (BRIT), mold (US)
formação [forma'sãw] (*pl* **-ões**) F formation; (*antecedentes*) background; (*caráter*) make-up; (*profissional*) training
formado, -a [for'madu, a] ADJ (*modelado*): **ser ~ de** to consist of ▶ M/F graduate
formal [for'maw] (*pl* **-ais**) ADJ formal; **formalidade** [formali'dadʒi] F formality
formar [for'mar] VT to form; (*constituir*) to constitute, make up; (*educar*) to train; **formar-se** VR to form; (*Educ*) to graduate
formatar [forma'tar] VT (*Comput*) to format
formidável [formi'davew] (*pl* **-eis**) ADJ tremendous, great
formiga [for'miga] F ant
formigar [formi'gar] VI to abound; (*sentir comichão*) to itch
formoso, -a [for'mozu, ɔza] ADJ beautiful; (*esplêndido*) superb
fórmula ['fɔrmula] F formula
formular [formu'lar] VT to formulate; (*queixas*) to voice
formulário [formu'larju] M form; **formulários** MPL: **~s contínuos** (*Comput*) continuous stationery *sg*
fornecedor, a [fornese'dor(a)] M/F supplier ▶ F (*empresa*) supplier
fornecer [forne'ser] VT to supply, provide; **fornecimento** [fornesi'mẽtu] M supply
forno ['fornu] M (*Culin*) oven; (*Tec*) furnace; (*para cerâmica*) kiln; **alto ~** blast furnace

foro ['foru] M forum; (*Jur*) Court of Justice; **foros** MPL (*privilégios*) privileges
forro ['fohu] M covering; (*interior*) lining
forró [fo'hɔ] M *see note*

> **Forró** is a style of popular music and dance that originated in the north-east of Brazil, but which is now popular all over the country. The instruments which feature in **forró** are the accordion, the bass drum and the triangle, and it is danced with a partner. There are a number of different styles of **forró**, such as the faster-paced *forró universitário*, which has attracted a considerable following among the younger generation in Brazil's cities.

fortalecer [fortale'ser] VT to strengthen
fortaleza [forta'leza] F fortress; (*força*) strength; (*moral*) fortitude
forte ['fɔrtʃi] ADJ strong; (*pancada*) hard; (*chuva*) heavy; (*som*) loud; (*dor*) sharp ▸ ADV strongly; (*som*) loud(ly) ▸ M fort; (*talento*) strength; **ser ~ em algo** (*versado*) to be good at sth *ou* strong in sth
fortuito, -a [for'twitu, a] ADJ accidental
fortuna [for'tuna] F fortune, (good) luck; (*riqueza*) fortune, wealth
fórum ['forũ] (*pl* **-ns**) M (*Comput*) forum; **~ de discussão** discussion forum, message board
fosco, -a ['fosku, a] ADJ dull; (*opaco*) opaque
fósforo ['fɔsforu] M match
fossa ['fɔsa] F pit
fosse ['fosi] VB *ver* **ir, ser**
fóssil ['fɔsiw] (*pl* **-eis**) M fossil
fosso ['fosu] M trench, ditch
foto ['fɔtu] F photo
fotocópia [foto'kɔpja] F photocopy; **fotocopiadora** [fotokopja'dora] F photocopier; **fotocopiar** [fotoko'pjar] VT to photocopy
fotografar [fotogra'far] VT to photograph
fotografia [fotogra'fia] F photography; (*uma foto*) photograph
fotógrafo, -a [fo'tɔgrafu, a] M/F photographer
foz [fɔz] F mouth (*of river*)
fração [fra'sãw] (*pl* **-ões**) F fraction
fracassar [fraka'sar] VI to fail; **fracasso** [fra'kasu] M failure
fraco, -a ['fraku, a] ADJ weak; (*sol, som*) faint
frágil ['fraʒiw] (*pl* **-eis**) ADJ (*débil*) fragile; (*Com*) breakable; (*pessoa*) frail; (*saúde*) delicate, poor
fragmento [frag'mẽtu] M fragment
fragrância [fra'grãsja] F fragrance, perfume
fralda ['frawda] F (*da camisa*) shirt tail; (*para bebê*) nappy (BRIT), diaper (US); (*de montanha*) foot
framboesa [frãbo'eza] F raspberry
França ['frãsa] F France
francamente [frãka'mẽtʃi] ADV (*abertamente*) frankly; (*realmente*) really
francês, -esa [frã'ses, eza] ADJ French ▸ M/F Frenchman/woman ▸ M (*Ling*) French
franco, -a ['frãku, a] ADJ frank; (*isento de pagamento*) free; (*óbvio*) clear ▸ M franc; **entrada franca** free admission

frango ['frãgu] M chicken
franja ['frãʒa] F fringe (BRIT), bangs *pl* (US)
franquia [frã'kia] F (*Com*) franchise; (*isenção*) exemption
franzino, -a [frã'zinu, a] ADJ skinny
fraqueza [fra'keza] F weakness
frasco ['frasku] M bottle
frase ['frazi] F sentence; **~ feita** set phrase
fratura [fra'tura] F fracture, break;
fraturar [fratu'rar] VT to fracture
freada [fre'ada] (BR) F: **dar uma ~** to slam on the brakes
frear [fre'ar] (BR) VT to curb, restrain; (*veículo*) to stop ▶ VI (*veículo*) to brake
freezer ['frizer] M freezer
freguês, -guesa [fre'ges, 'geza] M/F customer; (PT) parishioner;
freguesia [frege'zia] F customers *pl*; (PT) parish
freio ['freju] M (BR: *veículo*) brake; (*de cavalo*) bridle; (*bocado do freio*) bit; **~ de mão** handbrake
freira ['frejra] F nun
frenesi [frene'zi] M frenzy;
frenético, -a [fre'nɛtʃiku, a] ADJ frantic, frenzied
frente ['frẽtʃi] F front; (*rosto*) face; (*fachada*) façade; **~ a ~** face to face; **de ~ para** facing; **em ~ de** in front of; (*defronte a*) opposite; **para a ~** ahead, forward; **porta da ~** front door; **seguir em ~** to go straight on; **na minha (*ou* sua *etc*) ~** in front of me (*ou* you *etc*); **sair da ~** to get out of the way; **pra ~** (*col*) fashionable, trendy
frequência [fre'kwẽsja] F frequency; **com ~** often, frequently
frequentar [frekwẽ'tar] VT to frequent
frequente [fre'kwẽtʃi] ADJ frequent
fresco, -a ['fresku, a] ADJ fresh; (*vento, tempo*) cool; (*col: efeminado*) camp; (: *afetado*) pretentious; (: *cheio de luxo*) fussy ▶ M (*ar*) fresh air
frescobol [fresko'bɔw] M (kind of) racketball (*played mainly on the beach*)
frescura [fres'kura] F freshness; (*frialdade*) coolness; (*col: luxo*) fussiness; (: *afetaçao*) pretentiousness
frete ['frɛtʃi] M (*carregamento*) freight, cargo; (*tarifa*) freightage
frevo ['frevu] M *improvised Carnival dance*
fria ['fria] F: **dar uma ~ em alguém** to give sb the cold shoulder; **estar/ entrar numa ~** (*col*) to be in/get into a mess
fricção [frik'sãw] F friction; (*ato*) rubbing; (*Med*) massage;
friccionar [friksjo'nar] VT to rub
frieza ['frjeza] F coldness; (*indiferença*) coolness
frigideira [friʒi'dejra] F frying pan
frigorífico [frigo'rifiku] M refrigerator; (*congelador*) freezer
frio, -a ['friu, a] ADJ cold ▶ M coldness; **frios** MPL (*Culin*) cold meats; **estou com ~** I'm cold; **faz *ou* está ~** it's cold
frisar [fri'zar] VT (*encrespar*) to curl; (*salientar*) to emphasize
fritar [fri'tar] VT to fry
fritas ['fritas] FPL French fries, chips (BRIT)
frito, -a ['fritu, a] ADJ fried; (*col*): **estar ~** to be done for
frívolo, -a ['frivolu, a] ADJ frivolous
fronha ['froɲa] F pillowcase
fronteira [frõ'tejra] F frontier, border
frota ['frɔta] F fleet

frouxo, -a ['froʃu, a] ADJ loose; (*corda*) slack; (*fraco*) weak; (*col: condescendente*) soft

frustrar [frus'trar] VT to frustrate

fruta ['fruta] F fruit; **frutífero, -a** [fru'tʃiferu, a] ADJ (*proveitoso*) fruitful; (*árvore*) fruit-bearing

fruto ['frutu] M (*Bot*) fruit; (*resultado*) result, product; **dar ~** (*fig*) to bear fruit

fubá [fu'ba] M corn meal

fugir [fu'ʒir] VI to flee, escape; (*prisioneiro*) to escape

fui [fuj] VB *ver* **ir, ser**

fulano, -a [fu'lanu, a] M/F so-and-so

fulminante [fuwmi'nãtʃi] ADJ devastating; (*palavras*) scathing

fulo, -a ['fulu, a] ADJ: **estar** *ou* **ficar ~ de raiva** to be furious

fumaça [fu'masa] (BR) F (*de fogo*) smoke; (*de gás*) fumes *pl*

fumador, a [fuma'dor(a)] (PT) M/F smoker

fumante [fu'mãtʃi] M/F smoker

fumar [fu'mar] VT, VI to smoke

fumo ['fumu] M (PT: *de fogo*) smoke; (: *de gás*) fumes *pl*; (BR: *tabaco*) tobacco; (*fumar*) smoking

função [fũ'sãw] (*pl* **-ões**) F function; (*ofício*) duty; (*papel*) role; (*espetáculo*) performance

funcionalismo [fũsjona'lizmu] M: **~ público** civil service

funcionamento [fũsjona'mẽtu] M functioning, working; **pôr em ~** to set going, start

funcionar [fũsjo'nar] VI to function; (*máquina*) to work, run; (*dar bom resultado*) to work

funcionário, -a [fũsjo'narju, a] M/F official; **~ (público)** civil servant

funções [fũ'sõjs] FPL *de* **função**

fundação [fũda'sãw] (*pl* **-ões**) F foundation

fundamental [fũdamẽ'taw] (*pl* **-ais**) ADJ fundamental, basic

fundamento [fũda'mẽtu] M (*fig*) foundation, basis; (*motivo*) motive

fundar [fũ'dar] VT to establish, found; (*basear*) to base; **fundar-se** VR: **~-se em** to be based on

fundir [fũ'dʒir] VT to fuse; (*metal*) to smelt, melt down; (*Com: empresas*) to merge; (*em molde*) to cast; **fundir-se** VR to melt; (*juntar-se*) to merge

fundo, -a ['fũdu, a] ADJ deep; (*fig*) profound ▶ M (*do mar, jardim*) bottom; (*profundidade*) depth; (*base*) basis; (*da loja, casa, do papel*) back; (*de quadro*) background; (*de dinheiro*) fund ▶ ADV deeply; **fundos** MPL (*Com*) funds; (*da casa etc*) back *sg*; **a ~** thoroughly; **no ~** at the bottom; (*da casa etc*) at the back; (*fig*) basically

fúnebre ['funebri] ADJ funeral *atr*, funereal; (*fig*) gloomy

funeral [fune'raw] (*pl* **-ais**) M funeral

funil [fu'niw] (*pl* **-is**) M funnel

furacão [fura'kãw] (*pl* **-ões**) M hurricane

furado, -a [fu'radu, a] ADJ perforated; (*pneu*) flat; (*orelha*) pierced

furão, -rona [fu'rãw, 'rɔna] (*pl* **-ões/-s**) M ferret ▶ M/F (*col*) go-getter ▶ ADJ (*col*) hard-working, dynamic

furar [fu'rar] VT to perforate; (*penetrar*) to penetrate; (*frustrar*) to foil; (*fila*) to jump ▶ VI (*col: programa*) to fall through

fúria ['furja] F fury, rage; **furioso, -a** [fu'rjozu, ɔza] ADJ furious

furo ['furu] M hole; (*num pneu*) puncture

furões [fu'rõjs] MPL *de* **furão**

furona [fu'rɔna] F *de* **furão**

furor [fu'ror] M fury, rage; **fazer ~** to be all the rage

furtar [fur'tar] VT, VI to steal; **furtar-se** VR: **~-se a** to avoid

furtivo, -a [fur'tʃivu, a] ADJ furtive, stealthy

furto ['furtu] M theft

fusível [fu'zivew] (*pl* **-eis**) M (*Elet*) fuse

fuso ['fuzu] M (*Tec*) spindle; **~ horário** time zone

futebol [futʃi'bɔw] M football; **~ de salão** indoor football

futevôlei [futʃi'volej] M *see note*

> **Futevôlei** is a type of volleyball in which the ball is allowed to touch only the feet, legs, trunk and head of the players. It is very popular on the beaches of Rio de Janeiro, where tournaments take place during the summer, in which many famous footballers take part.

fútil ['futʃiw] (*pl* **-eis**) ADJ (*pessoa*) shallow; (*insignificante*) trivial

futilidade [futʃili'dadʒi] F (*de pessoa*) shallowness; (*insignificância*) triviality; (*coisa fútil*) trivial thing

futuro, -a [fu'turu, a] ADJ future ▶ M future; **no ~** in the future

fuzil [fu'ziw] (*pl* **-is**) M rifle; **fuzilar** [fuzi'lar] VT to shoot

fuzis [fu'zis] MPL *de* **fuzil**

g. ABR (= *grama*) gr.

gabar [ga'bar] VT to praise; **gabar-se** VR: **~-se de** to boast about

gabinete [gabi'netʃi] M (*Com*) office; (*escritório*) study; (*Pol*) cabinet

gado ['gadu] M livestock; (*bovino*) cattle; **~ leiteiro** dairy cattle; **~ suíno** pigs *pl*

gafanhoto [gafa'ɲotu] M grasshopper

gafe ['gafi] F gaffe, faux pas

gagueira [ga'gejra] F stutter

gaguejar [gage'ʒar] VI to stammer, stutter

gaiato, -a [ga'jatu, a] ADJ funny

gaiola [ga'jɔla] F cage; (*cadeia*) jail ▶ M (*barco*) riverboat

gaita ['gajta] F harmonica; **~ de foles** bagpipes *pl*

gaivota [gaj'vɔta] F seagull

gajo ['gaʒu] (PT *col*) M guy, fellow

gala ['gala] F: **traje de ~** evening dress; **festa de ~** gala

galão [ga'lãw] (*pl* **-ões**) M (*Mil*) stripe; (*medida*) gallon; (PT: *café*) white coffee; (*passamanaria*) braid
Galápagos [ga'lapagus] N: **(as) Ilhas ~** (the) Galapagos Islands
galáxia [ga'laksja] M galaxy
galera [ga'lɛra] F (*Náut*) galley; (*col: pessoas, público*) crowd
galeria [gale'ria] F gallery; (*Teatro*) circle
Gales ['galis] M: **País de ~** Wales
galho ['gaʎu] M (*de árvore*) branch
galinha [ga'liɲa] F hen; (*Culin*) chicken; **galinheiro** [gali'ɲejru] M hen-house
galo ['galu] M cock, rooster; (*inchação*) bump; **missa do ~** midnight mass
galões [ga'lõjs] MPL *de* **galão**
galopar [galo'par] VI to gallop; **galope** [ga'lɔpi] M gallop
gama ['gama] F (*Mús*) scale; (*fig*) range; (*Zool*) doe
gambá [gã'ba] M (*Zool*) opossum
game ['geimi] M computer game
Gana ['gana] M Ghana
gana ['gana] F craving, desire; (*ódio*) hate; **ter ~s de (fazer) algo** to feel like (doing) sth; **ter ~ de alguém** to hate sb
ganância [ga'nãsja] F greed; **ganancioso, -a** [ganã'sjozu, ɔza] ADJ greedy
gancho ['gãʃu] M hook; (*de calça*) crotch
gangue ['gãgi] (*col*) F gang
ganhador, a [gaɲa'dor(a)] ADJ winning ▶ M/F winner
ganha-pão ['gaɲa-] (*pl* **-pães**) M living, livelihood
ganhar [ga'ɲar] VT to win; (*salário*) to earn; (*adquirir*) to get; (*lugar*) to reach; (*lucrar*) to gain ▶ VI to win; **~ de alguém** (*num jogo*) to beat sb; **ganho** ['gaɲu] PP *de* **ganhar** ▶ M profit, gain; **ganhos** MPL (*ao jogo*) winnings
ganso, -a ['gãsu, a] M/F goose
garagem [ga'raʒẽ] (*pl* **-ns**) F garage
garantia [garã'tʃia] F guarantee; (*de dívida*) surety
garçom [gar'sõ] (BR) (*pl* **-ns**) M waiter
garçonete [garso'netʃi] (BR) F waitress
garçons [gar'sõs] MPL *de* **garçom**
garfo ['garfu] M fork
gargalhada [garga'ʎada] F burst of laughter; **rir às ~s** to roar with laughter; **dar** *ou* **soltar uma ~** to burst out laughing
gargalo [gar'galu] M (*tb fig*) bottleneck
garganta [gar'gãta] F throat; (*Geo*) gorge, ravine
gargarejo [garga'reʒu] M (*ato*) gargling; (*líquido*) gargle
gari [ga'ri] M/F (*na rua*) road sweeper (BRIT), street sweeper (US); (*lixeiro*) dustman (BRIT), garbage man (US)
garoa [ga'roa] F drizzle; **garoar** [ga'rwar] VI to drizzle
garotada [garo'tada] F: **a ~** the kids *pl*
garoto, -a [ga'rotu, a] M/F boy/girl ▶ M (BR: *chope*) small beer; (PT: *café*) coffee with milk
garoupa [ga'ropa] F (*peixe*) grouper
garrafa [ga'hafa] F bottle
garupa [ga'rupa] F (*de cavalo*) hindquarters *pl*; (*de moto*) back seat; **andar na ~** (*de moto*) to ride pillion
gás [gajs] M gas; **gases** MPL (*do*

g

intestino) wind *sg*; **~ natural** natural gas; **~ de efeito estufa** greenhouse gas

gasóleo [ga'zɔlju] M diesel oil

gasolina [gazo'lina] F petrol (BRIT), gas(oline) (US)

gasosa [ga'zɔza] F fizzy drink

gasoso, -a [ga'zozu, ɔza] ADJ (*água*) sparkling; (*bebida*) fizzy

gastador, -deira [gasta'dor, 'dejra] ADJ, M/F spendthrift

gastar [gas'tar] VT to spend; (*gasolina, electricidade*) to use; (*roupa, sapato*) to wear out; (*salto, piso etc*) to wear down; (*saúde*) to damage; (*desperdiçar*) to waste ▸VI to spend; to wear out; to wear down; **gastar-se** VR to wear out; to wear down

gástrico, -a ['gastriku, a] ADJ gastric

gata ['gata] F (she-)cat

gatilho [ga'tʃiʎu] M trigger

gato ['gatu] M cat; **~ montês** wild cat

gatuno, -a [ga'tunu, a] ADJ thieving ▸M/F thief

gaveta [ga'veta] F drawer

geada ['ʒjada] F frost

geladeira [ʒela'dejra] (BR) F refrigerator, icebox (US)

gelado, -a [ʒe'ladu, a] ADJ frozen ▸M (PT: *sorvete*) ice cream

gelar [ʒe'lar] VT to freeze; (*vinho etc*) to chill ▸VI to freeze

gelatina [ʒela'tʃina] F gelatine; (*sobremesa*) jelly (BRIT), Jell-O® (US)

geleia [ʒe'lɛja] F jam

gélido, -a ['ʒɛlidu, a] ADJ chill, icy

gelo ['ʒelu] ADJ INV light grey (BRIT) *ou* gray (US) ▸M ice; (*cor*) light grey (BRIT) *ou* gray (US)

gema ['ʒɛma] F yolk; (*pedra preciosa*) gem

gêmeo, -a ['ʒemju, a] ADJ, M/F twin; **Gêmeos** MPL (*Astrologia*) Gemini *sg*

gemer [ʒe'mer] VI (*de dor*) to groan, moan; (*lamentar-se*) to wail; (*animal*) to whine; (*vento*) to howl;

gemido [ʒe'midu] M groan, moan; (*lamento*) wail; (*de animal*) whine

gene ['ʒɛni] M gene

Genebra [ʒe'nɛbra] N Geneva

general [ʒene'raw] (*pl* **-ais**) M general

generalizar [ʒenerali'zar] VT to propagate ▸VI to generalize; **generalizar-se** VR to become general, spread

gênero ['ʒeneru] M type, kind; (*Bio*) genus; (*Ling*) gender; **gêneros** MPL (*produtos*) goods; **~s alimentícios** foodstuffs; **~ humano** humankind, human race

generosidade [ʒenerozi'dadʒi] F generosity

generoso, -a [ʒene'rozu, ɔza] ADJ generous

genética [ʒe'nɛtʃika] F genetics *sg*

gengibre [ʒẽ'ʒibri] M ginger

gengiva [ʒẽ'ʒiva] F (*Anat*) gum

genial [ʒe'njaw] (*pl* **-ais**) ADJ inspired, brilliant; (*col*) terrific, fantastic

gênio ['ʒenju] M (*temperamento*) nature; (*irascibilidade*) temper; (*talento, pessoa*) genius; **de bom ~** good-natured; **de mau ~** bad-tempered

genital [ʒeni'taw] (*pl* **-ais**) ADJ: **órgãos genitais** genitals *pl*

genoma [ʒe'noma] M genome

genro ['ʒẽhu] M son-in-law

gente ['ʒẽtʃi] F people *pl*; (*col*) folks *pl*; (*col: alguém*): **tem ~ batendo à porta** there's somebody knocking at the door; **a ~** (*nós: suj*) we; (*: obj*) us; **a casa da ~** our house; **toda a ~** everybody; **~ grande** grown-ups *pl*

gentil [ʒẽ'tʃiw] (*pl* **-is**) ADJ kind; **gentileza** [ʒẽtʃi'leza] F kindness; **por gentileza** if you please; **tenha a gentileza de fazer ...** would you be so kind as to do ...?

genuíno, -a [ʒe'nwinu, a] ADJ genuine

geografia [ʒeogra'fia] F geography

geometria [ʒeome'tria] F geometry

geração [ʒera'sãw] (*pl* **-ões**) F generation

gerador, a [ʒera'dor(a)] M/F (*produtor*) creator ▶ M (*Tec*) generator

geral [ʒe'raw] (*pl* **-ais**) ADJ general ▶ F (*Teatro*) gallery; **em ~** in general, generally; **de um modo ~** on the whole; **geralmente** [ʒeraw'mẽtʃi] ADV generally, usually

gerânio [ʒe'ranju] M geranium

gerar [ʒe'rar] VT to produce; (*eletricidade*) to generate

gerência [ʒe'rẽsja] F management; **gerenciar** [ʒerẽ'sjar] VT, VI to manage

gerente [ʒe'rẽtʃi] ADJ managing ▶ M/F manager

gerir [ʒe'rir] VT to manage, run

germe ['ʒɛrmi] M (*embrião*) embryo; (*micróbio*) germ

gesso ['ʒesu] M plaster (of Paris)

gesticular [ʒestʃiku'lar] VI to make gestures, gesture

gesto ['ʒɛstu] M gesture

Gibraltar [ʒibraw'tar] F Gibraltar

gigabyte [ʒiga'bajtʃi] M gigabyte

gigante, -a [ʒi'gãtʃi, a] ADJ gigantic, huge ▶ M giant;

gigantesco, -a [ʒigã'tesku, a] ADJ gigantic

gim [ʒĩ] (*pl* **-ns**) M gin

ginásio [ʒi'nazju] M gymnasium; (*escola*) secondary (BRIT) *ou* high (US) school

ginástica [ʒi'nastʃika] F gymnastics *sg*; (*para fortalecer o corpo*) keep-fit

ginecologia [ʒinekolo'ʒia] F gynaecology (BRIT), gynecology (US)

ginecologista [ʒinekolo'ʒista] M/F gynaecologist (BRIT), gynecologist (US)

ginjinha [ʒĩ'ʒiɲa] (PT) F cherry brandy

gira-discos (PT) M INV record-player

girafa [ʒi'rafa] F giraffe

girar [ʒi'rar] VT to turn, rotate; (*como pião*) to spin ▶ VI to go round; to spin; (*vaguear*) to wander

girassol [ʒira'sɔw] (*pl* **-óis**) M sunflower

gíria ['ʒirja] F (*calão*) slang; (*jargão*) jargon

giro[1] ['ʒiru] M turn; **dar um ~** to go for a wander; (*em veículo*) to go for a spin; **que ~!** (PT) great!

giro[2] VB *ver* **gerir**

giz [ʒiz] M chalk

glacê [gla'se] M icing

glacial [gla'sjaw] (*pl* **-ais**) ADJ icy

glamouroso, -a [glamu'rozu, ɔza] ADJ glamorous

glândula ['glãdula] F gland

global [glo'baw] (*pl* **-ais**) ADJ global; (*total*) overall; **quantia ~** lump sum; **globalização** [globaliza'sãw] F globalization

globo ['globu] M globe; **~ ocular** eyeball

glória ['glɔrja] F glory; **glorificar**

[glorifi'kar] VT to glorify; **glorioso, -a** [glo'rjozu, ɔza] ADJ glorious
glossário [glo'sarju] M glossary
gnomo ['gnomu] M gnome
goiaba [go'jaba] F guava;
goiabada [goja'bada] F guava jelly
gol [gow] (*pl* **gols**) M goal
gola ['gɔla] F collar
gole ['gɔli] M gulp, swallow; (*pequeno*) sip; **dar um ~** to have a sip
goleiro [go'lejru] (BR) M goalkeeper; (*col*) goalie
golfe ['gowfi] M golf; **campo de ~** golf course
golfinho [gow'fiɲu] M (*Zool*) dolphin
golfo ['gowfu] M gulf
golinho [go'liɲu] M sip; **beber algo aos ~s** to sip sth
golo ['golu] (PT) M = **gol**
golpe ['gɔwpi] M (*tb fig*) blow; (*de mão*) smack; (*de punho*) punch; (*manobra*) ploy; (*de vento*) gust; **de um só ~** at a stroke; **dar um ~ em alguém** to hit sb; (*fig: trapacear*) to trick sb; **~ (de estado)** coup (d'état); **~ de mestre** masterstroke; **golpear** [gow'pjar] VT to hit; (*com navalha*) to stab; (*com o punho*) to punch
goma ['gɔma] F gum, glue; (*de roupa*) starch; **~ de mascar** chewing gum
gomo ['gomu] M (*de laranja*) slice
gordo, -a ['gordu, a] ADJ fat; (*gordurento*) greasy; (*carne*) fatty; (*fig: quantia*) considerable, ample ▶ M/F fat man/woman
gordura [gor'dura] F fat; (*derretida*) grease; (*obesidade*) fatness; **gorduroso, -a** [gordu'rozu, ɔza] ADJ (*pele*) greasy; (*comida*) fatty
gorila [go'rila] M gorilla
gorjeta [gor'ʒeta] F tip, gratuity
gorro ['gohu] M cap; (*de lã*) hat
gosma ['gɔzma] F spittle; (*fig*) slime
gostar [gos'tar] VI: **~ de** to like; (*férias, viagem etc*) to enjoy; **gostar-se** VR to like each other; **~ mais de ...** to prefer ..., to like ... better
gosto ['gostu] M taste; (*prazer*) pleasure; **a seu ~** to your liking; **com ~** willingly; (*vestir-se*) tastefully; (*comer*) heartily; **de bom/mau ~** in good/bad taste; **ter ~ de** to taste of; **gostoso, -a** [gos'tozu, ɔza] ADJ tasty; (*agradável*) pleasant; (*cheiro*) lovely; (*risada*) good; (*col: pessoa*) gorgeous
gota ['gota] F drop; (*de suor*) bead; (*Med*) gout; **~ a ~** drop by drop
goteira [go'tejra] F (*cano*) gutter; (*buraco*) leak
gourmet [gur'me] (*pl* **-s**) M/F gourmet
governador, a [governador(a)] M/F governor
governamental [governamẽ'taw] (*pl* **-ais**) ADJ government *atr*
governante [gover'nãtʃi] ADJ ruling ▶ M/F ruler ▶ F governess
governar [gover'nar] VT to govern, rule; (*barco*) to steer
governo [go'vernu] M government; (*controle*) control
gozação [goza'sãw] (*pl* **-ões**) F enjoyment; (*zombaria*) teasing; (*uma gozação*) joke
gozado, -a [go'zadu, a] ADJ funny; (*estranho*) strange, odd
gozar [go'zar] VT to enjoy; (*col: rir de*) to make fun of ▶ VI to enjoy o.s.; **~ de** to enjoy; to make fun of;
gozo ['gozu] M (*prazer*) pleasure; (*uso*) enjoyment, use; (*orgasmo*) orgasm

GPS ABR M (= *global positioning system*) GPS

Grã-Bretanha [grã-bre'taɲa] F Great Britain

graça ['grasa] F (*Rel*) grace; (*charme*) charm; (*gracejo*) joke; (*Jur*) pardon; **de ~** (*grátis*) for nothing; (*sem motivo*) for no reason; **sem ~** dull, boring; **fazer** *ou* **ter ~** to be funny; **ficar sem ~** to be embarrassed; **~s a** thanks to

gracejar [grase'ʒar] VI to joke; **gracejo** [gra'seʒu] M joke

gracioso, -a [gra'sjozu, ɔza] ADJ (*pessoa*) charming; (*gestos*) gracious

grade ['gradʒi] F (*no chão*) grating; (*grelha*) grill; (*na janela*) bars *pl*; (*col: cadeia*) prison

gradear [gra'dʒjar] VT (*janela*) to put bars up at; (*jardim*) to fence off

graduação [gradwa'sãw] (*pl* **-ões**) F (*classificação*) grading; (*Educ*) graduation; (*Mil*) rank

gradual [gra'dwaw] (*pl* **-ais**) ADJ gradual

graduar [gra'dwar] VT (*classificar*) to grade; (*luz, fogo*) to regulate; **graduar-se** VR to graduate

gráfica ['grafika] F graphics *sg*; *ver tb* **gráfico**

gráfico, -a ['grafiku, a] ADJ graphic ▶ M/F printer ▶ M (*Mat*) graph; (*diagrama*) diagram, chart; **gráficos** MPL (*Comput*) graphics; **~ de barras** bar chart

grã-fino, -a [grã'finu, a] (*col*) ADJ posh ▶ M/F nob, toff

grama ['grama] M gramme ▶ F (BR: *capim*) grass

gramado [gra'madu] (BR) M lawn; (*Futebol*) pitch

gramática [gra'matʃika] F grammar

grampear [grã'pjar] VT to staple

grampo ['grãpu] M staple; (*no cabelo*) hairgrip; (*de carpinteiro*) clamp; (*de chapéu*) hatpin

grande ['grãdʒi] ADJ big, large; (*alto*) tall; (*notável, intenso*) great; (*longo*) long; (*adulto*) grown-up; **mulher ~** big woman; **~ mulher** great woman; **grandeza** [grã'deza] F size; (*fig*) greatness; (*ostentação*) grandeur

grandioso, -a [grã'dʒjozu, ɔza] ADJ magnificent, grand

granito [gra'nitu] M granite

granizo [gra'nizu] M hailstone; **chover ~** to hail; **chuva de ~** hailstorm

granulado, -a [granu'ladu, a] ADJ grainy; (*açúcar*) granulated

grão ['grãw] (*pl* **grãos**) M grain; (*semente*) seed; (*de café*) bean; **grão-de-bico** (*pl* **grãos-de-bico**) M chickpea

gratidão [gratʃi'dãw] F gratitude

gratificar [gratʃifi'kar] VT to tip; (*dar bônus a*) to give a bonus to; (*recompensar*) to reward

grátis ['gratʃis] ADJ free

grato, -a ['gratu, a] ADJ grateful; (*agradável*) pleasant

gratuito, -a [gra'twitu, a] ADJ (*grátis*) free; (*infundado*) gratuitous

grau [graw] M degree; (*nível*) level; (*Educ*) class; **em alto ~** to a high degree; **ensino de primeiro/segundo ~** primary (BRIT) *ou* elementary (US) /secondary education

gravação [grava'sãw] F (*em madeira*) carving; (*em disco, fita*) recording

gravador, a [grava'dor(a)] M tape

g

recorder ▶ M/F engraver; **~ de CD/DVD** CD/DVD burner, CD/DVD writer

gravar [gra'var] VT to carve; (*metal, pedra*) to engrave; (*na memória*) to fix; (*disco, fita*) to record

gravata [gra'vata] F tie; **~ borboleta** bow tie

grave ['gravi] ADJ serious; (*tom*) deep; **gravemente** [grave'mẽtʃi] ADV (*doente, ferido*) seriously

grávida ['gravida] ADJ pregnant

gravidade [gravi'dadʒi] F gravity

gravidez [gravi'dez] F pregnancy

gravura [gra'vura] F (*em madeira*) engraving; (*estampa*) print

graxa ['graʃa] F (*para sapatos*) polish; (*lubrificante*) grease

Grécia ['grɛsja] F: **a ~** Greece; **grego, -a** ['gregu, a] ADJ, M/F Greek ▶ M (*Ling*) Greek

grelha ['grɛʎa] F grill; (*de fornalha*) grate; **bife na ~** grilled steak; **grelhado, -a** [gre'ʎadu, a] ADJ grilled ▶ M (*prato*) grill

grêmio ['gremju] M (*associação*) guild; (*clube*) club

grená [gre'na] ADJ, M dark red

greve ['grɛvi] F strike; **fazer ~** to go on strike; **~ branca** go-slow; **grevista** [gre'vista] M/F striker

grilo ['grilu] M cricket; (*Auto*) squeak; (*col: de pessoa*) hang-up; **qual é o ~?** what's the matter?; **não tem ~!** (*col*) (there's) no problem!

gringo, -a ['grĩgu, a] (*col, pej*) M/F foreigner

gripado, -a [gri'padu, a] ADJ: **estar/ficar ~** to have/get a cold

gripe ['gripi] F flu, influenza; **~ aviária** bird flu; **~ suína** swine flu

grisalho, -a [gri'zaʎu, a] ADJ (*cabelo*) grey (BRIT), gray (US)

gritante [gri'tãtʃi] ADJ (*hipocrisia*) glaring; (*desigualdade*) gross; (*mentira*) blatant; (*cor*) loud, garish

gritar [gri'tar] VT to shout, yell ▶ VI to shout; (*de dor, medo*) to scream; **~ com alguém** to shout at sb; **gritaria** [grita'ria] F shouting, din; **grito** ['gritu] M shout; (*de medo*) scream; (*de dor*) cry; (*de animal*) call; **dar um grito** to cry out; **falar/protestar aos gritos** to shout/shout protests

Groenlândia [grwẽ'lãdʒja] F: **a ~** Greenland

grosseiro, -a [gro'sejru, a] ADJ rude; (*piada*) crude; (*modos*) coarse; **grosseria** [grose'ria] F rudeness; (*ato*): **fazer uma grosseria** to be rude; (*dito*): **dizer uma grosseria** to be rude, say something rude

grosso, -a ['grosu, 'grɔsa] ADJ thick; (*áspero*) rough; (*voz*) deep; (*col: pessoa, piada*) rude ▶ M: **o ~ de** the bulk of; **grossura** [gro'sura] F thickness

grotesco, -a [gro'tesku, a] ADJ grotesque

grudar [gru'dar] VT to glue, stick ▶ VI to stick

grude ['grudʒi] F glue; **grudento, -a** [gru'dẽtu, a] ADJ sticky

grunhir [gru'ɲir] VI (*porco*) to grunt; (*tigre*) to growl; (*resmungar*) to grumble

grupo ['grupu] M group

guarda ['gwarda] M/F policeman/woman ▶ F (*vigilância*) guarding; (*de objeto*) safekeeping ▶ M (*Mil*) guard; **estar de ~** to be on guard; **pôr-se em ~** to be on one's guard; **a G~ Civil** the Civil Guard; **guarda-chuva** (*pl* **-s**) M umbrella; **guarda-costas** M INV (*Náut*) coastguard boat; (*capanga*) bodyguard; **guardados**

[gwar'dadus] MPL keepsakes, valuables; **guarda-fogo** (*pl* **-s**) M fireguard; **guarda-louça** [gwarda'losa] (*pl* **-s**) M sideboard; **guardanapo** [gwarda'napu] M napkin; **guarda-noturno** (*pl* **guardas-noturnos**) M night watchman; **guardar** [gwar'dar] VT to put away; (*zelar por*) to guard; (*lembrança, segredo*) to keep; **guardar-se** VR (*defender-se*) to protect o.s.; **guardar-se de** (*acautelar-se*) to guard against; **guarda-redes** (PT) M INV goalkeeper; **guarda-roupa** (*pl* **-s**) M wardrobe; **guarda-sol** (*pl* **-sóis**) M sunshade, parasol

guardião, -diã [gwar'dʒjãw, 'dʒjã] (*pl* **-ães/-s**) M/F guardian

guarnição [gwarni'sãw] (*pl* **-ões**) F (*Mil*) garrison; (*Náut*) crew; (*Culin*) garnish

Guatemala [gwate'mala] F: **a ~** Guatemala

gude ['gudʒi] M: **bola de ~** marble; (*jogo*) marbles *pl*

guerra ['gɛha] F war; **em ~** at war; **fazer ~** to wage war; **~ civil** civil war; **~ mundial** world war; **guerreiro, -a** [ge'hejru, a] ADJ (*espírito*) fighting; (*belicoso*) warlike ▶ M warrior

guerrilha [ge'hiʎa] F (*luta*) guerrilla warfare; (*tropa*) guerrilla band; **guerrilheiro, -a** [gehi'ʎejru, a] M/F guerrilla

guia ['gia] F guidance; (*Com*) permit, bill of lading; (*formulário*) advice slip ▶ M (*livro*) guide(book) ▶ M/F (*pessoa*) guide

Guiana ['gjana] F: **a ~** Guyana

guiar [gjar] VT to guide; (*Auto*) to drive ▶ VI to drive; **guiar-se** VR: **~-se por** to go by

guichê [gi'ʃe] M ticket window; (*em banco, repartição*) window, counter

guinada [gi'nada] F: **dar uma ~** (*com o carro*) to swerve

guindaste [gĩ'dastʃi] M hoist, crane

guisado [gi'zadu] M stew

guitarra [gi'taha] F (electric) guitar

guloso, -a [gu'lozu, ɔza] ADJ greedy

h

há [a] VB *ver* **haver**
hábil ['abiw] (*pl* **-eis**) ADJ competent, capable; (*astucioso, esperto*) clever; (*sutil*) diplomatic; **em tempo ~** in reasonable time; **habilidade** [abili'dadʒi] F skill, ability; (*astúcia, esperteza*) shrewdness; (*tato*) discretion; **habilidoso, -a** [abili'dozu, ɔza] ADJ skilful (BRIT), skillful (US), clever
habilitação [abilita'sãw] (*pl* **-ões**) F competence; (*ato*) qualification; **habilitações** FPL (*conhecimentos*) qualifications
habilitar [abili'tar] VT to enable; (*dar direito a*) to qualify, entitle; (*preparar*) to prepare
habitação [abita'sãw] (*pl* **-ões**) F dwelling, residence; (*alojamento*) housing
habitante [abi'tãtʃi] M/F inhabitant
habitar [abi'tar] VT to live in; (*povoar*) to inhabit ▶ VI to live
hábito ['abitu] M habit; (*social*) custom; (*Rel: traje*) habit
habituado, -a [abi'twadu, a] ADJ: **~ a (fazer) algo** used to (doing) sth
habituar [abi'twar] VT: **~ alguém a** to get sb used to, accustom sb to; **habituar-se** VR: **~-se a** to get used to
hacker ['haker] (*pl* **-s**) M (*Comput*) hacker
Haia ['aja] N the Hague
haja ['aʒa] VB *ver* **haver**
hálito ['alitu] M breath
hall [hɔw] (*pl* **halls**) M hall; (*de teatro, hotel*) foyer; **~ de entrada** entrance hall
hambúrguer [ã'burger] (*pl* **-s**) M hamburger
hão [ãw] VB *ver* **haver**
hardware ['hadwer] M (*Comput*) hardware
harmonia [armo'nia] F harmony
harmonioso, -a [armo'njozu, ɔza] ADJ harmonious
harmonizar [armoni'zar] VT (*Mús*) to harmonize; (*conciliar*): **~ algo (com algo)** to reconcile sth (with sth); **harmonizar-se** VR: **~(-se) (com algo)** (*ideias etc*) to coincide (with sth); (*pessoas*) to be in agreement (with sth)
harpa ['arpa] F harp
Havaí [avaj'i] M: **o ~** Hawaii

PALAVRA-CHAVE

haver [a'ver] VB AUX **1** (*ter*) to have; **ele havia saído/comido** he had left/eaten
2: **quem haveria de dizer que ...** who would have thought that ...
▶ VB IMPESS **1** (*existência*): **há** (*sg*) there is; (*pl*) there are; **o que é que há?** what's the matter?; **o que é que houve?** what happened?, what was that?; **não há de quê** don't

mention it, you're welcome; **haja o que houver** come what may
2 (*tempo*): **há séculos/cinco dias que não o vejo** I haven't seen him for ages/five days; **há um ano que ela chegou** it's a year since she arrived; **há cinco dias (atrás)** five days ago
haver-se VR: **haver-se com alguém** to sort things out with sb
▶ M (*Com*) credit; **haveres** MPL (*pertences*) property *sg*, possessions; (*riqueza*) wealth *sg*

haxixe [a'ʃiʃi] M hashish
hebraico, -a [e'brajku, a] ADJ Hebrew ▶ M (*Ling*) Hebrew
Hébridas ['ɛbridas] FPL: **as (ilhas) ~** the Hebrides
hediondo, -a [e'dʒjõdu, a] ADJ vile, revolting; (*crime*) heinous
hei [ej] VB *ver* **haver**
hélice ['ɛlisi] F propeller
helicóptero [eli'kɔpteru] M helicopter
hematoma [ema'tɔma] M bruise
hemorragia [emoha'ʒia] F haemorrhage (BRIT), hemorrhage (US); **~ nasal** nosebleed
hemorróidas [emo'hɔjdas] FPL haemorrhoids (BRIT), hemorrhoids (US), piles
hepatite [epa'tʃitʃi] F hepatitis
hera ['ɛra] F ivy
herança [e'rãsa] F inheritance; (*fig*) heritage
herdar [er'dar] VT: **~ algo (de)** to inherit sth (from); **~ a** to bequeath to
herdeiro, -a [er'dejru, a] M/F heir(ess)
herói [e'rɔj] M hero
heroína [ero'ina] F heroine; (*droga*) heroin
hesitação [ezita'sãw] (*pl* **-ões**) F hesitation
hesitante [ezi'tãtʃi] ADJ hesitant
hesitar [ezi'tar] VI to hesitate
heterossexual [eterosek'swaw] (*pl* **-ais**) ADJ, M/F heterosexual
híbrido, -a ['ibridu, a] ADJ hybrid
hidratante [idra'tãtʃi] M moisturizer
hidrato [i'dratu] M: **~ de carbono** carbohydrate
hidráulico, -a [i'drawliku, a] ADJ hydraulic
hidrelétrico, -a [idre'lɛtriku, a] ADJ hydroelectric
hidro... [idru] PREFIXO hydro..., water... *atr*
hidrogênio [idro'ʒenju] M hydrogen
hidroginástica [idroʒi'nastʃika] F aquaerobics
hífen ['ifẽ] (*pl* **hífens**) M hyphen
higiene [i'ʒjeni] F hygiene; **higiênico, -a** [i'ʒjeniku, a] ADJ hygienic; (*pessoa*) clean; **papel higiênico** toilet paper
hindu [ĩ'du] ADJ, M/F Hindu
hino ['inu] M hymn; **~ nacional** national anthem
hipermercado [ipermer'kadu] M hypermarket
hipertensão [ipertẽ'sãw] F high blood pressure
hipismo [i'pizmu] M (*turfe*) horse racing; (*equitação*) (horse) riding
hipocrisia [ipokri'zia] F hypocrisy; **hipócrita** [i'pɔkrita] ADJ hypocritical ▶ M/F hypocrite
hipódromo [i'pɔdromu] M racecourse
hipopótamo [ipo'pɔtamu] M hippopotamus
hipoteca [ipo'tɛka] F mortgage; **hipotecar** [ipote'kar] VT to mortgage

hipótese [i'pɔtezi] F hypothesis; **na ~ de** in the event of; **em ~ alguma** under no circumstances; **na melhor/pior das ~s** at best/worst

hispânico, -a [is'paniku, a] ADJ Hispanic

histeria [iste'ria] F hysteria; **histérico, -a** [is'tɛriku, a] ADJ hysterical

história [is'tɔrja] F history; (*conto*) story; **histórias** FPL (*chateação*) bother *sg*, fuss *sg*; **isso é outra ~** that's a different matter; **que ~ é essa?** what's going on?; **historiador, a** [istorja'dor(a)] M/F historian; **histórico, -a** [is'tɔriku, a] ADJ historical; (*fig: notável*) historic ▶ M history

hobby ['hɔbi] (*pl* **-bies**) M hobby

hoje ['oʒi] ADV today; (*atualmente*) now(adays); **~ à noite** tonight

Holanda [o'lãda] F: **a ~** Holland; **holandês, -esa** [olã'des, eza] ADJ Dutch ▶ M/F Dutchman/woman ▶ M (*Ling*) Dutch

holocausto [olo'kawstu] M holocaust

homem ['omẽ] (*pl* **-ns**) M man; (*a humanidade*) mankind; **~ de empresa** *ou* **negócios** businessman; **~ de estado** statesman; **homem-bomba** (*pl* **homens-bomba**) M suicide bomber

homenagear [omena'ʒjar] VT (*pessoa*) to pay tribute to, honour (BRIT), honor (US)

homenagem [ome'naʒẽ] F tribute; (*Rel*) homage; **prestar ~ a alguém** to pay tribute to sb

homens ['omẽs] MPL *de* **homem**

homeopático, -a [omjo'patʃiku, a] ADJ homoeopathic (BRIT), homeopathic (US)

homicida [omi'sida] ADJ homicidal ▶ M/F murderer; **homicídio** [omi'sidʒju] M murder; **homicídio involuntário** manslaughter

homologar [omolo'gar] VT to ratify

homólogo, -a [o'mɔlogu, a] ADJ homologous; (*fig*) equivalent ▶ M/F opposite number

homossexual [omosek'swaw] (*pl* **-ais**) ADJ, M/F homosexual

Honduras [õ'duras] F Honduras

honestidade [onestʃi'dadʒi] F honesty; (*decência*) decency; (*justeza*) fairness

honesto, -a [o'nɛstu, a] ADJ honest; (*decente*) decent; (*justo*) fair, just

honorário, -a [ono'rarju, a] ADJ honorary; **honorários** [ono'rarjus] MPL fees

honra ['õha] F honour (BRIT), honor (US); **em ~ de** in hono(u)r of

honrado, -a [õ'hadu, a] ADJ honest; (*respeitado*) honourable (BRIT), honorable (US)

honrar [õ'har] VT to honour (BRIT), honor (US)

honroso, -a [õ'hozu, ɔza] ADJ honourable (BRIT), honorable (US)

hóquei ['hɔkej] M hockey; **~ sobre gelo** ice hockey

hora ['ɔra] F (*60 minutos*) hour; (*momento*) time; **a que ~s?** (at) what time?; **que ~s são?** what time is it?; **são duas ~s** it's two o'clock; **você tem as ~s?** have you got the time?; **fazer ~** to kill time; **de ~ em ~** every hour; **na ~** on the spot; **chegar na ~** to be on time; **de última ~** *adj* last-minute; *adv* at the last minute; **~ do almoço** lunch hour; **meia ~** half an hour; **~s extras** overtime *sg*; **horário, -a** [o'rarju, a] ADJ: **100 km horários**

100 km an hour ▸ M timetable; (*hora*) time; **horário de expediente** working hours *pl*; (*de um escritório*) office hours *pl*

horizontal [orizõ'taw] (*pl* **-ais**) ADJ horizontal

horizonte [ori'zõtʃi] M horizon

horóscopo [o'rɔskopu] M horoscope

horrível [o'hivew] (*pl* **-eis**) ADJ awful, horrible

horror [o'hor] M horror; **que ~!** how awful!; **ter ~ a algo** to hate sth; **horrorizar** [ohori'zar] VT to horrify, frighten; **horroroso, -a** [oho'rozu, ɔza] ADJ horrible, ghastly

hortaliças [orta'lisas] FPL vegetables

hortelã [orte'lã] F mint; **~ pimenta** peppermint

horticultor, a [ortʃikuw'tor(a)] M/F market gardener (BRIT), truck farmer (US)

hortifrutigranjeiros [ortʃifrutʃigrã'ʒejrus] MPL fruit and vegetables

horto ['ortu] M market garden (BRIT), truck farm (US)

hospedagem [ospe'daʒẽ] F guest house

hospedar [ospe'dar] VT to put up; **hospedar-se** VR to stay, lodge; **hospedaria** [ospeda'ria] F guest house

hóspede ['ɔspedʒi] M (*amigo*) guest; (*estranho*) lodger

hospedeira [ospe'dejra] F landlady; (PT: *de bordo*) stewardess, air hostess (BRIT)

hospício [os'pisju] M mental hospital

hospital [ospi'taw] (*pl* **-ais**) M hospital

hospitalidade [ospitali'dadʒi] F hospitality

hostil [os'tʃiw] (*pl* **-is**) ADJ hostile; **hostilizar** [ostʃili'zar] VT to antagonize; (*Mil*) to wage war on

hotel [o'tɛw] (*pl* **-éis**) M hotel; **hoteleiro, -a** [ote'lejru, a] M/F hotelier

houve ['ovi] VB *ver* **haver**

humanidade [umani'dadʒi] F (*os homens*) man(kind); (*compaixão*) humanity

humanitário, -a [umani'tarju, a] ADJ humane

humano, -a [u'manu, a] ADJ human; (*bondoso*) humane

humildade [umiw'dadʒi] F humility; (*pobreza*) poverty

humilde [u'miwdʒi] ADJ humble; (*pobre*) poor

humilhar [umi'ʎar] VT to humiliate

humor [u'mor] M mood, temper; (*graça*) humour (BRIT), humor (US); **de bom/mau ~** in a good/bad mood; **humorista** [umo'rista] M/F comedian; **humorístico, -a** [umo'ristʃiku, a] ADJ humorous

húngaro, -a ['ũgaru, a] ADJ, M/F Hungarian

Hungria [ũ'gria] F: **a ~** Hungary

hurra ['uha] M cheer ▸ EXCL hurrah!

h

I

ia ['ia] VB *ver* **ir**
iate ['jatʃi] M yacht; **~ clube** yacht club
ibérico, -a [i'bɛriku, a] ADJ, M/F Iberian
ibero-americano, -a [iberu-] ADJ, M/F Ibero-American
ICMS (BR) ABR M (= *Imposto sobre Circulação de Mercadorias e Prestação de Serviços*) ≈ VAT
icone ['ikoni] M (*ger, Comput*) icon
ida ['ida] F going, departure; **~ e volta** round trip, return; **a (viagem de) ~** the outward journey; **na ~** on the way there
idade [i'dadʒi] F age; **ter cinco anos de ~** to be five (years old); **de meia ~** middle-aged; **qual é a ~ dele?** how old is he?; **na minha ~** at my age; **ser menor/maior de ~** to be under/of age; **pessoa de ~** elderly person; **I~ Média** Middle Ages *pl*
ideal [ide'jaw] (*pl* **-ais**) ADJ, M ideal; **idealista** [idea'lista] ADJ idealistic ▶ M/F idealist
ideia [i'dɛja] F idea; (*mente*) mind; **mudar de ~** to change one's mind; **não ter a mínima ~** to have no idea; **não faço ~** I can't imagine; **estar com ~ de fazer** to plan to do
idem ['idẽ] PRON ditto
idêntico, -a [i'dẽtʃiku, a] ADJ identical
identidade [idẽtʃi'dadʒi] F identity
identificação [idẽtʃifika'sãw] F identification
identificar [idẽtʃifi'kar] VT to identify; **identificar-se** VR: **~-se com** to identify with
idioma [i'dʒɔma] M language
idiota [i'dʒɔta] ADJ idiotic ▶ M/F idiot
ido, -a ['idu, a] ADJ past
ídolo ['idolu] M idol
idoso, -a [i'dozu, ɔza] ADJ elderly, old
ignorado, -a [igno'radu, a] ADJ unknown
ignorância [igno'rãsja] F ignorance; **ignorante** [igno'rãtʃi] ADJ ignorant, uneducated ▶ M/F ignoramus
ignorar [igno'rar] VT not to know; (*não dar atenção a*) to ignore
igreja [i'greʒa] F church
igual [i'gwaw] (*pl* **-ais**) ADJ equal; (*superfície*) even ▶ M/F equal
igualar [igwa'lar] VT to equal; (*fazer igual*) to make equal; (*nivelar*) to level ▶ VI: **~ a** *ou* **com** to be equal to, be the same as; (*ficar no mesmo nível*) to be level with; **igualar-se** VR: **~-se a alguém** to be sb's equal
igualdade [igwaw'dadʒi] F equality; (*uniformidade*) uniformity
igualmente [igwaw'mẽtʃi] ADV equally; (*também*) likewise, also; **~!** (*saudação*) the same to you!

ilegal [ile'gaw] (*pl* **-ais**) ADJ illegal
ilegítimo, -a [ile'ʒitʃimu, a] ADJ illegitimate; (*ilegal*) unlawful
ilegível [ile'ʒivew] (*pl* **-eis**) ADJ illegible
iletrado, -a [ile'tradu, a] ADJ illiterate
ilha ['iʎa] F island; **ilhéu, ilhoa** [i'ʎɛw, i'ʎoa] M/F islander
ilícito, -a [i'lisitu, a] ADJ illicit
ilimitado, -a [ilimi'tadu, a] ADJ unlimited
iluminar [ilumi'nar] VT to light up; (*estádio etc*) to floodlight; (*fig*) to enlighten
ilusão [ilu'zãw] (*pl* **-ões**) F illusion; (*quimera*) delusion; **ilusório, -a** [ilu'zɔrju, a] ADJ deceptive
ilustração [ilustra'sãw] (*pl* **-ões**) F illustration
ilustrado, -a [ilus'tradu, a] ADJ illustrated; (*instruído*) learned
ilustrar [ilus'trar] VT to illustrate; (*instruir*) to instruct
ilustre [i'lustri] ADJ illustrious; **um ~ desconhecido** a complete stranger
ímã ['imã] M magnet
imagem [i'maʒẽ] (*pl* **-ns**) F image; (*semelhança*) likeness; (*TV*) picture; **imagens** FPL (*Literatura*) imagery *sg*
imaginação [imaʒina'sãw] (*pl* **-ões**) F imagination
imaginar [imaʒi'nar] VT to imagine; (*supor*) to suppose; **imaginar-se** VR to imagine o.s.; **imagine só!** just imagine!; **imaginário, -a** [imaʒi'narju, a] ADJ imaginary
imaturo, -a [ima'turu, a] ADJ immature
imbatível [ĩba'tʃivew] (*pl* **-eis**) ADJ invincible
imbecil [ĩbe'siw] (*pl* **-is**) ADJ stupid ▶ M/F imbecile; **imbecilidade** [ĩbesili'dadʒi] F stupidity
imediações [imedʒa'sõjs] FPL vicinity *sg*, neighbourhood *sg* (BRIT), neighborhood *sg* (US)
imediatamente [imedʒata'mẽtʃi] ADV immediately, right away
imediato, -a [ime'dʒatu, a] ADJ immediate; (*seguinte*) next; **~ a** next to; **de ~** straight away
imenso, -a [i'mẽsu, a] ADJ immense, huge; (*ódio, amor*) great
imigração [imigra'sãw] (*pl* **-ões**) F immigration
imigrante [imi'grãtʃi] ADJ, M/F immigrant
iminente [imi'nẽtʃi] ADJ imminent
imitação [imita'sãw] (*pl* **-ões**) F imitation
imitar [imi'tar] VT to imitate; (*assinatura*) to copy
imobiliária [imobi'ljarja] F estate agent's (BRIT), real estate broker's (US)
imobiliário, -a [imobi'ljarju, a] ADJ property *atr*
imobilizar [imobili'zar] VT to immobilize; (*fig*) to bring to a standstill
imoral [imo'raw] (*pl* **-ais**) ADJ immoral
imortal [imor'taw] (*pl* **-ais**) ADJ immortal
imóvel [i'mɔvew] (*pl* **-eis**) ADJ motionless, still; (*não movediço*) immovable ▶ M property; (*edifício*) building; **imóveis** MPL (*propriedade*) real estate *sg*, property *sg*
impaciência [ĩpa'sjẽsja] F impatience; **impacientar-se**

[ĩpasjẽ'tarsi] VR to lose one's patience; **impaciente** [ĩpa'sjẽtʃi] ADJ impatient
impacto [ĩ'paktu], (PT) **impacte** M impact
ímpar ['ĩpar] ADJ (*número*) odd; (*sem igual*) unique, unequalled
imparcial [ĩpar'sjaw] (*pl* **-ais**) ADJ fair, impartial
impecável [ĩpe'kavew] (*pl* **-eis**) ADJ perfect, impeccable
impeço [ĩ'pɛsu] VB *ver* **impedir**
impedido, -a [ĩpe'dʒidu, a] ADJ (*Futebol*) offside; (PT *Tel*) engaged (BRIT), busy (US)
impedimento [ĩpedʒi'mẽtu] M impediment
impedir [ĩpe'dʒir] VT to obstruct; (*estrada, passagem, tráfego*) to block; (*movimento, execução, progresso*) to impede; **~ alguém de fazer algo** to prevent sb from doing sth; (*proibir*) to forbid sb to do sth; **~ (que aconteça) algo** to prevent sth (happening)
impenetrável [ĩpene'travew] (*pl* **-eis**) ADJ impenetrable
impensado, -a [ĩpẽ'sadu, a] ADJ thoughtless; (*não calculado*) unpremeditated; (*imprevisto*) unforeseen
imperador [ĩpera'dor] M emperor
imperativo, -a [ĩpera'tʃivu, a] ADJ imperative ▶ M imperative
imperatriz [ĩpera'triz] F empress
imperdoável [ĩper'dwavew] (*pl* **-eis**) ADJ unforgivable, inexcusable
imperfeito, -a [ĩper'fejtu, a] ADJ imperfect ▶ M (*Ling*) imperfect (tense)
imperial [ĩpe'rjaw] (*pl* **-ais**) ADJ imperial
imperícia [ĩpe'risja] F inability; (*inexperiência*) inexperience
império [ĩ'pɛrju] M empire
impermeável [ĩper'mjavew] (*pl* **-eis**) ADJ: **~ a** (*tb fig*) impervious to; (*à água*) waterproof ▶ M raincoat
impessoal [ĩpe'swaw] (*pl* **-ais**) ADJ impersonal
ímpeto ['ĩpetu] M (*Tec*) impetus; (*movimento súbito*) start; (*de cólera*) fit; (*de emoção*) surge; (*de chamas*) fury; **agir com ~** to act on impulse; **levantar-se num ~** to get up with a start
impiedoso, -a [ĩpje'dozu, ɔza] ADJ merciless, cruel
implacável [ĩpla'kavew] (*pl* **-eis**) ADJ (*pessoa*) unforgiving
implantação [ĩplãta'sãw] (*pl* **-ões**) F introduction; (*Med*) implant
implementar [ĩplemẽ'tar] VT to implement
implicar [ĩpli'kar] VT (*envolver*) to implicate; (*pressupor*) to imply ▶ VI: **~ com alguém** (*chatear*) to tease sb, pick on sb; **implicar-se** VR to get involved; **~ (em) algo** to involve sth
implícito, -a [ĩ'plisitu, a] ADJ implicit
implorar [ĩplo'rar] VT: **~ (algo a alguém)** to beg *ou* implore (sb for sth)
impopular [ĩpopu'lar] ADJ unpopular; **impopularidade** [ĩpopulari'dadʒi] F unpopularity
impor [ĩ'por] (*irreg: como* **pôr**) VT to impose; (*respeito*) to command; **impor-se** VR to assert o.s.; **~ algo a alguém** to impose sth on sb
importação [ĩporta'sãw] (*pl* **-ões**) F (*ato*) importing; (*mercadoria*) import
importador, a [ĩporta'dor(a)] ADJ import *atr* ▶ M/F importer
importância [ĩpor'tãsja] F importance; (*de dinheiro*) sum,

amount; **não tem ~** it doesn't matter, never mind; **ter ~** to be important; **sem ~** unimportant; **importante** [ĩpor'tãtʃi] ADJ important ▶ M: **o (mais) importante** the (most) important thing

importar [ĩpor'tar] VT (*Com*) to import; (*trazer*) to bring in; (*causar: prejuízos etc*) to cause; (*implicar*) to imply, involve ▶ VI to matter, be important; **importar-se** VR: **~-se com algo** to mind sth; **não me importo** I don't care

importunar [ĩportu'nar] VT to bother, annoy

importuno, -a [ĩpor'tunu, a] ADJ annoying; (*inoportuno*) inopportune ▶ M/F nuisance

impossibilitado, -a [ĩposibili'tadu, a] ADJ: **~ de fazer** unable to do

impossibilitar [ĩposibili'tar] VT: **~ algo** to make sth impossible; **~ alguém de fazer, ~ a alguém fazer** to prevent sb doing; **~ algo a alguém, ~ alguém para algo** to make sth impossible for sb

impossível [ĩpo'sivew] (*pl* **-eis**) ADJ impossible; (*insuportável: pessoa*) insufferable; (*incrível*) incredible

imposto [ĩ'postu] M tax; **antes/depois de ~s** before/after tax; **~ ambiental** green tax, environmental tax; **~ de renda** (BR) income tax; **~ predial** rates *pl*; **I~ sobre Circulação de Mercadorias (e Serviços)** (BR), **~ sobre valor agregado** value added tax (BRIT), sales tax (US)

impotente [ĩpo'tẽtʃi] ADJ powerless; (*Med*) impotent

impraticável [ĩpratʃi'kavew] (*pl* **-eis**) ADJ impracticable; (*rua, rio etc*) impassable

impreciso, -a [ĩpre'sizu, a] ADJ vague; (*falto de rigor*) inaccurate

imprensa [ĩ'prẽsa] F printing; (*máquina, jornais*) press

imprescindível [ĩpresĩ'dʒivew] (*pl* **-eis**) ADJ essential, indispensable

impressão [impre'sãw] (*pl* **-ões**) F impression; (*de livros*) printing; (*marca*) imprint; **causar boa ~** to make a good impression; **ficar com/ter a ~ (de) que** to get/have the impression that

impressionante [ĩpresjo'nãtʃi] ADJ impressive

impressionar [ĩpresjo'nar] VT to affect ▶ VI to be impressive; (*pessoa*) to make an impression; **impressionar-se** VR: **~-se (com algo)** (*comover-se*) to be moved (by sth)

impresso, -a [ĩ'prɛsu, a] PP *de* **imprimir** ▶ ADJ printed ▶ M (*para preencher*) form; (*folheto*) leaflet; **impressos** MPL (*formulário*) printed matter *sg*

impressões [impre'sõjs] FPL *de* **impressão**

impressora [ĩpre'sora] F (*Comput*) printer; **~ jato de tinta** ink-jet printer

imprestável [ĩpres'tavew] (*pl* **-eis**) ADJ (*inútil*) useless; (*pessoa*) unhelpful

imprevisível [ĩprevi'zivew] (*pl* **-eis**) ADJ unforeseeable

imprevisto, -a [ĩpre'vistu, a] ADJ unexpected, unforeseen ▶ M: **um ~** something unexpected

imprimir [ĩpri'mir] VT to print; (*marca*) to stamp; (*infundir*) to instil (BRIT), instill (US)

impróprio, -a [ĩ'prɔprju, a] ADJ inappropriate; (*indecente*) improper
improvável [ĩpro'vavew] (*pl* **-eis**) ADJ unlikely
improviso [ĩpro'vizu] M: **de ~** (*de repente*) suddenly; (*sem preparação*) without preparation
imprudente [ĩpru'dẽtʃi] ADJ (*irrefletido*) rash; (*motorista*) careless
impulsivo, -a [ĩpuw'sivu, a] ADJ impulsive
impulso [ĩ'puwsu] M impulse; (*fig: estímulo*) urge, impulse
impune [ĩ'puni] ADJ unpunished; **impunidade** [ĩpuni'dadʒi] F impunity
imundície [imũ'dʒisji] F filth; **imundo, -a** [i'mũdu, a] ADJ filthy; (*obsceno*) dirty
imune [i'muni] ADJ: **~ a** immune to; **imunidade** [imuni'dadʒi] F immunity
inábil [i'nabiw] (*pl* **-eis**) ADJ incapable; (*desajeitado*) clumsy
inabitado, -a [inabi'tadu, a] ADJ uninhabited
inacabado, -a [inaka'badu, a] ADJ unfinished
inacreditável [inakredʒi'tavew] (*pl* **-eis**) ADJ unbelievable, incredible
inadequado, -a [inade'kwadu, a] ADJ inadequate; (*impróprio*) unsuitable
inadiável [ina'dʒjavew] (*pl* **-eis**) ADJ pressing
inadimplência [inadʒĩ'plẽsja] F (*Jur*) breach of contract, default
inaptidão [inaptʃi'dãw] (*pl* **-ões**) F inability
inatingível [inatʃĩ'ʒivew] (*pl* **-eis**) ADJ unattainable
inativo, -a [ina'tʃivu, a] ADJ inactive; (*aposentado, reformado*) retired
inauguração [inawgura'sãw] (*pl* **-ões**) F inauguration; (*de exposição*) opening; **inaugural** [inawgu'raw] (*pl* **-ais**) ADJ inaugural; **inaugurar** [inawgu'rar] VT to inaugurate; (*exposição*) to open
incapacidade [ĩkapasi'dadʒi] F incapacity; (*incompetência*) incompetence
incapacitado, -a [ĩkapasi'tadu, a] ADJ (*inválido*) disabled, handicapped ▶ M/F handicapped person; **estar ~ de fazer** to be unable to do
incapaz [ĩka'pajz] ADJ, M/F incompetent; **~ de fazer** incapable of doing; **~ para** unfit for
incendiar [ĩsẽ'dʒjar] VT to set fire to; (*fig*) to inflame; **incendiar-se** VR to catch fire
incêndio [ĩ'sẽdʒju] M fire; **~ criminoso** *ou* **premeditado** arson
incenso [ĩ'sẽsu] M incense
incentivar [ĩsẽtʃi'var] VT to stimulate, encourage
incentivo [ĩsẽ'tʃivu] M incentive; **~ fiscal** tax incentive
incerteza [ĩser'teza] F uncertainty
incerto, -a [ĩ'sɛrtu, a] ADJ uncertain
incesto [ĩ'sɛstu] M incest
inchado, -a [ĩ'ʃadu, a] ADJ swollen; (*fig*) conceited
inchar [ĩ'ʃar] VT, VI to swell
incidência [ĩsi'dẽsja] F incidence, occurrence
incidente [ĩsi'dẽtʃi] M incident
incisivo, -a [ĩsi'zivu, a] ADJ cutting, sharp; (*fig*) incisive
incitar [ĩsi'tar] VT to incite; (*pessoa, animal*) to drive on
inclinação [ĩklina'sãw] (*pl* **-ões**) F inclination; **~ da cabeça** nod
inclinar [ĩkli'nar] VT to tilt; (*cabeça*)

to nod ▶ VI to slope; (*objeto*) to tilt; **inclinar-se** VR to tilt; (*dobrar o corpo*) to bow, stoop; **~-se sobre algo** to lean over sth
incluir [ĩ'klwir] VT to include; (*em carta*) to enclose; **incluir-se** VR to be included
inclusão [ĩklu'zãw] F inclusion; **inclusive** [ĩklu'zivi] PREP including ▶ ADV inclusive; (*até mesmo*) even
incoerente [ĩkoe'rẽtʃi] ADJ incoherent; (*contraditório*) inconsistent
incógnita [ĩ'kɔgnita] F (*Mat*) unknown; (*fato incógnito*) mystery
incógnito, -a [ĩ'kɔgnitu, a] ADJ unknown ▶ ADV incognito
incolor [ĩko'lor] ADJ colourless (BRIT), colorless (US)
incomodar [ĩkomo'dar] VT to bother, trouble; (*aborrecer*) to annoy ▶ VI to be bothersome; **incomodar-se** VR to bother, put o.s. out; **~-se com algo** to be bothered by sth, mind sth; **não se incomode!** don't worry!
incômodo, -a [ĩ'komodu, a] ADJ uncomfortable; (*incomodativo*) troublesome; (*inoportuno*) inconvenient
incompetente [ĩkõpe'tẽtʃi] ADJ, M/F incompetent
incompreendido, -a [ĩkõprjẽ'dʒidu, a] ADJ misunderstood
incomum [ĩko'mũ] ADJ uncommon
incomunicável [ĩkomuni'kavew] (*pl* **-eis**) ADJ cut off; (*privado de comunicação, fig*) incommunicado; (*preso*) in solitary confinement
inconformado, -a [ĩkõfor'madu, a] ADJ bitter; **~ com** unreconciled to
inconfundível [ĩkõfũ'dʒivew] (*pl* **-eis**) ADJ unmistakeable
inconsciência [ĩkõ'sjẽsja] F (*Med*) unconsciousness; (*irreflexão*) thoughtlessness
inconsciente [ĩkõ'sjẽtʃi] ADJ unconscious ▶ M unconscious
inconsequente [ĩkõse'kwẽtʃi] ADJ inconsistent; (*contraditório*) illogical; (*irresponsável*) irresponsible
inconsistente [ĩkõsis'tẽtʃi] ADJ inconsistent; (*sem solidez*) runny
inconstante [ĩkõs'tãtʃi] ADJ fickle; (*tempo*) changeable
incontrolável [ĩkõtro'lavew] (*pl* **-eis**) ADJ uncontrollable
inconveniência [ĩkõve'njẽsja] F inconvenience; (*impropriedade*) inappropriateness
inconveniente [ĩkõve'njẽtʃi] ADJ inconvenient; (*inoportuno*) awkward; (*grosseiro*) rude; (*importuno*) annoying ▶ M disadvantage; (*obstáculo*) difficulty, problem
incorreto, -a [ĩko'hɛtu, a] ADJ incorrect; (*desonesto*) dishonest
incrédulo, -a [ĩ'krɛdulu, a] ADJ incredulous; (*cético*) sceptical (BRIT), skeptical (US) ▶ M/F sceptic (BRIT), skeptic (US)
incrível [ĩ'krivew] (*pl* **-eis**) ADJ incredible
incumbência [ĩkũ'bẽsja] F task, duty
incumbir [ĩkũ'bir] VT: **~ alguém de algo** *ou* **algo a alguém** to put sb in charge of sth ▶ VI: **~ a alguém** to be sb's duty; **incumbir-se** VR: **~-se de** to undertake, take charge of
indagação [ĩdaga'sãw] (*pl* **-ões**) F

investigation; (*pergunta*) inquiry, question

indagar [ĩda'gar] VT to investigate ▸ VI to inquire; **indagar-se** VR: **~-se a si mesmo** to ask o.s.; **~ algo de alguém** to ask sb about sth

indecente [ĩde'sẽtʃi] ADJ indecent, improper; (*obsceno*) rude, vulgar

indecoroso, -a [ĩdeko'rozu, ɔza] ADJ indecent, improper

indefinido, -a [ĩdefi'nidu, a] ADJ indefinite; (*vago*) vague, undefined; **por tempo ~** indefinitely

indelicado, -a [ĩdeli'kadu, a] ADJ impolite, rude

indenização [indeniza'sãw], (PT) **indemnização** (*pl* **-ões**) F compensation; (*Com*) indemnity

indenizar [ĩdeni'zar], (PT) **indemnizar** VT: **~ alguém por** *ou* **de algo** (*compensar*) to compensate sb for sth; (*por gastos*) to reimburse sb for sth

independência [ĩdepẽ'dẽsja] F independence; **independente** [ĩdepẽ'dẽtʃi] ADJ independent

indesejável [ĩdeze'ʒavew] (*pl* **-eis**) ADJ undesirable

indevido, -a [ĩde'vidu, a] ADJ (*imerecido*) unjust; (*impróprio*) inappropriate

Índia ['ĩdʒa] F: **a ~** India; **as ~s Ocidentais** the West Indies; **indiano, -a** [ĩ'dʒjanu, a] ADJ, M/F Indian

indicação [indʒika'sãw] (*pl* **-ões**) F indication; (*de termômetro*) reading; (*para um cargo, prêmio*) nomination; (*recomendação*) recommendation; (*de um caminho*) directions *pl*

indicado, -a [ĩdʒi'kadu, a] ADJ appropriate

indicador, a [ĩdʒika'dor(a)] ADJ: **~ de** indicative of ▸ M indicator; (*Tec*) gauge; (*dedo*) index finger; (*ponteiro*) pointer

indicar [ĩdʒi'kar] VT to indicate; (*apontar*) to point to; (*temperatura*) to register; (*recomendar*) to recommend; (*para um cargo*) to nominate; (*determinar*) to determine; **~ o caminho a alguém** to give sb directions

índice ['indʒisi] M (*de livro*) index; (*taxa*) rate

indício [in'dʒisju] M (*sinal*) sign; (*vestígio*) trace; (*Jur*) clue

indiferença [ĩdʒife'rẽsa] F indifference; **indiferente** [ĩdʒife'rẽtʃi] ADJ: **indiferente (a)** indifferent (to); **isso me é indiferente** it's all the same to me

indígena [ĩ'dʒiʒena] ADJ, M/F native; (*índio: da América*) Indian

indigência [ĩdʒi'ʒẽsja] F poverty; (*fig*) lack, need

indigestão [ĩdʒiʒes'tãw] F indigestion

indigesto, -a [ĩdʒi'ʒɛstu, a] ADJ indigestible

indignação [ĩdʒigna'sãw] F indignation; **indignado, -a** [ĩdʒig'nadu, a] ADJ indignant

indignar [ĩdʒig'nar] VT to anger, incense; **indignar-se** VR to get angry

índio, -a ['ĩdʒju, a] ADJ, M/F (*da América*) Indian; **o Oceano Í~** the Indian Ocean

indireto, -a [ĩdʒi'rɛtu, a] ADJ indirect

indiscreto, -a [ĩdʒis'krɛtu, a] ADJ indiscreet

indiscutível [ĩdʒisku'tʃivew] (*pl* **-eis**) ADJ indisputable

indispensável [ĩdʒispẽ'savew] (*pl* **-eis**) ADJ essential, vital ▸ M: **o ~** the essentials *pl*

indispor [ĩdʒis'por] (*irreg: como* **pôr**) VT (*de saúde*) to make ill; (*aborrecer*) to upset; **indisposto, -a** [ĩdʒis'postu, 'pɔsta] ADJ unwell, poorly
indistinto, -a [ĩdʒis'tʃĩtu, a] ADJ indistinct
individual [ĩdʒivi'dwaw] (*pl* **-ais**) ADJ individual
indivíduo [ĩdʒi'vidwu] M individual; (*col: sujeito*) person
indócil [ĩ'dɔsiw] (*pl* **-eis**) ADJ unruly, wayward; (*impaciente*) restless
índole ['ĩdoli] F (*temperamento*) nature; (*tipo*) sort, type
indolor [ĩdo'lor] ADJ painless
Indonésia [ĩdo'nɛzja] F: **a ~** Indonesia
indústria [ĩ'dustrja] F industry; **industrial** [ĩdus'trjaw] (*pl* **-ais**) ADJ industrial ▶ M/F industrialist; **industrializar** [ĩdustrjali'zar] VT (*país*) to industrialize; (*aproveitar*) to process
induzir [ĩdu'zir] VT to induce; (*persuadir*): **~ alguém a fazer** to persuade sb to do
inédito, -a [i'nɛdʒitu, a] ADJ (*livro*) unpublished; (*incomum*) unheard-of, rare
inegável [ine'gavew] (*pl* **-eis**) ADJ undeniable
inelutável [inelu'tavew] (*pl* **-eis**) ADJ inescapable
inepto, -a [i'nɛptu, a] ADJ inept, incompetent
inequívoco, -a [ine'kivoku, a] ADJ (*evidente*) clear; (*inconfundível*) unmistakeable
inércia [i'nɛrsja] F lethargy; (*Fís*) inertia
inerente [ine'rẽtʃi] ADJ: **~ a** inherent in *ou* to
inerte [i'nɛrtʃi] ADJ lethargic; (*Fís*) inert
inesgotável [inezgo'tavew] (*pl* **-eis**) ADJ inexhaustible; (*superabundante*) boundless
inesperado, -a [inespe'radu, a] ADJ unexpected, unforeseen ▶ M: **o ~** the unexpected
inesquecível [ineske'sivew] (*pl* **-eis**) ADJ unforgettable
inestimável [inestʃi'mavew] (*pl* **-eis**) ADJ invaluable
inexato, -a [ine'zatu, a] ADJ inaccurate
inexistência [inezis'tẽsja] F lack
inexperiência [inespe'rjẽsja] F inexperience; **inexperiente** [inespe'rjẽtʃi] ADJ inexperienced; (*ingênuo*) naive
inexpressivo, -a [inespre'sivu, a] ADJ expressionless
infância [ĩ'fãsja] F childhood
infantil [ĩfã'tʃiw] (*pl* **-is**) ADJ (*ingênuo*) childlike; (*pueril*) childish; (*para crianças*) children's
infarto [ĩ'fartu] M heart attack
infecção [ĩfek'sãw] (*pl* **-ões**) F infection; **infeccionar** [ĩfeksjo'nar] VT (*ferida*) to infect; **infeccioso, -a** [ĩfek'sjozu, ɔza] ADJ infectious
infelicidade [ĩfelisi'dadʒi] F unhappiness; (*desgraça*) misfortune
infeliz [ĩfe'liz] ADJ unhappy; (*infausto*) unlucky; (*ação, medida*) unfortunate; (*sugestão, ideia*) inappropriate ▶ M/F unhappy person; **infelizmente** [ĩfeliz'mẽtʃi] ADV unfortunately
inferior [ĩfe'rjor] ADJ: **~ (a)** (*em valor, qualidade*) inferior (to); (*mais baixo*) lower (than) ▶ M/F inferior, subordinate; **inferioridade** [ĩferjori'dadʒi] F inferiority

infernal [ĩfer'naw] (*pl* **-ais**) ADJ infernal
inferno [ĩ'fɛrnu] M hell; **vá pro ~!** (*col*) piss off!
infetar [ĩfe'tar] VT to infect
infiel [ĩ'fjɛw] (*pl* **-éis**) ADJ disloyal; (*marido*) unfaithful; (*texto*) inaccurate ▶ M/F (*Rel*) non-believer
ínfimo, -a ['ĩfimu, a] ADJ lowest; (*qualidade*) poorest
infindável [ĩfĩ'davew] (*pl* **-eis**) ADJ unending, constant
infinidade [ĩfini'dadʒi] F infinity; **uma ~ de** countless
infinitivo, -a [ĩfini'tʃivu, a] ADJ, M (*Ling*) infinitive
inflação [ĩfla'sãw] F inflation; **inflacionário, -a** [ĩflasjo'narju, a] ADJ inflationary
inflamação [ĩflama'sãw] (*pl* **-ões**) F inflammation; **inflamado, -a** [ĩfla'madu, a] ADJ (*Med*) inflamed; (*discurso*) heated
inflamar [ĩfla'mar] VT (*madeira, pólvora*) to set fire to; (*Med, fig*) to inflame; **inflamar-se** VR to catch fire; (*fig*) to get worked up; **~-se de algo** to be consumed with sth
inflamável [ĩfla'mavew] (*pl* **-eis**) ADJ inflammable
inflar [ĩ'flar] VT to inflate, blow up; **inflar-se** VR to swell (up)
inflexível [ĩflek'sivew] (*pl* **-eis**) ADJ stiff, rigid; (*fig*) unyielding
influência [ĩ'flwẽsja] F influence; **sob a ~ de** under the influence of; **influenciar** [ĩflwẽ'sjar] VT to influence ▶ VI: **influenciar em algo** to influence sth, have an influence on sth; **influenciar-se** VR: **influenciar-se por** to be influenced by; **influente** [ĩ'flwẽtʃi] ADJ influential; **influir** [ĩ'flwir] VI to matter, be important; **influir em** *ou* **sobre** to influence, have an influence on
informação [ĩforma'sãw] (*pl* **-ões**) F (piece of) information; (*notícia*) news; **informações** FPL (*detalhes*) information *sg*; **Informações** FPL (*Tel*) directory enquiries (BRIT), information (US); **pedir informações sobre** to ask about, inquire about
informal [ĩfor'maw] (*pl* **-ais**) ADJ informal
informar [ĩfor'mar] VT: **~ alguém (de/sobre algo)** to inform sb (of/about sth) ▶ VI to inform, be informative; **informar-se** VR: **~-se de** to find out about, inquire about; **~ de** to report on
informática [ĩfor'matʃika] F IT, information technology
informativo, -a [ĩforma'tʃivu, a] ADJ informative
informatizar [ĩformatʃi'zar] VT to computerize
infortúnio [ĩfor'tunju] M misfortune
infração [ĩfra'sãw] (*pl* **-ões**) F breach, infringement; (*Esporte*) foul
infrator, a [ĩfra'tor(a)] M/F offender
infrutífero, -a [ĩfru'tʃiferu, a] ADJ fruitless
ingênuo, -a [ĩ'ʒenwu, a] ADJ ingenuous, naïve; (*comentário*) harmless ▶ M/F naïve person
ingerir [ĩʒe'rir] VT to ingest; (*engolir*) to swallow
Inglaterra [ĩgla'tɛha] F: **a ~** England; **inglês, -esa** [ĩ'gles, eza] ADJ English ▶ M/F Englishman/woman ▶ M (*Ling*) English; **os ingleses** MPL the English
ingrediente [ĩgre'dʒjẽtʃi] M ingredient

íngreme [ĩgremi] ADJ steep
ingressar [ĩgre'sar] VI: **~ em** to enter, go into; (*um clube*) to join
ingresso [ĩ'grɛsu] M (*entrada*) entry; (*admissão*) admission; (*bilhete*) ticket
inibição [inibi'sãw] (*pl* **-ões**) F inhibition
inibido, -a [ini'bidu, a] ADJ inhibited
inibir [ini'bir] VT to inhibit
inicial [ini'sjaw] (*pl* **-ais**) ADJ, F initial
iniciar [ini'sjar] VT, VI (*começar*) to begin, start; **~ alguém em algo** (*arte, seita*) to initiate sb into sth
iniciativa [inisja'tʃiva] F initiative; **a ~ privada** (*Econ*) private enterprise
início [i'nisju] M beginning, start; **no ~** at the start
inimigo, -a [ini'migu, a] ADJ, M/F enemy
injeção [inʒe'sãw] (*pl* **-ões**) F injection
injetar [ĩʒe'tar] VT to inject
injúria [ĩ'ʒurja] F insult
injustiça [ĩʒus'tʃisa] F injustice
inocência [ino'sẽsja] F innocence
inocentar [inosẽ'tar] VT: **~ alguém (de algo)** to clear sb (of sth)
inocente [ino'sẽtʃi] ADJ innocent ▶ M/F innocent man/woman
inofensivo, -a [inofẽ'sivu, a] ADJ harmless, inoffensive
inovação [inova'sãw] (*pl* **-ões**) F innovation
inquérito [ĩ'kɛritu] M inquiry; (*Jur*) inquest
inquietação [ĩkjeta'sãw] F anxiety, uneasiness; (*agitação*) restlessness
inquietante [ĩkje'tãtʃi] ADJ worrying, disturbing
inquietar [ĩkje'tar] VT to worry, disturb; **inquietar-se** VR to worry, bother; **inquieto, -a** [ĩ'kjɛtu, a] ADJ anxious, worried; (*agitado*) restless
inquilino, -a [ĩki'linu, a] M/F tenant
insalubre [ĩsa'lubri] ADJ unhealthy
insanidade [ĩsani'dadʒi] F madness, insanity; **insano, -a** [ĩ'sanu, a] ADJ insane
insatisfatório, -a [ĩsatʃisfa'tɔrju, a] ADJ unsatisfactory
insatisfeito, -a [ĩsatʃis'fejtu, a] ADJ dissatisfied, unhappy
inscrever [ĩskre'ver] VT to inscribe; (*aluno*) to enrol (BRIT), enroll (US); (*em registro*) to register
inscrito, -a [ĩ'skritu, a] PP *de* **inscrever**
insegurança [ĩsegu'rãsa] F insecurity; **inseguro, -a** [ĩse'guru, a] ADJ insecure
insensato, -a [ĩsẽ'satu, a] ADJ unreasonable, foolish
inserir [ĩse'rir] VT to insert, put in; (*Comput: dados*) to enter
inseticida [ĩsetʃi'sida] M insecticide
inseto [ĩ'sɛtu] M insect
insípido, -a [ĩ'sipidu, a] ADJ insipid
insiro [ĩ'siru] VB *ver* **inserir**
insistência [ĩsis'tẽsja] F: **~ (em)** insistence (on); (*obstinação*) persistence (in); **insistente** [ĩsis'tẽtʃi] ADJ (*pessoa*) insistent; (*apelo*) urgent
insistir [ĩsis'tʃir] VI: **~ (em)** to insist (on); (*perseverar*) to persist (in); **~ (em) que** to insist that

insolação [insola'sãw] F sunstroke; **pegar uma ~** to get sunstroke
insólito, -a [ĩ'sɔlitu, a] ADJ unusual
insônia [ĩ'sonja] F insomnia
insosso, -a [ĩ'sosu, a] ADJ unsalted; (*sem sabor*) tasteless; (*pessoa*) uninteresting, dull
inspeção [ĩspe'sãw] (*pl* **-ões**) F inspection, check; **inspecionar** [ĩspesjo'nar] VT to inspect
inspetor, a [ĩspe'tor(a)] M/F inspector
inspirar [ĩspi'rar] VT to inspire; (*Med*) to inhale; **inspirar-se** VR to be inspired
INSS (BR) ABR M (= *Instituto Nacional do Seguro Social*) ≈ DSS (BRIT), ≈ Welfare Dept (US)
instalação [ĩstala'sãw] (*pl* **-ões**) F installation; **~ elétrica** (*de casa*) wiring
instalar [ĩsta'lar] VT to install; (*estabelecer*) to set up; **instalar-se** VR (*numa cadeira*) to settle down
instantâneo, -a [ĩstã'tanju, a] ADJ instant, instantaneous ▶ M (*Foto*) snap
instante [ĩs'tãtʃi] ADJ urgent ▶ M moment; **num ~** in an instant, quickly; **só um ~!** just a moment!
instável [ĩs'tavew] (*pl* **-eis**) ADJ unstable; (*tempo*) unsettled
instintivo, -a [ĩstʃĩ'tʃivu, a] ADJ instinctive
instinto [ĩs'tʃĩtu] M instinct; **por ~** instinctively
instituição [ĩstʃitwi'sãw] (*pl* **-ões**) F institution
instituto [ĩstʃi'tutu] M (*escola*) institute; (*instituição*) institution; **~ de beleza** beauty salon
instrução [ĩstru'sãw] (*pl* **-ões**) F education; (*erudição*) learning; (*diretriz*) instruction; (*Mil*) training; **instruções** FPL (*para o uso*) instructions (for use)
instruído, -a [ĩs'trwidu, a] ADJ educated
instruir [ĩs'trwir] VT to instruct; (*Mil*) to train; **instruir-se** VR: **~-se em algo** to learn sth; **~ alguém de** *ou* **sobre algo** to inform sb about sth
instrumento [ĩstru'mẽtu] M instrument; (*ferramenta*) implement; (*Jur*) deed, document; **~ de cordas/percussão/sopro** stringed/percussion/wind instrument; **~ de trabalho** tool
instrutivo, -a [ĩstru'tʃivu, a] ADJ instructive
instrutor, a [ĩstru'tor(a)] M/F instructor; (*Esporte*) coach
insubordinação [ĩsubordʒina'sãw] F rebellion; (*Mil*) insubordination
insubstituível [ĩsubistʃi'twivew] (*pl* **-eis**) ADJ irreplaceable
insuficiência [ĩsufi'sjẽsja] F inadequacy; (*carência*) shortage; (*Med*) deficiency; **~ cardíaca** heart failure; **insuficiente** [ĩsufi'sjẽtʃi] ADJ insufficient; (*Educ: nota*) ≈ fail; (*pessoa*) incompetent
insulina [ĩsu'lina] F insulin
insultar [ĩsuw'tar] VT to insult; **insulto** [ĩ'suwtu] M insult
insuportável [ĩsupor'tavew] (*pl* **-eis**) ADJ unbearable
insurgir-se [ĩsur'ʒirsi] VR to rebel, revolt
insurreição [ĩsuhej'sãw] (*pl* **-ões**) F rebellion, insurrection
intato, -a [ĩ'tatu, a] ADJ intact
íntegra ['ĩtegra] F: **na ~** in full
integral [ĩte'graw] (*pl* **-ais**) ADJ whole ▶ F (*Mat*) integral; **pão ~** wholemeal (BRIT) *ou* wholewheat

(US) bread; **integralmente** [ĩtegraw'mẽtʃi] ADV in full, fully
integrar [ĩte'grar] VT to unite, combine; (*completar*) to form, make up; (*Mat, raças*) to integrate; **integrar-se** VR to become complete; **~-se em** *ou* **a algo** to join sth; (*adaptar-se*) to integrate into sth
integridade [ĩtegri'dadʒi] F entirety; (*fig: de pessoa*) integrity
íntegro, -a ['ĩtegru, a] ADJ entire; (*honesto*) upright, honest
inteiramente [ĩtejra'mẽtʃi] ADV completely
inteirar [ĩtej'rar] VT (*completar*) to complete; **inteirar-se** VR: **~-se de** to find out about; **~ alguém de** to inform sb of
inteiro, -a [ĩ'tejru, a] ADJ whole, entire; (*ileso*) unharmed; (*não quebrado*) undamaged
intelecto [ĩte'lɛktu] M intellect; **intelectual** [ĩtelek'twaw] (*pl* **-ais**) ADJ, M/F intellectual
inteligência [ĩteli'ʒẽsja] F intelligence; **inteligente** [ĩteli'ʒẽtʃi] ADJ intelligent
inteligível [ĩteli'ʒivew] (*pl* **-eis**) ADJ intelligible
intenção [ĩtẽ'sãw] (*pl* **-ões**) F intention; **segundas intenções** ulterior motives; **ter a ~ de** to intend to; **intencionado, -a** [ĩtẽsjo'nadu, a] ADJ: **bem intencionado** well-meaning; **mal intencionado** spiteful; **intencional** [ĩtẽsjo'naw] (*pl* **-ais**) ADJ intentional, deliberate; **intencionar** [ĩtẽsjo'nar] VT to intend
intensificar [ĩtẽsifi'kar] VT to intensify; **intensificar-se** VR to intensify
intensivo, -a [ĩtẽ'sivu, a] ADJ intensive
intenso, -a [ĩ'tẽsu, a] ADJ intense; (*emoção*) deep; (*impressão*) vivid; (*vida social*) full
interação [ĩtera'sãw] F interaction
interativo, -a [ĩtera'tʃivu, a] ADJ (*Comput*) interactive
intercâmbio [ĩter'kãbju] M exchange
interdição [ĩterdʒi'sãw] (*pl* **-ões**) F (*de estrada, porta*) closure; (*Jur*) injunction
interditar [ĩterdʒi'tar] VT (*importação etc*) to ban; (*estrada, praia*) to close off; (*cinema etc*) to close down
interessado, -a [ĩtere'sadu, a] ADJ interested; (*amizade*) self-seeking
interessante [ĩtere'sãtʃi] ADJ interesting
interessar [ĩtere'sar] VT to interest ▸ VI to be interesting; **interessar-se** VR: **~-se em** *ou* **por** to take an interest in, be interested in; **a quem possa ~** to whom it may concern
interesse [ĩte'resi] M interest; (*próprio*) self-interest; (*proveito*) advantage; **no ~ de** for the sake of; **por ~ (próprio)** for one's own ends; **interesseiro, -a** [ĩtere'sejru, a] ADJ self-seeking
interface [ĩter'fasi] F (*Comput*) interface
interferência [ĩterfe'rẽsja] F interference
interferir [ĩterfe'rir] VI: **~ em** to interfere in; (*rádio*) to jam
interfone [ĩter'fɔni] M intercom
interior [ĩte'rjor] ADJ inner, inside; (*Com*) domestic, internal ▸ M inside, interior; (*do país*): **no ~**

inland; **Ministério do I~** ≈ Home Office (BRIT), ≈ Department of the Interior (US)

interjeição [ĩterʒej'sãw] (*pl* **-ões**) F interjection

interlocutor, a [ĩterloku'tor(a)] M/F speaker; **meu ~** the person I was speaking to

intermediário, -a [ĩterme'dʒjarju, a] ADJ intermediary ▶ M/F (*Com*) middleman; (*mediador*) intermediary, mediator

intermédio [ĩter'mɛdʒu] M: **por ~ de** through

internação [ĩterna'sãw] (*pl* **-ões**) F (*de doente*) admission

internacional [ĩternasjo'naw] (*pl* **-ais**) ADJ international

internações [ĩterna'sõjs] FPL *de* **internação**

internar [ĩter'nar] VT (*aluno*) to put into boarding school; (*doente*) to take into hospital; (*Mil, Pol*) to intern

internauta [ĩter'nawta] M/F internet user, web *ou* net surfer (*col*)

Internet [ĩter'nɛtʃi] F internet

interno, -a [ĩ'tɛrnu, a] ADJ internal; (*Pol*) domestic ▶ M/F (*tb*: **aluno ~**) boarder; (*Med: estudante*) houseman (BRIT), intern (US); **de uso ~** (*Med*) for internal use

interpretação [ĩterpreta'sãw] (*pl* **-ões**) F interpretation; (*Teatro*) performance

interpretar [ĩterpre'tar] VT to interpret; (*um papel*) to play;

intérprete [ĩ'tɛrpretʃi] M/F interpreter; (*Teatro*) performer, artist

interrogação [ĩtehoga'sãw] (*pl* **-ões**) F interrogation; **ponto de ~** question mark

interrogar [ĩteho'gar] VT to question, interrogate; (*Jur*) to cross-examine

interromper [ĩtehõ'per] VT to interrupt; (*parar*) to stop; (*Elet*) to cut off

interruptor [ĩtehup'tor] M (*Elet*) switch

interseção [ĩterse'sãw] (*pl* **-ões**) F intersection

interurbano, -a [ĩterur'banu, a] ADJ (*Tel*) long-distance ▶ M long-distance *ou* trunk call

intervalo [ĩter'valu] M interval; (*descanso*) break; **a ~s** every now and then

intervir [ĩter'vir] (*irreg: como* **vir**) VI to intervene; (*sobrevir*) to come up

intimação [ĩtʃima'sãw] (*pl* **-ões**) F (*ordem*) order; (*Jur*) summons

intimar [ĩtʃi'mar] VT (*Jur*) to summon; **~ alguém a fazer** *ou* **a alguém que faça** to order sb to do

íntimo, -a ['ĩtʃimu, a] ADJ intimate; (*sentimentos*) innermost; (*amigo*) close; (*vida*) private ▶ M/F close friend; **no ~** at heart

intolerante [ĩtole'rãtʃi] ADJ intolerant

intolerável [ĩtole'ravew] (*pl* **-eis**) ADJ intolerable, unbearable

intoxicação [ĩtoksika'sãw] F poisoning; **~ alimentar** food poisoning

intoxicar [ĩtoksi'kar] VT to poison

intranet [ĩtra'nɛtʃi] F intranet

intransitável [ĩtrãsi'tavew] (*pl* **-eis**) ADJ impassable

intratável [ĩtra'tavew] (*pl* **-eis**) ADJ (*pessoa*) contrary, awkward; (*doença*) untreatable; (*problema*) insurmountable

intriga [ĩ'triga] F intrigue; (*enredo*) plot; (*fofoca*) piece of gossip; **intrigas** FPL (*fofocas*) gossip *sg*;

~ **amorosa** (PT) love affair; **intrigante** [ĩtri'gãtʃi] M/F troublemaker ▶ ADJ intriguing; **intrigar** [ĩtri'gar] VT to intrigue ▶ VI to be intriguing

introdução [ĩtrodu'sãw] (*pl* **-ões**) F introduction

introduzir [ĩtrodu'zir] VT to introduce

intrometer-se [ĩtrome'tersi] VR to interfere, meddle; **intrometido, -a** [ĩtrome'tʃidu, a] ADJ interfering; (*col*) nosey ▶ M/F busybody

introvertido, -a [ĩtrover'tʃidu, a] ADJ introverted ▶ M/F introvert

intruso, -a [ĩ'truzu, a] M/F intruder

intuição [ĩtwi'sãw] (*pl* **-ões**) F intuition

intuito [ĩ'tuito] M intention, aim

inúmero, -a [i'numeru, a] ADJ countless, innumerable

inundação [inũda'sãw] (*pl* **-ões**) F (*enchente*) flood; (*ato*) flooding

inundar [inũ'dar] VT to flood; (*fig*) to inundate ▶ VI to flood

inusitado, -a [inuzi'tadu, a] ADJ unusual

inútil [i'nutʃiw] (*pl* **-eis**) ADJ useless; (*esforço*) futile; (*desnecessário*) pointless; **inutilizar** [inutʃili'zar] VT to make useless, render useless; (*incapacitar*) to put out of action; (*danificar*) to ruin; (*esforços*) to thwart; **inutilmente** [inutʃiw'mẽtʃi] ADV in vain

invadir [ĩva'dʒir] VT to invade; (*suj: água*) to overrun; (: *sentimento*) to overcome

inválido, -a [ĩ'validu, a] ADJ, M/F invalid

invasão [ĩva'zãw] (*pl* **-ões**) F invasion

inveja [ĩ'vɛʒa] F envy; **invejar** [ĩve'ʒar] VT to envy; (*cobiçar*) to covet ▶ VI to be envious; **invejoso, -a** [ĩve'ʒozu, ɔza] ADJ envious

invenção [ĩvẽ'sãw] (*pl* **-ões**) F invention

inventado, -a [ĩvẽ'tadu, a] ADJ (*história, personagem*) made-up

inventar [ĩvẽ'tar] VT to invent

inventivo, -a [ĩvẽ'tʃivu, a] ADJ inventive

inventor, a [ĩvẽ'tor(a)] M/F inventor

inverno [ĩ'vɛrnu] M winter

inverossímil [ĩvero'simiw], (PT) **inverosímil** (*pl* **-eis**) ADJ unlikely, improbable; (*inacreditável*) implausible

invés [ĩ'vɛs] M: **ao ~ de** instead of

investigação [ĩvestʃiga'sãw] (*pl* **-ões**) F investigation; (*pesquisa*) research

investigar [ĩvestʃi'gar] VT to investigate; (*examinar*) to examine

investimento [ĩvestʃi'mẽtu] M investment

investir [ĩves'tʃir] VT (*dinheiro*) to invest

inviável [ĩ'vjavew] (*pl* **-eis**) ADJ impracticable

invisível [ĩvi'zivew] (*pl* **-eis**) ADJ invisible

invisto [ĩ'vistu] VB *ver* **investir**

invocar [ĩvo'kar] VT to invoke

ioga ['jɔga] F yoga

iogurte [jo'gurtʃi] M yogurt

IR (BR) ABR M = **imposto de renda**

PALAVRA-CHAVE

ir [ir] VI **1** to go; (*a pé*) to walk; (*a cavalo*) to ride; (*viajar*) to travel; **ir caminhando** to walk; **fui de trem** I went *ou* travelled by train; **vamos (embora)!, vamos nessa!**

(*col*) let's go!; **já vou!** I'm coming!; **ir atrás de alguém** (*seguir*) to follow sb; (*confiar*) to take sb's word for it
2 (*progredir: pessoa, coisa*) to go; **o trabalho vai muito bem** work is going very well; **como vão as coisas?** how are things going?; **vou muito bem** I'm very well; (*na escola etc*) I'm getting on very well
▶ VB AUX 1 (+ *infin*): **vou fazer** I will do, I am going to do
2 (+ *gerúndio*): **ir fazendo** to keep on doing
ir-se VR to go away, leave

ira ['ira] F anger, rage
Irã [i'rã] M: **o ~** Iran
iraniano, -a [ira'njanu, a] ADJ, M/F Iranian
Irão [i'rãw] (PT) M = **Irã**
Iraque [i'raki] M: **o ~** Iraq;
iraquiano, -a [ira'kjanu, a] ADJ, M/F Iraqi
ir e vir M INV comings and goings *pl*
Irlanda [ir'lãda] F: **a ~** Ireland; **a ~ do Norte** Northern Ireland;
irlandês, -esa [irlã'des, eza] ADJ Irish ▶ M/F Irishman/woman ▶ M (*Ling*) Irish
irmã [ir'mã] F sister; **~ gêmea** twin sister; **~ de criação** adoptive sister
irmão [ir'mãw] (*pl* **irmãos**) M brother; (*fig: similar*) twin; (*col: companheiro*) mate; **~ de criação** adoptive brother; **~ gêmeo** twin brother
ironia [iro'nia] F irony
irra! ['iha] (PT) EXCL damn!
irracional [ihasjo'naw] (*pl* **-ais**) ADJ irrational
irreal [ihe'aw] (*pl* **-ais**) ADJ unreal
irregular [ihegu'lar] ADJ irregular; (*vida*) unconventional; (*feições*) unusual; (*aluno, gênio*) erratic
irremediável [iheme'dʒjavew] (*pl* **-eis**) ADJ irremediable; (*sem remédio*) incurable
irrequieto, -a [ihe'kjɛtu, a] ADJ restless
irresistível [ihezis'tʃivew] (*pl* **-eis**) ADJ irresistible
irresponsável [ihespõ'savew] (*pl* **-eis**) ADJ irresponsible
irrigar [ihi'gar] VT to irrigate
irritação [ihita'sãw] (*pl* **-ões**) F irritation
irritadiço, -a [ihita'dʒisu, a] ADJ irritable
irritante [ihi'tãtʃi] ADJ irritating, annoying
irritar [ihi'tar] VT to irritate;
irritar-se VR to get angry, get annoyed
irromper [ihõ'per] VI (*entrar subitamente*): **~ (em)** to burst in(to)
isca ['iska] F (*Pesca*) bait; (*fig*) lure, bait
isenção [izẽ'sãw] (*pl* **-ões**) F exemption
isentar [izẽ'tar] VT to exempt; (*livrar*) to free
Islã [iz'lã] M Islam
Islândia [iz'lãdʒa] F: **a ~** Iceland
isolado, -a [izo'ladu, a] ADJ isolated; (*solitário*) lonely
isolamento [izola'mẽtu] M isolation; (*Elet*) insulation
isotônico, -a [izo'toniku, a] ADJ isotonic
isqueiro [is'kejru] M (cigarette) lighter
Israel [izha'ɛw] M Israel;
israelense [izhae'lẽsi] ADJ, M/F Israeli
isso ['isu] PRON that; (*col: isto*) this; **~ mesmo** exactly; **por ~** therefore, so; **por ~ mesmo** for that very reason; **só ~?** is that all?

isto ['istu] PRON this; **~ é** that is, namely
Itália [i'talja] F: **a ~** Italy;
italiano, -a [ita'ljanu, a] ADJ, M/F Italian ▶ M (*Ling*) Italian
Itamarati [itamara'tʃi] M: **o ~** the Brazilian Foreign Ministry

> The Palace of **Itamarati** was built in 1855 in Rio de Janeiro. It became the seat of government when Brazil became a republic in 1889, and was later the Foreign Ministry. It ceased to be this when the Brazilian capital was transferred to Brasília, but **Itamarati** is still used to refer to the Foreign Ministry.

item ['itẽ] (*pl* **-ns**) M item
itinerário [itʃine'rarju] M itinerary; (*caminho*) route

J

já [ʒa] ADV already; (*em perguntas*) yet; (*agora*) now; (*imediatamente*) right away; (*agora mesmo*) right now ▶ CONJ on the other hand; **até já** bye; **desde já** from now on; **já não** no longer; **já que** as, since; **já se vê** of course; **já vou** I'm coming; **já até** even; **já, já** right away
jabuti [ʒabu'tʃi] M giant tortoise
jabuticaba [ʒabutʃi'kaba] F jaboticaba (*type of berry*)
jaca ['ʒaka] F jack fruit
jacaré [ʒaka'rɛ] (BR) M alligator
jaguar [ʒa'gwar] M jaguar
jaguatirica [ʒagwatʃi'rika] F leopard cat
Jamaica [ʒa'majka] F: **a ~** Jamaica
jamais [ʒa'majs] ADV never; (*com palavra negativa*) ever
janeiro [ʒa'nejru] M January
janela [ʒa'nɛla] F window
jangada [ʒã'gada] F raft
jantar [ʒã'tar] M dinner ▶ VT to have for dinner ▶ VI to have dinner

Japão [ʒa'pãw] M: **o ~** Japan; **japonês, -esa** [ʒapo'nes, eza] ADJ, M/F Japanese ▶ M (*Ling*) Japanese
jararaca [ʒara'raka] F jararaca (*snake*)
jardim [ʒar'dʒĩ] (*pl* **-ns**) M garden; **~ de infância** kindergarten; **~ zoológico** zoo; **jardinagem** [ʒardʒi'naʒẽ] F gardening
jardineira [ʒardʒi'nejra] F (*caixa*) trough; (*calça*) dungarees *pl*; *ver tb* **jardineiro**
jardineiro, -a [ʒardʒi'nejru, a] M/F gardener
jardins [ʒar'dʒĩs] MPL *de* **jardim**
jargão [ʒar'gãw] M jargon
jarra ['ʒaha] F pot
jarro ['ʒahu] M jug
jasmim [ʒaz'mĩ] M jasmine
jato ['ʒatu] M jet; (*de luz*) flash; (*de ar*) blast; **a ~** at top speed
jaula ['ʒawla] F cage
jazigo [ʒa'zigu] M grave; (*monumento*) tomb
jazz [dʒɛz] M jazz
jeito ['ʒejtu] M (*maneira*) way; (*aspecto*) appearance; (*aptidão, habilidade*) skill, knack; (*modos pessoais*) manner; **ter ~ de** to look like; **não ter ~** (*pessoa*) to be awkward; (*situação*) to be hopeless; **dar um ~ em algo** (*pé*) to twist sth; (*quarto, casa, papéis*) to tidy sth up; (*consertar*) to fix sth; **dar um ~** to find a way; **o ~ é ...** the thing to do is ...; **é o ~** it's the best way; **ao ~ de** in the style of; **com ~** tactfully; **daquele ~** (in) that way; (*col: em desordem, mal*) anyhow; **de qualquer ~** anyway; **de ~ nenhum!** no way!
jejuar [ʒe'ʒwar] VI to fast
jejum [ʒe'ʒũ] (*pl* **-ns**) M fast; **em ~** fasting
Jesus [ʒe'zus] M Jesus ▶ EXCL heavens!
jiboia [ʒi'bɔja] F boa (constrictor)
jiló [ʒi'lɔ] M *kind of vegetable*
jingle ['dʒĩgew] M jingle
joalheria [ʒoaʎe'ria] F jeweller's (shop) (BRIT), jewelry store (US)
joaninha [ʒwa'niɲa] F ladybird (BRIT), ladybug (US)
joelho [ʒo'eʎu] M knee; **de ~s** kneeling; **ficar de ~s** to kneel down
jogada [ʒo'gada] F move; (*lanço*) throw; (*negócio*) scheme; move
jogador, a [ʒoga'dor(a)] M/F player; (*de jogo de azar*) gambler
jogar [ʒo'gar] VT to play; (*em jogo de azar*) to gamble; (*atirar*) to throw; (*indiretas*) to drop ▶ VI to play; to gamble; (*barco*) to pitch; **~ fora** to throw away
jogging ['ʒɔgĩŋ] M jogging; (*roupa*) track suit; **fazer ~** to go jogging, jog
jogo ['ʒogu] M game; (*jogar*) play; (*de azar*) gambling; (*conjunto*) set; (*artimanha*) trick; **~ de computador** computer game; **J~s Olímpicos** Olympic Games
joia ['ʒɔja] F jewel
Jordânia [ʒor'danja] F: **a ~** Jordan; **Jordão** [ʒor'dãw] M: **o (rio) Jordão** the Jordan (River)
jornada [ʒor'nada] F journey; **~ de trabalho** working day
jornal [ʒor'naw] (*pl* **-ais**) M newspaper; (*TV, Rádio*) news *sg*; **jornaleiro, -a** [ʒorna'lejru, a] M/F newsagent (BRIT), newsdealer (US)
jornalismo [ʒorna'lizmu] M journalism; **jornalista** [ʒorna'lista] M/F journalist
jovem ['ʒɔvẽ] (*pl* **-ns**) ADJ young ▶ M/F young person
jovial [ʒo'vjaw] (*pl* **-ais**) ADJ jovial, cheerful

Jr ABR = **Júnior**
judaico, -a [ʒu'dajku, a] ADJ Jewish
judeu, judia [ʒu'dew, ʒu'dʒia] ADJ Jewish ▶ M/F Jew
judiar [ʒu'dʒjar] VI: **~ de alguém/algo** to ill-treat sb/sth
judicial [ʒudʒi'sjaw] (*pl* **-ais**) ADJ judicial
judiciário, -a [ʒudʒi'sjarju, a] ADJ judicial; **o (poder) ~** the judiciary
judô [ʒu'do] M judo
juiz, juíza [ʒwiz, -'iza] M/F judge; (*em jogos*) referee; **~ de paz** justice of the peace; **juizado** [ʒwi'zado] M court
juízo ['ʒwizu] M judgement; (*parecer*) opinion; (*siso*) common sense; (*foro*) court; **perder o ~** to lose one's mind; **não ter ~** to be foolish; **tomar** *ou* **criar ~** to come to one's senses; **chamar/levar a ~** to summon/take to court; **~!** behave yourself!
julgamento [ʒuwga'mẽtu] M judgement; (*audiência*) trial; (*sentença*) sentence
julgar [ʒuw'gar] VT to judge; (*achar*) to think; (*Jur: sentenciar*) to sentence; **julgar-se** VR: **~-se algo** to consider o.s. sth, think of o.s. as sth
julho ['ʒuʎu] M July
jumento, -a [ʒu'mẽtu, a] M/F donkey
junção [ʒũ'sãw] (*pl* **-ões**) F (*ato*) joining; (*junta*) join
junco ['ʒũku] M reed, rush
junções [ʒũ'sõjs] FPL *de* **junção**
junho ['ʒuɲu] M June
júnior ['ʒunjor] (*pl* **juniores**) ADJ younger, junior ▶ M/F (*Esporte*) junior; **Eduardo Autran J~** Eduardo Autran Junior
juntar [ʒũ'tar] VT to join; (*reunir*) to bring together; (*aglomerar*) to gather together; (*recolher*) to collect up; (*acrescentar*) to add; (*dinheiro*) to save up ▶ VI to gather; **juntar-se** VR to gather; (*associar-se*) to join up; **~-se a alguém** to join sb
junto, -a ['ʒũtu, a] ADJ joined; (*chegado*) near; **ir ~s** to go together; **~ a/de** near/next to; **segue ~** (*Com*) please find enclosed
jura ['ʒura] F vow
jurado, -a [ʒu'radu, a] ADJ sworn ▶ M/F juror
juramento [ʒura'mẽtu] M oath
jurar [ʒu'rar] VT, VI to swear; **jura?** really?
júri ['ʒuri] M jury
jurídico, -a [ʒu'ridʒiku, a] ADJ legal
juros ['ʒurus] MPL (*Econ*) interest *sg*; **~ simples/compostos** simple/compound interest
justamente [ʒusta'mẽtʃi] ADV fairly, justly; (*precisamente*) exactly
justiça [ʒus'tʃisa] F justice; (*poder judiciário*) judiciary; (*equidade*) fairness; (*tribunal*) court; **com ~** justly, fairly; **ir à ~** to go to court
justificar [ʒustʃifi'kar] VT to justify
justo, -a ['ʒustu, a] ADJ just, fair; (*legítimo: queixa*) legitimate, justified; (*exato*) exact; (*apertado*) tight ▶ ADV just
juvenil [ʒuve'niw] (*pl* **-is**) ADJ youthful; (*roupa*) young; (*livro*) for young people; (*Esporte: equipe, campeonato*) youth *atr*, junior
juventude [ʒuvẽ'tudʒi] F youth; (*jovialidade*) youthfulness; (*jovens*) young people *pl*, youth

K

kg ABR (= *quilograma*) kg
kit ['kitʃi] (*pl* **-s**) M kit
kitchenette [kitʃe'nɛtʃi] F studio flat
km ABR (= *quilômetro*) km
km/h ABR (= *quilômetros por hora*) km/h

L

lá [la] ADV there ▶ M (*Mús*) A; **lá fora** outside; **lá em baixo** down there; **por lá** (*direção*) that way; (*situação*) over there; **até lá** (*no espaço*) there; (*no tempo*) until then
lã [lã] F wool
-la [la] PRON her; (*você*) you; (*coisa*) it
labia ['labja] F (*astúcia*) cunning; **ter ~** to have the gift of the gab
lábio ['labju] M lip
labirinto [labi'rĩtu] M labyrinth, maze
laboratório [labora'tɔrju] M laboratory
laca ['laka] F lacquer
laçar [la'sar] VT to bind, tie
laço ['lasu] M bow; (*de gravata*) knot; (*armadilha*) snare; (*fig*) bond, tie; **dar um ~** to tie a bow
lacrar [la'krar] VT to seal (with wax); **lacre** ['lakri] M sealing wax
lacuna [la'kuna] F gap; (*omissão*) omission; (*espaço em branco*) blank
ladeira [la'dejra] F slope
lado ['ladu] M side; (*Mil*) flank; (*rumo*) direction; **ao ~** (*perto*) close

by; **a casa ao ~** the house next door; **ao ~ de** beside; **deixar de ~** to set aside; (*fig*) to leave out; **de um ~ para outro** back and forth
ladra ['ladra] F thief, robber; (*picareta*) crook
ladrão, -ona [la'drãw, ɔna] (*pl* **-ões/-s**) ADJ thieving ▶ M/F thief, robber; (*picareta*) crook
ladrilho [la'driʎu] M tile; (*chão*) tiled floor, tiles *pl*
ladrões [la'drõjs] MPL *de* **ladrão**
lagarta [la'garta] F caterpillar
lagartixa [lagar'tʃiʃa] F gecko
lagarto [la'gartu] M lizard
lago ['lagu] M lake; (*de jardim*) pond
lagoa [la'goa] F pool, pond; (*lago*) lake
lagosta [la'gosta] F lobster
lagostim [lagos'tʃĩ] (*pl* **-ns**) M crayfish
lágrima ['lagrima] F tear
lama ['lama] F mud
lamaçal [lama'saw] (*pl* **-ais**) M quagmire; (*pântano*) bog, marsh
lamber [lã'ber] VT to lick; **lambida** [lã'bida] F: **dar uma lambida em algo** to lick sth
lambuzar [lãbu'zar] VT to smear
lamentar [lamẽ'tar] VT to lament; (*sentir*) to regret; **lamentar-se** VR: **~-se (de algo)** to lament (sth); **~ (que)** to be sorry (that); **lamentável** [lamẽ'tavew] (*pl* **-eis**) ADJ regrettable; (*deplorável*) deplorable; **lamento** [la'mẽtu] M lament; (*gemido*) moan
lâmina ['lamina] F (*chapa*) sheet; (*placa*) plate; (*de faca*) blade; (*de persiana*) slat
lâmpada ['lãpada] F lamp; (*tb*: **~ elétrica**) light bulb; **~ de mesa** table lamp
lançar [lã'sar] VT to throw; (*navio, produto, campanha*) to launch; (*disco, filme*) to release; (*Com: em livro*) to enter; (*em leilão*) to bid
lancha ['lãʃa] F launch; **~ torpedeira** torpedo boat
lanchar [lã'ʃar] VI to have a snack ▶ VT to have as a snack; **lanche** ['lãʃi] M snack
lanchonete [lãʃo'nɛtʃi] (BR) F snack bar
LAN house [lã'hawzi] F internet café
lanterna [lã'tɛrna] F lantern; (*portátil*) torch (BRIT), flashlight (US)
lápide ['lapidʒi] F (*tumular*) tombstone; (*comemorativa*) memorial stone
lápis ['lapis] M INV pencil; **~ de cor** coloured (BRIT) *ou* colored (US) pencil, crayon; **~ de olho** eyebrow pencil; **lapiseira** [lapi'zejra] F propelling (BRIT) *ou* mechanical (US) pencil; (*caixa*) pencil case
lapso ['lapsu] M lapse; (*de tempo*) interval; (*erro*) slip
lar [lar] M home
laranja [la'rãʒa] ADJ INV orange ▶ F orange ▶ M (*cor*) orange; **laranjada** [larã'ʒada] F orangeade; **laranjeira** [larã'ʒejra] F orange tree
lareira [la'rejra] F hearth, fireside
larga ['larga] F: **à ~** lavishly; **dar ~s a** to give free rein to; **viver à ~** to lead a lavish life
largada [lar'gada] F start; **dar a ~** to start; (*fig*) to make a start
largar [lar'gar] VT to let go of, release; (*deixar*) to leave; (*deixar cair*) to drop; (*risada*) to let out; (*velas*) to unfurl; (*piada*) to tell; (*pôr em liberdade*) to let go ▶ VI (*Náut*) to set sail; **largar-se** VR (*desprender-se*)

to free o.s.; (*ir-se*) to go off; (*pôr-se*) to proceed

largo, -a ['largu, a] ADJ wide, broad; (*amplo*) extensive; (*roupa*) loose, baggy; (*conversa*) long ▸ M (*praça*) square; (*alto-mar*) open sea; **ao ~** at a distance, far off; **passar de ~ sobre um assunto** to gloss over a subject; **passar ao ~ de algo** (*fig*) to sidestep sth; **largura** [lar'gura] F width, breadth

laringite [larĩ'ʒitʃi] F laryngitis

lasanha [la'zaɲa] F lasagna

laser ['lejzer] M laser; **raio ~** laser beam

lástima ['lastʃima] F pity, compassion; (*infortúnio*) misfortune; **é uma ~ (que)** it's a shame (that); **lastimar** [lastʃi'mar] VT to lament; **lastimar-se** VR to complain, feel sorry for o.s.

lata ['lata] F can, tin (BRIT); (*material*) tin-plate; **~ de lixo** rubbish bin (BRIT), garbage can (US); **~ velha** (*col: carro*) old banger (BRIT) *ou* clunker (US)

latão [la'tãw] M brass

lataria [lata'ria] F (*Auto*) bodywork; (*enlatados*) canned food

latejar [late'ʒar] VI to throb

latente [la'tẽtʃi] ADJ latent

lateral [late'raw] (*pl* **-ais**) ADJ side, lateral ▸ F (*Futebol*) sideline ▸ M (*Futebol*) throw-in

latido [la'tʃidu] M bark(ing), yelp(ing)

latifundiário, -a [latʃifũ'dʒjarju, a] M/F landowner

latifúndio [latʃi'fũdʒju] M large estate

latim [la'tʃĩ] M (*Ling*) Latin; **gastar o seu ~** to waste one's breath

latino, -a [la'tʃinu, a] ADJ Latin; **latino-americano, -a** ADJ, M/F Latin-American

latir [la'tʃir] VI to bark, yelp

latitude [latʃi'tudʒi] F latitude; (*largura*) breadth; (*fig*) scope

latrocínio [latro'sinju] M armed robbery

laudo ['lawdu] M (*Jur*) decision; (*resultados*) findings *pl*; (*peça escrita*) report

lava ['lava] F lava

lavabo [la'vabu] M toilet

lavadeira [lava'dejra] F washerwoman

lavagem [la'vaʒẽ] F washing; **~ a seco** dry cleaning; **~ cerebral** brainwashing

lavanda [la'vãda] F (*Bot*) lavender; (*colônia*) lavender water; (*para lavar os dedos*) finger bowl

lavar [la'var] VT to wash; (*culpa*) to wash away; **~ a seco** to dry clean

lavatório [lava'tɔrju] M washbasin; (*aposento*) toilet

lavoura [la'vora] F tilling; (*agricultura*) farming; (*terreno*) plantation

laxativo, -a [laʃa'tʃivu, a] ADJ, M laxative

lazer [la'zer] M leisure

leal [le'aw] (*pl* **-ais**) ADJ loyal; **lealdade** [leaw'dadʒi] F loyalty

leão [le'ãw] (*pl* **-ões**) M lion; **L~** (*Astrologia*) Leo

lebre ['lɛbri] F hare

lecionar [lesjo'nar] VT, VI to teach

legal [le'gaw] (*pl* **-ais**) ADJ legal, lawful; (*col*) fine; (*: pessoa*) nice ▸ ADV (*col*) well; **(tá) ~!** OK!; **legalidade** [legali'dadʒi] F legality, lawfulness; **legalizar** [legali'zar] VT to legalize; (*documento*) to authenticate

legendado, -a [leʒẽ'dadu, a] ADJ (*filme*) subtitled

legendário, -a [leʒẽ'darju, a] ADJ legendary
legislação [leʒizla'sãw] F legislation
legislar [leʒiz'lar] VI to legislate ▶ VT to pass
legislativo, -a [leʒizla'tʃivu, a] ADJ legislative ▶ M legislature
legitimar [leʒitʃi'mar] VT to legitimize; (*justificar*) to legitimate
legume [le'gumi] M vegetable
lei [lej] F law; (*regra*) rule; (*metal*) standard
leigo, -a ['lejgu, a] ADJ (*Rel*) lay, secular ▶ M layman; **ser ~ em algo** (*fig*) to be no expert at sth, be unversed in sth
leilão [lej'lãw] (*pl* **-ões**) M auction; **vender em ~** to sell by auction, auction off; **leiloar** [lej'lwar] VT to auction
leio ['leju] VB *ver* **ler**
leitão, -toa [lej'tãw, 'toa] (*pl* **-ões/-s**) M/F sucking (BRIT) *ou* suckling (US) pig
leite ['lejtʃi] M milk; **~ em pó** powdered milk; **~ desnatado** *ou* **magro** skimmed milk; **~ de magnésia** milk of magnesia; **~ semidesnatado** semi-skimmed milk; **leiteira** [lej'tejra] F (*para ferver*) milk pan; (*para servir*) milk jug; **leiteiro, -a** [lej'tejru, a] ADJ (*vaca, gado*) dairy ▶ M/F milkman/ woman
leitões [lej'tõjs] MPL *de* **leitão**
leitor, a [lej'tor(a)] M/F (*pessoa*) reader; (*professor*) lector ▶ M (*objeto*) reader; **~ de livros digitais** e-reader
leitura [lej'tura] F reading; (*livro etc*) reading matter
lema ['lɛma] M motto; (*Pol*) slogan
lembrança [lẽ'brãsa] F recollection, memory; (*presente*) souvenir; **lembranças** FPL (*recomendações*): **~s a sua mãe!** regards to your mother!
lembrar [lẽ'brar] VT, VI to remember; **lembrar-se** VR: **~(-se) de** to remember; **~(-se) (de) que** to remember that; **~ algo a alguém, ~ alguém de algo** to remind sb of sth; **~ alguém de que, ~ a alguém que** to remind sb that; **ele lembra meu irmão** he reminds me of my brother, he is like my brother; **lembrete** [lẽ'bretʃi] M reminder
leme ['lɛmi] M rudder; (*Náut*) helm; (*fig*) control
lenço ['lẽsu] M handkerchief; (*de pescoço*) scarf; (*de cabeça*) headscarf; **~ de papel** tissue; **~ umedecido** baby wipe
lençol [lẽ'sɔw] (*pl* **-óis**) M sheet; **estar em maus lençóis** to be in a fix
lenda ['lẽda] F legend; (*fig: mentira*) lie; **lendário, -a** [lẽ'darju, a] ADJ legendary
lenha ['lɛɲa] F firewood
lente ['lẽtʃi] F lens *sg*; **~ de aumento** magnifying glass; **~s de contato** contact lenses
lentidão [lẽtʃi'dãw] F slowness
lento, -a ['lẽtu, a] ADJ slow
leoa [le'oa] F lioness
leões [le'õjs] MPL *de* **leão**
leopardo [ljo'pardu] M leopard
lepra ['lɛpra] F leprosy
leque ['lɛki] M fan; (*fig*) array
ler [ler] VT, VI to read
lesão [le'zãw] (*pl* **-ões**) F harm, injury; (*Jur*) violation; (*Med*) lesion; **~ corporal** (*Jur*) bodily harm
lesar [le'zar] VT to harm, damage; (*direitos*) to violate

lésbica ['lɛzbika] F lesbian
lesma ['lezma] F slug; (*fig: pessoa*) slowcoach
lesões [le'zõjs] FPL *de* **lesão**
lesse ['lesi] VB *ver* **ler**
leste ['lɛstʃi] M east
letal [le'taw] (*pl* **-ais**) ADJ lethal
letargia [letar'ʒia] F lethargy
letivo, -a [le'tʃivu, a] ADJ school *atr*; **ano ~** academic year
letra ['letra] F letter; (*caligrafia*) handwriting; (*de canção*) lyrics *pl*; **Letras** FPL (*curso*) language and literature; **à ~** literally; **ao pé da ~** literally, word for word; **~ de câmbio** (*Com*) bill of exchange; **~ de imprensa** print; **letrado, -a** [le'tradu, a] ADJ learned, erudite ▶ M/F scholar; **letreiro** [le'trejru] M sign, notice; (*inscrição*) inscription; (*Cinema*) subtitle
leu [lew] VB *ver* **ler**
léu [lɛw] M: **ao ~** (*à toa*) aimlessly; (*à mostra*) uncovered
leucemia [lewse'mia] F leukaemia (BRIT), leukemia (US)
levado, -a [le'vadu, a] ADJ mischievous; (*criança*) naughty
levantador, a [levãta'dor(a)] ADJ lifting ▶ M/F: **~ de pesos** weightlifter
levantamento [levãta'mẽtu] M lifting, raising; (*revolta*) uprising, rebellion; (*arrolamento*) survey
levantar [levã'tar] VT to lift, raise; (*voz, capital*) to raise; (*apanhar*) to pick up; (*suscitar*) to arouse; (*ambiente*) to brighten up ▶ VI to stand up; (*da cama*) to get up; (*dar vida*) to brighten; **levantar-se** VR to stand up; (*da cama*) to get up; (*rebelar-se*) to rebel
levar [le'var] VT to take; (*portar*) to carry; (*tempo*) to pass, spend; (*roupa*) to wear; (*lidar com*) to handle; (*induzir*) to lead; (*filme*) to show; (*peça teatral*) to do, put on; (*vida*) to lead ▶ VI to get a beating; **~ a** to lead to; **~ a mal** to take amiss
leve ['lɛvi] ADJ light; (*insignificante*) slight; **de ~** lightly, softly
leviandade [levjã'dadʒi] F frivolity
leviano, -a [le'vjanu, a] ADJ frivolous
lha [ʎa] = **lhe + a**
lhas [ʎas] = **lhe + as**
lhe [ʎi] PRON (*a ele*) to him; (*a ela*) to her; (*a você*) to you
lhes [ʎis] PRON PL (*a eles/elas*) to them; (*a vocês*) to you
lho [ʎu] = **lhe + o**
lhos [ʎus] = **lhe + os**
li [li] VB *ver* **ler**
Líbano ['libanu] M: **o ~** Lebanon
libélula [li'bɛlula] F dragonfly
liberação [libera'sãw] F liberation
liberal [libe'raw] (*pl* **-ais**) ADJ, M/F liberal
liberar [libe'rar] VT to release; (*permitir*) to allow
liberdade [liber'dadʒi] F freedom; **liberdades** FPL (*direitos*) liberties; **pôr alguém em ~** to set sb free; **~ condicional** probation; **~ de palavra** freedom of speech; **~ sob palavra** parole
libertação [liberta'sãw] F release
libertino, -a [liber'tʃinu, a] ADJ loose-living ▶ M/F libertine
Líbia ['libja] F: **a ~** Libya
libidinoso, -a [libidʒi'nozu, ɔza] ADJ lecherous, lustful
líbio, -a ['libju, a] ADJ, M/F Libyan
libra ['libra] F pound; **L~** (*Astrologia*) Libra
lição [li'sãw] (*pl* **-ões**) F lesson
licença [li'sẽsa] F licence (BRIT), license (US); (*permissão*) permission;

(*do trabalho, Mil*) leave; **com ~** excuse me; **estar de ~** to be on leave; **dá ~?** may I?
licenciado, -a [lisẽ'sjadu, a] M/F graduate
licenciar [lisẽ'sjar] VT to license; **licenciar-se** VR (*Educ*) to graduate; (*ficar de licença*) to take leave; **licenciatura** [lisẽsja'tura] F (*título*) degree; (*curso*) degree course
liceu [li'sew] (PT) M secondary (BRIT) *ou* high (US) school
lições [li'sõjs] FPL *de* **lição**
licor [li'kor] M liqueur
lidar [li'dar] VI: **~ com** (*ocupar-se*) to deal with; (*combater*) to struggle against; **~ em algo** to work in sth
líder ['lider] M/F leader; **liderança** [lide'rãsa] F leadership; (*Esporte*) lead; **liderar** [lide'rar] VT to lead
ligado, -a [li'gadu, a] ADJ (*Tec*) connected; (*luz, rádio etc*) on; (*metal*) alloy
ligadura [liga'dura] F bandage
ligamento [liga'mẽtu] M ligament
ligar [li'gar] VT to tie, bind; (*unir*) to join, connect; (*luz, TV*) to switch on; (*afetivamente*) to bind together; (*carro*) to start (up) ▸ VI (*telefonar*) to ring; **ligar-se** VR to join; **~-se com alguém** to join with sb; **~-se a algo** to be connected with sth; **~ para alguém** to ring sb up; **~ para** *ou* **a algo** (*dar atenção*) to take notice of sth; (*dar importância*) to care about sth; **eu nem ligo** it doesn't bother me; **não ligo a mínima (para)** I couldn't care less (about)
ligeiro, -a [li'ʒejru, a] ADJ light; (*ferimento*) slight; (*referência*) passing; (*conhecimentos*) scant; (*rápido*) quick, swift; (*ágil*) nimble ▸ ADV swiftly, nimbly
lilás [li'las] ADJ, M lilac
lima ['lima] F (*laranja*) *type of orange*; (*ferramenta*) file; **~ de unhas** nailfile
limão [li'mãw] (*pl* **-ões**) M lime; (*tb*: **~-galego**) lemon
limiar [li'mjar] M threshold
limitação [limita'sãw] (*pl* **-ões**) F limitation, restriction
limitar [limi'tar] VT to limit, restrict; **limitar-se** VR: **~-se a** to limit o.s. to; **~(-se) com** to border on; **limite** [li'mitʃi] M limit, boundary; (*fig*) limit; **passar dos limites** to go too far
limo ['limu] M (*Bot*) water weed; (*lodo*) slime
limoeiro [li'mwejru] M lemon tree
limões [li'mõjs] MPL *de* **limão**
limonada [limo'nada] F lemonade (BRIT), lemon soda (US)
limpar [lĩ'par] VT to clean; (*lágrimas, suor*) to wipe away; (*polir*) to shine, polish; (*fig*) to clean up; (*roubar*) to rob
limpo, -a ['lĩpu, a] PP *de* **limpar** ▸ ADJ clean; (*céu, consciência*) clear; (*Com*) net; (*fig*) pure; (*col: pronto*) ready; **passar a ~** to make a fair copy; **tirar a ~** to find out the truth about, clear up; **estar ~ com alguém** (*col*) to be in with sb
linchar [lĩ'ʃar] VT to lynch
lindo, -a ['lĩdu, a] ADJ lovely
lingerie [lĩʒe'ri] M lingerie
língua ['lĩgwa] F tongue; (*linguagem*) language; **botar a ~ para fora** to stick out one's tongue; **dar com a ~ nos dentes** to let the cat out of the bag; **estar na ponta da ~** to be on the tip of one's tongue

linguado [lĩ'gwadu] M (*peixe*) sole
linguagem [lĩ'gwaʒẽ] (*pl* **-ns**) F (*tb*: *Comput*) language; **~ de máquina** (*Comput*) machine language
linguarudo, -a [lĩgwa'rudu, a] ADJ gossiping ▶ M/F gossip
linguiça [lĩ'gwisa] F sausage
linha ['liɲa] F line; (*para costura*) thread; (*barbante*) string, cord; **linhas** FPL (*carta*) letter *sg*; **em ~** in line, in a row; (*Comput*) on line; **fora de ~** out of production; **manter/perder a ~** to keep/lose one's cool; **o telefone não deu ~** the line was dead; **~ aérea** airline; **~ de apoio** (PT) helpline; **~ de mira** sights *pl*; **~ de montagem** assembly line; **~ férrea** railway (BRIT), railroad (US)
linho ['liɲu] M linen; (*planta*) flax
liquidação [likida'sãw] (*pl* **-ões**) F liquidation; (*em loja*) (clearance) sale; (*de conta*) settlement; **em ~** on sale
liquidar [liki'dar] VT to liquidate; (*conta*) to settle; (*mercadoria*) to sell off; (*assunto*) to lay to rest ▶ VI (*loja*) to have a sale; **liquidar-se** VR (*destruir-se*) to be destroyed; **~ (com) alguém** (*fig*: *arrasar*) to destroy sb; (: *matar*) to do away with sb
liquidificador [likwidʒifika'dor] M liquidizer
líquido, -a ['likidu, a] ADJ liquid, fluid; (*Com*) net ▶ M liquid
lira ['lira] F lyre; (*moeda*) lira
lírio ['lirju] M lily
Lisboa [liz'boa] N Lisbon; **lisboeta** [liz'bweta] ADJ Lisbon *atr* ▶ M/F inhabitant *ou* native of Lisbon
liso, -a ['lizu, a] ADJ smooth; (*tecido*) plain; (*cabelo*) straight; (*col*: *sem dinheiro*) broke
lisonjear [lizõ'ʒjar] VT to flatter
lista ['lista] F list; (*listra*) stripe; (PT: *menu*) menu; **~ negra** blacklist; **~ telefônica** telephone directory;
listar [lis'tar] VT to list
listra ['listra] F stripe; **listrado, -a** [lis'tradu, a] ADJ striped
literal [lite'raw] (*pl* **-ais**) ADJ literal
literário, -a [lite'rarju, a] ADJ literary
literatura [litera'tura] F literature; **Literatura de cordel** *see note*

> **Literatura de cordel** is a type of literature typical of the north-east of Brazil, and published in the form of cheaply printed booklets. Their authors hang these booklets from wires attached to walls in the street so that people can look at them. While they do this, the authors sing their stories aloud. **Literatura de cordel** deals both with local events and people, and with everyday public life, almost always in an irreverent manner.

litoral [lito'raw] (*pl* **-ais**) ADJ coastal ▶ M coast, seaboard
litro ['litru] M litre (BRIT), liter (US)
livrar [li'vrar] VT to release, liberate; (*salvar*) to save; **livrar-se** VR to escape; **~-se de** to get rid of; (*compromisso*) to get out of; **Deus me livre!** Heaven forbid!
livraria [livra'ria] F bookshop (BRIT), bookstore (US)
livre ['livri] ADJ free; (*lugar*) unoccupied; (*desimpedido*) clear, open; **~ de impostos** tax-free; **livre-arbítrio** M free will
livro ['livru] M book; **~ brochado** paperback; **~ de bolso** pocket-sized book; **~ de cheques** cheque book (BRIT), check book (US); **~ de consulta** reference book;

~ eletrônico e-book;
~ encadernado *ou* **de capa dura** hardback

lixa ['liʃa] F sandpaper; (*de unhas*) nailfile; (*peixe*) dogfish; **lixar** [li'ʃar] VT to sand

lixeira [li'ʃejra] F dustbin (BRIT), garbage can (US)

lixeiro [li'ʃejru] M dustman (BRIT), garbage man (US)

lixo ['liʃu] M rubbish, garbage (US); **ser um ~** (*col*) to be rubbish; **~ atômico** nuclear waste

-lo [lu] PRON him; (*você*) you; (*coisa*) it

lobo ['lobu] M wolf

locação [loka'sãw] (*pl* **-ões**) F lease; (*de vídeo etc*) rental

locador, a [loka'dor(a)] M/F (*de casa*) landlord; (*de carro, filme*) rental agent ▶ F rental company; **~a de vídeo** video rental shop

local [lo'kaw] (*pl* **-ais**) ADJ local ▶ M site, place ▶ F (*notícia*) story; **localidade** [lokali'dadʒi] F (*lugar*) locality; (*povoação*) town; **localização** [lokaliza'sãw] (*pl* **-ões**) F location; **localizar** [lokali'zar] VT to locate; (*situar*) to place; **localizar-se** VR to be located; (*orientar-se*) to get one's bearings

loção [lo'sãw] (*pl* **-ões**) F lotion; **~ após-barba** aftershave (lotion)

locatário, -a [loka'tarju, a] M/F (*de casa*) tenant; (*de carro, filme*) hirer

loções [lo'sõjs] FPL *de* **loção**

locomotiva [lokomo'tʃiva] F railway (BRIT) *ou* railroad (US) engine, locomotive

locomover-se [lokomo'versi] VR to move around

locutor, a [loku'tor(a)] M/F (*TV, Rádio*) announcer

lógica ['lɔʒika] F logic; **lógico, -a** ['lɔʒiku, a] ADJ logical; **(é) lógico!** of course!

logo ['lɔgu] ADV (*imediatamente*) right away, at once; (*em breve*) soon; (*justamente*) just, right; (*mais tarde*) later; **~, ~** in no time; **~ mais** later; **~ no começo** right at the start; **~ que, tão ~** as soon as; **até ~!** bye!; **~ antes/depois** just before/shortly afterwards; **~ de saída** *ou* **de cara** straightaway, right away

logotipo [logo'tʃipu] M logo

lograr [lo'grar] VT (*alcançar*) to achieve; (*obter*) to get, obtain; (*enganar*) to cheat; **~ fazer** to manage to do

loiro, -a ['lojru, a] ADJ = **louro**

loja ['lɔʒa] F shop; **~ de presentes** gift shop (BRIT), gift store (US); **lojista** [lo'ʒista] M/F shopkeeper

lombo ['lõbu] M back; (*carne*) loin

lona ['lɔna] F canvas

Londres ['lõdris] N London; **londrino, -a** [lõ'drinu, a] ADJ London *atr* ▶ M/F Londoner

longa-metragem (*pl* **longas-metragens**) M: **(filme de) ~** feature (film)

longe ['lõʒi] ADV far, far away ▶ ADJ distant; **ao ~** in the distance; **de ~** from far away; (*sem dúvida*) by a long way; **~ de** a long way *ou* far from; **~ disso** far from it; **ir ~ demais** (*fig*) to go too far

longínquo, -a [lõ'ʒĩkwu, a] ADJ distant, remote

longitude [lõʒi'tudʒi] F (*Geo*) longitude

longo, -a ['lõgu, a] ADJ long ▶ M (*vestido*) long dress, evening dress; **ao ~ de** along, alongside

lotação [lota'sãw] F capacity; (*de funcionários*) complement; (BR: *ônibus*) bus; **~ completa** *ou* **esgotada** (*Teatro*) sold out

lotado, -a [lo'tadu, a] ADJ (*Teatro*) full; (*ônibus*) full up; (*bar, praia*) packed, crowded

lotar [lo'tar] VT to fill, pack; (*funcionário*) to place ▸ VI to fill up

lote ['lɔtʃi] M portion, share; (*em leilão*) lot; (*terreno*) plot; (*de ações*) parcel, batch

loteria [lote'ria] F lottery; **~ esportiva** football pools *pl* (BRIT), lottery (US)

louça ['losa] F china; (*conjunto*) crockery; (*tb*: **~ sanitária**) bathroom suite; **de ~** china *atr*; **~ de barro** earthenware; **~ de jantar** dinner service; **lavar a ~** to do the washing up (BRIT) *ou* the dishes

louco, -a ['loku, a] ADJ crazy, mad; (*sucesso*) runaway; (*frio*) freezing ▸ M/F lunatic; **~ varrido** raving mad; **~ de fome/raiva** ravenous/hopping mad; **~ por** crazy about; **deixar alguém ~** to drive sb crazy;

loucura [lo'kura] F madness; (*ato*) crazy thing; **ser loucura (fazer)** to be crazy (to do); **ser uma loucura** to be crazy; (*col: ser muito bom*) to be fantastic

louro, -a ['loru, a] ADJ blond, fair ▸ M laurel; (*Culin*) bay leaf; (*papagaio*) parrot; **louros** MPL (*fig*) laurels

louva-a-deus ['lova-] M INV praying mantis

louvar [lo'var] VT, VI: **~ (a)** to praise; **louvável** [lo'vavew] (*pl* **-eis**) ADJ praiseworthy

louvor [lo'vor] M praise

LP ABR M LP (record)

Ltda. ABR (= *Limitada*) Ltd

lua ['lua] F moon; **estar** *ou* **viver no mundo da ~** to have one's head in the clouds; **estar de ~** (*col*) to be in a mood; **ser de ~** (*col*) to be moody; **~ cheia/nova** full/new moon; **~ de mel** honeymoon

luar ['lwar] M moonlight

lubrificante [lubrifi'kãtʃi] M lubricant

lúcido, -a ['lusidu, a] ADJ lucid

lúcio ['lusju] M (*peixe*) pike

lucrar [lu'krar] VT (*tirar proveito*) to profit from *ou* by; (*dinheiro*) to make; (*gozar*) to enjoy ▸ VI to make a profit; **~ com** *ou* **em** to profit by

lucrativo, -a [lukra'tʃivu, a] ADJ lucrative, profitable

lucro ['lukru] M gain; (*Com*) profit; **~s e perdas** (*Com*) profit and loss

lugar [lu'gar] M place; (*espaço*) space, room; (*para sentar*) seat; (*emprego*) job; (*ocasião*) opportunity; **em ~ de** instead of; **dar ~ a** (*causar*) to give rise to; **~ comum** commonplace; **em primeiro ~** in the first place; **em algum/nenhum/todo ~** somewhere/nowhere/everywhere; **em outro ~** somewhere else, elsewhere; **ter ~** (*acontecer*) to take place; **~ de nascimento** place of birth;

lugarejo [luga'reʒu] M village

lula ['lula] F squid

lume ['lumi] M fire; (*luz*) light

luminária [lumi'narja] F lamp; **luminárias** FPL (*iluminações*) illuminations

luminosidade [luminozi'dadʒi] F brightness

luminoso, -a [lumi'nozu, ɔza] ADJ luminous; (*fig: raciocínio*) clear; (*: ideia, talento*) brilliant; (*letreiro*) illuminated

lunar [lu'nar] ADJ lunar ▶ M (*na pele*) mole
lunático, -a [lu'natʃiku, a] ADJ mad
lusitano, -a [luzi'tanu, a] ADJ Portuguese, Lusitanian
luso, -a ['luzu, a] ADJ Portuguese; **luso-brasileiro, -a** (*pl* **luso-brasileiros**) ADJ Luso-Brazilian
lustre ['lustri] M gloss, sheen; (*fig*) lustre (BRIT), luster (US); (*luminária*) chandelier
luta ['luta] F fight, struggle; **~ de boxe** boxing; **~ livre** wrestling; **lutador, a** [luta'dor(a)] M/F fighter; (*atleta*) wrestler; **lutar** [lu'tar] VI to fight, struggle; (*luta livre*) to wrestle ▶ VT (*caratê, judô*) to do; **lutar contra/por algo** to fight against/for sth; **lutar para fazer algo** to fight *ou* struggle to do sth; **lutar com** (*dificuldades*) to struggle against; (*competir*) to fight with
luto ['lutu] M mourning; (*tristeza*) grief; **de ~** in mourning; **pôr ~** to go into mourning
luva ['luva] F glove; **luvas** FPL (*pagamento*) payment *sg*; (*ao locador*) fee *sg*
Luxemburgo [luʃẽ'burgu] M: **o ~** Luxembourg
luxo ['luʃu] M luxury; **de ~** luxury *atr*; **dar-se ao ~ de** to allow o.s. to; **luxuoso, -a** [lu'ʃwozu, ɔza] ADJ luxurious
luxúria [lu'ʃurja] F lust
luz [luz] F light; (*eletricidade*) electricity; **à ~ de** by the light of; (*fig*) in the light of; **a meia ~** with subdued lighting; **dar à ~ (um filho)** to give birth (to a son); **deu-me uma ~** I had an idea

m

ma [ma] PRON = **me + a**
má [ma] ADJ F *de* **mau**
maca ['maka] F stretcher
maçã [ma'sã] F apple; **~ do rosto** cheekbone
macabro, -a [ma'kabru, a] ADJ macabre
macacão [maka'kãw] (*pl* **-ões**) M (*de trabalhador*) overalls *pl* (BRIT), coveralls *pl* (US); (*da moda*) jump-suit
macaco, -a [ma'kaku, a] M/F monkey ▶ M (*Mecânica*) jack; **(fato) ~** (PT) overalls *pl* (BRIT), coveralls *pl* (US); **~ velho** (*fig*) old hand
macacões [maka'kõjs] MPL *de* **macacão**
maçador, a [masa'dor(a)] (PT) ADJ boring
maçaneta [masa'neta] F knob
maçante [ma'sãtʃi] (BR) ADJ boring
macarrão [maka'hãw] M pasta; (*em forma de canudo*) spaghetti;

macarronada [makaho'nada] F pasta with cheese and tomato sauce
macete [ma'setʃi] M mallet
machado [ma'ʃadu] M axe (BRIT), ax (US)
machista [ma'ʃista] ADJ chauvinistic, macho ▶ M male chauvinist
macho ['maʃu] ADJ male; (*fig*) virile, manly; (*valentão*) tough ▶ M male; (*Tec*) tap
machucado, -a [maʃu'kadu, a] ADJ hurt; (*pé, braço*) bad ▶ M injury; (*área machucada*) sore patch
machucar [maʃu'kar] VT to hurt; (*produzir contusão*) to bruise ▶ VI to hurt; **machucar-se** VR to hurt o.s.
maciço, -a [ma'sisu, a] ADJ solid; (*espesso*) thick; (*quantidade*) massive
macio, -a [ma'siu, a] ADJ soft; (*liso*) smooth
maço ['masu] M (*de folhas, notas*) bundle; (*de cigarros*) packet
maçom [ma'sõ] (*pl* **-ns**) M (free)mason
maconha [ma'kɔɲa] F dope; **cigarro de ~** joint
maçons [ma'sõs] MPL *de* **maçom**
má-criação (*pl* **-ões**) F rudeness; (*ato, dito*) rude thing
mácula ['makula] F stain, blemish
macumba [ma'kũba] F ≈ voodoo; (*despacho*) *macumba* offering;
macumbeiro, -a [makũ'bejru, a] ADJ ≈ voodoo *atr* ▶ M/F follower of *macumba*
madama [ma'dama] F = **madame**
madame [ma'dami] F (*senhora*) lady; (*col: dona de casa*) lady of the house
madeira [ma'dejra] F wood ▶ M Madeira (wine); **de ~** wooden; **bater na ~** (*fig*) to touch (BRIT) *ou* knock on (US) wood; **~ compensada** plywood
madeirense [madej'rẽsi] ADJ, M/F Madeiran
madeixa [ma'dejʃa] F (*de cabelo*) lock
madrasta [ma'drasta] F stepmother
madrepérola [madre'pɛrola] F mother of pearl
Madri [ma'dri] N Madrid
Madrid [ma'drid] (PT) N Madrid
madrinha [ma'driɲa] F godmother
madrugada [madru'gada] F (early) morning; (*alvorada*) dawn, daybreak
madrugar [madru'gar] VI to get up early; (*aparecer cedo*) to be early
maduro, -a [ma'duro, a] ADJ ripe; (*fig*) mature; (*: prudente*) prudent
mãe [mãj] F mother; **~ adotiva** *ou* **de criação** adoptive mother
maestro, -trina [ma'ɛstru, 'trina] M/F conductor
má-fé F malicious intent
magia [ma'ʒia] F magic
mágica ['maʒika] F magic; (*truque*) magic trick; *ver tb* **mágico**
mágico, -a ['maʒiku, a] ADJ magic ▶ M/F magician
magistério [maʒis'tɛrju] M (*ensino*) teaching; (*profissão*) teaching profession; (*professorado*) teachers *pl*
magnético, -a [mag'nɛtʃiku, a] ADJ magnetic
magnífico, -a [mag'nifiku, a] ADJ splendid, magnificent
mago ['magu] M magician; **os reis ~s** the Three Wise Men, the Three Kings
mágoa ['magwa] F (*tristeza*) sorrow, grief; (*fig: desagrado*) hurt
magoado, -a [ma'gwadu, a] ADJ hurt

magoar [ma'gwar] VT, VI to hurt; **magoar-se** VR: **~-se com algo** to be hurt by sth
magro, -a ['magru, a] ADJ (*pessoa*) slim; (*carne*) lean; (*fig: parco*) meagre (BRIT), meager (US); (*leite*) skimmed
maio ['maju] M May
maiô [ma'jo] (BR) M swimsuit
maionese [majo'nɛzi] F mayonnaise
maior [ma'jɔr] ADJ (*compar: de tamanho*) bigger; (*: de importância*) greater; (*superl: de tamanho*) biggest; (*: de importância*) greatest ▶ M/F adult; **~ de idade** of age, adult; **~ de 21 anos** over 21; **maioria** [majo'ria] F majority; **a maioria de** most of; **maioridade** [majori'dadʒi] F adulthood

PALAVRA-CHAVE

mais [majs] ADV **1** (*compar*): **mais magro/inteligente (do que)** thinner/more intelligent (than); **ele trabalha mais (do que eu)** he works more (than me)
2 (*superl*): **o mais ...** the most ...; **o mais magro/inteligente** the thinnest/most intelligent
3 (*negativo*): **ele não trabalha mais aqui** he doesn't work here any more; **nunca mais** never again
4 (*+ adj, valor intensivo*): **que livro mais chato!** what a boring book!
5: **por mais que** however much; **por mais que se esforce ...** no matter how hard you try ...; **por mais que eu quisesse ...** much as I should like to ...
6: **a mais: temos um a mais** we've got one extra
7 (*tempo*): **mais cedo ou mais tarde** sooner or later; **a mais tempo** sooner; **logo mais** later on; **no mais tardar** at the latest
8 (*frases*): **mais ou menos** more or less; **mais uma vez** once more; **cada vez mais** more and more; **sem mais nem menos** out of the blue
▶ ADJ **1** (*compar*): **mais (do que)** more (than); **ele tem mais dinheiro (do que o irmão)** he's got more money (than his brother)
2 (*superl*): **ele é quem tem mais dinheiro** he's got most money
3 (*+ números*): **ela tem mais de dez bolsas** she's got more than ten bags
4 (*negativo*): **não tenho mais dinheiro** I haven't got any more money
5 (*adicional*) else; **mais alguma coisa?** anything else?; **nada/ninguém mais** nothing/no-one else
▶ PREP: **2 mais 2 são 4** 2 and 2 *ou* plus 2 is 4
▶ M: **o mais** the rest

maisena [maj'zena] F cornflour (BRIT), corn starch (US)
maiúscula [ma'juskula] F capital letter
majestade [maʒes'tadʒi] F majesty; **majestoso, -a** [maʒes'tozu, ɔza] ADJ majestic
major [ma'ʒɔr] M (*Mil*) major
majoritário, -a [maʒori'tarju, a] ADJ majority *atr*
mal [maw] (*pl* **males**) M harm; (*Med*) illness ▶ ADV badly; (*quase não*) hardly ▶ CONJ hardly; **~ desliguei o fone, a campainha tocou** I had hardly put the phone down when the doorbell rang;

falar ~ de alguém to speak ill of sb, run sb down; **não faz ~** never mind; **estar ~** (*doente*) to be ill; **passar ~** to be sick; **estar de ~ com alguém** not to be speaking to sb; **~ de Alzheimer** Alzheimer's (disease)
mal- [maw] PREFIXO badly, mis-
mala ['mala] F suitcase; (BR *Auto*) boot, trunk (US); **malas** FPL (*bagagem*) luggage *sg*; **fazer as ~s** to pack
malabarismo [malaba'rizmu] M juggling; **malabarista** [malaba'rista] M/F juggler
mal-acabado, -a ADJ badly finished; (*pessoa*) deformed
malagueta [mala'geta] F chilli (BRIT) *ou* chili (US) pepper
Malaísia [mala'izja] F: **a ~** Malaysia
malandragem [malã'draʒẽ] F (*patifaria*) double-dealing; (*preguiça*) idleness; (*esperteza*) cunning
malária [ma'larja] F malaria
mal-arrumado, -a [-ahu'madu, a] ADJ untidy
malcomportado, -a [mawkõpor'tadu, a] ADJ badly behaved
malcriado, -a [maw'krjadu, a] ADJ rude ▶ M/F slob
maldade [maw'dadʒi] F cruelty; (*malícia*) malice
maldição [mawdʒi'sãw] (*pl* **-ões**) F curse
maldizer [mawdʒi'zer] (*irreg: como* **dizer**) VT to curse
maldoso, -a [maw'dozu, ɔza] ADJ wicked; (*malicioso*) malicious
maledicência [maledʒi'sẽsja] F slander
mal-educado, -a ADJ rude ▶ M/F slob
malefício [male'fisju] M harm;
maléfico, -a [ma'lɛfiku, a] ADJ (*pessoa*) malicious; (*prejudicial*) harmful
mal-entendido, -a ADJ misunderstood ▶ M misunderstanding
mal-estar M indisposition; (*embaraço*) awkward situation
malfeito, -a [maw'fejtu, a] ADJ (*roupa*) poorly made; (*corpo*) misshapen
malfeitor, -a [mawfej'tor(a)] M/F wrongdoer
malha ['maʎa] F (*de rede*) mesh; (*tecido*) jersey; (*suéter*) sweater; (*de ginástica*) leotard; **fazer ~** (PT) to knit; **artigos de ~** knitwear; **vestido de ~** jersey dress
malhar [ma'ʎar] VT (*bater*) to beat; (*cereais*) to thresh; (*col: criticar*) to knock, run down
mal-humorado, -a [-umo'radu, a] ADJ grumpy, sullen
maligno, -a [ma'lignu, a] ADJ evil, malicious; (*danoso*) harmful; (*Med*) malignant
malograr [malo'grar] VT (*planos*) to upset; (*frustrar*) to thwart, frustrate ▶ VI (*planos*) to fall through; (*fracassar*) to fail; **malograr-se** VR to fall through; to fail
malpassado, -a [mawpa'sadu, a] ADJ underdone; (*bife*) rare
malsucedido, -a [mawsuse'dʒidu, a] ADJ unsuccessful
Malta ['mawta] F Malta
malta ['mawta] (PT) F gang, mob
maltrapilho, -a [mawtra'piʎu, a] ADJ in rags, ragged ▶ M/F ragamuffin
maluco, -a [ma'luku, a] ADJ crazy, daft ▶ M/F madman/woman
malvadeza [mawva'deza] F

wickedness; (*ato*) wicked thing
malvado, -a [maw'vadu, a] ADJ wicked
Malvinas [maw'vinas] FPL: **as (ilhas) ~** the Falklands, the Falkland Islands
mama ['mama] F breast
mamadeira [mama'dejra] (BR) F feeding bottle
mamãe [ma'mãj] F mum, mummy
mamão [ma'mãw] (*pl* **-ões**) M papaya
mamar [ma'mar] VT to suck; (*dinheiro*) to extort ▶ VI to be breastfed; **dar de ~ a um bebê** to (breast)feed a baby
mamífero [ma'miferu] M mammal
mamilo [ma'milu] M nipple
mamões [ma'mõjs] MPL *de* **mamão**
manada [ma'nada] F herd, drove
mancada [mã'kada] F (*erro*) mistake; (*gafe*) blunder; **dar uma ~** to blunder
mancar [mã'kar] VT to cripple ▶ VI to limp; **mancar-se** VR (*col*) to get the message, take the hint
Mancha ['mãʃa] F: **o canal da ~** the English Channel
mancha ['mãʃa] F stain; (*na pele*) mark, spot; **sem ~s** (*reputação*) spotless; **manchado, -a** [mã'ʃadu, a] ADJ soiled; (*malhado*) mottled, spotted; **manchar** [mã'ʃar] VT to stain, mark; (*reputação*) to soil
manchete [mã'ʃɛtʃi] F headline
manco, -a ['mãku, a] ADJ crippled, lame ▶ M/F cripple
mandado [mã'dadu] M order; (*Jur*) writ; (*tb*: **~ de segurança**) injunction; **~ de prisão/busca** arrest/search warrant; **~ de segurança** injunction
mandão, -dona [mã'dãw, 'dɔna] ADJ (*pl* **-ões/-s**) ADJ bossy, domineering
mandar [mã'dar] VT (*ordenar*) to order; (*enviar*) to send ▶ VI to be in charge; **mandar-se** VR (*col*: *partir*) to make tracks, get going; (*fugir*) to take off; **~ buscar** *ou* **chamar** to send for; **~ fazer um vestido** to have a dress made; **~ que alguém faça, ~ alguém fazer** to tell sb to do; **o que é que você manda?** (*col*) what can I do for you?; **~ em alguém** to boss sb around
mandato [mã'datu] M mandate; (*ordem*) order; (*Pol*) term of office
mandioca [mã'dʒjɔka] F cassava, manioc
mandões [mã'dõjs] MPL *de* **mandão**
mandona [mã'dɔna] F *de* **mandão**
maneira [ma'nejra] F (*modo*) way; (*estilo*) style, manner; **maneiras** FPL (*modos*) manners; **à ~ de** like; **de ~ que** so that; **de ~ alguma** *ou* **nenhuma** not at all; **desta ~** in this way; **de qualquer ~** anyway; **não houve ~ de convencê-lo** it was impossible to convince him
maneiro, -a [ma'nejru, a] ADJ (*ferramenta*) easy to use; (*roupa*) attractive; (*trabalho*) easy; (*pessoa*) capable; (*col*: *bacana*) great, brilliant
manejar [mane'ʒar] VT (*instrumento*) to handle; (*máquina*) to work; **manejo** [ma'neʒu] M handling
manequim [mane'kĩ] (*pl* **-ns**) M (*boneco*) dummy ▶ M/F model
manga ['mãga] F sleeve; (*fruta*) mango; **em ~s de camisa** in (one's) shirt sleeves

mangueira [mã'gejra] F hose(pipe); (*árvore*) mango tree
manha ['maɲa] F guile, craftiness; (*destreza*) skill; (*ardil*) trick; (*birra*) tantrum; **fazer ~** to have a tantrum
manhã [ma'ɲã] F morning; **de** *ou* **pela ~** in the morning; **amanhã/hoje de ~** tomorrow/this morning
manhoso, -a [ma'ɲozu, ɔza] ADJ crafty, sly; (*criança*) whining
mania [ma'nia] F (*Med*) mania; (*obsessão*) craze; **estar com ~ de ...** to have a thing about ...; **maníaco, -a** [ma'niaku, a] ADJ manic ▶ M/F maniac
manicômio [mani'komju] M asylum, mental hospital
manifestação [manifesta'sãw] (*pl* **-ões**) F show, display; (*expressão*) expression, declaration; (*política*) demonstration
manifestante [manifes'tãtʃi] M/F demonstrator
manifestar [manifes'tar] VT to show, display; (*declarar*) to express, declare
manifesto, -a [mani'fɛstu, a] ADJ obvious, clear ▶ M manifesto
manipulação [manipula'sãw] F handling; (*fig*) manipulation
manipular [manipu'lar] VT to manipulate; (*manejar*) to handle
manjericão [mãʒeri'kãw] M basil
manobra [ma'nɔbra] F manoeuvre (BRIT), maneuver (US); (*de mecanismo*) operation; (*de trens*) shunting; **manobrar** [mano'brar] VT to manoeuvre (BRIT), maneuver (US); (*mecanismo*) to operate, work; (*governar*) to take charge of; (*manipular*) to manipulate ▶ VI to manoeuvre *ou* maneuver
manso, -a ['mãsu, a] ADJ gentle; (*mar*) calm; (*animal*) tame
manta ['mãta] F blanket; (*xale*) shawl; (*agasalho*) cloak
manteiga [mã'tejga] F butter; **~ de cacau** cocoa butter
manter [mã'ter] (*irreg: como* **ter**) VT to maintain; (*num lugar*) to keep; (*uma família*) to support; (*a palavra*) to keep; (*princípios*) to abide by; **manter-se** VR to support o.s.; (*permanecer*) to remain;
mantimento [mãtʃi'mẽtu] M maintenance; **mantimentos** MPL (*alimentos*) provisions
manual [ma'nwaw] (*pl* **-ais**) ADJ manual ▶ M handbook, manual
manufatura [manufa'tura] F manufacture; **manufaturar** [manufatu'rar] VT to manufacture
manusear [manu'zjar] VT to handle; (*livro*) to leaf through
mão [mãw] (*pl* **mãos**) F hand; (*de animal*) paw; (*de pintura*) coat; (*de direção*) flow of traffic; **à ~** by hand; (*perto*) at hand; **de segunda ~** second-hand; **em ~** by hand; **dar a ~ a alguém** to hold sb's hand; (*cumprimentar*) to shake hands with sb; **dar uma ~ a alguém** to give sb a hand, help sb out; **~ única/dupla** one-way/two-way traffic; **rua de duas ~s** two-way street; **~ de obra** labour (BRIT), labor (US)
mapa ['mapa] M map; (*gráfico*) chart
maquiagem [ma'kjaʒẽ] F = **maquilagem**
maquiar [ma'kjar] VT to make up; **maquiar-se** VR to make o.s. up, put on one's make-up
maquilagem [maki'laʒẽ], (PT) **maquilhagem** F make-up; (*ato*) making up
máquina ['makina] F machine; (*de trem*) engine; (*fig*) machinery; **~ de**

costura sewing machine; **~ fotográfica** camera; **~ de lavar (roupa)** washing machine; **~ de lavar louça** dishwasher; **escrito à ~** typewritten

maquinar [maki'nar] VT to plot ▸VI to conspire

maquinista [maki'nista] M (*Ferro*) engine driver; (*Náut*) engineer

mar [mar] M sea; **por ~** by sea; **fazer-se ao ~** to set sail; **pleno ~**, **~ alto** high sea; **o ~ Morto** the Dead Sea; **o ~ Negro** the Black Sea

maracujá [maraku'ʒa] M passion fruit; **pé de ~** passion flower

maratona [mara'tona] F marathon

maravilha [mara'viʎa] F marvel, wonder; **maravilhoso, -a** [maravi'ʎozu, ɔza] ADJ wonderful

marca ['marka] F mark; (*Com*) make, brand; (*carimbo*) stamp; **~ de fábrica** trademark; **~ registrada** registered trademark

marcação [marka'sãw] (*pl* **-ões**) F marking; (*em jogo*) scoring; (*de instrumento*) reading; (*Teatro*) action; (PT *Tel*) dialling

marcador [marka'dor] M marker; (*de livro*) bookmark; (*Esporte: quadro*) scoreboard; (*: jogador*) scorer

marca-passo [marka'pasu] (*pl* **-s**) M (*Med*) pacemaker

marcar [mar'kar] VT to mark; (*hora, data*) to fix, set; (PT *Tel*) to dial; (*gol, ponto*) to score ▸VI to make one's mark; **~ uma consulta, ~ hora** to make an appointment; **~ um encontro com alguém** to arrange to meet sb

marcha ['marʃa] F march; (*de acontecimentos*) course; (*passo*) pace; (*Auto*) gear; (*progresso*) progress; **~ à ré** (BR), **~ atrás** (PT) reverse (gear); **pôr-se em ~** to set off

marchar [mar'ʃar] VI to go; (*andar a pé*) to walk; (*Mil*) to march

marco ['marku] M landmark; (*de janela*) frame; (*fig*) frontier; (*moeda*) mark

março ['marsu] M March

maré [ma'rɛ] F tide

marechal [mare'ʃaw] (*pl* **-ais**) M marshal

maremoto [mare'mɔtu] M tidal wave

marfim [mar'fĩ] M ivory

margarida [marga'rida] F daisy

margarina [marga'rina] F margarine

margem ['marʒẽ] (*pl* **-ns**) F (*borda*) edge; (*de rio*) bank; (*litoral*) shore; (*de impresso*) margin; (*fig: tempo*) time; (*: lugar*) space; **à ~ de** alongside

marginal [marʒi'naw] (*pl* **-ais**) ADJ marginal ▸M/F delinquent

marido [ma'ridu] M husband

marimbondo [marĩ'bõdu] M hornet

marinha [ma'riɲa] F (*tb*: **~ de guerra**) navy; **~ mercante** merchant navy; **marinheiro** [mari'ɲejru] M seaman, sailor

marinho, -a [ma'riɲu, a] ADJ sea *atr*, marine

mariposa [mari'poza] F moth

marítimo, -a [ma'ritʃimu, a] ADJ sea *atr*

marketing ['marketʃĩŋ] M marketing

marmelada [marme'lada] F quince jam

m

marmelo [mar'mɛlu] M quince
marmita [mar'mita] F (*vasilha*) pot
mármore ['marmori] M marble
marquês, -quesa [mar'kes, 'keza] M/F marquis/marchioness
marqueteiro, -a [marke'tejru, a] M/F (*col*) spin doctor
marquise [mar'kizi] F awning, canopy
Marrocos [ma'hɔkus] M: **o ~** Morocco
marrom [ma'hõ] (*pl* **-ns**) ADJ, M brown
martelar [marte'lar] VT to hammer; (*amolar*) to bother ▶ VI to hammer; (*insistir*): **~ (em algo)** to keep *ou* harp on (about sth); **martelo** [mar'tɛlu] M hammer
mártir ['martʃir] M/F martyr; **martírio** [mar'tʃirju] M martyrdom; (*fig*) torment
marxista [mar'ksista] ADJ, M/F Marxist
mas [ma(j)s] CONJ but ▶ PRON = **me + as**
mascar [mas'kar] VT to chew
máscara ['maskara] F mask; (*para limpeza de pele*) face pack; **sob a ~ de** under the guise of; **mascarar** [maska'rar] VT to mask; (*disfarçar*) to disguise; (*encobrir*) to cover up
mascote [mas'kɔtʃi] F mascot
masculino, -a [masku'linu, a] ADJ masculine; (*Bio*) male
massa ['masa] F (*Fís, fig*) mass; (*de tomate*) paste; (*Culin: de pão*) dough; (*: macarrão etc*) pasta
massacrar [masa'krar] VT to massacre; **massacre** [ma'sakri] F massacre
massagear [masa'ʒjar] VT to massage; **massagem** [ma'saʒẽ] (*pl* **-ns**) F massage
mastigar [mastʃi'gar] VT to chew
mastro ['mastru] M (*Náut*) mast; (*para bandeira*) flagpole
masturbar-se [mastur'barsi] VR to masturbate
mata ['mata] F forest, wood
matadouro [mata'doru] M slaughterhouse
matança [ma'tãsa] F massacre; (*de reses*) slaughter(ing)
matar [ma'tar] VT to kill; (*sede*) to quench; (*fome*) to satisfy; (*aula*) to skip; (*trabalho: não aparecer*) to skive off; (*: fazer rápido*) to dash off; (*adivinhar*) to guess ▶ VI to kill; **matar-se** VR to kill o.s.; (*esfalfar-se*) to wear o.s. out; **um calor/uma dor de ~** stifling heat/excruciating pain
mate ['matʃi] ADJ matt ▶ M (*chá*) maté tea; (*xeque-mate*) checkmate
matemática [mate'matʃika] F mathematics *sg*, maths *sg* (BRIT), math (US); **matemático, -a** [mate'matʃiku, a] ADJ mathematical ▶ M/F mathematician
matéria [ma'tɛrja] F matter; (*Tec*) material; (*Educ: assunto*) subject; (*tema*) topic; (*jornalística*) story, article; **em ~ de** on the subject of
material [mate'rjaw] (*pl* **-ais**) ADJ material; (*físico*) physical ▶ M material; (*Tec*) equipment; **materialista** [materja'lista] ADJ materialistic; **materializar** [materjali'zar] VT to materialize; **materializar-se** VR to materialize
maternal [mater'naw] (*pl* **-ais**) ADJ motherly, maternal; **escola ~** nursery (school); **maternidade** [materni'dadʒi] F motherhood, maternity; (*hospital*) maternity hospital
materno, -a [ma'tɛrnu, a] ADJ

motherly, maternal; (*língua*) native
matinê [matʃi'ne] F matinée
matiz [ma'tʃiz] M (*de cor*) shade
mato ['matu] M scrubland, bush; (*plantas agrestes*) scrub; (*o campo*) country
matraca [ma'traka] F rattle
matrícula [ma'trikula] F (*lista*) register; (*inscrição*) registration; (*pagamento*) enrolment (BRIT) *ou* enrollment (US) fee; (PT *Auto*) registration number (BRIT), license number (US); **fazer a ~** to enrol (BRIT), enroll (US)
matrimonial [matrimo'njaw] (*pl* **-ais**) ADJ marriage *atr*, matrimonial
matrimônio [matri'monju] M marriage
matriz [ma'triz] F (*Med*) womb; (*fonte*) source; (*molde*) mould (BRIT), mold (US); (*Com*) head office
maturidade [maturi'dadʒi] F maturity
mau, má [maw, ma] ADJ bad; (*malvado*) evil, wicked ▶ M bad; (*Rel*) evil; **os ~s** bad people; (*num filme*) the baddies
maus-tratos MPL ill-treatment *sg*
maxila [mak'sila] F jawbone
maxilar [maksi'lar] M jawbone
máxima ['masima] F maxim
máximo, -a ['masimu, a] ADJ (*maior que todos*) greatest; (*o maior possível*) maximum ▶ M maximum; (*o cúmulo*) peak; (*temperature*) high; **no ~** at most; **ao ~** to the utmost
me [mi] PRON (*direto*) me; (*indireto*) (to) me; (*reflexivo*) (to) myself
meado ['mjadu] M middle; **em** *ou* **nos ~s de julho** in mid-July
Meca ['mɛka] N Mecca
mecânica [me'kanika] F (*ciência*) mechanics *sg*; (*mecanismo*) mechanism; *ver tb* **mecânico**
mecânico, -a [me'kaniku, a] ADJ mechanical ▶ M/F mechanic
mecanismo [meka'nizmu] M mechanism
meço ['mɛsu] VB *ver* **medir**
medalha [me'daʎa] F medal;
medalhão [meda'ʎãw] (*pl* **-ões**) M medallion
média ['mɛdʒja] F average; (*café*) coffee with milk; **em ~** on average
mediano, -a [me'dʒjanu, a] ADJ medium; (*médio*) average; (*medíocre*) mediocre
mediante [me'dʒjãtʃi] PREP by (means of), through; (*a troco de*) in return for
medicamento [medʒika'mẽtu] M medicine
medicina [medʒi'sina] F medicine
médico, -a ['mɛdʒiku, a] ADJ medical ▶ M/F doctor; **receita médica** prescription
medida [me'dʒida] F measure; (*providência*) step; (*medição*) measurement; (*moderação*) prudence; **à ~ que** while, as; **na ~ em que** in so far as; **feito sob ~** made to measure; **ir além da ~** to go too far; **tirar as ~s de alguém** to take sb's measurements; **tomar ~s** to take steps; **tomar as ~s de** to measure
medieval [medʒje'vaw] (*pl* **-ais**) ADJ medieval
médio, -a ['mɛdʒju, a] ADJ (*dedo, classe*) middle; (*tamanho, estatura*) medium; (*mediano*) average; **ensino ~** secondary education
medir [me'dʒir] VT to measure; (*atos, palavras*) to weigh; (*avaliar: consequências, distâncias*) to weigh up ▶ VI to measure; **quanto você mede? — meço 1.60 m** how tall

are you? — I'm 1.60 m (tall)
meditar [medʒi'tar] VI to meditate; **~ sobre algo** to ponder (on) sth
mediterrâneo, -a [medʒite'hanju, a] ADJ Mediterranean ▶ M: **o M~** the Mediterranean
medo ['medu] M fear; **com ~** afraid; **meter ~ em alguém** to frighten sb; **ter ~ de** to be afraid of
medonho, -a [me'doɲu, a] ADJ terrible, awful
medroso, -a [me'drozu, ɔza] ADJ (*com medo*) frightened; (*tímido*) timid
megabyte [mega'bajtʃi] M megabyte
meia ['meja] F stocking; (*curta*) sock; (*meia-entrada*) half-price ticket ▶ NUM six; **meia-idade** F middle age; **pessoa de meia-idade** middle-aged person; **meia-noite** F midnight
meigo, -a ['mejgu, a] ADJ sweet
meio, -a ['meju, a] ADJ half ▶ ADV a bit, rather ▶ M middle; (*recurso*) means; (*social, profissional*) environment; (*tb*: **~ ambiente**) environment; **meios** MPL (*recursos*) means *pl*; **~ quilo** half a kilo; **um mês e ~** one and a half months; **cortar ao ~** to cut in half; **dividir algo ~ a ~** to divide sth in half *ou* fifty-fifty; **em ~ a** amid; **no ~ (de)** in the middle (of); **~s de comunicação (de massa)** (mass) media *pl*; **~s de comunicação social** social media *pl*; **por ~ de** through; **meio-dia** M midday, noon; **meio-fio** (*pl* **meios-fios**) M kerb (BRIT), curb (US); **meio-termo** (*pl* **meios-termos**) M (*fig*) compromise
mel [mɛw] M honey
melaço [me'lasu] M treacle (BRIT), molasses *sg* (US)
melancia [melã'sia] F watermelon
melancolia [melãko'lia] F melancholy, sadness; **melancólico, -a** [melã'kɔliku, a] ADJ melancholy, sad
melão [me'lãw] (*pl* **-ões**) M melon
melhor [me'ʎɔr] ADJ, ADV (*compar*) better; (*superl*) best; **~ que nunca** better than ever; **quanto mais ~** the more the better; **seria ~ começarmos** we had better begin; **tanto ~** so much the better; **ou ~ …** (*ou antes*) or rather …; **melhora** [me'ʎɔra] F improvement; **melhoras!** get well soon!;
melhorar [meʎo'rar] VT to improve, make better; (*doente*) to cure ▶ VI to improve, get better
melodia [melo'dʒia] F melody; (*composição*) tune
melões [me'lõjs] MPL *de* **melão**
melro ['mɛwhu] M blackbird
membro ['mẽbru] M member; (*Anat: braço, perna*) limb
memória [me'mɔrja] F memory; **memórias** FPL (*de autor*) memoirs; **de ~** by heart
memorizar [memori'zar] VT to memorize
mencionar [mẽsjo'nar] VT to mention
mendigar [mẽdʒi'gar] VT to beg for ▶ VI to beg; **mendigo, -a** [mẽ'dʒigu, a] M/F beggar
menina [me'nina] F: **~ do olho** pupil; **ser a ~ dos olhos de alguém** (*fig*) to be the apple of sb's eye; *ver tb* **menino**
meninada [meni'nada] F kids *pl*
menino, -a [me'ninu, a] M/F boy/girl
menopausa [meno'pawza] F menopause

menor [me'nɔr] ADJ (*mais pequeno: compar*) smaller; (*: superl*) smallest; (*mais jovem: compar*) younger; (*: superl*) youngest; (*o mínimo*) least, slightest; (*tb*: **~ de idade**) under age ▶ M/F juvenile, young person; (*Jur*) minor; **não tenho a ~ ideia** I haven't the slightest idea

PALAVRA-CHAVE

menos ['menus] ADJ **1** (*compar*): **menos (do que)** (*quantidade*) less (than); (*número*) fewer (than); **com menos entusiasmo** with less enthusiasm; **menos gente** fewer people
2 (*superl*) least; **é o que tem menos culpa** he is the least to blame
▶ ADV **1** (*compar*): **menos (do que)** less (than); **gostei menos do que do outro** I liked it less than the other one
2 (*superl*): **é o menos inteligente da classe** he is the least bright in his class; **de todas elas é a que menos me agrada** out of all of them she's the one I like least; **pelo menos** at (the very) least
3 (*frases*): **temos sete a menos** we are seven short; **não é para menos** it's no wonder; **isso é o de menos** that's nothing
▶ PREP (*exceção*) except; (*números*) minus; **todos menos eu** everyone except (for) me; **5 menos 2** 5 minus 2
▶ CONJ: **a menos que** unless; **a menos que ele venha amanhã** unless he comes tomorrow
▶ M: **o menos** the least

menosprezar [menuspre'zar] VT (*subestimar*) to underrate; (*desprezar*) to despise, scorn

mensageiro, -a [mẽsa'ʒejru, a] M/F messenger

mensagem [mẽ'saʒẽ] (*pl* **-ns**) F message; **~ de texto** text (message); **mandar uma ~ de texto para alguém** to text sb

mensal [mẽ'saw] (*pl* **-ais**) ADJ monthly; **ele ganha £2000 mensais** he earns £2000 a month; **mensalidade** [mẽsali'dadʒi] F monthly payment; **mensalmente** [mẽsaw'mẽtʃi] ADV monthly

menstruação [mẽstrwa'sãw] F period; (*Med*) menstruation

menta ['mẽta] F mint

mental [mẽ'taw] (*pl* **-ais**) ADJ mental; **mentalidade** [mẽtali'dadʒi] F mentality

mente ['mẽtʃi] F mind; **de boa ~** willingly; **ter em ~** to bear in mind

mentir [mẽ'tʃir] VI to lie

mentira [mẽ'tʃira] F lie; (*ato*) lying; **parece ~ que** it seems incredible that; **de ~** not for real; **~!** (*acusação*) that's a lie!, you're lying; (*de surpresa*) you don't say!, no!; **mentiroso, -a** [mẽtʃi'rozu, ɔza] ADJ lying ▶ M/F liar

menu [me'nu] M (*tb: Comput*) menu

mercado [mer'kadu] M market; **M~ Comum** Common Market; **~ negro** *ou* **paralelo** black market

mercadoria [merkado'ria] F commodity; **mercadorias** FPL (*produtos*) goods

mercearia [mersja'ria] F grocer's (shop) (BRIT), grocery store

mercúrio [mer'kurju] M mercury

merda ['mɛrda] (!) F shit (!) ▶ M/F (*pessoa*) jerk; **a ~ do carro** the bloody (BRIT) *ou* goddamn (US) car (!)

merecer [mere'ser] VT to deserve; (*consideração*) to merit; (*valer*) to be worth ▶ VI to be worthy; **merecido, -a** [mere'sidu, a] ADJ deserved; (*castigo, prêmio*) just
merenda [me'rẽda] F packed lunch
merengue [me'rẽgi] M meringue
mergulhador, a [merguʎa'dor(a)] M/F diver
mergulhar [mergu'ʎar] VI to dive; (*penetrar*) to plunge ▶ VT: **~ algo em algo** (*num líquido*) to dip sth into sth; (*na terra etc*) to plunge sth into sth; **mergulho** [mer'guʎu] M dip(ping), immersion; (*em natação*) dive; **dar um mergulho** (*na praia*) to go for a dip
mérito ['mɛritu] M merit
mero, -a ['mɛru, a] ADJ mere
mês [mes] M month
mesa ['meza] F table; (*de trabalho*) desk; (*comitê*) board; (*numa reunião*) panel; **pôr/tirar a ~** to lay/clear the table; **à ~** at the table; **~ de cabeceira** bedside table; **~ de toalete** dressing table; **~ telefônica** switchboard
mesada [me'zada] F monthly allowance; (*de criança*) pocket money
mesmo, -a ['mezmu, a] ADJ same; (*enfático*) very ▶ ADV (*exatamente*) right; (*até*) even; (*realmente*) really ▶ M/F: **o ~/a mesma** the same (one); **o ~** (*a mesma coisa*) the same (thing); **este ~ homem** this very man; **ele ~ o fez** he did it himself; **dá no ~** *ou* **na mesma** it's all the same; **aqui/agora/hoje ~** right here/right now/this very day; **~ que** even if; **é ~** it's true; **é ~?** really?; **(é) isso ~!** exactly!; **por isso ~** that's why; **nem ~** not even; **só ~** only; **por si ~** by oneself
mesquinho, -a [mes'kiɲu, a] ADJ mean
mesquita [mes'kita] F mosque
mestre, -a ['mɛstri, a] ADJ (*chave, viga*) master; (*linha, estrada*) main ▶ M/F master/mistress; (*professor*) teacher; **obra mestra** masterpiece
meta ['mɛta] F (*em corrida*) finishing post; (*gol*) goal; (*objetivo*) aim
metade [me'tadʒi] F half; (*meio*) middle
metáfora [me'tafora] F metaphor
metal [me'taw] (*pl* **-ais**) M metal; **metais** MPL (*Mús*) brass *sg*; **metálico, -a** [me'taliku, a] ADJ metallic; (*de metal*) metal *atr*
meteorologia [meteorolo'ʒia] F meteorology; **meteorologista** [meteorolo'ʒista] M/F meteorologist; (*TV, Rádio*) weather forecaster
meter [me'ter] VT (*colocar*) to put; (*envolver*) to involve; (*introduzir*) to introduce; **meter-se** VR (*esconder-se*) to hide; **~-se a fazer algo** to decide to have a go at sth; **~-se com** (*provocar*) to pick a quarrel with; (*associar-se*) to get involved with; **~-se em** to get involved in; (*intrometer-se*) to interfere in
meticuloso, -a [metʃiku'lozu, ɔza] ADJ meticulous
metido, -a [me'tʃidu, a] ADJ (*envolvido*) involved; (*intrometido*) meddling; **~ (a besta)** snobbish
metódico, -a [me'tɔdʒiku, a] ADJ methodical
método ['mɛtodu] M method
metralhadora [metraʎa'dora] F machine gun
métrico, -a ['mɛtriku, a] ADJ metric
metro ['mɛtru] M metre (BRIT), meter (US); (PT: *metropolitano*)

underground (BRIT), subway (US)
metrô [me'tro] (BR) M underground (BRIT), subway (US)
metrópole [me'trɔpoli] F metropolis; (*capital*) capital
meu, minha [mew, 'miɲa] ADJ my ▶ PRON mine; **os meus** MPL (*minha família*) my family *ou* folks (*col*); **um amigo ~** a friend of mine
mexer [me'ʃer] VT to move; (*cabeça: dizendo sim*) to nod; (*: dizendo não*) to shake; (*misturar*) to stir; (*ovos*) to scramble ▶ VI to move; **mexer-se** VR to move; (*apressar-se*) to get a move on; **~ em algo** to touch sth; **mexa-se!** get going!, move yourself!
mexerico [meʃe'riku] M piece of gossip; **mexericos** MPL (*fofocas*) gossip *sg*
México ['mɛʃiku] M: **o ~** Mexico
mexido, -a [me'ʃidu, a] ADJ (*papéis*) mixed up; (*ovos*) scrambled
mexilhão [meʃi'ʎãw] (*pl* **-ões**) M mussel
mi [mi] M (*Mús*) E
miau [mjaw] M miaow
micro... [mikru] PREFIXO micro...; **microblog, microblogue** [mikro'blɔgi] M microblog; **microfone** [mikro'fɔni] M microphone; **micro-ondas** [mikro'õdas] M INV microwave; **microprocessador** [mikroprosesa'dor] M microprocessor; **microscópio** [mikro'skɔpju] M microscope
mídia ['midʒja] F media *pl*; **~s sociais** social media *pl*
migalha [mi'gaʎa] F crumb; **migalhas** FPL (*restos, sobras*) scraps
migrar [mi'grar] VI to migrate
mijar [mi'ʒar] (*col*) VI to pee; **mijar-se** VR to wet o.s.
mil [miw] NUM thousand; **dois ~** two thousand
milagre [mi'lagri] M miracle; **por ~** miraculously; **milagroso, -a** [mila'grozu, ɔza] ADJ miraculous
milhão [mi'ʎãw] (*pl* **-ões**) M million; **um ~ de vezes** hundreds of times
milhar [mi'ʎar] M thousand; **turistas aos ~es** tourists in their thousands
milho ['miʎu] M maize (BRIT), corn (US)
milhões [miʎ'õjs] MPL *de* **milhão**
miligrama [mili'grama] M milligram(me)
milionário, -a [miljo'narju, a] M/F millionaire
milionésimo, -a [miljo'nɛzimu, a] NUM millionth
militar [mili'tar] ADJ military ▶ M soldier ▶ VI to fight; **~ em** (*Mil: regimento*) to serve in; (*Pol: partido*) to belong to, be active in; (*profissão*) to work in
mim [mĩ] PRON me; (*reflexivo*) myself; **de ~ para ~** to myself
mímica ['mimika] F mime
mimo ['mimu] M gift; (*pessoa, coisa encantadora*) delight; (*carinho*) tenderness; (*gentileza*) kindness; **cheio de ~s** (*criança*) spoiled, spoilt (BRIT); **mimoso, -a** [mi'mozu, ɔza] ADJ (*delicado*) delicate; (*carinhoso*) tender, loving; (*encantador*) delightful
mina ['mina] F mine
mindinho [mĩ'dʒiɲu] M (*tb*: **dedo ~**) little finger
mineiro, -a [mi'nejru, a] ADJ mining *atr* ▶ M/F miner
mineral [mine'raw] (*pl* **-ais**) ADJ, M mineral
minério [mi'nɛrju] M ore

míngua ['mĩgwa] F lack; **à ~ de** for want of; **viver à ~** to live in poverty;
minguado, -a [mĩ'gwadu, a] ADJ scant; (*criança*) stunted; **minguado de algo** short of sth
minguar [mĩ'gwar] VI (*diminuir*) to decrease, dwindle; (*faltar*) to run short
minha ['miɲa] F *de* **meu**
minhoca [mi'ɲɔka] F (earth)worm
mini... [mini] PREFIXO mini...
miniatura [minja'tura] ADJ, F miniature
mínima ['minima] F (*temperatura*) low; (*Mús*) minim
mínimo, -a ['minimu, a] ADJ minimum ▶ M minimum; (*tb*: **dedo ~**) little finger; **não dou** *ou* **ligo a mínima para isso** I couldn't care less about it; **a mínima importância/ideia** the slightest importance/idea; **no ~** at least
minissaia [mini'saja] F miniskirt
ministério [minis'tɛrju] M ministry; **M~ da Fazenda** ≈ Treasury (BRIT), ≈ Treasury Department (US); **M~ das Relações Exteriores** ≈ Foreign Office (BRIT), ≈ State Department (US)
ministro, -a [mi'nistru, a] M/F minister
minoria [mino'ria] F minority
minto ['mĩtu] VB *ver* **mentir**
minucioso, -a [minu'sjozu, ɔza] ADJ (*indivíduo, busca*) thorough; (*explicação*) detailed
minúsculo, -a [mi'nuskulu, a] ADJ minute, tiny; **letra minúscula** lower case letter
minuta [mi'nuta] F draft
minuto [mi'nutu] M minute
miolo ['mjolu] M inside; (*polpa*) pulp; (*de maçã*) core; **miolos** MPL (*cérebro, inteligência*) brains
míope ['miopi] ADJ short-sighted
mira ['mira] F (*de fuzil*) sight; (*pontaria*) aim; (*fig*) aim, purpose; **à ~ de** on the lookout for; **ter em ~** to have one's eye on
miragem [mi'raʒẽ] (*pl* **-ns**) F mirage
miserável [mize'ravew] (*pl* **-eis**) ADJ (*digno de compaixão*) wretched; (*pobre*) impoverished; (*avaro*) stingy, mean; (*insignificante*) paltry; (*lugar*) squalid; (*infame*) despicable ▶ M wretch; (*coitado*) poor thing; (*pessoa infame*) rotter
miséria [mi'zɛrja] F misery; (*pobreza*) poverty; (*avareza*) stinginess
misericórdia [mizeri'kɔrdʒja] F (*compaixão*) pity, compassion; (*graça*) mercy
missa ['misa] F (*Rel*) mass
missão [mi'sãw] (*pl* **-ões**) F mission; (*dever*) duty
míssil ['misiw] (*pl* **-eis**) M missile
missionário, -a [misjo'narju, a] M/F missionary
missões [mi'sõjs] FPL *de* **missão**
mistério [mis'tɛrju] M mystery;
misterioso, -a [miste'rjozu, ɔza] ADJ mysterious
mistificar [mistʃifi'kar] VT, VI to fool
misto, -a ['mistu, a] ADJ mixed; (*confuso*) mixed up ▶ M mixture;
misto-quente (*pl* **mistos-quentes**) M toasted cheese and ham sandwich
mistura [mis'tura] F mixture; (*ato*) mixing; **misturar** [mistu'rar] VT to mix; (*confundir*) to mix up;
misturar-se VR: **misturar-se com** to mingle with
mito ['mitu] M myth

miudezas [mju'dezas] FPL minutiae; (*bugigangas*) odds and ends; (*objetos pequenos*) trinkets
miúdo, -a ['mjudu, a] ADJ tiny, minute ▶ M/F (PT: *criança*) youngster, kid; **miúdos** MPL (*dinheiro*) change *sg*; (*de aves*) giblets; **dinheiro ~** small change
mm ABR (= *milímetro*) mm
mo [mu] PRON = **me + o**
moa ['moa] VB *ver* **moer**
móbil ['mɔbiw] (*pl* **-eis**) ADJ = **móvel**
móbile ['mɔbili] M mobile
mobília [mo'bilja] F furniture; **mobiliar** [mobi'ljar] (BR) VT to furnish; **mobiliário** [mobi'ljarju] M furnishings *pl*
moça ['mosa] F girl, young woman
Moçambique [mosã'biki] M Mozambique
moção [mo'sãw] (*pl* **-ões**) F motion
mochila [mo'ʃila] F rucksack
mochilão [moʃi'lãw] M backpacking trip
mocidade [mosi'dadʒi] F youth; (*os moços*) young people *pl*
moço, -a ['mosu, a] ADJ young ▶ M young man, lad
moções [mo'sõjs] FPL *de* **moção**
moda ['mɔda] F fashion; **estar na ~** to be in fashion, be all the rage; **fora da ~** old-fashioned; **sair da** *ou* **cair de ~** to go out of fashion
modalidade [modali'dadʒi] F kind; (*Esporte*) event
modelo [mo'delu] M model; (*criação de estilista*) design; (*pessoa admirada*) role-model ▶ M/F (*manequim*) model
modem ['modẽ] (*pl* **-ns**) M modem
moderar [mode'rar] VT to moderate; (*violência*) to control, restrain; (*velocidade*) to reduce; (*voz*) to lower; (*gastos*) to cut down
modernizar [moderni'zar] VT to modernize; **modernizar-se** VR to modernize
moderno, -a [mo'dɛrnu, a] ADJ modern; (*atual*) present-day
modéstia [mo'dɛstʃja] F modesty
módico, -a ['mɔdʒiku, a] ADJ moderate; (*preço*) reasonable; (*bens*) scant
modificar [modʒifi'kar] VT to modify, alter
modista [mo'dʒista] F dressmaker
modo ['mɔdu] M (*maneira*) way, manner; (*método*) way; (*Mús*) mode; **modos** MPL (*comportamento*) manners; **de (tal) ~ que** so (that); **de ~ nenhum** in no way; **de qualquer ~** anyway, anyhow; **~ de emprego** instructions *pl* for use
módulo ['mɔdulu] M module
moeda ['mwɛda] F (*uma moeda*) coin; (*dinheiro*) currency; **uma ~ de 50p** a 50p piece; **~ corrente** currency; **Casa da M~** ≈ the (Royal) Mint (BRIT), ≈ the (US) Mint (US)
moedor [moe'dor] M (*de café*) grinder; (*de carne*) mincer
moer [mwer] VT (*café*) to grind; (*cana*) to crush
mofado, -a [mo'fadu, a] ADJ mouldy (BRIT), moldy (US)
mofo ['mofu] M (*Bot*) mould (BRIT), mold (US); **cheiro de ~** musty smell
mogno ['mɔgnu] M mahogany
mói [mɔj] VB *ver* **moer**
moía [mo'ia] VB *ver* **moer**
moído, -a [mo'idu, a] ADJ (*café*) ground; (*carne*) minced; (*cansado*) tired out; (*corpo*) aching

moinho ['mwiɲu] M mill; (*de café*) grinder; **~ de vento** windmill
mola ['mɔla] F (*Tec*) spring; (*fig*) motive, motivation
moldar [mow'dar] VT to mould (BRIT), mold (US); (*metal*) to cast; **molde** ['mɔwdʒi] M mould (BRIT), mold (US); (*de papel*) pattern; (*fig*) model; **molde de vestido** dress pattern
moldura [mow'dura] F (*de pintura*) frame
mole ['mɔli] ADJ soft; (*sem energia*) listless; (*carnes*) flabby; (*col: fácil*) easy; (*lento*) slow; (*preguiçoso*) sluggish ▶ ADV (*lentamente*) slowly
moleque [mo'lɛki] M (*de rua*) urchin; (*menino*) youngster; (*pessoa sem palavra*) unreliable person; (*canalha*) scoundrel ▶ ADJ (*levado*) mischievous; (*brincalhão*) funny
molestar [moles'tar] VT to upset; (*enfadar*) to annoy; (*importunar*) to bother
moléstia [mo'lɛstʃja] F illness
moleza [mo'leza] F softness; (*falta de energia*) listlessness; (*falta de força*) weakness; **ser (uma) ~** (*col*) to be easy; **na ~** without exerting oneself
molhado, -a [mo'ʎadu, a] ADJ wet, damp
molhar [mo'ʎar] VT to wet; (*de leve*) to moisten, dampen; (*mergulhar*) to dip; **molhar-se** VR to get wet
molho¹ ['mɔʎu] M (*de chaves*) bunch; (*de trigo*) sheaf
molho² ['moʎu] M (*Culin*) sauce; (*: de salada*) dressing; (*: de carne*) gravy; **pôr de ~** to soak; **estar/deixar de ~** (*roupa etc*) to be/leave to soak
momentâneo, -a [momẽ'tanju, a] ADJ momentary
momento [mo'mẽtu] M moment; (*Tec*) momentum; **a todo ~** constantly; **de um ~ para outro** suddenly; **no ~ em que** just as
Mônaco ['monaku] M Monaco
monarquia [monar'kia] F monarchy
monitor [moni'tor] M monitor
monopólio [mono'pɔlju] M monopoly; **monopolizar** [monopoli'zar] VT to monopolize
monotonia [monoto'nia] F monotony; **monótono, -a** [mo'nɔtonu, a] ADJ monotonous
monstro, -a ['mõstru, a] ADJ INV giant ▶ M (*tb fig*) monster; **monstruoso, -a** [mõ'strwozu, ɔza] ADJ monstrous; (*enorme*) gigantic, huge
montagem [mõ'taʒẽ] (*pl* **-ns**) F assembly; (*Arq*) erection; (*Cinema*) editing; (*Teatro*) production
montanha [mõ'taɲa] F mountain; **montanha-russa** F roller coaster
montante [mõ'tãtʃi] M amount, sum; **a ~** (*nadar*) upstream
montar [mõ'tar] VT (*cavalo*) to mount, get on; (*colocar em*) to put on; (*cavalgar*) to ride; (*peças*) to assemble, put together; (*loja, máquina*) to set up; (*casa*) to put up; (*peça teatral*) to put on ▶ VI to ride; **~ a** *ou* **em** (*animal*) to get on; (*cavalgar*) to ride; (*despesa*) to come to
monte ['mõtʃi] M hill; (*pilha*) heap, pile; **um ~ de** (*muitos*) a lot of, lots of; **gente aos ~s** loads of people
montra ['mõtra] (PT) F shop window
monumento [monu'mẽtu] M monument
moqueca [mo'kɛka] F *fish or seafood simmered in coconut cream and palm oil*; **~ de camarão** prawn *moqueca*

morada [mo'rada] F home, residence; (PT: *endereço*) address; **moradia** [mora'dʒia] F home, dwelling; **morador, a** [mora'dor(a)] M/F resident; (*de casa alugada*) tenant
moral [mo'raw] (*pl* **-ais**) ADJ moral ▶ F (*ética*) ethics *pl*; (*conclusão*) moral ▶ M (*de pessoa*) sense of morality; (*ânimo*) morale; **moralidade** [morali'dadʒi] F morality
morango [mo'rãgu] M strawberry
morar [mo'rar] VI to live, reside
mórbido, -a ['mɔrbidu, a] ADJ morbid
morcego [mor'segu] M (*Bio*) bat
mordaça [mor'dasa] F (*de animal*) muzzle; (*fig*) gag
morder [mor'der] VT to bite; (*corroer*) to corrode; **mordida** [mor'dʒida] F bite
mordomia [mordo'mia] F (*de executivos*) perk; (*col: regalia*) luxury, comfort
mordomo [mor'dɔmu] M butler
moreno, -a [mo'renu, a] ADJ dark(-skinned); (*de cabelos*) dark(-haired); (*de tomar sol*) brown ▶ M/F dark person
mormaço [mor'masu] M sultry weather
morno, -a ['mornu, 'mɔrna] ADJ lukewarm, tepid
morrer [mo'her] VI to die; (*luz, cor*) to fade; (*fogo*) to die down; (*Auto*) to stall
morro ['mohu] M hill; (*favela*) slum
mortadela [morta'dɛla] F salami
mortal [mor'taw] (*pl* **-ais**) ADJ mortal; (*letal, insuportável*) deadly ▶ M mortal
mortalidade [mortali'dadʒi] F mortality
morte ['mɔrtʃi] F death
mortífero, -a [mor'tʃiferu, a] ADJ deadly, lethal
morto, -a ['mortu, 'mɔrta] PP *de* **matar, morrer** ▶ ADJ dead; (*cor*) dull; (*exausto*) exhausted; (*inexpressivo*) lifeless ▶ M/F dead man/woman; **estar ~** to be dead; **ser ~** to be killed; **estar ~ de inveja** to be green with envy; **estar ~ de vontade de** to be dying to
mos [mus] PRON = **me + os**
mosca ['moska] F fly; **estar às ~s** (*bar etc*) to be deserted
Moscou [mos'kow] (BR) N Moscow
Moscovo [mos'kovu] (PT) N Moscow
mosquito [mos'kitu] M mosquito
mostarda [mos'tarda] F mustard
mosteiro [mos'tejru] M monastery; (*de monjas*) convent
mostrador [mostra'dor] M (*de relógio*) face, dial
mostrar [mos'trar] VT to show; (*mercadorias*) to display; (*provar*) to demonstrate, prove; **mostrar-se** VR to show o.s. to be; (*exibir-se*) to show off
motel [mo'tɛw] (*pl* **-éis**) M motel
motivar [motʃi'var] VT (*causar*) to cause, bring about; (*estimular*) to motivate; **motivo** [mo'tʃivu] M (*causa*): **motivo (de** *ou* **para)** cause (of), reason (for); (*fim*) motive; (*Arte, Mús*) motif; **por motivo de** because of, owing to
moto ['mɔtu] F motorbike ▶ M (*lema*) motto
motoboy [moto'bɔj] M motorcycle courier
motocicleta [motosi'kleta] F motorcycle, motorbike

m

motociclista [motosi'klista] M/F motorcyclist
motociclo [moto'siklu] (PT) M = **motocicleta**
motor, motriz [mo'tor, mo'triz] ADJ, M motor; (*de carro, avião*) engine; **força motriz** driving force; **~ de explosão** internal combustion engine; **~ diesel** diesel engine; **~ de pesquisa** (PT *Comput*) search engine
motorista [moto'rista] M/F driver
móvel ['mɔvew] (*pl* **-eis**) ADJ movable ▶ M piece of furniture; **móveis** MPL (*mobília*) furniture *sg*
mover [mo'ver] VT to move; (*cabeça*) to shake; (*mecanismo*) to drive; (*campanha*) to start (up); **mover-se** VR to move
movimentado, -a [movimẽ'tadu, a] ADJ (*rua, lugar*) busy; (*pessoa*) active; (*show, música*) up-tempo
movimentar [movimẽ'tar] VT to move; (*animar*) to liven up
movimento [movi'mẽtu] M movement; (*Tec*) motion; (*na rua*) activity, bustle; **de muito ~** busy
MST (BR) ABR M (= *Movimento dos Trabalhadores Rurais Sem Terra*) *pressure group for land reform*
muamba ['mwãba] (*col*) F (*contrabando*) contraband; (*objetos roubados*) loot
muçulmano, -a [musuw'manu, a] ADJ, M/F Moslem
muda ['muda] F (*planta*) seedling; (*vestuário*) outfit; **~ de roupa** change of clothes
mudança [mu'dãsa] F change; (*de casa*) move; (*Auto*) gear; **~s climáticas** climate change
mudar [mu'dar] VT to change; (*deslocar*) to move ▶ VI to change; (*ave*) to moult (BRIT), molt (US); **mudar-se** VR (*de casa*) to move (away); **~ de roupa/de assunto** to change clothes/the subject; **~ de casa** to move (house); **~ de ideia** to change one's mind
mudo, -a ['mudu, a] ADJ dumb; (*calado, filme*) silent; (*telefone*) dead ▶ M/F mute

PALAVRA-CHAVE

muito, -a ['mwĩtu, a] ADJ (*quantidade*) a lot of; (*em frase negativa ou interrogativa*) much; (*número*) lots of, a lot of, many; **muito esforço** a lot of effort; **faz muito calor** it's very hot; **muito tempo** a long time; **muitas amigas** lots *ou* a lot of friends; **muitas vezes** often
▶ PRON a lot; (*em frase negativa ou interrogativa: sg*) much; (*: pl*) many; **tenho muito que fazer** I've got a lot to do; **muitos dizem que ...** a lot of people say that ...
▶ ADV **1** a lot; (*+ adj*) very; (*+ compar*): **muito melhor** much *ou* far *ou* a lot better; **gosto muito disto** I like it a lot; **sinto muito** I'm very sorry; **muito interessante** very interesting
2 (*resposta*) very; **está cansado? — muito** are you tired? — very
3 (*tempo*): **muito depois** long after; **há muito** a long time ago; **não demorou muito** it didn't take long

mula ['mula] F mule
mulato, -a [mu'latu, a] ADJ, M/F mulatto
muleta [mu'leta] F crutch; (*fig*) support
mulher [mu'ʎer] F woman; (*esposa*) wife; **mulher-bomba** (*pl* **mulheres-bomba**) F suicide bomber
multa ['muwta] F fine; **levar uma**

~ to be fined; **multar** [muw'tar] VT to fine; **multar alguém em $1000** to fine sb $1000
multi... [muwtʃi] PREFIXO multi...
multidão [muwtʃi'dãw] (*pl* **-ões**) F crowd; **uma ~ de** (*muitos*) lots of
multimídia [muwtʃi'midʒja] ADJ multimedia
multinacional [muwtʃinasjo'naw] (*pl* **-ais**) ADJ, F multinational
multiplicar [muwtʃipli'kar] VT to multiply; (*aumentar*) to increase
múltiplo, -a ['muwtʃiplu, a] ADJ, M multiple
múmia ['mumja] F mummy
mundial [mũ'dʒjaw] (*pl* **-ais**) ADJ worldwide; (*guerra, recorde*) world *atr* ▶ M world championship
mundo ['mũdu] M world; **todo o ~** everybody; **um ~ de** lots of, a great many
munição [muni'sãw] (*pl* **-ões**) F (*de armas*) ammunition; (*chumbo*) shot; (*Mil*) munitions *pl*, supplies *pl*
municipal [munisi'paw] (*pl* **-ais**) ADJ municipal
município [muni'sipju] M local authority; (*cidade*) town; (*condado*) county
munições [muni'sõjs] FPL *de* **munição**
munir [mu'nir] VT: **~ de** to provide with, supply with; **munir-se** VR: **~-se de** (*provisões*) to equip o.s. with
muralha [mu'raʎa] F (*de fortaleza*) rampart; (*muro*) wall
murchar [mur'ʃar] VT (*Bot*) to wither; (*sentimentos*) to dull; (*pessoa*) to sadden ▶ VI to wither, wilt; (*fig*) to fade
murmurar [murmu'rar] VI to murmur, whisper; (*queixar-se*) to mutter, grumble; (*água*) to ripple; (*folhagem*) to rustle ▶ VT to murmur; **murmúrio** [mur'murju] M murmuring, whispering; (*queixa*) grumbling; (*de água*) rippling; (*de folhagem*) rustling
muro ['muru] M wall
murro ['muhu] M punch; **dar um ~ em alguém** to punch sb
musa ['muza] F muse
musculação [muskula'sãw] F weight training
músculo ['muskulu] M muscle; **musculoso, -a** [musku'lozu, ɔza] ADJ muscular
museu [mu'zew] M museum; (*de pintura*) gallery
musgo ['muzgu] M moss
música ['muzika] F music; (*canção*) song; *ver tb* **músico**;
músico, -a ['muziku, a] ADJ musical ▶ M/F musician
mútuo, -a ['mutwu, a] ADJ mutual

m

n

N ABR (= *norte*) N
na [na] = **em + a**
-na [na] PRON her; (*coisa*) it
nabo ['nabu] M turnip
nação [na'sãw] (*pl* **-ões**) F nation
nacional [nasjo'naw] (*pl* **-ais**) ADJ national; (*carro, vinho etc*) domestic, home-produced; **nacionalidade** [nasjonali'dadʒi] F nationality; **nacionalismo** [nasjona'lizmu] M nationalism; **nacionalista** [nasjona'lista] ADJ, M/F nationalist
nações [na'sõjs] FPL *de* **nação**
nada ['nada] PRON nothing ▶ ADV at all; **antes de mais ~** first of all; **não é ~ difícil** it's not at all hard, it's not hard at all; **~ mais** nothing else; **~ de novo** nothing new; **obrigado — de ~** thank you — not at all *ou* don't mention it
nadador, a [nada'dor(a)] M/F swimmer
nadar [na'dar] VI to swim
nádegas ['nadegas] FPL buttocks
nado ['nadu] M: **atravessar a ~** to swim across; **~ borboleta** butterfly (stroke); **~ de costas** backstroke; **~ de peito** breaststroke
naipe ['najpi] M (*cartas*) suit
namorado, -a [namo'radu, a] M/F boyfriend/girlfriend
namorar [namo'rar] VT (*ser namorado de*) to be going out with
namoro [na'moru] M relationship
não [nãw] ADV not; (*resposta*) no ▶ M no; **~ sei** I don't know; **~ muito** not much; **~ só ... mas também** not only ... but also; **agora ~** not now; **~ tem de quê** don't mention it; **~ é?** isn't it?, won't you?; **eles são brasileiros, ~ é?** they're Brazilian, aren't they?
não... [nãw] PREFIXO non-
naquele(s), naquela(s) [na'keli(s), na'kɛla(s)] = **em + aquele(s), aquela(s)**
naquilo [na'kilu] = **em + aquilo**
narina [na'rina] F nostril
nariz [na'riz] M nose
narração [naha'sãw] (*pl* **-ões**) F narration; (*relato*) account
narrar [na'har] VT to narrate
narrativa [naha'tʃiva] F narrative; (*história*) story
nas [nas] = **em + as**
-nas [nas] PRON them
nascença [na'sẽsa] F birth; **de ~** by birth; **ele é surdo de ~** he was born deaf
nascente [na'sẽtʃi] M East, Orient ▶ F (*fonte*) spring
nascer [na'ser] VI to be born; (*plantas*) to sprout; (*o sol*) to rise; (*ave*) to hatch; (*fig: ter origem*) to come into being ▶ M: **~ do sol** sunrise; **ele nasceu para médico** *etc* he was born to be a doctor *etc*;
nascimento [nasi'mẽtu] M birth; (*fig*) origin; (*estirpe*) descent

nata ['nata] F cream
natação [nata'sãw] F swimming
natais [na'tajs] ADJ PL *de* **natal**
Natal [na'taw] M Christmas; **Feliz ~!** Merry Christmas!
natal [na'taw] (*pl* **-ais**) ADJ (*relativo ao nascimento*) natal; (*país*) native; **cidade ~** home town
natalino, -a [nata'linu, a] ADJ Christmas *atr*
nativo, -a [na'tʃivu, a] ADJ, M/F native
natural [natu'raw] (*pl* **-ais**) ADJ natural; (*nativo*) native ▶ M/F native; **ao ~** (*Culin*) fresh, uncooked; **naturalidade** [naturali'dadʒi] F naturalness; **de naturalidade paulista** *etc* born in São Paulo *etc*; **naturalizar** [naturali'zar] VT to naturalize; **naturalizar-se** VR to become naturalized; **naturalmente** [naturaw'mẽtʃi] ADV naturally; **naturalmente!** of course!
natureza [natu'reza] F nature; (*espécie*) kind, type
nau [naw] F (*literário*) ship
náusea ['nawzea] F nausea; **dar ~s a alguém** to make sb feel sick; **sentir ~s** to feel sick
náutico, -a ['nawtʃiku, a] ADJ nautical
naval [na'vaw] (*pl* **-ais**) ADJ naval; **construção ~** shipbuilding
navalha [na'vaʎa] F (*de barba*) razor; (*faca*) knife
nave ['navi] F (*de igreja*) nave
navegação [navega'sãw] F navigation, sailing; **~ aérea** air traffic; **companhia de ~** shipping line
navegar [nave'gar] VT to navigate; (*mares*) to sail ▶ VI to sail; (*dirigir o rumo*) to navigate
navio [na'viu] M ship; **~ cargueiro** cargo ship, freighter; **~ de guerra** warship; **~ petroleiro** oil tanker
nazi [na'zi] (PT) ADJ, M/F = **nazista**
nazista [na'zista] (BR) ADJ, M/F Nazi
NB ABR (= *note bem*) NB
neblina [ne'blina] F fog, mist
nebuloso, -a [nebu'lozu, ɔza] ADJ foggy, misty; (*céu*) cloudy; (*fig*) vague
necessário, -a [nese'sarju, a] ADJ necessary ▶ M: **o ~** the necessities *pl*
necessidade [nesesi'dadʒi] F need, necessity; (*o que se necessita*) need; (*pobreza*) poverty, need; **ter ~ de** to need; **em caso de ~** if need be
necessitado, -a [nesesi'tadu, a] ADJ needy, poor; **~ de** in need of
necessitar [nesesi'tar] VT to need, require ▶ VI: **~ de** to need
neerlandês, -esa [neerlã'des, eza] ADJ Dutch ▶ M/F Dutchman/woman
Neerlândia [neer'lãdʒa] F the Netherlands *pl*
negar [ne'gar] VT to deny; (*recusar*) to refuse; **negar-se** VR: **~-se a** to refuse to
negativa [nega'tʃiva] F (*Ling*) negative; (*recusa*) denial
negativo, -a [nega'tʃivu, a] ADJ negative ▶ M (*Tec, Foto*) negative ▶ EXCL (*col*) nope!
negligência [negli'ʒẽsja] F negligence, carelessness; **negligente** [negli'ʒẽtʃi] ADJ negligent, careless
negociação [negosja'sãw] (*pl* **-ões**) F negotiation
negociante [nego'sjãtʃi] M/F businessman/woman

negociar [nego'sjar] VT to negotiate; (*Com*) to trade ▶ VI: **~ (com)** to trade *ou* deal (in); to negotiate (with)

negócio [ne'gɔsju] M (*Com*) business; (*transação*) deal; (*questão*) matter; (*col: troço*) thing; (*assunto*) affair, business; **homem de ~s** businessman; **a ~s** on business; **fechar um ~** to make a deal

negro, -a ['negru, a] ADJ black; (*raça*) Black; (*fig: lúgubre*) black, gloomy ▶ M/F Black man/woman

nele(s), nela(s) ['neli(s), 'nɛla(s)] = **em + ele(s), ela(s)**

nem [nẽj] CONJ nor, neither; **~ (sequer)** not even; **~ que** even if; **~ bem** hardly; **~ um só** not a single one; **~ estuda ~ trabalha** he neither studies nor works; **~ eu** nor me; **sem ~** without even; **~ todos** not all; **~ tanto** not so much; **~ sempre** not always

nenê [ne'ne] M/F baby

neném [ne'nẽj] (*pl* **-ns**) M/F = **nenê**

nenhum, a [ne'ɲũ, 'ɲuma] ADJ no, not any ▶ PRON (*nem um só*) none, not one; (*de dois*) neither; **~ lugar** nowhere

nervo ['nervu] M (*Anat*) nerve; (*fig*) energy, strength; (*em carne*) sinew; **nervosismo** [nervo'zizmu] M (*nervosidade*) nervousness; (*irritabilidade*) irritability; **nervoso, -a** [ner'vozu, ɔza] ADJ nervous; (*irritável*) touchy, on edge; (*exaltado*) worked up; **isso/ele me deixa nervoso** he gets on my nerves

nesse(s), nessa(s) ['nesi(s), 'nɛsa(s)] = **em + esse(s), essa(s)**

neste(s), nesta(s) ['nestʃi(s), 'nɛsta(s)] = **em + este(s), esta(s)**

neto, -a ['nɛtu, a] M/F grandson/ daughter; **netos** MPL grandchildren

neurose [new'rɔzi] F neurosis; **neurótico, -a** [new'rɔtʃiku, a] ADJ, M/F neurotic

neutro, -a ['newtru, a] ADJ (*Ling*) neuter; (*imparcial*) neutral

nevar [ne'var] VI to snow; **nevasca** [ne'vaska] F snowstorm; **neve** ['nɛvi] F snow

névoa ['nɛvoa] F fog; **nevoeiro** [nevo'ejru] M thick fog

nexo ['nɛksu] M connection, link; **sem ~** disconnected, incoherent

Nicarágua [nika'ragwa] F: **a ~** Nicaragua

nicotina [niko'tʃina] F nicotine

Nigéria [ni'ʒɛrja] F: **a ~** Nigeria

Nilo ['nilu] M: **o ~** the Nile

ninguém [nĩ'gẽj] PRON nobody, no-one

ninho ['niɲu] M nest; (*toca*) lair; (*lar*) home

nisso ['nisu] = **em + isso**

nisto ['nistu] = **em + isto**

nitidez [nitʃi'dez] F (*clareza*) clarity; (*brilho*) brightness; (*imagem*) sharpness

nítido, -a ['nitʃidu, a] ADJ clear, distinct; (*brilhante*) bright; (*imagem*) sharp, clear

nível ['nivew] (*pl* **-eis**) M level; (*fig: padrão*) standard; (*: ponto*) point, pitch; **~ de vida** standard of living

nº ABR (= *número*) no.

no [nu] = **em + o**

nó [nɔ] M knot; (*de uma questão*) crux; **nós dos dedos** knuckles; **dar um nó** to tie a knot

-no [nu] PRON him; (*coisa*) it

nobre ['nɔbri] ADJ, M/F noble; **horário ~** prime time; **nobreza** [no'breza] F nobility

noção [no'sãw] (*pl* **-ões**) F notion; **noções** FPL (*rudimentos*) rudiments, basics; **~ vaga** inkling; **não ter a**

menor ~ de algo not to have the slightest idea about sth
nocaute [no'kawtʃi] M knockout ▶ ADV: **pôr alguém ~** to knock sb out
nocivo, -a [no'sivu, a] ADJ harmful
noções [no'sõjs] FPL *de* **noção**
nódoa ['nɔdwa] F spot; (*mancha*) stain
nogueira [no'gejra] F (*árvore*) walnut tree; (*madeira*) walnut
noite ['nojtʃi] F night; **à** *ou* **de ~** at night, in the evening; **boa ~** good evening; (*despedida*) good night; **da ~ para o dia** overnight; **tarde da ~** late at night
noivado [noj'vadu] M engagement
noivo, -a ['nojvu, a] M/F (*prometido*) fiancé/fiancée; (*no casamento*) bridegroom/bride; **os noivos** MPL (*prometidos*) the engaged couple; (*no casamento*) the bride and groom; (*recém-casados*) the newly-weds
nojento, -a [no'ʒẽtu, a] ADJ disgusting
nojo ['noʒu] M nausea; (*repulsão*) disgust, loathing; **ela é um ~** she's horrible; **este trabalho está um ~** this work is messy
no-la(s) = **nos + a(s)**
no-lo(s) = **nos + o(s)**
nome ['nɔmi] M name; (*fama*) fame; **de ~** by name; **escritor de ~** famous writer; **um restaurante de ~** a restaurant with a good reputation; **em ~ de** in the name of; **~ de batismo** Christian name
nomear [no'mjar] VT to nominate; (*conferir um cargo a*) to appoint; (*dar nome a*) to name
nono, -a ['nonu, a] NUM ninth
nora ['nɔra] F daughter-in-law
nordeste [nor'dɛstʃi] M, ADJ northeast
norma ['nɔrma] F standard, norm; (*regra*) rule; **como ~** as a rule
normal [nor'maw] (*pl* **-ais**) ADJ normal; (*habitual*) usual;
normalizar [normali'zar] VT to bring back to normal;
normalizar-se VR to return to normal
noroeste [nor'wɛstʃi] ADJ northwest, northwestern ▶ M northwest
norte ['nɔrtʃi] ADJ northern, north; (*vento, direção*) northerly ▶ M north; **norte-americano, -a** ADJ, M/F (North) American
Noruega [nor'wɛga] F Norway;
norueguês, -esa [norwe'ges, geza] ADJ, M/F Norwegian ▶ M (*Ling*) Norwegian
nos¹ [nus] = **em + os**
nos² [nus] PRON (*direto*) us; (*indireto*) us, to us, for us; (*reflexivo*) (to) ourselves; (*recíproco*) (to) each other
nós [nɔs] PRON we; (*depois de prep*) us; **~ mesmos** we ourselves
-nos [nus] PRON them
nosso, -a ['nɔsu, a] ADJ our ▶ PRON ours; **um amigo ~** a friend of ours; **Nossa Senhora** (*Rel*) Our Lady
nostalgia [nostaw'ʒia] F nostalgia; **nostálgico, -a** [nos'tawʒiku, a] ADJ nostalgic
nota ['nɔta] F note; (*Educ*) mark; (*conta*) bill; (*cédula*) banknote; **~ de venda** sales receipt; **~ fiscal** receipt
notar [no'tar] VT to notice, note; **notar-se** VR to be obvious; **fazer ~** to call attention to; **notável** [no'tavew] (*pl* **-eis**) ADJ notable, remarkable

n

notícia [no'tʃisja] F *(uma notícia)* piece of news; *(TV etc)* news item; **notícias** FPL *(informações)* news *sg*; **pedir ~s de** to inquire about; **ter ~s de** to hear from; **noticiário** [notʃi'sjarju] M *(de jornal)* news section; *(Cinema)* newsreel; *(TV, Rádio)* news bulletin
notório, -a [no'tɔrju, a] ADJ well-known
noturno, -a [no'turnu, a] ADJ nocturnal, nightly; *(trabalho)* night *atr* ▶ M *(trem)* night train
nova ['nɔva] F piece of news; **novas** FPL *(novidades)* news *sg*
novamente [nova'mẽtʃi] ADV again
novato, -a [no'vatu, a] ADJ inexperienced, raw ▶ M/F beginner, novice; *(Educ)* fresher
nove ['nɔvi] NUM nine
novela [no'vɛla] F short novel, novella; *(Rádio, TV)* soap opera
novelo [no'velu] M ball of thread
novembro [no'vẽbru] M November
noventa [no'vẽta] NUM ninety
novidade [novi'dadʒi] F novelty; *(notícia)* piece of news; **novidades** FPL *(notícias)* news *sg*
novilho, -a [no'viʎu, a] M/F young bull/heifer
novo, -a ['novu, 'nɔva] ADJ new; *(jovem)* young; *(adicional)* further; **de ~** again
noz [nɔz] F nut; *(da nogueira)* walnut; **~ moscada** nutmeg
nu, a [nu, 'nua] ADJ naked; *(braço, arvore, sala, parede)* bare ▶ M nude
nublado, -a [nu'bladu, a] ADJ cloudy, overcast
nuclear [nu'kljar] ADJ nuclear
núcleo ['nuklju] M nucleus *sg*; *(centro)* centre (BRIT), center (US)
nudez [nu'dez] F nakedness, nudity; *(de paredes etc)* bareness
nudista [nu'dʒista] ADJ, M/F nudist
nulo, -a ['nulu, a] ADJ *(Jur)* null, void; *(nenhum)* non-existent; *(sem valor)* worthless; *(esforço)* vain, useless
num [nũ] = **em + um**
numa(s) ['numa(s)] = **em + uma(s)**
numeral [nume'raw] (*pl* **-ais**) M numeral
numerar [nume'rar] VT to number
numérico, -a [nu'mɛriku, a] ADJ numerical
número ['numeru] M number; *(de jornal)* issue; *(Teatro etc)* act; *(de sapatos, roupa)* size; **sem ~** countless; **~ de matrícula** registration (BRIT) *ou* license plate (US) number; **numeroso, -a** [nume'rozu, ɔza] ADJ numerous
nunca ['nũka] ADV never; **~ mais** never again; **quase ~** hardly ever; **mais que ~** more than ever
nuns [nũs] = **em + uns**
núpcias ['nupsjas] FPL nuptials, wedding *sg*
nutrição [nutri'sãw] F nutrition
nuvem ['nuvẽj] (*pl* **-ns**) F cloud; *(de insetos)* swarm

O

PALAVRA-CHAVE

o, a [u, a] ART DEF **1** the; **o livro/a mesa/os estudantes** the book/table/students
2 (*com n abstrato, não se traduz*): **o amor/a juventude** love/youth
3 (*posse, traduz-se muitas vezes por adj possessivo*): **quebrar o braço** to break one's arm; **ele levantou a mão** he put his hand up; **ela colocou o chapéu** she put her hat on
4 (*valor descritivo*): **ter a boca grande/os olhos azuis** to have a big mouth/blue eyes
▶ PRON DEMOSTRATIVO: **meu livro e o seu** my book and yours; **as de Pedro são melhores** Pedro's are better; **não a(s) branca(s) mas a(s) verde(s)** not the white one(s) but the green one(s); **o que** (*etc*)
▶ PRON RELATIVO **1** (*indef*): **os que quiserem podem sair** anyone who wants to can leave; **leve o que mais gostar** take the one you like best
2 (*def*): **o que comprei ontem** the one I bought yesterday; **os que saíram** those who left
3: **o que** what; **o que eu acho/mais gosto** what I think/like most
▶ PRON PESSOAL **1** (*pessoa: m*) him; (*: f*) her; (*: pl*) them; **não consigo vê-lo(s)** I can't see him/them; **vemo-la todas as semanas** we see her every week
2 (*animal, coisa: sg*) it; (*: pl*) them; **não consigo vê-lo(s)** I can't see it/them; **acharam-nos na praia** they found them on the beach

obedecer [obede'ser] VI: **~ a** to obey; **obediência** [obe'dʒẽsja] F obedience; **obediente** [obe'dʒẽtʃi] ADJ obedient
óbito ['ɔbitu] M death; **atestado de ~** death certificate
objeção [obʒe'sãw] (*pl* **-ões**) F objection; **fazer** *ou* **pôr objeções a** to object to
objetivo, -a [obʒe'tʃivu, a] ADJ objective ▶ M objective
objeto [ob'ʒɛtu] M object
obra ['ɔbra] F work; (*Arq*) building, construction; (*Teatro*) play; **em ~s** under repair; **ser ~ de alguém** to be the work of sb; **~ de arte** work of art; **~s públicas** public works; **obra-prima** (*pl* **obras-primas**) F masterpiece
obrigação [obriga'sãw] (*pl* **-ões**) F obligation; (*Com*) bond
obrigado, -a [obri'gadu, a] ADJ obliged, compelled ▶ EXCL thank you; (*recusa*) no, thank you
obrigar [obri'gar] VT to oblige, compel; **obrigar-se** VR: **~-se a**

fazer algo to undertake to do sth; **obrigatório, -a** [obriga'tɔrju, a] ADJ compulsory, obligatory

obsceno, -a [obi'sɛnu, a] ADJ obscene

obscurecer [obiskure'ser] VT to darken; (*entendimento, verdade etc*) to obscure ▶ VI to get dark

obscuro, -a [obi'skuru, a] ADJ dark; (*fig*) obscure

observação [obiserva'sãw] (*pl* **-ões**) F observation; (*comentário*) remark, comment; (*de leis, regras*) observance

observador, a [obiserva'dor(a)] M/F observer

observar [obiser'var] VT to observe; (*notar*) to notice; **~ algo a alguém** to point sth out to sb

observatório [observa'tɔrju] M observatory

obsessão [obise'sãw] (*pl* **-ões**) F obsession; **obsessivo, -a** [obise'sivu, a] ADJ obsessive

obsoleto, -a [obiso'lɛtu, a] ADJ obsolete

obstinado, -a [obistʃi'nadu, a] ADJ obstinate, stubborn

obstrução [obistru'sãw] (*pl* **-ões**) F obstruction; **obstruir** [obi'strwir] VT to obstruct; (*impedir*) to impede

obter [obi'ter] (*irreg: como* **ter**) VT to obtain, get; (*alcançar*) to gain

obturação [obitura'sãw] (*pl* **-ões**) F (*de dente*) filling

obtuso, -a [obi'tuzu, a] ADJ (*ger*) obtuse; (*fig: pessoa*) thick

óbvio, -a ['ɔbvju, a] ADJ obvious; **(é) ~!** of course!

ocasião [oka'zjãw] (*pl* **-ões**) F opportunity, chance; (*momento, tempo*) occasion; **ocasionar** [okazjo'nar] VT to cause, bring about

oceano [o'sjanu] M ocean

ocidental [osidẽ'taw] (*pl* **-ais**) ADJ western ▶ M/F westerner

ocidente [osi'dẽtʃi] M west

ócio ['ɔsju] M (*lazer*) leisure; (*inação*) idleness; **ocioso, -a** [o'sjozu, ɔza] ADJ idle; (*vaga*) unfilled

oco, -a ['oku, a] ADJ hollow, empty

ocorrência [oko'hẽsja] F incident, event; (*circunstância*) circumstance

ocorrer [oko'her] VI to happen, occur; (*vir ao pensamento*) to come to mind; **~ a alguém** to happen to sb; (*vir ao pensamento*) to occur to sb

octogésimo, -a [okto'ʒɛzimu, a] NUM eightieth

oculista [oku'lista] M/F optician

óculo ['ɔkulu] M spyglass; **óculos** MPL glasses, spectacles; **~s de proteção** goggles

ocultar [okuw'tar] VT to hide, conceal; **oculto, -a** [o'kuwtu, a] ADJ hidden; (*desconhecido*) unknown; (*secreto*) secret; (*sobrenatural*) occult

ocupação [okupa'sãw] (*pl* **-ões**) F occupation

ocupado, -a [oku'padu, a] ADJ (*pessoa*) busy; (*lugar*) taken, occupied; (BR: *telefone*) engaged (BRIT), busy (US); **sinal de ~** (BR *Tel*) engaged tone (BRIT), busy signal (US)

ocupar [oku'par] VT to occupy; (*tempo*) to take up; (*pessoa*) to keep busy; **ocupar-se** VR: **~-se com** *ou* **de** *ou* **em algo** (*cuidar de*) to look after sth; (*passar seu tempo com*) to occupy o.s. with sth

odiar [o'dʒjar] VT to hate; **ódio** ['ɔdʒju] M hate, hatred; **odioso, -a** [o'dʒjozu, ɔza] ADJ hateful

odor [o'dor] M smell

oeste ['wɛstʃi] M west ▶ ADJ INV (*região*) western; (*direção, vento*) westerly

ofegante [ofe'gãtʃi] ADJ breathless, panting
ofender [ofẽ'der] VT to offend; **ofender-se** VR to take offence (BRIT) *ou* offense (US)
ofensa [o'fẽsa] F insult; (*à lei, moral*) offence (BRIT), offense (US); **ofensiva** [ofẽ'siva] F offensive; **ofensivo, -a** [ofẽ'sivu, a] ADJ offensive
oferecer [ofere'ser] VT to offer; (*dar*) to give; (*jantar*) to give; (*propor*) to propose; (*dedicar*) to dedicate; **oferecer-se** VR (*pessoa*) to offer o.s., volunteer; (*oportunidade*) to present itself, arise; **~-se para fazer** to offer to do; **oferecimento** [oferesi'mẽtu] M offer; **oferta** [o'fɛrta] F offer; (*dádiva*) gift; (*Com*) bid; (*em loja*) special offer
oficial [ofi'sjaw] (*pl* **-ais**) ADJ official ▶ M/F official; (*Mil*) officer; **~ de justiça** bailiff
oficina [ofi'sina] F workshop; **~ mecânica** garage
ofício [o'fisju] M trade; (*Rel*) service; (*carta*) official letter; (*função*) function; (*encargo*) job, task
oitavo, -a [oj'tavu, a] NUM eighth
oitenta [oj'tẽta] NUM eighty
oito ['ojtu] NUM eight
olá [o'la] EXCL hello!
olaria [ola'ria] F (*fábrica: de louças de barro*) pottery; (*: de tijolos*) brickworks *sg*
óleo ['ɔlju] M (*lubricante*) oil; **~ de bronzear** suntan oil; **~ diesel** diesel oil; **oleoso, -a** [o'ljozu, ɔza] ADJ oily; (*gorduroso*) greasy
olfato [ow'fatu] M sense of smell
olhada [o'ʎada] F glance, look; **dar uma ~** to have a look
olhadela [oʎa'dɛla] F peep
olhar [o'ʎar] VT to look at; (*observar*) to watch; (*ponderar*) to consider; (*cuidar de*) to look after ▶ VI to look ▶ M look; **olhar-se** VR to look at o.s.; (*duas pessoas*) to look at each other; **~ fixamente** to stare at; **~ para** to look at; **~ por** to look after; **~ fixo** stare
olho ['oʎu] M (*Anat, de agulha*) eye; (*vista*) eyesight; **~ nele!** watch him!; **~ vivo!** keep your eyes open!; **a ~** (*medir, calcular etc*) by eye; **~ mágico** (*na porta*) peephole; **~ roxo** black eye; **num abrir e fechar de ~s** in a flash
olimpíada [olĩ'piada] F: **as O~s** the Olympics
oliveira [oli'vejra] F olive tree
ombro ['õbru] M shoulder; **encolher os ~s, dar de ~s** to shrug one's shoulders
omelete [ome'letʃi] F omelette (BRIT), omelet (US)
omissão [omi'sãw] (*pl* **-ões**) F omission; (*negligência*) negligence
omitir [omi'tʃir] VT to omit
omoplata [omo'plata] F shoulder blade
onça ['õsa] F ounce; (*animal*) jaguar
onda ['õda] F wave; (*moda*) fashion; **~ curta/média/longa** short/medium/long wave; **~ de calor** heat wave
onde ['õdʒi] ADV where ▶ CONJ where, in which; **de ~ você é?** where are you from?; **por ~** through which; **por ~?** which way?; **~ quer que** wherever
ondulado, -a [õdu'ladu, a] ADJ wavy
ônibus ['onibus] (BR) M INV bus; **ponto de ~** bus stop

O

ontem ['õtẽ] ADV yesterday; **~ à noite** last night
ONU ['onu] ABR F (= *Organização das Nações Unidas*) UNO
ônus ['onus] M INV onus; (*obrigação*) obligation; (*Com*) charge; (*encargo desagradável*) burden
onze ['õzi] NUM eleven
opaco, -a [o'paku, a] ADJ opaque; (*obscuro*) dark
opção [op'sãw] (*pl* **-ões**) F option, choice; (*preferência*) first claim, right
ópera ['ɔpera] F opera
operação [opera'sãw] (*pl* **-ões**) F operation; (*Com*) transaction
operador, a [opera'dor(a)] M/F operator; (*cirurgião*) surgeon; (*num cinema*) projectionist
operar [ope'rar] VT to operate; (*produzir*) to effect, bring about; (*Med*) to operate on ▶ VI to operate; (*agir*) to act, function; **operar-se** VR (*suceder*) to take place; (*Med*) to have an operation
operário, -a [ope'rarju, a] ADJ working ▶ M/F worker; **classe operária** working class
opinar [opi'nar] VT to think ▶ VI to give one's opinion
opinião [opi'njãw] (*pl* **-ões**) F opinion; **mudar de ~** to change one's mind
oponente [opo'nẽtʃi] ADJ opposing ▶ M/F opponent
opor [o'por] (*irreg: como* **pôr**) VT to oppose; (*resistência*) to put up, offer; (*objeção, dificuldade*) to raise; **opor-se** VR: **~-se a** to object to; (*resistir*) to oppose
oportunidade [oportuni'dadʒi] F opportunity
oportunista [oportu'nista] ADJ, M/F opportunist
oportuno, -a [opor'tunu, a] ADJ (*momento*) opportune, right; (*oferta de ajuda*) well-timed; (*conveniente*) convenient, suitable
oposição [opozi'sãw] F opposition; **em ~ a** against; **fazer ~ a** to oppose
opressão [opre'sãw] (*pl* **-ões**) F oppression; **opressivo, -a** [opre'sivu, a] ADJ oppressive
oprimir [opri'mir] VT to oppress; (*comprimir*) to press
optar [op'tar] VI to choose; **~ por** to opt for; **~ por fazer** to opt to do
ora ['ɔra] ADV now ▶ CONJ well; **por ~** for the time being; **~ ..., ~ ...** one moment ..., the next ...; **~ bem** now then
oração [ora'sãw] (*pl* **-ões**) F prayer; (*discurso*) speech; (*Ling*) clause
oral [o'raw] (*pl* **-ais**) ADJ oral ▶ F oral (exam)
orar [o'rar] VI (*Rel*) to pray
órbita ['ɔrbita] F orbit; (*do olho*) socket
Órcades ['ɔrkadʒis] FPL: **as ~** the Orkneys
orçamento [orsa'mẽtu] M (*do estado etc*) budget; (*avaliação*) estimate
orçar [or'sar] VT to value, estimate ▶ VI: **~ em** (*gastos etc*) to be valued at, be put at
ordem ['ordẽ] (*pl* **-ns**) F order; **até nova ~** until further notice; **de primeira ~** first-rate; **estar em ~** to be tidy; **por ~** in order, in turn; **~ do dia** agenda; **~ pública** public order, law and order
ordenado, -a [orde'nadu, a] ADJ (*posto em ordem*) in order; (*metódico*) orderly ▶ M salary, wages *pl*
ordens ['ordẽs] FPL *de* **ordem**
ordinário, -a [ordʒi'narju, a] ADJ ordinary; (*comum*) usual; (*medíocre*)

mediocre; (*grosseiro*) coarse, vulgar; (*de má qualidade*) inferior; **de ~** usually
orelha [o'reʎa] F ear; (*aba*) flap
orelhão [ore'ʎãw] (*pl* **-ões**) M payphone
órfão, -fã ['ɔrfãw, fã] (*pl* **-s/-s**) ADJ, M/F orphan
orgânico, -a [or'ganiku, a] ADJ organic
organismo [orga'nizmu] M organism; (*entidade*) organization
organização [organiza'sãw] (*pl* **-ões**) F organization; **organizar** [organi'zar] VT to organize
órgão ['ɔrgãw] (*pl* **-s**) M organ; (*governamental etc*) institution, body
orgasmo [or'gazmu] M orgasm
orgia [or'ʒia] F orgy
orgulho [or'guʎu] M pride; **orgulhoso, -a** [orgu'ʎozu, ɔza] ADJ proud
orientação [orjẽta'sãw] F guidance; (*posição*) position; **~ educacional** training, guidance
oriental [orjẽ'taw] (*pl* **-ais**) ADJ eastern; (*do Extremo Oriente*) oriental
orientar [orjẽ'tar] VT to orientate; (*indicar o rumo*) to direct; (*aconselhar*) to guide; **orientar-se** VR to get one's bearings; **~-se por algo** to follow sth
oriente [o'rjẽtʃi] M: **o O~** the East; **Extremo O~** Far East; **O~ Médio** Middle East
origem [o'riʒẽ] (*pl* **-ns**) F origin; (*ascendência*) lineage, descent; **lugar de ~** birthplace
original [oriʒi'naw] (*pl* **-ais**) ADJ original; (*estranho*) strange, odd ▸ M original; **originalidade** [oriʒinali'dadʒi] F originality; (*excentricidade*) eccentricity
originar [oriʒi'nar] VT to give rise to, start; **originar-se** VR to arise; **~-se de** to originate from
oriundo, -a [o'rjũdu, a] ADJ: **~ de** arising from; (*natural*) native of
orla ['ɔrla] F: **~ marítima** seafront
ornamento [orna'mẽtu] M adornment, decoration
orquestra [or'kɛstra], (PT) **orquesta** F orchestra
orquídea [or'kidʒja] F orchid
ortodoxo, -a [orto'dɔksu, a] ADJ orthodox
ortografia [ortogra'fia] F spelling
orvalho [or'vaʎu] M dew
os [us] ART DEF *ver* **o**
osso ['osu] M bone
ostensivo, -a [ostẽ'sivu, a] ADJ ostensible
ostentar [ostẽ'tar] VT to show; (*alardear*) to show off, flaunt
ostra ['ostra] F oyster
OTAN ['otã] ABR F (= *Organização do Tratado do Atlântico Norte*) NATO
ótica ['ɔtʃika] F optics *sg*; (*loja*) optician's; (*fig: ponto de vista*) viewpoint; *ver tb* **ótico**
ótico, -a ['ɔtʃiku, a] ADJ optical ▸ M/F optician
otimista [otʃi'mista] ADJ optimistic ▸ M/F optimist
ótimo, -a ['ɔtʃimu, a] ADJ excellent, splendid ▸ EXCL great!, super!
ou [o] CONJ or; **ou este ou aquele** either this one or that one; **ou seja** in other words
ouço ['osu] VB *ver* **ouvir**
ouriço [o'risu] M (*europeu*) hedgehog; (*casca*) shell
ouro ['oru] M gold; **ouros** MPL (*Cartas*) diamonds
ousadia [oza'dʒia] F daring;

O

ousado, -a [o'zadu, a] ADJ daring, bold
ousar [o'zar] VT, VI to dare
outono [o'tɔnu] M autumn

PALAVRA-CHAVE

outro, -a ['otru, a] ADJ **1** (*distinto: sg*) another; (: *pl*) other; **outra coisa** something else; **de outro modo, de outra maneira** otherwise; **no outro dia** the next day; **ela está outra** (*mudada*) she's changed
2 (*adicional*): **quer outro café?** would you like another coffee?; **outra vez** again
▸ PRON **1**: **o outro** the other one; **(os) outros** (the) others; **de outro** somebody else's
2 (*recíproco*): **odeiam-se uns aos outros** they hate one another *ou* each other
3: **outro tanto** the same again; **comer outro tanto** to eat the same *ou* as much again; **ele recebeu uma dezena de telegramas e outras tantas chamadas** he got about ten telegrams and as many calls

outubro [o'tubru] M October
ouvido [o'vidu] M (*Anat*) ear; (*sentido*) hearing; **de ~** by ear; **dar ~s a** to listen to
ouvinte [o'vĩtʃi] M/F listener; (*estudante*) auditor
ouvir [o'vir] VT to hear; (*com atenção*) to listen to; (*missa*) to attend ▸ VI to hear; to listen; **~ dizer que ...** to hear that ...; **~ falar de** to hear of
ova ['ɔva] F roe
oval [o'vaw] (*pl* **-ais**) ADJ, F oval
ovário [o'varju] M ovary
ovelha [o'veʎa] F sheep
óvni ['ɔvni] M flying saucer
ovo ['ovu] M egg; **~ pochê** (BR) *ou* **escalfado** (PT) poached egg; **~ estrelado** *ou* **frito** fried egg; **~s mexidos** scrambled eggs; **~ cozido** *ou* **quente** boiled egg; **~s de granja** free-range eggs
oxidar [oksi'dar] VT to rust;
oxidar-se VR to rust, go rusty
oxigenado, -a [oksiʒe'nadu, a] ADJ (*cabelo*) bleached; **água oxigenada** peroxide
oxigênio [oksi'ʒenju] M oxygen
ozônio [o'zonju] M ozone; **camada de ~** ozone layer

P

P. ABR (= *Praça*) Sq.
pá [pa] F shovel; (*de remo, hélice*) blade ▸ M (PT) pal, mate; **pá de lixo** dustpan
paca ['paka] F (*Zool*) paca
pacato, -a [pa'katu, a] ADJ (*pessoa*) quiet; (*lugar*) peaceful
paciência [pa'sjẽsja] F patience;
paciente [pa'sjẽtʃi] ADJ, M/F patient
pacífico, -a [pa'sifiku, a] ADJ (*pessoa*) peace-loving; (*aceito sem discussão*) undisputed; (*sossegado*) peaceful; **o (Oceano) P~** the Pacific (Ocean)
pacote [pa'kɔtʃi] M packet; (*embrulho*) parcel; (*Econ, Comput, Turismo*) package
pacto ['paktu] M pact; (*ajuste*) agreement
padaria [pada'ria] F bakery, baker's (shop)
padeiro [pa'dejru] M baker
padiola [pa'dʒjɔla] F stretcher
padrão [pa'drãw] (*pl* **-ões**) M standard; (*medida*) gauge; (*desenho*) pattern; (*fig: modelo*) model; **~ de vida** standard of living
padrasto [pa'drastu] M stepfather
padre ['padri] M priest
padrinho [pa'driɲu] M godfather; (*de noivo*) best man; (*patrono*) sponsor
padroeiro, -a [pa'drwejru, a] M/F patron; (*santo*) patron saint
padrões [pa'drõjs] MPL *de* **padrão**
pães [pãjs] MPL *de* **pão**
pagador, a [paga'dor(a)] ADJ paying ▸ M/F payer; (*de salário*) pay clerk; (*de banco*) teller
pagamento [paga'mẽtu] M payment; **~ a prazo** *ou* **em prestações** payment in instal(l)ments; **~ à vista** cash payment; **~ contra entrega** (*Com*) COD, cash on delivery
pagar [pa'gar] VT to pay; (*compras, pecados*) to pay for; (*o que devia*) to pay back; (*retribuir*) to repay ▸ VI to pay; **~ por algo** (*tb fig*) to pay for sth; **~ a prestações** to pay in instal(l)ments; **~ de contado** (PT) to pay cash
página ['paʒina] F page; **~ (da) web** web page; **~ inicial** home page; **P~s Amarelas** Yellow Pages®
pago, -a ['pagu, a] PP *de* **pagar** ▸ ADJ paid; (*fig*) even ▸ M pay
pai [paj] M father; **pais** MPL parents
painel [paj'nɛw] (*pl* **-éis**) M panel; (*quadro*) picture; (*Auto*) dashboard; (*de avião*) instrument panel; **~ solar** solar panel
país [pa'jis] M country; (*região*) land; **~ natal** native land

paisagem [paj'zaʒẽ] (*pl* **-ns**) F scenery; landscape
paisano, -a [paj'zanu, a] ADJ civilian ▶ M/F (*não militar*) civilian; (*compatriota*) fellow countryman
Países Baixos MPL: **os ~** the Netherlands
paixão [paj'ʃãw] (*pl* **-ões**) F passion
palácio [pa'lasju] M palace; **~ da justiça** courthouse; **Palácio do Planalto** *see note*

> **Palácio de Planalto** is the seat of the Brazilian government, in Brasília. The name comes from the fact that the Brazilian capital is situated on a plateau. It has come to be a byword for central government.

paladar [pala'dar] M taste; (*Anat*) palate
palafita [pala'fita] F (*estacaria*) stilts *pl*; (*habitação*) stilt house
palavra [pa'lavra] F word; (*fala*) speech; (*promessa*) promise; (*direito de falar*) right to speak; **dar a ~ a alguém** to give sb the chance to speak; **ter ~** (*pessoa*) to be reliable; **~s cruzadas** crossword (puzzle) *sg*;
palavrão [pala'vrãw] (*pl* **-ões**) M swearword
palco ['pawku] M (*Teatro*) stage; (*fig: local*) scene
Palestina [pales'tʃina] F: **a ~** Palestine; **palestino, -a** [pales'tʃinu, a] ADJ, M/F Palestinian
palestra [pa'lɛstra] F chat, talk; (*conferência*) lecture
paletó [pale'tɔ] M jacket
palha ['paʎa] F straw
palhaço [pa'ʎasu] M clown
pálido, -a ['palidu, a] ADJ pale
palito [pa'litu] M stick; (*para os dentes*) toothpick
palma ['pawma] F (*folha*) palm leaf; (*da mão*) palm; **bater ~s** to clap;
palmada [paw'mada] F slap
palmeira [paw'mejra] F palm tree
palmo ['pawmu] M span; **~ a ~** inch by inch
palpável [paw'pavew] (*pl* **-eis**) ADJ tangible; (*fig*) obvious
pálpebra ['pawpebra] F eyelid
palpitação [pawpita'sãw] (*pl* **-ões**) F beating, throbbing; **palpitações** FPL (*batimentos cardíacos*) palpitations
palpitante [pawpi'tãtʃi] ADJ beating, throbbing; (*fig: emocionante*) thrilling; (*: de interesse atual*) sensational
palpitar [pawpi'tar] VI (*coração*) to beat
palpite [paw'pitʃi] M (*intuição*) hunch; (*Jogo, Turfe*) tip; (*opinião*) opinion
pampa ['pãpa] F pampas
Panamá [pana'ma] M: **o ~** Panama; **o canal do ~** the Panama Canal
pancada [pã'kada] F (*no corpo*) blow, hit; (*choque*) knock; (*de relógio*) stroke; **dar ~ em alguém** to hit sb;
pancadaria [pãkada'ria] F (*surra*) beating; (*tumulto*) fight
pandeiro [pã'dejru] M tambourine
pandemia [pãde'mia] F pandemic
pane ['pani] F breakdown
panela [pa'nɛla] F (*de barro*) pot; (*de metal*) pan; (*de cozinhar*) saucepan; (*no dente*) hole; **~ de pressão** pressure cooker
panfleto [pã'fletu] M pamphlet
pânico ['paniku] M panic; **entrar em ~** to panic
pano ['panu] M cloth; (*Teatro*) curtain; (*vela*) sheet, sail; **~ de pratos** tea towel; **~ de pó** duster; **~ de fundo** (*tb fig*) backdrop

panorama [pano'rama] M view
panqueca [pã'kɛka] F pancake
pantanal [pãta'naw] (*pl* **-ais**) M swampland
pântano ['pãtanu] M marsh, swamp
pantera [pã'tɛra] F panther
pão [pãw] (*pl* **pães**) M bread; **o P~ de Açúcar** (*no Rio*) Sugarloaf Mountain; **~ árabe** pitta (BRIT) *ou* pita (US) bread; **~ torrado** toast;
pão-duro (*pl* **pães-duros**) (*col*) ADJ mean, stingy ▶ M/F miser;
pãozinho [pãw'ziɲu] M roll
papa ['papa] M Pope
papagaio [papa'gaju] M parrot; (*pipa*) kite
papai [pa'paj] M dad, daddy; **P~ Noel** Santa Claus, Father Christmas
papel [pa'pɛw] (*pl* **-éis**) M paper; (*Teatro*) part; (*função*) role; **~ de embrulho** wrapping paper; **~ de escrever/de alumínio** writing paper/tinfoil; **~ de parede** wallpaper; **~ de seda/ transparente** tissue paper/ tracing paper; **~ filme** Clingfilm® (BRIT), Saran Wrap® (US); **~ higiênico** toilet paper;
papelada [pape'lada] F pile of papers; (*burocracia*) paperwork, red tape; **papelão** [pape'lãw] M cardboard; (*fig*) fiasco; **papelaria** [papela'ria] F stationer's (shop);
papel-carbono M carbon paper
papinha [pa'piɲa] F: **~ de bebê** baby food
papo ['papu] M (*col*) double chin; (*: conversa*) chat; (*: papo furado*) hot air; **bater** *ou* **levar um ~** (*col*) to have a chat; **bater ~** (*col*) to chat (*also internet*); **ficar de ~ para o ar** (*fig*) to laze around
paquerar [pake'rar] (*col*) VI to flirt ▶ VT to chat up
paquistanês, -esa [pakista'nes, eza] ADJ, M/F Pakistani
Paquistão [pakis'tãw] M: **o ~** Pakistan
par [par] ADJ (*igual*) equal; (*número*) even ▶ M pair; (*casal*) couple; (*pessoa na dança*) partner; **~ a ~** side by side, level; **sem ~** incomparable
para ['para] PREP for; (*direção*) to, towards; **~ que** so that, in order that; **~ quê?** what for?, why?; **ir ~ casa** to go home; **~ com** (*atitude*) towards; **de lá ~ cá** since then; **~ a semana** next week; **estar ~** to be about to; **é ~ nós ficarmos aqui?** should we stay here?
parabens [para'bẽjs] MPL congratulations; (*no aniversário*) happy birthday; **dar ~ a** to congratulate
para-brisa ['para-] (*pl* **-s**) M windscreen (BRIT), windshield (US)
para-choque ['para-] (*pl* **-s**) M (*Auto*) bumper
parada [pa'rada] F stop; (*Com*) stoppage; (*militar, colegial*) parade
parado, -a [pa'radu, a] ADJ (*imóvel*) standing still; (*sem vida*) lifeless; (*carro*) stationary; (*máquina*) out of action; (*olhar*) fixed; (*trabalhador, fábrica*) idle
paradoxo [para'dɔksu] M paradox
parafuso [para'fuzu] M screw
paragem [pa'raʒẽ] (*pl* **-ns**) F (PT) stop; **paragens** FPL (*lugares*) parts; **~ de elétrico** (PT) tram (BRIT) *ou* streetcar (US) stop
parágrafo [pa'ragrafu] M paragraph
Paraguai [para'gwaj] M: **o ~**

Paraguay; **paraguaio, -a** [para'gwaju, a] ADJ, M/F Paraguayan
paraíso [para'izu] M paradise
para-lama ['para-] (*pl* **-s**) M wing (BRIT), fender (US); (*de bicicleta*) mudguard
paralelepípedo [paralele'pipedu] M cobblestone
paralelo, -a [para'lɛlu, a] ADJ
parapeito [para'pejtu] M wall, parapet; (*da janela*) windowsill
parapente [para'pẽjtʃi] M (*Esporte*) paragliding; (*equipamento*) paraglider
paraquedas [para'kɛdas] M INV parachute
parar [pa'rar] VI to stop; (*ficar*) to stay ▶ VT to stop; **fazer ~** (*deter*) to stop; **~ na cadeia** to end up in jail; **~ de fazer** to stop doing
para-raios ['para-] M INV lightning conductor
parasita [para'zita] M parasite
parceiro, -a [par'sejru, a] ADJ matching ▶ M/F partner
parcela [par'sɛla] F piece, bit; (*de pagamento*) instalment (BRIT), installment (US); (*de terra*) plot; (*do eleitorado etc*) section; (*Mat*) item
parceria [parse'ria] F partnership
parcial [par'sjaw] (*pl* **-ais**) ADJ partial; (*feito por partes*) in parts; (*pessoa*) biased; (*Pol*) partisan;
parcialidade [parsjali'dadʒi] F bias, partiality
pardal [par'daw] (*pl* **-ais**) M sparrow
pardieiro [par'dʒjejru] M ruin, heap
pardo, -a ['pardu, a] ADJ (*cinzento*) grey (BRIT), gray (US); (*castanho*) brown; (*mulato*) mulatto
parecer [pare'ser] VI (*ter a aparência de*) to look, seem; **parecer-se** VR: **~-se com alguém** to look like sb; **~ alguém/algo** to look like sb/sth; **ao que parece** apparently; **parece-me que** I think that, it seems to me that; **que lhe parece?** what do you think?; **parece que** (*pelo visto*) it looks as if; (*segundo dizem*) apparently
parecido, -a [pare'sidu, a] ADJ alike, similar; **~ com** like
parede [pa'redʒi] F wall
parente [pa'rẽtʃi] M/F relative, relation; **parentesco** [parẽ'tesku] M relationship; (*fig*) connection
parêntese [pa'rẽtezi] M parenthesis; (*na escrita*) bracket; (*fig: digressão*) digression
páreo ['parju] M race; (*fig*) competition
parir [pa'rir] VT to give birth to ▶ VI to give birth; (*mulher*) to have a baby
Paris [pa'ris] N Paris; **parisiense** [pari'zjẽsi] ADJ, M/F Parisian
parlamentar [parlamẽ'tar] ADJ parliamentary ▶ M/F member of parliament
parlamento [parla'mẽtu] M parliament
paróquia [pa'rɔkja] F (*Rel*) parish
parque ['parki] M park; **~ industrial** industrial estate; **~ nacional** national park; **~ de diversões** amusement park
parte ['partʃi] F part; (*quinhão*) share; (*lado*) side; (*ponto*) point; (*Jur*) party; (*papel*) role; **a maior ~ de** most of; **à ~** aside; (*separado*) separate; (*separadamente*) separately; (*além de*) apart from; **da ~ de alguém** on sb's part; **em alguma/qualquer ~** somewhere/ anywhere; **em ~ alguma** nowhere; **por toda (a) ~** everywhere; **pôr de ~**

to set aside; **tomar ~ em** to take part in; **dar ~ de alguém à polícia** to report sb to the police
participar [partʃisi'par] VT to announce, notify of ▶ VI: **~ de** *ou* **em** to participate in, take part in; (*compartilhar*) to share in
participio [partʃi'sipju] M participle
particular [partʃiku'lar] ADJ particular, special; (*privativo, pessoal*) private ▶ M particular; (*indivíduo*) individual; **particulares** MPL (*pormenores*) details; **em ~** in private; **particularmente** [partʃikular'mẽtʃi] ADV privately; (*especialmente*) particularly
partida [par'tʃida] F (*saída*) departure; (*Esporte*) game, match
partidário, -a [partʃi'darju, a] ADJ supporting ▶ M/F supporter, follower
partido, -a [par'tʃidu, a] ADJ broken ▶ M (*Pol*) party; **tirar ~ de** to profit from; **tomar o ~ de** to side with
partilhar [partʃi'ʎar] VT to share; (*distribuir*) to share out
partir [par'tʃir] VT to break; (*dividir*) to split ▶ VI (*pôr-se a caminho*) to set off, set out; (*ir-se embora*) to leave, depart; **partir-se** VR to break; **a ~ de** (starting) from; **~ para outra** (*col*) to move on
parto ['partu] M (child)birth; **estar em trabalho de ~** to be in labour (BRIT) *ou* labor (US)
Páscoa ['paskwa] F Easter; (*dos judeus*) Passover
pasmo, -a ['pazmu, a] ADJ astonished ▶ M amazement
passa ['pasa] F raisin
passadeira [pasa'dejra] F (*tapete*) stair carpet; (*mulher*) ironing lady; (PT: *para peões*) zebra crossing (BRIT), crosswalk (US)
passado, -a [pa'sadu, a] ADJ past; (*antiquado*) old-fashioned; (*fruta*) bad; (*peixe*) off ▶ M past; **o ano ~** last year; **bem ~** (*carne*) well done
passageiro, -a [pasa'ʒejru, a] ADJ passing ▶ M/F passenger
passagem [pa'saʒẽ] (*pl* **-ns**) F passage; (*preço de condução*) fare; (*bilhete*) ticket; **~ de ida e volta** return ticket, round trip ticket (US); **~ de nível** level (BRIT) *ou* grade (US) crossing; **~ de pedestres** pedestrian crossing (BRIT), crosswalk (US); **~ subterrânea** underpass, subway (BRIT)
passaporte [pasa'pɔrtʃi] M passport
passar [pa'sar] VT to pass; (*exceder*) to go beyond, exceed; (*a ferro*) to iron; (*o tempo*) to spend; (*a outra pessoa*) to pass on; (*pomada*) to put on ▶ VI to pass; (*na rua*) to go past; (*tempo*) to go by; (*dor*) to wear off; (*terminar*) to be over; **passar-se** VR (*acontecer*) to go on, happen; **~ bem** (*de saúde*) to be well; **passava das dez horas** it was past ten o'clock; **~ alguém para trás** to con sb; (*cônjuge*) to cheat on sb; **~ por algo** (*sofrer*) to go through sth; (*transitar, estrada*) to go along sth; (*ser considerado como*) to be thought of as sth; **~ sem** to do without
passarela [pasa'rɛla] F footbridge
pássaro ['pasaru] M bird
passatempo [pasa'tẽpu] M pastime
passe ['pasi] M pass
passear [pa'sjar] VT to take for a walk ▶ VI (*a pé*) to go for a walk; (*sair*) to go out; **~ a cavalo/de**

P

carro to go for a ride/a drive;
passeata [pa'sjata] F (*marcha coletiva*) protest march; **passeio** [pa'seju] M walk; (*de carro*) drive, ride; (*excursão*) outing; (*calçada*) pavement (BRIT), sidewalk (US); **dar um passeio** to go for a walk; (*de carro*) to go for a drive *ou* ride
passível [pa'sivew] (*pl* **-eis**) ADJ: **~ de** (*dor etc*) susceptible to; (*pena, multa*) subject to
passivo, -a [pa'sivu, a] ADJ passive ▶ M (*Com*) liabilities *pl*
passo ['pasu] M step; (*medida*) pace; (*modo de andar*) walk; (*ruído dos passos*) footstep; (*sinal de pé*) footprint; **ao ~ que** while; **ceder o ~ a** to give way to
pasta ['pasta] F paste; (*de couro*) briefcase; (*de cartolina*) folder; (*de ministro*) portfolio; **~ dentifrícia** *ou* **de dentes** toothpaste
pastar [pas'tar] VT to graze on ▶ VI to graze
pastel [pas'tɛw] (*pl* **-éis**) ADJ INV (*cor*) pastel ▶ M samosa
pastelão [paste'lãw] M slapstick
pastelaria [pastela'ria] F cake shop; (*comida*) pastry
pasteurizado, -a [pastewri'zadu, a] ADJ pasteurized
pastilha [pas'tʃiʎa] F (*Med*) tablet; (*doce*) pastille
pastor, a [pas'tor(a)] M/F shepherd(ess) ▶ M (*Rel*) clergyman, pastor
pata ['pata] F (*pé de animal*) foot, paw; (*ave*) duck; (*col: pé*) foot
patamar [pata'mar] M (*de escada*) landing; (*fig*) level
pateta [pa'tɛta] ADJ stupid, daft ▶ M/F idiot
patético, -a [pa'tɛtʃiku, a] ADJ pathetic, moving
patife [pa'tʃifi] M scoundrel, rogue
patim [pa'tʃĩ] (*pl* **-ns**) M skate; **~ de rodas** roller skate; **patins em linha** Rollerblades®; **patinar** [patʃi'nar] VI to skate; (*Auto: derrapar*) to skid
patins [pa'tʃĩs] MPL *de* **patim**
pátio ['patʃju] M (*de uma casa*) patio, backyard; (*espaço cercado de edifícios*) courtyard; (*tb*: **~ de recreio**) playground; (*Mil*) parade ground
pato ['patu] M duck; (*macho*) drake
patologia [patolo'ʒia] F pathology; **patológico, -a** [pato'lɔʒiku, a] ADJ pathological
patrão [pa'trãw] (*pl* **-ões**) M (*Com*) boss; (*dono de casa*) master; (*proprietário*) landlord; (*Náut*) skipper
pátria ['patrja] F homeland
patrimônio [patri'monju] M (*herança*) inheritance; (*fig*) heritage; (*bens*) property
patriota [pa'trjɔta] M/F patriot
patrocinar [patrosi'nar] VT to sponsor; (*proteger*) to support; **patrocínio** [patro'sinju] M sponsorship, backing; (*proteção*) support
patrões [pa'trõjs] MPL *de* **patrão**
patrulha [pa'truʎa] F patrol; **patrulhar** [patru'ʎar] VT, VI to patrol
pau [paw] M (*madeira*) wood; (*vara*) stick; **paus** MPL (*Cartas*) clubs; **~ a ~** neck and neck; **~ de bandeira** flagpole
pausa ['pawza] F pause; (*intervalo*) break; (*descanso*) rest
pauta ['pawta] F (*linha*) (guide)line; (*ordem do dia*) agenda; (*indicações*) guidelines *pl*; **sem ~** (*papel*) plain; **em ~** on the agenda
pavão, -voa [pa'vãw, 'voa] (*pl* **-ões/-s**) M/F peacock/peahen

pavilhão [pavi'ʎãw] (*pl* **-ões**) M tent; (*de madeira*) hut; (*no jardim*) summerhouse; (*em exposição*) pavilion; (*bandeira*) flag

pavimento [pavi'mẽtu] M (*chão, andar*) floor; (*da rua*) road surface

pavões [pa'võjs] MPL *de* **pavão**

pavor [pa'vor] M dread, terror; **ter ~ de** to be terrified of; **pavoroso, -a** [pavo'rozu, ɔza] ADJ dreadful, terrible

paz [pajz] F peace; **fazer as ~es** to make up, be friends again

PC ABR M PC

Pça. ABR (= *Praça*) Sq.

pé [pɛ] M foot; (*da mesa*) leg; (*fig: base*) footing; (*de milho, café*) plant; **ir a pé** to walk, go on foot; **ao pé de** near, by; **ao pé da letra** literally; **estar de pé** (*festa etc*) to be on; **em** *ou* **de pé** standing (up); **dar no pé** (*col*) to run away, take off; **não ter pé nem cabeça** (*fig*) to make no sense

peão [pjãw] (*pl* **-ões**) M (PT) pedestrian

peça ['pɛsa] F piece; (*Auto*) part; (*aposento*) room; (*Teatro*) play; **~ de reposição** spare part; **~ de roupa** garment

pecado [pe'kadu] M sin

pecar [pe'kar] VI to sin; **~ por excesso de zelo** to be over-zealous

pechincha [pe'ʃĩʃa] F (*vantagem*) godsend; (*coisa barata*) bargain; **pechinchar** [peʃĩ'ʃar] VI to bargain, haggle

peço ['pɛsu] VB *ver* **pedir**

peculiar [peku'ljar] ADJ special, peculiar; (*particular*) particular; **peculiaridade** [pekuljari'dadʒi] F peculiarity

pedaço [pe'dasu] M piece; (*fig: trecho*) bit; **aos ~s** in pieces

pedágio [pe'daʒju] (BR) M (*pagamento*) toll

pedal [pe'daw] (*pl* **-ais**) M pedal; **pedalar** [peda'lar] VT, VI to pedal

pedante [pe'dãtʃi] ADJ pretentious ▶ M/F pseud

pedestre [pe'dɛstri] (BR) M pedestrian

pedicuro, -a [pedʒi'kuru, a] M/F chiropodist (BRIT), podiatrist (US)

pedido [pe'dʒidu] M request; (*Com*) order; **~ de demissão** resignation; **~ de desculpa** apology

pedinte [pe'dʒĩtʃi] M/F beggar

pedir [pe'dʒir] VT to ask for; (*Com, comida*) to order; (*exigir*) to demand ▶ VI to ask; (*num restaurante*) to order; **~ algo a alguém** to ask sb for sth; **~ a alguém que faça, ~ para alguém fazer** to ask sb to do

pedófilo, -a [pe'dɔfilu, a] M/F paedophile (BRIT), pedophile (US)

pedra ['pɛdra] F stone; (*rochedo*) rock; (*de granizo*) hailstone; (*de açúcar*) lump; (*quadro-negro*) slate; **~ de gelo** ice cube; **pedreiro** [pe'drejru] M stonemason

pegada [pe'gada] F (*de pé*) footprint; (*Futebol*) save; **~ de carbono** carbon footprint

pegado, -a [pe'gadu, a] ADJ stuck; (*unido*) together

pegajoso, -a [pega'ʒozu, ɔza] ADJ sticky

pegar [pe'gar] VT to catch; (*selos*) to stick (on); (*segurar*) to take hold of; (*hábito, mania*) to get into; (*compreender*) to take in; (*trabalho*) to take on; (*estação de rádio*) to pick up, get ▶ VI to stick; (*planta*) to take; (*moda*) to catch on; (*doença*) to be catching; (*motor*) to start;

P

~ em (*segurar*) to grab, pick up; **ir ~** (*buscar*) to go and get; **~ um emprego** to get a job; **~ fogo a algo** to set fire to sth; **~ no sono** to get to sleep

pego, -a ['pɛgu, a] PP *de* **pegar**

peito ['pejtu] M (*Anat*) chest; (*de ave, mulher*) breast; (*fig*) courage

peitoril [pejto'riw] (*pl* **-is**) M windowsill

peixada [pej'ʃada] F *fish cooked in a seafood sauce*

peixaria [pejʃa'ria] F fish shop, fishmonger's (BRIT)

peixe ['pejʃi] M fish; **Peixes** MPL (*Astrologia*) Pisces *sg*

pela ['pɛla] = **por + a**

pelada [pe'lada] F football game

> **Pelada** is an improvised, generally short, game of football, which in the past was played with a ball made out of socks, or an inflatable rubber ball. It is still played today on any piece of open land, or even in the street.

pelado, -a [pe'ladu, a] ADJ (*sem pele*) skinned; (*sem pelo, cabelo*) shorn; (*nu*) naked, in the nude; (*sem dinheiro*) broke

pelar [pe'lar] VT (*tirar a pele*) to skin; (*tirar o pelo*) to shear

pelas ['pɛlas] = **por + as**

pele ['pɛli] F skin; (*couro*) leather; (*como agasalho*) fur; (*de animal*) hide

película [pe'likula] F film

pelo¹ ['pɛlu] = **por + o**

pelo² ['pelu] M hair; (*de animal*) fur, coat; **nu em ~** stark naked

pelos ['pɛlus] = **por + os**

peludo, -a [pe'ludu, a] ADJ hairy; (*animal*) furry

pena ['pena] F feather; (*de caneta*) nib; (*escrita*) writing; (*Jur*) penalty, punishment; (*sofrimento*) suffering; (*piedade*) pity; **que ~!** what a shame!; **dar ~** to be upsetting; **ter ~ de** to feel sorry for; **~ de morte** death penalty

pênalti ['penawtʃi] M (*Futebol*) penalty (kick)

penar [pe'nar] VT to grieve ▶ VI to suffer

pendência [pẽ'dẽsja] F dispute, quarrel

pendente [pẽ'dẽtʃi] ADJ hanging; (*por decidir*) pending; (*inclinado*) sloping; (*dependent*): **~ de** dependent on ▶ M pendant

pêndulo ['pẽdulu] M pendulum

pendurar [pẽdu'rar] VT to hang

penedo [pe'nedu] M rock, boulder

peneira [pe'nejra] F sieve;

peneirar [penej'rar] VT to sift, sieve ▶ VI (*chover*) to drizzle

penetrar [pene'trar] VT to get into, penetrate; (*compreender*) to understand ▶ VI: **~ em** *ou* **por** *ou* **entre** to penetrate

penhasco [pe'ɲasku] M cliff, crag

penhorar [peɲo'rar] VT (*dar em penhor*) to pledge, pawn

penicilina [penisi'lina] F penicillin

península [pe'nĩsula] F peninsula

pênis ['penis] M INV penis

penitência [peni'tẽsja] F penitence; (*expiação*) penance;

penitenciária [penitẽ'sjarja] F prison

penoso, -a [pe'nozu, ɔza] ADJ (*assunto, tratamento*) painful; (*trabalho*) hard

pensamento [pẽsa'mẽtu] M thought; (*mente*) mind; (*opinião*) way of thinking; (*ideia*) idea

pensão [pẽ'sãw] (*pl* **-ões**) F (*tb*: **casa de ~**) boarding house; (*comida*) board; **~ completa** full board; **~ de**

aposentadoria (retirement) pension

pensar [pẽ'sar] VI to think; (*imaginar*) to imagine; **~ em** to think of *ou* about; **~ fazer** to intend to do; **pensativo, -a** [pẽsa'tʃivu, a] ADJ thoughtful, pensive

pensionista [pẽsjo'nista] M/F pensioner

pensões [pẽ'sõjs] FPL *de* **pensão**

pente ['pẽtʃi] M comb; **penteado, -a** [pẽ'tʃjadu, a] ADJ (*cabelo*) in place; (*pessoa*) smart ▶ M hairdo, hairstyle; **pentear** [pẽ'tʃjar] VT to comb; (*arranjar o cabelo*) to do, style; **pentear-se** VR to comb one's hair; to do one's hair

penúltimo, -a [pe'nuwtʃimu, a] ADJ last but one, penultimate

penumbra [pe'nũbra] F twilight, dusk; (*sombra*) shadow; (*meia-luz*) half-light

penúria [pe'nurja] F poverty

peões [pjõjs] MPL *de* **peão**

pepino [pe'pinu] M cucumber

pequeno, -a [pe'kenu, a] ADJ small; (*mesquinho*) petty ▶ M boy

Pequim [pe'kĩ] N Beijing

pera ['pera] F pear

perambular [perãbu'lar] VI to wander

perante [pe'rãtʃi] PREP before, in the presence of

per capita [pɛr'kapita] ADV, ADJ per capita

perceber [perse'ber] VT to realize; (*por meio dos sentidos*) to perceive; (*compreender*) to understand; (*ver*) to see; (*ouvir*) to hear; (*ver ao longe*) to make out; (*dinheiro: receber*) to receive

percentagem [persẽ'taʒẽ] F percentage

percepção [persep'sãw] F perception; **perceptível** [persep'tʃivew] (*pl* **-eis**) ADJ perceptible, noticeable; (*som*) audible

percevejo [perse'veʒu] M (*inseto*) bug; (*prego*) drawing pin (BRIT), thumbtack (US)

perco ['perku] VB *ver* **perder**

percorrer [perko'her] VT (*viajar por*) to travel (across *ou* over); (*passar por*) to go through, traverse; (*investigar*) to search through

percurso [per'kursu] M (*espaço percorrido*) distance (covered); (*trajeto*) route; (*viagem*) journey

percussão [perku'sãw] F (*Mús*) percussion

perda ['perda] F loss; (*desperdício*) waste; **~s e danos** damages, losses

perdão [per'dãw] M pardon, forgiveness; **~!** sorry!, I beg your pardon!

perder [per'der] VT to lose; (*tempo*) to waste; (*trem, show, oportunidade*) to miss ▶ VI to lose; **perder-se** VR to get lost; (*arruinar-se*) to be ruined; (*desaparecer*) to disappear; **~-se de alguém** to lose sb

perdido, -a [per'dʒidu, a] ADJ lost; **~s e achados** lost and found, lost property

perdiz [per'dʒiz] F partridge

perdoar [per'dwar] VT to forgive

perdurar [perdu'rar] VI to last a long time; (*continuar a existir*) to still exist

perecível [pere'sivew] (*pl* **-eis**) ADJ perishable

peregrinação [peregrina'sãw] (*pl* **-ões**) F (*viagem*) travels *pl*; (*Rel*) pilgrimage

peregrino, -a [pere'grinu, a] M/F pilgrim

P

peremptório, -a [perẽp'tɔrju, a] ADJ final; (*decisivo*) decisive
perene [pe'rɛni] ADJ everlasting; (*Bot*) perennial
perfeição [perfej'sãw] F perfection
perfeitamente [perfejta'mẽtʃi] ADV perfectly ▸ EXCL exactly!
perfeito, -a [per'fejtu, a] ADJ perfect ▸ M (*Ling*) perfect
perfil [per'fiw] (*pl* **-is**) M profile; (*silhueta*) silhouette, outline; (*Arq*) (cross) section
perfume [per'fumi] M perfume; scent
perfurar [perfu'rar] VT (*o chão*) to drill a hole in; (*papel*) to punch (a hole in)
pergunta [per'gũta] F question; **fazer uma ~ a alguém** to ask sb a question; **perguntar** [pergũ'tar] VT to ask; (*interrogar*) to question ▸ VI: **perguntar por alguém** to ask after sb; **perguntar-se** VR to wonder; **perguntar algo a alguém** to ask sb sth
perícia [pe'risja] F expertise; (*destreza*) skill; (*exame*) investigation
periferia [perife'ria] F periphery; (*da cidade*) outskirts *pl*
perigo [pe'rigu] M danger; **perigoso, -a** [peri'gozu, ɔza] ADJ dangerous; (*arriscado*) risky
período [pe'riodu] M period; (*estação*) season
periquito [peri'kitu] M parakeet
perito, -a [pe'ritu, a] ADJ expert ▸ M/F expert; (*quem faz perícia*) investigator
permanecer [permane'ser] VI to remain; (*num lugar*) to stay; (*continuar a ser*) to remain, keep; **~ parado** to keep still
permanência [perma'nẽsja] F permanence; (*estada*) stay;
permanente [perma'nẽtʃi] ADJ (*dor*) constant; (*cor*) fast; (*residência, pregas*) permanent ▸ M (*cartão*) pass ▸ F perm
permissão [permi'sãw] F permission, consent; **permissivo, -a** [permi'sivu, a] ADJ permissive
permitir [permi'tʃir] VT to allow, permit
perna ['pɛrna] F leg; **~s tortas** bow legs
pernil [per'niw] (*pl* **-is**) M (*de animal*) haunch; (*Culin*) leg
pernilongo [perni'lõgu] M mosquito
pernis [per'nis] MPL *de* **pernil**
pernoitar [pernoj'tar] VI to spend the night
pérola ['pɛrola] F pearl
perpendicular [perpẽdʒiku'lar] ADJ, F perpendicular
perpetuar [perpe'twar] VT to perpetuate; **perpétuo, -a** [per'pɛtwu, a] ADJ perpetual
persa ['pɛrsa] ADJ, M/F Persian
perseguição [persegi'sãw] F pursuit; (*Rel, Pol*) persecution
perseguir [perse'gir] VT to pursue; (*correr atrás*) to chase (after); (*Rel, Pol*) to persecute; (*importunar*) to harass, pester
perseverante [perseve'rãtʃi] ADJ persistent
perseverar [perseve'rar] VI to persevere
Pérsia ['pɛrsja] F: **a ~** Persia
persiana [per'sjana] F blind
Pérsico, -a ['pɛrsiku, a] ADJ: **o golfo ~** the Persian Gulf
persigo [per'sigu] VB *ver* **perseguir**
persistir [persis'tʃir] VI to persist
personagem [perso'naʒẽ] (*pl* **-ns**) M/F famous person, celebrity; (*num livro, filme*) character

personalidade [personali'dadʒi] F personality
perspectiva [perspek'tʃiva] F perspective; (*panorama*) view; (*probabilidade*) prospect
perspicácia [perspi'kasja] F insight, perceptiveness; **perspicaz** [perspi'kajz] ADJ perceptive; (*sagaz*) shrewd
persuadir [perswa'dʒir] VT to persuade; **persuadir-se** VR to convince o.s.; **persuasão** [perswa'zãw] F persuasion; **persuasivo, -a** [perswa'zivu, a] ADJ persuasive
pertencente [pertẽ'sẽtʃi] ADJ: **~ a** pertaining to
pertencer [pertẽ'ser] VI: **~ a** to belong to; (*referir-se*) to concern
pertences [per'tẽsis] MPL (*de uma pessoa*) belongings
pertinência [pertʃi'nẽsja] F relevance; **pertinente** [pertʃi'nẽtʃi] ADJ relevant; (*apropriado*) appropriate
perto, -a ['pɛrtu, a] ADJ nearby ▶ ADV near; **~ de** near to; (*em comparação com*) next to; **de ~** closely; (*ver*) close up; (*conhecer*) very well
perturbar [pertur'bar] VT to disturb; (*abalar*) to upset, trouble; (*atrapalhar*) to put off; (*andamento, trânsito*) to disrupt; (*envergonhar*) to embarrass; (*alterar*) to affect
Peru [pe'ru] M: **o ~** Peru
peru, a [pe'ru(a)] M/F turkey
peruca [pe'ruka] F wig
perverso, -a [per'vɛrsu, a] ADJ perverse; (*malvado*) wicked
perverter [perver'ter] VT to corrupt, pervert; **pervertido, -a** [perver'tʃidu, a] ADJ perverted ▶ M/F pervert
pesadelo [peza'delu] M nightmare
pesado, -a [pe'zadu, a] ADJ heavy; (*ambiente*) tense; (*trabalho*) hard; (*estilo*) dull, boring; (*andar*) slow; (*piada*) coarse; (*comida*) stodgy; (*tempo*) sultry ▶ ADV heavily
pêsames ['pezamis] MPL condolences, sympathy *sg*
pesar [pe'zar] VT to weigh; (*fig*) to weigh up ▶ VI to weigh; (*ser pesado*) to be heavy; (*influir*) to carry weight; (*causar mágoa*): **~ a** to hurt, grieve ▶ M grief; **~ sobre** (*recair*) to fall upon
pesaroso, -a [peza'rozu, ɔza] ADJ sorrowful, sad; (*arrependido*) regretful, sorry
pesca ['pɛska] F fishing; (*os peixes*) catch; **ir à ~** to go fishing
pescada [pes'kada] F whiting
pescado [pes'kadu] M fish
pescador, a [peska'dor(a)] M/F fisherman/woman; **~ à linha** angler
pescar [pes'kar] VT (*peixe*) to catch; (*tentar apanhar*) to fish for; (*retirar da água*) to fish out ▶ VI to fish
pescoço [pes'kosu] M neck
peso ['pezu] M weight; (*fig: ônus*) burden; (*importância*) importance; **~ bruto/líquido** gross/net weight
pesquisa [pes'kiza] F research; **uma ~** a study; **pesquisar** [peski'zar] VT, VI to research
pêssego ['pesegu] M peach
pessimista [pesi'mista] ADJ pessimistic ▶ M/F pessimist
péssimo, -a ['pɛsimu, a] ADJ very bad, awful
pessoa [pe'soa] F person; **pessoas** FPL people; **pessoal** [pe'swaw] (*pl* **-ais**) ADJ personal ▶ M personnel *pl*, staff *pl*; (*col*) people *pl*, folks *pl*

pestana [pes'tana] F eyelash
peste ['pɛstʃi] F epidemic; (*bubônica*) plague; (*fig*) pest, nuisance
pétala ['pɛtala] F petal
petição [petʃi'sãw] (*pl* **-ões**) F request; (*documento*) petition
petisco [pe'tʃisku] M savoury (BRIT), savory (US), titbit (BRIT), tidbit (US)
petróleo [pe'trɔlju] M oil, petroleum; **~ bruto** crude oil
peúga ['pjuga] (PT) F sock
pevide [pe'vidʒi] (PT) F (*de melão*) seed; (*de maçã*) pip
p. ex. ABR (= *por exemplo*) e.g.
pia ['pia] F wash basin; (*da cozinha*) sink; **~ batismal** font
piada ['pjada] F joke
pianista [pja'nista] M/F pianist
piano ['pjanu] M piano
piar [pjar] VI (*pinto*) to cheep; (*coruja*) to hoot
picada [pi'kada] F (*de agulha etc*) prick; (*de abelha*) sting; (*de mosquito, cobra*) bite; (*de avião*) dive; (*de navalha*) stab; (*atalho*) path, trail
picante [pi'kãtʃi] ADJ (*tempero*) hot
picar [pi'kar] VT to prick; (*suj: abelha*) to sting; (*: mosquito*) to bite; (*: pássaro*) to peck; (*um animal*) to goad; (*carne*) to mince; (*papel*) to shred; (*fruta*) to chop up ▶ VI (*comichar*) to prickle
picareta [pika'reta] F pickaxe (BRIT), pickax (US) ▶ M/F crook
pico ['piku] M (*cume*) peak; (*ponta aguda*) sharp point; (PT: *um pouco*) a bit; **mil e ~** just over a thousand
picolé [piko'lɛ] M lolly
picotar [piko'tar] VT to perforate; (*bilhete*) to punch
piedade [pje'dadʒi] F piety; (*compaixão*) pity; **ter ~ de** to have pity on; **piedoso, -a** [pje'dozu, ɔza] ADJ pious; (*compassivo*) merciful
piercing ['pirsĩ] (*pl* **-s**) M piercing
pifar [pi'far] (*col*) VI (*carro*) to break down; (*rádio etc*) to go wrong; (*plano, programa*) to fall through
pijama [pi'ʒama] M pyjamas *pl* (BRIT), pajamas *pl* (US)
pilantra [pi'lãtra] (*col*) M/F crook
pilar [pi'lar] VT to pound, crush ▶ M pillar
pilha ['piʎa] F (*Elet*) battery; (*monte*) pile, heap
pilhar [pi'ʎar] VT to plunder, pillage; (*roubar*) to rob; (*surpreender*) to catch
pilotar [pilo'tar] VT (*avião*) to fly
piloto [pi'lotu] M pilot; (*motorista*) (racing) driver; (*bico de gás*) pilot light ▶ ADJ INV (*usina, plano*) pilot; (*peça*) sample *atr*
pílula ['pilula] F pill; **a ~ (anticoncepcional)** the pill
pimenta [pi'mẽta] F (*Culin*) pepper; **~ de Caiena** cayenne pepper; **pimenta-do-reino** F black pepper; **pimenta-malagueta** (*pl* **pimentas-malagueta**) F chilli (BRIT) *ou* chili (US) pepper; **pimentão** [pimẽ'tãw] (*pl* **-ões**) M (*Bot*) pepper
pinça ['pĩsa] F (*de sobrancelhas*) tweezers *pl*; (*de casa*) tongs *pl*; (*Med*) callipers *pl* (BRIT), calipers *pl* (US)
pincel [pĩ'sɛw] (*pl* **-éis**) M brush; (*para pintar*) paintbrush; **pincelar** [pĩse'lar] VT to paint
pinga ['pĩga] F (*cachaça*) rum; (PT: *trago*) drink
pingar [pĩ'gar] VI to drip
pingo ['pĩgu] M (*gota*) drop
pingue-pongue [pĩgi-'põgi] M ping-pong
pinguim [pĩ'gwĩ] (*pl* **-ns**) M penguin

pinheiro [pi'ɲejru] M pine (tree)
pinho ['piɲu] M pine
pino ['pinu] M (*peça*) pin; (*Auto: na porta*) lock; **a ~** upright
pinta ['pĩta] F (*mancha*) spot
pintar [pĩ'tar] VT to paint; (*cabelo*) to dye; (*rosto*) to make up; (*descrever*) to describe; (*imaginar*) to picture ▶ VI to paint; **pintar-se** VR to make o.s. up
pintarroxo [pĩta'hoʃu] M (BR) linnet; (PT) robin
pinto ['pĩtu] M chick; (!) prick (!)
pintor, a [pĩ'tor(a)] M/F painter
pintura [pĩ'tura] F painting; (*maquiagem*) make-up
piolho ['pjoʎu] M louse
pioneiro, -a [pjo'nejru, a] M/F pioneer
pior ['pjɔr] ADJ, ADV (*compar*) worse; (*superl*) worst ▶ M: **o ~** worst of all;
piorar [pjo'rar] VT to make worse, worsen ▶ VI to get worse
pipa ['pipa] F barrel, cask; (*de papel*) kite
pipi [pi'pi] (*col*) M pee; **fazer ~** to have a pee
pipoca [pi'pɔka] F popcorn
pipocar [pipo'kar] VI to pop up
piquenique [piki'niki] M picnic
pirâmide [pi'ramidʒi] F pyramid
piranha [pi'raɲa] F piranha (fish)
pirata [pi'rata] M pirate
pires ['piris] M INV saucer
Pirineus [piri'news] MPL: **os ~** the Pyrenees
pirulito [piru'litu] (BR) M lollipop
pisar [pi'zar] VT to tread on; (*esmagar, subjugar*) to crush ▶ VI to step, tread
pisca-pisca [piska-'piska] (*pl* **-s**) M (*Auto*) indicator
piscar [pis'kar] VT to blink; (*dar sinal*) to wink; (*estrelas*) to twinkle ▶ M: **num ~ de olhos** in a flash
piscina [pi'sina] F swimming pool
piso ['pizu] M floor
pisotear [pizo'tʃjar] VT to trample (on)
pista ['pista] F (*vestígio*) trace; (*indicação*) clue; (*de corridas*) track; (*Aer*) runway; (*de estrada*) lane; (*de dança*) (dance) floor
pistola [pis'tɔla] F pistol
pitada [pi'tada] F (*porção*) pinch
pivete [pi'vɛtʃi] M child thief
pivô [pi'vo] M pivot; (*fig*) central figure, prime mover
pizza ['pitsa] F pizza
placa ['plaka] F plate; (*Auto*) number plate (BRIT), license plate (US); (*comemorativa*) plaque; (*na pele*) blotch; **~ de sinalização** road sign
placar [pla'kar] M scoreboard
plácido, -a ['plasidu, a] ADJ calm; (*manso*) placid
plágio ['plaʒu] M plagiarism
planalto [pla'nawtu] M tableland, plateau
planar [pla'nar] VI to glide
planear [pla'njar] (PT) VT = **planejar**
planejamento [planeʒa'mẽtu] M planning; **~ familiar** family planning
planejar [plane'ʒar] (BR) VT to plan; (*edifício*) to design
planeta [pla'neta] M planet
planície [pla'nisi] F plain
planilha [pla'niʎa] F spreadsheet
plano, -a ['planu, a] ADJ flat, level; (*liso*) smooth ▶ M plan; **~ de saúde** health insurance; **em primeiro/ em último ~** in the foreground/ background
planta ['plãta] F plant; (*de pé*) sole; (*Arq*) plan

P

plantação [plãta'sãw] F (*ato*) planting; (*terreno*) planted land; (*safra*) crops *pl*
plantão [plã'tãw] (*pl* **-ões**) M duty; (*noturno*) night duty; (*plantonista*) person on duty; (*Mil: serviço*) sentry duty; (*: pessoa*) sentry; **estar de ~** to be on duty
plantar [plã'tar] VT to plant; (*estaca*) to drive in; (*estabelecer*) to set up
plantões [plã'tõjs] MPL *de* **plantão**
plástico, -a ['plastʃiku, a] ADJ, M plastic
plataforma [plata'fɔrma] F platform; **~ de exploração de petróleo** oil rig; **~ de lançamento** launch pad
plateia [pla'tɛja] F (*Teatro etc*) stalls *pl* (BRIT), orchestra (US); (*espectadores*) audience
platina [pla'tʃina] F platinum
platinados [platʃi'nadus] MPL (*Auto*) points
plausível [plaw'zivew] (*pl* **-eis**) ADJ credible, plausible
playground [plej'grãwdʒi] (*pl* **-s**) M play area
plenamente [plena'mẽtʃi] ADV fully, completely
pleno, -a ['plenu, a] ADJ full; (*completo*) complete; **em ~ dia** in broad daylight; **em ~ inverno** in the middle *ou* depths of winter
plural [plu'raw] (*pl* **-ais**) ADJ, M plural
pneu ['pnew] M tyre (BRIT), tire (US)
pneumonia [pnewmo'nia] F pneumonia
pó [pɔ] M powder; (*sujeira*) dust; **pó de arroz** face powder; **sabão em pó** soap powder; **tirar o pó (de algo)** to dust (sth)
pobre ['pɔbri] ADJ poor ▶ M/F poor person; **pobreza** [po'breza] F poverty
poça ['posa] F puddle, pool
poção [po'sãw] (*pl* **-ões**) F potion
poço ['posu] M well; (*de mina, elevador*) shaft
poções [po'sõjs] FPL *de* **poção**
pôde ['podʒi] VB *ver* **poder**

PALAVRA-CHAVE

poder [po'der] VI **1** (*capacidade*) can, be able to; **não posso fazê-lo** I can't do it, I'm unable to do it
2 (*ter o direito de*) can, may, be allowed to; **posso fumar aqui?** can I smoke here?; **pode entrar?** (*posso?*) can I come in?
3 (*possibilidade*) may, might, could; **pode ser** maybe; **pode ser que** it may be that; **ele poderá vir amanhã** he might come tomorrow
4: **não poder com: não posso com ele** I cannot cope with him
5 (*col: indignação*): **pudera!** no wonder!; **como é que pode?** you're joking!
▶ M power; (*autoridade*) authority; **poder aquisitivo** purchasing power; **estar no poder** to be in power; **em poder de alguém** in sb's hands

poderoso, -a [pode'rozu, ɔza] ADJ powerful
podre ['podri] ADJ rotten; **podridão** [podri'dãw] F decay, rottenness; (*fig*) corruption
põe [põj] VB *ver* **pôr**
poeira ['pwejra] F dust; **~ radioativa** fall-out; **poeirento, -a** [pwej'rẽtu, a] ADJ dusty
poema ['pwɛma] M poem
poesia [poe'zia] F poetry; (*poema*) poem

poeta ['pwɛta] M poet; **poético, -a** ['pwɛtʃiku, a] ADJ poetic; **poetisa** [pwe'tʃiza] F (woman) poet

pois [pojs] ADV (*portanto*) so; (PT: *assentimento*) yes ▶ CONJ as, since; (*mas*) but; **~ bem** well then; **~ é** that's right; **~ não!** (BR) of course!; **~ não?** (BR: *numa loja*) can I help you?; (PT) isn't it?, aren't you?, didn't they? *etc*; **~ sim!** certainly not!; **~ (então)** then

polaco, -a [po'laku, a] ADJ Polish ▶ M/F Pole ▶ M (*Ling*) Polish

polar [po'lar] ADJ polar

polegada [pole'gada] F inch

polegar [pole'gar] M (*tb*: **dedo ~**) thumb

polêmica [po'lemika] F controversy; **polêmico, -a** [po'lemiku, a] ADJ controversial

pólen ['pɔlẽ] M pollen

polícia [po'lisja] F police, police force ▶ M/F policeman/woman; **policial** [poli'sjaw] (*pl* **-ais**) ADJ police *atr* ▶ M/F (BR) policeman/woman; **novela** *ou* **romance policial** detective novel; **policiar** [poli'sjar] VT to police; (*instintos, modos*) to control, keep in check

polidez [poli'dez] F good manners *pl*, politeness

polido, -a [po'lidu, a] ADJ polished, shiny; (*cortês*) well-mannered, polite

pólio ['pɔlju] F polio

polir [po'lir] VT to polish

política [po'litʃika] F politics *sg*; (*programa*) policy; **político, -a** [po'litʃiku, a] ADJ political ▶ M/F politician

polo ['pɔlu] M pole; (*Esporte*) polo; **P~ Norte/Sul** North/South Pole

polonês, -esa [polo'nes, eza] ADJ Polish ▶ M/F Pole ▶ M (*Ling*) Polish

Polônia [po'lonja] F: **a ~** Poland

polpa ['powpa] F pulp

poltrona [pow'trɔna] F armchair

poluição [polwi'sãw] F pollution; **poluir** [po'lwir] VT to pollute

polvo ['powvu] M octopus

pólvora ['pɔwvora] F gunpowder

pomada [po'mada] F ointment

pomar [po'mar] M orchard

pomba ['põba] F dove

pombo ['põbu] M pigeon

ponderação [põdera'sãw] F consideration, meditation; (*prudência*) prudence

ponderado, -a [põde'radu, a] ADJ prudent

ponderar [põde'rar] VT to consider, weigh up ▶ VI to meditate, muse

ponho ['poɲu] VB *ver* **pôr**

ponta ['põta] F tip; (*de faca*) point; (*de sapato*) toe; (*extremidade*) end; (*Futebol: posição*) wing; (*: jogador*) winger; **uma ~ de** (*um pouco*) a touch of; **~ do dedo** fingertip; **de ~** (*tecnologia*) cutting-edge

pontapé [põta'pɛ] M kick; **dar ~s em alguém** to kick sb

pontaria [põta'ria] F aim; **fazer ~** to take aim

ponte ['põtʃi] F bridge; **~ aérea** air shuttle, airlift; **~ de safena** (heart) bypass operation

ponteiro [põ'tejru] M (*indicador*) pointer; (*de relógio*) hand

pontiagudo, -a [põtʃja'gudu, a] ADJ sharp, pointed

ponto ['põtu] M point; (*Med, Costura, Tricô*) stitch; (*pequeno sinal, do i*) dot; (*na pontuação*) full stop (BRIT), period (US); (*na pele*) spot; (*de ônibus*) stop; (*de táxi*) rank (BRIT), stand (US); (*matéria escolar*) subject; **estar a ~ de fazer** to be on the point of doing; **às cinco em ~** at five o'clock on the dot; **dois ~s** colon *sg*; **~ de admiração** (PT) exclamation mark; **~ de exclamação/interrogação** exclamation/question mark; **~ de vista** point of view, viewpoint; **~ e vírgula** semicolon

pontuação [põtwa'sãw] F punctuation

pontual [põ'twaw] (*pl* **-ais**) ADJ punctual

pontudo, -a [põ'tudu, a] ADJ pointed

popa ['popa] F stern

população [popula'sãw] (*pl* **-ões**) F population

popular [popu'lar] ADJ popular; **popularidade** [populari'dadʒi] F popularity

pôquer ['poker] M poker

PALAVRA-CHAVE

por [por] (*por + o(s)/a(s) = pelo(s)/a(s)*) PREP **1** (*objetivo*) for; **lutar pela pátria** to fight for one's country

2 (*+ infin*): **está por acontecer** it is about to happen, it is yet to happen; **está por fazer** it is still to be done

3 (*causa*) out of, because of; **por falta de fundos** through lack of funds; **por hábito/natureza** out of habit/by nature; **faço isso por ela** I do it for her; **por isso** therefore; **a razão pela qual ...** the reason why ...; **pelo amor de Deus!** for Heaven's sake!

4 (*tempo*): **pela manhã** in the morning; **por volta das duas horas** at about two o'clock; **ele vai ficar por uma semana** he's staying for a week

5 (*lugar*): **por aqui** this way; **viemos pelo parque** we came through the park; **passar por São Paulo** to pass through São Paulo; **por fora/dentro** outside/inside

6 (*troca, preço*) for; **trocar o velho pelo novo** to change old for new; **comprei o livro por dez libras** I bought the book for ten pounds

7 (*valor proporcional*): **por cento** per cent; **por hora/dia/semana/mês/ano** hourly/daily/weekly/monthly/yearly; **por cabeça** a *ou* per head; **por mais difícil** *etc* **que seja** however difficult *etc* it is

8 (*modo, meio*) by; **por correio/avião** by post/air; **por si** by o.s.; **por escrito** in writing; **entrar pela entrada principal** to go in through the main entrance

9: **por que** why; **por quê?** why?

10: **por mim tudo bem** as far as I'm concerned that's OK

PALAVRA-CHAVE

pôr [por] VT **1** (*colocar*) to put; (*roupas*) to put on; (*objeções, dúvidas*) to raise; (*ovos, mesa*) to lay; (*defeito*) to find; **põe mais forte** turn it up; **você põe açúcar?** do you take sugar?; **pôr de lado** to set aside

2 (*+ adj*) to make; **você está me pondo nervoso** you're making me nervous

pôr-se VR **1** (*sol*) to set

2 (*colocar-se*): **pôr-se de pé** to stand up; **ponha-se no meu lugar** put yourself in my position

3: **pôr-se a** to start to; **ela pôs-se a chorar** she started crying

▶ M: **o pôr do sol** sunset

porão [po'rãw] (*pl* **-ões**) M (*de casa*) basement; (*: armazém*) cellar

porca ['pɔrka] F (*animal*) sow

porção [por'sãw] (*pl* **-ões**) F portion, piece; **uma ~ de** a lot of
porcaria [porka'ria] F filth; (*dito sujo*) obscenity; (*coisa ruim*) piece of junk
porcelana [porse'lana] F porcelain
porcentagem [porsẽ'taʒẽ] (*pl* **-ns**) F percentage
porco, -a ['porku, 'pɔrka] ADJ filthy ▶ M (*animal*) pig; (*carne*) pork
porções [por'sõjs] FPL *de* **porção**
porém [po'rẽ] CONJ however
pormenor [porme'nor] M detail
pornografia [pornogra'fia] F pornography
poro ['pɔru] M pore
porões [po'rõjs] MPL *de* **porão**
porque [por'ke] CONJ because; (*interrogativo: PT*) why
porquê [por'ke] ADV (PT) why ▶ M reason, motive; **~?** (PT) why?
porrete [po'hetʃi] M club
porta ['pɔrta] F door; (*vão da porta*) doorway; (*de um jardim*) gate
portador, a [porta'dor(a)] M/F bearer
portagem [por'taʒẽ] (PT) (*pl* **-ns**) F toll
portal [por'taw] (*pl* **-ais**) M doorway
porta-luvas M INV (*Auto*) glove compartment
porta-malas M INV (*Auto*) boot (BRIT), trunk (US)
porta-níqueis M INV purse
portanto [por'tãtu] CONJ so, therefore
portão [por'tãw] (*pl* **-ões**) M gate
portar [por'tar] VT to carry;
portar-se VR to behave
portaria [porta'ria] F (*de um edifício*) entrance hall; (*recepção*) reception desk; (*do governo*) edict, decree
portátil [por'tatʃiw] (*pl* **-eis**) ADJ portable
porta-voz (*pl* **-es**) M/F (*pessoa*) spokesman, spokesperson
porte ['pɔrtʃi] M transport; (*custo*) freight charge, carriage; **~ pago** post paid; **de grande ~** far-reaching, important
porteiro, -a [por'tejru, a] M/F caretaker; **~ eletrônico** entry phone
pórtico ['pɔrtʃiku] M porch, portico
porto ['portu] M (*do mar*) port, harbour (BRIT), harbor (US); (*vinho*) port; **o P~** Oporto
portões [por'tõjs] MPL *de* **portão**
Portugal [portu'gaw] M Portugal;
português, -guesa [portu'ges, 'geza] ADJ Portuguese ▶ M/F Portuguese *inv* ▶ M (*Ling*) Portuguese
porventura [porvẽ'tura] ADJ by chance; **se ~ você ...** if you happen to ...
pôs [pos] VB *ver* **pôr**
posar [po'zar] VI (*Foto*) to pose
posição [pozi'sãw] (*pl* **-ões**) F position; (*social*) standing, status;
posicionar [pozisjo'nar] VT to position
positivo, -a [pozi'tʃivu, a] ADJ positive
possante [po'sãtʃi] ADJ powerful, strong; (*carro*) flashy
possessão [pose'sãw] F possession; **possessivo, -a** [pose'sivu, a] ADJ possessive
possibilidade [posibili'dadʒi] F

P

possibility; **possibilidades** FPL (*recursos*) means

possibilitar [posibili'tar] VT to make possible, permit

possível [po'sivew] (*pl* **-eis**) ADJ possible; **fazer todo o ~** to do one's best

posso ['posu] VB *ver* **poder**

possuidor, a [poswi'dor(a)] M/F owner

possuir [po'swir] VT (*casa, livro etc*) to own; (*dinheiro, talento*) to possess

post [post] (*pl* **-s**) M (*Comput*) post

postal [pos'taw] (*pl* **-ais**) ADJ postal ▶ M postcard

postar [pos'tar] VT to place, post; (*Comput*) to post

poste ['pɔstʃi] M pole, post

posterior [poste'rjor] ADJ (*mais tarde*) subsequent, later; (*traseiro*) rear, back; **posteriormente** [posterjor'mẽtʃi] ADV later, subsequently

postiço, -a [pos'tʃisu, a] ADJ false, artificial

posto, -a ['postu, 'pɔsta] PP *de* **pôr** ▶ M post, position; (*emprego*) job; **~ de gasolina** service *ou* petrol station; **~ que** although; **~ de saúde** health centre *ou* center

póstumo, -a ['pɔstumu, a] ADJ posthumous

postura [pos'tura] F posture; (*aspecto físico*) appearance

potável [po'tavew] (*pl* **-eis**) ADJ drinkable; **água ~** drinking water

pote ['pɔtʃi] M jug, pitcher; (*de geleia*) jar; (*de creme*) pot; **chover a ~s** (PT) to rain cats and dogs

potência [po'tẽsja] F power

potencial [potẽ'sjaw] (*pl* **-ais**) ADJ, M potential

potente [po'tẽtʃi] ADJ powerful, potent

PALAVRA-CHAVE

pouco, -a ['poku, a] ADJ **1** (*sg*) little, not much; **pouco tempo** little *ou* not much time; **de pouco interesse** of little interest, not very interesting; **pouca coisa** not much

2 (*pl*) few, not many; **uns poucos** a few, some; **poucas vezes** rarely; **poucas crianças comem o que devem** few children eat what they should

▶ ADV **1** little, not much; **custa pouco** it doesn't cost much; **dentro em pouco, daqui a pouco** shortly; **pouco antes** shortly before

2 (+ *adj, negativo*): **ela é pouco inteligente/simpática** she's not very bright/friendly

3: **por pouco eu não morri** I almost died

4: **pouco a pouco** little by little

5: **aos poucos** gradually

▶ M: **um pouco** a little, a bit; **nem um pouco** not at all

poupador, a [popa'dor(a)] ADJ thrifty

poupança [po'pãsa] F thrift; (*economias*) savings *pl*; (*tb*: **caderneta de ~**) savings bank

poupar [po'par] VT to save; (*vida*) to spare

pousada [po'zada] F (*hospedagem*) lodging; (*hospedaria*) inn

pousar [po'zar] VT to place; (*mão*) to rest ▶ VI (*avião, pássaro*) to land; (*pernoitar*) to spend the night

povo ['povu] M people; (*raça*) people *pl*, race; (*plebe*) common people *pl*; (*multidão*) crowd

povoação [povwa'sãw] (*pl* **-ões**) F (*aldeia*) village, settlement; (*habitantes*) population

povoado [po'vwadu] M village

povoar [po'vwar] VT (*de habitantes*) to people, populate; (*de animais etc*) to stock

pra [pra] (*col*) PREP = **para a**; *ver* **para**

praça ['prasa] F (*largo*) square; (*mercado*) marketplace; (*soldado*) soldier; **~ de touros** bullring

praga ['praga] F nuisance; (*maldição*) curse; (*desgraça*) misfortune; (*erva daninha*) weed

pragmático, -a [prag'matʃiku, a] ADJ pragmatic

praia ['praja] F beach

prancha ['prãʃa] F plank; (*de surfe*) board

prata ['prata] F silver; (*col: cruzeiro*) ≈ quid (BRIT), ≈ buck (US)

prateleira [prate'lejra] F shelf

prática ['pratʃika] F practice; (*experiência*) experience, know-how; (*costume*) habit, custom; *ver tb* **prático**

praticante [pratʃi'kãtʃi] ADJ practising (BRIT), practicing (US) ▶ M/F apprentice; (*de esporte*) practitioner

praticar [pratʃi'kar] VT to practise (BRIT), practice (US); (*roubo, operação*) to carry out; **prático, -a** ['pratʃiku, a] ADJ practical ▶ M/F expert

prato ['pratu] M plate; (*comida*) dish; (*de uma refeição*) course; (*de toca-discos*) turntable; **pratos** MPL (*Mús*) cymbals

praxe ['praʃi] F custom, usage; **de ~** usually; **ser de ~** to be the norm

> Student life in Portugal follows the traditions set out in a written set of rules known as the 'código da **praxe**'. It begins in freshers' week, where freshers are jeered at by their seniors, and are subjected to a number of humiliating practical jokes, such as having their hair cut against their will and being made to walk around town in fancy dress.

prazer [pra'zer] M pleasure; **muito ~ em conhecê-lo** pleased to meet you

prazo ['prazu] M term, period; (*vencimento*) expiry date, time limit; **a curto/médio/longo ~** in the short/medium/long term; **comprar a ~** to buy on hire purchase (BRIT) *ou* on the installment plan (US)

precário, -a [pre'karju, a] ADJ precarious; (*escasso*) failing

precaução [prekaw'sãw] (*pl* **-ões**) F precaution

precaver-se [preka'versi] VR: **~ (contra** *ou* **de)** to be on one's guard (against); **precavido, -a** [preka'vidu, a] ADJ cautious

prece ['prɛsi] F prayer; (*súplica*) entreaty

precedente [prese'dẽtʃi] ADJ preceding ▶ M precedent

preceder [prese'der] VT, VI to precede; **~ a algo** to precede sth; (*ter primazia*) to take precedence over sth

precioso, -a [pre'sjozu, ɔza] ADJ precious

precipício [presi'pisju] M precipice; (*fig*) abyss

precipitação [presipita'sãw] F haste; (*imprudência*) rashness

precipitado, -a [presipi'tadu, a] ADJ hasty; (*imprudente*) rash

precisamente [presiza'mẽtʃi] ADV precisely

precisar [presi'zar] VT to need;

P

(*especificar*) to specify; **precisar-se** VR: **"precisa-se"** "needed"; **~ de** to need; **não precisa você se preocupar** you needn't worry

preciso, -a [pre'sizu, a] ADJ precise, accurate; (*necessário*) necessary; (*claro*) concise; **é ~ você ir** you must go

preço ['presu] M price; (*custo*) cost; (*valor*) value; **a ~ de banana** (BR) *ou* **de chuva** (PT) dirt cheap

preconceito [prekõ'sejtu] M prejudice

predador [preda'dor] M predator

predileto, -a [predʒi'lɛtu, a] ADJ favourite (BRIT), favorite (US)

prédio ['prɛdʒju] M building; **~ de apartamentos** block of flats (BRIT), apartment house (US)

predispor [predʒis'por] (*irreg: como* **pôr**) VT: **~ alguém contra** to prejudice sb against; **predispor-se** VR: **~-se a/para** to get o.s. in the mood to/for

predominar [predomi'nar] VI to predominate, prevail

preencher [preẽ'ʃer] VT (*formulário*) to fill in (BRIT) *ou* out, complete; (*requisitos*) to fulfil (BRIT), fulfill (US), meet; (*espaço, vaga, tempo, cargo*) to fill

prefácio [pre'fasju] M preface

prefeito, -a [pre'fejtu, a] M/F mayor; **prefeitura** [prefej'tura] F town hall

preferência [prefe'rẽsja] F preference; (*Auto*) priority; **de ~** preferably; **ter ~ por** to have a preference for; **preferencial** [preferẽ'sjaw] (*pl* **-ais**) ADJ (*rua*) main ▸ F main road (*with priority*)

preferido, -a [prefe'ridu, a] ADJ favourite (BRIT), favorite (US)

preferir [prefe'rir] VT to prefer

prefiro [pre'firu] VB *ver* **preferir**

prefixo [pre'fiksu] M (*Ling*) prefix; (*Tel*) code

prega ['prɛga] F pleat, fold

pregar[1] [prɛ'gar] VT, VI to preach

pregar[2] [pre'gar] VT (*com prego*) to nail; (*fixar*) to pin, fasten; (*cosendo*) to sew on; **~ uma peça** to play a trick; **~ um susto em alguém** to give sb a fright

prego ['prɛgu] M nail; (*col: casa de penhor*) pawn shop

preguiça [pre'gisa] F laziness; (*animal*) sloth; **estar com ~** to feel lazy; **preguiçoso, -a** [pregi'sozu, ɔza] ADJ lazy

pré-histórico, -a ADJ prehistoric

preia-mar (PT) F high tide

prejuízo [pre'ʒwizu] M damage, harm; (*em dinheiro*) loss; **em ~ de** to the detriment of

prematuro, -a [prema'turu, a] ADJ premature

premiado, -a [pre'mjadu, a] ADJ prize-winning; (*bilhete*) winning ▸ M/F prize-winner

premiar [pre'mjar] VT to award a prize to; (*recompensar*) to reward

prêmio ['premju] M prize; (*recompensa*) reward; (*Seguros*) premium

prenda ['prẽda] F gift, present; (*em jogo*) forfeit; **~s domésticas** housework *sg*

prendedor [prẽde'dor] M fastener; (*de cabelo, gravata*) clip; **~ de roupa** clothes peg; **~ de papéis** paper clip

prender [prẽ'der] VT to fasten, fix; (*roupa*) to pin; (*cabelo*) to tie back; (*capturar*) to arrest; (*atar, ligar*) to tie; (*atenção*) to catch; (*afetivamente*) to tie, bind; (*reter: doença, compromisso*) to keep; (*movimentos*) to restrict; **prender-se**

VR to get caught, stick; **~-se a alguém** (*por amizade*) to be attached to sb
preocupação [preokupa'sãw] (*pl* **-ões**) F preoccupation; (*inquietação*) worry, concern
preocupar [preoku'par] VT to preoccupy; (*inquietar*) to worry; **preocupar-se** VR: **~-se com** to worry about, be worried about
preparação [prepara'sãw] (*pl* **-ões**) F preparation
preparar [prepa'rar] VT to prepare; **preparar-se** VR to get ready; **preparativos** [prepara'tʃivus] MPL preparations, arrangements
preponderante [prepõde'rãtʃi] ADJ predominant
preposição [prepozi'sãw] (*pl* **-ões**) F preposition
prepotente [prepo'tẽtʃi] ADJ predominant; (*despótico*) despotic; (*atitude*) overbearing
prescrever [preskre'ver] VT to prescribe; (*prazo*) to set
presença [pre'zẽsa] F presence; (*frequência*) attendance; **ter boa ~** to be presentable; **presenciar** [prezẽ'sjar] VT to be present at; (*testemunhar*) to witness
presente [pre'zẽtʃi] ADJ present; (*fig: interessado*) attentive; (*: evidente*) clear, obvious ▶ M present ▶ F (*Com: carta*): **a ~** this letter; **os presentes** MPL (*pessoas*) those present; **presentear** [prezẽ'tʃjar] VT: **presentear alguém (com algo)** to give sb (sth as) a present
preservação [prezerva'sãw] F preservation
presidente, -a [prezi'dẽtʃi, ta] M/F president
presidiário, -a [prezi'dʒjarju, a] M/F convict
presídio [pre'zidʒju] M prison
presidir [prezi'dʒir] VT, VI: **~ (a)** to preside over; (*reunião*) to chair; (*suj: leis, critérios*) to govern
preso, -a ['prezu, a] ADJ imprisoned; (*capturado*) under arrest; (*atado*) tied ▶ M/F prisoner; **estar ~ a alguém** to be attached to sb
pressa ['prɛsa] F haste, hurry; (*rapidez*) speed; (*urgência*) urgency; **às ~s** hurriedly; **estar com ~** to be in a hurry; **ter ~ de** *ou* **em fazer** to be in a hurry to do
presságio [pre'saʒju] M omen, sign; (*pressentimento*) premonition
pressão [pre'sãw] (*pl* **-ões**) F pressure; **(colchete de) ~** press stud, popper
pressentimento [presẽtʃi'mẽtu] M premonition
pressentir [presẽ'tʃir] VT to foresee; (*suspeitar*) to sense
pressionar [presjo'nar] VT (*botão*) to press; (*coagir*) to pressure ▶ VI to press, put on pressure
pressões [pre'sõjs] FPL *de* **pressão**
pressupor [presu'por] (*irreg: como* **pôr**) VT to presuppose
prestação [presta'sãw] (*pl* **-ões**) F instalment (BRIT), installment (US); (*por uma casa*) repayment
prestar [pres'tar] VT (*cuidados*) to give; (*favores, serviços*) to do; (*contas*) to render; (*informações*) to supply; (*uma qualidade a algo*) to lend ▶ VI: **~ a alguém para algo** to be of use to sb for sth; **prestar-se** VR: **~-se a** to be suitable for; (*admitir*) to lend o.s. to; (*dispor-se*) to be willing to;

P

~ atenção to pay attention
prestes ['prɛstʃis] ADJ INV ready; (*a ponto de*): **~ a partir** about to leave
prestígio [pres'tʃiʒu] M prestige
presunção [prezũ'sãw] (*pl* **-ões**) F presumption; (*vaidade*) conceit, self-importance; **presunçoso, -a** [prezũ'sozu, ɔza] ADJ vain, self-important
presunto [pre'zũtu] M ham
pretender [pretẽ'der] VT to claim; (*cargo, emprego*) to go for; **~ fazer** to intend to do
pretensão [pretẽ'sãw] (*pl* **-ões**) F claim; (*vaidade*) pretension; (*propósito*) aim; (*aspiração*) aspiration; **pretensioso, -a** [pretẽ'sjozu, ɔza] ADJ pretentious
pretérito [pre'tɛritu] M (*Ling*) preterite
pretexto [pre'testu] M pretext
preto, -a ['pretu, a] ADJ black
prevalecer [prevale'ser] VI to prevail; **prevalecer-se** VR: **~-se de** (*aproveitar-se*) to take advantage of
prevenção [prevẽ'sãw] (*pl* **-ões**) F prevention; (*preconceito*) prejudice; (*cautela*) caution; **estar de ~ com** *ou* **contra alguém** to be bias(s)ed against sb
prevenido, -a [preve'nidu, a] ADJ cautious, wary
prevenir [preve'nir] VT to prevent; (*avisar*) to warn; (*preparar*) to prepare
prever [pre'ver] (*irreg: como* **ver**) VT to predict, foresee; (*pressupor*) to presuppose
prévio, -a ['prɛvju, a] ADJ prior; (*preliminar*) preliminary
previsão [previ'zãw] (*pl* **-ões**) F foresight; (*prognóstico*) prediction, forecast; **~ do tempo** weather forecast
previsível [previ'zivew] (*pl* **-eis**) ADJ predictable
previsões [previ'zõjs] FPL *de* **previsão**
prezado, -a [pre'zadu, a] ADJ esteemed; (*numa carta*) dear
prezar [pre'zar] VT (*amigos*) to value highly; (*autoridade*) to respect; (*gostar de*) to appreciate
primário, -a [pri'marju, a] ADJ primary; (*elementar*) basic, rudimentary; (*primitivo*) primitive ▶ M (*curso*) elementary education
primavera [prima'vɛra] F spring; (*planta*) primrose
primeira [pri'mejra] F (*Auto*) first (gear)
primeiro, -a [pri'mejru, a] ADJ, ADV first; **de primeira** first-class
primo, -a ['primu, a] M/F cousin; **~ irmão** first cousin
princesa [prĩ'seza] F princess
principal [prĩsi'paw] (*pl* **-ais**) ADJ principal; (*entrada, razão, rua*) main ▶ M head, principal; (*essencial, de dívida*) principal
príncipe ['prĩsipi] M prince
principiante [prĩsi'pjãtʃi] M/F beginner
principiar [prĩsi'pjar] VT, VI to begin
princípio [prĩ'sipju] M beginning, start; (*origem*) origin; (*legal, moral*) principle; **princípios** MPL (*de matéria*) rudiments
prioridade [prjori'dadʒi] F priority
prisão [pri'zãw] (*pl* **-ões**) F imprisonment; (*cadeia*) prison, jail; (*detenção*) arrest; **~ de ventre** constipation; **prisioneiro, -a** [prizjo'nejru, a] M/F prisoner
privacidade [privasi'dadʒi] F privacy
privada [pri'vada] F toilet

privado, -a [pri'vadu, a] ADJ private; (*carente*) deprived
privar [pri'var] VT to deprive
privativo, -a [priva'tʃivu, a] ADJ (*particular*) private; **~ de** peculiar to
privilegiado, -a [privile'ʒjadu, a] ADJ privileged; (*excepcional*) unique, exceptional
privilegiar [privile'ʒjar] VT to privilege; (*favorecer*) to favour (BRIT), favor (US)
privilégio [privi'lɛʒu] M privilege
pró [prɔ] ADV for, in favour (BRIT) *ou* favor (US) ▶ M advantage; **os ~s e os contras** the pros and cons; **em ~ de** in favo(u)r of
pró- [prɔ] PREFIXO pro-
proa ['proa] F prow, bow
probabilidade [probabili'dadʒi] F probability; **probabilidades** FPL (*chances*) odds
problema [prob'lɛma] M problem
procedência [prose'dẽsja] F origin, source; (*lugar de saída*) point of departure
proceder [prose'der] VI to proceed; (*comportar-se*) to behave; (*agir*) to act ▶ M conduct;
procedimento [prosedʒi'mẽtu] M conduct, behaviour (BRIT), behavior (US); (*processo*) procedure; (*Jur*) proceedings *pl*
processamento [prosesa'mẽtu] M processing; (*Jur*) prosecution; (*verificação*) verification; **~ de texto** word processing
processar [prose'sar] VT (*Jur*) to take proceedings against, prosecute; (*requerimentos, dados*) to process
processo [pro'sɛsu] M process; (*procedimento*) procedure; (*Jur*) lawsuit, legal proceedings *pl*; (*: autos*) record; (*conjunto de documentos*) documents *pl*
procissão [prosi'sãw] (*pl* **-ões**) F procession
Proclamação da República *see note*

> Commemorated on 15 November, which is a public holiday, the proclamation of the republic in 1889 was a military coup, led by Marshal Deodoro da Fonseca. It brought down the empire which had been established after independence and installed a federal republic in Brazil.

proclamar [prokla'mar] VT to proclaim
procura [pro'kura] F search; (*Com*) demand
procuração [prokura'sãw] (*pl* **-ões**) F: **por ~** by proxy
procurador, a [prokura'dor(a)] M/F attorney; **P~ Geral da República** Attorney General
procurar [proku'rar] VT to look for, seek; (*emprego*) to apply for; (*ir visitar*) to call on; (*contatar*) to get in touch with; **~ fazer** to try to do
produção [produ'sãw] (*pl* **-ões**) F production; (*volume de produção*) output; (*produto*) product; **~ em massa** *ou* **série** mass production
produtivo, -a [produ'tʃivu, a] ADJ productive; (*rendoso*) profitable
produto [pro'dutu] M product; (*renda*) proceeds *pl*, profit
produtor, a [produ'tor(a)] ADJ producing ▶ M/F producer
produzir [produ'zir] VT to produce; (*ocasionar*) to cause, bring about; (*render*) to bring in
proeminente [proemi'nẽtʃi] ADJ prominent

P

proeza [pro'eza] F achievement, feat
profanar [profa'nar] VT to desecrate, profane; **profano, -a** [pro'fanu, a] ADJ profane ▸ M/F layman/woman
profecia [profe'sia] F prophecy
professor, a [profe'sor(a)] M/F teacher; (*universitário*) lecturer
profeta, -tisa [pro'fɛta, profe'tʃiza] M/F prophet; **profetizar** [profetʃi'zar] VT, VI to prophesy, predict
profissão [profi'sãw] (*pl* **-ões**) F profession; **profissional** [profisjo'naw] (*pl* **-ais**) ADJ, M/F professional; **profissionalizante** [profisjonali'zãtʃi] ADJ (*ensino*) vocational
profundidade [profũdʒi'dadʒi] F depth
profundo, -a [pro'fũdu, a] ADJ deep; (*fig*) profound
profusão [profu'zãw] F profusion, abundance
prognóstico [prog'nɔstʃiku] M prediction, forecast
programa [pro'grama] M programme (BRIT), program (US); (*Comput*) program; (*plano*) plan; (*diversão*) thing to do; (*de um curso*) syllabus; **programação** [programa'sãw] F planning; (*TV, Rádio, Comput*) programming; **programador, a** [programa'dor(a)] M/F programmer; **programar** [progra'mar] VT to plan; (*Comput*) to program
progredir [progre'dʒir] VI to progress; (*avançar*) to move forward; (*infecção*) to progress
progressista [progre'sista] ADJ, M/F progressive
progressivo, -a [progre'sivu, a] ADJ progressive; (*gradual*) gradual
progresso [pro'grɛsu] M progress
progrido [pro'gridu] VB *ver* **progredir**
proibição [proibi'sãw] (*pl* **-ões**) F prohibition, ban
proibir [proi'bir] VT to prohibit; (*livro, espetáculo*) to ban; **"é proibido fumar"** "no smoking"; **~ alguém de fazer, ~ que alguém faça** to forbid sb to do
projeção [proʒe'sãw] (*pl* **-ões**) F projection
projetar [proʒe'tar] VT to project
projétil [pro'ʒɛtʃiw] (*pl* **-eis**) M projectile, missile
projeto [pro'ʒɛtu] M project; (*plano*) plan; (*Tec*) design; **~ de lei** bill
projetor [proʒe'tor] M (*Cinema*) projector
proliferar [prolife'rar] VI to proliferate
prolongação [prolõga'sãw] F extension
prolongado, -a [prolõ'gadu, a] ADJ prolonged; (*alongado*) extended
prolongar [prolõ'gar] VT to extend, lengthen; (*decisão etc*) to postpone; (*vida*) to prolong; **prolongar-se** VR to extend; (*durar*) to last
promessa [pro'mɛsa] F promise
prometer [prome'ter] VT, VI to promise
promíscuo, -a [pro'miskwu, a] ADJ disorderly, mixed up; (*comportamento sexual*) promiscuous
promissor, a [promi'sor(a)] ADJ promising
promoção [promo'sãw] (*pl* **-ões**) F promotion; **fazer ~ de alguém/algo** to promote sb/sth
promotor, a [promo'tor(a)] M/F promoter; (*Jur*) prosecutor

promover [promo'ver] VT to promote; (*causar*) to bring about
pronome [pro'nɔmi] M pronoun
pronto, -a [prõtu, a] ADJ ready; (*rápido*) quick, speedy; (*imediato*) prompt ▶ ADV promptly; **de ~** promptly; **estar ~ a ...** to be prepared *ou* willing to ...;
pronto-socorro (*pl* **prontos-socorros**) M (BR) casualty (BRIT), emergency room (US); (PT: *reboque*) tow truck
pronúncia [pro'nũsja] F pronunciation; (*Jur*) indictment
pronunciar [pronũ'sjar] VT to pronounce; (*discurso*) to make, deliver; (*Jur: réu*) to indict; (: *sentença*) to pass
propaganda [propa'gãda] F (*Pol*) propaganda; (*Com*) advertising; (: *uma propaganda*) advert, advertisement; **fazer ~ de** to advertise
propagar [propa'gar] VT to propagate; (*fig: difundir*) to disseminate
propensão [propẽ'sãw] (*pl* **-ões**) F inclination, tendency; **propenso, -a** [pro'pẽsu, a] ADJ: **propenso a** inclined to; **ser propenso a** to be inclined to, have a tendency to
propina [pro'pina] F (*gorjeta*) tip; (PT: *cota*) fee
propor [pro'por] (*irreg: como* **pôr**) VT to propose; (*oferecer*) to offer; (*um problema*) to pose; **propor-se** VR: **~-se (a) fazer** (*pretender*) to intend to do; (*visar*) to aim to do; (*dispor-se*) to decide to do; (*oferecer-se*) to offer to do
proporção [propor'sãw] (*pl* **-ões**) F proportion; **proporções** FPL (*dimensões*) dimensions;
proporcional [proporsjo'naw] (*pl* **-ais**) ADJ proportional;
proporcionar [proporsjo'nar] VT to provide, give; (*adaptar*) to adjust, adapt
proposição [propozi'sãw] (*pl* **-ões**) F proposition, proposal
proposital [propozi'taw] (*pl* **-ais**) ADJ intentional
propósito [pro'pɔzitu] M (*intenção*) purpose; (*objetivo*) aim; **a ~** by the way; **a ~ de** with regard to; **de ~** on purpose
proposta [pro'pɔsta] F proposal; (*oferecimento*) offer
propriamente [proprja'mẽtʃi] ADV properly, exactly; **~ falando** *ou* **dito** strictly speaking
propriedade [proprje'dadʒi] F property; (*direito de proprietário*) ownership; (*o que é apropriado*) propriety
proprietário, -a [proprje'tarju, a] M/F owner, proprietor
próprio, -a ['prɔprju, a] ADJ own, of one's own; (*mesmo*) very, selfsame; (*hora, momento*) opportune, right; (*nome*) proper; (*característico*) characteristic; (*sentido*) proper, true; (*depois de pronome*) -self; **~ (para)** suitable (for); **eu ~** I myself; **por si ~** of one's own accord; **ele é o ~ inglês** he's a typical Englishman; **é o ~** it's him himself
prorrogação [prohoga'sãw] (*pl* **-ões**) F extension
prosa ['prɔza] F prose; (*conversa*) chatter; (*fanfarrice*) boasting, bragging ▶ ADJ full of oneself
prospecto [pros'pɛktu] M leaflet; (*em forma de livro*) brochure
prosperar [prospe'rar] VI to prosper, thrive; **prosperidade** [prosperi'dadʒi] F prosperity;

P

(*bom êxito*) success; **próspero, -a** ['prɔsperu, a] ADJ prosperous; (*bem sucedido*) successful; (*favorável*) favourable (BRIT), favorable (US)
prosseguir [prose'gir] VT, VI to continue; **~ em** to continue (with)
prostíbulo [pros'tʃibulu] M brothel
prostituta [prostʃi'tuta] F prostitute
prostrado, -a [pros'tradu, a] ADJ prostrate
protagonista [protago'nista] M/F protagonist
proteção [prote'sãw] F protection
proteger [prote'ʒer] VT to protect; **protegido, -a** [prote'ʒidu, a] M/F protégé(e)
proteína [prote'ina] F protein
protejo [pro'teʒu] VB *ver* **proteger**
protestante [protes'tãtʃi] ADJ, M/F Protestant
protestar [protes'tar] VT, VI to protest; **protesto** [pro'tɛstu] M protest
protetor, a [prote'tor(a)] ADJ protective ▶ M/F protector; **~ solar** sunscreen; **~ de tela** (*Comput*) screensaver
protuberância [protube'rãsja] F bump; **protuberante** [protube'rãtʃi] ADJ sticking out
prova ['prɔva] F proof; (*Tec: teste*) test, trial; (*Educ: exame*) examination; (*sinal*) sign; (*de comida, bebida*) taste; (*de roupa*) fitting; (*Esporte*) competition; (*Tip*) proof; **prova(s)** F(PL) (*Jur*) evidence *sg*; **à ~ de bala/fogo/água** bulletproof/fireproof/waterproof; **pôr à ~** to put to the test
provar [pro'var] VT to prove; (*comida*) to taste, try; (*roupa*) to try on ▶ VI to try
provável [pro'vavew] (*pl* **-eis**) ADJ probable, likely
provedor, a [prove'dor(a)] M/F provider; **~ de acesso à Internet** internet service provider
proveito [pro'vejtu] M advantage; (*ganho*) profit; **em ~ de** for the benefit of; **fazer ~ de** to make use of; **proveitoso, -a** [provej'tozu, ɔza] ADJ profitable, advantageous; (*útil*) useful
proveniente [prove'njẽtʃi] ADJ: **~ de** originating from; (*que resulta de*) arising from
prover [pro'ver] (*irreg: como* **ver**) VT to provide, supply; (*vaga*) to fill ▶ VI: **~ a** to take care of, see to
provérbio [pro'vɛrbju] M proverb
providência [provi'dẽsja] F providence; **providências** FPL (*medidas*) measures, steps; **providencial** [providẽ'sjaw] (*pl* **-ais**) ADJ opportune; **providenciar** [providẽ'sjar] VT to provide; (*tomar providências*) to arrange ▶ VI to make arrangements, take steps; **providenciar para que** to see to it that
província [pro'vĩsja] F province; **provinciano, -a** [provĩ'sjanu, a] ADJ provincial
provisório, -a [provi'zɔrju, a] ADJ provisional, temporary
provocador, a [provoka'dor(a)] ADJ provocative
provocante [provo'kãtʃi] ADJ provocative
provocar [provo'kar] VT to provoke; (*ocasionar*) to cause; (*atrair*) to tempt, attract; (*estimular*) to rouse, stimulate
próximo, -a ['prɔsimu, a] ADJ (*no espaço*) near, close; (*no tempo*) close; (*seguinte*) next; (*amigo, parente*)

close; (*vizinho*) neighbouring (BRIT), neighboring (US) ▶ ADV near ▶ M fellow man; **~ a** *ou* **de** near (to), close to; **até a próxima!** see you again soon!
prudência [pru'dẽsja] F care, prudence; **prudente** [pru'dẽtʃi] ADJ prudent
prurido [pru'ridu] M itch
psicanálise [psika'nalizi] F psychoanalysis
psicologia [psikolo'ʒia] F psychology; **psicológico, -a** [psiko'lɔʒiku, a] ADJ psychological; **psicólogo, -a** [psi'kɔlogu, a] M/F psychologist
psique ['psiki] F psyche
psiquiatra [psi'kjatra] M/F psychiatrist
psiquiatria [psikja'tria] F psychiatry
psíquico, -a ['psikiku, a] ADJ psychological
puberdade [puber'dadʒi] F puberty
publicação [publika'sãw] F publication
publicar [publi'kar] VT to publish; (*divulgar*) to divulge; (*proclamar*) to announce
publicidade [publisi'dadʒi] F publicity; (*Com*) advertising; **publicitário, -a** [publisi'tarju, a] ADJ publicity *atr*; (*Com*) advertising *atr*
público, -a ['publiku, a] ADJ public ▶ M public; (*Cinema, Teatro etc*) audience
pude ['pudʒi] VB *ver* **poder**
pudera [pu'dɛra] VB *ver* **poder**
pudim [pu'dʒĩ] (*pl* **-ns**) M pudding
pudor [pu'dor] M bashfulness, modesty; (*moral*) decency
pular [pu'lar] VI to jump; (*no Carnaval*) to celebrate ▶ VT to jump (over); (*páginas, trechos*) to skip; **~ Carnaval** to celebrate Carnival; **~ corda** to skip
pulga ['puwga] F flea
pulmão [puw'mãw] (*pl* **-ões**) M lung
pulo[1] ['pulu] M jump; **dar um ~ em** to stop off at
pulo[2] VB *ver* **polir**
pulôver [pu'lover] (BR) M pullover
pulsação [puwsa'sãw] F pulsation, beating; (*Med*) pulse
pulseira [puw'sejra] F bracelet; (*de sapato*) strap
pulso ['puwsu] M (*Anat*) wrist; (*Med*) pulse; (*fig*) vigour (BRIT), vigor (US), energy
punha ['puɲa] VB *ver* **pôr**
punhado [pu'ɲadu] M handful
punhal [pu'ɲaw] (*pl* **-ais**) M dagger
punho ['puɲu] M fist; (*de manga*) cuff; (*de espada*) hilt
punição [puni'sãw] (*pl* **-ões**) F punishment
punir [pu'nir] VT to punish
pupila [pu'pila] F (*Anat*) pupil
purê [pu're] M purée; **~ de batatas** mashed potatoes
pureza [pu'reza] F purity
purificar [purifi'kar] VT to purify
puritano, -a [puri'tanu, a] ADJ puritanical; (*seita*) puritan ▶ M/F puritan
puro, -a ['puru, a] ADJ pure; (*uísque etc*) neat; (*verdade*) plain; (*intenções*) honourable (BRIT), honorable (US); (*estilo*) clear
pus[1] [pus] M pus
pus[2] [pujs] VB *ver* **pôr**
puser [pu'zer] VB *ver* **pôr**
puta ['puta] (!) F whore; *ver tb* **puto**

P

puto, -a ['putu, a] (!) M/F (*sem-vergonha*) bastard ▸ ADJ (*zangado*) furious; (*incrível*): **um ~ ...** a hell of a ...; **o ~ de ...** the bloody ...
pútrido, -a ['putridu, a] ADJ putrid, rotten
puxador [puʃa'dor] M handle, knob
puxão [pu'ʃãw] (*pl* **-ões**) M tug, jerk
puxar [pu'ʃar] VT to pull; (*sacar*) to pull out; (*assunto*) to bring up; (*conversa*) to strike up; (*briga*) to pick ▸ VI: **~ de uma perna** to limp; **~ a** to take after
puxões [pu'ʃõjs] MPL *de* **puxão**

q

QG ABR M (= *Quartel-General*) HQ
QI ABR M (= *Quociente de Inteligência*) IQ
quadra ['kwadra] F (*quarteirão*) block; (*de tênis etc*) court; (*período*) time, period
quadrado, -a [kwa'dradu, a] ADJ square ▸ M square ▸ M/F (*col*) square
quadril [kwa'driw] (*pl* **-is**) M hip
quadrinho [kwa'driɲu] M: **história em ~s** (BR) cartoon, comic strip
quadris [kwa'dris] MPL *de* **quadril**
quadro ['kwadru] M painting; (*gravura, foto*) picture; (*lista*) list; (*tabela*) chart, table; (*Tec: painel*) panel; (*pessoal*) staff; (*time*) team; (*Teatro, fig*) scene; **~ branco** whiteboard; **~ interativo** interactive whiteboard;
quadro-negro (*pl* **quadros-negros**) M blackboard
quadruplicar [kwadrupli'kar] VT, VI to quadruple

qual [kwaw] (*pl* **-ais**) PRON which ▸CONJ as, like ▸EXCL what!; **o ~** which; (*pessoa: suj*) who; (*: objeto*) whom; **seja ~ for** whatever *ou* whichever it may be; **cada ~** each one

qualidade [kwali'dadʒi] F quality

qualificação [kwalifika'sãw] (*pl* **-ões**) F qualification

qualificado, -a [kwalifi'kadu, a] ADJ qualified

qualificar [kwalifi'kar] VT to qualify; (*avaliar*) to evaluate; **qualificar-se** VR to qualify; **~ de** *ou* **como** to classify as

qualquer [kwaw'ker] (*pl* **quaisquer**) ADJ, PRON any; **~ pessoa** anyone, anybody; **~ um dos dois** either; **~ que seja** whichever it may be; **a ~ momento** at any moment

quando ['kwãdu] ADV when ▸CONJ when; (*interrogativo*) when?; (*ao passo que*) whilst; **~ muito** at most

quantia [kwã'tʃia] F sum, amount

quantidade [kwãtʃi'dadʒi] F quantity, amount

PALAVRA-CHAVE

quanto, -a ['kwãtu, a] ADJ
1 (*interrogativo: sg*) how much?; (*: pl*) how many?; **quanto tempo?** how long?
2 (*o que for necessário*) all that, as much as; **daremos quantos exemplares ele precisar** we'll give him as many copies as *ou* all the copies he needs
3: **tanto/tantos ... quanto** as much/many ... as
▸PRON 1 how much?; how many?; **quanto custa?** how much is it?; **a quanto está o jogo?** what's the score?
2: **tudo quanto** everything that, as much as
3: **tanto/tantos quanto ...** as much/as many as ...
4: **um tanto quanto** somewhat, rather
▸ADV 1: **quanto a** as regards; **quanto a mim** as for me
2: **quanto antes** as soon as possible
3: **quanto mais** (*principalmente*) especially; (*muito menos*) let alone; **quanto mais cedo melhor** the sooner the better
4: **tanto quanto possível** as much as possible; **tão ... quanto ...** as ... as ...
▸CONJ: **quanto mais trabalha, mais ele ganha** the more he works, the more he earns; **quanto mais, (tanto) melhor** the more, the better

quarenta [kwa'rẽta] NUM forty

quarentena [kwarẽ'tɛna] F quarantine

quaresma [kwa'rezma] F Lent

quarta ['kwarta] F (*tb*: **~-feira**) Wednesday; (*parte*) quarter; (*Auto*) fourth (gear); **quarta-feira** (*pl* **quartas-feiras**) F Wednesday; **quarta-feira de cinzas** Ash Wednesday

quarteirão [kwartej'rãw] (*pl* **-ões**) M (*de casas*) block

quartel [kwar'tɛw] (*pl* **-éis**) M barracks *sg*; **quartel-general** M headquarters *pl*

quarteto [kwar'tetu] M quartet(te)

quarto, -a ['kwartu, a] NUM fourth ▸M quarter; (*aposento*) bedroom; **~ de banho** bathroom; **~ de dormir** bedroom; **três ~s de**

hora three quarters of an hour
quase ['kwazi] ADV almost, nearly; **~ nunca** hardly ever
quatorze [kwa'torzi] NUM fourteen
quatro ['kwatru] NUM four

PALAVRA-CHAVE

que [ki] CONJ **1** (*com oração subordinada: muitas vezes não se traduz*) that; **ele disse que viria** he said (that) he would come; **não há nada que fazer** there's nothing to be done; **espero que sim/não** I hope so/not; **dizer que sim/não** to say yes/no
2 (*consecutivo: muitas vezes não se traduz*) that; **é tão pesado que não consigo levantá-lo** it's so heavy (that) I can't lift it
3 (*comparações*): **(do) que** than; *ver tb* **mais, menos, mesmo**
▶ PRON **1** (*coisa*) which, that; (*+ prep*) which; **o chapéu que você comprou** the hat (that *ou* which) you bought
2 (*pessoa: suj*) who, that; (*: complemento*) whom, that; **o amigo que me levou ao museu** the friend who took me to the museum; **a moça que eu convidei** the girl (that *ou* whom) I invited
3 (*interrogativo*) what?; **o que você disse?** what did you say?
4 (*exclamação*) what!; **que pena!** what a pity!; **que lindo!** how lovely!

quê [ke] M (*col*) something ▶ PRON what; **~!** what!; **não tem de ~** don't mention it; **para ~?** what for?; **por ~?** why?
quebra ['kɛbra] F break, rupture; (*falência*) bankruptcy; (*de energia elétrica*) cut; **de ~** in addition;
quebra-cabeça (*pl* **quebra-cabeças**) M puzzle, problem; (*jogo*) jigsaw puzzle
quebrado, -a [ke'bradu, a] ADJ broken; (*cansado*) exhausted; (*falido*) bankrupt; (*carro, máquina*) broken down; (*telefone*) out of order
quebrar [ke'brar] VT to break ▶ VI to break; (*carro*) to break down; (*Com*) to go bankrupt; (*ficar sem dinheiro*) to go broke
queda ['kɛda] F fall; (*fig*) downfall; **ter ~ para algo** to have a bent for sth; **~ de barreira** landslide;
queda-d'água (*pl* **quedas-d'água**) F waterfall
queijo ['kejʒu] M cheese
queimado, -a [kej'madu, a] ADJ burnt; (*de sol: machucado*) sunburnt; (*: bronzeado*) brown, tanned; (*plantas, folhas*) dried up
queimadura [kejma'dura] F burn; (*de sol*) sunburn
queimar [kej'mar] VT to burn; (*roupa*) to scorch; (*com líquido*) to scald; (*bronzear a pele*) to tan; (*planta, folha*) to wither ▶ VI to burn;
queimar-se VR (*pessoa*) to burn o.s.; (*bronzear-se*) to tan
queima-roupa F: **à ~** point-blank, at point-blank range
queira ['kejra] VB *ver* **querer**
queixa ['kejʃa] F complaint; (*lamentação*) lament; **fazer ~ de alguém** to complain about sb
queixar-se [kej'ʃarsi] VR to complain; **~ de** to complain about; (*dores etc*) to complain of
queixo ['kejʃu] M chin; (*maxilar*) jaw; **bater o ~** to shiver
quem [kẽj] PRON who; (*como objeto*) who(m); **de ~ é isto?** whose is this?; **~ diria!** who would have thought (it)!; **~ sabe** (*talvez*) perhaps

Quênia ['kenja] M: **o ~** Kenya
quente ['kẽtʃi] ADJ hot; (*roupa*) warm
quentinha [kẽ'tʃiɲa] F heatproof carton (*for food*); (*de restaurante*) doggy bag
quer [ker] CONJ: **~ ... ~ ...** whether ... or ...; **~ chova ~ não** whether it rains or not; **onde/quando/quem ~ que** wherever/whenever/whoever; **o que ~ que seja** whatever it is

PALAVRA-CHAVE

querer [ke'rer] VT **1** (*desejar*) to want; **quero mais dinheiro** I want more money; **queria um chá** I'd like a cup of tea; **quero ajudar/que vá** I want to help/you to go; **você vai querer sair amanhã?** do you want to go out tomorrow?; **eu vou querer uma cerveja** (*num bar etc*) I'd like a beer; **por/sem querer** intentionally/unintentionally; **como queira** as you wish
2 (*perguntas para pedir algo*): **você quer fechar a janela?** will you shut the window?; **quer me dar uma mão?** can you give me a hand?
3 (*amar*) to love
4 (*convite*): **quer entrar/sentar** do come in/sit down
5: **querer dizer** (*significar*) to mean; (*pretender dizer*) to mean to say; **quero dizer** I mean; **quer dizer** (*com outras palavras*) in other words
▶ VI: **querer bem a** to be fond of
querer-se VR to love one another
▶ M (*vontade*) wish; (*afeto*) affection

querido, -a [ke'ridu, a] ADJ dear ▶ M/F darling; **Q~ João** Dear John
querosene [kero'zɛni] M kerosene
questão [kes'tãw] (*pl* **-ões**) F question; (*problema*) issue, question; (*Jur*) case; (*contenda*) dispute, quarrel; **fazer ~ (de)** to insist (on); **em ~** in question; **há ~ de um ano** about a year ago; **questionar** [kestʃjo'nar] VI to question ▶ VT to question, call into question; **questionário** [kestʃjo'narju] M questionnaire; **questionável** [kestʃjo'navew] (*pl* **-eis**) ADJ questionable
quicar [ki'kar] VT, VI to bounce
quieto, -a ['kjɛtu, a] ADJ quiet; (*imóvel*) still; **quietude** [kje'tudʒi] F calm, tranquillity
quilate [ki'latʃi] M carat
quilo ['kilu] M kilo; **quilobyte** [kilo'bajtʃi] M kilobyte; **quilograma** [kilo'grama] M kilogram; **quilometragem** [kilome'traʒẽ] F number of kilometres *ou* kilometers travelled, ≈ mileage; **quilômetro** [ki'lometru] M kilometre (BRIT), kilometer (US); **quilowatt** [kilo'watʃi] M kilowatt
química ['kimika] F chemistry
químico, -a ['kimiku, a] ADJ chemical ▶ M/F chemist
quina ['kina] F corner; (*de mesa etc*) edge; **de ~** edgeways (BRIT), edgewise (US)
quindim [kĩ'dʒĩ] M *sweet made of egg yolks, coconut and sugar*
quinhão [ki'ɲãw] (*pl* **-ões**) M share, portion
quinhentos, -as [ki'ɲẽtus, as] NUM five hundred
quinhões [ki'ɲõjs] MPL *de* **quinhão**

q

quinquilharias [kĩkiʎa'rias] FPL odds and ends; (*miudezas*) knick-knacks, trinkets
quinta ['kĩta] F (*tb*: **~-feira**) Thursday; (*propriedade*) estate; (PT) farm; **quinta-feira** ['kĩta-'fejra] (*pl* **quintas-feiras**) F Thursday
quintal [kĩ'taw] (*pl* **-ais**) M back yard
quinteto [kĩ'tetu] M quintet(te)
quinto, -a ['kĩtu, a] NUM fifth
quinze ['kĩzɪ] NUM fifteen; **duas e ~** a quarter past (BRIT) *ou* after (US) two; **~ para as sete** a quarter to (BRIT) *ou* of (US) seven
quinzena [kĩ'zɛna] F two weeks, fortnight (BRIT); **quinzenal** [kĩze'naw] (*pl* **-ais**) ADJ fortnightly; **quinzenalmente** [kĩzenaw'mẽtʃi] ADV fortnightly
quiosque ['kjɔski] M kiosk
quis [kiz] VB *ver* **querer**
quiser [ki'zer] VB *ver* **querer**
quisto ['kistu] M cyst
quitanda [ki'tãda] F grocer's (shop) (BRIT), grocery store (US)
quitar [ki'tar] VT (*dívida: pagar*) to pay off; (*: perdoar*) to cancel; (*devedor*) to release
quite ['kitʃi] ADJ (*livre*) free; (*com um credor*) squared up; (*igualado*) even; **estar ~ (com alguém)** to be quits (with sb)
quitute [ki'tutʃi] M titbit (BRIT), tidbit (US)
quota ['kwɔta] F quota; (*porção*) share, portion
quotidiano, -a [kwotʃi'dʒjanu, a] ADJ everyday

r

R ABR (= *rua*) St
R$ ABR = **real**
rã [hã] F frog
rabanete [haba'netʃi] M radish
rabiscar [habis'kar] VT to scribble; (*papel*) to scribble on ▶ VI to scribble; (*desenhar*) to doodle; **rabisco** [ha'bisku] M scribble
rabo ['habu] M tail
rabugento, -a [habu'ʒẽtu, a] ADJ grumpy
raça ['hasa] F breed; (*grupo étnico*) race; **cão/cavalo de ~** pedigree dog/thoroughbred horse
racha ['haʃa] F (*fenda*) split; (*greta*) crack; **rachadura** [haʃa'dura] F crack; **rachar** [ha'ʃar] VT to crack; (*objeto, despesas*) to split; (*lenha*) to chop ▶ VI to split; (*cristal*) to crack; **rachar-se** VR to split; to crack
racial [ha'sjaw] (*pl* **-ais**) ADJ racial
raciocínio [hasjo'sinju] M reasoning
racional [hasjo'naw] (*pl* **-ais**) ADJ rational; **racionalizar**

[hasjonali'zar] VT to rationalize
racionamento [hasjona'mẽtu] M rationing
racismo [ha'sizmu] M racism; **racista** [ha'sista] ADJ, M/F racist
radar [ha'dar] M radar
radiação [hadʒja'sãw] F radiation
radiador [hadʒja'dor] M radiator
radical [hadʒi'kaw] (*pl* **-ais**) ADJ radical
radicar-se [hadʒi'karsi] VR to take root; (*fixar residência*) to settle
rádio ['hadʒju] M radio; (*Quím*) radium; **radioativo, -a** [hadʒjua'tʃivu, a] ADJ radioactive; **radiodifusão** [hadʒjodʒifu'zãw] F broadcasting; **radiografar** [hadʒjogra'far] VT to X-ray; **radiografia** [hadʒjogra'fia] F X-ray
raia ['haja] F (*risca*) line; (*fronteira*) boundary; (*limite*) limit; (*de corrida*) lane; (*peixe*) ray
raiar [ha'jar] VI to shine
rainha [ha'iɲa] F queen
raio ['haju] M (*de sol*) ray; (*de luz*) beam; (*de roda*) spoke; (*relâmpago*) flash of lightning; (*distância*) range; (*Mat*) radius; **~s X** X-rays
raiva ['hajva] F rage, fury; (*Med*) rabies *sg*; **estar/ficar com ~ (de)** to be/get angry (with); **ter ~ de** to hate; **raivoso, -a** [haj'vozu, ɔza] ADJ furious
raiz [ha'iz] F root; (*origem*) source; **~ quadrada** square root
rajada [ha'ʒada] F (*vento*) gust
ralado, -a [ha'ladu, a] ADJ grated; **ralador** [hala'dor] M grater
ralar [ha'lar] VT to grate
ralhar [ha'ʎar] VI to scold; **~ com alguém** to tell sb off
rali [ha'li] M rally
ralo, -a ['halu, a] ADJ (*cabelo*) thinning; (*tecido*) flimsy; (*vegetação*) sparse; (*sopa*) thin, watery; (*café*) weak ▶ M (*de regador*) rose, nozzle; (*de pia, banheiro*) drain
rama ['hama] F branches *pl*, foliage; **pela ~** superficially; **ramagem** [ha'maʒẽ] F branches *pl*, foliage; **ramal** [ha'maw] (*pl* **-ais**) M (*Ferro*) branch line; (*Tel*) extension; (*Auto*) side road
ramificar-se [hamifi'karsi] VR to branch out
ramo ['hamu] M branch; (*profissão, negócios*) line; (*de flores*) bunch; **Domingo de R~s** Palm Sunday
rampa ['hãpa] F ramp; (*ladeira*) slope
ranger [hã'ʒer] VI to creak ▶ VT: **~ os dentes** to grind one's teeth
ranhura [ha'ɲura] F groove; (*para moeda*) slot
rapar [ha'par] VT to scrape; (*a barba*) to shave; (*o cabelo*) to shave off
rapariga [hapa'riga] F girl
rapaz [ha'pajz] M boy; (*col*) lad
rapidez [hapi'dez] F speed
rápido, -a ['hapidu, a] ADJ quick, fast ▶ ADV fast, quickly ▶ M (*trem*) express
rapina [ha'pina] F robbery; **ave de ~** bird of prey
raptar [hap'tar] VT to kidnap; **rapto** ['haptu] M kidnapping; **raptor** [hap'tor] M kidnapper
raquete [ha'ketʃi] F racquet
raquítico, -a [ha'kitʃiku, a] ADJ (*franzino*) puny; (*vegetação*) poor
raramente [hara'mẽtʃi] ADV rarely, seldom
raro, -a ['haru, a] ADJ rare ▶ ADV rarely, seldom

rasgado, -a [haz'gadu, a] ADJ (*roupa*) torn, ripped
rasgão [haz'gãw] (*pl* **-ões**) M tear, rip
rasgar [haz'gar] VT to tear, rip; (*destruir*) to tear up, rip up; **rasgar-se** VR to split; **rasgo** ['hazgu] M tear, rip
rasgões [haz'gõjs] MPL *de* **rasgão**
raso, -a ['hazu, a] ADJ (*liso*) flat, level; (*não fundo*) shallow; (*baixo*) low; **soldado ~** private
raspa ['haspa] F (*de madeira*) shaving; (*de metal*) filing
raspão [has'pãw] (*pl* **-ões**) M scratch, graze
raspar [has'par] VT to scrape; (*alisar*) to file; (*tocar de raspão*) to graze; (*arranhar*) to scratch; (*pelos, cabeça*) to shave; (*apagar*) to rub out ▶ VI: **~ em** to scrape
raspões [has'põjs] MPL *de* **raspão**
rasteira [has'tejra] F: **dar uma ~ em alguém** to trip sb up
rasteiro, -a [has'tejru, a] ADJ crawling; (*planta*) creeping
rastejar [haste'ʒar] VI to crawl; (*furtivamente*) to creep; (*fig: rebaixar-se*) to grovel ▶ VT (*fugitivo etc*) to track
rasto ['hastu] M (*pegada*) track; (*de veículo*) trail; (*fig*) sign, trace; **andar de ~s** to crawl
rastro ['hastru] M = **rasto**
rata ['hata] F rat; (*pequena*) mouse
ratificar [hatʃifi'kar] VT to ratify
rato ['hatu] M rat; (*rato pequeno*) mouse; **~ de hotel/praia** hotel/beach thief; **ratoeira** [ha'twejra] F rat trap; (*pequena*) mousetrap
ravina [ha'vina] F ravine
razão [ha'zãw] (*pl* **-ões**) F reason; (*argumento*) reasoning; (*Mat*) ratio ▶ M (*Com*) ledger; **à ~ de** at the rate of; **em ~ de** on account of; **dar ~ a alguém** to support sb; **ter/não ter ~** to be right/wrong; **razoável** [ha'zwavew] (*pl* **-eis**) ADJ reasonable
r/c (PT) ABR = **rés do chão**
ré [hɛ] F (*Auto*) reverse (gear); **dar (marcha à) ré** to reverse, back up; *ver tb* **réu**
reabastecer [heabaste'ser] VT (*avião*) to refuel; (*carro*) to fill up; **reabastecer-se** VR: **~-se de** to replenish one's supply of
reação [hea'sãw] (*pl* **-ões**) F reaction
reagir [hea'ʒir] VI to react; (*doente, time perdedor*) to fight back; **~ a** (*resistir*) to resist; (*protestar*) to rebel against
reais [he'ajs] ADJ PL *de* **real**
reaja [he'aʒa] VB *ver* **reagir**; **reaver**
reajuste [hea'ʒustʃi] M adjustment
real [he'aw] (*pl* **-ais**) ADJ real; (*relativo à realeza*) royal ▶ M (*moeda*) real

> The Brazilian currency, the **real**, was introduced in 1994 as part of a comprehensive economic stabilization package known as the **Plano Real**. This brought an end to some thirty years of hyperinflation which saw successive devaluations and name-changes to the Brazilian currency, from *cruzeiro* to *cruzado* (1986), to *cruzado novo* (1989), back to *cruzeiro* (1990), to *cruzeiro real* (1993) and finally to *real* (1994). The *real* is subdivided into 100 *centavos*. The currency symbol is R$ and a comma is used to separate *reais* and *centavos*, e.g. R$ 2,40 (two *reais* and forty *centavos*).

realçar [heaw'sar] VT to highlight;

realce [he'awsi] M emphasis; (*mais brilho*) highlight; **dar realce a** to enhance
realeza [hea'leza] F royalty
realidade [heali'dadʒi] F reality; **na ~** actually, in fact; **~ virtual** virtual reality
realista [hea'lista] ADJ realistic ▶ M/F realist
realização [healiza'sãw] F fulfilment (BRIT), fulfillment (US), realization; (*de projeto*) execution, carrying out
realizador, a [healiza'dor(a)] ADJ enterprising
realizar [heali'zar] VT to achieve; (*projeto*) to carry out; (*ambições, sonho*) to fulfil (BRIT), fulfill (US), realize; (*negócios*) to transact; (*perceber, convertir en dinheiro*) to realize; **realizar-se** VR to take place; (*ambições*) to be realized; (*sonhos*) to come true
realmente [heaw'mẽtʃi] ADV really; (*de fato*) actually
reanimar [heani'mar] VT to revive; (*encorajar*) to encourage; **reanimar-se** VR to cheer up
reatar [hea'tar] VT to resume, take up again
reaver [hea'ver] VT to recover, get back
rebaixar [hebaj'ʃar] VT to lower; (*reduzir*) to reduce; (*time*) to relegate; (*funcionário*) to demote; (*humilhar*) to put down ▶ VI to drop; **rebaixar-se** VR to demean o.s.
rebanho [he'baɲu] M (*de carneiros, fig*) flock; (*de gado, elefantes*) herd
rebelar-se [hebe'larsi] VR to rebel; **rebelde** [he'bɛwdʒi] ADJ rebellious; (*indisciplinado*) unruly, wild ▶ M/F rebel; **rebeldia** [hebew'dʒia] F rebelliousness; (*fig: obstinação*) stubbornness; (*: oposição*) defiance
rebelião [hebe'ljãw] (*pl* **-ões**) F rebellion
rebentar [hebẽ'tar] VI (*guerra*) to break out; (*louça*) to smash; (*corda*) to snap; (*represa*) to burst; (*ondas*) to break ▶ VT to smash; to snap; (*porta, ponte*) to break down
rebocador [heboka'dor] M tug(boat)
rebocar [hebo'kar] VT (*paredes*) to plaster; (*dar reboque a*) to tow
rebolar [hebo'lar] VT to swing ▶ VI to sway
reboque[1] [he'bɔki] M tow; (*veículo: tb*: **carro ~**) trailer; (*cabo*) towrope; (BR: *de socorro*) tow truck; **a ~** on *ou* in (US) tow
reboque[2] VB *ver* **rebocar**
rebuçado [hebu'sadu] (PT) M sweet, candy (US)
recado [he'kadu] M message; **deixar ~** to leave a message
recair [heka'ir] VI (*doente*) to relapse
recalcar [hekaw'kar] VT to repress
recalque VB *ver* **recalcar**
recanto [he'kãtu] M corner, nook
recapitular [hekapitu'lar] VT to sum up, recapitulate; (*fatos*) to review; (*matéria escolar*) to revise
recarga [he'karga] F (*de celular*) top-up; **preciso fazer a ~ do meu celular** I need to top up my mobile
recarregar [hekahe'gar] VT (*celular*) to top up; (*bateria*) to recharge; (*cartucho*) to refill
recatado, -a [heka'tadu, a] ADJ (*modesto*) modest; (*reservado*) reserved
recauchutado, -a [hekawʃu'tadu, a] ADJ: **pneu ~**

(*Auto*) retread, remould (BRIT)

recear [he'sjar] VT to fear ▶ VI: **~ por** to fear for; **~ fazer/que** to be afraid to do/that

receber [hese'ber] VT to receive; (*ganhar*) to earn, get; (*hóspedes*) to take in; (*convidados*) to entertain; (*acolher bem*) to welcome ▶ VI (*receber convidados*) to entertain; **recebimento** [hesebi'mẽtu] (BR) M reception; (*de uma carta*) receipt; **acusar o recebimento de** to acknowledge receipt of

receio [he'seju] M fear; **ter ~ de que** to fear that

receita [he'sejta] F income; (*do Estado*) revenue; (*Med*) prescription; (*culinária*) recipe; **R~ Federal** ≈ Inland Revenue (BRIT), ≈ IRS (US); **receitar** [hesej'tar] VT to prescribe

recém [he'sẽ] ADV recently, newly; **recém-casado, -a** ADJ: **os recém-casados** the newlyweds; **recém-chegado, -a** M/F newcomer; **recém-nascido, -a** M/F newborn child

recente [he'sẽtʃi] ADJ recent; (*novo*) new ▶ ADV recently; **recentemente** [hesẽtʃi'mẽtʃi] ADV recently

receoso, -a [he'sjozu, ɔza] ADJ frightened, fearful; **estar ~ de (fazer)** to be afraid of (doing)

recepção [hesep'sãw] (*pl* **-ões**) F reception; (PT: *de uma carta*) receipt; **acusar a ~ de** (PT) to acknowledge receipt of; **recepcionista** [hesepsjo'nista] M/F receptionist

receptivo, -a [hesep'tʃivu, a] ADJ receptive; (*acolhedor*) welcoming

receptor [hesep'tor] M receiver

recessão [hese'sãw] (*pl* **-ões**) F recession

recessões [hese'sõjs] FPL *de* **recessão**

recheado, -a [he'ʃjadu, a] ADJ (*ave, carne*) stuffed; (*empada, bolo*) filled; (*cheio*) full, crammed

rechear [he'ʃjar] VT to fill; (*ave, carne*) to stuff; **recheio** [he'ʃeju] M stuffing; (*de empada, de bolo*) filling; (*o conteúdo*) contents *pl*

rechonchudo, -a [heʃõ'ʃudu, a] ADJ chubby, plump

recibo [he'sibu] M receipt

reciclar [hesi'klar] VT to recycle

reciclável [hesi'klavew] (*pl* **-eis**) ADJ recyclable

recinto [he'sĩtu] M enclosure; (*lugar*) area

recipiente [hesi'pjẽtʃi] M container, receptacle

recíproco, -a [he'siproku, a] ADJ reciprocal

recitar [hesi'tar] VT to recite

reclamação [heklama'sãw] (*pl* **-ões**) F complaint

reclamar [hekla'mar] VT to demand; (*herança*) to claim ▶ VI: **~ (de)** (*comida etc*) to complain (about)

reclinar [hekli'nar] VT to rest, lean; **reclinar-se** VR to lie back; (*deitar-se*) to lie down

recobrar [heko'brar] VT to recover, get back; **recobrar-se** VR to recover

recolher [heko'ʎer] VT to collect; (*gado, roupa do varal*) to bring in; (*juntar*) to collect up; **recolhido, -a** [heko'ʎidu, a] ADJ (*lugar*) secluded; (*pessoa*) withdrawn; **recolhimento** [hekoʎi'mẽtu] M retirement; (*arrecadação*) collection; (*ato de levar*) taking

recomeçar [hekome'sar] VT, VI to restart

recomendação [hekomẽda'sãw] (*pl* **-ões**) F recommendation; **recomendações** FPL (*cumprimentos*) regards

recomendar [hekomẽ'dar] VT to recommend; **recomendável** [hekomẽ'davew] (*pl* **-eis**) ADJ advisable
recompensa [hekõ'pẽsa] F reward; **recompensar** [hekõpẽ'sar] VT to reward
recompor [hekõ'por] (*irreg: como* **pôr**) VT to reorganize; (*restabelecer*) to restore
reconciliar [hekõsi'ljar] VT to reconcile
reconhecer [hekoɲe'ser] VT to recognize; (*Mil*) to reconnoitre (BRIT), reconnoiter (US); **reconhecido, -a** [hekoɲe'sidu, a] ADJ recognized; (*agradecido*) grateful, thankful; **reconhecimento** [hekoɲesi'mẽtu] M recognition; (*admissão*) admission; (*gratidão*) gratitude; (*Mil*) reconnaissance; **reconhecível** [hekoɲe'sivew] (*pl* **-eis**) ADJ recognizable
reconstruir [hekõs'trwir] VT to rebuild
recordação [hekorda'sãw] (*pl* **-ões**) F (*reminiscência*) memory; (*objeto*) memento
recordar [hekor'dar] VT to remember; **recordar-se** VR: **~-se de** to remember; **~ algo a alguém** to remind sb of sth
recorde [he'kɔrdʒi] ADJ INV record *atr* ▶ M record
recorrer [heko'her] VI: **~ a** to turn to; (*valer-se de*) to resort to
recortar [hekor'tar] VT to cut out; **recorte** [he'kɔrtʃi] M (*ato*) cutting out; (*de jornal*) cutting, clipping
recreação [hekrja'sãw] F recreation
recreio [he'kreju] M recreation
recriminar [hekrimi'nar] VT to reproach, reprove
recrutamento [hekruta'mẽtu] M recruitment
recrutar [hekru'tar] VT to recruit
recuar [he'kwar] VT to move back ▶ VI to move back; (*exército*) to retreat
recuperar [hekupe'rar] VT to recover; (*tempo perdido*) to make up for; (*reabilitar*) to rehabilitate; **recuperar-se** VR to recover
recurso [he'kursu] M resource; (*Jur*) appeal; **recursos** MPL (*financeiros*) resources
recusa [he'kuza] F refusal; (*negação*) denial; **recusar** [heku'zar] VT to refuse; to deny; **recusar-se** VR: **recusar-se a** to refuse to
redação [heda'sãw] (*pl* **-ões**) F (*ato*) writing; (*Educ*) composition, essay; (*redatores*) editorial staff
redator, a [heda'tor(a)] M/F editor
rede ['hedʒi] F net; (*de dormir*) hammock; (*Ferro, Tec, Comput, TV, fig*) network; **a ~** (*a Internet*) the web; **~ de área local** local area network; **~ sem fio** wireless network; **~ social** social network, social networking site
rédea ['hɛdʒja] F rein
redentor, a [hedẽ'tor(a)] ADJ redeeming
redigir [hedʒi'ʒir] VT, VI to write
redobrar [hedo'brar] VT (*aumentar*) to increase; (*esforços*) to redouble
redondamente [hedõda'mẽtʃi] ADV (*completamente*) completely
redondeza [hedõ'deza] F roundness; **redondezas** FPL surroundings
redondo, -a [he'dõdu, a] ADJ round

r

redor [he'dor] M: **ao** *ou* **em ~ (de)** around, round about
redução [hedu'sãw] (*pl* **-ões**) F reduction
redundância [hedũ'dãsja] F redundancy; **redundante** [hedũ'dãtʃi] ADJ redundant
reduzido, -a [hedu'zidu, a] ADJ reduced; (*limitado*) limited; (*pequeno*) small
reduzir [hedu'zir] VT to reduce; **reduzir-se** VR: **~-se a** to be reduced to; (*fig: resumir-se em*) to come down to
reembolsar [heẽbow'sar] VT to recover; (*restituir*) to reimburse; (*depósito*) to refund; **reembolso** [heẽ'bowsu] M (*de depósito*) refund; (*de despesa*) reimbursement
reencontro [heẽ'kõtru] M reunion
refeição [hefej'sãw] (*pl* **-ões**) F meal; **refeitório** [hefej'tɔrju] M refectory
refém [he'fẽ] (*pl* **-ns**) M hostage
referência [hefe'rẽsja] F reference; **referências** FPL (*informaçoes para emprego*) references; **fazer ~ a** to make reference to, refer to
referente [hefe'rẽtʃi] ADJ: **~ a** concerning, regarding
referir [hefe'rir] VT to relate, tell; **referir-se** VR: **~-se a** to refer to
REFESA F (= *Rede Ferroviária SA*) *Brazilian rail network*
refinamento [hefina'mẽtu] M refinement
refinaria [hefina'ria] F refinery
refiro [he'firu] VB *ver* **referir**
refletir [hefle'tʃir] VT to reflect ▸ VI: **~ em** *ou* **sobre** to consider, think about
reflexão [heflek'sãw] (*pl* **-ões**) F reflection
reflexo, -a [he'flɛksu, a] ADJ (*luz*) reflected; (*ação*) reflex ▸ M reflection; (*Anat*) reflex; (*no cabelo*) streak
reflexões [heflek'sõjs] FPL *de* **reflexão**
reflito [he'flitu] VB *ver* **refletir**
reforçado, -a [hefor'sadu, a] ADJ reinforced; (*pessoa*) strong; (*café da manhã, jantar*) hearty
reforçar [hefor'sar] VT to reinforce; (*revigorar*) to invigorate; **reforço** [he'forsu] M reinforcement
reforma [he'fɔrma] F reform; (*Arq*) renovation; **reformado, -a** [hefor'madu, a] ADJ reformed; renovated; (*Mil*) retired; **reformar** [hefor'mar] VT to reform; to renovate; **reformar-se** VR to reform
refrão [he'frãw] (*pl* **-ões**) M chorus, refrain; (*provérbio*) saying
refratário, -a [hefra'tarju, a] ADJ (*Tec*) heat-resistant; (*Culin*) ovenproof
refrear [hefre'ar] VT (*cavalo*) to rein in; (*inimigo*) to contain, check; (*paixões, raiva*) to control; **refrear-se** VR to restrain o.s.
refrescante [hefres'kãtʃi] ADJ refreshing
refrescar [hefres'kar] VT (*ar, ambiente*) to cool; (*pessoa*) to refresh ▸ VI to cool down
refresco [he'fresku] M cool fruit drink, squash; **refrescos** MPL (*refrigerantes*) refreshments
refrigerador [hefriʒera'dor] M refrigerator, fridge (BRIT)
refrigerante [hefriʒe'rãtʃi] M soft drink
refugiado, -a [hefu'ʒjadu, a] ADJ, M/F refugee
refugiar-se [hefu'ʒjarsi] VR to take refuge; **refúgio** [he'fuʒju] M refuge
refugo [he'fugu] M rubbish,

garbage (US); (*mercadoria*) reject
rega ['hɛga] F (PT) irrigation
regador [hega'dor] M watering can
regalia [hega'lia] F privilege
regar [he'gar] VT (*plantas, jardim*) to water; (*umedecer*) to sprinkle
regatear [hega'tʃjar] VT (*o preço*) to haggle over, bargain for ▶ VI to haggle
regenerar [heʒene'rar] VT to regenerate
reger [he'ʒer] VT to govern; (*orquestra*) to conduct; (*empresa*) to run ▶ VI to rule; (*maestro*) to conduct
região [he'ʒjãw] (*pl* **-ões**) F region, area
regime [he'ʒimi] M (*Pol*) regime; (*dieta*) diet; (*maneira*) way; **estar de ~** to be on a diet
regimento [heʒi'mẽtu] M regiment
regiões [he'ʒjõjs] FPL *de* **região**
regional [heʒjo'naw] (*pl* **-ais**) ADJ regional
registrar [heʒis'trar], (PT) **registar** VT to register; (*anotar*) to record
registro [he'ʒistru], (PT) **registo** M (*ato*) registration; (: *anotação*) recording; (*livro, Ling*) register; (*histórico, Comput*) record; **~ civil** registry office
regra ['hɛgra] F rule; **regras** FPL (*Med*) periods
regravável [hegra'vavew] (*pl* **-eis**) ADJ rewritable
regressar [hegre'sar] VI to come (*ou* go) back, return; **regresso** [he'grɛsu] M return
régua ['hɛgwa] F ruler; **~ de calcular** slide rule
regulador [hegula'dor] M regulator
regulamento [hegula'mẽtu] M rules *pl*, regulations *pl*
regular [hegu'lar] ADJ regular; (*estatura*) average, medium; (*tamanho*) normal; (*razoável*) not bad ▶ VT to regulate; (*reger*) to govern; (*máquina*) to adjust; (*carro, motor*) to tune ▶ VI to work, function; **regularidade** [hegulari'dadʒi] F regularity
rei [hej] M king; **Dia de R~s** Epiphany; **R~ Momo** carnival king
reinado [hej'nadu] M reign
reinar [hej'nar] VI to reign
reino ['hejnu] M kingdom; (*fig*) realm; **o R~ Unido** the United Kingdom
reivindicação [hejvĩdʒika'sãw] (*pl* **-ões**) F claim, demand
reivindicar [rejvĩdʒi'kar] VT to claim; (*aumento salarial, direitos*) to demand
rejeição [heʒej'sãw] (*pl* **-ões**) F rejection
rejeitar [heʒej'tar] VT to reject; (*recusar*) to refuse
rejo ['heju] VB *ver* **reger**
rejuvenescer [heʒuvene'ser] VT to rejuvenate
relação [hela'sãw] (*pl* **-ões**) F relation; (*conexão*) connection; (*relacionamento*) relationship; (*Mat*) ratio; (*lista*) list; **com** *ou* **em ~ a** regarding, with reference to; **relações públicas** public relations; **relacionamento** [helasjona'mẽtu] M relationship; **relacionar** [helasjo'nar] VT to make a list of; (*ligar*): **relacionar algo com algo** to connect sth with sth, relate sth to sth; **relacionar-se** VR to be connected *ou* related
relâmpago [he'lãpagu] M flash of

lightning; **relâmpagos** MPL (*clarões*) lightning *sg*
relance [he'lãsi] M glance; **olhar de ~** to glance at
relapso, -a [he'lapsu, a] ADJ (*negligente*) negligent
relatar [hela'tar] VT to give an account of
relativo, -a [hela'tʃivu, a] ADJ relative
relato [he'latu] M account
relatório [hela'tɔrju] M report
relaxado, -a [hela'ʃadu, a] ADJ relaxed; (*desleixado*) slovenly, sloppy; (*relapso*) negligent
relaxante [hela'ʃãtʃi] ADJ relaxing
relaxar [hela'ʃar] VT, VI to relax
relegar [hele'gar] VT to relegate
relembrar [helẽ'brar] VT to recall
relevante [hele'vãtʃi] ADJ relevant
relevo [he'levu] M relief
religião [heli'ʒãw] (*pl* **-ões**) F religion; **religioso, -a** [heli'ʒozu, ɔza] ADJ religious ▸ M/F religious person; (*frade/freira*) monk/nun
relíquia [he'likja] F relic; **~ de família** family heirloom
relógio [he'lɔʒu] M clock; (*de gás*) meter; **~ (de pulso)** (wrist)watch; **~ de sol** sundial
relutante [helu'tãtʃi] ADJ reluctant
relva ['hɛwva] F grass; (*terreno gramado*) lawn
relvado [hew'vadu] (PT) M lawn
remar [he'mar] VT, VI to row
rematar [hema'tar] VT to finish off; **remate** [he'matʃi] M (*fim*) end; (*acabamento*) finishing touch
remediar [heme'dʒjar] VT to put right, remedy
remédio [he'mɛdʒju] M (*medicamento*) medicine; (*recurso, solução*) remedy; (*Jur*) recourse; **não tem ~** there's no way
remendar [hemẽ'dar] VT to mend; (*com pano*) to patch; **remendo** [he'mẽdu] M repair; patch
remessa [he'mɛsa] F shipment; (*de dinheiro*) remittance
remetente [heme'tẽtʃi] M/F sender
remexer [heme'ʃer] VT (*papéis*) to shuffle; (*sacudir: braços*) to wave; (*folhas*) to shake; (*revolver: areia, lama*) to stir up ▸ VI: **~ em** to rummage through
reminiscência [hemini'sẽsja] F reminiscence
remo ['hɛmu] M oar; (*Esporte*) rowing
remoção [hemo'sãw] F removal
remorso [he'mɔrsu] M remorse
remover [hemo'ver] VT to move; (*transferir*) to transfer; (*demitir*) to dismiss; (*retirar, afastar*) to remove; (*terra*) to churn up
renal [he'naw] (*pl* **-ais**) ADJ renal, kidney *atr*
Renascença [hena'sẽsa] F: **a ~** the Renaissance
renascer [hena'ser] VI to be reborn; (*fig*) to revive
renascimento [henasi'mẽtu] M rebirth; (*fig*) revival; **o R~** the Renaissance
renda ['hẽda] F income; (*nacional*) revenue; (*de aplicação, locação*) yield; (*tecido*) lace
render [hẽ'der] VT (*lucro, dinheiro*) to bring in, yield; (*preço*) to fetch; (*homenagem*) to pay; (*graças*) to give; (*serviços*) to render; (*armas*) to surrender; (*guarda*) to relieve; (*causar*) to bring ▸ VI (*dar lucro*) to pay; **render-se** VR to surrender; **rendição** [hẽdʒi'sãw] F surrender
rendimento [hẽdʒi'mẽtu] M income; (*lucro*) profit; (*juro*) yield, interest

renegar [hene'gar] VT (*crença*) to renounce; (*detestar*) to hate; (*trair*) to betray; (*negar*) to deny; (*desprezar*) to reject
renomado, -a [heno'madu, a] ADJ renowned
renovar [heno'var] VT to renew; (*Arq*) to renovate
rentabilidade [hẽtabili'dadʒi] F profitability
rentável [hẽ'tavew] (*pl* **-eis**) ADJ profitable
renúncia [he'nũsja] F resignation
renunciar [henũ'sjar] VT to give up, renounce ▶VI to resign; (*abandonar*): **~ a algo** to give sth up
reouve [he'ovi] VB *ver* **reaver**
reouver [heo'ver] VB *ver* **reaver**
reparação [hepara'sãw] (*pl* **-ões**) F mending, repairing; (*de mal, erros*) remedying; (*fig*) amends *pl*, reparation
reparar [hepa'rar] VT to repair; (*forças*) to restore; (*mal, erros*) to remedy; (*prejuízo, danos, ofensa*) to make amends for; (*notar*) to notice ▶VI: **~ em** to notice; **reparo** [he'paru] M repair; (*crítica*) criticism; (*observação*) observation
repartição [hepartʃi'sãw] (*pl* **-ões**) F distribution
repartir [hepar'tʃir] VT (*distribuir*) to distribute; (*dividir entre vários*) to share out; (*dividir em várias porções*) to divide up
repelente [hepe'lẽtʃi] ADJ, M repellent
repente [he'pẽtʃi] M outburst; **de ~** suddenly; (*col: talvez*) maybe
repentino, -a [hepẽ'tʃinu, a] ADJ sudden
repercussão [heperku'sãw] (*pl* **-ões**) F repercussion
repercutir [heperku'tʃir] VT to echo ▶VI to reverberate, echo; (*fig*): **~ (em)** to have repercussions (on)
repertório [heper'tɔrju] M list; (*coleção*) collection; (*Mús*) repertoire
repetidamente [hepetʃida'mẽtʃi] ADV repeatedly
repetir [hepe'tʃir] VT to repeat ▶VI (*ao comer*) to have seconds; **repetir-se** VR to happen again; (*pessoa*) to repeat o.s.; **repetitivo, -a** [hepetʃi'tʃivu, a] ADJ repetitive
repito [he'pitu] VB *ver* **repetir**
repleto, -a [he'plɛtu, a] ADJ replete, full up
réplica ['hɛplika] F replica; (*contestação*) reply, retort
replicar [hepli'kar] VT to answer, reply to ▶VI to reply, answer back
repolho [he'poʎu] M cabbage
repor [he'por] (*irreg: como* **pôr**) VT to put back, replace; (*restituir*) to return; **repor-se** VR to recover
reportagem [hepor'taʒẽ] (*pl* **-ns**) F reporting; (*notícia*) report
repórter [he'pɔrter] M/F reporter
repousar [hepo'zar] VI to rest; **repouso** [he'pozu] M rest
representação [heprezẽta'sãw] (*pl* **-ões**) F representation; (*Teatro*) performance; **representante** [heprezẽ'tãtʃi] M/F representative
representar [heprezẽ'tar] VT to represent; (*Teatro: papel*) to play ▶VI to act; **representativo, -a** [heprezẽta'tʃivu, a] ADJ representative
repressão [hepre'sãw] (*pl* **-ões**) F repression
reprimir [hepri'mir] VT to repress
reprodução [heprodu'sãw] (*pl* **-ões**) F reproduction

reproduzir [heprodu'zir] VT to reproduce; (*repetir*) to repeat; **reproduzir-se** VR to breed

reprovar [hepro'var] VT to disapprove of; (*aluno*) to fail

réptil ['hɛptʃiw] (*pl* **-eis**) M reptile

república [he'publika] F republic; **republicano, -a** [hepubli'kanu, a] ADJ, M/F republican

repudiar [hepu'dʒjar] VT to repudiate; **repúdio** [he'pudʒju] M repudiation

repulsivo, -a [hepuw'sivu, a] ADJ repulsive

reputação [reputa'sãw] (*pl* **-ões**) F reputation

requeijão [hekej'ʒãw] M cheese spread

requerer [heke'rer] VT (*emprego*) to apply for; (*pedir*) to request; (*exigir*) to require; **requerimento** [hekeri'mẽtu] M application; request; (*petição*) petition

requintado, -a [hekĩ'tadu, a] ADJ refined, elegant

requinte [he'kĩtʃi] M refinement, elegance; (*cúmulo*) height

requisito [heki'zitu] M requirement

rés do chão [hɛzdu'ʃãw] (PT) M INV ground floor (BRIT), first floor (US)

reserva [he'zɛrva] F reserve; (*para hotel, fig*) reservation ▶ M/F (*Esporte*) reserve

reservado, -a [hezer'vadu, a] ADJ reserved

reservar [hezer'var] VT to reserve; (*guardar de reserva*) to keep; (*forças*) to conserve; **reservar-se** VR to save o.s.

reservatório [hezerva'tɔrju] M reservoir

resfriado, -a [hes'frjadu, a] (BR) ADJ: **estar ~** to have a cold ▶ M cold, chill; **ficar ~** to catch (a) cold

resgatar [hezga'tar] VT (*salvar*) to rescue; (*retomar*) to get back, recover; **resgate** [hez'gatʃi] M rescue; (*para livrar reféns*) ransom

residência [hezi'dẽsja] F residence; **residencial** [hezidẽ'sjaw] (*pl* **-ais**) ADJ residential; (*computador, telefone etc*) home *atr*; **residente** [hezi'dẽtʃi] ADJ, M/F resident

residir [hezi'dʒir] VI to live, reside

resíduo [he'zidwu] M residue

resignação [hezigna'sãw] (*pl* **-ões**) F resignation

resignar-se [hezig'narsi] VR: **~ com** to resign o.s. to

resina [he'zina] F resin

resistente [hezis'tẽtʃi] ADJ resistant; (*material, objeto*) hard-wearing, strong

resistir [hezis'tʃir] VI to hold; (*pessoa*) to hold out; **~ a** to resist; (*sobreviver*) to survive

resmungar [hezmũ'gar] VT, VI to mutter, mumble

resolução [hezolu'sãw] (*pl* **-ões**) F resolution; (*de um problema*) solution; **resoluto, -a** [hezo'lutu, a] ADJ decisive

resolver [hezow'ver] VT to sort out; (*problema*) to solve; (*questão*) to resolve; (*decidir*) to decide; **resolver-se** VR: **~-se (a fazer)** to make up one's mind (to do), decide (to do)

respectivo, -a [hespek'tʃivu, a] ADJ respective

respeitar [hespej'tar] VT to respect; **respeitável** [hespej'tavew] (*pl* **-eis**) ADJ respectable; (*considerável*) considerable

respeito [hes'pejtu] M: **~ (a** *ou* **por)**

respect (for); **respeitos** MPL (*cumprimentos*) regards; **a ~ de, com ~ a** as to, as regards; (*sobre*) about; **dizer ~ a** to concern; **em ~ a** with respect to
respiração [hespira'sãw] F breathing
respirar [hespi'rar] VT, VI to breathe
respiro [hes'piru] M breath
resplandecente [hesplãde'sẽtʃi] ADJ resplendent
responder [hespõ'der] VT to answer ▶VI to answer; (*ser respondão*) to answer back; **~ por** to be responsible for, answer for
responsabilidade [hespõsabili'dadʒi] F responsibility
responsabilizar [hespõsabili'zar] VT: **~ alguém (por algo)** to hold sb responsible (for sth); **responsabilizar-se** VR: **~-se por** to take responsibility for
responsável [hespõ'savew] (*pl* **-eis**) ADJ: **~ (por)** responsible (for); **~ a** answerable to, accountable to
resposta [hes'pɔsta] F answer, reply
resquício [hes'kisju] M (*vestígio*) trace
ressabiado, -a [hesa'bjadu, a] ADJ wary; (*ressentido*) resentful
ressaca [he'saka] F undertow; (*mar bravo*) rough sea; (*fig: de quem bebeu*) hangover
ressalva [he'sawva] F safeguard
ressentido, -a [hesẽ'tʃidu, a] ADJ resentful
ressentimento [hesẽtʃi'mẽtu] M resentment
ressentir-se [hesẽ'tʃirsi] VR: **~ de** (*ofender-se*) to resent; (*magoar-se*) to be hurt by; (*sofrer*) to suffer from, feel the effects of
ressurgimento [hesurʒi'mẽtu] M resurgence, revival
ressuscitar [hesusi'tar] VT, VI to revive
restabelecer [hestabele'ser] VT to re-establish, restore; **restabelecer-se** VR to recover, recuperate; **restabelecimento** [hestabelesi'mẽtu] M re-establishment; restoration; recovery
restante [hes'tãtʃi] ADJ remaining ▶M rest
restar [hes'tar] VI to remain, be left
restauração [hestawra'sãw] (*pl* **-ões**) F restoration; (*de costumes, usos*) revival
restaurante [hestaw'rãtʃi] M restaurant
restaurar [hestaw'rar] VT to restore
restituição [hestʃitwi'sãw] (*pl* **-ões**) F restitution, return; (*de dinheiro*) repayment
restituir [hestʃi'twir] VT to return; (*dinheiro*) to repay; (*forças, saúde*) to restore; (*usos*) to revive; (*reempossar*) to reinstate
resto ['hɛstu] M rest; (*Mat*) remainder; **restos** MPL (*sobras*) remains; (*de comida*) scraps
restrição [hestri'sãw] (*pl* **-ões**) F restriction
resultado [hezuw'tadu] M result
resultante [hezuw'tãtʃi] ADJ resultant; **~ de** resulting from
resultar [hezuw'tar] VI: **~ (de/em)** to result (from/in) ▶VI (*vir a ser*) to turn out to be
resumir [hezu'mir] VT to summarize; (*livro*) to abridge; (*reduzir*) to reduce; (*conter em resumo*) to sum up; **resumo**

[he'zumu] M summary, résumé; **em resumo** in short, briefly
retaguarda [heta'gwarda] F rearguard; (*posição*) rear
retaliação [hetalja'sãw] (*pl* **-ões**) F retaliation
retângulo [he'tãgulu] M rectangle
retardar [hetar'dar] VT to hold up, delay; (*adiar*) to postpone
reter [he'ter] (*irreg*: *como* **ter**) VT (*guardar, manter*) to keep; (*deter*) to stop; (*segurar*) to hold; (*ladrão, suspeito*) to detain; (*na memória*) to retain; (*lágrimas, impulsos*) to hold back; (*impedir de sair*) to keep back
reticente [hetʃi'sẽtʃi] ADJ reticent
retificar [hetʃifi'kar] VT to rectify
retirada [hetʃi'rada] F (*Mil*) retreat; (*salário, saque*) withdrawal
reto, -a ['hɛtu, a] ADJ straight; (*fig: justo*) fair; (: *honesto*) honest, upright ▶ M (*Anat*) rectum
retorcer [hetor'ser] VT to twist; **retorcer-se** VR to wriggle, writhe
retornar [hetor'nar] VI to return, go back; **retorno** [he'tornu] M return; **dar retorno** to do a U-turn; **retorno (do carro)** (*Comput*) (carriage) return
retraído, -a [hetra'idu, a] ADJ (*tímido*) reserved, timid
retrair [hetra'ir] VT to withdraw; (*contrair*) to contract; (*pessoa*) to make reserved
retrato [he'tratu] M portrait; (*Foto*) photo; (*fig: efígie*) likeness; (: *representação*) portrayal; **~ falado** Identikit® picture
retribuir [hetri'bwir] VT to reward, recompense; (*pagar*) to remunerate; (*hospitalidade, favor, sentimento, visita*) to return
retroceder [hetrose'der] VI to retreat, fall back; **retrocesso** [hetro'sɛsu] M retreat; (*ao passado*) return
retrógrado, -a [he'trɔgradu, a] ADJ retrograde; (*reacionário*) reactionary
retrospecto [hetro'spɛktu] M: **em ~** in retrospect
retrovisor [hetrovi'zor] ADJ, M: **(espelho) ~** rear-view mirror
réu, ré [hɛw, hɛ] M/F defendant; (*culpado*) culprit, criminal
reumatismo [hewma'tʃizmu] M rheumatism
reunião [heu'njãw] (*pl* **-ões**) F meeting; (*ato, reencontro*) reunion; (*festa*) get-together, party; **~ de cúpula** summit (meeting)
revanche [he'vãʃi] F revenge
reveillon [heve'jõ] M New Year's Eve
revelação [hevela'sãw] (*pl* **-ões**) F revelation
revelar [heve'lar] VT to reveal; (*Foto*) to develop; **revelar-se** VR to turn out to be
revelia [heve'lia] F default; **à ~** by default; **à ~ de** without the knowledge *ou* consent of
revendedor, a [hevẽde'dor(a)] M/F dealer
rever [he'ver] (*irreg*: *como* **ver**) VT to see again; (*examinar*) to check; (*revisar*) to revise
reverência [heve'rẽsja] F reverence, respect; (*ato*) bow; (: *de mulher*) curtsey; **fazer uma ~** to bow; to curtsey
reverso [he'vɛrsu] M reverse
reverter [hever'ter] VT to revert
revestir [heves'tʃir] VT (*paredes etc*) to cover; (*interior de uma caixa etc*) to line
revezar [heve'zar] VT to take turns with ▶ VI to take turns; **revezar-se**

VR to take it in turns
revidar [hevi'dar] VT (*soco, insulto*) to return; (*retrucar*) to answer; (*crítica*) to rise to, respond to ▶ VI to hit back; (*retrucar*) to respond
revirar [hevi'rar] VT to turn round; (*gaveta*) to turn out, go through
revisão [hevi'zãw] (*pl* **-ões**) F revision; (*de máquina*) overhaul; (*de carro*) service; (*Jur*) appeal
revisar [hevi'zar] VT to revise
revisões [hevi'zõjs] FPL *de* **revisão**
revista [he'vista] F (*busca*) search; (*Mil, exame*) inspection; (*publicação*) magazine; (: *profissional, erudita*) journal; (*Teatro*) revue
revisto [he'vistu] VB *ver* **revestir**
revogar [hevo'gar] VT to revoke
revolta [he'vɔwta] F revolt; (*fig: indignação*) disgust; **revoltado, -a** [hevow'tadu, a] ADJ in revolt; (*indignado*) disgusted; (*amargo*) bitter; **revoltante** [hevow'tãtʃi] ADJ disgusting; revolting
revoltar [hevow'tar] VT to disgust; **revoltar-se** VR to rebel, revolt; (*indignar-se*) to be disgusted
revolto, -a [he'vowtu, a] PP *de* **revolver** ▶ ADJ (*década*) turbulent; (*mundo*) troubled; (*cabelo*) dishevelled; (*mar*) rough; (*desarrumado*) untidy
revolução [hevolu'sãw] (*pl* **-ões**) F revolution; **revolucionar** [hevolusjo'nar] VT to revolutionize; **revolucionário, -a** [hevolusjo'narju, a] ADJ, M/F revolutionary
revolver [hevow'ver] VI to revolve, rotate
revólver [he'vɔwver] M revolver
reza ['hɛza] F prayer; **rezar** [he'zar] VI to pray
riacho ['hjaʃu] M stream, brook
ribeiro [hi'bejru] M brook, stream
rico, -a ['hiku, a] ADJ rich; (PT: *lindo*) beautiful; (: *excelente*) splendid ▶ M/F rich man/woman
ridicularizar [hidʒikulari'zar] VT to ridicule
ridículo, -a [hi'dʒikulu, a] ADJ ridiculous
rifa ['hifa] F raffle
rifle ['hifli] M rifle
rigidez [hiʒi'dez] F rigidity, stiffness; (*austeridade*) severity, strictness
rígido, -a ['hiʒidu, a] ADJ rigid, stiff; (*fig*) strict
rigor [hi'gor] M rigidity; (*meticulosidade*) rigour (BRIT), rigor (US); (*severidade*) harshness, severity; (*exatidão*) precision; **ser de ~** to be essential *ou* obligatory; **rigoroso, -a** [higo'rozu, ɔza] ADJ rigorous; (*severo*) strict; (*exigente*) demanding; (*minucioso*) precise, accurate; (*inverno*) hard, harsh
rijo, -a ['hiʒu, a] ADJ tough, hard; (*severo*) harsh, severe
rim [hĩ] (*pl* **-ns**) M kidney; **rins** MPL (*parte inferior das costas*) small *sg* of the back
rima ['hima] F rhyme; (*poema*) verse, poem; **rimar** [hi'mar] VT, VI to rhyme
rímel® ['himew] (*pl* **-eis**) M mascara
ringue ['hĩgi] M ring
rins [hĩs] MPL *de* **rim**
Rio ['hiu] M: **o ~ (de Janeiro)** Rio (de Janeiro)
rio ['hiu] M river
riqueza [hi'keza] F wealth, riches *pl*; (*qualidade*) richness
rir [hir] VI to laugh; **~ de** to laugh at

risada [hi'zada] F laughter
risca ['hiska] F stroke; (*listra*) stripe; (*no cabelo*) parting
riscar [his'kar] VT (*marcar*) to mark; (*apagar*) to cross out; (*desenhar*) to outline
risco ['hisku] M (*marca*) mark, scratch; (*traço*) stroke; (*desenho*) drawing, sketch; (*perigo*) risk; **correr o ~ de** to run the risk of
riso ['hizu] M laughter; **risonho, -a** [hi'zoɲu, a] ADJ smiling; (*contente*) cheerful
ríspido, -a ['hispidu, a] ADJ brusque; (*áspero*) harsh
ritmo ['hitʃmu] M rhythm
rito ['hitu] M rite
ritual [hi'twaw] (*pl* **-ais**) ADJ, M ritual
rival [hi'vaw] (*pl* **-ais**) ADJ, M/F rival; **rivalidade** [hivali'dadʒi] F rivalry; **rivalizar** [hivali'zar] VT to rival ▶ VI: **rivalizar com** to compete with, vie with
roa ['hoa] VB *ver* **roer**
robô [ho'bo] M robot
roça ['hɔsa] F plantation; (*no mato*) clearing; (*campo*) country
rocha ['hɔʃa] F rock; (*penedo*) crag
rochedo [ho'ʃedu] M crag, cliff
rock-and-roll [-ã'hɔw] M rock and roll
roda ['hɔda] F wheel; (*círculo, grupo de pessoas*) circle; **~ dentada** cog(wheel); **em** *ou* **à ~ de** round, around
rodada [ho'dada] F (*de bebidas, Esporte*) round
rodar [ho'dar] VT to turn, spin; (*viajar por*) to tour, travel round; (*quilômetros*) to do; (*filme*) to make; (*imprimir*) to print; (*Comput: programa*) to run ▶ VI to turn round; (*Auto*) to drive around; **~ por** (*a pé*) to wander around; (*de carro*) to drive around
rodela [ho'dɛla] F (*pedaço*) slice
rodízio [ho'dʒizju] M rota; **em ~** on a rota basis
rodopiar [hodo'pjar] VI to whirl around, swirl
rodovia [hodo'via] F highway, ≈ motorway (BRIT), ≈ interstate (US)
rodoviária [hodo'vjarja] F (*tb*: **estação ~**) bus station; *ver tb* **rodoviário**
rodoviário, -a [hodo'vjarju, a] ADJ road *atr*; (*polícia*) traffic *atr*
roer [hwer] VT to gnaw, nibble; (*enferrujar*) to corrode; (*afligir*) to eat away
rogar [ho'gar] VI to ask, request; **~ a alguém que faça** to beg sb to do
rói [hɔj] VB *ver* **roer**
roía [ho'ia] VB *ver* **roer**
rolar [ho'lar] VT, VI to roll
roleta [ho'leta] F roulette; (*borboleta*) turnstile
rolha ['hoʎa] F cork
roliço, -a [ho'lisu, a] ADJ (*pessoa*) plump, chubby; (*objeto*) round, cylindrical
rolo ['holu] M (*de papel etc*) roll; (*para nivelar o solo, para pintura*) roller; (*para cabelo*) curler; (*col: briga*) brawl, fight; **cortina de ~** roller blind; **~ compressor** steamroller
Roma ['homa] N Rome
romã [ho'mã] F pomegranate
romance [ho'mãsi] M novel; (*caso amoroso*) romance; **~ policial** detective story
romano, -a [ho'manu, a] ADJ, M/F Roman
romântico, -a [ho'mãtʃiku, a] ADJ romantic
rombo ['hõbu] M (*buraco*) hole; (*fig: desfalque*) embezzlement; (*: prejuízo*) loss, shortfall

Romênia [ho'menja] F: **a ~** Romania; **romeno, -a** [ho'mɛnu, a] ADJ, M/F Rumanian ▸ M (*Ling*) Rumanian
romper [hõ'per] VT to break; (*rasgar*) to tear; (*relações*) to break off ▸ VI: **~ em pranto** *ou* **lágrimas** to burst into tears; **rompimento** [hõpi'mẽtu] M breakage; (*fenda*) break; (*de relações*) breaking off
roncar [hõ'kar] VI to snore; **ronco** ['hõku] M snore
ronda ['hõda] F patrol, beat; **fazer a ~** to go the rounds; **rondar** [hõ'dar] VT to patrol; (*espreitar*) to prowl ▸ VI to prowl, lurk; (*fazer a ronda*) to patrol; **a inflação ronda os 10% ao ano** inflation is in the region of 10% a year
rosa ['hɔza] ADJ INV pink ▸ F rose; **rosado, -a** [ho'zadu, a] ADJ rosy, pink
rosário [ho'zarju] M rosary
rosbife [hoz'bifi] M roast beef
roseira [ho'zejra] F rosebush
rosnar [hoz'nar] VI (*cão*) to growl, snarl; (*murmurar*) to mutter, mumble
rosto ['hostu] M face
rota ['hɔta] F route, course
roteiro [ho'tejru] M itinerary; (*ordem*) schedule; (*guia*) guidebook; (*de filme*) script
rotina [ho'tʃina] F routine; **rotineiro, -a** [hotʃi'nejru, a] ADJ routine
roto, -a ['hotu, a] ADJ broken; (*rasgado*) torn
rotular [hotu'lar] VT to label; **rótulo** ['hɔtulu] M label
roubar [ho'bar] VT to steal; (*loja, casa, pessoa*) to rob ▸ VI to steal; (*em jogo, no preço*) to cheat; **~ algo a alguém** to steal sth from sb;
roubo ['hobu] M theft, robbery
rouco, -a ['roku, a] ADJ hoarse
round ['hãwdʒi] (*pl* **-s**) M (*Boxe*) round
roupa ['hopa] F clothes *pl*, clothing; **~ de baixo** underwear; **~ de cama** bedclothes *pl*, bed linen
roupão [ho'pãw] (*pl* **-ões**) M dressing gown
rouxinol [hoʃi'nɔw] (*pl* **-óis**) M nightingale
roxo, -a ['hoʃu, a] ADJ purple, violet
royalty ['hɔjawtʃi] (*pl* **-ies**) M royalty
rua ['hua] F street; **~ principal** main street; **~ sem saída** no through road, cul-de-sac
rubéola [hu'bɛola] F (*Med*) German measles
rubi [hu'bi] M ruby
rubor [hu'bor] M blush; (*fig*) shyness, bashfulness
ruborizar-se [hubori'zarsi] VR to blush
rubrica [hu'brika] F (signed) initials *pl*
rubro, -a ['hubru, a] ADJ (*faces*) rosy, ruddy
ruço, -a ['husu, a] ADJ grey (BRIT), gray (US), dun; (*desbotado*) faded
rúcula ['hukula] F rocket (BRIT), arugula (US)
ruela ['hwɛla] F lane, alley
ruga ['huga] F (*na pele*) wrinkle; (*na roupa*) crease
ruge ['huʒi] M rouge
rugido [hu'ʒidu] M roar
rugir [hu'ʒir] VI to roar
ruído ['hwidu] M noise; **ruidoso, -a** [hwi'dozu, ɔza] ADJ noisy
ruim [hu'ĩ] (*pl* **-ns**) ADJ bad; (*defeituoso*) defective
ruína ['hwina] F ruin; (*decadência*) downfall

r

ruins [hu'ĩs] ADJ PL *de* **ruim**
ruir ['hwir] VI to collapse, go to ruin
ruivo, -a ['hwivu, a] ADJ red-haired ▸ M/F redhead
rum [hũ] M rum
rumo ['humu] M course, bearing; (*fig*) course; **~ a** bound for; **sem ~** adrift
rumor [hu'mor] M noise; (*notícia*) rumour (BRIT), rumor (US), report
ruptura [hup'tura] F break, rupture
rural [hu'raw] (*pl* **-ais**) ADJ rural
rush [hʌʃ] M rush; **(a hora do) ~** rush hour
Rússia ['husja] F: **a ~** Russia;
russo, -a ['husu, a] ADJ, M/F Russian ▸ M (*Ling*) Russian

S

S. ABR (= *Santo/a, São*) St
SA ABR (= *Sociedade Anônima*) plc (BRIT), Inc. (US)
sã [sã] F *de* **são**
Saara [sa'ara] M: **o ~** the Sahara
sábado ['sabadu] M Saturday
sabão [sa'bãw] (*pl* **-ões**) M soap
sabedoria [sabedo'ria] F wisdom; (*erudição*) learning
saber [sa'ber] VT, VI to know; (*descobrir*) to find out ▸ M knowledge; **a ~** namely; **~ fazer** to know how to do, be able to do; **que eu saiba** as far as I know
sabiá [sa'bja] M/F thrush
sabido, -a [sa'bidu, a] ADJ knowledgeable; (*esperto*) shrewd
sabões [sa'bõjs] MPL *de* **sabão**
sabonete [sabo'netʃi] M toilet soap
sabor [sa'bor] M taste, flavour (BRIT), flavor (US); **saborear** [sabo'rjar] VT to taste, savour (BRIT), savor (US); **saboroso, -a** [sabo'rozu, ɔza] ADJ tasty, delicious
sabotagem [sabo'taʒẽ] F sabotage

sabotar [sabo'tar] VT to sabotage
SAC ['saki] ABR M (= *serviço de atendimento ao cliente*) customer service
saca ['saka] F sack
sacar [sa'kar] VT to take out; (*dinheiro*) to withdraw; (*arma, cheque*) to draw; (*Esporte*) to serve; (*col: entender*) to understand ▸ VI (*col: entender*) to understand
saca-rolhas M INV corkscrew
sacerdote [saser'dɔtʃi] M priest
saciar [sa'sjar] VT (*fome etc*) to satisfy; (*sede*) to quench
saco ['saku] M bag; (*enseada*) inlet; **~ de café** coffee filter; **~ de dormir** sleeping bag
sacode [sa'kɔdʒi] VB *ver* **sacudir**
sacola [sa'kɔla] F bag
sacramento [sakra'mẽtu] M sacrament
sacrificar [sakrifi'kar] VT to sacrifice; **sacrificar-se** VR to sacrifice o.s.; **sacrifício** [sakri'fisju] M sacrifice
sacrilégio [sakri'lɛʒju] M sacrilege
sacro, -a ['sakru, a] ADJ sacred
sacudida [saku'dʒida] F shake
sacudir [saku'dʒir] VT to shake; **sacudir-se** VR to shake
sádico, -a ['sadʒiku, a] ADJ sadistic
sadio, -a [sa'dʒiu, a] ADJ healthy
safado, -a [sa'fadu, a] ADJ shameless; (*imoral*) dirty; (*travesso*) mischievous ▸ M rogue
safira [sa'fira] F sapphire
safra ['safra] F harvest
Sagitário [saʒi'tarju] M Sagittarius
sagrado, -a [sa'gradu, a] ADJ sacred, holy
saia ['saja] F skirt
saiba ['sajba] VB *ver* **saber**
saída [sa'ida] F exit, way out; (*partida*) departure; (*ato: de pessoa*) going out; (*fig: solução*) way out; (*Comput: de programa*) exit; (*: de dados*) output; **~ de emergência** emergency exit
sair [sa'ir] VI to go (*ou* come) out; (*partir*) to leave; (*realizar-se*) to turn out; (*Comput*) to exit; **sair-se** VR: **~-se bem/mal de** to be successful/unsuccessful in
sal [saw] (*pl* **sais**) M salt; **sem ~** (*comida*) salt-free; (*pessoa*) lacklustre (BRIT), lackluster (US)
sala ['sala] F room; (*num edifício público*) hall; (*classe, turma*) class; **~ (de aula)** classroom; **~ de bate-papo** (*Internet*) chatroom; **~ de espera** waiting room; **~ (de estar)** living room; **~ de jantar** dining room; **~ de operação** (*Med*) operating theatre (BRIT) *ou* theater (US)
salada [sa'lada] F salad; (*fig*) confusion, jumble
sala e quarto (*pl* **-s, salas e quarto**) M two-room flat (BRIT) *ou* apartment (US)
salão [sa'lãw] (*pl* **-ões**) M large room, hall; (*exposição*) show; **~ de beleza** beauty salon
salário [sa'larju] M wages *pl*, salary
saldo ['sawdu] M balance; (*sobra*) surplus
saleiro [sa'lejru] M salt cellar
salgadinho [sawga'dʒiɲu] M savoury (BRIT), savory (US), snack
salgado, -a [saw'gadu, a] ADJ salty, salted
salgueiro [saw'gejru] M willow; **~ chorão** weeping willow
salientar [saljẽ'tar] VT to point out; (*acentuar*) to stress, emphasize; **saliente** [sa'ljẽtʃi] ADJ

S

prominent; (*evidente*) clear, conspicuous; (*importante*) outstanding; (*assanhado*) forward
saliva [sa'liva] F saliva
salmão [saw'mãw] (*pl* **-ões**) M salmon
salmoura [saw'mora] F brine
salões [sa'lõjs] MPL *de* **salão**
salsa ['sawsa] F parsley
salsicha [saw'siʃa] F sausage; **salsichão** [sawsi'ʃãw] (*pl* **-ões**) M sausage
saltar [saw'tar] VT to jump (over), leap (over); (*omitir*) to skip ▸ VI to jump, leap; (*sangue*) to spurt out; (*de ônibus, cavalo*): **~ de** to get off
salto ['sawtu] M jump, leap; (*de calçado*) heel; **~ de vara** pole vault; **~ em altura** high jump; **~ em distância** long jump
salubre [sa'lubri] ADJ healthy, salubrious
salvamento [sawva'mẽtu] M rescue; (*de naufrágio*) salvage
salvar [saw'var] VT to save; (*resgatar*) to rescue; (*objetos, de ruína*) to salvage; (*honra*) to defend; **salvar-se** VR to escape
salva-vidas M INV (*boia*) lifebuoy ▸ M/F INV (*pessoa*) lifeguard; **barco ~** lifeboat
salvo, -a ['sawvu, a] ADJ safe ▸ PREP except, save; **a ~** in safety
samba ['sãba] M samba

> The greatest form of musical expression of the Brazilian people, the **samba** is a type of music and dance of African origin. It embraces a number of rhythmic styles, such as *samba de breque*, *samba-enredo*, *samba-canção* and *pagode*, among others. Officially, the first samba, entitled *Pelo telefone*, was written in Rio in 1917.

SAMU (BR) ABR M (= *Serviço de Atendimento Móvel de Urgência*) *emergency ambulance service*
sanar [sa'nar] VT to cure; (*remediar*) to remedy
sanção [sã'sãw] (*pl* **-ões**) F sanction; **sancionar** [sansjo'nar] VT to sanction
sandália [sã'dalja] F sandal
sandes ['sãdəs] (PT) F INV sandwich
sanduíche [sand'wiʃi] (BR) M sandwich
saneamento [sanja'mẽtu] M sanitation
sanear [sa'njar] VT to clean up
sangrar [sã'grar] VT, VI to bleed; **sangrento, -a** [sã'grẽtu, a] ADJ bloody; (*Culin: carne*) rare
sangue ['sãgi] M blood
sanguinário, -a [sãgi'narju, a] ADJ bloodthirsty
sanguíneo, -a [sã'ginju, a] ADJ: **grupo ~** blood group; **pressão sanguínea** blood pressure; **vaso ~** blood vessel
sanidade [sani'dadʒi] F (*saúde*) health; (*mental*) sanity
sanita [sa'nita] (PT) F toilet, lavatory
sanitário, -a [sani'tarju, a] ADJ sanitary; **vaso ~** toilet, lavatory (bowl); **sanitários** [sani'tarjus] MPL toilets
santo, -a ['sãtu, a] ADJ holy ▸ M/F saint
santuário [sã'twarju] M shrine, sanctuary
São [sãw] M Saint
são, sã [sãw, sã] (*pl* **-s/-s**) ADJ healthy; (*conselho*) sound; (*mentalmente*) sane; **~ e salvo** safe and sound
São Paulo [-'pawlu] N São Paulo
sapataria [sapata'ria] F shoe shop

sapateiro [sapa'tejru] M shoemaker; (*vendedor*) shoe salesman; (*que conserta*) shoe repairer; (*loja*) shoe repairer's
sapatilha [sapa'tʃiʎa] F (*de balé*) shoe; (*sapato*) pump; (*de atleta*) running shoe
sapato [sa'patu] M shoe
sapo ['sapu] M toad
saque¹ ['saki] M (*de dinheiro*) withdrawal; (*Com*) draft, bill; (*Esporte*) serve; (*pilhagem*) plunder, pillage; **~ a descoberto** (*Com*) overdraft
saque² VB *ver* **sacar**
saquear [sa'kjar] VT to pillage, plunder
sarampo [sa'rãpu] M measles *sg*
sarar [sa'rar] VT to cure; (*ferida*) to heal ▶ VI to recover
sarcasmo [sar'kazmu] M sarcasm
sarda ['sarda] F freckle
Sardenha [sar'dɛɲa] F: **a ~** Sardinia
sardinha [sar'dʒiɲa] F sardine
sargento [sar'ʒẽtu] M sergeant
sarjeta [sar'ʒeta] F gutter
Satã [sa'tã] M Satan
Satanás [sata'nas] M Satan
satélite [sa'tɛlitʃi] M satellite
sátira ['satʃira] F satire
satisfazer [satʃisfa'zer] (*irreg*: *como* **fazer**) VT to satisfy ▶ VI to be satisfactory; **satisfazer-se** VR to be satisfied; (*saciar-se*) to fill o.s. up; **~ a** to satisfy; **satisfeito, -a** [satʃis'fejtu, a] ADJ satisfied; (*saciado*) full; **dar-se por satisfeito com algo** to be content with sth
saudação [sawda'sãw] (*pl* **-ões**) F greeting
saudade [saw'dadʒi] F longing, yearning; (*lembrança nostálgica*) nostalgia; **deixar ~s** to be greatly missed; **ter ~s de** (*desejar*) to long for; (*sentir falta de*) to miss; **~s (de casa** *ou* **da família** *ou* **da pátria)** homesickness *sg*
saudar [saw'dar] VT to greet; (*dar as boas vindas*) to welcome; (*aclamar*) to acclaim
saudável [saw'davew] (*pl* **-eis**) ADJ healthy; (*moralmente*) wholesome
saúde [sa'udʒi] F health; (*brinde*) toast; **~!** (*brindando*) cheers!; (*quando se espirra*) bless you!; **beber à ~ de** to drink to, toast; **estar bem/mal de ~** to be well/ill
saudosismo [sawdo'zizmu] M nostalgia
saudoso, -a [saw'dozu, ɔza] ADJ (*nostálgico*) nostalgic; (*da família ou terra natal*) homesick; (*de uma pessoa*) longing; (*que causa saudades*) much-missed
sauna ['sawna] F sauna
saxofone [sakso'fɔni] M saxophone
sazonal [sazo'naw] (*pl* **-ais**) ADJ seasonal
scanner ['skaner] M scanner

PALAVRA-CHAVE

se [si] PRON **1** (*reflexivo: impess*) oneself; (: *m*) himself; (: *f*) herself; (: *coisa*) itself; (: *você*) yourself; (: *pl*) themselves; (: *vocês*) yourselves; **ela está se vestindo** she's getting dressed
2 (*uso recíproco*) each other, one another; **olharam-se** they looked at each other
3 (*impess*): **come-se bem aqui** you can eat well here; **sabe-se que ...** it is known that ...; **vende(m)-se jornais naquela loja** they sell newspapers in that shop

▶ CONJ if; *(em pergunta indireta)* whether; **se bem que** even though

sê [se] VB *ver* **ser**
sebe ['sɛbi] (PT) F fence; **~ viva** hedge
sebo ['sebu] M tallow; **seboso, -a** [se'bozu, ɔza] ADJ greasy; *(sujo)* dirty
seca ['seka] F drought
secador [seka'dor] M: **~ de cabelo/roupa** hairdryer/clothes horse
seção [se'sãw] (*pl* **-ões**) F section; *(em loja, repartição)* department
secar [se'kar] VT to dry; *(planta)* to parch ▶ VI to dry; to wither; *(fonte)* to dry up
seco, -a ['seku, a] ADJ dry; *(ríspido)* curt, brusque; *(magro)* thin; *(pessoa: frio)* cold; *(: sério)* serious
seções [se'sõjs] FPL *de* **seção**
secretaria [sekreta'ria] F general office; *(de secretário)* secretary's office; *(ministério)* ministry
secretária [sekre'tarja] F writing desk; **~ eletrônica** answering machine; *ver tb* **secretário**
secretário, -a [sekre'tarju, a] M/F secretary; **S~ de Estado de ...** Secretary of State for ...
século ['sɛkulu] M century; *(época)* age
secundário, -a [sekũ'darju, a] ADJ secondary
seda ['seda] F silk
sedativo [seda'tʃivu] M sedative
sede¹ ['sɛdʒi] F *(de empresa, instituição)* headquarters *sg*; *(de governo)* seat; *(Rel)* see, diocese
sede² ['sedʒi] F thirst; **estar com** *ou* **ter ~** to be thirsty; **sedento, -a** [se'dẽtu, a] ADJ thirsty
sediar [se'dʒjar] VT to base
sedução [sedu'sãw] (*pl* **-ões**) F seduction
sedutor, a [sedu'tor(a)] ADJ seductive; *(oferta etc)* tempting
seduzir [sedu'zir] VT to seduce; *(fascinar)* to fascinate
segmento [seg'mẽtu] M segment
segredo [se'gredu] M secret; *(sigilo)* secrecy; *(de fechadura)* combination
segregar [segre'gar] VT to segregate
seguidamente [segida'mẽtʃi] ADV *(sem parar)* continuously; *(logo depois)* soon afterwards
seguido, -a [se'gidu, a] ADJ following; *(contínuo)* continuous, consecutive; **~ de** *ou* **por** followed by; **três dias ~s** three days running; **horas seguidas** for hours on end; **em seguida** next; *(logo depois)* soon afterwards; *(imediatamente)* immediately, right away
seguimento [segi'mẽtu] M continuation; **dar ~ a** to proceed with; **em ~ de** after
seguinte [se'gĩtʃi] ADJ following, next; **eu lhe disse o ~** this is what I said to him
seguir [se'gir] VT to follow; *(continuar)* to continue ▶ VI to follow; *(continuar)* to continue, carry on; *(ir)* to go; **seguir-se** VR: **~-se (a)** to follow; **logo a ~** next; **~-se (de)** to result (from)
segunda [se'gũda] F (*tb*: **~-feira**) Monday; *(Auto)* second (gear); **de ~** second-rate; **segunda-feira** (*pl* **segundas-feiras**) F Monday
segundo, -a [se'gũdu, a] ADJ second ▶ PREP according to ▶ CONJ as, from what ▶ ADV secondly ▶ M second; **de segunda mão** second-hand; **de segunda (classe)** second-class; **~ ele disse** according to what he said; **~ dizem** apparently; **~ me consta** as far as I

know; **segundas intenções** ulterior motives
seguramente [segura'mẽtʃi] ADV certainly; (*muito provavelmente*) surely
segurança [segu'rãsa] F security; (*ausência de perigo*) safety; (*confiança*) confidence ▶ M/F security guard; **com ~** assuredly
segurar [segu'rar] VT to hold; (*amparar*) to hold up; (*Com: bens*) to insure ▶ VI: **~ em** to hold; **segurar-se** VR: **~-se em** to hold on to
seguro, -a [se'guru, a] ADJ safe; (*livre de risco, firme*) secure; (*certo*) certain, assured; (*confiável*) reliable; (*de si mesmo*) confident; (*tempo*) settled ▶ ADV confidently ▶ M (*Com*) insurance; **estar ~ de/de que** to be sure of/that; **fazer ~** to take out an insurance policy; **~ contra acidentes/incêndio** accident/fire insurance; **seguro-saúde** (*pl* **seguros-saúde**) M health insurance
sei [sej] VB *ver* **saber**
seio ['seju] M breast, bosom; (*âmago*) heart; **~ paranasal** sinus
seis [sejs] NUM six
seita ['sejta] F sect
seixo ['sejʃu] M pebble
seja ['seʒa] VB *ver* **ser**
sela ['sɛla] F saddle
selar [se'lar] VT (*carta*) to stamp; (*documento oficial, pacto*) to seal; (*cavalo*) to saddle
seleção [sele'sãw] (*pl* **-ões**) F selection; (*Esporte*) team
selecionar [selesjo'nar] VT to select
seleções [sele'sõjs] FPL *de* **seleção**
seleto, -a [se'lɛtu, a] ADJ select
selim [se'lĩ] (*pl* **-ns**) M saddle
selo ['selu] M stamp; (*carimbo, sinete*) seal
selva ['sɛwva] F jungle
selvagem [sew'vaʒẽ] (*pl* **-ns**) ADJ wild; (*feroz*) fierce; (*povo*) savage; **selvageria** [sewvaʒe'ria] F savagery
sem [sẽ] PREP without ▶ CONJ: **~ que eu peça** without my asking; **estar/ficar ~ dinheiro/gasolina** to have no/have run out of money/petrol
semáforo [se'maforu] M (*Auto*) traffic lights *pl*; (*Ferro*) signal
semana [se'mana] F week; **semanal** [sema'naw] (*pl* **-ais**) ADJ weekly; **semanário** [sema'narju] M weekly (publication)
semear [se'mjar] VT to sow;
semelhante [seme'ʎãtʃi] ADJ similar; (*tal*) such ▶ M fellow creature
sêmen ['semẽ] M semen
semente [se'mẽtʃi] F seed
semestral [semes'traw] (*pl* **-ais**) ADJ half-yearly, bi-annual
semestre [se'mɛstri] M six months; (*Educ*) semester
semi... [semi] PREFIXO semi..., half...; **semicírculo** [semi'sirkulu] M semicircle; **semifinal** [semi'finaw] (*pl* **-ais**) F semi-final
seminário [semi'narju] M seminar; (*Rel*) seminary
sem-número M: **um ~ de coisas** loads of things
sempre ['sẽpri] ADV always; **você ~ vai?** (PT) are you still going?; **~ que** whenever; **como ~** as usual; **a comida/hora** *etc* **de ~** the usual food/time *etc*
sem-terra ADJ INV landless ▶ M/F

S

INV landless labourer (BRIT) *ou* laborer (US)
sem-teto ADJ INV homeless ▸ M/F INV homeless person; **os ~** the homeless
sem-vergonha ADJ INV shameless ▸ M/F INV (*pessoa*) rogue
senado [se'nadu] M senate; **senador, a** [sena'dor(a)] M/F senator
senão [se'nãw] (*pl* **-ões**) CONJ otherwise; (*mas sim*) but, but rather ▸ PREP except ▸ M flaw, defect
senha ['sɛɲa] F sign; (*palavra de passe, Comput*) password; (*de caixa eletrônico*) PIN number; (*recibo*) receipt; (*passe*) pass
senhor, a [se'ɲor(a)] M (*homem*) man; (*formal*) gentleman; (*homem idoso*) elderly man; (*Rel*) lord; (*dono*) owner; (*tratamento*) Mr(.); (*tratamento respeitoso*) sir ▸ F (*mulher*) lady; (*esposa*) wife; (*mulher idosa*) elderly lady; (*dona*) owner; (*tratamento*) Mrs(.), Ms(.); (*tratamento respeitoso*) madam; **o ~/a ~a** (*você*) you; **nossa ~a!** (*col*) gosh; **sim, ~(a)!** yes indeed
senhorita [seɲo'rita] F young lady; (*tratamento*) Miss, Ms(.); **a ~** (*você*) you
senil [se'niw] (*pl* **-is**) ADJ senile
senões [se'nõjs] MPL *de* **senão**
sensação [sẽsa'sãw] (*pl* **-ões**) F sensation; **sensacional** [sẽsasjo'naw] (*pl* **-ais**) ADJ sensational
sensível [sẽ'sivew] (*pl* **-eis**) ADJ sensitive; (*visível*) noticeable; (*considerável*) considerable; (*dolorido*) tender
senso ['sẽsu] M sense; (*juízo*) judgement
sensual [sẽ'swaw] (*pl* **-ais**) ADJ sensual
sentado, -a [sẽ'tadu, a] ADJ sitting
sentar [sẽ'tar] VT to seat ▸ VI to sit; **sentar-se** VR to sit down
sentença [sẽ'tẽsa] F (*Jur*) sentence; **sentenciar** [sẽtẽ'sjar] VT (*julgar*) to pass judgement on; (*condenar por sentença*) to sentence
sentido, -a [sẽ'tʃidu, a] ADJ (*magoado*) hurt; (*choro, queixa*) heartfelt ▸ M sense; (*direção*) direction; (*atenção*) attention; (*aspecto*) respect; **~!** (*Mil*) attention!; **em certo ~** in a sense; **"~ único"** (PT: *sinal*) "one-way"
sentimental [sẽtʃimẽ'taw] (*pl* **-ais**) ADJ sentimental; **vida ~** love life
sentimento [sẽtʃi'mẽtu] M feeling; (*senso*) sense; **sentimentos** MPL (*pêsames*) condolences
sentinela [sẽtʃi'nɛla] F sentry, guard
sentir [sẽ'tʃir] VT to feel; (*perceber, pressentir*) to sense; (*ser afetado por*) to be affected by; (*magoar-se*) to be upset by ▸ VI to feel; (*sofrer*) to suffer; **sentir-se** VR to feel; (*julgar-se*) to consider o.s. (to be); **~ (a) falta de** to miss; **~ cheiro/gosto (de)** to smell/taste; **~ vontade de** to feel like; **sinto muito** I am very sorry
separação [separa'sãw] (*pl* **-ões**) F separation
separado, -a [sepa'radu, a] ADJ separate; **em ~** separately, apart
separar [sepa'rar] VT to separate; (*dividir*) to divide; (*pôr de lado*) to put aside; **separar-se** VR to separate; to be divided
sepultamento [sepuwta'mẽtu] M burial
sepultar [sepuw'tar] VT to bury; **sepultura** [sepuw'tura] F grave, tomb

sequência [se'kwẽsja] F sequence
sequer [se'kɛr] ADV at least; **(nem) ~** not even
sequestrar [sekwes'trar] VT (*bens*) to seize, confiscate; (*raptar*) to kidnap; (*avião etc*) to hijack; **sequestro** [se'kwɛstru] M seizure; (*rapto*) abduction, kidnapping; (*de avião etc*) hijack

PALAVRA-CHAVE

ser [ser] VI **1** (*descrição*) to be; **ela é médica/muito alta** she's a doctor/very tall; **é Ana** (*Tel*) Ana speaking *ou* here; **ela é de uma bondade incrível** she's incredibly kind; **ele está é danado** he's really angry; **ser de mentir/briga** to be the sort to lie/fight
2 (*horas, datas, números*): **é uma hora** it's one o'clock; **são seis e meia** it's half past six; **é dia 1º de junho** it's the first of June; **somos/são seis** there are six of us/them
3 (*origem, material*): **ser de** to be *ou* come from; (*feito de*) to be made of; (*pertencer*) to belong to; **sua família é da Bahia** his (*ou* her *etc*) family is from Bahia; **a mesa é de mármore** the table is made of marble; **é de Pedro** it's Pedro's, it belongs to Pedro
4 (*em orações passivas*): **já foi descoberto** it had already been discovered
5 (*locuções com subjun*): **ou seja** that is to say; **seja quem for** whoever it may be; **se eu fosse você** if I were you; **se não fosse você, ...** if it hadn't been for you ...
6 (*locuções*): **a não ser** except; **a não ser que** unless; **é** (*resposta afirmativa*) yes; **..., não é?** isn't it?, don't you? *etc*; **ah, é?** really?; **que foi?** (*o que aconteceu?*) what happened?; (*qual é o problema?*) what's the problem?; **será que ...?** I wonder if ...?
▶ M being; **seres** MPL (*criaturas*) creatures

sereia [se'reja] F mermaid
série ['sɛri] F series; (*sequência*) sequence, succession; (*Educ*) grade; (*categoria*) category; **fora de ~** out of order; (*fig*) extraordinary
seriedade [serje'dadʒi] F seriousness; (*honestidade*) honesty
seringa [se'rĩga] F syringe
sério, -a ['sɛrju, a] ADJ serious; (*honesto*) honest, decent; (*responsável*) responsible; (*confiável*) reliable; (*roupa*) sober
▶ ADV seriously; **a ~** seriously; **~?** really?
sermão [ser'mãw] (*pl* **-ões**) M sermon; (*fig*) telling-off
serpente [ser'pẽtʃi] F snake
serra ['sɛha] F (*montanhas*) mountains *pl*; (*Tec*) saw
serralheiro, -a [seha'ʎejru, a] M/F locksmith
serrano, -a [se'hanu, a] ADJ highland *atr* ▶ M/F highlander
serrar [se'har] VT to saw
sertanejo, -a [serta'neʒu, a] ADJ rustic, country ▶ M/F inhabitant of the *sertão*
sertão [ser'tãw] (*pl* **-ões**) M backwoods *pl*, bush (country)
servente [ser'vẽtʃi] M/F servant; (*operário*) labourer (BRIT), laborer (US)
serviçal [servi'saw] (*pl* **-ais**) ADJ obliging, helpful ▶ M/F servant;

(*trabalhador*) wage earner
serviço [ser'visu] M service; (*de chá etc*) set; **estar de ~** to be on duty; **prestar ~** to help
servidor, a [servi'dor(a)] M/F servant; (*funcionário*) employee ▶ M (*Comput*) server; **~ público** civil servant
servil [ser'viw] (*pl* **-is**) ADJ servile
servir [ser'vir] VT to serve ▶ VI to serve; (*ser útil*) to be useful; (*ajudar*) to help; (*roupa: caber*) to fit;
servir-se VR: **~-se (de)** (*comida, café*) to help o.s. (to); **~-se de** (*meios*) to use, make use of; **~ de** (*prover*) to supply with, provide with; **você está servido?** (*num bar*) are you all right for a drink?; **~ de algo** to serve as sth; **qualquer ônibus serve** any bus will do
servis [ser'vis] ADJ PL *de* **servil**
sessão [se'sãw] (*pl* **-ões**) F (*do parlamento etc*) session; (*reunião*) meeting; (*de cinema*) showing
sessenta [se'sẽta] NUM sixty
sessões [se'sõjs] FPL *de* **sessão**
sesta ['sɛsta] F siesta, nap
seta ['sɛta] F arrow
sete ['sɛtʃi] NUM seven
setembro [se'tẽbru] M September

Brazil's independence from Portugal is commemorated on 7 September (**7 de setembro**). Independence was declared in 1822 by the Portuguese prince regent, Dom Pedro, who rebelled against several orders from the Portuguese crown, among them the order to swear loyalty to the Portuguese constitution. It is a national holiday and the occasion for processions and military parades through the main cities.

setenta [se'tẽta] NUM seventy
sétimo, -a ['sɛtʃimu, a] NUM seventh
setor [se'tor] M sector
seu, sua [sew, 'sua] ADJ (*dele*) his; (*dela*) her; (*de coisa*) its; (*deles, delas*) their; (*de você, vocês*) your ▶ PRON (*dele*) his; (*dela*) hers; (*deles, delas*) theirs; (*de você, vocês*) yours ▶ M (*senhor*) Mr(.)
severidade [severi'dadʒi] F severity
severo, -a [se'vɛru, a] ADJ severe
sexo ['sɛksu] M sex
sexta ['sesta] F (*tb*: **~-feira**) Friday;
sexta-feira (*pl* **sextas-feiras**) F Friday; **Sexta-feira Santa** Good Friday
sexto, -a ['sestu, a] NUM sixth
sexual [se'kswaw] (*pl* **-ais**) ADJ sexual; (*vida, ato*) sex *atr*
sexualidade [sekswali'dadʒi] F sexuality
sexy ['sɛksi] (*pl* **-s**) ADJ sexy
s.f.f. (PT) ABR = **se faz favor**
short ['ʃɔrtʃi] M (pair of) shorts *pl*
si [si] PRON oneself; (*ele*) himself; (*ela*) herself; (*coisa*) itself; (PT: *você*) yourself, you; (: *vocês*) yourselves; (*eles, elas*) themselves
SIDA ['sida] (PT) ABR F (= *síndrome de deficiência imunológica adquirida*) AIDS
siderúrgica [side'rurʒika] F steel industry
sigilo [si'ʒilu] M secrecy
sigla ['sigla] F acronym; (*abreviação*) abbreviation
significado [signifi'kadu] M meaning
significar [signifi'kar] VT to mean, signify; **significativo, -a** [signifika'tʃivu, a] ADJ significant
signo ['signu] M sign

sigo ['sigu] VB *ver* **seguir**
sílaba ['silaba] F syllable
silenciar [silẽ'sjar] VT to silence
silêncio [si'lẽsju] M silence, quiet; **silencioso, -a** [silẽ'sjozu, ɔza] ADJ silent, quiet ▸ M (*Auto*) silencer (BRIT), muffler (US)
silhueta [si'ʎweta] F silhouette
silvestre [siw'vɛstri] ADJ wild
sim [sĩ] ADV yes; **creio que ~** I think so
símbolo ['sĩbolu] M symbol
simetria [sime'tria] F symmetry
similar [simi'lar] ADJ similar
simpatia [sĩpa'tʃia] F liking; (*afeto*) affection; (*afinidade, solidariedade*) sympathy; **simpatias** FPL (*inclinações*) sympathies; **simpático, -a** [sĩ'patʃiku, a] ADJ (*pessoa, decoração etc*) nice; (*lugar*) pleasant, nice; (*amável*) kind; **simpatizante** [sĩpatʃi'zãtʃi] ADJ sympathetic ▸ M/F sympathizer; **simpatizar** [sĩpatʃi'zar] VI: **simpatizar com** (*pessoa*) to like; (*causa*) to sympathize with
simples ['sĩplis] ADJ INV simple; (*único*) single; (*fácil*) easy; (*mero*) mere; (*ingênuo*) naïve ▸ ADV simply; **simplicidade** [sĩplisi'dadʒi] F simplicity; **simplificar** [sĩplifi'kar] VT to simplify
simular [simu'lar] VT to simulate
simultaneamente [simuwtanja'mẽtʃi] ADV simultaneously
simultâneo, -a [simuw'tanju, a] ADJ simultaneous
sinagoga [sina'gɔga] F synagogue
sinal [si'naw] (*pl* **-ais**) M sign; (*gesto, Tel*) signal; (*na pele*) mole; (: *de nascença*) birthmark; (*depósito*) deposit; (*tb*: **~ de tráfego luminoso**) traffic light; **por ~** (*por falar nisso*) by the way; (*aliás*) as a matter of fact; **~ de chamada** (*Tel*) ringing tone; **~ de discar** (BR) *ou* **de marcar** (PT) dialling tone (BRIT), dial tone (US); **~ de ocupado** (BR) *ou* **de impedido** (PT) engaged tone (BRIT), busy signal (US); **sinalização** [sinaliza'sãw] F (*ato*) signalling; (*para motoristas*) traffic signs *pl*
sincero, -a [sĩ'sɛru, a] ADJ sincere
sindicalista [sĩdʒika'lista] M/F trade unionist
sindicato [sĩdʒi'katu] M trade union; (*financeiro*) syndicate
síndrome ['sĩdromi] F syndrome; **~ de Down** Down's syndrome
sinfonia [sĩfo'nia] F symphony
singular [sĩgu'lar] ADJ singular; (*extraordinário*) exceptional; (*bizarro*) odd, peculiar
sino ['sinu] M bell
sintaxe [sĩ'tasi] F syntax
síntese ['sĩtezi] F synthesis; **sintético, -a** [sĩ'tɛtʃiku, a] ADJ synthetic; **sintetizar** [sĩtetʃi'zar] VT to synthesize
sinto ['sĩtu] VB *ver* **sentir**
sintoma [sĩ'tɔma] M symptom
sinuca [si'nuka] F snooker
sinuoso, -a [si'nwozu, ɔza] ADJ (*caminho*) winding; (*linha*) wavy
siri [si'ri] M crab
sirvo ['sirvu] VB *ver* **servir**
sistema [sis'tɛma] M system; (*método*) method; **~ imunológico** immune system
site ['sajtʃi] M (*na Internet*) website; **~ de relacionamentos** social networking site
sítio ['sitʃju] M (*Mil*) siege;

(*propriedade rural*) small farm; (PT: *lugar*) place
situação [sitwa'sãw] (*pl* **-ões**) F situation; (*posição*) position
situado, -a [si'twadu, a] ADJ situated
situar [si'twar] VT to place, put; (*edifício*) to situate, locate;
situar-se VR to position o.s.; (*estar situado*) to be situated
slogan [iz'lɔgã] (*pl* **-s**) M slogan
smoking [iz'mokĩs] (*pl* **-s**) M dinner jacket (BRIT), tuxedo (US)
só [sɔ] ADJ alone; (*único*) single; (*solitário*) solitary ▶ ADV only; **a sós** alone
soar [swar] VI to sound ▶ VT (*horas*) to strike; (*instrumento*) to play; **~ a** to sound like; **~ bem/mal** (*fig*) to go down well/badly
sob [sob] PREP under; **~ juramento** on oath; **~ medida** (*roupa*) made to measure
sobe ['sɔbi] VB *ver* **subir**
soberano, -a [sobe'ranu, a] ADJ sovereign; (*fig: supremo*) supreme ▶ M/F sovereign
sobra ['sɔbra] F surplus, remnant; **sobras** FPL remains; (*de tecido*) remnants; (*de comida*) leftovers; **ter algo de ~** to have sth extra; (*tempo, comida, motivos*) to have plenty of sth; **ficar de ~** to be left over
sobrado [so'bradu] M (*andar*) floor; (*casa*) house (*of two or more storeys*)
sobrancelha [sobrã'seʎa] F eyebrow
sobrar [so'brar] VI to be left; (*dúvidas*) to remain
sobre ['sobri] PREP on; (*por cima de*) over; (*acima de*) above; (*a respeito de*) about
sobrecarregar [sobrikahe'gar] VT to overload
sobremesa [sobri'meza] F dessert
sobrenatural [sobrinatu'raw] (*pl* **-ais**) ADJ supernatural
sobrenome [sobri'nɔmi] (BR) M surname, family name
sobrepor [sobri'por] (*irreg: como* **pôr**) VT: **~ algo a algo** to put sth on top of sth
sobressair [sobrisa'ir] VI to stand out; **sobressair-se** VR to stand out
sobressalente [sobrisa'lẽtʃi] ADJ, M spare
sobressalto [sobri'sawtu] M start; (*temor*) trepidation; **de ~** suddenly
sobretaxa [sobri'taʃa] F surcharge
sobretudo [sobri'tudu] M overcoat ▶ ADV above all, especially
sobrevivência [sobrivi'vẽsja] F survival; **sobrevivente** [sobrivi'vẽtʃi] ADJ surviving ▶ M/F survivor
sobreviver [sobrivi'ver] VI: **~ (a)** to survive
sobrinho, -a [so'briɲu, a] M/F nephew/niece
sóbrio, -a ['sɔbrju, a] ADJ sober; (*moderado*) moderate, restrained
socar [so'kar] VT (*esmurrar*) to hit, strike; (*calcar*) to crush, pound; (*massa de pão*) to knead
social [so'sjaw] (*pl* **-ais**) ADJ social; **socialista** [sosja'lista] ADJ, M/F socialist
sociedade [sosje'dadʒi] F society; (*Com: empresa*) company; (*associação*) association; **~ anônima** limited company (BRIT), incorporated company (US)
sócio, -a ['sɔsju, a] M/F (*Com*) partner; (*de clube*) member
soco ['soku] M punch; **dar um ~ em** to punch
socorrer [soko'her] VT to help, assist; (*salvar*) to rescue;

socorrer-se VR: **~-se de** to resort to, have recourse to; **socorro** [so'kohu] M help, assistance; (*reboque*) breakdown (BRIT) *ou* tow (US) truck; **socorro!** help!; **primeiros socorros** first aid *sg*
soda ['sɔda] F soda (water)
sofá [so'fa] M sofa, settee; **sofá-cama** (*pl* **sofás-camas**) M sofa-bed
sofisticado, -a [sofistʃi'kadu, a] ADJ sophisticated; (*afetado*) pretentious
sofrer [so'frer] VT to suffer; (*acidente*) to have; (*aguentar*) to bear, put up with; (*experimentar*) to undergo ▶ VI to suffer; **sofrido, -a** [so'fridu, a] ADJ long-suffering; **sofrimento** [sofri'mẽtu] M suffering
software [sof'twer] M (*Comput*) software
sogro, -a ['sogru, 'sɔgra] M/F father-in-law/mother-in-law
sóis [sɔjs] MPL *de* **sol**
soja ['sɔʒa] F soya (BRIT), soy (US)
sol [sɔw] (*pl* **sóis**) M sun; (*luz*) sunshine, sunlight; **fazer ~** to be sunny; **pegar ~** to get the sun
sola ['sɔla] F sole
solar [so'lar] ADJ solar; **energia/painel ~** solar energy/panel
soldado [sow'dadu] M soldier
soleira [so'lejra] F doorstep
solene [so'lɛni] ADJ solemn; **solenidade** [soleni'dadʒi] F solemnity; (*cerimônia*) ceremony
soletrar [sole'trar] VT to spell
solicitar [solisi'tar] VT to ask for; (*emprego etc*) to apply for; (*amizade, atenção*) to seek; **~ algo a alguém** to ask sb for sth
solícito, -a [so'lisitu, a] ADJ helpful
solidão [soli'dãw] F solitude; (*sensação*) loneliness
solidariedade [solidarje'dadʒi] F solidarity
solidário, -a [soli'darju, a] ADJ (*pessoa*) supportive; **ser ~ a** *ou* **com** (*pessoa*) to stand by; (*causa*) to be sympathetic to, sympathize with
sólido, -a ['sɔlidu, a] ADJ solid
solitário, -a [soli'tarju, a] ADJ lonely, solitary ▶ M hermit
solo ['sɔlu] M ground, earth; (*Mús*) solo
soltar [sow'tar] VT to set free; (*desatar*) to loosen; (*largar*) to let go of; (*emitir*) to emit; (*grito, risada*) to let out; (*cabelo*) to let down; (*freio, animais*) to release; **soltar-se** VR to come loose; (*desinibir-se*) to let o.s. go
solteirão, -rona [sowtej'rãw, rɔna] (*pl* **-ões/-s**) ADJ unmarried ▶ M/F bachelor/spinster
solteiro, -a [sow'tejru, a] ADJ single ▶ M/F single man/woman
solteirões [sowtej'rõjs] MPL *de* **solteirão**
solto, -a ['sowtu, a] PP *de* **soltar** ▶ ADJ loose; (*livre*) free; (*sozinho*) alone
solução [solu'sãw] (*pl* **-ões**) F solution
soluçar [solu'sar] VI (*chorar*) to sob; (*Med*) to hiccup
solucionar [solusjo'nar] VT to solve; (*decidir*) to resolve
soluço [so'lusu] M sob; (*Med*) hiccup
soluções [solu'sõjs] FPL *de* **solução**
som [sõ] (*pl* **-ns**) M sound; **~ cd** compact disc player
soma ['sɔma] F sum; **somar**

[so'mar] VT (*adicionar*) to add (up); (*chegar a*) to add up to, amount to ▶ VI to add up
sombra ['sõbra] F shadow; (*proteção*) shade; (*indício*) trace, sign
sombrinha [sõ'briɲa] F parasol, sunshade
some ['sɔmi] VB *ver* **sumir**
somente [sɔ'mẽtʃi] ADV only
somos ['somos] VB *ver* **ser**
sonâmbulo, -a [so'nãbulu, a] M/F sleepwalker
sondar [sõ'dar] VT to probe; (*opinião etc*) to sound out
soneca [so'nɛka] F nap, snooze
sonegar [sone'gar] VT (*dinheiro, valores*) to conceal, withhold; (*furtar*) to steal, pilfer; (*impostos*) to dodge, evade; (*informações, dados*) to withhold
soneto [so'netu] M sonnet
sonhar [so'ɲar] VT, VI to dream; **~ com** to dream about; **sonho** ['sɔɲu] M dream; (*Culin*) doughnut
sono ['sɔnu] M sleep; **estar com** *ou* **ter ~** to be sleepy
sonolento, -a [sono'lẽtu, a] ADJ sleepy, drowsy
sonoro, -a [so'nɔru, a] ADJ resonant
sons [sõs] MPL *de* **som**
sonso, -a ['sõsu, a] ADJ sly, artful
sopa ['sopa] F soup
soporífero, -a [sopo'riferu, a] ADJ soporific ▶ M sleeping drug
soprar [so'prar] VT to blow; (*balão*) to blow up; (*vela*) to blow out; (*dizer em voz baixa*) to whisper ▶ VI to blow; **sopro** ['sopru] M blow, puff; (*de vento*) gust
sórdido, -a ['sɔrdʒidu, a] ADJ sordid; (*imundo*) squalid
soro ['soru] M (*Med*) serum
sorridente [sohi'dẽtʃi] ADJ smiling
sorrir [so'hir] VI to smile; **sorriso** [so'hizu] M smile
sorte ['sɔrtʃi] F luck; (*casualidade*) chance; (*destino*) fate, destiny; (*condição*) lot; (*espécie*) sort, kind; **de ~ que** so that; **dar ~** (*trazer sorte*) to bring good luck; (*ter sorte*) to be lucky; **estar com** *ou* **ter ~** to be lucky
sortear [sor'tʃjar] VT to draw lots for; (*rifar*) to raffle; (*Mil*) to draft; **sorteio** [sor'teju] M draw; (*rifa*) raffle; (*Mil*) draft
sortido, -a [sor'tʃidu, a] ADJ (*abastecido*) supplied, stocked; (*variado*) assorted; (*loja*) well-stocked
sortudo, -a [sor'tudu, a] (*col*) ADJ lucky
sorvete [sor'vetʃi] (BR) M ice cream
SOS ABR SOS
sossegado, -a [sose'gadu, a] ADJ peaceful, calm
sossegar [sose'gar] VT to calm, quieten ▶ VI to quieten down
sossego [so'segu] M peace (and quiet)
sótão ['sɔtãw] (*pl* **-s**) M attic, loft
sotaque [so'taki] M accent
soterrar [sote'har] VT to bury
sou [so] VB *ver* **ser**
soube ['sobi] VB *ver* **saber**
soutien [su'tʃjã] M = **sutiã**
sova ['sɔva] F beating, thrashing
sovaco [so'vaku] M armpit
sovina [so'vina] ADJ mean, stingy ▶ M/F miser
sozinho, -a [sɔ'ziɲu, a] ADJ (all) alone, by oneself; (*por si mesmo*) by oneself
spam [is'pã] (*pl* **-s**) M (*Comput*) spam
squash [is'kwɛʃ] M squash
Sr. ABR (= *senhor*) Mr
Sra. (BR), **Sr.a** (PT) ABR (= *senhora*) Mrs

Srta. (BR), **Sr.ta** (PT) ABR (= *senhorita*) Miss
sua ['sua] F *de* **seu**
suar [swar] VT, VI to sweat
suave ['swavi] ADJ gentle; (*música, voz*) soft; (*sabor, vinho*) smooth; (*cheiro*) delicate; (*dor*) mild; (*trabalho*) light; **suavidade** [suavi'dadʒi] F gentleness; softness
subalterno, -a [subaw'tɛrnu, a] ADJ, M/F subordinate
subconsciente [subkõ'sjẽtʃi] ADJ, M subconscious
subdesenvolvido, -a [subdʒizẽvow'vidu, a] ADJ underdeveloped
subentender [subẽtẽ'der] VT to understand, assume; **subentendido, -a** [subẽtẽ'dʒidu, a] ADJ implied ▶ M implication
subestimar [subestʃi'mar] VT to underestimate
subida [su'bida] F ascent, climb; (*ladeira*) slope; (*de preços*) rise
subir [su'bir] VI to go up; (*preço, de posto etc*) to rise ▶ VT to raise; (*ladeira, escada, rio*) to climb, go up; **~ em** to climb, go up; (*cadeira, palanque*) to climb onto, get up onto; (*ônibus*) to get on
súbito, -a ['subitu, a] ADJ sudden ▶ ADV (*tb*: **de ~**) suddenly
subjetivo, -a [subʒe'tʃivu, a] ADJ subjective
subjuntivo, -a [subʒũ'tʃivu, a] ADJ, M subjunctive
sublime [su'blimi] ADJ sublime
sublinhar [subli'ɲar] VT to underline; (*destacar*) to emphasize, stress
submarino, -a [subma'rinu, a] ADJ underwater ▶ M submarine
submeter [subme'ter] VT to subdue; (*plano*) to submit; (*sujeitar*): **~ a** to subject to; **submeter-se** VR: **~-se a** to submit to; (*operação*) to undergo
submisso, -a [sub'misu, a] ADJ submissive
subnutrição [subnutri'sãw] F malnutrition
subornar [subor'nar] VT to bribe; **suborno** [su'bornu] M bribery
subsequente [subse'kwẽtʃi] ADJ subsequent
subserviente [subser'vjẽtʃi] ADJ obsequious, servile
subsidiária [subsi'dʒjarja] F (*Com*) subsidiary (company)
subsidiário, -a [subsi'dʒjarju, a] ADJ subsidiary
subsídio [sub'sidʒu] M subsidy; (*ajuda*) aid
subsistência [subsis'tẽsja] F subsistence
subsistir [subsis'tʃir] VI to exist; (*viver*) to subsist
subsolo [sub'sɔlu] M (*de prédio*) basement
substância [sub'stãsja] F substance; **substancial** [substã'sjaw] (*pl* **-ais**) ADJ substantial
substantivo, -a [substã'tʃivu, a] ADJ substantive ▶ M noun
substituir [substʃi'twir] VT to substitute
subtil [sub'tiw] (PT) = **sutil** *etc*
subtrair [subtra'ir] VT to steal; (*deduzir*) to subtract ▶ VI to subtract
subumano, -a [subu'manu, a] ADJ subhuman; (*desumano*) inhuman
suburbano, -a [subur'banu, a] ADJ suburban
subúrbio [su'burbju] M suburb

subvenção [subvẽ'sãw] (*pl* **-ões**) F subsidy, grant
subversivo, -a [subver'sivu, a] ADJ, M/F subversive
sucata [su'kata] F scrap metal
sucção [suk'sãw] F suction
suceder [suse'der] VI to happen ▶ VT to succeed; **~ a** (*num cargo*) to succeed; (*seguir*) to follow
sucessão [suse'sãw] (*pl* **-ões**) F succession; **sucessivo, -a** [suse'sivu, a] ADJ successive
sucesso [su'sɛsu] M success; (*música, filme*) hit; **fazer** *ou* **ter ~** to be successful
sucinto, -a [su'sĩtu, a] ADJ succinct
suco ['suku] (BR) M juice
suculento, -a [suku'lẽtu, a] ADJ succulent
sucumbir [sukũ'bir] VI to succumb; (*morrer*) to die, perish
sucursal [sukur'saw] (*pl* **-ais**) F (*Com*) branch
Sudão [su'dãw] M: **o ~** (the) Sudan
sudeste [su'dɛstʃi] M south-east
súdito ['sudʒitu] M (*de rei etc*) subject
sudoeste [sud'wɛstʃi] M south-west
Suécia ['swɛsja] F: **a ~** Sweden; **sueco, -a** ['swɛku, a] ADJ Swedish ▶ M/F Swede ▶ M (*Ling*) Swedish
suéter ['swɛter] (BR) M *ou* F sweater
suficiente [sufi'sjẽtʃi] ADJ sufficient, enough
sufixo [su'fiksu] M suffix
sufocar [sufo'kar] VT, VI to suffocate
sugar [su'gar] VT to suck
sugerir [suʒe'rir] VT to suggest
sugestão [suʒes'tãw] (*pl* **-ões**) F suggestion; **dar uma ~** to make a suggestion; **sugestivo, -a** [suʒes'tʃivu, a] ADJ suggestive
sugiro [su'ʒiru] VB *ver* **sugerir**
Suíça ['swisa] F: **a ~** Switzerland
suíças ['swisas] FPL sideburns; *ver tb* **suíço**
suicida [swi'sida] ADJ suicidal ▶ M/F suicidal person; (*morto*) suicide; **suicidar-se** [swisi'darsi] VR to commit suicide; **suicídio** [swi'sidʒju] M suicide
suíço, -a ['swisu, a] ADJ, M/F Swiss
suíte ['switʃi] F (*Mús, em hotel*) suite
sujar [su'ʒar] VT to dirty ▶ VI to make a mess; **sujar-se** VR to get dirty
sujeira [su'ʒejra] F dirt; (*estado*) dirtiness; (*col*) dirty trick
sujeito, -a [su'ʒejtu, a] ADJ: **~ a** subject to ▶ M (*Ling*) subject ▶ M/F man/woman
sujo, -a ['suʒu, a] ADJ dirty; (*fig: desonesto*) dishonest ▶ M dirt
sul [suw] ADJ INV south, southern ▶ M: **o ~** the south; **sul-africano, -a** ADJ, M/F South African; **sul-americano, -a** ADJ, M/F South American
sulco [suw'ku] M furrow
suma ['suma] F: **em ~** in short
sumário, -a [su'marju, a] ADJ (*breve*) brief, concise; (*Jur*) summary; (*biquíni*) skimpy ▶ M summary
sumiço [su'misu] M disappearance
sumir [su'mir] VI to disappear, vanish
sumo, -a ['sumu, a] ADJ (*importância*) extreme; (*qualidade*) supreme ▶ M (PT) juice
sunga ['sũga] F swimming trunks *pl*
suor [swɔr] M sweat
super... [super-] PREFIXO super-, over-
superado, -a [supe'radu, a] ADJ (*ideias*) outmoded
superar [supe'rar] VT (*rival*) to

surpass; (*inimigo, dificuldade*) to overcome; (*expectativa*) to exceed
superfície [super'fisi] F surface; (*extensão*) area; (*fig: aparência*) appearance
supérfluo, -a [su'pɛrflwu, a] ADJ superfluous
superior [supe'rjor] ADJ superior; (*mais elevado*) higher; (*quantidade*) greater; (*mais acima*) upper ▶ M superior; **superioridade** [superjori'dadʒi] F superiority
superlotado, -a [superlo'tadu, a] ADJ crowded; (*excessivamente cheio*) overcrowded
supermercado [supermer'kadu] M supermarket
superpotência [superpo'tẽsja] F superpower
superstição [superstʃi'sãw] (*pl* **-ões**) F superstition; **supersticioso, -a** [superstʃi'sjozu, ɔza] ADJ superstitious
supervisão [supervi'zãw] F supervision; **supervisionar** [supervizjo'nar] VT to supervise; **supervisor, a** [supervi'zor(a)] M/F supervisor
suplemento [suple'mẽtu] M supplement
súplica ['suplika] F supplication, plea; **suplicar** [supli'kar] VT, VI to plead, beg
suplício [su'plisju] M torture
supor [su'por] (*irreg: como* **pôr**) VT to suppose; (*julgar*) to think
suportar [supor'tar] VT to hold up, support; (*tolerar*) to bear, tolerate; **suportável** [supor'tavew] (*pl* **-eis**) ADJ bearable; **suporte** [su'pɔrtʃi] M support
suposto, -a [su'postu, 'pɔsta] ADJ supposed ▶ M assumption, supposition
supremo, -a [su'prɛmu, a] ADJ supreme
suprimir [supri'mir] VT to suppress
surdo, -a ['surdu, a] ADJ deaf; (*som*) muffled, dull ▶ M/F deaf person; **surdo-mudo, surda-muda** ADJ deaf and dumb ▶ M/F deaf-mute
surfe ['surfi] M surfing
surfista [sur'fista] M/F surfer
surgir [sur'ʒir] VI to appear; (*problema, dificuldade*) to arise
surjo ['surʒu] VB *ver* **surgir**
surpreendente [surprjẽ'dẽtʃi] ADJ surprising
surpreender [surprjẽ'der] VT to surprise; **surpreender-se** VR: **~-se (de)** to be surprised (at); **surpresa** [sur'preza] F surprise; **surpreso, -a** [sur'prezu, a] PP *de* **surpreender** ▶ ADJ surprised
surra ['suha] F: **dar uma ~ em** to thrash; **levar uma ~ (de)** to get thrashed (by); **surrar** [su'har] VT to beat, thrash
surtar [sur'tar] VI to freak out
surtir [sur'tʃir] VT to produce, bring about
surto ['surtu] M (*de doença*) outbreak; (*ataque*) outburst
SUS [sus] (BR) ABR M (= *Sistema Único de Saúde*) *national health service*
suspeita [sus'pejta] F suspicion; **suspeitar** [suspej'tar] VT to suspect ▶ VI: **suspeitar de algo** to suspect sth; **suspeito, -a** [sus'pejtu, a] ADJ, M/F suspect
suspender [suspẽ'der] VT (*levantar*) to lift; (*pendurar*) to hang; (*trabalho, pagamento etc*) to

suspend; (*encomenda*) to cancel; (*sessão*) to adjourn, defer; (*viagem*) to put off; **suspensão** [suspẽ'sãw] (*pl* **-ões**) F (*ger, Auto*) suspension; (*de trabalho, pagamento*) stoppage; (*de viagem, sessão*) deferment; (*de encomenda*) cancellation; **suspense** [sus'pẽsi] M suspense; **filme de suspense** thriller; **suspenso, -a** [sus'pẽsu, a] PP *de* **suspender**

suspensórios [suspẽ'sɔrjus] MPL braces (BRIT), suspenders (US)

suspirar [suspi'rar] VI to sigh; **suspiro** [sus'piru] M sigh; (*doce*) meringue

sussurrar [susu'har] VT, VI to whisper; **sussurro** [su'suhu] M whisper

sustentar [sustẽ'tar] VT to sustain; (*prédio*) to hold up; (*padrão*) to maintain; (*financeiramente, acusação*) to support; **sustentável** [sustẽ'tavew] (*pl* **-eis**) ADJ sustainable; **sustento** [sus'tẽtu] M sustenance; (*subsistência*) livelihood; (*amparo*) support

susto ['sustu] M fright, scare

sutiã [su'tʃjã] M bra(ssiere)

sutil [su'tʃiw] (*pl* **-is**) ADJ subtle; **sutileza** [sutʃi'leza] F subtlety

t

ta [ta] = **te + a**

tabacaria [tabaka'ria] F tobacconist's (shop)

tabaco [ta'baku] M tobacco

tabela [ta'bɛla] F table, chart; (*lista*) list; **por ~** indirectly

taberna [ta'bɛrna] F tavern, bar

tablet [tablitʃ] (*pl* **-s**) M (*Comput*) tablet

tablete [ta'blɛtʃi] M (*de chocolate*) bar

tabu [ta'bu] ADJ, M taboo

tábua ['tabwa] F plank, board; (*Mat*) table; **~ de passar roupa** ironing board

tabuleiro [tabu'lejru] M tray; (*Xadrez*) board

tabuleta [tabu'leta] F (*letreiro*) sign, signboard

taça ['tasa] F cup

tacha ['taʃa] F tack

tachinha [ta'ʃiɲa] F drawing pin (BRIT), thumb tack (US)

taco ['taku] M (*Bilhar*) cue; (*Golfe*) club

tagarela [taga'rɛla] ADJ talkative ▶ M/F chatterbox; **tagarelar** [tagare'lar] VI to chatter
Tailândia [taj'lãdʒja] F: **a ~** Thailand
tal [taw] (*pl* **tais**) ADJ such; **~ e coisa** this and that; **um ~ de Sr. X** a certain Mr. X; **que ~?** what do you think?; (PT) how are things?; **que ~ um cafezinho?** what about a coffee?; **que ~ nós irmos ao cinema?** what about (us) going to the cinema?; **~ pai, ~ filho** like father, like son; **~ como** such as; (*da maneira que*) just as; **~ qual** just like; **o ~ professor** that teacher; **a ~ ponto** to such an extent; **de ~ maneira** in such a way; **e ~** and so on; **o/a ~** (*col*) the greatest; **o Pedro de ~** Peter what's-his-name; **na rua ~** in such and such a street; **foi um ~ de gente ligar lá para casa** there were people ringing home non-stop
talão [ta'lãw] (*pl* **-ões**) M (*de recibo*) stub; **~ de cheques** cheque book (BRIT), check book (US)
talco ['tawku] M talcum powder; **pó de ~** (PT) talcum powder
talento [ta'lẽtu] M talent; (*aptidão*) ability
talha ['taʎa] F carving; (*vaso*) pitcher; (*Náut*) tackle
talher [ta'ʎer] M set of cutlery; **talheres** MPL cutlery *sg*
talo ['talu] M stalk, stem
talões [ta'lõjs] MPL *de* **talão**
talvez [taw'vez] ADV perhaps, maybe
tamanco [ta'mãku] M clog, wooden shoe
tamanduá [tamã'dwa] M anteater
tamanho, -a [ta'maɲu, a] ADJ such (a) great ▶ M size
tâmara ['tamara] F date
também [tã'bẽj] ADV also, too, as well; (*além disso*) besides; **~ não** not ... either, nor
tambor [tã'bor] M drum
tamborim [tãbo'rĩ] (*pl* **-ns**) M tambourine
Tâmisa ['tamiza] M: **o ~** the Thames
tampa ['tãpa] F lid; (*de garrafa*) cap
tampão [tã'pãw] (*pl* **-ões**) M tampon
tampar [tã'par] VT (*lata, garrafa*) to put the lid on; (*cobrir*) to cover
tampinha [tã'piɲa] F lid, top
tampo ['tãpu] M lid
tampões [tã'põjs] MPL *de* **tampão**
tampouco [tã'poku] ADV nor, neither
tangerina [tãʒe'rina] F tangerine
tanque ['tãki] M tank; (*de lavar roupa*) sink
tanto, -a ['tãtu, a] ADJ, PRON (*sg*) so much; (: *+ interrogativa/negativa*) as much; (*pl*) so many; (: *+ interrogativa/negativa*) as many ▶ ADV so much; **~ ... como ...** both ... and ...; **~ ... quanto ...** as much ... as ...; **~ tempo** so long; **quarenta e ~s anos** forty-odd years; **~ faz** it's all the same to me, I don't mind; **um ~ (quanto)** (*como adv*) rather, somewhat; **~ (assim) que** so much so that
tão [tãw] ADV so; **~ rico quanto** as rich as; **~ só** only
tapa ['tapa] M slap
tapar [ta'par] VT to cover; (*garrafa*) to cork; (*caixa*) to put the lid on; (*orifício*) to block up; (*encobrir*) to block out
tapear [ta'pjar] VT, VI to cheat
tapeçaria [tapesa'ria] F tapestry

tapete [ta'petʃi] M carpet, rug
tardar [tar'dar] VI to delay; (*chegar tarde*) to be late ▸VT to delay; **sem mais ~** without delay; **~ a** *ou* **em fazer** to take a long time to do; **o mais ~** at the latest
tarde ['tardʒi] F afternoon ▸ADV late; **mais cedo ou mais ~** sooner or later; **antes ~ do que nunca** better late than never; **boa ~!** good afternoon!; **à** *ou* **de ~** in the afternoon
tardio, -a [tar'dʒiu, a] ADJ late
tarefa [ta'rɛfa] F task, job; (*faina*) chore
tarifa [ta'rifa] F tariff; (*para transportes*) fare; (*lista de preços*) price list; **~ alfandegária** customs duty
tartaruga [tarta'ruga] F turtle
tasca ['taska] (PT) F cheap eating place
tática ['tatʃika] F tactics *pl*
tático, -a ['tatʃiku, a] ADJ tactical
tato ['tatu] M touch; (*fig: diplomacia*) tact
tatu [ta'tu] M armadillo
tatuagem [ta'twaʒẽ] (*pl* **-ns**) F tattoo
taxa ['taʃa] F (*imposto*) tax; (*preço*) fee; (*índice*) rate; **~ de câmbio** exchange rate; **~ de juros** interest rate; **taxação** [taʃa'sãw] F taxation; **taxar** [ta'ʃar] VT (*fixar o preço de*) to fix the price of; (*lançar impostos sobre*) to tax
táxi ['taksi] M taxi
taxista [tak'sista] M/F taxi driver
tchau [tʃaw] EXCL bye!
tcheco, -a ['tʃɛku, a] ADJ, M/F Czech; **a República Tcheca** the Czech Republic
te [tʃi] PRON you; (*para você*) (to) you
teatro ['tʃjatru] M theatre (BRIT), theater (US); (*obras*) plays *pl*, dramatic works *pl*; (*gênero, curso*) drama; **peça de ~** play
tecer [te'ser] VT, VI to weave; **tecido** [te'sidu] M cloth, material; (*Anat*) tissue
tecla ['tɛkla] F key; **teclado** [tek'ladu] M keyboard
técnica ['tɛknika] F technique; *ver tb* **técnico**
técnico, -a ['tɛkniku, a] ADJ technical ▸M/F technician; (*especialista*) expert
tecnologia [teknolo'ʒia] F technology; **tecnológico, -a** [tekno'lɔʒiku, a] ADJ technological
tédio ['tɛdʒju] M tedium, boredom; **tedioso, -a** [te'dʒjozu, ɔza] ADJ tedious, boring
teia ['teja] F web; **~ de aranha** cobweb
teimar [tej'mar] VI to insist, keep on; **~ em** to insist on
teimosia [tejmo'zia] F stubbornness; **~ em fazer** insistence on doing
teimoso, -a [tej'mozu, ɔza] ADJ obstinate; (*criança*) wilful (BRIT), willful (US)
Tejo ['teʒu] M: **o (rio) ~** the (river) Tagus
tela ['tɛla] F fabric, material; (*de pintar*) canvas; (*Cinema, TV*) screen
tele... ['tele] PREFIXO tele...; **telecomunicações** [telekomunika'sõjs] FPL telecommunications; **teleconferência** [telekõfe'rẽsja] F teleconference
teleférico [tele'fɛriku] M cable car
telefonar [telefo'nar] VI: **~ para alguém** to (tele)phone sb
telefone [tele'fɔni] M phone, telephone; (*número*) (tele)phone

number; (*telefonema*) phone call; **~ celular** cellphone, mobile phone; **~ de carro** carphone; **~ fixo** landline; **telefonema** [telefo'nɛma] M phone call; **dar um telefonema** to make a phone call; **telefônico, -a** [tele'foniku, a] ADJ telephone *atr*; **telefonista** [telefo'nista] M/F telephonist; (*na companhia telefônica*) operator

tele...: telegrama [tele'grama] M telegram, cable; **telejornal** [teleʒor'naw] (*pl* **-ais**) M television news *sg*; **telemóvel** [tele'mɔvel] (PT) (*pl* **-eis**) M mobile (phone) (BRIT), cellphone (US); **telenovela** [teleno'vɛla] F (TV) soap opera; **telescópio** [tele'skɔpju] M telescope; **telespectador, a** [telespekta'dor(a)] M/F viewer **televendas** [tele'vẽdas] FPL telesales; **televisão** [televi'zãw] F television; **~ por assinatura** pay television; **~ a cabo** cable television; **~ a cores** colo(u)r television; **~ digital** digital television; **~ via satélite** satellite television; **aparelho de ~** television set; **televisionar** [televizjo'nar] VT to televise; **televisivo, -a** [televi'zivu, a] ADJ television *atr*; **televisor** [televi'zor] M (*aparelho*) television (set), TV (set)

telha ['teʎa] F tile; (*col: cabeça*) head; **ter uma ~ de menos** to have a screw loose

telhado [te'ʎadu] M roof

tema ['tɛma] M theme; (*assunto*) subject; **temática** [te'matʃika] F theme

temer [te'mer] VT to fear, be afraid of ▶ VI to be afraid

temeroso, -a [teme'rozu, ɔza] ADJ fearful, afraid; (*pavoroso*) dreadful

temido, -a [te'midu, a] ADJ fearsome, frightening

temível [te'mivew] (*pl* **-eis**) ADJ = **temido**

temor [te'mor] M fear

temperado, -a [tẽpe'radu, a] ADJ (*clima*) temperate; (*comida*) seasoned

temperamento [tẽpera'mẽtu] M temperament, nature

temperar [tẽpe'rar] VT to season

temperatura [tẽpera'tura] F temperature

tempero [tẽ'peru] M seasoning, flavouring (BRIT), flavoring (US)

tempestade [tẽpes'tadʒi] F storm; **tempestuoso, -a** [tẽpes'twozu, ɔza] ADJ stormy

templo ['tẽplu] M temple; (*igreja*) church

tempo ['tẽpu] M time; (*meteorológico*) weather; (*Ling*) tense; **o ~ todo** the whole time; **a ~** on time; **ao mesmo ~** at the same time; **a um ~** at once; **com ~** in good time; **de ~ em ~** from time to time; **nesse meio ~** in the meantime; **quanto ~?** how long?; **mais ~** longer; **há ~s** for ages; (*atrás*) ages ago; **~ livre** spare time; **primeiro/segundo ~** (*Esporte*) first/second half

temporada [tẽpo'rada] F season; (*tempo*) spell

temporal [tẽpo'raw] (*pl* **-ais**) M storm, gale

temporário, -a [tẽpo'rarju, a] ADJ temporary, provisional

tenacidade [tenasi'dadʒi] F tenacity

tencionar [tẽsjo'nar] VT to intend, plan

t

tenda ['tẽda] F tent
tendão [tẽ'dãw] (*pl* **-ões**) M tendon
tendões [tẽ'dõjs] MPL *de* **tendão**
tenebroso, -a [tene'brozu, ɔza] ADJ dark, gloomy; (*fig*) horrible
tenho ['teɲu] VB *ver* **ter**
tênis ['tenis] M INV tennis; (*sapatos*) training shoes *pl*; (*um sapato*) training shoe; **~ de mesa** table tennis; **tenista** [te'nista] M/F tennis player
tenor [te'nor] M (*Mús*) tenor
tenro, -a ['tẽhu, a] ADJ tender; (*macio*) soft; (*delicado*) delicate; (*novo*) young
tensão [tẽ'sãw] F tension; (*pressão*) pressure, strain; (*rigidez*) tightness; (*Elet: voltagem*) voltage
tenso, -a ['tẽsu, a] ADJ tense; (*sob pressão*) under stress, strained
tentação [tẽta'sãw] F temptation
tentáculo [tẽ'takulu] M tentacle
tentar [tẽ'tar] VT to try; (*seduzir*) to tempt ▸ VI to try; **tentativa** [tẽta'tʃiva] F attempt; **tentativa de homicídio/suicídio/roubo** attempted murder/suicide/ robbery; **por tentativas** by trial and error
tênue ['tenwi] ADJ tenuous; (*fino*) thin; (*delicado*) delicate; (*luz, voz*) faint; (*pequeníssimo*) minute
teor [te'or] M (*conteúdo*) tenor; (*sentido*) meaning, drift
teoria [teo'ria] F theory; **teoricamente** [teorika'mẽtʃi] ADV theoretically, in theory; **teórico, -a** [te'ɔriku, a] ADJ theoretical ▸ M/F theoretician
tépido, -a ['tɛpidu, a] ADJ tepid

PALAVRA-CHAVE

ter [ter] VT **1** (*possuir, ger*) to have; (*na mão*) to hold; **você tem uma caneta?** have you got a pen?; **ela vai ter neném** she is going to have a baby
2 (*idade, medidas, estado*) to be; **ela tem 7 anos** she's 7 (years old); **a mesa tem 1 metro de comprimento** the table is 1 metre long; **ter fome/sorte** to be hungry/lucky; **ter frio/calor** to be cold/hot
3 (*conter*) to hold, contain; **a caixa tem um quilo de chocolates** the box holds one kilo of chocolates
4: **ter que** *ou* **de fazer** to have to do
5: **ter a ver com** to have to do with
6: **ir ter com** to (go and) meet
▸ VB IMPESS **1**: **tem** (*sg*) there is; (*pl*) there are; **tem 3 dias que não saio de casa** I haven't been out for 3 days
2: **não tem de quê** don't mention it

terapeuta [tera'pewta] M/F therapist
terapia [tera'pia] F therapy
terça ['tersa] F (*tb*: **~-feira**) Tuesday; **terça-feira** (*pl* **terças-feiras**) F Tuesday; **terça-feira gorda** Shrove Tuesday
terceiro, -a [ter'sejru, a] NUM third; **terceiros** MPL (*os outros*) outsiders; *ver tb* **quinto**
terço ['tersu] M third (part)
termas ['tɛrmas] FPL bathhouse *sg*
térmico, -a ['tɛrmiku, a] ADJ thermal; **garrafa térmica** (Thermos®) flask
terminal [termi'naw] (*pl* **-ais**) ADJ terminal ▸ M (*de rede, Elet, Comput*) terminal ▸ F terminal; **~ (de vídeo)** monitor, visual display unit
terminar [termi'nar] VT to finish ▸ VI (*pessoa*) to finish; (*coisa*) to end; **~ de fazer** to finish doing; (*ter feito há pouco*) to have just done; **~ por**

algo/fazer algo to end with sth/ end up doing sth
término ['tɛrminu] M end, termination
termo ['termu] M term; (*fim*) end, termination; (*limite*) limit, boundary; (*prazo*) period; (PT: *garrafa*) (Thermos®) flask; **meio ~** compromise; **em ~s (de)** in terms (of)
termômetro [ter'mometru] M thermometer
terno, -a ['tɛrnu, a] ADJ gentle, tender ▶ M (BR: *roupa*) suit; **ternura** [ter'nura] F gentleness, tenderness
terra ['tɛha] F earth, world; (*Agr, propriedade*) land; (*pátria*) country; (*chão*) ground; (*Geo*) soil; (*pó*) dirt
terraço [te'hasu] M terrace
terramoto [teha'mɔtu] (PT) M = **terremoto**
terreiro [te'hejru] M yard, square
terremoto [tehe'mɔtu] M earthquake
terreno, -a [te'hɛnu, a] M ground, land; (*porção de terra*) plot of land ▶ ADJ earthly
térreo, -a ['tɛhju, a] ADJ: **andar ~** (BR) ground floor (BRIT), first floor (US)
terrestre [te'hɛstri] ADJ land *atr*
território [tehi'tɔrju] M territory
terrível [te'hivew] (*pl* **-eis**) ADJ terrible, dreadful
terror [te'hor] M terror, dread; **terrorista** [teho'rista] ADJ, M/F terrorist; **terrorista suicida** suicide bomber
tese ['tɛzi] F proposition, theory; (*Educ*) thesis; **em ~** in theory
teso, -a ['tezu, a] ADJ (*cabo*) taut; (*rígido*) stiff
tesouraria [tezora'ria] F treasury
tesouro [te'zoru] M treasure; (*erário*) treasury, exchequer; (*livro*) thesaurus
testa ['tɛsta] F brow, forehead
testar [tes'tar] VT to test; (*deixar em testamento*) to bequeath
teste ['tɛstʃi] M test
testemunha [teste'muɲa] F witness; **testemunhar** [testemu'ɲar] VI to testify ▶ VT to give evidence about; (*presenciar*) to witness; (*confirmar*) to demonstrate; **testemunho** [teste'muɲu] M evidence
testículo [tes'tʃikulu] M testicle
teta ['tɛta] F teat
tétano ['tɛtanu] M tetanus
teto ['tɛtu] M ceiling; (*telhado*) roof; (*habitação*) home
teu, tua [tew, 'tua] ADJ your ▶ PRON yours
teve ['tevi] VB *ver* **ter**
têxtil ['testʃiw] (*pl* **-eis**) M textile
texto ['testu] M text
textura [tes'tura] F texture
thriller ['triler] (*pl* **-s**) M thriller
ti [tʃi] PRON you
tia ['tʃia] F aunt
Tibete [tʃi'bɛtʃi] M: **o ~** Tibet
TIC [tʃik] ABR F (= *Tecnologia de Informação e Comunicação*) ICT
tido, -a ['tʃidu, a] PP *de* **ter** ▶ ADJ: **~ como** *ou* **por** considered to be
tigela [tʃi'ʒɛla] F bowl
tigre ['tʃigri] M tiger
tijolo [tʃi'ʒolu] M brick
til [tʃiw] (*pl* **tis**) M tilde
timbre ['tʃĩbri] M insignia, emblem; (*selo*) stamp; (*Mús*) tone, timbre; (*de voz*) tone; (*em papel de carta*) heading
time ['tʃimi] (BR) M team; **de segundo ~** (*fig*) second-rate
tímido, -a ['tʃimidu, a] ADJ shy, timid

t

tímpano ['tʃĩpanu] M eardrum; (*Mús*) kettledrum
tingir [tʃĩ'ʒir] VT to dye; (*fig*) to tinge
tinha ['tʃiɲa] VB *ver* **ter**
tinjo ['tʃĩʒu] VB *ver* **tingir**
tinta ['tʃĩta] F (*de pintar*) paint; (*de escrever*) ink; (*para tingir*) dye; (*fig: vestígio*) shade, tinge
tinto, -a ['tʃĩtu, a] ADJ dyed; (*fig*) stained; **vinho ~** red wine
tintura [tʃĩ'tura] F dye; (*ato*) dyeing; (*fig*) tinge, hint
tinturaria [tʃĩtura'ria] F dry-cleaner's
tio ['tʃiu] M uncle
típico, -a ['tʃipiku, a] ADJ typical
tipo ['tʃipu] M type; (*de imprensa*) print; (*de impressora*) typeface; (*col: sujeito*) guy, chap; (*pessoa*) person
tipografia [tʃipogra'fia] F printing; (*estabelecimento*) printer's
tíquete ['tʃiketʃi] M ticket
tira ['tʃira] F strip ▶ M (BR *col*) cop
tira-gosto (*pl* **-s**) M snack, savoury (BRIT)
tirano, -a [tʃi'ranu, a] ADJ tyrannical ▶ M/F tyrant
tirar [tʃi'rar] VT to take away; (*de dentro*) to take out; (*de cima*) to take off; (*roupa, sapatos*) to take off; (*arrancar*) to pull out; (*férias*) to take, have; (*boas notas*) to get; (*salário*) to earn; (*curso*) to do, take; (*mancha*) to remove; (*foto, cópia*) to take; (*mesa*) to clear; **~ algo a alguém** to take sth from sb
tiritar [tʃiri'tar] VI to shiver
tiro ['tʃiru] M shot; (*ato de disparar*) shooting; **~ ao alvo** target practice; **trocar ~s** to fire at one another
tiroteio [tʃiro'teju] M shooting, exchange of shots
tis [tʃis] MPL *de* **til**
titular [tʃitu'lar] ADJ titular ▶ M/F holder
título ['tʃitulu] M title; (*Com*) bond; (*universitário*) degree; **~ de propriedade** title deed
tive ['tʃivi] VB *ver* **ter**
to [tu] = **te + o**
toa ['toa] F towrope; **à ~** at random; (*sem motivo*) for no reason; (*inutilmente*) for nothing
toalete [twa'lɛtʃi] M (*banheiro*) toilet ▶ F: **fazer a ~** to have a wash
toalha [to'aʎa] F towel
toca ['tɔka] F burrow, hole
toca-discos (BR) M INV record-player
tocador [toka'dor] M player; **~ MP3** MP3 player
toca-fitas M INV cassette player
tocaia [to'kaja] F ambush
tocante [to'kãtʃi] ADJ moving, touching; **no ~ a** regarding, concerning
tocar [to'kar] VT to touch; (*Mús*) to play ▶ VI to touch; (*Mús*) to play; (*campainha, sino, telefone*) to ring; **tocar-se** VR to touch (each other); **~ a** (*dizer respeito a*) to concern, affect; **~ em** to touch; (*assunto*) to touch upon; **~ para alguém** (*telefonar*) to ring sb (up), call sb (up); **pelo que me toca** as far as I am concerned
tocha ['tɔʃa] F torch
todavia [toda'via] ADV yet, still, however

PALAVRA-CHAVE

todo, -a ['todu, 'tɔda] ADJ **1** (*com artigo sg*) all; **toda a carne** all the meat; **toda a noite** all night, the whole night; **todo o Brasil** the whole of Brazil; **a toda (velocidade)** at full speed; **todo o**

mundo (BR), **toda a gente** (PT) everybody, everyone; **em toda (a) parte** everywhere
2 (*com artigo pl*) all; (: *cada*) every; **todos os livros** all the books; **todos os dias/todas as noites** every day/night; **todos os que querem sair** all those who want to leave; **todos nós** all of us ▶ ADV: **ao todo** altogether; (*no total*) in all; **de todo** completely ▶ PRON: **todos** everybody *sg*, everyone *sg*

todo-poderoso, -a ADJ all-powerful ▶ M: **o T~** the Almighty
toicinho [toj'siɲu] M bacon fat
tolerância [tole'rɐ̃sja] F tolerance; **tolerante** [tole'rɐ̃tʃi] ADJ tolerant
tolerar [tole'rar] VT to tolerate; **tolerável** [tole'ravew] (*pl* **-eis**) ADJ tolerable, bearable; (*satisfatório*) passable; (*falta*) excusable
tolice [to'lisi] F stupidity, foolishness; (*ato, dito*) stupid thing
tom [tõ] (*pl* **-ns**) M tone; (*Mús: altura*) pitch; (: *escala*) key; (*cor*) shade
tomada [to'mada] F capture; (*Elet*) socket
tomar [to'mar] VT to take; (*capturar*) to capture, seize; (*decisão*) to make; (*bebida*) to drink; **~ café** (*de manhã*) to have breakfast
tomara [to'mara] EXCL: **~!** if only!; **~ que venha hoje** I hope he comes today
tomate [to'matʃi] M tomato
tombadilho [tõba'dʒiʎu] M deck
tombar [tõ'bar] VI to fall down, tumble down ▶ VT to knock down, knock over; **tombo** ['tõbu] M tumble, fall
tomilho [to'miʎu] M thyme
tona ['tɔna] F surface; **vir à ~** to come to the surface; (*fig*) to emerge; **trazer à ~** to bring up; (*recordações*) to bring back
tonalidade [tonali'dadʒi] F (*de cor*) shade
tonelada [tone'lada] F ton
tônica ['tonika] F (*água*) tonic (water); (*fig*) keynote
tônico, -a ['toniku, a] ADJ tonic ▶ M tonic; **acento ~** stress
tons [tõs] MPL *de* **tom**
tonteira [tõ'tejra] F dizziness
tonto, -a ['tõtu, a] ADJ stupid, silly; (*zonzo*) dizzy, lightheaded; (*atarantado*) flustered
topar [to'par] VT to agree to ▶ VI: **~ com** to come across; **topar-se** VR (*duas pessoas*) to run into one another; **~ em** (*tropeçar*) to stub one's toe on; (*esbarrar*) to run into; (*tocar*) to touch
tópico, -a ['tɔpiku, a] ADJ topical ▶ M topic
topless [tɔp'lɛs] ADJ INV topless
topo ['topu] M top; (*extremidade*) end, extremity
toque VB *ver* **tocar**
Tóquio ['tɔkju] N Tokyo
tora ['tɔra] F (*pedaço*) piece; (*de madeira*) log; (*sesta*) nap
toranja [to'rɐ̃ʒa] F grapefruit
torção [tor'sɐ̃w] (*pl* **-ões**) M twist; (*Med*) sprain
torcedor, a [torse'dor(a)] M/F supporter, fan
torcer [tor'ser] VT to twist; (*Med*) to sprain; (*desvirtuar*) to distort, misconstrue; (*roupa: espremer*) to wring; (: *na máquina*) to spin; (*vergar*) to bend ▶ VI: **~ por** (*time*) to support; **torcer-se** VR to

t

squirm, writhe
torcicolo [torsi'kɔlu] M stiff neck
torcida [tor'sida] F (*pavio*) wick; (*Esporte: ato de torcer*) cheering; (: *torcedores*) supporters *pl*
torções [tor'sõjs] MPL *de* **torção**
tormenta [tor'mẽta] F storm
tormento [tor'mẽtu] M torment; (*angústia*) anguish
tornar [tor'nar] VI to return, go back ▶ VT: **~ algo em algo** to turn *ou* make sth into sth; **tornar-se** VR to become; **~ a fazer algo** to do sth again
torneio [tor'neju] M tournament
torneira [tor'nejra] F tap (BRIT), faucet (US)
tornozelo [torno'zelu] M ankle
torpedo [tor'pedu] M (*bomba*) torpedo; (*col: mensagem*) text (message)
torrada [to'hada] F toast; **uma ~** a piece of toast; **torradeira** [toha'dejra] F toaster
torrão [to'hãw] (*pl* **-ões**) M turf, sod; (*terra*) soil, land; (*de açúcar*) lump
torrar [to'har] VT to toast; (*café*) to roast
torre ['tohi] F tower; (*Xadrez*) castle, rook; (*Elet*) pylon; **~ de controle** (*Aer*) control tower
tórrido, -a ['tɔhidu, a] ADJ torrid
torrões [to'hõjs] MPL *de* **torrão**
torso ['torsu] M torso
torta ['tɔrta] F pie, tart
torto, -a ['tortu, 'tɔrta] ADJ twisted, crooked; **a ~ e a direito** indiscriminately
tortuoso, -a [tor'twozu, ɔza] ADJ winding
tortura [tor'tura] F torture; (*fig*) anguish; **torturar** [tortu'rar] VT to torture; to torment
tos [tus] = **te + os**
tosco, -a ['tosku, a] ADJ rough, unpolished; (*grosseiro*) coarse, crude
tosse ['tɔsi] F cough; **~ de cachorro** whooping cough; **tossir** [to'sir] VI to cough
tosta ['tɔsta] (PT) F toast; **~ mista** toasted cheese and ham sandwich
tostão [tos'tãw] M cash
tostar [tos'tar] VT to toast; (*pele, pessoa*) to tan; **tostar-se** VR to get tanned
total [to'taw] (*pl* **-ais**) ADJ, M total
touca ['toka] F bonnet; **~ de banho** bathing cap
tourada [to'rada] F bullfight; **toureiro** [to'rejru] M bullfighter
touro ['toru] M bull; **T~** (*Astrologia*) Taurus
tóxico, -a ['tɔksiku, a] ADJ toxic ▶ M poison; (*droga*) drug; **toxicômano, -a** [toksi'komanu, a] M/F drug addict
TPM ABR F (= *tensão pré-menstrual*) PMT
trabalhador, a [trabaʎa'dor(a)] ADJ hard-working, industrious; (*Pol: classe*) working ▶ M/F worker
trabalhar [traba'ʎar] VI to work ▶ VT (*terra*) to till; (*madeira, metal*) to work; (*texto*) to work on; **~ com** (*comerciar*) to deal in; **~ de** *ou* **como** to work as; **trabalhista** [traba'ʎista] ADJ labour *atr* (BRIT), labor *atr* (US); **trabalho** [tra'baʎu] M work; (*emprego, tarefa*) job; (*Educ: tarefa*) assignment; **trabalho braçal** manual work; **trabalho doméstico** housework; **trabalhoso, -a** [traba'ʎozu, ɔza] ADJ laborious, arduous
traça ['trasa] F moth
traçado [tra'sadu] M sketch, plan
tração [tra'sãw] F traction

traçar [tra'sar] VT to draw; (*determinar*) to set out, outline; (*planos*) to draw up; (*escrever*) to compose
tradição [tradʒi'sãw] (*pl* **-ões**) F tradition; **tradicional** [tradʒisjo'naw] (*pl* **-ais**) ADJ traditional
tradução [tradu'sãw] (*pl* **-ões**) F translation
tradutor, a [tradu'tor(a)] M/F translator
traduzir [tradu'zir] VT to translate
trafegar [trafe'gar] VI to move, go
tráfego ['trafegu] M traffic
traficante [trafi'kãtʃi] M/F trafficker, dealer
traficar [trafi'kar] VI: **~ (com)** to deal (in)
tráfico ['trafiku] M traffic
tragar [tra'gar] VT to swallow; (*fumaça*) to inhale; (*suportar*) to tolerate ▶ VI to inhale
tragédia [tra'ʒɛdʒja] F tragedy; **trágico, -a** ['traʒiku, a] ADJ tragic
trago[1] ['tragu] M mouthful
trago[2] VB *ver* **trazer**
traiçoeiro, -a [traj'swejru, a] ADJ treacherous
traidor, a [traj'dor(a)] M/F traitor
trailer ['trejler] (*pl* **-s**) M trailer; (*tipo casa*) caravan (BRIT), trailer (US)
trair [tra'ir] VT to betray; (*mulher, marido*) to be unfaithful to; (*esperanças*) not to live up to; **trair-se** VR to give o.s. away
trajar [tra'ʒar] VT to wear
traje ['traʒi] M dress, clothes *pl*; **~ de banho** swimsuit
trajeto [tra'ʒɛtu] M course, path
trajetória [traʒe'tɔrja] F trajectory, path; (*fig*) course
tralha ['traʎa] F fishing net
trama ['trama] F (*tecido*) weft (BRIT), woof (US); (*enredo, conspiração*) plot
tramar [tra'mar] VT (*tecer*) to weave; (*maquinar*) to plot ▶ VI: **~ contra** to conspire against
trâmites ['tramitʃis] MPL procedure *sg*, channels
trampolim [trãpo'lĩ] (*pl* **-ns**) M trampoline; (*de piscina*) diving board; (*fig*) springboard
tranca ['trãka] F (*de porta*) bolt; (*de carro*) lock
trança ['trãsa] F (*cabelo*) plait; (*galão*) braid
trancar [trã'kar] VT to lock
tranquilidade [trãkwili'dadʒi] F tranquillity; (*paz*) peace
tranquilizante [trãkwili'zãtʃi] M (*Med*) tranquillizer
tranquilizar [trãkwili'zar] VT to calm, quieten; (*despreocupar*): **~ alguém** to reassure sb, put sb's mind at rest; **tranquilizar-se** VR to calm down
tranquilo, -a [trã'kwilu, a] ADJ peaceful; (*mar, pessoa*) calm; (*criança*) quiet; (*consciência*) clear; (*seguro*) sure, certain
transação [trãza'sãw] (*pl* **-ões**) F transaction
transar [trã'zar] (BR *col*) VI (*ter relação sexual*) to have sex
transbordar [trãzbor'dar] VI to overflow
transbordo [trãz'bordu] M (*de viajantes*) change, transfer
transe ['trãzi] M ordeal; (*lance*) plight; (*hipnótico*) trance
transeunte [trã'zjũtʃi] M/F passer-by
transferência [trãsfe'rẽsja] F transfer
transferir [trãsfe'rir] VT to

transfer; (*adiar*) to postpone
transformação [trãsforma'sãw] (*pl* **-ões**) F transformation
transformador [trãsforma'dor] M (*Elet*) transformer
transformar [trãsfor'mar] VT to transform; **transformar-se** VR to turn
transfusão [trãsfu'zãw] (*pl* **-ões**) F transfusion
transgênico, -a [trãz'ʒeniku, a] ADJ (*planta, alimento*) genetically modified, GM
transição [trãzi'sãw] (*pl* **-ões**) F transition
transitivo, -a [trãzi'tʃivu, a] ADJ (*Ling*) transitive
trânsito ['trãzitu] M transit, passage; (*na rua: veículos*) traffic; (*: pessoas*) flow; **transitório, -a** [trãzi'tɔrju, a] ADJ transitory; (*período*) transitional
transmissão [trãzmi'sãw] (*pl* **-ões**) F transmission; (*transferência*) transfer; **~ ao vivo** live broadcast
transmissor, a [trãzmi'sor(a)] ADJ transmitting ▶ M transmitter
transmitir [trãzmi'tʃir] VT to transmit; (*Rádio, TV*) to broadcast; (*transferir*) to transfer; (*recado, notícia*) to pass on
transparente [trãspa'rẽtʃi] ADJ transparent; (*roupa*) see-through; clear
transpirar [trãspi'rar] VI to perspire; (*divulgar-se*) to become known; (*verdade*) to come out ▶ VT to exude
transplante [trãs'plãtʃi] M transplant
transportar [trãspor'tar] VT to transport; (*levar*) to carry; (*enlevar*) to entrance, enrapture
transporte [trãs'pɔrtʃi] M transport; (*Com*) haulage
transtorno [trãs'tornu] M upset, disruption
trapalhão, -lhona [trapa'ʎãw, 'ʎɔna] (*pl* **-ões/-s**) M/F bungler, blunderer
trapo ['trapu] M rag
trarei [tra'rej] VB *ver* **trazer**
trás [trajs] PREP, ADV: **para ~** backwards; **por ~ de** behind; **de ~** from behind
traseira [tra'zejra] F rear; (*Anat*) bottom
traste ['trastʃi] M thing; (*coisa sem valor*) piece of junk
tratado [tra'tadu] M treaty
tratamento [trata'mẽtu] M treatment
tratar [tra'tar] VT to treat; (*tema*) to deal with; (*combinar*) to agree ▶ VI: **~ com** to deal with; (*combinar*) to agree with; **~ de** to deal with; **de que se trata?** what is it about?
trato ['tratu] M treatment; (*contrato*) agreement, contract; **tratos** MPL (*relações*) dealings
trator [tra'tor] M tractor
trauma ['trawma] M trauma
travão [tra'vãw] (PT) (*pl* **-ões**) M brake
travar [tra'var] VT (*roda*) to lock; (*iniciar*) to engage in; (*conversa*) to strike up; (*luta*) to wage; (*carro*) to stop; (*passagem*) to block; (*movimentos*) to hinder ▶ VI (PT) to brake
trave ['travi] F beam; (*Esporte*) crossbar
través [tra'vɛs] M slant, incline; **de ~** across, sideways
travessa [tra'vɛsa] F crossbeam, crossbar; (*rua*) lane, alley; (*prato*) dish; (*para o cabelo*) comb, slide
travessão [trave'sãw] (*pl* **-ões**) M

(*de balança*) bar, beam; (*pontuação*) dash
travesseiro [trave'sejru] M pillow
travessia [trave'sia] F (*viagem*) journey, crossing
travessões [trave'sõjs] MPL *de* **travessão**
travessura [trave'sura] F mischief, prank
travões [tra'võjs] MPL *de* **travão**
trazer [tra'zer] VT to bring
trecho ['treʃu] M passage; (*de rua, caminho*) stretch; (*espaço*) space
trégua ['trɛgwa] F truce; (*descanso*) respite
treinador, a [trejna'dor(a)] M/F trainer
treinamento [trejna'mẽtu] M training
treinar [trej'nar] VT to train; **treinar-se** VR to train; **treino** ['trejnu] M training
trejeito [tre'ʒejtu] M gesture; (*careta*) grimace, face
trem [trẽj] (*pl* **-ns**) M train; **~ de aterrissagem** (*avião*) landing gear
tremendo, -a [tre'mẽdu, a] ADJ tremendous; (*terrível*) terrible, awful
tremer [tre'mer] VI to shudder, quake; (*terra*) to shake; (*de frio, medo*) to shiver
trêmulo, -a ['tremulu, a] ADJ shaky, trembling
trenó [tre'nɔ] M sledge, sleigh (BRIT), sled (US)
trens [trẽjs] MPL *de* **trem**
trepar [tre'par] VT to climb ▸ VI: **~ em** to climb
trepidar [trepi'dar] VI to tremble, shake
três [tres] NUM three; *ver tb* **cinco**
trevas ['trɛvas] FPL darkness *sg*
treze ['trezi] NUM thirteen
triângulo ['trjãgulu] M triangle
tribal [tri'baw] (*pl* **-ais**) ADJ tribal
tribo ['tribu] F tribe
tribuna [tri'buna] F platform, rostrum; (*Rel*) pulpit
tribunal [tribu'naw] (*pl* **-ais**) M court; (*comissão*) tribunal
tributo [tri'butu] M tribute; (*imposto*) tax
tricô [tri'ko] M knitting; **tricotar** [triko'tar] VT, VI to knit
trigo ['trigu] M wheat
trilha ['triʎa] F (*caminho*) path; (*rasto*) track, trail; **~ sonora** soundtrack
trilhão [tri'ʎãw] (*pl* **-ões**) M billion (BRIT), trillion (US)
trilho ['triʎu] M (BR *Ferro*) rail; (*vereda*) path, track
trilhões [tri'ʎõjs] MPL *de* **trilhão**
trimestral [trimes'traw] (*pl* **-ais**) ADJ quarterly; **trimestralmente** [trimestraw'mẽtʃi] ADV quarterly
trimestre [tri'mɛstri] M (*Educ*) term; (*Com*) quarter
trincar [trĩ'kar] VT to crunch; (*morder*) to bite; (*dentes*) to grit ▸ VI to crunch
trinco ['trĩku] M latch
trinta ['trĩta] NUM thirty
trio ['triu] M trio; **~ elétrico**

> **Trios elétricos** are lorries, carrying floats equipped for sound and/or live music, which parade through the streets during *carnaval*, especially in Bahia. Bands and popular performers on the floats draw crowds by giving frenzied performances of various types of music.

tripa ['tripa] F gut, intestine; **tripas** FPL (*intestinos*) bowels; (*vísceras*) guts; (*Culin*) tripe *sg*

tripé [tri'pɛ] M tripod
triplicar [tripli'kar] VT, VI to treble; **triplicar-se** VR to treble
tripulação [tripula'sãw] (*pl* **-ões**) F crew
tripulante [tripu'lãtʃi] M/F crew member
triste ['tristʃi] ADJ sad; (*lugar*) depressing
tristeza [tris'teza] F sadness; (*de lugar*) gloominess
triturar [tritu'rar] VT to grind
triunfar [trjũ'far] VI to triumph; **triunfo** ['trjũfu] M triumph
trivial [tri'vjaw] (*pl* **-ais**) ADJ common(place), ordinary; (*insignificante*) trivial
triz [triz] M: **por um ~** by a hair's breadth
troca ['trɔka] F exchange, swap
trocadilho [troka'dʒiʎu] M pun, play on words
trocado [tro'kadu] M: **~(s)** (small) change
trocador, a [troka'dor(a)] M/F (*em ônibus*) conductor
trocar [tro'kar] VT to exchange, swap; (*mudar*) to change; (*inverter*) to change *ou* swap round; (*confundir*) to mix up; **trocar-se** VR to change; **~ dinheiro** to change money
troco ['troku] M (*dinheiro*) change; (*revide*) retort, rejoinder
troféu [tro'fɛw] M trophy
tromba ['trõba] F (*do elefante*) trunk; (*de outro animal*) snout
trombeta [trõ'beta] F trumpet
trombone [trõ'bɔni] M trombone
trombose [trõ'bɔzi] F thrombosis
tronco ['trõku] M trunk; (*ramo*) branch; (*de corpo*) torso, trunk
trono ['trɔnu] M throne
tropa ['trɔpa] F troop; (*exército*) army; **ir para a ~** (PT) to join the army
tropeçar [trope'sar] VI to stumble, trip; (*fig*) to blunder
tropical [tropi'kaw] (*pl* **-ais**) ADJ tropical
trotar [tro'tar] VI to trot; **trote** ['trɔtʃi] M trot; (*por telefone etc*) hoax call
trouxe ['trosi] VB *ver* **trazer**
trovão [tro'vãw] (*pl* **-ões**) M clap of thunder; (*trovoada*) thunder; **trovejar** [trove'ʒar] VI to thunder; **trovoada** [tro'vwada] F thunderstorm
truque ['truki] M trick; (*publicitário*) gimmick
truta ['truta] F trout
tu [tu] PRON you
tua ['tua] F *de* **teu**
tuba ['tuba] F tuba
tubarão [tuba'rãw] (*pl* **-ões**) M shark
tuberculose [tuberku'lɔzi] F tuberculosis
tubo ['tubu] M tube, pipe; **~ de ensaio** test tube
tucano [tu'kanu] M toucan
tudo ['tudu] PRON everything; **~ quanto** everything that; **antes de ~** first of all; **acima de ~** above all
tufão [tu'fãw] (*pl* **-ões**) M typhoon
tuitar [twi'tar] VT, VI to tweet
tulipa [tu'lipa] F tulip
tumba ['tũba] F tomb; (*lápide*) tombstone
tumor [tu'mor] M tumour (BRIT), tumor (US)
túmulo ['tumulu] M tomb; (*sepultura*) burial
tumulto [tu'muwtu] M uproar, trouble; (*grande movimento*) bustle; (*balbúrdia*) hubbub; (*motim*) riot;

tumultuado, -a [tumuw'twadu, a] ADJ riotous, heated; **tumultuar** [tumuw'twar] VT to disrupt; (*amotinar*) to rouse, incite
túnel ['tunew] (*pl* **-eis**) M tunnel
túnica ['tunika] F tunic
Tunísia [tu'nizja] F: **a ~** Tunisia
tupi [tu'pi] M Tupi (tribe); (*Ling*) Tupi ▸ M/F Tupi Indian
tupi-guarani [-gwara'ni] M *see note*

> **Tupi-guarani** is an important branch of indigenous languages from the tropical region of South America. It takes in thirty indigenous peoples and includes Tupi, Guarani, and other languages. Before Brazil was discovered by the Portuguese it had 1,300 indigenous languages, 87% of which are now extinct due to the extermination of indigenous peoples and the loss of territory.

tupiniquim [tupini'kĩ] (*pej*) (*pl* **-ns**) ADJ Brazilian (Indian)
turbilhão [turbi'ʎãw] (*pl* **-ões**) M (*de vento*) whirlwind; (*de água*) whirlpool
turbina [tur'bina] F turbine; **~ eólica** wind turbine
turbulência [turbu'lẽsja] F turbulence; **turbulento, -a** [turbu'lẽtu, a] ADJ turbulent
turco, -a ['turku, a] ADJ Turkish ▸ M/F Turk ▸ M (*Ling*) Turkish
turismo [tu'rizmu] M tourism; **turista** [tu'rista] M/F tourist ▸ ADJ (*classe*) tourist *atr*
turma ['turma] F group; (*Educ*) class
turquesa [tur'keza] ADJ INV turquoise
Turquia [tur'kia] F: **a ~** Turkey
tusso ['tusu] VB *ver* **tossir**
tutela [tu'tɛla] F protection; (*Jur*) guardianship
tutor, a [tu'tor(a)] M/F guardian
tutu [tu'tu] M (*Culin*) *beans, bacon and manioc flour*
TV [te've] ABR F (= *televisão*) TV

U

UE ABR F (= *União Europeia*) EU
Uganda [u'gãda] M Uganda
uísque ['wiski] M whisky (BRIT), whiskey (US)
uivar [wi'var] VI to howl; (*berrar*) to yell; **uivo** ['wivu] M howl; (*fig*) yell
úlcera ['uwsera] F ulcer
ultimamente [uwtʃima'mẽtʃi] ADV lately
ultimato [uwtʃi'matu] M ultimatum
último, -a ['uwtʃimu, a] ADJ last; (*mais recente*) latest; (*qualidade*) lowest; (*fig*) final; **por ~** finally; **nos ~s anos** in recent years; **a última** (*notícia*) the latest (news)
ultra... [uwtra-] PREFIXO ultra-
ultrajar [uwtra'ʒar] VT to outrage; (*insultar*) to insult, offend; **ultraje** [uw'traʒi] M outrage; (*insulto*) insult, offence (BRIT), offense (US)
ultramar [uwtra'mar] M overseas
ultrapassado, -a [uwtrapa'sadu, a] ADJ (*ideias etc*) outmoded
ultrapassar [uwtrapa'sar] VT (*atravessar*) to cross, go beyond; (*ir além de*) to exceed; (*transgredir*) to overstep; (*Auto*) to overtake (BRIT), pass (US); (*ser superior a*) to surpass
▸ VI (*Auto*) to overtake (BRIT), pass (US)
ultrassom [uwtra'sõ] M ultrasound
ultravioleta [uwtravjo'leta] ADJ ultraviolet

PALAVRA-CHAVE

um, a [ũ, 'uma] (*pl* **uns/umas**) NUM one; **um e outro** both; **um a um** one by one; **à uma (hora)** at one (o'clock)
▸ ADJ: **uns cinco** about five; **uns poucos** a few
▸ ART INDEF **1** (*sg*) a; (*antes de vogal ou 'h' mudo*) an; (*pl*) some; **um livro** a book; **uma maçã** an apple
2 (*dando ênfase*): **estou com uma fome!** I'm so hungry!; **ela é de uma beleza incrível** she's incredibly beautiful
3: **um ao outro** one another; (*entre dois*) each other

umbigo [ũ'bigu] M navel
umbilical [ũbili'kaw] (*pl* **-ais**) ADJ: **cordão ~** umbilical cord
umedecer [umede'ser] VT to moisten, wet; **umedecer-se** VR to get wet
umidade [umi'dadʒi] F dampness; (*clima*) humidity
úmido, -a ['umidu, a] ADJ wet, moist; (*roupa*) damp; (*clima*) humid
unânime [u'nanimi] ADJ unanimous
unha ['uɲa] F nail; (*garra*) claw; **unhada** [u'ɲada] F scratch
união [u'njãw] (*pl* **-ões**) F union; (*ato*) joining; (*unidade, solidariedade*)

unity; *(casamento)* marriage; *(Tec)* joint; **a U~ Europeia** the European Union
unicamente [unika'mẽtʃi] ADV only
único, -a ['uniku, a] ADJ only; *(sem igual)* unique; *(um só)* single
unidade [uni'dadʒi] F unity; *(Tec, Com)* unit; **~ central de processamento** *(Comput)* central processing unit; **~ de disco** *(Comput)* disk drive
unido, -a [u'nidu, a] ADJ joined, linked; *(fig)* united
unificar [unifi'kar] VT to unite; **unificar-se** VR to join together
uniforme [uni'fɔrmi] ADJ uniform; *(semelhante)* alike, similar; *(superfície)* even ▶ M uniform; **uniformizado, -a** [uniformi'zadu, a] ADJ uniform, standardized; *(vestido de uniforme)* in uniform; **uniformizar** [uniformi'zar] VT to standardize
uniões [u'njõjs] FPL *de* **união**
unir [u'nir] VT to join together; *(ligar)* to link; *(pessoas, fig)* to unite; *(misturar)* to mix together; **unir-se** VR to come together; *(povos etc)* to unite
uníssono [u'nisonu] M: **em ~** in unison
universal [univer'saw] *(pl* **-ais***)* ADJ universal; *(mundial)* worldwide
universidade [universi'dadʒi] F university; **universitário, -a** [universi'tarju, a] ADJ university *atr* ▶ M/F *(professor)* lecturer; *(aluno)* university student
universo [uni'vɛrsu] M universe; *(mundo)* world
uns [ũs] MPL *de* **um**
untar [ũ'tar] VT *(esfregar)* to rub; *(com óleo, manteiga)* to grease
urbanismo [urba'nizmu] M town planning
urbano, -a [ur'banu, a] ADJ *(da cidade)* urban; *(fig)* urbane
urgência [ur'ʒẽsja] F urgency; **com toda ~** as quickly as possible; **urgente** [ur'ʒẽtʃi] ADJ urgent
urina [u'rina] F urine; **urinar** [uri'nar] VI to urinate ▶ VT *(sangue)* to pass; *(cama)* to wet; **urinar-se** VR to wet o.s.; **urinol** [uri'nɔw] *(pl* **-óis***)* M chamber pot
urna ['urna] F urn; **~ eleitoral** ballot box
urrar [u'har] VT, VI to roar; *(de dor)* to yell
ursa ['ursa] F bear
urso ['ursu] M bear
urtiga [ur'tʃiga] F nettle
Uruguai [uru'gwaj] M: **o ~** Uruguay
urze ['urzi] M heather
usado, -a [u'zadu, a] ADJ used; *(comum)* common; *(roupa)* worn; *(gasto)* worn out; *(de segunda mão)* second-hand
usar [u'zar] VT *(servir-se de)* to use; *(vestir)* to wear; *(gastar com o uso)* to wear out; *(barba, cabelo curto)* to have, wear ▶ VI: **~ de** to use; **modo de ~** directions *pl*
usina [u'zina] F *(fábrica)* factory; *(de energia)* plant
uso ['uzu] M use; *(utilização)* usage; *(prática)* practice
usual [u'zwaw] *(pl* **-ais***)* ADJ usual; *(comum)* common
usuário, -a [u'zwarju, a] M/F user
usufruir [uzu'frwir] VT to enjoy ▶ VI: **~ de** to enjoy
úteis ['utejs] PL *de* **útil**
utensílio [utẽ'silju] M utensil
útero ['uteru] M womb, uterus
útil ['utʃiw] *(pl* **-eis***)* ADJ useful;

(*vantajoso*) profitable, worthwhile; **utilidade** [utʃili'dadʒi] F usefulness; **utilização** [utʃiliza'sãw] F use; **utilizador, a** [utʃiliza'dor(a)] (PT) M/F user; **utilizar** [utʃili'zar] VT to use; **utilizar-se** VR: **utilizar-se de** to make use of

uva ['uva] F grape

V

V ABR (= *volt*) V

vá [va] VB *ver* **ir**

vã [vã] F *de* **vão²**

vaca ['vaka] F cow; **carne de ~** beef

vacina [va'sina] F vaccine; **vacinar** [vasi'nar] VT to vaccinate

vácuo ['vakwu] M vacuum; (*fig*) void; (*espaço*) space

vaga ['vaga] F wave; (*em hotel, trabalho*) vacancy

vagão [va'gãw] (*pl* **-ões**) M (*de passageiros*) carriage; (*de cargas*) wagon; **vagão-leito** (*pl* **vagões-leitos**) (PT) M sleeping car; **vagão-restaurante** (*pl* **vagões-restaurantes**) M buffet car

vagar [va'gar] VI to wander about; (*barco*) to drift; (*ficar vago*) to be vacant

vagaroso, -a [vaga'rozu, ɔza] ADJ slow

vagina [va'ʒina] F vagina

vago, -a ['vagu, a] ADJ vague; (*desocupado*) vacant, free

vagões [va'gõjs] MPL *de* **vagão**

vai [vaj] VB *ver* **ir**
vaia ['vaja] F booing; **vaiar** [va'jar] VT, VI to boo, hiss
vaidade [vaj'dadʒi] F vanity; (*futilidade*) futility
vaidoso, -a [vaj'dozu, ɔza] ADJ vain
vaivém [vaj'vẽj] M to-ing and fro-ing
vala ['vala] F ditch
vale ['vali] M valley; (*escrito*) voucher; **~ postal** postal order
valer [va'ler] VI to be worth; (*ser válido*) to be valid; (*ter influência*) to carry weight; (*servir*) to serve; (*ser proveitoso*) to be useful; **valer-se** VR: **~-se de** to use, make use of; **~ a pena** to be worthwhile; **~ por** (*equivaler*) to be worth the same as; **para ~** (*muito*) very much, a lot; (*realmente*) for real, properly; **vale dizer** in other words; **mais vale ... (do que ...)** it would be better to ... (than ...)
valeta [va'leta] F gutter
valha ['vaʎa] VB *ver* **valer**
validade [vali'dadʒi] F validity; (*de cartão de crédito*) expiry date (BRIT), expiration date (US); (*de alimento*) best-before date
validar [vali'dar] VT to validate; **válido, -a** ['validu, a] ADJ valid
valioso, -a [va'ljozu, ɔza] ADJ valuable
valise [va'lizi] F case, grip
valor [va'lor] M value; (*mérito*) merit; (*coragem*) courage; (*preço*) price; (*importância*) importance; **valores** MPL (*morais*) values; (*num exame*) marks; (*Com*) securities; **dar ~ a** to value; **valorizar** [valori'zar] VT to value
valsa ['vawsa] F waltz
válvula ['vawvula] F valve
vampiro, -a [vã'piru, a] M/F vampire
vandalismo [vãda'lizmu] M vandalism
vândalo, -a ['vãdalu, a] M/F vandal
vangloriar-se [vãglo'rjarsi] VR: **~ de** to boast of *ou* about
vanguarda [vã'gwarda] F vanguard; (*arte*) avant-garde
vantagem [vã'taʒẽ] (*pl* **-ns**) F advantage; (*ganho*) profit, benefit; **tirar ~ de** to take advantage of; **vantajoso, -a** [vãta'ʒozu, ɔza] ADJ advantageous; (*lucrativo*) profitable; (*proveitoso*) beneficial
vão[1] [vãw] VB *ver* **ir**
vão[2]**, vã** [vãw, vã] (*pl* **-s/-s**) ADJ vain; (*fútil*) futile ▶ M (*intervalo*) space; (*de porta etc*) opening
vaqueiro [va'kejru] M cowboy
vara ['vara] F stick; (*Tec*) rod; (*Jur*) jurisdiction; (*de porcos*) herd; **salto de ~** pole vault; **~ de condão** magic wand
varal [va'raw] (*pl* **-ais**) M clothes line
varanda [va'rãda] F verandah; (*balcão*) balcony
varar [va'rar] VT to pierce; (*passar*) to cross
varejista [vare'ʒista] (BR) M/F retailer ▶ ADJ (*mercado*) retail
varejo [va'reʒu] (BR) M (*Com*) retail trade; **a ~** retail
variação [varja'sãw] (*pl* **-ões**) F variation
variado, -a [va'rjadu, a] ADJ varied; (*sortido*) assorted
variar [va'rjar] VT, VI to vary; **variável** [va'rjavew] (*pl* **-eis**) ADJ variable; (*tempo, humor*) changeable
varicela [vari'sɛla] F chickenpox

variedade [varje'dadʒi] F variety
varinha [va'riɲa] F wand; **~ de condão** magic wand
vário, -a ['varju, a] ADJ (*diverso*) varied; (*pl*) various, several; (*Com*) sundry
varizes [va'rizis] FPL varicose veins
varrer [va'her] VT to sweep; (*fig*) to sweep away
vaselina® [vaze'lina] F Vaseline®
vasilha [va'ziʎa] F (*para líquidos*) jug; (*para alimentos*) dish; (*barril*) barrel
vaso ['vazu] M pot; (*para flores*) vase
vassoura [va'sora] F broom
vasto, -a ['vastu, a] ADJ vast
vatapá [vata'pa] M *fish or chicken with coconut milk, shrimps, peanuts, palm oil and spices*
Vaticano [vatʃi'kanu] M: **o ~** the Vatican
vazamento [vaza'mẽtu] M leak
vazão [va'zãw] (*pl* **-ões**) F flow; (*venda*) sale; **dar ~ a** (*expressar*) to give vent to; (*atender*) to deal with; (*resolver*) to attend to
vazar [va'zar] VT to empty; (*derramar*) to spill; (*verter*) to pour out ▶ VI to leak
vazio, -a [va'ziu, a] ADJ empty; (*pessoa*) empty-headed, frivolous; (*cidade*) deserted ▶ M emptiness; (*deixado por alguém/algo*) void
vazões [va'zõjs] FPL *de* **vazão**
vê [ve] VB *ver* **ver**
veado ['vjadu] M deer; **carne de ~** venison
vedado, -a [ve'dadu, a] ADJ (*proibido*) forbidden; (*fechado*) enclosed
vedar [ve'dar] VT to ban, prohibit; (*buraco*) to stop up; (*entrada, passagem*) to block; (*terreno*) to close off
vegetação [veʒeta'sãw] F vegetation
vegetal [veʒe'taw] (*pl* **-ais**) ADJ vegetable *atr*; (*reino, vida*) plant *atr* ▶ M vegetable
vegetalista [veʒeta'lista] ADJ, M/F vegan
vegetariano, -a [veʒeta'rjanu, a] ADJ, M/F vegetarian
veia ['veja] F vein
veículo [ve'ikulu] M (*tb: fig*) vehicle
veio¹ ['veju] M (*de rocha*) vein; (*na mina*) seam; (*de madeira*) grain
veio² VB *ver* **vir¹**
vejo ['veʒu] VB *ver* **ver**
vela ['vɛla] F candle; (*Auto*) spark plug; (*Náut*) sail; **barco à ~** sailing boat
velar [ve'lar] VT to veil; (*ocultar*) to hide; (*vigiar*) to keep watch over; (*um doente*) to sit up with ▶ VI (*não dormir*) to stay up; (*vigiar*) to keep watch; **~ por** to look after
veleiro [ve'lejru] M sailing boat
velejar [vele'ʒar] VI to sail
velhaco, -a [ve'ʎaku, a] ADJ crooked ▶ M/F crook
velhice [ve'ʎisi] F old age
velho, -a ['vɛʎu, a] ADJ old ▶ M/F old man/woman
velocidade [velosi'dadʒi] F speed, velocity; (*PT Auto*) gear
velório [ve'lɔrju] M wake
veloz [ve'lɔz] ADJ fast
vem [vẽj] VB *ver* **vir¹**
vêm [vẽj] VB *ver* **vir¹**
vencedor, a [vẽse'dor(a)] ADJ winning ▶ M/F winner
vencer [vẽ'ser] VT (*num jogo*) to beat; (*competição*) to win; (*inimigo*) to defeat; (*exceder*) to surpass; (*obstáculos*) to overcome; (*percorrer*) to pass ▶ VI (*num jogo*) to win;
vencido, -a [vẽ'sidu, a] ADJ: **dar-se**

por vencido to give in;
vencimento [vẽsi'mẽtu] M (*Com*) expiry; (*data*) expiry date; (*salário*) salary; (*de gêneros alimentícios etc*) sell-by date; **vencimentos** MPL (*ganhos*) earnings
venda ['vẽda] F sale; (*pano*) blindfold; (*mercearia*) general store; **à ~** on sale, for sale
vendaval [vẽda'vaw] (*pl* **-ais**) M gale
vendedor, a [vẽde'dor(a)] M/F seller; (*em loja*) sales assistant; (*de imóvel*) vendor; **~ ambulante** street vendor
vender [vẽ'der] VT, VI to sell; **~ por atacado/a varejo** to sell wholesale/retail
veneno [ve'nɛnu] M poison; **venenoso, -a** [vene'nozu, ɔza] ADJ poisonous
venerar [vene'rar] VT to revere; (*Rel*) to worship
venéreo, -a [ve'nɛrju, a] ADJ: **doença venérea** venereal disease
Venezuela [vene'zwɛla] F: **a ~** Venezuela
venha ['vɛɲa] VB *ver* **vir**
ventania [vẽta'nia] F gale
ventar [vẽ'tar] VI: **está ventando** it is windy
ventilação [vẽtʃila'sãw] F ventilation
ventilador [vẽtʃila'dor] M ventilator; (*elétrico*) fan
vento ['vẽtu] M wind; (*brisa*) breeze; **ventoinha** [vẽ'twiɲa] F weathercock, weather vane; (*PT Auto*) fan
ventre ['vẽtri] M belly
ver [ver] VT to see; (*olhar para, examinar*) to look at; (*televisão*) to watch ▶ VI to see ▶ M: **a meu ~** in my opinion; **vai ~ que ...** maybe ...; **não tem nada a ~ (com)** it has nothing to do (with)
veracidade [verasi'dadʒi] F truthfulness
veraneio [vera'neju] M summer holidays *pl* (BRIT) *ou* vacation (US)
verão [ve'rãw] (*pl* **-ões**) M summer
verba ['vɛrba] F allowance; **verba(s)** F(PL) (*recursos*) funds *pl*
verbal [ver'baw] (*pl* **-ais**) ADJ verbal
verbete [ver'betʃi] M (*num dicionário*) entry
verbo ['vɛrbu] M verb
verdade [ver'dadʒi] F truth; **na ~** in fact; **de ~** (*falar*) truthfully; (*ameaçar etc*) really; **para falar a ~** to tell the truth; **verdadeiro, -a** [verda'dejru, a] ADJ true; (*genuíno*) real; (*pessoa*) truthful
verde ['verdʒi] ADJ green; (*fruta*) unripe ▶ M green; (*plantas etc*) greenery
verdura [ver'dura] F (*hortaliça*) greens *pl*; (*Bot*) greenery; (*cor verde*) greenness
verdureiro, -a [verdu'rejru, a] M/F greengrocer (BRIT), produce dealer (US)
vereador, a [verja'dor(a)] M/F councillor (BRIT), councilor (US)
veredicto [vere'dʒiktu] M verdict
verga ['verga] F (*vara*) stick; (*de metal*) rod
vergonha [ver'gɔɲa] F shame; (*timidez*) embarrassment; (*humilhação*) humiliation; (*ato indecoroso*) indecency; (*brio*) self-respect; **ter ~** to be ashamed; (*tímido*) to be shy; **vergonhoso, -a** [vergo'ɲozu, ɔza] ADJ shameful; (*indecoroso*) disgraceful
verídico, -a [ve'ridʒiku, a] ADJ true, truthful
verificar [verifi'kar] VT to check;

(*confirmar, Comput*) to verify
verme ['vɛrmi] M worm
vermelho, -a [ver'meʎu, a] ADJ red ▶ M red
verniz [ver'niz] M varnish; (*couro*) patent leather
verões [ve'rõjs] MPL *de* **verão**
verossímil [vero'simiw], (PT) **verosímil** (*pl* **-eis**) ADJ likely, probable; (*crível*) credible
verruga [ve'huga] F wart
versão [ver'sãw] (*pl* **-ões**) F version; (*tradução*) translation
versátil [ver'satʃiw] (*pl* **-eis**) ADJ versatile
verso ['vɛrsu] M verse; (*linha*) line of poetry
versões [ver'sõjs] FPL *de* **versão**
verter [ver'ter] VT to pour; (*por acaso*) to spill; (*traduzir*) to translate; (*lágrimas, sangue*) to shed ▶ VI: **~ de** to spring from; **~ em** (*rio*) to flow into
vertical [vertʃi'kaw] (*pl* **-ais**) ADJ vertical; (*de pé*) upright, standing ▶ F vertical
vespa ['vespa] F wasp
véspera ['vɛspera] F: **a ~ (de)** the day before; **a ~ de Natal** Christmas Eve
vestiário [ves'tʃjarju] M (*em casa, teatro*) cloakroom; (*Esporte*) changing room (BRIT), locker-room (US); (*de ator*) dressing room
vestíbulo [ves'tʃibulu] M hall(way), vestibule; (*Teatro*) foyer
vestido, -a [ves'tʃidu, a] ADJ: **~ de branco** *etc* dressed in white *etc* ▶ M dress
vestígio [ves'tʃiʒju] M (*rastro*) track; (*fig*) sign, trace
vestimenta [vestʃi'mẽta] F garment
vestir [ves'tʃir] VT (*uma criança*) to dress; (*pôr sobre si*) to put on; (*trajar*) to wear; (*comprar, dar roupa para*) to clothe; (*fazer roupa para*) to make clothes for; **vestir-se** VR to get dressed
vestuário [ves'twarju] M clothing
veterano, -a [vete'ranu, a] ADJ, M/F veteran
veterinário, -a [veteri'narju, a] M/F vet(erinary surgeon)
veto ['vɛtu] M veto
véu [vɛw] M veil
vexame [ve'ʃami] F shame, disgrace; (*tormento*) affliction; (*humilhação*) humiliation; (*afronta*) insult
vez [vez] F time; (*turno*) turn; **uma ~** once; **algumas ~es, às ~es** sometimes; **~ por outra** sometimes; **cada ~ (que)** every time; **de ~ em quando** from time to time; **em ~ de** instead of; **uma ~ que** since; **3 ~es 6** 3 times 6; **de uma ~ por todas** once and for all; **muitas ~es** many times; (*frequentemente*) often; **toda ~ que** every time; **um de cada ~** one at a time; **uma ~ ou outra** once in a while
vi [vi] VB *ver* **ver**
via[1] ['via] F road, route; (*meio*) way; (*documento*) copy; (*conduto*) channel ▶ PREP via, by way of; **em ~s de** in the process of; **por ~ terrestre/marítima** by land/sea
via[2] VB *ver* **ver**
viaduto [vja'dutu] M viaduct
viagem ['vjaʒẽ] (*pl* **-ns**) F journey, trip; (*o viajar*) travel; (*Náut*) voyage; **viagens** FPL (*jornadas*) travels; **~ de ida e volta** return trip, round trip
viajante [vja'ʒãtʃi] ADJ travelling (BRIT), traveling (US) ▶ M traveller (BRIT), traveler (US)

viajar [vja'ʒar] VI to travel
viável ['vjavew] (*pl* **-eis**) ADJ feasible, viable
víbora ['vibora] F viper
vibração [vibra'sãw] (*pl* **-ões**) F vibration; (*fig*) thrill
vibrante [vi'brãtʃi] ADJ vibrant; (*discurso*) stirring
vibrar [vi'brar] VT to brandish; (*fazer estremecer*) to vibrate; (*cordas*) to strike ▶ VI to vibrate; (*som*) to echo
vice ['visi] M/F deputy
vice- [visi-] PREFIXO vice-; **vice-presidente, -a** M/F vice president; **vice-versa** [-'vɛrsa] ADV vice versa
viciado, -a [vi'sjadu, a] ADJ addicted; (*ar*) foul ▶ M/F addict; **~ em algo** addicted to sth
viciar [vi'sjar] VT (*falsificar*) to falsify; **viciar-se** VR: **~-se em algo** to become addicted to sth
vício ['visju] M vice; (*defeito*) failing; (*costume*) bad habit; (*em entorpecentes*) addiction
viço ['visu] M vigour (BRIT), vigor (US); (*da pele*) freshness
vida ['vida] F life; (*duração*) lifetime; (*fig*) vitality; **com ~** alive; **ganhar a ~** to earn one's living; **modo de ~** way of life; **dar a ~ por algo/por fazer algo** to give one's right arm for sth/to do sth; **estar bem de ~** to be well off
videira [vi'dejra] F grapevine
vidente [vi'dẽtʃi] M/F clairvoyant
vídeo ['vidʒju] M video; **videocassete** [vidʒjuka'sɛtʃi] M video cassette *ou* tape; (*aparelho*) video (recorder); **videoteipe** [vidʒju'tejpi] M video tape
vidraça [vi'drasa] F window pane
vidrado, -a [vi'dradu, a] ADJ glazed; (*porta*) glass *atr*; (*olhos*) glassy
vidro ['vidru] M glass; (*frasco*) bottle; **fibra de ~** fibreglass (BRIT), fiberglass (US); **~ de aumento** magnifying glass
vier [vjer] VB *ver* **vir¹**
viés [vjɛs] M slant; **ao** *ou* **de ~** diagonally
vieste ['vjɛstʃi] VB *ver* **vir¹**
Vietnã [vjet'nã] M: **o ~** Vietnam; **vietnamita** [vjetna'mita] ADJ, M/F Vietnamese
vigiar [vi'ʒjar] VT to watch; (*ocultamente*) to spy on; (*presos, fronteira*) to guard ▶ VI to be on the lookout
vigilância [viʒi'lãsja] F vigilance; **vigilante** [viʒi'lãtʃi] ADJ vigilant; (*atento*) alert
vigor [vi'gor] M energy; **em ~** in force; **entrar/pôr em ~** to take effect/put into effect; **vigoroso, -a** [vigo'rozu, ɔza] ADJ vigorous
vil [viw] (*pl* **vis**) ADJ vile
vila ['vila] F town; (*casa*) villa
vilão, -lã [vi'lãw, 'lã] (*pl* **-ões/-s**) M/F villain
vilarejo [vila'reʒu] M village
vim [vĩ] VB *ver* **vir¹**
vime ['vimi] M wicker
vinagre [vi'nagri] M vinegar
vinco ['vĩku] M crease; (*sulco*) furrow; (*no rosto*) line
vincular [vĩku'lar] VT to link, tie; **vínculo** ['vĩkulu] M bond, tie; (*relação*) link
vinda ['vĩda] F arrival; (*regresso*) return; **dar as boas ~s a** to welcome
vingança [vĩ'gãsa] F vengeance, revenge; **vingar** [vĩ'gar] VT to avenge; **vingar-se** VR: **vingar-se de** to take revenge on; **vingativo, -a**

[vĩga'tʃivu, a] ADJ vindictive
vinha¹ ['viɲa] F vineyard; (*planta*) vine
vinha² VB *ver* **vir¹**
vinho ['viɲu] M wine; **~ branco/ rosado/tinto** white/rosé/red wine; **~ seco/doce** dry/sweet wine; **~ do Porto** port
vinte ['vĩtʃi] NUM twenty
viola ['vjɔla] F viola
violão [vjo'lãw] (*pl* **-ões**) M guitar
violar [vjo'lar] VT to violate; (*a lei*) to break
violência [vjo'lẽsja] F violence; **violentar** [vjolẽ'tar] VT to force; (*mulher*) to rape; **violento, -a** [vjo'lẽtu, a] ADJ violent
violeta [vjo'leta] F violet
violino [vjo'linu] M violin
violões [vjo'lõjs] MPL *de* **violão**
violoncelo [vjolõ'sɛlu] M cello
vir¹ [vir] VI to come; **~ a ser** to turn out to be; **a semana que vem** next week
vir² VB *ver* **ver**
viral [vi'raw] ADJ viral
vira-lata ['vira-] (*pl* **vira-latas**) M (*cão*) mongrel
virar [vi'rar] VT to turn; (*página, disco, barco*) to turn over; (*copo*) to empty; (*transformar-se em*) to become ▶ VI to turn; (*barco*) to capsize; (*mudar*) to change; **virar-se** VR to turn; (*voltar-se*) to turn round; (*defender-se*) to fend for o.s.
virgem ['virʒẽ] (*pl* **-ns**) F virgin; **V~** (*Astrologia*) Virgo
vírgula ['virgula] F comma; (*decimal*) point
viril [vi'riw] (*pl* **-is**) ADJ virile
virilha [vi'riʎa] F groin
viris [vi'ris] ADJ PL *de* **viril**
virtual [vir'twaw] (*pl* **-ais**) ADJ virtual; (*potencial*) potential
virtude [vir'tudʒi] F virtue; **em ~ de** owing to, because of; **virtuoso, -a** [vir'twozu, ɔza] ADJ virtuous
virulento, -a [viru'lẽtu, a] ADJ virulent
vírus ['virus] M INV virus
vis [vis] ADJ PL *de* **vil**
visão [vi'zãw] (*pl* **-ões**) F vision; (*Anat*) eyesight; (*vista*) sight; (*maneira de perceber*) view
visar [vi'zar] VT (*alvo*) to aim at; (*ter em vista*) to have in view; (*ter como objetivo*) to aim for
vísceras ['viseras] FPL innards, bowels
visita [vi'zita] F visit, call; (*pessoa*) visitor; (*na Internet*) hit; **fazer uma ~ a** to visit; **~ guiada** guided tour; **visitante** [vizi'tãtʃi] ADJ visiting ▶ M/F visitor; **visitar** [vizi'tar] VT to visit
visível [vi'zivew] (*pl* **-eis**) ADJ visible
vislumbrar [vizlũ'brar] VT to glimpse, catch a glimpse of; **vislumbre** [viz'lũbri] M glimpse
visões [vi'zõjs] FPL *de* **visão**
visse ['visi] VB *ver* **ver**
vista ['vista] F sight; (*Med*) eyesight; (*panorama*) view; **à** *ou* **em ~ de** in view of; **dar na ~** to attract attention; **dar uma ~ de olhos em** to glance at; **fazer ~ grossa (a)** to turn a blind eye (to); **ter em ~** to have in mind; **à ~** visible, showing; (*Com*) in cash; **até a ~!** see you!
visto¹, -a ['vistu, a] PP *de* **ver** ▶ ADJ seen ▶ M (*em passaporte*) visa; (*em documento*) stamp; **pelo ~** by the looks of things
visto² VB *ver* **vestir**
vistoria [visto'ria] F inspection
vistoso, -a [vis'tozu, ɔza] ADJ eye-catching

visual [vi'zwaw] (*pl* **-ais**) ADJ visual; **visualizar** [vizwali'zar] VT to visualize

vital [vi'taw] (*pl* **-ais**) ADJ vital; **vitalício, -a** [vita'lisju, a] ADJ for life

vitamina [vita'mina] F vitamin; (*para beber*) fruit crush

vitela [vi'tɛla] F calf; (*carne*) veal

vítima ['vitʃima] F victim

vitória [vi'tɔrja] F victory; **vitorioso, -a** [vito'rjozu, ɔza] ADJ victorious

vitrina [vi'trina] F = **vitrine**

vitrine [vi'trini] F shop window; (*armário*) display case

viúvo, -a ['vjuvu, a] M/F widower/ widow

viva ['viva] M cheer; **~!** hurray!

viva-voz [viva'vɔz] M (BR *Tel: em telefone*) speakerphone; (*para celular*) hands-free kit

viveiro [vi'vejru] M nursery

vivência [vi'vẽsja] F existence; (*experiência*) experience

vivenda [vi'vẽda] F (*casa*) residence

viver [vi'ver] VI, VT to live ▶ M life; **~ de** to live on

vívido, -a ['vividu, a] ADJ vivid

vivo, -a ['vivu, a] ADJ living; (*esperto*) clever; (*cor*) bright; (*criança, debate*) lively ▶ M: **os ~s** the living

vizinhança [vizi'ɲãsa] F neighbourhood (BRIT), neighborhood (US)

vizinho, -a [vi'ziɲu, a] ADJ neighbouring (BRIT), neighboring (US); (*perto*) nearby ▶ M/F neighbour (BRIT), neighbor (US)

vó [vɔ] (*col*) F gran

vô [vo] (*col*) M grandad, grandpa

voar [vo'ar] VI to fly; (*explodir*) to blow up, explode

vocabulário [vokabu'larju] M vocabulary

vocábulo [vo'kabulu] M word

vocal [vo'kaw] (*pl* **-ais**) ADJ vocal

você [vo'se] PRON you

vocês [vo'ses] PRON PL you

vodca ['vɔdʒka] F vodka

vogal [vo'gaw] (*pl* **-ais**) F (*Ling*) vowel

vol. ABR (= *volume*) vol

volante [vo'lãtʃi] M steering wheel

vôlei ['volej] M volleyball

voleibol [volej'bɔw] M = **vôlei**

volt ['vɔwtʃi] (*pl* **-s**) M volt

volta ['vɔwta] F turn; (*regresso*) return; (*curva*) bend, curve; (*circuito*) lap; (*resposta*) retort; **dar uma ~** (*a pé*) to go for a walk; (*de carro*) to go for a drive; **estar de ~** to be back; **na ~ do correio** by return (post); **por ~ de** about, around; **à** *ou* **em ~ de** around; **na ~** (*no caminho de volta*) on the way back

voltagem [vow'taʒẽ] F voltage

voltar [vow'tar] VT to turn ▶ VI to return, go (*ou* come) back; **voltar-se** VR to turn round; **~ a fazer** to do again; **~ a si** to come to; **~-se para** to turn to; **~-se contra** to turn against

volume [vo'lumi] M volume; (*pacote*) package; **volumoso, -a** [volu'mozu, ɔza] ADJ bulky, big

voluntário, -a [volũ'tarju, a] ADJ voluntary ▶ M/F volunteer

volúvel [vo'luvew] (*pl* **-eis**) ADJ fickle

vomitar [vomi'tar] VT, VI to vomit; **vômito** ['vomitu] M (*ato*) vomiting; (*efeito*) vomit

vontade [võ'tadʒi] F will; (*desejo*) wish; **com ~** (*com prazer*) with

pleasure; (*com gana*) with gusto; **estar com** *ou* **ter ~ de fazer** to feel like doing
voo ['vou] M flight; **levantar ~** to take off; **~ livre** (*Esporte*) hang-gliding
voraz [vo'rajz] ADJ voracious
vos [vus] PRON you
vós [vɔs] PRON you
vosso, -a ['vɔsu, a] ADJ your ▶ PRON: **(o) ~** yours
votação [vota'sãw] (*pl* **-ões**) F vote, ballot; (*ato*) voting
votar [vo'tar] VT (*eleger*) to vote for; (*aprovar*) to pass; (*submeter a votação*) to vote on ▶ VI to vote;
voto ['vɔtu] M vote; (*promessa*) vow; **votos** MPL (*desejos*) wishes
vou [vo] VB *ver* **ir**
vovó [vo'vɔ] F grandma
vovô [vo'vo] M grandad
voz [vɔz] F voice; (*clamor*) cry; **a meia ~** in a whisper; **de viva ~** orally; **ter ~ ativa** to have a say; **em ~ baixa** in a low voice; **em ~ alta** aloud; **~ de comando** command
vulcão [vuw'kãw] (*pl* **-ões**) M volcano
vulgar [vuw'gar] ADJ common; (*pej: pessoa etc*) vulgar
vulnerável [vuwne'ravew] (*pl* **-eis**) ADJ vulnerable
vulto ['vuwtu] M figure; (*volume*) mass; (*fig*) importance; (*pessoa importante*) important person

W

walkie-talkie [wɔki'tɔki] (*pl* **-s**) M walkie-talkie
watt ['wɔtʃi] (*pl* **-s**) M watt
web ['wɛbi] F, ADJ (*Comput*) web
webcam [wɛb'cã] F webcam
windsurfe M windsurfing

X

indigenous people. Situated in the north of the state of Mato Grosso, it aims to preserve indigenous culture. It brings together sixteen communities, a total of two thousand Indians.

xadrez [ʃa'drez] M chess; (*tabuleiro*) chessboard; (*tecido*) checked cloth
xampu [ʃã'pu] M shampoo
xarope [ʃa'rɔpi] M syrup; (*para a tosse*) cough syrup
xeque ['ʃɛki] M (*soberano*) sheikh; **pôr em ~** (*fig*) to call into question; **xeque-mate** (*pl* **xeques-mate**) M checkmate
xerocar [ʃero'kar] VT to photocopy, Xerox®
xerox® [ʃe'rɔks] M (*copia*) photocopy; (*máquina*) photocopier
xícara ['ʃikara] (BR) F cup
xingar [ʃĩ'gar] VT to swear at ▶ VI to swear
Xingu [ʃĩ'gu] M *see note*

The **Xingu** National Park was created in 1961 by the federal government and directed by the brothers Orlando and Cláudio Vilasboas, who were known internationally for their efforts to preserve Brazil's

Z

zagueiro [za'gejru] M (*Futebol*) fullback
Zâmbia ['zãbja] F Zambia
zangado, -a [zã'gadu, a] ADJ angry; annoyed; (*irritadiço*) bad-tempered
zangar [zã'gar] VT to annoy, irritate ▶ VI to get angry; **zangar-se** VR (*aborrecer-se*) to get annoyed; **~-se com** to get cross with
zarpar [zar'par] VI (*navio*) to set sail; (*ir-se*) to set off; (*fugir*) to run away
zebra ['zebra] F zebra
zelador, a [zela'dor(a)] M/F caretaker
zelar [ze'lar] VT, VI: **~ (por)** to look after
zerar [ze'rar] VT (*conta, inflação*) to reduce to zero; (*déficit*) to pay off, wipe out
zero ['zɛru] M zero; (*Esporte*) nil; **zero-quilômetro** ADJ INV brand new
ziguezague [zigi'zagi] M zigzag
Zimbábue [zĩ'babwi] M: **o ~** Zimbabwe
-zinho, -a [-'ziɲu, a] SUFIXO little; **florzinha** little flower
zíper ['ziper] M zip (BRIT), zipper (US)
zodíaco [zo'dʒiaku] M zodiac
zoeira ['zwejra] F din
zombar [zõ'bar] VI to mock; **~ de** to make fun of; **zombaria** [zõba'ria] F mockery, ridicule
zona ['zɔna] F area; (*de cidade*) district; (*Geo*) zone; (*col: local de meretrício*) red-light district; (*: confusão*) mess; (*: tumulto*) free-for-all; **~ eleitoral** electoral district, constituency
zonzo, -a ['zõzu, a] ADJ dizzy
zoo ['zou] M zoo
zoológico, -a [zo'lɔʒiku, a] ADJ zoological; **jardim ~** zoo
zumbido [zũ'bidu] M buzz(ing); (*de tráfego*) hum
zunzum [zũ'zũ] M buzz(ing)